The A.E. Nordenskiöld Collection
in the Helsinki University Library

Annotated Catalogue of Maps
made up to 1800

Compiled by

Ann-Mari Mickwitz

and

Leena Miekkavaara

Vol. 1
ATLASES A–J

Published by

HELSINKI UNIVERSITY LIBRARY

Distributed by

ALMQVIST & WIKSELL INTERNATIONAL
STOCKHOLM·SWEDEN

HUMANITIES PRESS
ATLANTIC HIGHLANDS · N.J., U.S.A.

© 1979 Helsinki University Library, Finland
All rights reserved

The printing of this catalogue
has been made possible through
a grant from
Koneen Säätiö

ISBN 951-45-1703-2
ISBN 951-45-1702-4 (Vols. 1—5)
ISBN 91-22-00275-8
ISBN 91-22-00291-X (Vols. 1—5)

First published 1979

Distributed outside the U.S.A. by Almqvist & Wiksell
International, Stockholm, Sweden
Distributed in the U.S.A. by
Humanities Press Inc.
Atlantic Highlands, N.J. 07716
ISBN 0-391-01393-9

Colour plates printed by Amer-Yhtymä Oy
Weilin + Göös
Printed in Finland by
Helsingin yliopiston monistuspalvelu, Helsinki 1979

The A.E. Nordenskiöld Collection

Vol. 1

Contents

Acknowledgements
VII
Introduction
IX
Notes for Use
XXIX
List of Atlases
XXX
Catalogue of Maps
1—250

Acknowledgements

The cataloguing of the A.E. Nordenskiöld map collection has taken much longer than Nordenskiöld took to acquire it. The map collection, together with the present analytical catalogue, form one of the cornerstones of cartographic history, which can perhaps without undue exaggeration be characterised in Horace's words *Monumentum aere perennius*.

The preparation of the catalogue has been an enormous task, both as a research and a bibliographical project, and it would not have succeeded without the effort and co-operation of a large number of people and institutions; it is my happy duty as the person responsible for the work to thank all these. The conclusion of this huge task, is accompanied not only by professional satisfaction, but also by private sorrow. My thanks can no longer reach Mrs Ann-Mari Mickwitz, the real editor of the catalogue, its heart and soul, who died on 6th December 1978, the day after her seventy-fifth birthday. She cannot see the result of her many years of unflagging effort. The Library of the University of Helsinki remembers Ann-Mari Mickwitz with gratitude; she devoted the last years of her life to Adolf Nordenskiöld, and with her irresistable charm and cultivated knowledge gained friends both for herself and for our Library among cartographic specialists and map librarians throughout the world.

It is not possible to mention here all the people and institutions who have helped in the preparation of the catalogue. It was largely thanks to the Nordenskiöld-Samfundet [Nordenskiöld Society] and its chairman, Professor Stig Jaatinen, that the work was restarted after a long period during which it had come to a complete halt. Ann-Mari Mickwitz and Leena Miekkavaara were fortunate in gaining the help of the international circle of experts in cartography whose members include Dr Ulla Ehrensvärd (Stockholm), Dr Cornelius Koeman (Utrecht), Dr Walter Ristow (Washington, D.C.) and Dr Helen Wallis (London) in the establishment of the research and bibliographical principles according to which the cataloguing was conducted, as well as in solving the problems which continually arose as the work progressed. In addition, I should like to thank the many libraries and other institutions which so kindly assisted Ann-Mari Mickwitz in her cartographic investigations and comparative work.

I should like also to mention the close co-operation which, thanks to Dr Helen Wallis, developed between the British Library Map Room and the editors of this catalogue. Mrs Gillian Hill and Mr John Huddy of the British Library Map Room carefully examined the notes and helped with the linguistic style of the catalogue at manuscript stage and have thus significantly advanced the progress of the work, and its result. I should like to offer both of them my sincerest thanks on behalf of the Helsinki University Library.

The raising of monuments also requires the raising of funds. The Helsinki University Library had the good fortune to obtain the patronage of the Koneen Säätiö [Kone Foundation], which is maintained by Kone Ltd. The Foundation has assisted with funds for the the preparation of the work and has also taken responsibility for the entire printing costs of this five-part catalogue. Without this help, it is difficult to imagine that the catalogue would ever have seen the light of day. In offering the Library's thanks to the Kone Foundation, I should like especially to express my gratitude to the Chairman of the Board of Trustees of the Foundation, the former managing director of Kone Ltd., Dr Heikki H. Herlin, who in his personal interests is no stranger to historical research, books and the advancement of Finnish culture.

The printing of this demanding work was carried out by Helsingin yliopiston monistuspalvelu, and Amer-Yhtymä Weilin + Göös Oy has kindly printed the facsimile maps included in the catalogue. Of the many people who have helped in the last stages of the project, I should like especially to mention Mrs Tuula Rantanen, who with great care and skill has supervised the printing, proof-reading and corrections to the work. In the preparation of my Introduction, I have always been able to rely on the help of Mrs Eeva Mäkelä-Henriksson, Chief of the Department of Printed Books and Manuscripts of our Library. Dr Wilhelm Odelberg, Librarian of the Royal Swedish Academy of Sciences in Stockholm, was always ready to with help, both in word and deed, when I was studying Nordenskiöld's life, his archives and other collections in Sweden. In conclusion, I must mention my debt of gratitude to the numerous people in London and Helsinki who helped in the various stages of translating the Introduction.

Helsinki, July 1979

Esko Häkli
Librarian, Helsinki University Library

Introduction

by
Esko Häkli

The private library of Adolf Erik Nordenskiöld is the extraordinary creation of a remarkable man, and a testament to his scientific curiosity and to his profound devotion to the development of the study of the history of ideas and bibliography. Nordenskiöld himself said that in the field of ancient geographical and cartographic literature, only three or four of the world's great national libraries bore comparison to his own collection. In twenty or thirty years Nordenskiöld, at considerable financial sacrifice, singlehandedly accumulated a collection to compare with those which great libraries, even with all their financial resources, had taken sometimes centuries to acquire. In the way he bought books, Nordenskiöld has been compared to a renaissance prince, but in fact his only financial resources were what he earned through his work and his writing.

Characteristic of Nordenskiöld was his persistence: he never gave up in the pursuit of the goals he set himself, nor would he be content with second best. Once he had decided to create as complete as possible a cartographic collection, he held fast to his idea. The result was a unique collection which is internationally known amongst specialists in cartographic history. Nordenskiöld's library is comparable to his other achievements, and a catalogue of the maps in this huge collection is not simply the catalogue of yet another interesting library: it is also a valuable contribution to the bibliography of cartography.

The present publication is a catalogue of only one part of Nordenskiöld's library; it deals only with his maps. It must also be emphasised that the catalogue does not contain all the cartographic material in the Helsinki University Library, but only that contained in the Nordenskiöld Collection. The Library, as the Finnish National Library, possesses a wide selection of Finnish maps; in addition the Library's Slavonic collection contains an important number of Russian maps which came into its possession during the years 1828—1917 when it had the status of a copyright library in the autonomous Grand Duchy of Finland under Russia.

The Man

When Adolf Erik Nordenskiöld died on 12th August 1901, his name was known throughout the civilised world. He was a member of over a hundred learned societies and academies of science. He was the most famous Swede of his day, and at the same time the best-known Swedish scientist, following in the great tradition of Carl von Linné, Carl Wilhelm Scheele and Jakob Berzelius. Since his death, however, his name has been largely forgotten; the reasons for this include the progress which has been made in the sciences and, in particular the specialisation which has developed since Nordenskiöld's day. A short description of his life and work is therefore necessary to gain an understanding of Nordenskiöld as a man, and to serve as a background for his cartographic investigations and the shaping of his library. (1)

Adolf Erik Nordenskiöld was a Swede only by chance; he was born in Helsinki in Finland, on 18th November 1832. His father, Nils Gustav Nordenskiöld, was a learned mineralogist whose work was widely known outside Finland. He was a member of many learned societies abroad, amongst them the Royal Geographical Society. In his own country he was the originator of the idea of founding the *Suomen Tiedeseura*, (*Societas Scientiarum Fennica*), and was its chairman in 1841—2. He is considered, with reason, to be the 'father of Finnish mineralogy'. Despite his learning, he was not a university man. He studied in Stockholm under Berzelius, in 1817 he gained a university qualification in mining engineering from Upsala and in 1823 he was made Director of Finland's Office of Mines. As a practical mineralogist, however, he was less successful than as an scholar: he poured government funds into impractical projects and was also deeply in debt in his private life.

Nordenskiöld was thus in touch with the latest developments in mineralogy from his early childhood. At home there was what by the standards of the times was a large library, from which he learned his first facts about the natural sciences. At the same time he saw how scientific advances are built on the achievements of earlier generations. His father had, in addition to the library, a fine mineral collection, to which he added constantly. He took his son with him on increasingly longer field trips and instilled in him a sound knowledge of Finland's minerals. At that time Nils Gustav Nordenskiöld was the outstanding authority in Finland on geology and mineralogy, a man who kept abreast of the latest developments in his subject and was without rival even among the specialists at the University; his son later remarked with gratitude on the importance of his father as his first teacher. The training he received at home showed itself in later years in his phenomenal ability to make finds on field trips even outside his own specialist subject of mineralogy, especially in palaeobotany.

Adolf Erik Nordenskiöld received his university education in Helsinki, where he gained his doctorate in 1855.

In the same year he published his *Beskrifning öfver de i Finland funna mineralier,* an extensive study of minerals which had been found in Finland, and of which a second edition with revisions by the author was published in 1863.

In 1809 Finland, which had until then been part of Sweden, became an autonomous Grand Duchy of Russia under the Tsar. Although Finland had its own government, and a Minister Secretary of State in St Petersburg brought Finnish matters directly to the Tsar for decision, a Russian Governor General looked after the Tsar's interests in Finland. Nordenskiöld completed his studies in the heady atmosphere of the Crimean War and — never one to practise judicious moderation — became involved in certain incidents which displeased the Governor General. In 1855 he was dismissed from two minor official posts, and in 1857 he was forced to leave the University, which had offered him the Chair of Geology and Mineralogy. In 1857—8 he had spent a term in Stockholm at the National Museum of Natural History (*Naturhistoriska riksmuséet*), an institution under the auspices of the Royal Swedish Academy of Sciences. In the autumn of 1858 he was invited to take up the post of Director and Professor in the Museum's mineralogical department, which had suddenly become vacant. He held this post until his death over forty years later.

Nordenskiöld attempted to return to Finland in 1867, when the University again offered him the Chair, which was still unfilled. He was excited by this possibility, and began to investigate how he would continue his research in Helsinki. But political reasons made this impossible. When the opportunity arose again in 1874, he was too involved in his work in Sweden to be able to consider moving back to Finland. All the same, his ties with Finland remained very strong. He always considered himself a Finnish emigrant, in his house Finland was always referred to as 'home', and through his many friends and relatives he was able to keep in touch with all that was happening in Finland. In 1863 he found himself a Finnish bride, Miss Anna Mannerheim, daughter of Carl Mannerheim, a former President of the Court of Appeal in Viipuri. The Marshal of Finland, Carl Gustav Mannerheim (1867—1951), was Anna Nordenskiöld's nephew. Nordenskiöld was also intensely interested in Finland's fate as a nation. When the programme of russification began in Finland at the end of the century, a petition was organised in 1899 amongst the intelligentsia of Europe, and sent directly to the Tsar. Among those who took the petition to St Petersburg was Nordenskiöld, who had often been celebrated as an explorer in Russia, who was an honorary member of nearly all the important Imperial Russian learned societies, and whom the Tsar himself had rewarded with high honours. But none of this helped: the delegation was not even given an audience. In front of the Hôtel de l'Europe in St Petersburg Sven Hedin met an old and broken man sitting on a bench. He could not believe that the Tsar had refused to see him, and for long afterwards he could hardly speak of anything else. (2)

In examining Nordenskiöld's Finnish origins and his continuing close contact with Finland, it should be borne in mind that contacts between Finland and Sweden were not severed as with a knife after 1809. For instance Swedish currency continued to be legal tender in Finland alongside the Russian rouble until 1840. Many families were divided, with branches in both Sweden and Finland; of the Nordenskiöld family, two branches were already living in Sweden and one in Germany when Adolf Erik Nordenskiöld moved to Sweden, in addition to which the founding father of the Nordenskiöld family had been born in Sweden.

The Explorer

To the European public at large, as well as to leading scholars and scientists of the time, Nordenskiöld was essentially a courageous and successful explorer. It was he who established the so-called Swedish school: its prime object was scientific research, rather than newsworthy adventure or territorial ambition, and the leader of the expedition was always a scientist accompanied by a good number of assistants with adequate scientific equipment. This has since become standard practice, but was by no means usual before Nordenskiöld's time.

Another feature, which became more important as exploration became more difficult, was the detailed advance planning of expeditions. Navigational problems were of course considered carefully — there was a great deal of experience in this field — but Nordenskiöld directed attention to two new aspects of planning. First, he examined all available accounts, old and new, of the climate, flora and fauna of the area under exploration; second, on the basis of these, he made a detailed scientific plan which concentrated on the problems which were peculiar to the area, or about which little was known.

An example of the way Nordenskiöld set out his aims is given by the concluding words of his plan for the Vega expedition, which he presented to King Oscar II of Sweden. He writes:

'In the Siberian Polar sea, the animal and vegetable types, so far as we can judge beforehand, exclusively consist of survivals from the glacial period, which next preceded the present, which is not the case in the Polar Sea, where the Gulf Stream distributes its waters, and whither it thus carries types from more southerly regions. But a complete and exact knowledge of which animal types are of glacial, and which of Atlantic origin, is of the greatest importance, not only for zoology and the geography of animals, but also for the geology of Scandinavia, and especially for the knowledge of our loose earthy layers [i.e. superficial deposits].

'Taking a general view of the subject, we see that an investigation, as complete as possible, of the geology of the Polar countries, so difficult of access, is a condition indispensable to a knowledge of the former history of our globe. In order to prove this I need only point to the epoch-making influence which has been exerted on geological theories by the discovery, in the rocks and earthy layers of the Polar countries, of beautiful fossil plants from widely separated geological periods. In this field too our expedition to the north coast of Siberia ought to expect to reap abundant harvests. There are besides to be found in Siberia, strata which have been deposited almost contemporaneously with the coal-bearing formations of South Sweden, and which therefore contain animal and vegetable petrifications which just now are of very special interest for geological science in our own country, with reference to the discoveries of splendid fossil plants which of late years have been made at several places among us, and give us so lively an idea of the subtropical vegetation which in former times covered the Scandinavian peninsula.' (3)

Nordenskiöld refers to the many finds which had been made in Skåne in Sweden and which, together with the fossil plants which had been systematically collected in the arctic area, Siberia and Japan, had stimulated the first serious scientific discussions about the earth's climate. A later scientist has said, 'There is no exaggeration in the assertion that the Swedish Riksmuseum toward the close of Nordenskiöld's era had incomparable arctic treasures, among them collections of prehistoric plants which gave foundation to the first discussions of the earth's perplexing climate variations during tens of millions of years before our time.' (4)

But the plan for the Vega expedition contains the key to the understanding of all Nordenskiöld's and the Swedish school's northern explorations: the purpose of the Vega exploration was to gather material to add to the information about the superficial deposits of the Scandinavian soil. This had actually also been the purpose of the first exploration in which Nordenskiöld had taken part, in 1858. The aim of the leader of the expedition, Dr Otto Torell, had been to answer questions about the possible ice age in Scandinavia and to solve the problem of Scandinavia's superficial deposits. In the fields of both geography and geology there was a clear common thread running through all the northern expeditions.

Nordenskiöld himself had started as a geologist and mineralogist; it is true that he also studied chemistry, botany and physics, but it is difficult to imagine that he could have gained very much from these sciences as they then were after his own very first expeditions. His younger colleague, Professor A.G. Nathorst, wrote the following of Nordenskiöld as a scientist: 'Having been from the beginning a mineralogist, he very soon became also a geologist, and he was extraordinarily good at spotting strata containing fossils. He developed an eye for fossils, especially fossil plants, on field trips, and although he was anything but a professional palaeobotanist, he knew a great deal about the fossils of the arctic region. He was especially interested in botanical and zoological research, particularly in entomology, but sometimes he was altogether too sanguine, for instance when he wanted us to find out about species which simply did not exist in the areas in which we were working. Trawling techniques and hydrographic work interested him a great deal. He carried out his own stellar navigation, neither was he a stranger to the art of photography. He was also fascinated by ethnographic research, whether about the Eskimos, Samoyeds or Chukchi. Taking into account the opportunities for the study of natural phenomena and ethnic groups which he had on his homeward journey from the Vega expedition from the Bering Straits, and on his many other travels, it can be said that few explorers can have had the chance to carry out such diverse research as Nordenskiöld.' (5)

Nordenskiöld was interested in so many different fields that his researches may seem to lack coherence. But on closer examination, it is not difficult to find clear groups of scientific problems which he wished to solve. This is evidently one reason why he moved on from his own original field of mineralogy. Apart from the fact that he did not have the patience to spend hours in the laboratory carrying out time-consuming and, in his opinion, not very productive, analyses of minerals, he had found himself a research project which was broad enough in its scope not to become bogged down in details. The earth as a whole had started to interest him: he was interested in the climate of the earth, and the development of its plant life in the past tens and hundreds of millions of years; he was interested in the shape of the earth and, above all, he was constantly concerned with the problem of the origin of the earth and its evolution. These were big questions, and speculations or analyses of detail were not enough to answer them. They also forced him to move into areas of research in which he had no formal qualifications.

Nordenskiöld never kept his research material selfishly to himself, but made it freely available to fellow scientists; he was also generous with his own vast knowledge. Once he realised how important palaeobotany was becoming in the search for answers to questions about the development of the earth's climate, he worked for a time with the European authority on the subject, Professor Oswald Heer of Zurich, who examined and published research on many of the fossil plants Nordenskiöld had found on his expeditions. At that time Nordenskiöld was also training a Swedish scientist to continue the work of Heer in this field; he secured for him a post in his own laboratory and after ten years of persistent effort persuaded the government to establish a department of palaeobotany in the National Museum of Natural History and to appoint as its director and professor this same man, Dr A.G. Nathorst.

Nordenskiöld gained his worldwide fame as a result of his expeditions to the arctic regions. In the quarter century between 1858 and 1883 he made ten expeditions, summarised below. (6)

1858	Spitsbergen, with three scientists, on the Norwegian yacht *Frithiof*
1861	Spitsbergen, with eight scientists, on the Norwegian brigantine *Aeolus* and the yacht *Magdalena*
1864	Spitsbergen and Storfjord, with three scientists, on the Norwegian schooner *Axel Thordsen*
1868	Spitsbergen, the northern and western parts of the islands, with eight scientists, on the Swedish steamship *Sofia*; an ambitious project among whose aims was to approach the North Pole as closely as possible, and which

	succeeded in setting a record for the most northerly latitude (81°42′) then reached by man
1870	Greenland, the western part of the island, with four scientists, on the Danish brig *Hvalfisken;* an expedition to the inland ice fields
1872—3	Spitsbergen, the northern coast of the islands, with three scientists, on the Swedish steamship *Polhem* accompanied by the brig *Gladan* and the steamship *Onkel Adam*; expedition over the north-east mainland ice field during winter
1875	The Yenisey, with five scientists, on the Norwegian fishing vessel *Pröven*; Nordenskiöld returned home by land, the other members of the expedition by sea
1876	The Yenisey, with two scientists, and five other scientists who travelled by land intending to meet their colleagues, which they did not however succeed in doing; on the Swedish steamship *Ymer*
1878—80	North-east passage, with seven scientists, on the Swedish steamship *Vega,* accompanied to the delta of the river Lena by the steamship *Lena* and to the Yenisey, by the steamship *Fraser* and the sailing ship *Express*
1883	Greenland, the west coast of the island, with seven scientists, on the steamship *Sofia*

The first two expeditions, in 1858 and 1861, were led by Dr Otto Torell.

When he returned home from an expedition, Nordenskiöld always set in motion an examination of its results, though he himself published only a small amount of the research which was carried out following each journey. While in his later years Nordenskiöld doubted his own capacity to be a successful university lecturer, he was an outstanding teacher of practical research techniques, and on expeditions always found time to help his students and assistants in their scientific work. The expeditions provided a unique practical schooling for numerous young scientists. The number of studies published as a result of the explorations has never been counted, but there must be hundreds. Some of these publications are important; of special note is Dr Oswald Heer's extensive, lavishly-illustrated series *Flora fossilis arctica,* which was published in 1868—83, originally as part of the *Kungliga Svenska Vetenskapsakademiens Handlingar* (Proceedings of the Royal Swedish Academy of Sciences) series, although it later appeared as a separate series, and contains the most important research into the plant fossils found on the Swedish expeditions. Another monumental series was the 3000-page *Vega-Expeditionens vetenskapliga iakttagelser* [Scientific observations on the Vega expedition] 1—5 (1882—7) and whose preparation Nordenskiöld himself supervised. This series is one of the most important achievements in research into the polar regions and contains an incomparable amount of information which is presented scientifically in relation to earlier research and not simply left as a collection of material.

In spite of his early specialisation, Nordenskiöld was one of the last natural scientists of the old tradition, a man with an encylopaedic knowledge. His strengths lay in the breadth of his knowledge, his powers of synthesis, and above all, in his tirelessness and keen-sightedness in collecting research material. With the distance of years, it has been realised that not only did Nordenskiöld stimulate research in many diverse areas in the natural sciences, but that he also changed the course of international as well as Swedish research into the northern regions. His achievements in this field are not invalidated by his tendency to allow his fecund imagination to invent hypotheses which he energetically tried to substantiate, but which eventually proved false. In many matters he was ahead of his time; he saw problems in the context of many related disciplines and was able to draw together research problems and results from different disciplines. For instance, the English geographer W.R. Mead has written of the impulse he gave to the study of ice and snow: "Besides making 'great additions' to the 'geography, zoology, botany, geology and meteorology of the Arctic regions', Nordenskiöld's investigations generated a research interest in ice and snow. This research, lifted to new levels of relevance, was at once practical and academic. At the practical level Nordenskiöld was called in to advise on the establishment of permanent communications across the Baltic. Academically, the expedition (1878—80) laid the foundations of ice and snow studies for which Scandinavians have achieved world renown." (7)

No biography of Nordenskiöld has yet assessed his achievements in the different branches of the natural sciences from the point of view of current research into the same subjects. Thus evaluations of his work are generally based on the writings of his contemporaries or on later summary appraisals. It is clear that Nordenskiöld stimulated considerable changes in direction in research in many areas, but it would be interesting to see what his real importance in the development of the natural sciences was. One of the most interesting aspects of his research was his theory of the origin and evolution of the earth, for which he came under much adverse criticism in his own time — and even some wry amusement. But equally interesting is his part in solving the problem of the ice age of the Scandinavian peninsula, even though he himself was not interested in the ice age as such. The present theory about the ice sheet which once covered the entire Scandinavian area did not become established until the 1870s.

Scientific Collections

Nordenskiöld left to posterity large scientific collections covering various aspects of the natural sciences. A general outline of these will also explain the nature of his interest in collecting cartographic material and they are also an inseparable part of his life-long contribution to scientific knowledge. Nordenskiöld's successor as director of the mineralogical department of the National Museum of Natural History has said that the creation of the Museum's mineral collection was in itself an achievement of a lifetime.

As the director of the National Museum of Natural History's mineralogy department, Nordenskiöld's first responsibility was the collection and study of mineralogical specimens. This he did with exemplary organisation and perseverance. He did most of his own field work before his big expeditions, visiting various parts of Scandinavia as well as making a large number of trips in Finland with his father. When he became concerned with more ambitious expeditions, he left the Scandinavian - side of the work mainly to his assistants and colleagues. He had also set up a network of miners and mining engineers who ensured that anything of scientific interest which was discovered in the mines of Sweden and Norway was referred to an expert for analysis. Letters dating from Nordenskiöld's first years in Stockholm show that he exchanged mineral samples with his father; the National Museum of Natural History worked closely with Nils Gustav Nordenskiöld's collection at Frugård, and through this connection the Museum gained a comprehensive collection of specimens from the Urals, where Nils Gustav Nordenskiöld had done much field work. Nordenskiöld was also in close contact with all the important mineral merchants.

On his northern expeditions, Nordenskiöld collected a vast number of stone and mineral specimens. His ambitious project was to make the mineralogical department of the Museum into the world's leading collection of Scandinavian minerals — and this he achieved. But, as a result of his arctic journeys, he set his sights higher, and it has been justly said that the mineralogical collection in the National Museum of Natural History was also unique in the quality and scope of its arctic specimens.

Once he had started up the programme of field work and the systematic collection of specimens, Nordenskiöld himself was forced to admit that he no longer had the time to examine every new specimen himself. The most important thing was that the material should be collected sufficiently systematically to be of use to other scientists. Although his time was limited, he nevertheless provided a constant flow of new materials to the Museum of such proportions that not all of it could be examined. In the catalogue of the mineral collection of the National Museum of Natural History there are 548 specimens from the Vega expedition and 900 from Greenland which still await close examination. It is difficult to estimate the total number of specimens Nordenskiöld collected, as no inventory was kept; Nordenskiöld, unlike Mosander, did not record specimens which were added to the collection or given away.

Nordenskiöld gave generously from his collection to various universities and institutes of learning, including the universities of Lund and Upsala. Even his own old school at Porvoo received a selected mineral collection. But above all, the newly-founded mineralogical institute of the University of Stockholm was the beneficiary of Nordenskiöld's support, and in 1881—5 he presented it with a large collection of extremely valuable specimens.

The forty years of Nordenskiöld's directorship of the mineral collection of the Museum were extraordinarily rich in mineral discoveries, the largest and most important of which were made in the iron and manganese mines of Värmland in the mid 1870s and late 1880s.

In addition to the mineral specimens, Nordenskiöld collected a large number of meteorites. His interest in meteorites stemmed from his theories about the origin and evolution of the world, and he persisted in this interest despite much adverse criticism. He was convinced that his theories were right, and was apt to say, 'Sic, derisa diu, tandem bona causa triumphat.' He gathered such a large number of meteorites that he can be considered as the founder of the Museum's meteorite collection. Again he was criticised by those who felt that he was devoting too much of the mineralogical department's limited funds to this interest. (8)

As we have already remarked, Nordenskiöld became increasingly interested in palaeobotany as the years passed. He collected enormous numbers of fossil plants from Spitsbergen, Greenland and Siberia and added to his collection by exchanging specimens for samples from Alaska and Sakhalin. These specimens formed the basis of the department of palaeobotany under Professor A.G. Nathorst, who systematically developed the collection. Spitsbergen and Greenland were for Nordenskiöld a great stone herbarium where plants from millions of years ago were to be gathered for research. The collections Nordenskiöld assembled on his field trips are very nearly complete as they stand; later scientists have been unable to add very much, a tribute to his thorough and systematic work. As early as 1858 on his first voyage to Spitsbergen, he had found fossil plants from the Tertiary age. He made his most important finds on his 1868 voyage to Spitsbergen where he collected as many as 130 petrified plant species from this period. He also made finds from even more distant times, from the Devonian age, 400—350 million years ago.

The researches of Heer and Nathorst established beyond all doubt the importance of palaeobotany in solving the problem of the earth's former climate. Their research showed that the Scandinavian peninsula and even Greenland had once had almost tropical climates. In 1870 Nordenskiöld found petrified tropical ferns in Greenland. In 1883 he found chalk layers from the time of the dinosaurs, fruit and leaves from the breadfruit tree and walnuts from the later Tertiary age. On the other hand, it was possible to prove from the material collected on the Vega expedition from Japan that there the climate had once been colder. Palaeobotany undoubtedly occupies a special position in the scientific analysis of material which Nordenskiöld gathered on his journeys.

The papers published in the Vega expedition series show that other departments of the National Museum of Natural History besides the mineralogical department benefited from Nordenskiöld's expeditions. However, as the present catalogues of the museum are organised systematically to meet the requirements of scientific research, the full significance of Nordenskiöld's contribution is not readily apparent. (9)

Other Collections

Nordenskiöld left a large number of manuscripts which are preserved in the library of the Royal Swedish Academy of Sciences in Stockholm. The papers include manuscripts dealing with his scientific work, plans for expeditions, log books, and a valuable and large collection of letters and other manuscripts. They are the key to the understanding of his scientific work and his private life.

The Royal Library in Stockholm also holds Nordenskiöld's fairly large collection of Japanese literature. Nordenskiöld bought these books when he spent September and October 1879 in Japan on his homeward journey from the Vega expedition. His aim was to obtain a representative Japanese library, and he succeeded in obtaining the services of a young Japanese scientist who spoke French and who bought books on Nordenskiöld's behalf. The collection comprises some 1050 titles and 5500 volumes. Of these, 170 are historical works, 161 about Buddhism and education, 137 poetry, 76 geography and maps, 68 natural history, 18 dictionaries and grammars, 9 bibliographies and similar works; the remainder is almost equally divided among the other branches of literature. The collection was in its time perhaps the most important single library of Japanese literature in western Europe. Japan had only two years previously re-opened its doors to the outside world. Nordenskiöld wrote to his wife about the purchase of this library on 8th October 1879, saying that the books had been extremely difficult to obtain, and had been bought almost one by one. Nearly all of them had been written before Japan's ports had been opened to foreign trade; he added: 'It would be a good thing if some librarian were to start learning Japanese soon.' Oscar Dickson financed a printed catalogue of the library as early as 1883; but because the compiler of the catalogue lived in Paris and could not visit Stockholm, it has not proved satisfactory. A new catalogue is now in preparation. (10)

A second collection, the *Nordenskiöldska biblioteket,* is in the library of Åbo Academy in Finland. The Academy received this as a gift from Mme Henriette Nordenskiöld in 1960, and the greater part of the collection consists of the library which Adolf Erik Nordenskiöld himself used when he was a young man on the family estate, Frugård in Mäntsälä, although it also contains some more recent literature. The inscriptions on the flyleaves of the books show that the collection was assembled over several generations of the Nordenskiölds and reflects the family's interest in the natural sciences. This library comprises some 2400 volumes.

Nordenskiöld gave the Ethnographical Museum, which was then one of the institutions attached to the Royal Academy of Sciences, some remarkable material collected on his expeditions. He brought back numerous Eskimo artefacts from his trips to Greenland. There is no record of his having brought anything back from Spitsbergen, but this is hardly surprising. On the other hand, the Vega expedition acquired for the museum some extremely interesting material from the tribes of northern Asia, the Samoyeds and the Chukchi as well as the Alaskan Eskimos. The number of articles given to the museum by Nordenskiöld rose to well over a thousand, but of course this number says nothing of the value of the collection. The Chukchi artefacts are especially beautiful; they were gathered while the Vega was wintering in Chukchi territory outside Pitlekaj in 1878—9. The only comparable collections of material concerning this geographical area are in the Soviet Union and the United States, but these are much more recent than the collection in the Ethnographical Museum in Stockholm. (11)

The History of Geography and Cartography

Nordenskiöld's extensive geographical and cartographic library is of course in itself a monument to his interest in geography and the history of discovery. Above all, he was interested in how man's knowledge of his own planet had gradually grown, and so he was especially interested in those writers and cartographers who had extended the frontiers of this knowledge. Although he himself had no formal training in history, and although this lack of formal training was apparent in much of his work, he believed that the study of history was important, as his close colleague Dr E.W. Dahlgren has written: 'He believed that the great discoveries, and the victorious progress of civilised nations across the world, cannot be fully understood without the knowledge of the conceptions of land and sea prevalent in earlier times, and of the groping attempts of our forefathers to visualise these conceptions on maps.' (12)

Before he began to direct his attention towards the history of geography and cartography, Nordenskiöld had taken a passing and general interest in the history of the natural sciences. Although he spoke scornfully of 'scientists' dogmas', he showed an astonishing loyalty and admiration for the great Swedish natural scientists of the past. There was very little research into the history of science in Sweden in Nordenskiöld's time; perhaps because of the great break-through in the natural sciences, the new generation of scientists did not want to admit their debt to their predecessors. Nordenskiöld was one of the first who wished to place scientists of the past in the context of the advances of their own time, and to ascribe to them their proper recognition. As early as 1858, he had published a paper about the uplift of land in Stockholm, and drawn attention to earlier research on the same subject from the time of Swedenborg and Celsius. He was especially interested in the history of chemistry in Sweden, and gave a series of public lectures on the subject in 1861—2. His main interest, however, was in the work of Carl Wilhelm Scheele, an apothecary who died in the small town of Köping in central Sweden in 1876 and who was one of the pioneers of modern chemistry. As early as 1862 Nordenskiöld published a short monograph on Scheele and in 1877, in a longish article, 'Ett blad ur de svenska naturvetenskapernas historia' [A leaf from the history of Swedish natural science], he dwelt on Scheele at some length before going on to describe the natural history of Sweden's 'age of freedom', the eighteenth century, which he admired greatly. (13)

In 1886, as a centenary tribute, Nordenskiöld published some notes and correspondence which were preserved in the archives of the Royal Swedish Academy of Sciences together with a thoroughly prepared introduction and biography of Scheele. It was published simultaneously in Swedish and German. Later Nordenskiöld took an active part in campaigning for a memorial statue to Scheele.

In his first years in Sweden, Nordenskiöld gave most of his time to research in his own field, but after he had embarked on his arctic expeditions, he began to read the literature concerning the nature and earlier explorations of these regions. His interest in history grew only gradually. In the report of the 1864 expedition there is a short history of theories about the shape of the world, going back to Herodotus and Aristotle. The same report includes some important, and until then unpublished information about early Norwegian whaling trips in the Arctic Ocean. This was typical of Nordenskiöld: he often valued the experiences of uneducated seamen and travellers above the theories of scientists. Belief in authority and all kinds of narrow learning were foreign to him. For instance, when he was preparing for an expedition to the North, he was always ready to talk with the fishermen and whalers of the Arctic Ocean, to listen to their practical advice on sailing, wind and ice conditions, - routes, suitable seasons and so on. In the same way, he studied literature concerning expeditions made in past centuries, sifting out every grain of useful knowledge and adding it to what he had learned from other sources. It was not enough for him to know how far and by what routes earlier explorers had sailed; he also wanted to know where they had failed, and why.

Nordenskiöld showed some knowledge of the history of exploration in the report of the 1870 Spitsbergen expedition, but his knowledge reached its full flower in the plan for the Vega expedition which he presented to King Oscar II. Sven Hedin thought it the best that Nordenskiöld had ever written (14), and we can agree that he could not have written it without the most comprehensive knowledge of earlier literature. The story of the Vega expedition was published in two volumes as *The Voyage of the Vega round Asia and Europe* (London 1881: Macmillan and Co.) and contains an almost complete account of earlier discoveries and the pioneer explorers of those regions. Nordenskiöld himself, in reply to critical comment, later admitted that there had been some gaps in his knowledge of the relevant literature at that time; on the same occasion, however, he remarked emphatically more than once that he had assembled a more extensive collection of books about the exploration of Siberia and published in the Western languages than most of his predecessors had ever had at their disposal. (15) According to the expert opinion of T.E. Armstrong, '*The Voyage of the Vega,* I think, is still one of the best books written about polar exploration. Nordenskiöld combines the explorer and scholar in a way that I think nobody else does — with the exception of Nansen, his junior and in some ways his spiritual heir. *The Voyage of the Vega* is packed with historical information of the greatest interest, which was not available elsewhere at the time.' (16)

Nordenskiöld had not intended to write any very extensive general account of the Vega expedition, but his publishers made the project so financially attractive that he finally agreed. But he did not want to write an adventure story, and in fact there had not been very much excitement on the expedition, as everything had gone according to plan, except perhaps for the wintering in Pitlekaj, although preparations had been made for that eventuality too. 'So admirable were all the preparations that chance rarely entered into the calculations.' (17) Nordenskiöld considered a journalistic presentation vulgar and refused to agree to it; on the other hand, he considered a 'popular' account perfectly respectable from a scientific point of view. He tried to make his account more interesting to the layman by including some history of previous expeditions. He also considered it his duty to do honour to his predecessors. Nordenskiöld gave the accounts of uneducated seamen, labourers and whaling men a prominent place in his book; he was concerned only with pioneers, with those who had advanced further than other men. Of course, he also gave scientists their due, but this was one of the respects in which the book was criticised the most severely. Nordenskiöld had his answer ready: the work was not intended for a scientific audience. For scientists there was the extensive scientific report of the Vega expedition, in five volumes and some 3000 pages. But *The Voyage of the Vega,* too, is scientifically respectable in that its historical sections are based on a thorough knowledge of the literature, and that the source of every quotation is acknowledged and every reference identified. Some material appeared for the first time in this book: for instance, the portrait of the great English explorer Sir Hugh Willoughby was published from an authentic original for the first time.

Nordenskiöld's practical interest in cartography emerged on his first expeditions to Spitsbergen in 1861 and 1864. He and Dr N. Dunér made a map of Spitsbergen as the result of new surveys, which was published in 1865. An English map which had appeared in 1860 (Admiralty Chart No. 2751) had been used on the expeditions, but it was somewhat inadequate. Nordenskiöld's and Dunér's map was used as the basis for all subsequent maps, and despite its deficiencies was the most reliable chart of the area until the appearance of a more complete map in 1898. On the expeditions to the Yenisey in 1875 and 1876, Nordenskiöld made a new map of the Yenisey delta — to the great joy of Russian geographers. On the Vega expedition of 1879—80, Nordenskiöld's party examined the whole of the northern coastline of Siberia, and made numerous amendments to the existing map.

Several facsimiles of ancient maps of the polar regions are included as appendices to *The Voyage of the Vega.* Of these, it is worth mentioning a map of northern Europe from Ptolemy's *Cosmography,* published in Ulm in 1482, Jakob Ziegler's *Schondia* of 1532, published in Strasburg, Olaus Magnus' map of northern Europe, which appeared in the Basle edition of his historical work of 1567, J.I. Pontanus' map of Barents' third expedition, published in Amsterdam in 1611, and Isaac Mass' map, Russian in origin, of the Arctic Ocean, published in Holland in 1612.

In 1882 Nordenskiöld published at his own expense a facsimile edition of a thirteenth-century French manuscript, which is preserved in the Royal Library in Stockholm, and describes the journeys of Marco Polo. He published this facsimile in a limited edition of 250 copies, which he used to exchange with other collectors in return for new items for his own private library. In 1883, in association with an international congress of Americanists in Copenhagen, he brought out a facsimile edition of three pre-Columbian maps. In 1884 he published in the periodical *Ymer,* a paper entitled, 'Om en märklig globkarta från början af sextonde seklet' [Concerning an important globe from the beginning of the sixteenth centu_ _. (19) As he claimed, it contained one of the oldest extant world maps, which showed fairly clearly the main features of South America before Magellan. He had bought this map, which was designed to be stuck on to a globe, from a bouquiniste in Rome.

Nordenskiöld did not begin the systematic collection of maps until about 1883. He must have made a conscious decision at that time to concentrate on cartographic, rather than on scientific, research. His first works dealing directly with cartographic history appeared in 1883, and thereafter he published a new work on the subject almost every year. Curiously he had at his disposal at that time the entire vast collection of mineral samples which he had brought back from his northern expeditions — there must be an explanation, unknown to us, of why he chose cartography instead of examining these. One can of course venture various hypotheses, but there seems to have been a definite reason why Nordenskiöld turned from mineralogy and expeditions to cartographic research; however, it appears to be clear that when an end came to the opportunities to travel he turned to cartography as the branch of knowledge which most readily offered the broad perspectives and scope which were so essential to a man of his temperament and which exploration had provided. It is true that he advanced a great number of theories which did not stand up to critical analysis; this shows that, on the one hand, historical cartography was a difficult area in which little basic research had been done, while on the other, it illustrates the disadvantage Nordenskiöld suffered through his lack of formal training in history. Alongside his cartographic interests, he continued to develop his theories concerning the origin and evolution of the world, despite the fact that he encountered great opposition: so much indeed that in the end his critics ceased even to write about his theories. (20) Given that Nordenskiöld was driven to make his explorations by a desire to find answers to questions about the natural history of the entire world, cartography can perhaps be seen as an extension of these interests; it is difficult to believe that a man as strong-willed as Nordenskiöld would shift from the natural sciences into historical cartography without a good reason. At all events, he made for himself a brilliant career as a cartographic historian which lasted for almost twenty years, but he continued the collection of minerals alongside his cartographic work.

As he added to his library of old maps and prepared his various monographs, Nordenskiöld found that there was no systematic treatment of the history of cartography either in terms of published maps or cartographic literature or of mankind's attempts to improve his understanding of his planet by exploration, or of the effects of new discoveries on the cartographic picture men had of the world. Jomard and Santarém had published a facsimile collection of old maps, but this was without any kind of commentary; Lelewel's history of mediaeval geography was an enormous, unsystematic collection of facts with no attempt at chronological or scientific organisation. At this time, Nordenskiöld already had in his possession a unique private library. The reasons for the publication of his Facsimile Atlas are set out succinctly in its preface, but its aims appear still more clearly in a letter he sent to John Scott Keltie, who was secretary of the Royal Geographic Society from 1892 to 1915, on 14th September 1888. He wrote:

'For researches in the history of cartography, I have since several years become a passionate collector of old maps and I have by assiduity and perseverance succeeded in forming a large, in certain respects (for example as to the editions of Ptolemy) almost complete private collection of printed maps from the fifteenth and sixteenth century. When I, guided by the cartographical material thus collected, studied the history of geography, I found that even the most eminent authors never had any opportunity personally to examine many of the most important maps from the incunable period of cartography, or they only accidentally had seen them at a visit to one of the few public libraries where larger suites of such works are to be found. I have, for example, never seen mentioned in the geographical literature the first engraved modern (not Ptolemain) map of France (c. 1478), the first copper-plate modern map of Germany or of Scandinavia (1507 — wood-cut maps of these countries exist from 1482 and 1493 and are frequently cited), the first modern engraved map of England (wood-cut from 1513). It is much written about Vasco da Gama but as far as I know, no author mentions maps printed early in the sixteenth century, very rich in legends and based on coast-surveys during his first and second voyage. None of the many authors on the Italian or Catalan portolans seems to have known that a portolano from the beginning of the fourteenth century was engraved in copper 1595 to serve as a chart for the navigation in the Mediterranean Sea and that legends from this map of 1327 still are found almost word by word unaltered on the sea charts from the last century. The only exception in this respect is the diligently collected and well-known cartographic literature on America. I suppose, however, that relatively few geographers had the opportunity at their leisure to examine the important map of Stobnicza (1512), the *Nova Franzia* by Zalteri (1566), the maps in Hackluyt's *Petrus Martyr* (1587), or the edition of Mercator's double-cordiform map published in Rome c. 1560 by Lafreri. Evidently this depends on the extreme scarcity of these old geographical documents and the impossibility to get an effective acquaintance with them without being able to examine and re-examine them leisurely at one's own writing desk. This has induced me to publish a Facsimile Atlas of the most important printed maps from the incunable period of cartography, so far different from the celebrated but unfortunately unfinished works of Jomard and Santarém, that whereas these authors especially reproduced old manuscript maps, my aim will be to give as complete and systematic a collection as possible of old printed maps.' (21)

The Facsimile Atlas contains 165 facsimile maps. The collection starts with the 27 maps which were contained in the different editions of Ptolemy before new maps began to be added; Nordenskiöld's facsimile is based on the 1490 Rome edition. These maps are followed by other maps, many of them new ones which were added to the later editions of Ptolemy, but also maps of Ortelius, Mercator and Apianus. 80 of these maps appear in their original size, 85 reduced.

The *Facsimile Atlas* has been compared, in its own field, to the Vega expedition. It was an epoch-making publication in the science of cartography. Nordenskiöld gives a thorough account, based on the information available to him, of the Ptolemaic tradition of mapmaking, and a detailed description of all known editions of Ptolemy; he also purges from contemporary catalogues some of the editions which never actually appeared, but whose existence had been conjectured on the basis of printing errors in dates and second-hand sources, and identifies the publications which do not belong to the Ptolemaic tradition. He describes how the original Ptolemaic view of the world grew as new maps were added to new editions. The first maps of the New World and Africa, as well as the newly-discovered maps of Asia, have a chapter of their own, as do the cartographic projections of the fourteenth and early fifteenth centuries. The end of the age of early cartography in 1520—50 is the subject of a thorough examination, and the last chapter of the work is devoted to the dawn of the age of modern cartography, which began with the publication of Abraham Ortelius' *Theatrum Orbis Terrarum* and the passing of the Ptolemaic tradition into history. A more important representative of the new style than Ortelius was Gerard Mercator.

The facsimiles were printed using the latest techniques. Nordenskiöld made extremely rigorous technical demands, and Dr E.W. Dahlgren, who supervised the printing of the maps, was very experienced and gave the project his scrupulous attention. Thanks to them, the Facsimile Atlas still stands as a basic reference work for the study of cartographic history, and is still considered by scholars to be an extremely accurate facsimile edition. The technical standard of the edition is so high that it has been possible to issue a reprint which itself, though a reprint of a reprint, is an edition of outstanding quality. The Facsimile Atlas continues to be highly regarded by cartographic historians and to provide an important source of bibliographical detail.

The Facsimile Atlas was received with enthusiasm verging on ecstasy. Cartographic historians were overjoyed to have at their disposal a collection of the most important maps in an edition of a hitherto unattained standard. There was much criticism of individual points in Nordenskiöld's text, however, but this was only natural for a pioneer work in so vast and difficult a field. (22)

In the Atlas, Nordenskiöld describes the history of printed maps. There are a great many manuscript maps in the libraries of Europe, but few in Sweden. All the same, Nordenskiöld thought it imperative to extend his cartographic investigations to unpublished sea-charts. It was impossible for him to assemble a collection of manuscript maps as he had of printed maps, so he was forced to travel widely to study important maps in the great libraries of Europe. He also acquired the information and material he needed through correspondence and by employing paid assistants in various parts of Europe. Nordenskiöld considered this work all the more important because the material was so widely dispersed, and no one had any real idea of what existed. The result of this research was an even more monumental work than the Facsimile Atlas: *Periplus. An Essay on the Early History of Charts and Sailing Directions.* Stockholm 1897.

Periplus is an account of the hand-drawn maps of the sea-faring nations of southern Europe. It starts with the earliest maps, and includes the early history of printed sea-charts up to the middle of the eighteenth century. Nordenskiöld's own text is supplemented in the same way as in the Facsimile Atlas by facsimiles of the relevant maps. Sixty appear in their original size, one hundred reduced. A still more advanced printing technique was used for this work, allowing the different shades of the coloured sea-charts to be reproduced in a black-and-white facsimile.

Periplus is, as a source book, at least as important as the Facsimile Atlas. Its subject is considerably more difficult, and Nordenskiöld himself explained that his presentation could not attempt to be complete since the necessary materials were deposited in many different libraries and not even the largest of these had published their catalogues of manuscript sea-charts, or portolano maps. In his examination of the history of portolano maps, Nordenskiöld encountered major problems of research, and also put forward and 'proved' a great many hypotheses which even the cartographers of his own day, including his former colleague Dr E.W. Dahlgren, could not accept. Nordenskiöld's theory that the basis of portolano maps might have been the so-called 'normal portolano', drawn by a scholastic, Raimundus Lullus, born in Mallorca in 1235, was also rejected. Nordenskiöld also differed from prevailing opinion in his theory of the length of the portolan mile. The theory was shown to be wrong in his own lifetime, but has been the centre of controversy in more recent years. (23) Nor did his theory that the portolanos were of Catalan origin receive general approval; experts drew attention to the fact that the Catalans were not the teachers of the Italians, but their pupils. His theory that the portolano maps were made without a knowledge of the compass was also proved to be a mere hypothesis, and he gained only little support for his general theory of the Byzanto-Scandinavian origin of maps of the countries of the North. But he held to this theory, in spite of all criticism, until his death.

Although Nordenskiöld's contemporaries were often severe in their criticism of points of detail in Periplus, this did not obscure their appreciation of the great importance of the work. Thus, in spite of everything, the

Englishman C. Raymond Beazley wrote: 'But on nearly all matters which properly concern the later Mediaeval, and especially the Portolano, cartography, no student can afford to be without Baron Nordenskiöld's last work. It is even more essential than his Facsimile Atlas.' (24)

This is not the place for a thorough assessment of the scientific importance of the Facsimile Atlas and Periplus. While both works were epoch-making, it would be strange if no later study had been able to amplify and correct statements which appear in them, and of course new material has come to light since their appearance. Their importance lies in the fact that they prepared the way for subsequent cartographic research and provided a major corpus of material for this work, a clear proof of which is the recent publication of new reprints. (25) The assessment of more recent time was stated succinctly by the well-known cartographic historian Dr R.A. Skelton. Concurring with Leo Bagrow's affirmation that the works 'will never be superseded,' he continues, 'That is a remarkable fact, and perhaps it is rather a bold thing to say about books published over seventy years ago, but it is difficult to see that a good deal of this work need ever be done again, even if many of the conclusions drawn by Nordenskiöld himself no longer hold water. This is less because Nordenskiöld himself found the right answers to problems raised by Renaissance cartography, than because he asked the right questions. He was able to do this, first of all, by his genius as collector and collator of the materials for study; secondly by his exploration ... of the resources of photography and photolithography to assemble a corpus of materials for comparative study; and thirdly, by his scrupulous inductive analysis of the materials. — But the form in which he postulated these questions and the terminology he introduced still provide the framework in which they are and must be debated today.' (26)

Nordenskiöld's second career, in cartography, was as brilliant as his first in mineralogy, and in his twenty years as a cartographic historian his achievements as a collector of an extraordinarily complete library of printed maps and geographical literature as well as those as a bibliographer were unparalleled. Studies of Nordenskiöld's cartographic research have not generally discussed the problems associated with the publication of his two major works. The volumes were expensive: 170 Swedish Crowns is the equivalent of 615 U.S. dollars in present-day values, and at that time the sum would have purchased four bulls in Finland. For this reason, Nordenskiöld did not imagine that even all the major libraries would be able to buy copies of his works. A surprising fact is that Nordenskiöld had to act as his own publisher and alone bear the financial risk. He wrote to his friend Leo Mechelin in Helsinki on 22th November 1889, 'I am my own publisher, even if the Firma Beijer appears to be my publisher. Beijer has explained to me that it is very creditable to have been able to trace and collect such a large library of old maps; that, as he understands it, it is no doubt even more creditable to have written a book on the subject, but that the true criterion of the success of the venture is to be able to sell the books profitably.' Only the name of the distributor — John E. Bergsjö, Nybrogatan 6 B, Stockholm — appears on the title page of Periplus; Beijer's name is absent. Nordenskiöld wrote to Mechelin about Periplus. 'No expense has been spared in the attempt to produce a book of as high a standard as possible. Visits to great libraries, large photographs, generous fees have caused the cost of the publication to rise to 37,000 Crowns. It will cost at least as much as Facsimile Atlas.' The sum Nordenskiöld mentioned is equivalent today to 133,000 U.S. dollars, so it is not surprising that Nordenskiöld used all his contacts to secure buyers for his books. He had calculated that he would have to sell 300 copies of the Facsimile Atlas to cover his costs; he needed to sell still more copies of Periplus. During Mechelin's term as a senator, he arranged for the Finnish state to buy twenty copies of the Facsimile Atlas; the list of institutions which were allotted copies is still extant. Sweden could not but follow this example. The same happened when Periplus appeared, although Mechelin was no longer a senator. (27)

Examinations of the archives have not yet revealed the size of the editions of these works. In any case, the Facsimile Atlas was sold out by the time of Nordenskiöld's death, and there were only a couple of dozen unsold copies of Periplus, some of them unbound.

Apart from the Facsimile Atlas and Periplus, Nordenskiöld's most important publications were:

Om bröderna Zenos resor och de äldsta kartor över Norden. Med Claudii Clavi karta och beskrifning öfver norden i facsimile [On the travels of the Brothers Zeno and the oldest maps of the North. With the map of Claudius Clavus and his description of the North in facsimile]. Stockholm 1883. 53 pp., 1 facs. (Kungliga Vetenskapsakademiens Bihang, Vol. 8:2). Also included in the book: *Studier och forskningar föranledda af mina resor i höga norden* [Studies and researches arising from my travels in the far North]. Stockholm 1883.

Trois cartes précolombiennes représentant une partie de l'Amérique (Groenland). Fac-similes présentés au Congrès internationale des Américanistes à Copenhague 1883. Stockholm 1883.

'Om en märklig globkarta från början af sextonde seklet' [A remarkable globe map of the sixteenth century] in *Ymer* 4 (1884) pp. 167—175. For further details of the English translation see reference 19.

'Den första på verkliga iakttagelser grundade karta öfver norra Asien' [The first map of Northern Asia based on proper observations] in *Ymer* 7 (1887) pp. 133—144.

'Om ett aftryck från XV:de seklet af den i metall graverade verldskarta, som förvarats i kardinal Stephan Borgias museum i Velletri' [On a fifteenth-century offprint of the map of the world engraved in metal which is preserved in the Museum of Cardinal Stephan Borgia at Velletri] in *Ymer* 11 (1891) pp. 83—92.

Bidrag till Nordens äldsta kartografi vid

fyrahundraårsfesten till minne af nya verldens upptäckt, utgifna af Svenska sällskapet för antropologi och geografi [Contribution to the oldest cartography of the North in commemoration of the four-hundredth anniversary of the discovery of the New World, published by the Swedish Anthropological and Geographical Society]. Stockholm 1892. 3 pp., 9 maps.

Jemförelser af legender på portolaner [Comparisons of legends on portolanos]. Stockholm 1894. 64 pp.

'Om det inflytande MARCO POLOS reseberättelser utöfvat på GASTALDIS kartor öfver Asien' in *Ymer* 19 (1899) pp. 33—43. English translation: "The influence of the 'Travels of MARCO POLO' on JACOBO GASTALDI'S maps of Asia" in *Geographical Journal* 13 (1899) pp. 396—406.

'Randteckningar i gamla handskrifter af DATIS La sfera [Marginal notes in old manuscripts of DATI's La Sfera] in *Ymer* 20 (1900) pp. 15—23. Italian translation: 'Dei dissegni marginali negli antichi manoscritti della Sfera del DATI' in *La Bibliofilia* 3 (1901) pp. 49—55.

Nordenskiöld's Library and its Formation

Nordenskiöld's maps and atlases are only a part of his total extant library. In all that has been written and said about his library, too much attention has perhaps been given to his unique maps and atlases. His collection of books on geographical history, classics of travel literature, world-famous ethnographic works containing rare engravings, bibliographies and other scientific literature, are indisputably as important as the maps and atlases. It is especially necessary to stress the significance of this part of his library so that its omission from the present catalogue will not lead to its being overlooked.

Another observation which should be made here is that the present Nordenskiöld Library is not precisely the same as the one which Nordenskiöld owned during his lifetime. The present library contains scientific works: all other literature has been removed from it. It is probable that Nordenskiöld himself removed these books when he began to arrange the sale of his library. Fiction, for example, is completely absent — Nordenskiöld is known to have bought many works of fiction from many different countries — and so are general works on history, art and several other subjects.

The history of the formation of Nordenskiöld's geographical and cartographic library would itself make an interesting and extensive subject of study. Nordenskiöld was systematic enough to keep all his book bills, and there is reason to believe that nothing essential is missing from this collection. His correspondence also survives illuminating the extent of his contacts with booksellers throughout Europe and also containing valuable information about his contacts with individuals through whom he both obtained books and supplemented the bibliographical and other information he needed in his cartographic work. The place and date of purchase is inscribed in many of the books. Some short articles about the formation of Nordenskiöld's library have appeared, but a thorough study has yet to be made. (28) On this occasion it is possible only to give a short general account, and to hope that we shall have a more exhaustive treatment in the near future. It would illuminate the development of Nordenskiöld's research and would be invaluable in shedding light on the research which occupied the last twenty-five years of his life.

Nordenskiöld had been interested in books since his youth; at home, he had been in charge of the family library. His book bills show that he began to buy books very soon after he arrived in Stockholm in 1858. The first foreign invoices date from 1877, when he was preparing for his exploration of the North-East Passage. In Sweden, Nordenskiöld used Samson and Wallin's bookshop (now Nordiska Bokhandeln) and Klemming's antiquarian bookshop. He bought only a moderate twenty to thirty books a year, and there were few rare editions among them. He began to buy accounts of explorations, as well as books about his own subject, relatively early on. In 1877 the number of books he bought increased dramatically: 235 works, according to the invoices from Swedish bookshops — ten times his average annual amount in previous years — as well as 45 from Holland, mainly old books about America. After the Vega expedition, when he was working on *The Voyage of the Vega* in 1880—81, he continued to purchase on a large scale and extended his contacts to booksellers in Germany, Italy, Denmark and England.

On the Vega expedition, Nordenskiöld took with him a large library containing about 1,000 volumes. The source of these is not entirely clear; it is probable that at least some of the books were on loan from libraries such as that of the Royal Swedish Academy of Sciences, and the Royal Library. It is also clear that a large number of them were from Nordenskiöld's private collection; inscribed on the flyleaves of some of his books are the words 'Vega 1878—1880'. A detailed scrutiny of Nordenskiöld's books would undoubtedly clarify our picture of the library he had on the *Vega*, as well as of the extent of his personal library at that time. The following examples of books bearing the above inscription indicate the direction of Nordenskiöld's interest at the time:

WILLIAM COXE, *Account of the Russian Discoveries between Asia and America.* London 1780.
ROBERT KERR, *A General History and Collection of Voyages and Travels Arranged in Systematic Order* 1—18. Edinburgh 1811—1824.
OTTO VON KOTZEBUE, *Entdeckungs-Reise in die Süd-See und nach der Berings-Strasse.* 1—3. Weimar 1821.
A. FR. PREVOOT, *Histoire générale des voyages.* 1—17. Paris & Amsterdam 1746—1761.
MARTIN SAUER, *An Account of a Geographical and Astronomical Expedition to the Northern Parts of Russia ... performed by Commodore Joseph Billings in the Years 1785 to 1794.* London 1802.

In May 1880 Nordenskiöld wrote to his friend Professor August Ahlqvist in Helsinki asking him to send him all that had been written, in Finnish as well as Swedish, about Ahlqvist's journeys among the Ostyaks and Voguls in Siberia, and about the expeditions of M.A. Castrén, Georg August Wallin and Henrik Holmberg. He was of course prepared to pay for the books, and wanted to have as complete as possible a collection of works by these Finnish travellers in Siberia — 'for I need them for my account of the Vega expedition, and I have also in recent years become an extremely enthusiastic collector of geographical literature.' (29)

This letter shows that Nordenskiöld's interest in collecting geographical and travel literature dates from about the mid 1870s. It also shows that, before the Vega Expedition, he did not possess all the books that he considered necessary for his purposes, and which he used in his description of the expedition. This explains the large number of purchases which his invoices show to have been made after his return. Furthermore Nordenskiöld also had to rely on the collections of large libraries when he was writing the account of the Vega expedition, and here he found an efficient assistant in the librarian of the Academy of Sciences, Dr E.W. Dahlgren, who was responsible for checking the quotations and the references to source materials.

While returning from the Vega expedition, Nordenskiöld had already been interested enough in books to stop at several Mediterranean ports to visit the antiquarian bookshops in search of some of the books he wanted. He had occasionally bought maps at the end of the 1870s but in 1880 most of the books he acquired were travel accounts and works on the history of geography; the shift from geographical literature to maps is not really very great, especially considering the fact, for instance, that Ptolemy's work was a geographical description. As the story of the Vega expedition began to earn Nordenskiöld money, he was able to buy books on a grander scale. His publisher, Macmillan & Co., paid him the then unheard sum of £1,000. Sven Hedin recalls that the income from the Swedish edition reached the sum of 100,000 Crowns.

After the Vega expedition, Nordenskiöld travelled widely on the continent and had the opportunity of working in the great libraries of Europe. Although he enjoyed special privileges and was allowed to consult, and even to borrow books to which he did not have access in Sweden, he found it impossible to do serious work in this way. He produced his best work at his own desk in the peace of his own home, with all the material he needed constantly before him.

For nearly twenty years, from 1883 until his death, Nordenskiöld concentrated his efforts on the systematic acquisition of cartographic and geographical literature. His booksellers' invoices show that in the years 1858—1901 Nordenskiöld spent the equivalent of 130,000 dollars in present-day values simply on books and manuscripts. But this is undoubtedly less than the total sum, as there is no record of purchases Nordenskiöld made from private individuals. His sharp eye scrutinized every possible European collection, and he had contacts with 94 bookshops; of the extent of his personal contacts and of the contacts with institutions, monasteries, museums and similar bodies we have little knowledge.

Yet another source of Nordenskiöld's books was exchange, using for instance his beautiful facsimile edition of the account of Marco Polo's travels mentioned above. His invoices also show some occasions of his having exchanged copies of the facsimile with booksellers, although more often he exchanged it with individuals and libraries which were not free to buy and sell. Hence the printing costs of this facsimile edition must also be taken into account in estimating the sum he spent on books. To a much lesser extent Nordenskiöld used the 1889 Facsimile Atlas and the 1897 Periplus for exchange — since he had to try to recover his investment in the publication of these. On 1st April 1900, for example, he wrote in English to the Asiatic Society of Japan about certain volumes of the Society's transactions which, he had just noticed, were missing from his library. 'Would you be so kind,' he asks, 'to help me to complete my collection of Your transactions by sending me the wanting volumes, I shall have the pleasure to send to the Society in exchange my Periplus, containing two or three hundred reproductions of maps from fifteenth and sixteenth centuries. Several of them illustrate the cartographical history of Japan *from the European point of view,* and the old cartography of Asia from Ptolemy to the commencement of the XVIIth century.'

In his description of his library, written in French, probably in 1899, Nordenskiöld explains that he had started by attempting to assemble as complete a collection as possible of the geographical and cartographic literature which had appeared before 1570. (31) 1570 was decisive as the year which saw the appearance of Abraham Ortelius' *Theatrum Orbis Terrarum* and marked the beginning of a new era in map-making. Gradually Nordenskiöld extended his interests to the collection of seventeenth-century literature.

Although Nordenskiöld had had no formal training in the study of history, as E.W. Dahlgren, subsequently National Librarian of Sweden, reminds us in his 1902 review of Nordenskiöld as a historical cartographer, his collector's instinct and his talent for organisation guided him in the right direction. (32) One of the most important parts of his library consists of bibliographies, printed library catalogues, works on the history of science and learning, with the aid of which he knew what he had to look for. Another revealing section of his library is his collection of antiquarian booksellers' catalogues. He held the catalogues of the Amsterdam firm Frederik Muller & Co. in such high esteem that he had them bound in half-leather bindings, with his initials tooled in gold on the spines and his own ex libris inside. Of his other catalogues, only a small number of Leo Olschki's are accorded the same honour. Nordenskiöld went through antiquarian book lists making careful notes; unless he could visit the bookshop in question personally, he was obliged to buy all his books through catalogues. Once his reputation as a buyer of books had spread through Europe, together with the knowledge that if he was really interested in a book, he would not haggle over the price, a great many antiquarian booksellers began, unsolicited, to send him their catalogues and to inform him of books which they thought might be of interest. He acquired hundreds of valuable works in this way. On the other hand, he was annoyed by booksellers who sent him books for which he had not asked; a draft of one of his letters contains the following unequivocal statement: 'Ich kann nicht erlauben dass man mir Bücher per porto zur Ansicht zusendet — ich habe keine Zeit dieselben zurück zu senden — und es kann ja nur ausnahmsweise vorkommen dass ich die Bücher behalte...' On the other hand, Nordenskiöld paid for books he had ordered by return of post, and this made him valued as a good customer. It is clear that the Facsimile Atlas was studied closely in by the antiquarian booksellers of Europe; many of the offers of items Nordenskiöld received remarked that the map in question had not been mentioned in the Facsimile Atlas or that he had indicated a map as being from a source other than his own collection.

Nordenskiöld always knew what the books he ordered should contain. It was not always possible to know from the catalogues what condition a book was in, or even whether it was the book he wanted; notes on the invoices show that books which did not tally with what he had ordered were returned to the bookseller. On the other hand, his library contains defective editions of many rare works; he was prepared to buy incomplete editions of works which his library lacked. If he later saw another incomplete edition of the same work for sale, he would buy it if it supplemented the copy he already possessed, and if a complete edition of the same work later became available, he would buy that without giving up the incomplete editions already in his library. This explains the duplicates in his collection, especially among the incunabula.

The table below summarises the sums in present-day Finn marks which Nordenskiöld spent on books from eight different countries (U.S. dollar = 3.8 Finn marks)

Sweden	150,000
Italy	111,000
Germany	110,000
Holland	62,000
France	27,000
England	19,000
Denmark	6,000
Austria	3,300

The value of books acquired from other sources is less than 1,000 Fmk per country. The large sums Nordenskiöld spent in Sweden are partly explained by the fact that he ordered the major scientific and scholarly serials of the day through local bookshops. Klemming's antiquarian bookshop also acted as an agent for foreign antiquarian booksellers, especially during the 1870s.

Two individual antiquarian booksellers deserve special mention: Frederik Muller & Co. of Amsterdam, and Leo S. Olschki of Venice (and Verona). Nordenskiöld bought exclusively rare books from Muller and sent the bookshop a list of desiderata. Other important bookshops were Francesco Perrella (Naples), E. Dufosse (Paris), Bernard Quaritch (London), Silvio Bocca (Rome), Ludwig Rosenthal (Munich), J. Scheible (Stuttgart), J.A. Stargardt (Berlin), Gennaro Cioffi (Naples), Fr. Casella (Naples), H.H.J. Lynge (Copenhagen), and Ch. Chadenat (Paris).

Yet another source of contemporary materials was gifts. His contemporaries among geographical and cartographic scholars wished to show their respect for the man who was undoubtedly the greatest living expert on the polar regions and the most notable cartographic authority of the day. The dedications in the books — monographs and offprints — make up an impressive record of the esteem their authors felt for Nordenskiöld.

Size and Composition of the Collection

Nordenskiöld's library contains 123 different incunabula, but because many of them are duplicates, the number of volumes is about 140. Nordenskiöld himself estimated that most of the books in his library were printed before 1650, and that it contained about 4,000 maps printed before 1600. All in all, the collection comprises more than 24,000 pre-nineteenth-century maps, most of which are contained in the library's 500 atlases; the remainder are either loose sheets (234), or in geographical works.

To give a simple measure of the size of the collection is difficult, as it is almost impossible to use the same yardstick for all the material. The shelf length of the collection — depending on how, for instance, large atlases are positioned on the shelf — is about 400—430 metres. The catalogue lists 3,870 publications in over 5,000 volumes. A graphic picture of the size of the collection is given by the calculations of Volter Kilpi, who catalogued the library at the beginning of the present century, and deserves to be quoted in full:

'Nordenskiöld collection
On shelves
   a) separate works   7,989 vols*
   b) articles, catalogues
      brochures etc in
      bundles**   75 cardboard boxes
Placed in cupboards and showcases
   a) books and atlases   125 vols
   b) loose maps   234
   c) portfolios   22
Globes   8
Boards   15

Total 8468

I cannot completely guarantee the accuracy of the above figures; in particular, it has not always been easy to decide what constitutes a separate item. For instance, in the case of the unbound collection of *Beskrifningar till Sveriges Geologiska Undersöknings kartblad* [Commentaries on the Map-sheets of the Geological Survey of Sweden], which runs to over a hundred issues, I always arbitrarily counted ten numbers as one volume, and sometimes I found myself compelled to use similar summary procedures in some other cases too.
* There are about 1,000 volumes of small brochures, offprints, antiquarian booksellers' catalogues, etc.
** Should the number of *publications* be counted separately?' (33)

Kilpi does not mention any manuscripts although a few are included in the collection. The manuscript maps are not listed separately. However, the small number of oriental manuscripts in the collection was listed later in an other catalogue. (34)

The table below is Nordenskiöld's estimate of the value of his library at the turn of the century (sums given in Swedish Crowns). The Figures are of interest for the light they throw on Nordenskiöld's own idea of the relative values of the different parts of his library. (35)

'Ptolemy [editions]	30,000
Incunabula	15,000
Am. Vetust.	10,000
Lafreri	20,000
N-ds globe map	7,000
Atlases 200	20,000
Lafreri II	1,000
Munster, Reisch, Apianus, Honter	5,000
Herrera Bordone, Wytflieth	3,000
Hakluyt Cosm. Introd.	3,000
Hakluyt Society	2,000
Loose maps	4,000
Gronlandica, Islandica	2,000
Arctica, Antarctica	2,000
Rossica	3,000
Americana 1551—1650	5,000
Pius Papa, Marco Polo Gesta Dei	2,000
Facsimiles	3,000
Periodicals	3,000
Blaeu, Medina, Condado, Cres.	3,000
Portolanos, Datis	5,000
Scandinese, Caesar, Macrobius, Solinus, Mela	
Strabo	2,000'

It can be seen that Nordenskiöld himself considered five groups to be of considerably greater value than the rest. The most valuable in his own estimation are the lemy editions; it probably remains one of the most important collections in the world. It contains all the editions published in the fifteenth century and all the sixteenth-century editions with the exception of the 1522 Strasburg and the 1547 Basle editions (the latter was not known in Nordenskiöld's time). In the 1525 Strasburg edition, of which Nordenskiöld did have a copy, the maps were printed with one exception (Tabula V Asiae) from the same block as the 1522 edition. Nordenskiöld possessed five of the eight seventeenth-century editions and one of the two eighteenth-century editions, as well as all five nineteenth-century editions. Of the fifty-six known editions which appeared between 1475 and 1883, Nordenskiöld had in his library fifty-one.

Nordenskiöld considered the so-called Lafreri atlas the most valuable individual item in his collection. Antonio Lafreri, a French engraver who had settled in Rome and founded a publishing house, published a large number of individual maps and later collected them into atlases. He often even included items printed in the Netherlands, France and Germany in the same bindings as his own maps, either at his own whim or at the request of his customers. His atlases all had the same engraved title page. Nordenskiöld possessed two Lafreri atlases; Lafreri I, which Nordenskiöld held to be his most valuable single work, contains 72 maps, while Lafreri II contains 50 maps. Before Nordenskiöld, cartographic historians had not realised the importance of Lafreri. Only three or four of his collected atlases were known — two of them in Nordenskiöld's possession and one in the Collegio Romano which he had compared to his own in his Facsimile Atlas. Today over 50 of Lafreri's volumes have come to light. Nordenskiöld drew particular attention to the fact that Lafreri had preserved a great many important individual maps for posterity by including them in his own publications.

The third most important group in Nordenskiöld's list are his atlases, whose number he gives as 200. In fact the collection contains 500 atlases; his list of 200 are those which are not included in other groups. This is not the place for a detailed description of the contents of the atlases; the present catalogue gives an exhaustive survey of all the maps. Nordenskiöld acquired all the important atlases, and he generally tried to ensure that he had at his disposal the *editio princeps* as well as later editions. An almost endless list could be compiled of the cartographers represented in the Collection; they include Apianus, Gastaldi, Ortelius, Waghenaer, Mercator, Blaeu, Homan, to mention only the most important. There is also a large collection of sea-charts by such renowned cartographers as Jansonius, Doncker, Goos and van Keylen.

Most of the incunabula in the collection were acquired for their maps or for their general geographical significance. The Nordenskiöld collection contains many handwritten catalogues of the collection of incunabula, but here again we must satisfy ourselves with listing only a few. The pre-sixteenth-century Ptolemy editions have already been mentioned. The collection also contains the oldest incunabulum in the library of the University of Helsinki: Rabanus Maurus' *De sermonum proprietate, sive Opus de Universo,* printed in Strasburg in 1467. Special curiosities are the earliest known thematic atlases, the *Isolario* of Bartholomeo dali Sonnetti, printed in 1484, and Schedel's *Liber chronicarum* in both the 1493 and 1497 editions.

Nordenskiöld showed a particular interest after 1877 in the earliest literature about the American continent, although in this field he did not try to assemble so complete a collection as that of the atlases. He did not, for instance, try to acquire every edition of works which had appeared in more than one edition, nor did he try to buy all the works in the field; he restricted his purchases to those which had provided new information at the time of publication. Among the bibliographies which he used was Henry Harrisse's *Bibliotheca americana vetustissima (ante 1551).*

Nordenskiöld's acquisitions for all the sections of his library reflect his scientific and bibliographical knowledge and his judgement. The library contains works by all the most important cartographers and, on the basis of the books in his collection, one can conduct an exhaustive examination of the major turning-points in the history of cartography. The collection of ancient cosmography is especially important. Nordenskiöld also collected atlases, accounts of various tribes and nations and books on geography and the history of geography which served principally as text-books in the seventeenth century; he showed a particular interest in pictures of towns, and Bertelli's *Theatrum urbium terrarum* (Venetiis 1509) is among the works in his collection.

The collection of bibliographies in Nordenskiöld's library has already been mentioned. He himself does not include them in his estimate of the value of his library, but to present-day cartographic historians they are of enormous worth.

Nordenskiöld's interest in the northern regions extended to the literature of the inhabitants, and he also collected books from Greenland and Iceland; his library contains 55 volumes in Greenlandese.

The old catalogue of the collection was divided into the following sections (the figures in the right-hand column show the number of catalogued items in each category):

A. Bibliography	1—171
B. Encyclopaedic geography	172—292
C. History of geography	293—738
D. Topography	739—2745
E. Oceanography	2746—2795
F. Cartography	2796—2932
G. Maps and atlases	2933—3599
H. Physical geography	3600—4522
I. Biogeography	4523—4715
K. Anthropological geography	4716—5074
Incunabula	5075—5201
Manuscripts	5202—5215
Oriental prints	5216—5217
Varia	5218—5553
Nordenskiöldiana	5554—5604

These figures are larger than in the present catalogue, as they include geographical and cartographical brochures and offprints as well as the catalogues of prominent antiquarian booksellers. Nevertheless, they give a fairly accurate picture of Nordenskiöld's principal interests.

The Sale of the Collection

Early in 1902, news that the Nordenskiöld Collection was to be sold to Finland began to spread in Sweden. It was considered, for obvious reasons, that to sell the library outside Sweden would be an immense loss. The Nordenskiöld Collection was undoubtedly the best collection of geographical and cartographic literature in Sweden, and Nordenskiöld had purchased most of the books and maps with money he had earned in Sweden. The proposed sale became a matter of lively debate in the press as well as in academic circles, and attempts were made to buy the collection for Sweden.

It was not, however, the case that the sale of the library had been hurriedly arranged following Nordenskiöld's death. It had in fact been planned for two and a half years, and there had also been a real possibility of the library being sold to a purchaser outside Scandinavia or even Europe. Those who were so concerned about the sale in 1902 were not aware of this, and sofar little is known about the proposed sale of the collection or of the reasons behind it. (36)

The earliest documentary reference to the sale of the library is in Nordenskiöld's own hand and is dated 9th June 1899. A scrap of paper bears the following undertaking: 'The undersigned hereby promises to pay Director Ernst Beckman a commission of ten per cent if he brings about the sale of my geographical library for the price of 60,000 dollars — A.E.N.' It is not known whether Nordenskiöld's arrangement came into operation, but it shows however that he had accepted the idea that he might have to sell his library despite all the trouble and money expended in acquiring it. His second great cartographical work, Periplus, had appeared only two years before the writing of the note, and in 1899 and 1901 he continued to publish articles on the history of geography. In 1901 he became involved in an interesting research project, which owed its origin partly to his attempts to find evidence in support of his theory of the Byzanto-Scandinavian cartographic tradition. He had received copies of maps from the Sultan's library in Constantinople from a Dr Fr. Martin, who was attached to the Swedish embassy there, and had hoped that he might be able to prove that the Buondelmonte manuscript, which was preserved in the library, contained new information about northern countries which might have been brought to the court of the Byzantine Empire by the Varangians. But in fact he received 91 photographs of maps from Ptolemy's geographical works, which were in the *Old Seraglio* in Constantinople. In the Facsimile Atlas, Nordenskiöld had dealt thoroughly with Ptolemy's geography, but had concentrated on material in Latin rather than in Greek. He had already started work on his examination of this new material, and Nordenskiöld's last instructions to Dr Martin date from the beginning of August 1901, just a few days before his death. (37)

Thus it is clear that Nordenskiöld did not start procedures for the sale of his library because of any loss of interest in cartography. Certain misfortunes, and an attack of influenza in the spring of 1901 which impaired his energy, hardly explain his decision to sell. In a document drawn up in connection with the inventory of her husband's estate, Anna Nordenskiöld remarks, 'Taking into account that a number of commitments made before his death will draw upon the estate of my late husband Professor Baron A.E. Nordenskiöld, and that these will possibly lead to demands for payment, we thought it best that the most valuable part of the estate, the book collection, should be sold for the highest possible price, and without any undue delay.' (38)

In the closing years of his life nothing came of the arrangement with Beckman, and new booksellers were quick to offer their services. In a letter dated 12th July 1899, a bookseller from Leipzig, G.F. Fock, who said that he had seen a report of the proposed sale in the press intimated that he would like to buy the library. He promised 'einen besonders günstigen Vorschlag'. About three weeks later Nordenskiöld received a second letter from Leipzig, this time from Harrassowitz, who introduced himself as a specialist in cartographic and geographical literature, and promised to pay a good price, better than any Nordenskiöld could expect from a public auction. In the meantime, Nordenskiöld had heard from Muller & Co. in Amsterdam. A letter 17th July 1899 reveals Muller's great surprise at Nordenskiöld's decision to sell: 'We have read with deep regret in a certain bibliographical periodical that you have met with financial adversity. Is it really true that you intend to sell your magnificent library? We shall not believe it unless you tell us yourself. Would you be willing, if this is true, to tell us whether you have already decided whom to sell it to? Would you let us know how high you estimate the value of the collection to be?... If the sale is unavoidable, we might perhaps be able to find a buyer for your library in its entirety.'

Nordenskiöld replied a year later in December 1900. He wrote, 'Messrs Fr. Muller & Co, this is a private communication and I would ask you not to make its contents public. I have the intention of leaving Stockholm in a couple of years' time to settle in the country, or to travel. For this reason it is my intention to relinquish my geographical and cartographic library, for which there is no safe or suitable place at my country house. If I remember rightly, you made me an offer two or three years ago to sell the collection *as a whole,* an offer to which I paid little heed at the time, but to which I might now be ready to agree. My price is 300,000 francs. But I shall sell my collection only as a whole, and for the price I have set.' On 8th January 1901 Muller & Co. agreed to take the sale of the library into its hands, and in a letter of 17th January 1901 Nordenskiöld confirmed his price of 300,000 francs with a commission of ten per cent. The firm was enjoined not to release news of the sale to the press, and to mention Nordenskiöld's name only to individuals or institutions who were seriously considering the purchase of the library. After some discussion, the deadline of the sale was fixed for 1st September 1901; if Muller & Co. succeeded in arranging a sale after that date but before 2nd February 1902, they would receive a reduced commission of six per cent.

Nordenskiöld was notoriously impatient. He was unable to imagine that his directions, however difficult they were, could demand time and trouble, so when he heard nothing from Muller for six weeks, he wrote an impatient letter explaining that he intended to travel on the continent for rest and that, because of this, he wanted to know if there was any news about the sale. He continued: 'I begin to doubt whether Frederik Muller & Co. quite realise the importance of the collection. With the possible exception of one or two public libraries, I do not believe that it has a rival either in Europe or America.' Muller quickly replied and in a letter dated 23rd March 1901 explained that preparations that had been made for the sale, and pointed out that Nordenskiöld's conditions did not make matters easy. 'But all the answers we have had from the south (Sydney) as well as America have been the same: they would like to be able to choose, in a public sale they would buy many books, they would prefer to buy the volumes which are lacking from already established libraries, and so on ... There are great problems in selling the library: 1) The value of historical cartography is not yet widely enough appreciated — a scientific library, for instance, would be easier to sell. 2) In this field, buyers prefer literature which is concerned with their own countries. 3) The requirement not to inform the press of the sale.' Muller concludes his letter, 'Next week we shall make our last attempt and if the result is not more encouraging, I think it may be best to end our agreement, in which case you could place the project in happier hands, perhaps ....'

Muller's letter is quoted at length because it brings out several important points. One reason for Nordenskiöld's success in acquiring so large a library was evidently, as Muller says, because the value of historical cartographic literature had not risen to anything like the level it later attained and was much less than scientific books. It is interesting to note that Muller, who was well known for his efficiency and thoroughness, had already offered the library to a good number of possible buyers. It is known, for example, that is was offered to the predecessor of the New York Public Library, the Lenox, Astor and Tilden Foundation, which felt that the price was too high and did not wish to acquire the whole library. The offer had also been turned down by the purchaser in Sydney.

When Nordenskiöld died on 12th August 1901, Frederik Muller was among those who sent condolences. Some time later he wrote again saying that, although it was not the policy of his firm to ingratiate itself with the relatives of a customer in order to seek permission to sell his effects, 'we are impelled by duty to make an exception in the case of Baron Nordenskiöld's scientific legacy. As you know, we have been in contact with the Baron concerning the sale of his library in its entirety. We have taken a great deal of trouble over this, but the only result we have so far been able to achieve is that we have assurances from some rich amateurs and large libraries that, should the library be dispersed — in other words, if it were sold publicly ... Would it be in your interests to organise a special sale with descriptive catalogues in Amsterdam, a city where the monuments of ancient geography are continually being studied? The compilation of catalogues and the sale of Nordenskiöld's scientific legacy would be a unique event in the history of our house.'

In fact Nordenskiöld had already set in motion the cataloguing of his collection. He had given the task to an assistant at the University library in Upsala, J.M. Hulth. This catalogue is still extant, as are the receipts for the fee Nordenskiöld paid for the work. Hulth later became the chief librarian of the library of the University of Upsala (1918—1928).

Muller's offer arrived too late. The Finnish geographer Dr J.E. Rosberg had worked in the library under Nordenskiöld's direction in the spring of 1901. In conversations with Rosberg, Nordenskiöld had often emphasised the importance of his collection to scientific research, and it was plain to see how attached he was to his library. But, once he had accepted the idea that he might have to part with his collection completely, he began to think that his country of origin, Finland, might have some use for his collection — it was hardly likely that any literature of that kind was to be found there. If Finland would be prepared to accept the library, he for his part would be willing to offer favourable conditions, partly for patriotic reasons and partly because with the library in Finland, he himself would have easy access to it. Nordenskiöld hoped that this possibility would be explored through private channels.

Nordenskiöld's illness was one of the reasons why nothing had been done before his death in August. After this, everything looked uncertain from the Finnish side. But it soon became apparent that Nordenskiöld had made his wishes concerning the location of the library in Finland clear to his closest relatives. Aware of this, his old friend and colleague Professor J.A. Palmén of Helsinki, who had himself contributed the volume on birds in the scientific series on the Vega expedition, took up the cause with all the energy and enthusiasm which was so typical of him. (39) He tried to raise funds in Helsinki and at the same time tried to contact Nordenskiöld's heirs. Another close friend of the family, Professor Leo Mechelin, mentioned above, was staying in Stockholm at the time, and Palmén asked him to mediate between himself and the Nordenskiöld family, and to negotiate conditions of sale. The part Mechelin played was decisive. He conducted the negotiations with Anna Nordenskiöld and gave practical advice to Palmén. The funds for the purchase were not to be raised through a public subscription, but from the government. While willing to sell the collection to Finland, Anna Nordenskiöld held fast to the original price of 200,000 Crowns, and refused to accept an offer of 200,000 marks. At that time 200,000 Crowns was the equivalent of 280,000 Finn marks or, in present-day values, about two million Finn marks. Once they knew that Anna Nordenskiöld was in principle willing to sell the library to Finland, Palmén and Rosberg travelled to Sweden at the end of November 1901 to acquaint themselves with the library and to prepare the documents for the financial requirements. Mechelin took responsibility for the compilation of the necessary lists.

Despite her refusal to accept a lower price, Anna Nordenskiöld was enthusiastic about the idea of locating the entire collection in Finland. In a letter to her son at that time, she said, 'We are continuing the cataloguing of the books and shall perhaps print the result, even though it will be expensive. If the Finns do not buy the collection, we shall offer it to Berlin; all the same, Richthofen [director of the Geographishes Institut in Berlin] will probably be interested only in the geographical collection. What shall we do with all the other books if that happens? The price too would be much lower. Of course, it is possible that we shall have to leave the library in Sweden. Here they also want to disperse papa's books and keep some in the Academy Library, some in the Royal Library, some in Lund. I have been most eager to sell the books to Finland, for there they will treat them with respect and value them greatly for the fact that they belonged to papa and that he has made many notes in them ...' (40)

Attempts to raise the money to purchase the library were organised simultaneously in Finland and Sweden. In August 1901 the librarian of the Royal Swedish Academy of Sciences, Dr E.W. Dahlgren, had informed the Swedish Ministry of Education that the collection was for sale. The Ministry had intimated that it was prepared to bring up the matter in connection with the budget of 1902. But this procedure proved too slow, as Nordenskiöld's estate needed the money as soon as possible. The matter was discussed publicly, and it was suggested that the necessary money could have been raised more quickly privately had those concerned really wanted to avoid another national scandal comparable to the loss of Linné's papers and botanical collections to England after his death. Mechelin thought it imperative that the University of Finland should make its decision before the Swedish government put the question of the funding of the purchase of the Nordenskiöld library to parliament. Once this had happened, it would not be proper to ask Anna Nordenskiöld to make any decision about the sale before parliament's opinion was known. Mechelin assumed that the decision would be positive, because Sweden wanted to keep the collection, and Finland was known to be willing to buy. (41)

The University of Finland dealt quickly with the proposals put forward by Palmén and Rosberg, and declared itself to be prepared to meet part of the cost from its own funds. The major part of the sum, however, 200,000 marks, was still to be obtained from the state, and the University would also need a loan if it was to be able to pay its share in a lump sum. It was prepared to pay the money back over a fixed period of time. The University enjoyed far-reaching autonomy but was unable to turn directly to the Senate for aid. It is probable that representatives of the University followed Mechelin's advice and made contact privately with certain senators. The University made its request to the Chancellor, who was usually the Crown Prince of Russia. Evidently this method, often fraught with difficulties, proved the best possible in this case. Rulers of great empires are generally more generous in financial matters than the finance ministers of small countries. In this particular case, the proposal had the support of the Finnish Senate and the Tsar agreed to the University's request even before it had been put to him formally. On 30th January 1902 Palmén was able to telegraph Anna Nordenskiöld with the news that the matter had been favourably settled; however, he begged her not to make it public until an official statement had been received. This was issued by the Chancellor's office in St Petersburg on 6th February 1902.

Anna Nordenskiöld had followed the fund-raising activities in Finland with the greatest interest. Palmén had kept her informed of the course of events, and on 12th January 1902 she wrote to him, 'Most honourable Sir, Baron, I hasten to thank you for your two letters concerning the good news about the progress of the negotiations of the sale of the Library to Finland. We are most heartily grateful, myself and my children, for the valuable time you have devoted to this matter through your admirable interest.' And when the financing of the purchase had been officially settled, she wrote to the

Rector of the University of Finland, Professor Edvard Hjelt, to express her grateful satisfaction with the happy outcome of the matter.

The contract of sale was signed on 6th March 1902 in Stockholm. Professor Edvard Hjelt made a special journey to Stockholm to be present at the occasion. The packing of the library began immediately under the supervision of Palmén himself, together with an official from the University library. The library arrived by sea at Hanko in late March and contained, besides books, maps and globes, the part of Nordenskiöld's personal correspondence which relates directly to the library and its collection.

The conditions of sale which were agreed upon in addition to the price can be summarised as follows:

The collection was to be preserved as a whole. The disposal of any of its items was strictly forbidden. It was to be known as the Adolf Nordenskiöld Library.

The collection was to be open to scholars from Sweden and elsewhere, and not only to Finns.

A printed catalogue of the library was to be prepared and published.

The accounts of the sale have generally been accurate down to the smallest detail. All the same, it should perhaps be emphasised that the collection was not bought by the City of Helsinki, as one study states. Nor are there any documents which give substance to the opinion that Palmén himself might have travelled to St Petersburg to petition the Tsar. All available sources, including Palméns private correspondence, imply that he stayed in Helsinki to await the decision. The memorandum which he, together with Rosberg, had drawn up, left the University of Finland in no doubt of the value of the collection.

Another story which has appeared in various forms in different accounts concerns the gift from the Nordenskiöld Collection which the University presented to the Tsar: C. Iulius Solinus' geographical work, published in Basle in 1538 by Sebastian Münster and containing nineteen maps from that time. One of these was the earliest known map of Moscow, showing its waterways. The map was well known in Russia, and had been discussed in many publications. Nordenskiöld himself had published reproductions of it in the periodical *Ymer* in 1885 and in the Facsimile Atlas of 1889 (p. 108). The documents concerning the purchase, which the University had sent to the Tsar, contained many lists which clarified the contents of the library. One of these mentioned Solinus' work: 'Solinus 1532 (la première carte imprimée de Moscovia ...)'. The entry had caught the Tsar's eye, and the University was aware of his interest. In recognition of his generosity, the University authorities wished to present him with the work. But, under the conditions of the sale, it had to obtain Anna Nordenskiöld's permission. This permission was forthcoming when Palmén announced that he would obtain another copy of the work for the collection. So the Tsar received his gift, but only after he had made the decision to release the funds to buy the library. There was certainly no question of Palmén's having visited the Tsar, book in hand, to beg for funds for the purchase of the collection.

The first hint of the rarity of the works in the Nordenskiöld Collection came when Palmén began to search for a new copy of the Solinus work. He turned to Frederik Muller, and Muller promised to provide a copy for the price of 36 guilders. It seems that Palmén sent the money immediately and before long received the book, but it was incomplete. Muller promised to procure a new copy at once, if Palmén had the patience to wait. But a couple of days later he had to inform Palmén that this second copy was also incomplete; a large map was missing. At this stage Palmén's patience came to an end and he sent Muller an angry letter. On 25th April 1902 Muller replied in the same coin: 'Obschon wir Ihren Brief vom 22 April d.J. zurückweisen müssen, weil man solche Briefe nicht schreibt an Friedrich Muller, Cie, können wir doch einigerweise Ihnen entgegen kommen ...' Muller offered Palmén a third copy, for an additional ten florins, and promised to send the book on receipt of the extra money. In May of the same year Palmén received the book which is now in the Nordenskiöld Collection.

Palmén was extremely active in the purchase of the Nordenskiöld Collection for Finland, and his perseverance received its reward. Moreover he appears to have paid for the Solinus work out of his own pocket.

The Cataloguing of the Nordenskiöld Collection

The cataloguing of Nordenskiöld's library, which was begun as a preliminary to its sale, continued after his death and the library arrived in Helsinki complete with a card catalogue. This catalogue, drawn up by J.M. Hulth, did not remain the only one. In Helsinki the collection was reorganised on the basis of the *Anordnungsplan der Gesellschaft für Erdkunde zu Berlin* and described in P. Dinsen's *Zur Systematik der erdkundlichen Literatur*. Certain modifications to the system were introduced because Dinsen's classification was more relevant to the study of geography from a natural history point of view rather than to collections of the history of geography. In 1916 it was announced in the Annual Report of the University of Helsinki that the catalogue was ready and printing would begin as soon as funds could be found.

However, the First World War, the declaration of Finland's independence in 1917 and the ensuing civil war in 1918 caused the printing to be postponed. In the meantime, the titles of the works in Nordenskiöld's Collection were included in the main catalogue of the University Library. Owing to a lack of staff, work was done only when time could be spared from other tasks, and on occasions it came to a complete halt. When the cataloguing got properly under way again it was interrupted by the Second World War when the Collection was removed from Helsinki for safety. With the return of peace, the first task was to put Nordenskiöld's Collection back on to the shelves and the revision of the catalogue continued slowly alongside other work. The work stopped again in the 1950s for a long while, and when the Collection was moved to new quarters it was necessary to depart from the earlier systematic arrangement and to arrange the Collection according to a mechanical numerical system. At the same time, the idea of publishing the old systematic catalogue had to be abandoned.

Cataloguing started again in 1968, largely at the instigation of the Nordenskiöld-Samfundet [Nordenskiöld Society]. It was at this stage that the cataloguing method was changed. The old systematic catalogue, by then almost complete, and which was and continues to be in itself an excellent guide to the Nordenskiöld Collection, lists only works, the classification also used for atlases. Since even two copies of the same edition can differ fundamentally, not to mention cases like Lafreri, it was clearly necessary to find a new approach to the cataloguing of the collection. In place of atlases, the individual items to be catalogued were taken to be maps, and these are described in sufficient detail to permit some measure of research in comparative cartography on the basis of the catalogue alone. In this respect, the catalogue is like a bibliography. Its precursors include Philip Lee Phillips' *A List of Geographical Atlases in the Library of Congress* and C. Koeman's *Bibliography of Terrestrial, Maritime and Celestial Atlases and Pilot Books in the Netherlands up to 1880: Atlantes Neerlandici*. The cataloguing system has been reviewed and amended several times as the work has progressed; revisions include the changing of the chronological ordering of the maps for an alphabetical one and the standardisation of the analytic descriptions of the maps.

References

1. The following biographies give a good general picture of Nordenskiöld's life: GEORGE KISH, *North-east passage. Adolf Erik Nordenskiöld, his life and times*. Amsterdam: Israel 1973. 283 pp. The standard biography is still HENRIK RAMSAY, *Nordenskiöld. Sjöfararen*. Helsingfors: Schildts 1950. 315 pp. This work, unfortunately long out of print, is not a scientific biography as such; SVEN HEDIN, *Adolf Erik Nordenskiöld. En levnadsteckning*. Stockholm: Albert Bonnier 1926. 378 pp. In 1902 the periodical *Ymer* devoted a large issue to the description and evaluation of Nordenskiöld's life work. The contributors were scientists in their fields and had been colleagues of Nordenskiöld. The same issue contains a bibliography of Nordenskiöld's publications: J.M. HULTH, 'Nordenskiöld-bibliografi' in *Ymer* 22 (1902) pp. 277—303. This includes a list of biographical treatments of Nordenskiöld's life on pages 302—303.
2. HEDIN 1926 pp. 302, 304
3. A.E. NORDENSKIÖLD, *The Voyage of the Vega round Asia and Europe*, Vol. 1. London: Macmillan & Co 1881 pp. 29—30.
4. J. GUNNAR ANDERSSON, 'Adolf Erik Nordenskiöld 1832—1901' in *Swedish Men of Science 1650—1950*. Ed. and with an Introduction by STEN LINDROTH. Stockholm 1952 p. 211.
5. A.G. NATHORST, 'A.E. Nordenskiölds polarfärder' in *Ymer* 22 (1902) p. 199.
6. GEORGE KISH, 'Adolf Erik Nordenskiöld (1832—1901): Polar Explorer and Historian of Cartography' in *Geographical Journal* Part 134 (1968); pp. 487—495 contain a concise account of Nordenskiöld's expeditions. KISH 1973 contains a more detailed account. See also L.P. KIRWAN, *The White Road. A Survey of Polar Exploration*. London: Hollis & Carter 1959 pp. 190—195.
7. W.R. MEAD, 'Luminaries of the North. A reappraisal of the achievements and influence of six Scandinavian geographers' in Institute of British Geographers. *Transactions* No 57 (1972) p. 5. For research after Nordenskiöld, see e.g. WILHELM ODELBERG, 'Adolf Erik Nordenskiöld. Mineralogen — polarforskaren' in *Mot fjärran land. Berömda svenska upptäckare*. Stockholm 1975 p. 90.
8. HJALMAR SJÖGREN, 'Riksmuseets mineralogiska afdelning' in *Naturhistoriska riksmuseets historia. Dess uppkomst och utveckling*. Stockholm 1916 pp. 152—161; ANDERSSON 1952 p. 213; HARALD WIESELGREN, 'Nils Adolf Erik Nordenskiöld' in *Ymer* 22 (1902) p. 136. As a mineralogist, Nordenskiöld was always primarily a chemist. His knowledge of geology and his interest in it were slight. See HANS HAUSEN, *The History of Geology and Mineralogy in Finland 1828—1918*. Helsinki 1968. (*The History of Learning and Science in Finland 1828—1918*, Vol. 8a) p. 40.
9. See e.g. A.G. NATHORST, 'Riksmuseets Paleobotaniska afdelning' in *Naturhistoriska riksmuseets historia. Dess uppkomst och utveckling*. Stockholm 1916 pp. 245—255; BRITTA LUNDBLAD, 'Utvecklingslinjer i svensk paleobotanik 1870—1945' in *Fauna och Flora* 64 (1969) pp. 269—281 (17 references); EINAR LÖNNBERG, 'Riksmuseets vertebratafdelning 1841—1916' in *Naturhistoriska riksmuseets historia. Dess uppkomst och utveckling*. Stockholm 1916 pp. 76—77. The author would also like to thank Tor Ørvig of the Department of Palaeozoology of the National Museum for the information which he and his colleagues have supplied in this connection.
10. NORDENSKIÖLD 1881, vol. 2. pp. 363—365. LÉON DE ROSNY, *Catalogue de la bibliothèque Japonaise de Nordenskiöld*. Paris 1883. 359 pp.; J.S. EDGREN, 'Illustrated Early Japanese Fiction in the Nordenskiöld Collection' in *Biblis* 1977—78 pp. 9—62. This also contains general information about the collection and its cataloguing.
11. GERHARD LINDBLOM, 'Statens etnografiska museum' in *Blå boken*. Stockholm 1954 p. 83. The author would also like to thank Anne Murray of the Etnografiska muséet for information, especially extracts from catalogues, which she has supplied.
12. GERGE KISH, 'Adolf Erik Nordenskiöld (1832—1901) historian of science and bibliophile' in *Biblis* 1968 p. 178. The original text of the quotation is from E.W. DAHLGREN, 'A.E. Nordenskiöld såsom forskare i historisk geografi och kartografi' in *Ymer* 22 (1902) p. 276.

13. The article has also appeared in English: 'A leaf from the history of Swedish natural science' in *Nature* 21 (1879—80) pp. 518—521, 539—541, 563—565.
14. HEDIN 1926 pp. 136—137.
15. A.E. NORDENSKIÖLD, 'Bemötande af anmärkningar, som riktats mot min skildring af Vegas färd kring Asien och Europa' in *Ymer* 5 (1885) pp. 254, 259.
16. T.E. ARMSTRONG [in discussion] in *Geographical Journal* part 134 (1968) p. 504.
17. MEAD 1972 pp. 4—5, quoting Sir Clements Markham's presidential address to the Royal Geographical Society in 1879.
18. NORDENSKIÖLD 1885 pp. 253—254.
19. The article has appeared in English: 'A remarkable globe map of the sixteenth century' in *Bulletin of the American Geographical Society* 1884 pp. 222—233.
20. A.G. NATHORST, 'A.E. Nordenskiöld såsom geolog' in *Ymer* 22 (1902) p. 224. A later evaluation of these theories which does Nordenskiöld justice is given in L.H. BORGSTRÖM, 'Om A.E. Nordenskiöld som mineralog och om hans kosmogenetiska teori' in *Terra* 45 (1932) p. 152.
21. W.R. MEAD and C. WADEL, 'Scandinavia and the Scandinavians in the Annals of the Royal Geographical Society 1830—1914' in *Norsk Geografisk Tidsskrift* 18 (1961) pp. 137—8.
22. E.g. S. RUGE, 'Nordenskiölds Faksimile-Atlas' in *Deutsche Geographische Blätter* 14 (1891) pp. 35—43 and F.R. v. WIESER, 'A.E. v. Nordenskiölds Facsimile-Atlas' in *Petermann's Mitteilungen* 36 (1890) pp. 270—276.
23. E.g. SALVADOR GARCIA FRANCO, 'The "Portolan Mile" of Nordenskiöld' in *Imago Mundi* 12 (1955) pp. 89—91 and G.S. RITCHIE, '500 years of graphical and symbolical representation on marine charts' in *International Hydrographic Review* 53 (1976) p. 144. Ritchie also mentions in passing Nordenskiöld's theory that the portolano maps were made without knowledge of the compass p. 142.
24. C. RAYMOND BEAZLEY, 'Nordenskjöld's Periplus' in *Geographical Journal* 12 (1898) p. 376. A thorough description of the contents of Periplus as well as the criticism it received is given in S. RUGE, 'Der Periplus Nordenskiölds' in *Deutsche Geographische Blätter* 23 (1900) pp. 161—229.
25. The Facsimile Atlas has been reprinted twice, in an edition by Kraus, New York in 1961 and in a paperback edition, somewhat reduced in size, Dover Publications, New York, 1973. Periplus has been issued in a reprint edition by Burt Franklin, New York, in 1962.
26. R.A. SKELTON [in discussion] in *Geographical Journal* Part 134 (1968) p. 502.
27. The letters of A.E. Nordenskiöld to Leo Mechelin. Leo Mechelin Collection, Finnish State Archives.
28. EINO NIVANKA, 'Amsterdamilainen Fr. Mullerin antikvariaatti Nordenskiöldin kirjakokoelman päähankkijana [The role of the Amsterdam antiquarian bookseller Fr. Muller as a main supplier of books for the Nordenskiöld Collection] in *Miscellanea Bibliographica* 5. Helsinki 1947. (Publications of the University Library at Helsinki, 20) pp. 122—133; DAHLGREN 1902 pp. 263—276; KISH 1968 pp. 178—80.
29. A.E. Nordenskiöld's letters to August Ahlqvist. Finnish Literature Society, Helsinki.
30. HEDIN 1926 p. 272.
31. Preserved in the Nordenskiöld collection in the University Library in Helsinki together with the booksellers' invoices and correspondence.
32. DAHLGREN 1902 p. 276.
33. In the Nordenskiöld Collection
34. JUSSI ARO, *Die arabischen, persischen und türkischen Handschriften der Universitätsbibliothek zu Helsinki.* Helsinki 1958. (Publications of the University Library at Helsinki, 28) pp. 56—59.
35. ANN-MARI MICKWITZ, 'Några bokhistoriska anteckningar om Nordenskiölds bibliotek' in *Nordenskiöld-samfundets tidskrift* 34 (1974) pp. 3—19.
36. EINO NIVANKA, 'Marginalanteckningar rörande försäljningen av A.E. Nordenskiölds bibliotek' in *Nordisk tidskrift för bok- och biblioteksväsen* 46 (1959) pp. 93—102. Summary in French. Quotes the correspondence between Nordenskiöld and Frederik Muller in the original French.
37. DAHLGREN 1902 p. 275; LAURI O. TH. TUDEER, 'Ptolemaioksen Maantiede-teokseen liittyvistä kartoista' [On the maps in Ptolemy's Geography] in *Terra* 49 (1937) p. 73—74.
38. In the collection of Nordenskiöld manuscripts in the Library of the Royal Swedish Academy of Sciences, Stockholm.
39. J.A. P[ALMÉN]., 'Finland och Adolf Nordenskiölds minne' in *Fennia* 19:4 (1902) pp. 1—15. Contains a detailed account of the discussion of the matter in university circles in Helsinki and publishes a number of documents, including book catalogues preserved unpublished in the archives of the University of Helsinki. Minutes of meeting of the Consistorium [Senate] of the University on 12 December 1901 § 20 appendices.
40. NIVANKA 1959 pp. 97—8.
41. Leo Mechelin's letters to J.A. Palmén from Stockholm 22 October 1901, 28 October 1901, 14 November 1901, 17 February 1902. Nordenskiöld Collection, Helsinki University Library.
42. This version is given in LEO BAGROW, 'A.E. Nordenskiöld 1901 [in memoriam]' in *Imago Mundi* 8 (1951) p. 99. Bagrow was extremely well-acquainted with the Nordenskiöld collection, which makes it all the more surprising that he should repeat the story. KISH 1968 p. 181 also has the story. The question has been clarified in ANN-MARI MICKWITZ, 'Kejsaren och den gamla kartan' in *Miscellanea Bibliographica* 7. Helsingfors. (Publications of the University Library at Helsinki, 26) pp. 59—65. MICKWITZ also proves that the Solinus work was not used as a bribe, but that the University gave it to the Tsar as a gift in grateful recognition of the extraordinarily large sum of money it had received, which made the purchase of the Nordenskiöld collection possible.

Notes for Use

The catalogue lists all the pre-nineteenth-century maps in the Nordenskiöld Collection, contained in atlases, books, or as loose sheets. The facsimiles are also catalogued. The quotations in the catalogue follow the original text; printing and grammatical mistakes have not been corrected. Omissions from the original are marked by three dots (...); additions appear in square brackets [ ]. In addition to the area depicted on each map, all the important information concerning their preparation and identification has been taken into account for cataloguing purposes.

The atlases and general geographical accounts are catalogued in Volumes 1 and 2. Volumes 4 and 5 contain the indexes. The works are arranged in alphabetical order according to author or publisher; maps by the same maker or by the same family are in chronological order. Atlases whose authors are unknown are arranged alphabetically according to title; works in this category which lack a title are listed under 'Collection'.

The descriptive part of the catalogue falls into four sections: atlases and works, maps, notes, and references. Each atlas and book has been given its own running number. In the descriptive section this number appears first, before the name of the maker or author and the year of publication. In addition, each map included in an atlas or book has been provided with its own number which is indicated in square brackets in the left-hand margin next to the relevant item. The works are numbered in the order mentioned above and each separate atlas, book and loose map has its own number. In the description of each item, this number is given first, before the name of the maker and the date of first appearance. The title, colophon, and size of the item follow. Title-pages of works containing maps are usually described in full; if a work has more than one title-page, all are listed. The information is always arranged in the same order: 1) title, 2) half-title, engraved title-page. If a work has a colophon, it has been placed after the title and marked [Colophon:]. The lengths of the spines of atlases and books are given in centimetres.

Information about maps which are included in atlases and books is presented in the following order:
1) Map number.
2) Texts. Those without the initial signa [C:] and [T:] are taken from the verso, frame or margins of the map. Texts marked [C:] are taken from the cartouche; texts marked [T:] are taken from the map outside the cartouche. The end of each text is marked by a hyphen (-).
3) Type. The type of each map (i.e. map, chart, plan, view, profile, celestial chart) is shown in round brackets.
4) Location. The place of each map in the work is shown by the page or folio number which appears on the map or its verso, in the form of the original. Where a page number is lacking, the numbers of the pages between which it appears are given. Where a map is printed on a text page, the preposition 'on' is used.
5) Colour. The colour of the map is indicated by the code 'coloured' or 'uncoloured'. More detailed information about colouring will be found in the notes.
6) Verso. The verso of each map is described, e.g. 'verso blank' or 'text on verso'. A fuller description will be found in the notes.
7) Size. The size of each map is measured from the outer edges of the frame (height × width). Dimensions are given in millimetres. Dimensions of irregularly-shaped inset maps are followed by the code [irregular].
8) Inset maps. Information about these items is printed in the same order as for maps.
9) References. Where the Collection contains more than one edition of a work by the same author, more than one work by that author, or more than one work containing the same map, the various maps are compared; the oldest dated edition of each map is treated as the definitive version for purposes of comparison. All definitive maps are catalogued individually and in detail, whereas later editions of the same maps have only a short reference giving the main title, location, colour, and verso description. The reference is marked (=) if the items in question are identical, while if the later edition has minor changes the code (= with small alterations) is used. Where a special connection exists between two maps, this is indicated by the instruction 'see ...' followed by the year of printing and the map's catalogue number. Where more than one work by the same author appeared in one year, the year is preceded by the catalogue number of the item in round brackets.
10) Notes. The verso and colouring of the maps are usually described at the beginning of the notes. These also provide information about works or maps which came to light while cataloguing was in progress. Information about the outward appearance of the item, as well as any hand-written notes made in it after printing, is also given in the notes. Nordenskiöld's own annotations, his signature and *ex libris* are described at the end of the note.
11) Bibliography. Works consulted during the process of cataloguing are indicated by the code 'Lit.:'

List of Atlases

1	ADRICHEM, CHRISTIAAN VAN, Theatrvm terræ sanctæ et biblicarvm historiarvm	1590	1
2	ADRICHEM, CHRISTIAAN VAN, Theatrvm terræ sanctæ et biblicarvm historiarvm	1593	1
3	ALBERTI, LEANDER, Isole appartenenti alla Italia	1567	2
4	ANANIA, GIOVANNI LORENZO D', L'Vniversale Fabrica del Mondo	1582	2
5	ANVILLE, JEAN BAPTISTE BOURGUIGNON D', Nouvel Atlas de la Chine	1737	2
6	APIAN [APIANUS], PHILIPP, Bairische Landtaflen	1568	3
7	Atlante dell' America	1777	4
8	BARENTZOEN, WILLEM, Nieuwe beschryvinghe ende Caertboeck vande Midlandtsche Zee	1595	6
9	BARTOLOMEO DA LI SONETTI, [Isolario.]	[1485]	8
10	BELLIN, JACQUES NICOLAS, Le Petit Atlas Maritime	1764	8
11	BELLIN, JACQUES NICOLAS, Le Petit Atlas Maritime Vol. III	1764	21
12	BERTELLI, FERDINANDO, Civitatvm aliqvot insigniorvm ... delineatio	1568	24
13	BERTELLI, PIETRO, [Theatrum Urbium Italicarum.]	1599	25
14	BERTIUS, PETRUS, [P. Bertii Tabvlarvm Geographicarvm Contractarvm Libri Quatuor.]	[1600]	26
15	BERTIUS, PETRUS, P. Bertij Tabvlarvm Geographicarvm contractarvm Libri septem.	1616	30
16	BERTIUS, PETRUS, Geographia vetvs ex antiqvis, et melioris notæ scriptoribvs nvper collecta	1645	34
17	BLAEU, WILLEM JANSZOON, Zeespiegel, Inhoudende Een korte Onderwysinghe inde Konst der Zeevaert	1627—1629	35
18	BLAEU, WILLEM JANSZOON AND JOAN, Novvs Atlas	1635	36
19	BLAEU, WILLEM JANSZOON AND JOAN, Le Theatre dv Monde Vol. II	1645	43
20	BLAEU, WILLEM JANSZOON AND JOAN, [Novus Atlas] Vol. I	1647—1649	44
21	BLAEU, WILLEM JANSZOON AND JOAN, Novvs Atlas Vol. III	1647	47
22	BLAEU, JOAN, Novvs Atlas Vol. V	1654	49
23	BLAEU, JOAN, Novvs Atlas Vol. VI	1656	51
24	BLAEU, JOAN, Atlas Maior, Sive Cosmographia Blaviana	1662	52
25	BODENEHR, HANS GEORG, Provinciarum Europæ Geographica Descriptio	1679	73
26	BOISSEAU, JEAN, Tresor des Cartes Geographiqves	1643	74
27	BORDONE, BENEDETTO, Libro di Benedetto Bordone Nel qual si ragiona de tutte l'Isole del mondo	1528	74
28	BORDONE, BENEDETTO, Isolario	1534	75
29	BORDONE, BENEDETTO, Isolario	1534	77
30	BORDONE, BENEDETTO, Isolario	1547	77
31	BOSCHINI, MARCO, Il regno tvtto di Candia delineato à parte, à parte, et intagliato da Marco Boschini Venetiano	1651	78
32	BOSCHINI, MARCO, L'Arcipelago	1658	79
33	BOTERO, GIOVANNI, Allgemeine Weltbeschreibung	1596	80
34	BOTERO, GIOVANNI, Le Relationi Vniversali	1596	80
35	BOTERO, GIOVANNI, Relationi Vniversali	1599	80
36	BOXHORN, MARCUS ZUERIUS, Marci Zuerii Boxhornii Theatrum Sive Hollandiæ comitatus et vrbium Nova Descriptio	1632	82
37	BRAUN, GEORG AND HOGENBERG, FRANZ, [Liber qvartvs Vrbivm præcipvarvm totivs mvndi.]		83
38	BRIET, PHILIP, Parallela geographiæ veteris et novæ	1648—1649	86
39	BROUCKNER, ISAAC, Nouvel Atlas	1759	87
40	BUFFIER, CLAUDE, Geografia Vniversale	1775	88
41	CELLARIUS, CHRISTOPH, Notitia Orbis Antiqvi	1701	89
42	CELLARIUS, CHRISTOPH, Notitia Orbis Antiqvi	1731—1732	89
43	CHIQUET, JACQUES, La nouveau et curieux Atlas Geographique et historique	[1719]	90
44	CLUVER, PHILIP, Philippi Clüveri Germaniæ Antiqvæ libri tres	1616	91
45	CLUVER, PHILIP, Philippi Cluverii Introductio in Universam Geographiam	1697	91
46	CLUVER, PHILIP, Philippi Cluverii, Gedanensis, Sicilia Antiqua	[1723—1725]	92
47	CLUVER, PHILIP, Philippi Cluveri Introductionis in Universam Geographiam ... Libri VI	1729	93
48	[Collection of maps, mostly Italian, without title-page.]	1532—1570	94
49	[Collection of Dutch maps, without title-page.]	1624—1626	95
50	[Collection of Dutch maps, without title-page.]	1629—1659	96
51	[Collection of French maps, without title-page.]	1693—1746	97
52	[Collection of French maps, without title-page.]	1700—1793	100
53	COLOM, ARNOLD, Atlas Marin Ou Monde Maritime	[1659?]	102
54	CORONELLI, VINCENZO, Memorie Istoriografiche de' regni della Morea, Negroponte	[1687]	103
55	CORONELLI, VINCENZO, 1687 Memorie Istoriogeografiche della Morea riacqvistata dall' armi Venete del regno di Negroponte	1687	104
56	CORONELLI, VINCENZO, Isola di Rodi	1688	105
57	CORONELLI, VINCENZO, Epitome Cosmografica	1693	105

58	CORONELLI, VINCENZO, Globi del Padre Coronelli	[1705]	106
59	CORONELLI, VINCENZO, Teatro della Guerra	1706—1708	107
60	CORONELLI, VINCENZO, Arcipelago	[1707?]	125
61	CORONELLI, VINCENZO, [Teatro della Querra.]	[1707]	126
62	CRUYS, CORNELIUS, Nieuw pas-kaart boek behelsende De Groote Rivier Don of Tanais	[1703?]	127
63	DANCKWERTH, CASPAR, Newe Landesbeschreibung der Zweij Hertzogthümer Schleswich Vnd Holstein	1652	129
64	DELISLE, GUILLAUME, Atlante novissimo	1740—1750	133
65	DELISHE, JOSEPH NICOLAS, Russischer Atlas	1745	134
66	DONCKER, HENDRIK, Nieuw Groot Stuurmans Straets-Boeck	1664	135
67	DONCKER, HENDRIK, De Zee-Atlas ofte Water-wæreld	1666	137
68	DONCKER, HENDRIK, La Atlas del Mundo o El Mundo Aguado	[1669]	138
69	DU BOIS, ABRAHAM, La geographie moderne, Naturelle, Historique & Politique	1729	140
70	DUDLEY, ROBERT, Dell'Arcano del mare	1646—1647	143
71	DU PINET, ANTOINE, Plantz, povrtraitz et descriptions de plvsievrs villes et forteresses, tant de l'Europe, Asia & Afrique	1564	148
72	FER, NICOLAS DE, L'Atlas curieux	1725	150
73	FERRETTI, FRANCESCO, Diporti nottvrni	1580	156
74	FORESTI, JACOBUS PHILIPPUS BERGOMENSIS, Nouissime hÿstoriarum omniũ repercussiones	1503	157
75	FORESTI, JACOBUS PHILIPPUS BERGOMENSIS, Svpplementvm svpplementi	1524	157
76	GEDDA, PETTER, General Hydrographisk Chart-Book öfwer Östersiön, och Katte-Gatt	1694—1695	159
77	GEDDA, PETTER, [General Hydrographisk Chart-Book öfwer Östersiön, och Katte-Gatt]	1699	159
78	Geographia Classica: The geography of the ancients	1712	160
79	GOOS, PIETER, De Lichtende Colomne Ofte Zee-Spiegel	1658	161
80	GOOS, PIETER, L'Atlas de la Mer ou Monde Aquaticque	1673	165
81	GOSSELIN, PASCAL FRANÇOIS JOSEPH, Recherches sur la Géographie systématique et positive des Anciens:	1798	167
82	GOTTFRIED, JOHANN LUDWIG, Vermehrte Archontologia Cosmica	1695	167
83	GOUGH, RICHARD, British topography	1780	170
84	GUICCIARDINI, LODOVICO, Descrittione di M. Lodovico Gvicciardini Patritio Fiorentino, di tutti i Paesi Bassi	1567	170
85	GUICCIARDINI, LODOVICO, Descrittione di M. Lodovico Gvicciardini Patritio Fiorentino, di tvtti i Paesi Bassi	1581	171
86	GUICCIARDINI, LODOVICO, Belgicæ, sive Inferioris Germaniæ , Descriptio	1633—1635	172
87	GUTHRIE, WILLIAM, A New Geographical Historical, and Commercial Grammar	1779	173
88	HERMELIN, SAMUEL GUSTAV, Geographiske Chartor öfver Swerige	1797—1807	175
89	HERMELIN, SAMUEL GUSTAV, [Geographiske Chartor öfver Swerige.]	1797—1799	176
90	HOMANN, JOHANN BAPTIST AND HEIRS, [Collection of maps without title-page.]	1710—1750	177
91	HOMANN, JOHANN BAPTIST AND HEIRS, [Collection of maps without title-page.]	1720—1771	183
92	HOMANN, JOHANN BAPTIST AND HEIRS, [Collection of maps without title-page.]	1736—1788	193
93	HOMANN, JOHANN BAPTIST, Atlas Novus terrarum orbis imperia, regna et status ... demonstrans	[1752?]	197
94	HOMANN HEIRS, Atlas compendiarivs seu ita dictus scholasticvs minor in usum erudiendae juventutis	1753	198
95	HOMANN, JOHANNES BAPTIST AND HEIRS, Atlas Germaniae specialis sev systema tabvlarvm geographicarvm	1762	200
96	HOMANN, JOHANN BAPTIST, [Collection of town plans and views without title-page.]	[1762?]	205
97	HONTERUS, JOHANNES, Ioannis Honter Coronensis Rvdimentorvm Cosmographiæ libri duo	1530	212
98	HONTERUS, JOHANNES, Rvdimenta Cosmographica.	1546	213
99	HONTERUS, JOHANNES, Rvdimentorvm Cosmographicorum Ioan. Honteri Coronensis libri III	[1548?]	213
100	HONTERUS, JOHANNES, Rvdimentorvm Cosmographicorum Ioan. Honteri Coronensis libri III	1549	213
101	HONTERUS, JOHANNES, Rvdimentorvm Cosmographicorum Ioan. Honteri Coronensis libri III	1522	213
102	HONTERUS, JOHANNES, Rvdimentorvm Cosmographicorum Ioan. Honteri Coronensis libri III	1552	214
103	HONTERUS, JOHANNES, Ioannis Honteri Coronensis, de Cosmographiæ rudimentis	1561	214
104	HONTERUS, JOHANNES, Rvdimentorvm Cosmographicorum Ioan. Honteri Coronensis libri III	1583	214
105	HONTERUS, JOHANNES, Ioannis Honteri Coronensis, de Cosmographiæ rudimentis	1585	215
106	HONTERUS, JOHANNES, Enchiridion cosmographiae: Continens praecipvarvm orbis regionvm delineationes	1597	215
107	HORN, GEORG, Accuratissima orbis antiqvi delineatio. Sive geographia vetus, sacra & profana	1653	215
108	HORN, GEORG, Accuratissima orbis delineatio Sive geographia vetus, sacra & profana	1677	217
109	Isole famose	[1571]	219
110	JACOBSZ, THEUNIS, 't Nieuwe en Vergroote Zee-Boeck	1657	220
111	JACOBSZ, THEUNIS. Le Grand & Nouveau Miroir ou Flambeau, De la Mer	1666	222
112	JANSSONIUS, JOANNES, Novus Atlas Vol. I	1645	226
113	JANSSONIUS, JOANNES, [Novus Atlas] Vol. II	[1645?]	230
114	JANSSONIUS, JOANNES, Novus Atlas Vol. III	1645	235
115	JANSSONIUS, JOANNES, Novus Atlas, Vol. IV	1647	238
116	JANSSONIUS, JOANNES, Het vyfde deel Des Grooten Atlas	1657	240
117	JANSSONIUS, JOANNES, De Lichtende Colomne, ofte Zeespiegel Vol. I	1653	241
118	JANSSONIUS, JOANNES, De Lichtende Colomne ofte Zeespiegel Vol. II	1653	245
119	JODE, CORNELIS DE, Speculum Orbis Terræ	1593	246

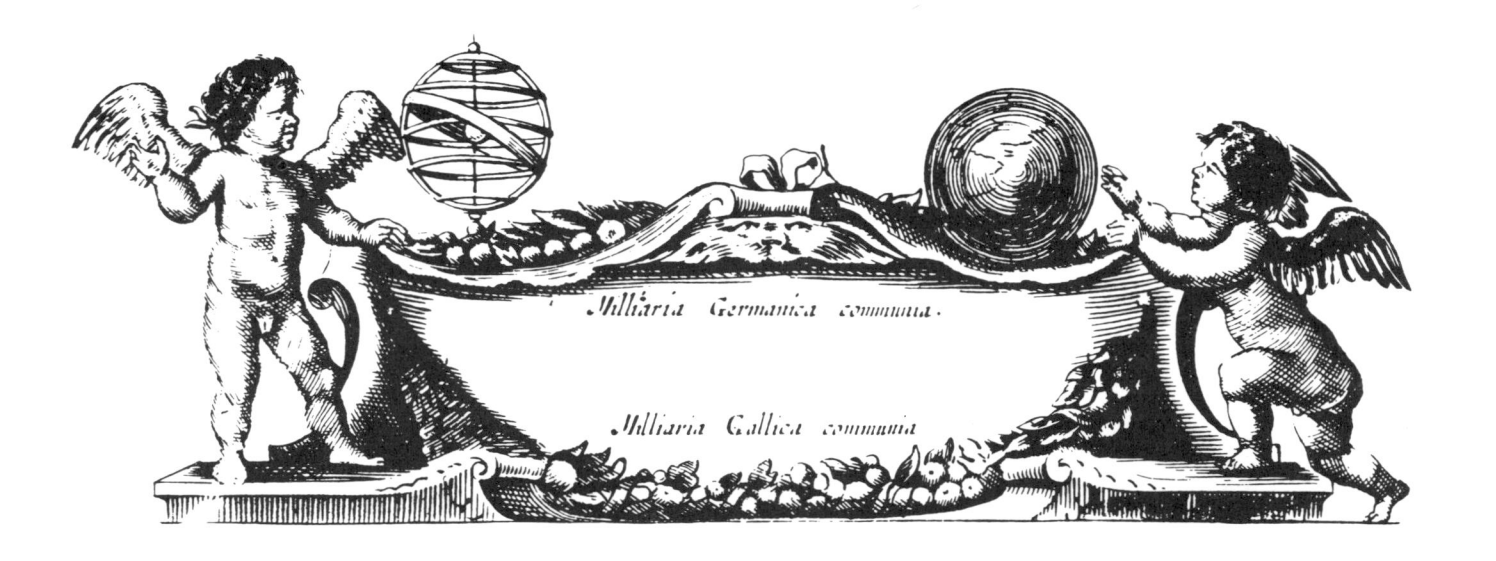

1 ADRICHEM, CHRISTIAAN VAN 1590

THEATRVM TERRÆ SANCTÆ ET BIBLICARVM HISTORIARVM cum tabulis geographicis ære expressis. AVCTORE, CHRISTIANO ADRICHOMIO, DELPHO. [Colophon:] COLONIÆ AGRIPPINÆ In Officina Birckmannica, sumptibus Arnoldi Mylij. Anno M. D. XC.
36,7 cm.

- [1] SITVS TERRÆ PROMISSIONIS SS BIBLIORVM INTELLIGENTIAM EXACTE APERIENS: PER CHRISTIANVM ADRICHOMIVM DELPHVM [C:] ADRICHOM — Before I 353 × 1009 mm.
- [2] [C:] TRIBVS ASER id est, portio illa Terræ Sanctæ, quæ Tribui Aser in diuisione regionis attributa fuit — Before I 220 × 389 mm.
- [3] [C:] TRIBVS EPHRAIM, BENIAMIN, ET, DAN, iste videlicet Terræ Sanctæ tractus, qui in regionis partitione istis tribus tribubus datus est. — Between pp. 24 and 25. 381 × 463 mm.
- [4] [C:] TRIBVS GAD nempe, ea Terræ Sanctę pars, quæ obtigit in partitione regionis tribui Gad. — Between pp. 32 and 33. 233 × 420 mm.
- [5] [C:] TRIBVS ZABVLON, ISACHAR, ET, DIMIDIA MANASSE altera, hoc est, illæ Terræ Sanctæ regiones, quas istę tribus in distribuendo possidendas acceperunt. — Between pp. 36 and 37. 358 × 396 mm.
- [6] [C:] TRIBVS IVDA id est, pars illa Terræ Sanctæ, quam in ingressu Tribus Iuda consecuta fuit. — Between pp. 38 and 39. 331 × 422 mm.
- [7] [C:] DIMIDIA TRIBVS MANASSE hoc est, ea Terræ Sanctæ pars, quam Manassæ dimidia tribus in regionis diuisione obtinuit. — Between pp. 76 and 77. 223 × 452 mm.
- [8] [C:] TRIBVS NEPTALIM videlicet, ea Terræ Sanctæ pars, quam in diuisione regionis tribus Neptalim accepit. — Between pp. 100 and 101. 208 × 366 mm.
- [9] [C:] PHARAN desertum, et confinia eius cum parte Ægypti, ea videlicet terræ regio, in qua filij Israël post exitum de Ægypto, triginta octo annis vagati sunt antequam terram promissam ingrederentur. — Between pp. 116 and 117. 345 × 493 mm.
- [10] [C:] TRIBVS RVBEN hoc est, ea Terræ Sanctæ regio, quę in diuidendo tribui Rubē assignata est. — Between pp. 126 and 127. 224 × 472 mm.
- [11] [C:] TRIBVS SIMEON nempe ea Terræ Sanctæ portio, quam tribus Simeon in ingressu nacta fuit. — Between pp. 132 and 133. 177 × 365 mm.
- [12] [C:] IERVSALEM[I], et suburbia eius, sicut tempore Christi floruit, cum locis in quibus Christǫ passus est: quæ religiose à Christianis obseruata, etiā nū Venerationi habentur. descripta per Christianum Adrichom Delphum. — [C:] ADRICHOM — [C:] ... Coloniæ Agrippinæ. Anno Christi. 1584. — [C:] R[mo] & Illustr[mo] D.D. Ernesto Archiep. Colon. S. Ro. ... Christ. Adrichō Delp. dedic. — (Plan). Between pp. 144 and 145. 507 × 737 mm.

Notes: All the maps are blank on the back and uncoloured. There is another plan of Jerusalem by Christiaan van Adrichem in Braun and Hogenberg's Civitates Orbis Terrarum, Part 4 no. 58—59. The atlas is bound in old vellum, with the same ornamentation on the front and back covers. Nordenskiöld's signature is on the inside of the front cover, with a note in another hand: Non è proibito affatto.

Lit.: ADB vol. 1, p. 125, Jöcher vol. 1, p. 106, Tooley, Dictionary p. 11.

2 ADRICHEM, CHRISTIAAN VAN 1593

THEATRVM TERRÆ SANCTÆ ET BIBLICARVM HISTORIARVM cum tabulis geographicis ære expressis. AVCTORE, CHRISTIANO ADRICHOMIO, DELPHO. [Colophon:] COLONIÆ AGRIPPINÆ In Officina Birckmannica, sumptibus Arnoldi Mylij. Anno M. D. XCIII.
38,9 cm.

- [1] SITVS TERRÆ PROMISSIONIS ... Before I = 1590:[1].
- [2] [C:] TRIBVS ASER ... — Before I = 1590:[2].
- [3] [C:] TRIBVS EPHRAIM, BENIAMIN, ET, DAN, ... — Between pp. 24 and 25. = 1590:[3].
- [4] [C:] TRIBVS GAD ... — Between pp. 30 and 31. = 1590:[4].
- [5] [C:] TRIBVS ZABVLON, ISACHAR, ET, DIMIDIA MANASSE ... — Between pp. 34 and 35. = 1590:[5].
- [6] [C:] TRIBVS IVDA ... — Between pp. 38 and 39. = 1590:[6].
- [7] [C:] DIMIDIA TRIBVS MANASSE ... — Between pp. 74 and 75. = 1590:[7].
- [8] [C:] TRIBVS NEPTALIM ... — Between pp. 100 and 101. = 1590:[8].
- [9] [C:] PHARAN desertum, ... — Between pp. 116 and 117. = 1590:[9].
- [10] [C:] TRIBVS RVBEN ... — Between pp. 126 and 127. = 1590:[10].

- [11] [C:] TRIBVS SIMEON ... — Between pp. 130 and 131. = 1590:[11].
- [12] [C:] IERVSALEM¹, ... — Between pp. 144 and 145. = 1590:[12].

Notes: All the maps are blank on the back and uncoloured. This edition is identical to that of 1590. Maps [2,3,5,6,9] have been cropped to the neat lines, and map [12], IERUSALEM, is in bad repair. The atlas is bound in old vellum, with Nordenskiöld's signature on the inside of the front cover.

Lit.: See Adrichem (1) 1590.

3 ALBERTI, LEANDER 1567

ISOLE APPARTENENTI ALLA ITALIA, DI F. LEANDRO ALBERTI, BOLOGNESE. Aggiuntoui di nuouo i disegni di quelle, & collocati alli suoi luoghi, a commune utilità, & sodisfattione de i Lettori. ... IN VENETIA, Appresso Lodouico Auanzi. M. D. LXVII.   20,8 cm.

- [1] CORSICA:
  [T:] L'ISOLA DI CORSICA — 5 A 5   Verso blank. 245 × 168 mm.
- [2] SARDIGNA.
  [T:] SARDEGNA — 18 C   Verso blank.   244 × 167 mm.
- [3] SICILIA.
  [T:] SICILIA ISOLA — 31 D 3   Verso blank.   172 × 246 mm.
- [4] Isole del mare Adriatico.
  [T:] ABRVZZO — 77   Verso blank.   172 × 248 mm.
- [5] VENETIA. (Plan). 79 K   Text on verso.   170 × 245 mm.

Notes: All the maps are uncoloured. Isolarios were popular in the 16th century; this one contains fewer maps than is usual, but in other respects has all the characteristics of the isolario, and may be treated as such. Bagrow states that there should be seven maps in this work, but this copy has only five. According to him, Alberti uses many maps by Antonius Ferrari (= Galateus), physician from Naples. The collection also contains a copy of the 1596 edition, bound with the same author's 'Descrittione di tutta l'Italia', but it has no maps. According to Castellani the 1567 edition is also associated with an edition of the 'Descrittione', published in 1568, but our copy is without it. The author was a Dominican of Bologna. In this copy there is a stamp on the title-page consisting of a cross surrounded by the letters S P B C. The volume was bound for Nordenskiöld by G. Hedberg of Stockholm. The initials A.E.N. are in gold on the spine, and Nordenskiöld's bookplate is pasted on the inside of the front cover.

Lit.: Bagrow, Geschichte p. 329, 342, Bonacker p. 28, Castellani, p. 75—76, Jöcher vol. 1, c. 195—196, Tooley, Dictionary, p. 13.

4 ANANIA, GIOVANNI LORENZO D' 1582

L'VNIVERSALE FABRICA DEL MONDO, OVERO COSMOGRAFIA Dell'Ecc. Gio. Lorenzo d'Anania, Diuisa in quattro Trattati: Ne' quali distintamente si misura il Cielo, e la Terra, & si descriuono particolarmente le Prouincie, Città, Castella, Monti, Mari, Laghi, Fiumi, & Fonti. Et si tratta delle Leggi, & Costumi di molti Popoli: de gli Alberi, & dell'Herbe, e d'altre cose pretiose, & Medicinali, & de gl'Inuentori di tutte le cose. Di nuouo ornata con le figure delle quattro parti del Mondo in Rame: Et dal medesimo Auttore con infinite aggiuntioni per ogni parte dell'opera, ampliata. ... IN VENETIA, Presso il Muschio. M D LXXXII. Ad instanza di Aniello San Vito di Napoli.   21,8 cm.

- [1] [T:] ORBIS DESCRIPTIO. — 178 × 257 mm. The hemispheres with 125 mm. diam.
- [2] EVROPA. 178 × 248 mm.
- [3] ASIA. 177 × 246 mm.
- [4] AFRICA. 176 × 244 mm.
- [5] AMERICA. 175 × 245 mm.

Notes: All the maps are blank on the back and uncoloured. They are all bound between the 'Prohemio al lettore' and the 'Indice delle piu notabil cose...' This is the third edition. The collection also has the second edition, published in Venice in 1576, but without maps. Bagrow states that Anania made three maps for his 'L'Universale fabrica del mondo' of 1582; Tooley, on the other hand, refers to four maps (of the four continents) in three editions of 1576, 1582 and 1596. The 1576 title-page, however, does not mention maps; and, as stated above, there are none in our copy. The world map in two hemispheres, which is the first map in our copy of the 1582 edition, is not mentioned in any of the descriptions I have seen. On the inside of the front cover of the 1576 edition, Nordenskiöld has written 'Lorenzo d'Anania Italiensk lärd — Vistades under skydd af Kardinal Caraffa i Napoli till dennes dod 1576. Dog sjelf 1582. Skref i Daemonologi.' [Lorenzo d'Anania Italian scholar. Lived in Naples under Cardinal Caraffa's protection until the cardinal died 1576. He himself died 1582. He wrote on daemonology.] Our copy of the 1582 edition is bound in half calf by the Swedish bookbinder Alfr. Lundin of Stockholm. Nordenskiöld's initials are in gold on the spine; his signature is on the first blank leaf, and his bookplate on the inside of the front cover.

Lit.: Bagrow, Geschichte, p. 330, Castellani, p. 9, nr 16 and 17, Graesse, vol. I, p. 114, Nouv. Biogr. Gener. vol. 2, c. 472, Tooley, Dictionary, p. 17.

5 ANVILLE, JEAN BAPTISTE BOURGUIGNON D' 1737

NOUVEL ATLAS DE LA CHINE, DE LA TARTARIE CHINOISE, ET DU THIBET: CONTENANT Les Cartes générales & particulieres de ces Pays, ainsi que la Carte du Royaume de CORÉE; La plupart levées sur les lieux par ordre de l'Empereur CHANG-HI avec toute l'exactitude imaginable, soit par les PP. Jésuites Missionaires à la Chine, soit par des Tartares du Tribunal des Mathématiques, & toutes revûes par les mêmes Peres: Rédigées PAR M^R. D'ANVILLE, GÈOGRAPHE ORDINAIRE DE SA MAJESTÉ TRÈS-CHRÉTIENNE, Precédé d'une DESCRIPTION DE LA BOUCHARIE, Par un Officier Suedois qui a fait quelque sejour dans ce Pays. ... A LA HAYE, Chez HENRI SCHEURLEER. M D C C X X X V I I.   55,8 cm.

- [1] [C:] CARTE LA PLUS GENERALE ET QUI COMPREND LA CHINE, LA TARTARIE CHINOISE, ET LE THIBET DRESSÉE SUR LES CARTES PARTICULIERES DES RR PP JESUITES, PAR LE S^R D'ANVILLE GEOGRAPHE ORD^RE DU ROI, QUI Y A JOINT LE PAYS COMPRIS ENTRE KASHGAR ET LA MER CASPIENNE tiré des Geographes et des Historiens Orientaux M DCC XXXIV. — G. Kondet fesit et scrip. Coloured.   468 × 686 mm.
- [2] [C:] CARTE GENERALE DE LA CHINE DRESSÉE SUR LES CARTES PARTICULIERES QUE L'EMPEREUR CHANG-HI A FAIT LEVER SUR LES LIEUX PAR LES R.R.P.P. JESUITES MISSIOÑAIRES DANS CET EMPIRE PAR LE S^r D'ANVILLE GEOGRAPHE ORD^re DU ROI. — Coloured.   585 × 506 mm.
- [3] [C:] PROVINCE DE PE-TCHE-LI   C.de Putter Sculp. — [T:] Tom I Page —   375 × 285 mm.
- [4] [C:] PROVINCE DE KIANG-NAN — [T:] Tom. I. Pag. —   356 × 337 mm.
- [5] [C:] PROVINCE DE KIANG-SI —   335 × 270 mm.
- [6] [C:] PROVINCE DE FO-KIEN —   376 × 319 mm.
- [7] [C:] PROVINCE DE TCHE KIANG —   255 × 234 mm.
- [8] [C:] PROVINCE DE HOU-QUANG. —   486 × 406 mm.
- [9] [C:] PROVINCE DE HO-NAN —   319 × 315 mm.
- [10] [C:] PROVINCE DE CHAN-TONG —   231 × 372 mm.
- [11] [C:] PROVINCE DE CHAN-SI —   352 × 243 mm.
- [12] [C:] PROVINCE DE CHEN-SI —   457 × 525 mm.
- [13] [C:] PROVINCE DE SE-TCHUEN —   401 × 476 mm.

[14] [C:] PROVINCE DE QUANG-TONG. — 420 × 528 mm.
[15] [C:] PROVINCE DE QUANG-SI — 264 × 403 mm.
[16] [C:] PROVINCE D'YUN-NAN — 365 × 430 mm.
[17] [C:] PROVINCE DE KOEI-TCHEOU — 265 × 304 mm.
[18] [C:] CARTE GENERALE DE LA TARTARIE CHINOISE DRESSÉE SUR LES CARTES PARTICULIERES FAITES SUR LES LIEUX PAR LES RRPP JESUITES ET SUR LES MEMOIRES PARTICULIERS DU P GERBILLON PAR LE S.r D'ANVILLE GEOGRAPHE ORD.re DU ROI MARS MDCCXXXII. — Coloured. 502 × 780 mm.
[19] [C:] I.e Feuille de la TARTARIE CHINOISE contenant le Leao tong, et les environs de Kirin Oula, le Pays de Cartchin et autres quartiers des MONGOUS — 285 × 473 mm.
[20] [C:] II.e Feuille particuliere de la TARTARIE CHINOISE contenant les environs de NIMGOUTA, qui est proprement l'ancien paÿs des MANTCHEOUX, et l'extrêmité la plus Septentrionale de la Corée. — 285 × 472 mm.
[21] [C:] III.e feuille particuliere de la TARTARIE CHINOISE, contenantles quartiers occupés par les MONGOUS au Nord de la Gr: Muraille et le Païs D'ORTOUS, environé de la Riviere HOANG-HO. — 288 × 477 mm.
[22] [C:] IV.e Feuille particuliere de la TARTARIE CHINOISE, occupée par une partie du COBI ou CHA-MO désert sabloneux, jusques à la Ville de HAMI. — 290 × 476 mm.
[23] [C:] V.e Feuille de la TARTARIE CHINOISE, contenant les environs de Tcitcicar et de Merguen, les Païs de TAGOURI et des SOLONS, et l'extremité Orientale du grand désert de Sable. — 288 × 474 mm.
[24] [C:] VI.e Feuille particuliere de la TARTARIE CHINOISE, contenant le Païs des Tartares YUPI et ILAN-HALA. qui est de l'ancien Païs MANTCHEOU. — 286 × 475 mm.
[25] [C:] VII.e Feuille particuliere de la TARTARIE CHINOISE, qui contient la plus grande partie du Païs occupé par les Tartares KALKAS. — 286 × 473 mm.
[26] [C:] VIII.e feuille de la TARTARIE CHINOISE, qui est le commencement du Païs des Tartares ELUTS, de l'extremité occidentale de celui des KALKAS. — 285 × 469 mm.
[27] [C:] IX.e Feuille particuliere de la TARTARIE CHINOISE, où ses Limites avec la TARTARIE RUSSIENNE sont exposés. — 287 × 472 mm.
[28] [C:] X.e feuille de la TARTARIE CHINOISE, contenant le Païs de KE-TCHING, l'embouchure du SAGHALIEN-OULA dans la Mer Orientale, et la grande Isle qui est au dedans. — 290 × 570 mm.
[29] [C:] Onzieme Feuille particul. de la TARTARIE CHINOISE, qui contient un Pays dependant de la Russie au Couchant de NIPTCHOU — 288 × 478 mm.
[30] [C:] XII.e derniere feuille DE LA TARTARIE CHINOISE. — 288 × 286 mm.
[31] [C:] ROYAUME DE CORÉE — [T:] G. Kondet fecit. — C. Kondet scrip. 514 × 351 mm.
[32] [C:] CARTE GENERALE DU THIBET OU BOUT-TAN ET DES PAYS DE KASHGAR ET HAMI DRESSÉE SUR LES CARTES ET MEMOIRES DE RR PP JESUITES DE LA CHINE et accordée avec la situation constante de quelques Pays voisins. PAR LE S.R D'ANVILLE Geographe Ord.re du Roi. Avril 1733. — [C:] ... C: et G: Kondet sculp. — 453 × 578 mm.
[33] [C:] I.re FEUILLE Comprise dans la Carte Générale du THIBET qui contient en particulier L'Extrêmité Occidentale du grand DESERT de SABLE et le PAYS AUX ENVIRONS DE HAMI. — 286 × 473 mm.
[34] [C:] II.e Feuille comprise dans la Carte Generale DU THIBET, et qui contient en particulier le Paÿs qui est au Couchant de TOURFAN. — 398 × 281 mm.
[35] [C:] III.e Feuille comprise dans la Carte Générale DU THIBET, et qui contient en particulier les Environs de KASHGAR. — 402 × 285 mm.
[36] [C:] IV.e Feuille Comprise dans la Carte générale du THIBET, et qui contient en particulier le Pais des TARTARES de HOHO-NOR — [T:] F:M LaCave sculp — 287 × 479 mm.
[37] [C:] V.e feuille qui est proprement la premiere DU TIBET, et qui contient LE SI-FAN et Païs Limitrophe. — 488 × 310 mm.
[38] [C:] VI.e Feuille, qui est la seconde DU THIBET et qui contient le Pays qui est au Levant DE LASA. — 492 × 316 mm.
[39] [C:] VII.e feuille qui est proprement la troisieme DU THIBET, et qui contient le pais des environs DU TSANPOU au couchant DE LASA. — 494 × 316 mm.
[40] [C:] VIII.e feuille qui est proprement la quatriéme DU THIBET, et qui donne l'origine DU TSANPON et DU GANGE. — 488 × 312 mm.
[41] [C:] IX.e et derniere feuille de celles qui sont comprises dans la Carte generale DU THIBET, et ou se trouve LATAC. — 493 × 316 mm.
[42] [C:] CARTE DES PAYS traversés par le Cap.ne BEERINGS depuis la Ville de TOBOLSK jusqú à KAMTSCHATKA. — G. Kondet fecit et scrip. 232 × 532 mm.

Notes: All the maps are blank on the back and uncoloured except the maps [1,2,18]. The words 'D de Putter sculp' on map [3] and 'F.M. Le Cave Sculp' on map [36] probably refer only to the cartouches. This is the first publication of the map of Bering's voyage [42]. The atlas is bound in the original boards, with Nordenskiöld's signature on the inside of the front cover.

Lit.: Koeman vol. 1, p. 48—49, Anv 1, Nordenskiöld, Vega vol. 2, p. 182, note 1, Thieme-Becker vol. 7, p. 293, vol. 21, p. 260.

6 APIAN [APIANUS], PHILIPP   1568

Bairische Landtaflen. XXIIII. Darinnē das Hochlöblich Furstenthumb Obern vnnd Nidern Bayrn/sambt der Obern Pfaltz/Ertz vnnd Stifft Saltzburg/Eichstet/vnnd andern mehrern anstossenden Herschafftē/mit vleiss beschribē/vnd in druck gegebē. Durch Philippum Apianum. Zu Inngolstat MDLXVIII.
39 cm.

[1]   Ein klaine Landtafel des Lands Obern vnd Nidern Bayrn. [T:] Ein kurtze Beschreibung des gantzen Fürstentumbs Obern vnd Nidern Bayrn / sambt den anstossenden Lendern. — [C:] BREVIS TOTI9 BAVARIAE DESCRIPTIO AVTORE PHIL. APIANO — [T:] HF — 316 × 321 mm.
[2—3] Die Erst Landtafel Begreifft in sich. Stett/ Altorff Herschprück Laüff Nürmberg ...
Die Annder Landtafel Helt in sich. Stett/ Amberg Nabprück Pfreimbt Sültzbach ...
1 [C:] ILLVSTRISSIMO ET SERENISS. PRINCIPI AC DN.D. ALBERTO COM. PALATINO RHENI SVPERIORIS INFER. QVE BAVARIAE DVCI. PHIL. APIANVS DD. ANN. SAL. M. D. LXVI. — 157 × 417 mm.
2 [T:] PALATINATVS SVPERIOR — A I 157 × 417 mm.
[4—5] Die Dritte vnd Vierde Landtafel Begreifft in sich. Stett/ Schonsee ...
3 [C:] CHOROGRAPHIA BAVARIÆ. — 155 × 148 mm.
4 [C:] AD ILLVSTRISS. ET SERENISS. PRINCIPEM AC DOMINVM: DOMIN. ALBERTVM COMITEM PALATINVM RHENI: VTRIVSQVE BAVARIAE DVCEM: DO. SVVM CLEMENTISS. PHILIPPI APIANI PRAEFATIO. ... — A II 157 × 417 mm.
[6]   5 Die Fünfft Landtafel Begreifft in sich. Stett/ Freyenstat Greding Güntzenhausn Heidegkh Hiltpoltstain Rott Schwabach Weissenbürg ... B I 323 × 415 mm.
[7]   6 Die Sechst Landtafel Helt in sich. Stett/ Berching Berngries Burcklengfeldt Dietfurt Hemmaw Neumarckht Regenspurg Schwandorf Velburg ... B ij 324 × 414 mm.
[8]   7 Die Sibendt Landtafel Begreifft in sich. Stett/ Cham

Fürt Neüburg vorm walt Retz Walt münchen ... B III 323 × 417 mm.

[9] 8 Die Acht Landtafel Helt in sich. Herschafft/ Zwisel ... [C:] Beschreibung Des Lands vnd Fürstenthumbs Obern vnd Nidern Baiern, sambt den vmbligenden anstössen anderer herrschaften Darinnen die Stet Märckt Clöster Schlösser auch etlich dörffer gebürg Wäldt wasserflüss See Weÿer vnd anders auf das vleissigest verzaichnet seyen. Dürch Philippum. Apianum. — B IIII 325 × 418 mm.

[10] 9 Die Neündt Landtafel Helt in sich. Stett/ Aichstet Dünawert Harburg Ingolstat Küpferberg Monhaim Neüburg Oeting Pappenheim Rain Wembding ... C I 323 × 413 mm.

[11] 10 Die Zehendt Landtafel Helt in sich. Stett/ Abensperg Ingolstat Kelhaim Newstat ... C II 324 × 415 mm.

[12] 11 Die Ailfft Landtafel Begreifft in sich. Stett/ Deckendorff Dingelfing Landaw Osterhouen Sträubing ... C III 325 × 417 mm.

[13] 12 Die Zwölfft Landtafel Begreifft in sich. Stett/ Graüenaw Vilsshouen ... C IIII 323 × 414 mm.

[14] 13 Die Dreizehend Landtafel Helt in sich. Stett/ Aichach Augspurg Fridberg Schröbĕhausn ... D I 324 × 413 mm.

[15] 14 Die Viertzehendt Landtafel Begreifft in sich. Stett/ Aerding Freising Landsshuet Mospurg Pfaffenhouen ... D II 324 × 417 mm.

[16] 15 Die Funfftzehend Landtafel Helt in sich. Stett/ Braünaw Oeting Müldorff ... D III 324 × 414 mm.

[17] 16 Die Sechtzehen Landtafel Helt in sich. Stett/ Passaw Scherding ... D IIII 323 × 415 mm.

[18] 17 Die Sibentzehendt Landtafel Begreifft in sich. Stett/ Landsperg ... E I 324 × 415 mm.

[19] 18 Die Achtzehend Landtafel Begreifft in sich. Stett/ München Wasserburg ... E II 324 × 415 mm.

[20] 19 Die Neüntzehendt Landtafel Helt in sich. Stett/ Burgkhausen Ditmaning Lauffen Traünstain Wasserburg ... E III 324 × 413 mm.

[21] 20 Die Zwaintzigist Landtafel Helt in sich. Märckt/ ... E IIII 324 × 416 mm.

[22] 21 Die Ain vnnd Zwaintzigist Landtafel Helt in sich. Stett/ Füessen Schonga Weilhaim ... [C:] CAVTVM EST CAESEREAE MAIESTATIS GRATIA ET PRIVILEGIO: NON SOLVM, NE QVIS HANC BAVARIAE DESCRIPTIONEM INTRA TRIGINTA ANNOS EXCVDAT, AVT IMPRIMI FACIAT, ALIBIVE IMPRESSAM VENDAT: SED ETIAM, NE VLLO MODO ALIAVE FORMA IMITETVR AC DIVVLGET. ABSOL. ET EXCVSA INGOLST. ANNO SAL. MDLXVIII. — F I 324 × 417 mm.

[23] 22 Die Zway vnnd zwaintzigist Landtafel Begreifft in sich. Stett/ Küpfstain ... F II 323 × 413 mm.

[24] 23 Die Drey vnnd zweintzigist Landtafel Begreifft in sich. Stett/ Reichenhall ... F III 325 × 414 mm.

[25] 24 Die Vier vnnd zwaintzigist Landtafel Helt in sich. Stett/ Hellel Saltzburg ... [C:] IN CHOROGRAPHIAM BAVARIAE, PHI. APIANI ACCVRATISS. HIERON. VVOLFIVS. ... — [T:] 1567. W. S. H. F. — 323 × 418 mm.

Notes: All the maps are blank on the verso, and uncoloured. This is the second edition of the Landtafeln; the first was published in 1563. On the title-page, in manuscript, are the words 'Ex libris I.H. LeFors Scutarij Nobilis Reg. Arm. Sac^{ae} Caes^{ae} et Cath. Maj.$^{ti's}$,; on the back of the last map, 'Delbroud'. Nordenskiöld's signature, in ink, is on the inside of the front cover, with the date 1887. A pencil note in his hand reads 'Den första kartan hör möjligen ej till arbetet och torde vara en stor r.r. [The first map may not belong to the work, and seems to be very rare.] (Jemf Günther Peter u. Ph. Apian. Prag 1882. s. 120.)' It is, however, clear from the text on the map that it is an index to the whole work, although it is lacking in many of the known extant copies; in this example it is in worse condition than the rest of the volume.

Lit.: Bagrow, Ortelius vol. 1, p. 36—41, Bonacker p. 32 and 47, BM Maps vol. 2, c. 451, Günther, Peter und Philipp Apian.

7 ATLANTE DELL' AMERICA 1777

ATLANTE DELL' AMERICA CONTENENTE LE MIGLIORI CARTE GEOGRAFICHE, E TOPOGRAFICHE DELLE PRINCIPALI CITTÀ, LAGHI, FIUMI, E FORTEZZE DEL NUOVO MONDO Con una succinta Relazione dei diversi Stabilimenti Europèi in quella parte di Globo, e principalmente dei Luoghi, che servono adesso di Teatro alla presente Guerra fra i Coloni Inglesi, e la Madre Patria. LIVORNO MDCCLXXVII. PRESSO GIO. TOMMASO MASI, E COMP. CON APPROVAZIONE. 35,6 cm.

[1] [C:] Nuova ed esatta Carta Della AMERICA Ricavata dalle MAPPE, e CARTE piu approvate — [T:] Andrea Scacciati scolpi — [T:] Giuseppe Pazzi scrisse. — 341 × 275 mm.

[2] [C:] CARTA DELLA NUOVA INGHILTERRA NUOVA IORK, E PENSILVANIA — 204 × 294 mm.

[3] [C:] Carta Rappresentante il Porto di Boston — G M Terreni s. 192 × 175 mm.

[4] [T:] PORTI DELLA NUOVA YORK E PERTHAMBOY — Giuseppe M. Terreni sc. Livorno 197 × 161 mm.

[5] [C:] Carta rappresentante i cinque Laghi del Canada' — Andr Scacciati sc Giusep. Pazzi scrisse 251 × 183 mm.

[6] [C:] CADUTA DI NIAGARA — G.M.T. sc. (View). 239 × 178 mm.

[7] [T:] PIANO DELLA CITTA DI QUEBEC — D. Ver. Rossi M.V. sc. (Plan). 240 × 234 mm.

[8] [C:] QUEBEC ... — (View). 183 × 272 mm.

[9] [T:] CARTA RAPPRESENTANTE IL GOLFO DEL FIUME S.LORENZO — Andrea Scacciati sc Giu. Pazzi scrisse. 252 × 191 mm.

[10] [C:] Nuova, e corretta Carta dell' Isola di Terra Nuova. — [T:] D. Verem. Rossi sc. — 218 × 162 mm.

[11] [C:] CARTA rappresentante una parte dlla BAJA D'HUDSON, e le Regioni a Maestro DELL'AMERICA SETTENTR^{LE} — D. Ver. Rossi M.V. sc. (Chart). 208 × 268 mm.

[12] [C:] PIANO di GUANTANIMO Chiamato dagl' Inglesi Porto di Cumberland — Viol: Vanni sc Giusep. Pazzi scrisse. (Chart). 260 × 192 mm.

[13] [C:] Carta Rappresentante la PENISOLA della FLORIDA — Andrea Scacciati sc Giu. Pazzi scrise. 225 × 209 mm.

[14] [T:] PIANO del PORTO, e degli STABILIMENTI di PENSACOLA — Viol. Vanni sc Giusep. Pazzi scrisse. (Chart). 180 × 258 mm.

[15] [C:] PIANO della CITTÀ, e PORTO di SANT' AGOSTINO — Viol. Vanni sc Giusep Pazzi Scrisse (Chart). 200 × 285 mm.

[16] [C:] NUOVO MESSICO — Violante Vanni sc. (View). 177 × 258 mm.

[17] [C:] NUOVA e corretta Carta dell' INDIE OCCIDENTALI cavata dalle migliori autorità — [T:] D.Veremondo Rossi Monaco Val.$^{O.}$ incise — 271 × 346 mm.

[18] [C:] CARTA ESATTA rappresentante l'ISOLA di CUBA estratta dalle Carte del Sig:^{re} Poppler — [T:] G.M.Terreni sc. — 258 × 318 mm.

[19] [T:] PIANO della CITTÀ e PORTO dell' HAVANA — Viol. Vanni sc Giusep. Pazzi scrisse 202 × 259 mm.

[20] [C:] CARTA esatta rappresentante l'ISOLA di S.DOMINGO o sia HISPANIOLA — [T:] G.M.Terreni sc — 253 × 308 mm.

[21] [T:] PIANO della CITTA di S.DOMINGO ... — Viol. Vanni sc Giusep. Pazzi scrisse (Plan). 181 × 257 mm.

[22] [C:] CARTA rappresentante l'ISOLA della GIAMMAICA — D. Ver. Rossi M.V. sc. 203 × 313 mm.

[23] [T:] VEDVTA DI S.EVSTACHIO — [T:] N. Matraini del. — [T:] I. Ottauiani inc. — (View). 176 × 345 mm.

[24] [C:] CARTA ESATTA Rappresentante l'Isola della GUADALUPA — Andrea Scacciati sc Giusep Pazzi scrisse 218 × 293 mm.

[25] [C:] CARTA rappresentante l'ISOLA DELLA

MARTINICCA — And. Scacciati scolpi D.V.Rossi scrisse 216 × 292 mm.

[26] [C:] CARTA esatta rappresentante l'Isola di BARBADOS — D. Verem. Rossi M.V. sc. 223 × 179 mm.

[27] [C:] CARTA ESATTA Rappresentante L'ISOLA DI GRANATA — 228 × 183 mm.

[28] [T:] PIANO DELLA RADA, E DELLA CITTÀ DELLA VERA CRUZ ... — Violante Vanni fe: (Chart). 226 × 167 mm.

[29] [C:] PIANTA DEL PORTO D'ACAPULCO Sopra la Costa de Messico nel Mar del Sud — G.M.T.sc. (Chart). 218 × 162 mm.

[30] [C:] CARTA RAPPRESENTANTE LA BAIA DI CAMPEGGIO E L'JUCATAN — 245 × 214 mm.

[31] [C:] CARTA RAPPRESENTANTE L'ISTMO DI DARIEN O'SIA DI PANAMA — G. Terreni sc. 248 × 209 mm.

[32] [T:] PIANO di PORTO BELLO — Violante Vanni sc Giusep. Pazzi scrisse. (Chart). 192 × 256 mm.

[33] [T:] PIANO della CITTÀ RADA, e PORTO di CHAGRE — Viol. Vanni sc Giusep. Pazzi scrisse. (Chart). 258 × 195 mm.

[34] [C:] CARTA rappresentante L'AMERICA MERIDIONALE — D:Verem:Rossi sc. 218 × 167 mm.

[35] [C:] CARTA rappresentante le Provincie di CARTAGENA S MARTA E VENEZUELA — [T:] D.Veremondo Rossi sc. — 205 × 290 mm.

[36] [T:] PIANO della CITTÀ, e SOBBORGHI di CARTAGENA — Viol. Vanni sc Giusep. Pazzi scrisse (Plan). 189 × 256 mm.

[37] [T:] Piano della Città e Contorni di S.FRANCESCO DI QUITO ... — D.Verem: Rossi M.V. sc. (Plan). 242 × 267 mm.

[38] [C:] CARTA DEL CORSO DEL MARAGNONE O SIA DEL GRAN FIVME DELL'AMAZZONI Ricavata dalla carta che fu' fatta nel 1743. e 1744. e sottoposta all' osservazioni astronomiche dal Sig^{re} de la Condamine della Accademia Reale delle Scienze accresciuta col corso del Fiume Nero, e altre notizie cavate dalle memorie dei piu' moderni Viaggiatori. — D.Verem.Rossi M.V. sc. 215 × 311 mm.

[39] [T:] Piano Scenografico della Città dei RE, ò sia di LIMA Capitale del Regno del PERÙ — D.Verem.Rossi M.V. sc. (Plan). 256 × 269 mm.

[40] [T:] PIANTA DI CUSCO nel tempo della Conquista chenesecero gli Spagnoli — G.M.T.sc. (Plan). 202 × 165 mm.

[41] [C:] Veduta della Citta, e della Montagna del Potosi — G.M.T.sc. (View). 249 × 183 mm.

[42] [T:] PIANTA DELLA CITTA DI SANT'IAGO Capitale del Regno del CHILI — [T:] D.Verem.Rossi M.V. sc. — (Plan). 233 × 203 mm.

[43] [C:] CARTA ESATTA RAPPRESENTANTE IL CORSO DEL FIUME PARAGUAY E DI PAESI AD ESSO VICINI — D:Verem:Rossi sc. 229 × 256 mm.

[44] [a] [T:] Veduta della Citta di S.Salvadore dalla parte della Baia — (View). 50 × 290 mm.
[b] [T:] PIANTA DELLA CITTA DI S.SALVADORE Capitale del Bresile — (Plan). 135 × 290 mm.
[The whole map:] Viol. Vanni sc Giusep. Pazzi scrisse 187 × 290 mm.

Notes: All the maps are blank on the back, and uncoloured. The index lists only 43 maps, taking [7] and [8] together as VII, PIANO E VEDUTA DELLA CITTÀ DI QUEBECK; Philips numbers them 7 and 7½. In the Library of Congress copy p. 15 of the text is misnumbered p. 8; our copy has p. 15. Map [18] is a part of Henry Popple's map of the British Empire in America, printed in London in 1732. All the maps are taken from Il Gazzettiere Americano..., Livorno, M. Cotellini, 1763. Nordenskiöld has written his initials, AEN, in ink on the first blank leaf.

Lit.: BM Maps vol. 11, c. 727, Enciclopedia Italiana vol. 33, p. 644, LC List vol. 1, p. 596—597, nr 1167.

Cum Privilegio ad decennium.

8 BARENTZOEN, WILLEM 1595

Nieuwe beschryvinghe ende CAERTBOECK VANDE MIDLANDTSCHE ZEE WAER-IN meerckelick afgebeeld en beschreven worden alle custen vande Midlandsche Zee. Beginnende van Gibraltar langs Granada, Valentia, Catalonia, Proventia en Italia, door de Golfe van Venetia, voorby de custen van Apúlia, Venetia, Istria, Slavonia, en Græcia. Item alle de principale tvmaerde havenen, als Constantinopolis, Tripolis, Iaffæ, Alexandriæ ende meer andere, naer het leven afgheteekent. Midschaders de streckinghen vande gansche Midlandsche Zee. Ooc alle eylanden der selfder, als Eviça, Majorca, Minorca, Sicilia, Malta, ende de Eylanden inde golfe van Venetia ect. Desghelicx particulierlick de Eylanden van Canarien ende Madera. ALLES in sekere Caerten met hare beschryvingen ende opdoeningen, met grooter neerstichetit ende aerbeyt gedaen, door Willem Barentzoen. TOT AMSTELREDAM, Ghedruct by Cornelis Claesz. op 't Water in't Schrijf-boeck/ by d'oude Brugghe. Met Privilegie. M. D. XCV. 41 cm.

[1] [T:] GENVA. — (View). On the title-page. Verso blank. 340 × 255 mm.

[2] [C:] Thalassographica Tabula totius Maris Mediterranei; necnon Oceani Atlantici, Hispanici, Gallici & Britãnici; in qua omnes Europæ, Asiæ & Africæ oræ maritimæ, quæ and hæ maria sunt sitæ: Portus item, Sinus, Promontoria, Insulæ, Profunda, Vada, Brevia et Syrtes fideliter describuntur. Quæ omnia magna diligentia ac labore sub veros Latitudinis gradus, & iustam Poli elevationem iuxta normam directorij nautici communis, idque sine ulla mutilatione sunt redacta. A.P.Plancio
Compascaerte van Fransche, Hispanische Canarische ende geheele Middenlãdsche Zee: Warin de zeecusten van Europa, Asia, en Africa, die aen dese Zeen sijn gelegen; metten Havenẽ, Inwycken, Capen, Eylanden, Sanden, Clippen ende andere ondiepten getrouwelic beschreven worden. Het welcke alles door groote neerstlicheide ende aerbeit onder de oprechte graden der Breedde en hoogde des Polus, na de regelmate des gemeynẽ compas, sonder eenige vercortĩge der lãdẽ, is gebracht Beschreven door Willem Barentsoen — [T:] Iudocus Hondius fec. — Blank on the back. 413 × 848 mm.
[Insets:]
[T:] Pennon de Veles — 38 × 66 mm. [T:] Oran — 38 × 64 mm. [T:] Alger — 38 × 67 mm. [T:] Constantinopolis — 38 × 66 mm. [T:] Goletta — 38 × 64 mm. [T:] Alexandria — 38 × 66 mm. [T:] Iaffa — 34 × 66 mm. [T:] Tripoli — 34 × 66 mm. (All insets plans).

[3] + Beschryvinghe der Zee custen van Barbaria/ beginnende van S. uVes hoeck voorby de C. S. Vincent langhs de Condado van Tanger, langs de Custen van Barbaria, tot C. de Bolador, midtsgaders de streckinghen van d'Eylanden van Canariën ende Madera.
[C:] Tabula Hydrographica, in qua Hispaniæ oræ maritimæ a Civitate Setubal usq3. ad promontorium S. Vincentij, & hinc ad Fretum Gaditanum, notantur, à quo usque ad promontorium Bojador dictum, insularum item Canariarum oræ maritimæ, portus, etiam promontoria, brevia et Syrtes accuratè summaqg diligentia discribuntur, a Guilielmo Barentsono.
Beschryvinghe der Zeecusten van Spaingnen, van ande Stadt Setubal, anders S. uves, tot Cabo S Vincent, van daer tot de Strate ende alsoo de custen van Barbarien tot Cabo Bojador ende voort aller Eylanden van Canariën, met alle havenen, hoecken, sanden ende ondipten seer neerstich beschreven door Willem Barentsoen. 1594. Pieter Vanden Keere fecit. — + 389 × 541 mm.
[Insets:]
[T:] Setubal. — 51 × 63 mm. [T:] S. Lucas. — 51 × 63 mm. [T:] Masagan — 51 × 64 mm. [T:] Garrachica — 51 × 64 mm. [T:] Portus Canariæ — 48 × 63 mm. [T:] Tangiara. — 47 × 63 mm. [T:] Septa. — 48 × 63 mm. [T:] Arzilla — 48 × 64 mm.

[4] GOMERA. TENERIFE. PALMA. PALMA. TENERIFE. (5 profiles). +

[5] 1 Beschryvinghe vande Zee Custen van Spangien/ beghinnende van Calis Malis door de Straet tot Cabo de Gata, met alle zijn Havenen/Bayen ende Reeden/ die tusschen beyden gheleghen zijn. Alles ghemaeckt op Spaensche mylen.
[C:] Hydrographica descriptio maris Mediterranei à freto Gaditano, usque ad C. dictum, de Gates; In qua oræ maritimæ Hispaniæ, & Barbariæ, Portus item & promontoria, insulæ, vada, brevia, necnon loca in quibus tuto anchoras figere liceat, evidenter et summa diligentia designantur, à peritissimo nauclero Guilielmo Barensono.
Beschrivinge der Zeecusten, beginnende van Calis af door de Straet tot aen Cabo de Gates, met alle de reeden ende bayen die tuschen beyden gelegen syn ende op wat plaetsen datmen magh reede maken. Oock de Barbarische custen tot voor by Cabo de Treforce, neerstich beschreven door Willem Barentsoen — [T:] J Hondius sculpsit — I 335 × 527 mm.

[6] Hier volghen de Opdoeninghen vande Landen/ die tusschen de Straet ende de C. Dagata gheleghen zijn/ beginnende vande Straet af tot C. de Gata ... (76 profiles). 1 I ij.

[7] 2 Beschryvinge der Zee Custen van Spangien/ beghinnende van Cabo de Gata voorby Cabo de Palos, tot Cabo S. Martin, hoemen in alle Havenen/ Bayen ende Reeden seylen sal.
[C:] Hydrographica descriptio maris Mediterran. in qua oræ maritimæ Hispaniæ a Charidemo, usq₃. ad Artemisium promontorium, Ebusus item insula, & Barbariæ oræ a promont. (quod dicit. Cap. de Hone) Iuliā Cæsaream usq₃, necnon & portus, promontoria, ins. adjacentes, vada, brevia & syrtes accuratissime describuntur.
Beschryvinge vandē Zeecusten van Spaengen beginnende van Cabo dagata tot de C. Martin, midschaders het eyland Yviça ende ooc de Barbarissche custē van Caep de Hone tot de stad van Alger, met alle havenen, reeden, bayen, ondiepten, clippē, sanden, ende ander drooghten seer neerstigh beschrevē door Willem Barentsoen — 2 370 × 526 mm.

[8] Hier nae volghen d'Opdoeningen/ beginnende van Cabo Dagata tot Cabo de Martin, van alle de landen die tusschen beyde de Capen gheleghen zijn. (59 profiles). 2 2ij.
Hier volghen d'Opdoeninghen van de Barbarische Cust. MOSTAGAN. (10 profiles).

[9] 3 Beschryvinghe der ZeeCusten van Valentia ende Catalonia/ beghinnende van Cabo Martin tot Cabo Dragonis, anders Cabo Dago fredi ghenaemt: Ende oock mede d'Eylanden van Majorca, Minorca, ende Yvica, met alle de Havenen/Bayen ende Reeden/die daer in gheleghen zijn.
[C:] Hydrographica descriptio, in qua Hispaniæ oræ maritimæ à Capite S. Martini usq₃ ad Caput Dragonis, item & insularum Yvicæ, Majorcæ & Minorcæ, accurate designantur, earumq̃₃ etiam promontoria, portus, insulæ, vada, brevia, syrtes, necnon et loca, in quibus tuto anchoras figere liceat, suis quæq̃₃ signis notantur, à peritissimo nauclero Guilielmo, Barentsono.
Beschryvinge vande Zeecusten van Spaengen van Cabo S. Martin tot Cabo Dragonis, ende ooc vande Eylanden vā Yvica, Majorca, ende Minorca, met alle hare Capen, hauenen, Eylanden, ondiepten ende sanden, ende ooc de plaetsen daermen reede maken magh, onder scheydelick afghebildet, doer den ervaren stierman Willem Barentsoen. Pieter Vanden Keere fecit anno 1593. — 3 335 × 517 mm.

[10] Opdoeninghe der Landen van Valencia ende Catalonia, beghinnende van Cabo Martijn, tot Cabo Dago Fredi, oft Cabo Dragonis, hoe die selvighe Landen haer opdoen/ midtsgaders d'Eylanden van Yviça, Majorca ende Minorca. (12 profiles). 3
Opdoeninghe vande Eylanden Majorca, Minorca ende Yviça (31 profiles).

[11] 4 Beschryvinghe vande ZeeCusten van Catalonia/ Languedoc/ Provencen/ ende een deel van Italien/ beghinnende van Cabo Dragonis tot Cabo delle Melle, met alle zijn Havenen/Bayen ende Reeden/die tusschen beyden gheleghen zijn/ende hoe datmen alle Clippen ende Ondiepten schouwen sal.
[C:] Hydrographica descriptio in qua oræ maritimæ Regionis Provinciæ, à Capite Dragonis usque ad C. delle Melle, unà cum portubus, fluvijs, promontorijs, adjacentibus insulis, brevijs, et vadis; locis item in quibus tuto anchoras figere liceat; summa cura et diligentia notantur à Guilielmo Barentsono
Beschryvinge vande Seecusten van Provincien, beginnende van Cabo Dragonis tot C. delle Melle, met alle hauenen, rijvieren, hoofden, Eylanden daerontrent, ondiepten ende clijppen ende ooc de plaetsen daermen reede maken magh; seer neerstich beschreven door Willem Barentsoen —
[T:] Pieter Vanden Keere fecit. 1593. — 4 331 × 521 mm.

[12] Opdoeninghen der Zee-custen van Provencen ende Italia/ beghinnende van Cabo de Tollon, langs de custen tot Cabo Delle Melle. (24 profiles). 4

[13] 5 Beschryvinghe der Zee Custen van Italien/beginnende van Cabo delle Melle tot Monte Argentato, hoemen in alle Havenen/Reeden/ende Baeyen seylen sal.
[C:] ITALIÆ ORÆ Maritime à Portu Herculis dicto, usque ad C. delle melle, unà cum promontorijs, portubus & insulis adjacentibus, in quibus profunda, vada et brevia accuratè designantur.
Italiaensche Zeecustē, beginnende van t'port Herculis tot C. delle melle toe, t'samen met alle haere capen, havenen, eylanden daer ontrent, sanden, ende andere ondiepten, seer neerstelick afgeteckēt — By Willem Barentzoen. 5 333 × 525 mm.

[14] Opdoeninghen van Italien/ beginnende van Cabo de Melle, tot den hoeck Pionbino, ende 't Eyland Corsica met d'ander cleyne Eylandekens daer ontrent gheleghen. (33 profiles). 5

[15] 6 Hoe datmen in alle de Havenen ende Bayen van Italien seylen sal/die tusschen Porto Hercole ende Napolis gheleghen zijn.
[C:] Hydrographica descriptio, in qua oræ maritimæ Italiæ à monte Argentato Napolim usq₉, promontoria item & portus, ajacentes insulæ, brevia & vada, accuratissimè a peritissimo nauclero Guiljelmo Barentsono designantur.
Beschrivinge der Zeecusten van Italien, beginnende van Monte Argentato tot Napolis, met alle hoofden, havenē, ende eylanden daer ontrent, ooc de ondiepten ende de sanden; seer neerstigh beschreven door den ervaren Piloot Willem Barentsoen. 1593. — 6 336 × 528 mm.

[16] Opdoeninghen van Sardinia/ ende vande eylanden Vulcani. (12 profiles). 6

[17] 7 Verclaringhe/hoe datmen in alle die Havenen van Cicilien seylen sal/midtsgaders oock tot sommighe plaetsen van Calabria.
[C:] HYDROGRAPHICA TABVLA, in qua Siciliæ, Maltæ confiniumq́ue insularum, necnon & partis Calabriæ, meridionalis Sardiniæ & Tunetani regni oræ maritimæ, unà cum suis portubus, insulis promontorijs & brevijs accuratè describuntur; quarum etiam portus præcipui topographicè summa diligentia designantur, à Guilielmo, Barentsono
Beschryvinge der Seecusten van Sicilien ende van Malta, midschaders aller eylanden daer ontrent, ende een deel van Calabria de Suythoeck van Sardinia ende een deel van Africa met alle havenen, bayen, hoecken ende plaetsen daermen reede maken magh: Ende noch de principale havenen hier boven int groote ghestelt so sy in haer wesen ghedaen syn. Alles seer neerstich Beschreven door Willem Barentsoen. Pieter vanden Keere fecit Anno 1594. — 7 410 × 551 mm.
[Insets:]
[T:] De hauen van Palermo in Sicilien — 61 × 61 mm.
[T:] De hauen Messina in Sicilien. — 61 × 54 mm.
[T:] De hauen Trapano in Sicilien. — 61 × 72 mm.
[T:] De hauen van Malta — 61 × 80 mm.

[18] Opdoeninghen van't Eyland van Cicilien ende Malta/ midtsgaders alle d'ander cleyne Eylanden daer ontrent ghelegen. (34 profiles). 7

[19] Beschryvinghe der Zee custen van Italien/ beginnende van Cabo Spartivento/ door de mont vande Golfe van Venetia/ langhs de Custen van Apulia/Venetia/Istria/Dalmatia/ Slavonia/ eñ Grecia/tot d'Eylanden Corfu eñ Xiphalonia/ alles seer naerstich beschreven naer onse gemeyne duytsch Compas/eñ ghestelt op duytsche mylen.
[C:] Tabula Hydrographica, IN qua Italiæ, oræ maritimæ; Item Venetiæ, Istriæ, Dalmatiæ, Slauoniæ, Græciæ, et oræ maritimæ Corfu, Chephaloniæ, et adjacentium Insularum: earum etiam omnium quæ in Mari Supero habentur: necnon & portus, Promontoria profunda & syrtes, Portus Item præcipui, topographicè summa diligentia designantur à Guiljelmo Barentsono.
Pascaerte, WAER inne beschreven Worden de Zeecosten van Italia, Venetia, Istria, Dalmatia, Slavonia, Grecia, Teijlant Corfu, ende Chephalonia, mitsgaders alle deijlanden daer ontrent ende in de Golfe ghelegen, met alle de hauenen reeden bayen ende ondieptē die in de selfde

Golfe ghelegen Zyn oock mede die princepaelste hauen̄ int groot. Zeer neerstich beschreuen doer Willem Barentsoe̅ — [T:] Pieter Vanden Keere fecit anno 1595 — 8   400 × 537 mm.
[Insets:]
[T:] La Vilona in Turckia — 61 × 68 mm. [T:] De hauen Trau in Dalmatia — 61 × 68 mm. [T:] De hauen Catarro in Dalmatia — 61 × 68 mm. [T:] De Stadt ende hauen Ragusa — 61 × 72 mm. [T:] De hauen Rouigno in Istria — 57 × 69 mm. [T:] S. Pedro — 57 × 72 mm. [C:] VENETIA. — 104 × 133 mm. [T:] De hauen Ancona — 47 × 77 mm. [T:] Brūdicio — 47 × 77 mm. [T:] Galipoli — 47 × 77 mm.

[20] Opdoeninghen vande Custen van Italien/ van C. Spartivento, tot C. de Otranto: Item van daer voorts langs de Custen van Puglia, Abruzzo, Marcda de Ancona, Romagna, Dalmatia, ende Istria tot Venetia. (96 profiles). 8 8ij.

Notes: All the maps have text on the verso except where otherwise specified and they are uncoloured. The profiles are printed on both sides of the leaves. The atlas is bound in old vellum. Nordenskiöld's signature is on the first blank leaf, with the note 'Ytterst sällsynt vigtig såsom det första? tryckta sjökort öfver Medelhafvet — och den första reproduktion i tryck af en Medelhafs portulankarta.' ['Very rare, important as the first? printed chart of the Mediterranean — and the first printed reproduction of a Mediterranean portolan.'] 'Complt. 10 Karten' is written on the inside of the front cover, and 'L. OL li Meno' on the verso of the last blank leaf. Nordenskiöld apparently doubted that this was the first printed chart of the Mediterranean, but it is confirmed by Koeman: 'For nearly twenty years, it was the first and the only printed chartbook of the Mediterranean coasts.' (Koeman vol. 4, p. 22.)

Lit.: Koeman vol. 4, p. 21—24, Bar 1.

9 BARTOLOMEO DA LI SONETTI   [1485]

[Isolario. Venezia, Guilelmus de Panceretto Tridinensis dit Anima mia, 1485].   24,8 cm.

[1] cerigo cecerigo
[2] rodi
[3] carchi e limonia
[4] piscopia
[5] Nisari
[6] candia   Text on the back.   238 × 348 mm.
[7] scarpanto
[8] stampalia
[9] namphio
[10] sancta erini
[11] sicandro e policantro
[12] milo
[13] siphano
[14] serphino
[15] fermenia
[16] zea
[17] andre
[18] tine   Map on verso.
[19] micone   On verso of tine.
[20] sdiles
[21] hyera
[22] pario
[23] nicsia
[24] Pira chiero raclia
[25] nio
[26] amorgo
[27] zinara e leuita
[28] caloiero
[29] lango
[30] calamo
[31] lero
[32] pactamos
[33] crusia mandria
[34] fermacusa
[35] samo
[36] nicaria
[37] psara
[38] sio
[39] metelin
[40] tenedo
[41] stalimene
[42] monte sancto
[43] limine pelegise
[44] sciro
[45] dromo
[46] sciati e scopolo
[47] negroponte   Text on the back.   238 × 351 mm.
[48] poci e altre isule
[49] cipro   Verso blank.

Notes: All the maps have text on the verso, except where otherwise specified. They are all uncoloured. There is no text on any of the maps; even the names of the islands are taken from the accompanying verses. The leaves measure 238 × 177 mm; the maps themselves are difficult to measure, as they have no neat lines, and only the sizes of the two larger maps are given above. The author's name appears in the second sonnet on f.3, beginning
  'Par aprobar questa operta fata
    per me bartolomeo da li sonetti
    intendo de monstrar con veri effetti
    quanto che londa egeia abia cerchatta...'
He has not yeat been satisfactorily identified. Brunet adds 'Zamberto' in brackets after his name, and this has been taken as his real name by others; 'Bartolomeo the Turk' has also been suggested. The atlas is a book of sailing directions for the Aegean Sea, written in sonnets. It lacks both title and imprint; the information given here is taken from Destombes's catalogue. It is the first printed special atlas. The maps are bound in the wrong order: the leaves from the 'Therzo soneto per Grete' to the text 'Per rodi' appear between the sonnets on Stampalia and the map they refer to. Destombes in his catalogue and Bagrow in his Essay list the maps in different order. Many of the maps bear the watermark 'fleur à six pétales'. In his Periplus Nordenskiöld states that his copy contains 48 maps, but in fact it has all 49. It is bound in old wood with wormholes, with gold-tooled leather covering the spine and about one third of the boards. There are holes left by the original clasps. There are a few MS notes in the atlas: on the first blank leaf is written 'Pelago d'Egeo di Bartol° dalli Sonetti Veneti[no]'; on the inside of the back cover, in pencil, 'Bartolommeo dalli Sonetti (Zamberto) Isolario in versi' and a note in Nordenskiöld's hand; 'köpt i. Dec. 1892 af Hoepli i Milano för 350 fr. Backfords Auct. L 29.' Hoepli's invoice, '19 Dicemb. 1892 Cat.83 N.232 Bartolomeo Isolario fs 350:— Aff. 85 fs 350 85,' is among Nordenskiöld's papers, with the note in his hand 'Postanvisn. 27,Dec.92.' Nordenskiöld's bookplate is on the inside of the front cover, and his signature appears on the first blank leaf.

Lit.: Bagrow, Imago Mundi vol. 7, 1951, p. 107, Beans, Imago Munde vol. 7, p. 91, Brunet vol. 1, c. 679—680, Castellani p. 66—68, Destombes, Catalogue p. 77—78, nr 52, Hain nr 253890, Nordenskiöld, Facsimile Atlas p. 36, Nordenskiöld, Periplus p. 71—72.

10 BELLIN, JACQUES NICOLAS   1764

LE PETIT ATLAS MARITIME RECUEIL DE CARTES ET PLANS DES QUATRE PARTIES DU MONDE. en Cinq Volumes. I. VOLUME. Amerique Septentrionale et Isles Antilles. II. VOLUME. Amérique Meridionale. Mexique Terre-Ferme, Bresil, Perou, Chily. III. VOLUME. Asie et Afrique. IV. ET V. VOLUMES. Europe et les Etats qu'elle contient. Par Ordre de M. Le Duc de Choiseul, Colonel Général des Suisses et Grisons Ministre de la Guerre et de la Marine Par le S. Bellin Ingenieur de la Marine 1764.

Vol. I
LE PETIT ATLAS MARITIME RECUEIL DE CARTES ET PLANS DES QUATRE PARTIES DU MONDE Premier Volume Contenant L'AMREIQUE SEPTENTRIONALE ET LES ISLES ANTILLES. 32 cm.

[1] Tome I.N° 1.
[C:] CARTE RÉDUITE DU GLOBE TERRESTRE ... — 222 × 345 mm.

[2] Tome I.N° 2. et Tome II.N° 2.
[C:] CARTE DE L'AMERIQUE et DES MERS VOISINES 1763 — 455 × 286 mm.

[3] Tome I.N° 3.
[C:] BAYE DE HUDSON et Pays Voisins ... 1763. — 218 × 338 mm.

[4] Tome I.N° 4.
[C:] LA NOUVELLE FRANCE où CANADA ... — 198 × 348 mm.

[5] Tome I.N° 5.
[C:] COURS DU FLEUVE DE SAINT LAURENT depuis la Mer jusqu'à Quebec. ... — 215 × 352 mm.

[6] Tome I.N° 6.
[C:] CARTE DES CINQ GRANDS LACS DU CANADA ... — 216 × 332 mm.

[7] Tome I.N° 7.
[C:] PARTIE DU FLEUVE S.T LAURENT avec le Passage de la Traverse et les Isles Voisines. ... — 208 × 301 mm.

[8] Tome I.N° 8.
[C:] PARTIE DU FLEUVE DE SAINT LAURENT avec le Bassin de Quebec et l'Isle d'Orleans ... — 206 × 298 mm.

[9] Tome I.N° 9.
[T:] PLAN DE LA VILLE DE QUEBEC — (Plan). 209 × 345 mm.

[10] Tome I.N° 10.
[a] [C:] PARTIE DU FLEUVE S.T LAURENT depuis Quebec jusqu'au Lac S.t Francois. ... — 125 × 315 mm.
[b] [C:] CARTE DU LAC CHAMPLAIN ... — 84 × 315 mm.
[The whole map:] 210 × 315 mm.

[11] Tome I.N° 11.
[C:] L'ISLE DE MONTREAL et ses Environs. ... — 215 × 346 mm.
[Inset:] [T:] PLAN DE LA VILLE DE MONTREAL ou VILLE MARIE ... — (Plan). 143 × 95 mm.

[12] Tome I.N° 12.
[C:] LA RIVIERE DU DÉTROIT Depuis le Lac Sainte Claire, jusqu'au Lac Erié ... — 205 × 316 mm.
[Inset:] [T:] PLAN DU FORT DÉTROIT ... — (Plan). 110 × 181 mm.

[13] Tome I.N° 13.
[C:] LE GOLPHE DE SAINT LAURENT ET L'ISLE DE TERRE-NEUVE ... — 212 × 342 mm.

[14] Tome I.N° 14.
[C:] LE DÉTROIT DE BELLE-ISLE ... — 207 × 158 mm.

[15] Tome I.N° 15.
[C:] IDEE DE LA RADE DU MINGAN Suivant le Journal de la Fregate du Roy La Diane en 1755. — 191 × 165 mm.

[16] Tome I.N° 16.
[C:] CARTE DES ISLES DE MIQUELON ET DE S.T PIERRE et la Coste de Terre-neuve voisine. ...— 217 × 159 mm.

[17] Tome I.N° 17.
[C:] CARTE DES ISLES DE S.T PIERRE ET DE MIQUELON ...— 210 × 168 mm.

[18] Tome I.N° 18.
[C:] CARTE DE L'ISLE S.T PIERRE ...— 206 × 163 mm.

[19] Tome I N° 19.
[C:] PLAN DE LA RADE ET PORT DE L'ISLE S.T PIERRE ... — 216 × 329 mm.

[20] Tome I.N° 20.
[C:] CARTE DES BAYES, RADES, ET PORT DE PLAISANCE dans l'Isle de Terre-Neuve. ... — croisey sculp 216 × 350 mm.

[21] Tome I.N° 21.
[C:] CARTE DU HAVRE DE SAINT JEAN dans l'Isle de Terre-neuve. ... — 204 × 159 mm.

[22] Tome I.N° 22.
[C:] L'ISLE ROYALE Située a l'Entrée du Golphe de Saint Laurent ... — 214 × 303 mm.

[23] Tome I.N° 23.
[C:] PORT DE LOUISBOURG dans l'Isle Royale. ... — 206 × 312 mm.

[24] Tome I.N° 24.
[C:] PLAN DE LA VILLE DE LOUISBOURG dans l'Isle Royale ... — (Plan). 210 × 341 mm.

[25] Tome I.N° 25.
[C:] BAYE S.TE ANNE ou LE PORT DAUPHIN dans l'Isle Royale ... — Groisey Sculp. 207 × 310 mm.

[26] Tome I.N° 26.
[C:] CARTE DE L'ACADIE et Pays Voisins ... — 207 × 310 mm.

[27] Tome I.N° 27.
[C:] PLAN DU PORT ROYAL dans l'Acadie, Appellé Aujourd' par les Anglois ANNAPOLIS ROYAL ... — 196 × 334 mm.

[28] Tome I.N° 28.
[C:] PLAN DE LA BAYE DE CHIBOUCTOU nommée par les Anglois HALIFAX ... 1763. — 220 × 348 mm.
[Inset:] [T:] Plan de la Ville d'Halifax ... — (Plan). 92 × 124 mm.

[29] Tome I.N° 29.
[C:] CARTE DE LA NOUVELLE ANGLETERRE NEW YORK PENSILVANIE ET NOUVEAU JERSAY Suivant les Cartes Angloises ... — 323 × 370 mm.

[30] Tome I.N° 30
[T:] CARTE DE LA BAYE DE BASTON Située dans la Nouvelle Angleterre. ... — 208 × 162 mm.

[31] Tome I.N° 31
[T:] PLAN DE LA VILLE DE BOSTON ... — (Plan). 208 × 152 mm.

[32] Tome I.N° 32.
[C:] BAYE ET PORT D'YORC Capitale de la Nouvelle Yorc ... — 213 × 166 mm.

[33] Tome I.N° 33.
[T:] VILLE DE MANATHE ou NOUVELLE-YORC ... — (Plan). 209 × 162 mm.

[34] Tome I.N° 34.
[C:] PLAN DE PHILADELPHIE ET ENVIRONS ... — 207 × 162 mm.

[35] Tome I.N° 35.
[C:] CARTE DE LA VIRGINIE MARI-LAND &a Tirée des meilleures Cartes Angloises ... — 190 × 299 mm.

[36] Tome I.N° 36.
[C:] LA CAROLINE dans l'Amérique Septentrionale Suivant les Cartes Angloises ... — 223 × 355 mm.

[37] Tome I.N° 37.
[C:] PORT ET VILLE DE CHARLES-TOWN dans la Caroline. ...— (Plan). 210 × 150 mm.

[38] Tome I.N° 38.
[C:] CARTE DE LA NOUVELLE GEORGIE. ... — 211 × 149 mm.

[39] Tome I.N° 39.
[C:] PLAN DU PORT DE S.T AUGUSTIN dans la Floride. ... — 206 × 158 mm.

[40] Tome I.N° 40.
[C:] LA LOUISIANE et Pays Voisins. ... — 209 × 345 mm.

[41] Tome I.N° 41.
[C:] CARTE DE LA COSTE DE LA FLORIDE depuis la Baye de la Mobile jusqu'aux Cayes de S.t Martin ... — 212 × 340 mm.

[42] Tome I.N° 42.
[C:] PLAN DE LA BAYE DE PENSACOLA dans la Floride ... — 211 × 135 mm.

[43] Tome I.N° 43.
[C:] COURS DU FLEUVE SAINT LOUIS depuis ses

Embouchures jusqu'a la Rivie^re d'Iberville et Costes Voisines. ... — 215 × 353 mm.

[44] Tome I.N° 44.
[C:] EMBOUCHURES DU FLEUVE S.^T LOUIS ou MISSISSIPI ... 1763 — 212 × 168 mm.

[45] Tome I.N° 45.
[T:] PLAN DE LA NOUVELLE ORLEANS — (Plan). 207 × 293 mm.

[46] Tome I.N° 46.
[C:] SUITE DU COURS DU FLEUVE S.^T LOUIS depuis la Riviere d'Iberville jusqua celle des Yasous. et les Parties connues de la Riviere Rouge et la Riviere Noire. ... — 216 × 347 mm.
[Inset:] [C:] CARTE DE L'ETABLISSEMENT FRANCOIS SUR LA RIVIERE ROUGE ... — 125 × 96 mm.

[47] Tome I.N° 47.
[C:] CARTE REDUITE DU GOLPHE DU MEXIQUE ET DES ISLES DE L'AMERIQUE Par M.B. Ing.^r de la Marine. — 209 × 307 mm.

[48] Tome I.N° 48.
[C:] CARTE DES ISLES BERMUDES OU DE SOMMER Tiré de l'Anglois. — 202 × 327 mm.

[49] Tome I.N° 49.
[C:] CARTE DES ISLES LUCAYES Par M.B. Ing.^r de la Marine. — 211 × 267 mm.

[50] Tome I.N° 50.
[C:] ISLE DE CUBE ... — 200 × 314 mm.

[51] Tome I.N° 51.
[C:] PORT DE LA HAVANE dans l'Isle de Cube ... — 217 × 160 mm.

[52] Tome I.N° 52.
[C:] BAYE DE MATANCE dans l'Isle de Cube. ... — 208 × 164 mm.

[53] Tome I.N° 53.
[C:] LE PORT MARIANNE dans l'Isle de Cube. ... — Croisey. c 220 × 160 mm.

[54] Tome I.N° 54
[C:] PLAN DE LA BAYE DE S.^T YAGO dans l'Isle de Cube. ... — 210 × 160 mm.

[55] Tome I.N° 55.
[C:] ENTRÉE DE LA BAYE DE S.^T YAGO, dans l'Isle de Cube ... — 215 × 167 mm.

[56] Tome I.N° 56.
[C:] CARTE DE L'ISLE DE LA JAMAIQUE ... — 203 × 314 mm.

[57] Tome I.N° 57
[C:] CARTE DES HAVRES DE KINGSTOWN ET DE PORT ROYAL. ... — 193 × 296 mm.

[58] Tome I.N° 58.
[C:] PLAN DE LA VILLE DE PORT ROYAL ... — (Plan). 196 × 150 mm.

[59] Tome I.N° 59.
[T:] PLAN DE LA VILLE DE KINGSTON Suivant le projet donné par le Colonel Christian Lilly. — (Plan). 196 × 294 mm.

[60] Tome I.N° 60.
[T:] Plan des Havres de Port Antonio et de Saint Francois Situés a la Coste du Nord Est de l'Isle de la Jamaique. ... — 199 × 153 mm.

[61] Tome I.N° 61.
[C:] ISLE DE SAINT DOMINGUE ... — 207 × 344 mm.

[62] Tome I.N° 62.
[C:] CARTE DES ISLES SITUÈES AU NORD DE S.^T DOMINGUE Avec les Passages pour le retour appellés Débouquemens. ... — 225 × 375 mm.

[63] Tome I.N° 63.
[T:] CARTE DES ENVIRONS DU CAP FRANÇOIS ET DES PAROISSES QUI EN DEPENDENT. — 215 × 352 mm.

[64] Tome I.N° 64.
[C:] PLAN DU PORT DU CAP dans L'ISLE DE S.^T DOMINGUE ... — 229 × 357 mm.

[65] Tome I.N° 65.
[C:] VILLE DU CAP dans l'Isle de St Domingue ... — Croisey. c. (Plan). 221 × 351 mm.

[66] Tome I.N° 66.
[C:] BAYE ET VILLE DE BAYAHA ou PORT-DAUPHIN dans l'Isle de St Domingue. ... — 212 × 348 mm.

[67] Tome I.N° 67.
[C:] LA PARTIE FRANCOISE DE L'ISLE DE SAINT DOMINGUE ... — 214 × 345 mm.

[68] Tome I.N° 68.
[C:] ENVIRONS DE LEOGANE ET DU PORT AU PRINCE dans l'Isle de St Domingue. ... — 221 × 356 mm.

[69] Tome I.N° 69.
[C:] LE PORT AU PRINCE dans l'Isle de St DOMINGUE ... — 214 × 170 mm.

[70] Tome I.N° 70.
[C:] PLAN DE LA RADE ET VILLE DU PETIT GOAVE dans l'Isle de St Domingue. ... — 214 × 302 mm.

[71] Tome I.N° 71.
[C:] PLAN DE LA BAYE SAINT LOUIS dans L'ISLE DE S.^T DOMINGUE ... — 226 × 345 mm.

[72] Tome I.N° 72.
[C:] CARTE DES BAYES DU MESLE DES FLAMANDS ET DE CAVAILLON dans l'Isle de St Domingue ... — 219 × 330 mm.

[73] Tome I.N° 73
[C:] PLAN DE L'ISLE A VACHE a la Coste du Sud de S.Domingue. ... — 210 × 163 mm.

[74] Tome I.N° 74.
[C:] VILLE DE S.DOMINGUE dans l'Isle de ce Nom. ... — (Plan). 215 × 162 mm.

[75] Tome I.N° 75.
[a] [T:] CARTE DE L'ISLE DE SAINTE CROIX au Sud des Isles des Vierges. — 98 × 169 mm.
[b] [T:] CARTE DE L'ISLE DE SAINT JEAN DE PORTORICO — 107 × 160 mm.
[The whole map:] 216 × 169 mm.

[76] Tome I.N° 76.
[C:] PORT ET VILLE DE PORTO-RICO dans l'Isle de ce nom ... — 207 × 314 mm.

[77] Tome I.N° 77.
[C:] CARTE DES ISLES DES VIERGES Par le S.^r B Ingen.^r de la Marine. — 202 × 244 mm.

[78] Tome I.N° 78.
[C:] CARTE DE L ISLE S.^T THOMAS l'Une des Vierges. ... — 221 × 357 mm.

[79] Tome I.N° 79.
[C:] LES PETITES ANTILLES ou Les Isles du Vent ... — Croiséy. Scup 220 × 162 mm.

[80] Tome I.N° 80.
[C:] PARTIE DES ISLES ANTILLES I.Partie ... — 215 × 158 mm.

[81] Tome I.N° 81.
[C:] SUITE DES ISLES ANTILLES 2. Partie ... — 221 × 170 mm.

[82] Tome I.N° 82.
[C:] PETITES ANTILLES ou ISLES DU VENT 3.e Partie. ... — 220 × 322 mm.

[83] Tome I.N° 83.
[C:] CARTE DE L'ISLE DE S.^T CHRISTOPHE — 202 × 337 mm.

[84] Tome I.N° 84.
[T:] CARTE D L'ISLE DE NIEVES — 212 × 161 mm.

[85] Tome I.N° 85.
[C:] CARTE DE L'ISLE D'ANTIGUE ... — 197 × 142 mm.

[86] Tome I.N° 86.
[C:] ISLE DE LA GUADELOUPE LES SAINTES et MARIE GALANTE ... — Croisey Sculp 225 × 347 mm.

[87] Tome I.N° 87.
[C:] PARTIE OCCIDENTALE DE L'ISLE DE LA GUADELOUPE, Appellée la Basse Terre ... — Croisey Scu 223 × 357 mm.

[88] Tome I.N° 88.
[C:] PARTIE ORIENTALE DE L'ISLE DE LA

GUADELOUPE Appellée la Grande-Terre ... — Croisey. 220 × 350 mm.

[89] Tome I.N° 89.
[C:] ENVIRONS DU FORT LOUIS de la Guadeloupe. ... — Croisey.Sc. 213 × 167 mm.

[90] Tome I.N° 90.
[T:] CARTE DE L'ISLE DE MARI-GALANTE — Croisey Scu. 212 × 163 mm.

[91] Tome I.N° 91.
[C:] ISLE DE LA MARTINIQUE ... — 215 × 347 mm.

[92] Tome I.N° 92.
[C:] PARTIE SEPTENTRIONALE DE LA MARTINIQUE ... — [T:] Croisey Sc — 217 × 355 mm.

[93] Tome I.N° 93.
[C:] PARTIE MÉRIDIONALE DE LA MARTINIQUE ... — Croisey Sc 216 × 353 mm.

[94] Tome I.N° 94.
[C:] PLAN DU CUL DE SAC ROYAL DE LA MARTINIQUE ... — 165 × 212 mm.

[95] Tome I.N° 95.
[C:] CARTE DE L'ISLE DE SAINTE LUCIE ... — 204 × 310 mm.

[96] Tome I.N° 96.
[T:] PLAN DU PORT DU CARENAGE où PETIT CUL DE SAC DE L'ISLE S^E.LUCIE. — 212 × 161 mm.

[97] Tome I.N° 97.
[C:] PLAN DU CUL DE SAC DES ROSEAUX dans l'Isle de Ste Lucie. ... 1763 — 212 × 166 mm.

[98] Tome I.N° 98.
[C:] CARTE DE L'ISLE DE LA BARBADE ... — 196 × 149 mm.

[99] Tome I.N° 99.
[T:] CARTE DE L'ISLE DE SAINT VINCENT. — 211 × 161 mm.

[100] Tome I.N° 100.
[T:] PLAN DU PORT ET DU CARENAGE DE CARIACOUA Situé dans la Partie du Sud de l'Isle de S^t.Vincent — (Plan). 168 × 218 mm.

[101] Tome I.N° 101.
[C:] CARTE DE L'ISLE DE LA GRENADE — 213 × 166 mm.

[102] Tome I.N° 102.
[C:] PORT ET FORT ROYAL DE LA GRENADE ... — 215 × 168 mm.

Notes: All the maps are blank on the back. The coastlines are coloured blue. There is no text in the body of the atlas, but between the first and second title-pages is a page bearing a dedication to 'Monseigneur le Duc de Choiseul', signed 'Votre tres humble et trés Obeissant Serviteur Bellin'. There is a four-page 'Table des Cartes et Plans du Ier Volume'. Maps [47] and [49] are signed by Bellin: 'M.B. Ing^r. de la Marine', and map [77]: 'S^r B Ingen^r. de la Marine'. The maps on double leaves are all numbered by hand on the back, in ink. The collection has all five volumes of the atlas, leather bound, with gold tooling and a coat-of-arms an front and back covers. The volumes were damaged by water during World War II. Nordenskiöld's bookplate is on the coloured blank leaf at the beginning; on the verso of this leaf is pencilled: 'Exempl. en grand papier et avec les planches colorier très rare 5 vol. 981002 284', and on the verso of the last leaf '5 vol. 8372'. Our five volumes contain all 575 maps listed in the Tables des Cartes et Plans.

Lit.: Bonacker p.43, LC List vol. 3, 348—362, nr 3508, Nat. Mar. Mus. vol. 3:1, p. 242—257, nr 211, Poggendorff vol. 2, c. 141.

Vol. II
LE PETIT ATLAS MARITIME RECUEIL DE CARTES ET PLANS DES QUATRE PARTIES DU MONDE. Second Volume. Contenant L'AMERIQUE MÉRIDIONALE et ses Details. 32 cm.

[1] Tome I.N° 1.
[C:] CARTE RÉDUITE DU GLOBE TERRESTRE ... — = I:[1].

[2] Tome I.N° 2. et Tome II.N° 2.
[C:] CARTE DE L'AMERIQUE et DES MERS VOISINES 1763. — = I:[2].

[3] Tome II.N° 3.
[C:] AMERIQUE MERIDIONALE. ... — 198 × 164 mm.

[4] Tome II.N° 4.
[C:] CARTE DU MEXIQUE ... — 218 × 285 mm.

[5] Tome II.N° 5.
[C:] CARTE DES ENVIRONS DE LA VILLE DE MEXICO — 211 × 167 mm.

[6] Tome II.N° 6.
[C:] PLAN DE LA RADE ET VILLE DE LA VERA-CRUZ ... — 205 × 152 mm.

[7] Tome II.N° 7.
[C:] LA VERA-CRUZ Ville du Mexique — (Plan). 212 × 165 mm.

[8] Tome II.N° 8.
[C:] CARTE DES PROVINCES DE TABASCO, CHIAPA, VERAPAZ, GUATIMALA, HONDURAS ET YUCATAN. ... — 206 × 339 mm.

[9] Tome II.N° 9.
[C:] CARTE DES PROVINCES DE NICARAGUA ET COSTA RICA ... — 195 × 164 mm.

[10] Tome II.N° 10.
[C:] CARTE DE L'ISTHME DE PANAMA ET DES PROVINCES DE VERAGUA TERRE FERME ET DARIEN ... — Croisey 204 × 293 mm.

[11] Tome II.N° 11.
[C:] CARTE DES PROVINCES DE TIERRA FIRME, DARIEN, CARTHAGENE ET NOUVELLE GRENADE ... Tirée des meilleures Cartes et en particulier de l'Amerique de M. d'Anville. — 200 × 260 mm.

[12] Tome II.N° 12.
[C:] CARTE DE L'ISTHME DE PANAMA ... — 218 × 308 mm.

[13] Tome II.N° 13.
[C:] PORT ET VILLE DE CHAGRE ... — 203 × 163 mm.

[14] Tome II.N° 14.
[C:] BAYE DE PORTO-BELO et Costes Voisines ... — 204 × 269 mm.

[15] Tome II.N° 15.
[C:] BAYE DE PORTO BELLO. ... — 212 × 166 mm.

[16] Tome II.N° 16.
[C:] RADE DU DARIEN et les Isles voisines ... — Croisey 220 × 167 mm.

[17] Tome II.N° 17.
[C:] CARTE DES PROVINCES DE CARTAGENE, S^E MARTHE ET VENEZUELA ... — Croisey Sc 210 × 304 mm.

[18] Tome II.N° 18.
[C:] PLAN DE LA BAYE DE ZISAPATA a la Coste de Terre ferme ... — 210 × 166 mm.

[19] Tome II.N° 19.
[C:] BAYE DE CARTHAGENE dans l'Amerique Meridionale. ... — 217 × 352 mm.

[20] Tome II.N° 20.
[T:] VILLE DE CARTAGENE dans l'Amerique Meridionale. ... — (Plan). 217 × 173 mm.

[21] Tome II.N° 21.
[C:] PLAN DE LA BAYE ET VILLE DE SAINTE MARTHE et de la Coste aux Environs. ... — 211 × 170 mm.

[22] Tome II.N° 22.
[C:] PLAN DU PORT DE S^{TE}MARTHE dans l'Amerique Meridionale ... — 216 × 168 mm.

[23] Tome II.N° 23.
[C:] CARTE DES PROVINCES DE CARACAS, COMANA, ET PARIA. ... — 199 × 294 mm.

[24] Tome II.N° 24.
[C:] PLAN DU PORT CABELLO a la Coste de Caraque. ... — 209 × 167 mm.

[25] Tome II.N° 25.
[C:] PORT DE LA GUAIRA A la Coste de Caraque ... — (Plan). 207 × 170 mm.

[26] Tome II.N° 26.
[C:] ISLE DE CURACAO ou CORASSOL ... — 214 × 168 mm.
[Inset:] [T:] Fort d'Amsterdam/ Entrée de la Baye S^e Anne — 214 × 168 mm.

[27] Tome II.N° 27.
[C:] COURS DE L'ORENOQUE Depuis ses sources jusqu'à la Mer Avec les Revieres qui s'y déchargent ... — 226 × 442 mm.

[28] Tome II.N° 28.
[a] [T:] CARTE D'UNE PARTIE DU COURS DE L'ORENOQUE Depuis sa principale Embouchure jusqu'a la Ville de S^t. Thomas de Guyane. Suivant les Cartes Angloises et Hollandoisea — 82 × 282 mm.
[b] [T:] CARTE DU BRAS PRINCIPAL DE LA RIVIERE D'ORENOQUE Depuis la Pointe de Barime a son Embouchure jusqu'au Fort de S.Thomas Suivant un Manuscrit Francoice. — 97 × 282 mm.
[The whole map:] 208 × 284 mm.

[29] Tome II.N° 29.
[C:] CARTE DE LA GUIANE ... — 191 × 334 mm.

[30] Tome II.N° 30.
[C:] CARTE DE L'ENTRÉE DE LA RIVIERE DE POUMARON Suivant les Plans des Hollandois ... — 210 × 165 mm.

[31] Tome II.N° 31.
[C:] CARTE DES ENTRÉES DES RIVIERES DE DEMERARY ET D'ESSEQUEBÉ Suivant les Plans des Hollandois ... — 208 × 163 mm.

[32] Tome II.N° 32.
[C:] CARTE DE L'EMBOUCHURE DES RIVIERES DE COPENAME ET SARAMECA ... Tiré des Hollandois — 211 × 164 mm.

[33] Tome II.N° 33.
[C:] CARTE DE L'ENTRÉE DE LA RIVIERE DE BERBICHE Suivant les Plans des Hollandois ... — 208 × 166 mm.

[34] Tome II.N° 34.
[C:] CARTE DE L'ENTRÉE DE LA RIVIERE DE CORENTYN Sur ce que les Anglois et les Hollandois en ont publiée. ... — 213 × 165 mm.

[35] Tome II.N° 35
[C:] CARTE D'UNE GRANDE PARTIE DE LA COLONIE DE SURINAM. Sur les Rivieres de Surinam Commewine et Cottica. Tiré de la Carte et Arpentage publié par les Hollandois. ... — 211 × 415 mm.

[36] Tome II.N° 36.
[C:] PLAN DE LA VILLE DE PARAMARIBO Suivant les Plans Hollandois ... — (Plan). 210 × 165 mm.

[37] Tome II.N° 37.
[C:] CARTE DE L'ENTRÉE DE LA RIVIERE DE MARONY Par le S. Bellin Ing^r. de la Marine 1762. ... — 211 × 163 mm.

[38] Tome II.N° 38.
[C:] CARTE DES COSTES DE LA GUYANE FRANCOISE Par le S. Bellin Ing^r. de la Marine 1762. — 219 × 302 mm.

[39] Tome II.N° 39.
[a] [C:] CARTE DE L'ENTREE DE LA RIVIERE DE KOUROU. Par le S. Bellin Ing^r. de la Marine 1762. — 210 × 164 mm.
[b] [C:] CARTE DES ISLES DU SALUT Autrefois LES ISLES AU DIABLE. ... — 216 × 174 mm.

[40] Tome II.N° 40.
[C:] CARTE DE L'ISLE DE CAYENNE et de ses Environs. ... — 204 × 284 mm.

[41] Tome II.N° 41.
[C:] CARTE DE L'ISLE DE CAYENNE ... — 237 × 315 mm.

[42] Tome II.N° 42.
[T:] PLAN DE LA VILLE DE CAYENNE ... — (Plan). 218 × 179 mm.

[43] Tome II.N° 43.
[C:] PORT DE CAYENNE et son Entrée ... — 211 × 168 mm.

[44] Tome II.N° 44.
[C:] ENTRÉE DE LA RIVIERE D'APROUAK Située dans la Gyane. ... — 215 × 172 mm.

[45] Tome II.N° 45
[C:] Entrée des Rivieres D'OUYAPOCO ET DE COURIPI. ... — 210 × 165 mm.

[46] Tome II.N° 46.
[C:] GUYANE PORTUGAISE et Partie du Cours de la Riviere des Amazones ... — 205 × 451 mm.

[47] Tome II.N° 47.
[C:] CARTE DU BRESIL. Prem. Partie Depuis la Riviere des Amazones jusqu'à la Baye de Tous les Saints. ... Tiré de la Carte de l'Amerique de M^r. Danville — 223 × 302 mm.

[48] Tome II.N° 48.
[C:] SUITE DU BRESIL Depuis la Baye de Tous les Saints jusqu'a St Paul Tiré de l'Amerique de M Danville — 227 × 163 mm.

[49] Tome II.N° 49.
[C:] SUITE DU BRESIL. ... Tiré de la Carte de l'Amerique de M d'Anville. — 226 × 164 mm.

[50] Tome II.N° 50.
[C:] PLAN DE FERNAMBOUC a la Coste de Bresil ... — 217 × 171 mm.

[51] Tome II.N° 51.
[C:] CARTE DE LA BAYE DE TOUS LES SAINTS a la Coste du Bresil ... — 209 × 171 mm.

[52] Tome II.N° 52.
[C:] VILLE DE SAINT SALVADOR Capitale du Bresil. ... — [T:] Croisey Sculp — (Plan). 162 × 315 mm.

[53] Tome II.N° 53.
[C:] ENTRÉE DE LA RIVIERE DE S^T FRANCOIS à la Coste de Bresil ... — 217 × 165 mm.

[54] Tome II.N° 54.
[C:] PLAN DE LA BAYE DE RIO-JANEIRO ... — 215 × 320 mm.

[55] Tome II.N° 55
[C:] ISLE DE SAINT SEBASTIEN a la Coste du Bresil ... — 219 × 162 mm.

[56] Tome II.N° 56.
[C:] CARTE DE L'ISLE-GRANDE et Coste de Bresil aux environs ... — 218 × 170 mm.

[57] Tome II.N° 57.
[C:] CARTE DE L'ISLE DE S^{TE} CATHERINE Située a la Coste du Bresil. ... — 216 × 174 mm.

[58] Tome II.N° 58.
[C:] CARTE DE LA RIVIERE DE LA PLATA ... — 207 × 288 mm.

[59] Tome II.N° 59.
[C:] VILLE DE BUENOS-AYRES ... — (Plan). 214 × 166 mm.

[60] Tome II.N° 60.
[C:] CARTE DU PARAGUAY et des Pays Voisins. ... — 202 × 301 mm.

[61] Tome II.N° 61.
[T:] CARTE REDUITE DE LA PARTIE LA PLUS MERIDIONALE DE L'AMERIQUE — 210 × 165 mm.

[62] Tome II.N° 62.
[T:] CARTE RÉDUITE DU DÉTROIT DE MAGELLAN Dressée sur les Journaux des Navigateurs Remarque J'ay dressé cette Carte sur les Memoires et les Plans qui ont eté levés par le S^r. Labat Ingenieur embarqué sur le Vaisseau de M^r. de Beauchesne en 1699. et suivantes, ... — 198 × 341 mm.

[63] Tome II.N° 63.
[C:] CARTE DU DETROIT DE LA MAIRE. ... — 214 × 162 mm.

[64] Tome II.N° 64.
[C:] CARTE REDUITE DE LA MER DU SUD — 205 × 349 mm.

[65] Tome II.N° 65.
[C:] CARTE DU CHILI. ... — 241 × 170 mm.

[66] Tome II.N° 66.
[C:] ISLE DU CHILOÉ. et Environs. ... — 215 × 173 mm.

[67] Tome II.N° 67.

[67] [C:] CARTE DE L'ENTRÉE DU GOLPHE DU CHILOÉ et du Port de Cachao au Chili ... — 212 × 165 mm.
[68] Tome II.N° 68.
[C:] CARTE DE L'ISLE DE JUAN FERNANDÉS ... — 217 × 166 mm.
[69] Tome II.N° 69.
[C:] PORT DE BALDIVIA à la Coste du Chili. ... — Croisey. Sculp. 211 × 170 mm.
[70] Tome II.N° 70.
[C:] PINCO ou Port de la Conception au Chili. ... — 211 × 167 mm.
[71] Tome II.N° 71.
[C:] PLAN DE LA VILLE DE SANTIAGO Capitale du Chili ... — (Plan). 212 × 166 mm.
[72] Tome II.N° 72.
[C:] PLAN DU PORT DE VALPARAISO ... — 212 × 165 mm.
[73] Tome II.N° 73.
[C:] PLAN DU PORT DE COQUIMBO a la Coste du Chili. .. — 209 × 167 mm.
[Inset:] [T:] VILLE DE LA SERENA — 100 × 155 mm. (Irregular).
[74] Tome II.N° 74.
[C:] SUITE DU PEROU AUDIENCE DE LIMA ... Tiré des meilleures Cartes et en particuli[er] de celles de M[r]. Danville. — 201 × 285 mm.
[75] Tome II.N° 75.
[C:] SUITE DU PEROU AUDIENCE DE CHARCAS ... Tiré des meilleures Cartes et en particulier de l'Amerique de M. d'Anville. — 214 × 298 mm.
[76] Tome II.N° 76.
[C:] RADE D'ARICA et Environs. Située a la Coste du Perou ... — 212 × 169 mm.
[Inset:] [T:] Ville d'Arica — 130 × 89 mm. (Irregular).
[77] Tome II.N° 77.
[C:] PLAN DE LA RADE DE PISCO a la Coste du Perou. ... — 212 × 167 mm.
[Inset:] [T:] Ville de Pisco — (Plan). 58 × 88 mm.
[78] Tome II.N° 78.
[C:] LIMA ET SES ENVIRONS PORT DU CALLAO, avec la Côte et les Isles voisines. ... — 221 × 354 mm.
[79] Tome II.N° 79
[C:] PLAN DE LA VILLE DE LIMA où DES ROIS Capitale du Perou. ... — Croisey Sc. (Plan). 207 × 342 mm.
[80] Tome II.N° 80.
[C:] CARTE DE LA BAYE DE GUAJAQUIL. ... — Croisey. Sculp. 208 × 167 mm.
[81] Tome II.N° 81.
[C:] Ire Feuille PROVINCE DE QUITO AU PEROU. ... — 224 × 343 mm.
[82] Tome II.N° 82.
[C:] 2[e] Feuille SUITE DE LA PROVINCE DE QUITO AU PEROU ... — 227 × 351 mm.
[83] Tome II.N° 83.
[C:] 3[e] Feuille SUITE DE LA PROVINCE DE QUITO AU PEROU ... — 179 × 353 mm.
[84] Tome II.N° 84.
[C:] PLAN DE LA VILLE DE S[T] FRANÇOIS DE QUITO ... — (Plan). 175 × 314 mm.
[85] Tome II.N° 85.
[C:] CARTE DE LA BAYE DE PANAMA dans l'Amerique Meridionale ... — 219 × 171 mm.
[86] Tome II.N° 86.
[C:] PLAN DU PORT D'ACAPULCO Sur la Côte du Mexique dans la Mer du Sud. ... — 206 × 162 mm.
[87] Tome II.N° 87.
[C:] CARTE DES ISLES AÇORES ou TERCERÉS Partie Occidentale ... — 195 × 323 mm.
[88] Tome II.N° 88.
[C:] Partie Orientale DES ISLES AÇORES ... — 206 × 162 mm.
[89] Tome II.N° 89.
[C:] PORT ET VILLE D'ANGRA dans l'Isle de Tercere. ... — 207 × 164 mm.

Notes: All the maps are blank on the back and lightly coloured. The title-page is for this volume only, and is followed by a four-page 'Table des Cartes et Plans du IIe Volume'. The first two maps are numbered Tome I.N° 1 and 2, and are the same as those in the first volume. Nordenskiöld's bookplate is on the inside of the front cover.
Lit.: See also notes for vol. I.

Vol. III.
LE PETIT ATLAS MARITIME RECEUIL DE CARTES ET DE PLANS DES QUATRE PARTIES DU MONDE. TOME III. Contenant I°. L'ASIE. II°. L'AFRIQUE. avec les Détails interessans de ces Deux Parties. M.DCC.LXIV.   32 cm.

[1] Tome I.N° 1.
[C:] CARTE REDUITE DU GLOBE TERRESTRE ... — = 1:1.
[2] Tome III.N° 2.
[C:] L'ASIE ... — 196 × 236 mm.
[3] Tome III.N° 3.
[C:] CARTE RÉDUITE DE LA MOSCOVIE SIBERIE TARTARIE et Pais Voisins. — 220 × 329 mm.
[4] Tome III.N° 4.
[a] [C:] CARTE DE LA MER NOIRE ... — 127 × 170 mm.
[b] [C:] CARTE DU CANAL DE LA MER NOIRE ... — 81 × 170 mm.
[The whole map:] 213 × 173 mm.
[5] Tome III.N° 5.
[C:] CARTE DE LA MER CASPIENNE et ses Environs. ... — 212 × 170 mm.
[6] Tome III.N° 6.
[C:] PLAN DE LA VILLE D'ASTRACAN ... — Croisey Scu (Plan). 215 × 176 mm.
[7] Tome III.N° 7.
[C:] LA PERSE ... — 240 × 348 mm.
[8] Tome III.N° 8.
[C:] CARTE DU GOLPHE PERSIQUE ... — 161 × 214 mm.
[9] Tome III.N° 9.
[C:] CARTE DES EMBOUCHURES DE L'EUPHRATE ... — 208 × 172 mm.
[10] Tome III.N° 10.
[C:] CARTE DE L'ASIE MINEURE aujourd'huy Caramanie Anadolie et Roum. — 205 × 303 mm.
[11] Tome III.N° 11.
[C:] CARTE DE L'ARMENIE GEORGIE et Pays Voisins ... — 204 × 341 mm.
[12] Tome III.N° 12.
[C:] CARTE DE LA SYRIE. ... — 206 × 164 mm.
[13] Tome III.N° 13.
[C:] CARTE DE L'ISLE DE CYPRE. ... — 207 × 165 mm.
[14] Tome III.N° 14.
[C:] CARTE DU GOLPHE D'ALEXANDRETTE. ... — 210 × 167 mm.
[15] Tome III.N° 15.
[C:] PLAN DE TRIPOLI DE SYRIE. ... — Croisey 211 × 170 mm.
[16] Tome III.N° 16.
[C:] PLAN DE SEIDE EN SYRIE. ... — 212 × 165 mm.
[17] Tome III.N° 17.
[C:] PLAN DE LA RADE DE SOUR EN SYRIE. ... — Croisey scu 209 × 170 mm.
[18] Tome III.N° 18.
[C:] PLAN DE LA RADE DE S[T] JEAN D'ACRE a la Coste de Syrie. ... — 208 × 162 mm.
[19] Tome III.N° 19.
[C:] CARTE DE LA MER ROUGE et Partie de L'ARABIE. ... — 208 × 353 mm.
[20] Tome III.N° 20.
[T:] PLAN DE LA VILLE DE MOKA Située sur la Mer Rouge. ... — (Plan). 216 × 168 mm.
[21] Tome III.N° 21.
[C:] CARTE DE L'INDOUSTAN I[e] Feuille ... — 216 × 308 mm.

[22] Tome III.N°. 22.
[C:] Suite de la Carte de L'INDOUSTAN. II.ᵉ Feuille, Comprenant LA PRESQU'ISLE DE L'INDE. ... — 210 × 170 mm.

[23] Tome III.N°. 23.
[C:] CARTE DES ISLES MALDIVES. ... — 211 × 151 mm.

[24] Tome III.N°. 24.
[C:] CARTE DU GOLPHE DE CAMBAYE. ... — Croisey 216 × 174 mm.

[25] Tome III.N°. 25.
[C:] PLAN DE BOMBAY et ses Environs. ... — 209 × 165 mm.

[26] Tome III.N°. 26.
[C:] CARTE DES COSTES DE CONCAN ET DECAN Depuis Goa jusqu'au Cap S. Jean. ... — Croisey.S. [Divided into two parts]. 212 × 176 mm.

[27] Tome III.N°. 27.
[a] [C:] COSTE DE CANARA depuis Mangalor jusqua Goa. ... — 213 × 98 mm.
[b] [C:] SUITE DE LA COSTE DE MALABAR Depuis Cranganor jusqua Mangalor ... — 213 × 125 mm.
[c] [C:] COSTE DE MALABAR Depuis le Cap Comorin jusqu'a Cranganor ... — 213 × 127 mm.
[The whole map:] 213 × 354 mm.

[28] Tome III.N°. 28.
[C:] BAYE VILLE ET FORTS D'ANDARAJAPOUR à la Coste de Malabar. ... — 206 × 169 mm.

[29] Tome III.N°. 29.
[C:] CARTE DU PORT DE GOA et ses Environs ... — 211 × 171 mm.

[30] Tome III.N°. 30.
[C:] PLAN DE MAYÉ à la Coste de Malabar ... — 211 × 170 mm.

[31] Tome III.N°. 31.
[C:] CARTE DE L'ISLE DE CEYLAN ... — 263 × 198 mm.

[32] Tome III.N°. 32.
[C:] CARTE DE LA BAYE DE TRINQUEMALE dans l'Isle de Ceylan. ... — 217 × 173 mm.

[33] Tome III.N°. 33.
[C:] PLAN DE LA VILLE ET FORT DE JAFFA NEPATAN dans l'Isle de Ceylan. ... — (Plan). 210 × 166 mm.

[34] Tome III.N°. 34.
[C:] CARTE DU GOLPHE DE BENGALE ... — Croisey. 213 × 264 mm.

[35] Tome III.N°. 35.
[T:] PLAN DE LA VILLE DE PONDICHERI — Croisey (Plan). 200 × 160 mm.

[36] Tome III.N°. 36.
[C:] CARTE DU DISTRICT DE TRANQUEBAR ... — 221 × 170 mm.

[37] Tome III.N°. 37.
[C:] PLAN DE MADRAS a la Coste de Coromandel ... — Croisey (Plan). 214 × 174 mm.

[38] Tome III.N°. 38.
Théâtre de la Guerre dans l'Inde.
[C:] COSTE DE COROMANDEL et les Pays de Tonda, Mandalum et Tanjaor ... — 228 × 176 mm.

[39] Tome III.N°. 39.
[C:] COSTE DE COROMANDEL depuis Gondagamas jusqu'a Narzapour ... — 208 × 325 mm.
[Inset:] [T:] Mazulipatam — 75 × 133 mm.

[40] Tome III.N°. 40.
[C:] NOUVELLE CARTE DU ROYAUME DE BENGALE. ... — Croisey.S. 269 × 332 mm.

[41] Tome III.N°. 41.
[C:] CARTE DE L'ENTRÉE DU GANGE Et son Cours jusqu'à Ugli ... — 216 × 171 mm.
[Inset:] [T:] Carte de l'Entrée de la Riviere d'Aracam — 127 × 84 mm.

[42] Tome III.N°. 42.
[C:] ARCHIPEL DE MERGUI. dans le Golphe de Bengale ... — 212 × 169 mm.

[43] Tome III.N°. 43.
[C:] PORT ET BOURG DE MERGUI ... — 212 × 169 mm.

[44] Tome III.N°. 44
[C:] CARTE des Isles de JAVA SUMATRA BORNEO &ᵃ Les Detroits de la Sonde Malaca et Banca &ᵃ ... — 239 × 281 mm.

[45] Tome III.N°. 45.
[C:] CARTE DE L'ISLE DE SUMATRA ... — 211 × 347 mm.

[46] Tome III.N°. 46.
[C:] PLAN DE LA VILLE DE MALACA ... — (Plan). 210 × 170 mm.

[47] Tome III.N°. 47.
[C:] CARTE DE L'ISLE DE JAVA ... — Croisey Sculp. 194 × 418 mm.

[48] Tome III.N°. 48.
[C:] CARTE DES ENVIRONS DE BATAVIA Tirée des Hollandois ... — 214 × 167 mm.

[49] Tome III.N°. 49.
[C:] CARTE DES ROYAUMES DE SIAM DE TUNQUIN Pegu, Ava Aracan &c ... — 261 × 261 mm.

[50] Tome III.N°. 50.
[C:] CARTE DU COURS DU MENAN, Depuis Siam Jusqu'a la Mer, Levée sur les Lieux par Ingenieur Francois ... — 206 × 142 mm.

[51] Tome III.N°. 51.
[T:] VILLE DE SIAM ou JUTHIA. ... — (Plan). 165 × 205 mm.

[52] Tome III.N°. 52.
[C:] PLAN DE LA VILLE DE LOUVO demeure ordinaire des Rois de Siam. ... — Croisey Sc (Plan). 214 × 173 mm.

[53] Tome III.N°. 53.
[C:] CARTE DU COURS DE LA RIVIERE DE TUNQUIN, depuis Cacho jusqu'à la Mer. Levé par un Navigateur Anglois. ... — 202 × 152 mm.

[54] Tome III.N°. 54.
[C:] L'EMPIRE DE LA CHINE. ... — 282 × 400 mm.

[55] Tome III.N°. 55.
[C:] CARTE DU ROYAUME DE KAU-LI ou CORÉE Copiée sur la Carte Angloise ... — [T:] Croisey Sc — 202 × 176 mm.

[56] Tome III.N°. 56.
[C:] CARTE DES ISLES qui sont a l'Entrée de la RIVIERE DE CANTON ... — 210 × 171 mm.

[57] Tome III.N°. 57.
[T:] PLAN DE LA VILLE ET DU PORT DE MACAO. ... — 215 × 168 mm.

[58] Tome III.N°. 58.
[C:] CARTE DE L'ENTRÉE DE LA RIVIERE DE CANTON dans la Chine. ... — 212 × 166 mm.

[59] Tome III.N°. 59.
[C:] CARTE DE L'ISLE FORMOSE Aux Costes de la Chine ... — 218 × 168 mm.

[60] Tome III.N°. 60.
[C:] CARTE DE LA BAYE D'HOCSIEU et des Entrées de la Riviere de Chang, Dans la Province de Fokyen, en Chine. ... — 208 × 164 mm.

[61] Tome III.N°. 61.
[C:] ISLE DE CHEU-CHAN ou ISLE CHUSAN avec les Costes et Isles voisines. ... — Croisey 220 × 170 mm.

[62] Tome III.N°. 62.
[C:] CARTE DE L'EMPIRE DU JAPON. ... — 208 × 304 mm.

[63] Tome III.N°. 63.
[C:] PLAN DU PORT ET DE LA VILLE DE NANGASAKI. ... — (Plan). 195 × 332 mm.

[64] Tome III.N°. 64.
[C:] CARTE DES ISLES PHILIPPINES CELEBES ET MOLUQUES ... — 214 × 165 mm.

[65] Tome III.N°. 65.
[C:] CARTE DES ISLES PHILIPPINES, Dressée sur la Carte Espagnole du R.P.Murillo de Velarde. Iʳᵉ Feuille. ... — 213 × 153 mm.

[66] Tome III.N°. 66.
[C:] CARTE DES ISLES PHILIPPINES Dressée sur la Carte Espagnole du R.P.Murillo de Velarde 2.e Feuille ... — 212 × 295 mm.

[67] Tome III.N°. 67.
[C:] PLAN DE LA BAYE DE MANILLE Située dans l'Isle de Luçon. ... — 216 × 170 mm.

[68] Tome III.N°. 68.
[T:] CARTE PARTICULIERE DES ISLES MOLUQUES. — 213 × 152 mm.

[69] Tome III.N°. 69.
[T:] CARTE DE L'ARCHIPEL DE S.T LAZARE OU LES ISLES MARIANES Sur les Cartes du P. Alonso Lopez Et le Mémoire du P. Morales, Jesuites Espagnols, Missionaires dans ces Isles. — 216 × 151 mm.
[Inset:] [T:] Isle de Guahan ou Isle S.t Jean. — 113 × 65 mm. (Irregular).

Tome III.Page 70.
SECONDE PARTIE DU TOME III. Contenant L'AFRIQUE avec ses Détails tant sur la Mer Mediterranée que sur l'Ocean, ET LES ISLES QUI EN DÉPENDENT. M.DCC.LXIV.

[70] Tome III.N°. 70.
[C:] CARTE DE L'AFRIQUE. ... — 211 × 172 mm.

[71] Tome III.N°. 71.
[C:] COSTES DE BARBARIE Contenant LES ROYAUMES D'ALGER ET DE TUNIS ... — 199 × 390 mm.

[72] Tome III.N°. 72.
[C:] CARTE DU DÉTROIT DE GIBRALTAR. ... — 212 × 171 mm.

[73] Tome III.N°. 73.
[C:] RADE ET VILLE DE CEUTE ... — (Plan). 210 × 166 mm.

[74] Tome III.N°. 74.
[C:] PLAN DE LA VILLE DE MELLILA ... — (Plan). 212 × 170 mm.

[75] Tome III.N°. 75.
[C:] PLAN D'ORAN et ses Environs. ... — 213 × 165 mm.

[76] Tome III.N°. 76.
[C:] PLAN DU CHATEAU ET PORT DE MARZALQUIVIR ... — 212 × 169 mm.

[77] Tome III.N°. 77
[C:] PLAN DE LA BAYE D'ALGER et ses Environs. ... — 226 × 349 mm.

[78] Tome III.N°. 78.
[C:] PLAN DE LA VILLE FORTS ET PORT D'ALGER ... — 209 × 168 mm.

[79] Tome III.N°. 79.
[C:] PLAN DE L'ISLE DE TABARQUE à la Coste de Barbarie. ... — (Plan). 214 × 172 mm.

[80] Tome III.N°. 80.
[C:] PLAN DE PORT FARINE. ... — 213 × 169 mm.

[81] Tome III.N°. 81.
[C:] GOLPHE DE TUNIS ... — 222 × 172 mm.

[82] Tome III.N°. 82.
[C:] PLAN DE LA VILLE DE TUNIS et ses Environs ... — Croisey 212 × 171 mm.

[83] Tome III.N°. 83.
[C:] PLAN DES FORTS ET CANAL DE LA GOULETTE ... — Croisey 213 × 172 mm.

[84] Tome III.N°. 84.
[C:] PLAN DE LA RADE ET VILLE DE TRIPOLI. à la Coste de Barbarie ... — 211 × 174 mm.

[85] Tome III.N°. 85.
[C:] COSTES D'EGYPTE, depuis Alexandrie jusqu'à Rosette. ... — 203 × 349 mm.

[86] Tome III.N°. 86.
[C:] PLAN DES PORTS ET VILLE D'ALEXANDRIE. ... — 211 × 174 mm.

[87] Tome III.N°. 87.
[C:] RADE DU BEQUIER — Croisey 215 × 169 mm.

[88] Tome III.N°. 88.
[C:] PLAN DU FORT ET DU VILLAGE DU BEQUIER ... — Croisey 214 × 172 mm.

[89] Tome III.N°. 89.
[C:] CARTE DES EMBOUCHURES DU NIL, ET PARTIE DE SON COURS Le Delta et l'Isthme de Suez. ... — 214 × 164 mm.

[90] Tome III.N°. 90.
[C:] CARTE EXACTE DU COURS DU NIL. ... — [Divided in two parts]. 208 × 163 mm.

[91] Tome IV.N°. 58. et Tome III.N°
[C:] CARTE RÉDUITE DE LA MER MÉDITERRANÉE. ... — 230 × 500 mm.

[92] Tome III.N°. 92.
[C:] CARTE DES ROYAUMES DE FEZ ET DE MAROC. ... — 214 × 172 mm.

[93] Tome III.N°. 92.*
[C:] ISLE DE MOGADOR Ses Mouillages et son Port ... — 213 × 168 mm.

[94] Tome III.N°. 93.
[C:] CARTE DES ISLES CANARIES ... — 170 × 217 mm.

[95] Tome III.N°. 94.
[T:] CARTE DE L'ISLE DE TENERIFFE Suivant les Observations Astronomiques Et les Journaux de Navigateurs — 206 × 147 mm.

[96] Tome III.N°. 95.*
[C:] COSTES DU SENEGAL depuis le Cap Blanc jusqu'à la Riviere de Gambie ... — 207 × 164 mm.

[97] Tome III.N°. 95.
[C:] CARTE de l'Entrée de la RIVIERE DE SANAGA ou SENEGAL. ... — [T:] Croisey Scul — 216 × 167 mm.

[98] Tome III.N°. 96.
[a] [C:] COURS DE LA RIVIERE DE SANAGA ou SENEGAL. Depuis son Embouchure Jusqu'à l'Isle de Bilbas Levé par un Ingenieur Francois en 1718. — 108 × 286.
[b] [C:] SUITE DU COURS DE LA RIVIERE DE SENEGAL Depuis l'Isle de Bilbas, Jusqu'au Sault du Rocher de Govina — 103 × 286 mm.
[The whole map:] 211 × 286 mm.

[99] Tome III.N°. 97.
[C:] PLAN DE LA BAYE ET Isle D'ARGUIM. Levé par un Pilote Francois ... — Croisey 216 × 162 mm.

[100] Tome III.N°. 98.
[C:] COSTES D'AFRIQUE depuis le Cap Verd jusqu'au Cap Verga. ... — Croisey 214 × 173 mm.

[101] Tome III.N°. 99.
[C:] PLAN DE L'ISLE DE GORÉ Avec ses Fortifications ... — 195 × 263 mm.

[102] Tome III.N°. 100.
[C:] CARTE DES ISLES DU CAP VERD ... — 210 × 298 mm.

[103] Tome III.N°. 101.
[C:] CARTE DE LA RIVIERE DE GAMBRA ou GAMBIE depuis son Embouchure jusqu'a Eropina. ... — 202 × 321 mm.

[104] Tome III.N°. 102.
[C:] CARTE DU COURS DE LA RIVIERE DE GAMBRA ou GAMBIE depuis Eropina jusqu'à Barrakonda ... — 201 × 322 mm.

[105] Tome III.N°. 103.
[a] [T:] CARTE DE L'ENTRÉE DE LA RIVIERE DE SIERRA LEONA — 142 × 166 mm.
[b] [T:] PLAN DE L'ISLE DE BENSE. — 65 × 166 mm.
[The whole map:] 212 × 169 mm.

[106] Tome III.N°. 104.
[a] [T:] ENTRÉE DE LA RIVIERE DE SESTOS. — 105 × 158 mm.
[b] [T:] VUE DU CAP MESURADO et ses Environs. — 105 × 158 mm.
[The whole map:] [T:] Croisey — 217 × 162 mm.

[107] Tome III.N°. 105
[C:] PARTIE DE LA COSTE DE GUINÉE depuis la Riviere de Sierra Leona jusqu'au Cap das Palmas. ... — 224 × 305 mm.

[108] Tome III.N°. 106.

[109] Tome III.N° 107.
[C:] COSTE DE GUINÉE Depuis le Cap Apollonia jusqu'a la Riviere de Volta OU LA COSTE D'OR. ... — 223 × 432 mm.

[109] Tome III.N° 107.
[C:] CARTE DU GOLFE DE BENIN ET PARTIE DE LA CÔTE DE GUINEE Depuis la Riviere de Volta Jusquau C.Formosa. ... — Croisey 217 × 298 mm.

[110] Tome III.N° 108.
[C:] CARTE DE LA RIVIERE DE KALBAR, Appellée communément Kalabar où Rio Réal; avec les côtes voisines. Tirées des Remaques de plusieurs Pilotes en 1699. ... Copie sur l'Anglois — 201 × 344 mm.

[111] Tome III.N° 109.
[C:] CARTE DES ROYAUMES DE CONGO ANGOLA et BENGUELA Avec les Pays Voisins Tiré de l'Anglois ... — 214 × 306 mm.

[112] Tome III.N° 110.
[C:] RADE DE BENGUELA ET RIVIERE DE CANTONBELLE ... — 214 × 166 mm.

[113] Tome III.N° 111.
[C:] CARTE DU PAIS DES HOTTENTOTS aux Environs du Cap de Bonne Esperance ... — 218 × 171 mm.

[114] Tome III.N° 112.
[C:] VILLE ET FORT DU CAP DE BONNE ESPERANCE ... — (Plan). 215 × 169 mm.

[115] Tome III.N° 113.
[T:] CARTE DE LA BAYE DE LA TABLE, ET RADE DU CAP DE BONNE ESPERANCE ... — 215 × 168 mm.

[116] Tome III.N° 114.
[C:] BAYE DE SALDANE au Nord-Ouest du Cap de Bonne Esperance. ... — 209 × 168 mm.

[117] Tome III.N° 115.
[C:] CARTE DE L'ISLE DE MADAGASCAR et du Canal de Mozambique ... — 213 × 350 mm.

[118] Tome III.N° 116.
[C:] CARTE DE L'ANCE DAUPHINE dans l'Isle de Madagascar ... — 217 × 344 mm.

[119] Tome III.N° 117.
[C:] CARTE DE LA BAYE D'ANTONGIL. dans l'Isle de Madagascar ... — 212 × 172 mm.

[120] Tome III.N° 118.
[C:] CARTE DE LA BAYE DE MOSAMBIQUE. ... — 202 × 156 mm.

[121] Tome III.N° 119.
[C:] CARTE DE L'ISLE DE FRANCE — 210 × 343 mm.

[122] Tome III.N° 120.
[C:] PLAN DU PORT BOURBON, dans l'Isle de France. ... — Croisey Scu 215 × 168 mm.

[123] Tome III.N° 121.
[C:] PLAN DU PORT LOUIS dans l'Isle de France. ... — 213 × 170 mm.

[124] Tome III.N° 122.
[C:] CARTE DE L'ISLE DE BOURDON autrefois MASCAREIGNE ... — 196 × 234 mm.

[125] Tome III.N° 123.
[C:] PLAN DE L'ISLE S.^{TE}HELENE ... — 214 × 260 mm.

[126] Tome 3.N° 124
[C:] PLAN DE LA FORTERESSE ET BOURG, DE LISLE DE S.^{TE}HELENE ... — 217 × 174 mm.

Notes: All the maps are blank on the back and lightly coloured. The first map is the same as that in vols. 1 and 2. All the maps are numbered in ink on the back, in addition to the printed numbers. There is a five-page. Table des Cartes et Plans du Troisieme Volume. L'ASIE'; it does not include maps 92* [93] and 95* [96]. Nordenskiöld's bookplate is on the inside of the front cover.

Lit.: See also notes for vol. 1.

Vol. IV.
LE PETIT ATLAS MARITIME TOME IV. Contenant L'EUROPE ET LES DIVERS ETATS QU'ELLE RENFERME Excepté la France. 33 cm.

[1] Tome IV.N° 1.
[C:] CARTE DE L'EUROPE. ... — 233 × 276 mm.

[2] Tome IV.N° 2.
[T:] ISLES BRITANNIQUES — 198 × 138 mm.

[3] Tome IV.N° 3.
[C:] ANGLETERRE ... — 190 × 189 mm.

[4] Tome IV.N° 4.
[C:] CARTE DES ENTRÉES DE LA TAMISE. ... — 213 × 175 mm.

[5] Tome IV.N° 5.
[C:] PLAN DE LA VILLE DE LONDRES. et ses Fauxbourgs. ... — (Plan). 226 × 172 mm.

[6] Tome IV.N° 6.
[C:] CARTE DE L'ISLE DE WIGHT ... — 212 × 345 mm.

[7] Tome IV.N° 7.
[C:] PLAN DE PORTSMOUTH et environs Avec les Rades de Spit Head et de Ste Helène. ... — 215 × 175 mm.

[8] Tome IV.N° 8.
[T:] CARTE DE L'ISLE DE PORTSEY, ET HAVRE DE PORTSMOUTH. — 208 × 152 mm.

[9] Tome IV.N° 9.
[C:] PLAN DU HAVRE DE RYE et de ses environs. ... — 213 × 168 mm.

[10] Tome IV.N° 10.
[C:] CARTE DE LA BAYE ET PORT DE PLIMOUTH ... — Croisey S 213 × 173 mm.

[11] Tome IV.N° 11.
[C:] PLAN DES VILLE ET CITADELLE DE PLYMOUTH — (Plan). 212 × 165 mm.

[12] Tome IV.N° 12.
[C:] PLAN DE LA VILLE D'YARMOUTH et Environs ... — 210 × 160 mm.

[13] Tome IV.N° 13
[C:] CARTE DE L'ECOSSE. ... — 204 × 162 mm.

[14] Tome IV.N° 14.
[C:] CARTE DU GOLPHE D'EDINBURG ... — 187 × 264 mm.

[15] Tome IV.N° 15.
[C:] CARTE DES ISLES D'ORKNEY ou ORCADES. ... — 211 × 167 mm.

[16] Tome IV.N° 16.
[C:] CARTE DES ISLES DE HETLAND où SCHETLAND ... — 209 × 173 mm.

[17] Tome IV.N° 17
[C:] CARTE DE L'IRLANDE ... — 220 × 166 mm.

[18] Tome IV.N° 18.
[C:] PLAN DE LA VILLE DE DUBLIN ... — (Plan). 209 × 285 mm.

[19] Tome IV.N° 19.
[C:] PORT ET VILLE DE KINGSAILL en Irlande ... — 211 × 168 mm.

[20] Tome IV.N° 20.
[C:] PLAN DE GALLOWAY et ses Environs. ... — 206 × 175 mm.

[21] Tome IV.N° 21.
[C:] CARTE DE LA NORWEGE, SUEDE ET LAPONIE. ... — 225 × 175 mm.

[22] Tome IV.N° 22.
[C:] CARTE DU SPITS-BERG Suivant les Hollandois. ... — 216 × 174 mm.

[23] Tome IV.N° 23.
[C:] CARTE DE L'ISLANDE ... — 213 × 160 mm.

[24] Tome IV.N° 24
[C:] CARTE DE LA MER BLANCHE ... — 210 × 168 mm.

[25] Tome IV.N° 25.
[C:] CARTE DE LA MOSCOVIE EUROPEENE. I. Feuille. ... — 235 × 290 mm.

[26] Tome IV.N° 26.
[C:] CARTE DE LA MOSCOVIE EUROPEENNE IIe Feuille ... — 231 × 292 mm.

[27] Tome IV.N° 27.
[C:] CARTE DU GOLPHE DE FINLANDE Suivant les Cartes Russes ... — 183 × 330 mm.

[28] Tome IV.N°. 28.
[C:] PLAN DE KROONSTAD et la Passe pour aller a Petersburg ... — 212 × 171 mm.
[29] Tome IV.N°. 29.
[C:] PLAN DE LA VILLE ET PORT DE S.T PETERSBOURG. ... — (Plan). 210 × 166 mm.
[30] Tome IV.N°. 30.
[C:] CARTE DE LA MER BALTIQUE. ... — 220 × 273 mm.
[31] Tome IV.N°. 31.
[C:] CARTE DU GOLPHE DE BOTHNIE. ... — 212 × 171 mm.
[32] Tome IV.N°. 32.
[C:] SUITE DU GOLPHE DE BOTHNIE. Tiré des Cartes Suedoises. ... — 216 × 171 mm.
[33] Tome IV.N°. 33.
[C:] CARTE DES ENVIRONS DE TORNEA ... — 215 × 168 mm.
[34] Tome IV.N°. 34.
[C:] PLAN DE STOCKHOLM ...— (Plan). 224 × 175 mm.
[35] Tome IV.N°. 35.
[C:] CARTE DU PASSAGE Depuis la Tour de Landsor jusqu'a Stockholm ... — 221 × 171 mm.
[36] Tome IV.N°. 36.
[C:] CARTE DU DANNEMARC ... — 210 × 167 mm.
[37] Tome IV.N°. 37.
[C:] CARTE DU PASSAGE DU SOND ... — 213 × 172 mm.
[38] Tome IV.N°. 38.
[C:] CARTE DE L'ISLE D'AMAK Et les Passes de Copenhague ... — Croisey 214 × 173 mm.
[39] Tome IV.N°. 39.
[T:] PLAN DE COPENHAGUE ... — Croisey (Plan). 215 × 172 mm.
[40] Tome IV.N°. 40.
[C:] CARTE DU COMTÉ DE HOLLANDE ... — 225 × 173 mm.
[41] Tome IV.N°. 41.
[C:] CARTE DES ENTRÉES DE TEXEL ET DE FLIE Ou l'on a marqué les Tonnes et les Balises qui indiquent les Passes avec la quantité de Pieds d'eau qu'on y trouve. ... — 205 × 338 mm.
[42] Tome IV.N°. 42.
[C:] IDÉE DE LA VILLE D'AMSTERDAM. ... — (Plan). 217 × 170 mm.
[43] Tome IV.N°. 43.
[C:] PLAN DE ROTERDAM et Environs. ... — (Plan). 222 × 168 mm.
[44] Tome IV.N°. 44.
[C:] CARTE DE LA ZEELANDE ... — 207 × 230 mm.
[45] Tome IV.N°. 45.
[T:] PLAN D'OSTENDE ... — (Plan). 218 × 165 mm.
[46] Tome IV.N°. 46.
[C:] PLAN DE LA VILLE DE NIEUPORT ... — (Plan). 218 × 172 mm.
[47] Tome IV.N°. 47.
[C:] COSTES DE FRANCE depuis Brest jusqu'a Dunkerque et celles d'Angleterre qui leur sont opposées. Par le S.B. Ingenieur de la Marine. 1761. — 214 × 350 mm.
[48] Tome IV N° 48. et Tome V N°
[C:] CARTE DES COSTES DE FRANCE depuis Brest jusqu'a Bayone. Par le S.B. Ingen.r de la Marine. 1761. — 350 × 228 mm.
[49] Tome IV.N°. 49. et Tome V.N°
[C:] CARTE RÉDUITE DES COSTES DE FRANCE ET D'ESPAGNE Par le S.r B..... Ing.r de la Marine. 1761 — 387 × 303 mm.
[50] Tome IV.N°. 50.
[C:] PLAN DE S.T SEBASTIEN ... — 219 × 176 mm.
[51] Tome IV.N°. 51.
[C:] PLAN DU PORT DE FERROL. ... — 218 × 172 mm.
[52] Tome IV.N°. 52.
[C:] CARTE DE LA BAYE DE CORCUBION ... — 205 × 165 mm.
[53] Tome IV.N°. 53.
[C:] PLAN DE LA BAYE ET PORT DE LA COROGNE ... — 211 × 164 mm.
[54] Tome IV.N°. 54.
[C:] CARTE DE LA BAYE DE VIGO. et Isles de Bayone. ... — 215 × 170 mm.
[55] Tome IV.N°. 55
[C:] PLAN DU PORT DE LISBONNE ... — 218 × 172 mm.
[56] Tome IV.N°. 56.
[C:] PLAN DE LA BAYE DE CADIX ... — Croisey 212 × 170 mm.
[57] Tome IV.N°. 57.
[C:] PLAN DE LA VILLE DE CADIX ... — (Plan). 231 × 335 mm.
[58] Tome IV.N°. 58. et Tome III.N°. 91.
[C:] CARTE RÉDUITE DE LA MER MÉDITERRANÉE. ... — = 1764:III:[91].
[59] Tome IV.N°. 59.
[C:] CARTE DE LA BAYE DE GIBRALTAR ... — 215 × 173 mm.
[60] Tome IV.N°. 60.
[C:] PLAN DE GIBRALTAR ... — 180 × 350 mm.
[61] Tome IV.N°. 61.
[C:] PLAN DE LA RADE ET VILLE D'ALICANT ... — 225 × 174 mm.
[62] Tome IV.N°. 62.
[C:] PLAN DU PORT ET VILLE DE CARTAGENE en Espagne. ... — 215 × 342 mm.
[63] Tome IV.N° 63.
[C:] PLAN DE BARCELONE Capitale de Catalogne. ... — Croisey Sc. (Plan). 223 × 176 mm.
[64] Tome IV.N°. 64.
[C:] PLAN DE PALAMOS ... — 206 × 171 mm.
[65] Tome IV.N°. 65.
[C:] PLAN DU PORT DE CADEQUIE ... — 218 × 174 mm.
[66] Tome IV.N°. 66.
[a] [C:] L'ISLE DE MAIORQUE ... — 235 × 212 mm.
[b] [C:] L'ISLE DE MINORQUE ... — 85 × 130 mm.
[c] [C:] CARTE DE L'ISLE D'YVICE et des Fromentieres. ... — 148 × 130 mm.
[The whole map:] 235 × 344 mm.
[67] Tome IV.N°. 67.
[C:] PLAN DU PORT ET VILLE DE MAHON Avec ses Forts ... — 214 × 170 mm.
[68] Tome IV.N°. 68.
[C:] CARTE DES COSTES D'ITALIE et les Isles de Corse, Sardaigne Sicile &.a ... — 340 × 286 mm.
[69] Tome IV.N°. 69.
[C:] PLAN DE NICE. ... — (Plan). 213 × 171 mm.
[70] Tome IV.N°. 70.
[C:] PLAN DE LA BAYE DE VILLE-FRANCHE ... — Croisey Sc. 215 × 172 mm.
[71] Tome IV.N°. 71.
[C:] PLAN DU PORT VILLE ET CHATEAU DE VILLE-FRANCHE. ... — Croisey.Sc. 214 × 172 mm.
[72] Tome IV.N°. 72.
[C:] PLAN DE MONACO ... — 216 × 178 mm.
[73] Tome IV.N°. 73.
[C:] CARTE DE L'ETAT DE GENES ... — Croisey. S. 242 × 431 mm.
[74] Tome IV.N°. 74.
[C:] PLAN DE LA VILLE DE SAVONE. ... — Croisey 217 × 172 mm.
[75] Tome IV.N°. 75.
[C:] PLAN DE LA VILLE DE GENES et de ses Environs ... — Croisey Sculp 218 × 176 mm.
[76] Tome IV.N°. 76.
[C:] CARTE DU GOLPHE DE L'ESPECY. ... — 211 × 167 mm.
[77] Tome IV.N°. 77.
[C:] PLAN DE PORTO-VENERE ... — 223 × 173 mm.

[78] Tome IV.N° 78.
[C:] PLAN DE LA VILLE DE LIVOURNE ... — (Plan). 207 × 168 mm.

[79] Tome IV.N° 79.
[C:] PLAN DU PORT ET VILLE DE CIVITA-VECCHIA. ... — 215 × 167 mm.

[80] Tome IV.N° 80
[C:] PLAN DE PORT-HERCULE. ... — 207 × 175 mm.

[81] Tome IV.N° 81.
[C:] PLAN DE L'ISLE D'ELBE ... — 216 × 171 mm.

[82] Tome IV.N° 82.
[C:] PLAN DE PORT FERRARE dans l'Isle d'Elbe. ... — Croisey, Sc. 214 × 174 mm.

[83] Tome IV.N° 83.
[C:] PLAN DE PORTO LONGON ... — 210 × 169 mm.

[84] Tome IV.N° 84.
[C:] PLAN DU GOLPHE VILLE ET ENVIRONS DE NAPLES. ... — 218 × 350 mm.

[85] Tome IV.N° 85.
[C:] PLAN DE BAYES ET POUSSOLE ... — 211 × 168 mm.

[86] Tome IV.N° 86.
[C:] PLAN DE LA BAYE DE GAYETTE ... — 211 × 174 mm.

[87] Tome IV.N° 87.
[C:] CARTE DE LA BAYE DE TARANTE. ... — 210 × 175 mm.

[88] Tome IV.N° 88.
[C:] CARTE DU ROYAUME DE NAPLES. ... — 266 × 312 mm.

[89] Tome IV.N° 89.
[C:] CARTE DE L'ISLE DE CORSE ... — Croisey — Sc 394 × 221 mm.

[90] Tome IV.N° 90.
[C:] PLAN DE LA BAYE DE CALVI. dans l'Isle de Corse. — 218 × 158 mm.

[91] Tome IV.N° 91.
[C:] PLAN DE LA VILLE DE CORTE dans l'Isle de Corse ... — 215 × 176 mm.

[92] Tome IV.N° 92.
[C:] GOLPHE DE CAMPO-MORO ET VALINCO. ... — 213 × 176 mm.

[93] Tome IV.N° 93.
[C:] PLAN DE PORTO VECCHIO ... — 217 × 176 mm.

[94] Tome IV.N° 94
[C:] PLAN DU PORT ET VILLE DE BONIFACE dans l'Isle de Corse. ... — Croisey 213 × 173 mm.

[95] Tome IV.N° 95.
[C:] CARTE DES BOUCHES DE BONIFACE entre la Corse et la Sardaigne ... — 209 × 165 mm.

[96] Tome IV.N° 96.
[C:] L'ISLE DE SARDAIGNE. ... — Croisey .Sc. 204 × 165 mm.

[97] Tome IV.N° 97.
[C:] PLAN DE LA BAYE DE LA HIACE ... — 207 × 170 mm.

[98] Tome IV.N° 98.
[C:] CARTE DE LA BAYE DE L'ORISTAN ... — 204 × 170 mm.

[99] Tome IV.N° 99
[C:] ISLE DE SICILE. ... — [T:] Croisey .S — 221 × 347 mm.

[100] Tome IV.N° 100.
[C:] CARTE DE L'ENTRÉE DU PHARE DE MESSINE ... — 226 × 334 mm.

[101] Tome IV.N° 101.
[C:] PLAN DE LA VILLE DE MESSINE dans l'Isle de Sicile ... — 212 × 165 mm.

[102] Tome IV.N° 102.
[C:] PLAN DE LA VILLE DE PALERME dans l'Isle de Sicile. ... — Croisey (Plan). 214 × 171 mm.

[103] Tome IV.N° 103.
[C:] PLAN DE MILAZZO dans l'Isle de Sicile. ... — 214 × 169 mm.

[104] Tome IV.N° 104.
[C:] PLAN DE LA VILLE DE TRAPANO dans l'Isle de Sicile. ... — Croisey 208 × 175 mm.

[105] Tome IV.N° 105.
[C:] PLAN DE SIRACUSE ... — 210 × 170 mm.

[106] Tome IV.N° 106.
[C:] CARTE DE L'ISLE DE MALTE ... — 215 × 164 mm.

[107] Tome IV.N° 107.
[C:] PLAN DES PORT ET VILLE DE MALTHE ... — Croisey Sc 219 × 177 mm.

[108] Tome IV.N° 108.
[C:] CARTE de la Partie Septentrionale DU GOLFE DE VENISE ... — 217 × 167 mm.

[109] Tome IV.N° 109.
[C:] CARTE DES ENVIRONS DE VENISE ... — 212 × 170 mm.

[110] Tome IV.N° 110.
[C:] PLAN DE TRIESTE dans l'Istrie. ... — (Plan). 219 × 172 mm.

[111] Tome IV.N° 111.
[C:] PLAN DU PORT DE POLE dans l'Istrie. ... — 220 × 166 mm.

[112] Tome IV.N° 112.
[C:] CARTE DE L'ETAT DE RAGUSE et Isles Voisines ... — 209 × 166 mm.

[113] Tome IV.N° 113.
[C:] PLAN DE ZARA Capitale de la Dalmatie ... — 217 × 173 mm.

[114] Tome IV.N° 114.
[C:] CARTE DES VILLE ET CITADELLE D'ANCONE ... — 209 × 167 mm.

[115] Tome IV.N° 115.
[C:] PLAN DE LA VILLE ET PORT DE BRINDISI Dans le Golphe de Venise. ... — 208 × 162 mm.

[116] Tome IV.N° 116.
[C:] CARTE DE LA GRECE ET DE LA MORÉE ... — 225 × 180 mm.

[117] Tome IV.N° 117.
[C:] CARTE DE LA PARTIE MERIDIONALE DE LA GRECE. ... — 216 × 290 mm.

[118] Tome IV.N° 118.
[C:] PLAN DE L'ISLE DE CANDIE ... — 227 × 345 mm.

[119] Tome IV.N° 119.
[T:] PLAN DE LA VILLE DE CANDIE. ... — (Plan). Croisey Sculp 218 × 173 mm.

[120] Tome IV.N° 120.
[T:] PLAN DE LA VILLE DE LA CANÉE dans l'Isle de Candie. ... — Croisey Scul (Plan). 218 × 176 mm.

[121] Tome IV.N° 121.
[C:] CARTE DE L'ARCHIPEL ... — 212 × 168 mm.

[122] Tome IV.N° 122.
[C:] CARTE DE L'ENTRÉE DU CANAL DES DARDANELLES ... — 201 × 173 mm.

[123] Tome IV.N° 123.
[C:] CARTE DE LA MER DE MARMARA ... — 218 × 351 mm.

[124] Tome IV.N° 124.
[C:] PLAN DE LA VILLE ET CHATEAU DE GALLIPOLI. ... — (Plan). 217 × 168 mm.

[125] Tome IV.N° 125.
[C:] PLAN DE LA VILLE DE CONSTANTINOPLE ... — (Plan). 209 × 345 mm.

[126] Tome IV.N° 126.
[C:] CARTE DE LA CRIMÉE. ... — 212 × 169 mm.

[127] Tome IV.N° 127.
[C:] CARTE DES EMBOUCHURES DU TANAIS. Et des Environs depuis Taigan, jusqu'a Nova-Krepa. ... — Croisey Scul. 234 × 167 mm.
[Inset:] [T:] PLAN DE NOVA-KREPA ... — 117 × 88 mm.

[128] Tome IV.N° 128.
[C:] PLAN D'AZAK où AZOF. ... — Croisey. Scs 212 × 164 mm.

Notes: All the maps are blank on the back and lightly coloured.

All the double-leaf maps are numbered in ink on the back, in addition to the printed numbers. There is a five-page 'Table des Cartes et Plans du Quatrieme Volume EUROPE'. Nordenskiöld's bookplate is on the inside of the front cover.
Lit.: See also notes for vol. 1.

Vol. V.
LE PETIT ATLAS MARITIME RECUEIL DE CARTES ET PLANS DES QUATRE PARTIES DU MONDE Cinquieme Volume Contenant LES COSTES DE FRANCE ET LES PLACES MARITIMES Sur l'Ocean et sur la Méditerranée 1764 32 cm.

[1] Tome V.N°. 1.
[C:] CARTE DE LA FRANCE — 228 × 276 mm.
[2] Tome IV.N°. 49. et Tome V.N°
[C:] CARTE RÉDUITE DES COSTES DE FRANCE ET D'ESPAGNE Par le S.r B..... Ing.r de la Marine 1761 — = 1764:IV:[49].
[3] Tome IV N°. 47.
[C:] COSTES DE FRANCE depuis Brest jusqu'a Dunkerque ... — = 1764:IV:[47].
[4] Tome V.N°. 4.
[C:] COSTES DE FLANDRES ET DE PICARDIE depuis Nieuport jusqua Calais ... — 214 × 312 mm.
[5] Tome V.N°. 5.
[C:] CARTE DE LA RADE DE DUNKERQUE et ses Bancs ... — 226 × 167 mm.
[6] Tome V.N°. 6.
[C:] DUNKERQUE et Canal de Mardick ... — 223 × 165 mm.
[7] Tome V.N°. 7.
[C:] PLAN DE DUNKERQUE ... — (Plan). 210 × 337 mm.
[8] Tome V.N°. 8.
[C:] PLAN DE GRAVELINES a la Coste de Flandres. ... — (Plan). 194 × 268 mm.
[9] Tome V.N°. 9.
[C:] COSTES DE PICARDIE, depuis Calais jusqu'à la Pointe des Grofiliers ... — 213 × 314 mm.
[10] Tome V.N°. 10.
[C:] PLAN DE CALAIS Coste voisine ET ENVIRONS. ... — 219 × 159 mm.
[11] Tome V.N°. 11.
[C:] PLAN DE CALAIS ... — (Plan). 220 × 269 mm.
[12] Tome V.N°. 12.
[C:] FORT DE NIEULET près de Calais ... — (Plan). 222 × 159 mm.
[13] Tome V.N°. 13.
[C:] PLAN D'AMBLETEUSE. ... — 225 × 167 mm.
[14] Tome V.N°. 14.
[C:] PLAN DE BOULOGNE Et des Environs ... — 227 × 165 mm.
[15] Tome V.N°. 15.
[C:] PLAN DE LA VILLE DE BOULOGNE ... — (Plan). 220 × 165 mm.
[16] Tome V.N°. 16.
[C:] CARTE DES ENTRÉES DE LA RIVIERE DE CANCHE et de ses Environs, jusqu'a Montreuil. ... — 236 × 163 mm.
[17] Tome V.N°. 17
[C:] SUITE DES COSTES DE PICARDIE ET PARTIE DE NORMANDIE depuis la Pointe de Groofiliers jusqu'à Criel ... — 227 × 163 mm.
[18] Tome V.N°. 18.
[C:] CARTE DES ENTRÉES DE LA RIVIERE DE SOMME, et de la Coste depuis S.t Vallery jusqu'a Treport ... — 213 × 322 mm.
[19] Tome V.N°. 19.
[C:] CARTE DU COURS DE LA SOMME depuis Abbeville jusqu'a S.t Vallery ... — 224 × 163 mm.
[20] Tome V.N°. 20.
[C:] ENVIRONS DU CROTOY ET S.T VALERY ... — 225 × 168 mm.
[21] Tome V.N°. 21.
[C:] CARTE DE LA NORMANDIE ET DE LA BRETAGNE ... — 218 × 292 mm.
[22] Tome V.N°. 22.
[C:] PLAN DE TREPORT ... — 223 × 166 mm.
[23] Tome V.N°. 23.
[C:] COSTE DE NORMANDIE Depuis Dieppe jusqu'au Havre. ... — 210 × 159 mm.
[24] Tome V.N°. 24
[C:] PLAN DE DIEPPE et Environs. ... — 209 × 165 mm.
[25] Tome V.N°. 25.
[C:] PLAN DE LA VILLE DE DIEPPE ... — (Plan). 214 × 327 mm.
[26] Tome V.N°. 26.
[C:] PLAN DU PORT ET BOURG DE S.T VALERY. en Caux. ... — (Plan). 214 × 164 mm.
[27] Tome V.N°. 27
[C:] PLAN DE FECAMP ... — (Plan). 230 × 167 mm.
[28] Tome V.N°. 28.
[C:] COSTE DE NORMANDIE, depuis le Havre, jusqu'à la Hougue. ... — 165 × 239 mm.
[Inset:] [T:] LE GRAND ET LE PETIT VAY. — 82 × 115 mm.
[29] Tome V.N°. 29.
[C:] ENTRÉE DE LA RIVIERE DE SEINE et son Cours jusqu'a Quillebeuf. ... — Croisey 218 × 367 mm.
[30] Tome V.N°. 30.
[C:] COURS DE LA RIVIERE DE SEINE depuis Quillebeuf jusques au Port S.t Ouen. ... — 216 × 346 mm.
[31] Tome V.N°. 31.
[C:] PLAN DU HAVRE ET DES ENVIRONS ... — 214 × 323 mm.
[32] Tome V.N°. 32.
[T:] PLAN DE LA VILLE ET CITADELLE DU HAVRE — (Plan). 240 × 173 mm.
[33] Tome V.N°. 33.
[C:] PLAN DE ROUEN ET DES ENVIRONS ... — (Plan). Croisey 213 × 324 mm.
[34] Tome V.N°. 34
[T:] PLAN DE LA VILLE et Port de HONFLEUR ... — (Plan). 228 × 180 mm.
[35] Tome V.N°. 35
[C:] PARTIE DU COTENTIN Depuis Tourlaville jusqu'à la Hougue. ... — 220 × 327 mm.
[36] Tome V.N°. 36.
[C:] COSTE DE NORMANDIE depuis l'Ance de Vauville et Cap de la Hague jusqu'à Cherbourg ... — 220 × 324 mm.
[37] Tome V.N°. 37
[C:] PLAN DE CHERBOURG et de ses Environs. ... — 214 × 324 mm.
[38] Tome V.N°. 38.
[C:] PLAN DE CHERBOURG ... — 211 × 166 mm.
[39] Tome V.N°. 39
[C:] COSTE DE NORMANDIE Depuis l'Ance de Vauville jusqu'á Surville Avec les Isles de Grenesey et d'Aurigny. ... — 173 × 221 mm.
[40] Tome V.N°. 40.
[C:] SUITE DE LA COSTE DE NORMANDIE, Depuis Surville jusqu'au Mont S.Michel: Avec l'Isle de Jersey. ... — 221 × 175 mm.
[41] Tome V.N°. 41.
[C:] PLAN DE GRANVILLE ... — (Plan). 222 × 165 mm.
[42] Tome V.N°. 42.
[T:] PLAN DU MONT S.T MICHEL — (Plan). 219 × 163 mm.
[43] Tome V.N°. 43.
[C:] PARTIE DE LA COSTE DE BRETAGNE depuis Cancale jusqu'au Cap de Frehel. ... — 201 × 361 mm.
[44] Tome V.N°. 44
[C:] S.T MALO et Environs. ... — 216 × 326 mm.
[45] Tome V.N°. 45.
[C:] PARTIE DE LA COSTE DE BRETAGNE depuis le Cap de Frehel jusqu'a S.t Quay. ... — 216 × 345 mm.

[46] Tome V.Nº 46.
[C:] PARTIE DE LA COSTE DE BRETAGNE, Depuis les Isles de Brehat jusqu'aux sept Isles ... — 212 × 354 mm.

[47] Tome V.Nº 47.
[C:] CARTE DE L'ISLE DE BREHAT avec ses Mouillages et les Costes Roches et Isles Voisines. ... — 212 × 159 mm.

[48] Tome V.Nº 48.
[C:] COSTE DE BRETAGNE depuis les Sept Isles jusqu'a l'Isle Molene et Lanion ... — 218 × 163 mm.

[49] Tome V.Nº 49
[a] [C:] CARTE DES SEPT ISLES à la coste de Bretagne ... — 90 × 156 mm.
[b] [C:] Plan de L'ISLE AUX MOINES et ses Mouillages ... — 115 × 156 mm.
[The whole map:] 210 × 160 mm.

[50] Tome V.Nº 50.
[C:] COSTE DE BRETAGNE depuis l'Isle Molene jusqu'a l'Isle de Bas ... — 222 × 324 mm.

[51] Tome V.Nº 51
[C:] CARTE DE L'ENTRÉE DES RIVIERES DE MORLAIX, DE S.T PAUL DE LEON, ET ISLE DE BAS Avec les Roches, Basses, et Isles ... — 211 × 316 mm.

[52] Tome V.Nº 52
[C:] COSTE DE BRETAGNE depuis l'Isle de Bas jusqua la Pointe de Landegavan. ... — 200 × 299 mm.

[53] Tome V.Nº 53
[C:] COSTE DE BRETAGNE Depuis la Pointe de Landegavan jusqu'à Aberilduc. ... — 216 × 322 mm.

[54] Tome V.Nº 54.
[C:] COSTE DE BRETAGNE depuis Aberilduc jusqu'à S.Mathieu ET LE PASSAGE DU FOUR ... — 226 × 173 mm.

[55] Tome V.Nº 55.
[C:] PLAN DE L'ISLE D'OUESSANT. ... — 208 × 165 mm.

[56] Tome IV.Nº 48 et Tome V.Nº
[C:] CARTE DES COSTES DE FRANCE depuis Brest jusqu'a Bayone ... — = 1764:IV:[48].

[57] Tome V.Nº 57.
[C:] CARTE DE LA RADE DE BREST et celles de Bertheaume et de Camaret ... — 210 × 326 mm.

[58] Tome V.Nº 58.
[C:] PLAN DU PORT ET VILLE DE BREST ... — (Plan). 241 × 352 mm.

[59] Tome V.Nº 59.
[C:] CARTE DE LA BAYE DE DOVARNENEZ et la Coste de Bretagne depuis Dinant jusqu'au Bec du Ras ... — 221 × 340 mm.
[Inset:] [T:] le Grand Stevenet — 70 × 113 mm.

[60] Tome V.Nº 60
[C:] COSTE DE BRETAGNE depuis Plouan et Roches de Pennemark jusqua la Baye de la Forest. ... — 221 × 326 mm.

[61] Tome V.Nº 61.
[C:] LES ISLES DE GLENAN et Partie de la Coste de Bretagne qui est opposée. ... — 218 × 165 mm.

[62] Tome V.Nº 62
[C:] COSTE DE BRETAGNE Depuis la Baye de la Forest, Jusqu'à la Rivière de Quimperlay ... — 214 × 316 mm.

[63] Tome V.Nº 63.
[C:] PLAN DE CONCARNEAU ... — 226 × 166 mm.

[64] Tome V.Nº 64.
[C:] COSTE DE BRETAGNE depuis la Riviere de Quimperlay jusqu'aupres de Quiberon. Contenant l'Isle de Grois, Port Louis et Port l'Orient. ... — 215 × 325 mm.

[65] Tome V.Nº 65
[C:] CARTE DE L'ISLE DE GROIS a la Coste de Bretagne. ... — 203 × 341 mm.

[66] Tome V.Nº 66.
[C:] CARTE DE L'ORIENT ET DU PORT LOUIS ... — 205 × 340 mm.

[67] Tome V.Nº 67
[T:] VILLE DU PORT LOUIS — (Plan). 217 × 172 mm.

[68] Tome V.Nº 68
[C:] VILLE DE L'ORIENT ... — (Plan). 226 × 169 mm.

[69] Tome V.Nº 69.
[C:] CARTE DU MORBIAN et la Presqu'Isle de Quiberon ... — 217 × 326 mm.

[70] Tome V.Nº 70
[C:] CARTE DE BELLE-ISLE ET LES ISLES D'HOUAT ET D'HEDIC ... — 215 × 324 mm.

[71] Tome V.Nº 71
[C:] CARTE DE L'ISLE DE BELLE ISLE ... — 212 × 350 mm.

[72] Tome V.Nº 72
[C:] CARTE DU CROISIC, et des Entrèes de la Riviere La-Vilaine. ... — 214 × 163 mm.

[73] Tome V.Nº 73.
[C:] COURS DE LA RIVIERE DE LOIRE Depuis la Mer jusqu'à Nantes. ... — 210 × 327 mm.

[74] Tome V.Nº 74.
[C:] PLAN DE LA VILLE DE NANTES ... — (Plan). 214 × 321 mm.

[75] Tome V.Nº 75.
[C:] CARTE DE LA BAYE DE BOURNEUF et des Isles de Bouin et de Noirmoutier ... — 211 × 152 mm.

[76] Tome V.Nº 76.
[C:] POITOU AUNIS ET SAINTONGE ... — 208 × 170 mm.

[77] Tome V.Nº 77.
[C:] PLAN DU BOURG ET FORT DE LA CHAUME et DES SABLES D'OLONNE. ... — (Plan). 215 × 325 mm.

[78] Tome V.Nº 78.
[C:] CARTE DE L'ISLE DE RÉ. ... — 217 × 167 mm.

[79] Tome V.Nº 79.
[C:] PLAN DE S.T MARTIN DE RÉ ... — (Plan). 226 × 166 mm.

[80] Tome V.Nº 80.
[C:] CARTE DE L'ISLE D'OLLERON ... — 244 × 171 mm.
[Inset:] [C:] VILLE ET CHATEAU D'OLLERON — (Plan). 86 × 55 mm.

[81] Tome V.Nº 81.
[C:] PLAN DES VILLE CITADELLE DE L ISLE D Olleron ... — (Plan). 212 × 161 mm.

[82] Tome V.Nº 82.
[C:] CARTE DES RADES DE LA ROCHELLE et Environs. ... — 228 × 167 mm.

[83] Tome V.Nº 83.
[C:] PLAN DE LA ROCHELLE ... — 214 × 324 mm.

[84] Tome V.Nº 84.
[C:] PLAN DE L'ISLE DAIX ... — 225 × 166 mm.

[85] Tome V.Nº 85.
[C:] CARTE DE L'ENTRÉE DE LA CHARENTE et Environs de Rochefort. ... — 215 × 174 mm.

[86] Tome V.Nº 86.
[C:] PLAN DE ROCHEFORT ... — (Plan). 215 × 325 mm.

[87] Tome V.Nº 87.
[C:] PERTUIS DE MAUMUSSON et Riviere de Seudre. ... — 222 × 168 mm.

[88] Tome V.Nº 88.
[C:] GUYENNE ET GASCOGNE ET BEARN ... — 209 × 256 mm.

[89] Tome V.Nº 89.
[C:] EMBOUCHURE DE LA RIVIERE DE GIRONDE depuis la Mer jusqu'au Banc de Bey ... — 223 × 165 mm.

[90] Tome V.Nº 90.
[C:] COURS DE LA RIVIERE DE GIRONDE, et Parties de la Dordogne et de la Garonne depuis Bourdeaux jusqu'au Banc de Bey ... — 217 × 325 mm.

[91] Tome V.Nº 91.
[C:] PLAN DE BLAYE. ... — (Plan). 222 × 165 mm.

[92] Tome V.Nº 92.
[C:] PLAN DE BORDEAUX et de ses Environs. ... — (Plan). 215 × 162 mm.

[93] Tome V.N° 93.
 [C:] PLAN DE BORDEAUX: ... — (Plan). 218 × 329 mm.
[94] Tome V.N° 94
 [C:] COURS DE LA RIVIERE DE L'ADOUR depuis la Mer jusqu a Bayonne ... — 213 × 328 mm.
[95] Tome V.N° 95.
 [C:] PLAN DE BAYONNE ... — (Plan). 216 × 326 mm.
[96] Tome V.N° 96.
 [C:] CARTE DES ENVIRONS DE BAYONNE et les Costes jusqu'a Fontarabie ... — 220 × 167 mm.
[97] Tome V.N° 97.
 [C:] PLAN DE FONTARABIE ET DE LA REDOUTE D'ANDAYE. ... — 217 × 321 mm.
[98] Tome V.N° 98.
 [C:] LANGUEDOC ET PROVENCE. ... — 185 × 280 mm.
[99] Tome V.N° 99.
 [C:] COSTE DE ROUSSILLON Depuis Port Vendres, Jusqu'au Golphe de Rozes ... — 226 × 166 mm.
[100] Tome V.N° 100.
 [C:] COSTE DE LANGUEDOC ET ROUSSILLON Depuis Leucate Jusqu'a Port Vendres ... — 225 × 166 mm.
[101] Tome V.N° 101.
 [C:] PLAN DE PORT VENDRE en Roussillon. ... — 205 × 167 mm.
[102] Tome V.N° 102.
 [C:] PLAN DU PORT ET VILLE DE COLLIOURE en Roussillon. ... — 200 × 157 mm.
[103] Tome V.N° 103.
 [C:] COSTE DE LANGUEDOC depuis l'Etang de Leucate jusqu'à Gruissan. ... — 220 × 326 mm.
[104] Tome V.N° 104.
 [C:] CARTE DU CANAL DE LANGUEDOC depuis le Port de Cette jusqu'a l'Etang de Marceillette ... — 214 × 368 mm.
[105] Tome V.N° 105.
 [C:] CARTE DU CANAL DE LANGUEDOC Depuis Toulouse jusqu'à l'Etang de Marceillette. ... — 218 × 372 mm.
[106] Tome V.N° 106.
 [C:] SUITE DE LA COSTE DE LANGUEDOC depuis Gruissan jusqu'a Brescon ... — 189 × 395 mm.
[107] Tome V.N° 107.
 [C:] PLAN DE NARBONE ... — 221 × 168 mm.
[108] Tome V.N° 108.
 [C:] COSTE DE LANGUEDOC depuis Agde jusqu a Cette ... — 220 × 168 mm.
[109] Tome V.N° 109.
 [C:] COSTE DE LANGUEDOC depuis Cette jusqu'a l'Etang de Repousset ... — 213 × 366 mm.
[110] Tome V.N° 110.
 [C:] PLAN DU PORT ET VILLE D'AGDE a la Coste de Languedoc ... — 216 × 298 mm.
[111] Tome V.N° 111.
 [C:] PORT DE CETTE et Entree du Canal de Languedoc ... — 224 × 163 mm.
[112] Tome V.N° 112.
 [C:] CARTE DES COSTES DE PROVENCE depuis l'Embouchure du Rhône jusqu'au Var. ... — 212 × 347 mm.
[113] Tome V.N° 113.
 [C:] ENVIRONS D'AIGUEMORTES DE PECCAIS &[a] et la Petite Camargue. ... — 213 × 173 mm.
[114] Tome V.N° 114.
 [C:] PLAN D'AIGUESMORTES et Environs ... — (Plan). 228 × 169 mm.
[115] Tome V.N° 115.
 [C:] CARTE DES ETANGS DE BERRE DE MARTIGUE et Environs ... — 212 × 163 mm.
[116] Tome V.N° 116.
 [C:] ETANG DE MARTIGUE et Environs ... — 228 × 165 mm.
[117] Tome V.N° 117.
 [C:] CARTE DE LA BAYE DE MARSEILLE ... — 210 × 171 mm.
[118] Tome V.N° 118.
 [C:] PLAN DE MARSEILLE et ses Environs. ... — Croisey .S. 212 × 171 mm.
[119] Tome V.N° 119.
 [C:] CARTE DES ISLES DE ROTONAU S.[T] JEAN et Chateau d'If. ... — 213 × 162 mm.
[120] Tome V.N° 120.
 [C:] PLAN DE CASSIS ET ENVIRONS. ... — 216 × 167 mm.
[121] Tome V.N° 121.
 [C:] CARTE DE LA RADE DU BRUSC ... — 213 × 171 mm.
[122] Tome V.N° 122
 [C:] GOLFE DE LA CIOTAT ... — 207 × 320 mm.
[123] Tome V.N° 123.
 [C:] PLAN DES RADES DE TOULON ... — Croisey .S. 225 × 309 mm.
[124] Tome V.N° 124.
 [T:] CARTE DES ISLES D'HIERES — Croisey S 207 × 342 mm.
[125] Tome V.N° 125
 [C:] PLAN DE LA RADE DE CAVALAIRE ... — 220 × 168 mm.
[126] Tome V.N° 126.
 [C:] PLAN DE S.[T] TORPEZ ET ENTRÉE DU GOLFE DE GRIMAUD ... — 226 × 169 mm.
[127] Tome V.N° 127
 [C:] PLAN DE S.[T] TORPÉS ... — (Plan). 215 × 174 mm.
[128] Tome V.N° 128
 [C:] GOLFE DE FREJUS ... — 213 × 172 mm.
[129] Tome V.N° 129.
 [C:] PORT DE NAGAYE ET COSTE VOISINES ... — 224 × 171 mm.
[130] Tome V.N° 130.
 [C:] PLAN DE LA RADE DE GOURJEAN ... — 218 × 339 mm.
[131] Tome V.N° 131.
 [C:] PLAN D'ANTIBES ET ENVIRONS ... — 217 × 167 mm.
[132] Tome V.N° 132.
 [C:] PLAN D'ANTIBES ... — 217 × 175 mm.

Notes: All the maps are blank on the back and lightly coloured. There is a six-page "Table des Cartes et Plans" for this volume. All the double-leaf maps are numbered in ink on the back. Three maps from vol. 4 reappear in this volume as [2], [3] and [56]. Nordenskiöld's bookplate is on the inside of the front cover.

Lit.: See also notes for vol. 1.

11 BELLIN, JACQUES NICOLAS   1764

Vol. III
LE PETIT ATLAS MARITIME RECUEIL DE CARTES ET DE PLANS DES QUATRE PARTIES DU MONDE. TOME III. Contenant I°. L'ASIE. II°. L'AFRIQUE. avec les Details interessans de ces Deux Parties. M. DCC. LXIV.   32,3 cm.

[1] Tome I.N° 1.
 [C:] CARTE REDUITE DE GLOBE TERRESTRE... — = 1764:I:[1].
[2] Tome III.N° 2.
 [C:] L'ASIE ... — = 1764:III:[2].
[3] Tome III.N° 3.
 [C:] CARTE RÉDUITE DE LA MOSCOVIE... — = 1764:III:[3].
[4] [C:] CARTE RÉDUITE DES DÉCOUVERTES DES RUSSES, Entre l'Asie et l'Amerique Pour servir à l'Histoire générale des Voyages — 198 × 288 mm.

[5] Tome III.N? 4.
[a] [C:] CARTE DE LA MER NOIRE ... — [b] [C:] CARTE DU CANAL DE LA MER NOIRE ... — = 1764:III:[4].
[6] Tome III.N? 5.
[C:] CARTE DE LA MER CASPIENNE et ses Environs ... — = 1764:III:[5].
[7] Tome III.N? 6.
[C:] PLAN DE LA VILLE D'ASTRACAN ... — = 1764:III:[6].
[8] Tome III.N? 7.
[C:] LA PERSE ... — = 1764:III:[7].
[9] Tome III.N? 8.
[C:] CARTE DU GOLPHE PERSIQUE ... — = 1764:III:[8].
[10] Tome III.N? 9.
[C:] CARTE DES EMBOUCHURES DE L'EUPHRATE ... — = 1764:III:[9].
[11] Tome III.N? 10.
[C:] CARTE DE L'ASIE MINEURE ... — = 1764:III:[10].
[12] Tome III.N? 11.
[C:] CARTE DE L'ARMENIE GEORGIE ... — = 1764:III:[11].
[13] Tome III.N? 12.
[C:] CARTE DE LA SYRIE. ... — = 1764:III:[12].
[14] Tome III.N? 13.
[C:] CARTE DE L'ISLE DE CYPRE. ... — = 1764:III:[13].
[15] Tome III.N? 14.
[C:] CARTE DU GOLPHE D'ALEXANDRETTE. ... — = 1764:III:[14].
[16] Tome III.N? 15.
[C:] PLAN DE TRIPOLI DE SYRIE. ... — = 1764:III:[15].
[17] Tome III.N? 16.
[C:] PLAN DE SEIDE EN SYRIE. ... — = 1764:III:[16].
[18] Tome III.N? 17.
[C:] PLAN DE LA RADE DE SOUR EN SYRIE. ... — = 1764:III:[17].
[19] Tome III.N? 18.
[C:] PLAN DE LA RADE DE S.T JEAN D'ACRE a la Coste de Syrie. ... — = 1764:III:[18].
[20] Tome III.N? 19.
[C:] CARTE DE LA MER ROUGE ... — = 1764:III:[19].
[21] Tome III.N? 20.
[C:] PLAN DE LA VILLE DE MOKA Située sur la Mer Rouge. ... — = 1764:III:[20].
[22] Tome III.N? 21.
[C:] CARTE DE L'INDOUSTAN I.e Feuille ... — = 1764:III:[21].
[23] Tome III.N? 22.
[C:] Suite de la Carte de L'INDOUSTAN. II.e Feuille, ... — = 1764:III:[22].
[24] Tome III.N? 23.
[C:] CARTE DES ISLES MALDIVES. ... — = 1764:III:[23].
[25] Tome III.N? 24.
[C:] CARTE DU GOLPHE DE CAMBAYE. ... — = 1764:III:[24].
[26] Tome III.N? 25.
[C:] PLAN DE BOMBAY et ses Environs. ... — = 1764:III:[25].
[27] Tome III.N? 26.
[C:] CARTE DES COSTES DE CONCAN ET DECAN ... — = 1764:III:[26].
[28] Tome III.N? 27.
[a] [C:] COSTE DE CANARA ... — [b] [C:] SUITE DE LA COSTE DE MALABAR ... — [c] [C:] COSTE DE MALABAR ... — = 1764:III:[27].
[29] Tome III.N? 28.
[C:] BAYE VILLE ET FORTS D'ANDARAJAPOUR ... — = 1764:III:[28].
[30] Tome III.N? 29.
[C:] CARTE DU PORT DE GOA ... — = 1764:III:[29].
[31] Tome III.N? 30.
[C:] PLAN DE MAYÉ à la Coste de Malabar ... — = 1764:III:[30].
[32] Tome III.N? 31.
[C:] CARTE DE L'ISLE DE CEYLAN ... — = 1764:III:[31].
[33] Tome III.N? 32
[C:] CARTE DE LA BAYE DE TRINQUEMALE ... — = 1764:III:[32].
[34] Tome III.N? 33.
[C:] PLAN DE LA VILLE ET FORT DE JAFFA NEPATAN ... — = 1764:III:[33].
[35] Tome III.N? 34.
[C:] CARTE DU GOLPHE DE BENGALE ... — = 1764:III:[34].
[36] Tome III.N? 35.
[T:] PLAN DE LA VILLE DE PONDICHERI — = 1764:III[35].
[37] Tome III.N? 36.
[C:] CARTE DU DISTRICT DE TRANQUEBAR ... — = 1764:III:[36].
[38] Tome III.N? 37.
[C:] PLAN DE MADRAS ... — = 1764:III:[37].
[39] Tome III.N? 38.
Theâtre de la Guerre dans l'Inde.
[C:] COSTE DE COROMANDEL ... — = 1764:III:[38].
[40] Tome III.N? 39.
[C:] COSTE DE COROMANDEL ... — = 1764:III:[39].
[41] Tome III.N? 40.
[C:] NOUVELLE CARTE DU ROYAUME DE BENGALE. ... — = 1764:III:[40].
[42] Tome III.N? 41.
[C:] CARTE DE L'ENTRÉE DU GANGE ... — = 1764:III:[41].
[43] Tome III.N? 42.
[C:] ARCHIPEL DE MERGUI, ... — = 1764:III:[42].
[44] Tome III.N? 43.
[C:] PORT ET BOURG DE MERGUI ... — = 1764:III:[43].
[45] Tome III.N? 44.
[C:] CARTE des Isles de JAVA SUMATRA BORNEO &.a ... — = 1764:III:[44].
[46] Tome III.N? 45.
[C:] CARTE DE L'ISLE DE SUMATRA ... — = 1764:III:[45].
[47] Tome III.N? 46.
[C:] PLAN DE LA VILLE DE MALACA ... — = 1764:III:[46].
[48] Tome III.N? 47.
[C:] CARTE DE L'ISLE DE JAVA ... — = 1764:III:[47].
[49] Tome III.N? 48.
[C:] CARTE DES ENVIRONS DE BATAVIA ... — = 1764:III:[48].
[50] Tome III.N? 49.
[C:] CARTE DES ROYAUMES DE SIAM DE TUNQUIN Pegu, Ava Arcan, &c ... — = 1764:III:[49].
[51] Tome III.N? 50.
[C:] CARTE DU COURS DU MENAN, ... — = 1764:III:[50].
[52] Tome III.N? 51.
[T:] VILLE DE SIAM ou JUTHIA. ... — = 1764:III:[51].
[53] Tome III.N? 52.
[C:] PLAN DE LA VILLE DE LOUVO ... — = 1764:III:[52].
[54] Tome III.N? 53.
[C:] CARTE DU COURS DE LA RIVIERE DE TUNQUIN, ... — = 1764:III:[53].
[55] Tome III.N? 54.
[C:] L'EMPIRE DE LA CHINE. ... — = 1764:III:[54].
[56] Tome III.N? 55.
[C:] CARTE DU ROYAUME DE KAU-LI ou CORÉE ... — = 1764:III:[55].
[57] Tome III.N? 56.
[C:] CARTE DES ISLES qui sont a l'Entrée de la RIVIERE DE CANTON ... — = 1764:III:[56].

[58] Tome III.N.° 57.
[T:] PLAN DE LA VILLE ET DU PORT DE MACAO. ... — = 1764:III:[57].
[59] Tome III.N.° 58.
[C:] CARTE DE L'ENTRÉE DE LA RIVIERE DE CANTON dans la Chine. ... — = 1764:III:[58].
[60] Tome III.N.° 59.
[C:] CARTE DE L'ISLE FORMOSE ... — = 1764:III:[59].
[61] Tome III.N.° 60.
[C:] CARTE DE LA BAYE D'HOCSIEU ... — = 1764:III:[60].
[62] Tom. III.N.° 61.
[C:] ISLE DE CHEU-CHAN ou ISLE CHUSAN ... — = 1764:III:[61].
[63] Tome III.N.° 62.
[C:] CARTE DE L'EMPIRE DU JAPON. ... — = 1764:III:[62].
[64] Tome III.N° 63.
[C:] PLAN DU PORT ET DE LA VILLE DE NANGASAKI. ... — = 1764:III:[63].
[65] Tome III.N.° 64.
[C:] CARTE DES ISLES PHILIPPINES CELEBES ET MOLUQUES ... — = 1764:III:[64].
[66] Tome III.N.° 65.
[C:] CARTE DES ISLES PHILIPPINES, ... — = 1764:III:[65].
[67] Tome III.N.° 66.
[C:] CARTE DES ISLES PHILIPPINES ... 2.e Feuille ... — = 1764:III:[66].
[68] Tome III.N.° 67.
[C:] PLAN DE LA BAYE DE MANILLE ... — = 1764:III:[67].
[69] Tome III.N.° 68.
[C:] CARTE PARTICULIERE DES ISLES MOLUQUES. — = 1764:III:[68].
[70] Tome III.N.° 69.
[T:] CARTE DE L'ARCHIPEL DE S.T LAZARE OU LES ISLES MARIANES ... — = 1764:III:[69].
Tome III. Page 70
SECONDE PARTIE DU TOME III. Contenant L'AFRIQUE avec ses Détails tant sur la Mer Mediterranée que sur l'Ocean, ET LES ISLES QUI EN DÉPENDENT. M. DCC.LXIV.
[71] Tome III.N.° 70.
[C:] CARTE DE L'AFRIQUE. ... — = 1764:III:[70].
[72] Tome III.N.° 71.
[C:] COSTES DE BARBARIE Contenant LES ROYAUMES D'ALGER ET DE TUNIS ... — = 1764:III:[71].
[73] Tome III.N.° 72.
[C:] CARTE DU DÉTROIT DE GIBRALTAR. ... — = 1764:III:[72].
[74] Tome III.N.° 73.
[C:] RADE ET VILLE DE CEUTE ... — = 1764:III:[73].
[75] Tome III.N.° 74.
[C:] PLAN DE LA VILLE DE MELLILA ... — = 1764:III:[74].
[76] Tome III.N.° 75.
[C:] PLAN D'ORAN ... — = 1764:III:[75].
[77] Tome III.N.° 76.
[C:] PLAN DU CHATEAU ET PORT DE MARZALQUIVIR ... — = 1764:III:[76].
[78] Tome III.N.° 77.
[C:] PLAN DE LA BAYE D'ALGER ... — = 1764:III:[77].
[79] Tome III.N.° 78.
[C:] PLAN DE LA VILLE FORTS ET PORT D'ALGER ... — = 1764:III:[78].
[80] Tome III.N.° 79.
[C:] PLAN DE L'ISLE DE TABARQUE ... — = 1764:III:[79].
[81] Tome III.N.° 80.
[C:] PLAN DE PORT FARINE. ... — = 1764:III:[80].
[82] Tome III.N.° 81.
[C:] GOLPHE DE TUNIS ... — = 1764:III:[81].

[83] Tome III.N.° 82.
[C:] PLAN DE LA VILLE DE TUNIS ... — = 1764:III:[82].
[84] Tome III.N.° 83.
[C:] PLAN DES FORTS ET CANAL DE LA GOULETTE ... — = 1764:III:[83].
[85] Tome III.N.° 84.
[C:] PLAN DE LA RADE ET VILLE DE TRIPOLI, ... — = 1764:III:[84].
[86] Tome III.N.° 85.
[C:] COSTES D'EGYPTE, ... — = 1764:III:[85].
[87] Tome III.N.° 86.
[C:] PLAN DES PORTS ET VILLE D'ALEXANDRIE. ... — = 1764:III:[86].
[88] Tome III.N.° 87.
[C:] RADE DU BEQUIER ... — = 1764:III:[87].
[89] Tome III.N.° 88.
[C:] PLAN DU FORT ET DU VILLAGE DU BEQUIER ... — = 1764:III:[88].
[90] Tome III.N.° 89.
[C:] CARTE DES EMBOUCHURES DU NIL, ... — = 1764:III:[89].
[91] Tome III.N.° 90.
[C:] CARTE EXACTE DU COURS DU NIL. ... — = 1764:III:[90].
[92] Tome IV.N.°58. et Tome III.N.° 91.
[C:] CARTE RÉDUITE DE LA MER MÉDITERRANÉE. ... — = 1764:III:[91].
[93] Tome III.N.° 92.
[C:] CARTE DES ROYAUMES DE FEZ ET DE MAROC. ... — = 1764:III:[92].
[94] Tome III.N.° 92*.
[C:] ISLE DE MOGADOR ... — = 1764:III:[93].
[95] Tome III.N.° 93.
[C:] CARTE DES ISLES CANARIES ... — = 1764:III:[94].
[96] Tome III.N.° 94.
[T:] CARTE DE L'ISLE DE TENERIFFE ... — = 1764:III:[95].
[97] Tome III.N.° 95.
[C:] CARTE de l'Entrée de la RIVIERE DE SANAGA ou SENEGAL. ... — = 1764:III:[97].
[98] Tome III.N.° 95*.
[C:] COSTES DU SENEGAL ... — = 1764:III:[96].
[99] Tome III.N° 96.
[a] [C:] COURS DE LA RIVIERE DE SANAGA ou SENEGAL ... — [b] [C:] SUITE DU COURS DE LA RIVIERE DE SENEGAL. ... — = 1764:III:[98].
[100] Tome III.N.° 97.
[C:] PLAN DE LA Baye et Isle D'ARGUIM. ... — = 1764:III:[99].
[101] Tome III.N.° 98
[C:] COSTES D'AFRIQUE ... — = 1764:III:[100].
[102] Tome III.N° 99.
[C:] PLAN DE L'ISLE DE GORÉ ... — = 1764:III:[101].
[103] Tome III.N.° 100.
[C:] CARTE DES ISLES DU CAP VERD ... — = 1764:III:[102].
[104] Tome III.N.° 101.
[C:] CARTE DE LA RIVIERE DE GAMBRA ou GAMBIE ... — = 1764:III:[103].
[105] Tome III.N.° 102.
[C:] CARTE DU COURS DE LA RIVIERE DE GAMBRA ou GAMBIE ... — = 1764:III:[104].
[106] Tome III.N.° 103.
[a] [T:] CARTE DE L'ENTRÉE DE LA RIVIERE DE SIERRA LEONA ... — [b] [T:] PLAN DE L'ISLE DE BENSE. — = 1764:III:[105].
[107] Tome III.N.° 104.
[a] [T:] ENTRÉE DE LA RIVIERE DE SESTOS. ... — [b] [T:] VUE DU CAP MESURADO ... — = 1764:III:[106].
[108] Tome III.N.° 105.
[C:] PARTIE DE LA COSTE DE GUINÉE ... — = 1764:III:[107].

[109] Tome III.N°. 106.
[C:] COSTE DE GUINÉE ... — = 1764:III:[108].

[110] Tome III.N° 107.
[C:] CARTE DU GOLFE DE BENIN ... — = 1764:III:[109].

[111] Tome III.N°. 108.
[C:] CARTE DE LA RIVIERE DE KALBAR, ... — = 1764:III:[110].

[112] Tome III.N°. 109.
[C:] CARTE DES ROYAUMES DE CONGO ANGOLA et BENGUELA ... — = 1764:III:[111].

[113] Tome III.N°. 110.
[C:] RADE DE BENGUELA ... — = 1764:III:[112].

[114] Tome III.N°. 111.
[C:] CARTE DU PAIS DES HOTTENTOTS ... — = 1764:III:[113].

[115] Tome III.N°. 112.
[C:] BAYE DE SALDANE ... — = 1764:III:[116].

[116] Tome III.N°. 113.
[C:] CARTE DE LA BAYE DE LA TABLE, ... — = 1764:III:[115].

[117] Tome III.N°. 114.
[C:] VILLE ET FORT DU CAP DE BONNE ESPERANCE ... — = 1764:III:[114].

[118] Tome III.N°. 115.
[C:] CARTE DE L'ISLE DE MADAGASCAR ... — = 1764:III:[117].

[119] Tome III.N°. 116.
[C:] CARTE DE L'ANCE DAUPHINE ... — = 1764:III:[118].

[120] Tome III.N°. 117.
[C:] CARTE DE LA BAYE D'ANTONGIL. ... — = 1764:III:[119].

[121] Tome III.N°. 118.
[C:] CARTE DE LA BAYE DE MOSAMBIQUE. ... — = 1764:III:[120].

[122] Tome III.N°. 119.
[C:] CARTE DE L'ISLE DE FRANCE ... — = 1764:III:[121].

[123] Tome III.N°. 120.
[C:] PLAN DU PORT BOURBON. ... — = 1764:III:[122].

[124] Tome III.N°. 121.
[C:] PLAN DU PORT LOUIS ... — = 1764:III:[123].

[125] Tome III.N°. 122.
[C:] CARTE DE L'ISLE DE BOURBON ... — = 1764:III:[124].

[126] Tome III.N°. 123.
[C:] PLAN DE L'ISLE S.^{TE} HELENE ... — = 1764:III:[125].

[127] Tome 3.N°. 124.
[C:] PLAN DE LA FORTERESSE ET BOURG, DE LISLE DE S.^{TE} HELENE ... — = 1764:III:[126].

Notes: All the maps are blank on the back and lightly coloured. This second copy of vol. 3 of the atlas contains one map [4] that is not in our complete set, the "Carte réduite des decouvertes des Russes..." In the copy in the National Maritime Museum at Greenwich this map is printed as an inset to the "Carte réduite de la Moscovie Sibirie Tartarie ..."; in our copy it is neither numbered not listed in the Table. In addition to the printed number, all the double-leaf maps are numbered in ink on the back; this map bears the number 3bis. Two other maps, nos.[92] and [95], are not listed in the Table; the atlas thus contains 127 maps, not 124 as listed. The volume is bound in old leather. Nordenskiöld's bookplate is on the inside of the front cover, and that of Gabriel Cramer is on the verso of the second blank leaf. The title-page bears a relief stamp reading 'E. Dufossé 27. Rue Guénégaud Paris Librairie Américaine et coloniale.'

Lit.: See also notes for vol. 1.

12 BERTELLI, FERDINANDO 1568

CIVITATVM ALIQVOT INSIGNIORVM, et locor, magis munitor exacta delineatio: Cum additione aliquot Insularum principalium. DISEGNI di alcune piu illustri città, et fortezze del mondo, con aggionta di alcune Isole principali. Venetiis M.D.LXVIII Ferrandi Bertelli formis.   26 cm.

[1] [T:] MESSINA — [T:] F B — 154 × 284 mm.

[2] [C:] ROMA ANTIQVA — 180 × 247 mm.

[3] [T:] L: Porti di Malta, di nuouo ristaurati doppo partito l'assedio d'infideli, ridotto in picciola forma ... In merzaria al segno della.I. — 167 × 130 mm.

[4] [T:] VALLETTA NOVA CITTA DI MALTA — [T:] Al segno della colonna — 170 × 130 mm.

[5] [C:] AGRIA, fortezza nel paese di Ongheria nel modo che al presente si troua, la quale è di grande importanzza. l'anno 1568. — [T:] L.B. — 182 × 256 mm.

[6] [C:] Fortezza nouamente fatta da Turchi detta Turchartogli Olimionàs, che in greco dice fortezza de Mani et in turchescho Monige al porto delle Quaglie, et Mayna al' capo Mattapan nella Morea presa dal' CL^{mo}Cap^{o}de Colfo Quiriui cō l'armata di Candia alli di lulio 1570 e poi spionata. ... IN VENETIA, A presso Gio.Franc.^{o} Camocio. 1570 — 296 × 216 mm.

[7] [T:] Vitenbergo. — [T:] F.F. F L — 167 × 236 mm.

[8] [T:] FORTEZZA DI SAPOTO — [C:] Sapoto presa dal Cl^{mo} m sabastian Venul. procurator et proueditor general de l'isola di corfù insieme col clar^{mo} proueditor zelsi et ali 7. giugno sino ali 10. sa presero. D.Z. — (View). 160 × 236 mm.

[9] [T:] MILO — [T:] NB — (Map). 193 × 154 mm.

[10] [T:] SIO — [An empty cartouche]. (Map). 208 × 151 mm.

[11] [T:] MAIORICA — [C:] DE MAIORICA INSVLA ... Ferando bertelli. Exc. — (Map). 254 × 190 mm.

[12] [T:] ELBA — [C:] ILBA siue ILVA insula est immari tusco continet distans mill.X. pasuum et nascuntur minerales metalli bene munita et forti situ impetui turcarum resistit. Ferando bertelli. — (Map). 250 × 177 mm.

[13] [T:] RHODI — [T:] 1570 — (Map). 260 × 177 mm.

[14] [T:] NICSIA — [T:] NB — (Map). 250 × 169 mm.

[15] [T:] MINORICA — [C:] DE MINORICA INSVLA ... Ferando Bertelli Exc. — (Map). 248 × 198 mm.

[16] [T:] HIBERNIA — [C:] HIBERNIA siue IRLANDA insula maxima inter britanniam et hispaniam ... — (Map). 256 × 170 mm.

[17] [T:] ISLANDA — [C:] DE ISLANDA INSVLA ... anno 1566 FERANDO BERTELI EXC — (Map). 263 × 193 mm.

[18] [T:] GOTLANDIA — [C:] FERANDO Bertelli [in an empty cartouche]. — (Map). 255 × 190 mm.

[19] [T:] CRETA CANDIA — [C:] CANDIDO LECTORI HAEC est illa insignis creta in medio ponto sita, ... VENETIÆ. M. D. LXII. Ferrandus bertellus Exc. — [T:] Marius cartarus fec — (Map). 175 × 244 mm.

[20] [T:] ISOLA DI CIPRO — [C:] CYPRVS Insula olim Macherio, ... ROMÆ. M.D.LXII. Ferandus bertelli excude. — [T:] MK — (Map). 181 × 245 mm.

[21] [T:] AVGVSTA — [Two empty cartouches]. [T:] E B — 206 × 294 mm.

[22] [T:] GRAVELINGA IN FIANDRA. — 153 × 204 mm.

[23] [C:] Il uero disegno del sito' e della fortezza di Comar'terra parta sopra un'isola fatta dal Danubio fiume nella parte del Vngaria, ferando bertelli Excudebat. — 185 × 247 mm.

[24] [T:] DISEGNO DELLA FORTEZZA ET CITTA DI GOTTA IN SASSONIA — [T:] L:P. — 192 × 262 mm.

[25] [T:] ROMA — 168 × 265 mm.

[26] [T:] IL CASTELLO DI SANT ANGELO — 200 × 285 mm.

[27] [T:] LION — [T:] ABF — 195 × 284 mm.

[28] [C:] VIENNA, Città principál d'Ongheria nel modo che al presente s'ē fortificata. in uenetia 1566. Domenico Zenoi cum priuilegio. — 145 × 199 mm.

[29] [T:] GENOVA — 185 × 290 mm.
[30] [T:] NAPOLI — [T:] F.B. — [T:] L.P. — 172 × 256 mm.
[31] [T:] GENEVR — [T:] A.B F — 199 × 229 mm.
[32] [T:] CHALES — [C:] CHALES — [T:] A.B. — 176 × 209 mm.
[33] [C:] ZIGET, fortezza innespugnabile, si come ogi di è ueramēte situata, con li pōti per l'intrata et uscita, si della terra come d'ùna fortezza al altra quali pōti suo leuatori, e cinto d'acqua et paludi come nel presente disegno si uede: et hora assediato dal grā Turco cō iooooo. Turchi l'anno.M.D.LXVI. In Ven.merzaria alla .I. — 137 × 181 mm.
[34] [C:] Verò disegno di Giula, si come è ueramēte situata ogi di cō l'assedio d'infideli l'anno M.D.LXVI. — [T:] Paolo Furlani Veronese intagliatore in Ven all'insegna della colonna — 134 × 172 mm.
[35] [T:] CRESCENTINO — [T:] E B — 175 × 226 mm.
[36] [T:] [The Eastern part of Cypros with] Nicosia Famagosta — [T:] .S.Z. — (Map). 145 × 198 mm.
[37] [T:] CIVITAS HIERVSALEM — [T:] .L.P. — 185 × 262 mm.
[38] [T:] GABATA CITTA IN ARABIA — [T:] N[?] — 132 × 168 mm.
[39] [T:] CORSICA — [C:] CIRNVS siue CORSICA insula est in mari Ligustico ... Ferando Berteli excidebat. 1562 — (Map). 305 × 197 mm.
[40] [T:] SARDEGNA — [C:] Sardinia insula inter africū et tirrenum pellagus sita ... FER. BER. EXC. 1562. — (Map). 293 × 185 mm.
[41] [T:] TRIPOLI DE BARBARIA — [T:] L.P. — 193 × 257 mm.
[42] [T:] LA GRAN CITTA DEL CAIRO — [T:] JON & NFS [?] — [T:] . Æ.— 200 × 285 mm.
[43] [C:] PARIGI. — [T:] Appresso Ferrádo Bertelli. — 191 × 248 mm.
[44] [T:] BOVRDEAVX Citta nobilissima di studio posta nella francia — [T:] ℔ — 199 × 284 mm.
[45] [T:] MIRANDOLA — [T:] L P — 172 × 257 mm.
[46] [T:] LA NOBILE CITA DI FIORENZA — 128 × 272 mm.
[47] [T:] CVI T NES — [T:] .A.B. — 158 × 211 mm.
[48] [T:] ALBA DE GRATIA — 199 × 285 mm.
[49] [T:] IL VERO ET RITRATTO DI SIENA. — [T:] A.B. — 171 × 241 mm.
[50] [T:] LA FORTEZZA DI FANO — 173 × 222 mm.
[51] [T:] MONICHO — 152 × 267 mm.
[52] [C:] Toquay fortezza ne 'i confini d'Ongaria, uerso Transiluania, si ueramente come ogi di si troua — 137 × 179 mm.
[53] [T:] PARMA — 163 × 246 mm.
[54] [T:] PIASEZA — 200 × 290 mm.
[55] [T:] ALGIERI — 131 × 185 mm.
[56] [C:] Il uero disegno della Pianta de MILANO si come egi di si ritroua Ferando Berteli exa: — 153 × 178 mm.
[57] [T:] IL GERBI — 175 × 239 mm.
[58] [T:] CORFV — [An empty cartouche]. (Map). 206 × 153 mm.
[59] [T:] NEGROPONTE — [T:] NB — [An empty cartouche]. (Map). 206 × 158 mm.
[60] [T:] L'ASSEDIO DI GOTTA — (View). 179 × 269 mm.
[61] [T:] IL PIGNON — (View). 175 × 244 mm.
[62] [C:] MOREA peninsula anticamēte detta poloponesse, apia, e pelagia. oratio berteli — (Map). 148 × 195 mm.
[63] [T:] AИVERSA — [T:] F— 192 × 317 mm.
[64] [T:] FRANCKFORT — 175 × 253 mm.
[65] [T:] FORTEZZA DI IAVARIN doue si troua hora il campo de l'impator — 141 × 178 mm.
[66] [T:] THION VILLE — 210 × 213 mm.

Notes: There is no text in the atlas, on the verso of the maps or elsewhere. The maps are uncoloured. The title page and maps [62] and [66] have been trimmed along the edges and pasted on old paper. The title-page is dated 1568, but two of the maps are dated 1570. Map [8] is signed 'D.Z.', i.e. Domenico Zeno, whose name appears in full on map [28].

Some of the other maps are also signed with initials: map [5] with L.B. (= Luca Bertelli ?), [14] & [59] with NB (= Nicolò Bertelli), [30] with F.B. (= Francesco Bertelli). Other initials have not been identified. On the first old blank leaf 'G. M.' (?) is written in old ink, which has eaten through the paper, and in pencil '66 Karten Titel die letzten 2 Blatt aufgez.'; then in Nordenskiöld's hand 'En upplaga med tryckår 1569 utbjudes i L. Rosenthals Catalog 100 för 100 M. innehåller endast hälften så många tafl. som denna.' [An edition dated 1569 offered in L. Rosenthal's Catalog 100 for 100 M contains only half as many plates as this one.] Nordenskiöld's signature is on the following blank leaf, and on the last old blank leaf at the end he has written : '1897 köpt från I. Halles Antiquarit i München för 100 M.' [1897 bought from I. Haller's antiquarian bookshop in Munich for 100 M.] A coat-of-arms is stamped on the title-page.

Lit.: BM Maps vol. 2, c. 714, Nagler vol. 2, p. 718, nr 1945.

13 BERTELLI, PIETRO 1599

[Theatrum Urbium Italicarum. Venetiis 1599]. [Colophon:] VENETIIS. M D X C I X. APVD PETRVM BERTELLIVM BIBLIOPOLAM PATAVINVM. 16,7 cm.

[1] [T:] VENETIA — A 2 121 × 176 mm.
[2] [T:] LA GRAN CITA DI MILANO — 116 × 172 mm.
[3] [T:] NAPOLI — 4 B 2 111 × 170 mm.
[4] [T:] FIORENZA — 6 119 × 173 mm.
[5] [T:] GENOVA — 8 117 × 173 mm.
[6] [T:] PALERMO — 112 × 172 mm.
[7] [T:] LA NOBILE CITTA DI MESSINA. — 11 D 112 × 168 mm.
[8] [T:] CATANIA IN SICILIA PATRIA DI S:AGATA — 13 114 × 172 mm.
[9] [C:] DROPANVM VRBS EST SICILIÆ TRANS LILYPÆVM: PROMONTORIVM NON PROCVL AB IRICE MONTE — [T:] TRAPANO — 16 E 2 118 × 172 mm.
[10] [T:] TRIDNTVM — 18 118 × 167 mm.
[11] [T:] MALTA. — 21 117 × 171 mm.
[12] [T:] CALIARI — [C:] CALARIS SARDINE PRIMARIA CIVITAS — 22 112 × 166 mm.
[13] [T:] TVRINO — [C:] AVGVSTA TAVRINORVM IN SABAVDIE — 23 G 120 × 180 mm.
[14] [T:] PARMA — 24 G 2 114 × 171 mm.
[15] [T:] L'ANTICHISS. E NOBILSS. CITTA DI PIACENZA — 25 114 × 172 mm.
[16] [T:] CREMONA — [C:] Cremonac abitus qui nunc moenibus septus est cubitos undicim M. Ducentos quiquaginta complectitur — 26 111× 168 mm.
[17] [T:] BOLOGNA — 27 H 119 × 175 mm.
[18] [T:] MANTOVA — [C:] MANTVA, LOMBARDIE TRANSPADANE, VRBS CLARISS. ETANTITQVISS. VENVSTISSIMV IN MEDIO PALVDIVM. SITV OPTINET — 30 113 × 170 mm.
[19] [T:] REGGIO — [C:] REGIVN LEPIDI VRBS NOBILISIMA IN LOMBARDIA — 33 121 × 173 mm.
[20] [T:] FERRARA — 34 130 × 182 mm.
[21] [T:] PAVIA — 35 K 117 × 176 mm.
[22] [T:] MIRANDOLA — 36 K 2 116 × 174 mm.
[23] [T:] LVCA. — 37 113 × 169 mm.
[24] [T:] SIENA — 40 L 2 119 × 173 mm.
[25] [T:] PERVGIA — 41 111 × 169 mm.
[26] [T:] VITERBO CITTA METROPOLI DELLA PROVINCIA DEL PATRIMONIO — 44 M 2 116 × 174 mm.
[27] [T:] RIMINI — [C:] ARIMINVM VALIDVM ET MVNITVM ROMANDI OLAE OPP. — 45 116 × 175 mm.
[28] [C:] SVLMONA. OVIDII PARTIA BRVTIORVM PELIGNE REGIONIS OPPIDVM — [T:] SVLMONA. — 120 × 175 mm.

[29] [T:] NETVNO — 49 118 × 180 mm.
[30] [T:] FANO — 50 115 × 174 mm.
[31] [T:] VRBINO — [C:] Vrbinum. piceni urbs. alto In Monte inter albin siue sapim. — 51 O 117 × 178 mm.
[32] [T:] CITTA D'VDINE — 53 113 × 170 mm.
[33] [T:] TREVISO — 54 130 × 183 mm.
[34] [T:] PALMA — 117 × 174 mm.
[35] [T:] SERAVAL — [C:] SERAVALVM CELEBERRIMVM MARCHIAE TARVISINA IN AGRO FORO IVLIENSIS PPO. — 57 117 × 177 mm.
[36] [T:] VICENZA — [C:] IACOBVS MONTICVLVS INVENTOR. — [C:] VICETIA VENETIAI VRBS NOBILISSIMA ET ANTIQVISSIMA — 125 × 180 mm.
[37] [T:] PADOA — 61 114 × 171 mm.
[38] [T:] VERONA — 112 × 171 mm.
[39] [T:] BRESCIA — 66 121 × 171 mm.
[40] [T:] LA ROCCA CONTRADA — 69 121 × 178 mm.
[41] [T:] ORVIETO — [C:] VRBS VETVS ITALIÆ ETRVSCORṼ CIVITAS — 70 119 × 179 mm.
[42] [T:] BERGAMO — [C:] IN LOMBARDIA FERTILISIMA — 67 S 120 × 180 mm.
[43] [T:] CREMA — 68 S 2 116 × 172 mm.
[44] [T:] AQVA PENDENTE — 71 T 117 × 177 mm.
[45] [T:] ANCONA — 72 T 2 119 × 180 mm.
[46] [T:] LAVRETVM — [C:] LAVRETVM. AGRI RECENATEN IN ITALIA CELEBRE OPP: AD MARIÆ ATIQVISSIMA IBI SITA Æ DE ILLVSTRTV — 74 118 × 173 mm.
[47] [T:] NOCERRA In Appennino Monte — 127 × 184 mm.
[48] [T:] MOLA — [C:] TV QVOQ LITTORIB̲NOS TRIS ÆNLIA NVTRIXÆ, TRNA MORIENS FAMA CAIETA DEDISTI — 77 119 × 177 mm.
[49] [T:] BELITRI — [C:] Velitræ, Antiguissima LatY, initalia Vrbs. in monte. mænibus — 79 X 117 × 181 mm.
[50] [T:] CALATIA. — 129 × 184 mm.
[51] [T:] PVTEOLI — 124 × 180 mm.
[52] [T:] TERRACINA — [C:] VETVSTISS AD MARE THIIRRHENVM TERRACINAE OPPIDVM — 86 120 × 179 mm.
[53] [T:] TIVOLI — [C:] TYBVR VENVSTALA: VRBS VVLGO TIVOLI — 88 Z 2 110 × 165 mm.
[54] [T:] GALLIPOLI — [C:] CALLIPOLIS VRBS VETVSTISSIMA FORTISSIMA ATQVE FIDELTS — 90 119 × 177 mm.
[55] [T:] FONDI — 92 Aa 2 128 × 184 mm.
[56] [T:] TARANTO — 94 123 × 178 mm.
[57] [T:] ROMA ANTIQVA. — [96] 137 × 186 mm.

Notes: All the maps have text on the verso. They are uncoloured. They all bear either one or two coats-of-arms, except [57] Roma antiqua. The first map, Roma, is missing; fol. 69 and 70 are bound before fol. 67 and 68. The title-page is also missing; the title has been written in ink on the first blank leaf. The atlas is bound in soft leather with blind tooling. Nordenskiöld's signature in on the inside of the front cover.

Lit.: BM Maps vol. 2, c. 714, Tooley, Dictionary p. 36 (Bertellius).

14 BERTIUS, PETRUS [1600]

[P. BERTII TABVLARVM GEOGRAPHICARVM CONTRACTARVM Libri Quatuor. Cum luculentis Tabularum singularum explicationibus. Amstelodami, apud Cornelium Nicolai. Anno M.DC. Veneunt autem Arnhemij apud Ioannem Ioannis.] 12,3 cm.

[1] [C:] TYPUS ORBIS TERRARUM — [T:] I. Hondius cælavit — Before p. a 3. 83 × 122 mm. = Langenes 1599:I:[1].
[2] DE SPHÆRA CÆLESTI. (Celestial chart). 18 84 × 122 mm. = Langenes 1599:I:[2].
[3] EVROPÆ VNIVERSALIS DESCRIPTIO. [C:] EUROPA Iodocus Hondius cæla. — 35 C 2 86 × 123 mm. = Langenes 1599:I:[4].
[4] ASIÆ DESCRIPTIO. [C:] ASIA — 39 C 4 86 × 124 mm. = Langenes 1599:I:[5] and [114] in this ed.
[5] DESCRIPTIO AFRICÆ. [C:] AFRICA — 43 85 × 123 mm. = Langenes 1599:I:[6].
[6] DESCRIPTIO AMERICÆ. [T:] AMERICA — 50 84 × 122 mm. = Langenes 1599:I:[7].
[7] DESCRIPTIO ANGLIÆ. [C:] ANGLIA Pe. Kærius fecit. — 57 D 5 83 × 122 mm. = Langenes 1599:I:[8], scale of lat. added.
[8] DESCRIPTIO CAMBRIÆ SIVE WALLIÆ. [C:] CAMBRIA — 62 86 × 123 mm. = Langenes 1599:I:[9], scale of lat. added.
[9] DESCRIPTIO SCOTIÆ. [C:] SCOTIA — 64 83 × 121 mm. = Langenes 1599:I:[10], scale of lat. added.
[10] DESCRIPTIO HIBERNIÆ. [C:] HIBERNIA — 70 83 × 122 mm. = Langenes 1599:I:[11], scale of lat. added.
[11] DESCRIPTIO HISPANIÆ. [C:] HISPANIA — 76 84 × 122 mm. = Langenes 1599:I:[12], scale of lat. added.
[12] DESCRIPTIO ANDALVSIÆ. [C:] ANDALUZIA — 84 83 × 123 mm. = Langenes 1599:I:[13], scale of lat. added.
[13] DESCRIPTIO VALENTIÆ. [C:] VALENTIA — 88 Coloured. 83 × 122 mm. = Langenes 1599:I:[14], scale of lat. added.
[14] DESCRIPTIO GADIVM. [T:] Baia de Cadiz — 90 85 × 122 mm. = Langenes 1599:I:[15].
[15] DESCRIPTIO MAIORICÆ ET MINORICÆ. [C:] Majorcæ et Minorcæ descrip. — 94 84 × 123 mm. = Langenes 1599:I:[16], scale of lat. added.
[16] DESCRIPTIO PORTVGALLIÆ. [C:] PORTUGALLIA. Petrus Kærius fecit. — 104 Coloured. 83 × 122 mm. = Langenes 1599:I:[17], scale of lat. added.
[17] DESCRIPTIO GALLIÆ. [C:] GALLIA — [T:] Petrus Kærius fc. — 108 84 × 122 mm. = Langenes 1599:I:[18], scale of lat. added.
[18] DESCRIPTIO VASCONIÆ. [C:] GASCONIA — 113 H 83 × 122 mm. = Langenes 1599:I:[19], scale of lat. added.
[19] DESCRIPTIO PICTAVIÆ. [C:] POICTOU — 115 H 2 83 × 121 mm. = Langenes 1599:I:[20], scale of lat. added.
[20] DESCRIPTIO BITVRIGVM. [C:] BITURIGUM — 118 183 × 124 mm. = Langenes 1599:I:[21], scale of lat. added.
[21] DESCRIPTIO LEMOVICVM. [C:] LIMANIA — 120 83 × 122 mm. = Langenes 1599:I:[22].
[22] DESCRIPTIO PROVINCIÆ. [C:] Galliæ Narbonẽsis descriptio — 122 85 × 123 mm. = Langenes 1599:I:[23], scale of lat. added.
[23] DESCRIPTIO COMITATVS VENIESSINI. [C:] Venuxinus Comitatus — 127 84 × 123 mm. = Langenes 1599:I:[24], scale of lat. added.
[24] DESCRIPTIO SABAVDIÆ. [C:] SAVOIE — 129 I Coloured. 83 × 122 mm. = Langenes 1599:I:[25].
[25] DESCRIPTIO COMITATVS BVRGVNDIÆ. BURGUNDIÆ COM — 134 Coloured. 85 × 123 mm. = Langenes 1599:I:[26], scale of lat. added.
[26] DESCRIPTIO BVRGVNDIÆ DVCATVS. [C:] BURGUNDIÆ DUCATUS — 136 Coloured. 85 × 123 mm. = Langenes 1599:I:[27].
[27] DESCRIPTIO DVCATVS ANDEGAVENSIS. [C:] ANIOU — 139 85 × 122 mm. = Langenes 1599:I:[28], scale of lat. added.
[28] DESCRIPTIO BRITANNIÆ. [C:] BRITANNIA — 141 84 × 124 mm. = Langenes 1599:I:[29], scale of lat. added.

[29] DESCRIPTIO NORMANNIÆ.
[T:] NORMANDIA — 145 K 84 × 122 mm. = Langenes 1599:I:[30], scale of lat. added.

[30] DESCRIP. CALETENS. ET BONONIENSIVM.
[C:] Caletensium et Bononiesium des. — 149 K 3 84 × 122 mm. = Langenes 1599:I:[31].

[31] DESCRIPTIO PICARDIÆ.
[C:] PICARDIA — 152 Coloured. 84 × 122 mm. = Langenes 1599:I:[32], scale of lat. added.

[32] DESCRIPTIO VEROMANDVORVM.
[C:] VEROMĀDUI — 154 85 × 122 mm. = Langenes 1599:I:[33].

[33] DESCRIPTIO DVCATVS LOTHARINGIÆ.
[C:] LOTHARINGIA — 156 Coloured. 85 × 122 mm. = Langenes 1599:I:[34], scale of lat. added.

[34] DESCRIPTIO GERMANIÆ.
[C:] GERMANIA — 163 L 2 84 × 122 mm. = Langenes 1599:I:[35], scale of lat. added.

[35] DESCRIPTIO GERMANIÆ INFERIORIS.
[C:] Inferior Germania. — 154 (pro 172). 85 × 124 mm. = Langenes 1599:I:[36], scale of lat. added.

[36] DESCRIPTIO LEODIENSIS DIOECESIS.
[C:] Leodiensis Dioecesis — 179 M 2 Coloured. 85 × 123 mm. = Langenes 1599:I:[37], scale of lat. added.

[37] DESCRIPTIO COMITATVS NAMVRCI.
[C:] NAMUR — 185 M 5 Coloured. 84 × 125 mm. = Langenes 1599:I:[38].

[38] DESCRIPTIO DVCATVS LVTZENBVRGI.
[C:] Lutzenburg — 187 Coloured. 85 × 123 mm. = Langenes 1599:I:[39], scale of lat. added.

[39] DESCRIPTIO COMITATVS HANNONIÆ.
[C:] HANNONIA — 190 Coloured. 85 × 121 mm. = Langenes 1599:I:[40].

[40] DESCRIPTIO COMITATVS ARTESIÆ.
[C:] ARTESIA — 194 85 × 121 mm. = Langenes 1599:I:[41], scale of lat. added.

[41] DESCRIPTIO COMITATVS FLANDRIÆ.
[C:] FLANDRIA — 199 N 4 86 × 123 mm. = Langenes 1599:I:[42], scale of lat. added.

[42] DESCRIPTIO DVCATVS BRABANTIÆ.
[C:] BRABANTIA — 205 86 × 123 mm. = Langenes 1599:I:[43], scale of lat. added.

[43] DESCRIPTIO ZELANDIÆ.
[C:] SELANDIA — 213 O 3 86 × 123 mm. = Langenes 1599:I:[44], scale of lat. added.

[44] DESCRIPTIO HOLLANDIÆ.
[C:] HOLLANDIA — 220 85 × 123 mm. = Langenes 1599:I:[45], scale of lat. added.

[45] DESCRIPTIO HOLLANDIÆ AVSTRALIS.
[C:] 1597 HOLLANDIA SEPTEN. ... Petrus Kærius cælavit — 236 85 × 123 mm. = Langenes 1599:I:[48], scale of lat. added.

[46] DESCRIPTIO ARCIS BRITANNICA
[T:] P.K. cælavit. — 242 84 × 123 mm. = Langenes 1599:I:[47].

[47] DESCRIPTIO HOLLANDIÆ BOREALIS.
[C:] Zuydhollād — 246 88 × 124 mm. = Langenes 1599:I:[46], scale of lat. added.

[48] DESCRIPTIO ZIPÆ.
[C:] Die Zyp — 248 86 × 124 mm. = Langenes 1599:I:[49].

[49] DESCRIPTIO EPISCOPATVS VLTRAIECTINI.
[C:] Ultrajectum — 250 87 × 125 mm. = Langenes 1599:I:[50].

[50] DESCRIPTIO GELRIÆ DVCATVS
[C:] GELDRIA — 254 87 × 124 mm. = Langenes 1599:I:[51].

[51] DESCRIPTIO TRANSISALANIÆ.
[C:] Trans-Isula.D. — 258 Coloured. 86 × 123 mm. = Langenes 1599:I:[52], scale of lat. added.

[52] DESCRIPTIO FRISIÆ ORIENTALIS.
[C:] FRISIA — 262 Coloured. 85 × 124 mm. = Langenes 1599:I:[53].

[53] DESCRIPTIO COMITATVS EMBDANI.
[T:] FRISIA ORIENTALIS — [T:] Petrus Kærius cælavit — 265 R 5 Coloured. 85 × 123 mm. = Langenes 1599:I:[54], scale of lat. added.

[54] DESCRIPTIO WESTPHALIÆ.
[C:] Westphalia — 267 85 × 122 mm. = Langenes 1599:I:[55], scale of lat. added.

[55] DESCRIPTIO DIETMARSIÆ.
[C:] THIETMARSIA — 270 86 × 121 mm. = Langenes 1599:I:[56].

[56] DESCRIPTIO DANIÆ.
[C:] DANIA Pe Kærius fecit — 273 S 85 × 122 mm. = Langenes 1599:I:[57], scale of lat. added.

[57] DESCRIPTIO ISLANDIÆ.
[C:] ISLANDIA — [T:] Petrus Kærius cælavit. — 276 85 × 124 mm. = Langenes 1599:I:[58], scale of lat. added.

[58] DESCRIPTIO NORWEGIÆ ET SWETIÆ.
[C:] Septentrionalum regionū descrip. — [T:] Petrus Kærius fecit et cælavit — 281 S 5 84 × 121 mm. = Langenes 1599:I:[59].

[59] DESCRIPTIO GOTHIÆ.
[C:] GOTIA — 286 85 × 122 mm. = Langenes 1599:I:[60], scale of lat. added.

[60] DESCRIPTIO HYPERBOREORVM.
[C:] Nortcaep — [T:] Norwegia Suedia — 290 Coloured. 84 × 124 mm. = Langenes 1599:I:[61], scale of lat. added.

[61] DESCRIPTIO RVSSIÆ ET MOSCHOVIÆ.
[C:] RUSSIA — [T:] Petrus Kærius cælavit — 296 84 × 122 mm. = Langenes 1599:I:[62], scale of lat. added.

[62] DESCRIPTIO LIVONIÆ.
[C:] Livoniæ descrip. — 305 V 87 × 123 mm. = Langenes 1599:I:[63], scale of lat. added.

[63] DESCRIPTIO INSVLÆ GOTHLANDIÆ.
[T:] Gotland — 308 84 × 122 mm. = Langenes 1599:I:[64].

[64] DESCRIPTIO BORVSSIÆ.
[C:] PRUSSIA — 310 87 × 123 mm. = Langenes 1599:I:[65], scale of lat. added.

[65] DESCRIPTIO POLONIÆ.
[C:] POLONIA — 319 86 × 123 mm. = Langenes 1599:I:[66], scale of lat. added.

[66] DESCRIPTIO DVCAT. OZWIEC. ET ZATOR.
[C:] Oswieczimēsis et Zatoriensis Duc. — 326 86 × 124 mm. = Langenes 1599:I:[67], scale of lat. added.

[67] DESCRIPTIO POMERANIÆ.
[C:] POMERANIA — 328 86 × 124 mm. = Langenes 1599:I:[68], scale of lat. added.

[68] DESCRIPTIO MARCH. BRANDENBVRGICÆ.
[C:] Brandenburg — 331 85 × 123 mm. = Langenes 1599:I:[69], scale of lat. added.

[69] DESCRIPTIO SAXONIÆ.
[C:] SAXONIA THURINGIA MISNIA — 334 85 × 122 mm. = Langenes 1599:I:[70], scale of lat. added.

[70] DESCRIPTIO SILESIÆ.
[C:] SILESIA — 338 84 × 124 mm. = Langenes 1599:I:[71], scale of lat. added.

[71] DESCRIPTIO BOHEMIÆ.
[C:] BOHEMIA — 340 84 × 123 mm. = Langenes 1599:I:[72], scale of lat. added.

[72] DESCRIPTIO FRANCONIÆ.
[C:] FRANCONIA — 345 Y 5 85 × 122 mm. = Langenes 1599:I:[73], scale of lat. added.

[73] DESCRIPTIO NORICI.
[C:] NORICUM — 348 84 × 121 mm. = Langenes 1599:I:[74], scale of lat. added.

[74] DESCRIPTIO BAVARIÆ.
[C:] BAVARIA — 350 85 × 123 mm. = Langenes 1599:I:[75], scale of lat. added.

[75] DESCRIPTIO SALISBVRGENIS DIOECES.
[C:] Salisburgensis Dioecesis — 353 Z 85 × 123 mm. = Langenes 1599:I:[76], scale of lat. added.

[76] DESCRIPTIO ARCHIDVCATVS AVSTRIÆ.
[C:] Austria — 355 Z 2 85 × 122 mm. = Langenes 1599:I:[77], scale of lat. added.

[77] DESCRIPTIO TRANSSYLVANIÆ.
[C:] Trāssilvania — 358 87 × 124 mm. = Langenes 1599:I:[78], scale of lat. added.

[78] DESCRIPTIO REGNI HVNGARIÆ.
[C:] HUNGARIA — 361 Z 5 Coloured. 86 × 123 mm. = Langenes 1599:I:[79], scale of lat. added.
[79] DESCRIPTIO ILLYRICI.
[C:] Illyricum — 364 84 × 123 mm. = Langenes 1599:I:[80], scale of lat. added.
[80] DESCRIPTIO LIBVRNIÆ.
[C:] SARA et ZEBENIC — 367 85 × 124 mm. = Langenes 1599:I:[81].
[81] DESCRIPTIO COMITATVS TIROLENSIS.
[C:] TIROLIS COMITA — 369 Aa 84 × 122 mm. = Langenes 1599:I:[82], scale of lat. added.
[82] DESCRIPTIO HELVETIÆ.
[C:] HELVETIA — 372 84 × 123 mm. = Langenes 1599:I:[83], scale of lat. added.
[83] DESCRIPTIO ITALIÆ.
[C:] ITALIA — 375 Aa 4 83 × 122 mm. = Langenes 1599:I:[84], scale of lat. added.
[84] DESCRIPTIO ISTRIÆ.
[C:] HISTRIA — 382 Coloured. 84 × 122 mm. = Langenes 1599:I:[85], scale of lat. added.
[85] DESCRIPTIO FORI IVLII.
[C:] FORUM IULIII — 384 84 × 121 mm. = Langenes 1599:I:[86].
[86] DESCRIPTIO AGRI PATAVINI.
[C:] PATAVINUM. Ter. — [T:] P. Kærius fe. — 388 Coloured. 84 × 121 mm. = Langenes 1599:I:[87], scale of lat. added.
[87] DESCRIPTIO AGRI VERONENSIS.
[C:] VERONENSIS AGER. Petrus Kærius cælavit. — 391 Bb 4 Coloured. 85 × 121 mm. = Langenes 1599:I:[88].
[88] DESCRIPTIO TERRIT. BRIXIENSIS.
[C:] BRESCIANO — [T:] Petrus Kærius cælavit — 394 Coloured. 86 × 122 mm. = Langenes 1599:I:[89], scale of lat. added.
[89] DESCRPTIO CREMENSIS TERRITORII.
[C:] CREMAE AGER. P. Kærius cælavit. — 396 Coloured. 84 × 121 mm. = Langenes 1599:I:[90].
[90] DESCRIPTIO DVCATVS MEDIOLANENSIS.
[C:] Ducatus Mediolanensis finitimarū que regionū Descriptio. à 1596 — [T:] P. Kærius sculpsit. — 398 85 × 123 mm. = Langenes 1599:I:[91].
[91] DESCRIPTIO AGRI CREMONENSSI.
[C:] CREMONENSIS. AGER. — [T:] Petrus Kærius cælavit. — 403 Cc 2 87 × 122 mm. = Langenes 1599:I:[92].
[92] DESCRIPTIO LACVS COMENSIS.
[C:] LARIUS LACUS. — [T:] P. Kærius scul. — [T:] ... Paul. Iovius. — 406 84 × 123 mm. = Langenes 1599:I:[93].
[93] DESCRIPTIO PEDEMONTII.
[C:] Pedemontii descriptio. — 408 84 × 122 mm. = Langenes 1599:I:[94].
[94] DESCRIPTIO ETRVRIÆ.
[C:] TUSCIA. Petrus Kærius cælavit. — 412 85 × 123 mm. = Langenes 1599:I:[95], scale of lat. added.
[95] DESCRIPTIO TRACTVS SENENSIS.
[C:] SIENA. ... — [C:] P.K. sculp. — 414 Coloured. 85 × 123 mm. = Langenes 1599:I:[96].
[96] DESCRIPTIO TRACTVS PERVSINI.
[C:] Petrus Kærius cælavit PERUSIA — 417 Dd Coloured 85 × 122 mm. = Langenes 1599:I:[97].
[97] DESCRIPTIO AGRI ORIVETANI.
[C:] Petrus Kærius sc. ORVIETUM — 419 Dd 2 Coloured. 86 × 122 mm. = Langenes 1599:I:[98].
[98] DESCRIPTIO PICENI.
[C:] MARCHA ANCONÆ, OLIM PICENUM. 1572. — [T:] P. Kærius fe. — 421 Cc 3 Coloured. 84 × 122 mm. = Langenes 1599:I:[99], scale of lat. added.
[99] DESCRIPTIO LATII.
[C:] Romanum territorium — [T:] P. Kærius scul. — 425 Dd 5 84 × 122 mm. = Langenes 1599:I:[100].
[100] DESCRIPTIO REGNI NEAPOLITANI.
[C:] Petrus Kærius cælavit. REGNUM NEAPOLITANUM. — 430 84 × 122 mm. = Langenes 1599:I:[101], scale of lat. added.
[101] DESCRIPTIO APRVTII.
[C:] APRUTIUM — [T:] P. Kærius fe. — 434 86 × 123 mm. = Langenes 1599:I:[102], scale of lat. added.
[102] DESCRIPTIO SARDINIÆ.
[C:] SARDINIA — 436 85 × 121 mm. = Langenes 1599:I:[103], scale of lat. added.
[103] DESCRIPTIO CORSICÆ.
[C:] CORSICA — 439 Ee 4 86 × 121 mm. = Langenes 1599:I:[104], scale of lat. added.
[104] DESCRIPTIO ILVÆ.
[C:] ELBA. — [An empty cartouche]. 441 Ee 5 86 × 123 mm. = Langenes 1599:I:[105].
[105] DESCRIPTIO ISCHIÆ.
[C:] ISCHIA insula — 443 86 × 123 mm. = Langenes 1599:I:[106].
[106] DESCRIPTIO SICILIÆ.
[C:] SICILIA — 446 85 × 122 mm. = Langenes 1599:I:[107], scale of lat. added.
[107] DESCRIPTIO MELITÆ.
[C:] MALTA — 450 86 × 123 mm. = Langenes 1599:I:[108].
[108] DESCRIPTIO CORCYRÆ.
[C:] CORFU — 452 85 × 123 mm. = Langenes 1599:I:[109].
[109] DESCRIPTIO GRÆCIÆ.
[C:] GRÆCIA — 454 84 × 122 mm. = Langenes 1599:I:[110], scale of lat. added.
[110] DESCRIPTIO PELOPONNESI.
[T:] MOREA — [T:] Petrus Kærius cælavit — 460 86 × 122 mm. = Langenes 1599:I:[111], scale of lat. added.
[111] DESCRIPTIO CEPHALLENIÆ.
[C:] CEFALONIA — 464 86 × 124 mm. = Langenes 1599:I:[112].
[112] DESCRIPTIO ZASYNTHI.
[C:] ZANTE Insula — 466 86 × 125 mm. = Langenes 1599:I:[113].
[113] DESCRIPTIO CRETÆ.
[C:] CANDIA — 468 85 × 122 mm. = Langenes 1599:I:[114], scale of lat. added.
[114] [C:] ASIA — [472] 86 × 124 mm. = Langenes 1599:I:[5] and [4] in this ed.

P. BERTII TABVLARVM GEOGRAPHICARVM CONTRACTARVM Liber secundus, IN QVO ASIA Cum luculentis Tabularum singularum explicationibus.

[115] DESCRIPTIO IMPERII TVRCICI.
[C:] Petrus Kærius cælavit TURCICUM IMPERIUM... — 474 85 × 124 mm. = Langenes 1599:II:[1], scale of lat. added.
[116] DESCRIPTIO ASIÆ MINORIS.
[C:] NATOLIA — 484 85 × 123 mm. = Langenes 1599:II:[2], scale of lat. added.
[117] DESCRIPTIO CHII INS.
[C:] SCIO — 488 85 × 124 mm. = Langenes 1599:II:[3].
[118] DESCRIPTIO RHODI.
[C:] RHODI — [C:] Petrus Kærius cælavit — 490 84 × 123 mm. = Langenes 1599:II:[4].
[119] DESCRIPTIO CYPRI.
[C:] CYPRUS — 492 85 × 122 mm. = Langenes 1599:II:[5], scale of lat. added.
[120] DESCRIPTIO PALESTINÆ.
[C:] PALAESTINA ... Petrus Kærius cæla. — 495 86 × 123 mm. = Langenes 1599:II:[6], scale of lat. added.
[121] DESCRIPTIO ARABIÆ.
[C:] ARABIA — 500 85 × 119 mm. = Langenes 1599:II:[20], scale of lat. added.
[122] DESCRIPTIO PERSIÆ.
[C:] Petrus Kærius cælavit PERSIA — 502 84 × 123 mm. = Langenes 1599:II:[7], scale of lat. added.
[123] DESCRIPTIO REGNI ORMVZII.
[C:] ORMUS — 508 85 × 124 mm. = Langenes 1599:II:[19], scale of lat. added.
[124] DESCRIPTIO TARTARIÆ.
[C:] TARTARIA — 510 84 × 123 mm.
[125] DESCRIPTIO INSVLÆ ORIENTALIS.
[C:] INDIA ORIEN — 514 87 × 122 mm.

[126] DESCRIPTIO INSVLARVM IAPAN.
 [C:] IAPAN — 517 Kk 3 87 × 124 mm.
[127] DESCRIPTIO CHINÆ.
 [C:] CHINA Regio Asię. ... Petrus Kærius cælavit. — 520 85 × 122 mm. = Langenes 1599:II:[8].
[128] DESCRIPTIO PHILIPPINARVM.
 [C:] Insulæ Philippinae. ... Petrus Kærius cælavit — 523 86 × 124 mm. = Langenes 1599:II:[9], scale of lat. added.
[129] DESCRIPTIO MOLVCCARVM INSS.
 [C:] Moluccæ insulæ — 525 84 × 124 mm. = Langenes 1599:II:[10], scale of lat. added.
[130] DESCRIPTIO BORNEO INSVLÆ.
 [C:] BORNEO — [T:] Petrus Kærius cælavit. — 528 86 × 126 mm. = Langenes 1599:II:[11], scale of lat. added.
[131] DESCRIPTIO IAVÆ.
 [C:] IAVA MAIOR Beniamin Wright cælavit — 530 87 × 123 mm.
[132] DESCRIPTIO SVMATRÆ.
 [C:] SUMATRA INSULA — [T:] Beniamin Wright cælator — 532 86 × 123 mm.
[133] DESCRIPTIO MALACCÆ.
 [C:] MALACCA — 535 Ll 4 84 × 122 mm. = Langenes 1599:II:[12], scale of lat. added.
[134] DESCRIPTIO ARCAN ET PEGV.
 [C:] Petrus Kærius cælavit. ARACAM — 537 Ll 5 85 × 124 mm. = Langenes 1599:II:[13], scale of lat. added.
[135] DESCRIPTIO BENGALÆ.
 [C:] BENGALA — 539 84 × 124 mm. = Langenes 1599:II:[14], scale of lat. added.
[136] DESCRIPTIO ZEILAN, ET MALDIVARVM INSS.
 [C:] MALDIVAE INSULÆ — 541 84 × 123 mm. = Langenes 1599:II:[15], scale of lat. added.
[137] DESCRIPTIO REGNI MALABAR. 544 84 × 117 mm. See Langenes 1599:II:[16].
[138] DESCRIPTIO NARSINGÆ.
 [C:] Narsinga et Ceylon — [C:] ...Petrus Kærius cælavit — 538 85 × 124 mm. = Langenes 1599:II:[17], scale of lat. added.
[139] DESCRIPTIO CAMBAIÆ.
 [C:] GAMBAIA — 540 86 × 125 mm. = Langenes 1599:II:[18].

P. BERTII TABVLARVM GEOGRAPHICARVM CONTRACTARVM Liber tertius, IN QVO AFRICA. Cum luculentis Tabularum singularum explicationibus.

[140] DESCRIPTIO ÆGYPTI.
 [C:] AEGYPTUS — 544 85 × 122 mm. = Langenes 1599:II:[21], scale of lat. added.
[141] DESCRIPTIO MARIS RVBRI.
 [C:] Mare Rubrum — 551 Nn 84 × 123 mm. = Langenes 1599:II:[25], scale of lat. added.
[142] DESCRIPTIO ABYSSINORVM.
 [C:] Abissinorum Imperium — 554 84 × 123 mm. = Langenes 1599:II:[22], scale of lat. added.
[143] DESCRIPTIO ÆTHIOPIÆ INFERIORIS.
 [C:] AFRICÆ PARS meridionalior — Nn 4 85 × 122 mm. = Langenes 1599:II:[23], scale of lat. added.
[144] DESCRIPTIO REGNI MOZAMBIQVÆ.
 [C:] Insulæ & Ars Mosambique — [T:] Petrus Kærius cælavit — 560 86 × 124 mm. = Langenes 1599:II:[24].
[145] DESCRIPTIO INS. MADAGASCAR.
 [C:] I.S. Lauretij — 562 85 × 123 mm. = Langenes 1599:II:[26] with small alternations.
[146] DESCRIPTIO REGNI CONGI.
 [C:] Congi Regni. Christiani in Africa nova descriptio Auctore Philippo Pigafetta — 567 Oo 83 × 120 mm. = Langenes 1599:II:[27].
[147] DESCRIPTIO INSVLÆ S. HELENÆ.
 [C:] SANCTA HELENA — [T:] Beniamin W: cælator — 570 88 × 123 mm.
 [Insets:] [T:] West Zyde — (Profile). 14 × 30 mm. [T:] Noort Zyde — (Profile). 14 × 28 mm. See Langenes 1599:II:[28].
[148] DESCRIPTIO INSVLÆ S. THOMÆ.
 [T:] Ins. S^{ti} Thomę — 573 Oo 4 85 × 124 mm.
 [Insets:] [T:] Facies Insulæ Annobon ubi à te jacet ad borrhape liotem — (Profile). 17 × 33 mm. [T:] Facies Ins. Principis ubi à te abest fere 5 miliaribus ad Meseurum — (Profile). 14 × 37 mm. = Langenes 1599:II:[29].
[149] DESCRIPTIO GVINEÆ.
 [C:] GUINEA — 575 Oo 5 85 × 123 mm. = Langenes 1599:II:[30], scale of lat. added.
[150] DESCRIPTIO INSVLARVM CAPITIS VIRIDIS.
 [C:] Insulæ Capitis Viridis — 578 85 × 122 mm. = Langenes 1599:II:[31], scale of lat. added.
[151] DESCRIPTIO INSS. CANARIARVM.
 [T:] Insulæ Canariæ ol: Fortunatae — 580 84 × 120 mm. [Inset:] [T:] Portus Canaria — 30 × 39 mm. = Langenes 1599:II:[32], scale of lat. added.
[152] DESCRIPTIO BARBARIÆ AFRICANÆ.
 [C:] Barbaria — 584 86 × 123 mm. = Langenes 1599:II:[33], scale of lat. added.
[153] DESCRIPTIO REGNI TVRNETANI.
 [C:] Carthaginensis sinus — 586 87 × 123 mm. = Langenes 1599:II:[34], scale of lat. added.

P. BERTII TABVLARVM GEOGRAPHICARVM CONTRACTARVM Liber quartus, in quo AMERICA Et MAGELLANICA. Cum luculentis Tabularum singularum explicationibus.

[154] DESCRIPTIO TERCERÆ.
 [T:] TERCERA — [T:] Petrus Kærius fecit — 590 84 × 122 mm. = Langenes 1599:II:[35].
[155] DESCRIPTIO IVCATANÆ.
 [C:] Insularum Cubæ, Hispaniolæ Jucatanæ & circumjacentium descriptio. — 594 83 × 122 mm. = Langenes 1599:II:[36], scale of lat. added.
[156] DESCRIPTIO CVBÆ ET IAMAICÆ.
 [C:] CUBA INSULA ... Petrus Kærius cæla. — 586 (pro 596). 84 × 122 mm. = Langenes 1599:II:[37], scale of lat. added.
[157] DESCRIPTIO HISPANIOLÆ.
 [C:] AITY SIVE SPANIOLA — [T:] P. Kæri. cælavit — 598 86 × 122 mm. = Langenes 1599:II:[38], scale of lat. added.
[158] DESCRIPTIO AMERICÆ AVSTRALIS.
 [T:] PERUANA — 600 83 × 122 mm. = Langenes 1599:II:[39].
[159] DESCRIPTIO BRASILIÆ.
 [C:] BRASILIA — 604 83 × 124 mm. = Langenes 1599:II:[40], scale of lat. added.
[160] DESCRIPTIO REGNI CHILI.
 [C:] CHILI et PATAGONUM regio — 612 83 × 123 mm. = Langenes 1599:II:[41], scale of lat. added.
[161] DESCRIPTIO PERVVIÆ.
 [C:] PERU — 614 87 × 121 mm. = Langenes 1599:II:[43], scale of lat. added.
[162] DESCRIPTIO ARGENTI FODINARVM POTVSI.
 [T:] CERRO DE POTOSI — (View). 626 84 × 122 mm. = Langenes 1599:II:[42].
[163] DESCRIPTIO NOVÆ HISPANIÆ.
 [C:] MEXICANA — 628 83 × 122 mm. = Langenes 1599:II:[44].
[164] DESCRIPTIO TERRÆ NOVÆ.
 [C:] TERRA NOVA — 633 Ss 2 86 × 124 mm. = Langenes 1599:II:[45], scale of lat. added.
[165] DESCRIPTIO FRETI MAGELLANICI.
 [C:] FRETUM MAGELLANICUM... Petrus Kærius cælavit — 637 Ss 4 86 × 123 mm. = Langenes 1599:II:[46], scale of lat. added.
[166] DESCRIPTIO NOVÆ GVINEÆ ET INSS. SALOM.
 [C:] NOVA GUINEA ET IN. SALOMONIS ... Petrus Kærius cælavit — 640 87× 123 mm. = Langenes 1599:II:[47], scale of lat. added.
[167] DESCRIPTIO FRETI AVIGATS.
 [C:] INS. VAYGATS — 642 86 × 121 mm. = Langenes 1599:II:[48].

Notes: All the maps have text on the verso. Some of them are lightly coloured. Maps [45] and [47] have been transposed, so that map [45] [C:] HOLLANDIA SEPTEN. has the heading 'DESCRIPTIO HOLLANDIÆ AUSTRALIS', and map [47], [C:] Zuydhollād, has 'DESCRIPTIO

HOLLANDIÆ BOREALIS'. Map [46], DESCRIPTIO ARCIS BRITANNICA, is pasted on p.242 over a map of Britannia, and map [116] [C:] NATOLIA replaces another map, apparently of Asia. There are several manuscript notes in the margins of the text. Every tenth map has been numbered in pencil, but the numbers do not correspond with those given here. The pencil numbers go up to 173, but this number apparently includes two prints, COENOBIVM B. LAVRENTII on p.98 and DESCRIPTIO SYRTVM IVDAICARVM on p.564. It is possible that the map of the terrestrial hemispheres, now wanting, may have been in the volume at the time of numbering, and that the other numbers unaccounted for may also have appeared on leaves now wanting; but Tiele lists only 169 maps. The text of the atlas is by Bertius; the maps are the same as those in Langenes's Caert-Thresoor of 1598 and 1599. Koeman deals with these atlases together, under the heading Barent Langenes (vol. 2 p. 252—261); Tiele lists Langenes under Caert-Thresoor and Bertius under Bertius, but provides cross-references. The British Museum deals with them separately, without references. They are listed separately here, but references are provided for the maps in Bertius to those in Langenes's Caert-Thresoor. This edition of Bertius was bound for Nordenskiöld in half-leather; his initials AEN are in gold on the spine. His bookplate is on the inside of the front cover.

Lit.: BM Maps vol. 2, c. 716—717, and vol. 8, c. 786, Koeman vol. 1, p. 60—61, vol. 2, p. 256, Lan 4, Tiele p. 25, nr 100, and p. 56, nr 225, (Caert-Thresoor).

15 BERTIUS, PETRUS 1616

P. Bertij TABVLARVM GEOGRAPHICARVM CONTRACTARVM Libri septem. In quibus Tabulæ omnes gradibus distinctæ, descriptiones accuratæ, cætera supra priores editiones politiora, Auctioraq₃. ad Christianissimum Galliæ & Navarræ Regem LVDOVICVM XIII. Amsterodami excusum in ædibus Viduæ Iudoci Hondij. Anno 1616. 12,7 cm.

P. BERTII TABVLARVM GEOGRAPHICARVM CONTRACTARVM Liber primus, IN QVO DE ORBE VNIVERSO IN GENERE.
- [1] [T:] TYPVS ORBIS TERRARVM — 8 93 × 133 mm. See Langenes 1599:I:[3].
- [2] DE SPHÆRA CÆLESTI.
  [T:] GLOBUS COELESTIS. — (Celestial chart.) 28 Coloured. 93 × 136 mm. See [1600]:[2].
- [3] DE GLOBO TERRÆ.
  [T:] TYPVS ORBIS TERRARVM — 36 93 × 133 mm. See [1600]:[1].

P. BERTII TABVLARVM GEOGRAPHICARVM CONTRACTARVM Liber secundus, IN QVO TERRAE SEPTENTRIONALES Ptolemæo incognitæ.
- [4] REGIONES HYPERBOREÆ. 52 Coloured. 95 × 118 mm.
- [5] DESCRIPTIO SPITSBERGIÆ.
  [C:] delineatio SPITSBERGIÆ — 60 93 × 133 mm.
- [6] DESCRIPTIO GROENLANDIÆ.
  [C:] GROENLAND 64 92 × 131 mm.
- [7] DESCRIPTIO ISLANDIÆ.
  [C:] Islandia — 68 93 × 131 mm.
- [8] DESCRIPTIO NOVÆ ZEMLÆ.
  [C:] NOVÆ ZEMLAE delineatio — 72 92 × 133 mm.
- [9] DESCRIPTIO FRETI VAIGATS.
  [C:] Delineatio FRETI VAIGATS — 78 92 × 132 mm.

P. BERTII TABVLARVM GEOGRAPHICARVM CONTRACTARVM Liber tertius, IN QVO TERRA SVBAVSTRALIS Ptolemæo & priscis incognita.
- [10] DESCRIPTIO TERRÆ SVBAVSTRALIS.
  [T:] MAGALLANICA, sive TERRA AUSTRALIS INCOGNITA — 82 92 × 132 mm.
- [11] DESCRIPTIO NOVÆ GVINEÆ &c.
  [C:] NOVA GUINEA et Ins. Salomonis — 88 91 × 131 mm.
- [12] DESCRIPTIO FRETI MAGELLANICI.
  [C:] MAGELLANICI FRETI delineatio. — 90 94 × 134 mm.

P. BERTII TABVLARVM GEOGRAPHICARVM CONTRACTARVM Liber quartus, IN QVO EVROPA Cum luculentis singularum Tabularum explicationibus.
- [13] EVROPAE VNIVERSALIS DESCRIPTIO.
  [C:] EUROPA — 94 93 × 134 mm.
- [14] DESCRIPTIO INSVLARVM BRITANNICARVM.
  [C:] ANGLIA SCOTIA et Hibernia — 98 92 × 131 mm.
- [15] DESCRIPTIO HIBERNIÆ.
  [C:] HIBERNIA — [T:] S. Rogiers Sculp. 100 92 × 131 mm.
- [16] DESCRIPTIO VLTONIÆ IN HIBERNIA.
  [C:] Hibernia Septentr. in qua Ultonia Connatia — 104 92 × 131 mm.
- [17] DESCRIPTIO CONNACIÆ IN HIBERNIA.
  [C:] CONNATIA. 1616. — 106 93 × 134 mm.
- [18] DESCRIPTIO MEDIÆ IN HIBERNIA.
  [C:] MEDIA. — 108 94 × 134 mm.
- [19] DESCRIPTIO MOMONIÆ IN HIBERNIA.
  [C:] Hibernia Austral. in qua Momonia Lagenia — 110 92 × 131 mm.
- [20] DESCRIPTIO LAGENIÆ IN HIBERNIA.
  [C:] Lagenia — 112 92 × 133 mm.
- [21] DESCRIPTIO VDRONES BARONATVS IN HIBERNIA.
  [C:] UDRONE — 114 95 × 137 mm.
- [22] DESCRIPTIO BRITANNIÆ MAGNÆ.
  [C:] Magna Britannia — 116 97 × 136 mm.
- [23] DESCRIPTIO SCOTIÆ.
  [C:] SCOTIA — [T:] Salomon Rogiers Cælavit — 120 94 × 133 mm.
- [24] DESCRIPTIO SCOTIÆ SEPTENTRIONALIS.
  [C:] SCOTIA Septentrion. — 124 94 × 133 mm.
- [25] DESCRIPTIO SCOTIÆ AVSTRALIS.
  [C:] SCOTIA Australis — 128 94 × 132 mm.
- [26] DESCRIPTIO ANGLIÆ.
  [C:] ANGLIA — [T:] S. Rogiers Cælavit — 132 94 × 131 mm.
- [27] TAB. I. ANGLIÆ, IN QVA NORTHVMBRIA &c.
  [C:] Northumbr. Cumberlan. Dunelm. Episcop. — 138 94 × 134 mm.
- [28] TAB. II. PARTICVLARIS ANGLIÆ WESTMORLANDIÆ &c.
  [C:] Westmorlād: Lancastria Cestria etc. — 140 94 × 134 mm.
- [29] TAB. III. ANGLIÆ, IN QVA CAMBRIA SIVE WALLIA.
  [C:] CAMBRIA — 142 94 × 133 mm. See [1600]:[8].
- [30] TAB. IV. ANGLIÆ IN QVA CORNVBIA &c.
  [C:] Cornub. Devonia Somerset etc. — 144 93 × 133 mm.
- [31] TAB. V. ANGLIÆ, IN QVA EBORACVM &c.
  [C:] Eboracum Lincolnia Derbia Staffordia etc. — 146 93 × 133 mm.
- [32] TAB. VI. ANGLIÆ, IN QVA VVARVVICVM &c.
  [C:] Warwicum Northāpton Hunting. etc. — 148 94 × 134 mm.
- [33] TAB. VII. ANGLIÆ, IN QVA INSVLÆ &c. 150 90 × 132 mm.
  - [a] [C:] ANGLESEY INS. — 41 × 60 mm.
  - [b] [C:] WIGHT ol. Vectis — 41 × 60 mm.
  - [c] [C:] INS GARNESAY — 41 × 60 mm.
  - [d] [C:] Ins. IARSAY — 41 × 60 mm.
- [34] DESCRIPTIO HISPANIAE.
  [C:] HISPANIA — [T:] S. Rogiers sculpsit. — 152 92 × 132 mm.
- [35] DESCRIPTIO PORTVGALLIÆ.
  [C:] PORTUGALLIA — [T:] S. Rogiers sculpsit — 160 93 × 131 mm. See [1600]:[16].
- [36] DESCRIPTIO GALLECIÆ ET ASTVRIAE IN HISPANIA.
  [C:] GALECIA — 164 96 × 136 mm.
- [37] DESCRIPTIO LEGIONES IN HISP.
  [C:] LEGIO — 166 97 × 136 mm.

[38] DESCRIPTIO BISCAIÆ ET GVIPISCOÆ IN HISPANIA.
[C:] Guipuscoa et Biscaia — 168   96 × 134 mm.
[39] DESCRIPTIO GADIVM.
[T:] BAIA DE CADIS — 170   92 × 128 mm. See [1600]:[14].
[40] DESCRIPTIO ANDALVSIÆ.
[C:] ANDALUZIA — 174   94 × 132 mm. See [1600]:[12].
[41] DESCRIPTIO ESTREMADVRÆ IN HISP.
[C:] ESTREMADURA — 178   96 × 137 mm.
[42] DESCRIPTIO CASTELLÆ VET. ET NOVÆ IN HISP.
[C:] CASTILIA VETUS et NOVA — 180   97 × 136 mm.
[43] DESCRIPTIO GRANATÆ ET MVRCIAE IN HISP.
[C:] Granada et Murcia — 186   96 × 136 mm.
[44] DESCRIPTIO VALENTIAE IN HISP.
[C:] VALENTIA — 188   94 × 134 mm. See [1600:]:[13].
[45] DESCRIPTIO ARRAGONIÆ ET CATALONIÆ.
[C:] CATALONIA et ARAGONIA — 192   96 × 136 mm.
[46] DESCRIPTIO REGNI NAVARRÆ.
[C:] NAVARRA — 194   96 × 135 mm.
[47] DESCRIPTIO MAIORICÆ ET MINORICÆ.
[C:] Majorcæ et Minorcæ descrip — 196   93 × 132 mm.
[48] DESCRIPTIO GALLIÆ.
[C:] GALLIA — 200   93 × 134 mm.
[49] DESCRIPT. BENEARNIÆ ET BIGORNIÆ IN AQVIT.
[C:] BENEARNIA et BIGORNIA — 206   95 × 134 mm.
[50] DESCRIPTIO VASCONIÆ IN GALL. AQVIT.
[C:] Guascogne — 208   94 × 133 mm.
[51] DESCRIPTIO PICTAVIÆ IN GALL. AQVIT.
[C:] Poictou — 212   94 × 134 mm.
[52] DESCRIPTIO BITVRIGVM IN GALL. AQVIT.
[C:] BITURIGUM BORBONIUM et TURENA in Gallia Aqui. — 216   93 × 134 mm.
[53] DESCRIPTIO LEMOVICVM IN GALL. AQVIT.
[C:] LEMOVICUM — 218   94 × 133 mm.
[54] DESCRIPTIO LANGVEDOCIÆ IN GALL. NARB.
[C:] LANGVEDOC — 220   93 × 134 mm.
[55] DESCRIPTIO PROVINCIÆ IN GALL. NARB.
[C:] Provence — 222   93 × 136 mm.
[56] DESCRIPT. COMITATVS AVENIONENSIS IN GALL. NARB.
[C:] COMIT. AVENIONENSIS — 226   96 × 133 mm.
[57] DESCRIPTIO DELPHINATVS IN GALL. NARB.
[C:] DAVPHINE — 228   94 × 137 mm.
[58] DESCRIPTIO SABAVDIÆ IN GALL. NARB.
[C:] SABAVDIA — 230   94 × 136 mm.
[59] DESCRIPTIO GALLÆ LVGDVNENSIS.
[C:] Lionnois — 234   94 × 137 mm.
[60] DESCRIPTIO BRITANNIÆ IN GALL. LVGD.
[C:] Britannia — 236   94 × 133 mm.
[61] DESCRIPTIO NORMANNIÆ IN GALL. LVGD.
[C:] NORMANDIA — 240   93 × 133 mm.
[62] DESCRIPT. ANDEVAV. ET CENOMAN. IN GALL. LVGD.
[C:] ANIOU et LEMAINE — 244   94 × 134 mm.
[63] DESCRIPTIO BELSIÆ IN GALL. LVGD.
[C:] BELSIA — 246   94 × 134 mm.
[64] DESCRIPT. FRANCIÆ COMITAT. IN GALL. LVGD.
[C:] FRANCIÆ Comitatus. — 250   93 × 134 mm.
[65] DESCRIPTIO CAMPANIÆ IN GALL. LVGD.
[C:] CHAMPAIGNE. — 252   93 × 132 mm.
[66] DESCRIPTIO COMITATVS BVRGVNDIÆ.
[C:] BURGUDIA Comitatus. — 244   94 × 133 mm.
[67] DESCRIPTIO BVRGVNDIÆ DVCATVS.
[C:] BURGUNDIA DUCATUS — 258   93 × 132 mm.
[68] DESCRIPTIO GALLIÆ BELGICAE
[C:] GALLIÆ BELGICÆ veteris accurata descriptio P. Bertio auctori, amico suo colendo cælavit I. Hondius. — 260   86 × 126 mm.
[69] DESCRIPT. CALET. ET BONON. IN GALL. BELG.
[C:] CALETUM et BOLONIA — 264   94 × 132 mm.
[70] DESCRIPTIO PICARDIÆ IN GALL. BELG.
[C:] PICARDIA. — 268   93 × 130 mm.
[71] DESCRIPTIO COMIT. ARTESIÆ IN GALL. BELG.
[C:] ARTESIA — 270   92 × 131 mm. See [1600]:[40].
[72] DESCRIPTIO COMIT. FLANDRIÆ IN GALL. BELG.
[C:] FLANDRIA — 274   91 × 131 mm. See [1600]:[41].
[73] DESCRIPT. DVCATVS BRABANTIÆ IN GALL. BELG.
[C:] BRABANTIA — 280   95 × 131 mm. See [1600]:[42].
[74] DESCRIPTIO ZELANDIÆ IN GALL. BELG.
[C:] ZEELANDIA — 286   92 × 132 mm. See [1600]:[43].
[75] DESCRIPTIO HOLLANDIAE IN GALL. BELG.
[C:] HOLLANDIA — 294   94 × 132 mm.
[76] DESCRIPT. HOLLAND. AVSTRALIS IN GALL. BELG.
[C:] HOLLANDIA MERIDIONAL. — 308   Coloured. 92 × 131 mm.
[77] DESCRIPTIO ARCIS BRITANNIÆ IN HOLLANDIA. 314   Coloured.   92 × 131 mm. See [1600]:[46].
[78] DESCRIPT. HOLLAND. BOREALIS IN GALL. BELG.
[C:] HOLLANDIA SEPTENTR — 318   93 × 132 mm.
[79] DESCRIPTIO ZIPÆ IN HOLLANDIA.
[C:] DE ZYPE — 322   87 × 127 mm. See [1600]:[48].
[80] DESCRIPTIO VEROMANDVORVM IN GALL. BELG.
[C:] VEROMANDUI — 324   91 × 132 mm.
[81] DESCRIPTIO COMIT. HANNONIÆ IN GALL. BELG.
[C:] HANNONIA — 326   92 × 131 mm. See [1600]:[39].
[82] DESCRIPT. COMIT. NAMVRCENSIS IN GALL. BELG.
[C:] NAMUR — 330   92 × 132 mm. See [1600]:[37].
[83] DESCRIPT. LEODIENSIS DIOECES. IN GALL. BELG.
[C:] Leodiensis Dioecesis — 332   94 × 132 mm. See [1600]:[36].
[84] DESCRIPT. DVCAT. LOTHARINGIÆ IN GALL. BELG.
[C:] LOTARINGIA Ducatus — 340   93 × 132 mm.
[85] DESCRIPT. DVCAT. LVTZENBVRGENSIS IN GALL. BELG.
[C:] Lutzenburg — 344   94 × 131 mm. See [1600]:[38].
[86] DESCRIPT. DVCAT. LIMBVRGENSIS IN GALL. BELG.
[C:] LIMBURGUM — 348   93 × 131 mm.
[87] DESCRIPT. DVCAT. IVLIACENSIS IN GALL. BELG.
[C:] GULICK — 350   92 × 130 mm.
[88] DESCRIPTIO DVCAT. CLIVIÆ IN GALL. BELG.
[C:] CLIVIA — 352   92 × 131 mm.
[89] DESCRIPTIO DVCATVS GELRIÆ.
[C:] GELDRIA — 356   93 × 131 mm. See [1600]:[50].
[90] DESCRIPTIO HELVETIÆ.
[C:] HELVETIA — 360   91 × 131 mm. See [1600]:[82].
[91] DESCRIPTIO VALESIÆ IN HELVETIA.
[C:] VALESIA — 364   97 × 136 mm.
[92] DESCRIPT. DITIONIS BERNATIVM ET FRIBVRG. IN HELVET.
[C:] WIFLISPURGERGOW. — 368   95 × 135 mm.
[93] DESCRIPTIO ARGOVIÆ IN HELVETIA.
[C:] ARGOW — 370   93 × 131 mm.
[94] DESCRIPTIO PAGI TIGVRINI IN HELVETIA.
[C:] ZVRICHGOW — 372   94 × 133 mm.
[95] DESCRIPTIO ALSATIÆ IN GALL. BELG.
[C:] Alsatia — 374   93 × 131 mm.
[96] DESCRIPTIO WESTRASIÆ IN GALL. BELG.
[C:] Westrasia — 376   93 × 131 mm.
[97] DESCRIPTIO TREVIRENSIVM IN GALL. BELG.
[C:] PROVINCIA Trevirensis — 378   94 × 132 mm.
[98] DESCRIPT. EPISCOP. COLON. IN GALL. BELG.
[C:] COLONIENSIS Dioecesis — 380   91 × 132 mm.
[99] DESCRIPTIO GERMANIÆ.
[C:] GERMANIA — 382   94 × 131 mm. See [1600]:[34].
[100] DESCRIPT. PROVINCIARVM XVII. GERM. INFER.
[C:] INFERIOR GERMANIA — 392   94 × 131 mm.
[101] DESCRIPTIO EPISCOPATVS VLTRAIECTINI.
[C:] Ultrajectum — 398   93 × 132 mm. See [1600]:[49].
[102] DESCRIPTIO TRANSISALANIÆ.
[C:] Trans-Isula D. — 402   92 × 131 mm. See

[1600]:[51].
- [103] DESCRIPTIO FRISIÆ ORIENTALIS.
  [C:] FRISIA — 406 93 × 132 mm.
- [104] DESCRIPTIO COMITATVS EMDANI.
  [T:] FRISIA ORIENTALIS. — 410 92 × 131 mm.
- [105] DESCRIPTIO WESTPHALIÆ.
  [C:] WESTPHALIA — 414 92 × 131 mm. See [1600]:[54].
- [106] DESCRIPTIO HASSIÆ.
  [C:] HASSIÆ descriptio — 416 96 × 134 mm.
- [107] DESCRIPTIO COMITATVS NASSOVICI.
  [C:] Descriptio Comitatus Nassovi Cattimeliboci — 420 95 × 133 mm.
- [108] DESCRIPTIO DIETMARSIÆ.
  [C:] THIETMARSIA — 93 × 131 mm. See [1600]:[55].
- [109] DESCRIPTIO DANIÆ.
  [C:] DANIA — 424 92 × 130 mm.
- [110] DESCRIPTIO NORWEGIÆ ET SVECIÆ.
  [C:] SUECIA et Norvegia ect. — 428 90 × 130 mm.
- [111] DESCRIPTIO GOTHIÆ.
  [C:] GOTIA — 432 Coloured. 93 × 132 mm.
- [112] DESCRIPTIO POMERANIÆ.
  [C:] POMERANIA — 436 92 × 131 mm. See [1600]:[67].
- [113] DESCRIPTIO MARCH. BRANDENBVRGICI.
  [C:] BRANDENBURG — 440 95 × 133 mm.
- [114] DESCRIPTIO SAXONIÆ.
  [C:] SAXONIA — 442 93 × 131 mm.
- [115] DESCRIPTIO SILESIÆ.
  [C:] SILESIA — 446 93 × 130 mm. See [1600]:[70].
- [116] DESCRIPTIO BOHEMIÆ.
  [C:] BOHEMIA — 448 95 × 133 mm. See [1600]:[71].
- [117] DESCRIPTIO FRANCONIAE.
  [C:] FRANCONIA. — 454 94 × 132 mm. See [1600]:[72].
- [118] DESCRIPTIO PALATINATVS RHENI.
  [C:] Palatinatus Rheni ... — 456 91 × 131 mm.
- [119] DESCRIPTIO SALISBVRGENSIS DIOECES.
  [C:] SALTZBURG et Carinthia — 458 92 × 132 mm.
- [120] DESCRIPTIO ARCHIDVCATVS AVSTRIÆ.
  [C:] AUSTRIA — 460 91 × 132 mm. See [1600]:[76].
- [121] DESCRIPTIO BAVARIÆ.
  [C:] BAVARIA Ducatus — 464 92 × 132 mm.
- [122] DESCRIPTIO NORICI.
  [C:] NORICI. — 466 92 × 131 mm.
- [123] DESCRIPTIO REGNI HVNGARIÆ.
  [C:] HUNGARIA — 470 90 × 130 mm.
- [124] DESCRIPTIO TRANSSYLVANIÆ.
  [C:] Trãssilvania — 474 93 × 131 mm.
- [125] DESCRIPTIO ILLYRICI.
  [C:] ILLYRICUM — 478 91 × 131 mm.
- [126] DESCRIPTIO LIBVRNIÆ.
  [C:] LIBURNIA. — 480 91 × 129 mm.
- [127] DESCRIPTIO COMITATVS TIROLENSIS.
  [C:] FORUM IULII — 482 94 × 131 mm. See [1600]:[85].
- [128] DESCRIPTIO ITALIÆ.
  [C:] ITALIA — 484 95 × 131 mm. See [1600]:[83].
- [129] DESCRIPTIO ISTRIÆ.
  [C:] HISTRIA — 492 94 × 131 mm. See [1600]:[84].
- [130] DESCRIPTIO FORI IVLII.
  [C:] TIROL — 494 93 × 132 mm.
- [131] DESCRIPTIO AGRI PATAVINI.
  [C:] PATAVINUM. Ter. ... — 498 93 × 131 mm. See [1600]:[86].
- [132] DESCRIPTIO AGRI VERONENSIS.
  [C:] VERONENSIS AGER — 502 94 × 131 mm.
- [133] DESCRIPTIO TERRIT. BRIXIENSIS.
  [C:] BRIXIENSIS Episcopatus — 504 92 × 131 mm.
- [134] DESCRIPTIO CREMENSIS TERRITORII.
  [C:] Crema — 508 93 × 131 mm.
- [135] DESCRIPTIO DVCATVS MEDIOLANENSIS.
  [C:] MILANESE — 510 89 × 129 mm.
- [136] DESCRIPTIO AGRI CREMONENSIS.
  [C:] CREMONENSIS Ager — 514 92 × 130 mm.
- [137] DESCRIPTIO LACVS COMENSIS.
  [C:] LARIUS Lacus. — 518 90 × 132 mm.
- [138] DESCRIPTIO PEDEMONTII.
  [C:] PIEDMONT — 520 92 × 131 mm.
- [139] DESCRIPTIO ETRVRIÆ.
  [C:] THUSCIA — 524 92 × 131 mm.
- [140] DESCRIPTIO TRACTVS SENENSIS.
  [C:] SENENSE Territorium. — 526 93 × 131 mm.
- [141] DESCRIPTIO TRACTVS PERVSINI.
  [C:] TRACTUS Perusinus. — 530 Coloured. 90 × 128 mm.
- [142] DESCRIPTIO AGRI ORIVETANI.
  [C:] AGER Orivetanus — 532 Coloured. 92 × 131 mm.
- [143] DESCRIPTIO PICENI.
  [C:] MARCHIA ANCONITANA — 534 93 × 132 mm.
- [144] DESCRIPTIO LATII.
  [C:] LATIUM sive Campania di ROMA — 538 Coloured. 93 × 131 mm.
- [145] DESCRIPTIO REGNI NEAPOLITANI.
  [C:] REGNUN Neapolitanũ — 542 94 × 131 mm.
- [146] DESCRIPTIO APRVTII.
  [C:] ABRUZZO — 548 93 × 132 mm.
- [147] DESCRIPTIO SARDINIÆ.
  [C:] SARDINIA. — 550 91 × 128 mm.
- [148] DESCRIPTIO CORSICÆ.
  [C:] CORSICA — 554 93 × 131 mm.
- [149] DESCRIPTIO ILVÆ.
  [C:] ELBA — 556 Coloured. 94 × 132 mm. See [1600]:[104].
- [150] DESCRIPTIO ISCHIÆ.
  [C:] ISCHIA Insula. — 558 Coloured. 92 × 128 mm. See [1600]:[105].
- [151] DESCRIPTIO SICILIÆ.
  [C:] SICILIA — 560 93 × 133 mm. See [1600]:[106].
- [152] DESCRIPTIO MELITAE.
  [C:] MALTA — 566 94 × 132 mm. See [1600]:[107].
- [153] DESCRIPTIO LIVONIÆ.
  [C:] LIVONIÆ DESCRIP. — 568 93 × 132 mm. See [1600]:[62].
- [154] DESCRIPTIO INSVLÆ GOTHLAND.
  [T:] Gotland — 572 93 × 132 mm. See [1600]:[63].
- [155] DESCRIPTIO BORVSSIÆ.
  [C:] PRUSSIA — 574 91 × 132 mm.
- [156] DESCRIPTIO POLONIÆ.
  [C:] POLONIA — 580 92 × 131 mm. See [1600]:[65].
- [157] DESCRIPTIO DVCAT. OZWIEC. ET ZATOR.
  [C:] Oswieczimensis et Zatoriensis Ducat. —590 92 × 130 mm. See [1600]:[66].
- [158] DESCRIPTIO CORCYRÆ.
  [C:] CORFU — 592 94 × 132 mm. See [1600]:[108].
- [159] DESCRIPTIO GRÆCIÆ.
  [C:] GRAECIA — 594 95 × 131 mm.
- [160] DESCRIPTIO PELOPONNESI.
  [C:] Morea — 602 95 × 132 mm.
- [161] DESCRIPTIO CEPHALLENIÆ.
  [C:] CEFALONIA — 606 Coloured. 94 × 133 mm. See [1600]:[111].
- [162] DESCRIPTIO ZACYNTHI.
  [C:] ZANTE Insula — 608 Coloured. 93 × 132 mm.
- [163] DESCRIPTIO CRETAE.
  [C:] CANDIA — 610 92 × 131 mm.

P. BERTII TABVLARVM GEOGRAPHICARVM CONTRACTARVM Liber quintus, IN QVO AFRICA Cum luculentis singularum Tabularum explicationibus.
- [164] DESCRIPTIO AFRICÆ.
  [C:] AFRICA — 616 94 × 132 mm.
- [165] DESCRIPTIO ÆGYPTI.
  [C:] AEGYPTUS. — 624 95 × 132 mm.
- [166] DESCRIPTIO MARIS RVBRI.
  [C:] MARE RVBRVM — 932 (pro 632) 91 × 129 mm.
- [167] DESCRIPTIO ABISSINORVM.
  [C:] ABISSINORVM Imperium — 636 94 × 133 mm.
- [168] DESCRIPTIO ÆTHIOPIÆ INFERIORIS.
  [C:] AFRICÆ pars meridional. — 640 92 × 131 mm.

[169] DESCRIPTIO REGNI MOZAMBIQVÆ.
   [C:] Insula & Arx MOSAMBIQVE — 642 93 × 133 mm. See [1600]:[144].
[170] DESCRIPTIO INS. MADAGASCAR.
   [C:] I. S. Laurētij sive Madagascar — 644 91 × 129 mm.
[171] DESCRIPTIO BARBARIÆ AFRICANÆ.
   [C:] Barbaria — 646 92 × 131 mm.
[172] DESCRIPTIO REGNI TVNETANI.
   [C:] Tunetanum REGNUM. — 650 92 × 132 mm.
[173] DESCRIPTIO GVINEÆ.
   [C:] GVINEA — 652 90 × 130 mm.
[174] DESCRIPTIO REGNI CONGI.
   [C:] CONGO Regnum Christian. in Africa — 656 93 × 133 mm.
[175] DESCRIPTIO INSVLARVM CANARIARVM.
   [C:] Canariæ I. — 658 93 × 131 mm.
[176] DESCRIPTIO INSS. CAPITIS VIRIDIS.
   [C:] Insulæ Capitis Viridis — 662 91 × 130 mm.
[177] DESCRIPTIO INSVLÆ S. HELENÆ.
   [C:] Sancta HELENA. — 664 93 × 133 mm.
[178] DESCRIPTIO INSVLÆ S. THOMÆ.
   [C:] Insula S.t THOMÆ — 666 93 × 132 mm.
P. BERTII TABVLARVM GEOGRAPHICARVM CONTRACTARVM Liber sextus, IN QVO ASIA Cum luculentis singularum Tabularum explicationibus.
[179] ASIÆ DESCRIPTIO.
   [C:] ASIA — 670 94 × 133 mm.
[180] DESCRIPTIO ASIÆ MINORIS.
   [C:] NATOLIA — 674 92 × 132 mm. See [1600]:[116].
[181] DESCRIPTIO CHII INS.
   [C:] SCIO — 680 Coloured. 90 × 128 mm. See [1600]:[117].
[182] DESCRIPTIO RHODI.
   [C:] RHODI — 682 91 × 129 mm. See [1600]:[118].
[183] DESCRIPTIO RVSSIÆ ET MOSCHOVIÆ.
   [C:] RUSSIA — 684 91 × 132 mm. See [1600]:[61].
[184] DESCRIPTIO TARTARIÆ.
   [C:] TARTARIA — 694 92 × 132 mm.
[185] DESCRIPTIO CYPRI.
   [C:] CYPRUS — 698 93 × 132 mm. See [1600]:[119].
[186] DESCRIPTIO PALÆSTINÆ.
   [C:] Tabula CANANÆÆ prout tempore Christi et Apostolorum divisa fuit — 702 93 × 130 mm.
[187] DESCRIPTIO ARABIÆ.
   [C:] ARABIA — 706 95 × 131 mm. See [1600]:[121].
[188] DESCRIPTIO PERSIÆ.
   [C:] Persicum Regnum — 710 93 × 132 mm.
[189] DESCRIPTIO REGNI ORMVZII.
   [C:] ORMUS regnum — 716 94 × 132 mm.
[190] DESCRIPTIO INDIÆ ORIENTALIS.
   [C:] INDIA Orientalis. — 718 96 × 131 mm.
[191] DESCRIPTIO CAMBAIÆ.
   [C:] CAMBAIA — 722 93 × 133 mm.
[192] DESCRIPTIO REGNI MALABAR.
   [C:] Malabar — 724 95 × 131 mm.
[193] DESCRIPTIO NARSINGIÆ.
   [C:] NARSINGA — 730 95 × 131 mm.
[194] DESCRIPTIO BENGALÆ.
   [C:] BENGALA — 732 94 × 131 mm.
[195] DESCRIPTIO ARACHAN ET PEGV.
   [C:] ARACHAN & PEGV — 734 Coloured. 91 × 132 mm.
[196] DESCRIPTIO MALACCÆ.
   [C:] MALACCA — 736 91 × 131 mm.
[197] DESCRIPTIO CHINÆ.
   [C:] CHINA — 738 94 × 131 mm.
[198] DESCRIPTIO ZEILAN, ET MALDIVARVM INSS. 742 Coloured. 95 × 130 mm.
   [a] [T:] INSUL. MALDIVÆ. — 86 × 57 mm.
   [b] [C:] CEYLON.I. — 86 × 62 mm.
[199] DESCRIPTIO SVMATRÆ.
   [C:] SVMATRA insula — 744 91 × 131 mm.
[200] DESCRIPTIO BORNEO INSVLÆ.
   [C:] BORNEO insula ... — 746 91 × 131 mm.
[201] DESCRIPTIO IAVÆ.
   [T:] IAVA MAIOR — 748 94 × 129 mm.
[202] DESCRIPTIO MOLVCCARVM INSS.
   [C:] MOLVCCÆ insulæ — 750 91 × 130 mm.
[203] DESCRIPTIO PHILIPPINARVM.
   [C:] PHILIPPINÆ INSULÆ — 754 94 × 134 mm.
[204] DESCRIPTIO INSVLARVM IAPAN.
   [C:] IAPAN. — 756 95 × 130 mm.
[205] DESCRIPTIO IMPERII TVCICI.
   [C:] TURCICUM IMPERIUM — 758 95 × 130 mm.
P. BERTII TABVLARVM GEOGRAPHICARVM CONTRACTARVM Liber septimus. IN QVO AMERICA, Cum luculentis Tabularum singularum explicationibus.
[206] DESCRIPTIO AMERICÆ.
   [C:] AMERICA — 770 92 × 133 mm.
[207] DESCRIPTIO TERRÆ NOVÆ.
   [C:] VIRGINIA et Nova Francia — 787 (pro 778). 93 × 134 mm.
[208] DESCRIPTIO TERCERÆ.
   [C:] TERCERA. — 782 94 × 132 mm.
[209] DESCRIPTIO AMERICÆ.
   [C:] IUCATANA. — 786 95 × 129 mm.
[210] DESCRIPTIO CVBÆ ET IAMAICÆ.
   [C:] CUBA et Iamaica — 788 94 × 129 mm.
[211] DESCRIPTIO CVBÆ ET IAMAICÆ.
   [C:] HISPANIOLA. — 790 95 × 130 mm.
[212] DESCRIPTIO HISPANIOLÆ.
   [C:] NOVA HISPANIA — 792 95 × 129 mm.
[213] DESCRIPTIO NOVÆ HISPANIÆ.
   [T:] MEXICO — 764 (pro 794) Coloured. 91 × 129 mm.
[214] DESCRIPTIO NOVÆ HISPANIÆ.
   [C:] AMERICA Meridionalis — 798 95 × 130 mm.
[215] DESCRIPTIO PERVVIÆ.
   [C:] PERU — 802 95 × 130 mm.
[216] DESCRIPTIO NOVÆ HISPANIÆ.
   [T:] CERRO de POTOSI — (View). 812 Coloured. 95 × 124 mm. See [1600]:[162].
[217] DESCRIPTIO AMERICÆ.
   [C:] CHILI — 816 94 × 129 mm.
[218] DESCRIPTIO REGNI CHILI.
   [C:] BRASILIA — 818 95 × 129 mm.
[219] DESCRIPTIO ORBIS PTOLEMAICÆ.
   [T:] DESCRIPTIO ORBIS PTOLOMAICA. — [T:] Excusum et cælatum apud filios I. Hondij Amsterodami in platea Vitulina prope Senatoriam. Anno 1616. — 807 (pro 828). 94 × 133 mm.
[220] DESCRIPTIO ORBIS NOSTRA.
   [T:] TYPUS ORBIS TERRARUM — 808 (pro 829) = [3] in this ed.
COMPARATIO OPERIS PRÆSENTIS CVM PTOLEMAICO.

Notes: All the maps have text on the verso and they are uncoloured, except where otherwise specified. Koeman (vol. 2, p. 258—260) describes a copy of this edition with the imprint: 'Amsterodami Sumptibus et typus Iodoci Hondij. Anno 1616': our copy has: 'Amsterodami excusum in ædibus Viduæ Iodici Hondij. Anno 1616'. The year is printed in the decorative part of the title-page, not with the rest of the text inside the cartouche. In the copy described by Koeman, maps [2] and [3] are signed Iodoco Hondio, but his name does not appear on our maps. In our copy of map [68], the text in the cartouche reads: "GALLIÆ BELGICÆ veteris accurata descriptio P. Bertio auctori, amico suo colendo cælavit I. Hondius." In the copy described by Koeman (which belongs to the U.B. Amsterdam), the last part reads: "amico colendo d P Bertio, I Hondius Dt." Maps [127] and [130] in our copy have been transposed on pp.482 and 494, so that the map of Forum Julii has the heading 'DESCRIPTIO COMITATVS TIROLENSIS', and the map of TIROL has 'DESCRIPTIO FORI IVLII'. On map [219], p.807, "DESCRIPTIO ORBIS PTOLOMAICA", the text under the map in our copy reads: 'Excusum et cælatum apud filios I. Hondij Amsterodami in platea Vitulina prope Senatorium. Anno 1616'; the text given by Koeman is: 'Excusum et caelatum a

Iodoco Hondio Amsterodami in platea Vitulina prope Euriam'. However, the maps is printed on the same page in both copies. Tiele (p.25) gives the same text as Koeman. Some of the pages are misnumbered, and some of the headings do not correspond with the maps: [103] FRISIA has the heading of DESCRIPTIO FRISIÆ ORIENTALIS, but the map depicts Frisia occidentalis, map [211], HISPANIOLA, has the heading 'DESCRIPTIO CVBÆ ET IAMAICÆ', and map [218], BRASILIA, has 'DESCRIPTIO REGNI CHILI.' The maps in this edition are only partly the same as those in the earlier editions in the collection (Langenes 1599 and Bertius 1600). Maps [15] [26] [36] are signed by S. Rogiers in our copy, but not in Koeman (16,27,36). Some of the new maps are by Mercator. The atlas is bound in old vellum. Nordenskiöld's signature is on the recto of the blank leaf preceding the title-page, and on the verso is written in old ink: "Schruyver deses is gebooren to Beveren een dorp in Vlaanderen den 14 Novenber 1565 Zie Vaderl. Woordenbook dln 4. pag: 4 alwoor mede een portret van hem te vinden is".

Lit.: Koeman vol. 2, p. 258—260, Lan 11A, Tiele p. 25, nr 101.

16 BERTIUS, PETRUS 1645

GEOGRAPHIA VETVS EX ANTIQVIS, ET MELIORIS NOTÆ SCRIPTORIBVS NVPER COLLECTA, Per Clarissimum virum P. Bertium Regis Galliarum Christianissimi Geographum, nunc prodit, & prostat. PARS PRIMA. ... A PARIS, Chez IEAN BOISSEAV, Enlumineur du Roy, és Cartes Geographiques, sur le Quay qui regarde la Mégisserie, à la Fontaine de Iouuance Royalle. M. DC. XLV. 19,5 cm.

[1] 1 AD TYPVM ORBIS A POMPONIO MELA PROPOSITVM.
[T:] ORBIS TERRARVM EX MENTE POMPONII MELAE DELINEATVS A P. BERTIO. Christianissimi Regis Geographo — [T:] Cælauit MELCHIOR TAVERNIER Lutetiæ Parisiorum. Anno MDCXXVIII. — Circular map with 143 mm. diam.

[2] 2 AD FVNDAM POSSIDONII.
[T:] ΣΦΕΝΔΟΝΗ [SFENDONE], hoc est, FVNDA POSIDONII DELINEATA A P. BERTIO Christianissimi Regis LVDOVICI XIII Geographo & Professore. — [T:] Cælauit LVTETIAE PARISIOR. MELCHIOR TAVERNIER Anno MDCXXVIII — Oval map 86 × 187 mm.

[3] 3 Artificium conficiendi Tabulam vniuersalem. EX CL. PTOLEMÆI GEOGRAPHIÆ, lib. I. cap. XXIV.
[T:] PINAX PTOLEMAICVS CHLMYDOEIDES continens contractam ex ipsius mente orbis tunc cogniti descriptionem delineatus a P. BERTIO Christianissimi Regis Cosmographo — 152 × 205 mm.

[4] 4 ORBIS STANS QVOMODO IN DVOBVS HEMISPHÆRIIS PLANIS DESCRIBATVR, ita vt Poli pro centro sint, Æquator pro peripheria.
[T:] ORBIS STANS, SECTVS PER AEQVATOREM, Opera P. BERTII Cosmographi Regij. HEMISPHÆRIVM ANTARCTICVM HEMISPHÆRIVM ARCTOVM — [T:] Cælauit LVTETIAE PARISIOR Melchior Tauernier, Anno MDC XXVIII apud quem etiam prostat. — 150 × 190 mm.

[5] 5 ORBIS STANS SIVE MORALIS VT DESCRIBATVR, SECTVS per Primum Meridianum in duo Hemesphæria, Nostrum, & Americanum.
[T:] ORBIS STANS SIVE MOLARIS SECTVS PER PRIMVM MERIDIANVM PTOLEMAICVM IN DVO PLANISPHAERIA. OPERA P.Bertij Geographi Regij HEMISPHAERIVM AMERICANVM HEMI-SPHAERIVM NOSTRVM — [T:] Cælauit Melchior Tauernier Lut. Paris. A° 1628. — 144 × 193 mm.

[6] 6 AD INSVLAS BRITANNICAS.
[C:] BRITANNICARVM delineatio Ptolemaica ad naturalem locorum situm restituta. Delineata a P Bertio. A 1628. — [T:] Melchior Tauernier sculpcit & excudit — 141 × 182 mm.

[7] 7 HISPANIA PLINII SECVNDI.
[C:] HISPANIAE C. PLINII Secundi, delineatæ a P Bertio. ... M. Tauernier sculpcit & excudit. — 146 × 189 mm.

[8] 8 AD TABVLAM GALLIÆ.
[C:] GALLIA C. Iulij Caesaris delineata a P. Bertio Melchior Tauernier Fecit & excudit, A° 1628. — 150 × 199 mm.

[9] 9 AD ITALIAM OCTAVII AVGVSTI CÆSARIS.
[C:] ITALIA Augusti ex C. Plinio, delineata a P. Bertio Christianiss. Regis Geographo. A° 1628. — [C:] ... M. Tauernier Fecit et ex. — 160 × 194 mm.

[10] 10 AD TABVLAM GRÆCIÆ.
[C:] GRAECIA siue Hellas Cl. Ptolemæi. A° 1628. Melchior Tauernier scul — 149 × 193 mm.

[11] 11 ASIA INTER SINVM AMISENVM ET ISSENVM, ex Plinio & Strabone.
[C:] ASIA intra Sinum Amisenum & Issicum ex Plinio et Strabone. — 148 × 196 mm.

[12] 12 EVPHRATES ET TIGRIS, ex Plinij libri V. cap. 24. & VI. cap. 27.
[C:] TERRA CHANAAN DESIGNATA A BVRCHARDO MONACHO. Anno MCCLXXXIII Delineata a P. Bertio — [C:] ... Melchior Tauernier sculpcit & excudit A° 1628. — 143 × 193 mm.

[13] 13 AD TABVLAM ARABIAE FÆLICIS, ex Plinio lib. VI. cap. XXVIII.
[C:] ARABIA EVDAEMON ex Plinio lib VI cap. 28. — 144 × 193 mm.

[14] 14 AD TABVLAM TERRÆ SANCTÆ.
[C:] EVRHRATIS et TIGRIS Cursus cum Regionibus Vicinis ex Plinij lib. V. Cap. 24 & lib VI Cap 26 & 27. 1628 — 147 × 193 mm.

[15] 15 ORA ASIÆ CIRCA PONTVM EVXINVM ET MÆOTIM. ex Plin. lib. VI. cap.1.2.3.4.5.6.
[C:] ASIA circa PONTVM EVXINVM et MAEOTIM, ex Plinio lib. V. cap. 1.2.3.4.5. — 143 × 193 mm.

[16] 16 AD AFRICÆ PERIPLVM.
[C:] AFRICAE PERIPLVS ex Hannone. Polybio. Mela. Plinio. Ptolemæ° Arriano~ — 147 × 199 mm.

[17] 17 MAVRITANIÆ duae, Extima siue Tingitana vel Bogudiana; & Bochi, quæ posteà Cæsariensis, ex Plinio.
[C:] MAVRITANIAE DVAE BOGVDIANA ET BOCHIANA ex Plinio. — [T:] Melchior Tauernier sculp. A.° 1628 — 139 × 191 mm.

[18] 18 AFRICA propriè dicta, siue ZEVGITANA, & LIBYA Plinij.
[C:] AFRICA Proprie dicta, ex Plinio — [T:] Melchior Tauernier sculpsit — 139 × 194 mm.
[Inset:] [T:] SITVS CARTHAGINIS — 35 × 41 mm.

[19] 19 CYRENAICA PLINII. ex libro V. cap. V.
[C:] CYRENAICA siue PENTAPOLIS cum LIBYA MARMARICA a Syrti maiore vsq₃ ad Aegÿptum ex Plin. lib. V. cap 5 & 6. 1628 — 149 × 197 mm.

[20] 20 ÆGYPTVS INFERIOR EX AMMIANI MARCELLINI libro XXII.
[C:] AEGIPTVS INFERIOR CVM AVGVSTAMNICA ex Ammiano Marcellius libro XXII. — Verso blank. 147 × 199 mm.

Notes: All the maps have text on the verso, except map [20]. They are uncoloured. The text given above before [C:] or [T:] is opposite the map. Our collection has only this first part of the atlas. Koeman describes a 1630 edition, Ber 3, which contains the same maps as this copy; of the 1645 edition, Ber 4, he says only that the British Museum has a copy. He does not mention the second part of the atlas, referred to on the title-page of the first part. The atlas is bound in old, soft vellum. Nordenskiöld's signature is on the first blank leaf.

Lit.: BM, Maps vol. 2, c. 716, Koeman vol. I, p. 65—66, Ber 3 and Ber 4.

17 BLAEU, WILLEM JANSZOON   1627—1629

Zeespiegel, Inhoudende Een korte Onderwysinghe inde KONST DER ZEEVAERT, En Beschryvinghe der Seen en kusten van de Oostersche/ Noordsche/ en Westersche SCHIPVAERT. Wt ondervindinghen van veel ervaren Zeevaerders vergadert/ en t'samen ghestelt Door Willem Iansz Blaeu. Tot AMSTERDAM, Ghedruckt by Willem Iansz Blaeuw, inde vergulde Sonnewyser. 1627.   31 cm.

EERSTE DEEL DER Zeespiegel, Inhoudende Een korte Onderwysinghe inde KONST DER ZEEVAERT, ...

No maps.

Tweede Deel Der Zeespiegel, ... [wanting].

's Derden Deels Eerste Boeck der ZEESPIEGEL Vande Westersche SCHIPVAERT: Inhoudende De Beschryvinghe der Seekusten van Hollandt/ Zeelandt/ en Vlaenderen. Van Tessel tot de Hoofden. ...

[1]   57 [C:] Pascaart vande Noord-Zee, van het Tessel tot de Hoofden — 257 × 357 mm.
[2]   58 [C:] De Tesselstroom met de Gaten van 't Marsdiep. — 255 × 352 mm.
      [Inset:] [C:] Caarte vande Reede ende Haven van Medenblick hoemen die Coomende soo van 'tWieringer als Vriesche vlack bezeijlē mogen tot dienst ende nut voor alle Zeevarende luijden perfectelije gemeten afgepeijlt ende beschreven A° 1614 uijt speciale lastvande E.H. Burgemeesteren ende Regeerders der voorss'. Stadt Medenblick — 110 × 250 mm.
[3]   Van de Tesselstroom en gaten van Tessel.   (2 profiles). On 7
[4]   Kust van Hollandt tusschen Wijck en de Maes.   (2 profiles). On 10
[5]   59 [C:] De Mase met het Goereesche gat — 255 × 347 mm.
[6]   Opdoeninghen vande Mase en Goereesche gat.   (10 profiles). 15—16
[7]   60 [C:] De Gaten van Brouwershaven Ziericzee en Der Veere — 255 × 351 mm.
[8]   De gaten van Bouwershaven ...   (2 profiles). On 20
[9]   61 [C:] Pascaart vande Gaten van Wielinge — 254 × 352 mm.
[10] Van de Wielinghe.   (2 profiles). On 25   D
[11] 62 [C:] De Cust van Vlaenderē en Engelandt van Oostende tot deur de Hoofden — 254 × 350 mm.
[12] De kust van't Voorlandt tot Deveren.   (4 profiles). On 32

Das derden Deels Tweede Boeck der ZEESPIEGEL Vande Westersche SCHIPVAERT: Inhoudende De Beschryvinghe der Seekusten van Vranckrijck/ Van Cales tot aen Heysant: Ende van Engelandt/ Van Doveren om Englandts eyndt, tot de hoeck van S. David. ...

[13] 63 [C:] Het Canael tusschen Engelandt en Vrancrijck — Text on verso. 257 × 358 mm.
[14] 64 [C:] De Custen van Picardie en Normandie, van Swartenes tot de Seine — 254 × 354 mm.
[15] Van Calis [to] Struysaert.   (6 profiles). On 5   A 3—6
[16] 65 [C:] De Cust van Normandie tusschen Seynhooft en de Kiscassen — 255 × 353 mm.
[17] Van Caen [to] Ornay.   (5 profiles). On 9   B
[18] 66 [C:] Pascaarte vande Zeecusten van Normandie en Bretaigne tusschen de C. de Hagu en Roscou — 255 × 352 mm.
[19] S. Malo.
      [C:] De Haven van S. Malo — On 13   B 3   Text on verso. 170 × 161 mm.
[20] Garnzey.   (3 profiles). On 17   C
[21] 67 [C:] De Cust van Engelandt tusschen de Singels en de droogthen van Weembrugh — 255 × 352 mm.
[22] Fierley [to] Bevesier.   (4 profiles). 20
[23] 68 [C:] De Custen van Engelandt tusschen de droogtē van Weembrugh en Poortlandt — 255 × 353 mm.
[24] De Kusten van Enghelandt, tusschen Wicht en Poortlandt. (5 profiles). On 24.
[25] 69 [C:] De Cust van Engelandt tusschē Poortlādt en Goutstart. — 254 × 352 mm.
[26] Poortlant tot Dortmuyen.   (7 profiles). 27 D 2 —28
[27] 70 [C:] De Custen van Engelandt tusschē Goutstart en Lezard — 256 × 354 mm.
[28] Goutstaert [to] Lezart.   (13 profiles). 32 —35 E 2
[29] 71 [C:] De Engelsche Cust val Lezart af tot de C. de Cornwal en d'Eijlanden van de Sorlinges — 257 × 355 mm.
[30] Van Lezart [to] Sorrels.   (12 profiles). On 38—40
[31] 72 [C:] De Custen van Engelandt tusschē C. Corwal en het eijlandt Londey — 256 × 353 mm.
[32] Engelants-eynd [to] Londay.   (9 profiles). On 45 F 3 —46
[33] 73 [C:] T'Canael van Bristou met de Zuijd-Cust van Wals-Engelandt. — 256 × 354 mm.
[34] Ilfraycombe [to]Muylfoort en Zinbuy.   (8 profiles). 51 G 2 — 52

Das derden deels Derde Boeck der ZEESPIEGEL Vande Westersche SCHIPVAERT: Inhoudende De Beschryvinghe der Seekusten Van Yerlandt. ... 1629

[35] 74 [C:] Zeekarte van Yerlandt. — Text on the back. 257 × 358 mm.
[36] 75 [C:] De Zuijdoost hoeck can Yerlandt tusschen Waterfoort en Glaskarick — 254 × 351 mm.
[37] Bovenlandt ofte t'hooghe landt over den hoeck van Grenoort. 't Vlacke voorlandt van Grenoort.   (Profile). On 4
[38] Waterfoort [to] Grenoort.   (5 profiles). 9 B
[39] 76 [C:] De oost Cust van Yerlandt tusschen Glaskarick en Dubling. — 254 × 352 mm.
[40] Suyckerbroodt [to]Bay van Dublin.   (4 profiles). 14
[41] 77 [C:] De Custen van Yerlandt van Dublingh tot Stranghfoort. — 256 × 354 mm.
[42] Het Eylandt Lambey [to] Carlingfoort.   (3 profiles). On 16
[43] 78 [C:] De Kust van Vlster tusschen Strang foort en Bandthaven met de Custen van Schotlandt daer tegen over — 255 × 356 mm.
[44] Hoeck van Shotlandt [to] de C.Cantyr.   (5 profiles). 21 C 3
[45] 79 [C:] De Noord-Cust van Yerlandt tusschen Bandthaven on C. de Telling — 255 × 353 mm.
[46] 80 [C:] De West-Cust van Yerlandt tusschen C.Tellin en Slijnehooft — 255 × 353 mm.
[47] Kelbeg en Slego [to] Blackrock.   (12 profiles). 26 —28
[48] 81 [C:] West-Cust van Yerlandt tusschen Slijnhooft en de Blasques — 256 × 355 mm.
      [Inset:] [C:] 'tVervolgh vande Rievier van Limrick vant Eijlandt Qowine tot de Stadt — 106 × 82 mm.
[49] C. Kiery ofte Brandonhil [to] De Blasques.   (7 profiles). 31
[50] 82 [C:] De Zuijdwest hoeck van Yerlandt tusschen Blasques en Mesanhooft — 253 × 353 mm.
[51] De Blasques [to] Mesanhead.   (12 profiles). 35 E 2 —37 E 3
[52] 83 [C:] De Eijlanden en Havenen ontrent de Cabo Clare bijde zuijdwesthoeck van Ierlandt. — 255 × 354 mm.
      [Inset:] [C:] De Cust tusschen Baltimoer en Oldhooft — 96 × 156 mm. (Irregular)
[53] C. de Clear [to] Hoeck van Rossen.   (8 profiles). 40 —41 F
[54] 84 [C:] De Zuijdcust van Yerlandt tusschen Oldhooft en Waterfoort — 256 × 355 mm.
[55] Oldhooft [to] Dongarvan.   (12 profiles). 44 —46

Des derden Deels Vierde Boeck der ZEESPIEGEL Vande Westersche SCHIPVAERT: Inhoudende De Beschryvinghe der Seekusten van Vranckrijck en Biscayen. Tusschen Heyssant en Caep de Ortegael. ...

[56] 85 [C:] Pascaarte van Vrancrijck Biscaijen en Galissen tusschen Heissant en C. de Finesterre — Text on verso. 257 × 359 mm.
[57] 86 [C:] De Zeecusten en Eijlanden aent westeijnde van Bretaignen — 255 × 351 mm.
[58] Conquets oort.   (Profile). On 2
[59] Heyssant [and] Slaeplakens.   (14 profiles). 5 A 3 —6

[60] 87 [C:] De Zeecusten van Bretaignen tusschen de Westerpleimarques en de Riviervan Vannes. — 256 × 351 mm.
[61] Het landt tusschen de Wester en Ooster Pleymarckes [to] Boelyn. (8 profiles). On 11 B 2 — 10 (pro 12).
[62] 88 [C:] De Zeecusten van Bretaignen en Poictou tusschen Boelijn en S. Martens Eijlandt. — 256 × 351 mm.
[63] Het landt van Peictou [and] het Eylandt Heys. (2 profiles). On 16
[64] 89 [C:] De Kusten van Vranckrijck tusschen Olone en de Rivier van Bourdeaux — 256 × 352 mm.
[65] 't Eylandt van S.Martin [to] Het landt tusschen Olderdon ende de Riviere van Bordeaux. (12 profiles). 20 — 21 C 3
[66] 90 [C:] Caarte Van de Rivier van Bourdeaux en de haven van Arcachon. — 255 × 350 mm.
[67] 91 [C:] De Zeecusten van Vrancrijck en Biscaijen tusschen Arcachon en de C. de Machicaco — 254 × 350 mm.
[68] S. Jan de Luz [to] C. Machichaco. (9 profiles). 29 D 3 — 30
[69] 92 [C:] De Kust van Biscaijen tusschen de C. de Massichaco en C. de Pinas. — [Divided into two parts]. 254 × 351 mm.
[70] Bilbau [to] C. Pinas. (18 profiles). 33 E — 37 E 3
[71] 93 [C:] Zeecusten van Galissen tusschen C. de Pinas en C. de Ortegal. — 254 × 353 mm.
[72] Het landt van Aviles [to] C. Ortegael. (11 profiles). 41 —43

's Derden Deels Vijfde Boeck der ZEESPIEGEL Vande Westersche SCHIPVAERT: Inhoudende De Beschryvinghe der Seekusten van Galissen/ Portugael en Spangien/ Van de C. Ortegal tot de Straet van Gibraltar. ...

[73] 94 [C:] De Custen van Gallissen Portugal en Andalusien van de C. Ortegal tot de Strate van Gibraltar. — Text on verso. 256 × 359 mm.
[74] 95 [C:] De Zeekusten van Galissen tusschen de Cabe͂ Ortegal en Finisterre. — 254 × 350 mm.
[75] Ortegael [to] Cap de Finisterre. (16 profiles). 3 A 2 — 5 A 3
[76] 96 [C:] De Zeecusten van Galissen tusschen de Cabo Finisterre en Camino. — 254 × 350 mm.
[77] de Kapen de Coriane en Finisterre [to] S.Rego ende Bayone. (14 profiles). 10 — 13 B 3
[78] 97 [C:] De Zeecusten van Portugal van Viana tot Avero. — 253 × 350 mm.
[79] Kust van Portugael/ van Bayone [to] Port a Port. (13 profiles). 17 C — 19 C 2
[80] 98 [C:] De Custen van Portugael tusschen Avero en Roxent — 255 × 353 mm.
[81] De C. de Montego [to] Roxent. (8 profiles). 22 — 23
[82] 99 [C:] Zeecaart van de Rivier van Lisbon en de bancken voor S.t Vves — 255 × 352 mm.
[83] Roxent [to] S. Vves hoeck. (6 profiles). 26 — 27 D 2
[84] 100 [C:] De Custen van Algarve tusschen de C. S. Vincente en Aimonte — 255 × 351 mm.
[85] C. de S. Vincente [to] C. S. Maria. (9 profiles). 30 — 31
[86] 101 [C:] De Custe van Andaluzien tusschen Aimonte en de Strate van Gibraltar — 255 × 352 mm.
[87] Het landt tusschen Wolves en de Rivier van S. Lucas vertoont alsmen daer by langhs zeylt/ ghelyck in dese drie volghende figueren afghebeelt staet. [and] Alsmen nae Calis zeylt. (4 profiles). 35 E 2
[88] 102 [C:] De Strate van Gibraltar met de Spaensche Cust van daer tot Malaga. — 253 × 350 mm.
[89] De Spaensche kust van Malaga tot Modril. (Profile). On 38

's Derden Deels Seste Boeck der ZEESPIEGEL Vande Westersche SCHIPVAERT: Inhoudende De Beschryvinghe der Seekusten van Barbarien/ van de Straet van Gibraltar tot de Caep de Geer. Mitsgaders van de Canarische ende Vlaemsche Eylanden. ...

[90] 103 [C:] Pascaarte Vañ Barbarische cust mitsgaders van de Canarische en Vlamsche Eijlanden — Text on verso. 257 × 357 mm.
[91] 104 [C:] Dese drie stucken vertoonen de Barbarische Cust van de Straet tot C. Cantin. — [Divided into three parts]. 256 × 354 mm.
[92] De kust van Barbarien van C. de Spartel [to] Casa Cavalgero. (4 profiles). 5 A 3
[93] 105 [C:] De Custen van Barbarien van C. Cantin tot de C. de Geer — [Divided into two parts]. 254 × 352 mm.
[94] de noordhoeck van Saffia [to] C. de Geer. (6 profiles) On 8 — 10
[95] 106 [C:] De Eijlanden Lancerota Forteventura en Groot Canarien — 254 × 350 mm.
[Inset]: [C:] De tijhavens, Porto de Naos en Porto de Cavallos aen de Zuijdoostzyde van Lācerota — 109 × 136 mm.
[96] 107 [C:] De Eijlanden Tenerifa Palma Gomera en Ferro — 255 × 351 mm.
[97] de zuydkust van Forteventura [to] Madera. (15 profiles) 14 — 17 C
[98] 108 [a] [C:] d'Eijlanden Madera en Porto Santo — 146 × 352 mm.
[b] [C:] De Reede van Punte del Gada int eijlandt S. Michiels — 104 × 132 mm.
[Inset:] [Without names]. 50 × 51 mm.
[c:] [C:] De Reede voor de Stadt Angra int eijlandt Tercera — (Plan). 104 × 216 mm.
[The whole map:] 256 × 352 mm.
[99] het Eylandt S. Michiels [to] het Eylandt Gratiosa. (10 profiles). 20 —22

Notes: All the maps are blank on the back, except for the first map in each book, which is printed on the verso of the title-page. (Maps [1, 13, 35, 56, 78, 90].) They are uncoloured. There are errors in the signatures of the third book: '2 deel iij. b.' instead of '3 deel.' The third book is dated 1629: the first part contains no maps; the second part is wanting in our copy. This copy differs from those described by Koeman. The atlas in bound in old vellum. Nordenskiöd's signature is on the inside of the front cover, with the note: '1889. Köpt af Frederik Muller & C⁰ Del. I Compl. Del III. dito Del II saknas.' On the inside of the back cover is written in pencil "Outlevet 2ᵉ deel met karten 1—57. 1ᵉ deel Pag. 1—2 en ...".

Lit.: Keuning-Donkersloot-de Vrij p. 86—87, Koeman vol. 4, p. 84—91, M. Bl 32 I. II. III., Tiele p. 33, nr 124.

18 BLAEU, WILLEM JANSZOON AND JOAN 1635

NOVVS ATLAS, Das ist Abbildung und Beschreibung von allen Ländern des Erdreichs. Gantz vernewt vnd verbessert. AMSTERDAMI, Apud Guiljelmum Blaeuw, ANNO M DC XXXV.
48,2 cm.

Vol. I
[1] ASIA.
[C:] ASIA noviter delineata Auctore Guiljelmo Blaeuw. — C 408 × 559 mm.
[Insets:] [T:] CANDY — (Plan). [T:] CALECVTH — (View). [T:] GOA — (Plan). [T:] DAMASCO — (Plan). [T:] IERVSALEM — (Plan). [T:] ORMVS — (View). [T:] BANTAM — (Plan). [T:] ADEN — (View). [T:] MACAO — (Plan). All 9 oval. 41 × 58 mm.
[2] Eysslandt.
[C:] TABULA ISLANDIÆ Auctore Georgio Carolo Flandro. Amstelodami Guiljelmus Blaeuw excudit. — F 379 × 500 mm.
[3] BRITANNIA.
[C:] MAGNÆ BRITANNIÆ et HIBERNIÆ TABVLA — [C:] AMSTELODAMI, Guiljelmus Blaeuw excudit. — G 387 × 500 mm.
[Inset:] [T:] Orcades Insulæ — 54 × 83 mm.
[4] Königreich Engellandt.
[C:] ANGLIA REGNVM — H 383 × 496 mm.
[5] Schottland.
[C:] SCOTIA REGNVM — K 2 380 × 500 mm.
[Inset:] [T:] ORCADES INSVLÆ. — 110 × 78 mm.
[6] Irrlandt.
[C:] HIBERNIA REGNVM Vulgo IRELAND. — [T:] Apud Guiljelmum Blaeu. — K 3 381 × 498 mm.
[7] Mitternächtige Königreiche Dennemark/ Norwegen und Schweden.

[C:] SVECIA, DANIA, ET NORVEGIA, Regna Europæ Septentrionalia. Iuxta Archetypum Andreæ Buræi de Boo, Secretarÿ Regÿ, et supremi Regni Sueciæ Architecti. — L 424 × 530 mm.

[8] Das Hertzogthumb Litthow / Samogeten / schwartz Reussen vnd Volhinia.
[C:] Lectori S. Hunc Borysthenis tractum ut ad nostram Geographiæ tabulam adjiciamus duo nos præcipue impulerunt. ... — [Divided into two parts]. O (pro N). 321 × 745 mm.

[9] Reussen / Moscaw vnd Lieffland.
[C:] TABVLA RVSSIÆ ex autographo, quod delineandum curavit Foedor filius Tzaris Boris desumta; et ad fluvios Dwinam, Zuchanam, aliaque loca, quantum ex tabulis et notitiis ad nos delatis fieri potuit, amplificata: ac Magno Domino, Tzari et Magno Duci Michäeli Foedrowits omnium Russorum, Autocratori Wolodimeriæ, Moscoviæ et Novogardiæ, ... dedicata ab Hesselo Gerardo M.DC.XIIII — [T:] Amstelodami, Excusum Apud Guiljelmum Blaeu. — O 425 × 546 mm.
[Insets:] [T:] MOSCVA ad Architypum Foedori Borissowitsi — (Plan). 140 × 194 mm. [T:] ARCHANGELSCKAGORODA — (View). Oval 49 × 110 mm.

[10] CRIMEA, Oder Die Przecopenzer Tartarey / Und der Peninsel bey den Alten Taurica Chersonesus genänt.
[C:] TAVRICA CHERSONESVS. Nostra ætate PRZECOPSCA, et GAZARA dicitur. — O 3 377 × 496 mm.

[11] Siebenbürgen.
[C:] TRANSYLVANIA Sibenburgen. Amsterdami, Apud Guiljelmum et Ioannem Blaeu — P 381 × 499 mm.

[12] Walachia / Servia / Bulgaria vnd Romania.
[C:] WALACHIA SERVIA, BVLGARIA, ROMANIA. — [T:] Per Gerardum Mercatorem Guiljelmus Blaeu excudebat — Q 383 × 508 mm.

[13] Sclavonia / Croatia / Bossnia vnd ein Theil der Dalmacey.
[C:] SCLAVONIA, CROATIA, BOSNIA cum DALMATIÆ PARTE. Auct. Ger. Mercatore. — [T:] Apud Guiljel. Blaeu. — R 384 × 499 mm.

[14] Carniola oder Crain.
[C:] KARSTIA, CARNIOLA, HISTRIA et WINDORVM MARCHIA. Ger. Mercatore Auctore. — [T:] Guiljelm. Blaeu excudit. — S 382 × 498 mm.

[15] Königreich Ungern.
[C:] HVNGARIA REGNVM. — [T:] Amsterdami Apud Guiljelmum et Iohannem Blaeu. — T 418 × 510 mm.

[16] Königreich Polen.
[C:] POLONIA Regnum, et SILESIA Ducatus. — [T:] Guiljelm Blaeu excudit. — X 413 × 508 mm.

[17] Preussen.
[C:] PRVSSIÆ NOVA TABVLA. Auctore Gasparo Henneberg Erlichensi. — [C:] AMSTELODAMI, Ex officina Guilj. Blaeu. — Y 378 × 481 mm.

[18] Teutschland.
[T:] NOVA TOTIVS GERMANIÆ DESCRIPTIO. — Aa 389 × 497 mm.

[19] Pommern.
[C:] POMERANIÆ DVCATVS TABVLA. Auctore Eilhardo Lubino. — [T:] S. Rogiers sculpsit. — [C:] AMSTELODAMI, Guiljelm. Blaeu excudit. — Dd 378 × 491 mm.

[20] Insel Rügen.
[C:] RVGIA INSVLA AC DVCATVS accuratissimè descripta ab E. Lubino. ... — [T:] Amsterdami Apud Guiljelmum Blaeuw — Ee 380 × 497 mm.

[21] Hertzogthumb Mecklenburg.
[C:] MEKLENBVRG DVCATVS. Auctore Ioanne Laurenbergio. — [C:] AMSTELODAMI, Guiljelmus Blaeuw excudit. — [T:] S.Rogiers sculp. — Ff 364 × 485 mm.

[22] Marck Brandenburg.
[C:] BRANDEBVRGVM MARCHIONATVS, cum Ducatibus POMERANIÆ et MEKELENBVRGI. — [T:] Amstelodami, Apud Guiljelmum et Ioannem Blaeu. — Gg 393 × 524 mm.

[23] Hertzogthumb Braunschweig.
[C:] BRAVNSWYCK et MEYDBVRG cum terris adjacentibus. — [T:] Amsterdami, Guiljelmus Blaeuw Excud. — Hh 375 × 497 mm.

[24] Bischoffthumb Hildesheimb.
[C:] EPISCOPATVS HILDESIENSIS DESCRIPTIO NOVISSIMA Authore Ioanne Gigante D. Med. et Math. — Ii 411 × 498 mm.

[25] Hertzogthumb Luneburg.
[C:] DVCATVS LVNEBVRGENSIS Adiacentiumq$_3$ regionum delineatio. Auctore IOHANNE MELLINGERO. — [T:] Amstelodami, Guiljelm. Blaeuw excudit. — Kk 377 × 489 mm.

[26] Hertzogthumb Schlesswick.
[T:] DVCATVS HOLSATIÆ NOVA TABVLA — [C:] Amstelodami Guiljelmus Blaeuw excudit — Ll 381 × 516 mm.
[Insets:] [C:] Alluvies propè Detzbul, Incolis Inferioris Germaniæ, a Duce Holsatie concessa aggeribus cingi. Aenwas bÿ Detzbul den Nederlanders geconsenteert te bedÿcken van den Hartoch van Holsteÿn. — 108 × 131 mm. [C:] Tabula Barmerensis, Meggerensis, et Noortstaepplerensis maris: Incolis Inferioris Germãiæ concessum hæc maria aggeribus cingere, et desiccare. — 109 × 131 mm.

[27] Beschreibung der Elbe.
[C:] CELEBERRIMI FLVVII ALBIS nova delineatio Auctore Christiano Mollero. — [C:] Viris Magnificis Amplissimis et Consultissimis Dom^{ls} Consulibus et Senatoribus, florentissimæ Reipublicæ Hamburgensis tabulam, hanc Provinciarum et Insularum Hamburgum Circumiacentium officiose dedicat Guiljelm Blaeuw. Anno 1628. — [T:] Amstelodami Guilj. Blaeuw Excudit. — [Divided into two parts]. Mm 307 × 531 mm.

[28] Graffschafft Oldenburg.
[C:] OLDENBVRG COMITATVS — [T:] Amstelodami Guiljelm Blaeuw excudit. — [T:] E.Sijmonsz. Hamersveldt sculp. — [Oo] 375 × 493 mm.

[29] Ostfriesslandt.
[C:] TYPVS FRISIÆ ORIENTALIS. Auctore Vbbone Emmio. — [T:] Amstelodami Guiljelm Blaeuw excudit. — Pp 375 × 484 mm.
[Inset:] [C:] RIDERIÆ PORTIONIS facies, ante inundationem, quæ postea finus maris facta est. — [T:] Emden — 113 × 97 mm.

[30] Bischthumb Munster.
[C:] MONASTERIENSIS Episcopatus. Auctore Ioh. Gigante Medico et Mathematico. — [C:] Apud Guiljelmum Blaeuw. — Qq 372 × 493 mm.

[31] Die Grafschaften BENTHEM vnd STEINFVRT.
[C:] COMITATVS BENTHEIM et STEINFVRT. Auctore Ioanne Westenberg M.Doct. et Math. — [T:] Guljelm. Blaeu excudebat. — Rr Verso blank. 377 × 497 mm.

[32] Bischthumb Ossnabrugge.
[C:] OSNABRVGENSIS EPISCOPATVS. Auctore Ioanne Gigante. — [C:] Reverendissimo et Illmo Principi ac Domino D.^{no} FRANCISCO GVILIELMO Episc. OSNABRVGENSI S.ROM:IMP:PRIN: Comiti in Wartenberg etc. Principi suo longe clementissimo humillime offert IOANNES GIGAS MED. DOCT. — [T:] Amstelodami, Guilielm. Blaeuw Excudit. — Ss 369 × 484 mm.
[Insets:] [T:] OSENBRVGGE — (View). 55 × 170 mm. [C:] DISTRICTVS RECKENBERGENSIS. — 83 × 75 mm.

[33] Bischthumb Paderborn.
[C:] PADERBORNENSIS Episcopatus DESCRIPTIO NOVA Ioanne Gigante Ludense D.Med. et Math. auth. — [C:] Amstelodami Guiljelmus Blaeuw excudit. — Tt 372 × 491 mm.

[34] Hertzogthumb Westphalen.
[C:] WESTPHALIA Ducatus Auctore Ioh. Gigante Medico et Mathematico. — [C:] Guiljelmus Blaeuw excudit. — Uu 377 × 492 mm.

[35] Graffschafft Waldeck.

[C:] WALDECK COMITATVS. — [T:] Amsterdami Apud Guiljelmum Blaeu — Xx 380 × 500 mm.

[36] Hertzogthumb Franckenland Der Erste Kreiss des Römischen Reichs.
[C:] FRANCONIA Vulgo Franckenlandt. — [T:] Excudit Guiljelmus Blaeu. — Yy 378 × 496 mm.

[37] Landgrafschafft Hessen.
[C:] HASSIA Landgraviatus. — [T:] Amsterdami. Apud Guiljelmum et Johannem Blaeu. — Zz 387 × 495 mm.

[38] Beschreibung von dem Stifft Hirschfelt.
[C:] TERRITORIVM ABBATIÆ HERESFELDENSIS. 't Stift Hirszfeldt. Apud Guiljelmum Blaeu. — Zz 2 Verso blank. 382 × 496 mm.

[39] Landgraffschafft Thüringen.
[C:] THVRINGIA LANDGRAVIATVS Auct. Adolario Erichio Anderslebiano. — [C:] Amplissimo Doctissimo et Elegantissimi ingenii viro IOACHIMO A WICKEVOORT omnis politioris literaturæ, et Græcarum pariter ac Romanarum Antiquitatū Studiosissimo D.D.D. Joh: Blaeu. — Aaa 411 × 524 mm.

[40] Grafschafft Manssfeldt.
[C:] MANSFELDIA COMITATVS Auctore Tilemanno Stella Sig. — [T:] Apud Guiljelm. Blaeu. — Bbb 408 × 498 mm.

[41] Ober Sachsen.
[C:] SAXONIA SVPERIOR, CVM LVSATIA ET MISNIA. — Ccc 391 × 507 mm.

[42] Königreich vnd Chur Böhmen.
[C:] BOHEMIA — Ddd 409 × 545 mm.

[43] Schlesien Sampt dessen zugehörigen Hertzogthumben.
[C:] SILESIA DVCATVS A Martino Helwigio Nissense descriptus. — Eee 379 × 496 mm.

[44] Marggrafschafft Mähren.
[C:] MORAVIA MARCHIONATVS Auctore I. A. Comenio. — [T:] Amstelodami, Guiljelm Blaeuw Excudit. — Fff 377 × 487 mm.

[45] ErtzHertzogthumb Oesterreich. Der dritte Kreiss des Römischen Reichs in Oesterreich / ...
[C:] AVSTRIA ARCHIDVCATVS auctore Wolfgango Lazio — [C:] AMSTELODAMI Guiljelmus Blaeuw excudit. — Ggg 363 × 544 mm.

[46] Steyermarck.
[C:] STIRIA Steyrmarck. — [T:] Apud Guiljelmum Blaeuw. Amsterdami. — Hhh 375 × 502 mm.

[47] Bischthumb Saltzburg.
[C:] SALTZBVRG ARCHIEPISCOPATVS, et CARINTHIA DVCATVS. Auct. Ger. Mercatore. — [T:] Amsterdami Apud Guiljelmum Blaeu. — Iii 381 × 500 mm.

[48] Hertzogthumb Beyern. Der ander Kreiss des Römischen Reichs ist Beyerland.
[C:] BAVARIA DVCATVS, Per Ger. Mercatorem. — [T:] Apud Guiljelmum Blaeu. — Kkk 383 × 501 mm.

[49] Ober Pfaltz / oder Ober Bayern.
[C:] PALATINATVS BAVARIÆ. — [T:] Amsterdami Excudit Guiljelmus Blaeuw. — Lll 379 × 498 mm.

[50] [C:] TERRITORIVM NORIMBERGENSE. — [T:] Amstelodami Exc. Guiljelm. Blaeuw. — [C:] Nobilissimis Amplissimis Consultissimisque Viris Dominis D. Consulibus totique Senatui inclytæ reipublicæ Norimbergensis dedicabat Guiljelmus Blaeuw. — Blank on the back. 362 × 470 mm.
[Inset:] [T:] NVRNBERG — (Plan). 92 × 118 mm.

[51] Hertzogthumb Würtenberg.
[C:] WIRTENBERG DVCATVS. — Nnn 412 × 496 mm.

[52] Schwabenland. Der vierdte Kreyss des Römischen Reichs ist Schwaben.
[C:] SVEVIÆ NOVA TABVLA. — [C:] AMSTELODAMI, Apud Guiljelmum Blaeuw — Ooo 372 × 487 mm.

[53] Alemannia oder Ober Schwaben.
[C:] ALEMANNIA SIVE SVEVIA SVPERIOR A. Christophoro Hurtero. — Ppp 378 × 498 mm.

[54] [T:] TRACTVS DANVBII, FLVMINIS IN EVROPA MAXIMI, A FONTIBVS, PER GERMANIAM ET HVNGARIAM, BELGRADVM VSQVE. — Blank on the back. 409 × 885 mm.

[55] [C:] RHENVS, MOSELLA, VAHALIS, MOSA, & reliqui qui in illos se exonerant FLVVII. — [T:] Amstelredami apud Guilielmum Blaeu. — Blank on the back. 761 × 486 mm.

[56] Schweitzerland.
[C:] HELVETIA, cum finitimis regionibus confœderatis. — [T:] Describebat Gerard' Mercator, et excudebat Guiljelmus Blaeu. — Sss 385 × 504 mm.

[57] Grawpündten.
[C:] Alpinæ seu Fœderatæ RHAETIAE SUBDITARUMQUE ei Terrarum nova descriptio. Auctoribus Fortunato Sprechero à Berneck, Eq.aur.et I.V.D.Ret. AC PHIL. CLUVERIO. — [T:] Amstelodami Guiljelmus Blaeuw excudit — [T:] Evert Sijmons Z. Hamors Veldt sculp. — [C:] Nobilitate, eruditione & virtute Clarissimo viro, D. HADRIANO PAUW EQUITI, DOMINO DE HEEMSTEDE, CONSILIARIO ET SYNDICO REIPUBLICÆ AMSTELODAMENSIS, CURATORI ACADEMIÆ LUGDUNO BATAVÆ, HANC SUAM DE NOVO AUCTAM TABULAM RHÆTIÆ D.D. — Ttt 378 × 498 mm.

[58] Wiflispurgergow.
[C:] DAS WIFLISPVRGERGOW. Gerardo Mercatore Auctore. — [T:] Guiljel. Blaeu excudit. — Vuu 380 × 499 mm.

[59] Argow.
[C:] ARGOW cum parte merid. ZVRICHGOW Auctore Ger: Mercatore. — Xxx 384 × 499 mm.

[60] Zürichow.
[C:] ZVRICHGOW et Basiliensis provincia — Yyy 378 × 497 mm.

[61] Elsass. Der fünffte Kreiss des Reichs ist der Rheinische.
[C:] ALSATIA Landgraviatus, cum SVNTGOIA et BRISGOIA Ger. Mercatore Auctore. — [C:] ... Guiljelm. Blaeu excudit. — Aaaa 395 × 797 mm.

[62] Pfaltz am Rhein. Der sechste Kreyss des Reichs ...
[C:] PALATINATVS AD RHENVM — [T:] Apud Guiljelmum Blaeu. — Cccc 410 × 498 mm.

[63] Grafschfft Erpach.
[C:] ERPACH COMITATVS. — [C:] AMSTELODAMI Guiljelmus Blaeuw excudit. — Dddd Verso blank. 356 × 480 mm.

[64] Grafschafft Nassaw.
[C:] NASSOVIA Comitatus. — [T:] Amstelodami, Guiljelm. Blaeuw Excudit. — [T:] Salom Rogiers sculpsit. — Eeee 377 × 489 mm.

[65] ErtzBischthumb Cölln.
[C:] COLONIENSIS Archiepiscopatus Auctore Ioh. Gigante Medico et Mathematico. — [T:] Amstelodami Guiljelmus Blaeuw Excudit. — Gggg 376 × 490 mm.

[66] Die Hertzogthumber Gulich / Cleve / Bergen / Nebens den Grafschafften Marck vnd Ravensperg.
[C:] De Hertochdommen GULICK CLEVE BERGHE en de Graefschappen vander MARCK EN RAVENSBERGH. Midsgaders de grensen der omleggende landen daeraen palēde. Nu van nieus perfectelyck met vlydt beschreven. a' 1610 — [T:] T' Amsterdam Gedruckt by Hessel Gerritz z. Ende men vindtze te coop by Willem Ians z. opt Water In de Vergulde Sonnewyser — Hhhh 423 × 549 mm.
[Inset:] [T:] Om de landen van Gulick en Cleve in dese Caert soo groot van form als mogelijck was te vertoonen; soo en hebben Ravensberg en der Lippe met de oostelijckste deelen vander Marck daer niet in kōnen begrepē werden. Daerom die hier onder dē Leser voor ooghen gestelt zyn in mīder besteck. — 196 × 189 mm.

[67] Das Hertzogthumb Gülich.
[C:] IVLIACENSIS ET MONTENSIS DVCATVS. De Hertoghdomen GVLICK en BERGHE. — Hhhh 2 379 × 497 mm.

[68] Die Graffschafft Marck vnnd Ravensberg.
[C:] COMITATVS MARCHIA ET RAVENSBERG. — Hhhh 3 380 × 498 mm.
[Inset:] [T:] RAVENSBERG COMITATVS. — 190 × 152 mm.

[69] Das Hertzogthumb Cleve.
[C:] CLIVIA DVCATVS ET RAVESTEIN DOMINIVM. — Hhhh 4   378 × 506 mm.

[70] Alt Teutschland.
[C:] GERMANIAE VETERIS, typus. — [C:] DN. IACOBO MONAVIO SILESIO PATRICIO VRATISLAVIENSI, VIRO ET ERVDITIONE ET HVMANITATE ORNATISSIMO, ABRAHAMVS ORTELIVS HOC MVTVÆ AMICITIAE MONVMENTVM LIBENS DONABAT DEDICABATQVE. — [T:] AMSTERDAMI Apud Guilj. Blaeuw. — Iiii   378 × 480 mm.

[71] Nieder Landt.
[C:] NOVUS XVII INFERIORIS GERMANIÆ PROVINCIARUM TYPUS de integro multis in locis emendatus à Guliel. Ianssonio. ... — [C:] Ghedruckt t'Amsterdam, bÿ Willem Ianszoon op't Water inde vergulde Zonnewyser. — [T:] Josua vanden Ende sculp. — A   399 × 505 mm.

[72] Der Grabe S.MARIÆ Welcher auch FOSSA EVGENIANA genennet / Zwischen dem Rhein vnd Maass aussgeführt im jahr 1628.
[C:] FOSSA quæ a Rheno ad Mosam duci coepta est Anno M D C XXVII. Excudit Guilj. Ianssonius Blaeuw. — D   383 × 507 mm.

[73] Hertzogthumb Geldern / Grafschafft Sütphen vnd die Herrschafft Oberissel.
[C:] GELDRIA DVCATVS, et ZVTFANIA COMITATVS. — [T:] Amsterd. Apud Guilj. Blaeuw. — EF   380 × 498 mm.

[74] Die Grafschafft ZVTPHEN.
[C:] ZVTPHANIA COMITATVS. Excudit Guiljelmus Blaeuw. — On EF 2   218 × 263 mm.

[75] Gröninger Landt.
[C:] GRONINGA DOMINIVM. Auctore Bartholdo Wicheringe. — [C:] AMSTELODAMI Guiljelmus Blaeuw excudit. — G   376 × 487 mm.

[76] Westfriesslandt.
[C:] FRISIA OCCIDENTALIS Adriano Metio et Gerardo Freitag Auctoribus. Amstelodami Guiljelm. Blaeuw excudit. — H   378 × 492 mm.

[77] Grafschafft Holland.
[C:] HOLLANDIA COMITATVS. — [T:] Apud Guiljelmum Blaeu. — [An empty cartouche]. I   390 × 523 mm.
[Inset:] INSVLÆ Texel Vlielandt et der Schelling. — 100 × 161 mm.

[78] Noort Hollandt Oder West Friesslandt.
[C:] HOLLANDIÆ PARS SEPTENTRIONALIS, Vulgo WESTVRIESLAND en 'TNOORDER QVARTIER. — [T:] Amsterdami Apud Guiljelmum et Ioannem Blaeu. — I2   384 × 499 mm.

[79] Rheinlandt.
[C:] RHENOLANDIÆ et AMSTELLANDIÆ exactissima Tabula. — [T:] Exc. Guilj. Blaeuw. — I3   403 × 498 mm.

[80] Delfflandt / Schielandt / vnnd die beyligende Insulen.
[C:] DELFLANDIA, SCHIELANDIA, et Insulæ trans Mosam illis objacentes ut sunt VOORNA, OVERFLACKEA, GOEREA, YSELMONDA, etc. — [T:] Exc. Guilj Blaeuw. — Iiii 5   381 × 499 mm.

[81] Hollandt so gegen Mittag ligt / in gemein Zuydt-Hollandt.
[C:] ZVYDHOLLANDIA stricte sumta. — [T:] Amsterdami Guiljelmus Blaeuw excudit. — I Mmmm7   380 × 508 mm.

[82] Stifft Vtrecht.
[C:] VLTRAIECTVM DOMINIVM. Excudit Guiljelmus Blaeuw. — K   382 × 501 mm.

[83] Alt BATAVIA. Oder Ein Theil des Rheins zusampt der gantzen Maass.
[C:] Tractus RHENI et MOSÆ totusq$_3$ VAHALIS à Rhenoberca Gorcomium usque cum terris adjacentibus ducatus Cliviæ regno Noviomagensi et Bommelerwaert Parte insuper veteris Bataviæ quæ continet de Betouwe Tielerwaert et com: Buyren, Cuylenborch et Leerdam. — [T:] Exc: Guiljel: Blaeuw. — [Divided into two parts]. L   382 × 499 mm.

[84] Hertzogthumb Braband.
[C:] BRABANTIA DVCATVS. — [C:] ... Amsterdami Apud Guiljelmum Blaeuw. — M   380 × 498 mm.

[85] Hertzogenbusch. Kämpen. Peland. Maesland.
[C:] QVARTA PARS BRABANTIÆ cujus caput SYLVADVCIS. Willebordus vander Burght describ. — [T:] Apud Guiljelmum Blaeu. — O   414 × 522 mm.

[86] Das Erste Theil van Brabant / Dessen Hauptstatt ist Löven.
[C:] PRIMA PARS BRABANTIÆ cuius caput LOVANIVM Auctore Michaele Florentio a Langren Hispan. Regis Mathematico. — [C:] ... Guiljelmus Blaeu excudit — M   407 × 518 mm.

[87] Das Ander Theil von Brabandt / dessen Hauptstatt ist Brüssel.
[C:] SECVNDA PARS BRABANTIÆ cuius urbs primaria BRVXELLÆ Descr. Michaele Florentio a Langren Mathematico Regio. — [C:] ... Guiljelmus Blaeu excudit — M 3   410 × 522 mm.

[88] Der Dritte Theill von Brabant / dessen die Erste Stadt ist Antorff / ein Marggraffschafft des Röm. Reichs.
[C:] TERTIA PARS BRABANTIÆ qua continetur MARCHIONAT. S.R.I. horum urbs primaria ANTVERPIA Ex Archetypo Michaelis Florentÿ a Langren Reg. Maj. Mathematico. — [C:] ... Guiljelmus Blaeu excudit. — Mmmm 4   416 × 522 mm.

[89] Das Castel bey Santfliet.
[C:] TABVLA Castelli ad Sandflitam, qua simul inundati agri, alluviones, fossæ, alvei, quæ Bergas ad Zoman et Antverpiam interjacent, annotantur. Excudit Guiljelmus Blaeuw. — Mmmm 6   380 × 499 mm.

[90] Bergen-op-Soom / Steinbergen / sampt andern alda gemachten Wercken.
[C:] TABVLA Bergarum ad Zoman Stenbergæ et novorum ibi operum. Ad amussim fecit Francisc[9] van Schoten Math. Professor in Acad. Leidensi. — O Mmmm 7   223 × 537 mm.
[Inset:] [T:] Castra Pinsii — [T:] Exc. Guiljelmus Blaeuw. — 85 × 105 mm.

[91] Hertzogthumb Limburg.
[C:] DVCATVS LIMBVRGVM Auctore ÆGIDIO MARTINI. — [T:] Amsterdami Apud Guiljelmum et Joannem Blaeu — P   379 × 494 mm.

[92] Die Herrschafft Mechlen.
[C:] MECHLINIA DOMINIVM, et AERSCHOT DVCATVS Auctore Michaele Flor: a Langren Regis Catholici Mathematico. — Pppp 2   408 × 516 mm.

[93] Lütticher Gebiet.
[C:] LEODIENSIS DIOECESIS. — [T:] Amsterdami Apud Guiljelmum et Ioannem Blaeu — Q   378 × 497 mm.

[94] Hertzogthumb Lützelburg.
[C:] TREVIRENSIS ARCHIEPISCOPATVS, et LVTZENBVRGI DVCATVS. — [T:] Amsterdami Apud Guiljelmum et Ioannem Blaeu. — R   378 × 498 mm.

[95] Grafschafft Namen.
[C:] NAMVRCVM COMITATVS Auctore Iohann. Surhonio. — S   410 × 526 mm.

[96] Grafschafft Hennegow.
[C:] COMITATVVM HANNONIÆ ET NAMVRCI DESCRIPTIO. — [T:] Amsterdami Apud Guiljelmü. et Ioannem Blaeu — T   379 × 498 mm.

[97] Grafschafft Flandern.
[C:] FLANDRIA ET ZEELANDIA COMITATVS. Apud Guiljelmum Blaeuw. — V   417 × 531 mm.

[98] Das Occidentalische Theill Teutsch Flandern.
[C:] PARS FLANDRIÆ TEVTONICÆ OCCIDENTALIOR. [T:] Amsterdami Exc. Guiljelmus et Iohannes Blaeu. — Vuuu 2   390 × 496 mm.

[99] Duynkirchen.
[C:] Afbeeldinge vande vermaerde seehaven ende stadt van Duynkercken met der omliggende plaetsen sanden ende droochten afgeteeckent door Capiteijn Pieter Codde van Enchuysen Pourtraict de la fameuse ville et havre de Duynckercke et places voisines, sables etc. faict par le Capitaine Pierre Codde d'Enchuse — X   444 × 693 mm.
[Inset:] [T:] Calès — (View).   57 × 212 mm.

[100] Das Orientalische Theill Flammisch Flandern.
[C:] FLANDRIÆ TEVTONICÆ PARS ORIENTALIOR — [T:] Guiljelmus et Iohannes Blaeuw exc. Amsterdami. — X 2   377 × 496 mm.

[101] Welsch Flandern / In gemeiner Sprach FLANDRE WALLONNE.
[C:] GALLOFLANDRIA, in qua CASTELLANIÆ LILANA, DVACENA, & ORCHIESIA, cum dependentibus; necnon TORNACVM, & TORNACESIVM. Auctore Martino Doué Gallo-Flandro. — [T:] Guiljelmus Blaeu excudit. — X 3   385 × 501 mm.

[102] Reichs, vnd Eygen Flandern.
[C:] FLANDRIÆ Partes duæ, quarum altera PROPRIETARIA, altera IMPERIALIS vulgo dicitur. [C:] Nob.^{mo} Stren.^{mo} Prud.^{moq3} Viro D. IACOBO WIITS Exercitus Ordinum Belgicæ Fœderatæ Ephoro, et Concilii militaris Præsidi, ac præsidiariorum militum in urbe Amsteldamensi Præfecto, Viro de patria ac Reip. hujus salute præclare merito, et indies merenti, D.D. Guilj. et Joh. Blaeu. — X 4   410 × 520 mm.

[103] Grafschafft ARTESIA.
[C:] ARTESIA, COMITATVS. ARTOIS. — [T:] Amsterdami Apud Guiljelmū Blaeuw. — Z 379 × 498 mm.

[104] Grafschafft Seeland.
[C:] ZEELANDIA Comitatus. — [C:] Magnifico Amplissimo Doctissimoq$_3$ Viro D. SIMONI BELLIMONTIO Reipub. Middelburgensis Syndico, et in Potent.^{orum} Ord. Gener. Belg. Fœderatæ Consessu nomine Ordinum Zeelandiæ Assessori, nuper ad Poloniæ et Sueciæ Reges Legato D.D. Guiljelmus Blaeu. —Y 379 × 499 mm.

Notes: The maps have text on the verso, except where otherwise specified, and are uncoloured. Maps A Die gantze Welt, B Europa, D Africa and E America are wanting in this copy. Map [8], signed O (pro N), Das Hertzogthumb Litthow/ Samogeten/ schwartz Reussen vnd Volhinia, represents the river Dnjepr, divided into two parts. Koeman (vol. 1, p.97, B1 7 A) lists two maps under this title: no.12, Magni Ducatus Lithuaniae, and no.13, Borysthenes. Our map [9] is dated 1614, which according to Koeman (vol.1, B1 5 (14) p.89) indicates that it is the second state of the map. Some of the leaves have letters differing from those indicated in the Register:

[84] Braband   M   In the Register L 2
[85] Hertzogenbusch   O   L 4
[88] Dritte Theill von Brabant … Antorff Mmmm 4   M 6
[89] Castel bey Santfliet   Nmmm 6   N
[90] Bergen-op-Soom … O   Mmmm 7   O
[92] Die Herrschafft Mechlen Pppp 2   P 2
[98] … Teutsch Flandern   Vuuu 2   V 2

Map [20], RVGIA, has 30 coats-of-arms, 15 down each border. On map [66], De Hertochdommen GULICK CLEVE BERGHE …, there are two portraits: RUDOLPHUS II. ROMAN IMPERATOR AUG: and ERNESTUS D.G. MARCH. BRANDENBURG. etc. The title is printed on a separate slip of paper and pasted in the proper space on the engraved title-page. The atlas is bound in half vellum. On the inside of the front cover 'Lippests Catal. N° 213' is written in pencil.

Lit.: Koeman vol. 1, 97—99, B1 7 A, LC List vol. 3, p. 130, nr 3420, Tiele p. 34, nr 129.

Vol. II
Ander Theil NOVI ATLANTIS, Das ist Abbildung vnd Beschreibung von allen Ländern des Erdreichs. Gantz vernewt vnd verbessert. Durch Wilhelm vnd Iohann Blaeu. AMSTERDAMI, Apud Guiljelmum Blaeuw, ANNO MDCXXXV.   48 cm.

[1] Königreich Franckreich.
[C:] GALLIA LE ROYAVME DE FRANCE. I. vanden Ende fec. — [T:] Amsterodami Excudebat Guilielmus Blaeuw Sub Signo Solarii — C 375 × 494 mm.

[2] Grafschafft Boulogne vnd Guines.
[C:] COMITATVVM BOLONIÆ et GVINES DESCRIPTIO. — [T:] Guilielmus Blaeu excud. Amsterdami. — E 380 × 499 mm.

[3] Ertzbischthumb Cambray.
[C:] ARCHIEPISCOPATVS CAMERACENSIS. Archevesché de CAMBRAY. — [T:] AMSTERDAMI Apud Guiljelmum Blaeuw. — F 379 × 497 mm.

[4] Picardey.
[C:] PICARDIA Regio Belgica, Auctore Ioanne Surhonio. — [T:] Amsterdami Apud Guiljelmum et Joannem Blaeu. — G 381 × 533 mm.

[5] VERMANDOIS.
[a] [C:] DESCRIPTIO VEROMANDVORVM Auctore Ioanne Suthonio Gallice VERMANDOIS. — 386 × 249 mm.
[b] [C:] GOVVERNEMENT de la CAPPELLE Par P. petit Bourbon. — [T:] Amsterdami Apud Guiljelmum et Joannem Blaeuw. — 386 × 249 mm.
[The whole map:] H 386 × 508 mm.

[6] Das Gubernament von L'ISLE de FRANCE, vnnd sonderlich von HVREPOIS.
[C:] LE GOVVERNEMENT DE L'ISLE DE FRANCE Par Damien de Templeux Escuyer Sr du Frestoy — I 407 × 520 mm.

[7] Das Hertzogthumb Vales, In Frantzösisch: Le Duché de Valois.
[C:] VALESIVM Ducatus. VALOIS. — [T:] Guiljelmus Blaeu excudit. — I 2   388 × 497 mm.

[8] Die Graffschafft Bellovacum, In Frantzösisch: BEAVVOISIS.
[C:] COMITATVS BELLOVACVM, Vernaculé BEAVVAIS. — [T:] Amsterdami Apud Guiljelmum et Joannē Blaeu. — I 3   378 × 497 mm.

[9] Das Theil des Königreichs / so eygentlich Francia genennet.
[C:] AGER PARISIENSIS Vulgo L'ISLE DE FRANCE Fr. Guilloterius Bitur. Viu.describ. et CL.V.Petro Pithœo I.C. dedicabat. — [T:] Apud Guiljelmum Blaeu. — HIK 380 × 501 mm.

[10] Die Briensische Graffschafft In gemeiner Sprach COMTE de BRIE.
[C:] LE PAIS DE BRIE. — [T:] Guiljelmus Blaeu excudit. — L 388 × 499 mm.

[11] Belsia oder Beausse.
[C:] BELSIA, Vulgo LA BEAVSSE. — [T:] G. Blaeu excudit. — LMN 382 × 503 mm.

[12] GASTINOIS.
[C:] GASTINOIS ET SENONOIS. — [T:] Amsterdami Excud. Guiljelmus Blaeu. — O 380 × 498 mm.

[13] Schampanien.
[C:] CHAMPAGNE latine CAMPANIA, COMITATVS Amsterdami Apud Guiljelmum et Ioannem Blaeu. — P 383 × 500 mm.

[14] Das Rhemische Hertzogthumb / In gemeiner Sprach DVCHE' PAIRIE, vnd das Ertzbischthumb De Rheims.
[C:] DIOECESE de RHEIMS, et le païs de RETHEL. Par Iean Iubrien Chalonnois. — [T:] Amsterdami, Apud Guilj. et Joan. Blaeuw. — Ppppp 2   410 × 530 mm.

[15] Das Fürstenthumb SEDAN vnnd RAVCOVRT, sampt der Vogthey DONCHERI.
[C:] LES SOVVERAINETEZ DE SEDAN ET DE RAVCOVRT ET LA PREVOSTÉ DE DONCHERI. — [C:] AMSTERDAMI Apud Guiljelmum Blaeuw. ... — P 3 378 × 497 mm.

[16] Hertzogthumb Lothringen.
[T:] LOTHARINGIA DVCATVS; Vulgo LORRAINE. — [T:] Amsterdami Apud Guiljelmum Blaeuw. — Q 380 × 502 mm.

[17] Metz.
[C:] TERRITORIVM METENSE Auctore AB. FABERT Consule urbis Metensis. LE PAIS MESSIN. — [T:] Amsterdami Apud Guiljelmum et Johannem Blaeuw. — S 383 × 498 mm.

[18] CAROLOESIVM oder CHAROLOIS.
[C:] Les environs de L'ESTANG DE LONGPENDV Comprenant vne grande partie du COMTÉ de CHAROLOIS. Par Iean van Damme S.^{r} d'Amendale — T Verso blank.   377 × 499 mm.

[19] Grafschafft Burgund.
[C:] VTRIVSQVE BVRGVNDIÆ, tum Ducatus tum Comitatus, DESCRIPTIO. — [C:] ... Amsterdami Apud Guiljelmum Blaeu. — V 385 × 500 mm.

[20] Genffer See.
[C:] LACVS LEMANNI LOCORVMQVE CIRCVMIACENTIVM ACCVRATISSIMA DESCRIPTIO. Auctore IACOBO GOVLARTIO GENEVENSI. — [T:] Apud Guiljelmum Blaeu. — X 410 × 522 mm.

[21] BRESSIA Oder PAYS DE BRESSE.
[C:] BRESSIA Vulgo BRESSE — [T:] Amsterdami. Guiljelmus Blauw. excudit. — YX 379 × 498 mm.

[22] Das Fürstenthumb in gemeiner Sprach LA SOVVERAINETE DE DOMBES.
[C:] LA SOVVERAINETE DE DOMBES. — [T:] Apud Guiljelmum et Ioannem Blaeu. — Z 380 × 498 mm.

[23] Lion, Forest vnd Beaviolois.
[C:] LIONNOIS, FOREST, BEAVIOLOIS ET MASCONNOIS. — [T:] G. Blaeu excud. — Aa 379 × 501 mm.

[24] LEMOVICIVM. LIMANIA.
[a] [C:] LEMOVICVM, Auctore Jo. Faiano M.L. LYMOSIN. — 379 × 343 mm.
[b] [C:] TOPOGRAPHIA LIMANIÆ, Auctore Gabriele Simeoneo. — [C:] ... Amsterdami Excudebat Guiljelmus Blaeu. — 379 × 151 mm.
[The whole map:] Bb 379 × 503 mm.

[25] Hertzogthumb Nivers.
[C:] NIVERNIVM DVCATVS, Gallicè DVCHE DE NEVERS. — [C:] ... Amsterdami, Apud Guiljelmum et Iohannem Blaeu. — Dd Verso blank. 380 × 499 mm.

[26] Hertzogthumb Berry.
[C:] BITVRICVM DVCATVS. DVCHE DE BERRI. — [T:] Amsterdami Guiljelmus Blaeuw excudit. — Ee 380 × 499 mm.

[27] Grafschafften PERCHE vnd BLOIS.
[a] [C:] PERCHENSIS COMITATVS LA PERCHE COMTÉ — 385 × 227 mm.
[b] [C:] COMITATVS BLESENSIS, Auctore Ioanne Temporio. BLAISOIS. [T:] AMSTERDAMI Apud Guiljelmum Blaeuw. 385 × 258 mm.
[The whole map:] Ff 385 × 504 mm.

[28] Tours.
[C:] DVCATVS TVRONENSIS Perlustratus et descriptus ab ISAACO FRANCO, Ædili Regio, et in ea provincia viarum magistro. TOVRAINE. — [T:] Amsterdami, Apud Guiljelmum et Iohannem Blaeu. — Gg Hh 380 × 497 mm.

[29] Das Loudunenser Gebiet.
[a] [C:] LOVDONOIS. LAVDVNVM. — 380 × 340 mm.
[b] [C:] MIREBALAIS. — [C:] ... Amsterdami Apud Guiljelmum et Ioannem Blaeu — 379 × 158 mm.
[The whole map:] Hh 380 × 508 mm.

[30] Hertzogthumb Aniou.
[C:] DVCATVS ANDEGAVENSIS, Auctore Licimo Guÿeto Andegavense ANIOV. — [T:] Amsterdami Apud Guiljelmum Blaeuw. — Ii 378 × 497 mm.

[31] Grafschafft Mans.
[C:] CENOMANORVM Galliæ regionis typus: Vulgo LE MANS. Auct. Matheo Ogerio. — [T:] Apud Guiljemum Blaeu. — Kk Verso blank. 380 × 498 mm.

[32] Hertzogthumb Normandeyen.
[C:] NORMANDIA DVCATVS. — [T:] Excudit Guiljelmus Blaeu. — Ll Verso blank. 380 × 521 mm.

[33] Hertzogthumb Britannien.
[C:] BRITANNIA DVCATVS. Duché de Bretaigne. — [T:] Apud Guiljelmum Blaeu. — Mm 381 × 524 mm.

[34] Grafschafft Poictiers.
[C:] PICTAVIÆ DVCATVS DESCRIPTIO, Vulgo LE PAIS DE POICTOV. — [T:] Apud Guiljelmum Blaeu. — Nn 382 × 529 mm.

[35] Landschafft Santonien.
[C:] XAINTONGE et ANGOVMOIS. — [T:] Apud Guiljelmum Blaeu — Oo 392 × 504 mm.

[36] Insulæ S.Martini vnnd Vliarus, In gemeiner Sprach L'ISLE DE RE vnnd OLERON.
[C:] INSVLÆ DIVI MARTINI et VLIARVS, Vulgo L'ISLE DE RÉ et OLERON. — Pp 388 × 535 mm.

[37] Das Stifft SARLAT.
[C:] DIŒCESIS SARLATENSIS, Vernacule LE DIŒCESE DE SARLAT. IOANNES TARDO Canonicus Ecclesiæ Sarlati delineabat. — [T:] Amsterdami Apud Guiljelmum Blaeu. — Qq 378 × 495 mm.

[38] Bourdeaux.
[a] [C:] Carte du BOVRDELOIS, du pais de MEDOC, et de la prevosté de BORN. — 387 × 226 mm.
[b] [C:] PRINCIPATVS BENEARNIA. LA PRINCIPAVTE DE BEARN. — [T:] Guiljel. Blaeu exc. — 387 × 272 mm.
[The whole map:] Qq Rr 387 × 507 mm.

[39] Cadurch / In gemeiner Sprach QVERCY.
[C:] CADVRCIVM Vernaculé QVERCI. — [T:] Amsterdami Guiljelmus Janssonius, et Johannes Blaeuw Excudebant. — Rr 2 378 × 496 mm.

[40] Langedock.
[C:] LANGVEDOC — [T:] Amsterdami Guiljelmus Blaeuw excudit. — Ss 441 × 545 mm.

[41] Provintz.
[C:] PROVINCIA Auctore Petro Joanne Bompario. PROVENCE. — [T:] Amsterdami Apud Guiljelmum Iansonium et Johannem Blaeu. — Tt 385 × 537 mm.

[42] Fürstenthumb Oranien.
[C:] LA PRINCIPAVTE D'ORANGE et COMTAT de VENAISSIN Par Iaques de Chieze Orangeois. 1627. — [T:] Excudit Guiljelmus Ianssonius Cæsius. — [C:] A Treshaut et Puissant Seigneur FREDERIC HENRY Par la grace de Dieu, Prince d'Orange, Conte de Nassau, Catzenelbogē, Vianden, Dietz, Lingen, Meurs, Buren, Leerdam etc. IAQVES DE CHIEZE Orangeois D.D. — Vv 382 × 499 mm.

[43] Delphinat.
[C:] DELPHINATVS vulgo DAVPHINÉ Avec ses Confins des Pais et provinces voisines. Par Iean de Beins Geographe et Ingenieur du Roy. Apud Guiljelmum et Joannem Blaeum. — Xx 381 × 499 mm.

[44] Hertzogthumb Saphoyen.
[C:] SABAVDIA DVCATVS. SAVOYE — [T:] Amsterdami Apud Guiljelmum Blaeu. — Yy 380 × 499 mm.

[45] [C:] IMPERII CAROLI Magni et vicinarum regionum DESCRIPTIO. Dedicata et inscripta LVDOVICO, REGI, VICTORI, ET DEFENSORI ECCLESIÆ CHRISTI, ab Auctore Petro Bertio ejusdem Cosmographo. — Blank on the back. 643 × 982 mm.

[46] Franckreich so Strabo vnd andere alte Scribenten beschrieben.
[C:] TYPVS GALLIÆ VETERIS, Ex conatib[9] Geograph. ABRAH. ORTELII. Excudebat Guiljelmus Blaeu. — Bbb 393 × 504 mm.

[47] Franckreich so allein auss dem dem Iulio Cæsare gezogen.
[C:] GALLIA VETVS, Ad Iul Cæsaris Commentaria, ex Conatibus Geographicis Abrah Ortelii. — Fff 383 × 498 mm.

[48] Italia oder Welschland.
[C:] NOVA ITALIÆ DELINEATIO — A 378 × 498 mm.

[49] Fürstenthumb Piemont
[C:] PEDEMONTANA Regio cum GENVENSIVM territorio et MONTISFERRATI Marchionatu. — [T:] Amsterodami Guiljelmus Blaeuw Excudit. — C 382 × 498 mm.

[50] Hertzogthumb Montferrat.
[C:] MONTISFERRATI DVCATVS. — [C:] Doctrina et humanitate celebri Viro Domino Iacobo Backer, Vrbis Amstelodamensis Viro consulari dignissimo, in benevolentiæ testimonium dedicabat. Guiljelmus Blaeuw. Amstelodami, excudit Guiljelm. Blaeuw. — D 367 × 482 mm.

[51] Herrschafft Genua.
[C:] Genovesato SERENISSIMÆ REIPUBLICÆ GENUENSIS DUCATUS ET DOMINII. NOVA DESCRIPTIO. — [T:] Amstelodami apud Guiljelmum Blaeuw. — [T:] DGryp. Sculps. — E 370 × 493 mm.

[52] Hertzogthumb Meyland.
[C:] MEDIOLANVM Ducatus. — [T:] Amstelodami, Guiljelm. Blaeuw Excudit. — F 376 × 490 mm.

[53] Hertzogthumb Mantua.
[C:] MANTVA DVCATVS. — [C:] ... Amstelodami Guiljelm. Blaeuw Excudit. — G 350 × 473 mm.

[54] Fürstenthumb Trient.
[C:] TERRITORIO DI TRENTO. — [T:] AMSTERDAMI Apud Guiljelmum Blaeuw. — H 370 × 483 mm.

[55] Herrschafft Venedig.
[C:] DOMINIO VENETO NELL'ITALIA. — I 380 × 497 mm.

[56] Königreich Neopolis.
[C:] REGNO DI NAPOLI — L 380 × 498 mm.

[57] Das Bäbstliche Gebiet.
[C:] STATO DELLA CHIESA, CON LA TOSCANA. — [C:] ... Guiljelmus Blaeu excudit. — M 382 × 500 mm.

[58] Konigreich Sicilien.
[C:] SICILIA REGNVM. — [T:] Apud Guiljelmus Blaeu. — M2 378 × 496 mm.

[59] SARDINIA. — On N 177 × 240 mm.

[60] CORSICA. — On O 177 × 240 mm.

[61] Hispania.
[C:] REGNORVM HISPANIÆ nova descriptio. — [T:] Amstelodami Apud Guiljelmum Blaeuw. — A 377 × 495 mm.

[62] Königreich CATALONIA.
[C:] CATALONIA — [T:] Guiljelmus Blaeu excud. Amstelodami. — C 380 × 497 mm.

[63] Königreich Valentz.
[C:] VALENTIA REGNVM; Contestani, Ptol. Edentani, Plin. — [T:] AMSTERDAMI Apud Guiljelmum Blaeuw. — E 380 × 499 mm.

[64] Königreich ARAGON.
[C:] ARAGONIA ET NAVARRA. — FG 381 × 499 mm.

[65] BISCAIA vnd GVIPVSCOA.
[C:] BISCAIA ET GVIPVSCOA CANTABRIÆ VETERIS PARS. — H 381 × 500 mm.

[66] Königreich LEGIO Vnd das Fürstenthumb ASTVRIAS.
[C:] LEGIONIS REGNVM et ASTVRIARVM PRINCIPATVS. — I 380 × 498 mm.

[67] Königreich GALLICIA.
[C:] GALLÆCIA, REGNVM, descripta a F. Fer. Ojea Ord.Præd. et postmodum multis in locis emendata et aucta. — [T:] Apud Guilj Blaeu. — K 380 × 498 mm.

[68] Portugal vnd Algarbia.
[C:] PORTVGALLIA et ALGARBIA quæ olim LVSITANIA. Auctore Vernando Alvero Secco. — [T:] Amsterdami Apud Guiljelmum et Joannem Blaeuw. — L 383 × 499 mm.

[69] Alt vnd new Castilien.
[C:] VTRIVSQVE CASTILIÆ nova descriptio. — M 409 × 501 mm.

[70] Granaten.
[C:] GRANATA, ET MVRCIA REGNA. — N 376 × 498 mm.

[71] Die Insulen BALEARIDES vnnd PITIVSÆ.
[C:] INSVLÆ BALEARIDES et PYTIVSÆ. — Nn 2 378 × 496 mm.

[72] ANDALVZIA.
[C:] ANDALVZIA continens SEVILLAM et CORDVBAM. — O 378 × 499 mm.

[73] Indien gegen Orient.
[C:] INDIA quæ ORIENTALIS dicitur, ET INSVLÆ ADIACENTES. — [C:] Nob.^{mo} Fort.^{mo}q3 Viro et Heroi D. LAVRENTIO REAL Equiti, Indiæ Orient.ol.Gubernatori Supremo, nup. Thalassiarchæ classis Britannici Vicario, et nomine Ord.Belgicæ Fœd.ad Regem Daniæ Legato, Vrbis Amstelodamens. Senatori et Scabino, nec non Concilii Societatis Indicæ Orientalis Assessori, vario literarum ac doctrinæ genere claro, Tabulam hanc D.D. Guiljelmus Blaeu. — N 410 × 504 mm.

[74] Die Inseln Moluccæ.
[C:] MOLVCCÆ INSVLÆ CELEBERRIMÆ — [T:] AMSTELODAMI, Guiljelmus Blaeuw excudit. — O 371 × 487 mm.
[Inset:] [T:] BACHIAN I. — 84 × 86 mm.

[75] Das Chinesische Reich.
[C:] CHINA Veteribus SINARVM REGIO nunc Incolis TAME dicta. — [C:] Nobiliss.^{mo} Ampliss.^{mo} Spectatiss.^{mo}q3 Viro D. THEODORO BAS Equiti, Reip. Amstelodamensis Consuli ac Senatori, ad Suecorum Regem et Moschorum Ducem nuper Legato; Societatis quoq3 Indicæ quæ ad Orientem mercatur et militat assessori, Tab. hanc D.D. Guiljelmus et Johannes Blaeu. — R 409 × 497 mm.

[76] Tartarien.
[C:] TARTARIA sive MAGNI CHAMI IMPERIVM — T 379 × 498 mm.

[77] Persien.
[C:] PERSIA Sive SOPHORVM REGNVM — [C:] Ampliss.^{mo} Prudentiss^{q3} Viro D. THEODORO THOLING, Reip.Amstelod.Senatori et Gollegii Scabinorum Præsidi, nec non in Consessu Societatis Indicæ Orientalis adsessori, Tabulam hanc D.D. Guiljelmus Blaeu. 1634. — V 377 × 497 mm.

[78] Das Türckische Reich.
[C:] TVRCICVM IMPERIVM — [C:] Magnifico Prudent.^{mo} Spectat.^{mo}q3 Viro DAVIDI DE WILHEM I.V.L. Curiæ Brabanticæ Senatori, et Ill.^{mi} Arausionensiü Principis Consiliario, viro Orientalium linguarum peritissimo, studiorumq3 quotquot sunt, elegantiorum fautori serio, Tabulam hanc D.D.D. Guiljelmus et Iohannes Blaeu. — X 408 × 520 mm.

[79] Das Gelobte Land.
[C:] TERRA SANCTA quae in Sacris Terra Promissionis olim PALESTINA Amstelodami Ex officina Guiljelmi Blaeuw 1629 — Z 379 × 497 mm.

[80] Natolien oder Klein Asien.
[C:] NATOLIA, quæ olim ASIA MINOR. — Aa 379 × 496 mm.

[81] Die Insel CYPRVS.
[C:] CYPRVS INSVLA. — B6 380 × 506 mm.

[82] Das Königreich der Abissiner.
[C:] ÆTHIOPIA SVPERIOR vel INTERIOR; vulgo ABISSINORVM sive PRESBITERI IOANNIS IMPERIVM. — Cc 382 × 497 mm.

[83] Nieder-Morenlandt.
[C:] ÆTHIOPIA INFERIOR, vel EXTERIOR. Partes magis Septentrionales, quæ hic desiderantur, vide in tabula Æthiopiæ Superioris. — Dd 378 × 497 mm.

[84] GVINEA.
[C:] GVINEA — [C:] Ampliss.^{mo} Doctiss.^{mo}q3 Viro D. NICOLAO TVLP, Medicinæ Doctori Reip. Amsterdamensis Senatori et Scabino, Medico et Anatomico celeberrimo, Tab. hanc D.D. Guiljelmus Blaeu. — Ff 383 × 527 mm.

[85] Das Maurotanische Königreich.
[C:] FEZZÆ ET MAROCCHI REGNA AFRICÆ CELEBERRIMA, describebat Abrah: Ortelius. — Gg 382 × 500 mm.

[86] Bermudes.
[C:] Mappa ÆSTIVARVM Insularum, alias BARMVDAS dictarum, ... accurate descripta. — [C:] ... Amstelodami, Guiljelm. Blaeuw excudit. — A 400 × 533 mm.

[87] New Belgica vnnd New Anglia.
[C:] NOVA BELGICA ET ANGLIA NOVA — A 2 385 × 502 mm.

[88] Landschafft Virginia.
[C:] NOVA VIRGINIÆ TABVLA — [C:] ... Ex officina Guiljelmi Blaeuw. DGrijp, Sculpt. — B 373 × 479 mm.

[89] Süder Virginia / Florida / Honduras / Yucatan / vnd die Inseln vor America gelegen.
[C:] INSVLÆ AMERICANÆ IN OCEANO

SEPTENTRIONALI, cum Terris adiacentibus. — [C:] Ampl.^{mo} Prud.^{mo} Doct.^{moq3} Viro D.ALBERTO CONRADI VANDER BVRCH, I.C. Reip. Amsterdamensis Senatori, Collegii Scabinorum Præsidi, Societatis Indicæ, quæ ad Occidentem militat, asessori, et nuper ad Magnum Moscoviæ Ducem Legato, Tabulam hanc inscribit Guiljelmus Blaeu. — C 377 × 523 mm.

[90] TERRA FIRMA, NEVVA GRANADA, POPAYAN, &c.
[C:] TERRA FIRMA et NOVUM REGNUM GRANATENSE et POPAYAN — [T:] Amstelodami Guiljelmus Blaeuw excudit — D 374 × 488 mm.

[91] VENEZVELA.
[C:] VENEZVELA, cum parte Australi NOVÆ ANDALVSIÆ. — [C:] ... AMSTELODAMI, Guiljelmus Blaeuw excudit. — E 372 × 485 mm.

[92] GVYANA.
[C:] GVIANA siue AMAZONVM REGIO — [C:] AMSTELODAMI Guiljelmus Blaeuw excudit. — F 370 × 492 mm.

[93] Landschafft Brasilien.
[C:] NOVUS BRASILIÆ TYPVS — [T:] Amstelodami Guiljelmus Blaeuw excudit. — G 375 × 494 mm.
[Inset:] [T:] Baya de todos os Sanctos — 67 × 104 mm.

[94] Die Provintz von RIO DE LA PLATA. Mit den beyliggenden Länden.
[C:] PARAGVAY, Ó PROV. DE RIO DE LA PLATA cum regionibus adiacentibus TVCVMAN et S.^{TA} CRVZ DE LA SIERRA. — [C:] AMSTELODAMI, Guiljelmus Blaeuw excudit. — H 372 × 478 mm.

[95] FRETVM MAGELLANICVM.
[C:] FRETI MAGELLANICI ac novi FRETI vulgó LE MAIRE exactissima delineatio. — [T:] Guiljelmus Blaeuw excudit. — [T:] DGrijp Sculp. — I 372 × 491 mm.

[96] CHILI.
[C:] CHILI — [C:] AMSTELODAMI Guiljelmus Blaeuw excudit. — K 353 × 478 mm.

[97] Königreich Peru.
[C:] PERV ... — [T:] Amstelodami, Guiljelmus Blaeuw excudit. — L 375 × 490 mm.

[98] New Hispanien.
[C:] NOVA HISPANIA, ET NOVA GALICIA. — [C:] ... Guiljelmus Blaeuw excudit. — M 381 × 496 mm.

Notes: All the maps have text on the verso except [32] and the large map, [45], "Imperii Caroli Magni," which are blank on the back. All are uncoloured. One map is wanting: Co Bourbon. Some of the leaves have letters differing from those indicated in the Register:

[9] ...Francia...	H I K	in the Register K
[11] Belsia oder Beausse	L M N	M N
[14] Das Rhemische Hertzogthumb/	Ppppp 2	P 2
[21] BRESSIA...	Y X	Y
[28] Tours	Gg Hh	Gg
[38] Bourdeaux	Qq Rr	Rr
[39] ... QVERCY	Rr 2	Rr 3
[71] ... BALEARIDES	Nn 2	N 2
[73] Indien gegen Orient	N	P
[74] Die Inseln Moluccæ	O	Q
[88] Landschafft Virginia	B	B 2

Map [46], "Typus Galliæ Veteris", is signed Bbb both on the map itself and in the Register, Koeman gives no sign for it. Map [56], Regno di Napoli, bears 12 coats-of-arms, 6 down each side. The title is printed on a separate slip of paper and pasted in the proper place on the engraved title-page. The atlas is bound in half vellum.

Lit.: Koeman vol. 1, p.99—101, Bl 8A, LC List vol. 3, p. 130, nr 3420, Tiele p. 34, nr 129.

19 BLAEU, WILLEM JANSZOON AND JOAN 1645

Vol. II
LE THEATRE DV MONDE, ou NOVVEL ATLAS, Mis en lumiere par GVILLAVME & IEAN BLAEV. LA SECONDE PARTIE DE LA SECONDE A AMSTERDAM, Chez IEAN BLAEV. M D C XLV. 49,5 cm.

[1] DESCRIPTION DE L'ESPAGNE.
[C:] REGNORVM HISPANIÆ nova descriptio. — Espagne. A = 1635:II:[61].

[2] CATALOGNE.
[C:] CATALONIA — Espagne. C = 1635:II:[62].

[3] DESCRIPTION DV ROYAVME DE VALENCE.
[C:] VALENTIA REGNVM; ... — Espagne. D = 1635:II:[63].

[4] LE ROYAVME DE NAVARRE.
[C:] ARAGONIA ET NAVARRA. — Espagne. E2 = 1635:II:[64].

[5] ROYAVME D'ARAGON.
[C:] ... ARRAGONIA REGNVM. Auctore Joanne Baptista Labanna. — [C:] Amplissimo et Nobili Viro GASPARI CHARLES Sacri Romani Imperij Equiti aurato, Domino de Baerledoncq, cohortis liberæ Duci reformato, et Reg: Majestatis Catholicæ generali aggerum præfecto. Guilj: et Iohannes Blaeu. — ESPAGNE. Bb 413 × 516 mm.

[6] ROYAVME DE NAVARRE.
[C:] NAVARRA REGNVM. — [T:] G. Blaeu exc. — ESPAGNE. Aa 414 × 500 mm.

[7] BISCAYE, ET GVIPVSCOE.
[C:] BISCAIA ET GVIPVSCOA CANTABRIÆ VETERIS PARS. — Espagne. F = 1635:II:[65].

[8] LEON & ASTVRIE.
[C:] LEGIONIS REGNVM et ASTVRIARVM PRINCIPATVS. — Espagne, G = 1635:II:[66].

[9] LA GALLICE.
[C:] GALLÆCIA, REGNVM, ... — Espagne. H = 1635:II:[67].

[10] DESCRIPTION DES ROYAVMES DE PORTVGAL, ET D'ALGARBE.
[C:] PORTVGALLIA et ALGARBIA quæ olim LVSITANIA. ... — Espagne. I = 1635:II:[68].

[11] DESCRIPTION de l'ancienne & nouvelle CASTILLE.
[C:] VTRIVSQVE CASTILIÆ nova descriptio. — K2 = 1635:II:[69].

[12] GRENADE ET MVRCIE.
[C:] GRANATA, ET MVRCIA REGNA. — Espagne. L = 1635:II:[70].

[13] LES ISLES BALEARES, & PITIVSES.
[C:] INSVLÆ BALEARIDES et PYTIVSÆ. — Espagne. M = 1635:II:[71].

[14] DESCRIPTION DE L'ANDALOVSIE, comprenant les Royaumes DE SEVILLE ET DE CORDOVE.
[C:] ANDALVZIA continens SEVILLAM et CORDVBAM. — Espagne. N = 1635:II:[72].

[15] DESCRIPTION DE L'ASIE.
[C:] ASIA ... — Asie. A = 1635:I:[1].

[16] LES INDES.
[C:] INDIA quæ ORIENTALIS dicitur, ET INSVLÆ ADIACENTES. — B = 1635:II:[73].

[17] GRAND MOGOL.
[C:] MAGNI MOGOLIS IMPERIVM — [C:] Nob.^{mo} Spectat.^{moq3} viro D. IOHANNI HVYDEKOPER, Equiti, Domino in Thamen, Blocland, etc. Vrbis Amsterdamensis Senatori et Scabino, nec non Concilii Societatis Indicæ Assessori, Tabulam hanc D.D. Joh: et Corn. Blaeu. — Asie. Cc 415 × 518 mm.

[18] LES ISLES MOLVQVES.
[C:] MOLVCCÆ INSVLÆ CELEBERRIMÆ — D = 1635:II:[74].

[19] CHINE & IAPON.
[C:] CHINA ... — E = 1635:II:[75].

[20] TARTARIE.
[C:] TARTARIA sive MAGNI CHAMI IMPERIVM — G Qp = 1635:II:[76].

[21] PERSE.
[C:] PERSIA Sive SOPHORVM REGNVM — H = 1635:II:[77].

[22] L'EMPIRE DV TVRC.
[C:] TVRCICVM IMPERIVM — K = 1635:II:[78].

[23] CYPRE.
[C:] CYPRVS INSVLA. — Asie L = 1635:II:[81].

[24] LA NATOLIE. OV ASIE MINEVR.
 [C:] NATOLIA, quæ olim ASIA MINOR. — M = 1635:II:[80].
[25] LA PALESTINE.
 [C:] TERRA SANCTA ... — L'Asie. LN = 1635:II:[79].
[26] L'AFRIQVE.
 [C:] AFRICÆ nova descriptio. Auct: Guiljelmo Blaeuw. — L'Afrique. A 409 × 553 mm.
 [Insets:] [T:] TANGER — (Plan). [T:] CEVTA — (View). [T:] ALGER — (Plan). [T:] TVNIS — (Plan). [T:] ALEXANDRIA — (Plan). [T:] ALCAIR — (Plan). [T:] MOZAMBIQVE — (Plan). [T:] S.GEORGIVS della MINA — (View). [T:] CANARIA — (View). All 9 oval 41 × 58 mm.
[27] LE ROYAVME de MAROQVE.
 [C:] FEZZÆ ET MAROCCHI REGNA AFRICÆ CELEBERRIMA, ... — Afrique. C = 1635:II:[85].
[28] LA GVINEE.
 [C:] GVINEA — E = 1635:II:[84].
[29] LE ROYAVME DES ABISSINS.
 [C:] ÆTHIOPIA SVPERIOR vel INTERIOR; ... — F = 1635:II:[82].
[30] L'ETHIOPIE INFERIEVRE.
 [C:] ÆTHIOPIA INFERIOR, vel EXTERIOR. ... Afrique. G = 1635:II:[83].
[31] L'AMERIQVE.
 [C:] AMERICÆ nova Tabula. Auct: Guiljelmo Blaeuw. — L'Amerique. A 409 × 553 mm.
 [Insets:] [C:] Septentrionalissimas Americæ partes, Groenlandiam puta, Islandiâ et adjacentes, quod Americæ tabulæ commodè comprehendi non potuerint, peculiari hac tabella Spectatoribus exhibendas duximus. — 70 × 76 mm. [T:] HAVANA Portus — (View). [T:] St DOMINGO. — (Plan). [T:] CARTAGENA — (Plan). [T:] MEXICO — (Plan). [T:] CUSCO — (Plan). [T:] POTOSI — (View). [T:] I. LA MOCHA in Chili. — (View). [T:] RIO IANEIRO. — (View). [T:] OLINDA in Pharnambucco — (View). 9 oval 41 × 58 mm.
[32] LA NOVVELLE BELGIQVE, & la Nouvelle ANGLETERRE.
 [C:] NOVA BELGICA ET ANGLIA NOVA — C = 1635:II:[87].
[33] ISLES D'AMERIQVE.
 [C:] INSVLÆ AMERICANÆ IN OCEANO SEPTENTRIONALI, ... — Amerique. E = 1635:II:[89].
[34] L'ISLE DE BARMVDAS, avec ses voysines.
 [C:] Mappa ÆSTIVARVM Insularum, ... — G = 1635:II:[86].
[35] LA VERGINIE.
 [C:] NOVA VIRGINIÆ TABVLA — Amerique. I = 1635:II:[88].
[36] FLORIDE.
 [C:] VIRGINIÆ partis australis, et FLORIDÆ partis orientalis, interjacentiumq$_3$ regionum NOVA DESCRIPTIO. — AMERIQVE. Ee 385 × 501 mm.
[37] LA NOVVELLE ESPAGNE.
 [C:] NOVA HISPANIA ET NOVA GALICIA. — K = 1635:II:[98].
[38] DE LA TERRE FERME, & du nouveau Royaume de GRANADE, & de POPAYAN.
 [C:] TERRA FIRMA... — L = 1635:II:[90].
[39] VENEZVELA, &c.
 [C:] VENEZVELA, ... — N = 1635:II:[91].
[40] LA GVIANE, Ou pays DES AMAZONES.
 [C:] GVIANA siue AMAZONVM REGIO — O = 1635:II:[92].
[41] DESCRIPTION DE BRASIL PRISE DE MAFFÉE.
 [C:] NOVUS BRASILIÆ TYPVS — Q = 1635:II:[93].
[42] LE PARAGVAY, Ou la Province DV RIO DE LA PLATA, Avec les contrées voysines de Tucuman, & de S.Croix de la Serre.
 [C:] PARAGVAY, ... — R = 1635:II:[94].
[43] LE DESTROICT DE MAGELLANES, & celuy DE LE MAIRE.
 [C:] TABVLA MAGELLANICA, quâ Tierræ del fuego, cum celeberrimis fretis a F. Magellano et I. Le Maire detectis novissima et accuratissima descriptio exhibetur. — [T:] NOBILI, ET MAGNIFICO VIRO, D. CONSTANTINO HVGENIO EQVITI, DOMINO IN ZVYLICHEM, ET ILLVSTRISSIMO PRINCIPI AVRAICO À SECRETIS. Hanc exactissimam Terræ Magellanicæ descriptionem dedicat Guiljelmus Blaeuw. — S 412 × 536 mm.
[44] CHILI.
 [C:] CHILI — T = 1635:II:[96].
[45] LE PERV.
 [C:] PERV ... — V = 1635:II:[97].

Notes: All the maps have text on the verso. The frontiers and coastlines on the maps are coloured; the engraved title-page is uncoloured. The letterpress title is printed on slips pasted in the proper space of the title-page. Over the words 'La seconde partie de la seconde' is pasted another slip, bearing the works 'QUATRIEME PARTIE' written in old ink. In the same hand, in the empty space beneath, is written 'ESPAGNE. ASIE AFRIQVE AMERIQVE'. This copy corresponds to Koeman's Bl 17, La seconde partie de la Seconde, but the imprint is that of Bl 18 C. This French edition contains the maps of Africa and America which are wanting in our German edition of 1635. The map of Asia is the same as the one in the first volume of the German edition, but the map of the Strait of Magellan is different. Four of the maps were not published in the German edition: [5] ROYAVME D'ARAGON, [6] ROYAVME DE NAVARRE, [17] GRAND MOGOL, and [36] FLORIDE. The leaves are numbered in old ink from 1 to 63. The index is from another copy, cut into four and pasted in two columns on one of the blank leaves at the end of the volume, the numbers being written in old ink. The volume is bound in soft vellum, with linen ties. On the inside of the back cover Nordenskiöld has written in ink: 'Viktiga kartor öfver Asien. Am. kartan 61. Eldslandet. Merk. proj. Kartan 22 Mercators proj. Merklig karta öfver öarna i s. ö. Asien'. [Important maps of Asia. Am. map 61. Tierra del Fuego. Strange proj. Map 22 Mercator's proj. Strange map of the islands in South East Asia.] Nordenskiöld's signature is on the first blank leaf, with the year 1896.

Lit.: Koeman vol. 1, p. 120—121, Bl 17, p. 124, Bl 18 C, Tiele p. 134—135, nr 131, p. 135, nr 132.

20 BLAEU, WILLEM JANSZOON AND JOAN   1647—1649

Vol. I.
[NOVVS ATLAS, Das ist Welt-beschreibung Mit schönen newen aussführlichen Land-Taffeln in Kupffer gestochen vnd an den Tag gegeben Durch GVIL. vnd IOHANNEM BLAEV. Amsterdami, Apud Iohannem Guiljelmi F. Blaeu. Anno MDCXLVIIII.]
52.3 cm.

[1] Die Länder vnter POLVS ARCTICVS.
 [C:] REGIONES SVB POLO ARCTICO. Auctore Guiljelmo Blaeu. — [T:] Amplissimo Spectatissimo Prudentiss^{93} Viro GVILIELMO BACKER DE CORNELIIS, Reip. Amstelodamensis Consuli et Senatori, nec non in Consessu Societatis Indicæ Orientalis Assessori Tabulam hanc D:D. Joh: Blaeu. — 2 B 409 × 529 mm.
[2] Das Bischoffthumb STAVANGRIA, vnd dero angräntzende Oerther.
 [C:] DIŒCESIS STAVANGRIENSIS, & partes aliquot vicinæ, operâ L. SCAVENII, S.S. — Apud. Joh. et Cornel. Blaeu. — 6 F 412 × 498 mm.
[3] Dennemarck.
 [C:] DANIA REGNVM — 7 G 423 × 523 mm.
[4] FIONIA, sampt jhren vmbligenden Inseln.
 [C:] FIONIA vulgo FVNEN — 8 H 378 × 498 mm.
[5] Vplandt.
 [C:] DVCATVS VPLANDIA. Joh. et Cornelius Blaeu exc. — [C:] Amplissimo, Sagacissimoq$_3$ Viro, D. MICHAELI LE BLON, Serenissimæ M.^{tis} et Coronæ Sueciæ ad pariter

Sereniss.^{m} Magnæ Britanniæ Regem à mandatis, Tabulam hanc D.D.D. Joh. et Cornelius Blaeu. — 12 M   378 × 496 mm.
[6]   Liefflandt.
      [C:] LIVONIA, Vulgo Lyefland. — 13 N   383 × 498 mm.
[7]   Moscaw.
      [C:] TABVLA RVSSIÆ ... — O   = 1635:I:[9].
[8]   MOSCAW gegen Mitternacht vnd Osten.
      [C:] RVSSIÆ, vulgo MOSCOVIA dictæ, Partes Septentrionalis et Orientalis. Auctore Isaaco Massa. — [T:] Apud Ioannem et Cornelium Blaeu. — 15 P   417 × 539 mm.
[9]   Moscaw gegen Mittag.
      [C:] RVSSIÆ, vulgo MOSCOVIA, Pars Australis. Auctore Jsaaco Massa. — [T:] Apud Johan. et Cornelium Blaeu. — 17 R   386 × 530 mm.
[10] CRIMEA, Oder Die Przecopenser Tartarey / Vnd der Peninsel bey den Alten Taurica Chersonesus genant.
      [C:] TAVRICA CHERSONESVS, ... — 18 Asia. S = 1635:I:[10].
[11] [C:] MAGNI DVCATVS LITHVANIAE, CAETERARVMQVE REGIONVM ILLI ADIACENTIVM EXACTA DESCRIPTIO Jllss.$^{mi.}$ ac Excellss.$^{mi.}$ Prĩcipis et Dñi. D. Nicolai Christophori Radziwil. D.G.Olijcæ ac in Nieswies Ducis, S.Rom.Imperii Principis in Szylowiec ac Mir Comitis et S.Sepulchri Hierosolimitani Militis &c. Opera cura et impensis facta ac in lucem edita — [C:] ... Amsterodami Excudebat Guilhelmus Janssonius sub signo Solarij deaurati. Anno 1613. — [T:] Sculptum apud Hesselum Gerardum. — Blank on the back.   745 × 715 mm.
[12] Das Hertzogthumb Litthaw / Samogeten / schwartz Reussen vnd Volhinia.
      [C:] Lectori S. Hunc Borysthenis tractum ... — 19 T = 1635:I:[8].
[13] Das Königreich Polen.
      [C:] POLONIA Regnum, et SILESIA Ducatus. — 20 V = 1635:I:[16].
[14] Preussen.
      [C:] PRVSSIA ACCVRATE DESCRIPTA a Gasparo Henneberg Erlichensi. — [T:] Excud: Guiljelmus Janss: Cæsius. — 21 X   381 × 499 mm. See 1635:I:[17].
[15] Teutschlandt.
      [T:] NOVA TOTIVS GERMANIÆ DESCRIPTIO. — A = 1635:I:[18].
[16] Pommern.
      [C:] POMERANIÆ DVCATVS TABVLA. ... — 4 Teutschlandt. C = 1635:I:[19].
[17] Die Insel Rügen.
      [C:] RVGIA INSVLA ... — 5 Teutschlandt. D = 1635:I:[20].
[18] Das Hertzogthumb Meckelnburg.
      [C:] MEKLENBVRG DVCATVS. ... — 6 Teutschlandt. E = 1635:I:[21].
[19] Die Marck Brandenburg.
      [C:] BRANDEBVRGVM MARCHIONATVS, ... — 7 Teutschlandt. F = 1635:I:[22].
[20] Das Ertzbischthumb Magdenburg / sampt den dabey gelegenen orthen.
      [C:] ARCHIEPISCOPATVS MAGHDEBVRGENSIS, ET ANHALTINVS DVCATVS; Cum terris adjacentibus. — 8 Teutschlandt. G = 1635:I:[23], but a new text in the cartouche.
[21] Das Fürstenthumb Braunschweig.
      [C:] DVCATVS BRVNSVICENSIS fereq$_3$ LVNÆ BVRGENSIS, Cum adjacentibus Episcopatibus, Comit. Domin. etc. DESCRIPTIO GEOGRAPHICA, per annos aliquot concinnata, et Rev.^{mis} Ill.^{mis} ac Cels.^{mis} Principib. ac Ducib. Brunsvic. et Luneburg. dicata ab observatore et Elaboratore Casparo Dauthendeij Architecto et Mathematico Guelphico. ... — 17 (pro 9)   409 × 523 mm.
[22] Das Bischthumb Hildesheim.
      [C:] EPISCOPATVS HILDESIENSIS ... — 10 I = 1635:I:[24].
[23] Das Hertzogthumb Lüneburg.
      [C:] DVCATVS LVNEBVRGENSIS ... — 11 Teutschlandt. K = 1635:I:[25].
[24] Die Hertzogthumben Schlesswick vnd Holstein.
      [C:] DVCATVS HOLSATIÆ NOVA TABVLA — 12 Teutschlandt. L = 1635:I:[26].
[25] Beschreibung des Elbstroms.
      [C:] CELEBERRIMI FLVVII ALBIS nova delineatio ... — 13 Tutschlandt. M = 1635:I:[27].
[26] Der Westphalische Kreyss.
      [C:] CIRCVLVS WESTPHALICVS, Sive GERMANIÆ INFERIORIS. — 14 Teutschlandt. N   410 × 532 mm. [Inset:] [T:] Harborg Hamborg — Semicirle map with 75 mm diam.
[27] Die Grafschafft Oldenburg.
      [C:] OLDENBVRG COMITATVS — 15 Teutschlandt. O = 1635:I:[28].
[28] Ost-Friesslandt.
      [C:] TYPVS FRISIÆ ORIENTALIS. ... — 16 Teutschlandt. P = 1635:I:[29].
[29] Das Bischthumb Münster.
      [C:] MONASTERIENSIS Episcopatus. ... — 17 Tutschlandt. Q = 1635:I:[30].
[30] Die Graffschafften BENTHEM vnd STEINFVRT.
      [C:] COMITATVS BENTHEIM, et STEINFVRT. ... — 18 Teutschlandt. R   Verso blank. = 1635:I:[31].
[31] Das Bischthumb Paderborn.
      [C:] PADERBORNENSIS Episcopatus ... — 20 Teutschlandt. T = 1635:I:[33].
[32] Das Hertzogthumb Westphalen.
      [C:] WESTPHALIA Ducatus ... — 21 Teutschlandt. V = 1635:I:[34].
[33] Die Grafschaft Waldeck.
      [C:] WALDECK COMITATVS. — 22 Teutschlandt. X = 1635:I:[35].
[34] Das Hertzogthumb Franckenlandt.
      [C:] FRANCONIA Vulgo Franckenlandt. — 23 Teutschlandt. Y = 1635:I:[36].
[35] Beschreibung bon dem Stifft HIRSCHFELT.
      [C:] TERRITORIVM ABBATIÆ HERESFELDENSIS. ... — Verso blank. = 1635:I:[38].
[36] Landgrafschafft Hessen.
      [C:] HASSIA Landgraviatus. —Zz   447 × 560 mm.
[37] Die Landtgrafschafft Thüringen.
      [C:] THVRINGIA LANDGRAVIATVS ... — 27 Teutschlandt. Cc = 1635:I:[39].
[38] Die Grafschafft Manssfeldt.
      [C:] MANSFELDIA COMITATVS ... — 28 Teutschlandt. Dd = 1635:I:[40].
[39] Ober Sachsen.
      [C:] SAXONIA SVPERIOR, CVM LVSATIA ET MISNIA. — 29 Teutschlandt. Ee = 1635:I:[41].
[40] Die Obere Laussnitz.
      [C:] LVSATIA SVPERIOR. Authore Barthol:Sculteto Gorlitio. — 31 Teutschlandt. Ff   408 × 521 mm.
[41] Das Königreich vnd Chur Böhmen.
      [C:] BOHEMIA — 32 Teutschlandt. Gg = 1635:I:[42].
[42] Schlesien Sampt dessen zugehörigen Hertzogthumben.
      [C:] SILESIA DVCATVS ... — 33 Teutschlandt. Hh = 1635:I:[43].
[43] Nieder-Schlesien.
      [C:] SILESIA INFERIOR, Sereniss. ac Celsiss. Principibus ac Dominis Dn. GEORGIO, Dn. LVDOVICO, Dn. CHRISTIANO, Fratribus, Ducibus Silesiæ Ligniciens. ac Bergensibus, Dominis gratiosissimis Dicata à Jona Sculteto Sprotta-Silesio. — [T:] Joh: et Corn: Blaeu Excud. — 35 Teutschlandt. Kk   415 × 515 mm.
[44] Das Fürstenthumb Glogaw.
      [C:] DVCATVS SILESIÆ GLOGANI Vera Delineatio Secundâ curâ ac labore confecta A Iona Sculteto Sprotta Silesio. — 36 Teutschlandt. Ll   414 × 504 mm.
[45] Die Grafschafft Glatz.
      [C:] COMITATVS GLATZ Authore Jona Sculteto. — 37 Teutschlandt. Mm   Verso blank.   414 × 500 mm.
[46] Die Marckgrafschafft Mähren.
      [C:] MORAVIA MARCHIONATVS ... — 39 Teutschlandt. Nn = 1635:I:[44].

[47] [C:] DANVBIVS, FLUVIUS EUROPÆ MAXIMUS, A FONTIBVS AD OSTIA, Cum omnibus Fluminibus, ab utroque latere, in illum defluentibus. — Blank on the back. 411 × 960 mm.

[48] Das Königreich Vngern.
[C:] HVNGARIA REGNVM. — 40 Teutschlandt. Pp = 1635:I:[15].

[49] Siebenbürgen.
[C:] TRANSYLVANIA Sibenburgen. ... — 41 Teutschlandt. Rr = 1635:I:[11].

[50] Carniola oder Crain.
[C:] KARSTIA, CARNIOLA, HISTRIA et WINDORVM MARCHIA. ... — 42 Teutschlandt. Ss = 1635:I:[14].

[51] Wallachia / Servia / Bulgaria vnd Romania.
[C:] WALACHIA SERVIA, BVLGARIA, ROMANIA. — 43 Teutschlandt. Tt = 1635:I:[12].

[52] Sclavonia / Croatia / Bossnia / vnd ein theil von Dalmatien.
[C:] SCLAVONIA, CROATIA, BOSNIA cum DALMATIÆ PARTE. ... — 41 Teutschlandt. Vu = 1635:I:[13].

[53] Steyermarck.
[C:] STIRIA Steyrmarck. — 45 Teutschlandt. Xx = 1635:I:[46].

[54] Das Ertzhertzogthumb Oesterreich.
[C:] AVSTRIA ARCHIDVCATVS ... — 46 Teutschlandt. Yy = 1635:I:[45].

[55] Das Bischthumb Saltzburg.
[C:] SALTZBVRG ARCHIEPISCOPATVS, et CARINTHIA DVCATVS. ... — 47 Teutschlandt. Zz = 1635:I:[47].

[56] Das Hertzogthumb Beyern.
[C:] BAVARIA DVCATVS, ... — 48 Teutschlandt. Aaa = 1635:I:[48].

[57] Ober Pfaltz oder Ober Beyern.
[C:] PALATINATVS BAVARIÆ. — 49 Teutschlandt. Bbb = 1635:I:[49].

[58] Das Nürenberger Gebiet.
[C:] TERRITORIVM NORIMBERGENSE. — 50 Teutschlandt. Ccc = 1635:I:[50].

[59] Das Hertzogthumb Würtenberg.
[C:] WIRTENBERG DVCATVS. — 51 Teutschlandt. Ddd = 1635:I:[51].

[60] Schwabenlandt.
[C:] SVEVIÆ NOVA TABVLA. — 52 Teutschlandt. Eee = 1635:I:[52].

[61] Alemannia oder Ober Schwaben.
[C:] ALEMANNIA SIVE SVEVIA SVPERIOR ... — 53 Teutschlandt. Fff = 1635:I:[53].

[62] [C:] RHENVS Fluviorum Europæ celeberrimus, cum MOSA, MOSELLA, et reliquis, in illum se exonerantibus, fluminibus. — [C:] Amplissimo Spectatissimo, Prudentiss^{q}3. Viro D. ANDREÆ BICKERO I.V.D. Reip. Amstelodamensis Consuli et Senatori, nuper ad Poloniæ et Sueciæ Reges secundum Legato Tab. hanc D.D.D. Guiljelmus Blaeu. — Blank on the back. 413 × 958 mm.

[63] Schweitzerlandt.
[C:] HELVETIA, cum finitimis regionibus confœderatis. — 55 Teutschlandt. Hhh = 1635:I:[56].

[64] Grawpünten.
[C:] Alpinæ seu Fœderatæ RHAETIAE SUBDITARUMQUE ei Terrarum nova descriptio. — 56 Teutschlandt. Iii = 1635:I:[57].

[65] Wifflisburgergow.
[C:] DAS WIFLISPVRGERGOW. ... 57 Teutschlandt. Kkk = 1635:I:[58].

[66] Argow.
[C:] ARGOW cum parte merid. ZVRICHGOW. — 58 Teutschlandt. Lll = 1635:I:[59].

[67] Zürichow.
[C:] ZVRICHGOW et Basiliensis provincia — 59 Teutschlandt. Mmm = 1635:I:[60].

[68] Elsass.
[C:] ALSATIA Landgraviatus, cum SVNTGOIA et BRISGOIA ... — 60 Teutschlandt. Nnn = 1635:I:[61].

[69] Pfaltz am Rhein.
[C:] PALATINATVS AD RHENVM — 63 Teutschlandt. Ppp = 1635:I:[62].

[70] Die Grafschafft Erpach.
[C:] ERPACH COMITATVS. — 64 Teutschlandt. Qqq = 1635:I:[63].

[71] Die Grafschafft Nassaw.
[C:] NASSOVIA Comitatus. — 65 Teutschlandt. Rrr = 1635:I:[64].

[72] ErtzBischthumb Cölln.
[C:] COLONIENSIS Archiepiscopatus ... — Sss = 1635:I:[65].

[73] Das Hertzogthumb Gülich.
[C:] IVLIACENSIS ET MONTENSIS DVCATVS. ... — 67 Teutschlandt. Ttt = 1635:I:[67].

[74] Die Graffschafft Marck vnnd Ravensberg.
[C:] COMITATVS MARCHIA ET RAVENSBERG. — Teutschlandt. = 1635:I:[68].

[75] Das Hertzogthumb Cleve.
[C:] CLIVIA DVCATVS ET RAVESTEIN DOMINIVM. — Teutschlandt. = 1635:I:[69].

[76] Das Ertzbischthumb Trier.
[C:] ARCHIEPISCOPATVS TREVIRENSIS — [T:] Joh. et Cornelius Blaeu exc. — 19 Teutschlandt. Yyy 411 × 497 mm.

[77] Alt Teutschlandt.
[C:] GERMANIAE VETERIS typus. — 71 Teutschlandt. Zzz = 1635:I:[70].

NOVVS ATLAS, Das ist/ Welt-beschreibung / Mit schönen newen aussführlichen Land-Taffeln in Kupffer gestochen / vnd an den Tag gegeben Durch GVIL. vnd IOHANNEM BLAEV. Ersten Theils Ander Stuck. Zu Amsterdam / Bey IOHANNEM BLAEV. M D C XLVII

[78] Niderlandt.
[C:] NOVUS XVII INFERIORIS GERMANIÆ PROVINCIARUM TYPUS de integro multis in locis emendatus à Guliel. Blaeu. ... — [C:] Ghedruckt t'Amsterdam, bÿ Willem Blaeu op't Water inde vergulde Zonnewyser. — I Niderlandt. A = 1635:I:[71], but in the cartouches Blaeu instead of Ianssonio and Janszoon.

[79] Das Hertzogthumb Brabant.
[C:] BRABANTIA DVCATVS. — 6 Niderlandt. D = 1635:I:[84].

[80] Das erste theil von Brabant / dessen Hauptstadt ist Löven.
[C:] PRIMA PARS BRABANTIÆ cuius caput LOVANIVM ... — 8 Niderlandt. F = 1635:I:[86], but 9 of the 10 coats-of-arms in the cartouche filled up.

[81] Das ander theil von Brabant / dessen Hauptstadt ist Brüssel.
[C:] SECVNDA PARS BRABANTIÆ ... — 10 Niderlandt. G = 1635:I:[87], but all three coats-of-arms in the cartouche filled up.

[82] Der dritte theil von Brabant / dessen erste Stadt ist Antorff / ein Marckgrafschafft des Röm. Reichs.
[C:] TERTIA PARS BRABANTIÆ ... — 11 Niderlandt. H = 1635:I:[88].

[83] Bergen op-Soom / Steinbergen / sampt andern allda gemachten Wercken.
[C:] TABVLA Bergarum ad Zoman Stenbergæ et novorum ibi operum. ... — 13 Niderlandt. I = 1635:I:[90].

[84] Das Castel bey Santfliet.
[C:] TABVLA Castelli ad Sandflitam, ... — 14 Niderlandt. K = 1635:I:[89].

[85] Hertzogenbusch.
[C:] QVARTA PARS BRABANTIÆ ... — 15 I = 1635:I:[85], but the empty columns on the left and right filled up with 3 coats-of-arms each.

[86] Das Hertzogthumb Limburg.
[C:] DVCATVS LIMBVRGVM ... — 16 Niderlandt. M = 1635:I:[91].

[87] Das Hertzogthumb Lützelburg.
[C:] LVTZENBVRG DVCATVS — 17 Niederlandt. N = 1635:I:[94], but the cartouche is a new one.

[88] Das Lütticher Gebiet.
[C:] LEODIENSIS DIOECESIS. — 18 Niederlandt O = 1635:I:[93], but the coat-of-arms in the cartouche filled up.

[89] Die Grafschafft Namen.

[C:] NAMVRCVM COMITATVS Auctore Iohann. Surhonio. — [T:] Apud Guiljelmum et Johannem Blaeu. — 19 Niederlandt. P = 1635:I:[95].

[90] Die Grafschafft Hennegaw.
[C:] COMITATVVM HANNONIÆ ET NAMVRCI DESCRIPTIO. — 20 Niederlandt. Q = 1635:I:[96].

[91] Die Grafschafft ARTESIA.
[C:] ARTESIA, COMITATVS. ... 21 Niderlandt. R = 1635:I:[103].

[92] Die Grafschafft Flandern.
[C:] FLANDRIA ET ZEELANDIA COMITATVS. ... — 22 Niderlandt S = 1635:I:[97].

[93] Das Orientalische Theil Flammisch Flandern.
[C:] FLANDRIÆ TEVTONICÆ PARS ORIENTALIOR — 23 Niderland. = 1635:I:[100].

[94] Das Occidentalische Theil Teutsch Flandern.
[C:] PARS FLANDRIÆ TEVTONICÆ OCCIDENTALIOR. — 25 Niederlandt. X = 1635:I:[98].

[95] Duynkirchen.
[C:] Afbeeldinge vande vermaerde seehaven ende stadt van Duynkercken ... — 26 Niederlandt. Y = 1635:I:[99].

[96] Welsch Flandern / In gemeiner Sprach FLANDRE WALLONNE.
[C:] GALLOFLANDRIA. ... — 27 Niederlandt. Z = 1635:I:[101].

[97] Reichs: vnd eigen Flandern.
[C:] FLANDRIÆ Partes duæ, ... 28 Niederlandt. Aa = 1635:I:[102].

[98] Die Herrschafft Mecheln.
[C:] MECHLINIA DOMINIVM et AERSCHOT DVCATVS ... 29 Niederlandt. Bb = 1635:I:[92].

[99] Das Hertzogthumb Geldern / vnd die Grafschafft Sütphen.
[C:] GELDRIA DVCATVS et ZVTFANIA COMITATVS. — 30 Niederlandt. Cc = 1635:I:[73].

[100] Die Grafschafft ZVTPHEN.
[C:] ZVTPHANIA COMITATVS. ... — On 31 Nierderlandt. Dd = 1635:I:[74].

[101] Alt BATAVIA, Oder Ein theil des Rheins sampt der gantzen Maass.
[C:] Tractus RHENI et MOSÆ totusq$_3$ VAHALIS ... — 32 Niederlandt. Ee = 1635:I:[83].

[102] Der Graben S. MARIÆ, Sonsten FOSSA EVGENIANA, welcher zwischen dem Rhein vnd der Maass aussgeführet / im Jahr 1628.
[C:] FOSSA SANCTÆ MARIÆ, quæ et EVGENIANA dicitur Vulgo De Nieuwe Grift. — [C:] FOSSA hæc a Rheno ad Mosam duci cœpta est Anno M DC XXVII. Auspiciis Serenissimæ Principis ISABELLÆ, CLARÆ, EVGENIÆ, Hispaniarum Infantis Belgicæ Gubernatricis. Excudit Guilj. Janssonius Blaeu. — 33 Niederlandt. Ff = 1635:I:[72], but with more text in the cartouche and a new cartouche and coats-of arms added on the map.

[103] Die Grafschafft Hollandt.
[C:] HOLLANDIA COMITATVS. — 34 Niederlandt. Gg = 1635:I:[77].

[104] Nord-Hollandt Oder West Friesslandt.
[C:] HOLLANDIÆ PARS SEPTENTRIONALIS, ... — 35 Niederlandt. Hh = 1635:I:[78], with small alterations.

[105] Rheinlandt.
[C:] RHENOLANDIÆ et AMSTELLANDIÆ exactissima Tabula. — 36 Niederlandt. Ii = 1635:I:[79].

[106] Delfflandt / Schielandt / vnd die beyligende Inseln.
[C:] DELFLANDIA, SCHIELANDIA, ... — 38 Niederlandt. Ll = 1635:I:[80].

[107] Hollandt so gegen Mittag ligt / in gemein Zuydt-Hollandt.
[C:] ZVYDHOLLANDIA stricte sumta. — Niederlandt. = 1635:I:[81].

[108] Die Grafschafft Seelandt.
[C:] ZEELANDIA Comitatus. — 40 Niederlandt. Nn = 1635:I:[104].

[109] Das Stifft Vtrecht.
[C:] VLTRAIECTVM DOMINIVM ... — 41 Niederlandt Qq = 1635:I:[82].

[110] Westfriesslandt.
[C:] FRISIA OCCIDENTALIS ... — 42 Niederlandt. Pp = 1635:I:[76].

[111] Das Gröninger Landt.
[C:] GRONINGA DOMINIVM. ... — 43 Niederlandt. Qq = 1635:I:[75].

[112] TRANSISALANIA, auff Teutsch Ober-Yssel.
[C:] TRANSISELANIA DOMINIVM vernaculè OVER-YSSEL. — [C:] Nobiliss. Ampliss. Consultissimoq$_3$ viro, D.BARTOLDO WICHERINGE Toparchæ in Noorthorm, nuper in senatu Ordinum fœderati Belgij assessori prudent.^{mo} nunc verò alternis patriæ reip. in urbe Groninga Consuli, ac cameræ provincialis iudicij Hovetmanno grav.^{mo} ut et societat. Indicæ ad Occidentem pariter negotiant. atq$_3$ militantis curatori spectat.^{mo} Joh. et Corn. Blaeu. — 21 Niederlandt. Rr 412 × 519 mm.

[113] Die Grafschafft Drent / Vnd Herrschafft Westerwoldt.
[C:] DRENTIA COMITATVS. Transiselaniæ Tabula II. Auctore Cornelio Pynacker I.C. — 23 Niederlandt. Tt 378 × 526 mm.

Notes: The maps have text on the verso, except where otherwise specified. All the maps and the title-page of the second part are coloured. The printed title is pasted in the proper space. In our copy the title-page of the first part and seven maps are wanting: 1 A Die gantze Welt, 31 C Europa, 4 D Eyszlandt, 9 Europa I Das Königreich Schweden, 10 K Gothlandt, 19 Teutschl. S Das Bischthumb Osnabrück, 20 Teutschl. Z Das Gebiet der Stadt Franckfurth am Mayn. Maps [11] and [12] are parts of a foru-sheet map first published in Blaeu's Appendix Theatri A. Ortelii et Atlantis G. Mercatoris 1631, which is not in this collection. Map [12] was published earlier in the 1635 edition of the Novus Atlas. Each of the two maps is composed of two sheets of the original four. One part of map [12] is pasted on the verso of leaf 19 T; map [11] is bound between map [10] and p.19. Map [68], Alsatia, is also made up of two parts, so folded that the central part is pasted to leaf 60. In some cases the numbering of the leaves is not consistent with the numbering of the Register:

		In the Register
[21] Braunschweig.	17, altered to 9 in old ink.	9
	Koeman gives the same misprint.	
[35] Hirschfelt.	Unnumbered.	25
[36] Hessen.	Unnumbered; Zz Bb written in, in old ink.	26
[47] Donowstrom.	Blank on the back. The following text leaf unnumbered.	40
[52] Sclavonia etc.	41.	44
[72] Cölln.	Unnumbered. 66 added in pencil.	66
	Koeman has 'Kölln.'.	
[74] Marck vnnd Ravensberg.	Unnumbered.	68
[75] Cleve.	Unnumbered.	69
[76] Trier.	19.	70
[107] Hollandt gegen Mittag.	Unnumbered!	39
[112] Transiselania.	21.	44
[113] Drent.	23.	46

The atlas is bound in old vellum with gold tooling, but it is in bad repair. On the inside of the front cover is written in old ink: 'Till Georg Isaac Londicer, såsom Hugkomst af dess Morfar Isaac Berg.' [To Georg Isaac Londicer, as a memento of his grandfather, I.B.]

Lit.: Koeman vol. 1, p. 153—156, Bl 33, Tiele p. 35, nr 132.

21 BLAEU, WILLEM JANSZOON AND JOAN   1647

Vol III

NOVVS ATLAS, Das ist / Welt-beschreibung / Mit schönen newen ausszführlichen Land-Taffeln in Kupffer gestochen / vnd an den Tag gegeben Durch GVIL. vnd IOHANNEM BLAEV. Drittes Theil. Zu Amsterdam / Bey IOHANNEM BLAEV. M D C XLVII   51 cm.

[1] ITALIA.
[C:] NOVA ITALIÆ DELINEATIO — 1 Italia. A = 1635:II:[48].

[2] PIEMONT.
[C:] PIEMONTE ET MONFERRATO — Piemont. I 418 × 521 mm.

[3] PIEMONT.
[C:] STATO DEL PIEMONTE — 17 Italia. K 386 × 500 mm.
[4] Die Herrschafft VERCEIL.
[C:] SIGNORIA di VERCELLI — 20 Italia. M 411 × 498 mm.
[5] Das Hertzogthumb MONTFERRAT.
[C:] MONTISFERRATI DVCATVS. — 21 Italia. N = 1635:II:[50].
[6] LIGVRIA, Oder Dar Staat Genua.
[C:] LIGVRIA, ò Stato della Republica di GENOVA. — [C:] Ampl.^{mo} Spect.^{mo} gravissimoq$_3$ viro D.PETRO HASSELAER, Emporij Amstelodamensis Consulj ac Senatorj dignissimo, maris Septentrionalis Directorj vigilantissimo, viro avitis virtutibus, fide in patriam, humanitate in cives, claro celebriq$_3$, Tabulam hanc D.D.D. Guiljelmus Blaeu — 22 Italia. Q 377 × 524 mm.
[7] Der Staat Genua am Westen.
[C:] RIVIERA DI GENOVA DA PONENTE — 23 Italien. P 380 × 498 mm.
[8] Der Staat Genua am Osten.
[C:] RIVIERA DI GENOVA DI LEVANTE — 24 Italia. Q 384 × 495 mm.
[9] Die Insel CORSICA. On 25 Italia. R = 1635:II:[60].
[10] Der Staat von MEYLAND.
[C:] STATO DI MILANO — 26 Italia. S 408 × 525 mm.
[11] Meyland gegen Mitternacht.
[C:] PARTE ALPESTRE DELLO STATO DI MILANO, Con il LAGO MAGGIORE DI LUGANO, È DI COMO — 28 Italia. V 378 × 504 mm.
[12] Das Hertzogthumb MEYLAND.
[C:] DVCATO ouero TERRITORIO DI MILANO — 29 Italia. X 379 × 505 mm.
[13] Das Theyl MEYLAND Gegen Mittag.
[C:] TERRITORIO DI PAVIA, LODI, NOVARRA, TORTONA, ALESSANDRIA et altri vicini dello Stato di Milano. — 30 Italia. Y 378 × 498 mm.
[14] CREMONA.
[C:] TERRITORIO DI CREMONA. — 32 Italia. Aa 378 × 503 mm.
[15] Das Hertzogthumb MANTVA.
[C:] DVCATO DI MANTOVA — 33 Italia. Bb 378 × 497 mm.
[16] Das Hertzogthumb MVTINA Vnd RHEGIVM, Sampt den benachbarten Herrschafften.
[C:] DVCATO DI MODENA REGIO ET CARPI, Col Dominio della Carfagnana. — [T:] Apud Guiljelmum et Joannem Blaeu. — 34 Italia. Cc 397 × 463 mm.
[17] Das Hertzogthumb PARMA Vnd PLACENTIA.
[C:] DVCATO di PARMA et di PIACENZA — 35 Italien. Dd 379 × 499 mm.
[18] Die Herrschafft Venedig in Italien.
[C:] DOMINIO VENETO NELL' ITALIA. — 36 Italia. Ee = 1635:II:[55].
[19] Der Bergomensische Landkreyss / welchen sie nennen IL BERGAMASCO.
[C:] TERRITORIO DI BERGAMO — 42 Italia. Ii 378 × 497 mm.
[20] Die Brixiensische Landtschafft / welche sie nennen IL BRESCIANO.
[C:] TERRITORIO di BRESCIA et di CREMA — [T:] Apud Guiljelmum et Joannem Blaeu. — 43 Italia. Kk 378 × 498 mm.
[21] Das Cremensische Gebieth / Sonsten IL CREMASCO.
[C:] TERRITORIO CREMASCO. — 44 Italia. Ll 379 × 238 mm.
[22] Der Veronische Landtkreyss / Sonsten IL VERONESE.
[C:] TERRITORIO DI VERONA. — 45 Italia. Mm 380 × 500 mm.
[23] Das Vicenzische Gebiet.
[C:] TERRITORIO DI VICENZA — 47 Italia. Oo 414 × 498 mm.
[24] Das Paduanische Gebieth.
[C:] TERRITORIO PADOVANO — [C:] Ampliss.^{mo} Prudent.^{mo} Doctissimoq$_3$ viro D. ROBERTO VANDER HOVVE, Medico apud Amstelodamenses celeberrimo hanc tabulam D.D.D. Joh. et Cornelius Blaeu. — 49 Italia. Qq 382 × 505 mm.
[25] Das Hertzogthumb Venedig. [On verso:] Das Rhodiginische Gebieth.
[C:] POLESINO DI ROVIGO — 53 Italia. Tt 382 × 501 mm.
[26] Die Marck TREVISE.
[C:] TERRITORIO TREVIGIANO — 54 Italia. Vu 382 × 500 mm.
[27] Beschreibung Des Belluensisch: vnd Feltrinischen Bischoffthumbs.
[C:] IL BELLVNESE Con il FELTRINO — 55 Italia. Xx 381 × 499 mm.
[28] IL CADORINO.
[C:] IL CADORINO — 56 Italia. Yy 379 × 499 mm.
[29] FORVM- IVLIVM, Auff Italianisch FRIVLI.
[C:] Patria del FRIVLI olim FORVM IVLII — 57 Italia. Zz 408 × 500 mm.
[30] ISTRIA.
[C:] ISTRIA olim IAPIDIA — 58 Italia. Aaa 379 × 499 mm.
[31] Das Fürstenthumb Trient.
[C:] TERRITORIO DI TRENTO — [T:] Excudebat Guiljelmum Blaeu. — 59 Italia. Bbb 380 × 501 mm.
[32] Der Kirchen Herrschafft.
[C:] STATO DELLA CHIESA, CON LA TOSCANA — 60 Italia. Ccc = 1635:II:[57].
[33] Das Hertzogthumb FERRARA.
[C:] DVCATO DI FERRARA — [C:] Al Molto Ill.^{re} Sig.^{r} et Pron̄ nostro oss.^{mo} il Sig.^{re} ANDREA BRVGIOTTI Computista delle Spoglie di S.S.VRBANO VIII. et Stampatore della Camera Apostolica. in memoria de beneficii riceuti. Joh: et Corn̄. Blaeu. — 62 Italia. Eee 379 × 499 mm.
[34] Die Bononiensische Landtschafft.
[C:] TERRITORIO DI BOLOGNA — 63 Italia. Fff 440 × 540 mm.
[35] ROMANVLA, Vorzeiten FLAMINIA.
[C:] ROMAGNA olim FLAMINIA — 64 Italia. Ggg 379 × 498 mm.
[36] Das Hertzogthumb VRBINVM.
[C:] DVCATO DI VRBINO — 68 Italia. Iij.Kkk 380 × 502 mm.
[37] Die Anconitanische Marck / Vorzeiten genant PICENVM.
[C:] MARCA D'ANCONA olim PICENVM — 70 Italia. Mmm 416 × 507 mm.
[38] Die Perusinische Landtschafft.
[C:] TERRITORIO PERVGINO — 72 Italia. Ooo 378 × 497 mm.
[39] Die Orivetanische Landtschafft / genant Il ORVIETANO.
[C:] TERRITORIO DI ORVIETO — 73 Italia. Ppp 378 × 498 mm.
[40] VMBRIA, Oder Das Spoletanische Hertzogthumb.
[C:] VMBRIA OVERO DVCATO DI SPOLETO. — [C:] All.$^!$ Eminent.^{mo} et Reverend.^{mo} Principe FRANCESCO CARDINALE BARBERINO Vicecancellario e Nipote della S.S.Vrbano VIII. Gioanni et Cornelio Blaeu — 74 Italia. Qqq 380 × 500 mm.
[41] SABINA, Des H.Petri Patrimonium / Vnd Der Römische Landtkreyss/ vorzeiten LATIVM genant.
[C:] CAMPAGNA DI ROMA, olim Latium: PATRIMONIO DI S.PIETRO; et SABINA. — [C:] All.$^!$ Illustr.^{mo} et Rev.^{mo} mio Sig.^{r} et Pron̄e Col.^{mo} il Sig.^{r} CASSIANO DEL POZZO Cav.^{re} di S.Stefano in testimonio di debita osservanza. Cornelio di Guglielmo Blaeu. — 77 Italia. Sss 382 × 500 mm.
[42] ETRVRIA, Jetzo genant TOSCANA.
[C:] DOMINIO FIORENTINO. — [C:] Magnifico, prud.^{mo} fortissimoq$_3$ viro D. THEODORO HASSELAER, militiæ urbanæ Præfecto, Societatis Indiæ Orientalis Directorj sagacissimo, proavorum suisq$_3$, in patriam et urbem hanc meritis insignj, hanc Tabulam prono cultu animoq$_3$ D.D.D. Johan. et Corn. Blaeuw. — 88 Italia. Aaaa 380 × 499 mm.
[43] Das Senensische Gebieth.

[C:] TERRITORIO DI SIENA et DVCATO di CASTRO — 94 Italia. Eeee 378 × 497 mm.
- [44] ILVA, Heutiges Tags ELBA.
[C:] ELBA ISOLA olim ILVA. — On 97 Italia. Gggg 198 × 257 mm.
- [45] RESPVBLICA LVCENSIS.
[C:] STATO DELLA REPVBLICA DI LVCCA — [C:] Ampl.mo Prudent.moq3 Viro D.ALLARDO CLOECQ I.C. Senatori et Scabino Reipub. Amsterdamensis, nec non delectui militum ejusdem urbis præfecto, Tabulam hanc D.D. Guilj: et Joh: Blaeu. — 98 Italia. Hhhh 378 × 499 mm.
- [46] Das Königreich NEAPOLIS.
[C:] REGNO DI NAPOLI — 100 Italia. Kkkk = 1635:II:[56].
- [47] APRVTIVM, Sonsten genant ABRVZZO; Da die Sammtes wohnen.
[C:] ABRVZZO CITRA, ET VLTRA. — 105 Italia. Oooo 378 × 498 mm.
- [48] CAMPANIA FELIX, Jetzo genant TERRA DI LAVORO.
[C:] TERRA DI LAVORO, olim CAMPANIA FELIX — 108 Italia. Qqqq 378 × 500 mm.
- [49] Die Grafschafft MOLISO, Sampt PRINCIPATO VLTRA.
[C:] CONTADO DI MOLISE et PRINCIPATO VLTRA — 119 Italia. Yyyy — 379 mm.
- [50] CAPITANATA, Vor zeiten genant APVLIA DAVNIA.
[C:] CAPITANATA, olim MESAPIÆ et IAPYGIÆ PARS. Apud Guiljelmum Blaeu. — 120 Italia. Zzzz 379 × 499 mm.
- [51] PRINCIPATVS CITERIOR, Vor zeiten genant PICENTIA.
[C:] PRINCIPATO CITRA olim PICENTIA. — 121 Italia. Aaaaa 379 × 499 mm.
- [52] Das Landt BARI, Verzeiten genandt APVLIA PEVCETIA.
[C:] TERRA DI BARI ET BASILICATA — 123 Italia. Ccccc 378 × 498 mm.
- [53] HYDRVNTVM, Sonsten TERRA D'OTRANTO.
[C:] Terra di OTRANTO olim SALENTINA et IAPIGIA — [C:] Ill.mo ac Rev.mo Domino D. FABIO CHISIO Episc. Neritonensi, S.mi D.P.P. INNOCENTII X, ad tractum Rheni et Infer. Germ. partes, Ordinario, nec non, ad tractatus generalis pacis Monasterii, extraordinario, cum potestate de latere Legati, Nuncio, Patrono suo colendiss.mo D.D.D. Joh: Blaeu. — 124 Italia Ddddd 379 × 499 mm.
- [54] CALABRIA, Sonsten Gross Griechenlandt.
[C:] CALABRIA CITRA olim Magna Græcia. — 127 Italia. Fffff 380 × 498 mm.
- [55] CALABRIA.
[C:] CALABRIA VLTRA olim Altera Magnæ Græciæ pars. — 128 Italia. Ggggg 379 × 499 mm.
- [56] Die Insel ISCHIA.
[C:] ISCHIA Isola, olim ÆNARIA — [C:] ... Iulius Iasolinus describ. — [T:] Joh. et Cornelius Blaeu exc. — 131 Italia. Iiiii 374 × 492 mm.
- [57] Die Insel SARDINIA.
[T:] SARDINIA INSVLA — On p. 132 Italia. Kkkkk = 1635:II:[59].
- [58] Das Königreich Sicilien.
[C:] SICILIA REGNVM. — 132 Italia Lllll = 1635:II:[58].
- [59] Griechenlandt.
[C:] GRÆCIA. Joh. et Corn. Blaeu exc. — [C:] Illustri, & incomparab. viro CLAVDIO SALMASIO, Equiti, et Comiti Consistoriano, Tabulam hanc D.D.D. Joh. et Cornelius Blaeu. — I Gæcia. A 407 × 522 mm.
- [60] Macedonien / EPIRVS vnd ACHAIA.
[C:] MACEDONIA, EPIRVS ET ACHAIA. G.Blaeu exc. — 4 Græcia. C 407 × 497 mm.
- [61] MOREA, Sonsten PELOPONNESVS.
[C:] MOREA olim PELOPONNESVS. Guilj. Blaeu exc. — 6 Græcia. E 408 × 497 mm.
- [62] CANDIE.
[C:] CANDIA, olim CRETA. — 8 Gæcia. G 379 × 526 mm.

Notes: All the maps have text on the verso, and are beautifully coloured. The title is printed on a separate slip and pasted in the proper place on the engraved title-page. This copy is identical to Koeman's B1 41 A, wanting the supplement 'England' as in B1 41 B. The only difference between this copy and the two Koeman describes is in the title of map [23]; ours reads 'Das Vicenzische Gebiet' where Koeman has 'Das Virenzische Gebiet'. The atlas is bound in old vellum with gold tooling. On the inside of the front cover is written: 'Till Georg Isaac Londicer År 1818. Såsom Hugkomst af dess Morfar Isaac Berg.' [To G.I.L. as a memento of his grandfather I.B.]

Lit.: Koeman vol. 1, p. 171—172, B1 41 A, B1 41 B, Tiele p. 35, nr. 132.

22 BLAEU, JOAN 1654

Vol. V
NOVVS ATLAS, Das ist Weld-beschreibung / Mit schönen newen aussführlichen Land-Taffeln in Kupffer gestochen / Vnd an den Tag gegeben Durch JOAN BLAEU. Funfter Theil. AMSTELÆDAMI Apud IOANNEM BLAEV M DC LIV
51,6 cm.

- [1] ROBERT. GORDONIVS Bericht von der Insel THULE.
[C:] INSVLÆ A'LBION et HIBERNIA cum minoribus adjacentibus — 9 Schotland. C 380 × 444 mm.
- [2] ROBERTVS GORDONIVS Auff die Tafel des Alten SCHOTTLANDES Anmerckungen.
[C:] SCOTIA ANTIQVA, qualis priscis temporibus, Romanis præsertim, cognita fuit quam in lucem eruere conabatur R. Gordonius a Straloch M DC LIII. — [Divided into two parts]. 11 Schottland. D 418 × 543 mm.
- [3] SCHOTTLAND.
[a] [C:] SCOTIA REGNVM cum insulis adjacentibus. Robertus Gordonius a Straloch descripsit. — 418 × 356 mm.
[b] [C:] ORCADES et SHETLANDICÆ INSVLÆ ... — [C:] Exc.mo Emin.mo et vere Nobil.mo viro IACOBO DVCI HAMILTONII, et Castri Heraldi, Marchioni Cliddis-daliæ, Comiti Araniæ, et Cantabrigiæ, Vicecomiti Lanarci, Baroni Evenæ, Arbroth et Inner-daliæ, Magistro equorum serenissimi Magnæ Britanniæ Regis, eiq3 a camera cubili generoso, et a secretioribus consiliis Honoris regii de Hampton-court Seneschallo, nobilissimi ordinis Periscelidis Equiti liberalium artum et amœniorum ingeniorum summo fautori Robertus Gordonius a Straloch grati animi et debitæ observantiæ Symbolum L.M.D.C.Q. — 418 × 184 mm. [The whole map:] 17 Schottland. F 418 × 541 mm.
- [4] GADENI, oder LADENI. TEVIOTIA, sonst TEIFIDALE.
[C:] TEVIOTIA Vulgo TIVEDAIL — [T:] Auct. Tim. Pont. Io. Blaeu Excudit — 41 Schottland. N Verso blank. 424 × 530 mm.
- [5] Beschreibung TWEEDAIL, Vnd der Landschafft PEBLIS.
[C:] TVEDIA cum vicecomitatu Etterico Forestæ. etiam Selkirkæ dictus. TWEEDAIL with the Sherifdome of Etterik-Forrest called also Selkirk. — [T:] Auct. Timotheo Pont. — 43 Schottland. O 420 × 504 mm.
- [6] LAVDERDALIA.
[C:] LAVDELIA Sive LAVDERDALIA Scotis vulgo LAVDERDAIL. — [T:] Auct. Tim.Pont. — [C:] Ill. ac Nob.mo Dnō. D. IOANNI, Comiti Lauderdalliæ, Maitlandiæ Vicecomiti, Domino Thirlestainæ et Boltone, Tab. hanc D.D. J. Blaeu — 45 Schottland. P Verso blank. 390 × 505 mm.
- [7] MARCIA, oder MERCH.
[C:] MERCIA Vulgo VICECOMITATVS BERVICENSIS Auct Timothei Pont. — [C:] THE MERCE or Shirrefdome of BERWICK — 47 Schottland. Q 380 × 494 mm.
- [8] LAVDEN, oder LOTHIEN.
[C:] LOTHIAN and LINLITQVO — [T:] Joh. et Cornelius Blaeu exc. — [C:] Illustrissimo ac Nobilissimo D. GVILIELMO Lothianæ Comiti, Domino Kerr de Neubattle et Sedburg; Consilario Regio, et Scotici exercitus in Hibernia Præfecto, etc. Tabulam hanc D.D.D. J.B. — 49 Schottland. R 378 × 546 mm.
- [9] SELGOVÆ. LIDESDALE.

[C:] LIDALIA vel LIDISDALIA REGIO, LIDISDAIL. Auct. Timotheo Pont. — 55 Schottland. T 407 × 517 mm.

[10] EVIA vnd ESCIA, sonst EVSDAIL vnd ESKDAIL.
[C:] EVIA et ESCIA, Scotis EVSDAIL et ESKDAIL. — [T:] Auct. Tim. Pont. I. Blaeu Excud. — [C:] Illustrissimo Nobilissimo D. FRANCISCO, COMITI DE BACKLEVGH, DOMINO SCOTT DE WICHESTER et DALKIETH, etc. Tab. hanc D.D. J. Blaeu. — 57 Schottland. V 418 × 522 mm.

[11] Beschreibung der Vice-Graffschafft DRUMFREYS. ANNANDIA, sonst ANNANDAIL.
[C:] ANNANDIÆ Præfectura, Vulgo THE STEWARTRIE of ANNANDAIL. — [T:] Auct. Timotheo Pont. Excud. Io. Blaeu. — 59 Schottland. 418 × 504 mm.

[12] NITHIA, sonst NIDISDAIL. Auss dem Camdeno hie her genommen.
[C:] NITHIA VICECOMITATVS. The Shirifdome of NIDIS-DAIL. Auctore Timotheo Pont. — [C:] Nobilissimo Domino D. ARCHIBALDO, NATV MAXIMO MARCHIONIS DVGLASSIÆ, ANGVSIÆ COMITI, REGI à CONSIL. SECRETIS. — 61 Schottland. Y 386 × 531 mm.

[13] NOVANTES. GALLOVIDIA, sonst GALLOWAY. Auss der Beschreibung Camdeni.
[C:] GALLOVIDIA vernacule GALLOWAY Auct. Timoth: Pont. — [C:] Nobilissimo Domino D. ALEXANDRO, GALLOVIDIÆ COMITI, Domino GAIRLIS, etc. Consilario Regis, Tab. hanc D.D. I. Blaeu. — 63 Schottland. Z 415 × 525 mm.

[14] Beschreibung von GALLOWAY, durch IOAN MACLELLAN.
[C:] GALLOVIDIÆ Pars Occidentalior, in qua VICECOMITATVS VICTONIENSIS cum Regalitate Glenlucensi. — [T:] The Sherifdome of Wigtoun w^t the Regalitie of Glen-Luze both in Galloway. Auct. Timoth. Pont. — 65 Schottland. Aa 412 × 523 mm.

[15] GALLOWAY.
[C:] GALLOVIDIÆ PARS MEDIA, quæ Deam et Cream fluvios interjacet. The Middle-part of Galloway, whiche lyeth betweene the rivers Dee and Cree. — [T:] Auct. Tim. Pont. — 67 Schottland. Bb Verso blank. 423 × 542 mm.

[16] [C:] PRÆFECTVRA KIRCVBRIENSIS, quæ Gallovidiæ maxime orientalis pars est. The Steuartrie of Kircubright, The most easterlie part of Galloway. — [T:] Auct. Tim. Pont. — [An empty cartouche]. Blank on the back. 420 × 537 mm.

[17] CARRICK.
[C:] CARRICTA MERIDIONALIS. The South part of CARRICK. — [T:] Auct. Tim. Pont. — 69 Schottland. Cc Verso blank. 382 × 522 mm.

[18] [C:] CARICTA BOREALIS Vulgo The northpart of CARRICK. — [T:] Opus Timothei Pont. — Blank on the back. 419 × 524 mm.

[19] KOILA, oder KYLE.
[C:] COILA PROVINCIA. THE PROVINCE OF KYLE. Auct. Timoth: Pont. — [C:] Nobilissimo et ornatissimo Iuveni IACOBO, FRENDERETTI VICECOMITI, Crichtonii Domino, etc. matheseos, amœniorumq$_3$ studiorum summo fautori, tabulam hanc a Timotheo Pont quondam descriptam, a se vero nunc locupletatam in amicitiæ Symbolum R. Gordonius D.D. — 71 Schottland. Dd 450 × 566 mm.

[20] CVNNINGHAM. Auss dem CAMDENO.
[C:] CVNINGHAMIA. Ex schedis TIMOTHEO PONT. — [T:] Ioannes Blaeu excudebat — [C:] Illust.^{mo} ac Nob.^{mo} Domino, D ALEXANDRO, COMITI DE EGLINTOVN, Domino de Montgomerie et Kilwÿnning, Baroni Ardrossani, Hæreditario Cunningamiæ Bailivo. Tab. hanc D. D. J. Blaeu. — 73 Schottland. Ee Verso blank. 422 × 558 mm.

[21] KNAPDAIL.
[C:] KNAPDALIA PROVINCIA, que sub Argathelia censetur. The Province of KNAPDAIL which is accounted a member of Argyll. — [T:] Auct. Timoth. Pont. — 75 Schottland. Ff Verso blank. 419 × 529 mm.

[22] CANTYRE, Auss dem CAMDENO.
[C:] CANTYRA Chersonesus, CANTYR a Demie-yland Auctor Timoth. Pont. — 77 Schottland. Gg Verso blank. 411 × 496 mm.

[23] Die Insel GLOTTA, oder ARRAN. Auss dem CAMDENO.
[C:] ARANIA Insula in æstuario Glottæ THE YLE OF ARREN in the Fyrth of Clyd Thimotheo Pont Auctore. — 79 Schottland. Hh Verso blank. 387 × 519 mm.

[24] Die Insel BUTHE, oder BOOT. Auss dem CAMDENO.
[C:] BUTHE INSULA Vulgo THE YLE OF BOOT, Auct. Tim. Pont. — 81 Schottland. Ii Verso blank. 388 × 500 mm.

[25] DAMNII. Auss dem CAMDENO. CLVYDSDALE.
[C:] GLOTTIANA PRÆFECTVRA INFERIOR, CVM BARONIA GLASCVENSI. THE NETHER WARDE OF CLYDS-DAIL, and Baronie of Glasco. — [T:] Auct. Timoth. Pont. — 83 Schottland. Kk 387 × 535 mm.

[26] [C:] GLOTTIANA PRÆFECTVRA SVPERIOR. Auct. Timoth: Pont. — [C:] THE VPPER WARD of CLYDS-DAYL. — Blank on the back. 387 × 535 mm.

[27] REINFRAW. Auss dem CAMDENO.
[C:] PRÆFECTVRA RENFROANA Vulgo dicta BARONIA THE BARONIE OF RENFROW Timotheus Pont Auctor. — [An empty cartouche]. 85 Schottland. Ll 388 × 529 mm.

[28] LENNOX. Auss dem CAMDENO.
[C:] LEVINIA, VICECOMITATVS. The Province of LENNOX, called the Shyre of Dun-Britton. — [T:] Auct. Timoth: Pont. — 87 Schottland. Mm 390 × 523 mm.

[29] STERLING SHIRIFDOME. Auss dem CAMDENO.
[C:] STERLINENSIS PRÆFECTVRA STERLIN-SHYR. Auct. Timoth Pont. — [C:] Illustriss.^{mo} ac Nobiliss.^{mo} Domino D. IACOBO COMITI DE KALENDER Domino Amonte etc Tabulam hanc D.D. J. Blaeu. — 93 Schottland. Oo 408 × 518 mm.

[30] Beschreibung von FIFE. Auss dem CAMDENO.
[C:] FIFÆ VICECOMITATVS. The Sheriffdome of FYFE. — [C:] Illustrissimo Nobilissimoque Viro IOANNI CRAVFORDIÆ Comiti LYNDSAIÆ, et PERBROTHIÆ Baroni, fisci regni Scotiæ magno delegato, ejusdem regni consiliario, nec non electo præsidi supremi conventus ordinum habiti hoc anno 1645. amœniorum ingeniorum fautori summo Iacobus Gordonius Ecclesiastes Rothemayus hanc FIFÆ nobilissimæ provinciæ a se peragratæ descriptionem B.M.L.D.D. — 99 Schottland. Qq 416 × 522 mm.

[31] Newe Beschreibung von FIFE, durch ROBERT GORDONIVM.
[C:] FIFÆ PARS OCCIDENTALIS, THE WEST PART OF FIFE. — 101 Schottland. Rr 416 × 531 mm.

[32] FIFE.
[C:] FIFÆ PARS ORIENTALIS, THE EAST PART OF FIFE. — 103 Schottland. Ss 416 × 524 mm.

[33] Die Vice-Graffschafft ABERDONIA vnd BAMFIA, Zusamt denen Land- vnd Strichen die vnter ihnen begriffen werden. Auss CAMDENI Schrifften verfasset.
[C:] DVO VICECOMITATVS ABERDONIA & BANFIA, Una cum Regionibus & terrarum tractibus sub iis comprehensis. Auctore Roberto Gordonio à Straloch. A Description of the two Shyres ABERDENE and BANF, With such Countreys and Provinces as ar comprehended under them. — 121 Schottland. Zz 425 × 556 mm.

[34] BRAID ALBIN, oder ALBANI. Auss dem CAMDENO.
[C:] Scotiæ provinciæ mediterraneæ inter Taum flumen et Vararis æstuarium: Sunt autem BRAID-ALLABAN, ATHOLIA, MARRIA SVPERIOR. BADENOCHA, STRATH-SPEA, LOCHABRIA, cum Chersoneso qui ei ad occasum prætenditur; cum singulis earundem partibus. Opera Ro. Gordonii a Straloch. a Description of the inland provinces of SCOTLAND lying betueen Tay river and Murra fyrth, conteyning BRAID-ALLABAN, ATHOL, BRAE OF MAR, BADENOCH, STRATH-SPEY, LOCHABYR, w^t al ye lands which ley west from LOCHABYR, w^t all thair parts conteyned under them. — 127 Schottland. Bbb 418 × 528 mm.

[35] LORNA, Auss des CAMDENI Beschreibung.
[C:] LORNA cum insulis vicinis et provinciis eidem conterminis. LORN w^t the Yles and provinces bordering there-vpon. — [T:] Auct. Timoth. Pont. — [C:] Nob. Dño. D. IACOBO BALFOVRIO Militi Baroneti di Kynaird, Leoni Armorum Regis et Regni Scotiæ, nec non Insularum adjacentium, etc. Tab. hanc D.D. J. Blaeu. — 129 Schottland. Ccc Verso blank. 390 × 524 mm.

[36] Der Eusserste Strich SCHOTTLANDES, In welchem die Landschafften ROSSIA, SVTHERLAND, CATHANES, STRATHNAVERN, samt denen vntergebenen Ländlein / wie auch MORAVIA.
[C:] EXTIMA SCOTIÆ SEPTENTRIONALIS ORA, ubi Provinciæ sunt ROSSIA, SVTHERLANDIA, CATHENESIA, STRATH-NAVERNIÆ; cum vicinis regiunculis quæ eis subsunt, etiamque MORAVIA. R. Gordonius à Strath-loch collegit et descripsit. — 131 Schottland. Ddd 419 × 527 mm.

[37] MORAVIA.
[C:] MORAVIA SCOTIÆ provincia, ex Timothei Pont scedis descripta et aucta per Robert Gordonium à Strathloch. — 137 Schottland. Fff 415 × 553 mm.

[38] Wahre jedwertige Beschreibung von SVTHERLAND, Auss einer sehr köstlichem Handschrifft / bey H. ROBERTO GORDONIO, Pfleger von Sutherland, vnd Königlichen Vice-Kämmerer.
[C:] SOVTHERLANDIA — 143 Schottland. Hhh 380 × 527 mm.

[39] STRATH-NAVERN.
[C:] STRATH-NAVERNIA. STRATH-NAVERN. — [T:] Auct. Timotheo Pont. — [An empty cartouche]. 149 Schottland. Kkk 412 × 502 mm.

[40] CAITHNES.
[C:] CATHENESIA. CAITHNESS. — [T:] Auct. Timotheo Pont. — 153 Schottland. Mmm 381 × 521 mm.

[41] Beschreibung derer Inseln vmb vnd neben SCHOTTLAND. BVCHANANVS. Die Inseln ÆBVDÆ, gemeinlich HEBRIDES.
[C:] ÆBUDÆ INSULÆ Sive HEBRIDES; Quæ Scotiæ ad occasum prætenduntur, lustratæ et descriptæ a Timotheo Pont. THE WESTERNE ILES OF SCOTLAND. — 155 Schottland. Nnn 380 × 530 mm.

[42] ÆBVDÆ oder HEBRIDES. IVRA.
[C:] IVRA INSVLA The Yle of IVRA one of the westerne Iles of SCOTLAND. Auct. Timoth. Pont. — 157 Schottland. Ooo Verso blank. 408 × 522 mm.

[43] ILA.
[C:] ILA INSVLA. ex Æbudarum majoribus una. THE YLE OF ILA, being one of the biggest of the Westerne Yles. — [T:] Auct. Tim. Pont. — 159 Schottland. Ppp Verso blank. 400 × 522 mm.

[44] MULA.
[C:] MVLA INSVLA, quæ ex Æbudarum numero una est, et Lochabriæ ad occasum prætenditur. THE YLE OF MYL whiche is one of the westerne Yles and lyeth ovir against Lochabÿr. — [C:] Auct. Timoth. Pont. — 161 Schottland. Qqq 421 × 532 mm.

[45] RVMA, Zusamt den ümligenden Inseln.
[C:] INSVLÆ QVÆDAM MINORES ex Æbudis quæ MVLAM et SKIAM insulas interjacent. SOME OF THE SMALLER WESTERNE YLES, lÿing betweene the Yles of MVLE and SKYE. Timoth: Pont auctor. — 163 Scotland. Rrr Verso blank. 390 × 519 mm.

[46] SKIA.
[C:] SKIA vel SKIANA The Yle of SKIE Auct. Timotheo Pont. — 165 Schottland. Sss Verso blank. 412 × 524 mm.

[47] Die Eylanden / Nahe der Insel VISTO vom Mittag her gelegen.
[C:] VISTVS INSVLA vulgo VIIST. cum aliis minoribus EX ÆBVDARVM NVMERO ei ad meridiem adjacentibus. Auct. Timotheo Pont. — 167 Schottland. Ttt 450 × 580 mm.
[Inset:] [T:] BARRA — [and other islands]. 125 × 331 mm.

[48] HARRYS.
[C:] LEOGVS et HARAIA, insulæ ex Æbudarum numero, quæ, quamquam isthmo cohæreant, pro diversis habentur. LEWIS and HARRAY of the numbre of the Westerne Yles, which two although they ioyne be a necke of land ar accounted dyvers Ylands. — 169 Schottland. Vvv 390 × 523 mm.

[49] ORCADES.
[C:] ORCADVM et SCHETLANDIÆ INSVLARVM accuratissima descriptio. — 171 Schottland. Xxx 399 × 525 mm.
[a] [C:] ORCADES. — 399 × 225 mm.
[b] [C:] SCHETLANDIA. — [C:] Generis Nobilitate, ac Eruditionis Splendore Præstantissimo Heroi, D. IOANNI SCOTT Baroni de Scottis tarvet, Equiti Aurato, ac Ser.^{mi} magnæ Brittanniæ Regis Cancellariæ Directori, eidemque a privatis consiliis, et a fisco, viro vere hospitali, et Literatorum fautori summo; Dicat Guiljelmus Blaeuw. — 399 × 300 mm.

[50] HIBERNIA, Das ist / Irrland / Beschrieben durch GVILIELMVM CAMBDENVM.
[C:] HIBERNIA REGNVM Vulgo IRELAND. — I Irrland. A = 1635:I:[6].

[51] MOMONIA, Oder MOVNSTER.
[C:] MOMONIA Hibernice MOUN et WOUN; Anglice MOVNSTER — 11 Irrland. D 413 × 517 mm.

[52] LAGENIA, Oder LEINSTER.
[C:] LAGENIA; Anglis LEINSTER. — 19 Irrland. G 391 × 495 mm.

[53] [On verso:] Die Graffschafft CATERLOGH.
[C:] BARONIA UDRONE IN COMITATU CATHERLOVGHÆ — 22 381 × 252 mm.

[54] CONAGHT.
[C:] CONNACHTIA Vulgo CONNAVGHTY — 33 Irrland. L 393 × 495 mm.

[55] Irrland.
[C:] VLTONIA; Hibernis CVJ-GVJLLY; Anglis VLSTER. — 41 Irrland. O 412 × 493 mm.

Notes: The maps have text on the verso, except where otherwise specified. All the maps are coloured. The title is printed on a separate slip and pasted in the proper place on the engraved title-page. 17 of the maps are unsigned. This copy is complete, according to Koeman's description Bl 51. It is bound in old vellum. The inside of the front cover bears the same dedication as the other volumes of this set: 'Till Georg Isaac Londicer År 1818: såsom Hugkomst af dess Morfar Isaac Berg.' [To G.I.L. as a memento of his grandfather I.B.]

Lit.: Koeman vol. 1, p. 192—194, Bl 51, Koeman, Blaeu p. 70—76, LC List, vol. 5, p. 153—154, nr 5941, Skelton, County Atlases, MCS, 41, p. 97—110, nr. 58 and 60.

23 BLAEU, JOAN 1656

Vol. VI

NOVVS ATLAS, Das ist / Weld-beschreibung / Mit schönen newen aussführlichen Land-Taffeln in Kupffer gestochen / und an den Tag gegeben Durch JOAN BLAEU. Sechster Theil.
NOVVS ATLAS SINENSIS. Das ist ausfuhrliche Beschreibung des grossen Reichs SINA Durch P.M. MARTINIVM, der S.I. vnd aussgegeben Bey IOAN BLAEV MDCLVI. 51,2 cm.

[1] [C:] IMPERII SINARVM NOVA DESCRIPTIO. — Before p.I. 458 × 597 mm.

[2] [C:] PECHELI, SIVE PEKING, IMPERII SINARVM PROVINCIA PRIMA. — Between pp. 28 and 29. 397 × 485 mm.

[3] [C:] XANSI, IMPERII SINARVM PROVINCIA SECVNDA. — [T:] Exc. Ioannes Blaeu. — Between pp. 38 and 39. 394 × 481 mm.

[4] [C:] XENSI, IMPERII SINARVM PROVINCIA

TERTIA. — [T:] Excudebat Ioannes Blaeu. — Between pp. 44 and 45.   397 × 482 mm.
[5] [C:] XANTVNG, SINARVM IMPERII PROVINCIA QVARTA. — Between pp. 54 and 55.   395 × 484 mm.
[6] [C:] HONAN, IMPERII SINARVM PROVINCIA QVINTA. — Between pp. 62 and 63.   406 × 490 mm.
[7] [C:] SVCHVEN, IMPERII SINARVM PROVINCIA SEXTA. — [T:] Excudit Joannes Blaeu. — Between pp. 68 and 69.   399 × 481 mm.
[8] [C:] HVQVANG, IMPERII SINARVM PROVINCIA SEPTIMA. — [T:] Excud. Joannes Blaeu. — Between pp. 76 and 77.   401 × 486 mm.
[9] [C:] KIANGSI, IMPERII SINARVM PROVINCIA OCTAVA. — [T:] Excudebat Joannes Blaeu, ... — Between pp. 86 and 87.   395 × 490 mm.
[10] [C:] NANKING, SIVE KIANGNAN, IMPERII SINARVM PROVINCIA NONA. — [T:] J.Blaeu Excud. — Between pp. 96 and 97.   404 × 491 mm.
[11] [C:] CHEKIANG, IMPERII SINARVM PROVINCIA DECIMA. — [T:] J. Blaeu Excudebat. — Between pp. 112 and 113.   401 × 490 mm.
[12] [C:] FOKIEN IMPERII SINARVM PROVINCIA VNDECIMA. — [T:] Excud: Ioannes Blaeu. — Between pp. 124 and 125.   399 × 482 mm.
[13] [C:] QVANTVNG, IMPERII SINARVM PROVINCIA DVODECIMA. — [T:] Excudit Joannes Blaeu. — Between pp. 134 and 135.   403 × 490 mm.
[14] [C:] QVANGSI, SINARVM IMPERII PROVINCIA DECIMATERTIA. — [T:] Exc: Joannes Blaeu. ... — Between pp. 146 and 147.   403 × 491 mm.
[15] [C:] QVEICHEV, IMPERII SINARVM PROVINCIA DECIMAQVARTA. — [T:] Exc: I.Blaeu, ... — Between pp. 152 and 153.   391 × 487 mm.
[16] [C:] IVNNAN IMPERII SINARVM PROVINCIA DECIMAQVINTA. — [T:] Exc. Jo: Blaeu... — Between pp. 160 and 161.   404 × 492 mm.
[17] [T:] IAPONIA REGNVM. — Between pp. 176 and 177.   417 × 568 mm.

Notes: All the maps are blank on the back and coloured, as is the title-page. The title is printed on a separate slip and pasted in the proper place on the title-page, which bears the date 1656; the dedication and privileges are dated 1655. Koeman's B1 55 is dated 1655 on the title-page, but otherwise corresponds exactly with this copy, apart from four slight differences in the page signatures. This is the last of four volumes given by Isaac Berg to his grandson Georg Isaac Londicer in 1818: they are parts 1,3,5 and 6 of a six-volume edition of Blaeu's Novus Atlas, with German text. The atlas is bound in old vellum.

Lit.: Koeman, vol. 1, p. 197—198, B1 55, Tiele, p. 35, nr 132.

24   BLAEU, JOAN   1662

ATLAS MAIOR, SIVE COSMOGRAPHIA BLAVIANA, QVA SOLVM, SALVM, COELVM, ACCVRATISSIME DESCRIBVNTVR.

Vol. I
GEOGRAPHIA, QVÆ EST COSMOGRAPHIÆ BLAVIANÆ PARS PRIMA, QVA ORBIS TERRÆ TABVLIS ANTE OCVLOS PONITVR, ET DESCRIPTIONIBVS ILLVSTRATVR. AMSTELÆDAMI, Labore & Sumptibus IOANNIS BLAEV, MDCLXV.
[Engraved half title:]
GEOGRAPHIA BLAVIANA.   56,7 cm.

[1] ORBIS TERRARVM.
[C:] NOVA ET ACCVRATISSIMA TOTIVS TERRARVM ORBIS TABVLA. Auctore IOANNE BLAEV. — j g 407 × 540 mm. Two hemispheres with 276 mm. diam.
ARCTICA, QVÆ EST GEOGRAPHIÆ BLAVIANÆ PARS PRIMA, LIBER VNVS.

[2] HYPARCTICA, SIVE REGIONES SVB POLO BOREALI.
[C:] REGIONES SVB POLO ARCTICO. ... — I Hyparctica A = 1647—1949:I:[1].
[3] INSVLÆ IAN-MAJANÆ DESCRIPTIO.
[C:] INSVLA QVÆ À IOANNE MAYEN NOMEN SORTITA EST. — [An empty cartouche]. 19 Hyparctica. F   434 × 546 mm.
[4] SPITZBERGA.
[C:] SPITSBERGA. — 21 Hyparctica. G   379 × 495 mm.
[5] NOVA ZEMBLA.
[C:] NOVA ZEMLA. — 25 Hyparctica. I   378 × 498 mm.
[6] FRETVM WAIGATS, SIVE NASSAVICVM.
[C:] FRETVM NASSOVIVM Vulgo DE STRAET NASSOV. — On 32—33   246 × 552 mm.
[7] [T:] I. ORDINVM Vulgo STATEN EYLAND. — On 37   166 × 247 mm.
[8] [T:] I. MAVRITIVS. — On 39   Hyparctica. N   164 × 249 mm.
[9] YSLANDIA.
[C:] TABVLA ISLANDIÆ ... — 43 Hyparctica. O = 1635:I:[2].
EUROPA, QVÆ EST GEOGRAPHIÆ BLAVIANÆ PARS SECVNDA, LIBRI XVII.
[10] EUROPA.
[C:] EVROPA recens descripta à Guilielmo Blaeuw. — j Europa. a   406 × 549 mm.
[Insets:] [T:] AMSTERDAM — (View). [T:] PRAGA — (Plan). [T:] CONSTANTINOPOLIS — (Plan). [T:] VENETIA — (Plan). [T:] ROMA — (Plan). [T:] PARIS — (Plan). [T:] LONDON — (Plan). [T:] TOLEDO — (Plan). [T:] LISBONA — (Plan). All 9 oval 41 × 57 mm.
[11] [C:] EVROPA delineata et recens edita per NICOLAUM VISSCHER. — [C:] Nobilissimo Prudent.[moq3] Domino D. SIMONI VAN HOORN, Consuli et Senatori Vrbis Amstelædamensis, &c. Ordinum Belgicæ Foederatæ nomine ad Magnæ Britanniæ Regem nuper Legato extraordinario, Tabulam hanc D.D. Nicolaus Visscher. — Blank on the back.   433 × 542 mm.
NORVEGIA, QVÆ EST EUROPÆ LIBER PRIMVS.
[12] NORWEGIA.
[C:] NORVEGIA REGNVM Vulgo NOR-RYKE. — [C:] SERENISSIMO PRINCIPI CHRISTIANO, DANIÆ, NORVEGIÆ, VANDALORVM, GOTHORVMQ3 PRINCIPI, Duci Slesvici, Holsatiæ, Stormariæ, & Ditmarsiæ, Comiti in Oldenburgh & Delmenhorst. Tab. hanc. D.D.D. I. Blaeu. — I Norvegia. A 413 × 497 mm.
[13] EPISCOPATVS STAVANGRIÆ.
[C:] DIŒCESIS STAVANGRIENSIS, ... — 5 Norvegia C   Verso blank. = 1647—1649:I:[2].
[14] [C:] EPISCOPATVS STAVANGRIÆ PARS AVSTRALIS. — Blank on the back.   413 × 529 mm.
[15] [C:] EPISCOPATVS STAVANGRIÆ PARS BOREALIS. — Blank on the back.   383 × 497 mm.
[16] EPISCOPATVS BERGA.
[C:] DIŒCESIS BERGENSIS TABVLA. — 7 Norvegia. Verso blank.   435 × 532 mm.
[17] EPISCOPATVS DRVNTHEM.
[C:] DIŒCESIS TRVNDHEMIENSIS PARS AVSTRALIS. — 9 Norvegia. E Verso blank.   419 × 523 mm.
[18] FINMARCHIA.
[C:] FINMARCHIA — 11 Norvegia. F   394 × 553 mm.
DANIA, QVÆ EST EUROPÆ LIBER SECVNDVS.
[19] DESCRIPTIO DANIÆ, Auctore Ioanne Isaacio Pontano, Historiographo Regio.
[C:] DANIA REGNVM — I Dania. A 1647—1649:I: [3].
[20] [C:] REGNI DANIÆ, Novissima et Accuratissima TABVLA Per Nicolaum Visscher. — [C:] Potentissimo Invictissimoq3 D. Christiano V, Daniæ, Norvegiæ,

Joan Blaeu, 1665. 24:1 [6]

FRETVM NASSOVIVM
vulgo
DE STRAET NASSOV.

SIVE NASSAVICVM. 33

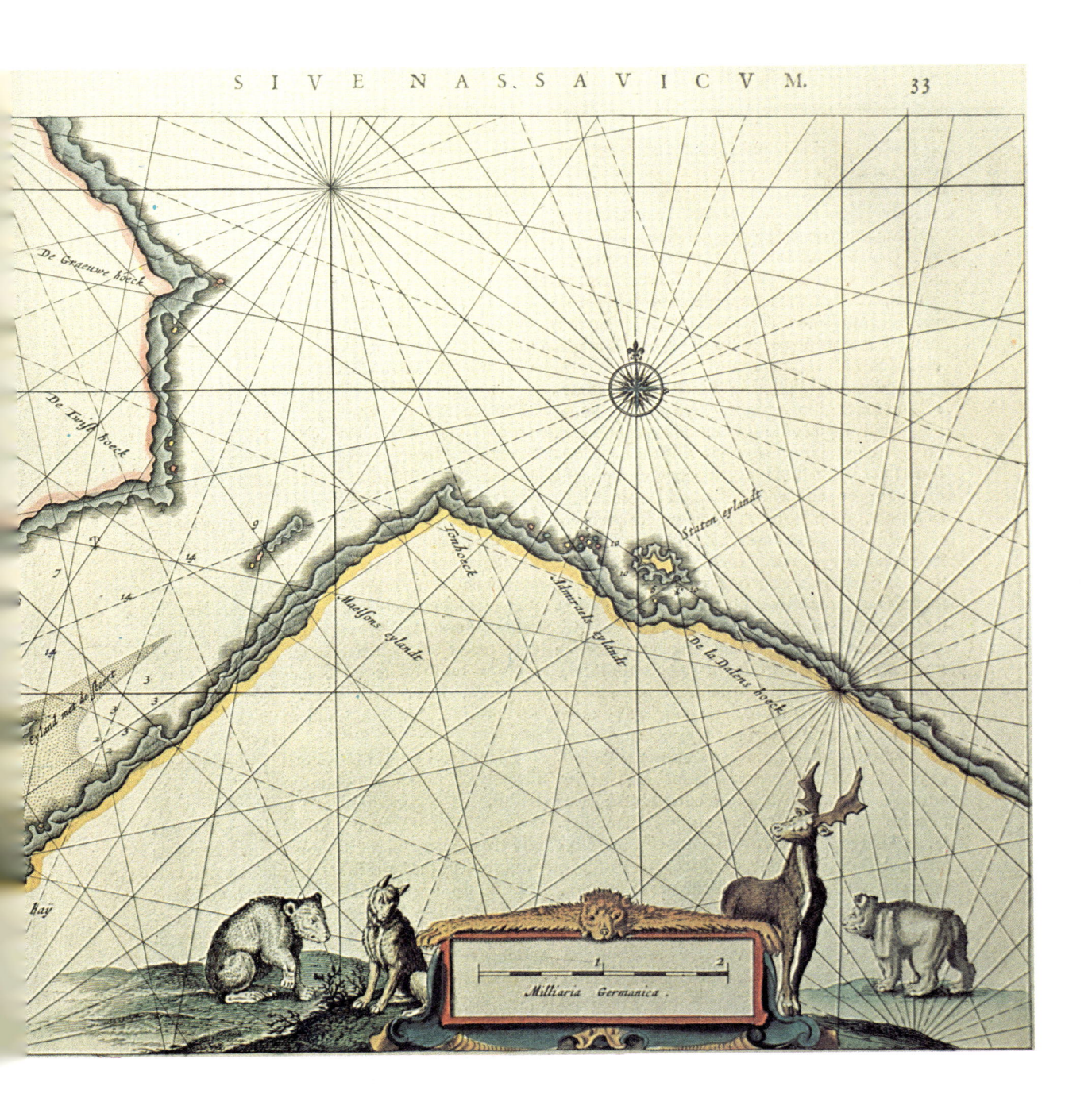

Milliaria Germanica.

Gotthor., Vandalorum Regi, etc. Hanc Daniæ Tabulam D.D.D. N: Visscher. — Blank on the back. 451 × 551 mm.

[21] IVTIA.
[C:] IVTIA, olim CIMBRICA CHERSONESVS. — [An empty cartouche]. 31 Dania. I 437 × 580 mm.

[22] IVTLANDIA SEPTENTRIONALIS.
[C:] PARS AVSTRALIOR IVTIÆ SEPTENTRIONALIS, in qua DIŒCESES RIPENSIS et ARHVSIENSIS. — 37 Dania. M 438 × 579 mm.

[23] IVTIÆ SEPTENT. PARS MERIDION.
[C:] PARS BOREALIOR IVTIÆ SEPTENTRIONALIS, in qua DIŒCESES ALBVRGENSIS et VIBVRGENSIS. — 39 Dania. N 436 × 578 mm.

[24] FIONIA.
[C:] FIONIA vulgo FVNEN — 43 Dania. P 1647—1649:I:[4].

[25] LALANDIA. FALSTRIA. MONA.
[C:] LALANDIA, FALSTRIA, et MONA, INSVLÆ IN MARI BALTHICO. — [T:] Joannes Blaeu Excudit. — 45 Dania. Q Verso blank. 388 × 521 mm.

[26] SELANDIA.
[C:] ZEELANDIA INSVLA Danicarum Maxima. — [C:] Nobil. Magnifico et Amplissimo D. PETRO CHARISIO, Ser. Reg. Maj. DANIÆ NORVEGIÆ, &c. Apud Ordd. General. Belgicæ Fœderatæ Consilario et Vicelegato Ordinario, Tabulam hanc D.D. J. Blaeu. — 47 Dania. R 433 × 535 mm.

[27] HVENA.
[C:] INSULA HVÆNA, sive VENUSIA, à GVILJELMO BLAEV, cum sub TYCHONE Astronomiæ operam daret, delineata. — [C:] Clarissimo Viro CHRISTIANO S. LONGOMONTANO, Astronomiæ in Regia Hafniensi Academia Professore, olim Parentis sui sub Tychone condiscipulo, Tab. hanc D.D. J. Blaeu. — 53 Dania. T Verso blank. 406 × 518 mm.

[28] DESCRIPTIO ARCIS URANIBVRGI quoad totam capacitatem.
[T:] ARCIS VRANIBVRGI, A TYCHONE BRAHE, DÑO DE KNVDSTRVP, IN INSVLA HELLESPONTI DANICI HVENNA CONSTRVCTÆ, QUO AD TOTAM CAPACITATEM, DESIGNATIO. — (Plan). 55 Dania. V Verso blank. 462 × 565 mm.

[29] SCANIA, vulgo SCHONEN.
[C:] SCANIA Vulgo SCHOONEN. — [An empty cartouche]. 99 Dania. Kk 491 × 508 mm.

[30] SLESVICENSIS DVCATVS.
[C:] DVCATVS SLESWICVM sive IVTIA AVSTRALIS. — [C:] Serenissimo et Potentissimo Principi ac Domino Dn. FRIDERICO III. Daniæ, Norwegiæ, Vandalorum, Gothorumq₃ Regi, V.Duci Slesw. Holsatiæ, Stormariæ & Dithmarsiæ, Comiti in Oldenborg & Delmenhorst. Et Serenissimo Celsissimoque Principi ac Domino Dn. FRIDERICO IV. Hæredi Norwegiæ, Duci Sleswici, Holsatiæ, Stormariæ et Dithmarsiæ, Comiti in Oldenburg et Delmenhorst, Dominis suis Clementissimis, Tabulam hanc Geographicam Ducat₉ Sleswicensis prorsus Novam subjectissimè Offert author Iohannes Mejer. Husum. — [T:] Matthias undt Nicolaus Peters Goldts. gebr. Hus: sculps. — j Slesvicum. a 419 × 553 mm.

[31] DVCATVS.
[C:] DVCATVS SLESWICI PARS BOREALIS. Sereniss.^{mo} Celsiss.^{mo} Principi ac Domino D. CHRISTIANO VI Dania,$^?$ Norvegia,$^?$ Vandalorum, Gothorumq₃ Principi Electo, Duci Slesvici, Holsatia,$^?$ Stormaria$^?$ & Dithmarsia,$^?$ Comiti in Oldenburg. et Delmenhorst, Domino meo Clementissimo, Tabulam hanc Geographicam subjectissimè Offert, author Iohannes Mejerus Husum: Cimber. — [C:] Matthias Und Nicola₉ Pet: Goldtschmide gebr: Hus: sculp. — iij Slesvicum. b 410 × 612 mm.

[32] SLESVICENSIS DVCATVS.
[C:] DVCATVS SLESWICI PARS MERIDIONALIS. — [C:] Illustrib₉, Magnificis ac Strenuissimis Dominis, Dño. Christiano Thomæo Seefeldt, Domino in Stowgard, &c. Equiti aurato, Reg. Maj. Cancellario Magno, Regni Daniæ Senatori prudentissimo, præfecto Cænobÿ s. Canuti in Odensee, Academiæq₃ Haffniensis Inspectori, Et Dño Andreæ Bilde, Domino in Dambsboe, &c. Equiti aurato, Regni Daniæ Mareschalto fortissimo, ac Senatori prudentissimo præfectoq₃ Schanderborgensi, patronis suis plurimum Observandis Tabulam hanc Geographicam submisse inscribit author Iohannes Mejer₃ Husum Reg.^{æ} Maj.^{ls} Mathematic₉. Matthias & Nicola₉ Peters Goldtschmide gebr. Hus. sculp. — v Slesvicum. c Verso blank. 405 × 617 mm.

[33] PRÆFECTVRA HADERSLEBEN.
[C:] PARS ORIENTALIS PRÆFECTVRÆ HADERSLEBEN Vulgo dictæ Baringsijssel. — [C:] Viro dignitate eminenti, Generoso, Magnifico ac Strenuo, Dn. Cajo Von Allfelde. Equiti aurato, Dn. in Mehlbeck. Saxdorff, &c. Ecclesiæ Sleswicensis Cathedralis Archidiacono, Reg.^{æ} Maj.^{ls} Consiliario Intimo, ac Senatori in Ducatib₉ Sleswicô et Holsatiâ, præfectoq₉ Haderslebiensi. Fautori suo Obseruando, hanc Diœcesis Baringsiliæ Tabulam Geographicam Officiosissimè dedicat, Author Iohannes Mejer₉. Husum= Reg.^{æ} Maj.^{ls} Mathematicus. Anno 1649. — [T:] Matthias Vnd Clauss Petersen. G S: gebr: Husumenss: sculps: — vij Slesvicum. d 402 × 538 mm.

[34] HADERSLEBIENSIS PRÆFECTVRÆ PARS OCCIDENTALIS.
[C:] PARS OCCIDENTALIS PRÆFECTVRÆ HADERSLEBEN cum adjacentibus RIPEN et LOHMCLOSTER PRÆFECTVRIS. — [C:] Illustri Magnifico ac Strenuo Dn.Dn. Gregorio Krabben. Equiti aurato Dn. in Tastlundt, Senatori Regni Daniæ. prudentissimo. præfectoq₃ Ripensi. & Generoso. Strenuo ac prudentissimo Viro. Dn. Ottoni Kraggen Hæreditario in Trutzholm Serenissimi Daniæ Regis Secretario magno. Præfectoq₃ Cænobÿ Halsted & præfecturæ Haranger in Norvegia, Patronis suis benignissimis. Tabulam hanc Geographicam Officiosissimè dedicat author Iohannes Mejerus, Hus. Reg.^{æ} Maj.^{ls} Mathematic₃. Matthias Und Clauss Petersen Goldtschmide gebr: Husumens: schulps: — ix Slesvicum e 413 × 534 mm.

[35] PRÆFECTVRA TONDEREN.
[C:] PRÆFECTVRA TONDERN sine Lundtofft Herde Anno 1648. — [C:] Christian Rothgiesser Husum sculps. — [C:] Viro Generoso, Magnifico et Strenuo Dnō. Wolff Blohm. Sereniss. et Celsissimi Ducis Sleswici & Holsatiæ, in ducatib₉ his Consiliario provinciali, præsectoq₃ Tunderensi, Domino in Testorp & Seedorp. Fautori suo honorando, Tabulam hanc Geographicam officiosissime inscribit author Iohannes Mejerus Husum. Reg.^{æ} Maj.^{ls} Mathematic₃ — xiij Slesvicum. g 433 × 589 mm.

[36] [C:] PRÆFECTVRÆ TONDERANÆ ORA MARITIMA. Generoso, Strenuo ac Splendido, Dn. Hans Blohm. Sereniss. nostræ Celsit. Supremo rei Venatoriæ præfecto, fautori suo observando, regionem hanc Præfecturæ Tonderensis maritimam et uliginosam Officiosè dedicat author Iohannes Mejerus Reg.^{æ} Maj.^{ls} Mathematic₉. — [T:] Matthias & Nicola₉ Peters Goldtschmide. gebr. Hus. sculps. — Blank on the back. 392 × 478 mm.

[37] FRISIA SEPTENTRIONALIS.
[a] [C:] FRISIA BOREALIS IN DVCATV SLESWICEN-SI sive FRISIA CIMBRICA Anno 1651. Viro Nobilissimo, Strenuo ac Magnifico Dñō Christophoro Von der Lippe Icto Regiæ Maj. Cancellario & Consiliario Intimo, Hæreditario in Sillimow & Swargen, fautori suo honorando. Tabulam hanc Frisiæ minoris Cimbricæ, Officiosissimè inscribit author Iohannes Mejerus Husum. Reg.^{æ} Maj.^{ls} Mathemati₉. — [T:] Matthias & Nicola₉ Peters Goltschmide. gbr. Husum. sculps. — 391 × 287 mm.

[b] [C:] FRISIA BOREALIS IN DVCATV SLESWICEN-SI Anno jz40. Frisia Cimbrica Antiqua Dignitate Eminenti Nobili amplissimo et prudentissimo Viro. Dñō Henrico Von Hatten Icto. Sereniss. Regiæ Majest. et Sereniss. et Celsit.

Consiliario jntimo, earundemq₃ in ducatib₉ Slesvico et Holsatia Cancellario provinciali Canonicoq₃ Slesvicensi, fautori suo Observando, Officiosissimè dedicata authore Iohanne Mejero Husum. Cimb. Reg.ᵅᵉ Maj.ˡˢ Mathematico. — 391 × 281 mm.

[The whole map:] xv Slesvicum. h Verso blank. 391 × 572 mm.

[38] PRÆFECTVRA APENRADE.
[C:] PRÆFECTVRA APENRADE et Luntoft herde. — [C:] Christian Rodtgiesser Husum sculpsit. — [C:] Viro Dignitate Eminenti generoso ac Strenuo, Dn. Iohanni Friderico Uon Winterfelt, Dnō in Dalmien, Garlien, et Stressaw, Ecclesiæ Cathedralis Lubecensis Præposito Canonico et Thesaurario, Ecclesiæ Collegialis Eutinensis Decano. Sereniss. et Celsiss. Ducis Sleswici & Holsatiæ Consiliario Intimo, ac præfecto Apenradensi, Fautori suo plurimum honorando. Tabulam hanc Geographicam officiosissimè inscribit. Author Iohannes Mejer Husum Reg.ᵅᵉ Maj.ˡˢ Mathematic₉. — xvij Slesvicum. i Verso blank. 448 × 604 mm.

[Inset:] [C:] Grundtriss der stat APENRADE mit dem schloss BRVNDLVNDT Aō 1648 — (Plan). 194 × 116 mm.

[39] PRINCIPATVS SONDERBVRGENSIS.
[C:] DVCATVS SONDERBORG cum adjacentibus Territoriis ALSSEN. SVNDEWITT, et Luxburgh. — [T:] Matthis Peterss. Gs. & Claus P. Goldtschmide Unt gbr. Huss. Cimb. sculp. — [C:] Illustrissimis et Celsissimis Principibus ac Dominis Dn. Friderico. Dn. Philippo. ac Dn. Iohanni Christiano, Hæredibus Norwegiæ, Ducibus Sleswici & Holsatiæ, Stormariæ & Dithmarsiæ, Comitibus in Oldenborg et Delmenhorst, Dominis suis Clementissimis, Tabulam hanc Geographicam submissè Offert, author Iohannes Meier, Reg.ᵅᵉ Maj.ˡˢ Mathematic₉, Husan₉ — xix Slesvicum k 424 × 563 mm.

[Inset:] [C:] Grundtriss der stadt undt d. slosses Sonderborg. ... — (Plan). 144 × 108 mm.

[40] PRÆFECTVRA FLENSBVRGENSIS.
[C:] PRÆFECTVRA FLENSBVRGENSIS absque Nordgoessherde. Matthias & Nicola₉ Peters Goldtschmide, gebr. Husum. sculps. — [C:] Viris Nobilib₉ amplissimis et prudentissimis, Dñō. Theodoro Lente Iᶜᵗᵒ Reg. Maj. Dan. et Norweg. Consiliario Jntimo et Secretario dexterrimo Et Dnō. Philippo Iulio Borneman Ejusdem Seren. Reg: Majest: Secretario Spectatissimo, Fautorib₉ suis honorandis. Tabulam hanc quatuor Nomorum. Præfecturæ Flensborgensis perofficiosè inscribit, Author Iohannes Mejer₉, Husum. Reg.ᵅᵉ Maj.ˡˢ Mathematic₉. — xxj Slesvicum. l 425 × 563 mm.

[Inset:] [T:] Grundtriss der stadt Flensborg — (Plan). 112 × 207 mm.

[41] PRÆFECTVRÆ GOTTORPIENSIS PARS BOREALIS.
[C:] PRÆFECTVRÆ GOTTORPIENSIS pars Borealis. — [C:] Matthias und Clauss Petersen, Goldtschmide, gebr. Hus. sculps. — [C:] Viro Nobilissimo. Strenuo ac Magnifico, Dn. Iohanni Adolpho Kielmann, ICᵗᵒ Eximio, Com. pal. Cæs. et sac. Rom. Imperÿ Exempto, Sereniss. Celsitud. Consiliario Intimo, Cancellario aulico, ac præcidi supremi dicasterÿ Gottorpiensis, præfectoq₃ Barmstedensi, patrono suo Observando, Tabulam hanc Geographicam Officiosissimè dedicat. author Iohannes Meier Husumens: Reg.ᵅᵉ Mai.ˡˢ Mathematic₉. — xxiij Slesvicum. m 378 × 566 mm.

[42] PARS BOREALIS.
[C:] ACCVRATISSIMA SLIÆ FLVMINIS DESCRIPTIO. — [T:] Christian Lorensen Rodtgiesser sculps. — [C:] Viris Generosis Strenuis & Splendidis Dñ. Heinrico Rumoer Hæreditario in Röste. Dn. Gerhardo Philippo Uon Alfeldt Hæradit. in Buckhagn. Dn. Wolff Uon der Wisch Hæredit. in Ohe. Tabulam hanc Geographicam Officiose dedicat. author Iohannes Mejer Husum. Reg.ᵅᵉ Maj.ˡˢ Mathematic₉. Aō 1649 — xxv Slesvicum. n Verso blank. 420 × 639 mm.

[Numerous insets of the fishing grounds].

[43] GOTTORPII PARS MERIDIONALIS.
[C:] PRÆFECTVRÆ GOTTORPIENSIS PARS AVSTRALIS. Viro Nobili amplissimo & prudentissimo Dn. Iohanni Hekelauer. Præfecturæ Gottorpiensis Inspectori et Serenissimæ Celsitudinis Structurarum Directori Generali Tabulam hanc Geographicam Officiosè dedicat author Iohannes Meier. Husumens. Reg.ᵅᵉ Mai.ˡˢ Mathemaitc₉. Anno 1649. — [C:] ... Matthis und Clauss Peters: Goldtschmide und gbr. sculp. Husumens. — xxvij Slesvicum. o Verso blank. 398 × 596 mm.

[Insets:] [C:] Grundtriss Von Fridrichstadt Anno 1649. — (Plan). 118 × 123 mm.   [C:] Grundtriss der stadt Eckernfoerde — (Plan). 121 × 153 mm.

[44] ANGLEN, ET SCHWANTZEN.
[C:] TERRITORIA ANGLEN ET SCHWANSEN Anno 1649. Viris Generosis Strenuis ac splendidis, Dn. Heinrico Brockdorff, Domino in Hemmelmarck Sereniss. ac Celsiss. Ducis Sleswici & Holsatiæ Tribuno militum fortissimo. et Dn. Nicolao Von Allfeldt, Hæreditario in Geltingen. Tabulam hanc Geographicam per Officiose dedicat author, Iohannes Meier. Husan. Reg.ᵅᵉ Mai.ˡˢ Mathematic₉. — [T:] Matthis und Clauss Petersen Goldtschmide und gebr: Hus. Cimb. sculps: — xxix Slesvicum. p Verso blank. 428 × 535 mm.

[45] PRÆFECTVRA HVSVMENSIS.
[C:] PRÆFECTVRA HVSVMENSIS LVNDERBERGH NORDSTRAND et NORDGOESHERDE. ... Viro Generoso, Strenuo ac splendido Dn. Lüdero Dessien, Sereniss. Celsit. Conjugis Serenissimæ, Aulæ magistro et præfecturæ Husumanæ directori, Hæreditario in Daschow & Suderholtz, Et Nobili amplissimo ac prudentissimo Viro Dn. Iohanni Wittemake, Centurioni Regio et Nomarchæ in Norgoesherde, fautorib₉ suis Colendis, Tabulam hanc Geographicam perofficiosè inscribit author Iohannes Mejer₉ Husumens. Reg.ᵅᵉ Maj.ˡˢ Mathematic₉. Anno 1649. — [T:] Matthias Vnd Clauss Petersen G S. gebr. Husumenss. sculps. — xxxj Slesvicum. q 425 × 606 mm.

[46] Præfectura seu Regio EYDERSTEDE, EVERSCHOP & VTHOLM.
[C:] TERRITORIA EŸDERSTEDE EVerschop et Uthholm. Viris Nobilib₉, amplissimis, doctissimis & prudentissimis Dn. Ioachimo Danckwerth, Hæreditario in Höÿersworth, Sereniss. Celsit. Ærarÿ præfecto dexterrimo Integerrimo, Fautori suo Multis Nominib₉ Colendo Et Dnō. Augusto Luth; Fautori suo Magno, Tabulam hanc Chorographicam Eÿderostadiæ Officiosè dedicat author Iohannes Mejerus Husum. Reg.ᵅᵉ Maj.ˡˢ Mathematic₉. Anno 1648. Matthias und Nicola₉ Pet: Goldtschmide gebr. Husum sculps. — xxxiij Slesvicum. r Verso blank. 422 × 611 mm.

[47] HELGOLANDIA INSVLA.
[a] [T:] HELGELANDIA A.° 1649. — 199 × 266 mm.
[b] [C:] HELGELADT. in annis Christi 800. 1300 & 1649. — [T:] Matthias Vnd Clauss Petersen, G S.gebr. Husumenss. sculps. — [C:] Viris Nobilibus, Amplissimis, doctissimis ac prudentissimis, Dn. Eberhardo Weidenkopff, IUD. Sereniss. Celsitud. Consiliario, ac supremi dicasterij Gottorpiensis assessori, Et Dn. Eilhardo Schachten. Sereniss. ac Celsissimi Ducis Sleswici et Holsatiæ, in supremo Dicasterio Gottorpiensi secretario, fautorib₉ suis Observandis, Tabulam hanc Simul Chorographicam & Topograhmicam, perofficiosè dedicat author Iohannes Mejer₉. Husum. Reg.ᵅᵉ Maj.ˡˢ Mathematic₉ — 209 × 267 mm.

[The whole map:] xxxv Slesvicum. s 424 × 275 mm.

[48] PRÆFECTVRA CHRISTIANPRIES, & DANISCH WOLDT.
[C:] SYLVA DANICA Vulgo DÆNISCHEN WALDE. — xxxix Slesvicum. t 239 × 301 mm.

[49] INSVLA FEMEREN.
[C:] FIMBRIÆ; Vulgo FEMEREN DELINEATIO GEOMETRICA — [C:] FEMBRIA Dignitate præcellenti, Nobili Amplissimo ac prudentissimo Viro Dn. Balthasart Gloxin I.V.D. Sereniss. Cels. Consiliario, ac supremi

dicastery Gottorpiensis assessori Canonicoq3 Lubecensi Fautori suo inscripta ab Authore Iohanne Mejero Husum Regæ Maj^{ls} Mathematico — XLj Slesvicum. u Verso blank. 231 × 298 mm.

[50] INSVLÆ ARROE, ROM, & MANDOE.
[C:] AROE INSVLÆ DELINEATIO GEOMETRICA —
[C:] Viro Generoso. Strenuo ac splendido Domino. Friderico Uon Buchwalde Equiti aurato. Hæreditario in Preissorth, siue Bulcke, Seekamp etc. Legato militari supremo fortissimo. Fautori suo. Tabulam hanc Chorographicam officiosissime dedic. Author Iohannes Mejer, Regæ Maj^{ls} Mathemati — XLiij Slesvicum. x Verso blank. 193 × 302 mm.

Notes: The maps have text on the verso, except where otherwise specified. They are all coloured. This is the second edition of vol.I, which was the only part of the Latin edition to be reissued. This copy contains two Visscher maps [11] and [20] which are not included in the index, nor in Koeman's description of the first edition, Bl 56. Only five of the 50 maps appear in earlier Blaeu atlases; this is his first publication of the others. In addition to the maps, the volume contains the following plates, which Koeman lists in the same sequence as the maps, and of which the Library of Congress List mentions only four:
MAIORIS DOMVS EXPRESSIO
[T:] ORTHOGRAPHIA PRÆCIPVÆ DOMVS ARCIS VRANIBVRGI in Insula Porthmi Danici Venusia, Vulgo Huenna, Astronomiæ instaurandæ gratia, circa annum MDLXXX, à TYCHONE BRAHE exædificatæ. — 57 Dania X Verso blank.
ICHNOGRAPHIA ET EXPLICATIO DOMVS PRÆCIPVÆ ARCIS URANIBVRGI.
[T:] ICHNOGRAPHIA PRÆCIPVÆ DOMVS ARCIS VRANIBVRGI in Insula Porthmi Danici Venusia, Vulgo Huenna, Astronomiæ instaurandæ gratia, circa annum M D L X X X, à TYCHONE BRAHE exædificatæ. — 59 Dania Y Verso blank.
TYCHONIS BRAHÆ INSTRVMENTA ASTRONOMICA.
[T:] SEXTANS ASTRONOMICVS PROUT ALTITUDINIBUS inservit. — 61 Dania Z.
ARMILLÆ ÆQVATORIÆ.
[T:] ARMILLÆ AEQVATORIÆ. — 65 Dania Aa.
INSTRVMENTVM PARALLATICVM, sive REGVLÆ PTOLEMAICÆ NIC. COPERNICI. —
[T:] INSTRVMENTVM PARALLATICVM TYCHONIS BRAHE. — [68].
ARMILLÆ ÆQVATORIÆ; in Observatorio S.
[T:] ARMILLÆ ÆQVATORIÆ. — 73 Dania Cc.
[C:] EFFIGIES TYCHONIS BRAHE O. F, ÆDIFICII ET INSTRUMENTORUM ASTRONOMICORUM STRUCTORIS. A.º DOMINI 1587, ÆTATIS SUÆ 40. — [76].
DESCRIPTIO STELLÆBVRGI, ET INSTRVMENTO-RVM In Cryptis subterraneis ibidem dispositorum.
[T:] STELLÆBURGUM sive OBSERVATORIUM SUBTERRANEVM, A TYCHONE BRAHE NOBILI DANO IN INSULA HVÆNA, EXTRA ARCEM URANIAM, EXTRVCTVM CIRCA ANNVM M D LXXXIIII. — [T:] Amstelædami, Joannes Blaeu excudebat. — 81 Dania Ee
ICNOGRAPHIA STELLÆBVRGI. 84
[T:] ARMILLÆ ÆQVATORIÆ MAXIMÆ SES QVIALTERO CONSTANTES CIRCULO. — [86].
SEXTANS ASTRONOMICVS Pro distantiis rimandis.
[T:] SEXTANS ASTRONOMICUS TRIGONICUS PRO DISTANTIIS RIMANDIS. — [89].
QVADRANS MAGNVS CHALYBEVS, ...
[T:] QVADRANS MAGNUS CHALIBEUS in Quadrato etiam chalibeo compræhensus, unaque AZIMUTHALIS. — 91 Dania Hh.
[T:] QVADRANS VOLUBILIS AZIMUTHALIS. — [94].
All the Mejer maps appear in Caspar Danckwerth's Newe Landesbeschreibung Der Zweij Hertzogthümer Schleswich Vnd Holstein... 1652. The text in the cartouches is in Latin in Blaeu, in German in Danckwerth; the dedications are in Latin in both. The following comparison of the maps is based on the copies in the Nordenskiöld collection:

Blaeu		Danckwerth
[30]	=	[5]
[31]	=	[6]
[32]	=	[7] a new dedication in Blaeu
[33]	=	[8]
[34]	=	[9] undated in Blaeu
[35]	=	[11]
[36]	=	[12] undated in Blaeu
[37]	=	[13]
[38]	=	[15]
[39]	=	[16]
[40]	=	[17] undated in Blaeu
[41]	=	[18] undated in Blaeu
[42]	=	[21]
[43]	=	[22] with a new dedication in Blaeu
[44]	=	[20]
[45]	=	[23]
[46]	=	[24]
[47]ab	=	[19]ab a without cartouche in Blaeu
[48]	=	[26:c]
[49]	=	[26:b]
[50]	=	[26:a]

This is the first of the eleven volumes of the Latin Atlas maior in the collection. The set is well preserved, bound in the original vellum of the Blaue printing-house; only the green silk ties are missing. Nordenskiöld's signature is on the first blank leaf.

Lit.: Koeman vol.11, p. 203—206, Bl 56, Koeman, Blaeu p. 41—48, LC List vol. 3 p. 146—150, nr 3430, Tiele p. 35, nr 133.

Vol. II
GEOGRAPHIÆ BLAVIANÆ VOLVMEN SECVNDVM, QVO LIB. III, IV, V, VI, VII, EUROPÆ CONTINENTVR. AMSTELÆDAMI, Labore & Sumptibus IOANNIS BLAEV, M DC LXII. 56,3 cm.

SUECIA, QVÆ EST EUROPÆ LIBER TERTIVS.
[1] DESCRIPTIO SCANDIÆ AVTORE ANDREA BVRÆO, Sueco.
[C:] SVECIA, DANIA, ET NORVEGIA, ... — I Suecia. A Verso blank. = 1635:I:[7].
[2] REGNORVM SVECIÆ DESCRIPTIO, AVCTORE ANDREA BVRÆO, SUECO.
[C:] SVECIA REGNVM, AVCT. ANDREA BVRÆO SVECO. — [C:] Sereniss.^{mo} Potentiss.^{mo} Principi ac Domino, D. CAROLO GVSTAVO, SVECORVM GOTHORVM VANDALORVMQ3 REGI AC PRINCIPI HÆRIDITARIO, Magno Duci Finlandiæ, Comiti Palatino Rheni, Duci Esthoniæ, Careliæ, Iuliæ, Cliviæ, ac Montium, Comiti in Veldentz, Marcæ & Ravensburgi, Domino Ingriæ & Ravenstein, &c. Tabulam hanc D.D. J. Blaeu. — 3 Sueciæ. B 428 × 490 mm.
[3] SUEONIA. VPLANDIA.
[C:] SUEONIA Proprie sic dicta. Auctore Andrea Buræo. — [C:] Perill. ac Generos.^{mo} Dño, D. AXELIO OXENSTIERNA Comiti Moreæ Australis, Libero Baroni in Kÿmitho, Dño. in Fiholm et Tÿdoen Equiti Aurato. S.R.M. Regnorumq3 Sueciæ Senatori et Cancellario, nec non Judici Provinciali Norlandiarum Occidentalium, etc. Tab. hanc D.D. I. Blaeu. — 17 Suecia. F 407 × 482 mm.
[4] SVEONIA.
[C:] DVCATVS VPLANDIA. Joh. et Cornelius Blaeu exc. — [C:] Illust.^{mo} et Exc.^{mo} Dño IACOBO DE LA GARDIE Comiti in Lachö, Libero Baroni in Eckholmen, Domino in Kalckha, Kyda, Hebsal, Dagdö et Reushe, Equiti S.R.M. et Regni Sueciæ Consiliario, Marescallo et Exercituum Præfecto seu Campiductori Generali, et in Regio militari Consilio Præsidi, nec non Vplandiæ Iudici provinciali,

Tabulam hanc dedicat Joannes Blaeu. — 19 Suecia. G Verso blank. = 1647—1649:I:[5], but with a new dedication.

[5] PROVINCIÆ NORDLANDICÆ Sunt Gestricia & Helsingia.
[C:] NORDLANDIÆ et quibies GESTRICIA et HELSINGICÆ REGIONES Auct: Andrea Buræo Sueco. — [C:] Illustrissimo Domino GABRIEL BENGTSON OXENSTIRNA Libero Baroni in Möreby̆ et Lindholm S.R.M. et Regni Sueciæ Consiliario et Archithalasso, nec non ditionis Tyharet in Smalandia Judici Provinciali Tabulam hanc D.D. J. Blaeu. — 21 Suecia. H 408 × 478 mm.

[6] LAPPONIA.
[C:] LAPPONIA, Auct. Andrea Buræo Sueco. — [An empty cartouche]. 25 Suecia. K 415 × 527 mm.

[7] GOTHIA, REGNVM.
[C:] GOTHIA Auctore Andrea Bareo Sueco. — [C:] Perill. ac Generos.^{mo} Dño. LEONHARDO TORSTENSTONIO, Comiti in Ortala, L.B. in Wirista, Dño in Forstena, Redsta et Rasigk, et S^{æ} R^{æ} M!^{tis} Regnorumq₃ Sueciæ Senatori, Campi Mareschallo, ac Vest. Goth. Dal. Werm. Hallandiæq₃ Gubernatori Generali. Tabulam hanc D.D. J. Blaeu. — 27 Suecia. L 413 × 526 mm.

[8] FINLANDIA.
[C:] MAGNVS DVCATVS FINLANDIÆ. Auct. Andrea Buræo Sueco. — [C:] Perill. ac Generos^{mo} Domino GVSTAVO HORN Comiti Biörneburgi, B. in Marienburgh, Dñ. in Hering et Malla, etc. S^{æ}R^{æ}M. Regnorumq₃ Sueciæ Senatori et Campi Mareschallo, Finlandiæ Australis Iudici Provinciali, Equiti Aurato. Tabulam hanc D.D. J. Blaeu. — 33 Suecia. N 432 × 522 mm.

[9] INGRIA.
[T:] INGRIA. — On 37 Verso blank. 160 × 206 mm.

[10] LIVONIA, vulgo LYFLAND.
[C:] LIVONIA, Vulgo LYEFLAND. — 38 Suecia. O 2 = 1647—1649:I:[6].

RVSSIA, QVÆ EST EUROPÆ LIBER QVARTVS.
[11] RVSSIA, SIVE MOSCOVIA.
[C:] TABVLA RVSSIÆ ... — I Russia. A = 1635:I:[9].

[12] REGIONES AVSTRALES MOSCOVIÆ.
[C:] RVSSIÆ vulgo MOSCOVIA, ... — 15 Russia. E = 1647—1649:I:[9].

[13] MOSKVA, IMPERII RVSSICI METROPOLIS.
[C:] Ц҃РСТВАЮЩОИ ГРАД М҃ОСКВА НАЧАЛЬНО͂ ГОРОД ВСѢ М҃ОСКВСКЍ ГСД҃РСТВ̃ [CARSTVA-JUŠČOI GRAD MOSKVA NAČAL'NOI GOROD VSEH MOSKOVSKIH GOSUDARSTV] —
[C:] Benevole Lector, in hac tabulâ VRBIS MOSKVÆ quadripartitam sectionem, aut murorum quatuor munitiones vides: ... — (Plan). 17 Russia. F 372 × 482 mm.

[14] PALATIVM ET CASTELLVM MAGNI DVCIS, VULGO KREMLENAGRAD.
[C:] КРЕМЛЕНАГРАДЪ.[KREMLENAGRAD]. KREMLENAGRAD, CASTELLVM VRBIS MOSKVÆ — [T:] MAGNO DOMINO CÆSARI, ET MAGNO DVCI ALEXIO MICHAELOVITS, DEI GRATIA, OMNIVM RVSSORVM AVTOKRATORI, ... — [C:] Privilegio Nobilissimorum et Præpotentum D.D. Ordinum Generalium Confœderatarum Regionum cautum est, ne quis has Tabulas Civitatis et Castelli Moskuæ aliquo modo imprimat, aut alibi impressas divendat. — (Plan). Russia. G 372 × 483 mm.

[15] REGION. OCCIDENT. MOSCOVIÆ.
[C:] RVSSIÆ, Vulgo MOSCOVIA dictæ, Pars Occidentalis. Auctore Isaaco Massa. — 25 Russia. I 384 × 486 mm.

[16] REGION. SEPTENT. MOSCOVIÆ.
[C:] RVSSIÆ, vulgo MOSCOVIA dictæ, ... — 29 Russia. L = 1647—1649:I:[8].

[17] WOLGA FLVVIVS.
[C:] NOVA & ACCVRATA WOLGÆ FLVMINIS, olim RHA dicti, DELINEATIO, Auctore ADAMO OLEARIO. — [Divided into two parts]. 37 Russia. O Verso blank. 475 × 560 mm.
[Inset:] [T:] WOLGÆ OSTIA. — 208 × 157 mm. (Irregular).

[18] DWINA FLVVIVS.
[C:] DWINA FLVVIVS. — [An empty cartouche]. [Divided into three parts.] 39 Russia P Verso blank. 421 × 538 mm.

POLONIA, QVÆ EST EUROPÆ LIBER QVINTVS.
[19] POLONIA, Auctore SALOMONE NEVGEBAVERO.
[C:] POLONIA Regnum, et SILESIA Ducatus. — I Polonia. A = 1635:I:[16].

[20] [C:] REGNI POLONIÆ et Ducatus LITHVANIÆ VOLINIÆ, PODOLIÆ VCRANIÆ PRVSSIÆ, LIVONIÆ et CVRLANDIÆ descriptio emendata per F. de Wit. Amstelodami. — Blank on the back. 481 × 556 mm.

[21] POLONIA MAJOR, Auctore SIMONE STAROVOLSCI.
[C:] PALATINATVS POSNANIENSIS, IN MAIORI POLONIA PRIMARII NOVA DELINEATIO. Per G.F.M. — [T:] AMSTERDAMI, Exc. Joannes Blaeu. — [T:] Gerard Coeck sculpsit. — [C:] Illmo et Exc.^{mo} Heroi ac Domino D. CHRISTOPHORO COMITI DE BNIN OPALINSKI, Palatino Posnaniensi, Regniq₃ Poloniæ primi Ordinis Senatori, Sremensi, Osecensi, Medilesensi Gubernatori, ad contrahendum nomine Sacræ Regiæ Maiestatis Poloniæ et Sueciæ, Matrimonium, Suprema cum potestate in Gallias Legato. Domino suo Clementissimo D.D.D. G. Freudenhamerus Medicus. — 25 Polonia. H 411 × 525 mm.

[22] POLONIA MINOR.
[C:] DVCATVS OSWIECZENSIS et ZATORIENSIS. — 31 Polonia. K 407 × 514 mm.

[23] PRVSSIA, EODEM AVCTORE.
[C:] PRVSSIA ACCVRATE DESCRIPTA ... — 39 Polonia. N = 1647—1649:I:[14].

[24] DESCRIPTIO TRIVM INSVLARVM, Germanice WERDERS, IN DVCATV BORVSSIÆ.
[C:] TRACTVS BORVSSIÆ, circa Gedanum et Elbingam, ab incolis WERDER appellati; cum adiuncta NERINGIA, nova et elaboratissima delineatio. Authore Olao Ioannis Gotho. — 45 Polonia. P Verso blank. 416 × 526 mm.

[25] LITHVANIA, EODEM AVCTORE.
[C:] MAGNI DVCATVS LITHVANIÆ et Regionum Adiacentium exacta Descriptio Ill.^{mi} ac Excell.^{mi} Principis et Dñi D.Nicolai Christophori Radziwil. D.G. Olÿcæ ac in Nieswies Ducis, S.Rom.Imp. Principis, in Szÿlowiec ac Mir Comitis et S.Sepulchri Hierosolimitani Militis etc. Opera, cura et impensis olim facta, ac nunc denuo hac forma edita a I. Blaeu. — [C:] Ioannes Blaeu Excudebat. — 47 Polonia. Q 444 × 529 mm.

[26] DESCRIPTIO BORYSTHENIS FLVVII, vulgo NIEPR, sive DNIEPR dicti: simul & de Moribus COSACORVM ZAPOROVIORVM.
[C:] TRACTVS BORYSTHENIS Vulgo DNIEPR et NIEPR dicti, à KIOVIA usque ad BOUZIN. — [T:] Amstelædami, Excud. I. BLAEV. — [Divided into two parts]. 51 Polonia. S 421 × 557 mm.

[27] BORYSTHENES.
[C:] TRACTVS BORYSTHENIS Vulgo DNIEPR et NIEPR dicti, à BOVZIN usque ad CHORTYCA OSTROW. — [T:] Amstelædami Excud. Joannes Blaeu. — [Divided into two parts]. 53 Polonia. T 422 × 558 mm.

[28] BORYSTHENES.
[C:] TRACTVS BORYSTHENIS, Vulgo DNIEPR et NIEPR dicti, A Civitate Czyrkassi ad ostia et Ilmien lacum, per quem in Pontum Euxinum se exonerat. Superiorem huj⁹ fluminis partem, a Czÿrkassi nimirum ad fontes usque, vide in Tabula Lithvaniæ. — [Divided into two parts]. 55 Polonia. V 378 × 540 mm.

[29] BORYSTHENES.
[C:] TRACTVS BORYSTHENIS Vulgo DNIEPR et NIEPR dicti, à CHORTICA OSTRO ad Urbem OCZAKOW ubi in PONTVM EUXINUM se exonerat. — [Divided into two parts]. 57 Polonia. X 462 × 543 mm.

REGIONES ORIENTALES VLTRA GERMANIAM CIRCA DANVBIVM. EUROPÆ LIBER SEXTVS.

[30] CHERSONESVS TAURICA, ET TARTARIA PRÆCOPENSIS, VEL CRIMEA.
[C:] TAVRICA CHERSONESVS, ... — I Partes Orient.Europæ ad Austrum. A = 1635:I:[10].
[31] VALACHIA.
[C:] WALACHIA SERVIA, BVLGARIA, ROMANIA. — 9 Part.Orient.Eur.ad Aust. D = 1635:I:[12].
[32] TRANSILVANIA.
[C:] TRANSYLVANIA Sibenburgen. ... — 29 Part.Orient. Eur.ad Austru. K = 1635:I:[11].
[33] HVNGARIA.
[C:] HVNGARIA REGNVM. — 33 Part.Orient. Eur.ad Austr. M = 1635:I:[15].
[34] [C:] Totius Regni HUNGARIÆ, Maximæque Partis DANUBII FLUMINIS, una cum adjacentibus et finitimis REGIONIBUS Novissima Delineatio, per Nicolaum Visscher. — Blank on the back. 431 × 801 mm.
[35] ILLYRICVM, SIVE SCLAVONIA.
[C:] SCLAVONIA, CROATIA, BOSNIA cum DALMATIÆ PARTE. ... — 47 Part. Orient. Eur. ad Austr. Q = 1635:I:[13].
[36] GRÆCIA.
[C:] GRAECIA. ... — I Græcia. A = 1647:III:[59].
[37] [C:] E‛ΛΛÀΣ [ELLÀS], Seu GRÆCIA UNIVERSA. Auctore J: Laurenbergio. — [T:] N: Visscher Excudit. — Blank on the back. 462 × 562 mm.
[38] MACEDONIA.
[C:] MACEDONIA, EPIRVS ET ACHAIA. ... — 9 Græcia. D = 1647:III:[60].
[39] PELOPONNESVS, SIVE MOREA.
[C:] MOREA olim PELOPONNESVS. ... — 19 Græcia. G = 1647:III:[61].
[40] CANDIA.
[C:] CANDIA, olim CRETA. — 25 Græcia. I = 1647:III:[62].
[41] [a] [C:] CANDIA — (View). 200 × 503 mm.
[b] [C:] INSULA CANDIA olim CRETA. N.Visscher exc. — 202 × 503 mm.
[The whole map:] Blank on the back. 405 × 503 mm.
[42] INSVLÆ ARCHIPELAGI.
[C:] CYCLADES INSVLÆ IN MARI ÆGÆO, hodie ARCHIPELAGO, Auctore I.LAVRENBERGIO. — [T:] Amsterdami, J. Blaeu excudit. — 43 Græcia. O 482 × 580 mm.
[43] INSVLÆ ARCHIPELAGI.
[C:] MARIS ÆGÆI, quod hodie ARCHIPELAGO nuncupatur, PARS SEPTENTRIONALIS. Auctore IOANNE LAVRENBERGIO. — 45 Græcia. P 481 × 576 mm.

Notes: The maps have text on the verso, except where otherwise specified. They are all coloured. This copy corresponds to Koeman's B1 56, with the addition of four maps [20], [34], [37] and [41] which are not mentioned either in the index or in Koeman. The Library of Congress copy contains 7 maps not listed in the index, of which the Visscher map of Hungary [34] is also in our copy. They have a map of Candia by de Wit; ours [41] is by Visscher. Our other two additional maps are not among those in the Library of Congress copy: Regni Poloniæ by de Wit [20], and a map of Greece by Laurenberg [37]. 16 of the maps in this volume are also in our copies of the 1635 or 1647 editions; the colourist of this volume has provided them with boundaries which do not appear on the black and white copies. Nordenskiöld's signature is on the first blank leaf.

Lit.: Keuning, Imago Mundi vol. 14, p. 87—89, Koeman vol. 1, p. 206—208, B1 56, Koeman, Blaeu, LC. List vol. 3, p.147, nr 3430, Tiele p. 35, nr 133.

Vol. III
GEOGRAPHIÆ BLAVIANÆ VOLVMEN TERTIVM, QVO GERMANIA. QVÆ EST EUROPÆ LIBER OCTAVVS, CONTINETVR. AMSTELÆDAMI, Labore & Sumptibus IOANNIS BLAEV, M DC LXII.   56,5 cm.

[1] GERMANIA.
[C:] GERMANIA, Vulgo Teutschlandt. — I Germania. A 485 × 566 mm.

[2] [C:] TABULA GERMANIÆ emendata recens per Nicolaum Joh Piscatorem — [T:] A.vanden Broeck sculp. — [C:] Claes Ianssen Visscher Excudebat. — Blank on the back. 466 × 548 mm.
[3] ARCHIDVCATVS AVSTRIA.
[C:] AVSTRIA ARCHIDVCATVS ... — 19 Germania. F = 1635:I:[45].
[4] AVSTRIA.
[C:] ARCHIDVCATCS AVSTRIÆ SVPERIORIS Vulgo SVPRA ANISVM cognominatæ NOVA DESCRIPTIO Juxta accuratissimas dimensiones ABRAHAMI HOLZWORMII. — [An empty cartouche]. 21 Germania. G 494 × 539 mm.
[5] BOHEMIA.
[C:] BOHEMIA — 25 Germania. I = 1635:I:[42].
[6] GLATZ COMITATVS.
[C:] COMITATVS GLATZ ... — 41 Germania. O = 1647—1649:I:[45].
[7] SILESIA DVCATVS.
[C:] SILESIA DVCATVS ... — 43 Germania. P = 1635:I:[43].
[8] SILESIA INFERIOR.
[C:] SILESIA INFERIOR, ... — 55 Germania. T = 1647—1649:I:[43].
[9] IAVRAVIENSIS DVCATVS.
[C:] DVCATVS SILESIÆ IAVRANI DELINEATIO Auctore Friderico Kuhnovio Bolcol: Siles. — [T:] Exc. I. Blaew. — [C:] Illustri, et Generoso Dnō, D. OTTONI, Lib: Baroni à Nostitz in Rockhitnitz, Seifersdorff, Hertzogswaldaw, Lobris, Prefen, Mangschütz et Neuendorff; Sacr. Cæs. Maj.[ti] à Consiliis, et Capitaneo Swidnicensis et Iaurani Ducatuum: ut et Plurimum Reverendis Præsulibus, Illustrissimis Generosis Comitibus et L.L.Baronibus, Nobilibus, Strenuis, Equestris Ord. D.D.Provincialibus universis Ducatus Iaurani, Dominis suis gratiosissimis, Delineationem hanc Ducat:Iaurani humillime D.D. Fridericus Kühn. — 59 Germania. X 421 × 527 mm.
[10] GLOGAW DVCATVS.
[C:] DVCATVS SILESIÆ GLOGANI ... — 61 Germania. Y = 1647—1649:I:[44].
[11] BARONATVS CAROLATH.
[C:] BARONATVS CAROLATO BETHANIENSIS IN SILESIA INFERIORE Illustr. ac Generos. Domini, D. GEORGII A SCHÖNAICH Liberi Baronis Bethaniæ Carolati, Milkaviensis, Sac. Cæs. Majest. Consilarii ac per Silesiam & Lusatiam utramque Cancellarii, dum viveret, procuratione delineatus. — [T:] Amstelædami Apud Joannem Blaeu. — [An empty cartouche]. 63 Germania. Z Verso blank. 413 × 504 mm.
[12] WOLAVIENSIS DVCATVS.
[C:] Ducatus SILESIÆ WOLANVS Authore Jona Sculteto Sprotta Silesio. — [T:] Amstelædami J. Blaeu escudebat. — [T:] Serenissimo et Celsissimo Principi ac Domino D. GEORGIO RODULPHO, DUCI SILESIÆ LIGNICENSI, BREGENSI, WOLAVIENSI, GOLTBERGENSI, DOMINO SUO AC PRINCIPI CLEMENTISSIMO, Delineationem istam Ducatus WOLANI humillime D.D. Jonas Scultetus. — 65 Germania. Aa Verso blank. 414 × 528 mm.
[13] LIGNICIVM DVCATVS.
[C:] DVCATVS SILESIÆ LIGNICIENSIS. Auctore Iona Sculteto Sprotta Silesio. — [T:] Amstelædami J. Blaeu excud. — [C:] Serenissimo et Celsissimo Principi ac Domino D. GEORGIO RODVLPHO, Duci Silesiæ Liniciensi, Bregensi, Goldbergensi Supremi per Utramq[3] Silesiam Capitaneatus Administratori, PRINCIPI ac DOMINO gratiosiss[o] D. â Ionâ Sculteto Silesio. — 67 Germania. Bb 411 × 526 mm.
[14] DVCATVS BRESLAVIENSIS.
[C:] DVCATVS BRESLANVS sive WRATISLAVIENSIS. Amstelædami, Apud Joan. Blaeu. — [C:] Nobil. Ampl.[mo] et Consultissimo viro D. BERNHARDO GULIELMO NUSLERO, Celsissimorum Lygio-Bergensium Duci à Consiliis ac secretis. Præcipuo operis hujus Promotori. A. Georgio Vechnero S.Th.D. et Iona Sculteto Sprotta Silesio. — 69 Germania. Cc 415 × 556 mm.

[15] SCHWIDNICENSIS DVCATVS.
[C:] DVCATVS SILESIÆ SCHWIDNICENSIS Authore Friduico Kuhnovio Bolco:lucano Silesio. — [C:] Illustri et Generoso Domino D. OTTONI, Lib: Baroni à Nostitz in Rockhitnitz, Seifersdorff, Hertzogswaldaw, Lobris, Profen, Mangschütz, et Neuendorff; Sacr. Cæs. Maj.^{ti} à Consiliis, et Capitaneo Swidnicensis et Iaurani Ducatuum: ut et Plurimum Reverendis Præsulibus, Illustrissimis Generosis Comitibus, et L.L. Baronibus, Nobilibus, Strenuis, Equestris Ord.D.D. Provincialibus universis Ducatus Swidnicensis, Dominis suis gratiosissimis, Delineationem hanc Ducat. Swidnicensis humillimè D.D. Frid. Kühn. — 71 Germania. Dd Verso blank. 419 × 527 mm.

[16] DVCATVS GROTKANVS, SIVE NISSENSIS.
[C:] DVCATVS SILESIÆ GROTGANVS cum Districtu Episcopali NISSENSI. — [T:] Amstelædami J. Blaeu excudit. — [T:] Generoso et Magnifico D. OTTONI HENRICO De Radschin, in Steina, Wolffsdorf, Gismansdorf, Zaupitz, etc. Operis hujus Patrono præcipuo, D. à Ionâ Sculteto Silesio. — 73 Germania. Ee Verso blank. 388 × 523 mm.

[17] MORAVIA.
[C:] MORAVIA MARCHIONATVS ... — 75 Germania. Ff = 1635:I:[44].

[18] STIRIA.
[C:] STIRIA Steyrmarck. — 77 Germania. Gg = 1635:I:[46].

[19] CARNIOLA, WINDORVM MARCHIA, ET CILIA.
[C:] CARNIOLA, CILIA COMITATVS, et WINDORVM MARCHIA. Ger. Mercatore Auctore. — [T:] Guiljelm. Blaeu excudit. — 79 Germania. Hh = 1635:I:[14], but the title altered.

[20] CARINTHIA.
[C:] SALTZBVRG ARCHIEPISCOPATVS, et CARINTHIA DVCATVS. ... — 81 Germania. Ii = 1635:I:[47].

[21] TIROLIS COMITATVS.
[C:] TYROLIS COMITATVS. — [C:] SERENISSIMO PRINCIPI FERDINANDO CAROLO, D.G.ARCHIDVCI AVSTRIÆ, DVCI BVRGVNDIÆ, COMITI TYROLIS, & GORITIÆ, LANDGRAVIO ALSATIÆ, &c. Tabulam hanc humillime offert et dedicat I.BLAEV. — 85 Germania. Ll 472 × 571 mm.

[22] BAVARIA DVCATVS.
[C:] BAVARIA DVCATVS, ... — 87 Germania. Mm = 1635:I:[48].

[23] BAVARIÆ PALATINATVS.
[C:] PALATINATVS BAVARIÆ. — 97 Germania. Pp = 1635:I:[49].

[24] Descriptio Territorii NOVOFORENSIS, In Superiori Palatinatu.
[C:] TERRITORII NOVOFORENSIS IN SVPERIORE PALATINATU ACCURATA DESCRIPTIO Auctore Nicolao Rittershusio D. — 99 Germania. Qq 424 × 546 mm.

[25] SVPERIORIS SAXONIÆ CIRCVLVS.
[C:] SAXONIA SVPERIOR, CVM LVSATIA ET MISNIA. — 101 Germania. Rr = 1635:I:[41].

[26] MARCHIONATVS MISNIÆ.
[C:] MISNIA MARCHIONATVS. Meissen. — [T:] Jo: Blaeu Excu. — 103 Germania. Ss 415 × 548 mm.

[27] TERRA ADVOCATORVM, SIVE VOYTLANDIA.
[C:] TERRA ADVOCATORVM Vulgo VOIGHTLAND. Descripta ab Olao Ioannis Gotho S.R.M. Sueciæ Geographo. — [T:] Amstelædami J. Blaeu excudebat. — 105 Germania. Tt 389 × 497 mm.

[28] THVRINGIA.
[C:] THVRINGIA LANDGRAVIATVS Auct. Adolario Erichio Anderslebiano. — [C:] Nobilissimo, Doctissimo, et Elegantissimi ingenii viro, IOACHIMO VICOFORTIO Equiti, Illustriss. Bernhardo Saxoniæ Duci à sanctioribus consiliis, D.D.D. Johan. et Cornelium Blaeu. — 107 Germania. Vv = 1635:I:[39], but the text in the dedication altered.

[29] MANSFELDIA COMITATVS.
[C:] MANSFELDIA COMITATVS ... — 113 Germania. Yy = 1635:I:[40].

[30] PRINCIPATVS ANHALTINVS.
[C:] PRINCIPATVS ANHALTINVS — 115 Germania. Zz 387 × 524 mm.

[31] SAXONIA DVCATVS.
[C:] SAXONIA SVPERIOR, & HALL EPISCOPATVS. — [C:] Serenissimo ac Celsissimo Principi IOANNI GEORGIO, D.G. SAXONIÆ DVCI, S.R.I. Electori Ensifero, et Archimarescallo, MARCHIONI MISNIÆ, THVRINGIÆ LANDGRAVIO, etc. Tab. hanc D.D. J. Blaeu. — [T:] Amstelædami J. Blaeu excudebat. — 117 Germania. Aaa 414 × 526 mm.

[32] LVSATIA.
[C:] LVSATIA SVPERIOR. ... — 121 Germania. Ccc = 1647—1649:I:[40].

[33] MARCHIONATVS BRANDENBVRG.
[C:] Marchionatus BRANDENBVRGICVS. Auth. Olao Iohannis Gotho, Gustaui Mag. R.S. Cosm. — [C:] Serenissimo ac Celsissimo Principi FREDERICO GVILIELMO D.G. MARCHIONI BRANDEBVRGICO, S.R.I. ELECTORI et ARCHICAMERARIO, Borussiæ, Iuliæ, Cliviæ, Montium, Stetini, Pomeraniæ, Cassubiorum, Vandalorum, et in Silesia Crossiæ, Carnoviæ ac Iagerndorfii Duci, Burggravio Norici, Rugiæ Principi, Marchiæ et Ravensbergii Comiti, Ravensteinii Toparchæ, etc. Tabulam hanc D.D. I. Blaeu. — 125 Germania. Eee 473 × 546 mm.

[34] MARCHIÆ VETERIS DESCRIPTIO.
[C:] MARCHIONATVS BRANDENBURGICI PARS, quæ MARCHIA VETUS, Vulgo ALTEMARCK, dicitur. — [An empty cartouche]. 129 Germania. Ggg 388 × 506 mm.

[35] MARCHIA MEDIA.
[C:] MARCH. BRANDENBURGICI PARS, quæ MARCHIA MEDIA Vulgo MITTELMARCK audit. — [T:] Amstelædami, Excud. Joannes Blaeu. — [An empty cartouche]. 133 Germania. Iii 391 × 525 mm.

[36] MARCHIA NOVA.
[C:] MARCHIONATVS BRANDENBURGICI PARTES DUÆ; NOVA MARCHIA et UCKERANA. Auctore OLAO JOANNIS GOTHO Gustavo Magni Cosmographo. — [Two empty cartouche]. 137 Germania. Lll 388 × 526 mm.

[37] COMITATVS RVPPINENSIS, ET DITIONIS PRIGNITZENSIS DESCRIPTIO.
[C:] MARCHIONATVS BRANDENBURGICI PARTES DUÆ, RUPPIN Comitatus & PRIGNITS Regiuncula. Auth. Olao Iohannis Gotho, Gustavo Magno Cosm. — [Two empty cartouches]. 139 Germania. Mmm Verso blank. 386 × 529 mm.

[38] DESCRIPTIO POMERANIÆ DVCATVS, Auct. EILHARDO LVBINO, in Acad. Rostochiensi nuper Professore.
[C:] POMERANIÆ DVCATVS TABVLA. ... — 141 Germania. Nnn = 1635:I:[19].

[39] [C:] Serenissimo, Celsissimo ac Invictissimo Principi FREDERICO GUILIELMO, D.G. Marchioni Brandenburgico, S.R.I. Electori et Archicamerario, etc̃. Pomeraniæ Ultori, Victori, Duci ac Reduci, Hanc POMERANIÆ DUCATUS Tabulam, D.D.D Nicolaus Visscher. — Blank on the back. 460 × 562 mm.

[40] RVGIA INSVLA.
[C:] RVGIA INSVLA AC DVCATVS ... — 147 Germania. Ppp = 1635:I:[20[.

[41] CIRCVLVS SAXONIÆ INFERIORIS.
[C:] INFERIORIS SAXONIÆ CIRCVLVS. — [C:] Joannes Blaeu Excudebat. — [C:] Serenissimo, Celsissimo Principi ac Domino, D. CHRISTIANO LUDOVICO, BRUNSVICENSIUM et LUNÆBURGENSIUM DUCI, &c. Circuli Inferioris Saxoniæ Capitaneo Generali; Tabulam hanc D.D.D. J. Blaeu. — 149 Germania. Qqq Verso blank. 417 × 523 mm.

[42] DVCATVS MECKELBVRGENSIS.
[C:] MEKLENBVRG DVCATVS. ... — 151 Germania. Rrr = 1635:I:[21].

[43] HOLSATIA DVCATVS.
[C:] Newe Landtcarte Von denbeiden Hertzogthümern SCHLESWIEG Und HOLSTEIN Zusamen. Anno 1650. —

[C:] Serenissimo et Potentissimo Principi ac Domino, Dnō. FRIDERICO III. Daniæ, Norwegiæ, Vandalorum, Gothorumq3 Regi. VDuci Sleswici Holsatiæ, Stormariæ & Dithmarsiæ, Comiti in Oldenborg et Delmenhorst. Et Serenissimo, Celsissimoq3 Principi ac Domino, Dño. FRIDERICO IV. Hæredi Norwegiæ, Duci Sleswici Holsatiæ, Storma= et Dithmarsiæ, Comiti in Oldenborg et Delmĕhor= Dominis suis Clementissimis, Tabulam hanc Geographicam, Ducatuum Slesswici & Holsatiæ Conjunctim exhibitorum, subjectissimè Offert author Iohannes Mejerus, Husumensis. Matthias und Nicola9 Pet= Goldtschmide gebr: Hus: Cimb: sculps. — 163 Germania. Yyy 417 × 588 mm.
[Insets:] [T:] Rÿpen. — 39 × 67 mm. [T:] Sleswieg. — 52 × 67 mm. [T:] Flensborg. — 38 × 67 mm. [T:] Haderschleben. — 38 × 67 mm. [T:] Husum. — 35 × 67 mm. [T:] Tondern. — 41 × 67 mm. [T:] Sonderborg — 32 × 67 mm. [T:] Apenrade. — 35 × 67 mm. [T:] Eckernförde — 42 × 67 mm. [T:] Tonning — 51 × 67 mm. [T:] Hamburg. — 55 × 66 mm. [T:] Kiel. — 58 × 66 mm. [T:] Rendssborg — 49 × 66 mm. [T:] Itzehoa. — 64 × 66 mm. [T:] Oldesloh. — 51 × 66 mm. [T:] Krempe — 37 × 66 mm. [T:] Gluckstadt. — 52 × 66 mm. [T:] Plōen, — 34 × 66 mm. (All insets plans).

[44] HOLSATIA PROPRIE SIC DICTA.
[C:] DUCATUS HOLSATIÆ DESCRIPTIO NOVISSIMA. — 167 Germania. Aaaa 440 × 542 mm.

[45] [C:] Landtcarte Von dem Lande WAGEREN. Welches ist das Ostertheil Von HOLSTEIN. aō 1651. ... — [T:] Matthias & Nicola9 Peters Goltschmide. gbr. Hus. sculps: — [C:] Eminentissimo, Illustrissimo et Celsissimo Principi ac Domino. Dnō. Iohanni Episcopo Lubecensi, Hæredi Norwegiæ, Duci Schlesswici, Holsatiæ Stormariæ, et Dithmarsiæ, Comiti in Oldenborg et Delmenhorst, Domino suo Clementissimo, Tabulam hanctoti9 Wagriæ subjectissimè Offert Author. Iohannes Mejerus Hus. Regæ Maj.ls Mathematic9. — Blank on the back. 420 × 511 mm.
[Insets:] [C:] Grundtriss Oldenburg. añ 1651. — (Plan). 156 × 123 mm. [C:] Grundtriss Oldenburg. Anno 1320 — (Plan). 175 × 154 mm.

[46] WAGRIA.
[C:] Nordertheill. Uon WAGEREN Worinnen auch die ämpter Cissmar Und Oldenborg Anno 1649 Illustrissimo & Celsissimo Principi ac Domino. Dnō Ioachimo Ernesto, Hæredi Norwegiæ, Duci Sleswici & Holsatiæ, Stormariæ & Dithmarsiæ, Comiti in Oldenburg et Delmenhorst Domino suo Clementissimo Tabulam hanc Geographicam submisse offert author Iohannes Mejer. Husumens. Regæ Maj.ls Mathematic9. — [T:] Christian Lorcnsen, Rodtgiesser sculps. — 171 Germania. Cccc 420 × 605 mm.
[Insets:] [C:] Grundtriss d. Statt Undt d. Schlosses PLÖEN. — 55 × 86 mm. [C:] Grundtriss Vom Flecken Preeƚe. — 115 × 68 mm. [T:] Grundriss Uon LVTKENBORG. — 60 × 95 mm. [C:] Grundtriss Uō HILLIGNHAVEN. aō 1649 — 60 × 84 mm. [T:] Grundtriss der Newstadt. — 81 × 106 mm. (All insets plans).

[47] [C:] Landtcarte Uom Süderntheil des WAGERLANDeS Und ein theil á Stormaria . Worinnen dass Stifft Lubeck. das Fürstenthumb PLÖEN Und das Ambt Segeberg begriffen Anno 1650 — [T:] Andres Lorenssen Rothgiesser Hus. sculps. — [C:] Viris Generosis, Strenuis ac splendidis Dn. Casparo Uon Buchwaldt Equiti aurato Reg. Maj. in ducatib9 Sleswicò & Holsatiá Consiliario ac præfecto Segebergensi, Domino in Pronstorp Dno. Nicolao Uon Qualen. Sereniss Celsit. in ducatib9 Sleswico & Holsatiæ Consiliario præfectoq3 Cissmariensi et Oldenborgensi Domino in Syggen, Tabulam hanc Geographicam Officiosissime dedicat author Iohannes Mejerus Husum Regæ Maj.ls Mathematicus. — Blank on the back. 419 × 626 mm.
[Insets:] [C:] Grundtriss der stadt Und dSchloss Eutÿn aō 1648. — (Plan). 75 × 112 mm. [C:] Grundris der stadt & schloss. segeberg aō 1648. — (Plan). 66 × 112 mm.

[T:] Segeberg Ieschnhagn — (View). 36 × 70 mm.
[T:] Grundriss Trauemünde — (Plan). 73 × 135 mm.

[48] STORMARIA DVCATVS.
[C:] Landtcarte Von dem Furstenthumbe STORMARN. Anno 1650. — [C:] Matthias & Nicola9 Peters. Goldtschmide gebr. Hus. sculp. — [C:] Illustri Generosissimoq3 Comiti ac domino, Dño Christiano, Sacri Romani Imperÿ Comiti in Rantzow, Dño. in Breitenburg. Lindewith.et Giesingholm. Ecquiti aurato, Sereniss.æ Regæ Majest. Dan. ac Norweg: Consiliario intimo, ejusdemq3 in ducatib3 Sleswicô & Holsatià Senatori ac Vicario honoratissimo Præfecto Langelandiæ, Dithmarsiæ Australis & Præfecturæ Steinborgensis, Dn. meo Clement. Tabulam hanc Stormariæ Submissè Offert author Iohannes Mejer9. Husum. Regæ Maj.ls Mathematic9. — 175 Germania. Eeee 394 × 550 mm.

[49] COMITATVS PINNENBERG.
[C:] Landt Carte Uon der Grafschaft PINNEN BERG aō. 1650. — [T:] Andres Lorensen Rodtgiesser Husum. sculps. — [C:] Viro Generoso. Strenuo ac Splendido. Dnō. Iasparo Von Orƚen. Reg. Mai. Consiliario Intimo ac præfecto Pinnenbergensi. et Nobili amplissimo Doctissimo ac prúdentissimo Viro Dnō Francisco Stapel I.V.D. Consiliario regio et præsidi Pinnēbergensi. Fautorib9 suis honorandis. Tabulam hanc Geographicam per officiosé inscribit. author Iohannes Mejer, Husum. Regæ Maj.ls Mathematic9 — 180, b Germania. Ffff2 420 × 540 mm.
[Inset:] [C:] Grundtris der statt Und Uehstung Krempe aō. 1648. — (Plan). 117 × 129 mm.

[50] [C:] Die Ämbter Trittow, Reinbeeck, Tremsbüttel Und Steinhorst Aō 1649. Dignitate Eminentib9, generosis et Strenuis Viris Dn Christophoro Iohanni Uon Bulow, præposito monostery Veteris in Ducatu Bremensi, Sereniss. ac Celsiss. Ducis Sleswici & Holsatiæ Consiliario Intimo, præfectoq3 Tremsbuttelensi et Steinhorstij. Et Dn. Friderico Uon Alfeldt Hæreditario in Sestermuhe, præposito monastery Vterssen, Sereniss. nostræ Celsitudinis in Ducatib9 Sleswico et Holsatiâ Senatori, et præfecto Trittouiensi, Fautorib9 suis, Tabulam hanc Geographicam perofficiose inscribit. Author Iohannes Mejer Husum Regæ Maj.ls Mathematic9 — [T:] Andres Lorensen Rodtgiesser Husum. sculps. — Blank on the back. 430 × 574 mm.
[Inset:] [C:] Grundriss Uon OLDESCHLOH Anno 1382 ... — 136 × 147 mm.

[51] [C:] Newe Landtcarte Von dem Ampte STEINBORG. Der Kremper, Vndt Wilstermarsch. Anno 1651. — [C:] Viro Nobilissimo, Magnifico ac Clarissimo Dño. Theodoro Reinking Icto Eximio Com.pal. Cæs. &c: Sereniss. Regiæ Majest. Consiliario Intimo. Cancellario ac præsidi Supremi Gluckstadiensis. Hæreditario in Wellingsbuttel. Et. Nobili amplissimo ac prudentissimo Viro Dnō. Iacobo Steinman Icto, Consiliario Regio & præfecturæ Steinborg: administratori dignissimo, Faurotib9 suis Colendis. Tabulam. hanc Geometricam Officiosissimè dedicat author Iohannes Mejerus. Husū. Regæ Maj.ls Mathematicus. Matthias & Nicaola9 Peters Goltdschmide gbr. Hus. sculps. — Blank on the back. 404 × 569 mm.
[Inset:] [C:] Grundtriss der Vehstung Gluckstadt. ... — (Plan). 127 × 144 mm.

[52] ALBIS FLUVIVS.
[C:] ALBIS Fluvius Germaniæ celebris A FONTIBUS AD OSTIA Cum fluminibus ab utroque latere in illum fluentibus, descriptus. — [C:] Amstelodami, Apud Joannem Janssonium. — [Divided into two parts]. 181 Germania. Gggg 391 × 491 mm.

[53] [a] [C:] Landtcarte Von DITHMARSCHEN Anno 1559. — [C:] Dignitate præcellenti, Nobili, amplissimo, prudentissimoq3 Viro Dnō. Reimaro Doren, ICto, Regæ Maj.ls Consiliario Intimo, Canonicoq3 Slesvicensi. Fautori suo Observando. Tabulam hanc Dithmarsiæ Veteris, perofficiosè dedicat author Iohannes Mejer9. Husum. Regæ Maj.ls Mathematicus. Anno 1651. — 406 × 303 mm.
[b] [C:] Landtcarte Von DITHMARSCHEN Anno 1651. ... — [C:] Matthias & Nicolaus Peters Goldtschmide.gbr.

[54] Hus. sculps: — [C:] Viro Nobili amplissimo, prudentissimoq₃ Dño. Iohanni Helmens, IUL, Regæ Majⁱˢ Consiliario, Intimo Fautori suo honorando, Tabulam hanc Dithmarsiæ peroffisiosè inscribit, Author Iohannes Mejer₉ Regæ Majⁱˢ Mathematicus. — 406 × 304 mm.
[The whole map:] Blank on the back. 406 × 607 mm.

[54] DITMARSIA.
[C:] Landtcarte Von dem Suderthiell DITHMARSCHEN. Anno 1648. Author Iohannes Mejer₉ Husum. Regæ Majⁱˢ Mathematicus. ... Matthias undt Nicolaus Peters Goldtsch: gebr. Hus. sculps. — [C:] Viris Nobilib₉ amplissimis, doctissimis et prudentissimis. Dnō. Iacobo Braun, I.U.L. Dithmarsiæ Australis, Satrapæ Regio dignissimo, Ut et Dño. Georgio Reichen. Iudicÿ provincialis Dithmarsiæ Meridionalis, Assessori ac Secretario Regio experientissimo, Nec Non Doctissimis, Prudentib₉ & honestis ejusdem Iudicÿ provincialis Dithmarsici Senatorib₉, Tabulam hanc Chorographicam perofficiosè inscribit author. — 183 Germania. Hhhh 400 × 591 mm.
[Insets:] [C:] Grundtriss der Festung BRUNSBUTTEL. Anno 1644. — (Plan). 102 × 122 mm. [C:] Delineatio Urbis MELDORPIÆ. Anno 1500. — (Plan). 128 × 126 mm.

[55] [C:] Landtcarte Von dem Nordertheill Dithmarschen. Nobili, amplissimo, doctissimo ac prudentissimo, Dn. Iohanni Boje, UID. præsidi Dithmarsiæ septentrionalis, fautori suo, Et Honestis ac prudentib₉ Ejusdem Regionis Senatorib₉, Tabulam hanc Geometricam perofficiosè inscribit author Iohannes Mejer₉ Husum. Regæ Majⁱˢ Mathematic₉. — [C:] ... Matthis Pet. & Clauss Peterss Goldtschmide Unt gb Hus. Cimb sculp. — Blank on the back. 400 × 590 mm.
[Insets:] [C:] Grundriss Von Wesslingburen. ... — 101 × 90 mm. [C:] Grundriss Uon Lunden. aō. 1648. — 106 × 83 mm. [C:] Grundriss Von der Heÿde ... — 125 × 142 mm. (All insets plans).

[56] BREMENSIS DVCATVS.
[C:] DUCATUS BREMÆ & FERDÆ a Ioanne Gorries Capitaneo Sueco Jussu Com. Ioan Christoph. a Coningsmarck accuratissime dimensi & in tabulam redacti. — [An empty cartouche]. 185 Germania. Iiii 507 × 620 mm.

[57] LVNÆBVRGVM DVCATVS.
[C:] DVCATVS LVNEBVRGENSIS ... — 189 Germania. Llll = 1635:I:[25].

[58] BRVNSVICENSIS DVCATVS.
[C:] DVCATVS BRVNSVICENSIS fereq₃ LVNÆBVRGENSIS, ... — 191 Germania. Mmmm = 1647—1649:I:[21].

[59] ARCHIEPISCOP. MAGDEBVRGENSIS.
[C:] MAGDEBVRGENSIS ARCHIEPISCOPATVS. — [T:] Amstelædami J. Blaeu excudebat — 195 Germania. Oooo 417 × 506 mm.

[60] HALBERSTADIENSIS EPISCOPATVS.
[C:] EPISCOPATVS HALBERSTAT. — [T:] Amstelædami apud Joannem Blaew. — 199 Germania. Qqqq 429 × 530 mm.

[61] EPISCOPATVS HILDESHEIMENSIS.
[C:] EPISCOPATVS HILDESIENSIS DESCRIPTIO NOVISSIMA ... — 201 Germania. Rrrr = 1635:I:[24].

[62] CIRCVLVS WESTPHALIÆ.
[C:] CIRCVLVS WESTPHALICVS, Sive GERMANIÆ INFERIORIS. — 203 Germania. Ssss = 1647—1649:I:[26].

[63] WESTPHALIA DVCATVS.
[C:] WESTPHALIA Ducatus ... — 205 Germania. Tttt = 1635:I:[34].

[64] MONASTERIENSIS EPISCOPATVS.
[C:] MONASTERIENSIS Episcopatus. ... — 207 Germania. Vuuu = 1635:I:[30].

[65] PADERBORNENSIS EPISCOPATVS.
[C:] PADERBORNENSIS Episcopatus DESCRIPTIO NOVA ... — 211 Germania. Yyyy = 1635:I:[33].

[66] DESCRIPTIO OSNABRVGENSIS EPISCOPATVS.
[C:] OSNABRVGENSIS EPISCOPATVS. ... — 215 Germania. Aaaaa = 1635:I:[32].

[67] COMITATVS BENTHEMENSIS ET STEINFVRTENSIS.
[C:] COMITATVS BENTHEIM, et STEINFVRT. ... — 219 Germania. Ccccc Verso blank = 1635:I:[31].

[68] OLDENBVRGVM COMITATVS.
[C:] OLDENBVRG COMITATVS — 221 Germania. Ddddd = 1635:I:[28] with small alterations.

[69] FRISIA ORIENTALIS.
[C:] TYPVS FRISIÆ ORIENTALIS. ... — 223 Germania. Eeeee = 1635:I:[29].

[70] CLIVIA DVCATVS, ET DOMINIVM RAVENSTEYN.
[C:] CLIVIA DVCATVS ET RAVESTEIN DOMINIVM. — 225 Germania. Fffff = 1635:I:[69].

[71] COMITATVS MARCKA, ET RAVENSBERG.
[C:] COMITATVS MARCHIA ET RAVENSBERG. — 229 Germania. Hhhhh = 1635:I:[68].

[72] DVCATVS IVLIACENSIS.
[C:] IVLIACENSIS ET MONTENSIS DVCATVS. ... — 231 Germania. Iiiii = 1635:I:[67].

[73] LEODIENSIS EPISCOPATVS.
[C:] LEODIENSIS DIOECESIS. — 233 Germania. Kkkkk = 1635:I:[93].

[74] ARCHIEPISCOPATVS COLONIENSIS.
[C:] COLONIENSIS Archiepiscopatus ... — 237 Germania. Mmmmm = 1635:I:[65].

[75] TERRITORIVM COLONIENSE.
[C:] DESCRIPTIO AGRI CIVITATIS COLONIENSIS, Cum suis limitibus, terminis, Viis, confiniis, interjacentibus et adjacentibus Pagis, Villis, Castris, etc. — 239 Germania. Nnnnn 374 × 523 mm.

[76] ARCHIEPISCOPATVS TREVIRENSIS.
[C:] ARCHIEPISCOPATVS TREVIRENSIS — 241 Germania. Ooooo = 1647—1649:I:[76].

[77] [C:] RHENVS Fluviorum Europæ celeberrimus, cum MOSA, MOSELLA. ... — Blank on the back. = 1647—1649:I:[62].

[78] [C:] Totius FLUMINIS RHENI Novissima DESCRIPTIO ex Officina N: Visscher. — [Divided into two parts]. Blank on the back. 466 × 515 mm.

[79] PALATINATVS RHENI.
[C:] PALATINATVS AD RHENVM — 253 Germania. Sssss = 1635:I:[62].

[80] HASSIA SVPERIOR.
[C:] HASSIA SVPERIOR et MOGVNTINVS ARCHIEPISCOPATVS. — 261 Xxxxx 423 × 533 mm.

[81] COMITATVS NASSOVIA.
[C:] NASSOVIA Comitatus. — 263 Germania. Yyyyy = 1635:I:[64].

[82] WETTERAVIA.
[C:] WETTERAVIA. Vulgo die Wetteraw. — 267 Germania. Aaaaaa 395 × 482 mm.

[83] TERRITORIVM FRANCOFVRTENSE AD MOENVM.
[C:] Novam Hanc TERRITORII FRANCOFVRTENSIS Tabulam Nobilissⁱˢ Magnificis, Amplissⁱˢ, Prudentissimisq₃ Dominis Dnn. PRÆTORI, CONSVLIBVS, SCABINIS ET SENATORIBVS inclÿtæ ejusdem vrbis et Reip. Francof. Viris prẹstantissimis, Humanissimis, integerrimisque, Domins fautoribus suis in reverentiæ signum merito D.D.D. Johan. et Cornel. Blaeu. — 269 Germania. Bbbbbb 450 × 550 mm.

[84] HASSIA LANTGRAVIATVS.
[C:] HASSIA Landgraviatus. — 271 Germania. Cccccc = 1647—1649:I:[36].

[85] ABBATIA HIRSCHFELDENSIS.
[C:] TERRITORIVM ABBATIÆ HERESFELDENSIS. ... — 275 Germania. Eeeeee = 1635:I:[38].

[86] WALDECK COMITATVS.
[C:] WALDECK COMITATVS. — 277 Germania. Ffffff = 1635:I:[35].

[87] FRANCONIA.
[C:] FRANCONIA Vulgo Franckenlandt. — 279 Germania. Gggggg = 1635:I:[36].

[88] HENNEBERGENSIS COMITATVS.
[C:] COMITATVS HENNEBERGENSIS. — 283 Germania. Iiiiii 416 × 527 mm.

[89] ERPACH COMITATVS.
[C:] ERPACH COMITATVS. — 285 Germania. Kkkkkk = 1635:I:[63].

[90] COMITATVS WERTHEIM.
[C:] COMITATVS WERTHEIM cum adjacentibus. — 287 Germania. Lllllll Verso blank. 384 × 508 mm.

[91] NORIMBERGENSE TERRITORIVM.
[C:] TERRITORIVM NORIMBERGENSE. — 289 Germania. Mmmmmm = 1635:I:[50].

[92] [C:] DANVBIVS, FLUVIUS EUROPÆ MAXIMUS, ... — Blank on the back = 1647—1649:I:[47].

[93] SVEVIA.
[C:] SVEVIÆ NOVA TABVLA. — 295 Germania. Oooooo = 1635:I:[52].

[94] SVEVIA SVPERIOR.
[C:] ALEMANNIA SIVE SVEVIA SVPERIOR ... — 299 Germania. Qqqqqq = 1635:I:[53].

[95] TERRITORIVM LINDAVIENSE.
[C:] CIVITATIS IMP. LINDAVIENSIS TERRITORIVM. ita Delineabat Iohannes Andreas Rauhen. — 301 Germania. Rrrrrr 460 × 584 mm.

[96] [C:] TERRITORII LINDAVIENSIS PARS SEPTENTRIONALIS. — Between pp. 302 and 303. Verso blank. 286 × 238 mm.

[97] DVCATVS WIRTEMBERGICVS.
[C:] WIRTENBERG DVCATVS. — 303 Germania. Ssssss = 1635:I:[51].

[98] ALSATIA.
[C:] ALSATIA Landgraviatus, ... — 307 Germania. Vuuuuu = 1635:I:[61].

[99] [C:] Utriusque ALSATIÆ, DUCATUS DUPONTII, et SPIRENSIS EPISCOPATUS Novissima Descriptio per F. de Wit. — Blank on the back. 485 × 565 mm.
[Inset:] [T:] DUCATUS DUPONTII PARS SEPTENTRIONALIS. — 137 × 170 mm.

Notes: The maps have text on the verso, except where otherwise specified, and they are all coloured. Pages 155—162 are wanting, but according to the index they contain no maps. There is no engraved title-page in this copy. The volume contains three Visscher maps, [1], [39] and [78], and one by F. de Wit, [99], which are not mentioned in the index or in Koeman. Three maps [49], Pinneberg [53], the first of the three maps of Ditmarschen, and [96], Territorii Lindauiensis pars septentrionalis are wanting in the index, but they do appear in Koeman. The 'Index & Ordo tabularum voluminis terti' has the verso blank; the copy described by Koeman has an 'Index alphabeticus'. The map of Elba, Albis Fluvius, [52], is by Johannes Jansonius; Koeman's is by Christian Moller. The maps by Johannes Mejer, [43]—[51] and [53], [54] have their titles in German; in Koeman they are in Latin. The dedications are in Latin in both copies. In this copy all the Mejer maps are dated; in Koeman, only the last two. The maps were published in Caspar Danckwerth's Newe Landesbeschreibung der Zweij Hertzogthümer Schleswich Vnd Holstein, 1652. The following comparison of the maps is based on the copies in the Nordenskiöld collection:

Blaeu	Danckwert
[43]	= [1]
[44]	cfr [27] different editions
[45]	= [30]
[46]	= [31]
[47]	= [32]
[48]	= [33]
[48]	= [33]
[49]	= [36]
[50]	= [34]
[51]	= [37]
[53 ab]	= [38 ab]
[54]	= [39]

50 of the maps appear in the earlier 1635 and 1647—1649 German text editions of the Novus Atlas in the Nordenskiöld collection. According to Koeman, 40 of the maps are published for the first time in this edition. Nordenskiöld's signature is on the first blank leaf.

Lit.: Keuning, Imago Mundi vol. 14, p. 87—89, Koeman vol. 1, p. 208—212, B1 56, Koeman Blaeu, LC List vol. 3, p. 151—154 nr 3430, Tiele p. 35, nr 133.

Vol. IV
GEOGRAPHIÆ BLAVIANÆ VOLVMEN QVARTVM, QVO LIBER IX, X, EUROPÆ CONTINENTVR. AMSTELÆDAMI, Labore & Sumptibus IOANNIS BLAEV, M DC LXII. 56,5 cm.

BELGICA REGIA, QVÆ EST EUROPÆ LIBER NONVS.
[1] BELGICA.
[C:] NOVUS XVII INFERIORIS GERMANIÆ PROVINCIARUM TYPUS ... — j Belgica. a = 1647—1649:I:[78].

[2] [C:] Novissima et accuratissima XVII PROVINCIARUM GERMANIÆ INFERIORIS Delineatio. Ex officina NICOLAI VISSCHER. — [T:] A.Deur sculpsit. — [T:] Spectatissimo Consultissimoq$_3$ Viro D^O IOHANNI MUNTER Consuli Urbis Amstelædamensis, nec non in Consessu Societatis Indicæ Orientalis Asessori gravissimo, Tabulam hanc D.D.D. Nicolaus Visscher. — Blank on the back. 462 × 561 mm.

[3] [C:] BELGII REGII accuratissima Tabula, Auctore NICOLAO VISSCHER — Blank on the back. 466 × 537 mm.

[4] BRABANTIA DVCATVS.
[C:] BRABANTIA DVCATVS. — I Belgica. A = 1635:I:[84].

[5] [C:] TABULA DUCATUS BRABANTIÆ continens MARCHIONATUM SACRI IMPERII et DOMINIUM MECHLINIENSE de novo accuratè emendata et in lucem edita Per NICOLAUM I. PISCATOREM. — [C:] ... Gedruckt by Claes Ianss Visscher — Blank on the back. 469 × 548 mm.

[6] Brabantiæ pars prima, cujus caput LOVANIVM.
[C:] PRIMA PARS BRABANTIÆ cuius caput LOVANIVM ... — 7 Belgica. C = 1635:I:[86].

[7] BRVXELLÆ.
[C:] SECVNDA PARS BRABANTIÆ cuius urbs primaria BRVXELLÆ ... — 11 Belgica. E = 1635:I:[87].

[8] Tertia pars Brabantiæ, cujus civitas primaria ANTVERPIA; ET MARCHIONATVS S.R. IMPERII.
[C:] TERTIA PARS BRABANTIÆ qua continetur MARCHIONAT.S.R.I. ... — 13 Belgica. F = 1635:I:[88].

[9] DESCRIPTIO CASTELLI AD SANTFLITAM, &c. ex Cl. Viri HVGONIS GROTII Historia de Obsidione Grollæ.
[C:] TABVLA Castelli ad Sandflitam, ... — 19 Belgica. H = 1635:I:[89].

[10] LIMBVRGVM DVCATVS, Et Ditiones Trans-Mosanæ.
[C:] DVCATVS LIMBVRGVM ... — 21 Belgica. I = 1635:I:[91].

[11] [C:] LIMBURGI Ducatus et Comitatus VALCKENBURGI Nova Descriptio Per N: Visscher. — Blank on the back. 463 × 562 mm.

[12] LVTZENBVRGENSIS DVCATVS.
[C:] LVTZENBVRG DVCATVS — 23 Belgica. K = 1647—1649:I:[87].

[13] [C:] DUCATUS LUTZENBURGI Novissima et accuratissima DELINEATIO. per Nicolaum Visscher. — Blank on the back. 462 × 561 mm.

[14] FLANDRIA COMITATVS.
[C:] FLANDRIA ET ZEELANDIA COMITATVS. ... — 29 Belgica. M = 1635:I:[97].

[15] [C:] FLANDRIÆ COMITATUS Accuratissima Descriptio, edita per Nicolaum Visscher. — [C:] ... t' Amsterdam by Nicolaes Visscher. — Blank on the back. 463 × 564 mm.

[16] EPISCOPATVS GANDAVENSIS.
[C:] EPISCOPATVS GANDAVENSIS: Iohannes et Cornelius Blaeu Excudebant. — [C:] Rev.^{mo} et Illmo Dño. D. ANTONIO TRIEST, Episcopo Gandavensi, Comiti de Heverghē, Eprendonck, Mendonck; Domino territorij Sancti Bavonis, etz. hanc accuratissimam sui Episcopatus tabulam D.D. Ioh. et Corn. Blaeu. — 41 Belgica. Q 420 × 523 mm.

[17] CASTELLANIA GANDENSIS.
[C:] NOBILIBUS AMPLISSIMISQ$_3$ DOMINIS D' GEORGIO DE LA FAILLE TOPARCHÆ DE NEUELE etc. PRÆTORI TOTIQ$_3$ COLLEGIO SUPREMÆ

CURIAE FEUDALIS REGIÆ VETERIS BURGI GANDENSIS Hanc Veteris Burgi novam tabulam D.D.Cq₃ Johan et Cornel. Blaeu. — [C:] ANNO DÑI. M . C LXXX: PHILIP COMES FLANDRIE & VIROMANDIE. FILIVS THEODERICI COMITIS & CIBILIE: FECIT HANC PORTAM... — 45 Belgica. S 411 × 489 mm.
[Inset:] [T:] PETRA COMITIS, vulgo het Graven Casteel — (View). 125 × 245 mm.

[18] CASTELLANIA ALDENARDENSIS.
[C:] CASTELLANIA ALDENARDENSIS. — [T:] Ampliss.^{mo} Nobilissimoq₃ MAGISTRATVI CASTELLANIÆ ALDENARDENSIS Geographicam hanc ejusdem ditionis Tabulam Observantiæ ergo D.D.D. ANT. SANDERVS Gandavensis. — On 48 176 × 303 mm.

[19] EPISCOPATVS BRVGENSIS
[C:] EPISCOPATVS BRVGENSIS. Ad Illustrissimum & Reverendissimum NICOLAVM HAVDION Episcopum Brugensium denominat. — 53 Belgica. X 364 × 486 mm.

[20] FRANCONATVS vulgo HET VRYE.
[C:] FRANCONATVS, Vulgo HET VRYE. — [T:] Guiljelmus et Iohannes Blaeuw exc. Amstelodami. — 57 Belgica. Z 377 × 496 mm.

[21] EPISCOPATVS IPRENSIS.
[C:] IPRENSIS Episcopatus. Perillustri et Re.^{mo} Dño D. IVDOCO BOVCKAERD IPRENSIS ECCLESIÆ EPISCOPO Tab. hanc ejusdem Episcopatus D.D. Joh: Blaeu. — [T:] Ioh: Blaeu excud. — 69 Belgica. Dd 405 × 496 mm.

[22] CASTELLANIA IPRENSIS.
[T:] NOVA ET EXACTA TABVLA GEOGRAPHICA SALÆ ET CASTELLANIÆ IPRENSIS. De Casselrie van Ipre. LA CHASTELENIE D'IPRE ANNO M DC XXXXI — [T:] Vedastus du Plouich fec. Henricus Hondius excudebat. — [C:] ILLUSTRIBUS AC GENEROSIS DOMINIS DOMINIS. PRÆTORI, SENATUI, AC NOBILIBUS VASALLIS.SALÆ REGIÆ ET CASTELLANIÆ YPRENSIS: VIRIS Prudentiæ ac æquitatis laude clarissimis, Hanc Geographicam eiusdem Castellaniæ Tabulam D.D. Antonius Sanderus. — 73 Belgica. Ff 390 × 487 mm.
[Insets:] (View) 110 × 340 mm. and 20 architectural drawings.

[23] CASTELLANIA CORTVRIACENSIS.
[C:] CASTELLANIÆ CORTVRIACENSIS TABVLA. — [T:] Generoso et Illustri viro D. PHILIPPO TRIEST, Equiti Ord. S.Iacobi Summo Vrbis et Castellaniæ Corturiacensis Prætori: Nobiliss. item et Ampliss. Dominis D. FLORENTIO DE GRIBOVAL, Equiti, Toparchæ de Sweveghem etc. D. CAROLO DE SCHIETERE Equiti, Toparchæ de Maelstaple, D. IOANNI DV FOREST Toparchæ de Heuverie. D. GVILIELMO DE VVLDER, Domino de Duderseele. Prudentibusque viris ac liberis ejusdem Castellaniæ Scabinis ... D.D. Ant. Sanderus. — 77 Belgica. Hh 362 × 489 mm.

[24] FLANDRIÆ TEVTONICÆ PARS OCCIDENTALIOR.
[C:] PARS FLANDRIÆ TEVTONICÆ OCCIDENTALIOR. — 83 Belgica. Kk = 1635:I:[98].

[25] CASTELLANIA CASLETENSIS.
[T:] DITIO CASLETANA IN COMITATU FLANDRIÆ Vulgo Cassel Ambacht. — [T:] Amstelodami Sumtibus Henrici Hondy. — [C:] ILLUSTRISSIMO VIRO D. LAMORALDO DE HORNES VICECOMITI FURNENSI SUMMO CASLETENSIUM PRÆTORI NOBILISSIMIS ITEM AC AMLISSIMIS D. VASSALLIS CÆTERISQUE CURIÆ AC DITIONIS CASLETANÆ MODERATORIBUS D.D. Anthonius Sanderus. Vedastus du Plouich invenit et fecit. — 85 Belgica. Ll 384 × 479 mm.

[26] CASTELLANIA FVRNENSIS.
[C:] CASTELLANIA FURNENSIS. — 9 Belgica. Nn 413 × 527 mm.

[27] CASTELLANIA BERGENSIS.
[T:] ACCURATA TERRITORII BERGENSIS ET AQUAEDUCTUUM DELINEATIO — [C:] Nobilibus ac Amplissimis Dominis Vrbis ac territorii BERGENSIS MAGISTRATIBUS Hosce primos suos ausus D D.C.Q. Iacobus de la Fontaine — 99 Belgica. Qq 369 × 487 mm.

[28] FLANDRIA IMPERIALIS ET PROPRIETARIA.
[C:] FLANDRIÆ ... — 103 Belgica. SS = 1635:I:[102].

[29] BORNHEM BARONATVS.
[C:] Castellaniæ Siue Baronat: Bornhemii Accurata delineatio. — On 110   155 × 230 mm.

[30] ALOSTANVS.
[C:] NOVA ET ACCVRATA COMITATVS ET DITIONIS ALOSTANÆ in Flandria Imperiali TABVLA. — [T:] Illustrissimo Domino D. PRÆTORI Cæterisque Amplissimis ac Nobilissimis MAGISTRATIBVS Comitatus et Ditionis Alostanæ Prudentissimis Æquissimisque IMPERIALIS FLANDRIÆ MODERATORIBVS Geographicam hanc eiusdem Ditionis Tabulam honoris et obseruantiæ ergo D.D. Antonius Sanderus Gandauensis. — 117 Belgica. Yy 364 × 465 mm.

[31] QVATERNA FLANDRIÆ AMBACTA.
[C:] KAERTE VAN DE VIER AMBACHTEN. — [T:] Geraerd Coeck sculp. — 121 Belgica. Aaa 413 × 528 mm.

[32] WASIA, vulgò HET LANDT VAN WAES.
[C:] WASIA. 'T Land van Waes. — [C:] Ampliss. Nobiliss. Prudentissimisq₃ viris D. MAXÆMILIANO vander GRACHT, Equiti, Domino de Vremde, Eechove, Schardā, etc. SVMMO PRÆTORI; D. GEORGIO DE BRACLE, Domino de Willecomme, Varebeke etc. D. IACOBO VANDER ELST D. CAROLO DE HARTOGHE Domino de Padeschot etc. D. FREDERICO VAN NIEVWELAND, Domino de Walle D. ÆGIDIO DANSAERT D.PHILIPPO LAMORAEL D.IOHANNI DOISTERLINCK SCABINIS TERRÆ WASIÆ Tabulam hanc D.D. Antonius Sanderus. — 123 Belgica. Bbb 369 × 451 mm.

[33] DITIVNCVLA DE LALEVE.
[C:] Ditiuncula in Confiniis Flandriæ Gallicanæ sita, vulgo LE PAYS DE LALLEVE Sub Dominio Abbatis S. Vedasti ad Atrebatum Vedasto du Plouich Auctore. — [T:] V. du Plouich Fecit — On 128   177 × 237 mm.

[34] GALLO-FLANDRIA.
[C:] GALLOFLANDRIA, ... — 129 Belgica. Ddd = 1635:I:[101].

[35] ARTESIA COMITATVS, vulgo ARTHOIS.
[C:] ARTESIA COMITATVS. ARTOIS. — 137 Belgica. Ggg = 1635:I:[103].

[36] [C:] GEOGRAPHICA ARTESIÆ COMITATUS TABULA, per NICOLAUM VISSCHER edita. — Blank on the back.   462 × 560 mm.

[37] HANNONIA COMITATVS.
[C:] COMITATVVM HANNONIÆ ET NAMVRCI DESCRIPTIO. — 141 Belgica. Iii = 1635:I:[96].

[38] [C:] COMITATUS HANNONIÆ et ARCHIEPISCOPATUS CAMERACENSIS TABULA, Per Nicolaum Visscher. — Blank on the back.   463 × 563 mm.

[39] NAMVRCVM COMITATVS.
[C:] NAMVRCVM COMITATUS ... — 145 Belgica. Lll = 1635:I:[95].

[40] [C:] COMITATUS NAMURCI Emendata Delineatio, Nuperrimè in lucem edita, Per Nicolaum Visscher. — Blank on the back.   462 × 561 mm.

[41] MECHLINIA DOMINIVM.
[C:] MECHLINIA DOMINIVM et AERSCHOT DVCATVS ... — 147 Belgica. Mmm = 1635:I:[92].

[42] [C:] MECHLINIA DOMINIUM et AERSCHOT DUCATUS Auctore Nicolao Visscher. — Blank on the back.   462 × 562 mm.

[43] GELRIÆ TETRARCHIA RVRÆMONDANA.
[C:] TETRARCHIA Ducatus Gelriæ RVRÆMVNDENSIS. — 151 Belgica. Ooo 407 × 528 mm.

[44] FOSSA S. MARIÆ, Quæ & EVGENIANA dicta, Rhenum Mosamque inter duci cæpta anno 1628.
[C:] FOSSA SANCTÆ MARIÆ, ... — 153 Belgica Ppp = 1647—1649:I:[102].

[45] CAMERACVM ET CAMERACESIVM.
[C:] ARCHIEPISCOPATVS CAMERACENSIS.

Archevesché de CAMBRAY. — [T:] AMSTERDAMI Apud Guiljelmum Blaeuw. — [C:] Illustrissimo ac Reverendissimo Domino D. FRANCISCO VA'NDER BVRGH Archiepiscopo ac Duci Cameracensi, Comiti Cameracesii, etc. Principi Sacri Romani Imperii Tabulam hanc D.D.D Johannes Blaeu. — 155 Belgica. Qqq = 1635:II:[3], but the dedication added.

BELGICA FOEDERATA, QVÆ EST EUROPÆ LIBER DECIMVS.

[46] BELGICA FOEDERATA.
[C:] BELGICA FŒDERATA. — j Belgica Fœderata. a 429 × 519 mm.
[Inset:] [T:] Mosa Flu [from] Wessem [to] Maestricht — 58 × 40 mm.

[47] GELDRIA DVCATVS.
[C:] GELDRIA DVCATVS et ZVTFANIA COMITATVS. — I Belgica Fœderata. A = 1635:I:[73].

[48] [C:] DUCATUS GELDRIA et ZUTPHANIA Comitatus. — [C:] ... 't Amsteldam gedruckt by NICOLAES VISSCHER In de Kalverstraet inde Visscher. — Blank on the back. 461 × 563 mm.

[49] NEOMAGVM.
[C:] TETRARCHIA Ducatus Gelriæ NEOMAGENSIS. — 7 Belgica Fœederata. C 380 × 524 mm.

[50] ZUTPHANIA COMITATVS, SIVE GELDRIÆ TETRARCHIA ZVTPHANIENSIS.
[C:] ZVTPHANIA COMITATVS, sive Ducatus Gelriæ TETRARCHIA Zutphaniensis. — 9 Belgica Fœderata. D 407 × 524 mm.

[51] [C:] Novissima COMITATUS ZUTPHANIÆ, Totiusq3 Fluminis ISULÆ DESCRIPTIO, Ex Officina Nicolai Visscher. — Blank on the back. 462 × 558 mm.

[52] ARNHEMIVM.
[C:] TETRARCHIA Ducatus Gelriæ ARNHEMIENSIS, sive VELAVIA. — 13 Belgica Fœderata. F 408 × 524 mm.

[53] VETERIS BATAVIÆ PARS, SIVE TRACTVS RHENI, & MOSÆ, TOTIVSQVE VAHALIS, ...
[C:] Tractus RHENI et MOSÆ totusq3 VAHALIS ... — 15 Belgica Fœderata. G = 1635:I:[83].

[54] HOLLANDIA COMITATVS.
[C:] HOLLANDIA COMITATVS. — 19 Belgica Fœderata. I = 1635:I:[77].

[55] [T:] COMITATUS HOLLANDIÆ TABULA PLURIBUS LOCIS RECENS EMENDATA A NICOLAO I. VISSCHERO. — [T:] Visscher excudit. — Blank on the back. 460 × 561 mm.
[Inset:] [T:] De resterende Eylanden van Hollant alhier dus bÿgevoecht om ons besteck soo groot te houden als t'papier konde lÿden — 105 × 100 mm. (Irregular).

[56] HOLLANDIA AVSTRALIS.
[C:] ZVYDHOLLANDIA stricte sumta. — 35 Belgica Fœderata. O = 1635:I:[81].

[57] SCHIELANDIA.
[C:] DELFLANDIA, SCHIELANDIA, ... — 39 Belgica Fœderata. Q = 1635:I:[80].

[58] RHENOLANDIA.
[C:] RHENOLANDIÆ et AMSTELLANDIÆ exactissima Tabula. — 41 Belgica Fœderata. R = 1635:I:[79].

[59] [C:] RHENOLANDIA, AMSTELANDIA Et Circumjacentia aliquot Territoria, cum Aggeribus omnibus, Terminisq3 suis, Accurate et distincte edita, per Nicolaum Visscher. — [C:] Amplissimo, Spectat.[mo] Consultissimoq3 Viro D. IOHANNI HUDDE, Rei Publ. Amstelædamensis Consuli, Senatori ac Thesaurario dignissimo etc. Mathematico Summo Hanc Tabulam D.D.D. Nicolaus Visscher. — Blank on the back. 460 × 563 mm.

[60] WEST-FRISIA.
[C:] HOLLANDIÆ PARS SEPTENTRIONALIS, ... — 47 Hollandia. T = 1635:I:[78].

[61] ZIPA.
[C:] AGRI ZYPANI Nova Descript. — 49 Belgica Fœderata. V 374 × 492 mm.

[62] BEEMSTRA.
[C:] AGRI BIEMSTRANI Descriptio a L.I.S. — 51 Belgica Fœderata. X 368 × 477 mm.

[63] [a] [C:] Kaarte vande Buyck-slooter, Broecker ende Belmer Meeren in Water-land. Gemeten door M[r] SNBoonacker. — 266 × 472 mm.
[Inset:] [C:] Kaerte van Water land Vertonende de gelegentheyt der Meeren onlangs bedyckt, als Purmer, Buyck-slooter, Broecker en Belmer Meer met de naest ghelegen Steeden. — 90 × 185 mm.
[b] [C:] CAERTE VAN DE Purmer, Gemeten ende getekent, door M[r] Luÿcas Ianss Sinck. Anno 1622. — 184 × 301 mm.
[c:] [C:] BYLLEMER-MEER — [T:] C.D. de Rij. 1626 — 172 × 224 mm. [The whole map:] Blank on the back.

[64] [C:] CAERTE VAN DE SCHER-MEER, Alsoo de selve is Bedyckt, ende by Cavels van 15 Morgen suyver landt door lotinge uytgedelt, op den 25 October Anno 1635. ende aldus met groote verbeteringe int licht gegeuen — Blank on the back. 463 × 561 mm.

[65] TRACTVS HOLLANDIÆ SEPTENTRIONALIS, Quem vulgo HET KOEGRAS vocant.
[C:] Kaerte van alle de Sanden, Gorsingen, Slicken, Waerden ende Kreecken, gelegen tusschen HUYSDUYNEN, WIERINGEN, WIERINGERWAERDT, ZYP ENDE KALANDS — OOGE, GENAEMT HET KOE-GRAS, Inde welcke d'Erfgenamen van S.[al] Isaack le Maire, als eygenaers vande gronden gelegen onder t'resort van Huysduynen, van meininge zijn (volgens haer Octroy) uyt te geven, ende te bedÿcken DE POLDER VAN LE MAIRE, alhier afgebeelt. — 52,b Belgica Fœderata. X2 Verso blank. 463 × 565 mm.

[66] BERGÆ IN KENNEMARIA.
[T:] TERRITORII BERGENSIS ACCVRATISSIMA DESCRIPTIO. — [T:] Joannes Dou, Geometra Lugduno-Batavus mensuravit & delineavit. — [C:] Nob.[mo] & Gen.[so] Dño. D. ANTONIO STVDLER EQVITI, Bergarum in Kennemaria TOPARCHÆ ; Sweyburgii Domino &c. Tab. hanc D.D. J.Blaeu. — 53 Belgica Fœderata. Y 414 × 550 mm.

[67] ZELANDIA COMITATVS.
[C:] ZEELANDIA Comitatus. — 55 Belgica Fœderata. Z = 1635:I:[104].

[68] [C:] COMITATVS ZELANDIÆ Novissima Delineatio per NICOLAUM VISSCHER. — [T:] Visscher Excudit — [C:] Viro Amplissimo prudentissimoque D. Adriano Veth , Jurisconsulto et illustrium Zelandiæ Ordinum Syndico Dignissimo Flandriæque Concilÿ Assessori, Tabulam hanc L.M.Q.D.D. N. Visscher. — Blank on the back. 461 × 549 mm.

[69] WALACHRIA, ZELANDIÆ CIS-SCALDINÆ INSVLA.
[C:] WALACHRIA, ZELANDIÆ CISSCALDINÆ INSVLA OCCIDENTALIS. — 59 Belgica Fœderata. Bb 444 × 543 mm.

[70] ZELANDIÆ CIS-SCALDINÆ PARS ORIENTALIOR.
[C:] VTRAQVE BEVELANDIA, & WOLFERSDYCK, INSVLÆ ORIENTALIORES ZELANDIÆ CISSCALDINÆ; Vernacule, De Oostelycke Eylanden van BEWESTER-Scheld. — 61 Belgica Fœderata. Cc 434 × 561 mm.

[71] ZELANDIA, TRANS-SCALDINA, vulgò BEOOSTER-SCHELD.
[C:] ZELANDIÆ PARS TRANSSCALDINA Vulgo BEOOSTER-SCHELD. — [C:] Nobiliss. Prudentiss. D. IODOCO DE HVYBERT, Syndico Civitatis Zirizeæ, AD CHRISTIANISS. GALLIARVM REGEM NOMINE ORDD.BELG. FŒDERATÆ LEGATO EXTRAORDINARIO Tabulam hanc D.D. I.BLAEV. — 63 Belgica Fœderata. Dd 453 × 572 mm.

[72] VLTRAIECTINVM DOMINIVM.
[C:] VLTRAIECTVM DOMINIVM. ... — 65 Belgica Fœderata. Ee = 1635:I:[82].

[73] [C:] ULTRAIECTINI DOMINII TABULA Multo aliis auctior et correctior, per Nic: Visscher. — [C:] R de Hooghe fecit — Blank on the back. 461 × 564 mm.

[74] FRISIA OCCIDENTALIS.
[C:] FRISIA OCCIDENTALIS... — 71 Belgica Fœderata. Gg = 1635:I:[76].

[75] [C:] DOMINII FRISIÆ Tabula, inter FLEVUM et

LAVICAM, Auctore B. Schotano à Sterringa. ex Officina Nicolai Visscher. — Blank on the back. 472 × 558 mm.
[Inset:] [T:] Caerte vande Vriese Eylanden — 50 × 77 mm.

[76] TRANSISALANIA, vulgo OVER-YSSEL.
[C:] TRANSISALANIA PROVINCIA; Vulgo OVER-YSSEL. Auct. N. Ten-Have. Sch.Zwol. Conrect. — [T:] Geraerd Coeck sculp. — 71 b Belgica Fœderata. Gg 2 436 × 554 mm.

[77] GRONINGA DOMINIVM.
[C:] GRONINGA DOMINIVM. ... — 73 Belgica Fœderata. Hh = 1635:I:[75].

[78] [C:] DOMINII GRONINGÆ nec non maximæ partis DRENTIÆ Novissima Delineatio, per Nicolaum Visscher. R. de H f. — [T:] Nicolaus Visscher excud: — Blank on the back. 460 × 560 mm.
[Inset:] [T:] Caerte vande Groeninger Eylanden ende Watte. — 102 × 116 mm.

[79] DRENTIA.
[C:] DRENTIA COMITATVS. Auctore Cornelio Pynacker I.C. — 79 Belgica Fœderata. Kk = 1647—1649:I:[113], but without "Transiselaniæ Tabula II" in the cartouche.

[80] Brabantiæ pars quarta, cujus caput SYLVA-DVCIS.
[C:] QVARTA PARS BRABANTIÆ cujus caput SYLVADVCIS. ... — 81 Belgica Fœderata. Ll = 1635:I:[85], but six coats-of arms added in the earlier empty places.

[81] DESCRIPTIO BERGARVM AD ZOMAM, STEENBERGÆ, & novorum ibi operum.
[C:] TABVLA Bergarum ad Zomam Stenbergæ ... — 83 Belgica Fœderata. Mm = 1635:I:[90].

Notes: The maps have text on the verso, except where otherwise specified, and they are all coloured. The engraved title-pages of Liber nonus and Liber decimus are also coloured, and the text has been printed separately and pasted in the proper spaces. This copy contains 18 maps by Nicolaus Visscher, bound in after the earlier maps of the same places; these are not present in the copy described by Koeman, and only the first two are in the Library of Congress copy. 31 of the other maps do not appear in earlier Blaeu atlases; 17 from Belgica Regia, Liber nonus, and 14 from Belgica Foederata, Liber Decimus. Map [27], Accurata Territorii Bergensis et Aquaeductuum delineatio, is pasted on p.99 and p.100. Map [63], Kaarte vande Buyck-slooter... is not listed in the index. On map [78], Dominii Groningæ... per Nicolaum Visscher, the signature'R de H f'stands for Romain de Hooghe, whose name also appears on map [73]. Nordenskiöld's signature is on the first blank leaf of the atlas.

Lit.: Keuning, Imago Mundi vol. 14, p. 87—89, Koeman, vol. 1, p. 213—215, Bl 56, Koeman, Blaeu, p. 64—68, LC List, vol. 3, p. 147, 154—155, nr 3430, Tiele p. 35, nr 133.

Vol. V
GEOGRAPHIÆ BLAVIANÆ VOLVMEN QVINTVM, QVO ANGLIA, QVÆ EST EUROPÆ LIBER UNDECIMVS, CONTINETVR. AMSTELÆDAMI, Labore & Sumptibus IOANNIS BLAEV, M DC LXII. 56,6 cm

ANGLIA, QVAE EST EUROPÆ LIBER XI. Amsterdami, Apud IOHANNEM BLAEV, M DC XLVIII.

[1] BRITANNIA.
[C:] MAGNÆ BRITANNIÆ et HIBERNIÆ TABVLA — I Britannia. A = 1635:I:[3].

[2] BRITANNIA.
[C:] BRITANNIA prout divisa fuit temporibus ANGLO-SAXONVM, præsertim durante illorum HEPTARCHIA. — 59 Britannia. Q 410 × 313 mm.

[3] BRITANNIA.
[C:] ANGLIA REGNVM — 73 Britannia. V = 1635:I:[4].

[4] DANMONII. CORNWALL.
[C:] CORNVBIA. sive CORNWALLIA. — 87 Britannia. Aa 386 × 497 mm.

[5] DENSHIRE.
[C:] DEVONIA Vulgo DEVON-SHIRE. — 95 Britannia. Dd 389 × 498 mm.

[6] DVROTRIGES. DORSET-SHIRE.
[C:] COMITATVS DORCESTRIA, sive DORSETTIA; Vulgo Anglice DORSET SHIRE. — 101 Britannia. Ff 379 × 500 mm.

[7] SOMERSET-SHIRE.
[C:] SOMERSETTENSIS COMITATVS. Somerset shire. — 107 Britannia. Hh 381 × 498 mm.

[8] WILSHIRE.
[C:] WILTONIA sive COMITATVS WILTONIENSIS; Anglis WIL SHIRE. — 117 Britannia. Ll 408 × 498 mm.

[9] HANT-SHIRE.
[C:] HANTONIA SIVE SOVTHANTONENSIS COMITATVS Vulgo HANT-SHIRE. — 123 Britannia. Nn 412 × 497 mm.

[10] VECTA INSVLA. ISLE OF WIGHT.
[C:] VECTIS INSVLA. Anglice THE ISLE OF WIGHT. — [T:] Ioh. Blaeu Excud. — 131 Britannia. Qq 381 × 501 mm.

[11] ATTREBATII. BARK-SHIRE
[C:] BERCHERIA Vernacule BARK SHIRE. — 133 Britannia. Rr 378 × 498 mm.

[12] SVT — REY.
[C:] SVRRIA Vernacule SVRREY. — 141 Britannia. Vu 377 × 496 mm.

[13] SVSSEX.
[C:] SVTHSEXIA; Vernacule SVSSEX. — 145 Britannia. Yy 377 × 521 mm.

[14] KENT.
[C:] CANTIVM Vernacule KENT. — 153 Britannia. Bbb 381 × 527 mm.

[15] GLOCESTER-SHIRE.
[C:] GLOCESTRIA DVCATVS; Vulgo GLOCESTER SHIRE. — 167 Britannia. Fff 408 × 498 mm.

[16] OXFORD-SHIRE.
[C:] OXONIVM Comitatus, Vulgo OXFORD SHIRE. — [T:] Ioh. Blaeu excud. — 173 Britannia. Hhh 379 × 502 mm.

[17] CATTIEVCHLANI. BVCKINGHAM-SHIRE.
[a] [C:] BEDFORDIENSIS COMITATVS; Anglis BEDFORD SHIRE. — 412 × 240 mm.
[b] [C:] BVCKINGHAMIENSIS COMITATVS; Anglis BVCKINGHAM SHIRE. — 413 × 266 mm.
[The whole map:] 181 Britannia. Lll 413 × 527 mm.

[18] HERTFORD-SHIRE.
[C:] HERTFORDIA COMITATVS. Vernacule HERTFORDSHIRE — 187 Britannia. Nnn 378 × 497 mm.

[19] TRINOBANTES.
[C:] MIDDLE-SEXIA. — 193 Britannia. Ppp 387 × 404 mm.

[20] ESSEX.
[C:] ESSEXIA COMITATVS. — 203 Britannia. Sss 414 × 522 mm.

[21] ICENI.
[C:] SVFFOLCIA, Vernacule SVFFOLKE. — 211 Britannia. Xxx 377 × 497 mm.

[22] NORTH-FOLKE.
[C:] NORTFOLCIA, NORFOLKE. — 219 Britannia. Aaaa 375 × 495 mm.

[23] NORTH-FOLKE.
[C:] REGIONES INVNDATÆ In finibus Comitatus NORFOLCIÆ, SVFFOLCIÆ, CANTABRIGIÆ, HVNTINGTONIÆ NORTHAMTONIÆ, ET LINCOLNIÆ — [An empty cartouche]. 221 Britannia. Bbbb 431 × 538 mm.

[24] CAMBRIDGE-SHIRE.
[C:] CANTABRIGIENSIS COMITATVS; CAMBRIDGE SHIRE. — 227 Britannia. Dddd 413 × 521 mm.

[25] HVNTINGDON-SHIRE.
[C:] HVNTINGDONENSIS COMITATVS; HVNTINGTON SHIRE. — 233 Britannia. Ffff 390 × 497 mm.

[26] NORTHAMPTON-SHIRE.
[C:] COMITATVS NORTHANTONENSIS; Vernacule NORTHAMTON SHIRE. — 237 Britannia. Hhhh 410 × 494 mm.

[27] LEICESTER-SHIRE.
[C:] LEICESTRENSIS COMITATVS. LEICESTER SHIRE. — 243 Britannia. Kkkk 379 × 496 mm.
[28] RVTHLAND-SHIRE.
[C:] RVTLANDIA COMITATVS. RVTLAND SHIRE. — 247 Britannia. Mmmm 378 × 497 mm.
[29] LINCOLNE-SHIRE.
[C:] LINCOLNIA COMITATVS. Anglis LINCOLN-SHIRE. — 249 Britannia. Nnnn 417 × 500 mm.
[30] NOTTINGHAM-SHIRE.
[C:] COMITATVS NOTTINGHAMIENSIS; NOTTINGHAM SHIRE. — 259 Britannia. Qqqq 379 × 497 mm.
[31] DARBY-SHIRE.
[C:] DARBIENSIS COMITATVS. Vernacule DARBIE SHIRE. — 261 Britannia. Rrrr 380 × 497 mm.
[32] WARWICK-SHIRE.
[C:] WIGORNIENSIS Comitatus et Comitatus WARWICENSIS; nec non COVENTRÆ LIBERTAS. WORCESTER, WARWIK SHIRE. and THE LIBERTY OF COVENTRE. — 265 Britannia. Tttt 408 × 501 mm.
[33] STAFFORD-SHIRE.
[C:] STAFFORDIENSIS COMITATVS; Vulgo STAFFORD SHIRE. — 273 Britannia. Yyyy 406 × 501 mm.
[34] SHROPP-SHIRE.
[C:] COMITATVS SALOPIENSIS; Anglice SHROP SHIRE. — 277 Britannia. Aaaaa — 378 × 497 mm.
[35] CHES-SHIRE.
[C:] CESTRIA COMITATVS PALATINVS. — 283 Britannia. Ccccc 378 × 498 mm.
[36] WALLIA. SILVRES.
[C:] WALLIA PRINCIPATVS Vulgo WALES. —
[C:] SEREN.^{mo} DOMINO CAROLO MAGNÆ BRITANNIÆ, etc. PRINCIPI. Ioh. Blaeu. — 289 Britannia. Eeeee 382 × 498 mm.
[37] HEREFORD-SHIRE.
[C:] HEREFORDIA COMITATVS. HEREFORD-SHIRE. — 291 Britannia. Fffff 407 × 496 mm.
[38] RADNOR-SHIRE.
[C:] RADNORIA COMITATVS RADNOR-SHIRE. — 293 Britannia. Ggggg 378 × 495 mm.
[39] BRECHNOCK-SHIRE.
[C:] COMITATVS BRECHINIÆ; BREKNOKE. — 295 Britannia. Hhhhh 373 × 505 mm.
[40] MONMOVTH-SHIRE.
[C:] MONVMETHENSIS COMITATVS. Vernacule MONMOVTH SHIRE. — [T:] I.Blaeu Exc. — 297 Britannia. Iiiii 378 × 496 mm.
[41] GLAMORGAN-SHIRE.
[C:] GLAMORGANENSIS COMITATVS; Vulgo GLAMORGAN SHIRE. — 301 Britannia. Lllll 379 × 506 mm.
[42] DIMETÆ.
[C:] PENBROCHIA Comitatus et Comitatus CAERMARIDVNVM. — 305 Britannia. Nnnnn 407 × 531 mm.
[43] CARDIGAN-SHIRE.
[C:] CERETICA; sive CARDIGANENSIS Comitatus; Anglis CARDIGAN SHIRE. — 309 Britannia. Ppppp 379 × 497 mm.
[44] MONTGOMERY-SHIRE.
[C:] MONTGOMERIA Comitatus et Comitatus MERVINIA. — 311 Britannia. Qqqqq 378 × 498 mm.
[45] CAERNARVON-SHIRE.
[C:] COMITATVS CAERNARVONIENSIS; Vernacule CARNARVON-SHIRE. et MONA INSVLA Vulgo ANGLESEY. — 313 Britannia. Rrrrr 378 × 496 mm.
[46] FLINT-SHIRE.
[C:] DENBIGIENSIS Comitatus et Comitatus FLINTENSIS; DENBIGH et FLINTSHIRE. — [An empty cartouche]. 317 Britannia. Ttttt 378 × 495 mm.
[47] YORKE-SHIRE.
[C:] DVCATVS EBORACENSIS Anglice YORK SHIRE. — [T:] SEREN.^{mo} PRINCIPI IACOBO EBORACENSIUM DVCI, etc. — 321 Britannia. Xxxxx 388 × 500 mm.
[48] YORKE-SHIRE.
[C:] DVCATVS EBORACENSIS PARS OCCIDENTALIS; THE WESTRIDING OF YORKE SHIRE. — 323 Britannia. Yyyyy 380 × 498 mm.
[49] EAST-RIDING.
[C:] DVCATVS EBORACENSIS PARS ORIENTALIS; The Eastriding of Yorkeshire. — 331 Britannia. Bbbbbb 378 × 499 mm.
[50] NORTH-RIDING.
[C:] DVCATVS EBORACENSIS PARS BOREALIS THE NORTHRIDING OF YORK SHIRE. — 335 Britannia. Dddddd 380 × 497 mm.
[51] BISHOPRICKE OF DURHAM.
[C:] EPISCOPATVS DVNELMENSIS. Vulgo The Bishoprike of DVRHAM. — 345 Britannia. Gggggg 379 × 498 mm.
[52] LANCA-SHIRE.
[C:] LANCASTRIA PALATINATVS Anglis LANCASTER et Lancas shire. — 349 Britannia. Iiiiii 349 × 506 mm.
[53] WESTMORE-LAND.
[C:] WESTMORIA COMITATVS; Anglice WESTMORLAND. — 357 Britannia. Mmmmmm 378 × 493 mm.
[54] CVMBER-LAND.
[C:] CVMBRIA; Vulgo CVMBERLAND. — 359 Britannia. Nnnnnn 408 × 495 mm.
[55] OTTADINI. NORTH-HVMBER-LAND.
[C:] COMITATVS NORTHVMBRIA Vernacule NORTHUMBERLAND. — [T:] Ioh: Blaeu Exc. — 373 Britannia. Rrrrrr 408 × 497 mm.
[56] [C:] MONA. — 377 × 271 mm.
[57] INSVLÆ BRITANNICÆ.
[C:] INSVLA SACRA; Vulgo HOLY ILAND; et FARNE. — 395 Britannia. Zzzzzz 387 × 469 mm.
[58] IARSEY & GARNSEY.
[C:] SARNIA INSVLA, Vulgo GARNSEY: et INSVLA CÆSAREA, Vernacule IARSEY. — 397 Britannia. Aaaaaaa 387 × 470 mm.

Notes: All the maps have text on the verso, and are coloured. The engraved title-page is the same as that in Blaeu's Theatrum, vol. 4; the year 1648 is that of the Dutch edition and of the second Latin edition of the Theatrum. The title is printed on a separate slip which has been pasted in the proper place on the engraved title-page. Maps [2] and [4]-[58] were published earlier in vol. 4 of the French 1645 edition of the Theatrum, and all the maps in this volume were published with the same pagination in the Latin edition of 1648. Koeman's description of this volume, in Bl 56, corresponds with our copy, but the pagination of the last three maps is different. In the index this pagination differs both from that in the atlas itself and from that given by Koeman. Nordenskiöld's signature is on the first blank leaf of the volume.

Lit.: Koening, Imago Mundi vol. 14, p. 87—89, Koeman vol. 1, p. 215—218, Bl 56, Koeman, Blaeu, p. 68—70, LC List vol.3, p. 155—157, 3430, Tiele p. 35, nr 133.

Vol. VI
GEOGRAPHIÆ BLAVIANÆ VOLVMEN SEXTVM, QVO LIBER XII, XIII, EUROPÆ CONTINENTVR. AMSTELÆDAMI, Labore & Sumptibus IOANNIS BLAEV, M DC LXII. 56,7 cm.

SCOTIA, QVÆ EST EUROPÆ LIBER XII. AMSTELÆDAMI Apud IOANNEM BLAEV M DC LIV.
[1] ROBERTI GORDONII DE THVLE INSVLA DISSERTATIO.
[C:] INSVLÆ ALBION et HIBERNIA ... — 7 Scotia. C = 1654:V:[1].
[2] ROBERTI GORDONII AD VETERIS SCOTIÆ TABVLAM ADNOTATA.
[C:] SCOTIA ANTIQVA, ... — [9] Scotia. D = 1654:V:[2].

[3] BREVISSIMA REGNI SCOTIÆ DESCRIPTIO, Ex lib. I Hist. GEORGII BVCHANANI Scoti desumpta.
[a] [C:] SCOTIA REGNVM ... — [b] [C:] ORCADES et SHETLANDICÆ INSVLÆ ... — 13 Scotia. F = 1654:V:[3].

[4] GADENI SIVE LADENI. TEVIOTIA, vulgo TEIFIDALE.
[C:] TEVIOTIA Vulgo TIVEDAIL — 31 Scotia. L Verso blank. = 1654:V:[4].

[5] TWEDIÆ ET PROVINCIÆ PEBLIANÆ DESCRIPTIO.
[C:] TVEDIA ... — 33 Scotia M = 1654:V:[5].

[6] LAVDERDALIA.
[C:] LAVDELIA ... — 35 Scotia. N Verso blank. = 1654:V:[6].

[7] MARCIA.
[C:] MERCIA ... — 37 Scotia. O Verso blank. = 1654:V:[7], but schips added.

[8] LAVDEN SIVE LOTHIEN.
[C:] LOTHIAN and LINLITQVO— 39 Scotia. P = 1654:V:[8], but ships added.

[9] SELGOVÆ. LIDESDALE.
[C:] LIDALIA vel LIDISDALIA REGIO, ... — 45 Scotia. R Verso blank. = 1654:V:[9].

[10] EVIA ET ESCIA, vulgo EVSDAIL & ESKDAIL.
[C:] EVIA et ESCIA, ... — 47 Scotia. S Verso blank. = 1654:V:[10].

[11] DESCRIPTIO DRVMFRIŞII VICECOMITATVS. ANNANDIA Senescallatus in Vicecomitatu de Dumfreis.
[C:] ANNANDIÆ Præfectura, ... — 49 Scotia. T = 1654:V:[11], but ships added.

[12] NITHIA, vulgo NIDISDALE.
[C:] NITHIA VICECOMITATVS. ... — 51 Scotia. V = 1654:V:[12].

[13] NOVANTES. GALLOVIDIA, vulgo GALLOWAY. EX CAMDENO.
[C:] GALLOVIDIA vernacule GALLOWAY. ... — 53 Scotia. X = 1654:V:[13], but ships, compass-rose and decorations added.

[14] GALLOVIDIÆ DESCRIPTIO, IOANNE MACLELLANO Autore.
[C:] GALLOVIDIÆ Pars Occidentalior, ... — 55 Scotia. Y = 1654:V:[15], but ships and compass-roses added.

[15] [C:] GALLOVIDIÆ PARS MEDIA, ... — Blank on the back. = 1654:V:[15], but ships added.

[16] [C:] PRÆFECTVRA KIRCVBRIENSIS, ... — Blank on the back. = 1654:V:[16], but ships added.

[17] CARRICTA.
[C:] CARRICTA MERIDIONALIS. ... — 57 Scotia. Z Verso blank. = 1654:V:[17], but a ship added.

[18] [C:] CARICTA BOREALIS... — Blank on the back. = 1654:V:[18].

[19] KOILA, SIVE KYLE.
[C:] COILA PROVINCIA. ... — 59 Scotia. Aa = 1654:V:[19], but ships added.

[20] CVNNINGHAM. EX CAMBDENO.
[C:] CVNINGHAMIA. ... — 61 Scotia. Bb Verso blank. = 1654:V:[20], but ships added.

[21] KNAPDALIA.
[C:] KNAPDALIA PROVINCIA, ... — 63 Scotia. Cc Verso blank. = 1654:V:[21], but ships added.

[22] CANTIRE. EX CAMBDENO.
[C:] CANTYRA Chersonesus, ... — 65 Scotia. Dd Verso blank. = 1654:V:[22], but ships and compass-roses added.

[23] GLOTA INSVLA, SIVE ARRAN. EX CAMBDENO.
[C:] ARANIA Insula in æstuario Glottæ... — 67 Scotia. Ee Verso blank. = 1654:V:[23], but ships added.

[24] BVTHE INSVLA, SIVE BOOT. EX CAMBDENO.
[C:] BUTHE INSULA ... — 69 Scotia. Ff Verso blank. = 1654:V:[24], but ships, compass-roses and sea animal added.

[25] DAMNII. EX CAMDENO. CLVYDSDALE.
[C:] GLOTTIANA PRÆFECTVRA INFERIOR, ... — 71 Scotia. Gg = 1654:V:[25].

[26] [C:] GLOTTIANA PRÆFECTVRA SVPERIOR. ... — Blank on the back. = 1654:V:[26].

[27] RENFRAW.
[C:] PRÆFECTURA RENFROANA ... — 73 Scotia. Hh Verso blank. = 1654:V:[27].

[28] LENNOX. EX CAMBDENO.
[C:] LEVINIA, VICE COMITATVS. ... — 75 Scotia. Ii = 1654:V:[28].

[29] STIRLING SHIRIFDOME. EX CAMBDENO.
[C:] STERLINENSIS PRÆFECTVRA. ... — 79 Scotia. Ll = 1654:V:[29].

[30] DESCRIPTIO FIFÆ. EX CAMBDENO.
[C:] FIFÆ PARS ORIENTALIS, ... — 83 Scotia. Nn = 1654:V:[32].

[31] NOVA FIFÆ DESCRIPTIO, Auctore ROBERTO GORDONIO.
[C:] FIFÆ PARS OCCIDENTALIS, ... — 85 Scotia. Oo = 1654:V:[31], but ships added.

[32] FIFÆ.
[C:] FIFÆ VICECOMITATVS. ... — 87 Scotia. Pp = 1654:V:[30], but ships and compass-rose added.

[33] VICECOMITATVS ABERDONIA ET BAMFIA, una cum Regionibus & terrarum tractibus sub iis comprehensis. EX CAMBDENO.
[C:] DVO VICECOMITATVS ABERDONIA & BANFIA, ... — 99 Scotia. Tt = 1654:V:[33], but lettering added in the sea.

[34] BRAID ALBIN. EX CAMBDENO.
[C:] Scotiæ provinciæ mediterraneæ... — 113 Scotia. Zz = 1654:V:[34].

[35] LORNA. EX CAMBDENO.
[C:] LORNA ... — 115 Scotia. Aaa Verso blank. = 1654:V:[35], but ships and compass-rose added.

[36] EXTIMA ORA SCOTIÆ, in qua Provinciæ aut Regiones sunt, Rossia, Sutherlandia, Cathanesia, Strath-Navernia, cum regiunculis quæ iis subsunt, itidemque Moravia.
[C:] EXTIMA SCOTIÆ SEPTENTRIONALIS ORA, ... — 117 Scotia. Bbb = 1654:V:[36], but ships added.

[37] MORAVIA, vulgo MVRRAY. EX CAMBDENO.
[C:] MORAVIA SCOTIÆ provincia, ... — 121 Scotia. Ddd = 1654:V:[37], but ships added.

[38] SOVTHERLANDIA.
[C:] SOVTHERLANDIA — 127 Scotia. Fff = 1654:V:[38].

[39] STRATH-NAVERNIA.
[C:] STRATH-NAVERNIA. ... — 131 Scotia. Hhh = 1654:V:[39], but ships added.

[40] CATHANESIÆ NOVA DESCRIPTIO.
[C:] CATHENESIA. ... — 133 Scotia. Iii = 1654:V:[40], but ships added.

[41] INSVLARVM CIRCA SCOTIAM DESCRIPTIO. BVCHANANVS. ÆBVDÆ INSVLÆ, vulgo HEBRIDES.
[C:] ÆBUDÆ INSULÆ Sive HEBRIDES; ... — 135 Scotia. Kkk = 1654:V:[41], but schips and compass-roses added.

[42] IVRA.
[C:] IVRA INSVLA ... — 137 Scotia. Lll Verso blank. = 1654:V:[42], but ships added.

[43] ILA.
[C:] ILA INSVLA, ... — 139 Scotia. Mmm Verso blank. = 1654:V:[43], but many ships and compass-roses added.

[44] MVLA.
[C:] MVLA INSVLA, ... — 141 Scotia. Nnn Verso blank. = 1654:V:[44], but ships added.

[45] RVMA, cum Insulis circumjacentibus.
[C:] INSVLÆ QVÆDAM MINORES ex Æbudis ... — 143 Scotia. Ooo Verso blank. = 1654:V:[45], but ships and compass-roses added.

[46] SKIA.
[C:] SKIA vel SKIANA ... — 145 Scotia. Ppp Verso blank. = 1654:V:[46], but ships and a compass-roses added.

[47] VISTVS INSVLA, ET INSVLÆ VISTO à Meridie adjacentes.
[C:] VISTVS INSVLA, ... — 147 Scotia. Qqq = 1654:V:[47], but ships and compass-roses added.

[48] LEOGVS ET HARRAYA vulgo LEWIS OR LODHVS, and HARRYS.
[C:] LEOGVS et HARAIA, ... — 149 Scotia. Rrr = 1654:V:[48], but ships and compass-roses added.
[49] ORCADES.
[C:] ORCADVM et SCHETLANDIÆ INSVLARVM accuratissima descriptio. — [a] [C:] ORCADES. — [b] [C:] SCHETLANDIA. — 151 Scotia. Sss = 1654:V:[49], but ships and compass-roses added.

HIBERNIA, QVÆ EST EUROPAE LIBER XIII.
[50] HIBERNIA.
[C:] HIBERNIA REGNVM ... — 1 Hibernia. A = 1635:I:[6], but ships added.
[51] MOMONIA, SIVE MOVNSTER.
[C:] MOMONIA, ... — 9 Hibernia. D = 1654:V:[51], but ships and decoration added.
[52] LAGENIA, SIVE LEINSTER.
[C:] LAGENIA; ... — 15 Hibernia. F = 1654:V:[52].
[53] [C:] BARONIA UDRONE IN COMITATU CATHERLOVGHÆ — Verso blank. = 1654:V:[53].
[54] CONNACHTIA. TWOMOND, SIVE COMITATVS CLARE.
[C:] CONNACHTIA ... — 23 Hibernia. I = 1654:V:[54], but ships added.
[55] VLTONIA, SIVE VLSTER.
[C:] VLTONIA; ... — 27 Hibernia. L = 1654:V:[55], but ships added.

Notes: The maps have text on the verso except where otherwise specified, and they are all coloured. The engraved title-page is dated 1654; the title is printed on a separate slip and pasted in the proper place. This title-page is the same as the one in our copy of vol. V of the German edition of the Novus Atlas; the maps are the same also, apart from the slight differences noted above. Nordenskiöld's signature is on the first blank leaf of the volume.
Lit.: Keuning, Imago Mundi vol. 14, p. 87—89, Koeman vol. 1, p. 218—220, Bl 56, Koeman, Blaeu, p. 70—76, LC List, vol. 3, p. 157—159, nr 3430, Tiele p. 35, nr 133.

Vol. VII
GEOGRAPHIÆ BLAVIANÆ VOLVMEN SEPTIMVM QVO LIBER XIV, XV, EUROPÆ CONTINENTVR. AMSTELÆDAMI, Labore & Sumptibus IOANNIS BLAEV, M DC LXII.   56,7 cm.

DVO PRO-TEGIT VNVS. GALLIA, QVÆ EST EUROPAE LIBER XIV.
[1] DESCRIPTIO GALLIÆ.
[C:] GALLIA, Vulgo LA FRANCE. — 1 Gallia. A 431 × 547 mm.
[2] Præfectura Vrbis & Agri PARISIENSIS, vulgo L'ISLE DE FRANCE.
[C:] LE GOVVERNEMENT DE L'ISLE DE FRANCE Par Damien de Templeux Escuyer S.r du Frestoy — 17 Gallia. F = 1635:II:[6] with small alterations.
[3] REGIO PARISIENSIS.
[C:] AGER PARISIENSIS Vulgo L'ISLE DE FRANCE ... — 19 Gallia. G = 1635:II:[9].
[4] REGIO GAST. ET HVREP.
[C:] GASTINOIS ET HVREPOIS. — 29 Gallia. K = 1635:II:[12] with small alterations.
[5] REGIO ET SILVA EQUALINA, vulgò PAYS & FOREST D'YVELINE.
[C:] CARTE DV PAYS et FOREST D'YVELINE, que quelques uns mettent pour la partie Septentrionale DE L'HUREPOIS. — 33 Gallia. M 412 × 510 mm.
[6] VELOCASSINVS COMITATVS, vulgò VEXIN LE FRANÇOIS.
[C:] CARTE DV PAYS VEXIN FRANÇOIS. — [C:] Amstelodami, Apud Ioannem Blaeu. — 35 Gallia. N 442 × 497 mm.
[7] REGIO BELLOVACENSIS, vulgò LE BEAVVOISIS.
[C:] COMITATVS BELLOVACVM, ... — 37 Gallia. O = 1635:II:[8], but a shield filled in.
[8] TRACTVS VALESIVS.
[C:] VALESIVM Ducatus. VALOIS. — 43 Gallia. Q = 1635:II:[7].
[9] CAMPANIA.
[C:] CHAMPAGNE ... — 53 Gallia. T = 1635:II:[13].
[10] RHEMENSIS DVCATVS, vulgò RHEIMS.
[C:] DIŒCESE de RHEIMS, et le païs de RETHEL. ... — 59 Gallia. X = 1635:II:[14].
[11] BRIONIA, vulgò LA BRIE.
[C:] LE PAIS DE BRIE. — 61 Gallia. Y = 1635:II:[10] with small alterations.
[12] SENONES, vulgò SENONOIS.
[C:] SENONOIS, & LA PARTIE MERIDIONALE DE LA CHAMPAGNE. — 63 Gallia. Z 397 × 543 mm.
[13] PICARDIA.
[C:] NOVA PICARDIÆ TABULA. — 67 Gallia. Bb 388 × 542 mm.
[14] REGIO VEROMANDVORVM.
[a] [C:] DESCRIPTIO VEROMANDVORVM... — [b] [C:] GOVVERNEMENT de la CAPPELLE ... — 69 Gallia. Cc = 1635:II:[5].
[15] BOLONIENSIS, ET GVINENSIS COMITATVS, vulgò Comtez de Boulogne, & de Guisnes.
[C:] COMITATVVM BOLONIÆ ET GVINES DESCRIPTIO. — 71 Gallia. Dd = 1635:II:[2].
[16] CALETVM.
[C:] LE GOUVERNEMENT DE CALAIS, & PAYS RECONQVIS. — 73 Gallia. Ee Verso blank. 461 × 559 mm.
[17] NORMANNIA, vulgò NORMANDIE.
[C:] NORMANDIA DVCATVS. — 75 Gallia. Ff = 1635:II:[32].
[18] NORMANNIA. EPISCOPATVS EBROICENSIS, vulgò L'EVESCHE' D'EVREUX.
[C:] DIŒCESIS EBROICENSIS, Vulgo L'EVESCHÈ D'EVREUX. — [C:] Illustr.mo Reverend.mo Domino D. ÆGIDIO BOVTAVLT, EBROICENSI EPISCOPO, Domino et Comiti Condeti, Illierii, Brosville, etc. Tabulam hanc dedicat Collegium Musarum Blavianum. — 79 Gallia. Hh 425 × 523 mm.
[19] CALETES, vulgò LE PAYS DE CAVX.
[C:] LE PAYS DE CAVX. — 85 Gallia. Kk 360 × 512 mm.
[20] COMITATVS PERCHENSIS.
[C:] PERCHENSIS COMITATVS ... — 87 Gallia. Ll = 1635:II:[27 a].
[21] BRITANNIA.
[C:] BRITANNIA DVCATVS. ... — 91 Gallia. Mm = 1635:II:[33].
[22] COMITATVS CENOMANENSIS, vulgò PAYS DV MAINE.
[C:] LE PAYS & DIOCESE DE MANS, Vulgairement LE MAINE ubi olim CENOMANNI. — [An empty cartouche]. 97 Gallia. Oo 442 × 576 mm.
[23] ANDEGAVVM.
[C:] DVCATVS ANDEGAVENSIS, ... — 101 Gallia. Qq = 1635:II:[30].
[24] TERRITORIVM LODONENSE.
[a] [C:] LOVDONOIS. LAVDVNVN. — [b] [C:] MIREBALAIS. — 103 Gallia. Rr = 1635:II:[29].
[25] BELSIA.
[C:] BELSIA, ... — 105 Gallia. Ss = 1635:II:[11].
[26] TERRITORIVM BLESENSE.
[C:] COMITATVS BLESENSIS, ... — 107 Gallia. Tt = 1635:II:[27 b].
[27] TVRONENSIS DVCATVS.
[C:] DVCATVS TVRONENSIS... — 111 Gallia. Vu = 1635:II:[28].
[28] AVRELIANENSIS PRÆFECTVRA. INFERIOR BELSIA, DVCATVS AVRELIANENSIS, ET SOLONIA.
[C:] GOUVERNEMENT GENERAL DV PAYS ORLEANOIS. — 113 Gallia. Xx 463 × 597 mm.
[29] BITVRIGVM REGIO, vulgò LE BERRY.
[C:] BITVRICVM DVCATVS. ... — 117 Gallia. Zz = 1635:II:[26].
[30] PICTAVIA, vulgò POICTOV.

[C:] PICTAVIÆ DVCATVS DESCRIPTIO, ... — 121 Gallia. Bbb = 1635:II:[34].
[31] SANTONIA, vulgò XAINTONGE.
[C:] XAINTONGE, avec LE PAYS D'AVLNIS, LE BROVAGEAIS, TERRE D'ARVERT, &c. — 125 Gallia. Ddd 479 × 531 mm.
[32] INSVLÆ S.MARTINI, ET VLIARVS, vulgò L'ISLE DE RÉ, & OLERON.
[C:] INSVLÆ DIVI MARTINI et VLIARVS, ... — 129 Gallia. Fff = 1635:II:[36].
[33] LEMOVICIUM.
[a] [C:] LEMOVICVM, ... — [b] [C:] TOPOGRAPHIA LIMANIÆ, ... — 131 Gallia. Ggg = 1635:II:[24].
[34] DVCATVS NIVERNENSIS, vulgò DVCHÉ DE NEVERS.
[C:] NIVERNIVM DVCATVS, ... — 133 Gallia. Hhh = 1635:II:[25].
[35] BORBONIVM vulgò LE BOVRBONOIS.
[C:] BORBONIVM DVCATVS. BOVRBONNOIS. — [T:] AMSTERDAMI Apud Guiljelmum et Ioannem Blaeuw. — 135 Gallia. Kkk 377 × 489 mm.
[36] ARVERNORVM PROVINCIA, ET LIMANIA.
[C:] AUVERGNE. — 137 Gallia. Lll 449 × 528 mm.
[37] PETROGORIENSE TERRITORIVM vulgò PERIGORD.
[C:] PETROCORIVM COMITATVS Vulgo LA COMTEE DE PERIGORT. — 143 Gallia. Nnn 383 × 510 mm.
[38] SARLATENSIS EPISCOPATVS, ET DITIO, vulgò SARLAT.
[C:] DIŒCESIS SARLATENSIS, ... — 145 Gallia. Ooo = 1635:II:[37].
[39] CADVRCIVM, vulgo QVERCY.
[C:] CADVRCIVM ... — 147 Gallia. Ppp = 1635:II:[39].
[40] AQVITANIA, vulgò LA GVYENNE.
[C:] GOVVERNEMENT DE LA GVIENNE & GASCOGNE. — 151 Gallia. Rrr 442 × 584 mm.
[41] [C:] Carte du BOVRDELOIS, ... — [153] Gallia. Sss = 1635:II:[38 a].
[42] AYRENSIS EPISCOPATVS. BAYONENSIS EPISCOPATVS.
[C:] L'EVESCHÉ D'AIRE, tracé par le S.^{R} PIERRE DE VAL Secretaire de Monseign.^{r} l'Evesque. — 155 Gallia. Ttt Verso blank. 424 × 529 mm.
[43] TERRITORIVM AGENNENSE.
[C:] LE DVCHÉ D'AIGVILLON Par le Sr PIERRE DU VAL, domestique de Monseigneur le Marquis de S.^{t}Sorlin, Abbe de S.^{t}Remy de Rheims. — [An empty cartouche]. 157 Vuu 378 × 488 mm.
[44] BENEARNENSIS PRINCIPATVS.
[C:] PRINCIPATVS BENEARNIA. ... — 163 Gallia. Yyy = 1635:II:[38 b].
[45] PROVINCIA LANGVEDOCIENSIS.
[C:] LANGVEDOC — 167 Gallia. Zzz = 1635:II:[40].
[46] LANGVEDOCIENSIS. Comitatus & Episcopatus ALBIGENSIS.
[C:] EPISCOPATVS ALBIENSIS, EVESCHÉ D'ALBY. — [T:] Amstelædami exc. Joannes Blaeu. — [C:] Illustrissimo, Reverendissimo Domino; D. GASPARDO DE DAILLON, Episcopo et Domino Albiensi, Abbati B. Mariæ de Castellariis Dioecesis Pictaviensis, Priori Commendatario S.Virginis de Castellis in Eremo, Tab. hanc dedicant Musæ Blavianæ. — 173 Gallia. Bbbb 463 × 590 mm.
[47] PROVINCIA.
[C:] PROVINCIA... — 187 Gallia. Ffff = 1635:II:[41].
[48] PRINCIPATVS ARAVSIONENSIS, Vulgò LA PRINCIPAVTÉ D'ORANGE. COMITATVS AVENIONENSIS, sive VENISSÆ.
[C:] La PINCIPAVTÉ D'ORANGE et COMTAT de VENAISSIN ... — 197 Gallia. Iiii = 1635:II:[42].
[49] DELPHINATVS.
[C:] DELPHINATVS vulgo DAVPHINÉ ... — 199 Gallia. Kkkk = 1635:II:[43].
[50] AGER LVGDVNENSIS.
[C:] LIONNOIS, FOREST, BEAVIOLOIS ET MASCONNOIS. — 209 Gallia. Nnnn = 1635:II:[23].
[51] [C:] GOUVERNEMENT GENERAL DV LYONNOIS. — [T:] AMSTELÆDAMI, Apud IOANNEM BLAEV. — Blank on the back. 409 × 576 mm.
[52] BRESSIA & BVGIA, vulgò LA BRESSE, & LE BVGEY.
[C:] BRESSIA ... — 213 Gallia. Pppp = 1635:II:[21].
[53] DOMBESII DOMINIVM.
[C:] LA SOVVERAINETE DE DOMBES. — 217 Gallia. Rrrr Verso blank. = 1635:II:[22].
[54] DVCATVS BVRGVNDIÆ.
[C:] BVRGVNDIA DVCATVS. — 219 Gallia. Ssss 452 × 553 mm.
[55] [C:] LA BRESSE CHALONNOISE. — Blank on the back. 386 × 497 mm.
[56] DVCATVS BVRGVNDIÆ.
[C:] Les environs de L'ESTANG DE LONGPENDV, ... — 225 Gallia. Vuuu = 1635:II:[18].
[57] BVRGVNDIÆ COMITATVS, vulgò LA FRANCHE COMTÉ.
[C:] BURGUNDIA COMITATUS Vulgo LA FRANCHE COMTÉ. — [T:] J. Blaeu Excudit — [C:] Illustriss.^{mo} Excellentissi.^{moq3} Domino D. ANTONIO DE BRVN, Baroni d'Apremont, et Toparchæ de Villeclair, Angiré, et Villers-chemin, Supremi in Belgio Financiarum Consilii Præfecto, et intimi ejusdem Belgii in Hispania Senatus Consiliario; nec non Regis Catholici ad Tractatus Pacis Generalis summa cum potestate tum apud Præpotentes Foederatarum Provinciarum Ordines ordinario Legato. &^{cc} Tab. hanc D.D. I.Blaeu. — 227 Gallia. Xxxx 431 × 562 mm.
[58] METENSIS EPISCOPATVS.
[C:] Nova & Accurata delineatio Geographica EPISCOPATVS METENSIS Quo ad Iurisdictionem temporalem. — 235 Gallia. Aaaaa 461 × 555 mm.
[59] EPISCOPATVS. METENSIS AGER, vulgo LE PAYS MESSIN.
[C:] TERRITORIVM METENSE... — 237 Gallia. Bbbbb = 1635:II:[17].
[60] LOTHARINGIA.
[C:] LOTHARINGIA DVCATVS; ... — 241 Gallia. Ddddd = 1635:II:[16].
[61] PRINCIPATVS SEDANENSIS, ET RAVCORTII, ac Præfectura DONCHERII.
[C:] LES SOVVERAINETEZ DE SEDAN ET DE RAVCOVRT ET LA PREVOSTÉ DE DONCHERI. — 245 Gallia. Fffff = 1635:II:[15].
[62] LACVS GENEVENSIS, Ac cognominis Ducatus descriptio.
[C:] LACVS LEMANNI ... — 247 Gallia. Ggggg = 1635:II:[20].
[63] COMITATVS RVSCINONENSIS, Coliovra, Perpignianum, Salça, &c.
[C:] COMITATVS RVSCINONIS, Vulgo ROVSSILLON, in quo EPISCOPATVS HELENENSIS; Gallicé EVESCHÉ d'ELNE ou de PERPIGNAN. — 251 Gallia. Iiiii 411 × 512 mm.
[64] SABAVDIÆ DVCATVS.
[C:] SABAVDIA DVCATVS. ... — 253 Gallia. Kkkkk = 1635:II:[44].
HELVETIA, QVÆ EST EUROPÆ LIBER XV.
[65] HELVETIA.
[C:] HELVETIA, ... — 1 Helvetia. A = 1635:I:[56].
[66] [C:] HELVETIÆ RHETIÆ & VALESIÆ cum omnibus finitimis regionibus Tabula Vulgo Schweitzerland. — [T:] Amstelodami Apud Ioannem Ianssonium. — Between pp. 2 and 3. Blank on the back. 415 × 530 mm.
[67] ZVRICHGOW. SALODORVM.
[C:] ZVRICHGOW et Basiliensis provincia — 19 Helvetia. F = 1635:I:[60].
[68] WIFLISPVRGERGOW.
[C:] DAS WIFLISPVRGERGOW. ... — 23 Helvetia. H = 1635:I:[58].
[69] ARGOW.
[C:] ARGOW cum parte merid. ZVRICHGOW ... — 33 Helvetia. L = 1635:I:[59].
[70] TERRITORIVM BASILEENSE.
[C:] TERRITORIVM BASILEENSE, cum adjacentibus. — 39 Helvetia. N 419 × 528 mm.

[71] RHÆTIA FŒDERATA, vulgo GRISONVM REGIO.
[C:] Alpinæ seu Fœderatæ RHAETIAE SUBDITARUM-
QUE ei Terrarum nova descriptio. ... — 41 Helvetia. O =
1635:I:[57].

Notes: The maps have text on the verso, except where otherwise specified, and all of them are coloured. The engraved title-page of Gallia has no imprint, and the title itself is printed an a separate slip of paper and pasted in the proper place in the engraving. Map [66], the Janssonius map of Switzerland, does not appear in the index and is not listed by Koeman, but is also found in the Library of Congress copy. The index lists a final map, p.59, which does not in fact appear in this copy, in Koeman, or in the Library of Congress copy. From map [19] onwards the signatures of the leaves differ from those described by Koeman, although the page-numbering is the same. In the second part, Helvetia, however, the lettering is the same as in our copy but the page-numbering is different. 23 of the maps have not been published in earlier editions. Nordenskiöld's signature is on the first blank leaf of the volume.

Lit.: Keuning, Imago Mundi vol. 14, p. 87—89, Koeman vol. 1, p. 220—222, Bl 57, Koeman, Blaeu, p. 78—80, LC List, vol. 3, p.147, 159—160, nr 3430, Tiele, p. 35, nr 133.

Vol. VIII
GEOGRAPHIÆ BLAVIANÆ VOLVMEN OCTAVVM, QVO ITALIA, QVÆ EST EUROPÆ LIBER DECIMVS SEXTVS, CONTINETVR. AMSTELÆDAMI, Labore & Sumptibus IOANNIS BLAEV, M DC LXII.   56,4 cm.

ITALIA, QVÆ EST EUROPÆ LIBER XVI.
[1]   ITALIA.
       [C:] ITALIA. — I Italia. A 420 × 514 mm.
[2]   PEDEMONTIVM.
       [C:] PIEMONTE ET MONFERRATO — 23 Italia. G
       = 1647:III:[2].
[3]   PEDEMONTIVM.
       [C:] STATO DEL PIEMONTE — 25 Italia. H =
       1647:III: [3].
[4]   DOMINIVM VERCELLENSE.
       [C:] SIGNORIA di VERCELLI — 29 Italia. K
       = 1647:III:[4].
[5]   MONTISFERRATVM, DVCATVS.
       [C:] MONTISFERRATI DVCATVS. — 31 Italia. L
       = 1635:II:[50].
[6]   LIGVRIA, SIVE STATVS REIPVBLICÆ GENVENSIS.
       [C:] LIGVRIA, ... — 33 Italia. M = 1647:III:[6].
[7]   ORÆ LIGVST. PARS OCCIDENTALIS.
       [C:] RIVIERA DI GENOVA DA PONENTE — 35 Italia.
       N = 1647:III:[7].
[8]   ORÆ LIGVST. PARS ORIENTALIS.
       [C:] RIVIERA DI GENOVA DI LEVANTE — 37 Italia.
       O = 1647:III:[8].
[9]   CORSICA.
       [C:] CORSICA INSVLA. — 39 Italia. P Verso blank.
       377 × 513 mm.
[10]   STATVS MEDIOLANENSIS.
       [C:] STATO DI MILANO — 41 Italia. Q =
       1647:III:[10].
[11]   STATVS MEDIOLANENSIS PARS ALPINA, SIVE SEPTENTRIONALIS.
       [C:] PARTE ALPESTRE DELLO STATO DI MILANO,
       ... — 43 Italia. R = 1647:III:[11].
[12]   DVCATVS MEDIOLANENSIS.
       [C:] DVCATO ouero TERRITORIO DI MILANO — 45
       Italia. S = 1647:III:[12].
[13]   STATVS MEDIOLANENSIS PARS MERIDIONALIS.
       [C:] TERRITORIO DI PAVIA, LODI, ... — 47 Italia. T
       = 1647:III:[13].
[14]   CREMONÆ TERRITORIVM.
       [C:] TERRITORIO DI CREMONA. — 49 Italia. V
       = 1647:III:[14].
[15]   MANTVA, DVCATVS.
       [C:] DVCATO DI MANTOVA — 51 Italia. X =
       1647:III:[15].
[16]   DVCATVS MVTINA, ET RHEGIVM, cum vicinis Dominiis.
       [C:] DVCATO DI MODENA REGIO ET CARPI, ... — 53
       Italia. Y = 1647:III:[16].
[17]   DVCATVS PARMA, ET PLACENTIA.
       [C:] DVCATO di PARMA et di PIACENZA — 55 Italia.
       Z = 1647:III:[17].
[18]   DOMINIVM VENETVM IN ITALIA.
       [C:] DOMINIO VENETO NELL' ITALIA. — 57 Italia.
       Aa = 1635:II:[55].
[19]   TERRITORIVM BERGOMENSE, vernaculè IL BERGAMASCO.
       [C:] TERRITORIO DI BERGAMO — 65 Italia. Dd
       = 1647:III:[19].
[20]   TERRITORIVM BRIXIENSE, incolis IL BRESCIANO.
       [C:] TERRITORIO di BRESCIA et di CREMA — 67
       Italia. Ee = 1647:III:[20].
[21]   [On verso:]   TERRITORIVM CREMENSE, Italis IL CREMASCO.
       [C:] TERRITORIO CREMASCO. — [69] Italia. Ff =
       1647:III: [21].
[22]   TERRITORIVM VERONENSE, vulgò IL VERONESE.
       [C:] TERRITORIO DI VERONA. — 71 Italia. Gg =
       1647:III:[22].
[23]   TERRITORIVM VICENTINVM.
       [C:] TERRITORIO DI VICENZA — 75 Italia. Ii =
       1647:III:[23].
[24]   TERRITORIVM PATAVINVM, vulgò IL PADOANO.
       [C:] TERRITORIO PADOVANO — 77 Italia. Kk
       = 1647:III:[24].
[25]   TERRITORIVM RHODIGINVM, vernaculè POLESINO DI ROVIGO.
       [C:] POLESINO DI ROVIGO — 83 Italia. Nn =
       1647:III:[25].
[26]   TERRITORIVM TARVISINVM, vulgò IL TRIVIGIANO.
       [C:] TERRITORIO TREVIGIANO — 85 Italia. Oo
       = 1647:III:[26].
[27]   DESCRIPTIO BELLVNENSIS ET FELTRINI EPISCOPATVVM.
       [C:] IL BELLVNESE Con il FELTRINO — 87 Italia. Pp
       Verso blank. = 1647:III:[27].
[28]   TERRITORIVM CADORINVM.
       [C:] IL CADORINO — 89 Italia. Qq Verso blank.
       = 1647:III:[28].
[29]   FORVM-JVLIVM, Italis FRIVLI.
       [C:] Patria del FRIVLI olim FORVM IVLII — 91 Italia.
       Rr = 1647:III:[29].
[30]   ISTRIA.
       [C:] ISTRIA olim IAPIDIA — 93 Italia. Ss =
       1647:III:[30].
[31]   DESCRIPTIO TRIDENTINI PRINCIPATVS.
       [C:] TERRITORIO DI TRENTO — 95 Italia. Tt
       = 1647:III:[31].
[32]   DOMINIVM ECCLESIASTICVM.
       [C:] STATO DELLA CHIESA, CON LA TOSCANA. —
       97 Italia. Vu = 1635:II:[57].
[33]   FERRARIA DVCATVS.
       [C:] DVCATO DI FERRARA — 103 Italia. Yy =
       1647:III:[33].
[34]   TERRITORIVM BONONIENSE.
       [C:] TERRITORIO DI BOLOGNA — 107 Italia. Aaa
       = 1647:III:[34].
[35]   ROMANVLA, olim FLAMINIA.
       [C:] ROMAGNA olim FLAMINIA — 109 Italia. Bbb
       = 1647:III:[35].
[36]   VRBINVM DVCATVS.
       [C:] DVCATO DI VRBINO — 113 Italia. Ddd =
       1647:III:[36].
[37]   MARCHIA ANCONITANA, olim PICENVM.
       [C:] MARCA D'ANCONA olim PICENVM — 117 Italia.
       Fff = 1647:III:[37].
[38]   TERRITORIVM PERVSINVM.
       [C:] TERRITORIO PERVGINO — 121 Italia. Hhh =
       1647:III:[38].
[39]   TERRITORIVM ORIVETANVM, vernaculè IL ORVIETANO.

[C:] TERRITORIO DI ORVIETO — 123 Italia. Iii = 1647:III:[39].
- [40] VMBRIA, sive DVCATVS SPOLETINVS.
[C:] VMBRIA overo DVCATO DI SPOLETO. — 125 Italia. Kkk = 1647:III:[40].
- [41] SABINA, TVSCIA SVBVRBICARIA, PATRIMONIVM S.PETRI, ET ROMÆ TERRITORIVM, olim LATIVM.
[C:] CAMPAGNA DI ROMA, olim LATIVM: TVSCIA SVBVRBICARIA, et in ea PATRIMONIVM S.PETRI; nec non SABINA. — 129 Italia. Mmm = 1647:III:[41], with small alterations.
- [42] TVSCIA SVBVRBICARIA.
[C:] DVCATVS BRACCIANVS olim SABATIÆ REGIO. — [An empty cartouche]. 131 Italia. Nnn 399 × 547 mm.
- [43] TOSCANA.
[C:] DOMINIO FIORENTINO. — 147 Italia. Sss = 1647:III:[42].
- [44] TERRITORIVM SENENSE.
[C:] TERRITORIO DI SIENA et DVCATO di CASTRO — 155 Italia. Xxx = 1647:III:[43].
- [45] ILVA, hodiè ELBA.
[C:] ELBA ISOLA, olim ILVA. — On 159 Italia. Zzz = 1647:III:[44].
- [46] RESPVBLICA LVCENSIS.
[C:] STATO DELLA REPVBLICA DI LVCCA — 161 Italia. Aaaa = 1647:III:[45].
- [47] REGNVM NEAPOLITANVM.
[C:] REGNO DI NAPOLI — 165 Italia. Cccc = 1635:II:[56].
- [48] APRVTIVM, vernaculè ABRVZZO; in quo SAMNITES.
[C:] ABRVZZO CITRA, ET VLTRA. — 169 Italia. Eeee = 1647:III:[47].
- [49] CAMPANIA FELIX, hodie TERRA di LAVORO.
[C:] TERRA DI LAVORO, ... — 173 Italia. Gggg = 1647:III:[48].
- [50] COMITATVS MOLISSINVS, ET PRINCIPATVS VLTERIOR.
[C:] CONTADO DI MOLISE et PRINCIPATO VLTRA — 189 Italia. Mmmm Verso blank. = 1647:III:[49].
- [51] CAPITANATA, olim APVLIA DAVNIA.
[C:] CAPITANATA, ... — 191 Italia. Nnnn = 1647:III:[50].
- [52] INSVLÆ DIOMEDEÆ, vulgo dictæ TREMITANÆ.
[C:] INSVLÆ TREMITANÆ olim DIOMEDEÆ dictæ. — 193 Italia. Oooo (View). Verso blank. 376 × 491 mm.
- [53] PRINCIPATVS CITERIOR, olim PICENTIA.
[C:] PRINCIPATO CITRA ... — 195 Italia. Pppp = 1647:III:[51].
- [54] TERRA BARIANA, olim APVLIA PEVCETIA: ET BASILICATA, antiquis LVCANIA.
[C:] TERRA DI BARI ET BASILICATA — 197 Italia. Qqqq = 1647:III:[52].
- [55] HYDRVNTVM, vulgò TERRA D'OTRANTO.
[C:] Terra di OTRANTO ... — 199 Italia. Rrrr = 1647:III:[53].
- [56] CALABRIA, SIVE MAGNA GRÆCIA.
[C:] CALABRIA CITRA... — 203 Italia. Tttt = 1647:III:[54].
- [57] CALABRIA.
[C:] CALABRIA VLTRA... — 205 Italia. Vuuu = 1647:III:[55].
- [58] INSVLA ISCHIA.
[C:] ISCHIA Isola, ... — 209 Italia. Yyyy Verso blank. = 1647:III:[56].
- [59] SARDINIA REGNVM.
[C:] ISOLA DI SARDEGNA. — 211 Italia. Zzzz 378 × 492 mm.
- [60] SICILIA.
[C:] SICILIA REGNVM. — 215 Italia. Bbbbb = 1647:III:[58].
- [61] [C:] REGNUM SICILIÆ Cum circumjacentibus REGNIS et INSULIS Nuperrime descriptum et editum per Nicolaum Visscher. — After 218. Blank on the back. 460 × 560 mm.

Notes: The maps have text on the verso, except where otherwise specified, and all of them are coloured. The title is printed on a separate slip of paper and pasted in the proper space on the engraved title-page. The last map, [61], Regnum Siciliæ by Nicolas Visscher, is not in the copy described by Koeman, but otherwise the two copies are the same. Maps [1], [9], [42] and [52] are not in earlier Blaeu atlases. Map [59] does not appear in any of our other Blaeu atlases. Nordenskiöld's signature is on the first blank leaf of the atlas.

Lit.: Keuning, Imago Mundi vol. 14, p. 87—89, Koeman vol. 1, p. 222—223, Bl 56, Koeman, Blaeu p. 80—81, LC List vol. 3, p. 160—161, nr 3430, Tiele p.35, nr133.

Vol. IX
GEOGRAPHIÆ BLAVIANÆ VOLVMEN NONVM, QVO EUROPÆ LIBER XVII, ET AFRICA, CONTINENTVR. AMSTELÆDAMI, Labore & Sumptibus IOANNIS BLAEV, M DC LXII. 56,4 cm.

HISPANIA, QVÆ EST EUROPÆ LIBER XVII.
- [1] HISPANIA.
[C:] REGNORVM HISPANIÆ nova descriptio. — I Hispania. A = 1635:II:[61].
- [2] [C:] Totius Regnorum HISPANIÆ et PORTUGALLIÆ descriptio, auct: F. de Wit. — [C:] Gedruckt tot Amsterdam by Frederick de Wit in de Kalverstraet in de Witte Paskaert. — Between pp. 2 and 3. Blank on the back. 454 × 552 mm.
- [3] CASTELLA REGNVM.
[C:] VTRIVSQVE CASTILIÆ nova descriptio. — 23 Hispania. G = 1635:II:[69].
- [4] LEGIO REGNVM, ET ASTVRIARVM PRINCIPATVS.
[C:] LEGIONIS REGNVM et ASTVRIARVM PRINCIPATVS. — 39 Hispania. N = 1635:II:[66].
- [5] GALLÆCIA.
[C:] GALLÆCIA, REGNVM, ... — 43 Hispania. P = 1635:II:[67].
- [6] BISCAIA, ET GVIPVSCOA.
[C:] BISCAIA, ALAVA et GVIPVSCOA CANTABRIÆ VETERIS PARTES. — 47 Hispania. R = 1635:II:[65], with small alterations.
- [7] ANDALVSIA, continens SEVILLIAM, CORDVBAM & IAEN.
[C:] ANDALVZIA continens SEVÌLLAM et CORDVBAM. — 49 Hispania. S = 1635:II:[72].
- [8] INSVLA GADITANA.
[C:] INSULA GADITANA Vulgo ISLA DE CADIZ. — [T:] Excud. Joannes Blaeu, Amstelodami. — 55 Hispania. V Verso blank. 379 × 496 mm.
- [9] GRANATA ET MVRCIA.
[C:] GRANATA, ET MVRCIA REGNA. — 57 Hispania. X = 1635:II:[70].
- [10] ARRAGONIA REGNVM.
[C:] ARRAGONIA REGNVM. ... — 63 Hispania. Z = 1645:II:[5].
- [11] ARRAGONIA.
[C:] Arçobispado de ÇARAGOSSA. — [C:] ARCHIEPISCOPATUS CÆSARAUGUSTANUS. ... — 65 Hispania. Aa 411 × 521 mm.
- [12] ARRAGONIA.
[C:] EPISCOPATUS OSCENSIS Vulgo HVESCA. Auct. I. Baptista Labanna. — 67 Hispania. Bb 377 × 515 mm.
- [13] ARRAGONIA.
[C:] EPISCOPATUS IACENSIS Vulgo IACA. — [C:] Auctore Joanne Baptista Labanna. ... — [An empty cartouche]. 69 Hispania. Cc 378 × 490 mm.
- [14] [C:] EPISCOPATUS TERVELENSIS et ALBARACINENSIS. — [C:] Auct. Joanne Baptista Labanna. ... — Blank on the back. 377 × 491 mm.
- [15] [C:] EPISCOPATUS BALBASTRENSIS, RIBAGORÇA COMIT. et SOBRARBE, Cum Adjacentibus. — [C:] AMSTELODAMI, Joannes Blaeu Excudit. — [C:] Auct. Joanne Baptista Labanna. ... — Blank on the back. 377 × 522 mm.
- [16] [C:] EPISCOPATUS TURIASSONENSIS Vulgo TARRAÇONA. — [C:] Auctore Joanne Baptista Labanna. ... — Blank on the back. 341 × 512 mm.

[17] CATALONIA PRINCIPATVS.
[C:] CATALONIA — 71 Hispania. Dd = 1635:II:[62].
[18] VALENTIA.
[C:] VALENTIA REGNVM; ... — 79 Hispania. Gg = 1635:II:[63].
[19] INSVLÆ BALEARES, ET PITIVSÆ.
[C:] INSVLÆ BALEARIDES et PYTIVSÆ. — 81 Hispania. Hh = 1635:II:[71].
[20] NAVARRA REGNVM.
[C:] NAVARRA REGNVM. — 83 Hispania. Ii = 1635:II:[6].
[21] PORTVGALLIA.
[C:] PORTVGALLIA et ALGARBIA quæ olim LVSITANIA. ... — 91 Hispania. Mm = 1635:II:[68].
[22] ASORES INSVLÆ.
[C:] INSULÆ AÇORES delineante LUDOVICO TEISERA Reg. Maj. Cosmographo. — [C:] Amstelædami, Excud. Joannes Blaeu. — 105 Hispania. Qq 377 × 490 mm.

AFRICA, QVÆ EST GEOGRAPHIÆ BLAVIANÆ PARS TERTIA, LIBER VNVS. AMSTELÆDAMI, Labore & Sumptibus IOANNIS BLAEV, M DC LXII.
[23] AFRICA.
[C:] AFRICÆ nova descriptio. ... — 1 Africa. A = 1635:II:[26].
[24] [C:] AFRICÆ ACCURATA TABULA ex officina NIC. VISSCHER. — [C:] Nob.^{mo} Spectat.^{mo} Prudent.^{moq}3 Viro D. GERARDO SCHAEP, I.V.D. Toparchæ in Cortenhoeff, Consuli ac Senatori Amstelædamensis: et ad Serenissimos Sueciæ Daniæque Reges quondam Legato dignissimo, Tabulam hanc D.D. N.Visscher. — Between pp. 2 and 3. Blank on the back. 432 × 541 mm.
[25] BARBARIA.
[a] [T:] BARBARIA — 222 × 585 mm.
[b] [C:] BARBARIA — 262 × 585 mm.
[The whole map:] 11 Africa. D 492 × 585 mm.
[26] REGNA MAVROCANVM, ET FESSANVM.
[C:] FEZZÆ ET MAROCCHI REGNA AFRICÆ CELEBERRIMA, ... — 35 Africa. L = 1635:II:[85].
[27] ÆGYPTVS.
[C:] NOVA ÆGYPTI TABVLA. — 55 Africa. R 440 × 533 mm.
[28] ABYSSINORVM IMPERIVM.
[C:] ÆTHIOPIA SVPERIOR vel INTERIOR; ... — 85 Africa. Bb = 1635:II:[82].
[29] NIGRITARVM REGIO.
[C:] NIGRITARVM REGIO. — [T:] Amstelædami Ioannis Blaeu Excud. — 101 Africa. Gg 379 × 571 mm.
[30] GVINEA.
[C:] GVINEA — 115 Africa. Ll = 1635:II:[84].
[31] ÆTHIOPIA INFERIOR.
[C:] ÆTHIOPIA INFERIOR, vel EXTERIOR. ... — 127 Africa. Pp = 1635:II:[83].
[32] CONGI REGNVM.
[C:] REGNA CONGO et ANGOLA. — 147 Africa. Xx 451 × 533 mm.
[33] MELITA INSVLA, vulgò MALTA.
[C:] MELITE INSVLA, Vulgo MALTA. — 153 Africa. Zz 440 × 552 mm.
[34] INSVLÆ CANARIÆ.
[C:] INSULÆ CANARIÆ Alias FORTUNATÆ dictæ. — 159 Africa. Bbb 380 × 498 mm.
[35] [C:] INSULÆ PROMONTORII VIRIDIS, Hispanis ISLAS DE CABO VERDE, Belgis DE SOUTE EYLANDEN. — Between pp. 164 and 165. Blank on the back. 380 × 489 mm.
[36] INSVLA D. LAVRENTII, vulgo MADAGASCAR.
[C:] INSVLA S.LAVRENTII, Vulgo MADAGASCAR. — 167 Africa. Eee 423 × 548 mm.

Notes: The maps have text on the verso, except where otherwise specified, and are all coloured. The title is printed on a separate slip and pasted in the proper space on the engraved title-page. In addition to the maps, the volume contains the following architectural drawings, which Koeman lists in the same sequence as the maps:

ESCVRIACVM, SIVE PALATIVM REGIVM, ET MONASTERIVM D. LAVRENTII.
[T:] SCENOGRAPHIA FABRICÆ S. LAVRENTII IN ESCVRIALI. — 33 Hispania. K
ESCVRIACVM.
[T:] ORTOGRAPHIA EXTERIOR MERIDIONAL DEL TEMPLO I CONVENTO DE S. LORENCIO EL REAL DEL ESCVRIAL I APOSENTOS REALES. — 35 Hispania. L
ESCVRIACVM
[T:] ORTOGRAPHIA I SECCION INTERIOR DEL TEMPLO DE S. LORENCIO EL REAL DEL ESCVRIAL I PARTE DEL CONVENTO I APOSENTOS REALES. — 37 Hispania. M Verso blank.
[T:] ORTOGRAPHIA DELA ENTRADA DEL TEMPLO DE S. LORENCIO EL REAL DEL ESCVRIAL I SECCION INTERIOR DEL CONVENTO I COLEGIO. — After 37 Hispania. M Blank on the back.
[T:] ORTOGRAPHIA I SECCION INTERIOR DEL TEMPLO DE S. LORENCIO EL REAL DEL ESCVRIAL CON SV RETABLO I ALTAR MAIOR I CLAVSTROS DEL CONVENTO I CASA REAL. — After 37 Hispania. M Blank on the back.
[T:] SECCION DEL SAGRARIO DEL ALTAR MAIOR DE SAN LORENCIO EL REAL DEL ESCVRIAL —
[T:] ORTOGRAPHIA DEL SAGRARIO DEL ALTAR MAIOR DE SAN LORENCIO EL REAL DEL ESCVRIAL. — After 37 Hispania. M Blank on the back.
[T:] PLANTA PRIMERA Y GENERAL DE TODO EL EDIFICIO DE S. LORENÇO EL REAL. — (Plan). After 37 Hispania. M Blank on the back.

The signatures and page-numbers in our copy differ from those given by Koeman throughout 'Hispania'. The de Wit map of Spain, no. [2], and the Visscher map of Africa, no. [24], are not in the copy described by Koeman. 17 of the maps have not been previously published by Blaeu. Nordenskiöld's signature is on the first blank leaf of the volume.

Lit.: Keuning, Imago Mundi vol.14, p. 87—89, Koeman vol. 1, p. 224—224, Bl 56, Koeman, Blaeu p. 81—83, LC List, vol. 3, p. 147, 162—163, nr 3430, Tiele p. 35, nr 133.

Vol. X
ASIA, QVÆ EST GEOGRAPHIÆ BLAVIANÆ PARS QVARTA; LIBRI DVO, VOLVMEN DECIMVM. AMSTELÆDAMI, Labore & Sumptibus IOANNIS BLAEV, M DC LXII. 56,5 cm.

ASIÆ LIBER PRIMVS.
[1] ASIA.
[C:] Asia... — 1 Asia. A = 1635:I:[1].
[2] [C:] ASIÆ NOVA DELINEATIO Auctore N.VISSCHER. — [C:] Spectat.^{mo} Consult.^{moq}3 Viro D. HENRICO SPIEGEL, Vrbis Amstelædamensis Consuli et Senatori, nec non in Consessu Indicæ Orientalis Assessori gravissimo, Tabulam hanc D.D. N.Visscher. — Between pp. 2 and 3. Blank on the back. 433 × 543 mm.
[3] IMPERIVM TVRCICVM.
[C:] TVRCICVM IMPERIVM — 3 Asia. B = 1635:II:[78].
[4] NATOLIA, SIVE ASIA MINOR.
[C:] NATOLIA, ... — 13 Asia. E = 1635:II:[80].
[5] CYPRVS INSVLA.
[C:] CYPRVS INSVLA — 25 Asia. I = 1635:II:[81].
[6] TERRA SANCTA, Sive PALÆSTINA.
[C:] TERRA SANCTA ... — 29 Asia. L = 1635:II:[79].
[7] ARABIA.
[C:] ARABIA. — 45 Asia. Q 416 × 521 mm.
[8] PERSIA.
[C:] PERSIA Sive SOPHORVM REGNVM — [C:] Nobilissimo Prudentissimoque Domino, D. SIMONI VAN HOORN, CONSVLI ET SENATORI urbis Amstelædamensis &c. Ordd. Belgicæ fœderatæ nomine ad Magnæ Britanniæ Regem LEGATO EXTRAORDINARIO, Tabulam hanc D.D. J.Blaeu. — 53 Asia. T = 1635:II:[77], but with a new dedication.

[9] MAGNI MOGOLIS IMPERIVM.
[C:] MAGNI MOGOLIS IMPERIVM — 65 Asia. Z = 1645:II:[17], but in the dedication on this map: ... D.IOHANNI HVYDEKOPER, Equiti, Domino in Marsenveen, Neerdyck etc. ...

[10] INDIA.
[C:] INDIA quæ ORIENTALIS dicitur ET INSVLÆ ADIACENTES. — 85 Asia. Ff = 1635:II:[73].

[11] [C:] INDIÆ ORIENTALIS, nec non INSULARUM ADIACENTIUM Nova Descriptio, Per Nicolaum Visscher. — Between pp. 88 and 89. Blank on the back. 463 × 562 mm.

[12] INSVLÆ MOLVCCÆ.
[C:] MOLVCCÆ INSVLÆ CELEBERRIMÆ — 89 Asia. Hh = 1635:II:[74].

[13] TARTARIA.
[C:] TARTARIA sive MAGNI CHAMI IMPERIVM — 93 Asia. Kk = 1635:II:[76].

NOVVS ATLAS SINENSIS A MARTINO MARTINIO SOC.IESV DESCRIPTVS ET SEREN.^{MO} ARCHIDVCI LEOPOLDO GVILIELMO AVSTRIACO DEDICATVS.

[14] [C:] IMPERII SINARVM NOVA DESCRIPTIO — Before 1 = 1656:VI:[1].

[15] [C:] PECHELI, SIVE PEKING, ... — Between pp. 26 and 27. = 1656:VI:[2].

[16] [C:] XANSI, ... — Between pp. 36 and 37. = 1656:VI:[3].

[17] [C:] XENSI, ... — Between pp. 42 and 43. = 1656:VI:[4].

[18] [C:] XANTVNG, ... — Between pp. 52 and 53. = 1656:VI:[5].

[19] [C:] HONAN, ... — Between pp. 58 and 59. = 1656:VI:[6].

[20] [C:] SVCHVEN, ... — Between pp. 64 and 65. = 1656:VI:[7].

[21] [C:] HVQVANG, ... — Between pp. 74 and 75. = 1656:VI:[8].

[22] [C:] KIANGSI, ... — Between pp. 84 and 85. = 1656:VI:[9].

[23] [C:] NANKING, SIVE KIANGNAN, ... — Between pp. 94 and 95. = 1656:VI:[10].

[24] [C:] CHEKIANG, ... — Between pp. 108 and 109. = 1656:VI:[11].

[25] [C:] FOKIEN... — Between pp. 120 and 121. = 1656:VI:[12].

[26] [C:] QVANTVNG, ... — Between pp. 132 and 133. = 1656:VI:[13].

[27] [C:] QVANGSI, ... — Between pp. 142 and 143. = 1656:VI:[14].

[28] [C:] QVEICHEV, ... — Between pp. 148 and 149. = 1656:VI:[15].

[29] [C:] IVNNAN ... — Between pp. 154 and 155. = 1656:VI:[16].

[30] [T:] IAPONIA REGNVM. — Between pp. 168 and 169. = 1656:VI:[17].

Notes: The maps in the first part have text on the verso, except the two Visscher maps [2] and [11] which are blank on the back. All the maps in the second part, Novus Atlas Sinensis, are blank on the back. The text on the engraved title-page of Asia Liber primus has been printed on a separate slip and pasted in the proper place in the engraving. A blank slip has been pasted over the open door; other copies of this engraving have text at this point. The maps in both parts are coloured. The first part of this volume corresponds with Koeman's description in Bl 56. The Chinese part is also the same, but in other respects there are differences between the two copies. The 'Index & Ordo Tabularum' is wanting. Nordenskiölds's signature is on the first blank leaf of the volume.

Lit.: Keuning, Imago Mundi vol. 14, p. 87—89, Koeman vol. 1, p. 225—226, Bl 56, Koeman, Blaeu, p. 983—88, LC List vol 3, p. 147, 163, nr 3430, Tiele p. 35, nr 133.

Vol. XI
AMERICA, QVÆ EST GEOGRAPHIÆ BLAVIANÆ PARS QVINTA, LIBER VNVS, VOLVMEN VNDECIMVM. AMSTELÆDAMI, Labore & Sumptibus IOANNIS BLAEV, M DC LXII.   56,4 cm.

[1] AMERICA.
[C:] AMERICÆ nova Tabula. ... — 1 America. A = 1645:II:[31].

[2] [C:] Novissima et Accuratissima TOTIUS AMERICÆ DESCRIPTIO. per N. VISSCHER. — [C:] Amplissimo Spectat^{mo} Prudent.^{mo}q3 Domino. D. CORNELIO WITSEN I.V.D. Consuli et Senatori Vrbis Amstelædam.^{sis} in Potent.^{mo} Ordinum Generalium Consessu Deputato, ac Consilii Societatis Indicæ Occidentalis Assessori dignissimo. Tabulam hanc D.D. N.Visscher. — Between pp. 2 and 3. Blank on the back. 432 × 542 mm.

[3] NOVA FRANCIA, & Terræ adjacentes.
[C:] EXTREMA AMERICÆ Versus Boream, ubi TERRA NOVA NOVA FRANCIA, Adjacentiaq3. — [C:] Amstelodami Io: Blaeu Exc. — 21 America. G 446 × 567 mm.

[4] ANGLIA NOVA.
[C:] NOVA BELGICA ET ANGLIA NOVA. — 35 America. L = 1635:II:[87].

[5] VIRGINIA.
[C:] NOVA VIRGINIÆ TABVLA — 39 America. N = 1635:II:[88].

[6] FLORIDA.
[C:] VIRGINIÆ partis australis, ... — 41 America. O = 1645:II:[36].

[7] NOVA HISPANIA.
[C:] NOVA HISPANIA. ET NOVA GALICIA. — 45 America. Q = 1635:II:[98].

[8] YVCATANA.
[C:] YVCATAN Conventus Iuridici Hispaniæ Novæ Pars Occidentalis, et GVATIMALA CONVENTVS IVRIDICVS. — 73 America. Aa 413 × 523 mm.

[9] INSVLÆ AMERICANÆ
[C:] INSVLÆ AMERICANÆ IN OCEANO SEPTENTRIONALI,... — 89 America. Ff = 1635:II:[89].

[10] [C:] INSULA MATANINO Vulgo MARTANICO in lucem edita per Nicolaum Visscher. — Between pp. 100 and 101. Blank on the back. 459 × 563 mm.

[11] CANIBALES INSVLÆ.
[T:] CANIBALES INSVLÆ. — 101 America. Kk 413 × 531 mm.

[12] BERMVDEZ INSVLÆ.
[C:] Mappa ÆSTIVARVM Insularum, ... — 103 America. Ll = 1635:II:[86].

[13] TERRA FIRMA.
[C:] TERRA FIRMA ... — 105 America. Mm = 1635:II:[90].

[14] PERUVIA.
[C:] PERV — 133 America. Vu = 1635:II:[97].

[15] CHILE.
[C:] CHILI — 183 America. Kkk = 1635:II:[96].

[16] MAGALLANICA.
[C:] TABVLA MAGELLANICA, ... — 191 America. Nnn = 1645:II:[43].

[17] PARAQVARIA, & Regiones adjacentes.
[C:] PARAQVARIA Vulgo PARAGVAY, Cum adjacentibus. — [T:] Gerard Coeck sculpsit. — [T:] Ioannes Blaeu Exc. Amstelædami. — [C:] Adm. R.^{do} P. Nrō. P. VINCENTIO CARRAFA Præposito Grafī Soc.^{tis} Jesv. ... — 201 America. Qqq 449 × 549 mm.

[18] BRASILIA.
[C:] BRASILIA Generis Nobilitate, armorum et litterarum Scientia prestant.^{mo} Heroi CHRISTOPH: AB ARTISCHAV ARCISZEWSKI, nuper in Brasilia per triennium Tribuno militum Prudentiss. Fortiss. Feliciss. tabulam hanc prono cultu D.D.D. Johannes Blaeu. Excudebat Johannes Blaeu. — 213 America. Vuu 381 × 490 mm.

[19] N.º 31. [C:] SINVS OMNIUM SANCTOR$\overline{V}$. — Between pp. 240 and 241. Blank on the back. 384 × 508 mm.
[Inset:] [T:] Civitas S.Salvatoris. — (Plan). 161 × 248 mm.

[20] BRASILIA.
[C:] PRÆFECTURA DE CIRÎÎÎ, vel SEREGIPPE

DELREY cum Itâpuáma. — 241 America. Eeee 415 × 536 mm.
[21] PRÆFECTVRA PERNAMBVCO.
[C:] PRÆFECTURÆ PARANAMBUCÆ PARS BOREALIS una cum PRÆFECTURA de ITÂMARACÂ — [C:] PERNAMBUCA — [C:] I. TAMARICA. — 243 America. Ffff 415 × 535 mm.
[22] PERNAMBVCO.
[C:] PRÆFECTURÆ PARANAMBUCÆ PARS MERIDIONALIS. — 245 America. Gggg 414 × 445 mm.
[23] PRÆFECTVRA PARAIBA.
[C:] PRÆFECTURÆ DE PARAIBA, ET RIO GRANDE. — [C:] PARAYBA. — [C:] RIO GRANDE — 247 America. Hhhh 414 × 534 mm.
[24] GVAIANA.
[C:] GVIANA siue AMAZONVM REGIO — 259 America. Mmmm = 1635:II:[92].
[25] NOVA ANDALVZIA.
[C:] VENEZVELA, ... — 277 America. Rrrr = 1635:II:[91].
[26] [Polus Antarcticus] After p. 287. Blank on the back. 435 × 493 mm.

Notes: The maps have text on the verso, except where otherwise specified, and they are all coloured. This copy contains three maps which are not in the index, nor in the copy described by Koeman. Two of them, [2] America and [10] Insula Matanino, are by Nicolas Visscher; the third map, the last in the volume, depicts the South Pole, and is printed without signature or title. The same map, in the same state, appears in our copy of vol.V of the Janssonius Novus Atlas, 1647, but it was published for the first time in the Mercator-Hondius Atlas, Appendix, in 1637, with the title Polus Antarcticus, Henricus Hondius excudit. In other respects this copy corresponds with Koeman's description of vol. 11 in Bl 56. Nordenskiöld's signature is on the first blank leaft of the volume.

Lit.: Keuning, Imago Mundi vol. 14, p. 87—89, Koeman vol. 1, p. 226—227, Bl 56, Koeman, Blaeu, p. 89—91, LC List, vol. 3, p. 147, 163—164, nr 3430, Tiele p. 35, nr 133.

25 BODENEHR, HANS GEORG   1679

PROVINCIARUM EUROPÆ Geographica Descriptio. EUROPA Mit Angrentzenden Welt-Theilen Denen Staats.Kriegs vnd Gelehrten Personen Auch Handels- und Reisenden Leuthen zu sonderbar bequemen Gebrauch in 32 auffeinander zutreffenden TABELLEN Vorgestellet. Sambt einem Vorbericht, und kurtzen Entwurff der Grentzen, auch vornemsten Ab- und Eintheilungen der darinn gelegnen Reiche, Königreiche, Lænder, und Provinzen Und dann zu end angehengtem Aussführlichen Register aller vorgekomenen Lænder, Meer, Seen, Flüss, Stædt und Orthen. AUGSPURG Bey Hans Georg Bodenehr, Kupfferstechern. ... Anno 1679.
[Half title:]
Europa Zu bequemen Gebrauch in 32 Tabellen Vorgestelt. Augspurg Beÿ Hanss Georg Bodenehr Kupferstechern ...
[Colophon:]... Augustæ Vindelicorum Apud Joh. Georg Bodenehr Calcograph. ...   17,2 cm.

[1] [T:] EUROPÆ Compendiosa Representatio Forstellung Europæ sampt dessen Fornehmbsten Theil- vnd Angrentzungen. — I.G.Bodenehr sculps. ... 145 × 198 mm.
[2] [T:] TYPUS EUROPÆ IN SEQQ. XXXII. TABULAS DIVISÆ. Anweÿsung über nachfolgende 32 Tabellen Europæ. — Uncoloured. 144 × 197 mm.
[3] 1 [Davis Strait and part of Greenland]   147 × 125 mm.
[4] 2 [T:] GRONLAND. — 147 × 124 mm.
[5] 3 [T:] INSUL.ISLAND — 147 × 123 mm.
[6] 4 [T:] NORWEGISCHE SEE. NORWEGEN — 149 × 125 mm.
[7] 5 [T:] LAPLAND KÖNIGREICHE SCHWEDEN — 148 × 125 mm.
[8] 6 [T:] NOVA ZEMBLA. RUSSISCH oder MOSCOVISCHE SEE CONDORA DWINA. — 148 × 124 mm.
[9] 7 [T:] MANAMO HASIAIEDZ. OBDORA SAMOIEDES. PETZORA. CONDORA. SIBERIEN PERMSKI — 147 × 123 mm.
[10] 8 [T:] GROSSE TARTAREY SIBERIEN — 146 × 124 mm.
[11] 9 [T:] C.Confort   C.Christian   C.Farwel   C.Discord C.Goede hoop — [Greenland.] 148 × 124 mm.
[12] 10 [T:] Elisabeth Forland DER GROSSE WEST OCEAN. — 148 × 124 mm.
[13] 11 [T:] BRITANNISCHE SEE   GROS BRITANNIEN — 147 × 123 mm.
[14] 12 [T:] DIE TEUTSCHE oder NORD SEE   GROS BRITANNIEN NORDISCHE KÖNIGREICH. DENEMARCK TEUTSCHLAND. — 148 × 125 mm.
[15] 13 [T:] DIE OOST SEE POHLEN TEUTSCHLAND — 149 × 124 mm.
[16] 14 [T:] MOSCAV — 147 × 125 mm.
[17] 15 [T:] MOSCAV oder RVSSLAND CASAN TARTAREY. — 149 × 123 mm.
[18] 16 [T:] RUSSLAND BVLGAR TARTAREY — 147 × 123 mm.
[19] 17 [T:] I.Gratiosa   I.Fayal   I.S.Georgio   I.Del Pico I.Tercera — 147 × 123 mm.
[20] 18 [T:] DER GROSSE WEST OCEAN. SPANISCHE SEE. — 146 × 123 mm.
[21] 19 [T:] FRANZÖSISCHE SEE   FRANCKREICH HISPANIEN — 146 × 123 mm.
[22] 20 [T:] FRANCKREICH   ITALIEN   SCHWEIZ SCHWABEN BAIREN — 148 × 125 mm.
[23] 21 [T:] HVNGARN TURCKEY in Europa ITALIEN — 151 × 125 mm.
[24] 22 [T:] VOKRAYNE od'COSACKISCHE LÆNDER PODOLIEN MOLDAU BVLGARIEN ROMANIEN MACEDONIEN — 147 × 123 mm.
[25] 23 [T:] KRIMISCHE TARTARN CYRCASSISCHE TARTARN   DAS SCHWARZE MEER. TURCKEY in ASIA — 148 × 123 mm.
[26] 24 [T:] ASIA   ASTRACHAN   CYRCASSISCHE TARTARN   GEORGIEN PERSIEN ARMENIEN — 148 × 123 mm.
[27] 25 [T:] INSULN   AZORES.   INS   MADERA CANARISCHE INSULN — 147 × 123 mm.
[28] 26 [T:] CANARISCHE INSULN   KÖNIGR. MAROCC. — 147 × 123 mm.
[29] 27 [T:] CUSTEN VON BARBARIE   KÖNIGR. FEZ. KÖNIGREICH ALGIER KÖNIGR. TAFILET. — 148 × 123 mm.
[30] 28 [T:] [CUSTEN] VON BARBARIE. ALGIER KÖNIGR.TVNIS — 148 × 124 mm.
[31] 29 [T:] KÖN.SICILIEN MITTELLÆNDISCHE SEE KÖNIGREICH TRIPOLI BARBARIE — 146 × 125 mm.
[32] 30 [T:] ACHAIA MOREA ARCHIPELAGO   INS: und KÖNIGR.CANDIA BARCA — 145 × 124 mm.
[33] 31 [T:] NATOLIA   INS: und KÖNIGR: CYPERN ÆGYPTEN. — 147 × 123 mm.
[34] 32 [T:] SIRIEN DIARBECH od' ASSIRIEN. DAS WÜSTE ARABIEN. ARABIEN. — 147 × 122 mm.

Notes: All the maps are blank on the verso. The first two are in bad repair. The index map is uncoloured; on all the other maps, the boundary lines are coloured. The first title-page, and the page with the colophon, are both engraved. This schoolroom atlas belonged in turn to several children of the Hazelius family of Stockholm: 'Gustaf Anton Hazelius den 30 Ianuarie År 1811 Stocholm Denna Bock har jag fått utav pappa Efter Jullottan 1810 Denna Geografie Tillhörer Gustaf Anton Hazelius 1810 Fredric Hazelius Axel Hazelius sedan har jag gifvit den Åt Agneta det TillHörer Agneta Sophie Hazelius Stockholm den 21 Juniÿ 1821 Axel Hazelius d 24/6 1821 Denna lok Har Jag fått utaf Axel Eduard Hazelius Hann Johan Hazelius fru Dorothea Lovisa Kåssen Jan Öhrner Stockh. 1786.' On the inside of the front cover are the initials AEN.

26 BOISSEAU, JEAN 1643

TRESOR DES CARTES GEOGRAPHIQVES DES PRINCIPAVX ESTATZ DE LVNIVERS .... A Paris chez Iean Boisseau, en l'Isle du Palais, a la Fontaine de Iouuence Royalle, Auec priuilege du Roy, 1643   15,3 cm.

[1] 4 [C:] POLE ARCTIQVE ou terres du Septentrion — 142 × 195 mm.
[2] [5] [C:] Nouuelle description de L'EVROPE 1643 — 140 × 188 mm.
[3] 6 [C:] ANGLETERRE ECOSSE et Hibernie. — 130 × 173 mm.
[4] 7 [C:] HESPAGNE — 133 × 174 mm.
[5] 8 [C:] PORTVGAL et ALGARVE — 132 × 192 mm.
[6] [9] [C:] FRANCE Nouuellement descripte 1641 — 133 × 174 mm.
[7] 10 [C:] ITALIE CORSE SARDAIGNE et Prouinces adiacentes — 131 × 177 mm.
[8] 11 [C:] NOVVELLE Carte DALEMAGNE 1641 — 133 × 178 mm.
[9] 12 [T:] LES DIXSET PROVINCE^S DES PAIS BAS — [C:] BELGIVM Sive Inferior GERMANIA — 120 × 167 mm.
[10] 13 [C:] DANEMARCK — 130 × 168 mm.
[11] 14 [C:] NORVEGE et SVEDE — 126 × 166 mm.
[12] 15 [C:] RVSSIE Auec ses confins 1643 — 138 × 190 mm.
[13] 16 [C:] MOSCOVI — 128 × 168 mm.
[14] 18 [C:] HONGRIE ... — 124 × 165 mm.
[15] 19 [C:] L'EMPIRE DES TVRCS — 132 × 170 mm.
[16] 20 [C:] GRECE — 140 × 177 mm.
[17] 21 [C:] MOREE jadis PELOPONESE — 130 × 188 mm.
[18] 22 [C:] CYPRE — 135 × 184 mm.
[Insets:] [T:] Stalimene — 38 × 22 mm. [T:] Chios — 38 × 25 mm. [T:] Mitilene — 38 × 32 mm. [T:] Negropont — 38 × 32 mm. [T:] Cerigo — 38 × 27 mm. [T:] Rhodes — 38 × 22 mm.
[19] 23 [C:] CANDIE — 130 × 190 mm.
[Insets:] [T:] CORFV — 42 × 26 mm. [T:] ZANTE — 42 × 30 mm. [T:] MILO — 42 × 36 mm. [T:] NICSIA — 42 × 33 mm. [T:] SATORINI — 42 × 17 mm. [T:] SCARPANTO — 42 × 34 mm.
[20] 24 [C:] ASIE — 138 × 188 mm.
[21] 25 [C:] NATOLIE ou Asie mineur ... — 131 × 188 mm.
[22] 26 [C:] TERRE SAINTE jadis Terre Promise ou PALESTINE — 133 × 188 mm.
[23] 27 [C:] Le grand Royaume du Sophi de PERSE — 126 × 187 mm.
[24] 28 [C:] INDES Orientalles ou du Gange — 140 × 190 mm.
[25] 29 [C:] Les ISLES des Indes Orientalles — 142 × 191 mm.
[26] 30 [C:] LA CHINE ... — 132 × 188 mm.
[27] 31 [C:] TARTARIE — 132 × 188 mm.
[28] 32 [C:] Nouuelle description DAFRIQVE — 135 × 190 mm.
[29] 33 [a] [C:] BARBARIE — 69 × 175 mm.
[b] [T:] SEIN DE CARTAGE — 58 × 91 mm.
[c:] [T:] ÆGYPTE — 58 × 80 mm.
[The whole map:] 140 × 183 mm.
[30] 34 [C:] LE ROYAVME DE FEZ — 130 × 185 mm.
[31] 35 [C:] Le Royaume de MARROC — 127 × 183 mm.
[32] 36 [C:] GVINEE — 130 × 178 mm.
[Inset:] [T:] I. S. THOMAS — 62 × 68 mm. (Irregular).
[33] 37 [C:] LE ROYAVME ABYSSIN ou l'Empire du PRESTE IEAN 1643 — 126 × 184 mm.
[34] 38 [C:] Nouuelle description de L'AMERIQVE — 138 × 192 mm.

Notes: All the maps are blank on the back. The boundaries, coasts and borders are coloured. There is no text in the atlas. According to the 'Table des Cartes' which appears on the titlepage maps 2, 3 and 17 (Globe Celeste en deux Hemispheres, Carte generalle du Monde en 2 Hemispheres and Pologne et Silesie), are wanting in our copy. Many of the maps have been badly cropped, so that parts of the borders are missing. The volume is paper bound, and the first plate, Orbes Celestes, has been pasted to the front cover, on which is written in ink 'Atlas 1643'. The last map, America, is pasted to the inside of the back cover. The Library of Congress and Tooley both mention this atlas among Boisseau's works, but neither Jöcher-Adelung, the French Grand Encyclopedia nor NBG does so.

Lit.: Bonacker p. 50, Jöcher-Adelung vol. 1, p. 1996, LC List vol. 3, p. 140, nr 3424, Tooley, Dictionary p. 42.

27 BORDONE, BENEDETTO 1528

LIBRO DI BENEDETTO BORDONE Nel qual si ragiona de tutte l'Isole del mondo con li lor nomi antichi & moderni, historie, fauole, & modi del loro uiuere, & in qual parte del mare stanno, & in qual parallelo & clima giacciono. CON IL BREVE DI PAPA Leone, Et gratia & priuilegio della Illustrissima Signoria com' in queli appare. M.D.XXVIII. [Colophon:] Impresse in Vinegia per Nicolo d'Aristotile, detto Zoppino, nel mese di Giugno, del M.D.XXVIII. ....   31,4 cm.

[1] [Zone-map] BB Circular map with 116 mm. diam.
[2] [T:] EVROPA — BB 283 × 383 mm.
[3] [World map] DD 215 × 381 mm.
[4] [T:] MARE EGEO ARCIPELAGO — CC 292 × 404 mm.
[5] [T:] ISLANDA — On I A 37 × 145 mm.
[6] [T:] Irlanda — On I A verso. 85 × 146 mm.
[7] Tauola secondo moderni.
[T:] inghilterra secõdo moderni — On III A iii 137 × 143 mm.
[8] Tauola secondo Tolomeo
[T:] inghilterra secondo tolemeo — III Aiii verso. 228 × 154 mm.
[9] [T:] di lugduno parte de eqtania pte — On IIII 82 × 146 mm.
[10] [T:] parte de hispagna — On IIII verso. 82 × 144 mm.
[11] [T:] datia norbegia gottia — On VI 141 × 147 mm.
[12] [T:] Terra de lauoratore — On VI verso. 80 × 145 mm.
[13] La gran citta di Temistitan. (Plan). On X 163 × 163 mm.
[14] [T:] iamaiqua spagnola chanchite curtana maria tambal paria — On XI verso. 83 × 145 mm.
[15] [T:] Jamaiqua — On XIII C 84 × 146 mm.
[16] [T:] Cuba — On XIII C verso. 83 × 147 mm.
[17] [T:] S.Maria antica s.maria rotonda mõferato santa✠ S,martino buchima dominica — On XVIII (pro XIIII) C ii 82 × 146 mm.
[18] [T:] guadalupe' — On XVIII (pro XIIII) C ii verso. 80 × 145 mm.
[19] [T:] matinina — On XVIII (pro XIIII) C ii verso. 82 × 143 mm.
[20] [T:] porto santo — On XV C iii verso. 82 × 145 mm.
[21] [T:] madera — On XVI 83 × 145 mm.
[22] [T:] ombrio iunone cisperia ninguaria canaria pĩturia — On XVI verso. 138 × 148 mm.
[23] [T:] astores S.georgio asmaida brasil samguimi S.maria. — On XVIII 82 × 145 mm.
[24] [T:] REGNO DE CASTIGLIA — On XVIII verso. 83 × 145 mm.
[25] [T:] dragonera ieuiza tagamago saniolaria formentaria — On XX D ii 82 × 145 mm.
[26] [T:] maiorica minorica — On XX D ii verso. 83 × 144 mm.
[27] [T:] m.cristi elba capraia ziglio gorgona corsica — On XXI 84 × 143 mm.
[28] [T:] capraia gorgona elba corsica palmosa — On XXI verso. 82 × 144 mm.
[29] [T:] Sardigna — On XXII verso. 83 × 146 mm.
[30] [T:] sicilia secondo tolemeo sicilia secondo moderni — On XXIIII E ii — XXV 135 × 324 mm.
[31] [T:] palmosa palmarola ischia — On XXVII (pro XXVI). 81 × 145 mm.

[32] [C:] VINEGIA — (Plan). XXIX F iii — XXX 228 × 327 mm.
[33] [T:] murano — (Plan). On XXX verso. 82 × 145 mm.
[34] [T:] mazorbo — (Plan). On XXVIII (pro XXXI). 80 × 145 mm.
[35] [T:] chiozza — (Plan). On XXVIII (pro XXXI). 83 × 144 mm.
[36] [T:] PARTE DE SCHIAVONIA — On XXVIII (pro XXXI) verso. 85 × 147 mm.
[37] [T:] istria uegia arbe cherso oscero nia — On XXXII 82 × 143 mm.
[38] [T:] trau brazza S. andrea lisa buxo — On XXXII verso. 84 × 144 mm.
[39] [T:] liezena — On XXXIII G 83 × 145 mm.
[40] [T:] curzola — On XXXIII G 84 × 145 mm.
[41] [T:] S.ᵐ de tremidi — On XXXIII G verso. 84 × 146 mm.
[42] [T:] corfu — On XXXIIII G ii 84 × 146 mm.
[43] [T:] pacsu — On XXXIIII G ii verso. 84 × 147 mm.
[44] [T:] S.maura — On XXXV G iii 83 × 145 mm.
[45] [T:] compare — On XXXV G iii 82 × 144 mm.
[46] [T:] EPIRO cuzolari diluchio — On XXXV G iii verso. 83 × 144 mm.
[47] [T:] zafalonia — On XXXVI 83 × 144 mm.
[48] [T:] zante — On XXXVI verso. 83 × 145 mm.
[49] [T:] striuali — On XXXVII 86 × 146 mm.
[50] [T:] P. DELLA MOREA — On XXXVII 83 × 144 mm.
[51] [T:] morea — On XXXVIII verso. 141 × 148 mm.
[52] [T:] albara flenda legina boetia — On XXXIX H 83 × 145 mm.
[53] [T:] cerigo cecerigo — On XXXIX H verso. 83 × 145 mm.
[54] [T:] SDILE — On XL H ii verso. 81 × 145 mm.
[55] [T:] Tino — On XLI H iii 82 × 145 mm.
[56] [T:] Andre — On XLI H iii 83 × 146 mm.
[57] [T:] Zea — On XLII 83 × 144 mm.
[58] [T:] fermene — On XLII 83 × 144 mm.
[59] [T:] siphano — On XLIII 83 × 145 mm.
[60] [T:] milo — On XLIII verso. 83 × 146 mm.
[61] [T:] nio — On XLIIII 83 × 145 mm.
[62] [T:] Amurgo — On XLIIII 83 × 144 mm.
[63] [T:] antipario pario — On XLIIII verso. 84 × 143 mm.
[64] [T:] nixia — On XLV I 83 × 145 mm.
[65] [T:] polimio policandro cardia sicino — On XLV I verso. 84 × 144 mm.
[66] [T:] fecussa scinussa heraclia chiero pyra — On XLV I verso. 83 × 144 mm.
[67] [T:] charusa zinara leuita — On XLVI I ii 83 × 143 mm.
[68] [T:] micole — On XLVI I ii 83 × 144 mm.
[69] [T:] stapodia nicaria fornelli — On XLVI I ii verso. 83 × 145 mm.
[70] [T:] palmosa — On XLVII 80 × 144 mm.
[71] [T:] iero — On XLVII 82 × 144 mm.
[72] [T:] calamo — On XLVII verso. 81 × 144 mm.
[73] [T:] stampalia — On XLVII verso. 83 × 144 mm.
[74] [T:] S. erini — On XLVII (pro XLVIII). 81 × 143 mm.
[75] [T:] namphio — On XLVII (pro XLVIII) verso. 81 × 144 mm.
[76] [T:] candia. — On L k ii — LI 51 × 331 mm.
[77] [T:] scarpanto — On LI verso. 82 × 143 mm.
[78] [T:] rhodo — On LII verso. 82 × 144 mm.
[79] [T:] simie — On LII verso. 82 × 144 mm.
[80] [T:] limonia carchi — On LIII L 81 × 144 mm.
[81] [T:] episcopia — On LIII L verso. 81 × 143 mm.
[82] [T:] nisaro chirana — On LIIII L ii 81 × 143 mm.
[83] [T:] caloiero — On LIIII ii verso. 82 × 144 mm.
[84] [T:] lango — On LV L iii 83 × 144 mm.
[85] [T:] fornoli mandria lipso crusia — On LV L iii verso. 83 ×. 145 mm.
[86] [T:] gatonisi fermaco theclida fermacusa — On LVI 82 × 143 mm.
[87] [T:] samo demoniar — On LVI verso. 82 × 145 mm.
[88] [T:] sio — On LVII 160 × 148 mm.
[89] [T:] psara piccilo psara — On LVII verso. 81 × 144 mm.
[90] [T:] metelin — On LVIII verso. 161 × 148 mm.
[91] [T:] tenedo lembro — On LIX M 81 × 144 mm.
[92] [T:] samotracia lembro — On LIX M 83 × 144 mm.
[93] [T:] el tasso monte santo — On LIX M verso. 142 × 148 mm.
[94] [T:] stalimene S. strati — On LX 148 × 144 mm.
[95] [T:] limene pelagisi larsura la iura ipiperi prasonisi — On LX verso. 81 × 144 mm.
[96] [T:] dromo sarachino el caloiero o uer.s.ilia — On LX verso. 81 × 143 mm.
[97] [T:] sciatos scopelos — On LIX (pro LXI) N 82 × 143 mm.
[98] [T:] schiropola sciro — On LIX N verso. 81 × 143 mm.
[99] [T:] negroponte — On LXII N ii — LXIII 138 × 331 mm.
[100] [T:] constantinopoli — On LXIII verso. 82 × 146 mm.
[101] [T:] taurica chersoneso — On LXIIII verso. 83 × 146 mm.
[102] [T:] Cipro — On LXVI O ii — LXVII 156 × 328 mm.
[103] [T:] ciampagu — On LXVIII 82 × 145 mm.
[104] [T:] iaua maggiore fondur condur — On LXVIII verso. 82 × 146 mm.
[105] [T:] iaua minore — On LXIX P verso. 82 × 146 mm.
[106] [T:] locaz necumera patera mahgama botegon — On LXIX P verso. 82 × 144 mm.
[107] [T:] scilam dondina — On LXX P ii 81 × 145 mm.
[108] [T:] maniole bazacata isole di satyri daruse inebila imangla ibadio — On LXX P ii verso. 82 × 146 mm.
[109] [T:] zanzibar maidegascar scorsia — On LXX P ii verso. 82 × 146 mm.
[110] [T:] taprobana — On LXXII verso. 193 × 145 mm.

Notes: All the maps have either text or another map on the verso, and they are all uncoloured. The title-page is printed in red and black. On the second blank leaf, in Nordenskiöld's handwriting, are the words 'Saknas Xii & XVII. Föröfrigt fullständing, med flerestädes finnes tryckfel i pagineringen och DD är inbundet före CC.' [Wanting XII & XVII. Otherwise complete, but many pages are misnumbered and DD is bound before CC.] i.e. the world map (DD) and the map of the Mare Egeo (CC) have been transposed. The atlas is quarter bound in leather. On the verso of the first blank leaf is written in pencil: 'Non compl XII', with 'XVII' added in red. A bookseller's label, 'J.A. Stargardt Buchhandlung Berlin, SW. Zimmerstrasse 19' is pasted on the upper left-hand corner of this leaf; and in Nordenskiöld's collection of invoices is a note from Stargardt, stating that he has sent the Bordone for the price of Rm.7.50 plus 1.00 carriage. On the inside of the back cover Nordenskiöld has written in pencil: 'Kat. Olschki 1896—125 fr.' His signature appears on the second blank leaf.

Lit.: Bagrow p. 334, Bagrow, Ortelius vol. 1, p. 47—49, LC List, vol. 1, p. 44, nr 162.

28 BORDONE, BENEDETTO 1534

ISOLARIO DI BENEDETTO BORDONE Nel qual si ragiona di tutte l'Isole del mondo, con li lor nomi antichi & moderni, historie, fauole, & modi del loro viuere, & in qual parte del mare stanno, & in qual parallelo & clima giaciono. Con la gionta del Monte del Oro nouamente ritrouato. CON IL BREVE DEL PAPA Et gratia & priuilegio della Illustrissima Signoria di Venetia come in quelli appare. M D XXXIIII. [Colophon:] Impresse in Vinegia per Nicolo d'Aristotile, detto Zoppino, nel mese di Giugno, del. .M.D.XXXIIII. 31,2 cm.

[1]   [Zone-map] BB = 1528:[1].
[2]   [T:] EVROPA — BB = 1528:[2].
[3]   [T:] MARE EGEO ARCIPELAGO — CC = 1528:[4].
[4]   [World map] DD = 1528:[3].
[5]   [T:] ISLANDA — On I A = 1528:[5].
[6]   [T:] Irlanda — On I A verso. = 1528:[6].
[7]   Tauola secondo moderni.
      [T:] inghilterra secōdo moderni — On III A iii = 1528:[7]
[8]   Tauola secondo Tolomeo.
      [T:] inghilterra secondo tolemeo — III A iii verso = 1528:[8].
[9]   [T:] di lugduno parte de eqtania pte — On IIII = 1528:[9].
[10] [T:] parte de hispagna — On IIII verso. = 1528:[10].
[11] [T:] datia norbegia gottia — On VI = 1528:[11].
[12] [T:] Terra de lauoratore — On VI verso. = 1528:[12].
[13] La gran citta di Temistitan. On X = 1528:[13].
[14] [T:] iamaiqua spagnola ... — On XI verso. = 1528:[14].
[15] [T:] spagnola — On XII verso.   85 × 146 mm.
[16] [T:] Jamaiqua — On XIII C = 1528:[15].
[17] [T:] Cuba — On XIII C verso. = 1528:[16].
[18] [T:] S.Maria antica S.maria rotonda ... — On XVIII (pro XIIII). C ii = 1528:[17].
[19] [T:] guadalupe — On XVIII (pro XIIII). C ii verso. = 1528:[18].
[20] [T:] matinina — On XVIII (pro XIIII). C ii verso. = 1528:[19].
[21] [T:] porto santo — On XV C iii verso. = 1528:[20].
[22] [T:] madera — On XVI = 1528:[21].
[23] [T:] ombrio iunone ... — On XVI verso. = 1528:[22].
[24] [T:] palma agore tinerif. canaria forte uentura lāzaroto S.antonio S.nicolo S.Jacopo S.uincemio i.bianca cuori i.delle gaze — On XVII verso. 83 × 145 mm.
[25] [T:] astores S.georgio ... — On XVIII = 1528:[23].
[26] [T:] REGNO DE CASTIGLIA — On XVIII verso. = 1528:[24].
[27] [T:] dragonera ieuiza... — On XX D Iii = 1528:[25].
[28] [T:] maiorica minorica — On XX D Iii verso. = 1528:[26].
[29] [T:] m.cristi elba ... — On XXI D iii = 1528:[27].
[30] [T:] capraia gorgona ... — On XXI D ii verso. = 1528:[28].
[31] [T:] Sardigna — On XXII verso. = 1528:[29].
[32] [T:] sicilia secondo tolemeo sicilia secondo moderni — On XXIIII — XXV E = 1528:[30].
[33] [T:] palmosa palmarola ischia — On XXVI E ii = 1528:[31].
[34] [C:] VINEGIA — XXIX F verso — XXX = 1528:[32].
[35] [T:] murano — On XXX verso. = 1528:[33].
[36] [T:] mazorbo — On XXXI G = 1528:[34].
[37] [T:] chiozza — On XXXI G = 1528:[35].
[38] [T:] PARTE DE SHIAVONIA — On XXXI G verso. = 1528:[36].
[39] [T:] istria uegia ... — On XXXII G ii = 1528:[37].
[40] [T:] trau brazza ... — On XXXII G ii verso. = 1528:[38].
[41] [T:] liezena — On XXXIII G iii = 1528:[39].
[42] [T:] curzola — On XXXIII G iii = 1528:[40].
[43] [T:] S.ā de tremidi — On XXXIII G iii verso. = 1528:[41].
[44] [T:] corfu — On XXXIIII = 1528:[42].
[45] [T:] pacsu — On XXXIIII verso. = 1528:[43].
[46] [T:] S.maura — On XXXV = 1528:[44].
[47] [T:] compare — On XXXV = 1528:[45].
[48] [T:] EPIRO cuzolari diluchio — On XXXV verso. = 1528:[46].
[49] [T:] zafalonia — On XXXVI = 1528:[47].
[50] [T:] zante — On XXXVI verso. = 1528:[48].
[51] [T:] striuali — On XXXVII H = 1528:[49].
[52] [T:] P. DELLA MOREA — On XXXVII H = 1528:[50].
[53] [T:] morea — On XXXVIII H iii verso. = 1528:[51].
[54] [T:] albara flenda ... — On XXXIX H ii = 1528:[52].
[55] [T:] cerigo cecerigo — On XXXIX H iii = 1528:[53].

[56] [T:] SDILE — On XL verso. = 1528:[54].
[57] [T:] Tino — On XLI = 1528:[55].
[58] [T:] Andre — On XLI = 1528:[56].
[59] [T:] Zea — On XLII = 1528:[57].
[60] [T:] fermene — On XLII = 1528:[58].
[61] [T:] siphano — On XLIII I = 1528:[59].
[62] [T:] milo — On XLIII I verso. = 1528:[60].
[63] [T:] nio — On XLIII (pro XLIIII) I ii = 1528:[61].
[64] [T:] Amurgo — On XLIII (pro XLIIII) I ii = 1528:[62].
[65] [T:] antipario pario — On XLIII (pro XLIIII) I ii verso. = 1528:[63].
[66] [T:] nixia — On XLV I iii = 1528:[64].
[67] [T:] polimio policandro ... — On XLV I iii verso. = 1528:[65].
[68] [T:] fecussa scinussa ... — On XLV I iii verso. = 1528:[66].
[69] [T:] charusa zinara leuita — On XLVI = 1528:[67].
[70] [T:] micole — On XLVI = 1528:[68].
[71] [T:] stapodia nicaria fornelli — On XLVI verso = 1528:[69].
[72] [T:] palmosa — On XLVII = 1528:[70].
[73] [T:] iero — On XLVII = 1528:[71].
[74] [T:] calamo — On XLVII verso. = 1528:[72].
[75] [T:] stampalia — On XLVII verso. = 1528:[73].
[76] [T:] S. erini — On XLVIII = 1528:[74].
[77] [T:] namphio — On XLVIII verso. = 1528:[75].
[78] [T:] candia — On L K ii — LI K iii = 1528:[76].
[79] [T:] scarpanto — On LI K iii verso. = 1528:[77].
[80] [T:] rhodo — On LII verso. = 1528:[78].
[81] [T:] simie — On LII verso. = 1528:[79].
[82] [T:] limonia carchi — On LIII = 1528:[80].
[83] [T:] episcopia — On LIII verso. = 1528:[81].
[84] [T:] nisaro chirana — On LIIII = 1528:[82].
[85] [T:] caloiero — On LIIII verso. = 1528:[83].
[86] [T:] lango — On LV L = 1528:[84].
[87] [T:] fornoli mandria ... — On LV L verso. = 1528:[85].
[88] [T:] gatonisi fermaco ... — On LVI L ii = 1528:[86].
[89] [T:] samo demoniar — On LVI L ii verso. = 1528:[87].
[90] [T:] sio — On LVII L iii = 1528:[88].
[91] [T:] psara piccilo psara — On LVII L iii verso. = 1528:[89].
[92] [T:] metelin — On LVIII verso. = 1528:[90].
[93] [T:] tenedo lembro — On LIX = 1528:[91].
[94] [T:] samotracia lembro — On LIX = 1528:[92].
[95] [T:] el tasso monte santo — On LIX verso. = 1528:[93].
[96] [T:] stalimene S.strati — On LX = 1528:[94].
[97] [T:] limene pelagisi ... — On LX verso. = 1528:[95].
[98] [T:] dromo sarachino ... — On LX verso. = 1528:[96].
[99] [T:] sciatos scopelos — On LXI M = 1528:[97].
[100] [T:] schiropola sciro — On LXI M verso. = 1528:[98].
[101] [T:] negroponte — On LXII M ii — LXIII M iii = 1528:[99].
[102] [T:] constantinopoli — On LXIII M iii verso. = 1528:[100].
[103] [T:] taurica chersoneso — On LXIIII verso. = 1528:[101].
[104] [T:] Cipro — On LXVI — LXVII N = 1528:[102].
[105] [T:] ciampagu — On LXVIII N ii = 1528:[103].
[106] [T:] iaua maggiore fondur condur — On LXVIII N ii = 1528:[104].
[107] [T:] iaua minore — On LXIX N iii = 1528:[105].
[108] [T:] locaz necumera ... — On LXIX N iii verso. = 1528:[106].
[109] [T:] scilam dondina — On LXX N iiii = 1528:[107].
[110] [T:] maniole bazacata ... — On LXX N iiii verso. = 1528:[108].
[111] [T:] zanzibar maidegascar scorsia — On LXX N iiii verso. = 1528:[109].
[112] [T:] taprobana — On LXXII verso. = 1528:[110].

Notes: All the maps have either text or another map on the verso, except for the world map, [4], which lacks the 'Erroti da glimpressori per inaduertenza fatti'. All the maps are uncoloured. The title-page is printed in red and black. Although this edition of Bordone's atlas has a different title from the edition of 1528, the text and maps are the same. This copy is complete; it includes both of the maps wanting in our copy of the 1528 edition. It is finely bound in blue leather by Gruel & Engelmann Relieurs A Paris, with a beautiful scrollwork border on the inside of the covers, and gilt edges. Nordenskiöld's bookplate is pasted on the inside of the front cover.

Lit.: Bagrow p. 334, Bagrow, Ortelius vol. 1, p. 47—49, LC List vol. 1, p. 45, nr 163.

29 BORDONE, BENEDETTO   1534

ISOLARIO DI BENEDETTO BORDONE Nel qual si ragiona di tutte l'Isole del mondo, con li lor nomi antichi & moderni, historie, fauole, & modi del loro viuere, & in qual parte del mare stanno, & in qual parallelo & clima giaciono. Con la gionta del Monte del Oro nouamente ritrouato. CON IL BREVE DEL PAPA Et gratia & priuilegio della Illustrissima Signoria di Venetia come in quelli appare. M D XXXIIII. [Colophon:] Impresse in Vinegia per Nicolo d'Aristotile, detto Zoppino, nel mese di Giugno, del..M.D.XXXIIII.   30 cm.

Notes: All the maps have text on the verso, and they are uncoloured. This is a second copy of the 1534 edition, in which the leaf BB with maps [1] and [2] is lacking, so that maps [1]—[110] correspond to maps [3]—[112] in the complete copy. There is a manuscript index of six pages, beginning on the verso of the world map and bearing the title 'TAVOLA DE'I NOMI DELLE ISOLE DESCRITTE DA BENEDETTO BORDONE ET ANCO DI MOLTI MARI, FIVMI, MONTI, SENI, GOLFI, SCOGLI, E FAMOSE CITTADI, DELLE QVALI SI FA MENTIONE NELL OPERA, CON I SVOI NOMI TANTO ANTICHI QVANTO MODERNI.' The atlas was bound for Nordenskiöld, and bears the initials AEN on the spine. His signature appears in ink on the verso of the first blank leaf and in pencil on the title-page.

30 BORDONE, BENEDETTO   1547

ISOLARIO DI BENEDETTO BORDONE Nel qual si ragiona di tutte l'Isole del mondo, con li lor nomi antichi & moderni, historie, fauole, & modi del loro viuere, & in qual parte del mare stanno, & in qual parallelo & clima giaciono. Ricoreto, & di Nuouo ristampato. Con la gionta del Monte del Oro nouamente ritrouato. CON IL BREVE DEL PAPA Et gratia & priuilegio della Illustrissima Signoria di Venetia come in quelli appare. M. D. XLVII. [Colophon:] In Vinegia ad instantia, & spese del Nobile huomo M.Federico Toresano. M. D. XLVII.   30,5 cm.

[1]   [Zone-map] BB = 1528:[1].
[2]   [T:] EVROPA — BB = 1528:[2].
[3]   [T:] MARE EGEO ARCIPELAGO — CC = 1528:[4].
[4]   [World map] DD = 1528:[3].
[5]   [T:] ISLANDA — On I   A = 1528:[5].
[6]   [T:] Irlanda — On I   A verso. = 1528:[6].
[7]   Tauola secondo moderni,
      [T:] inghilterra secōdo moderni — On III   A iii = 1528:[7]
[8]   Tauola secondo Tolomeo.
      [T:] inghilterra secondo tolomeo — III   A iii verso = 1528:[8]
[9]   [T:] di lugduno parte de eqtania pte — On IV = 1528:[9].
[10] [T:] parte de hispagna — On IV verso. = 1528:[10].
[11] [T:] datia   norbegia   gottia — On VI = 1528:[11].
[12] [T:] Terra de lauoratore — On VI verso. = 1528:[12].
[13] La gran Citta di Temistitan. On X = 1528:[13].
[14] [T:] iamaiqua   spagnola ... — On XI verso. = 1528:[14].
[15] [T:] spagnola — On XII verso. = 1534:[15].
[16] [T:] Jamaiqua — On XIII   C = 1528:[15].
[17] [T:] Cuba — On XIII   C verso. = 1528:[16].
[18] [T:] S.Maria antica S.Maria rotonda ... — On XIII   C ii = 1528:[17].
[19] [T:] guadalupe' — On XIIII   C ii verso. = 1528:[18].
[20] [T:] matinina — On XIII   C ii verso. = 1528:[19].
[21] [T:] porto santo — On XV   C iii verso. = 1528:[20].
[22] [T:] madera — On XVI = 1528:[21].
[23] [T:] ombrio   iunone ... — On XVI verso. = 1528:[22].
[24] [T:] palma   agore ... — On XVII verso. = 1534:[24]
[25] [T:] astores   S.georgio ... — On XVIII = 1528:[23].
[26] [T:] REGNO DE CASTIGLIA — On XVIII verso. = 1528:[24].
[27] [T:] dragonera   ieuiza... — On XX   D ii = 1528:[25].
[28] [T:] maiorica minorica — On XX Dii verso. = 1528:[26].
[29] [T:] m.cristi   elba ... — On XXI   D iii = 1528:[27].
[30] [T:] capraia   gorgona ... — On XXI   D ii verso. = 1528:[28].
[31] [T:] Sardigna — On XXII verso. = 1528:[29].
[32] [T:] sicilia secondo tolomeo   sicilia secondo moderni — On XXIIII — XXV   E = 1528:[30].
[33] [T:] palmosa   palmarola   ischia — On XXVI   E ii = 1528:[31].
[34] [C:] VINEGIA — XXIX   F — XXX = 1528:[32].
[35] [T:] murano — On XXX verso. = 1528:[33].
[36] [T:] mazorbo — On XXXI   G = 1528:[34].
[37] [T:] chiozza — On XXXI   G = 1528:[35].
[38] [T:] PARTE DE SHIAVONIA — On XXXI   G verso. = 1528:[36].
[39] [T:] istria   uegia ... — On XXXII   G ii = 1528:[37].
[40] [T:] trau   brazza ... — On XXXII   G ii verso. = 1528:[38].
[41] [T:] liezena — On XXXIII   G iii = 1528:[39].
[42] [T:] curzola — On XXXIII   G iii = 1528:[40].
[43] [T:] S.m̃ de tremidi — On XXXIII   G iii verso. = 1528:[41].
[44] [T:] corfu — On XXXIIII = 1528:[42].
[45] [T:] pacsu — On XXXIIII verso. = 1528:[43].
[46] [T:] S.maura — On XXXV = 1528:[44].
[47] [T:] compare — On XXXV = 1528:[45].
[48] [T:] EPIRO   cuzolari   diluchio — On XXXV verso. = 1528:[46].
[49] [T:] zafalonia — On XXXVI = 1528:[47].
[50] [T:] zante — On XXXVI verso. = 1528:[48].
[51] [T:] striuali — On XXXVII   H = 1528:[49].
[52] [T:] P. DELLA MOREA — On XXXVII   H = 1528:[50].
[53] [T:] morea — On XXXVIII   H iii verso. = 1528:[51].
[54] [T:] albara   flenda ... — On XXXIX   H iii = 1528:[52].
[55] [T:] cerigo   cecerigo — On XXXIX   H iii verso. = 1528:[53].
[56] [T:] SDILE — On XL verso. = 1528:[54].
[57] [T:] Tino — On XLI = 1528:[55].
[58] [T:] Andre — On XLI = 1528:[56].
[59] [T:] Zea — On XLII = 1528:[57].
[60] [T:] fermene — On XLII = 1528:[58].
[61] [T:] siphano — On XLIII   I = 1528:[59].
[62] [T:] milo — On XLIII   I verso. = 1528:[60].
[63] [T:] nio — On XLIII (pro XLIIII)   I ii = 1528:[61].
[64] [T:] Amurgo — On XLIII (pro XLIII)   I ii = 1528:[62].
[65] [T:] antipario   pario — On XLIII (pro XLIIII) I ii verso. = 1528:[63].
[66] [T:] nixia — On XLV   I iii = 1528:[64].
[67] [T:] polimio policandro ... — On XLV   I iii verso. = 1528:[65].
[68] [T:] fecussa scinussa ... — On XLV   I iiii verso. = 1528:[66].
[69] [T:] charusa   zinara   leuita — On XLVI = 1528:[67].
[70] [T:] micole — On XLVI = 1528:[68].
[71] [T:] stapodia   nicaria   fornelli — On XLVI verso = 1528:[69].
[72] [T:] palmosa — On XLVII = 1528:[70].
[73] [T:] iero — On XLVII = 1528:[71].
[74] [T:] calamo — On XLVII verso. = 1528:[72].
[75] [T:] stampalia — On XLVII verso. = 1528:[73].
[76] [T:] S. erini — On XLVIII = 1528:[74].
[77] [T:] namphio — On XLVIII verso. = 1528:[75].
[78] [T:] candia — On L   K ii — LI   K iii = 1528:[76].

[79] [T:] scarpanto — On LI K ii verso. = 1528:[77].
[80] [T:] rhodo — On LII verso. = 1528:[78].
[81] [T:] simie — On LII verso. = 1528:[79].
[82] [T:] limonia   carchi — On LIII = 1528:[80].
[83] [T:] episcopia — On LIII verso. = 1528:[81].
[84] [T:] nisaro chirana — On LIIII = 1528:[82].
[85] [T:] caloiero — On LIIII verso. = 1528:[83].
[86] [T:] lango — On LV L = 1528:[84].
[87] [T:] fornoli   mandria ... — On LV L verso. = 1528:[85].
[88] [T:] gatonisi   fermaco ... — On LVI L ii = 1528:[86].
[89] [T:] samo   demoniar — On LVI L ii verso. = 1528:[87].
[90] [T:] sio — On LVII L iii = 1528:[88].
[91] [T:] psara piccilo   psara — On LVII L iii verso. = 1528:[89].
[92] [T:] metelin — On LVIII verso. = 1528:[90].
[93] [T:] tenedo   lembro — On LIX = 1528:[91].
[94] [T:] samotracia   lembro — On LIX = 1528:[92].
[95] [T:] el tasso   monte santo — On LIX verso. = 1528:[93].
[96] [T:] stalimene   S.strati — On LX = 1528:[94].
[97] [T:] limene pelagisi ... — On LX verso. = 1528:[95].
[98] [T:] dromo   sarachino ... — On LX verso. = 1528:[96].
[99] [T:] sciatos   scopelos — On LXI M = 1528:[97].
[100] [T:] schiropola   sciro — On LXI M verso. = 1528:[98].
[101] [T:] negroponte — On LXII M ii — LXIII M iii = 1528:[99].
[102] [T:] constantinopoli — On LXIII M iii verso. = 1528:[100].
[103] [T:] taurica chersoneso — On LXIIII verso. = 1528:[101].
[104] [T:] Cipro — On LXVI — LXVII N = 1528:[102].
[105] [T:] ciampagu — On LXVIII N ii = 1528:[103].
[106] [T:] iaua maggiore   fondur   condur — On XLVIII N ii = 1528:[104].
[107] [T:] iaua minore — On LXIX N iii verso. = 1528:[105].
[108] [T:] locaz   necumera ... — On LXIX N iii verso. = 1528:[106].
[109] [T:] scilam   dondina — On LXX N iiii = 1528:[107].
[110] [T:] maniole   bazacata ... — On LXX N iiii verso. = 1528:[108].
[111] [T:] zanzibar   maidegascar — On LXX N iiii verso. = 1528:[109].
[112] [T:] taprobana — On LXXII verso. = 1528:[110].

Notes: All the maps have either text or a map on the verso except for the world map, which is blank on the verso, as is the one in the 1534 edition. They are all uncoloured. The signatures do not correspond with those in the 1528 edition, but are the same as those in the 1534 edition. The title-page is printed in red and black, and the engraved border is the same in all our three editions. The trade-mark of the new publisher of the 1547 edition appears between the M.D. and the XLVII. The volume is bound in soft vellum, with holes left by four pairs of leather straps. Nordenskiöld's signature is on the first blank leaf, with the note 'Karta öfver Skandinavien fol.VI' [Map of Scandinavia], which seems to indicate that this was the first edition of the Isolario that he bought, as the map appears in all of them.

Lit.: Bagrow p. 334, Bagrow, Ortelius vol. 1, p. 47—49, LC List vol. 1, p. 45, nr 164.

31 BOSCHINI, MARCO   1651

IL REGNO TVTTO DI CANDIA DELINEATO À PARTE, À PARTE, ET INTAGLIATO DA Marco Boschini VENETIANO. AL SERENISSIMO PRENCIPE E REGAL COLLEGIO DI VENETIA M. D. C. LI. ...   35,5 cm.

[1] 1 [C:] IL REGNO DI CANDIA — 222 × 426 mm.
[2] 2 [T:] SCOGLIO ET FOR^{ZA}. DI GARABVSE. — 214 × 394 mm.
[3] 3 [T:] GOLFO DEL CASTEL CHISSAMO. — 210 × 163 mm.
[4] 4 [T:] SCOGLIO ET FORTEZZE DI S. THODORO. — 210 × 162 mm.
[5] 5 [T:] SPIAGGIA DI S. Thodoro — 210 × 159 mm.
[6] 6 [T:] PIANTA DELLA CANEA. — 213 × 390 mm.
[7] 7 [T:] CANEA. — 210 × 159 mm.
[8] 8 [T:] PORTO, E FORTE^{ZA} D^{A} SVDA. — 214 × 165 mm.
[9] 9 [T:] FORTEZZA DELLA SVDA. — (Plan). 214 × 393 mm.
[10] 10 [T:] PORTO DI MARATHI. — 211 × 162 mm.
[11] 11 [T:] SPIAGGIA DEL C^{L} APICORONA. — 215 × 161 mm.
[12] 12 [T:] SPIAGGIA DEL C^{L} APICORONA VERSO LEVANTE. — 212 × 161 mm.
[13] 13 [T:] SPIAGGIA DELL ARMIRO. DI RETTIMO. — 213 × 160 mm.
[14] 14 [T:] FORTEZZA DI RETTIMO. — 218 × 396 mm.
[15] 15 [T:] RETTIMO. — 213 × 157 mm.
[16] 16 [T:] SPIAGGIA DELLA TORRE. — 213 × 160 mm.
[17] 17 [T:] CASTEL DI MILOPOTAMO. — 216 × 162 mm.
[18] 18 [T:] PORTO DI ATALÌ. — 208 × 160 mm.
[19] 19 [T:] GALINVS. — 212 × 159 mm.
[20] 20 [T:] SANTA PELAGIA. — 212 × 157 mm.
[21] 21 [T:] PONTA DELLA FRASCHIA. — 213 × 160 mm.
[22] 22 [T:] PALEOCASTRO. — 217 × 163 mm.
[23] 23 [T:] CITTA DI CANDIA. — (Plan). 220 × 390 mm.
[24] 24 [T:] CASTEL DI CANDIA. — 216 × 160 mm.
[25] 25 [T:] CITTA DI CANDIA ASSEDIATA. — (Plan). 418 × 558 mm.
[26] 26 [T:] STANDIA ISOLA. — 217 × 163 mm.
[27] 27 [T:] SPIAGGIA DEL CAZZABANO — 218 × 162 mm.
[28] 28 [T:] SPIAGGIA DI MESSOVVGNI. — 218 × 163 mm.
[29] 29 [T:] CACCO NOROS. — 216 × 161 mm.
[30] 30 [T:] PORTO DI TIGANI. — 217 × 163 mm.
[31] 31 [T:] SPIAGGIA DI MAGLIA. — 216 × 160 m.
[32] 32 [T:] PORTO DI SPINA LONGA. — 217 × 162 mm.
[33] 33 [T:] FORTEZZA DI SPINA LONGA. — (Plan). 215 × 396 mm.
[34] 34 [T:] CAVVSSI. — 216 × 162 mm.
[35] 35 [T:] PACHIANAMO. — 216 × 160 mm.
[36] 36 [T:] CASTEL MIRABEL. — 217 × 163 mm.
[37] 37 [T:] LEOPETRO. — 214 × 160 mm.
[38] 38 [T:] SETTIA. — 215 × 161 mm.
[39] 39 [T:] CITTA DI SETTIA. — 212 × 390 mm.
[40] 40 [T:] PALEOCASTRO. — 215 × 162 mm.
[41] 41 [T:] PORTO DI XACRO. — 213 × 161 mm.
[42] 42 [T:] XERO CAMBO. — 215 × 163 mm.
[43] 43 [T:] SPIAGGIA DI CVZZVRA. — 216 × 162 mm.
[44] 44 [T:] SPIAGGIA DI GERAPETRA. — 213 × 161 mm.
[45] 45 [T:] SPIAGGIA DI MIRTO. — 214 × 161 mm.
[46] 46 [T:] SPIAGGIA DI DERMATO. — 214 × 161 mm.
[47] 47 [T:] PORTO DI CALVSLIMIONES. — 214 × 161 mm.
[48] 48 [T:] SPIAGGIA DI ZVZZVRO. — 215 × 165 mm.
[49] 49 [T:] MESSAREA. — 210 × 160 mm.
[50] 50 [T:] CASTEL PROTISSA. — 215 × 161 mm.
[51] 51 [T:] CASTEL BELVEDER. — 214 × 163 mm.
[52] 52 [T:] PORTO DI LVTRO DELLA SFACHIA. — 215 × 161 mm.
[53] 53 [T:] ISOLA DE GOZZI DI CANDIA — 211 × 163 mm.
[54] 54 [T:] CASTEL FRANCO. — 217 × 163 mm.
[55] 55 [T:] CASTEL SFACCHIA. — 217 × 163 mm.
[56] 56 [T:] CASTEL SELINO. — 218 × 164 mm.
[57] 57 [T:] LASSITI. — 218 × 163 mm.
[58] 58 [T:] CASTEL PEDIADA. — 215 × 159 mm.
[59] 59 [T:] CASTEL TEMENE. — 216 × 162 mm.
[60] 60 [T:] CERIGO. — 215 × 161 mm.
[61] 61 [T:] THINE. — 217 × 162 mm.

Notes: All the maps are blank on the back and uncoloured. The title-page is printed on a small sheet which has been pasted to a full-size leaf. On the engraved leaf following the dedication is a map of Candia, 52 × 163 mm, which has no text. The Encl. ital. (vol. 7, p.538) mentions an edition of 1644, which does not seem to be recorded elsewhere; the number of maps is given as 41. Thieme-Becker lists only the Candia atlas under Boschini; Bagrow mentions also two 1646 maps, of Dalmatia and Albania, and a 1651 map of Venice. The volume is bound in paper. Nordenskiöld's signature is on the first blank leaf, with the year 1894, and on the first of the blank leaves at the back of the volume he has written 'Köpt hos S. Rosen Venezia. Aug. 1894 36 fr.'

Lit.: Bagrow, p. 334, Encl. ital. vol. 7, p. 538, Thieme-Becker vol. 4 p. 393.

32 BOSCHINI, MARCO   1658

L'ARCIPELAGO Con tutte le Isole, Scogli Secche, e Bassi Fondi, CON I MARI, GOLFI, SENI, PORTI, CITTA, E CASTELLI; NELLA FORMA, CHE SI VEDONO AL TEMPO PRESENTE. Con vna succinta narratiua de i loro nomi, Fauole, & Historie, tanto antiche quanto moderne. OPERA DI MARCO BOSCHINI. Non meno vtile alli Studiosi di Cosmografia, che dilettuole all'vniuersale. DEDICATA ALL'ALTEZZA SERENISSIMA DEL SIG PRENCIPE ALESSANDRO FARNESE. Per l'Augustissima Republica di Venetia, General della Cauallaria, control'armi Ottomane. IN VENETIA, Per Francesco Nicolini. MDCLVIII. ...
[Half title:]
L'ARCIPELAGO. [Colophon:] IN VENETIA, Appresso il Nicolini.   22,5 cm.

[1]   [T:] ARCIPELAGO. — Before 1. Verso blank. 236 × 279 mm.
[2]   [T:] REGNO DI CANDIA. — Between pp. 4 and [5]. Verso blank. 175 × 268 mm.
[3]   [T:] CERIGO. — [7]. 175 × 120 mm.
[4]   [T:] SCARPANTO. — 9. 175 × 118 mm.
[5]   [T:] RODI. — [11]. 173 × 118 mm.
[6]   [T:] LE SIMIE. — [13]. 176 × 120 mm.
[7]   [T:] CARCHI, E LIMONIA. — [15]. 174 × 113 mm.
[8]   [T:] PISCOPIA. — 17 174 × 116 mm.
[9]   [T:] NISARI. — 19 173 × 118 mm.
[10] [T:] STAMPALIA. — 21 175 × 119 mm.
[11] [T:] NAMPHIO. — 23 175 × 120 mm.
[12] [T:] SANTA ERINI. — 25 175 × 117 mm.
[13] [T:] SICANDRO E POLICANDRO. — 27 176 × 118 mm.
[14] [T:] MILO. — 29 175 × 118 mm.
[15] [T:] SIPHANO. — 31 175 × 117 mm.
[16] [T:] SERPHINO. — 33 173 × 115 mm.
[17] [T:] FERMENIA. — 35 173 × 116 mm.
[18] [T:] ZEA. — 37 173 × 117 mm.
[19] [T:] TINE. — 39 174 × 116 mm.
[20] [T:] ANDRO. — 41 173 × 116 mm.
[21] [T:] MICONE. — 43 174 × 115 mm.
[22] [T:] SDILE. — 45 173 × 117 mm.
[23] [T:] PARIS. — 47 173 × 115 mm.
[24] [T:] NIXIA. — 49 176 × 117 mm.
[25] [T:] ISOLETTE. — 51 174 × 117 mm.
[26] [T:] NIO. — 53 174 × 118 mm.
[27] [T:] AMORGO. — 55 175 × 117 mm.
[28] [T:] ZINARA E LEVITA. — 57 174 × 117 mm.
[29] [T:] CALOIERO. — 59 176 × 120 mm.
[30] [T:] LANGO. — 61 174 × 117 mm.
[31] [T:] CALAMO. — 63 173 × 119 mm.
[32] [T:] LERO. — 65 172 × 117 mm.
[33] [T:] PATMOS. — 67 172 × 118 mm.
[34] [T:] DIPSO, CRVSIA, FORNI. — 69 173 × 118 mm.
[35] [T:] GATONISI, FERMACO. — 71 173 × 117 mm.
[36] [T:] SAMO. — 73 170 × 118 mm.
[37] [T:] NICARIA. — 75 171 × 117 mm.
[38] [T:] PSARÀ. — 77 168 × 118 mm.
[39] [T:] SIO. — 79 171 × 118 mm.
[40] [T:] METELIN. — 81 175 × 117 mm.
[41] [T:] TENEDO. — 83 172 × 120 mm.
[42] [T:] STALIMINE. — 85 173 × 117 mm.
[43] [T:] MONTE SANTO. — 87 178 × 120 mm.
[44] [T:] LIMINE PELEGISE. — 89 177 × 121 mm.
[45] [T:] SCHIRO. — 91 176 × 117 mm.
[46] [T:] LI DROMI. — 93 172 × 118 mm.
[47] [T:] SCHIATTI SCOPOLI. — 95 Verso blank. 174 × 120 mm.
[48] [T:] NEGROPONTE. — Between pp. 96 and 67 (pro 97) Verso blank. 165 × 260 mm.
[49] [T:] DAMALÀ, E ALTREIS^{TE} — 101 Verso blank. 177 × 121 mm.

Notes: The maps have text on the verso, except where otherwise mentioned. They are uncoloured. The Enciclopedia italiana (vol. 7, p.538) states that there should be 50 maps in this work, but our copy has only 49. On the title-page is written, in ink, 'le carte geogr sono d. epoca d cinque cento'.
Someone has compared this work with Bartolomeo degli Sonetti's Isolario (Venezia, 1485) and written the numbers of the corresponding maps in pencil in the lower right-hand corner, as follows:

[3]   Sonetti 1
[4]   Sonetti 7 (should be 3)
[7]   Sonetti 3 (should be 5)
[10] Sonetti 8
[11] Sonetti 9
[12] Sonetti 10
[13] Sonetti 11
[14] Sonetti 12
[15] Sonetti 13
[16] Sonetti 14
[17] Sonetti 15
[18] Sonetti 16
[19] Sonetti 18
[20] Sonetti 17
[21] Sonetti 19
[22] Sonetti 20
[23] 22
[24] 23
[25] 24
[26] 25
[27] 25.6 (= 26)
[28] 26 (from now on the numbers differ from those in our edition of the Sonetti)
[29] 27
[30] 28
[31] 29
[32] 30
[33] 31
[34] 32
[35] 33
[36] 34
[37] 35
[38] 36
[39] 37
[40] 38
[41] 39
[42] 40
[43] 41
[44] 42
[45] 43
[46] 44
[47] 45
[48] 46
[49] 47

As can be seen Boschini has followed his almost two hundred years older compatriot very closely.
The copy is unbound, with a paper wrapper. On the inside of the back cover Nordenskiöld has written in ink: 'för 30 fr. 50 c. köpt hos S. Rosén. Venezia Juli 1894' — the same place where he bought Boschini's 'Il regno tutto di Candia'. His signature is on the inside of the front cover.

Lit.: Encl. ital. vol. 7, p. 538.

33 BOTERO, GIOVANNI 1596

Allgemeine Weltbeschreibung Das ist: Eigentliche vñ warhafftige Erzehlung/aller der gantzen Welt vornembster Landschafften/ Stätten vnnd Völckern ... Durch Den hoch vnd wolgelehrten Herrn IOANNEM BOTERVM den Beneser/erstlich in Italienischer Spraache beschrieben/vnnd in zweij Theile verfasset: Nun aber/zu grösserm Nutz allgemeiner Teutscher Nation/in Hochteutsch vbergesetzt/vnd jetzt erstmals im Truck aussgangen. Mit künstlichen Kupfferstücken vnd eigentlichen Landtafflen gezieret. 1596. Gedruckt zu Cölln/Durch Johan Gymnici Erben/zum Einhorn ... 24,5 cm.

Vol. I

[1] ORBIS TERRAE COMPENDIOSA DESCRIPTIO Quam ex Magna Vniuersali Gerardi Mercatoris Domino Richardo Gartho Geographię ac ceterarum bonarum artium amatori ac fautori summno, in veteris amicitię ac familiaritatis memoriã Rumoldus Mercator fieri curabat A. M. D. LXXXVII Before the title-page. 282 × 509 mm. The hemispheres with 250 mm diam.

[2] [C:] EVROPA, ad magnæ Europæ Gerardi Mercatoris P. imitationem, Rumoldi Mercatoris F. cura edita, seruato tamen initio longitudinis ex ratione magnetis, quod Pater in magna sua vniuersali posuit. — [T:] Duysburgi Cliuorum typis æneis. — Before I a. 379 × 465 mm.

[3] [C:] ASIA ex magna orbis terrę descriptione Gerardi Mercatoris desumpta studio et industria G. M. Iunioris. — Between pp. 158 and 159. 374 × 456 mm.

[4] [C:] AFRICA Ex magna orbis terrę descriptione Gerardi Mercatoris desumpta, Studio & industria G. M. Iunioris. — Between pp. 204 and 205. 374 × 461 mm.

[5] [C:] AMERICA siue INDIA NOVA, ad magnæ Gerardi Mercatoris aui Vniversalis imitationem in compendium redacta. Per Michaelem Mercatorem Duysburgensem. — Between pp. 250 and 251. 362 × 455 mm.
[Insets:] [T:] GOLFO MEXICANO — [T:] CVBA — [T:] HAITI nunc Hispaniola — All insets circular maps with 75 mm. diam.

Vol. II
No maps.

Notes: All the maps are blank on the back and uncoloured. Both volumes are bound together. This German edition of the Weltbeschreibung includes five maps by different members of the Mercator family. The map of America is the only known map by Gerard Mercator's grandson Michael. On map [1] the astrolabe between the two hemispheres has been cut away, and parts of the left and right-hand borders have been cropped to facilitate the folding of the map. Part of the upper left-hand corner of map [3] is wanting. On the title-page is written, in old ink, 'Exlibris Ludovisi Schumacheri Lucernensis C.B. 1615' and 'Loci Capucinorum Sursee'. On the inside of the front cover is a bookplate reading 'BIBLIOTHECAE P.P. Capucinorum SURLACI.' The volume is bound in old vellum with blind tooling and metal clasps.

Lit.: Bagrow, Geschichte p. 334, Bagrow-Ortelius part 2, p. 15.

34 BOTERO, GIOVANNI 1596

LE RELATIONI VNIVERSALI DI GIOVANNI BOTERO BENESE, DIVISE IN QVATTRO PARTI. ... In Venetia, Appresso Giorgio Angelieri. 1596. 20,4 cm.

Vol. I
[1] EVROPA. 173 × 247 mm. Before [1] A.
[2] ASIA. 172 × 242 mm. Between pp. 118 and [119].
[3] AFRICA. 174 × 245 mm. Between pp. 152 and [153].
[4] AMERICA. 173 × 242 mm. Between pp. 192 and [193].

Vol. II—IV
No maps.

Notes: All the maps are blank on the back and uncoloured. The four volumes are bound together. The first edition of this work was published in Rome in 1591, without maps; later it became bery popular, and appeared in many editions and translations, all of them with maps. The maps in this edition are from the 1582 edition of the Universale fabrica del mondo by Giovanni Lorenzo d'Anania, published in Venice. This copy was damaged during World War II.

Lit.: Bagrow, Geschichte p. 334, Tooley, Dictionary p.45.

35 BOTERO, GIOVANNI 1599

RELATIONI VNIVERSALI DI GIOVANNI BOTERO BENESE Diuise in quattro Parti. NOVAMENTE REVISTE, Corrette, & ampliate dall'Istesso Auttore. Et aggiontoui in questa vltima Impressione la figurata Descrittione intagliata in Rame, di tutti i Paesi del Mondo. IN BRESCIA PER LA COMPAGNIA BRESCIANA [1599]. 22,4 cm.

Vol. I
[1] [T:] EVROPA. — On I A 75 × 102 mm.
[2] SPAGNA.
[C:] REGNI HISPANIAE POST OMNIVM EDITIONES LOCVPLEISSIMA Descriptio — HISPANIA. On 4 72 × 103 mm.
[3] ANDALOGIA.
[T:] ANDALVZIA — ANDALVSIA On 15 70 × 98 mm.
[4] [T:] BAIA DE CADIZ — GADES On 16 71 × 100 mm.
[5] PORTOGALLO.
[C:] Portugalliae que olim Lusitania nouissima et exactissima descriptio — PORTVGALLIA On 27 74 × 102 mm.
[6] [T:] GVASCONIAE DESCRIPTIO — GASCONIA On 36 71 × 100 mm.
[7] PVETV.
[C:] POICTOV. — On 43 76 × 100 mm.
[8] BITVRIGES.
[C:] Regionis Biturigum exactis: descriptio — BITVRIGES On 44 72 × 102 mm.
[9] ALVERNIA.
[C:] LIMANIÆ DESCRIPTIO — LIMANIA On 45 73 × 103 mm.
[10] BERTAGNA.
[T:] BRITANNIA — BRITANNIA On 48 72 × 100 mm.
[11] NORMANDIA.
[T:] NORMANDIA — NORMANNIA On 49 D 70 × 98 mm.
[12] ANGIO.
[C:] ANIOV — ANDEGAVENSIS DVCATVS On 52 75 × 100 mm.
[13] LORENA.
[T:] LOTHARINGIAE TYPVS — LOTHARINGIA On 59 71 × 101 mm.
[14] BORGOGNA.
[C:] Caletēsiũ et bononiensium ditionis accurata — CALETES ET BONONIENSES On 60 71 × 100 mm.
[15] LA CONTEA DI BORGOGNA.
[T:] BOVRGOIGNE COMIT — BVRGVNDIÆ COMITATVS On 62 75 × 100 mm.
[16] BRESSA. SAVOIA.
[C:] SABAVDIA ET BVRGVDIAE COMITVS DESCRIPTIO. — SABAVDIA On 63 72 × 100 mm.
[17] ITALIA.
[T:] ITALIAE TYPVS — ITALIA On 67 E 2 71 × 100 mm.

[18] TOSCANA. Patrimonio di san Pietro.
[C:] THVSCIAE DESCRIPTIO AVCTORE HIERONIMO BELLARMATO — TVSCIA On 72 70 × 102 mm.

[19] SIENA.
[C:] SIENA — STATO DI SIENA On 76 70 × 101 mm.

[20] PERVGIA.
[C:] PERVSIA — TERRITORIO DI PERVGIA On 78 71 × 101 mm.

[21] REGNO DI NAPOLI.
[C:] REGNI NEAPOLITANI VERISSIMA SECVNDVM antiquorū et recentiorū traditionem descriptio Pirrho Ligorio auc. — REGNVM NEAPOLITANVM On 81 F 70 × 102 mm.

[22] PVGLIA.
[C:] APVLIA — PVGLIA O TERRA D'OTTRANTO On 89 67 × 101 mm.

[23] ABBRVZZO.
[C:] APRVTIVM — ABRVZZO VLTERIORE On 91 70 × 100 mm.

[24] MARCA D'ANCONA.
[C:] MARCA ANCONITANA. — MARCA D'ANCONA On 92 71 × 100 mm.

[25] LOMBARDIA. Marca Triuigiana.
[C:] DVCATVS MEDIOLANENSIS FINITIMARVMQVE REGIONIS — MEDIOLANEN. DVCATVS On 95 72 × 102 mm.

[26] IL BRESCIANO.
[C:] BRISCIANO — TERITORIO DI BRESCIA. On 97 G 71 × 100 mm.

[27] IL PADOVANO.
[C:] PATAVINVM TERITOR. — TERRITORIO DI PADOVA On 98 72 × 100 mm.

[28] IL VERONESE.
[C:] VERONENSIS AGER. — TERITORIO DI VERONA On 99 G 2 71 × 101 mm.

[29] IL CREMONESE.
[C:] CREMONENSIS AGER — TERITORIO DI CREMONA On 100 72 × 100 mm.

[30] IL CREMASCO.
[C:] CREMAE AGER — TERITORIO DI CREMA. On 101 G 3 70 × 99 mm.

[31] COMO.
[T:] Larij Lacus vulgo Comensis Descriptio auct Paulo Iouio — LACVS COMENSIS, OLIM LARIVS. On 102 72 × 100 mm.

[32] PIAMONTE. FRIVLI.
[T:] FORI IVLII VVLGO FRIVLI TYPVS — FORVM IVLII. On 104 69 × 100 mm.

[33] TVRINO.
[C:] PEDEMONTANAE VICINORVQVE — PEDEMONTIVM On 105 72 × 102 mm.

[34] PAESI BASSI.
[T:] GALLIA BELGICA — BELGICA On 109 71 × 99 mm.

[35] ARTOIS.
[C:] ARTOIS. — ARTESIA On 113 H 74 × 100 mm.

[36] HAILNAVLT.
[C:] HENAVLT — HANNONIA On 116 75 × 99 mm.

[37] NAMVR.
[C:] NAMVR Namen — NAMVRCVM On 118 77 × 101 mm.

[38] LIEGE. LEODIENSIS DIOECESIS On 119 H 4 71 × 99 mm.

[39] LVCIMBORGO.
[C:] LVTZEBVRG — LVTZENBVRGVM DVCATVS. On 121 76 × 99 mm.

[40] [C:] FLANDRIA — FLANDRIA On 123 74 × 103 mm.

[41] BRABANTE.
[C:] BRABANTIAE RECENS DESCRI — BRABANTIA On 125 72 × 98 mm.

[42] OLANDA.
[C:] OLLANDT — OLLANDIA On 128 73 × 104 mm.

[43] COLONIA, VVESFAGLIA.
[C:] MONASTERIENSIS OSNABVRGENSIS EPISCOPATVS DESCRIPTIO — VESTPHALIA. On 145 K 73 × 102 mm.

[44] HELVETIA.
[C:] HELVETIAE DESCRIPTIO AEGIDIO TSCHVDO AVTORE. — HELVETIA On 148 73 × 102 mm.

[45] BAVARIA.
[C:] TYPVS VINDELICIAE SIVE VTRIVSQVE BAVARIAE. — BAVARIA On 158 70 × 100 mm.

[46] SALZBVRC.
[T:] SALISBVRGENSIS IVRISDICTIO. — SALISBVRGVM On 156 71 × 102 mm.

[47] SVEVIA.
[C:] WIRTENBERGESIS DVCATVS VERA DESCRIPTIO TVBINGAE EDITA. — WIRTEMBVRGVM On 157 70 × 100 mm.

[48] NORIMBERGA. Franconia.
[C:] PALATINATVS BAVARIAE DESCRIPTIO ERHARDOREIICH TIROLESE AVCT — NORICVM On 159 70 × 100 mm.

[49] [C:] FRANCIAE ORIENTALIS VVLGO FRANCKENLANT DESCRIPTIO AVCTORE SEBAST: ROTENHAN. — FRANCONIA. On 161 L 69 × 98 mm.

[50] TVRINGIA.
[C:] SAXONIAE MISNIAE THVRINGIÆ NOVA EXACTISSIMA DESCRI. — SAXONIA On 163 L 2 73 × 102 mm.

[51] MARCA ANTICA. Marca nuoua.
[C:] BRANDEBVRGENS Marcha. — BRANDEBVRGENSIS MARCHIONATVS On 166 71 × 101 mm.

[52] PRVSSIA.
[C:] PRVSSIAE DESCRIP: — PRVSSIA. On 172. 73 × 102 mm.

[53] BOEMIA.
[C:] REGNI BOHEMIAE DESCRIPTIO — BOHEMIA On 174 72 × 102 mm.

[54] SLESIA.
[C:] SILESIÆ TYPVS DESCRIPTVS ET EDITVS A MARTINO HEILVIG NEISENSE ET NOBILI VIRO NICOLAO RHEDINGER DEDICAT. — [T:] Anno 1561 — SILESIA On 176 71 × 101 mm.

[55] [C:] AVSTRIAE DESCRIPTIO — AVSTRIA On 179 M2 72 × 100 mm.

[56] ONGHERIA.
[C:] HVNGARIAE DESCRIPTIO WOLFGANGO LASIO DESC: — HVNGARIA On 182 70 × 102 mm.

[57] TRANSILVANIA.
[C:] TRANSILVANIA. — TRANSSILVANIA On 185 71 × 101 mm.

[58] SCHIAVONIA. Dalmatia.
[C:] SLAVONIAE, CROATIAE, CARNIAE, ISTRIAE, BOSNIAE, DESCRI. — ILLYRICVM On 190 70 × 102 mm.

[59] GRECIA.
[C:] GRAECIAE VNIVERSÆ SECVNDVM HODIERNVM SITV NEOTERICA DESCRI. — GRÆCIA On 195 N 2 72 × 101 mm.

[60] BESSARABIA. Podolia.
[C:] Ducatus Osroiczensis et zatoriensis descriptio — OSWIEC. ET ZATORIEN. DVCATVS. On 205 71 × 100 mm.

[61] POLONIA.
[C:] POLONIAE DESCRIPTIO — POLONIA. On 207 73 × 101 mm.

[62] LIVONIA.
[C:] LIVONIÆ NOVA DESCRIPTIO IOANNE PORTANTIO AVTORE — LIVONIA On 209 O 71 × 102 mm.

[63] SCANDIA.
[C:] SEPTENTRIONALIVM REGIONVM DESCRIPTIO — SEPTENTRIONALES REGIONES. On 213 O 3 71 × 102 mm.

[64] MOSCOVIA.
[C:] RVSSIÆ MOSCOVIÆ ET TARTARIÆ

DESCRIPTIO AVTORE ANTONIO IENKENSONO — RVSSIA. On 219   71 × 102 mm.
[65] [C:] ASIAE NOVA DESC — ASIA. On 227 P2   72 × 100 mm.
[66] TARTARIA.
[C:] TARTARIAE SIVE MAGNI CHAMI REGNI TIPVS — TARTARIA. On 229 P 3 72 × 102 mm.
[67] CHINA.
[C:] CHINA REGIO ASIE — CHINA On 236 72 × 100 mm.
[68] INDONSTAN.
[C:] INDIAE ORIENTALIS INSVLARVMQVE ADIACIENTIVM TIIPVS. — INDIA On 247 Q 4. 70 × 101 mm.
[69] PERSIA.
[C:] PERCICI SIVE SOPHORVM REGNI TIPVS. — PERSIA On 259 R 2   71 × 100 mm.
[70] SIRIA.
[C:] PALESTINAE SIVE TOTIVS TERRAE PROMISSIONIS NOVA DESCRIPTIO AVCTORE TILEMANO STELIA SIGENENS. — PALÆSTINA On 274 70 × 100 mm.
[71] SORIA.
[C:] NATOLIAE QVAE OLIM ASIA MINOR NOVA DESCRIPTIO. — NATOLIA. On 227 S 3 70 × 101 mm.
[72] [C:] AFRICAE TABVLA NOVA. — AFRICA. On 285 72 × 101 mm.
[73] EGITTO.
[C:] ÆGYPTI RECENTIOR DESCRIPTIO. — ÆGIPTI. On 289 T   71 × 98 mm.
[74] BARBARIA.
[C:] BARBARIAE ET BILEDVLGERID NOVA DESCRIPTIO. — BARBARIA On 334 67 × 100 mm.
[75] PROVINCIA CARTAGINESE. Tunigi.
[C:] CARTHAGINIS CELEBERIMI SINVS TIPVS — CARTHAGINENSIS PORTVS On 341 Y 3 70 × 99 mm.
[76] ISOLE DI ZELANDA. e di Fiandra.
[C:] ZELANDICARVM INSVLARVM DESCRIPTIO — ZELANDIA On 483 Hh 2 73 × 105 mm.
[77] SCOTIA.
[T:] SCOTIAE DESCRIPTIO — SCOTIAE On 487 Hh 4 72 × 101 mm.
[78] INGHILTERRA.
INGILTERA On 490 72 × 101 mm.
[79] HIBERNIA.
[C:] IRLANDIA — Hirlandia On 498 72 × 101 mm.
[80] SARDEGNA.
[T:] SARDINIA — SARDINIA On 509 69 × 101 mm.
[81] ISOLE DEL GOLFO DI Pozzuolo, e di Napoli.
[C:] ISCHIA INS. — ISCHIA On 513 Kk 66 × 95 mm.
[82] SICILIA.
[T:] SICILIAE Descriptio — SICILIA On 515 Kk 2 70 × 102 mm.
[83] ISOLE DEL MAR IONIO.
[T:] CORFV — CORCYRA VEL CORFV On 522 68 × 100 mm.
[84] CANDIA.
[C:] CANDIA OLIM CRETA — On 525 70 × 102 mm.
[85] CIPRO.
[C:] CYPRVS INSVLA. — CYPRVS On 534 73 × 101 mm.

Vol. II
LA SECONDA PARTE DELLE RELATIONI VNIVERSALI DI GIOVANNI BOTERO BENESE. Nella quale si discorre della potenza de' maggior Prencipi, che siano al mondo: & delle cagioni della grandezza, e sicurezza de' loro stati. IN BRESCIA, M D XCIX. Appresso la Compagnia Bresciana. ...

[1] RE DI SVETIA.
[C:] SEPTENTRIONALIVM REGIONVM DESCRIPTIO — On 27 = [63] in this ed.
[2] RE DI POLONIA.
[C:] POLONIAE DESCRIPTIO — On 34 = [61] in this ed.
[3] IMPERIO ROMANO.
[T:] GERMANIA — GERMANIA On 61 71 × 100 mm.
[4] GRAN CAM DI TARTARIA.
[C:] TARTARIAE ... — On 79 = [66] in this ed.
[5] RE DELLA CHINA.
[C:] CHINA ... — On 89 = [67] in this ed.
[6] RE DI PERSIA.
[C:] PERCICI SIVE SOPHORVM REGNI TIPVS. — On 133 I 3 = [69] in this ed.
[7] IMPERIO DEL PRESTE GIANNI.
[C:] PRESBITERI IOHANNIS SIVE ABISSINOR IMPERII DESCRIPTIO — ABISSINORVM REGIO On 150 70 × 101 mm.
[8] GRAN TVRCO.
[C:] TVRCICI IMPERII DESCRIPTIO. — [T:] TVRCICVM IMPERIVM — On 173 70 × 100 mm.
[9] PONTEFICE ROMANO.
CAMPAGNA DI ROMA. On 216 71 × 101 mm.

Vol. III—IV
No maps.

Notes: All the maps have text on the verso, and are uncoloured. All four volumes are bound together. In this copy nine of the maps have not been printed in the spaces allotted to them, which are left blank. These are:
PICARDIA. p.55
VEROMANDVS. p.56
CALETES, ET BONONIENSES. p.57. This map has instead been printed on p.60, under the heading BORGOGNA.
PROVENZA. p. 65
OMBRIA. p. 79
LATIO. p. 80
AMBORGO. DANIA. p. 167
DITMARSIA. p. 168
LVBECH. MECHELBORGO. Pomerania. p. 170
All the maps are printed from the same plates as the 1598 edition of Ortelius, Il Theatro del mondo, and published by the same Compagnia Bresciana which published the Ortelius. Nordenskiöld's signature is on the first original blank leaf.

Lit.: Ersch-Gruber, Allgem. Enzyklopädie, Sect. I, vol. 12, p. 92, Encicl. Ital. 1930, vol. 7. c. 567—568.

36 BOXHORN, MARCUS ZUERIUS   1632

MARCI ZUERII BOXHORNII THEATRUM Sive HOLLANDIÆ COMITATUS ET VRBIUM Nova Descriptio. Qua omnium Civitatum, præcipuorumq₃ locorum Icones, Origines, Incrementa, Res domi forisq₃ gestæ, Iura, Privilegia, Immunitates, ipsis Principum tabulis expressa, et Viri illustres exhibentur. AMSTELODAMI, Sumptibus Henrici Hondii
[Colophon:] LUGDUNI BATAVORUM, Ex Officinâ WILHELMI CHRISTIANI, ANNO M DC XXXII. 21,7 cm. obl.

[1] [C:] COMITATVS HOLLANDIÆ novissima descriptio Designatore Balth. Flor. a Berckenr. ... — [T:] Amstelodami, Sumptibus Henrici Hondii. — [T:] fol.8 — (Map). 12   157 × 236 mm.
[2] [C:] NOVISSIMA DELFLANDIÆ, SCHIELANDIÆ et circumiacentium insularum ut VOORNÆ, OVERFLACKEÆ, GOEREÆ, ISELMONDÆ, aliarumque tabula. — [C:] AMSTELODAMI, Sumptibus Henrici Hondii. Anno 1632. — (Map). 18   160 × 233 mm.
[3] [C:] NOVISSIMA TABULA INSULAR. DORDRACENSIS, ALBLASSER, CRIMPER, CLUNDERT etc. Comprehendens item TERRITORIA VIANÆ, GORICOMII, LEERDAMI, ALTENÆ, HEUSDENÆ, ac Civitat. S.Geertrudisbergam, Sevenbergam, Willemstadium, et circumjacentes Regiones ad Holl. pertinentes. ... Amstelodami, Sumptibus Henrici

Hondij. Anno 1632. — (Map). 20   156 × 235 mm.
- [4] [C:] RHINOLANDIÆ AMSTELANDIÆ circumjacent. aliquot territoriorū, accurata descriptio. Auctore Balth. Florentio a Berckenrode. Amstelodami Sumptibus Henrici Hondij. Anno 1632. ... — (Map). 22   156 × 233 mm.
- [5] [C:] TOTIVS HOLLANDIÆ SEPTENTRIONALIS vulgo WESTFRISIÆ novissima tabula. Auct. Balth. Flor. a Berckenrode. — [T:] Amstelodami, Sumptibus Henrici Hondij. — (Map). 24   156 × 233 mm.
- [6] [C:] DORDRECHT ... — 92   145 × 223 mm.
- [7] [C:] HAERLEM ... — 124   150 × 229 mm.
- [8] [C:] DELFT ... — 158   151 × 230 mm.
- [9] [C:] LEYDEN ... — 180   153 × 232 mm.
- [10] [C:] AMSTELREDAM ... — 240   153 × 230 mm.
- [11] [C:] GOUDA ... — 268   153 × 231 mm.
- [12] [C:] ROTTERDAM ... — 282   150 × 228 mm.
- [13] [C:] GORCUM ... — 288   153 × 233 mm.
- [14] [C:] SCHIEDAM ... — 294   154 × 232 mm.
- [15] [C:] SCHOONHOVEN ... — 928 (pro 298).   153 × 230 mm.
- [16] [C:] BRIEL ... — 302   151 × 229 mm.
- [17] [C:] S.GEERTRUYDENBERG ... — 304   153 × 230 mm.
- [18] [C:] WILLEMSTADT ... — 308   146 × 223 mm.
- [19] [C:] CLUNDERT ... — 310   149 × 226 mm.
- [20] [C:] HEUSDEN ... — 312   148 × 226 mm.
- [21] [C:] WORCKUM ... — 316   151 × 229 mm.
- [22] [C:] VYANEN ... — 318   148 × 227 mm.
- [23] [C:] LEERDAM ... — 320   150 × 228 mm.
- [24] [C:] ASPEREN ... — 322   149 × 227 mm.
- [25] [C:] HOECKELUM ... — 324   148 × 227 mm.
- [26] [C:] YSELSTEIN ... — 326   150 × 227 mm.
- [27] [C:] WOERDEN ... — 328   150 × 228 mm.
- [28] [C:] OUDEWATER ... — 330   150 × 227 mm.
- [29] [C:] NAERDEN ... — 334   146 × 225 mm.
- [30] [C:] WEESP ... — 344   151 × 229 mm.
- [31] [C:] MUYDEN ... — 346   152 × 227 mm.
- [32] [C:] VLAERDINGEN ... — 348   149 × 226 mm.
- [33] [C:] HAGHE ... — 350   148 × 223 mm.
- [34] [C:] DELFSHAVEN ... — 354   148 × 226 mm.
- [35] [C:] BEVERWYCK ... — 356   146 × 222 mm.
- [36] [C:] GOEREE ... — 358   146 × 225 mm.
- [37] [C:] ALCKMAER ... — 364   154 × 231 mm.
- [38] [C:] SCHAGEN ... — 368   154 × 229 mm.
[Inset:] [T:] Schager Slodt — (View).   60 × 86 mm.
- [39] [C:] HOORN ... — 370   153 × 230 mm.
- [40] [C:] ENCKHUYSEN ... — 374   148 × 227 mm.
- [41] [C:] EDAM ... — 376   146 × 230 mm.
- [42] [C:] MONNEKEDAM ... — 378   148 × 225 mm.
- [43] [C:] PURMEREND ... — 380   156 × 234 mm.
- [44] [C:] MEDENBLICK ... — 382   156 × 233 mm.

Notes: All the maps have text on the verso and are uncoloured. According to Tiele, all five maps are by Balthasar Floris Berckenrode, although he signed only [1], [4] and [5]. The other 39 items are all town plans. The key to the numbers on plans has been omitted from the cartouches. All the maps are headed MARCI BOXHORN-ZVERII. There are 11 known copies of this atlas in different collections in the Netherlands, but it is not mentioned in Koeman's Atlantes Neerlandici. Our copy is bound in contemporary vellum. The paper is foxed. Nordenskiöld's signature is on the first blank leaf, and there is a small, illegible stamp on the inside of the front cover.

Lit.: Bagrow p. 332, (Berckenrode), Jöcher vol. 1, c. 1314—1316, Koeman, Collections p. 125, nr. 9.1 and p. 157, Lynam, Geogr. Journ. 67, 1926, p. 158—161, Nouv. Biogr. g-ener. vol. 7, c. 158—159, Tiele p. 46, nr 179.

37 BRAUN, GEORG AND HOGENBERG, FRANZ

[LIBER QVARTVS VRBIVM PRÆCIPVARVM TOTIVS MVNDI.]   38,5 cm.

Vol. IV
- [1] I CANTVARIA.
[C:] CANTVARBVRY — [C:] CANTVARIA Vrbs fertilissimae Angliae celebris; Archiepiscopati sede, commendata. — (Plan).   290 × 428 mm.
- [2] 2 HISPALIS.
[T:] SEVILLA — (Plan).   330 × 480 mm.
- [3] 3 VRSAO, NVNC OSVNA. MARCHENA OLIM MARTIA.
[a] [C:] MARCHENA. — [T:] G. Hoefnagel. — (View).   164 × 460 mm.
[b] [C:] ORCHVNA. — [T:] G. Hoefnagel. — (View).   166 × 460 mm.
[The whole plate:]   337 × 466 mm.
- [4] 4 MATISCONA. CABILLONVM.
[a] [C:] MATISCONA, Vulgo Mascon; ad Ararim flu: probe munitum Burgundiae Oppidum M.D. LXXX. — (Plan).   325 × 215 mm.
[b] [C:] CABILLINVM, Indigenis, Chalon, vt agri vberrimi, ita saluberrimi coeli, ac proinde eximié felix Burgundiæ Opp: conuehēdis mercimonijs, ob Araris, cui impēdet vicinitatē idoneū. — (Plan).   323 × 220 mm.
[The whole plate:]   325 × 440 mm.
- [5] 5 CAMERACVM.
[C:] CAMBRAY. — (View).   330 × 450 mm.
- [6] 6 HESDINVM.
[T:] HESDYN FORT — [C:] HESDINVM Oppidum et castrum in expugnabile, bello inter Cæsarea nos et Gallos æs fuante, excitatum. — (Plan).   332 × 457 mm.
- [7] 7 BETHVNIA.
[C:] BETHVNE — [C:] BETHVNAE VRBIS ARTESIAE GENVINA DESCRIP. — [T:] Quintinus vanden Gracht delineabat. — (View).   295 × 453 mm.
- [8] 8 S. AVDOMARI.
[T:] S. OMER — [C:] S. AVDOMARI FANVM. S. Ausmer. Omer. Jccius portus Abrahamo Orttelio, Artesij vrbs munitissima. — (Plan).   337 × 370 mm.
[9 — 11 wanting].
- [9] 12 BVSCVMDVCVM.
[T:] TSHERTOGENBOSCH — [C:] HADRIANVS BARLANDVS BVSCVMDVCIS Brabantiæ Opp. ludo litterario et pugnaci populo nobile. Horum arma semper annis haud semel Gelrij sensère, cum qua gente uario certatum est euentu nostris hominib. In hac vrbe templum est Deiparæ sacrum, opus visendo apparatu. — (Plan).   334 × 469 mm.
- [10] 13 ROTERODAMVM.
[T:] ROTTERDAM. — [C:] ROTERODAMVM, Hollandiae in Ostio Roteri flu: Opp. Magni illius Desiderij Erasmi Patria. — (Plan).   285 × 395 mm.
- [11] 14 GOVDA.
[C:] GOVDA, elegantiss. Hollandiæ Opp: ad Isalam amnem, vbi Goudam flu. à quo Oppidum nomen habet, absorbet. 1585. — (Plan).   325 × 482 mm.
- [12] 15 AMORFORTIA.
[a] [C:] AMORFOTIA Dioecesis Vltraiectensis Oppidum amoenitate loci solique fertilitate admodum insigne. — (Plan).   241 × 369 mm.
[b] [C:] AMORFORTIA. — (View).   114 × 369 mm.
[The whole plate:]   355 × 369 mm.
- [13] 16 ZVTPHANNIVM.
[T:] ZVTPHEN. — (Plan).   315 × 417 mm.
- [14] 17 BOLSVARDIA. STAVRIA. HARLINGA. HINDELOPIA.
[a] [C:] BOLZVARDIA vetus in Frisia Foederis Anzæ' teutonicæ Op. — (Plan).   215 × 215 mm.
[b] [C:] STAVRIA, vulgo Stauerē Frisiæ Op. in Stricto maris australis, cui ZuderSee nomen situm. — (Plan).   215 × 210 mm.
[c:] [C:] HARLINGA. — (Plan).   130 × 265 mm.
[d] [C:] HINDELOPIA. — (Plan).   130 × 162 mm.
[The whole plate:]   355 × 438 mm.
- [15] 18 SNECA. DOCCVM. SLOTENVM. ILSTA.
[a] [C:] SNEECHA, vulgo Sneeck Frisiæ Occidentalis Oppidum. — (Plan).   230 × 222 mm.
[b] [C:] DOCCVM. — (Plan).   184 × 183 mm.
[c:] [C:] SLOTEN. — (Plan).   111 × 222 mm.
[d] [C:] YLSTA. — (Plan).   156 × 183 mm.
[The whole plate:]   348 × 415 mm.

[16] 19 VVESALIA INFERIOR.
[T:] WESEL. — [C:] HERMANNVS HAMMELMAN WESALIA in Ducatu Cliuiensi vrbs clara opibus, dignitate, ædificijs, et mercatura, quam nauigio in flumine Rheno exercet. — (Plan). 342 × 472 mm.

[17] 20 ORIGINES VRBIS ET COMITATVS TREMONIENSIS.
[a] [T:] LIPPE — [C:] LIPPIA Opp. licet Comitib. de Lippia subsit, tamen eius dimidia pars est olim Comitib. de Marca concesla, vt eam nunc in totum possideant æquo iure cum Comitib. de Lippia. agricultura se sustentat et oblectationem vtilitatemque ex Lippia flumine capit. Hęc Hermannus Hammelmannus. — (View). 172 × 434 mm.
[b] [C:] DORTMVND — (View). 170 × 434 mm.
[The whole plate:] Text on verso. 350 × 440 mm.

[18] 21 SVSATVM
[C:] SOEST. — (View). 323 × 475 mm.

[19] 22 ARNSPERGVM.
[C:] ARNSBERG. — (View). 320 × 431 mm.

[20] 23 NOVESIVM.
[T:] NEVS — [C:] NOVESIVM, circa annum 1206. Romanor Rex Philippus capit, et deposito per pontificē Epō Adolpho, donat. ... Aliquot postmodum horis miserabili in incendio ferè tota consumitur. — [T:] . PP. — (Plan). 330 × 432 mm.

[21] 24 VVESALIA. BOPARDIA.
[a] [T:] Ober Wesell. — [C:] Vosauię alias Ficelię Ciuitatis ad Rhenum sitę exactissima delineatio, Que Germanico Idiomate Ober Wesell vocatur. — (View). 175 × 422 mm.
[b] [T:] Boppart — [C:] Bodobrigę Ciuitatis ad ripam Rheni collacatę peramænus situs, quę hodie Boppart dicitur. — (View). 138 × 422 mm.
[The whole plate:] 322 × 428 mm.

[22] 25 DANIA.
[C:] Danorum Marca, uel Cimbricum, aut Daniae Regnum, multis sui partib. marinis interseptum fluctib, ab ortu, Suedia; à meridie, Saxonia et Westphalia; ab Occidente, Oceano Germanico; à Septentrione, Nordwegià terminatur. Vbi Suediae uicina, Schaniam, Hallandiam, Blekingiam prouincias habet, amoenas, fertiles, populosas. Vnde breuis ex Helsenburgo in Sealandiam, locupletissimam insulam, traiectus, In qua teolonium illud famosum ad Cronenburgum arcem, Et Hafnia, Siue Copenhafnia, sędes regia. Sealandiae ad meridiem Lalandia, Falstria, et minores aliquot insulae subsunt, Et alia, sed occidentalior, Langelandia. Inde, Fionia, quae & ipsa vna ex praecipius Daniae insulis, sed, Sealandia minor, cui septem et triginta insulae minores adiacent. Ex Fionia, facilis est in ducatum Slesuicensem traiectus, cui Cimbrica Chersonesus, quae Jutia borealis, proxima. Dehinc Wenslia, regio peninsularis, Noruegiam uersus in cunei formam, ad Scagam Opp. Cimbrici promontorij caput, se extendit. In Cimbricam ex Saxonia, aditu est Holsatia, cum Wagria, Stormaria, et Dithmarsia. Ducatus sunt, qui Generosi ac Nobilis uiri HENRICI RANZOVII, bonis artib. et Marte Illustris gubernatione, Regi Daniae foeliciter parent. M. D. LXXXV. — [C:] HENRICVS RANZOVIVS, FRIDERICI II. Daniæ Regis intimus consiliarius, tam vtriusque Ducatus Slesuicensis et Holsatiæ, quam Dithmarsorum Gubernator &c. Fruditor singulare præsidiū, Sic patriam opusq₃ nostrū exornabat. — (Map). Text on verso. 380 × 464 mm.
[26 wanting].

[23] 27 TOPOGRAPHIA. INSVLÆ HVÆNÆ IN CELEBRI PORTHMOREGNI DANIAE, QVEM VVLGO OERSVNDT VOCANT, SITAE, IN QVA ARX VRANIBVRGVM dicta, quamplurimis, varia exactáq₃ ratione, elaboratis Machinis Astronomicis referta, in summæ illius scientiæ honorem et instaurationem à TYCHONE BRAHE nobili Dano, Domino de Knudsdrup, circa annum M. D. LXXX. exædificata est. ORTO-GRAPHIA. ARCIS VRANIENBVRG IN INSVLA PORTHMI DANICI HVAENA, ...
[C:] Topographia Insulæ Huenæ in celebri porthmo Regni Daniæ, quem Vulgo Oersunt uocant. Effigiata Coloniæ 1586. — (Map). 339 × 480 mm.

[Insets:] [T:] VRANIBVRGVM ... — 152 × 105 mm.
[T:] Totius Ambit[9] et capacitatis delineaio. — 127 × 111 mm.
[28 — 29 wanting].

[24] 30 FLENSBVRGVM. [On verso:] ITZOHOA.
[a] [T:] FLENSBVRGVM — (Plan). 170 × 487 mm.
[b] [C:] ITZOHOA Florentissimae Holsatiae Op. — (Plan). 173 × 487 mm.
[The whole plate:] Text on verso. 346 × 487 mm.
[31 — 32 wanting].

[25] 33 HVSENVM. HADERSLEBIA.
[a] [C:] HVSEMVM DVCATVS SLESVICENSIS AD SINVM HEVERAM OPP. — [C:] Ilustris viri HENRICI RANZOVII Regii gubernatoris etc. conatib[9] — (Plan). 170 × 450 mm.
[b] [C:] HADERSLEBIA in Ducatu Slesuicensi, uersus Fioniam, Opp. Arce Regia minitū, quæ forma quadrata aream exhibet, centū et quinquaginta passus longam, et totidem fere latam. 1585. Coloniæ Agripp. — (Plan). 170 × 450 mm.
[The whole plate:] 345 × 457 mm.

[26] 34 CHILONIVM.
[C:] CHILONIVM, Vulgo Kyell, lautum atque uetustum Holsatiae, ad Isthmum Maris Balthici Opp Situ, negotiationi peroportuno, et annuis, nobilitatis Cimbricæ Comitijs, comendatum. — (View). 327 × 478 mm.
[35 — 42 wanting].

[27] 43 MONACHIVM.
[C:] MONACHIVM VTRIVSQVE BAVARIAE CIVITAS PRIMAR: — [C:] SERENISSIMO PRINCIPI AC DOMINO .D. GWILHELMO COMITI PAL. RHENI VTRIVSQ BAVARIÆ DVCI DOŌ SVO CLEMENTISS: IN HVMILLIMI OBSEQVII SVI MONVM: GEORG: HOEFNAGLIVS D. — [C:] ... Anno doñi. M.D.LXXXVI. — (View). 283 × 485 mm.

[28] 44 POSONIVM PRESBURCH.
[T:] Pressburg — [C:] POSONIVM uel Pisonium vt Lazius Hungariae vrbs — (View). 295 × 487 mm.

[29] 45 BRIXINA. LAVBINGA.
[a] [T:] BRIXEN. — [C:] BRIXIA TYROLIS. — (View). 195 × 493 mm.
[b] [T:] LAVGINGEN. — [C:] LAVBINGA Sveuiæ Opp. Alberti Magni Patria. — (View). 126 × 493 mm.
[The whole plate:] 330 × 493 mm.

[30] 46 SERAVALLVM.
[T:] SERAVALLUM CELEBERRIMUM MARCHIAE TARVISINAE IN AGRO FORO JULIENSJ OPP. — [C:] SERAVALLI, quam vides, Spectator, iconem, operi huic nostro suis sumptib. inseri curauerat MINVTIVS HIERONYMI MINVTII F. vir nobilis, et amplissimis legationib. celebris. Eum nos Colonia disedentem; vbi ipsum secundo negotia Gregorij XIII. P.M. curantem aspeximus; dum votis comitamur, delatos à nobis honores respuentem, hac saltem memoria, vel inuitum, prosequi voluimus, vt virtutem etiam nossent, qui non viderunt, videbunt autem, et qui non norunt, si Deus O.M. peregrinantem animam non tam cito ad æternas beator sedes, reuocet. — (View). 333 × 482 mm.

[31] 47 VINCENTIA.
[T:] VICENZA — [C:] VICENTIA AMPLISSIMA MARCHIAE TARVISINAE CIVIT. — (Plan). 357 × 433 mm.

[32] 48 ARIMINVM.
[C:] RIMINI. — [C:] ARIMINVM VALIDVM ET MVNITVM ROMANDIOLAE OPP. — (View). 307 × 465 mm.

[33] 49 BONONIA.
[T:] BONONIA — [C:] BONONIA ALMA STVDIOR MATER — (Plan). 328 × 493 mm.

[34] 50 LVCA.
[T:] LVCA — [T:] Tuscia nobiliss. Italiae Regio LVCAM vrbem in mediterraneis ostentat. Romanor quondam Coloniam. — (Plan). 350 × 512 mm.

[35] 51 PERVSIA.
[C:] PERVSIA GRATVMSIS IN TVSCIA

DOMICILIVM. — (Plan). 364 × 436 mm.
[36] 52 VRBINVM. SVLMO.
 [a] [T:] VRBINO. — (View). 165 × 172 mm.
 [b] [C:] VRBINO. — (View). 155 × 172 mm.
 [c:] [C:] SVLMO OVIDII PATRIA. — (Plan). 320 × 280 mm.
 [The whole plate:] 328 × 457 mm.
[37] 53 VTRIVSQVE OSTIÆ PORTVS, HORATII TIGRINI DE MARIIS, DESCRIPTIO.
 [T:] OSTIA — (Plan). Verso blank. 295 × 494 mm.
[38] 54 ROMANA TRIVMPHANS ANDREÆ FVLVII ANTIQVQRII ROMAE, DE LAVDIBVS VRBIS. ORATIO AD QVIRITES.
 [C:] ANTIQVÆ VRBIS ROMÆ IMAGO ACCVRATISS: EX VETVSTIS MONVMENTIS, EX VESTIGIIS VIDELICET ÆDIFICIOR, MOENIVM RVINIS, FIDE NVMISMATVM, MONVMENTIS ÆNEIS, PLVMBEIS, SAXEIS TIGLINISQ, COLLECTA, VETER, DENQ AVCTORVM FIDE CONFIRMA^{TA}, IN HAC TABVLAM REDACTA ATQ DESCRIPTA A PYRRHO LIGORIO ROMANO PER XIIII REGIONES IN QVAS VRBEM DIVISIT IMP. CÆSAR AVGVSTVS. ... — [Part I]. (Plan). Text on verso. 328 × 493 mm.
[39] 55 [ANTIQVÆ VRBIS ROMÆ IMAGO] [Part II]. (Plan). 355 × 495 mm.
[40] 56 PANORMVS.
 [C:] PALERMO. — [C:] PANORMVS Corona Regis et Vrbium Sicularum maxima, Emporium celebratissimum. — (Plan). 324 × 493 mm.
[41] 57 CHIOS.
 [T:] CHIOS. — [C:] CHIOS Maris Aegæi eiusdem nominis Insulae Ciuitas. — (View). 320 × 458 mm.
[42] 58 IERVSALEM VRBS AITSINGERI DESCRIPTIONE, ILLVSTRATA.
 [T:] IERVSALEM, et suburbia eius, sic ut tempore Christi floruit, cū locis, in quib^9 Christ^9 pass^9 est: quæ religiose à Christianis obseruata, etiam nū Venerationi habent. descripta per Christianum Adrichum Delphum. — [Part I]. (Plan). Text on verso. 366 × 482 mm.
[43] 59 [IERVSALEM VRBS] [Part II]. (Plan). 370 × 482 mm.

Notes: The maps are blank on the verso, except where otherwise specified. All the maps are coloured. This incomplete fourth part of the famous Civitates Orbis Terrarum by Braun and Hogenberg is the only part in our collection. As the title-page is wanting, I have tried to find a similar copy elsewhere. I have examined about 40 copies in 21 different libraries, but nowhere could I find the same typographical layout as in our copy for the dedications which follow the title-page. It seemed appropriate, therefore, to provide an exact copy of these leaves:
SERENISSIMO ET/ ILLVSTRISSIMO/ PRINCIPI AC DO=/MINO D. VVILHELM=/MO COMITI PA=/LATINO RHENI/ VTRIVSQVE BAVA=/RIAE DVCI ET CAET./ DOMINO SVO CLE=/MENTISSIMO./ GEORGIVS BRAVN,/ ET/ FRANCISCVS/ HOGENBERGIVS/ DED. CONSE-/CRANTQ./ —
On verso:
S. CAESAREAE MAIESTATIS/ PRIVILEGIVM./ ... Datū in ciuitate nostra Vienna, die vigesima octaua mensis Au=/gusti, Anno Domini Millesimo Quingentesimo Septuagesimo secundo, Regnorum nostrorum, Romani/ decimo, Hungarici, nono, Boiemici verò vingesimo quarto./ Maximilianus./ V. Io. Bap. VVeber, &c. Ad mandatum Sac. Cæs./Maiestatis proprium/ Obernburger./
TENOR PRIVILEGII REGIS./ CATHOLICI./ (The end of the lines:) Hogen/ Bruin/ modo in-/ depictos/ apertè di/ ...Datum Bruxellæ, XXII Nouemb. M.D.LXXIIII./ Ex concilio./ I.De VVitte/
Leaf 2: GEORGIVS BRAVN/ AGRIPPINAS, LECTORIS./ EXHIBEMVS nunc tandem, Lectores beneuoli, quartum præci=/puarum totius mundi vrbium, oppidorumqúe Theatrum, quod/ partim amicorum, topographicas hasce delitias amantium, liberale/ & honestum studium, partim ea, ad quam, nescio quo genio rapi-/mur, in picturas & Geographica oblectamenta affectio, & sensus/ procliuis, extorsit. Eorum etiam amicitiæ & abseruantiæ aliquid/ concessum fuit, qui ad hosce conatus nostros, symbola contulerūt,/ quos hic omnes recensere, nimis longum foret. Quorum si nomi-/na, paucis quibusdam, qui Martem in lingua gerunt, &, quos liberalia hæc studia minus/ delectant, nota forent, reuerentius fortasse de hoc opere sentirent, neque caninos in id/ dentes acuerent. Sed elegantia & liberalia ingenia, æquius de eo iudicium ferunt, quorum/ pleraque sumptibus suis vrbium, quas patrias habent, icones & historias, nobis suppedita-/runt, vt, sine iusta multorum offensione, manum de tabula non potuerim amouere. Ita-/que amicis morem gerere, eorumqúe hic auctoritatem, curiosis & minus amicis quorun-/dam iudicijs, præferre debui. Qui cum nihil ipsi egregij operis præstent, aliorum labores/ nimia libertate carpunt, Peruagatum illud Dureri, balder thadlen/ dan besseren./
Ordinem fortasse alium, quarundam vrbium dispositio poscebat, ne saltu nimis re-/moto, diuersarum Regionum vrbes, immediatè se subsequerentur, & in plerisque Reg=/nis, Ducatibus & Prouincijs, nimis remoto situ dispares, mutuo foliorum decursu sibi/ substituerentur, non ignoro id quidem, vt mihi quandoque ipsi, hac in re minus satisfa=/ciam, Sed, quanta, obsecro, monstrosi operis molis hæc foret, quæ talem omnium Pro=/uinciarum & Regionum dispositionem suppeditaret. Mundus omninò vniuersus depin-/gendus hic esset, vt cuilibet Regioni separatum, & peculiare opus nuncupandum. Quod/ tamen, Deo benèfauente, proxima editione (si hæc studia porro colemus) futurum confi=/do, in qua accuratiore methodo vtemur. Primum, vt generalem eius vel Regni, vel Du-/catus, cuius deinde vrbes exhibituri sumus, typum demus. Tum rursus, vniuersales eiusdē/ Regni Ducatuum, Comitatuum & Beroniarum, descriptionem exhibentes, istorum de=/inde generalium typorum oppida, arces & celebriora loca absoluta methodo subijeia-/mus. Interim tamen, si qui impatientes more, quibus præsentis operis dispositio minus/ satisfacere videtur, hi, earum vrbium & oppidorum, quorum typos & enarrationes desi=/derant, vel etiam emendatiores habere vellent, vel ipsi nobis liberaliter suppeditent, quas/ suis locis interseri curabimus, vel Dominici Lampsonij nostri sequantur consilium, &/ Geographicas Abrahami Ortelij chartas, cum nostris vrbium Tomis coniungentes, ab-/solutum sibi opus, ipsi industria, quantacunque valent, perficiant./
Then follows a poem in 22 lines, printed in italics and on the bottom of the page the catchwords: IN GEOR- and on verso:
IN GEORGII BRAVNII/ VRBIVM ORBIS DESCRI-/PTIONES,/ IOANNIS POLITII, C. SERENIS./ ELECTORIS COLONIEN. HISTO-/ RICI CARMEN./ (Then follows the poem in ten lines) IANI MELLERI PALMERII IN TOPO-/GRAPHICOS BRAVNII, ET HOGENBER-/GII CONATVS CARMEN./ Both poems are printed in minuscles.
The INDEX. LIBRI QVARTI is printed on 15 pages, the verso of the last leaf being blank. Our copy is not only incomplete, it is unbound and in poor condition, although all the plates are well coloured. The numbering of the plates on the recto is the same as that in the facsimile edition of 1965 ([Publ. by] Theatrvm orbis terrarvm LTD. Amsterdam MCMLXV.), but the versos do not always correspond, as will be seen. The first edition of the Liber quarto was dedicated to King Christian IV of Denmark and published in 1588, according to Braun's correspondence. An edition with a dedication to Wilhelm, Pfalzgraf, Duke of Bavaria ('IV B' in Skelton), should have a colophon with the year 1594, but our copy has no colophon. Only three of the plates have the engraver's name on them: [3] 3, where both the pictured towns, Marchena and Orchuna, are signed G. Hoefnagel; the double plate [38—39] 54—55, Rome, is signed Pyrrho (= Pirro); and the double plate [42—43] 58—59, Jerusalem, is signed Christian Adrichom (= Adrichem).
In our copy:

plate [3] 3 is blank on the verso, in the facsimile there is text,
plate [4] 4 is blank on the verso, in the facsimile there is text,
plate [9] 9 is blank on the verso, in the facsimile there is text,
plate [15] 18 is blank on the verso, in the facsimile there is text,
plate [20] 23 is blank on the verso, in the facsimile there is text,
plate [21] 24 is blank on the verso, in the facsimile there is text,
plate [23] 27 is blank on the verso, in the facsimile there is text,
On the back of [24] 30, the text for Flensburgum is on the recto and that for Itzohoa on the verso; in the facsimile, the texts are transposed.
In our copy, plate [27] 43 is blank on the verso, in the facsimile there is text.
In our copy, plate [31] 47 is blank on the verso, in the facsimile there is text.
In our copy, plate [33] 49 is blank on the verso, in the facsimile there is text.
The misprint on plate 57 in the facsimile, 75 for 57, is not present in our copy; but on many of the plates the text in the facsimile edition is set quite differently from the text in our copy.

Lit.: Bachmann, Städtebilder p. 7—11 and Tabellen, Denucé vol. 1, p. 266—281, Keuning, Braun and Hogenberg, LC List, vol. 1, p. 14—15, nr 59, vol. 3, p. 16—25, nr 3292, Skelton, Braun & Hogenberg.

38 BRIET, PHILIP   1648—1649

PARALLELA GEOGRAPHIÆ VETERIS ET NOVÆ. Auctore PHILIPPO BRIETIO, Abbauillæo, Societatis IESV Sacerdote. PARISIIS, Sumptibus SEBASTIANI CRAMOISY, Regis & Reginæ Regentis Architypographi: ET GABRIELIS CRAMOISY. viâ Iacobæâ, sub Ciconiis. M. DC. XLVIII.

[Engraved half title:]
PARALLELA GEOGRAPHIÆ VETERIS ET NOVÆ. Authore PHILIPPO BRIETIO Societatis IESV Sacerdote. PARISIIS Apud SEB. et GAB. CRAMOISY. via Iacobea 1648.   25,8 cm.

Vol. I
[1] ANTIQVISSIMA ORBIS DELINEATIO. [85]. Oval 156 × 202 mm.
[2] AGATHI-DÆMONIS MECHANICI ALEXANDRINI ORBIS DESCRIPTIO ÈX LIBRIS GEOGRAPHICIS CLAVDII PTOLEMÆI   Inter pag. 86 et 87 Verso blank.   156 × 242 mm.
[3] ORBIS PARS VETERIBVS COGNITA   Inter pag. 88 et 89. Verso blank.   158 × 262 mm.
[4] [C:] ORBIS ROMANVS Seu Diuisio Romani IMPERII Ex Imperii Notitia — Inter pagin. 92 et 93.   Verso blank.   149 × 258 mm.
[5] HOC EST PVCTVM QVOD INTER TOT GENTES FERRO ET IGNE DIVIDITVR. O QVAM RIDICVLI SVNT MORTALIVM TERMINI. Sen. præ.nat. Quæst.
A PARIS, Chez Mich.van Lochom, Graueur et jmprimeur du Roy pour les tailles douces. demeurant rüe S.t Iacques, a la rose blanche couronnée. Inter pag. 98 et 99.   Verso blank.   156 × 220 mm. Two hemispheres with 95 mm. diam.
[6] [C:] VETVS OCEANI DIVISIO. — [101].   143 × 186 mm.
[Inset:] [C:] PARS MARIS SEPTENTRIONALIS. — 50 × 40 mm.
[7] MARIS MEDITERRANEI ANTIQVA DIVISIO. Iniectum Terris subitùm mare. Sil. Ital. lib. 3. [111].   128 × 196 mm.
[Insets:] [T:] MARE CASPIVM SEV HYRCANVM. — 46 × 67 mm. [T:] OS PONTI EVXINI. — 36 × 58 mm. [T:] OS MEDITERRANEI. — 25 × 42 mm.
[8] [T:] LES DIVISIONS DE LA MEDITERRANÉE SELON LES MODERNES — [129]. 137 × 201 mm.
[Insets:] [T:] LA MER CASPIENE — 45 × 70 mm. [T:] LA CANAL DE LA MER NOIRE — 36 × 61 mm. [T:] IONCTION LA L OCEAN ET DE LA MEDIT. — 25 × 44 mm.
[9] [C:] LA DIVISION DE NOSTRE OCEAN. — [135].   140 × 183 mm.
[10] [C:] LA DIVISION DE LOCEAN DV NOVVEAV MONDE. — [145]. 183 × 137 mm.
[11] [C:] EVROPÆ ANTIQVÆ DELINEATIO — [156]. 144 × 189 mm.
[12] [C:] L'EVROPE DIVISEE EN SES PRINCIPALES PARTIES — [166]. 145 × 189 mm.
[13] [C:] ALBION SEV BRITANNIA MAIOR. — [179]. 207 × 145 mm.
[14] [C:] HIBERNIA seu Britannia minor cum aliq.t jnsulis. — [187]   189 × 146 mm.
[Inset:] [T:] THVLE ET ORCADES. — 69 × 49 mm.
[15] [C:] LE ROYAVME DE LA GRANDE BRETAIGNE. — [203].   189 × 145 mm.
[16] [C:] LA VRAYE ANGLETERRE DICTE AVLTREMET LOEGRIE. — [207]. 191 × 143 mm.
[17] [C:] PRINCIPAVTÉ DE GALLES. — [C:] PARTIE OCCIDENTALE D'ANGLETERRE — [214]. 191 × 145 mm.
[Inset:] [T:] ISLE DE MAN. — 39 × 36 mm.
[18] [C:] LE ROYAVME DESCOSSE. — [220].   141 × 185 mm.
[19] [C:] LES ISLES DE SCHETLAND ou Thylinsel et ORKNAY — [226]. 87 × 109 mm.
[20] [C:] IRLANDE OV HIBERNIE. — [231]. 187 × 143 mm.
[21] [C:] HISPANIA VETVS — [257]. 146 × 197 mm.
[22] [C:] HISPANIÆ VETERIS PARS OCCIDENTALIS. — [260]. 189 × 150 mm.
[23] [C:] PARS ORIENTALIS ANTIQVÆ HISPANIÆ. — [261]. 189 × 149 mm.
[24] [C:] HISPANIÆ DIVISIO IN XIV. CONVENTVS. — [273]. 146 × 191 mm.
[Insets:] [T:] NOVA CARTHAGO — 48 × 55 mm. [T:] GADES. — 17 × 28 mm.
[25] [C:] HISPANIARVM DIVISIO PER CONSTANTINVM Siue Secundum IMPERII Notitiam. — [275]. 145 × 188 mm.
[26] [C:] HISPANIÆ NOVA DIVISIO — [287]. 147 × 192 mm.
[27] [C:] LE ROYAVME DE PORTVGAL AVEC SES DEPENDENCES. — [290]. 191 × 146 mm.
[28] [C:] LA CASTILLE SEPTENTRIONALE AUEC.SES. DEPENDENCES. — [297]. 146 × 191 mm.
[29] [C:] LA CASTILLE MERIDIONALE AVEC SES DEPENDÈCES. — [302]. 145 × 190 mm.
[30] [C:] LE ROYAVME DARRAGON AVEC SES DEPÈDANCES — [309]. 191 × 151 mm.
[31] [C:] GALLIÆ TABVLA ACCVRATIOR ad IVLII CÆSARIS commentaria — [T:] AB.de la plaects fec. — [333]. 145 × 190 mm.
[Inset:] [C:] BELGIVM CÆSARIS — 38 × 54 mm.
[32] [C:] GALLIÆ DIVISIO OCTAVIANA. — [339]. 145 × 190 mm.
[33] [C:] GALLIA NARBONENSIS SEU PROUINCIA ROMANORUM. — [343]. 143 × 186 mm.
[34] [C:] AQVITANIA — [349]. 188 × 143 mm.
[35] [C:] GALLIA LVGDVNENSIS. — Inter paginam 356 et 357. Verso blank. 142 × 263 mm.
[36] [C:] GALLIA BELGICA. — [363]. 144 × 190 mm.
[37] [C:] DIVISIO GALLIÆ SECVNDVM NOTITIAM IMPERII. — [371]. 144 × 188 mm.
[38] [C:] DESCRIPTION DV ROYAVME DE FRANCE — [381]. 145 × 191 mm.
[39] [C:] LANCIENNE FRANCE   Comprenant LA PICARDIE. LISLE DE FRANCE ET LA CHAMPAIGNE — [383]. 187 × 143 mm.

[40] [C:] LA NEUSTRIE Ou la France occidentale — [397]. 142 × 191 mm.

[41] [C:] LA GRANDE BEAVLSE Comprenant les pais CHARTRAIN, ORLEANOIS, LE PERCHE, LE MAINE, D'ANIOV, DE TOVRAINE, BLAISOIS, DE BRENNE, VENDOSMOIS, ET DVNOIS. — Entre les pages 398. et 399. Verso blank. 140 × 185 mm.

[42] [C:] LE ROYAVME DE BOVRGOGNE COMPRENANT LE DUCHÉ ET CONTÉ. LA BRESSE. LE NIVERNOIS. LAVXERROIS. DOMBES. ET PVYSAYE. — [407]. 146 × 191 mm.

[43] [C:] LE ROYAVME DARLES. Comprenant LA PROVENCE DAVLPHINÉ SAVOYE et LIONNOIS. — [417]. 188 × 145 mm.

[44] [C:] PARTIE ORIENTALE DE LA GRANDE AQVITAINE. LE BERRY BOVRBONOIS LIMOSIN AVVERGNE QVERCY ROVERGNE et le LANGVEDOC — [431]. 190 × 146 mm.

[45] [C:] LA PARTIE OCCIDENTALE DE LA GRĀDE AQVITAINE. — [C:] Comprenant LE POICTOV XAINTONGE ANGOVMOIS PERIGORD GVIENNE GASCOGNE — [445]. 191 × 145 mm.

[46] [C:] LES XVII. PROVINCES DV PAYS BAS. — [481]. 191 × 149 mm.

[47] [C:] LES ESTATS OV LES PROVINCES VNIE S DV PAYS BAS. — [487]. 143 × 188 mm.

[48] [C:] LA FLANDRE ESPAIGNOLE — [499]. 151 187.

Vol. II
PARALLELA GEOGRAPHIÆ VETERIS ET NOVÆ. Auctore PHILIPPO BRIETIO, Abbauillæo, Societatis IESV Sacerdote. TOMVS SECVNDVS. PARISIIS ... M. DC. XLIX.
[Engraved half title:]
PARALLELA GEOGRAPHIÆ ... 1649   26 cm.

[1] [C:] GERMANIA ANTIQVA. — Inter Pag. 8. et 9. Verso blank. 146 × 256 mm.

[2] [C:] SCANDIA. — [23]. 145 × 188 mm.

[3] [C:] GERMANIÆ ANTIQVÆ ADIECTA. — [27]. 143 × 189 mm.

[4] [C:] LES X'CERCLES D'ALLEMAIGNE. — [41]. 147 × 190 mm.

[5] [C:] L'ALLEMAIGNE. — [45]. 146 × 146 mm.

[6] [C:] PROVINCES LIGVÉES. — [53]. 161 × 207 mm.

[7] [C:] L'ALLEMAIGNE audeca du Rhin. — [67]. 195 × 149 mm.

[8] [C:] LA SVAVBE — [85]. 146 × 190 mm.

[9] [C:] LA FRANCONIE. — [93]. 146 × 188 mm.

[10] [C:] BAVIERE ET TIROL. — [103]. 195 × 147 mm.

[11] [C:] L'AVSTRICHE et ses dependances. — [109]. 189 × 145 mm.

[12] [C:] ROYAULME DE BOHEME. — [117]. 145 × 189 mm.

[13] [C:] PARTIE DE SAXE. — [132]. 145 × 190 mm.

[14] [C:] LA PARTIE OCCIDĒTALE DE LA GRANDE SAXE. — [133]. 190 × 152 mm.

[15] [C:] LA VESTPHALIE. — [147]. 189 × 146 mm.

[16] [C:] LES ROYAVMES SEPTENTRIONAVX. — [164]. 145 × 189 mm.

[17] [C:] LE DANEMARK SVEDE ET GOTIE. — [165]. 148 × 190 mm.

[18] [C:] GROENLAND ET LES NOVVELLES TERRES DES COVVERTES VERS LE SEPTENTRION — [188]. 146 × 190 mm.
[Insets:] [C:] ISLAND — 61 × 81 mm. [C:] SPITZ-BERGE — 26 × 46 mm.

[19] [C:] SARMATIÆ EVROPÆÆ DELINEATIO — [198]. 146 × 192 mm.
[Inset:] [C:] TAVRICA CHERSONESVS — 46 × 67 mm.

[20] [C:] LE ROYAVME DE POLOGNE. — [213]. 147 × 193 mm.

[21] [C:] LA RVSSIE OV MOSCOVIE. — [231]. 147 × 190 mm.

[22] [C:] PANNONIÆ ET ILLYRICUM. — [268]. 190 × 146 mm.

[23] [C:] ILLYRICI DIVISIO SECVNDVM NOTITIAM IMPERII — [278]. 141 × 185 mm.

[24] [C:] DACIÆ ET MYSIARV̂ DELINEATIO — [287]. 146 × 188 mm.

[25] [C:] DIOECESES THRACIÆ ET MACEDONIÆ IVXTA NOTITIAM IMPERII — [295] 188 × 146 mm.

[26] [C:] LE GRAND ROYAVME DE HONGRIE. — [315] 142 × 186 mm.

[27] [C:] LA TRANSILVANIE ou SIBENBVRGEN. — [323] 143 × 157 mm.

[28] [C:] GRÆCIÆ DELINEATIO — [337]. 144 × 190 mm.

[29] [C:] MACEDONIA THESSALIA EPIRVS. — [351]. 146 × 188 mm.

[30] [C:] THRACIÆ DELINEATIO. — [373]. 143 × 186 mm.

[31] [C:] ACHAIA SEV HELLAS — [407]. 144 × 187 mm.
[Insets:] [C:] HELICON MONS — 40 × 50 mm. [C:] ATHENÆ — 40 × 71 mm. [C:] THERMOPYLÆ — 40 × 48 mm.

[32] [C:] DELINEATIO PELOPŌNESI. — [419]. 143 × 190 mm.

[33] [a] [C:] DELOS ET RHENIA — 47 × 28 mm.
[b] [C:] EVBŒA — 43 × 101 mm.
[c] [T:] CORCYRA — 48 × 46 mm.
[d] [T:] CEPHALONIA ZACINTHVS ET VICINÆ — 52 × 35 mm.
[e] [C:] LEMNOS Insula — 25 × 43 mm.
[f] [C:] CYTHERA Insula — 24 × 43 mm.
[g] [T:] CRETA — 70 × 142 mm.
[The whole map:] [435] 187 × 143 mm.

[34] [C:] LA GRECE. — [451]. 145 × 190 mm.

[35] [a] [C:] LA ROMANIE OV LA THRACE. — 111 × 143 mm.
[b] [C:] STAMBOVL OV CONSTANTINOPLE. — (Plan). 71 × 135 mm.
[The whole map:] [469] 188 × 143 mm.

[36] [C:] LA MACEDOINE ET L'ALBANIE — [472]. 144 × 187 mm.

[37] [C:] LIUADIE. Liuadie Stramulipa. Duché d'Athenes. MORÉE. D.de Clarence. Beluedere Saccanie Tzaconie — [477]. 148 × 188 mm.

[38] [a] [C:] ISLES DE LA MER IONIENNE — 107 × 81 mm.
[b] [T:] STALIMENE — 55 × 55 mm.
[c] [T:] CERIGO — 49 × 55 mm.
[d] [T:] CANDIE — 78 × 144 mm.
[The whole map:] [481]. 188 × 144 mm.

Notes: All the maps have text on the verso, except those inserted between two leaves, which are blank on the back. All the maps are uncoloured. In both volumes the pagination includes the maps, although the number is not always printed on the page. This is indicated by brackets in the list above. In vol. 1, page 134 is misnumbered 135. The British Library Map Library has an edition of 1748—49 with 57 maps in vol.1 and 82 in vol.2. Our copy of vol.1 is half bound in leather; vol.2 is bound in vellum. The second title-page in both volumes is engraved in the same style. On the inside of the front cover of both volumes is marked in pencil 'Dupl. D.' and 'c. 22.5.' Nordenskiöld's signature is on the first blank leaf of each volume.

Lit.: BM Maps vol.3 C 319, Jöcher vol. 1 p.1379.

39 BROUCKNER, ISAAC   1759

NOUVEL ATLAS DU GLOBE TERRESTRE REPRESENTÉ EN UNE CARTE GÉNÉRALE Et XII. CARTES particulieres avec une courte Description, PAR MR BROUCKNER, Membre de l'Académie des Sciences de BERLIN. A LA HAYE, Chez PIERRE VAN OS, 1759.   47,3 cm.

[1] [T:] ISLES AÇORES IRLANDE PORTUGAL — On (3) * 2 Uncoloured. 184 × 148 mm.

[2] [T:] CARTE GENERALE du GLOBE TERRESTRE, dressée sur les Memoires les plus approuvés et les Observations les plus exactes. 1749 — N.F.Sauerbreÿ Sculpsit Berol. 438 × 511 mm.

[3] Nō: I [T:] CARTE MAR^NE de SUEDE, NORWEGE, NOUV^LE ZEMBLE et de SPITSBERGE. 1749. — 446 × 518 mm.

[4] Nō: II [T:] CARTE MARINE de la MER GLACIALE, et la SIBERIE SEPTENTRIONAL. 1749. — 446 × 517 mm.

[5] Nō: III [C:] NOUVEL ATLAS DE MARINE Composé d'une Carte Generale, et de XII Cartes Particulieres, qui Representent Le Globe Terrestre jusqu'au 82e Degré du Coté du Nord, et jusqu'au 60.e du Coté du Sud Le tout Dressé sur les Observations les plus Nouvelles et les plus approuvées Dedié A Son Excellence MGR LE COMTE DE SCHMETTAU Gen.Feld-Marechall, Grand-Maitre d'Artillerie et Chevalier de l'Ordre de l'Aigle noir etc. Qui a fourni pour Cet Atlas toutes les Cartes et touts les Memoires necessaires: par son tres humble et tres obeissant Serviteur Isaac Brouckner Geographe de S.M.T.C. et Correspondant de l'Academie Royale des Sciences de Paris. Approuvé par l'Academie Royale des Sciences a. Berlin l'Année 1749. — [T:] CARTE MARINE de la MER GLACIALE avec une Partie de la Province de JRKUCKI 1749. — 446 × 516 mm.

[6] Nō: IV [T:] CARTE MARINE, de la B. de BAFFIN, et une Partie D'HUDSON, D'ISLAND et GROENLAND. l'Année 1749. — 444 × 511 mm.

[7] Nō: V. [T:] CARTE MAR.^NE d'une Partie de L'EUROPE, de L'ASIE et de L'AFRIQUE. 1749 — 438 × 514 mm.

[8] Nō: VI [T:] CARTE MAR.^E d'une Partie de L'ASIE, ou des INDES ORIENT^ES et des ISL^ES au dessus de l'Equas.^r 1749. — 437 × 518 mm.

[9] Nō VII [T:] CARTE MARINE éntre CALIFORNIE et une Partie de L'ASIE la plus Orientale 1749 — 437 × 516 mm.

[10] Nō: VIII [T:] CARTE MARINE de L'AMERIQUE SEPTRIONALE et une Partie de la B^E D'HUDSON. 1749. — 440 × 518 mm.

[11] Nō IX [T:] CARTE Marine de L'AFRIQUE Meridionale 1749 — 438 × 513 mm.

[12] Nō X [T:] CARTE MARINE des ISLES MERID.^LE des INDES ORIENT.^LES et de la NOUV.^E HOLLANDE. 1749. — 438 × 516 mm.

[13] Nō: XI [T:] CARTE MAR^E de la NOUV^LLE ZELANDE des ISLES SALOMON et de plusieurs autres ISLES Merid^es 1749. — 437 × 515 mm.

[14] Nō: XII [T:] CARTE MARINE de L'AMERIQUE MERIDIONALE. l'Anné 1749. — 436 × 512 mm.

Notes: All the maps are blank on the back. The coastlines are lightly coloured. The form of the author's name varies: Brit. Mus. and Tooley, Dictionary, inter alia, give it as Brouckner; Bonacker and Hist. Biogr. Lexikon der Schweiz give it as Bruckner, and the American National Union Catalog, pre-1956 imprints, gives it as Brückner. The atlas seems to be quite rare; the only reference to it that I have traced is in the National Union Catalog, where it is recorded in the Yale University Library. Nordenskiöld's signature is at the beginning of the volume, with the year 1898.

Lit.: Bonacker p. 57 (Bruckner d.Ä.), BM Maps vol. 3 C.400, Nat. union cat. vol. 80 p. 267, Tooley, Dictionary p. 51.

40 BUFFIER, CLAUDE 1775

GEOGRAFIA UNIVERSALE DEL P. BUFFIER Edizione prima Romana Avmentata, corretta, e ridotta in miglior forma Con un nouvo Trattato della Sfera, e d una Dissertazione sopra l'origine, e progresso della Geografia DAL P. FRANCESCO JACQUIER.
IN ROMA MDCCLXXV. A Spese di Venanzio Monaldini Mercante di Libri.
IN ROMA L'Anno del Giubbileo 1775. Nella Stamperia di Ottavio Puccinelli incontro il Governo Vecchio. 17,6 cm.

[1] [T:] MAPPAMONDO — Petroschi inc. Between pp. 90 and 91. 127 × 167 mm. The hemispheres with 80 mm. diam.

[2] [C:] EUROPA Secondo le ultime osservazioni dell' Accademia Reale delle Scienze — Petroschi inc. Between pp. 98 and 99. 127 × 166 mm.

[3] [C:] ITALIA Secondo i gradi dell' Accademia delle Scienze di Parigi — Petroschi inc. Between pp. 98 and 99. 128 × 166 mm.

[4] [C:] MOSCOVIA — Gio.Petroschi inc. Between pp. 138 and 139. 130 × 160 mm.

[5] [C:] SVEZIA NORVEGIA, E DANIMARCA Secondo i gradi dell' Accademia delle Scienze di Parigi — Petroschi inc. Between pp. 144 and 145. 170 × 128 mm.

[6] [C:] CARTA DELLA GRAN BRETAGNA Sopra li gradi dell' Accademia di Parigi — Petroschi inc. Between pp. 156 and 157. 167 × 130 mm.

[7] [C:] POLONIA Secondo le osservazioni dell' Accademia di Parigi — Petroschi inc. Between pp. 166 and 167. 132 × 172 mm.

[8] [C:] IMPERIO D'ALLEMAGNA Diviso in dodici Circoli Secondo le Osservazioni dell' Accademia Reale delle Scienze, e di altri Autori antichi, e moderni — Petroschi inc. Between pp. 178 and 179. 129 × 168 mm.

[9] [C:] LI DUE CIRCOLI DELL'ALTO E BASSO RENO Secondo le Osservazioni dell' Accademia delle Scienze — Petroschi inc. Between pp. 200 and 201. 168 × 130 mm.

[10] [C:] FRANCIA Secondo le ultime osservazioni dell' Accademia Reale delle Scienze — Petroschi inc. Between pp. 232 and 233. 126 × 166 mm.

[11] [C:] LE XVII PROVINCIE DEI PAESI BASSI Secondo i gradi dell' Accademia delle Scienze di Parigi — Petroschi inc. Between pp. 316 and 317. 165 × 126 mm.

[12] [C:] CARTA DEL PAESE Degli Svizzeri, e DELLA SAVOJA Secondo i gradi dell' Accademia delle Scienze di Parigi — Gio.Petroschi inc. Between pp. 336 and 337. 130 × 168 mm.

[13] [C:] SPAGNA Secondo le ultime osservazioni dell' Accademia Reale delle Scienze — Petroschi inc. Between pp. 342 and 343. 133 × 169 mm.

[14] [C:] LA TURCHIA In Europa Sopra le osservazioni dell' Accademia delle Scienze di Parigi — Petroschi inc. Between pp. 360 and 361. 128 × 170 mm.

[15] [C:] GRECIA ANTICA, E MODERNA — Petroschi inc. Between pp. 368 and 369. 130 × 172 mm.

[16] [C:] ASIA Secondo le ultime Osservazioni dell' Accademia Reale di Parigi — Petroschi inc. Between pp. 376 and 377. 130 × 166 mm.

[17] [C:] TURCHIA NELL' ASIA ANTICA, E MODERNA — Petroschi inc. Between pp. 376 and 377. 168 × 130 mm.

[18] [C:] AMERICA Secondo le ultime osservazioni dell' Accademia Reale delle Scienze — Petroschi inc. Between pp. 428 and 429. 166 × 128 mm.

[19] [C:] AMERICA SETTENTRIONALE — Petroschi inc. Between pp. 428 and 429. 157 × 208 mm.

[20] [C:] AMERICA MERIDIONALE ... — [T:] Petroschi inc. — Between pp. 432 and 433. 212 × 182 mm.

Notes: All the maps are blank on the back and uncoloured. The map of Africa is wanting. Before p.1 is a plate showing an armillary sphere, signed 'G. Petroschi inc.' as are all the maps. The Library of Congress also has a copy of the Italian edition; the original language was French. Buffier was a theologian, historian and geographer from Warsaw, living in Paris. The volume is bound in contemporary vellum. The spine is full of worm-holes. On the inside of the front cover is pasted a card with mourning borders, with the words: 'Le Baron de Bildt. Envoyé Extraordinaire et Ministre Plénipotentiare de S.M. le Roi de Suède et de Norvège. Palazzo Capranica. Via Tr...' (The rest is covered by the black border.) It is possible that the volume was presented to Nordenskiöld by the Baron.

Lit.: Bonacker p. 59, Jöcher vol. 1, c. 1468—1469 Nat.union cat. vol. 83, p. 294, Nouv. Biogr. Gen. vol. 7, c. 733—734.

Isaac Brouckner, 1759. 39 [2]

CARTE GENERALE du GLOBE TERRESTRE, dreßée su

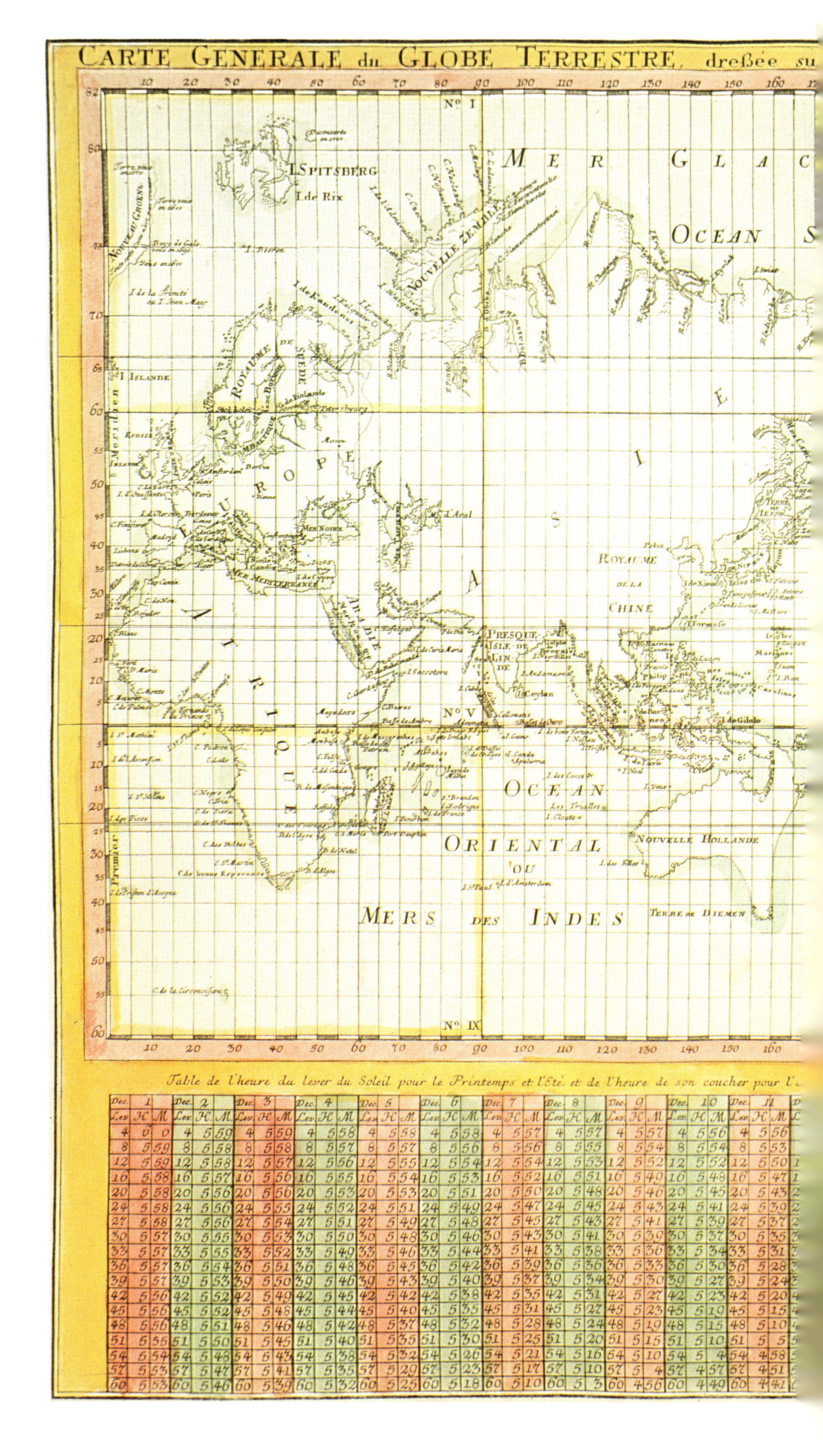

Table de l'heure du lever du Soleil pour le Printemps et l'Eté et de l'heure de son coucher pour l'

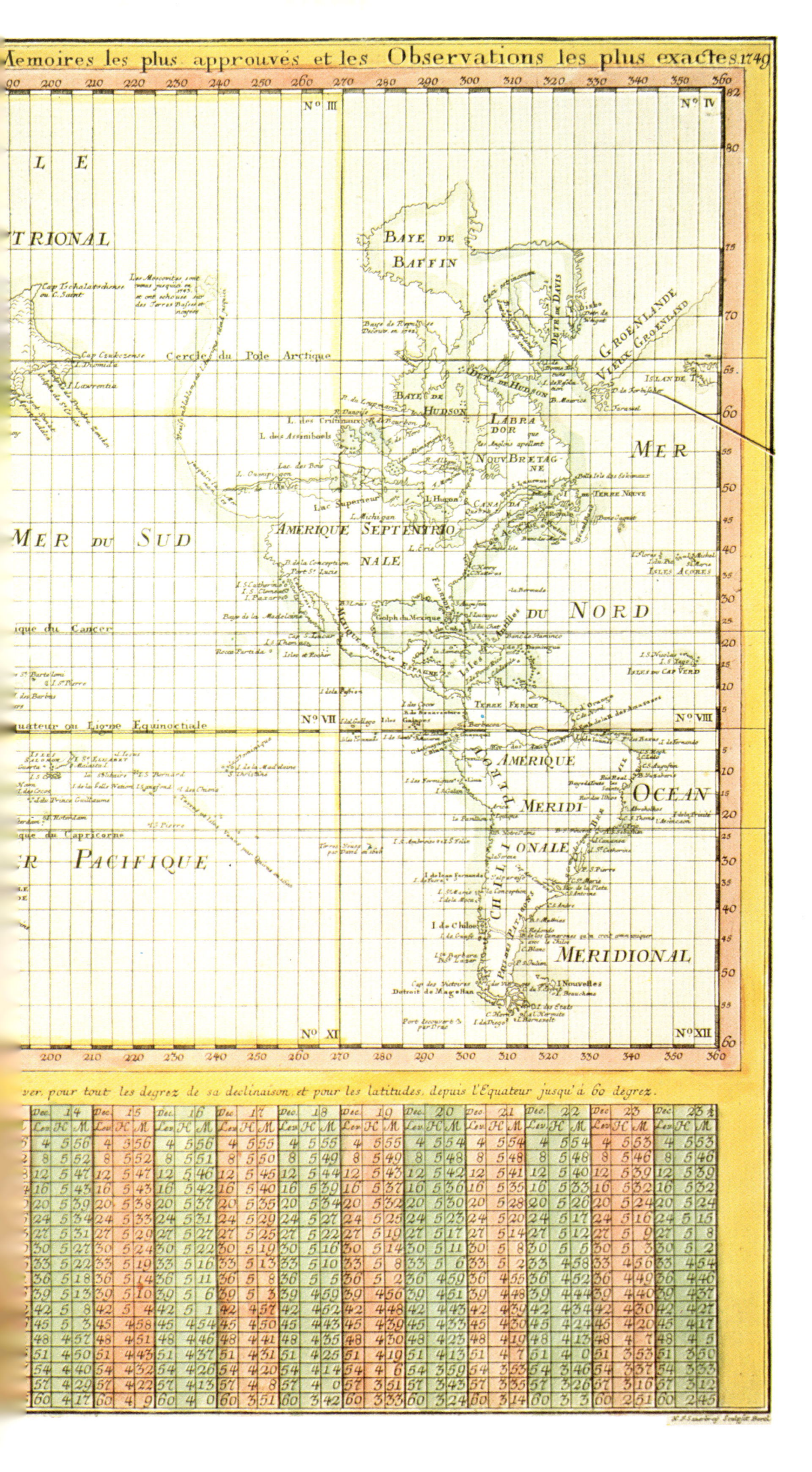

Mémoires les plus approuvés et les Observations les plus exactes 1749

41 CELLARIUS, CHRISTOPH 1701

NOTITIA ORBIS ANTIQVI, SIVE GEOGRAPHIA PLENIOR, ab Ortu Rerumpublicarum ad Constantinorum tempora Orbis terrarum faciem declarans. CHRISTOPHORVS CELLARIVS ex vetustis probatisque monimentis collegit, & NOVIS TABVLIS GEOGRAPHICIS, singulari cura & studio delineatis, illustrauit. Adiectus est Index copiosissimus locorum et aliarum rerum Geographicarum. LIPSIAE, Impensis GLEDITSCH, Senioris. M. DCCI. 24,7 cm.

Vol. I
- [1] [C:] INSVLARVM BRITANNICARVM FACIES ANTIQVA. — pag. 400. Uncoloured. Verso blank. 207 × 308 mm.
  [Inset:] [T:] THVLE INS. Orcades Insulæ — 75 × 54 mm.
- Notes: There should be 20 maps and a Tabula Ventorum in this volume, but 19 of the maps have been torn out. There are copies of these missing maps in our edition of 1731—32. In the 1701 edition there is a portrait of Cellarius as frontispiece. The book formerly belonged to 'Thodberg's Bibliothek', which is stamped on the title-page in blue. On the same page there is also a circular stamp with the words 'DE LICHTENBERG GERTH'. Nordenskiöld's signature is on the grey leaf at the beginning of the volume.
- Lit.: ADB vol. 4, p. 80, Bagrow p. 336, Bonacker p. 64 and 128, BM Maps vol. 4, c. 28, Jöcher vol. 1, c. 1796, Poggendorff vol. 1, c. 409.

42 CELLARIUS, CHRISTOPH 1731—1732

NOTITIA ORBIS ANTIQVI, SIVE GEOGRAPHIA PLENIOR, Ab Ortu Rerumpublicarum ad Constantinorum tempora Orbis terrarum faciem declarans. CHRISTOPHORVS CELLARIVS Ex vetustis probatisque monimentis collegit, & NOVIS TABVLIS GEOGRAPHICIS, singulari cura & studio delineatis, illustrauit. Alteram hanc editionem annotationibus varii generis partim e scriptis veterum, partim e recentiorum obseruationibus illustrauit & auxit L. IO. CONRADVS SCHWARTZ, Eloq. & Græc. Ling. P.P.O. in Casimiriano. Adiectus est Index copiosissimus locorum et aliarum rerum Geographicarum. LIPSIAE, Apud IOH. FRIDERICI GLEDITSCHII, B.FIL. M. DCC. XXXI. 25,3 cm.

Vol. I
- [1] VETERIS ORBIS CLIMATA EX STRABONE. pag.17 207 × 307 mm.
- [2] [C:] HISPANIA ANTIQVA — pag.51 205 × 306 mm.
- [3] [C:] GALLIA NARBONENSIS LVGDVNENSIS ET AQVITANIA — pag.129 205 × 308 mm.
- [4] [C:] GALLIA BELGICA. — pag.205 297 × 308 mm.
- [5] [C:] INSVLARVM BRITANNICARVM FACIES ANTIQVA. — pag.321 = 1701:[1].
- [6] [C:] GERMANIA ANTIQVA — pag.358 206 × 308 mm.
- [7] [C:] SARMATIA — pag.395. 207 × 308 mm.
- [8] [C:] VINDELICIA RHAETIA, ET NORICVM. — pag.412. 205 × 306 mm.
- [9] [C:] PANNONIA MOESIA, DACIA ILLYRICVM. — pag.437. 204 × 307 mm.
- [10] [C:] ITALIA ANTIQVA — pag.501. 203 × 304 mm.
- [11] [C:] GALLIA CISALPINA — pag.513. 205 × 307 mm.
- [12] [C:] ITALIA MEDIA siue PROPRIA — pag.568. 206 × 307 mm.
- [13] [C:] LATII VTRIVSQVE DELINEATIO. — pag.630. 205 × 304 mm.
- [14] [C:] GRAECIA MAGNA SIVE PARS VLTIMA ITALIAE — pag.665. 205 × 308 mm.
- [15] [C:] REGIONES ITALIAE EX AVGVSTI CAESARIS DIVISIONE. — pag.745. 204 × 307 mm.
- [16] [C:] SICILIA ANTIQVA. — pag.756. 204 × 306 mm.
  [Inset:] [T:] SICILIA Melite I. — 50 × 68 mm.
- [17] [C:] GRAECIAE ANTIQVAE ET INSVLARVM CONSPECTVS. — pag.820. 205 × 306 mm.
- [18] [C:] MACEDONIA, THESSALIA, EPIRVS. — pag.828. 206 × 308 mm.
- [19] [C:] HELLAS siue GRAECIA PROPRIA. — pag.887. 206 × 308 mm.
- [20] [C:] THRACIA ANTIQVA — pag.1055. 206 × 308 mm.
- Notes: All the maps are blank on the back and uncoloured. This is the first part of the Notitia, containing Liber I and Liber II. Our copy is complete, with all the maps, the Tabula Ventorum and the portrait of Cellarius. The Library of Congress, inter alia, uses the German form of the author's name, Keller; catalogue of the British Museum uses the Latin form. The book is bound in old vellum. Nordenskiöld's signature is on the first blank leaf.
- Lit.: See Cellarius, Christoph 1701.

Vol. II
NOTITIAE ORBIS ANTIQVI, SIVE GEOGRAPHIAE PLENIORIS TOMVS ALTER ASIAM ET AFRICAM

ANTIQVAM EXPONENS. CHRISTOPHORVS CELLARIVS ex vetustis probatisque monimentis collegit, ... LIPSIAE, Apud IOH. FRIDERICI GLEDITSCHII B. FIL. M. DCC. XXXII.
25 cm.

[1] [C:] ASIA MINOR — Libri III.pag.2. 203 × 305 mm.
[2] [C:] BOSPORVS, MAEOTIS, IBERIA, ALBANIA, ET SARMATIA ASIATICA — Lib. III.pag.301. 203 × 308 mm.
[3] [C:] SYRIA — Lib. III pag.335. 201 × 306 mm.
[4] [C:] PALAESTINA SEV TERRA SANCTA. — Lib. III.pag.390. 301 × 204 mm.
[5] [C:] ARABIA PETRAEA ET DESERTA. — Lib. III.pag.569.
[6] [C:] MESOPOTAMIA ET BABYLONIA FLVMINIBVS SECVNDVM VETEREM TABVLAM DVCTIS — [T:] Beck fe: — Lib. III pag.602. 203 × 309 mm.
[7] [C:] ORIENS, PERSIA, INDIA ec. — Lib. III pag.675. 205 × 309 mm.
[8] [C:] SCYTHIA ET SERICA — Lib. III.pag. 753. 207 × 307 mm.
[9] [C:] AEGYPTVS ET CYRENAICA — Lib. IV pag.764. 205 × 308 mm.
[10] [C:] AEGYPTI DELTA ET NILI OSTIA — Lib. IV pag.774. 202 × 305 mm.
[11] [C:] AFRICA PROPRIA. — Lib. IV pag.864. 204 × 305 mm.
[12] [C:] MAVRETANIA ET NVMIDIA — B Lib. IV pag.898 204 × 306 mm.
[13] [C:] AFRICA INTERIOR — [T:] J.G.Beck sculp: — Lib. IV pagin.939 205 × 311 mm.

Notes: All the maps are blank on the back, and uncoloured. This is the second part of the Notitia, containing Liber III and Liber IV. The signatures 'B' on map [12], 'Bock (or Beck) fe:' on map [6] and 'J.G. Beck sculp:' on map [13] probably refer to the same person; he may have been responsible only for the cartouches. The volume was damaged during World War II, and has been rebound, using some of the old vellum. Nordenskiöld's signature is on the first original blank leaf in the volume.

43 CHIQUET, JACQUES [1719]

Le nouveau et curieux ATLAS Geographique et historique, ou Le Divertissement des Empereurs, Roys, et Princes. Tant dans la Guerre que dans la Paix Dedié A Son A.R. MONSEIGNEUR le DUC D'ORLEANS Regent du Roïaume de France Par son tres humble et tres Obeissant et fidele serui. Iacq. Chiquet A Paris rue S.t Jacque, chez Chereanau Grand S.t Remy. prez l'Eglise des Mathurins. 22 cm.obl.

[1] [T:] LE GLOBE CELESTE REPRESENTÉ EN DEUX PLANS-HEMISPHERES PAR MONS.r DE LA HIRE PROFESSEUR ROYAL et de l'Academie des Sciences — [T:] A Paris chez I Chiquet 1719. — (Celestial chart). 9 Uncoloured. 165 × 216 mm. The hemispheres with 110 mm. diam.
[Insets:] Saturne Selon M.r Cassini. LE SOLEIL auec ses maculē selon le Per Kircher. Iupiter Selon M.r Cassini. Venus Selon Monsieur Cassini. Mars Selon M.r Cassini. Mercure Selon M.r Cassini. la Lune au sextil aspect selon Galilei. All seven circular maps with 26 mm. diam.
[2] [C:] LE GLOBE TERRESTRE REPRESENTÉ EN DEUX PLANS-HEMISPHERES dressée sur les Observations de M.r de l'Academie Royale des Sciences. 1719 A Paris Chez Chiquet — 11 162 × 215 mm. The hemispheres with 106 mm. diam.
[3] [C:] L'EUROPE Dressée sur les Observations de M.rs l'Academie Royale des Sciences. a Paris IChiquet 1719. — 13 164 × 223 mm.
[4] [C:] L'ASIE Dressée selon les Observations de M.rs de l'Academie Royale des Sciences. A Paris chez I.Chiquett1719. — 15 165 × 223 mm.
[5] [C:] L'AFRIQUE Dressée suivant les Auteurs les plus nouvea⁻. et Sur Observations de Messieurs de l'Academie Royale des Sciences. a Paris chez I.Chiquet 1719. — 17 164 × 224 mm.
[6] [C:] L'AMERIQUE SEPTENTRIONALE qui fait partie des Indes Occidentales. Dressée selon les dernieres Relations des Voiageurs et Suivant les nouvelles Observations de M.ur de l'Academie Royale des Sciences. a Pais Chez I. Chiquet 1719. — 19 162 × 217 mm.
[7] [C:] L'AMERIQUE MERIDIONALE qui fait l'autre Partie des Indes Occidentales Dressée tres Exactement Suivant les Observations de M.ur de l'Academie Royale des Sciences et sur les memoires les plus nouveaux A.Paris chez Chiquet 1719. — 21 164 × 216 mm.
[8] [C:] LES ROYAUMES DE PORTUGAL et D'ALGARVE. Le premier est divisé en ses cinq grandes Provinces. Ou se trouvent le détroit de Gibaltar avec les Frontieres d'Espagne Suivant les derniers Memoires. — [T:] a Paris chez I. Chiquet. — 23 218 × 162 mm.
[9] [C:] L'ESPAGNE nommée Par les Anciens Grecs IBERIA ou HESPERIA Dressée sur les memoires et Observations de Messieurs de l'Academie Royale des Sciences a Paris chez I.Chiquet 1719 — [T:] Grave par l'auteur. — 25 162 × 217 mm.
[10] [C:] LE ROYAUME DE FRANCE Suivant les Nouvelles Observations A Paris Chez I.Chiquet 1719. — 27 162 × 218 mm.
[11] [C:] LES XVII PROVINCES DES PAYS-BAS Divisées en Provinces Unies Connues sous le nom de Hollande, et en Pays Bas Catholiques Connues sous le nom de Flandre. Ou Sont. LE DUCHÉ DE LORAINE, PARTIE DE LA FRANCE &c. Dressée sur les Derniers memoires a Paris chez I.Chiquet. — 29 212 × 166 mm.
[12] [C:] L'EMPIRE D'ALLEMAGNE Divisé en ses dix Cercles et Autres Estats. Dressé sur les Memoires les plus Nouveaux A Paris chez I.Chiquet. 1719. — 31 162 × 220 mm.
[13] [C:] LES ESTATS DE LA COURONNE DE POLOGNE. Chez I. Chiquet A.Paris 1719. — 33 165 × 222 mm.
[14] [C:] ESTATS DU GRAND DUC DE MOSCOVIE ou de L'EMPEREUR de la RUSSIE BLANCHE Suivant les dernieres relations. 1719. — [T:] a Paris chez Chiquet. — 35 165 × 220 mm.
[15] [C:] Les Royavmes D'ANGLETERRE, D'ESCOSSE ET D'IRLANDE avec Partie de la France et des Pays Bas Chez Chiquet. a Paris. 1719. — 37 164 × 220 mm.
[16] [C:] LE ROYAUME de D'ANEMARK Subdivisée en ses quatre Dioceses Avec les Isles Adjacentes LE DUCHÉ DE SLEWICK &.c. Chez Iacq. Chiquet. A Paris 1719. — 39 166 × 220 mm.
[17] [C:] LE ROYAUME DE NORWEGE Divisé en ses cinq Principaux GOUVERNEMENTS Dressé sur les Derniers Memoires des plusieurs Auteurs à Paris chez Chiquet 1719. — 41 216 × 161 mm.
[18] [C:] ESTATS DE LA COURONNE DE SUEDE dans la SCANDINAVIE, ou sont Suede, Gotlande, Lapponie Suedoise, Finlande, Ingrie et Livonie. Subdivisées en leurs Provinces. Suivant les dernieres relations a Paris chez Chiquet 1719 — 43 162 × 218 mm.
[19] [C:] ESTATS DE L'EMPIRE DU GRAND SEIGNEUR dit SULTAN et OTTOMANS EMPEREUR des TURCS Dans trois partie.s du Monde Sçavoir. EN EUROPE, EN ASIE, et EN AFRIQUE. Chez Iacq. Chiquet. A Paris 1719. — 45 163 × 218 mm.
[Inset:] [T:] BARBARIE BILEDULGERID — 30 × 69 mm.
[20] [C:] LE ROYAUME DE HONGRIE ou se trouvent La Transilvanie, La Moldavie, La Valaquie, L'esclavonie, La Bosnie, La Servie, et la Bulgarie, &.c. chez Chiquet A Paris. 1719. — 47 161 × 219 mm.
[21] [C:] CARTE GENERALE D'ITALIE Et des Isles Adjacentes Tiré des Bons Auteurs Chez Iacq. Chiquet A Paris 1719. — 49 160 × 218 mm.
[22] [C:] LES ISLES et COSTE DE LA DALMATIE. ou se Trouvent la Republique de Raguse, et Partie de la Servie &c. chez Iacq. Chiquet Aaris 1719. — 51 164 × 221 mm.

[23] [C:] LA GRECE ou PARTIE MERIDIONALE DE LA TURQUIE D'EUROPE dressée sur les Dernieres Observations chez Chiquet A.Paris 1719. — 53 163 × 221 mm.

[24] [C:] ISLE ET ROYAUME DE CANDIE. — [T:] a Paris Chez I. Chiquet 1719. — 55 162 × 220 mm.

Notes: All the maps are blank on the verso. Only map [1], the celestial map, is uncoloured; all the other maps are coloured along the boundary lines. In most of the cartouches there are indications of erasures. It is not possible to read the original wording, but Chiquet's name appears to be replacing an earlier one. In some cases the year 1711 can be deciphered. The volume is bound in old, worn vellum with the author's name and 'Atlas 1719' written on it in ink. Nordenskiöld's signature is on the first blank leaf, with the date 1898.

Lit.: Bagrow p. 337, Tooley, Dictionary p. 70.

44 CLUVER, PHILIP   1616

PHILIPPI CLÜVERI GERMANIÆ ANTIQVÆ Libri tres. Opus post omnium curas elaboratissium, tabulis geographicis, et imaginibus, priscum Germanorum cultum moresque referentibus, exornatum. Adjectæ sunt VINDELICIA et NORICUM, ejusdem auctoris. LUGDUNI BATAVORUM Apud Ludovicum Elzevirium Anno M DC XVI.   33 cm.

PHILIPPI CLVVERI GERMANIAE ANTIQVAE LIBER PRIMUS: Quo situs universæ Germaniæ, & origo moresque priscum Germanorum describuntur.

[1] [C:] SEPTEMTRIONALIUM In EUROPÂ et ASIÂ terra[ru] descriptio, ad falsam veterum scriptorum mentem accommodata, autore PHILIP. CLÜVERIO — 265 × 349 mm.

[2] [C:] Summa EUROPÆ antiquæ descriptio; Auctore PHILIP. CLÜVERIO — [T:] Nicol. geilkerckio sc. — 265 × 349 mm.

PHILIPPI CLVVERI GERMANIAE ANTIQVAE LIBER SECVNDVS; Quo GERMANIA CISRHENANA describitur.

[3] [C:] GERMANIÆ CISRHENANÆ ut circa Julii Cæsaris fuit ætatem, descriptio; Auctore PHIL. CLÜVERIO. — [T:] Nic. geilk. s. — 263 × 349 mm.

[4] [C:] GERMANIÆ CISRHENANÆ ut inter I. Cæsaris et Trajani fuit imperia descriptio Auctore PHIL. CLÜVERIO — [T:] Nicolao Geilkerckio sculpsit — 264 × 349 mm.

[5] HELVETIÆ conterminarumque terrarum antiqua descriptio. Auctore PHIL. CLÜVERIO [T:] Nicolao geilkerckio scu. — 264 × 349 mm.

[6] [C:] SCALDIS, MOSAE, ac Rheni Ostiorum, gentiumque accolarum antiqua descriptio; Auctore PHILIPPO CLÜVERIO. — [T:] Nic. geilkerckio sc. — 266 × 351 mm.

PHILIPPI CLVVERI GERMANIAE ANTIQVAE LIBER TERTIVS; Quo GERMANIA TRANSRHENANA describitur.

[7] [a] [C:] Populorum GERMANIÆ inter Rhenum et albim descriptio, ut inter Cæsaris et Trajani imperia incoluerūt. Auct P. CLÜVERIO — 249 × 165 mm.
[b] [C:] Populorū GERMANIÆ inter Rhenum et Albim Descriptio, ut circa I. Cæsaris ævum incoluerunt: autore P. CLÜVERIO. — 249 × 165 mm.
[The whole map:] 262 × 348 mm.

[8] [C:] GERMANIÆ Populorum inter Rhenum et Albim amneis, ut à Trajani imperio, et circa Marcellini ætatem incoluerunt, descriptio; Auctore PHILIPPO CLÜVERIO. — [T:] Nicol. Geilkerckio sculpsit. — 262 × 350 mm.

[9] [C:] SVEVIÆ quæ cis Codânum fuit sinum, antiqua descriptio; Auctore PHIL. CLÜVE[rio] — [T:] Nicol. geilkerckio sc. — 263 × 348 mm.

[10] [C:] ANTIQVÆ GERMANIÆ[rio] SEPTEMTRIonalis descriptio; Auctore PHIL. CLÜVE[rio] — [T:] N. geilk. sc. — 263 × 348 mm.

PHILIPPI CLVVERI VINDELICIA ET NORICVM.

[11] [C:] VINDELICIÆ et NORICI Conterminarumque terrarum antiqua descriptio; auctore PHILIPPO CLÜVERIO. Nic. Geilkerckio sc. — 265 × 348 mm.

Notes: All the maps are blank on the back and uncoloured. The work consists of three parts, with the appropriate maps bound at the beginning of each; thus maps [1] and [2] are at the beginning of book 1, maps [3] — [6] at the beginning of book 2, and maps [7] — [10] at the beginning of book 3. Map [11] is placed at the beginning of the additional part, Vindelicia et Noricum. The name of the engraver, Nicolaus Geilkercken, appears on nine of the maps; it is wanting only on maps [1] and [7]. The volume is bound in the original vellum, with blind tooling. It is the first edition of the work.

Lit.: Bonacker p. 68, Tiele p. 61, nr 250.

45 CLUVER, PHILIP   1697

PHILIPPI CLUVERII INTRODUCTIO IN UNIVERSAM GEOGRAPHIAM Tam veterem quam novam Tabulis Geographicis XLVI. ac Notis olim ornata à JOHANNE BUNONE, Jam verò locupletata Additamentis & Annotationibus JOH. FRID. HEKELII & JOH. REISKII. ... Venduntur AMSTELÆDAMI, Apud JOANNEM WOLTERS, Bibliopolam op 't Water. M DC XCVII.
[Engraved half title:]
PHILIPPI CLUVERII INTRODUCTIONIS IN UNIVERSAM GEOGRAPHIAM Cum Notis I. BUNONIS HEKELII ET REISKII LIB. VI Venduntur AMSTELÆDAMI, Apud, JOANNEM WOLTERS, A.º 1697,   23,2 cm.

[1] Tab: 4. [C:] Typus ORBIS TERRARVM — Between pp. 42 and 43. 156 × 300 mm. The hemispheres with 145 mm. diam.

[2] Tab: 5. [C:] Summa EUROPÆ ANTIQUÆ Descriptio Auctore PHIL. CLUV. — Between pp. 60 and 61. 201 × 250 mm. See 1616:[2].

[3] Tab: 6. [C:] HISPANIÆ Veteris et NOVÆ Descriptio — Between pp. 62 and 63. 264 × 319 mm.
[Inset:] [T:] BALEARIDES INSULÆ DUÆ. — 38 × 71 mm.

[4] Tab. 7 [C:] GALLIA ANTIQUA et NOVA, — Between pp. 86 and 87. 268 × 324 mm.

[5] Tab: 8. [C:] GERMANIÆ CISRHENANÆ ut inter I.Cæsaris et Traiani fuit imperia SCALDIS Item MOSÆ ac RHENI Ostiorum antiqua Descriptio — Between pp. 92 and 93. 244 × 251 mm.

[6] Tab: 9. [C:] HELVETIA Conterminarumq3 terrarum antiqua Descriptio. Auctore PHIL: CLUVERIO. — Between pp. 116 and 117. 119 × 249 mm. See 1616:[5].

[7] Tab. 10 [C:] HODIERNÆ BELGICÆ sive GERMANIÆ INFERIORIS Tabula — Between pp. 124 and 125. 200 × 248 mm.

[8] Tab:. 11. [C:] VETERIS et NOVÆ BRITANNIÆ Descriptio — Between pp. 136 and 137. 212 × 257 mm.
[Inset:] [T:] Orcades Ins. — 32 × 41 mm.

[9] Tab: 12. [a] [C:] Populorum GERMANIÆ Inter Rhenum et Albim Descript: ut inter Cæsaris et Traiani imperia Incoluerunt — 190 × 117 mm.
[b] [C:] Populorum GERMANIÆ Inter Rhenum et Albim Descriptio ut circa I. Cæsaris ærum Incoluerunt — 190 × 123 mm.
[The whole map:] Between pp. 152 and 153. 201 × 252 mm. See 1616:[7].

[10] Tab: 13 [C:] SVEVIA, quæ cis Codanum fuit sinum Antiqua descriptio Auctore PHIL CLVVERIO. — Between pp. 158 and 159. 196 × 245 mm. See 1616:[9].

[11] Tab: 14 [C:] VINDELICIÆ et NORICI, Conterminarumq3 terrarum antiqua descriptio Auctore PHIL: CLUVERIO — Between pp. 160 and 161. 201 × 252 mm. See 1616:[11].

[12] Tab:15. [C:] Nova Totius GERMANIÆ DESCRIPTIO. — Between pp. 166 and 167. 259 × 321 mm.

[13] Tab:16. [C:] REGNI DANIÆ Accuratissima delineatio. — Between pp. 226 and 227. 207 × 250 mm.

[14] Tab:17. [C:] SVECIA DANIA et NORVEGIA. — Between pp. 230 and 231. 206 × 255 mm.

[15] Tab. 18 [C:] ITALIA ANTIQUA — Between pp. 236 and 237. 261 × 319 mm.
[16] Tab. 19 [C:] ITALIÆ GALLICÆ sive GALLIÆ CISALPINÆ Conterminarumque Terrarū Vetus et nova Descriptio — Between pp. 244 and 245. 202 × 250 mm.
[17] Tab:20. [C:] ETRURIÆ LATII UMBRIÆ PICENI SABINORUM et MARSORUM Vetus et Nova Descriptio — Between pp. 246 and 247. 204 × 249 mm.
[18] Tab: 21 [C:] CAMPANIÆ, SAMNII APULIÆ LUCANIÆ BRUTIORUM Vetus et Nova Descriptio, — Between pp. 260 and 261. 255 × 217 mm.
[19] Tab. 22. [C:] ITALIA NOVA — Between pp. 274 and 275. 260 × 303 mm.
[20] Tab: 23. [C:] SICILIAE ANTIQUAE Descriptio Auctore. PHILIP CLUVERIO. — Between pp. 302 and 303. 257 × 318 mm.
[21] Tab: 24 [C:] CORSICÆ Antiquæ Descriptio — [C:] SARDINIÆ Antiquæ Descriptio — Between pp. 308 and 309. 263 × 107 mm.
[22] Tab: 25 [C:] Veteris et Nova PANNONIÆ et ILLYRICI Descriptio — Between pp. 312 and 313. 206 × 241 mm.
[23] Tab: 26. [C:] HELLAS Seu GRÆCIA VNIVERSA — Between pp. 326 and 327. 225 × 252 mm.
[24] Tab:27. [C:] EPIRUS hodie CANINA cum Maris Ionii Insulis Corcyra seu Corfu Cephalenia seu Cefalogna etc. — Between pp. 328 and 329. 202 × 254 mm.
[25] Tab: 28 [C:] PELOPONNESUS nunc MOREA — Between pp. 330 and 331. 207 × 254 mm.
[Inset:] [T:] VETERIS CORINTHI ICHNOGRAPHIA — 68 × 46 mm.
[26] Tab: 29 [C:] ACHAIA quæ et HELLAS hodie LIVADIA. — Between pp. 336 and 337. 198 × 256 mm.
[Insets:] [C:] THEBÆ BOETICÆ — (Plan). 55 × 84 mm. [C:] ATHENÆ — 49 × 76 mm.
[27] Tab: 30 [C:] MACEDONIÆ et THESSALIÆ Regiones — Between pp. 346 and 347. 197 × 252 mm.
[28] Tab: 31. [C:] DACIARUM MOESIARUM et THRACIÆ Vetus et Nova. Descriptio — Between pp. 366 and 367. 202 × 241 mm.
[29] Tab: 32. [C:] SARMATIA et SCYTHIA, Russia et Tartaria Europæa — Between pp. 386 and 387. 233 × 251 mm.
[30] Tab.33 [C:] Veteris et Novæ REGNI POLONIÆ Magniq Ducatus, LITHUANIÆ Cum suis Palatinatibus ac Confinus Descriptio — Between pp. 390 and 391. 204 × 250 mm.
[31] Tab: 34. [C:] PRUSSIÆ NOVA TABULA — Between pp. 402 and 403. 268 × 333 mm.
[32] Tab: 35. [C:] ASIA Antiqua et NOVA — Between pp. 412 and 413. 208 × 257 mm.
[33] Tab: 36 [C:] SCYTHIA et TARTARIA ASIATICA. — Between pp. 414 and 415. 207 × 255 mm.
[34] Tab: 37. [C:] IMPERII SINARVM Nova Descriptio — Between pp. 424 and 425. 206 × 253 mm.
[35] Tab. 38. [C:] INDIÆ Orientalis et Insularum Adiacentium Antiqua et Nova Descriptio — Between pp. 428 and 429. 216 × 260 mm.
[36] Tab 39. [C:] PERSIA Sive SOPHORUM REGNUM cum ARMENIA ASSYRIA MESOPOTAMIA et BABILONIA — Between pp. 446 and 447. 204 × 254 mm.
[37] Tab. 40 [C:] CHERSONESI quæ hodie NATOLIA, Descriptio — Between pp. 464 and 465. 203 × 250 mm.
[38] Tab: 41 [C:] TOTIUS TERRÆ SANCTÆ Delineatio — Between pp. 478 and 479. 265 × 214 mm.
[39] Tab: 42 [C:] SYRIÆ Sive SORIÆ Descriptio — Between pp.. 492 and 493. 197 × 245 mm.
[40] Tab. 43. [C:] AFRICA, Antiqua, et NOVA. — Between pp. 510 and 511. 211 × 253 mm.
[41] Tab: 44. [C:] ÆGYPTVS et CYRENE — Between pp. 510 and 511. 127 × 214 mm.
[42] Tab: 45. [C:] MAURITANA et Africa Propria nunc BARBARIA — Between pp. 522 and 523. 129 × 218 mm.
[43] Tab: 46. [C:] AMERICA. — Between pp. 546 and 547. 206 × 257 mm.
Notes: All the maps are blank on the back and uncoloured. The title-page is printed in red and black. There is a portrait of Cluverius on the engraved half-title. The first edition of this work was published in 1624, Ex offic. Elzeviriana, and contained seven books; this edition contains only six. Tiele states that this was the most popular history book for over a century, and that it was published in many editions in the Netherlands and abroad. Our copy is complete, with all the maps and the three additional tables mentioned in the index. Five of the maps are signed by Cluverius. Our copy is bound in old vellum. There are wormholes in the centre of the volume. Nordenskiöld's signature, dated Napoli 1880, is on the first blank leaf.

Lit.: Tiele p. 60—61, nrs 245 and 246.

46 CLUVER, PHILIP   [1723—1725]

PHILIPPI CLUVERII, Gedanensis, SICILIA ANTIQUA, Ubi Primum universæ hujus Insulæ varia Nomina, Incolæ, Situs, Figura, Magnitudo, tum Orientale, Meridionale atque Septemtrionale Litora, dein Mediterranea ejus, ac tandem INSULÆ MINORES Ei adjacentes Variaque plurium locorum Memorabilia solidissime explicantur. Opus post omnium curas elaboratissimum, TABULIS GEOGRAPHICIS, Et nunc etiam aliis Figuris, ære expressis, Illustratum. Editio Novissima, Auctior, & Emendatior. LUGDUNI BATAVORUM, Sumptibus PETRI VANDER Aa, Bibliopolæ, Civitatis atque Academiæ Typographi.   40,7 cm.

[1] [C:] SICILIAE ANTIQVAE DESCRIPTIO Auctore PHIL. CLVVERIO. — (Map). Pag. 1. 280 × 357 mm. See 1697:[20].
[2] [C:] ΣΙΚΕΛΙΑΣ ΤΗΣΠΑΛΑΙΑΣ ΤΥΠΟΣ, χωρογραφοῦντος ΦΙΛΙΠΠΟΥ τοῦ ΚΛΥΒΕΡΙΟΥ. [SIKELIAS TĒSPALAIAS TUPOS, hōrografoũntos FILIPPOU toũ KLUBERIOU.] — (Map). Between pp. 56 and 57. 277 × 356 mm.
[3] [C:] MESSINA, Urbs Sicilia. — (Plan). Between pp. 96 and 97. 377 × 500 mm.
[4] [C:] ÆTNA, Mons Siciliæ. — (View). Between pp. 116 and 117. 174 × 288 mm.
[5] [C:] CATANA Urbs Siciliæ Clarissima. — (Plan). Between pp. 140 and 141. 365 × 484 mm.
[6] [C:] VETERVM SYRACVSARVM Typus. Auctore PHIL. CLVVERIO. — (Plan). Pag. 166. 279 × 355 mm.
[7] [C:] PANORMUS Urbs metropolis SICILIÆ. — (Plan). Between pp. 336 and 337. 322 × 459 mm.
[8] [a] [C:] INSVLARVM ORIENTALI SICILIÆ LATERI OBJACENTIUM TYPUS. Auctore PHIL. CLVVERIO. — (Map). 145 × 355 mm.
[b] [C:] MELITA. — (Map). 128 × 172 mm.
[c] [T:] MELITA INSULA — (Map). 128 × 171 mm.
[The whole map:] Between pp. 488 and 489. 280 × 355 mm.
[9] [C:] VALETTA CIVITAS NOVA MALTÆ Olim Millitæ — (Plan). Between pp. 536 and 537. 401 × 500 mm.
[Inset:] [T:] Malta Comene Gozzo — (Map). Oval 68 × 113 mm.

PHILIPPI CLUVERII, Gedanensis, SARDINIA ET CORSICA ANTIQUÆ, ... Editio Novissima, nitidior, & Indice locupletiori instructa. LUGDUNI BATAVORUM, Sumptibus PETRI VANDER Aa, Bibliopolæ, Civitatis atque Academiæ Typographi.

Notes: All the maps are blank on the back and uncoloured. The title-pages of both parts are printed in red and black. This new edition, published by van der Aa, is undated. The original Elzevir edition is part three of Italia antiqua, published in 1624. The British Museum Catalogue of Printed Books lists an 'Editio novissima' dated 1723, with 587 C. as in our copy. The second part, Sardinia, dated 1725, has 42 columns, as in our copy. There is a portrait of Cluverius preceding map [1], with the inscription 'PHILIPPUS CLUVERIUS. Geographorum Phoenix. Lugd. Bat ex Officina Petri Vander Aa.' The verso is blank. In the part 'SARDINIA ET CORSICA ANTIQUAE' there is a portrait of Vorstius, with the words 'ÆLIUS

EVERHARDUS VORSTIUS. Medicinæ Professor' and the page-number 4. The verso is blank. The volume is bound in paper, with a vellum spine. Nordenskiöld's bookplate is pasted to the inside of the front cover.

Lit.: BM Books, vol. BM Maps, Maps vol. 40 c. 959, Tiele p. 61—62, nr 252.

47 CLUVER, PHILIP   1729

PHILIPPI CLUVERI INTRODUCTIONIS IN UNIVERSAM GEOGRAPHIAM, TAM VETEREM QUAM NOVAM LIBRI VI. Cum integris JOHANNIS BUNONIS, JOH. FRID. HEKELII & JOH. REISKII, & selectis LONDINENSIBUS notis. Textum ad optimas Editiones recognovit; Pauca CLUVERII, multa interpretum sphalmata obelo notavit; Bunonianis Tabulis geographicis passim emendatis novas accuratiores addidit; Præfationemque de CLUVERII fatis & scriptis Historico-criticam; cum præcognitis geographicis, præfixit AUGUSTINUS BRUZEN LA MARTINIERE, Sapientissimi Hispaniarum Indiarumque Regis PHILIPPI V. Geographus. EDITIO OMNIUM LOCUPLETISSIMA. AMSTELÆDAMI, Apud JOANNEM PAULI. M D C C X X I X.
[Engraved half title:] PHILIPPI CLUVERII INTRODUCTIONIS IN UNIVERSAM GEOGRAPHIAM Cum Notis I. BUNONIS HEKELII ET REISKII LIB. VI   26,5 cm.

[1]   [C:] Typus ORBIS TERRARVM — Pag. 50. = 1697:[1].
[2]   [T:] ORBIS VETERIBUS NOTI TABULA NOVA Auctore GUILLELMO DEL'ISLE è Regiâ Scientiarum Academia et Christianissimi Francorum Regis Geographo primario. — I. Stemmers Iunior Sculp. Pag. 52. Circular map with 378 mm. diam.
[3]   [C:] Summa EUROPÆ ANTIQUÆ Descriptio Auctore PHIL. CLUV. — Pag. 73. = 1697:[2].
[4]   [C:] HISPANIÆ Veteris et NOVÆ Descriptio — Pag.76. = 1697:[3].
[5]   [C:] GALLIA ANTIQUA et NOVA, — Pag. 100. = 1697:[4].
[6]   [C:] GERMANIÆ CISRHENANÆ ut inter I. Cæsaris et Traiani fuit jmperia SCALDIS Item MOSÆ ac RHENI Ostiorum antiqua Descriptio — Pag. 112. = 1697:[5].
[7]   [C:] HELVETIA Conterminarumq₃ terrarum antiqua Descriptio. Auctore PHIL: CLUVERIO. — Pag. 142. = 1697:[6].
[8]   [C:] HODIERNÆ BELGICÆ sive GERMANIÆ INFERIORIS Tabula — Pag. 150. = 1697:[7].
[9]   [C:] VETERIS et NOVÆ BRITANNIÆ Descriptio — Pag. 165. = 1697:[8].
[10] [a] [C:] Populorum GERMANIÆ Inter Rhenum et Albin Descript ... — [b] [C:] Populorum GERMANIÆ Inter Rhenum et Albin Descriptio ... —
[The whole map:] Pag. 186., but bound between pp. 180 and 181. = 1697:[9].
[11] [C:] SVEVIA, quæ cis Codanum fuit sinum Antiqua descriptio Auctore PHIL CLVVERIO. — Pag. 193., but bound between pp. 188 and 189. = 1697:[10].
[12] [C:] VINDELICIÆ et NORICI, Conterminarumq₃ terrarum antiqua descriptio Auctore PHIL: CLUVERIO — Pag. 194. = 1697:[11].
[13] [C:] Nova Totius GERMANIÆ DESCRIPTIO. — Pag. 200. = 1697:[12].
[14] [C:] REGNI DANIÆ Accuratissima delineatio. — Pag. 279. = 1697:[13].
[15] [C:] SVECIA DANIA et NORVEGIA. — Pag. 284. = 1697:[14].
[16] [C:] ITALIA ANTIQUA — Pag. 291. = 1697:[15].
[17] [C:] TABULA ITALIÆ ANTIQUÆ in REGIONES XI ab Augusto divisæ et tum ad mensuras itinerarias tum ad observationes astronomicas exacta Accurante Guillelmo de l'Isle è Regiâ Scientiarum Academiâ et Christianissimi Francorum Regis Geographo primario. — Pag. 292.   380 × 481 mm.
[18] [C:] ITALIÆ GALLICÆ sive GALLIÆ CISALPINÆ Conterminarumque Terrarū Vetus et nova Descriptio — Pag. 301. = 1697:[16].
[19] [C:] ETRURIÆ LATII UMBRIÆ PICENI SABINORUM et MARSORUM Vetus et Nova Descriptio — Pag. 304. = 1697:[17].
[20] [C:] CAMPANIÆ SAMNII APULIÆ LUCANIÆ BRUTIORUM Vetus et Nova Descriptio, — Pag. 321. = 1697:[18].
[21] [C:] ITALIA NOVA — Pag. 339. = 1697:[19].
[22] [C:] SICILIAE ANTIQUAE Descriptio Auctore. PHILIP CLUVERIO — Pag. 379. = 1697:[20].
[23] [C:] CORSICÆ Antiquæ Descriptio — [C:] SARDINIÆ Antiquæ Descriptio — Pag. 383. = 1697:[21].
[24] [C:] Veteris et Nova PANNONIÆ et ILLYRICI Descriptio — Pag. 387. = 1697:[22].
[25] [C:] HELLAS Seu GRÆCIA VNIVERSA — Pag. 404. = 1697:[23].
[26] [C:] GRÆCIÆ PARS SEPTENTRIONALIS. Auctore Gullielmo Del'isle. — Pag. 404.   380 × 480 mm.
[27] [C:] EPIRUS hodie CANINA ... — Pag. 406. = 1697:[24].
[28] [C:] PELOPONNESUS nunc MOREA — Pag. 409. = 1697:[25].
[29] GRÆCIÆ PARS MERIDIONALIS.
[C:] GRÆCIÆ ANTIQUÆ TABULA NOVA in qua locorum situs tum ad distantias itinerarias, tum ad Observationes Astronomicas exactus litorum flexuræ et alia id genus ad accuratas recentiorum rationes accomodatæ sunt Auctore Guillelmo Delisle, ex Regia Scientiarum Academia. — Pag. 409.   364 × 477 mm.
[30] [C:] ACHAIA quæ et HELLAS hodie LIVADIA. — Pag. 416. = 1697:[26].
[31] MACEDONIÆ et THESSALIÆ Regiones   Pag. 447. = 1697:[27].
[32] [C:] DACIARUM MOESIARUM et THRACIÆ Vetus et Nova. Descriptio — Pag.451., but bound between pp. 452 and 453. = 1697:[28].
[33] [C:] SARMATIA et SCYTHIA, Russia et Tartaria Europæa — Pag. 477. = 1697:[29].
[34] [C:] Veteris et Novæ REGNI POLONIÆ Magniq Ducatus, LITHUANIÆ Cum suis Palatinatibus ac Confinus Descriptio — Pag. 481. = 1697:[30].
[35] [C:] PRUSSIÆ NOVA TABULA — Pag. 496. = 1697:[31].
[36] [C:] ASIA Antiqua et NOVA — Pag. 508. = 1697:[32].
[37] [C:] SCYTHIA et TARTARIA ASIATICA. — Pag. 510. = 1697:[33].
[38] [C:] IMPERII SINARVM Nova Descriptio — Pag. 522. = 1697:[34].
[39] [C:] INDIÆ Orientalis et Insularum Adiacentium Antiqua et Nova Descriptio — Pag. 527. = 1697:[35].
[40] [C:] PERSIA Sive SOPHORUM REGNUM ... — Pag. 547. = 1697:[36].
[41] [C:] CHERSONESI quæ hodie NATOLIA, Descriptio — Pag. 568. = 1697:[37].
[42] [C:] TOTIUS TERRÆ SANCTÆ Delineatio — Pag. 587., but bound between pp. 588 and 589. = 1697:[38].
[43] [C:] SYRIÆ Sive SORIÆ Descriptio — Pag. 603. = 1697:[39].
[44] [C:] AFRICA, Antiqua, et NOVA. — Pag. 623. = 1697:[40].
[45] [C:] ÆGYPTVS et CYRENE — Pag. 625. = 1697:[41].
[46] [C:] MAURITANA et Africa Propria nunc BARBARIA — Pag. 639. = 1697:[42].
[47] [C:] AMERICA. — Pag. 666. = 1697:[43].

Notes: All the maps are blank on the back and uncoloured. The title-page is printed in red and black. The engraved half-title is the same as in the earlier edition in the collection, except that it lacks the publisher's name, as this last edition of the work had a new publisher. The maps are the same as in the earlier edition, with the addition of four maps by Guillaume de l'Isle. Our copy corresponds in all particulars with Tiele's description of this edition. On the first blank leaf, in old ink, is written: 'Preis: 150 gr — (Extr: Provission) Leipziger (Hartung) Auction April 1863. H. Holberg Dr L 7/5 1863' and 'A.E. Nordenskiöld 1885'

Lit.: Tiele p. 60—61, nr 246.

48 [**Collection of maps, mostly Italian, without title-page.**]
1532—1570
49,5 cm.

[1] [T:] La uera descritione di tutta la Francia, et la Spagna, et la Fiandra ... M. D. LIIII. — 370 × 533 mm.

[2] [C:] BRITANNIÆ INSVLÆ QVÆ NVNC ANGLIÆ ET SCOTIÆ REGNA CONTINET CVM HIBERNIA ADIACENTE NOVA DESCRIPTIO. — [C:] ... ROMÆ Anglorum studio et diligentia. M D L VIII Sebastianus a Regibus Clodiensist in æs incidebat — 400 × 542 mm.

[3] [T:] BRITANNIA INSVLA QVAE DVO REGNA CONTINENT ANGLIAM ET SCOTIAM CVM HIBERNIA ADIACENTE. — [C:] I H S — [C:] ... M.D. LVI — 483 × 349 mm.

[4] [a] [C:] DE MAIORICA INSVLA. ... — 250 × 176 mm.
[b][C:] DE MINORICA INSVLA. ... — 240 × 173 mm.

[5] [T:] Nauigationi dil mondo nouo. — [T:] IN VENETIA per Gio. Franc.º Camocio M.D.L X. — [T:] opera dim. nicollo del dolfinatto cosmographo del xp̄anissimo P e. Paulo di forlani da Verona Fecit — (Chart). 241 × 359 mm.

[6] [C:] LA FRANZA. — [C:] L'anno 1557. — 490 × 425 mm.

[7] [A plan of a fortress]. 440 × 304 mm.

[8] [T:] TOTIVS GALLIÆ DESCRIPTIO, cum parte Angliæ, Germaniæ, Flandriæ, Brabantiæ, Italiæ, Romam usque. Pyrrho Ligorio Neap. auctore. ROMÆ. M.D.LVIII. Michaelis Tramezini formis. ... Sebastianus a Regibus Clodiensis incidebat. — 390 × 518 mm.

[9] [C:] La noua & uera descrittion della Gallia Beglica. — [C:] DESCRIPTIO TOTIVS GALLIÆ BELGICÆ. Pyrrho Ligorio Neapolit. auctore. ROMÆ M. D. LVIII. Michaelis TrameZini formis. ... Sebastianus de Regibus Clodiensis incidebat. — 371 × 530 mm.

[10] [C:] BRABANTIÆ BELGARVM PROVINCIAE RECENS EXACTAQVE DESCRIPTIO MICHAELIS TRAMEZINI FORMIS ... ∞ Ɖ LVIII. — [T:] Iacobus Bossius Belga, in æs incidebat. — 510 × 395 mm.

[11] [C:] HOLLANDIA. — [C:] HOLLANDIAE BATAVOR₃ VETERIS INSVLAE ET LOCORVM ADIACENTIVM EXACTA DESCRIPTIO. MICHAELIS TRAMEZINI FORMIS. ... ∞ . Ɖ. LVIII. — [T:] Iac. Bossius Bælga, in æ incidebat. — 530 × 380 mm.

[12] [C:] GELRIAE CLIVIAE IVLIAE NEC NON ALIARVM REGIONVM ADIACENTIVM NOVA DESCRIPTIO MICHAELIS TRAMEZINI FORMIS ... ∞ . Ɖ. LVIII. — [T:] Iac. Bossius Belga, in æs incidebat. — 502 × 390 mm.

[13] [C:] GERMANIA. — [C:] Opera di Iacopo di Gastaldi Cosmografo In Venetia M D L V IIII. — [T:] In Venetia appresso Donato Bertelli libraro al Segno del San Marco. — [T:] Dominico D Genoi Venetiano Fecit. — 283 × 409 mm.

[14] [C:] AVSTRIA E VNGARIA. — [T:] Alla libraria de l'insegna del.S. Marco Donato Bertelli domenego Venetiano F. M D LVIIII. — 284 × 415 mm.

[15] [T:] TABVLA MODERNA POLONIÆ VNGARIÆ BOEMIÆ GERMANIÆ RVSSIÆ LITHVÆ — [T:] Ant Sa Excu. — 390 × 516 mm.

[16] [C:] ITALIA NVOVA. — [C:] ... Alla libraria de l'Insegna del S. Marco Donato Bertelli 1558. Domenego. VE. F. — 407 × 572 mm.

[17] [C:] Opera de Iacomo gastaldo piamontese cosmographo in Venetia, nella quale e descritto la regione dil piamonte, et quella di Monferra, con la maggior parte della riuiera di Genoa, e il teritorio Astesano, Alexandrino, Tortonese, Nouarese, et la piu parte del Pauese, et parte del Milanese ... M. D. L. VI. — [C:] In Vinegia appresso Gabriel Giolito de'ferrari. ... — 375 × 505 mm.

[18] [T:] LA VERA DESCRITIONE DI TVTTA LA LOMBARDIA M. D. LX. — [C:] VENETIIS Jo. Francisci camocij æreis Formis. — 302 × 485 mm.

[19] [C:] La vera descritione del Friuli... In Vinegia per Giouanni Andrea Valuastorii detto Guadagnino. M. D. LVII. — 368 × 519 mm.

[20] [T:] en candidi Lectores, elegantioris Italiæ' partis, Tusciæ scilicet Topographiam, æneis nr̃is formis ... — 396 × 551 mm.

[21] [C:] TERRITORIO DI ROMA. — 320 × 476 mm.

[22] [C:] REGNO DI NAPOLI. — 332 × 490 mm.

[23] [C:] Sicilia insulårum omnium (ut inquit Diodorus) optima, ... — 371 × 495 mm.

[24] [T:] Malta — [C:] Gewisse verzaijchnüs der insel vnd Ports Malta mit aller seiner beuestigung vnd ortten ... Zu Nurmberg, bey Mathias Zündten auff S Katterina hoff von Neywem aufz gangen Ao 1565. — 318 × 491 mm.
[Inset:] EVROPA myt seynen lender vnd prouinczen ... 99 × 154 mm.

[25] [C:] MELITA Insula, quam hodie MALTAM uocant,... — [T:] ANT. LAFRERI ROMÆ 1551. — 330 × 476 mm.

[26] [T:] ISOLA DE CIPRO. — [C:] Questa e la uera descriptione et Geographia di tutta Iinsula de Cypre riditta alla uera forma secundo li moderni et nomi antiqui tratta dal uero sito de essa insula con monti paludi piani ouer mesarçe et casali sui et citadi. Stampata in Venetia ver Matheo pagano 1538 — 259 × 399 mm.

[27] [C:] La Uera descriptione de lisola de Cania ... Stāpata in Veneggia p Giouāni Andrea Uauasore detto Guadagninọ. M.D.xxxviii. — 275 × 395 mm.

[28] [a] [C:] Sardinia insula ... fabius. licinius. f. — 302 × 198 mm.
[b] [C:] CIRNVS siue CORSICA insula ... F. L ~ — 302 × 198 mm.

[29] [a] [C:] HIBERNIA siue IRLANDA insula ... — 248 × 172 mm.
[b] [C:] ILBA siue ILVA insula ... — 250 × 177 mm.

[30] [C:] M. D. L. IX. Il dissegno particolare delle' Regioni che sono da Constantinopoli à Venetia, da Venetia a Viena et da Viena a Constantinopoli ... fabius licinius fecit — 350 × 510 mm.

[31] [C:] PALESTINÆ SIVE TERRĘ SANCTĘ DESCRIPTIO. — [C:] ... M. D. LVII. ROMAE APVD IOANNEM FRANCISCIVM VVLGO DELLA GATTA — 367 × 550 mm.

[31] [C:] Anthonius Wied candido lectori S. MOSCOVIA quę & Alba Russia nō cōtenta Europę Sarmatię parte ... Vale ex Wilda Lithuaniæ anno 1555 Cal: Nouemb: — [C:] Fransiscus Hogenb: ex vero sculpsit 1570. — 342 × 475 mm.

[33] [T:] PERPIGNIAN CARCASONA NERBONA. — [T:] E. V. 1542. — 223 × 331 mm.

[34] [C:] S. QVINTINO. — [T:] Gallorum strages die X Augusti Expugnatio Vrbis die XXVII eiusdem. M D LVII. — 337 × 438 mm.

[35] [C:] BOLOGNA IN FRANCIA. — 292 × 444 mm.

[36] [C:] GOTTA. — In dem Jar 1567 den 25 Thag Januarij wart die gewaltige vestung Das Schloss Grimmenstein, Und die Statt Gotta belegert von Dem Haÿligen Ro: Prÿch vnd war Oberster veldtherr, Herrzog Augustus Churfuſt in Saxen, wardt auffgeben den 13 Mo Aprilij Mathias Zyndt. 260 × 361 mm.

[37] [C:] GVINES. — [C:] RITRATTO DELLA FORTEZZA di Ghines, presa per forza dallo essercito del Re Christianissimo. ... — 336 × 443 mm.

[38] [C:] Eccouj amants.mi lectorj il uero sito della Battaglia data nel Anno 1558. a di 13 di luglio intorno a Grauellina infra l'Campo de Philippo Re di Spagna, et di Inghliterra & et Henricho Re di Francia; ... — 296 × 430 mm.

[39] [T:] ANTVVERPIÆ CIVITATIS BELGICÆ TOTO ORBE COGNITI ET CELEBRATI EMPORII SIMVLACRVM. — (Plan). 326 × 437 mm.

[40] [T:] INGOLSTAD — [C:] Il VERO DESENG̃O VENVTO VLTIMAMENTE DE GERMANIA DE LE TRINCERE DEL CAMPO CESARIO ET DE LANGRAVIO — [C:] TOM.B. — 288 × 430 mm.

[41] [T:] AVGVSTA VLMA REIN NEVNBVRG INGELSTAD — [C:] IL DISEGNO DEL PAESE DOVE SE TROVANO I DVE ESERCITI DE SWA MAIESTA CESAREA ET DE LANGRAVIO CON LA DESCRITTI ON E DELLE CITTA ET FIVMI VICINI VENVTO CON

LE VLTIME LETTERE — [T:] TOMASSO. B. — 263 × 364 mm.

[42] [C:] VERISSIMO RETRATTO DELLI SITI ET LVOGHI DELLE PARTE DAVSTRIA ET VNGARIA CONLI NOMI DELLI FIVMI, PONTI, CITTA, ET, CASTELLE, DOVE NELANNO MDXXXII DEL MESE DI SEPTEMBRE, SE TROVAVA ... DAR LA BATTAGLIA, A, SOLYMANO RE DE TVRCHI,... — [T:] 1532 A. V. — [T:] Ant. Sal. exc. — 262 × 343 mm.

[43] [T:] BVDA. — [T:] E. V. 1542. — 290 × 405 mm.

[44] [T:] CIVITELLA. — [An empty cartouche]. 300 × 385 mm.

[45] [T:] VICOVARO. — [C:] IL VERO DISEGNO DI VICOVARO OCCVPATO DA IMPERIALI ET RECVPERATO DALLA CHIESA A DI XIIII FEBRARO. ∞ Đ.LVII. — [T:] Sebastianus f. — (Plan). 272 × 391 mm.

[46] [C:] IL VERO DISEGNO DEL SITO DI HOSTIA E, DI PORTO CON LI FORTI FATTI DAL CAMPO DI SVA SANTITA ET DELLI IMPERIALI QVALI SI RESERO ADI XXIIII GENNARO M.D.L.VII — 253 × 390 mm.

[47] [C:] ILLVSTRISS. ATQ. INTEGERRIMO OCTAVIO FARNESIO PLACENTIAE ET PARMAE DVCI FRANCISCVS PACIOTTVS VRBNAT MAECENATI. S. VRBIS ROMAE FORMAM ... EX TYPIS ET DILIGENTIA ANT LAFRERI SEQVANI AN ∞ Đ. LVII. ... — [C:] NB — (Plan). 467 × 527 mm.

[48] [T:] Vero disegno de la Mirandola con le citta casteli uille et poste nel suo sito. — [T:] A: S: EX. — (Plan). 405 × 308 mm.

[49] [T:] GENOA. — (View). 243 × 406 mm.

[50] [T:] TRIPOLI Città di Barbaria, ... — (Plan). 296 × 430 mm.

Notes: All the maps are blank on the back and uncoloured. The initials E.V., on maps [33] and [43], stand for Enea Vico; 'Ant. Sal.' and A.S. on maps [42] and [48] indicate Antonio Salamanca; and 'Sebastianus' on map [95] refers to Sebastiano di Re. Pasted on the inside of the back cover is a letter from M.A. Thury offering this volume for sale. It states that the collection was put together in Poland in 1570. Nordenskiöld purchased it through Gerhard & Hey of St Petersburg in November 1894. His signature is in the volume with the date Jan. 1895. There are several names written on the inside of the front cover, with early dates: 1574 Jeronimi L Anskoninsky Zbrezra na Wlodzyslawn Pogrzebon Krol Segismint August obranij Przijefal Do Crakowa Hinrih Obrani Korunowoni Anno 1575 Anno 1585 Anno domini 1601. The atlas is bound in old leather, and it is in bad condition.

Lit.: Bagrow, Geschichte, p. 161 and 362, Leithäuser p. 380.

49 [Collection of Dutch maps, without title-page.] 1624—1626
41,3 cm.

[1] [C:] NOVA HISPANIÆ DESCRIPTIO — [C:] Excusum in ædibus Iudoci Hondij Amsterodami in platea quæ dicitur de Calverstrate sub Cane Vigilanti. — 415 × 551 mm.
[Insets:] [T:] Alhama — [T:] Granada — [T:] Bilbao — [T:] Burgos — [T:] Veliz Malaga — [T:] Eçia — 6 oval views 26 × 85 mm. [T:] LISBONA — [T:] TOLEDO — [T:] SIVILIA — [T:] VALLA DOLID — 4 oval views 41 × 120 mm.

[2] [C:] DANIAE REGNI TYPUM Potentissimo, Invictissimoq₃ D. Christiano Daniæ, Norvegiæ, Gotthorum Vandalorum Regi, lubens offert Nicolaus Johann Piscator. — [T:] Abraham Goos schulp. — [C:] Claes Ianss Visscher excudit. — 448 × 543 mm.
[Insets:] [T:] COPPENHAGEN — [T:] ELSENOR — [T:] LANTSKROON — [T:] RIPEN — [T:] SLESWYCK — [T:] HAMBURGH — [T:] LUBECK — [T:] OLDENBORGH — 8 oval views 47 × 92 mm.

[3] [C:] DUCATUS HOLSATIÆ, SUMMÂ DILIGENTIÂ ACCURATÂQ₃ CENSURÂ NOVITER EDITUS, À Nicolao Iohannide Piscatore. — [T:] Abrahamum Goos sculpsit — 442 × 545 mm.
[Insets:] [C:] Alluvies propè Detzbul, Incolis Inferioris Germaniæ, a Duce Holsatiæ concessa aggeribus cingi. Aenwas bij Detzbul den Nederlanders geconsenteert te bedijcken van den Hartoch van Holsteyn. — 103 × 128 mm. [C:] Tabula Barmerensis, Meggerensis, et Noortstaepplerensis maris: ... — 104 × 128 mm. [T:] SLESWYCK — (View). Oval 35 × 91 mm. [T:] FLENSBORCH — (View). Oval 35 × 91 mm. [T:] HUSUM — (View). 35 × 56 mm. [T:] TONNINGEN — (View). 35 × 56 mm. [T:] RENSBORG — (View). 35 × 56 mm. [T:] KIEL — (View). 35 × 56 mm. [C:] VREDERYCKSTAT — (Plan). 35 × 52 mm. [T:] ITZEHOA — (View). 35 × 56 mm. [T:] CREMPE — (View). 35 × 56 mm.

[4] [C:] NOVA TOTIUS WESTPHALIÆ DESCRIPTIO, ex celeberrimis, et varijs Autoribus, in unam tabulam redacta, per Nicolaum Janssonium Visscher, aut Piscatorem. 1626. — 592 × 540 mm.

[5] [C:] POMERANIÆ DVCATVS TABVLA. Auctore Eilhardo Lubino. — [C:] ... AMSTELODAMI, Iudocus Hondius excudit. — [T:] S.Rogiers sculpsit. — 378 × 494 mm.

[6] [C:] INFERIOR GERMANIA ... — 409 × 553 mm.

[7] [C:] AVSTRIA ARCHIDVCATUS NOVA DESCRIPTIO. Anno .1625. — [C:] Petrus Kærius Cælavit. — [T:] Abrahamus Janssonius Excu. — 380 × 508 mm.
[Insets:] [T:] PASSAW — [T:] LINCZ — [T:] WIEN — [T:] PRESBURG — 4 oval views 45 × 106 mm.

[8] [C:] SAXONIAE superioris LVSATIAE MISNIÆQVE descriptio — [T:] Per Gerardum Mercatorem... — 348 × 488 mm.

[9] [C:] SAXONIA INFERIOR ET MEKLENBORG DVC. — [T:] Per Gerardum Mercatorem ... — 341 × 446 mm.

[10] [C:] HASSIA landtgrauiatus. — [T:] Per Gerardum Mercatorem... — 345 × 417 mm.

[11] [C:] FRANCKENLANDT. Francia orientalis. — [T:] Per Gerardum Mercatorem... — 339 × 500 mm.

[12] [C:] MONASTERIENSIS Episcopatus. — [C:] Judocus Hondius excudit. — 370 × 491 mm.

[13] [C:] PADERBORNENSIS Episcopatus DESCRIPTIO NOVA Ioanne Gigante Ludense D. Med. et Math. auth. — [C:] Amstelodami Judocus Hondius excudit. — 373 × 491 mm.

[14] [C:] TYPVS Frisiæ Orientalis à Dullarto sinu, atq₃ amasi ostio ad Iada usq₃ fl. singulari studio ac industria concinat'et ad vivum expressᵒ Authore vbbone — [T:] Visscher excudebat. 1624. — 393 × 501 mm.
[Inset:] [C:] EMBDEN — (Plan). 157 × 150 mm.

[15] [C:] DUCATUUM LIVONIÆ, et CURLANDIÆ. Nova Tabula, descripta, Divisa, et edita per F. de Witt Amstelodami ... — Coloured. 412 × 499 mm.

[16] [C:] Hæc Tabula nova POLONIÆ et SILESIÆ, Sigismondo Tertio, dei Gratia Regi Poloniæ, Magno Duci Lithuaniæ, Russiæ, Borussiæ, Masoviæ, Samogetarum, Livoniæ, nec non Suecorum, Gotthorum Hæriditario Regi D.D.D. a Nicolao Johannide Piscatore. — [C:] Impressa in ædibus Nicolaij Iohannis Visscher. — [T:] Sculptum apud AGoos. — 462 × 526 mm.
[Insets:] [T:] CRACOVIA — [T:] DANTZICK — 2 oval views 45 × 175 mm. [T:] POSNA — [T:] CROSSEN — [T:] SANDOMIRIA — [T:] BRESLAW — 4 oval views 25 × 82 mm.

[17] [C:] TURCICI IMPERII IMAGO. — 355 × 478 mm.

[18] [C:] NOVA AFRICÆ TABULA AUCTORE Jodoco Hondio — [T:] Excusum in ædibus Auctoris Amsterodammi — 370 × 500 mm.

[19] [C:] ASIÆ NOVA Descriptio Auctore Jodoco Hondio ... Excusum in ædibus auctoris. — 370 × 497 mm.

[20] [C:] AMERICA — [T:] Jodocus Hondius excudit Amsterodami — 371 × 496 mm.

[21] [C:] BRABANTIA DUCATUS MACHLINIÆ URBIS DOMINIUM — [C:] Petrus Kærius cælavit — 345 × 498 mm.

[Insets:] [T:] MECHELEN — [T:] ANTWERPEN — [T:] Toff van Brussel — Oval views 40 × 50 mm. [C:] MACHLINIÆ URBIS DOMINIUM — 45 × 56 mm.

Notes: All the maps are blank on the back and uncoloured, except map [15], which is slightly coloured. Most of the maps are in a bad state of preservation, with parts missing from maps [2], [3], [4] and [16]. In the cartouche of map [14] the author's name, Emmio [Emmius], has been erased. There are portraits on some of the maps: [1] PHILIPPUS, III REX HISPAN.; [2] CHRISTIANUS IV. D.G. DANIÆ ET NORVEGIAE REX DUX SLESW. STORM. and FREDER. CHRISTIAN. HÆRES NORVEG. CHRISTIANI IIII REX DANIÆ FILIUS etc.; [16] SIGISMUNDUS. III., STEPHANUS.I. and SIGISMUNDUS II (one portrait missing); and [17] SULTAN MAHUMET TURCORUM IMPERAT. The volume is bound in old vellum. An index to the volume is written in old ink on the verso of the blank leaf at the beginning: according to this there should be 22 maps, but map 22 [Acies & pugna Wahlhassiana.] is missing. On the same leaf is an illegible signature with the date 1822, and beneath that 'Skara 1828. Nordenskiöld's signature is on the inside of the front cover, with the note: Köpt 1884 hos Klemmings antiquariat som köpt samlingen hos fru Pettersson på Järfva. [Bought 1884 at Klemming's antiquarian bookshop, as a collection formerly belonging to Mrs. Pettersson in Järfva.]

50 [**Collection of Dutch maps, without title-page.**]   1629—1659
                                                                46,3 cm.

[1] [T:] NOVA TOTIVS TERRARVM ORBIS GEOGRAPHICA AC HYDROGRAPHICA TABVLA. Auct: Henr: Hondio. — [T:] Amstelodami Excudit Ioannes Ianssonius. — [C:] Doctissimis Ornatissimisq₃ Viris D.D. Davidi Sanclaro, Antonio de Willon, et D.Martinio, Matheseos in illustriss. Academia Parisiensi Professoribus eximiis in veræ amicitiæ μνημόσυνον [mnēmósunon] D.D. Henr. Hondius A.⁰ 1641 — 378 × 535 mm. The hemisphere with 280 mm. diam.

[2] [C:] CARTE GENERALE DES DIX ET SEPT PROVINCES DES Pays bas. — 364 × 508 mm.

[3] [C:] NOVA EVROPAE DESCRIPTIO. — [C:] Joannes Ianssonius Excudit. — 411 × 552 mm.
[Insets:] [T:] LISBONA — (View). [T:] TOLEDO — (View). [T:] LONDON — (Plan). [T:] PARIS — (Plan). [T:] ROMA — (Plan). [T:] Venetia — (Plan). All 9 oval 40 × 89 mm.

[4] [C:] ASIA noviter delineata Auctore Guiljelmo Blaeuw. — 407 × 549 mm.
[Insets:] [T:] CANDY — (Plan). [T:] CALECVTH — (View). [T:] GOA — (Plan). [T:] DAMASCO — (Plan). [T:] IERVSALEM — (Plan). [T:] ORMVS — (View). [T:] BANTAM — (Plan). [T:] ADEN — (View). [T:] MACAO — (View). All 9 oval 41 × 57 mm.

[5] [C:] AFRICÆ nova descriptio. Auct: Guiljelmo Blaeuw. — 410 × 553 mm.
[Insets:] [T:] TANGER — (Plan). [T:] CEVTA — (View). [T:] ALGER — (Plan). [T:] TVNIS — (Plan). [T:] ALEXANDRIA — (Plan). [T:] ALCAIR — (Plan). [T:] MOZAMBIQVE — (Plan). [T:] S.GEORGIVS della MINA — (View). [T:] CANARIA — (View). All 9 ova 41 × 57 mm.

[6] [C:] AMERICÆ nova Tabula. Auct: Guiljelmo Blaeuw. — 406 × 549 mm.
[Insets:] [T:] HAVANA Portus — (View). [T:] Sᵗ DOMINGO. — (Plan). [T:] CARTAGENA. — (Plan). [T:] MEXICO — (Plan). [T:] CUSCO. — (Plan). [T:] POTOSI — (View). [T:] I. LA MOCHA in Chili. — (View). [T:] RIO IANEIRO. — (View). [T:] OLINDA in Pharnambucco — (View). — 9 oval 41 × 57 mm. [C:] Septentrionalissimas Americæ partes, Groenlandiam puta, Islandiã et adjacentes, quod Americæ tabulæ commodé comprehendi non potuerint, peculiari hac tabella Spectatoribus exhibendas duximus. — 70 × 76 mm.

[7] [C:] Magnæ BRITANNIÆ et HIBERNIÆ TABULA. — [C:] Amstelodami Ex Officina et sumptibus Henrici Hondij. A.⁰ Domini 1631. — 377 × 504 mm.
[Inset:] [T:] Orcades Insulæ — 50 × 66 mm.

[8] [C:] Nova et accurata Tabula HISPANIÆ Præcipuis Urbibus Vestitu Insignibus, et Antiquitatibus exornata per Cornelium Dankerum. — 400 × 552 mm.
[Insets:] [T:] BARCELONA. — [T:] MADRID. — [T:] MONAST. S.LAVRENT in Escurial. — [T:] SEVILLA — [T:] LIXBONA — [T:] VALLADOLID. — 6 oval views 40 × 85 mm.

[9] [C:] GALLIÆ, Nova et accurata descriptio Vulgo ROYAVME DE FRANCE. — [T:] Amstelodami Apud Joannem Janssonium — 445 × 559 mm.

[10] [C:] Nova Totius GERMANIÆ DESCRIPTIO. — 440 × 520 mm.

[11] [T:] LEO BELGICVS — [C:] MICHAELIS Aitsingeri Austriaci ad leonem pro lectore introductio ... — 364 × 443 mm.

[12] [C:] COMITATVS HOLLANDIÆ novissima descriptio Designatore Balthazaro Florentio a Berckenrode. Anno Domini 1629. ... AMSTELODAMI, Sumptibus Henrici Hondii habitantis in Damo ad intersigne Atlantis. — [T:] Salomon Rogiers sculpsit — [C:] Clarissimis, Magnificis, Prudentissimisq₃ D.D.Prætori, Consulibus cæterisq₃ Senatorib⁹ Reipub. Amstelodamensis, hanc accuratissimam Hollandiæ tabulam de novo in lucem editam, lubens meritoq₃ dat, dicat, dedicat consecratq₃ Humill. Cl. vest. Henricus Hondius. — 393 × 508 mm.
[Inset:] [C:] d'Eÿlanden Texel, Vlielandt en der Schelling. — 98 × 161 mm.

[13] [C:] ZEELANDIA Comitatus. — [C:] Magnifico Amplissimo Doctissimoq₃ Viro D. SIMONI BELLIMONTIO Reipub. Middelburgensis Syndico, et in Potent.ᵒʳᵘᵐ Ord. Gener. Belg. Fœderatæ Consessu nomine Ordinum Zeelandiæ Assessori, nuper ad Poloniæ et Suecia Reges Legato D.D. C. Dankerio. — [T:] Cornelis Danckerts Excudit. — 397 × 503 mm.

[14] [C:] MAXIMI TOTIUS EUROPÆ FLUMINIS DANUBII CURSUS PER GERMANIAM HUNGARIAMQUE Nova Delineatio. Amstelodami, Sumpt. Ioannis Ianssonii. — [Divided into two parts].   447 × 514 mm.

[15] [C:] TOTIUS RHENI, ab eius capitibus ad Oceanũ usque Germanicum in quem se exonerat novissima descriptio. Auctore Henrico Hondio ... Amstelodami Sumptibus Ioannis Ianssonii. — [T:] Petrus Kærius Cælavit. — [C:] Doctrina et humanitate celebri Viro D. Ioachimo a Wickefoort Vrbis Amstelodamensis Mercatori Fidelissimo in beneuolentiæ testimonium dedicabat Henricus Hondius 1641 — [Divided into two parts].   447 × 517 mm.

[16] [C:] HELVETIA, cum finitimis regionibus confœderatis. — [T:] Describebat Gerard' Mercator, et excudebat Guiljelmus Blaeu. — 385 × 498 mm.

[17] [C:] BAVARIÆ Superioris et Inferioris nova descriptio. — [C:] Amstelodami Excudebat Ioannes Ianssonius — 380 × 462 mm.

[18] [C:] AVSTRIA ARCHIDVCATVS auctore Wolfgango Lazio — [C:] AMSTELODAMI Guiljelmus Blaeuw excudit. — 362 × 538 mm.

[19] [C:] HVNGARIA REGNVM. — [T:] Amsterdami Apud Iohannem Ianssonium. — 420 × 510 mm.

[20] [C:] NOVA ET ACCURATA TRANSYLVANIÆ DESCRIPTIO — [T:] AMSTELODAMI, Apud Ioannem Ianssonium. — 389 × 492 mm.

[21] [C:] POLONIA Regnum, et SILESIA Ducatus. — [T:] Guiljelmus Blaeu excudit. — 411 × 503 mm.

[22] [C:] DANIAE REGNI TYPUS — [C:] AMSTELODAMI, Apud Danckerum Danckerts. Anno 1657. — 380 × 491 mm.

[23] [C:] TABVLÆ ITALIÆ Corsicæ, Sardiniæ, et

adjacentium Regnorum. Nova et accurata delineatio Edita per IOANNEM IANSSONIVM. Amsterod A⁰ 1659. — [T:] Illustriss. Antiquissimæq₃ Reipublicæ Venetæ, hanc Novam et bene sculptā Italiæ totius Tabulam dicat, donat, consecrat. Ioannes Iansonius. — 458 × 540 mm.
[Insets:] [T:] ROMA — (View). [T:] NAPOLI — (View). [T:] VENETIA — (View). [T:] FIORENZA — (View). [T:] GENOVA — (View). [T:] VERONA — (View). [T:] PARMA — (Plan). [T:] SIENA — (View). [T:] POSSVOLO — (View). [T:] VELIITRI — (View). All 10 oval 40 × 62 mm.

[24] [C:] STATO DELLA CHIESA, CON LA TOSCANA. — [C:] ... Guiljelmus Blaeu excudit. — 382 × 498 mm.

[25] [C:] HELLAS seu GRÆCIA VNIVERSA. AUTORE J. Laurenbergio. — 466 × 568 mm.

[26] [T:] PALESTINA, SIUE TERRÆ SANCTÆ DESCRIPTIO — [C:] Amstelodami excudebat Joannes Joanssonius — 434 × 566 mm.
[Inset:] [T:] Ierusalem — (View). 54 × 65 mm.

[27] [C:] Doctrina et humanitate prædito D. Isaaco Bernart, rerum quæ per Moscoviam maxime trahuntur mercatori peritissimo, hanc Moscoviæ tabulā dedicat affinis suus Hen. Hondius. NOVISSIMA RUSSIÆ TABULA Authore Isaaco Massa. — [T:] Amstelodami sumptibus Ioannis Ianssonii. — 468 × 553 mm.

[28] [C:] MOSCOVIÆ PARS AVSTRALIS Auctore Isaaco Massa. — 381 × 502 mm.

[29] [C:] PERSIA Sive SOPHORVM REGNVM — [C:] Ampliss.ᵐᵒ Prudentiss.q³ . Viro D. THEODORO THOLING, Reip. Amstelod. Senatori et Collegii Scabinorum Præsidi, nec non in Consessu Societatis Indicæ Orientalis adsessori, Tabulam hanc D.D. Guiljelmus Blaeu. 1634. — 376 × 495 mm.

[30] [C:] TVRCICVM IMPERIVM — [T:] Sumpt: Ioannis Ianssonii, Priori multo accuratior ac emendatior. — 410 × 520 mm.

Notes: All the maps are blank on the back and uncoloured. Most of them appear also in the Blaeu, Janssonius and Mercator atlases in the Nordenskiöld collection. They are therefore described by Koeman, but there are some differences between our maps and those he describes. Map [3], for example, is described by Koeman Me 69:168* as being by Hondius, but the name does not appear on our copy; the imprint on his example is 'Ex officina et sumptibus Ioannis Ianssonij', on ours 'Joannes Ianssonius Excudit'. The river maps, [14] and [15], are new editions of Koeman's Me 35:296 and Me 35:295, with the imprint changed from Hondius to Janssonius. Map [20] is a later state of Koeman's Me 41A:75, without Mercator's name and with a coat-of-arms added in the upper right-hand corner. Map [27] is Koeman's Me 47:349*, but with an imprint not mentioned by him. Map [28] is another state of the map in our copy of Blaeu 1647—1649:I:[9], Koeman Bl 33:284*, the text in the cartouche being that described in Koeman Me 44:417. Map [30] is Koeman's Me 50:482 but with a slightly altered imprint. Our copy of the map in Janssonius 1645:III:[60] bears the same imprint as Koeman's example. Map [11], Michael Aitsinger's Leo Belgicus, was first published in 1583, with new editions appearing in 1584, 1585 and 1586. On our copy the arms of the Holy Roman Empire, with the name 'Anna', have been inserted below the Lion's tongue, and the arms of France, with the name 'Elizabeth', on its left hind foot. (See Tooley, Leo Belgicus.) Map [25] also appears in our copy of Blaeu's Atlas Major 1662:II:[37], with the name N. Visscher. Map [1] has portraits in the corners: IVLIVS CÆSAR, CLAVDIVS PTOLEMÆVS ALE:, GERARDVS MERCATOR Flander, and IODOCVS HONDIVS Flander. The only traces of a title for this collection can be deciphered on the spine of the volume, which has been damaged by water: TABUL... GEOG ... AC HYDEO ... On the first blank leaf there is a note in old ink: $\frac{1648}{IX}$. Nordenskiöld's signature is on the same leaf.

Lit.: Koeman vol. 1—2, Tooley, Leo Belgicus, An illustrated list.

51 **[Collection of French maps, without title-page.]** 1693—1746
56,4 cm

[1] [C:] NOUVELLE CARTE Qui Comprend les principaux Triangles qui servent de Fondement à la Description Géométrique de la FRANCE Levée par ordre du Roy. Par Messʳˢ Maraldi & Cassini de Thury, de l'Académie Royale des Sciences. Année 1744. — [T:] Tracé d'apres les Mesures, et gravé par Dheulland — [T:] Aubin Scripsit — A PARIS sur le Quay de l'Horloge, en la maison de feu Mʳ Delisle: ... Uncoloured. 570 × 897 mm.

[2] [C:] LE ROYAUME DE FRANCE distingué suivant l'Estendue de TOUTES SES PROVINCES ET SES ACQUISITIONS dans L'ESPAGNE dans L'ITALIE dans L'ALLEMAGNE et dans LES PAYS BAS Par le Sʳ SANSON, Geographe Ordinaire du Roy DEDIÉ AU ROY. Par son tres humble tres Obeissant, tres fidele, Sujet, et Seruiteur HUBERT IAILLOT, Geographe Ordinaire de sa Majesté — [C:] ... A Paris Chez H.Iaillot ... 1724 — [T:] Cordier Sculpsit — 454 × 641 mm.

[3] [C:] LE ROYAUME DE FRANCE et ses Païs circonvoisins Jusqu'à l'Etendue de L'Ancienne Gaule, Par les Sᴿˢ SANSON Géographe odr. du Roi. reveu et assujetti aux Observations Astronomiques Par le Sᴿ ROBERT Géog. ord.du Roi 1742. — [C:] ... A Paris chés le Sieur ROBERT ... — [T:] Delahaye sculpsit. — 495 × 676 mm.

[4] [C:] LE ROYAUME DE FRANCE dressé sur les memoires et nouvelles observations de Messieurs de l'Academie Royalle des Sciences; DIVISÉ EN TOUTES SES GENERALITEZ ET SES ACQUISITIONS. ... [T:] C.Simonneau f. — [C:] ... A PARIS Chez l'Auteur, le Sʳ IAILLOT, ... 1717 — [C:] Cordier Sculpsit — 664 × 887 mm.

[5] [C:] NOUVELLE CARTE DES POSTES DE FRANCE PAR ORDRE ET DEDIÉE a son Altesse Serenissime MONSEIGNEUR LE DUC Par son tres humble et tres obeissant Serviteur Bernard Jaillot Geographe ordinaire du Roy Corrigée et augmentée le Iᵉʳ Janvier 1738. — [C:] A PARIS Chez le Sʳ Jaillot ... 1726 — 512 × 647 mm.

[6] [C:] DEDIÉ A SON ALTESSE ROYALE MONSEIGNEUR LE DUC D'ORLEANS. Regent du Royaume. Par son tres humble et tres obeissant Serviteur B.JAILLOT, Geographe du ROY. — PARTIE DE LA PICARDIE, DE L'ARTOIS ET DE LA FLANDRES, ou sont les Villes de CALAIS, ARDRES, BOULOGNE, MONSTREUIL, RHUE, HESDIN, ARRAS, LENS, BETHUNE, AIRE, Sᵀ OMER, GRAVELINE, BOURBOURG, DONKERKE, BERGUE, FURNES, NIEUPORT, IPRES, CASSEL et LA BASSÉE. Par le Sʳ JAILLOT Geographe Ordinaire du Roy A PARIS Chez l'Auteur ... 405 × 557 mm.

[7] [C:] GOUVERNEMENT GENERAL DE PICARDIE qui comprend LA GENERALITÉ D'AMIENS divisée en ses Huit Elections. Avec L'ARTOIS, ET LES FRONTIERES DES PAYS BAS. Dréssé sur les Memoires lē plus Nouveaux Par le Sʳ Jaillot Geographe du Roy. — PARTIE DE LA FLANDRE, ET DU HAYNAUT, ou sont les Villes de DIXMUDE, IPRES, LILLE, DOUAY, COURTRAY, TOURNAY, OUDENARDE, GAND, DENDERMONDE, MONS, VALENCIENNES, CONDÉ, Sᵀ GUISLAIN, ATH, LE QUESNOY, et MAUBEUGE. Par le Sʳ JAILLOT Geographe ordinaire du Roy. A Paris ... 406 × 562 mm.

[8] LES ELECTIONS D'AMIENS, D'ABBEVILLE, DE DOURLENS, DE MONDIDIER ET PARTIE DE CELLE DE PERONE DANS LA GENERALITÉ D'AMIENS par le Sʳ JAILLOT Geographe ordinaire du Roy, A PARIS Chez l'Auteur ... 407 × 558 mm.

[9] L'ELECTION DE Sᵀ QUENTIN PARTIE DE CELLE DE PERONE DANS LA GENERALITÉ D'AMIENS AVEC LES ELECTIONS DE GUISE, DE LAON ET DE NOYON DANS LA GENERALITÉ DE SOISSONS. par le Sʳ JAILLOT Geographe ordinaire du Roy, A PARIS Chez l'Auteur ...
[C:] ... A PARIS Chez le Sʳ JAILLOT Geographe du Roy, ... 1717. — 407 × 560 mm.

[10] [C:] LE GOUVERNEMENT GENERAL DE NORMANDIE DIVISÉE EN SES TROIS GÉNÉRALITEZ, Sçavoir ROÜEN, CAEN ERT ALENÇON et Subdivisée en ses Trente deux Electioss. Dressée sur les Memoires les plus Nouveaux Dédiée a S.A.R. MONSEIGNEUR LE DUC D'ORLEANS REGENT DU ROYAUME Par son tres humble et tres obeissant Serviteur B. Jaillot Geographe du Roy. — [C:] P. Starck-man Sculpsit. — [C:] ... A Paris chez l'Auteur ... 1719. — [Part I]. 682 × 511 mm.

[11] [NORMANDIE] [Part II]. 683 × 516 mm.
[Inset:] [C:] LES ISLES ANGLOISES, Dans leur Juste position par raport a la Coste Occidentalle du Coutantin. ... — 199 × 180 mm.

[12] [C:] CARTE du GOUVERNEMENT MILITAIRE de L'ISLE de FRANCE. Dressée Sur les Memoires des Meilleurs Auteurs Suivant les Observations Astronomiques. Par le S^r. Janvier. A PARIS Chéz le S^r. J.B.Nolin ... 1746. Gravée par Chambon — [C:] Le GOUVERNEMENT MILITAIRE de L'ISLE DE FRANCE Dedié et Presenté a Monseigneur le Duc de Gesvres ... Par son tres humble et tres obéissant serviteur JANVIER. — 438 × 548 mm.

[13] [C:] LA GENERALITE' DE PARIS DIVISÉE EN SES ESLECTIONS. DÉDIÉE A MESSIRE IEAN IACQUES CHARRON ... Par son tres-humble et tres affectioñé Seruiteur A.H.IAILLOT, Geographe du Roy — [T:] S.f. — [C:] A Paris, Chez l'Autheur ... 1708. — 417 × 650 mm.

[14] [T:] Partie Septentrionale de la Generalité de Paris. — LE GOUVERNEMENT GENERAL DE L'ISLE DE FRANCE, Par le S^r. IAILLOT, Geographe Ordinaire du Roy. A PARIS, ... 1708 416 × 647 mm.

[15] [C:] LA GENERALITÉ DE SOISSONS Divisée en Sept Elections SCAVOIR SOISSONS LAON NOYON CRESPY CLERMONT GUISE en Picardie. CHATEAU = THIERY en Brie. Dressée sur les Nouvelles observations. Par le S^r. JAILLOT Geographe ord.^{re} du Roi. — [C:] A PARIS chez l'Auteur ... — [C:] ... 1723. — 497 × 647 mm.

[16] [C:] GOUVERNEMENT GENERAL DE CHAMPAGNE. ou sont diviseés LES ESLECTIONS, DE LA GENERALITÉ DE CHAALONS et celles qui sont partie DES GENERALITÉS DE PARIS, et DE SOISSONS PRESENTÉ A MONSEIGNEUR LE DAUPHIN Par son tres humble, tres obeissant, et tres-fidele Seruiteur HUBERT IAILLOT — [C:] ... A PARIS Chez H.IAILLOT, Geographe Ordinaire du Roy ... 1717. — 369 × 550 mm.

[17] [T:] PARTIE MERIDIONALE DE CHAMPAGNE, dans laquelle sont divisées les ESLECTIONS que comprennent les GENERALITÉZ DE PARIS et DE CHAALONS. A PARIS, Chez l'Autêur le S^r. IAILLOT, Geographe du Roy ... — 406 × 548 mm.

[18] 1. LE VERDUNOIS OU SONT LES PREVOTEZ DEPENDANS DU BALLIAGE DE L'EVESCHÉ DE VERDUN, ET DE SON CHAPITRE. PARTIE DU BARROIS DUCAL, OU BALLIAGE DE S^T. MIHEL, DANS LE DUCHÉ DE BAR, LES TERRES ADJACENTES DU CLERMONTOIS, DE STENAY, DUN et IAMETZ, &c. Par le S^r. IAILLOT, Geographe ordinaire du Roy 17 4 454 × 695 mm.

[19] 2. LE PAYS MESSIN, PARTIE DU TEMPOREL DE L'EVESCHÉ DE METZ. ET PARTIE DU BALLIAGE ALLEMAND, DANS LE DUCHÉ DE LORRAINE DIVISEZ PAR CHATELLENIES, PREVOTEZ, &c. par le S^r. IAILLOT, Geographe ordinaire du Roy.
[C:] LES ESTATS, DU DUC DE LORRAINE ou sont LES DUCHEZ DE LORRAINE et DE BAR. LE TEMPOREL DES EVESCHEZ DE METZ, TOUL ET VERDUN DEDIÉ AU ROY Par son tres humble, tres-obeissant, tres-fidele sujet et Serviteur HUBERT JAILLOT, Geographe ordinaire de Sa Majesté — 454 × 696 mm.

[20] 3. LE TOULOIS OU SONT LES CHATELLENIES et LES PREVOTÉS DU TEMPOREL DE L'EVECHÉ DE TOUL et de son CHAPITRE: PARTIE DU BALLIAGE DE L'EVÉCHÉ DE VERDUN. LE DUCHÉ DE BARROIS OU BALLIAGE DE BARLEDUC, et PARTIE DU BASSIGNY, DU BARROIS DUCAL ou BALLIAGE DE S^T. MIHEL dans le Duché de Bar, DU BALLIAGE DE NANCY dans le Duché de Lorraine: et LES TERRES ADJACENTES DE HATTONCHATEL, D'ASPREMONT, DE VAUDEMONT et DE COMMERCY. Par le S^r. IAILLOT, Geographe Ordinaire du Roy. 450 × 696 mm.

[21] 4. PARTIE MERIDIONALE DU TEMPOREL DE L'EVESCHÉ DE METZ; ET PARTIES DES BALLIAGES DE NANCY ET ALLEMAND, DANS LE DUCHÉ DE LORRAINE, DIVISEZ PAR CHATELLENIES, OFFICES, PREVOTEZ &c. LES TERRES ADJACENTES DE BLANMONT, DE SALME, DE SARBOURG, DE BICHE, &c. Par le S^r. IAILLOT, Geographe ordinaire du Roy 452 × 694 mm.

[22] 5. PARTIE DU BALLIAGE DE VOSGE ou DE MIRECOUR, DANS LE DUCHÉ DE LORRAINE PARTIE DU BALLIAGE DE BASSIGNY ou BARROIS MOUVANT DANS LE DUCHÉ DE BAR DIVISEZ PAR PREVÔTEZ, OFFICES, SENES CHAUSSÉES; ET AUTRES SUBDIVISIONS, OU SONT EXACTEMENT REMARQUÉES LES ENCLAVES ET DE QUI ELLES DEPENDENT. Par le S^r. IAILLOT Geographe ordinaire du Roy. 451 × 698 mm.

[23] 6. LES PREVOTEZ, OFFICES, SENÉCHAUSSÉE et COMTÉ, QUI FONT PARTIE DES BALLIAGES DE VOSGE ou MIRECOUR et DE NANCY, DANS LE DUCHÉ DE LORRAINE, LES TERRES ADJACENTES D'EPINAL, DE CHATÉ &c ET LES SOURCES DES RIVIERES DE LA MOSELLE, DE LA MEURTHE, DE MORTAGNE, DE VELOGNE &c DANS LES MONTAGNES DE VOSGES. Par le S^r. IAILLOT Geographe ordinaire du Roy.
[C:] ... A PARIS, Chez le S^r. IAILLOT, Geographe du Roy... Corrigé et Augmenté en 1743. — 452 × 699 mm.

[24] [C:] L'ALSACE DIVISÉE EN SES PRINCIPALES PARTIES SÇAVOIR LES LANDGRAVIATS DE LA HAUTE, ET BASSE ALSACE ET LE SUNTGAW. Par le S^r. SANSON Geographe Ordinaire du Roy. A PARIS Chez le S^r. IAILLOT, Geographe de Sa Majesté ... 1700. — [T:] S. f. — [T:] Cordier, Sculpsit — 649 × 456 mm.

[25] LE COMTÉ DE BOURGOGNE, ou LA FRANCHE COMTÉ, DIVISÉ EN TROIS GRANDS BALLIAGES, SÇAVOIR D'AMONT, D'AVAL, et DU MILIEU ou DE DOLE SUBDIVISÉS EN LEURS BALLIAGES, et IURIDICTIONS SUBALTERNES. LE COMTÉ DE MONBELIART. &c. Conquise par le Roy, pour la deusiesmefois en l'Année. 1674, et Reünie a sa Couronne par la Paix de Nimeque en l'Année. 1678 a Paris ... 1695. [C:] LA FRANCHE COMTÉ divisée en TROIS GRANDS BALLIAGES sçavoir D'AMONT, D'AVAL, et DU MILIEU ou DE DOLE subdivisés en leurs BALLIAGES, et IURIDICTIONS SUBALTERNES. dressé sur les Memoires les plus Nouveaux, et PRESENTÉ A MONSEIGNEUR LE DAUPHIN Par son tres-humble, tres-obeissant, et tres-Fidele Seruiteur, HUBERT IAILLOT. Geographe du Roy — [Part I]. 402 × 564 mm.

[26] [T:] PARTIE MERIDIONALE DU COMTÉ DE BOURGOGNE. A PARIS, Chez l'Auteur le S^r. IAILLOT, Geographe ordinaire du Roy, ... 1695. — [C:] ... A Paris, Chez H.IAILLOT, ... Auec Privilege du Roy pour Vingt Ans. 1695. — [Part II]. 400 × 564 mm.

[27] PARTIE MERIDIONALE DU DUCHÉ ET GOUVERNEMENT GENERAL DE BOURGOGNE; Par le S^r. JAILLOT Geographe ordinaire du Roy. A PARIS, ... [C:] LE GOUVERNEMENT GENERAL DU DUCHÉ DE BOURGOGNE ET DE LA BRESSE, ou sont divisez ONZE GRANDS BALLIAGES et DIX Balliages Subalternes DEDIÉ A TRES-HAUT TRES-EXCELLENT ET TRES-PUISSANT PRINCE MONSEIGNEUR LOUIS DUC DE BOURBON PRINCE DU SANG ... Par son tres-humble et tres-obeissant Serviteur H.JAILLOT Geographe ordinaire du ROY. — [T:] и .Sar. f. — 467 × 689 mm.

[28] PARTIE SEPTENTRIONALE DU DUCHÉ ET GOUVERNEMENT GENERAL DE BOURGOGNE; Par le S^r. JAILLOT, Geographe Ordinaire du Roy.

[C:] ... A PARIS Chez le Sr JAILLOT Geographe ordinaire du Roy. ..., avec Privilege de Sa Majesté, 1708. — 468 × 692 mm.

[29] [C:] LE GOUVERNEMENT GENERAL D'ORLEANS Qui Comprend l'Orleanois, le Blaisois la Touraine, l'Anjou, le Maine, le Perche la Beauce, le Vendosmois, le Gastinois le Nivernois, le Berry, l'Angoumois l'Aunis & le Haut et le Bas Poitou DEDIÉ A S.A.R. MONSEIGNEUR LE DUC D'ORLEANS REGENT DU ROYAUME. Par son tres humble et tres obeissant Serviteur B. Jaillot Geographe du Roy. 1721 — [T:] A PARIS Chez le Sr JAILLOT, ... — [T:] Gravé par Delahaye. — 533 × 772 mm.

[30] [C:] LA GENERALITE D'ORLEANS, DIVISÉE EN SES ESLECTIONS. DEDIÉE A MESSIRE IEAN DE CREIL, Chevalier Marquis de Creil-bournezeau .... Par son tres-humble et tres-Obeissant Serviteur HUBERT IAILLOT, Geographe Ordinaire du Roy 1719 — [C:] Cordier, Sculpsit — [C:] ... A PARIS, joignant les Grands Augustins, ... — 508 × 720 mm.

[31] [T:] CARTE DES PROVINCES DU MAINE ET DU PERCHE dans laquelle se trouve comprise LA PARTIE SEPTENTRIONALE DE LA GENERALITÉ DE TOURS PAR GUILLAUME DEL'ISLE PREMIER GEOGRAPHE DU ROY de l'Academie Royale des Sciences A Paris chez l'Auteur ... 25 Mai 1719. — 482 × 655 mm.

[32] [T:] CARTE PARTICULIERE D'ANJOU ET DE TOURAINE ou de la PARTIE MERIDIONALE DE LA GENERALITÉ DE TOURS Par Guillaume Delisle Premier Geographe du Roy de l'Academie R.^{le} des Sciences. — 482 × 656 mm.

[33] [C:] LA PROVINCE ou DUCHE de BRETAGNE Divisée en deux Grandes Parties, qui sont La HAUTE, et la BASSE BRETAGNE. Le Gouvernement General de BRETAGNE , Comprenant les LIEUTENANCES GENERALES de BRETAGNE et du COMTÉ NANTOIS. La Lieutenance Generale de BRETAGNE est partagée en LIEUTENANCES de ROY de HAUTE et de BASSE BRETAGNE qui sont subdivisées en plusieurs EVECHEZ. Dressée sur divers Memoires Nouveaux du Sr Tillemon et Dediée A SON ALTESSE ROYALE MONSIEUR FILS DE FRANCE, FRERE VNIQUE DU ROY, ET DUC D'ORLEANS. par son tres humble et tres obeissant serviteur Jean B. Nolin. A PARIS Chez I.B.Nolin ... 1703. — 446 × 603 mm.

[34] [C:] LA PROVINCE DE POITOU ET LE PAYS D'AUNIS. LAGENERALITÉ DE POITIERS, OU SONT LES ESLECTIONS DE POITIERS, DE CHATELLERAUD, DE THOUARS, DE S.^T MAIXENT, DE NIORT, DE FONTENAY LE COMTE, DE MAULEON, DES SABLES D'OLONNE, ET DE CONFOLENS. DEDIÉE AU ROY Par son tres-humble, tres-obeissant, tres-fidele sujet et Serviteur, AH. IAILLOT, Geographe Ordinaire de Sa Majesté, Corrigé et Augmenté sur les Observations de l'Académie. 1732. — [C:] ... A PARIS, CHez l'Auteur, le Sr IAILLOT, Geographe ordinaire du Roy... — 476 × 730 mm.

[35] [C:] LA GENERALITÉ DE LA ROCHELLE Comprenant LE PAYS D'AUNIS, LA SAINTONGE, &c. Divisée EN CINQ ELECTIONS Savoir LA ROCHELLE, SAINT IEAN-D'ANGELY, .MARENNES, COGNAC et SAINTES. Dressée sur les Memoires qui ont été comuniquez et Dediée A MONSIEUR BEGON ... Par Son tres-humble et tres-Obeissant Serviteur I.B.Nolin. Geographe ordinaire du Roy. A PARIS ... — [Part I]. 365 × 647 mm.
[Insets:] [T:] VEÜE DE LA ROCHELLE. — (View). 57 × 173 mm. [T:] VEÜE DE ROCHEFORT. — (View). 65 × 140 mm.

[36] [ROCHELLE]. [Part II]. 368 × 648 mm.

[37] [C:] LA GENERALITÉ DE LIMOGES DIVISÉE EN SES CINQ ELECTIONS, DE LIMOGES, DE BRIVE, DE TULLE, DE BOURGANEUF ET D'ANGOULESME. Par le Sieur.B.IAILLOT. Geographe Ordinaire du Roy. 1719. — [C:] ... A PARIS Chez le Sr Jaillot Geographe, ... — [T:] Desbruslins, Sc — 472 × 725 mm.

[38] [C:] LA PROVINCE DE BERRY. LA GENERALITÉ DE BOURGES, ou sont LES ESLECTIONS DE BOURGES, D'YSSOUDUN, DE CHAŨ-ROUX, DU BLANC, DELA CHASTRE, DE S.^T AMAND ET DE LA CHARITÉ. DÉDIÉE A MESSIRE NICOLAS ESTIENNE ROUJAULT, ... Par son tres-humble et tres-Obeissant Serviteur AHUBERT IAILLOT, Geographe ordinaire du Roy. — [C:] ... A PARIS, Chez l'Auteur le Sr IAILLOT, Geographe Ordinaire du Roy, ... 1707. — 461 × 672 mm.

[39] [C:] GOUVERNEM. GEN^{RAL} DU LYONNOIS, Suivant les derniers Estats Generaux ou sont LE LYONNOIS FOREZ BEAUIOLOIS, BOURBONOIS, AUVERGNE, LA MARCHE, NIVER.^{NOIS} en part Par le S. SANSON, d'Abbeville Géogr. du Roy A PARIS Chés le Sr Robert Geogr ord. du Roi ... 1726. — 378 × 517 mm.

[40] [C:] LA GENERALITÉ DE MOULINS ou sont LES ESLECTIONS de MOULINS, NEVERS, CHÂTEAU-CHINON, GAÑAT, MONTLUÇON, EVAUX, et GUERET, DEDIÉE A MESSIRE IEAN DE CREIL ... Par son tres-humble, et tres Obeissant Seruiteur H. IAILLOT, Geographe Ordinaire du Roy. — [T:] S.f. — [T:] A PARIS, Chez H.IAILLOT ... 1700. — 456 × 647 mm.

[41] [C:] LE GOUVERNEMENT GENERAL et MILITAIRE du LYONNOIS Comprenant les Provinces du LYONNOIS, du FOREZ, et du BEAUJOLOIS Partie du Gouvernement General de BOURGOGNE ou sont Le Bailliage de MACON, le Comté de CHAROLOIS, et vne grande partie de la BRESSE, divisée en ses MANDEMENS. La Principauté et Souveraineté de DOMBES, divisée en ses Chatellenies LA GENERALITÉ DE LYON qui Contient Les ELECTIONS DE LYON, de SAINT ESTIENNE, de MONTBRISON, de ROANNE, et de VILLEFRANCHE Dressé Selon les Memoires du R.P.MENESTRIER de la Compagnie de IESUS. et Dedié à M.^R LE PREVOST DES MARCHANDS et a M.^{RS} les ECHEVINS de la Ville de LYON. Par leur Tres humble Serviteur I.B.Nolin A Paris Chez I.B.Nolin Geographe de S.A. Royale MONSIEUR Frere Vnique du ROY ... — [Part I] 395 × 620 mm.

[42] [LYONNOIS]. [Part II]. 398 × 620 mm.
[Inset:] [C:] GOUVERNEMENT GENERAL DU LYONNOIS Suivant les Estats Generaux tenu à Paris en l'Année 1614. — [C:] Le Sr Nolin a fait les Cartes du DAUPHINÉ, du LANGUEDOC, et de la PROVENCE, tres particulieres. — 105 × 106 mm.

[43] [C:] LE DAUPHINÉ DIVISÉ EN SES PRINCIPALES PARTIES Nouvellement Corrigé avec ses Limites Suivant le traité de 1713. Dressée sur les Memoires les plus Nouveaux Par H.JAILLOT geographe du Roy 1728. — [C:] ... A PARIS Chez le Sr JAILLOT, Geographe Ordinaire du Roy ... 1728. — 516 × 722 mm.

[44] [C:] CARTE DU DIOCESE DE GRENOBLE Divisée en ses quatre Archipretré Dressée sur plusieurs Cartes levées sur les lieux et assujetie aux dernieres Observations Astronomiques de Messrs de l'Academie Royale des Sciences. Par Mr de Beaurain Geographe ord.^{re} du Roy DEDIÉ À MONSEIGNEUR JEAN DE CAULET EVÊQUE ET PRINCE DE GRENOBLE Par son trés Humble et trés Obeissant Serviteur de Beaurain. à Paris chés l'Auteur ... — [T:] Desbruslins sculpsit — [T:] ...1741. — 515 × 639 mm.

[45] [T:] CARTE DE PROVENCE et des Terres Adjacentes Par GUILLAU^{me} DELISLE Premier Geog. du Roy de l'Acade^{mie} R.^{le} des Sciences AParis Chez l'Auteur ... Octobre 1715. — [T:] Derozier fc. — 475 × 600 mm.

[46] [C:] GOUVERNEMENT GENERAL DE LANGUEDOC qui comprend deux Generalitéz Sçavoir LA GENERALITÉ DE TOULOUSE ET CELLE DE MONTPELLIER DIVISÉES EN VINGT DEUX DIOCESES OU RECETTES avec les Provinces adjacentes — [Part I] 771 × 460 mm.

[47] [LANGUEDOC]. [C:] ... A PARIS Chez le Sr JAILLOT Geographe du Roy.... 1721. — [Part II]. 771 × 458 mm.

[48] [C:] LA PROVINCE D'AUVERGNE DIVISÉE EN

HAUTE ET BASSE LA GENERALITÉ DE RIOM ou sont les ELECTIONS DE RIOM, CLERMONT, ISSOIRE, BRIOUDE, S.FLOUR, ET AURILLAC, Dressée sur les Memoires les plus Nouveaux Par B.JAILLOT Geographe ... 1715 — [T:] A PARIS chez B.JAILLOT ... — 470 × 707 mm.

[49] [C:] GOUVERNEMENT GENERAL DE GUIENNE et GASCOGNE DEDIÉ AU ROY Dressé Sur les Memoires et Nouvelles Observations de Messieurs de l'Accademie Royale des Sciences. Par Son tres Humble et tres Obeissant tres fidel Sujet et Serviteur Bernard Antoine Jaillot Geogr. Ord.^{re} de Sa Majesté. A Paris ... 1733. — [Part I]. 405 × 922 mm.

[50] Partie Meridionale de Guienne et Gascogne. [Part II]. 407 × 922 mm.

[51] [C:] DIOCESE, PREVOSTE, ET ESLECTION DE PARIS LE DIOCESE est diuisé en Archiprés, ou Doyennés Ruraux, LA PREVOSTÉ en Balliages, ou Prevostés subalternes, ET L'ESLECTION en Chastellenies, Et ces differentes divisions sont distiguées par différetes sortes de lettres, et de Points. — [C:] ILLVSTRISSIMO, AC REVERENDISSIMO DOMINO. DOMINO IOANNI FRANCISCO PAVLO GONDIO, CORINTHIORVM ARCHIEPISCOPO, ET IN ECCLESIA PARISIENSI COADIVTORI; HANC PARISIENSIS DIOECESIS TABVLAM D D D NICOLAVS SANSON Abbavillæus Christ^{f}nissimi Galliar. Regis Geograp. — [T:] Par N.Sanson d'Abbeville Geographe du Roy A Paris chez l'Autheur Et chez P. Mariette ... — [T:] A Peyrounin sculp. — 400 × 537 mm.

[52] [C:] Carte Geographicque des Postes qui trauersent la France Dediée — [An empty cartouche]. [C:] A PARIS, Par Melchior Tauernier, Graueur et Imprimeur ordinaire du Roy ... A.^{o} 1632 — 400 × 520 mm.

[53] [C:] NOVVELLE DESCRIPTION DV TERRITOIRE ET BANLIEVÉE DE LA VILLE CITTE ET VNIVERSITES DE PARIS. Par Jean Boisseau Enlumineur du Roy pour les Cartes Geographiques ... A Paris ... — 392 × 515 mm.

[54] [C:] LE ROUSSILLON — [C:] le Comte de Roussillon à pour ville Capitale Perpignan, ... A PARIS Chez Mr de Beaurin G. Or. du Roy ... — [T:] Gravé par Incelin. — 244 × 331 mm.

Notes: All the maps are blank on the back and slightly coloured, except where otherwise specified. Of the 54 maps in this collection, 29 are by the Jaillot family. The year 1690 or 1695 has been erased from map [17]. There is no text at all in the volume, which is bound in old paper with leather spine and corners.

52 [Collection of French maps, without title-page.] 1700—1793
53,5 cm

[1] [C:] MAPPEMONDE à l'usage du ROY Par Guillaume Delisle Ier Géographe de S.M. 1720, Augmentée en 1755. des Nouv.^{lles} Découvertes Par Philippe Buache Ier Géographe du Roi et de l'Académie des Sciences. — [C:] AVERTISSEMENT. On a ajouté à cette Mappemonde les Découvertes faites depuis 30. ans, soit au Sud du Cap de Bonne Espérance, &c. soit au Nord de la GRANDE MER appellée vulgairement la MER DU SUD. Selon les Plans de Philippe Buache approuvés par l'Académie des Sciences le 5.Sept.^{bre} 1739. le 6.Sept.^{bre} 1752, &c. 1.Dec.^{bre} 1753. 24.Juill. et 4.Sep.^{bre} 1754. avec les Considérations Géographiques, &c. qui en exposent les fondemens: comme Guill. Delisle l'a fait pour cette Mappemonde dans les Mémoires de l'Académie de 1720. — [T:] Ph.Buache P.G.d.R:dl'A.R.D.S. Gendre de l'Auteur. Avec Privilége du 30. Av. 1745. — 436 × 667 mm.

[2] [C:] CARTE D'EUROPE Dressée pour l'Usage du Roy sur les Itinéraires anciens et modernes et sur les Routiers de mer assujetis aux observations astronomiques Par G. Delisle Premier Géographe de S.M. de l'Académie Royale des Sciences. A PARIS, Chez l'Auteur,... May 1724. Augmentée des Nouv.^{les} connoiss.^{ces} Géographiques par Phil. Buache Gendre de l'Auteur Janvier 1760. — Ph. Buache P.G.d.R.d.l'A.R.d.S.Gendre de l'Auteur. ... 1745. 487 × 608 mm.

[Inset:] [T:] Nouv.^{lle} Zemle Samoîedes SIBÉRIE Partie d'ASIE Ostiakes — 76 × 71 mm.

[3] [C:] CARTE D'ASIE Dressée pour l'usage du ROY. Sur ce que les Arabes nous ont laissé de plus éxact des Pays Orientaux, sur les Routiers et Observ.^{ons} des Voyageurs Européens, et sur les Mémoires envoyés par le Czar Pierre le Grand à l'Académie des Sciences de PARIS: Publiée en 1723. par Guill. Delisle, P.^{er} Géographe de SA MAJESTE de l'Académie R.^{le} des Sciences. En 1762. Phil. Buache son Gendre a augmenté cette Carte des Nouv.^{lles} Découv.^{tes} faites en Géograph.^{e} depuis environ 30. ans dont il a rendu compte à l'Acad.^{e} L'Empire des Russes qui se termine au N. et au N-E. par les G.^{des} Mers, a été assujeti aux déterminations Astron., aux Mém. et Cartes publiées par l'Acad.^{e} Imp.^{le} de St Pétersbourg, et par Joseph De l'Isle l'Astronome. A Paris, ... Ph. Buache P.G.d.R.d.l'A.R.d.S. Gendre de l'Auteur. ... 30.Av. 1745. — 487 × 632 mm.

[Inset:] [T:] Detroits du Nord CANAL DU NORD — 70 × 110 mm. (Irregular).

[4] [C:] CARTE D'AFRIQUE Dressée pour l'usage du ROY. Par Guillaume Delisle, Premier Géographe de Sa MAJESTÉ, de l'Académie Royale des Sciences. A PARIS Se distribuë avec les Ouvrages Géographiques de l'Auteur et de Phil. Buache. ... 1765. — [T:] Ph. Buache P.G.d.R:d.l'A.R.d.S. Gendre de l'Auteur. ... 30.av. 1745. — 493 × 633 mm.

[5] [C:] CARTE D'AMERIQUE, dressée pour l'usage du ROY. Par Guillaume Delisle premier Géographe de SA MAJESTÉ de l'Académie Royale des Sciences. À PARIS, Chez l'Auteur ... 1722. — Ph. Buache P.G.d.R.d.l'A.d.S. Gendre de l'Auteur... 30 Av. 1745. 485 × 610 mm.

[6] [C:] L'ESPAGNE Dressée sur la Description qui en a été faite par Rodrigo Mendez Sylva et sur plusieurs Relations et Cartes Manuscrites ou unprimées de ce Royaume Rectifiées par les Observations de M.^{rs} de l'Academie des Sciences & autres Astronomes Par G DE L'ISLE Premier Geographe du Roy A PARIS Chez l'Auteur ... 1701. — [T:] Car. Simonneau inv et sculp — Ph.Buache P.G.d.R;d.l'A.R.d.S. Gendre de l'Auteur.... 30 Av. 1745 445 × 617 mm.

[7] [C:] L'ESPAGNE divisée en tous ses ROYAUMES ET PRINCIPAUTÉS Où sont exactement recueillies et observées toutes les Routes des Postes d'Espagne, sur les memoires des Courriers Majors de Madrid. Pr ordre de son Excellence Monseigneur le Marquis de Grimaldo Ministre et Secretaire d'Etat de sa Majesté Catholique. en 1721. ... — [T:] s.f. — [C:] ... A PARIS, Chez H.IAILLOT ... — 457 × 647 mm.

[8] [C:] CARTE DE FRANCE Dressée pour l'Usage du Roy, en Avril 1721. Par Feu Guillaume Delisle, Premier Géographe de SA MAJESTE De l'Académie R.^{le} des Sciences. Et augmentée en 1764. par Phil Buache A PARIS, se distribuë chés l'Auteur, ... — Ph. Buache P.G.d.R:d.l'A.R.d.S. Gendre de l'Auteur... 30 Av. 1745. 483 × 617 mm.

[9] [C:] LE ROYAUME DE FRANCE DIVISÉ en 84 DÉPARTEMENS, suivant les DÉCRETS de L'ASSEMBLÉE NATIONALE des 15 Janvier, 16 et 26 Fevrier 1790, et de la CONVENTION NATIONALE qui y a réuni la Savoie par un Décret du 17 Novembre 1792. PAR C.E.DELAMARCHE Successeur de M. de VAUGONDY Géographe 1793. ... — 478 × 595 mm.

[10] [C:] NOUVELLE CARTE DES POSTES DE FRANCE PAR ORDRE ET DEDIÉE a son Altesse Serenissime MONSEIGNEUR LE DUC Par son tres humble et tres obeissant Serviteur Bernard Jaillot Geographe ordinaire du Roy. Corrigée et augmentée le Ier Janvier 1738 — [C:] A PARIS Chez le Sr Jaillot. ... 1726. — 502 × 645 mm.

[11] [C:] PARTIE MERIDIONALE DES PAYS BAS qui comprend les Provinces de Brabant, Gueldre, Limbourg, Luxembourg, Hainaut, Namur, Flandre, Cambresis et

Artois. Partagées entre la France, la Maison d'Autriche et les Hollandois Par le S.ʳ Janvier Géographe . Chez Lattré ... — 478 × 656 mm.

[12] [C:] CARTE DES PROVINCES UNIES DES PAYS BAS Tirée des Cartes les plus correctea qui en ont eté faites sur les lieux Rectifieés par les Observations et Operations Geometriques de Snellius et par celles que M.ʳ Cassini y a faites en dernier lieu Par G. DE L'ISLE Geographe de l'Academie Royale des Sciences A PARIS Chez l'Auteur ... 1702 Gravée par Liébaux le fils — 473 × 615 mm.

[13] [T:] CARTE DE SUISSE où sont les Cantōs de Zurich Berne Lucerne Uri Schwitz Underwald Zug Glaris Basle Fribourg Soleurre Schaffouse et Appenzel; LES ALLIEZ quisont la Ville de Bienne, l'Abbé et la Ville de S.Gal les 3.Ligues des GRISONS, Grise de Cadee, et des Dix Droitures, LE PAYS de VALAIS, l'Evêché de Basle, Mulhausen, Neuchatel, et Geneve. Dressée sur les mémoires de M.ʳ Merveilleux Con.ᵉʳ Sécr.ᵉ Interprete de S.M.T.C. aux Grisons. Par GUILLAUME DE L'ISLE Prem. G.ᵉᵒ̄ du Roy, de l'Académie R.ˡᵉ des Sciēces [Augmentée en 1759. Par Phil: Buache] — [T:] Ph. Buache P.G.d.R:d.l'A.R.d.S. Gendre de l'Auteur. ... 30 Av: 1745. — [T:] A PARIS chez l'Auteur ... Août 1715. — 485 × 638 mm.

[14] [C:] CARTE NOUVELLE DE L'ISLE DE CORSE dressée, d'après une grande Carte manuscrite levée sur les lieux par ordre de M le MARECHAL DE MAILLEBOIS, par le S.ʳ Robert de Vaugondy Géographe ord. du Roi et de S. M.Pol.Duc de Lorraine et de Bar, de l'Académie royale des Sciences et Belles Lettres de Nancy. A LAUSANNE Chés François Grasset et Compagnie 1769 — [T:] Arrivet inv. & Sculp. — 573 × 438 mm.

[15] [C:] LA SAVOYE, DEDIEE AU ROY Sire Dans le temps que la valeur Françoise se fait voir auec tant d'Eclat, par tous les glorieux succéz des Armes de V.M. Il est bien Iuste qu'vn Geographe s'occupe a d'escrire vos conquestes, pour laisser a la Posterité un Monument Eternel de la benediction si visible et si constante qu'il a plû a Dieu de donner au Regne toûjours Victorieux de V.M. C'est dans cette veüe Sire que j'ay cru devoir donner au Public cette Carte de la Savoye, et que ie prens la Liberté de l'Offrir a V.M. comme une marque du Zele et du tres Profond respect auec le quel ie suis. Sire de V.M. le tres humble tres Obeissant et tres fidel Serviteur et Sujet le P.PLACIDE Augustin Déchaussé Geog.ˢ de V.M. — [C:] ... A PARIS Chez le S.ʳ JAILLOT Geographe du Roy ... — 570 × 426 mm.

[16] CARTE DU PIEMONT et du MONFERRAT Dressée sur plusieurs Cartes Manuscrites ou Imprimées Rectifiées par quelques Observations Par Guillaume De l'Isle de l'Académie Royale des Sciences A Paris Chez l'Auteur ... 1707.
[C:] ... Gravé par Liébaux le fils — [T:] Ph. Buache P.G.d.R:d.l'A.R.d.S. Gendre de l'Auteur. ... 30 Avril 1745. 479 × 635 mm.

[17] [T:] PARTIE MERIDIONALE DU PIEMONT ET DU MONFERRAT Par Guillaume De l'Isle de l'Academie R.ˡᵉ des Sciences — [T:] A Paris, Chez l'Auteur ... 1707 — [T:] Desrosiers sc. et se trouve a Amsterdam chez Loui Renard Libraire prez de la Bourse — Ph. Buache P.G.d.R.d.l'A.R.d.S. Gendre de l'Auteur. ... 30 Av. 1745. 487 × 632 mm.
[Inset:] [C:] Environs de Nice et de Ville-franche — 71 × 122 mm.

[18] [C:] LE ROYAUME DE SARDAIGNE Dréssé Sur les Cartes manuscrites Levées dans le Pays par les Ingenieurs Piemontois a Paris Par le Rouge Ing.ʳ Géographe du Roy ... 1753 ... — [T:] A Messieurs de l'Academie Royale des Sciences. Messieurs la délicatesse de vôtre gout pour la Geographie nouvelle me fait esperer que vous voudrés bien agréer l'homage que je vous fais des Manuscrits précieux que j'ay découverts sur l'Isle de Sardaigne, J'eus l'honneur de vous faire part il y a environ 10 ans un nombre prodigieux de Cartes manuscrittes et inconnuës que vous honorates de votre suffrage et dont le Roy fit l'acqisition, permettés que mon zele encouragé par vos bontés n'echappe aucune occasion de vous prouver le profond respect avec lequel je suis Messieurs Votre tres humble et trés obeissant Servıteur Le Rouge. — 701 × 411 mm.

[19] [C:] L'ITALIE divisée en ses principaux ESTATS, ROYAUMES, ET REPUBLIQUES. ou sont exactement remarquées TOUTES LES ROUTES DES POSTES suivant qu'elles sont presentement etablies. Dressée sur les Memoires les plus nouveaux, Par le S.ʳ IAILLOT, Geographe ordinaire du Roy. A PARIS Chez l'Auteur, ... 1718 — 510 × 610 mm.

[20] [C:] L'ITALIE Dressée sur les Observations de M.ʳˢ de l'Academie Royale des Sciences sur celles du RP.Riccioli de la Compagnie de Jesus, et autres Astronomes du pays, et sur plusieurs autres memoires. Par G. DE L'ISLE Géographe A PARIS Chez l'Auteur ... M.D.CC. — [T:] L.Simonneau inv. et fecit — [T:] Gravé par Berey — Ph. Buache P.G.d.R:d.l'A.R.d.S. Gendre de l'Auteur. ... 30 Av. 1745. 489 × 629 mm.

[21] [C:] PARTIE DU DUCHÉ DE MILAN, LA PRINCIPAUTÉ DE PIÉMONT, LE MONTFERRAT; et LA REPUBLI QUE DE GENES. DEDIÉ AU ROY Par son tres-humb; tres-obeissāt, tres-fidele Sujet et Serviteur HUBERT IAILLOT — [C:] ... A PARIS, Chez H.IAILLOT, Geographe Oridinaire du Roy; ... 1700 — 458 × 647 mm.

[22] [C:] L'ALLEMAGNE Dressée sur les Observations de Tycho-Brahé de Kepler de Snellius sur celles de Messieurs de l'Academie Royale des Sciences &c. Sur Zeiller et autres Auteurs anciens ou modernes Par G. DE L'ISLE Géographe A PARIS Chez l'Auteur ... 1701. Revüe et Augmentée en 1757. — [T:] Ph. Buache P.G.d.R; d.l'A.R.d.S. Gendre de l'Auteur. ... 30 av. 1745 — 482 × 625 mm.

[23] [C:] L'EMPIRE D'ALLEMAGNE divisé en ses principaux ETATS, ou sont exactement remarquées TOUTES LES ROUTES DES POSTES et Chariots de Poste de L'EMPIRE de la Hollande et des Pays-Bas, depuis les Confins de la France, jusque dans la Pologne et dans la Hongrie. Sur les Memoires les plus Nouveaux par le S.ʳ JAILLOT Geographe. ... — [C:] ... A PARIS chez le S.ʳ JAILLOT, ... 1718 Fait par Desbruslins. — 451 × 640 mm.

[24] [C:] LE ROYAUME DE HONGRIE ET LES ESTATS, QUI EN ONT ESTÉ SUJETS et qui sont presentement LA PARTIE SEPTENTRIONALE DE LA TURQUIE EN EUROPE Tiré des Memoires les plus Nouveaux Par le S.ʳ SANSON, Geographe ordinaire du Roy 1717. — [C:] ...A PARIS, Chez H.IAILLOT ... — [C:] Cordier Sculpsit — 457 × 652 mm.

[25] [C:] LA GRECE Tirée des Memoires de Monsieur l'ABBÉ BAUDRAND. A PARIS, Chez Le S.ʳ JAILLOT Geographe du Roy ... — [C:] DEDIÉE A MESSIRE NICOLAS LE CAMUS Chevalier, Seigneur de la Grange, et autres lieux, Conseillier du Roy en ses Conseils, et PREMIER PRESIDENT en la Cour des Aydes de Paris. 1716. — 456 × 544 mm.

[26] [C:] LE ROYAUME DE POLOGNE Par le S.ʳ ROBERT DE VAUGONDY Géog. ord. du Roi de S.M.Pol. Duc de Lorr. et de Bar, et de l'Académie royale de Nancy A PARIS Ches l'Auteur ... 1759. — 485 × 614 mm.

[27] [T:] IL REGNO DI POLONIA CON I SMEMBRAMENTI fattisi nel 1773 e 1793 — 202 × 228 mm.

[28] [C:] LA SCANDINAVIE, et les Environs ou sont LES ROYAUMES DE SUEDE, DE DANEMARCK, et DE NORWEGE: divisés en leurs principales PROVINCES. Par le S.ʳ SANSON, Geographe Ordinaire du Roy. DEDIÉ AU ROY Par son tres-humble, tres-obeissant, tres-fidele Sujet et Seruiteur HUBERT IAILLOT Geographe ordinaire de sa Majesté — [C:] ... A PARIS, Chez H.IAILLOT ... 1708. — [T:] Cordier, sculpsit — 457 × 649 mm.

[29] [C:] LA RUSSIE BLANCHE ou MOSCOVIE divisée suivant l'Estendüe DES ROYAUMES, DUCHÉS, PRINCIPAUTÉS, PROVINCES, et PEUPLES: qui sont presentement sous la Domination DU CZAR DE LA RUSSIE, connû sous le Nom de GRAND DUC DE

MOSCOVIE. Par le Sr SANSON, Geographe ordinaire du Roy DEDIÉ AU ROY Par son tres-humble, tres-Obeissant, tres-fidele Sujet et Seruiteur HUBERT IAILLOT, Geographe de sa Majesté — [C:] ... A PARIS Chez H.IAILLOT, ... 1717. — [T:] Cordier, Sculps. — 449 × 647 mm.

[30] [C:] LES ISLES BRITANNIQUES ou sont le R.^{me} d'ANGLETERRE tiré de Sped celuy d'ECOSSE tiré de Th. Pont &c. et celuy d'IRLANDE tire de Petti Le tout rectifié par diverses Observations Par G. DE L'ISLE Geographe, le l'Academie Royale des Sciences A PARIS Chéz l'Auteur ... Gravé par J.B.Lièbaux — [T:] C.Simonneau Inu. — Ph. Buache P.G.d.R.d.l'A.R.d.S. Gendre de l'Auteur.... 30 Av. 1745 468 × 606 mm.

[31] [C:] THEATRUM HISTORICUM ad annum Christi quadringentesimū in quo tum IMPERII ROMANI tū BARBARORUM circum incolentiū status ob oculos ponitur PARS OCCIDENTALIS Autore Guillemo Del'Isle Regiæ Scientiarū Academiæ Socio et Primo Regis Geographo Parisiis apud Auctorem ... 1705 — [T:] Des Rosiers sculp. — 484 × 647 mm.
[Inset:] SUPPLEMENTUM THEATRO HISTORICO [America]. Circular map with 190 mm diam.

[32] [C:] THEATRUM HISTORICUM ad annum Christi quadringentesimū in quo tū IMPERII ROMANI tū BARBARORUM circumincolentium status ob oculos ponitur PARS ORIENTALIS Autore Giullemo Delisle Regiæ Scientiarum Academiæ Socio et Prima Regis Geographo Parisiis Apud Autorem, ... 1705. — [T:] Des Rosiers sc' — Ph.Buache P.G.d.R.d.l'A.R.d.S. Gendre de l'Auteur. ... 30 Av. 1745. 482 × 648 mm.
[Inset:] SUPPLEMENTUM THEATRO HISTORICO [The old world]. Circular map with 190 mm. diam.

[33] [T:] PARTIE OCCIDENTALE DE LA CARTE DES ANCIENNES MONARCHIES. Que tout le monde soit soumis aux Puissances Superieures; car il n'y a point de Puissance qui ne vienne de Dieu, et c'est luy qui a etabli toutes celles qui sont sur la Terre. Aux Romains, ch.XIII.v.I. — [C:] CARTE POUR SERVIR A LA LECTURE DE L'HISTOIRE ANCIENNE DES EGYPTIENS, DES CARTHAGINOIS, DES ASSYRIENS, DES BABYLONIENS, DES MEDES, DES PERSES, DES MACEDONIENS, DES GRECS. Par M. ROLLIN ancien Recteur de l'Université de Paris, Professeur d'Eloquence au College Royal, et Associé à l'Academie Royale des Inscriptions et Belles=Lettres. Dressée par le Sr ROBERT Geographe ordinaire du Roy. 1737. — [T:] A PARIS, Chés le Sr ROBERT Geog. du Roy ... — Gravé par Le Tellier 503 × 654 mm.
[Inset:] [C:] Suplement pour LA GRECE. ... — 192 × 216 mm.

[34] [T:] PARTIE ORIENTALE DE LA CARTE DES ANCIENNES MONARCHIES Omnis anima Potestatibus sublimioribus subdita sit: Non est enim Potestas nisi à Deo: quæ autem sunt, à Deo ordinata sunt. Aux Romains, ch.XIII. v.I. — [T:] A PARIS, Ches le Sr ROBERT Geog. du Roy ... — Gravé par Le Tellier 503 × 656 mm.
[Inset:] SUPPLEMENT Pour L'ASIE et L'AFRIQUE Circular map with 210 mm. diam.

[35] [C:] TERRÆ SANCTÆ TABULA è Scripturæ Sacræ, Flavii Josephi, Eusebii et Divi Hieronymi, innumerisque aliorum Historicorum Commentatorum, Geographorum, Viatorum, sive veterum, sive recentium, Romanorum, Græcorum, Hebræorum, Arabum &c. Testimoniis et Relationibus delineata Opus postumum GUILLELMI DE L'ISLE, primarii Regis Geographi, Ex Archivo Geographico Rei navalis Gallicæ erutum, et editum à JOSEPHO NICOLAO DE L'ISLE, Auctoris Fratre, Rei navalis Astronomo Geographo. ANNO. M.DCC.LXIII. Sub Auspiciis Illustr. D.D. DUCIS DE CHOISEUL Summi rei navalis et bellicæ Administri. — [T:] marillier inv. — [T:] Berthault Sculp. — [T:] MONITUM. Hujus Tabulæ Elucidatio seorsim est edita, ex collectaneis Guillelmi De L'isle, propriá-que ejus manu scriptis in 2. vol. in 4° Quæ quidem collectanea in Rei Navalis Archivo Geographico conservantur, continent que tum veterum, tum recentium ex scripta et memorialia quæ ad hanc Tabulam conficiendam inservierunt, et locorum situs confirmant. — [T:] a Paris chez Lattré Graveur ... — [T:] Gravé par Lattré — 657 × 490 mm.

[36] [C:] LE ROYAUME DE NAPLES DIVISÉ EN SES DOUZE PROVINCES ou sont marquez TOUS LES ARCHEVECHEZ ET EVECHEZ Les Fiefs Royaux les Sieges des Audiences Royales Les Principautez les Duchez, Marquisats et Comtez Dressé sur les Memoires des meilleurs Auteurs et Dedié. A SA MAJESTÉ CATHOLIQUE PHILIPPE V. ROY D'ESPAGNE des INDES, de NAPLES, de SICILE, de SARDAIGNE et DUC de MILAN. &c. Par Son tres humble et tres obeissant Serviteur I.B.Nolin A Paris. Chez l'Auteur ... — 560 × 469 mm.

A loose map not belonging to the set:

[37] [C:] CARTA TOPOGRAFICA DIMOSTRATIVa dei Contorni DELLA CITTÀ DI TORINO e Campagne Reali DEDICATA À SUA MAESTÀ LA REGINA DI SARDEGNA Dall'Vmilissimo, e Fedelissimo Suddito De Caroly in Torino 1785 — 393 × 588 mm.

Notes: All the maps are blank on the back and slightly coloured. 17 of the maps are by Guillaume Delisle, and 8 are by Hubert Jaillot. A manuscript index is pasted to the verso of the first blank leaf, listing 34 maps, numbered 1—32 with the numbers 22 and 32 duplicated. Map [27] in our list is not mentioned in the index, nor is the last bound map, [36], nor of course the loose map. The maps are numbered on small vellum strips pasted to the back of the maps so that they can be seen on the fore-edge. On map [6] some of the text in the cartouche and below it has been erased, as has the year on map [30]. The loose map of Turin, [37], is incomplete, the upper part only being preserved; according to the CBM:III:846 the map should consist of two parst. The volume is half bound in old vellum. It is in bad condition.

Lit.: CBM:III:846.

53 COLOM, ARNOLD [1659 ?]

ATLAS MARIN, Ou MONDE MARITIME. Contenant une briefve DESCRIPTION De toutes les COSTES Cognuës de la TERRE. Nouvellement mis en lumiere, par ARNOLD COLOM. A AMSTERDAM, Sur l'Eau,proche le pont neuf, a l'enseigne de la Colomne Esclairante.   57,5 cm.

[1] [T:] NOVA DELINEATIO TOTIUS ORBIS TERRARUM AUCTORE A. COLOM. — [C:] WERELT CAARTE nieuwlijk uyt gegeven door ARNOLD COLOM t'Amsteldam op t'water inde Lichtende Colom. — (Map). 548 × 625 mm. The hemisphere with 310 mm. diam.

[2] 1 [C:] Pascaarte Van de NOORD ZEE — [C:] Door ARNOLD COLOM t Amsterdam op het Water by de Nieuwe-brugh inde Lichtende Colom — 541 × 623 mm.

[3] 2 [C:] OOST ZEE door Arnold Colom op het Water by de Nieuwe brugh inde Lichtende Colom. — 543 × 637 mm.
[Inset:] [The eastern part of the Gulf of Finland] 140 × 112 mm.

[4] 3 [C:] De Sondt en Belt uyt gegeven door Arnold Colom op het Water — 548 × 629 mm.
[Inset:] [T:] COPPENHAVEN. — (View). 94 × 136 mm.

[5] 4 [C:] Nieuwe Pascaart door ARNOLD COLOM tAmsterdam op het Water by de Nieuwe brugh inde Lichtende Colom. — [Arctic Ocean] 541 × 632 mm.
[Inset:] [T:] Ian Mayen Eylant — 80 × 151 mm.

[6] 5 [C:] Pascaarte vant CANAAL door ARNOLD COLOM tAmsterdam op het Water by de Nieuwe brugh inde LICHTENDE COLOM. — 539 × 630 mm.

[7] [C:] Pascaarte van HISPANGIEN van de Noord zyde van Yrlandt tot de Straet. — [C:] Door ARNOLD COLOM t Amsterdam op het Water by de Nieuwe brugh inde Lichtende Colom — 534 × 632 mm.

[8] 7 [C:] Middel-landtsche Zee Nieuwlix uytgegeven door ARNOLD COLOM op het Water by de Nieuwe brugh inde Lichtende Colom tot Amsterdam. — [Divided into two parts]. 529 × 624 mm.

[9] 8 [C:] de Vlaamsche en Canarische Eylanden door Arnold Colom. tot Amsterdam op de Texelsche kay inde Lichtende Colom. — 535 × 625 mm.

[10] 9 [T:] Pascaarte van GUINEA van Capo Verde tot Capo de bon Esperance tot Amsterdam by Arnold Colom — 635 × 549 mm.

[11] 10 [C:] OOST INDIEN Van Cabo de Bona Esperanca tot Ceilon Uÿt gegeven door ARNOLD COLOM Tot Amsterdam op het water inde Lichtende Colom — 624 × 534 mm.

[12] 11 [C:] OOSTERDEEL van OOST INDIEN door Arnold Colom tot Amsterdam inde Lichtende Colom — 627 × 547 mm.

[13] [C:] Pascaerte van Brazil en Nieu Nederlandt van Cuorvo en Flores tot de Barbados nu eerst uyt gegeven door Arnold Colom tot Amsterdam op t'Water by de Nieuwe brugh inde lichtende Colom. — 637 × 547 mm.

[14] 13 [C:] Zuyder deel van AMERICA uytgegeven door Arnold Colom. — 532 × 619 mm.
[Inset:] [C:] Vervattinge van Manta tot R.Verde. — 148 × c.192 mm.

[15] 14 [C:] De CARYBSCHE EYLANDEN van de Barbados tot de bocht van Mexico toe Nu eerst Vytgegeven door Arnold Colom tot Amsterdam op het Water by de Nieuwe brugh in de Lichtende Colom — 514 × 634 mm.

[16] 12 [C:] NIEUWE CARYBSCHE PASCAART The Carybes Ilands Newly setforth and amendid by Arnold Colom Amsterdam dwelling on the Water in the Lightning Colom — [C:] Pascaarte Nieuwelyx uytgegeven door ARNOLD COLOM tot Amsterdam op bet Water byde Nieuwe brugh inde lichtende Colom — 543 × 634 mm.

[17] 16 [C:] Pascaarte van NIEU NEDERLANDT uytgegeven door Arnold Colom. t'Amsterdam opt Water by de Nieuwe brugh in de Lichtende Colom. — 545 × 632 mm.

[18] [C:] MAR DEL ZUR HISPANIS MARE PACIFICUM. — [C:] ... D.D. GEORGIO BACKER ... Tabulam hanc D.D.D. Arnold Colom. — 538 × 608 mm.

Notes: All the maps are blank on the back. Coastlines and cartouches are coloured, as is the background of the world map, [1], with allegorical figures. The 'Preface au Lecteur' and 'Description maritime' are in French; the dedication and the text of the cartouches are in Dutch; map [16] 12 also bears text in English. The folios are numbered in old ink; ff.1—3 are the title-page and following text, ff.4—21 are double-page maps. In the same hand, on the last blank leaf, is an index to the maps: 'Table, ou Indice des Cartes contenues aupresant Volume, Du monde Vniversel.' Koeman describes three different editions of Colom's Zee-atlas. The first (A.Col.1) is in Latin, and was published c.1654; the other two are both in Dutch, and were published in 1658. A.Col.3 contains the same charts as this copy, but in a slightly different order. The atlas is bound in old vellum, with worn gilt or ornamentation on the front and back covers. There are traces of the original ties. A circular label with the numbers 3.. 3 5 is pasted to the inside of the front cover, which also bears Nordenskiöld's bookplate and signature.

Lit.: Koeman vol. 4, p. 114—117, A. Col 1—3, Nederl. Hist. Scheepv. Mus. Cat. bibl. vol. 1, p. 46, Tiele p. 62, nr 255.

54 CORONELLI, VINCENZO [1687]

MEMORIE ISTORIOGRAFICHE DE'REGNI DELLA MOREA, NEGROPONTE e Littorali fin'à Salonichi Accresciute in questa Terza edizione Nel Laboratorio del P.M.Coronelli Cosmog. Della Ser: Republica di Venezia... Si uende alla Libreria del Colosso sul Ponte di Rialto.
[Half title:]

MOREA, NEGROPONTE, &c. 16,3 cm.

[1] [C:] PATRASSO — (Plan). Between pp. 42 and 43. 134 × 177 mm.

[2] [C:] CAS: TORNESE (View). — Between pp. 48 and 49. 131 × 168 mm.

[3] [C:] NAUARINO — (View). Between pp. 48 and 49. 130 × 167 mm.

[4] [C:] CITTA DI MODONE — (Plan). Between pp. 52 and 53. 130 × 166 mm.

[5] [C:] PIANTA DELLA CITTA E FORTEZZA DI CORON cogl'accampamenti del 1685 — (Plan). Between pp. 60 and 61. 131 × 166 mm.

[6] [C:] CORON — (Plan). Between pp. 60 and 61. 131 × 169 mm.

[7] [C:] VEDUTA DI CORON DALLA PARTE DEL GOLFO — (View). Between pp. 60 and 61. 131 × 167 mm.

[8] [C:] CALAMATA — (View). Between pp. 80 and 81. 130 × 169 mm.

[9] [C:] LA BATTAGLIA SOTTO CALAMATA — (View). Between pp. 80 and 81. 131 × 170 mm.

[10] [C:] CHIELAFA — (Plan). Between pp. 84 and 85. 130 × 170 mm.

[11] [C:] ZARNATA — (View). Between pp. 84 and 85. 130 × 168 mm.

[12] [C:] VEDUTA DI ZARNATA DALLA PARTE DI GRECO — (View). Between pp. 84 and 85. 132 × 175 mm.

[13] [C:] PIANTA DI ZARNATA — (Plan). Between pp. 84 and 85. 130 × 172 mm.

[14] [C:] PASSAUA — (Plan). Between pp. 88 and 89. 131 × 167 mm.

[15] [C:] MISITRA ol: SPARTA — (View). Between pp. 90 and 91. 130 × 172 mm.

[16] [C:] PIANTA DI MAINA — (Plan). Between pp. 100 and 101. 130 × 167 mm.

[17] [C:] MALUASIA — (View). Between pp. 100 and 101. 131 × 172 mm.

[18] [C:] CAPO MATAPAN — (View). Between pp. 102 and 103. 130 × 167 mm.

[19] [C:] VEDUTA DI NAPOLI DI ROMANIA dalla parte del Porto — (View). Between pp. 114 and 115. 134 × 173 mm.

[20] [C:] ISOLA DI CORFV — (Map). Between pp. 144 and 145. 130 × 170 mm.

[21] [C:] FORT DI S MAURA — (Map). Between pp. 150 and 151. 130 × 172 mm.

[22] [C:] S MAURA — (Plan). Between pp. 150 and 151. 129 × 170 mm.

[23] [C:] CEFALONIA — (View). Between pp. 152 and 153. 130 × 168 mm.

[24] [T:] ISOLA DI CEFALONIA — (Map). Between pp. 152 and 153. 130 × 168 mm.

[25] [T:] FORTEZZA DI ASSO — (Plan). Between pp. 160 and 161. 132 × 170 mm.

[26] [C:] ISOLA DEL ZANTE — (Map). Between pp. 166 and 167. 130 × 163 mm.

[27] [C:] FORTEZZA DEL ZANTE — (Plan). Between pp. 166 and 167. 130 × 168 mm.

[28] [C:] FORT: DI CERIGO — (Plan). Between pp. 184 and 185. 130 × 168 mm.

[29] [C:] PORTO DI CERIGO — (View). Between pp. 184 and 185. 128 × 170 mm.

[30] [C:] MEGARA — (View). Between pp. 194 and 195. 130 × 166 mm.

[31] [C:] NEGROPONTE — (View). Between pp. 210 and 211. 129 × 166 mm.

[32] [C:] PIANT DELLA FORT: DI VOLO — (Plan). Between pp. 222 and 223. 131 × 168 mm.

[33] [C:] PROSPETTO DI VOLO — (View). Between pp. 222 and 223. 130 × 169 mm.

[34] [C:] DARDANELLI DI LEPANTO. — (Map). Between pp. 234 and 235. 130 × 170 mm.

Notes: All the maps are blank on the verso and uncoloured. On the inside of the back cover is written, in pencil, 'Rig[to] Complt

Gamba'; however, some of the maps listed in the Indice are lacking:

Venezia Trionfante a carte I	
Carta Generale Geografica della Morea	à carte I
Stendardo aquistato sotto Coron	carte 73
Code prese collo Stendardo sudetto	carte 73
Porto Lione	carte 200
Atene	carte 204
Lepanto	carte 234

The volume is undated; Armao describes this edition (no.38, p.85—86) with the comment 'Manca ogni indicazione di data ma la menzione del fatto d'arme di Lepanto avvenuto nel luglio 1687 permette di ritenere che l'opera uscì alla luce nel secondo semestre del 1687.' Our copy has been tightly bound so that the inner margin of many of the maps cannot be measured exactly, but all of them are about 130 × 170 mm. There is a second note on the inside of the back cover: 'Raro 5 913—14'. The signature 'Gius^e. Arcangli 1727' appears on the title-page, and 'A.E. Nordenskiöld 1898' on an inserted blank leaf at the beginning, together with a partly legible stamp beginning 'CLEMENTE FALS...'

Lit.: Armao, p. 85—86 nr 38, Bonacker, p. 70, Bagrow, p. 338.

55 CORONELLI, VINCENZO 1687

1687 MEMORIE ISTORIOGEOGRAFICHE DELLA MOREA RIACQVISTATA DALL' ARMI VENETE DEL REGNO DI NEGROPONTE E degli altri luoghi circonuicini, e di quelli c'hanno sottomesso nella Dalmacia, e nell' Epiro Dal principio della Guerra intimata al Turco in Constantinopoli nel 1684. sin'all'anno presente 1687. Colla Descrizione delle Fortezze di Gastel Nuouo, e Chnin. CONSACRATE ALL ECCELLENZA DEL SIGNOR PIETRO FOSCARINI IN VENEZIA M DC LXXXVII A'spese di Giuseppe Maria Ruinetti alla Libraria della Verità in Merzeria ... 39 cm.

[1] [C:] PATRASSO olim NEOPATRIA — (View). 12 273 × 441 mm.
[2] [C:] CITTA, E FORTEZZE DI NAUARINO Vecchio, e Nuouo Prese dall'Armi della SER: REP: DI VENEZIA ... — (View). 13 270 × 434 mm. See 1687:[3].
[3] [C:] PIANTA DELLA FORTEZZA, E CITTA DI MODONE Resa all'Armi Venete li 8 Lug: MDCLXXXVI sotto la prudentiss: condotta dell'Illm͞o, & Ecc: Sig: FRANCESCO MOROSINI Cau^r, e Proc^r di S.Marco, Cap: Generale da Mare — (Plan). 14. 270 × 439 mm.
[4] [C:] CITTA DI MODONE — (Plan). On [16]. Text on verso. 131 × 168 mm. = 1687:[4].
[5] [C:] CORON — (Plan). 21 267 × 438 mm. See 1687:[6].
[6] [C:] CITTÀ, E FORT DI CORON ASSEDIATA, E PRESA DELLA SERENIS: REPUB: M.DC.LXXXV. — (Plan). 22 273 × 439 mm. See 1687:[5].
[7] [C:] CITTA E FORTEZZA DI CORON Battuta, e presa dall'Armi Ven: l'An: 1685 — (View). 25 270 × 438 mm. See 1687:[7].
[8] [C:] PIAZZA DI CALAMATA — (View). 28. 273 × 437 mm. See 1687:[8].
[9] [C:] LA BATTAGLIA SOTTO CALAMATA — (View). 29 268 × 441 mm. See 1687:[9].
[10] [C:] ZARNATA — (Plan). 31 265 × 440 mm. See 1687:[13].
[11] [C:] ZARNATA — (View). On 32 verso. Text on verso. 128 × 170 mm. = Coronelli 1687:[11].
[12] [C:] FORT: DI CHIELAFA — (Plan). 33 270 × 438 mm. See 1687:[10].
[13] [C:] PASSAUA — (Plan). 33 270 × 436 mm. See 1687:[14].
[14] [C:] PIANTA DI MAINA — (Plan). On 34 Text on verso. 130 × 170 mm. = 1687:[16].
[15] [C:] MALUASIA — (View). On 35 K Text on verso. 131 × 171 mm. = 1687:[17].
[16] [C:] MISITRA ol: SPARTA — (View). On 34 L Text on verso. 130 × 170 mm. = 1687:[15].
[17] [C:] NAPOLI DI ROMANIA — (View). 38 266 × 436 mm. See 1687:[19].
[18] [C:] ISOLA DI CORFV — (Map). 41 O Text on verso. 130 × 170 mm. = 1687:[20].
[19] [C:] VEDUTA DELLA FORTEZZA VECCHIA DI CORFU VERSO OSTRO — (View). 43 130 × 438 mm.
[20] [C:] VEDUTA DELLA FORTEZZA VECCHIA DI CORFU VERSO TRAMONT. — (View). 43 125 × 438 mm.
[21] [C:] FORT DELLA PREUESA — (Plan). On 46 Q Text on verso. 130 × 170 mm.
[22] [C:] VEDVTA DELLE GOMENIZZE — (View). On 48. 131 × 172 mm.
[23] [C:] LE GOMENIZZE — (Plan). On 48 133 × 172 mm.
[24] [C:] FORT: DI S.MAURA — (Plan). 51 267 × 435 mm. See 1687:[22].
[25] [C:] SANTA MAURA — (Map). 52 270 × 440 mm. See 1687:[21].
[26] [C:] FORTEZZE DELLA PREUESA, E SANTA MAURA — (Map). 53 265 × 440 mm.
[27] [T:] ISOLA DI CEFALONIA — (Map). On 54 S Text on verso. 130 × 172 mm. = 1687:[24].
[28] [T:] FORTEZZA DI ASSO — (Plan). On [55] verso. Text on verso. 132 × 172 mm. = 1687:[25].
[29] [C:] CERIGO — (Plan). 58 269 × 434 mm. See 1687:[18].
[30] [C:] ISOLA DEL ZANTE — (Map). On 57 Text on verso. 130 × 168 mm. = 1687:[26].
[31] [C:] PORTO DI CERIGO — (View). On 61 verso. Text on verso. 130 × 171 mm. = 1687:[29].
[32] [C:] CITTA DI ATENE — (View). On 64 129 × 168 mm.
[33] [T:] GOLFO D'ENGIA SARONICUS SINUS Ptol — (Map). On 64 130 × 170 mm.
[34] [C:] CITTA DI NEGROPONTE CONSACRATO Al'Sig: Domenica Coscorleti D.S.Bat͞ta-Brespi — [T:] Palazzi Scul. — (View). Between 66 and 67. 290 × 393 mm.
[35] [C:] PROSPETTO DI VOLO — (View). On 69 Aa Text on verso. 128 × 168 mm. = 1687:[33].
[36] [C:] PIANT DELLA FORT: DI VOLO — (Plan). On 70 Text on verso. 130 × 168 mm. = 1687:[32].
[37] [C:] LEPANTO — (View). On 70 bB Text on verso. 132 × 172 mm.
[38] [C:] DARDANELLI DI LEPANTO — (Map). On 71 Text on verso. 131 × 171 mm. = 1687:[34].
[39] [C:] ZEMONICO — (View). On 75 130 × 171 mm.
[40] [C:] URANA — (View). On 75 132 × 171 mm.
[41] [C:] CARIN — (View). On 78 130 × 171 mm.
[42] [C:] SCARDONA — (View). On 78 130 × 168 mm.
[43] [C:] FORTEZZA DI DVARE — (Plan). On 80 130 × 170 mm.
[44] [C:] IL TERRITORIO DI DUARE — (View). On 80 130 × 170 mm.
[45] [C:] CANALE DI CATTARO — (Map). On 81 131 × 170 mm.
[46] [C:] RISANO — (View). On 81 130 × 170 mm.
[47] [C:] DERNIS — (View). On 82 verso. Text on verso. 132 × 171 mm.
[48] [C:] DISEGNO POTOMOGRAFICO Del Fiume Narenta da Ciclut fin al Mare — (Map). On 83 Ff Text on verso. 129 × 168 mm.
[49] [T:] FORTE OPUS — (Plan). On 84 Map on verso. 131 × 171 mm.
[50] [C:] NOIACH — (Plan). On 84 verso. Map on verso. 130 × 170 mm.
[51] [C:] Incontro de Veneti, e Turchi Sotto Budua 12. Ag. 1686. — (View). On 85 130 × 170 mm.
[52] [C:] CITTA DI BUDUA. — (View). On 85 131 × 170 mm.
[53] [C:] SIGN dalla Parte d'Ostro. — (View). Between 88 and 89. 131 × 171 mm.
[54] [C:] SIGN dalla parte di Ponente. — (View). Between 88 and 89. 130 × 170 mm.

[55] [C:] SIGN. dalla Parte di Sirocco. — (View). Between 88 and 89. 131 × 171 mm.

[56] [C:] SIGN della parte di Tramontana — (View). Between 88 and 89. 132 × 172 mm.

[57] [C:] FORTEZZA DI SIGN Colle Nuoue Fortificazioni. — (Plan). 89 264 × 432 mm.

[58] [C:] CHNIN — (View). On 90 132 × 172 mm.

[59] [C:] Vistade KNIN per Ponente Garbin — (View). On 90 130 × 172 mm.

[60] [C:] CASTELNOVO CITTA IN ALBANIA Preso d l armi Venete l 30. z$\overline{b}$re. 1687 CONSACRATO All' Ecc^{mo} Sig^{o} Carlo Poli, Medico e Cir^{to} Romano Vm^{o} De^{o} Se^{o} Ba$\overline{tt}$a Brespi — [T:] Palazzi Cul — [T:] Ba$\overline{tt}$a Brespi, forma Venetia — (View). Between 91 and 92. 300 × 435 mm.

[61] [C:] CASTEL NUOUO — (View). On 93 130 × 173 mm.

[62] [C:] FORTEZZA DI GORNIGRAD Distante passi 400 da Cast: Nuouo — (View). On 93 131 × 172 mm.

[63] [C:] DISEGNO IDROGRAFICO DE LITTORALI DELLA MOREA ET ADIACENZE Dedicato Al Molto Reu: Pre̅: Mr̅o̅:Gioseppe Ant: Muzzarelli Teologo del Ser:di Matoua Lettor Morale nel Conu: de Frari di Venezia — (Chart). At the end of the volume. 420 × 727 mm.

Notes: The plates are blank on the back, except where otherwise indicated, and are uncoloured. Coronelli's name does not appear in this edition. In our copy the title is Memorie istoriogeografiche, not istoriografiche, as given by Armao. Plates [2] and [4], Nauarino and Modone (in folio), appear at f.18 and f.14, but according to the index they should be the order way round. A number of the leaves are bound incorrectly. The Carta generale della Morea, with the number 4 on the back and in the index, is bound at the end of the volume. The views of Citta di Negroponte, [34], and of Castel Nuvo, [60], are not listed in the index, nor are they mentioned by Armao. Leaves 33—35 occur twice, but the signatures K,L,M etc. continue in one sequence independently. The view of Misitra ol: Sparta, map [16], on the second f.34, is not listed in the index. Our other copy of Morea, (54 [1687]), also includes this view, as [15], and it is indexed. The Fortezza dal Zante, Carte 58, is wanting. Armao states that some copies of this edition contain a corrected version of ff.59 and 60: f.59 of the original version ends with the words 'quando il terremoto', of the revised version 'fabbriche di gran rilevo'. This copy contains the original version. Fonzo states that there are 15 editions of this work, published between 1686 and 1688 in Italian, French, English, German and Dutch. Francesco Bonasera provides a list of these editions in his essay in Il P. Coronelli, 1951. Our copy was damaged during World War II, and the binding has been restored. On the third blank leaf at the beginning of the volume is a stamp bearing the words 'S. ROSEN Librairie Ancienne PADOVA', and Nordenskiöld's signature. His bookplate is pasted on the inside of the front cover.

Lit.: Armao p. 90—91, nr 42, Fonzo, p. 351, Bonasera, p. 72—73.

56 CORONELLI, VINCENZO 1688

ISOLA DI RODI Geografica-Storica, Antica, e Moderna, COLL' ALTRE ADIACENTI Già possedute da Caualieri Hospitalieri di S.Giouanni di Gerusalemme. Opera dé Padri Maestri Coronelli Cosmografo della Serenissima Republica di Venetia, e Parisotti Storiografo dell'Accademia Cosmografica degli Argonauti. TOMO PRIMO dell'Arcipelago. All'Eminentissimo, e Reuerendiss. Principe IL S. CARDINALE PANFILIO Gran Priore di Roma dell'Ordine Gerosolim, et c. In Venezia 1688. ... Alla Libraria della Geografia sopra il Ponte di Riolto. 18 cm.

[1] [C:] ISOLA DI RODI — (Map). Before p. I. 130 × 168 mm.

[2] [C:] CITTA DI RODI — (Plan). Between pp. 116 and 117. 131 × 173 mm.

[3] [T:] ISOLE DELLE SIMIE — (Map). Between pp. 254 and 255. 132 × 171 mm.

[4] [T:] ISOLA DI PISCOPIA nel Mare di Rodi posseduta Dalla Prosapia Cornari Sin l'an 1572 — (Map). Between pp. 264 and 265. 130 × 168 mm.

[5] [T:] ISOLA DI STNCHIÒ, ò LANGO — (Map). Between pp. 274 and 275. 131 × 172 mm.

[6] [C:] STANCHIÒ, ò STANGIÒ — (View). Between pp. 278 and 279. 130 × 170 mm.

[7] [T:] Rouine di Fabbriche nel Scoglio Capra, ò Anticlare del Mare di Mandria — (View). Between pp. 318 and 319. 130 × 170 mm.

[8] [T:] ISOLA DI CALAMO NEL ARCIPEL — (Map). Between pp. 334 and 335. 132 × 174 mm.

[9] [C:] FORTE CALAMO — (View). Between pp. 334 and 335. 131 × 172 mm.

[10] [C:] CALOIERO dalla parte d'Ostro — (View). Between pp. 336 and 337. 132 × 173 mm.

[11] [C:] CALOIERO dalla parte di Tramontana — (View). Between pp. 336 and 337. 130 × 170 mm.

[12] [C:] CALOIERO ... — Between pp. 336 and 337 = [10] in this ed. with very small alterations.

[13] [C:] FORTEZZA DI LERO — (View). Between pp. 336 and 337. 131 × 170 mm.

[14] [T:] I. DI NICARIA NELL' ARCIPEL: — (Map). Between pp. 350 and 351. 130 × 170 mm.

Notes: All the maps are blank on the back, and uncoloured. In addition to these 14 maps there are 4 plates in the volume. Armao mentions 3 further maps, which are wanting in our copy: 'una carta dell'Arcipelago meridionale', 'Le isole di Carchi e di Limonia,' 'L'Isola di Nissari'. He also gives the name of the printer, P.A. Brigonci, which appears in the privilege, on the page preceding the first map. Our copy is bound in old vellum. The first engraved page, with the imprint of the Argonauti, has had a piece cut out at the bottom, presumably to remove some previous owher's name or names. On the inside of the front cover are the notes 'Roma li 9. Luglio 1839 Baltz', 'Cronurand, Geogr. 27½ Dupl. D.' and Nordenskiöld's signature.

Lit.: Armao nr 94, p. 184—185, Fonzo, p. 351.

57 CORONELLI, VINCENZO 1693

EPITOME COSMOGRAFICA, O COMPENDIOSA INTRODUTTIONE All' Astronomia, Geografia, & Idrografia, Per l'Uso, Dilucidatione, e Fabbrica Delle SFERE, GLOBI, PLANISFERJ, ASTROLABJ, E TAVOLE GEOGRAFICHE, E particolarmente degli stampati, e spiegati nelle PUBLICHE LETTIONI DAL P. MAESTRO VINCENZO CORONELLI M.C. COSMOGRAFO DELLA SERENISSIMA REPUBLICA DI VENETIA, e Lettore di Geografia in quella Università, per l'Accademia Cosmografica DEGLI ARGONAUTI. COLONIA, M DC LXXXXIII. Ad istanza di Andrea Poletti in Venetia.
[Engraved half title:]
EPITOME COSMOGRAFICA Del P. Coronelli 18,5 cm.

[1] [The terrestrial globe of 2 inches.]
[T:] del P. Coronelli — On gores [4]—[6].
On the same plate a design for a still smaller globe.
[T:] Aut: il P. Cosmografo Coronelli in Venetia 1693 — 345 The globe consists of 12 gores on one plate. 126 × 171 mm.

[2] [C:] LA SPAGNA Suddiuisa Nè Suoi Regni e descritta Dal P. Cosmografo Coronelli — Between pp. 366 and 367. 118 × 164 mm.

Notes: The maps are blank on the back, and uncoloured. Fonzo describes this volume (p.357), and states that there are 40 + 420 pages and 38 plates. Our copy has 46 unnumbered pages, including the title and half-title, 418 numbered pages, and only 28 plates. The last leaf, with pp. 419—420, is wanting. The first six plates depict wind roses, nine others depict different world systems, 1 according to Ptolemy, 5 to Copernicus, 1 to Tycho Brahe and 2 to Descartes, and in addition to the two maps described above there are pictures illustrating the making of globes and maps. According to Armao (p.189) the Epitome can be described as the prototype of the modern handbook in physical, natural and political geography. Our copy is bound in old leather. The first blank leaf is entirely covered by a manuscript note in Swedish. On the title-page is the signature 'Er. V. Roland'; on the inside of the front cover 'F.W. Hultman Ups. 1859', 'A.E. Nordenskiöld erhållen af Dr. C. Browallius 1896' [A.E. Nordenskiöld received from Dr. C Browallis 1896] and 'N° 1' in old ink, with the somewhat obscure note, '4. ol: 9^{mk}'(?) A blue label, with the words 'CARLBERGS ANTIKVARIAT 17 Hamngatan, STOCKHOLM' is pasted to the inside of the back cover.

Lit.: Armao p. 189—191, Bonasera, p. 52—53, Fonzo, p. 357—358.

58 CORONELLI, VINCENZO   [1705]

GLOBI DEL PADRE CORONELLI
[Engraved half title:]
GLI ARGONAUTI, In Venetia   36,6 cm.

[1]—[50] [The terrestrial globe of 3½-foot, 1688.]
[C:] ALLA SERENISSIMO REPUBLICA, E SERENISSIMO PRENCIPE FRANCESCO MOROSINI, DOGE DI VENETIA, Capitan Gen: da Mare, & c. F. Vincenzo Coronelli M. C. Suddito, Cosmografo, e Lettore Publico, Generale de M. C. F. V. CORONELLI M. C. COSMOGR: PUBLI. BIBLIOT. UNIVER: ATLANTE VENETO — [Portrait of Coronelli] On gores [1]—[2].
[C:] IL GENIO della Virtù raccomandò all'Eternità il Nome di CESARE, Cardinale Eminentissimo D'ESTREES, Duca, e Pari di Francia, mentre fece elaborare Per LODOVICO IL MAGNO, Dal P. Coronelli Due Gran Globi, l'Idea dè quali hà poi epilogata in questi Per L'ACCADEMIA COSMOGRAFICA DEGLI ARGONAUTI, l'Anno MDCLXXXVIII in Venezia. — On gore [12].

[1]—[12] 12 gores of the Southern hemisphere from the latitude of 70° to the Tropic of Capricorn. To form the circumference beginning with the prime meridian the gores should be placed in the following order: 9, 5, 4, 3, 2, 1, 11, 10, 12, 8, 7, 6.

[13]—[24] 12 gores of the Northern hemisphere from the latitude of 70° to the Tropic of Cancer. Beginning from the prime meridian they should be placed in the following order: 13, 15, 14, 16, 17, 19, 18, 20—24.

[25]—[36] 12 gores of the Northern hemisphere from the Tropic of Cancer to the equator. Beginning from the prime meridian the gores should be placed in the following order: 30, 29, 28, 27, 26, 25, 36, 35, 34, 33, 32, 31.

[37]—[48] 12 gores of the Southern hemisphere from the Tropic of Capricorn to the equator. Beginning from the prime meridian the gores should be placed in the following order: 48, 47, 46, 40, 39, 38, 37, 42, 41, 45, 44, 43.

[49] [T:] POLO AUSTRALE, ò MERIDIONALE, & ANTARTICO. — Circular map with 355 mm. diam.

[50] [T:] POLO SETTENTRIONALE, ò BOREALE, ET ARTICO. — Circular map with 365 mm. diam.

[51]—[100] [The celestial globe of 3½-foot, 1700.]
[C:] EMINENTISSIMO, E REVERENDISSIMO PRINCIPE Risoluta dalla mia tenuità la struttura di due Globi, con aggiunta di uarie osseruationi, e tutte di una somma importanza, nel medesimo tempo, che pensai di darfreggio al Terrestre, marcandolo con il nome immortale della Veneta Serenissima Republica, diuisai pure d'accrescere un'Astro Regio al Celeste, e ueramente di prima grandezza, umiliandolo à piedi d'Alessandro Ottauo, che con applauso di tutto il Mondo occupaua uiuente la Sedia di Pietro. ... D.V.E. Umilissimo Seruitore F. Vinc: Coronelli M.C. Cosmog: della S.S. Repub: Alexander à Via Veronensis sculpsit. — On gores [54]—[55].

[51]—[86] 36 gores of the celestial globe.

[87] COSTELLATIONI CELESTI DEL POLO ANT[ARTICO DESC]RITTE DAL P. CORONELLI, COSMOGRAFO DELLA SERENISSIMA [REPUBLICA] DI VENETIA 1700. Circular map with 355 mm. diam.

[88] COSTELLATIONI CELESTI DE[L POLO ART]ICO DESCRITTE DAL P. CORONELLI, COSMOGRAFO DELLA [SERENISSIMA] REPUBLICA DI VENETIA 1700. Circular map with 360 mm. diam.

[89]—[100] 12 gores of the same globe.

[101]—[112] [The terrestrial globe of 1½-foot, 1699.] 2 gores on each plate.
[C:] D.D.D. Pater Magister Vincentius Coronelli Min: Com: S. Francisci Serenissimæ Venetorum Reipublicæ Cosmographus MDCLXXXXIX. — On gore [107b].

[101]—[106] 12 gores of the Northern hemisphere. Beginning from the prime meridian the gores should be placed in the following order: 103b, 102a, 102b, 101b, 101a, 106a, 106b, 105a, 105b, 104a, 104b, 103a.

[107]—[112] 12 gores of the Southern hemisphere. Beginning from the prime meridian the gores should be placed in the following order: 110b, 111a, 111b, 112b, 112a, 107a, 107b, 108b, 108a, 109a, 109b, 110a.

[113]—[124] [The celestial globe of 1½-foot, 1700.] 2 gores on each plate.
[C:] Amico Lettore Oltre ai molti Globi delineati dal P. Cosmografo Coronelli per Sourani diuersi deuarie, e uaste misure, ne hà ultimamente composti, e stampati di cinque grandezze à publico beneficio, fra quali i più commodi, ed esatti sono i presenti. I Numeri che accompagnano le Stelle calcolate all'Epoca del 1700; cosi l'altre notitie, ed uso de medesimi Globi, uengono nel suo Epitome Cosmografico diffusamente spiegati — On gores [122b]—[123a].

[125] [The terrestrial globe of 6 inches.]
[C:] Hos Globos Terracqueum, ac Cæelestem dicat, et donat Rm̄o P.D. Sigismundo Pollitio à Placentia Præposito Generali Monachorum Eremitarum S. Hyeronimi Congreg: Lombardiæ P.M. Coronelli Cosmographus P. — On gore [7]. The globe consists of 12 connected gores on one plate 240 × 464 mm.

[126] [The celestial globe of 6 inches.]
[C:] Auct: P. Mag: Vincentio Coronelli Cosmog Publi — On gore [7].
[C:] Venetijs In Accademia Cosmog Argon — On gores [4]—[5].
[C:] Stellæ supput fuerunt ad annum 1700 — On gores [5]—[6].
[C:] Rm̄o Patri D. Sigismundo Pollitio Præp: Generali Mon: Erem S. Hyeron: — On gores [8]—[9]. The globe consists of 12 connected gores on one plate 245 × 470 mm.

[127] [a] [The celestial globe of 4 inches.].
[C:] Auc. P. M. Coronelli — On gore [7]. [C:] Illustris: D.D. Ant: de V-Comitib, G. P. N-Comi — On gore [5]. The globe consists of 12 connected gores on one plate 138 × 274 mm.
[b] [The terrestrial globe of 4 inches.]
[C:] Auctore P. Cosmographo Coronelli Venetijs 1697 — On gore [3]. An empty cartouche on gore [6]. The globe consists of 12 connected gores on one plate 138 × 275 mm.

[128] [a] [The celestial globe of 2 inches.]
[C:] All' Illustriss: S. Franc: Gasparoli Nobile Fanese — On gore [6]. The globe consists of 12 gores on one plate 130 × 168 mm.
[b] [The terrestrial globe of 2 inches.]
[C:] All' Illustriss: S. Franc: Gasparoli Nobile Fanese — On gore [4].
[T:] del P. Coronelli — On gores [4]—[6].

On the same plate a design for a still smaller globe.
[T:] Aut: il P. Cosmografo Coronelli in Venetia 1693 — 345
The globe consists of 12 gores on one plate   125 × 170 mm.
See 1693:[1].
[The whole plate:] [C:] Autore Il P. Coronelli ad uso dell' Accademia Cosmografica degli Argonauti —   395 × 260 mm.

Notes: All the plates are blank on the back and uncoloured. Our copy contains material from both the first (1697, with a later issue) and second (1705) editions. A facsimile of the second edition, with an introduction by Helen Wallis, was published in 1969. Helen Wallis states that each of the seven known copies differs from the others. Three of these are of the first edition, four are of the second. It is perhaps appropriate to give a more detailed description of our copy here. The preliminary leaves are as follows:

1. GLOBI DEL PADRE CORONELLI   Printed from an engraved plate, with the text printed separately and pasted on. = 3 in both first and second editions.
2. GLI ARGONAUTI, In Venetia. = 1 in both editions. The year is wanting.
3. Allegorical design representing the Accademia Cosmografica degli Argonauti. [C:] GLI ARGONAUTI — [C:] Lodouico Lanberti del: Allessandro Dalla Via Sc. — = 2 in both editions.
4. PALESTRA LITTERARIA, O INVITO Dell'Accademia Cosmografica a' suoi Argonauti, Et ad ogn' altro Accademista di qualunque Università, e Nazione, PROFESSORI DI GEOGRAFIA, ED ASTRONOMIA, A di nuovo CENSURARE; E CONFRONTARE Con qualunque altro Globo pubblicato, I Globi Celesti, e Terracqueo, elaborati già in Parigi. DAL P. M. CORONELLI, Generale LXXVIII. di tutto l'Ordine di S. Francesco de' Minori Conventuali, Cosmografo della Serenissima Republica di Venezia, Al presente collocati nella Real Galeria di Varsaglia, in luogo a tal' effetto espressamente fabbricato da S. M. Cristianissima, Che coll'annesso suo Reggio Diploma li ha parimente dichiarati, dopo discusso Esame, li più Esatti, li più Arrichiti di Novità, & i Maggiori di quanti sin' ora ne siano stati pubblicati, A questo fine nel presente Volume epilogati, ED IN MAPPE ESPOSTI Nella rinomata Libreria di S. Marco di quest' inclita Dominante, ed in altre cospicue dell'Europa. Pubblicata in continuazione dell'Atlante Veneto SOTTO I GLORIOSI AUSPICJ Dell' Illustrissimo, et Eccellentissimo Signore VETTOR ZANE, SAVIO GRANDE, &c. — See Armao, p. 131.
5. ILLUSTRISSIMO, ET ECCELLENTISSIMO SIGNORE. ... Umilissimi Serv. Obblig. Gli Argonauti. (Included in the John Carter Brown Library's copy.)
6. Diploma del Rè Cristianissimo alle Opere del P. Cosmografo CORONELLI. ... Dato à Versaglie a' 28. Decembre 1686. ... GIUDIZIO DELL' ACCADEMIA FISICOMATEMATICÀ DI ROMA, Stampato a' 7. Decembre M. DC. VIIIC. = Tav. 6, 2nd ed. See Armao, p.131.
7. A CHI LEGGE L'ACCADEMIA DEGLI ARGONAUTI. = Tav.5, 2nd ed. See Armao, p.131.
8. Coronelli's portrait, surrounded by the names of the 79 generals of the Franciscan order, beginning with S. Franciscus and ending with Coronelli himself.
9. GLI ARGONAUTI. Emblem of the Accademia Cosmografica degli Argonauti, centred on a terrestrial globe surmounted by a ship, surrounded by a decorative border of scientific instruments. = Tav.4, 2nd ed.
10. [a] Globi publicati alle Stampe della misura dell'ingionlta Scala dal P. Cosmografo Coronelli ad uso dell'Accademia Cosmografica degli Argonauti in Venetia 1689   405
    [b] Piede inuentato dall'Ill.mo et Ecc.mo S. Gio: Batta Donà Sauio Grande per li di lui Globi destinatagli dall' Accademia degli Argonauti promossa da S. E. 405 = part 2 of Tav. 6, 2 nd ed.
    Autore Il P. Coronelli ad uso dell'Accademia Cosmografica degli Argonauti. The first part of this plate is different in the copy in the British Library, as is the border of the whole plate.
11. [a] Globe stands 334
    [b] Altro modo di collocare gli Globi publicati alle stampe dal P. Cosmografo Coronelli ad uso dell'Accademia Cosmografica degli Argonauti Autore Il P. Coronelli ad uso dell'Accademia Cosmografica degli Argonauti 405 — Cf. Tav.5 of the copy in the British Library.

The following numbers of the facsimile edition are wanting in our copy: 7—13, 42 (the dedicatory cartouche for the 3½-foot celestial globe). The groups of plates are bound in the opposite order to those in the second edition, so that our numbers [1]—[50] = 91—138, [51]—[100] = 43—90 (2 gores wanting), [101]—[112] = 12—23, and [113]—[124] = 24—35 of the 1st ed., [125]—[128] = 17, 16, 15, 14 of the 2nd ed. Our copy is bound so that the leaves are folded to the size of 360 × 265 mm. The binding is dark blue buckram, with gold tooling and lettering on the spine. On the first blank leaf is Nordenskiöld's signature, with the date 1898, and a note in his hand: 'Ett isolerat på väf uppklistradt exemplar af den stora jordgloben utbjuds (421 Catal. 1900) af Jos. Baer för 120 M.' [A copy of the big terrestrial globe, mounted on cloth, is offered at 120 M by Jos. Baer (421 Catal. 1900].

Lit.: Almagia p. 80—87, Armao, nr. 59 and 60, p. 127—132, Muris p. 167—173, Fiorini p. 36, and 358, Wallis, Helen, Introduction.

59   CORONELLI, VINCENZO   1706—1708

TEATRO DELLA GUERRA, DIVISO IN XXXXVIII PARTI, In cui sono esattamente delineati, e compendiosamente descritti fin l'Anno M. D C C. I REGNI, LE PROVINCIE, LE CITTA', LE FORTEZZE, LE PIAZZE, I PORTI, E GLI ALTRI LUOGHI PRINCIPALI, DELL' EUROPA, ASIA, AFRICA, E DELL'UNA, E L'ALTRA AMERICA, In Pianta, in Veduta, o in Elevazione, colle nuove loro Fortificazioni. Pubblicato secondo gli Originali DEL P. CORONELLI, Dall' Accademia Cosmografica ad uso de'suoi Argonauti, Ed a maggior dilucidazione di quanto vien spiegato dall' Autor medesimo Ne' XXXXV. Tomi della di lui Biblioteca Universale. In Napoli con licenza de'Superiori 1706.
[Engraved half titles:]
TEATRO DELLA GUERRA
GLI ARGONAUTI

Vol. I
TEATRO DELLA GUERRA, In cui sono esattamente delineate, e compendiosamente descritte fin l'Anno M. D C C. LE XVII. PROVINCIE DEL BELGIO, E LE CITTA', LE FORTEZZE, I PORTI, ED ALTRI LUOGHI LORO PRINCIPALI, In Pianta, in Veduta, ò in Elevazione, colle nuove loro Fortificazioni, DIVISE Conforme i Trattati i varj tempi segnati di Pace, Nelle possedute dalla Spagna, Francia, & Olanda. Pubblicato secondo gli Originali DEL P. CORONELLI, Dall'Accademia Cosmografica ad uso de'suoi Argonauti, Ed a maggior dilucidazione di quanto vien spiegato dall'Autor medesimo Ne'XXXXV. Tomi della di lui Biblioteca Universale. PARTE I, In Napoli ... 1706.   18,5 cm obl.

[Engraved half title:] BELGIO
[1]   [C:] BELGIO Descritto Dal P. CORONELLI ... — (Map). 125 × 177 mm.
[2]   [C:] POTAMOGRAFIA DEL BELGIO Esposta Dal P. CORONELLI a uso de' Suo' Argonauti ... — (Map).   126 × 176 mm.
CORSO DEL RENO
[3]   [C:] CORSO DEL RENO — (Map).   123 × 175 mm.
IL BELGIO CATTOLICO
[4]   [C:] FORTEZZE Riservatesi da LODOVICO XIV. Nel Belgio, ed altrove Per il Trattato di Nimega MDCLXXVIII.

Valenciennes. Cambrai. Mont-Cassel. Sant-Omer. Condé. Ypri. Bailleul. Bouchain. Poperinque. Varwick. Bavay. Friburgo. Varneton. Maubege. Tutta la Franca-Contea. Vedi Trattato di Reswich MDCLXXXXVII. ... — (View). 125 × 177 mm.

LA FIANDRA SPAGNUOLA
- [5] [C:] GAND — (View). 132 × 173 mm.
- [6] [T:] CITTA DI GAND — (Plan). 325 131 × 168 mm.
- [7] [T:] SASSO DI GANT — (Plan). 134 × 167 mm.
- [8] [C:] BRUGGES — 126 × 176 mm.
  [a] (View). 43 × 176 mm.
  [b] (Plan). 83 × 176 mm.
- [9] [C:] OSTENDA Nella Fiandra — (Plan). 125 × 177 mm.
- [10] [C:] NIEUPORT — (Plan). 125 × 177 mm.
- [11] [C:] DAMA — (Plan). 124 × 176 mm.
  [Inset:] [C:] PROFILO — (Profile). 11 × 103 mm. (Irregular).
- [12] [T:] DISMUDA — 124 × 176 mm.
  [a] (View). 35 × 176 mm.
  [b] (Plan). 89 × 176 mm.
- [13] [C:] DENDERMONDE. — (Plan). 125 × 177 mm.
- [14] [a] [C:] ALOST, e DENDERMOND — (Map). 87 × 177 mm.
  [b] [T:] DENDERMOND — (View). 36 × 177 mm.
  [The whole plate:] 123 × 177 mm.
- [15] [C:] COURTRAY — (Plan). 123 × 174 mm.
- [16] [C:] FURNES — 124 × 177 mm.
  [a] (View). 26 × 177 mm.
  [b] (Plan). 98 × 177 mm.
- [17] [C:] GLEMBOURS — (Map). 39 124 × 177 mm.

LA FIANDRA GALLICANA
- [18] [C:] LILLA — 124 × 178 mm.
  [a] (View). 29 × 173 mm.
  [b] (Plan). 90 × 173 mm.
- [19] [C:] La Cittadella DI LILA Fabbricata da Lodouico XIV — (Plan). 125 × 171 mm.
- [20] [a] [T:] Chisoing — (View). 39 × 171 mm.
  [b] [C:] Orchies — (View). 40 × 85 mm.
  [c] [C:] Commincs — (View). 40 × 85 mm.
  [d] [C:] Marchiennes — (View). 39 × 85 mm.
  [e] [C:] Lannoy — (View). 39 × 85 mm.
  [The whole plate:] 45 122 × 174 mm.
- [21] [a] [T:] Phalempin — (View). 40 × 172 mm.
  [b] [T:] Waurain — (View). 40 × 86 mm.
  [c] [T:] La Bassée — (View). 40 × 86 mm.
  [d] [T:] Descarpe — (View). 39 × 86 mm.
  [e] [T:] Armentieres — (View). 39 × 86 mm.
  [The whole plate:] 46 123 × 175 mm.
- [22] [C:] IPRI — (Plan). 126 × 177 mm.
- [23] [a] [C:] IPRI — (View). 38 × 170 mm.
  [b] [C:] OUDENARDE — (View). 37 × 170 mm.
  [c] [C:] COURTRAY — (View). 37 × 170 mm.
  [The whole plate:] 122 × 174 mm.
- [24] [a] [T:] DUNQUERKE — (View). 38 × 175 mm.
  [b] [C:] Contorni di Dunquerke, Furnes, e Nieuport ... — (Map). 81 × 175 mm.
  [The whole plate:] 125 × 178 mm.
- [25] [a] [C:] DONCHERKEN — (Plan). 76 × 173 mm.
  [b] [C:] RISBAN — (View). 46 × 173 mm.
  [The whole plate:] 126 × 177 mm.
- [26] [T:] DONKERKEN — (Plan). 326 130 × 168 mm.
- [27] [T:] RISBAN DI DONCHERCHEM — (View). 141 × 281 mm.
- [28] [C:] GRAVELINES — (Plan). 125 × 176 mm.
- [29] [C:] GRAVELINES — 123 × 175 mm.
  [a] (Plan). 76 × 172 mm.
  [b] (View). 43 × 172 mm.
- [30] [C:] BERGUE S.VINOX — 124 × 176 mm.
  [a] (View). 27 × 171 mm.
  [b] (Plan). 91 × 171 mm.
- [31] [C:] TOURNAY — (Plan). 124 × 176 mm.
- [32] [C:] PIANTA ICONOGRAFICA DELLA CITTADELLA DI TOURNAY, Descritta, e Dedicata dal P. Maestro Coronelli Cosmografo della SS.Republica di Venetia All Illustrissimo S.re GIO: BATTISTA VITOLINI, Accademico Argonauta — (Plan). 170 × 238 mm.
- [33] [C:] BOURBOURG — (Plan). 125 × 176 mm.
- [34] [T:] LINCK — (Plan). 133 × 167 mm.
- [35] [a] [T:] DOVAY — (View). 38 × 173 mm.
  [b] [T:] DOVAY — (Plan). 81 × 86 mm.
  [c] [T:] ARMENTIERS — (Plan). 81 × 84 mm.
  [The whole plate:] 125 × 176 mm.
- [36] [C:] OUDENARDE — (Plan). 126 × 178 mm.
- [37] [T:] WATTE — (Plan). 132 × 167 mm.
- [38] [C:] MENEIM — (Plan). 125 × 175 mm.
- [39] [a] [T:] F.REBUS — (Plan). 122 × 83 mm.
  [b] [T:] F.HENNUIN — (Plan). 122 × 90 mm.
  [The whole plate:] 125 × 176 mm.
- [40] [a] [C:] FORT-FRANCOIS Sul Canale, che vá á DoncherKen — (Plan). 121 × 87 mm.
  [b] [C:] F. LUIGI Sul Canale, che vá á DoncherKen — (Plan). 121 × 84 mm.
  [The whole plate:] 124 × 177 mm.
- [41] [C:] KENOQUE Colle Proposizioni del 1692. — (Plan). 124 × 177 mm.

IL DUCATO DI BRABANTE
- [42] [C:] LOVANIO — 123 × 177 mm.
  [a] (View). 29 × 173 mm.
  [b] (Plan). 90 × 173 mm.
- [43] [T:] TILEMONT — (View). 124 × 176 mm.
- [44] [C:] CITTA, e CITTADELLA DI LEWE — (Plan). 130 × 171 mm.
- [45] [C:] Contorni di BRUSSELLES — (Map). 124 × 178 mm.
  [Inset:] [Brussels]. (View). 40 × 99 mm.
- [46] [T:] BRUSSELLES — (View). 125 × 176 mm.
- [47] [C:] BRUSSELLES — (Plan). 123 × 174 mm.
- [48] [C:] BRUSSELLES Prima Delle Nuove Fortificazioni — (Plan). 131 × 170 mm.

IL MARCHESATO DEL S.ROMANO IMPERO
- [49] [C:] Contorni d'ANVERSA — (Map). 125 × 178 mm.
- [50] [C:] D'ANVERSA Capitale del Brabante Descritta e Dedicata Del P.Cosmografo Coronelli All Illustrissimo Sig: Conte CAMILLO SILVESTRI Nobile di Rouigo ... — (Plan). 175 × 266 mm.

LA SIGNORIA DI MALINES.
- [51] [C:] Contorni tra MALINES, e LIER — (Map). 124 × 176 mm.
- [52] [C:] MALINES — (Plan). 126 × 178 mm.
  [The whole plate:] 124 × 178 mm.
- [53] [a] [T:] MALINES — (View). 57 × 175 mm.
  [b] [T:] LIRA — (View). 60 × 175 mm.
  [The whole plate:] 124 × 178 mm.
- [54] [a] [C:] FILIPPINE Nel Brabante — (Plan). 124 × 84 mm.
  [b] [C:] STEENBERG Nel Brabante — (Plan). 124 × 90 mm.
  [The whole plate:] 127 × 178 mm.

IL DUCATO DI LIMBURGO
- [55] [a] [T:] LIMBURGO — (View). 43 × 173 mm.
  [b] [T:] LIMBURGO — (Plan). 77 × 173 mm.
  [The whole plate:] 125 × 178 mm.

IL DUCATO DI LUXEMBURGO
- [56] [C:] LUCEMBURGO — (Plan). 124 × 176 mm.
- [57] [C:] THIONVILLE Nel Luxemburgo — (Plan). 124 × 177 mm.
- [58] [C:] MONMIDY — (Plan). 123 × 175 mm.
- [59] [C:] DANVILLIERS — (Plan). 124 × 177 mm.

IL DUCATO DI GUELDRIA
- [60] [a] [T:] GELDRIA — (View). 44 × 172 mm.
  [b] [T:] GELDRIA — (Plan). 76 × 85 mm.
  [c] [T:] BIEVOORT — (Plan). 76 × 84 mm.
  [The whole plate:] 123 × 174 mm.
- [61] [a] [T:] WACHTENDONCH — (View). Oval 34 × 42 mm.
  [b] [T:] RUREMONDE — (View). Oval 41 × 82 mm.
  [c] [T:] BREEFOORT — (View). Oval 34 × 42 mm.
  [d] [T:] VAGENINGEN — (Plan). 71 × 74 mm.
  [e] [T:] RUREMONDA — (Plan). 71 × 99 mm.
  [The whole plate:] 124 × 177 mm.

[62] [T:] WACHTENDONC — 125 × 178 mm.
    [a] (View). 50 × 175 mm.
    [b] (Plan). 72 × 117 mm.
[63] [a] [T:] VEENLO — (View). Oval 31 × 39 mm.
    [b] [T:] HARDERWICH — (View). Oval 40 × 89 mm.
    [c] [T:] GROLLE — (View). 31 × 40 mm.
    [d] [T:] S.STEFANO — (Plan). 80 × 80 mm.
    [e] [T:] GROLLE — (Plan). 80 × 92 mm.
    [The whole plate:] 125 × 176 mm.

IL CONTADO D'HAINAUT

[64] [C:] MONS ASSEDIATO li 22. Marzo, e' reso a'S.Maesta' Cristianissima li 10.Aprile 1691 — (Map). 128 × 177 mm.
[65] [C:] MONS — (Plan). 132 × 168 mm.
[66] [C:] VALENCIENNES — (Plan). 125 × 176 mm.
[67] [C:] BOVIGNES Nel Contado di Namur — (Map). 123 × 174 mm.
[68] [a] [T:] VALENZIENNES — (View). 33 × 174 mm.
    [b] [C:] VALENZIENNES — (Plan). 85 × 75 mm.
    [c] [C:] LANDRECY — (Plan). 85 × 86 mm.
    [The whole plate:] 124 × 178 mm.
[69] [C:] ATH come é oggidi — (Plan). 166 × 187 mm.
[70] [C:] ATH Colle Fortificazioni rappresentate dal C.Gualdo — (Plan). 127 × 180 mm.
[71] [C:] CONDÈ — (Plan). 126 × 178 mm.
[72] [C:] AVENES — (Plan). 179 × 201 mm.
[73] [a] [T:] LANDRECY — (View). 49 × 174 mm.
    [b] [T:] AVESNES — (View). 58 × 174 mm.
    [The whole plate:] 124 × 174 mm.
[74] [C:] QUENOY Nell' Hainaut — (Plan). 126 × 176 mm.
[75] [C:] MAUBEUGE — (Plan). 126 × 179 mm.
[76] [C:] PHILIPPEVILLE Nell' HAINAUT — (Plan). 124 × 178 mm.
[77] [T:] MINE DI FILIPPEVILLE — (Plan). 124 × 178 mm.
    [Inset:] [T:] PROFILO — (Profile). 22 × 168 mm. (Irregular).
[78] [C:] Contorni di PHILIPPEVILLE Nell' Hannonia — (Map). 110—2 123 × 172 mm.
[79] [T:] MARIEBURG — 125 × 177 mm.
    [a] (View). 45 × 173 mm.
    [b] (Plan). 76 × 117 mm.
[80] [T:] Fortezza di Charleroij — (Plan). 127 × 180 mm.
[81] [C:] CHARLE-ROY Bonbardato Da Francesi nel 1692 e nel 1693 ed acquistato ii Ott: dell anno stesso — (Plan). 125 × 167 mm.

IL CONTADO D'ARTESIA

[82] [C:] ARRAS — (Plan). 123 × 177 mm.
[83] [C:] BETHUNE — (Plan). 124 × 176 mm.
[84] [C:] AIRE nell'Artesia — (View). 135 × 243 mm.
[85] [C:] S.OMER — (Plan). 125 × 177 mm.
    [Inset:] [View of S.Omer]. 13 × 102 mm.
[86] [T:] LENS —
    [a] (View). 20 × 85 mm.
    [b] (Plan). 98 × 85 mm.
    [T:] HESDIN —
    [c] (View). 20 × 83 mm.
    [d] (Plan). 98 × 83 mm.
    [The whole plate:] 124 × 177 mm.
[87] [a] [T:] BAPPAVME — (View). 25 × 175 mm.
    [b] [C:] BAPPAVME — (Plan). 95 × 121 mm.
    [The whole plate:] 124 × 177 mm.
[88] [C:] LILLERS Nel Artesia — (View). 133 × 238 mm.

IL CONTADO DI NAMUR

[89] [T:] Conteè de Namurs — (Map). 107 × 130 mm.
[90] [C:] VEDUTA DELLA CITTA, e Pianta de CASTELLO DI NAMUR ... — 125 × 176 mm.
    [a] [T:] Veue de NAMUR — (View). 57 × 145 mm.
    [b] (Plan). 68 × 176 mm.
[91] [C:] NAMUR Capitale del Ducato dello stesso Nome — (Plan). 128 × 180 mm.
[92] [C:] CASTELLO DI NAMUR — (Plan). 126 × 175 mm.
[93] [C:] CHARLEMONT Nella C. di Namur — (Plan). 125 × 177 mm.

IL CAMBRESI

[94] [C:] CAMBRAY — (Plan). 125 × 178 mm.

Notes: All the maps are blank on the verso and uncoloured. This is the first volume of Coronelli's Teatro della Guerra, described by Armao under no.62 (pp. 138—140). Two of the maps do not appear in the index: [67] Bovignes Nel Contado di Namur and [78] Contorni di Philippeville Nell' Hannonia. The volume contains three portraits: 1. before the title Belgio, P. MAGISTER VINCENTIUS CORONELLI VENETUS Minister Generalis totius Seraphici Ordinis Min. Conu. LXVIII post S. Franciscum, Serenissimæq. Reipublicæ Cosmographij; 2. following the title La Fiandra Spagnuola, Ritratto del Ré di Spagna (title taken from the Indice); and following the title La Fiandra Gallicana, 3. Ritratto di Lodovico XIV (title taken from the Indice). Some of the maps in this copy are badly cropped, and map [28] is bound upside-down. Armao gives the text on the title-page as '... Pubblicato dal P. Coronelli secondo gli originali dell'Accademia Cosmografic', but in our copy the passage reads '...Pubblicato secondo gli Originali Del P. Coronelli, Dall'Accademia Cosmografica.' The leaves are numbered in old ink in accordance with the Indice, but certain maps do not fully correspond with those listed. Nordenskiöld's signature is on the inside of the front cover. All 13 volumes are bound in leather.

Fonzo ends his description of the different parts of the Teatro della guerra with an 'Annotazioni sul TG', in which he examines the whole series (pp.362—374). Nordenskiöld bought all 13 volumes of the Teatro della Guerra in our collection from Silvio Bocca in Rome. Among Nordenskiöld's papers is Bocca's invoice, on a postcard, dated 19.1.1900. The price was 80 fr. Bocca mentions that the Coronelli was no. 269 in his catalogue CLXVI, which is also in our collection; on the front cover Nordenskiöld has noted, in ink, 'Best. Jan 13— No 125 — 8 269 —80.' No. 125 is a two-volume work by Franc. Bernier, printed in Amsterdam in 1711. It also appears on the postcard, with the price 8 fr. The postage for the whole parcel was 6 fr.

Lit.: Armao nr 62, p. 138—140, Fonzo p. 360—363, nr 45.

Vol. II
TEATRO DELLA GUERRA
IL BELGIO CONFEDERATO [1706]. 18,5 cm obl.

[1] [C:] BELGIO CONFEDERATO Altrimenti detto L'OLANDA, Delineato, e Descritto dal P. CORONELLI — (Map). 4 123 × 175 mm.
[2] [a] [T:] ROTTERDAM — (Plan).
    [b] [T:] AMSTERDAM — (Plan).
    [c] [T:] HAJA — (View).
    [d] [T:] MIDDELBURGO — (Plan).
    [e] [T:] S. ANDREA — (Plan).
    [f] [T:] NIMEGA — (Plan).
    [g] [T:] ZUTPHEN — (Plan).
    [h] [T:] LOVESTEIN — (Plan).
    [i] [T:] ISABELLA — (Plan).
    [k] [T:] RAMMEXENS — (Plan).
    [l] [T:] ISENDYCX — (Plan).
    [m] [T:] SASSO — (Plan). Circular maps with 42 mm. diam.
    [The whole plate:] 7 125 × 178 mm.

CONTADO D'OLANDA

[3] [T:] AMSTERDAM — (View). 17 127 × 177 mm.
[4] [C:] AMSTERDAM — (Plan). 18 133 × 172 mm.
[5] [C:] CANALE D'AMSTERDAM DA HARLEM — (Map). 19 124 × 177 mm.
    [Inset:] [T:] AMSTERDAM (View). — 36 × 97 mm.

ROTERDAM, Rappresentato in Differenti Vedute

[6] [a] [T:] ROTTERDAM — (View). 54 × 173 mm.
    [b] [T:] GORCUM — (View). 65 × 173 mm.
    [The whole plate:] 25 123 × 177 mm.
[7] [T:] Veduta di Rotterdam — (View). 26 128 × 167 mm.
[8] [T:] Veduta di Rotterdam — (View). 27 134 × 170 mm.
[9] [T:] Veduta di Rotterdam — (View). 28 132 × 164 mm.
[10] [T:] Veduta di Rotterdam — (View). 29 133 × 171 mm.
[11] [C:] HAJA — (View). 31 123 × 176 mm.

[12] [a] [T:] DERGOU — (View). 66 × 175 mm.
 [b] [T:] BRIEL — (View). 54 × 175 mm.
 [The whole plate:] 33 124 × 177 mm.
[13] [C:] BRIEL — (Plan). 34 127 × 180 mm.
[14] [a] [C:] LA BRIELLE — (Plan). 125 × 84 mm.
 [b] [C:] SLUIS — (Plan). 125 × 85 mm.
 [The whole plate:] T.2. 46 126 × 172 mm.
[15] [T:] Esclusa — 36 124 × 177 mm.
 [a] (View). 56 × 174 mm.
 [b] (Plan). 65 × 175 mm.
[16] [a] [T:] HOORN — (View). 51 × 172 mm.
 [b] [T:] DENCHVYSEN — (View). 70 × 173 mm.
 [The whole plate:] 37 126 × 177 mm.
[17] [C:] NAERDEN — (Plan). 38 126 × 178 mm.
[18] [C:] DELFT CITTA DELL'OLLANDA ... — (Plan). 39 114 × 156 mm.
[19] [a] [C:] SCHENELINGUE — (View). 124 × 91 mm.
 [b] [C:] LEIDEM — (Plan). 124 × 90 mm.
 [The whole plate:] 40 124 × 184 mm.
[20] [a] [T:] DELFT — (View). 53 × 172 mm.
 [b] [T:] LEYDEN — (View). 67 × 172 mm.
 [The whole plate:] 42 123 × 176 mm.
[21] [T:] MEDENBLICK — (Plan). 43 125 × 177 mm.
[22] [a] [T:] OUDE WATER — (Plan). 122 × 84 mm.
 [b] [T:] WOERDEN — (Plan). 122 × 88 mm.
 [The whole plate:] 44 125 × 176 mm.
[23] [a] [T:] HARLLM — (View). 74 × 172 mm.
 [b] [T:] DORDRECHT — (View). 45 × 172 mm.
 [The whole plate:] 45 124 × 175 mm.
[24] [a] [C:] HARLEM — (Plan). 125 × 90 mm.
 [b] [C:] ALCKMAR — (Plan). 125 × 85 mm.
 [The whole plate:] T.2.96 46 126 × 178 mm.
[25] [a] [T:] SCHOOVEN — (View). 58 × 175 mm.
 [b] [T:] ALCKMAER — (View). 64 × 175 mm.
 [The whole plate:] 47 126 × 178 mm.
[26] [T:] S.GEERTRUYDEN-BERG — 48 125 × 174 mm.
 [a] (View). 54 × 174 mm.
 [b] (Plan). 68 × 174 mm.
[27] [a] [C:] WORCKUM — (Plan). 124 × 91 mm.
 [b] [C:] GORCKUM — (Plan). 124 × 91 mm.
 [The whole plate:] T II 49 126 × 187 mm.

CONTADO DI ZELANDA
[28] [C:] CONTADO DI ZELANDA — (Map). 52 124 × 176 mm.
[29] [a] [T:] MIDDELBVRGO — (View). 52 × 171 mm.
 [b] [T:] MIDDELBURGO — (Plan). 67 × 87 mm.
 [c] [T:] GOES — (Plan). 67 × 86 mm.
 [The whole plate:] 53 122 × 174 mm.
[30] [a] [C:] FLESINGUE — (Plan). 121 × 85 mm.
 [b] [C:] TOLLEN — (Plan). 121 × 85 mm.
 [The whole plate:] 54 125 × 175 mm.
[31] [a] [T:] ULISSINGEN — (View). 56 × 175 mm.
 [b] [T:] ARMUYDEN — (View). 63 × 175 mm.
 [The whole plate:] 56 124 × 178 mm.
[32] [T:] VEERE — 57 124 × 175 mm.
 [a] (View). 52 × 173 mm.
 [b] (Plan). 68 × 172 mm.

DUCATO DI GUELDRIA Del P. Coronelli
[33] [C:] ARNHEM — (Plan). 125 × 177 mm.
[34] [a] [T:] BOMMEL — (View). Oval 40 × 85 mm.
 [b] [T:] TIEL — (View). Oval 40 × 84 mm.
 [c] [T:] ARNEM — (View). 75 × 172 mm.
 [The whole plate:] 60 123 × 176 mm.
[35] [a] [C:] NIMEGA — (Plan). 124 × 82 mm.
 [b] [T:] BOMMEL — (Plan). 125 × 86 mm.
 [The whole plate:] T.2 61 126 × 177 mm.
[36] [a] [C:] VENLO — (Plan). 122 × 87 mm.
 [b] [C:] HARDEWICH — (Plan). 122 × 87 mm.
 [The whole plate:] 62 124 × 178 mm.
[37] [a] [T:] ISENDICHE — (Plan). 62 × 175 mm.
 [b] [C:] ARDENBURCH — (Plan). 60 × 88 mm.
 [c] [C:] TERNEUSE — (Plan). 60 × 86 mm.
 [The whole plate:] 63 125 × 177 mm.
[38] [C:] SCHINCKSCHANS Assediato Nel 1635. e 1636. — (Map). 64 125 × 178 mm.

[Inset:] [T:] PROFILO — (Profile).
[39] [C:] SCHINCKSCHANS — (Plan). 65 125 × 176 mm.

CONTEA DI ZUTPHEN 66
[40] [C:] CONTADO DI ZUTPHSN — (Map). 67 124 × 176 mm.
[41] [a] [T:] Ysel-oort — (Plan). Oval 31 × 41 mm.
 [b] [T:] Lochem — (View). Oval 33 × 43 mm.
 [c] [T:] Kaodsenborgh — (View). Oval 32 × 43 mm.
 [d] [T:] Wageningen — (View). Oval 33 × 42 mm.
 [e] [T:] ZUTPHEN — (View). Oval 40 × 86 mm.
 [f] [T:] ZUTPHEN — (Plan). 73 × 85 mm.
 [The whole plate:] [68] 124 × 176 mm.
[42] [C:] FRISIA ORIENTALE — (Map). 68 * 124 × 175 mm.
[43] [T:] EMBDEN — (View). 69 124 × 176 mm.
[44] [C:] EMDEN — (Plan). 69 125 × 175 mm.
[45] [C:] BOLZVARDIA — (Plan). 70 123 × 175 mm.
[46] [a] [C:] STAVEREN — (Plan). 121 × 84 mm.
 [b] [C:] BOURTANGE — (Plan). 121 × 86 mm.
 [The whole plate:] 71 124 × 175 mm.
[47] [a] [C:] DELFZIL — (Plan). 121 × 87 mm.
 [b] [C:] HARLINGEN — (Plan). 121 × 87 mm.
 [The whole plate:] 72 125 × 177 mm.
[48] [a] [T:] LEEUWARDEN — (View). 57 × 174 mm.
 [b] [T:] FRANCHER — (View). 65 × 173 mm.
 [The whole plate:] 73 124 × 176 mm.
[49] [a] [C:] LIEROORT — (Plan). 121 × 84 mm.
 [b] [C:] GRIETZIL — (Plan). 121 × 86 mm.
 [The whole plate:] 74 125 × 174 mm.

SIGNORIA D'OVERISSEL, Ó TRANSISSELANA
[50] [C:] OWER-VSSEL, ó TRANSISELLANA — (Map). 76 124 × 174 mm.
[51] [a] [T:] DEVENTER — (View). 44 × 173 mm.
 [b] [T:] OLDENZAL — (Plan). 76 × 88 mm.
 [c] [T:] DEVENTER — (Plan). 76 × 85 mm.
 [The whole plate:] 77 123 × 175 mm.
[52] [C:] CAMPEN — (Plan). 78 125 × 177 mm.
[53] [a] [T:] CAMPEN — (View). 73 × 172 mm.
 [b] [T:] CAMPEN — (Plan). 47 × 85 mm.
 [c] [T:] HASSELT — (Plan). 47 × 86 mm.
 [The whole plate:] 79 125 × 174 mm.
[54] [T:] ZWOL — (View). 80 125 × 176 mm.
[55] [a] [T:] SWOL — (Plan). 123 × 85 mm.
 [b] [T:] STEENWICK — (Plan). 123 × 86 mm.
 [The whole plate:] 81 125 × 176 mm.
[56] [C:] BLOCZIL — (Plan). 82 125 × 176 mm.
[57] [T:] COUORDEN — (Plan). T.II.83 67. 130 × 170 mm.

SIGNORIA D'UTRECHT
[58] [C:] SIGNORIA D'UTRECNT — (Map). 85 124 × 178 mm.
[59] [a] [T:] HINDERDAN — (Plan). 62 × 43 mm.
 [b] [T:] Nieuwer Sluys — (Plan). 62 × 44 mm.
 [c] [T:] MUYDEN — (Plan). 63 × 88 mm.
 [d] [T:] UTRECHT — (Plan). 126 × 88 mm.
 [The whole plate:] T.2.122 87 126 × 177 mm.
[60] [C:] SIGNORIA DI GRONINGUE — (Map). 88 123 × 173 mm.
[61] [T:] GROENINGHEN — (View). 89 125 × 176 mm.
[62] [C:] GRONINGEN — (Plan). 90 125 × 177 mm.
[63] [a] [C:] LANGACNER SCHANS — (Plan). 123 × 87 mm.
 [b] [C:] BELLINGWOLDER SCHANS — (Plan). 123 × 87 mm.
 [The whole plate:] 91 126 × 177 mm.

FIANDRA
[64] [C:] HULST, Assediato Nel 1645. — (Plan). 93 125 × 175 mm.
[65] [C:] FLANDRIÆ AMBACTA QVATERNA — [T:] AXEL — (Plan). 94 126 × 176 mm.
[66] [a] [C:] CASSANT — 122 × 90 mm.
 [b] [C:] OOSTBURG — 122 × 84 mm.
 [The whole plate:] 95 124 × 177 mm.

BRABANTE
[67] [C:] BRABANTE — (Map). 97 125 × 175 mm.

[68] [a] [C:] MASTRICK Colle Proposte del Blondel — (Plan). 124 × 73 mm.
[b] [C:] MASTRICK com'è Oggidi — (Plan). 124 × 99 mm.
[The whole plate:] 98   125 × 176 mm.
[69] [C:] GRAVE Città del Brabante Descritto, e Dedicato dal Padre Cosmografo Coronelli — (Plan). 99   185 × 235 mm.
[70] [a] [T:] GRAVE — (View). 59 × 174 mm.
[b] [T:] HELMOND — (View). 62 × 174 mm.
[The whole plate:] 100   125 × 177 mm.
[71] [a] [C:] BOIS LE DUC — (View). 56 × 173 mm.
[b] [C:] LILLO — (Plan). 63 × 77 mm.
[c] [C:] BOIS-LE-DUC — (Plan). 63 × 95 mm.
[The whole plate:] 101   124 × 176 mm.
[72] [C:] GENEP — (Plan). 102   124 × 177 mm.
[73] [a] [C:] CLUNDERT — (Plan). 123 × 85 mm.
[b] [C:] WILLEMSTAT — (Plan). 123 × 89 mm.
[The whole plate:] 203 (pro 103).   125 × 177 mm.
[74] [T:] BERGOPZOM — 104   126 × 177 mm.
[a] (View). 36 × 176 mm.
[b] (Plan). 87 × 176 mm.
[75] [T:] DOESBURG prima delle Nuoue Fortificazioni ... — (Plan). 352   105   131 × 171 mm.
[76] [C:] DOESBURG Modernamente fortificato — (Plan). 106   125 × 177 mm.
[77] [C:] BREDA Assediata Nel 1624. — (Plan). 107   126 × 176 mm.
[78] [C:] BREDA — (Plan). 175 × 226 mm.
[79] [T:] LIEFKENS — (Plan). 109   131 × 165 mm.
[80] [C:] CREVECOR — (Plan). 110   126 × 179 mm.
[81] [a] [C:] HEUSDEM. — (Plan). 125 × 87 mm.
[b] [C:] Forte S.Andrea — (Plan). 71 × 87 mm.
[c] [C:] F.Nassau, ó Voorn — (Plan). 54 × 87 mm.
[The whole plate:] T 2 III   124 × 178 mm.
[82] [a] [T:] EMMERICK — (View). 32 × 174 mm.
[b] [T:] BURICK — (Plan). 86 × 82 mm.
[c] [T:] EMMERICK — (Plan). 86 × 88 mm.
[The whole plate:] 112   125 × 177 mm.
[83] [a] [C:] WESEL — (Plan). 123 × 90 mm.
[b] [C:] REES — (Plan). 123 × 90 mm.
[The whole plate:] 113   126 × 184 mm.
[84] [C:] Forti fabbricati dagli Stati Vniti Sù le Frontiere di Olanda — 114   125 × 177 mm.
[a] [T:] GOUDSESLUYS — (Plan). 50 × 88 mm.
[b] [T:] PAINEVIN — (Plan). 35 × 83 mm.
[c] [T:] NIEWERBRUGH — (Plan). 62 × 88 mm.
[d] [T:] WIERICHE — (Plan). 77 × 83 mm.

LUOGHI POSSEDUTI DAL BELGIO CONFEDERATO Fuori dell'Europa
[85] [C:] ISOLA GOREE — (View). 119   172 × 244 mm.
[86] [C:] ISOLA GOREE — (Plan). 120   131 × 166 mm.
[87] [C:] MONTE TAVOLA Situato al Capo di Buona Speranza degli Olandèsi — (View). 121   130 × 164 mm.
[88] [C:] I DI CERNE, ò MAURITIO Scoperta 18 Settembre 1695 — (View). 123   130 × 164 mm.
[89] [C:] BATTAVIA — (Plan). 167 × 223 mm.
[90] [T:] BATAVIA — (Plan). 125   123 × 176 mm.
[91] [T:] ISOLE DI BANDA NELLE MOLUCCHE — (Map). 126   129 × 166 mm.
[92] [T:] NUOVA ZELANDIA, ò TERRA DEGLI STATI, detta dagl' Hollandesi HET NIEW ZELANDT Scoperta dagli Medemi L'annó 1654 — (Map). 127   120 × 160 mm.
[93] [C:] ISOLA DI SOLOR — (View). 128   133 × 166 mm.
[94] [a] [C:] I.COCOS — (View). 121 × 84 mm.
[b] [C:] I.HORN — (View). 121 × 86 mm.
[The whole plate:] 129   125 × 178 mm.
[95] [a] [C:] BATAVIA — (View). 42 × 83 mm.
[b] [C:] BATAVIA — (View). 77 × 83 mm.
[c] [C:] ISOLE MOLUCCHE — (Map). 121 × 87 mm.
[The whole plate:] 130   124 × 177 mm.
[96] [a] [C:] GAMMALAMME — (View). 120 × 87 mm.
[b] [T:] COLOMBO — (Plan). 58 × 82 mm.
[c] [C:] GALLE — (View). 60 × 82 mm.
[The whole plate:] 132   125 × 178 mm.

Notes: All the maps are blank on the verso and uncoloured. The frontispiece mentioned by Armao (p.140) is wanting in our copy. This is the second volume of the whole Teatro della guerra, and the second volume of Belgico. Following map [1], Belgico Confederato, is a portrait of Guglielmo di Nassau Rè d'Inghilterra (title taken from the index). Some of the maps are badly cropped and nos. [65] and [76] have been bound upside-down, as has the title-page of Signoria d'Overissel. The volume is no.63 in Armao (pp.140—141); our copy does not quite correspond to Armao's description. Some of the plates have two different numbers, the first referring to this volume, the other, in a lower corner, apparently referring to some other work. F.11, with text, appears twice in our copy. Nordenskiöld's initials are written on the inside of the front cover.

Lit.: Armao p. 140—141, Fonzo, p. 360, nr 45, T.II.

Vol. III wanting
Vol. IV wanting

Vol. V
LA FRANCIA Divisa in XII. PREFETTURE Delineata dal P. CORONELLI P.I. [1706].
[Half title:]
FRANCIA   18,5 cm obl.

[1] [C:] FRANCIA — (Map). 128 × 180 mm.
[2] [C:] LA FRANCIA ANTICA, e MODERNA Dedicata All' Illustrissimo Signore Marchese Michiele Sagramoso, Accademico degli Argonauti, già Inuiato di S.A. del S. Duca di Mantoa, appresso S.M.Cristianissima Descritta dal P. Maestro Coronelli, Cosmografo della S.S. Republica di Venetia — [Part I]. (Map). 604 × 444 mm.
[3] [La Francia antica] [Part II]. 608 × 446 mm.
[4] [C:] VEDUTE D'ALCUNE CITTA PRINCIPALI DELLA FRANCIA — 13   122 × 179 mm.
[a] [T:] LION — (View). Oval 39 × 59 mm.
[b] PARIGI — (Plan). Oval 41 × 55 mm.
[c] [T:] VIENNA — (View). Oval 40 × 59 mm.
[d] [T:] ORLEANS — (View). Oval 38 × 58 mm.
[e] [T:] POICTIERS — (View). Oval 38 × 58 mm.
[f] [T:] BOURGES — (View). Oval 40 × 60 mm.
[g] [T:] CALES — (View). Oval 40 × 58 mm.
[h] [T:] MONPELLIER — (View). Oval 38 × 58 mm.

ISOLA DI FRANCIA
[5] [C:] PARTE OCCIDENTALE DELLI CONTORNI DI PARIGI Dedicata All'Ill.mo, et ECC.mo Sig.r D.Donato de Gubernatis — (Map). 607 × 445 mm.
[6] [C:] PARTE ORIENTALE DELLI CONTORNI DI PARIGI Dedicata All'Ill.mo et Ecc.mo Sig.r D.Donato de Gubernatis di Ventimiglia Cauaiiere, e Comend: dell' Ord' Militare de S.S. Mauritio, e Lazaro — (Map). 607 × 437 mm.
[7] [C:] PARIGI — 19   121 × 177 mm.
[a] (View). 38 × 172 mm.
[b] (View). 38 × 85 mm.
[8] [C:] PARIGI — (Plan). 123 × 178 mm.
[9] [C:] CORBEIL — 123 × 178 mm.
[a] (Plan). 58 × 176 mm.
[b] (Map). 63 × 176 mm.
[10] [T:] GOVERNO DI MONTARGIS — (Map). 124 × 180 mm.
[11] [T:] CONFLANS — (View). 320   133 × 176 mm.
[12] [C:] MONTFORT L'AMAULERY — (View). 27   124 × 181.
[13] [T:] CORSO DEL F. LOIRE — (Map). 28   123 × 179 mm.
[14] [C:] AMBOISE — 123 × 179 mm.
[a] (View). 33 × 177 mm.
[b] (Map). 87 × 177 mm.
[15] [C:] ANGERS — 122 × 177 mm.
[a] (View). 41 × 174 mm.
[b] (Map). 74 × 174 mm.
[16] [T:] GOVERNO DI NEVERS — (Map). 31   124 × 180 mm.

VERSAGLIA

[17] [T:] Castello, e Giardino di Versaglia — (View). 33   123 × 177 mm.
BORGOGNA
[18] [C:] DUCATO DI BORGOGNA Descritto dal P. Coronelli — (Map). 109   123 × 175 mm.
[19] [T:] GOVERNO DI DIJON — (Map). 47   123 × 178 mm.
[20] [T:] DIJON — (Plan). 48   126 × 182 mm.
[21] [T:] GOVERNO DI BEAULNE — (Map). 49   123 × 178 mm.
[22] [T:] S. JEAN DE LAUNE — (Plan). 57   124 × 179 mm.
[23] [T:] GOVERNO D'AUTUN — (Map). 50   122 × 177 mm.
[24] [T:] GOVERNO D'AUXONNE — (Map). 51   123 × 178 mm.
[25] [T:] GOVERNO DI CHAALONS SVR SAONE — (Map). 122 × 178 mm.
[26] [T:] CHAALONS — (Plan). 35 (pro 53).   124 × 178 mm.
[27] [T:] Governo di Bellegarde — (Map). 54   123 × 178 mm.
[28] [C:] BELLEGARDE Nella Borgogra — (Plan). 122 × 179 mm.
[29] [T:] GOVERNO DI S. JEAN DE LAUNE — (Map). 56   121 × 175 mm.
[30] [C:] TOURNUS —   121 × 175 mm.
 [a] (View).   39 × 175 mm.
 [b] (Map).   75 × 172 mm.
[31] [T:] GOVERNO DI MACON — (Map). 59   123 × 177 mm.
[32] [C:] VERDUN — (Plan).   124 × 178 mm.
[33] [C:] BESANÇON — (Plan). 61   122 × 177 mm.
NORMANDIA
[34] [C:] DUCATO DI NORMANDIA. Dedicato All'Illustriss, et Eccelletissimo S. PIETRO DONA Frattello dell'Eccellentiss. S. Proc: Lunando dal P. Coronelli — (Map).   445 × 611 mm.
[35] [C:] DIEPPE — (Plan).   125 × 160 mm.
[36] [C:] ROAN — 65   124 × 179 mm.
 [a] (View).   38 × 177 mm.
 [b] (Plan).   82 × 177 mm.
[37] [C:] ROAN — 65   124 × 179 mm.
 [a] (Plan).   76 × 176 mm.
 [b] (View). Oval 44 × 156 mm.
[38] [C:] HAVRE DE GRACE — (Plan). 66   122 × 178 mm.
GUENNA
[39] [C:] LA GUIENNA, MEDOC, SAINTONGE, AUNIS, e Paesi Conuicini, Dedicati Al Padre Reuerendissimo Don Mattia Toscani, della Congregatione de Monaci di S. Girolamo di Lombardia, Accademico degli Argonauti — (Map).   608 × 446 mm.
 [Inset:] [T:] BORDO, ò BORDEAUX — (Plan).   136 × 265 mm.
[40] [T:] GOVERNO DI BAJONNA — (Map). 69   122 × 177 mm.
[41] [C:] BAJONNA — (Plan).   121 × 177 mm.
[42] [C:] BOURG Sopra La Garonna — 74   123 × 177 mm.
 [a] (Plan).   58 × 173 mm.
 [b] (Map).   62 × 173 mm.
[43] [T:] GOVERNO DI CAHORS — (Map). 72   123 × 177 mm.
[44] [C:] CAHORS — (Plan). 73   121 × 176 mm.
[45] [a] [T:] BOURG — (Plan).   48 × 175 mm.
 [b] [C:] BOURG — (Map).   71 × 175 mm.
 [The whole plate:] 71   122 × 178 mm.
[46] [T:] BOVRG — (Plan). 324   129 × 172 mm.
[47] [T:] GOVERNO DI BERGERAC — (Map). 76   122 × 176 mm.
[48] [a] [T:] FRONSAC — (Plan).   121 × 85 mm.
 [b] [T:] BERGERAC — (Plan).   121 × 88 mm.
 [The whole plate:] 77   124 × 178 mm.
[49] [T:] GOVERNO DI LIBOURNE, & FRONSAC — (Map). 78   123 × 176 mm.
[50] [T:] LIBOURNE — (Plan). 79   122 × 178 mm.
[51] [T:] S. JEAN D'ANGELY — (Plan). 80   122 × 177 mm.
Notes: All the maps are blank on the verso and uncoloured. Armao states that the three volumes of Coronelli's Francia are not held by the Bibliothèque Nationale in Paris. There are two portraits in the volume, immediately following the title-page: 4 LVDOVICVS MAGNVS FRANC. ET NAV. REX. P.P., and LODOVICO IL GRANDE. The index includes all three volumes. Some of the plates are incorrectly bound: no.57 appears between 49 and 50, and 70 is followed by 74, 72, 73, 71. No. [13] is bound upside-down. 'A.E.N.' is written in pencil on the inside of the front cover.

Lit.: Armao p. 143—144, nr 66, Fonzo, p. 360.

Vol. VI
LA FRANCIA Divisa in XII. PREFETTURE Delineata dal P. CORONELLI P.I[I]. [1706].   18,5 cm obl.

SCIAMPAGNA
[1] [C:] SEDAN — (Plan).   124 × 179 mm.
[2] [T:] S.t DEZIER — (Plan). 347   135 × 177 mm.
[3] [C:] MEZIERS Colle Nuove Fortificazioni — (Plan).   125 × 180 mm.
[4] [T:] MESIERES Prima delle Nuove Fortificazioni — (Plan). 160   130 × 168 mm.
[5] [a] [C:] ESPERNAY Sul F.Marne — (View).   58 × 172 mm.
 [b] [C:] JAMETZ — (View).   58 × 172 mm.
 [The whole plate:] 101   121 × 175 mm.
[6] [C:] CHASTILLON Sur Marne — (View). 102   123 × 178 mm.
[7] [T:] LA FERE — (Plan). 321   130 × 171 mm.
[8] [C:] DONCHERY — (View).   123 × 179 mm.
[9] [T:] LANGRES — (Plan).   129 × 169 mm.
[10] [C:] CHARLEVILLE — [T:] CHARLEVILLE, Dedicato Al'Monto Reu: PreBacc. Giuseppe Cesena dalla Pergola, Padre della Gran Casa de Frari — (Plan).   128 × 173 mm.
LINGUADOCCA
[11] [T:] COSTA DI LINGUADOCCA, PROVENZA, E PARTE D'ITALIA A.P.Coronelli. — (Chart). 108   124 × 178 mm.
[12] [T:] PROVINCIA DI LINGUADOCCA — (Map). 109   124 × 178 mm.
[13] [C:] LINGUADOCCA SUPERIORE, Descritta Dal P. Coronelli — (Map).   124 × 177 mm.
[14] [T:] PARTE OCCIDENTALE DELLA LINGUADOCCA — (Map). 111   124 × 178 mm.
[15] [C:] DISEGNO IDROGRAFICO DEL CANALE REALE Dell'Vnione di due Mari In Lingua docca Descritto — [C:] DEDICATO Agli Illustrissimi Signori GIO. FRANCESCO, GIROLAMO, E GIOVANNI QVERINI Figli dell'Illustrissimo, et Eccellentissimo Signore PAOLO Procuratore di S.Marco dal P. Maestro Coronelli Cosmografo della Serenissima Republica e Lettore Publico. — (Map).   432 × 598 mm.
[16] [T:] GOVERNO DI TOLOSA — (Map). 113   124 × 179 mm.
[17] [C:] TOLOSA — (Plan). 114   124 × 180 mm.
[18] [a] [T:] BOURDEAUX — (View).   54 × 174 mm.
 [b] [C:] CONTORNI DI BOURDEAUX — (Map).   66 × 174 mm.
 [The whole plate:] 71   124 × 178 mm.
[19] [C:] BOURDEAUX — (Plan).   124 × 179 mm.
[20] [C:] NARBONNA —   124 × 179 mm.
 [a] (View).   35 × 177 mm.
 [b] (Map).   86 × 177 mm.
[21] [T:] NARBONNA — (Plan). 118   125 × 178 mm.
[22] [C:] Bocca del Fiume Garonna — (Map).   115 × 163 mm.
[23] [C:] MONPELLIER — 184   122 × 178 mm.
 [a] (View).   35 × 176 mm.
 [b] (Map).   84 × 176 mm.
[24] [T:] CITTADELLA DI MONTPELLIER — (Plan). 122   122 × 178 mm.
[25] [T:] Governo di Nismes — (Map). 123   122 × 177 mm.
[26] [T:] NISMES — (Plan). 124   123 × 178 mm.
[27] [T:] CLERAC — (Plan). 125   123 × 178 mm.
[28] [T:] Governo di Montauban — (Map). 126   123 × 178 mm.
[29] [C:] MONTAUBAN — (Plan).   123 × 178 mm.
[30] [T:] Pont S.Esprit — (Map). 128   124 × 179 mm.

[31] [T:] PONT S.ESPRIT — (View). 129 123 × 180 mm.
[32] [T:] CITTA DI S.SPIRITO — (Plan). 130 123 × 178 mm.
[33] [T:] GOVERNO DI REALMONT — (Map). 131 123 × 178 mm.
[34] [T:] REALMONT — (Plan). 132 123 × 178 mm.
[35] [T:] Governo di Castres — (Map). 123 × 178 mm.
[36] [T:] CASTRES — (Plan). 134 123 × 178 mm.
[37] [T:] GOVERNO DI ROQUECOURBE — (Map). 135 123 × 179 mm.
[38] [T:] ROQUECOURBE — (Plan). 136 124 × 177 mm.
[39] [T:] Governo di Pezenas — (Map). 137 126 × 179 mm.
[40] [C:] PEZENAS — (View). 123 × 177 mm.
[41] [a] [T:] ALEZ — (Plan). 62 × 174 mm.
     [b] [C:] ALEZ — (Map). 59 × 174 mm.
     [The whole plate:] 139 125 × 178 mm.
[42] [C:] LEYTOVRE — 124 × 179 mm.
     [a] (Plan). 57 × 176 mm.
     [b] (Map). 63 × 177 mm.
[43] [C:] NAVARINS — 141 124 × 179 mm.
     [a] (Plan). 72 × 177 mm.
     [b] (Map). 49 × 177 mm.
[44] [C:] PRIVAS — 122 × 175 mm.
     [a] (View). 38 × 172 mm.
     [b] (Map). 77 × 172 mm.
[45] [C:] S.MATHURIN DE L'ARQUAN — 123 × 176 mm.
     [a] (View). 49 × 173 mm.
     [b] (Map). 67 × 174 mm.
[46] [T:] Gouerni di Lunel, e Sommieres — (Map). 144 122 × 178 mm.
[47] [T:] LUNEL — (Plan). 145 124 × 180 mm.
[48] [T:] GOVERNO D'ANGOULESME — (Map). 146 124 × 179 mm.
[49] [T:] ANGOULESME — (Plan). 147 122 × 180 mm.
[50] [T:] FOIX — (Map). 123 × 178 mm.
[51] [T:] GOVERNO DI LAUCATTE — (Map). 149 123 × 180 mm.
[52] [T:] Governo di Uzez — (Map). 150 123 × 178 mm.
[53] [C:] UZEZ — (Plan). 151 123 × 179 mm.
[54] [T:] Governo di Caussade — (Map). 152 123 × 178 mm.
[55] [T:] DUCATO DI RICHELIEU — (Map). 153 123 × 180 mm.
[56] [T:] GOVERNO DI BROUAGE — (Map). 124 × 179 mm.
[57] [a] [C:] CARLAT — (View). 64 × 176 mm.
     [b] [C:] SAVEDUN — (View). 55 × 176 mm.
     [The whole plate:] 123 × 179 mm.
[58] [C:] CITTA, E CITTADELLA DI PERPIGNAN colle antiche Fortificazioni — (Plan). 125 × 175 mm.
[59] [C:] PERPIGNAN Modernamente fortificato — (Plan). 123 × 178 mm.
[60] [C:] PRATS DEMOLIOU Nel Rossiglione — (Plan). 125 × 180 mm.
[61] [C:] COLLIOURE — (Plan). 125 × 178 mm.
[62] [C:] CITTADELLA DI SALLES, ò SALCES Nel Rossiglione Descritta, e Dedicata Dal P. Cosmografo Coronelli Al M.R.P.D. Giuseppe Maria Cigala Chierico Regolare, Predicatore, etc. — (Plan). 161 223 × 294 mm.
[63] [C:] MONT-LOUIS Fabbricato nel 1678. ... — (Plan). 162 123 × 179 mm.
[64] [C:] TROMPETTE — (Plan). 125 × 181 mm.

PICARDIA

[65] [T:] PICARDIA — (Map). 165 125 × 180 mm.
[66] [T:] GOVERNO DI GUISE — (Map). 166 123 × 180 mm.
[67] [T:] GVIZE — (Plan). 322 130 × 172 mm.
[68] [a] [C:] GUISE — (View). 62 × 177 mm.
     [b] [C:] HAN — (View). 58 × 177 mm.
     [The whole plate:] 158 (pro 168). 124 × 179 mm.
[69] [a] [Amiens]. (View). 28 × 177 mm.
     [b] [C:] GOVERNO D'AMIENS — (Map). 92 × 178 mm.
     [The whole plate:] 124 × 180 mm.
[70] [C:] AMIENS — (Plan). 170 123 × 179 mm.
[71] [T:] GOVERNO DI BOLOGNA — (Map). 171 124 × 179 mm.
[72] [C:] BOLOGNA — 172 123 × 180 mm.
     [a] (View). 36 × 176 mm.
     [b] (Plan). 82 × 176 mm.
[73] [a] [T:] HAN — (Plan). 59 × 177 mm.
     [b] [C:] GOVERNO D'HAN — (Map). 61 × 177 mm.
     [The whole plate:] 124 × 179 mm.
[74] [T:] GOVERNO D'ARDRES — (Map). 179 (pro 174). 123 × 179 mm.
[75] [C:] ARDRES — (Plan). 175 123 × 179 mm.
[76] [T:] GOVERNO DI PERONNE — (Map). 176 125 × 180 mm.
[77] [C:] PERONNE — (Plan). 177 125 × 180 mm.
[78] [T:] GOVERNO D'ABBEVILLE — (Map). 178 125 × 177 mm.
[79] [C:] ABBEVILLE — 179 172 × 127 mm.
     [a] (View). 50 × 123 mm.
     [b] (Plan). 121 × 123 mm.
[80] [a] [C:] LA-FERE — (View). 48 × 177 mm.
     [b] [C:] ESTAPLES — (View). 71 × 177 mm.
     [The whole plate:] 123 × 177 mm.
[81] [C:] CATELET — 181 125 × 180 mm.
     [a] (Plan). 38 × 178 mm.
     [b] (Map). 84 × 178 mm.
[82] [C:] LAON — (View). 182 121 × 176 mm.
[83] [C:] Contorni di CORBIE — 123 × 180 mm.
     [a] (Plan). 67 × 177 mm.
     [b] (Map). 53 × 178 mm.
[84] [a] [C:] MONTREVIL — (View). 52 × 175 mm.
     [b] [C:] MONTREVIL — (Plan). 68 × 175 mm.
     [The whole plate:] 184 124 × 180 mm.
[85] [C:] RVE — 185 123 × 178 mm.
     [a] (Plan). 59 × 176 mm.
     [b] (Map). 62 × 176 mm.
[86] [T:] PONT DE REMY com'é presentemente — (Plan). 186 124 × 178 mm.
[87] [T:] PONT DE REMY — (Plan). 214 131 × 172 mm.
[88] [a] [T:] CONTORNI D'ESTAPLE — (Map). 120 × 90 mm.
     [b] [C:] ESTAPLE — [T:] PIANTA D'ESTAPLE — (Plan). 120 × 85 mm.
     [The whole plate:] 123 × 179 mm.
[89] [a] [C:] DOURLANS — (Plan). 48 × 176 mm.
     [b] [C:] GOVERNO DI DOURLANS — (Map). 75 × 176 mm.
     [The whole plate:] 124 × 178 mm.
[90] [T:] GOVERNO DI CALAIS — (Map). 190 123 × 180 mm.
[91] [T:] Contorni di Cales, o di Calais. — (Map). 191 123 × 178 mm.
[92] [C:] CALES — 193 (pro 192). 123 × 179 mm.
     [a] (View). 58 × 175 mm.
     [b] (Plan). 70 × 175 mm.
[93] [C:] CALAIS — (Plan). 193 123 × 179 mm.
[94] [a] [C:] DOWER — (Plan). 123 × 92 mm.
     [b] [C:] CALAIS — (Plan). 123 × 91 mm.
     [The whole plate:] T.2.185 124 × 187 mm.
[95] [C:] FORTE NIEULAY — (Plan). 195 124 × 179 mm.
[96] [C:] AMBLETEUSE — (Plan). 196 124 × 179 mm.

DELFINATO

[97] [C:] DELFINATO, Descritto Dal P. Coronelli — (Map). 198 125 × 170 mm.
[98] [C:] IL DELFINATO Diuiso in Baillaggi Dal P. Cosmografo Coronelli — [C:] Dedicato, e Presentato ALL' ILL.mo SIGNORE IL SIGNORE PIETRO BUSINELLO Residente per la Serenissima Republica di Venetia in Milano — (Map). 438 × 607 mm.
[99] [C:] VIENNA — 123 × 179 mm.
     [a] (View). 43 × 178 mm.
     [b] (Map). 77 × 178 mm.
[100] [C:] GOVERNO D'EMBRUN Ò AMBRUN — (Map). 130 × 171 mm.
[101] [C:] Città, e Fortezza D'AMBRUN Nel Delfinato, Dedicata All'Illustrissimo Signore ANGELO BERTONCELLI Dal P. Coronelli — (Plan). 130 × 176 mm.

[102] [T:] GOVRNO DI VALENZA — (Map). 203 125 × 180 mm.
[103] [T:] VALENZA — (Plan). 204 122 × 177 mm.
[104] [C:] CITTA e FORTEZZA DI BRIANZON Dedicata All'Illustris: Sig: Conte e Cauallier Matteo Alberti — (View). 128 × 169 mm.
[105] [C:] GOVERNO DI QUIRIEU — 206 123 × 177 mm.
  [a] (View). 52 × 174 mm.
  [b] (Map). 67 × 174 mm.
[106] [a] [T:] CONTORNI DI MONTELIMAR — (Map). 121 × 90 mm.
  [b] [T:] PIANTA DI MONTELIMAR — (Plan). 121 × 84 mm.
  [The whole plate:] 123 × 178 mm.
[107] [a] [T:] GAP — (Plan). 46 × 174 mm.
  [b] [C:] GAP, e PUYMORE — (Map). 72 × 174 mm.
  [The whole plate:] 298 (pro 208). 123 × 177 mm.
[108] [a] [C:] PUYMORE — (View). 55 × 173 mm.
  [b] [C:] GAP — (View). 66 × 173 mm.
  [The whole plate:] 209 124 × 178 mm.

Notes: All the maps are blank on the verso and uncoloured. The title-page is the same as that in vol. V i.e. Francia I, even including the number. The first part of the volume should be Bretagna, but this has been bound into vol. III instead. The title-page for Rossiglione is wanting. The numbers on several of the plates have been wrongly printed, as can be seen from the list above. Some of the maps are badly cropped, and no. [32] is bound upside-down. The initials 'A.E.N.' are written on the inside of the front cover.

Lit.: Armao, p. 143—144, nr 66, Fonzo, p. 360.

Vol. VII
LA FRANCIA Divisa in XII. PREFETTURE Delineata dal P. CORONELLI P.I[II]. [1706]. 18,8 cm obl.

PROVENZA
[1] [C:] MARSEGLIA — 212 124 × 178 mm.
  [a] (View). 55 × 175 mm.
  [b] (Map). 65 × 175 mm.
[2] [C:] Ingresso del Porto di MARSIGLIA — (Map). 313 (pro 213) 124 × 178 mm.
[3] [T:] FORTE DE LA CROSETTE — (Plan). 30 130 × 164 mm.
[4] [C:] PIANO del CAPO, e Porto di CETTE — (Plan). 308 130 × 173 mm.
[5] [C:] PORTO DI TOLON Descritto Dal P. Cosmografo, e Lettore Coronelli. — (Map). 315 127 × 172 mm.
[6] [C:] TOLON colle Proposte, e Nuove Fortificazioni. — (Plan). 131 × 171 mm.
[7] [C:] Forte di Brigançon, ed Isole di yeres — (Map). 132 × 168 mm.
[8] [C:] BRIGANCON FORTE' — (View). 221 (pro 220). 124 × 179 mm.
[9] [T:] ISOLE D'HIERES O' D'OR NEL MEDITERRANEO — (Map). 221 122 × 177 mm.
[10] [T:] GOVERNO D'ANTIBES — (Map). 174 124 × 179 mm.
[11] [C:] ANTIBES Colle moderne Fortificazioni — (Plan). 125 × 180 mm.
[12] [C:] ANTIBES Auanti l'ultime Fortificazioni — (Map). 130 × 160 mm.
[13] [T:] ISOLE DI S.MARGARITA — (Chart). 225 123 × 177 mm.
[14] [T:] I. S. HONORATO DI LERIN — (Map). 226 123 × 178 mm.
[15] [C:] ISOLE DI IONQUIERES e TORRE DI BUC Nel Canale di Martegues. — (Map). 121 × 160 mm.
[16] [C:] CASTELLO DIF — (Plan). 228 124 × 176 mm.
[17] [T:] STAGNO DI VENDRES — (Map). 229 124 × 177 mm.
[18] [T:] GOVERNO DI S.TROPEZ — (Map). 310 (pro 230). 123 × 178 mm.
[19] [C:] GOLFO DI GRIMAUT — (Map). 231 125 × 178 mm.
[20] [T:] CANALE DI MARTEGUES, E MARE DI BERRE — (Map). 232 123 × 179 mm.
[21] [T:] Capo d'Agde, olim Agathæ Prom: — [T:] FORTE BRESCON, olim BLASCON — (View). 134 × 225 mm.
[22] [T:] GOVERNO D'AIX. — (Map). 234 124 × 178 mm.
[23] [T:] AIX — (Plan). 235 123 × 178 mm.
[24] [T:] GOVERNO DI CISTERON — (Map). 236 124 × 179 mm.
[25] [a] [T:] CISTERON — (Plan). 120 × 88 mm.
  [b] [T:] EXILLES — (Plan). 120 × 84 mm.
  [The whole plate:] 237 123 × 177 mm.

CONTADI D'AVIGNONE, E VENASSINO
[26] [T:] Prencipato d'Oranges, e Contado Venassino — (Map). 242 124 × 178 mm.
[27] [C:] CONTADO DE VENASSINO, E PRENCIPATO D'ORANGES, Dedicato All'Illustriss: Sig: Abbate DOMENICO DI CABANES Dal P. Maestro Coronelli Lettore, e Cosmografo della Serenissima Republica di Venetia, 1690 — (Map). 440 × 603 mm.
[28] [T:] AVIGNONE Già Seggio de Sommi Pontefici — (Plan). 392 130 × 165 mm.
[29] [C:] ORANGES — 242 124 × 179 mm.
  [a] (View). 42 × 177 mm.
  [b] (Plan). 80 × 177 mm.

LIONESE
[30] [a] [T:] LION — (View). 39 × 175 mm.
  [b] [T:] LION — (Map). 80 × 175 mm.
  [The whole map:] 244 124 × 179 mm.
[31] [T:] LION — (Plan). 245 125 × 178 mm.

POITÚ
[32] [a] [T:] POITÙ — (View). 56 × 173 mm.
  [b] [C:] POICTIERES — (Map). 58 × 173 mm.
  [The whole plate:] 247 121 × 177 mm.
[33] [C:] ESTAMPES — 248 123 × 178 mm.
  [a] (View). 48 × 172 mm.
  [b] (Map). 70 × 173 mm.
[34] [T:] GOVERNO DELLA GARNACHE — (Map). 249 122 × 179 mm.
[35] [C:] LA GARNACHE — (Plan). 130 × 168 mm.
[36] [C:] C.REGNARD — 251 124 × 178 mm.
  [a] (View). 53 × 175 mm.
  [b] (Map). 68 × 175 mm.
[37] [C:] ISOLA DI NARMOUSTIER, alle Bocche del Fiume Loira. — (Map). 129 × 162 mm.

SANTONIA, Ó SANTOIGNE
[38] [T:] SANTONIA ó GOVERNO DI XAINTES — (Map). 153 123 × 178 mm.
[39] [C:] XAINTES — (Plan). 255 122 × 178 mm.
[40] [C:] ISOLA DERE — (Map). 314 130 × 172 mm.
[41] [T:] S.MARTIN DEL RE' — (Plan). 257 124 × 179 mm.
[42] [C:] FORTE DI S.MARTINO Descritto Dal P. Cosmografo Coronelli — (Plan). 128 × 167 mm.
[43] [T:] ISOLA D'OLERON — (View). 100 × 191 mm.
[44] [C:] LA CITTADELLA D'OLERON — (Plan). 132 × 161 mm.
[45] [C:] LA ROCHELLE — 121 × 176 mm.
  [a] (View). 40 × 173 mm.
  [b] (Map). 75 × 173 mm.
[46] [T:] ROCELLA — (Plan). 262 125 × 179 mm.
  [Inset:] (View). Oval 44 × 55 mm.
[47] [C:] S.GIO: D'ANGELI — 263 124 × 180 mm.
  [a] (View). 40 × 178 mm.
  [b] (Map). 80 × 178 mm.
[48] [C:] ROCHEFORT Nella Saintonge — (Plan). 124 × 178 mm.

ANIOU
[49] [a] [T:] PIANTA DI SAUMUR — (Plan). 122 × 83 mm.
  [b] [T:] CONTORNI DI SAUMUR — (Map). 122 × 92 mm.
  [The whole plate:] 125 × 179 mm.
[50] [T:] BLESENSE ó GOVERNO DI BLOIS — (Map). 298 (pro 268). 124 × 180 mm.
[51] [T:] Governo di Chartres — (Map). 269 123 × 178 mm.
[52] [C:] CHARTRES — 270 122 × 178 mm.
  [a] (View). 44 × 174 mm.

[b] (Plan). 75 × 175 mm.
- [53] [C:] LA CHAPELLE — 123 × 178 mm.
  - [a] (Plan). 43 × 176 mm.
  - [b] (Map) 76 × 176 mm.
- [54] [C:] DAMPIERRE — (View). 297 (pro 272) 123 × 179 mm.
- [55] [T:] MAROUSSY C. — (View). 273 122 × 177 mm.

ORLEANESE
- [56] [C:] ORLEANS — 275 124 × 178 mm.
  - [a] (View). 53 × 174 mm.
  - [b] (Map). 68 × 174 mm.
- [57] [C:] ORLEANS Dedicato Al M.R.P.Maestro Carlo Bernardi M.C, già Prouinciale di Sassonia — (View). 192 131 × 174 mm.
- [58] [C:] ORLEANS — (Plan). 130 × 175 mm.
- [59] [C:] GALLARDON — 278 121 × 176 mm.
  - [a] (View). 52 × 173 mm.
  - [b] (Map). 63 × 174 mm.
- [60] [C:] TOURS — 249 (pro 279). 125 × 180 mm.
  - [a] (View). 42 × 177 mm.
  - [b] (Map). 80 × 177 mm.
- [61] [T:] ISOLA BOUCHART — (View). 99 × 204 mm.

LORENA
- [62] [C:] NANCY Capitale della LORENA — (Plan). 124 × 168 mm.
- [63] [C:] CHASTILLON Sur Seine. — (View). 284 123 × 179 mm.
- [64] [C:] LONGWY — (Plan). 124 × 179 mm.
- [65] [C:] METZ — (Plan). 286 125 × 178 mm.
- [66] [C:] SAARLOUIS — (Plan). 124 × 178 mm.

ARTESIA
- [67] [T:] NELL'ARTESIA GOVERNO DI MONTHULIN — (Map). 290 123 × 177 mm.
- [68] [C:] LENS NEL ARTESIA — (View). 291 125 × 429 mm.
- [69] [C:] 20 Agos 1648 BATTAGLIA DI LENS — (View). 292 134 × 430 mm.
- [70] [C:] CLERMONT — (View). 293 123 × 178 mm.

ALSAZIA
- [71] [C:] BRISACH Capitale del BRISGOW — (Plan). 123 × 177 mm.
- [72] [C:] BEFFORT — (Plan). 296 123 × 180 mm.
- [73] [T:] STRASBOURG — (Map). 297 123 × 178 mm.
  [Inset:] (View). Oval 28 × 93 mm.
- [74] [C:] STRASBURGO, o ARGENTINA — (Plan). 122 × 178 mm.
- [75] [C:] FORTE KELL — (Plan). 317 129 × 174 mm.
- [76] [C:] HUNNINGEN FORTEZZA Fabbricata da S.M.Cristianissima l'anno M D C LXXXIX — (Plan). 131 × 168 mm.
- [77] [C:] FORTE LUIGI — (Plan). 123 × 178 mm.
- [78] [C:] LANDAU — (Plan). 123 × 177 mm.
- [79] [C:] PHALSBOURG Nell'Alsazia — (Plan). 123 × 178 mm.
- [80] [C:] HAGUENAU — (Plan). 125 × 180 mm.
- [81] [C:] FREBOURG Nel Palatinato — (Plan). 124 × 178 mm.
- [82] [C:] FILISBURGO Modernamente fortificato — (Plan). 305 124 × 177 mm.
- [83] [T:] FILISBORGO Prima delle ultime Fortificazioni — (Plan). 127 × 177 mm.
- [84] [C:] FRIBURGO Colle Moderne Fortificazioni — (Plan). 124 × 178 mm.
- [85] [C:] SCHLESTAT — (Plan). 309 125 × 178 mm.
- [86] [C:] HOMBOURG Nella Contea di Sarbriek — (Plan). 308 123 × 178 mm.

BRETAGNA 82
- [87] [C:] CITTA, PORTO, e RADA DI BREST, e Luoghi conuicini nella Bretagna, oue Attualmente si troua l'Armata di Sua Maestà Cristianissima, Descritte Dal P. Maestro Coronelli, Lettore, e Cosmografo della Serenissima Republica di Venetia — [C:] Dedicata All. Ill.mo; et Eccell: Sig: FRANCESCO SANVDO, Senatore Amplissimo nella Serenissima, Republica di Venetia — [C:] ... in Venetia 1689 Ad uso dell'Accademia Cosmografica degli Argonauti — (Chart). 610 × 444 mm.
  [Inset:] [T:] BREST — (Plan). 90 × 153 mm.
- [88] [C:] BREST — (Plan). 37 125 × 170 mm.
- [89] [C:] BREST Nuovamente fortificato — (Plan). 123 × 177 mm.
- [90] [C:] Governo di S.QUENTIN — (Map). 125 × 177 mm.
- [91] [C:] S.QUENTIN — (Plan). 87 122 × 177 mm.
- [92] [C:] CONQUERNAU — (Map). 88 124 × 178 mm.
- [93] [C:] PORTO LUIGI Nella Bretagna — (Plan). 124 × 180 mm.
- [94] [C:] BELL'ISLE — (Plan). 124 × 178 mm.
- [95] [T:] LE CONQUET Porto della Bretagna — (Map). 124 × 159 mm.
- [96] [T:] PORTO D'ABEURAYE — (Map). 309 127 × 169 mm.
- [97] [C:] S.MALO — (View). 105 × 220 mm.
- [98] [C:] S.MALO — (Plan). 94 125 × 179 mm.
- [99] [C:] BLAIE — (Plan). 125 × 179 mm.

Notes: All the maps are blank on the verso and uncoloured. The title-page is the same as in vol. V i.e. Francia I, including the number. This is the seventh volume of the Teatro della guerra, and the third of Francia. This copy contains Bretagna, which should be in the second volume of Francia. Armao mentions only three parts of this volume: Provenza, Lionese and Orleanese. In this copy there are seven further parts: Contadi d'Avignone e Venassino, Poitú, Santonia ó Santoigne, Aniou, l'Orena, Artesia and Alsazia. Two maps listed in the index are wanting: 216, Governo di Tolon, and 238, Altra detta Tavola in foglio Imperiale. There is a large map between pp. 240 and 241, however, which is not mentioned in the indice; it appears to be the one listed at 238. Plate [21] is apparently part of a larger plate, as is has an upper border only. Most of the larger maps are badly cropped. The initials 'A.E.N.' are on the inside of the front cover.

Lit.: Armao p. 143—144, nr 66, Fonzo, p. 360.

Vol. VIII
SPAGNA [1707].   19,1 cm obl.

- [1] [C:] LA SPAGNA Suddiuisa Nè Suoi Regni, e descritta Dal P. Cosmografo Coronelli — (Map). 366 118 × 164 mm. = 1693:[2].
- [2] [C:] PARTE ORIENTALE DELLA SPAGNA Descritta, e Dedicata All'Illustris:, et Eccellentiss: S.Carlo Ruzini Ambasciatore della Serenissima Republica di Venetia à S.M. Cattolica dal P.M. Coronelli Cosmografo, e Lettore Publico 1691 — [Part I]. (Map). 299 × 452 mm.
- [3] [Parte Orientale della Spagna.] [Part II]. (Map). 310 × 452 mm.
- [4] [C:] PARTE OCCIDENTALE DELLA SPAGNA Descritta, e Dedicata Dal. P. Maestro Coronelli Cosmografo, e Lettore Publico All'Illustrissimo, et Eccellentissimo Signore Carlo Ruzini Ambasciatore à S.M. Cattolica per la Serenissima Republica di Venetia — (Map). 610 × 444 mm.
- [5] [C:] POSTE DALLA SPAGNA A PARIGI — (Map). 11 128 × 263 mm.
- [6] [a] [T:] MADRID — 40 × 85 mm.
  [b] [T:] ESCURIAL — 40 × 88 mm.
  [c] [T:] MONISERRAT — 34 × 50 mm.
  [d] [T:] SIVIGLIA — 33 × 64 mm.
  [e] [T:] M.S.ADRIANO — 35 × 51 mm.
  [f] [T:] VAILADOLID — 40 × 87 mm.
  [g] [T:] TOLEDO — 41 × 86 mm. (All oval views).
  [The whole plate:] 12 124 × 175 mm.
- [7] [a] [T:] BARCELLONA — 40 × 88 mm.
  [b] [T:] BURGOS — 40 × 88 mm.
  [c] [T:] CISTERNA DI GRANADA — 41 × 50 mm.
  [d] [T:] GRANADA — 40 × 74 mm.
  [e] [T:] PONTE DI SEGOVIA — 41 × 50 mm.
  [f] [T:] SIVIGLIA — 42 × 88 mm.
  [g] [T:] LISBONA — 42 × 87 mm. (All oval views).
  [The whole plate:] 13 127 × 176 mm.
- [8] [a] [C:] MADRID — (Plan). 125 × 90 mm.

[b] [C:] D.DI MADRID — (View). 125 × 85 mm.
[The whole plate:] 14   125 × 175 mm.
[9] [C:] MADRID ... A P. CORONELLI — (Plan). 15   179 × 382 mm.
[10] [T:] MONT-SERRAT — (View). 21   124 × 174 mm.
[11] [C:] Casa, e Camera Angelica di Maria V. DI MONT SERRAT — (View). 22   125 × 176 mm.
[12] [T:] SPAGNA DAL RIO DI SIVIGLIA A MALACCA; E COSTA DI BARBARIA DA LAPACHE A PENON DI VELEZ — (Chart). 23   125 × 175 mm.
[13] [a] [C:] Passaggio di Francia in Spagna nella Bijcaia — (Map).   119 × 86 mm.
[b] [C:] Passaggio dall'Africa in Europa per lo Stretto di Gibraltar — (Map).   120 × 87 mm.
[The whole plate:]   122 × 177 mm.
[14] [C:] GIBALTAR Attaccata DA' GALLO-HISPANI 22 Ottobre 1704 — (Plan). 25   126 × 175 mm.
[15] [C:] GIBALTAR Attaccato da' Gallo Spani 22. Ottobre 1704. Sino 18. Maggio 1705. — (Plan). 26   124 × 358 mm.
[16] [C:] GIBRALTAR — (View). 27   132 × 359 mm.
[17] [C:] PARTE OCCIDENTALE DEL MEDITERRANEO — (Chart). 28   124 × 175 mm.
[18] [C:] ISOLA E PORTO DI CADIZE — (Map). 43   129 × 164 mm.
[19] [a] [T:] BARCELLONA — (View).   81 × 125 mm.
[b] [T:] CADIZ — (View).   81 × 125 mm.
[The whole plate:] 51   178 × 125 mm.
[20] [a] [T:] CEUTA — (View).   82 × 125 mm.
[b] [T:] CASCALE — (View).   78 × 125 mm.
[The whole plate:} 31   178 × 125 mm.
[21] [T:] COSTA DI VALENZA, E CATALOGNA DA C.S. MARTIN A'C.DRAGONIS, E ISOLE MAJORCA, MINORCA, E IVIZA — (Chart). 32   124 × 176 mm.
[22] [T:] I. IVICA — (Chart). 33   126 × 176 mm.
[23] [C:] ISOLA DI MAIORICA — (Map).   168 × 242 mm.
[24] [a] [T:] BILBAO — (View).   83 × 123 mm.
[b] [T:] XERE DE LA FRONTERA — (View).   82 × 123 mm.
[The whole plate:] 35   177 × 123 mm.
[25] [a] [T:] CORDUBA — (View).   84 × 124 mm.
[b] [T:] BURGOS — (View).   81 × 124 mm.
[The whole plate:] 36   178 × 124 mm.
[26] [a] [T:] LOXA — (View).   88 × 125 mm.
[b] [T:] OSUNA — (View).   79 × 125 mm.
[The whole plate:] 37   178 × 125 mm.
[27] [a] [T:] ANTIQUERA — (View).   82 × 126 mm.
[b] [T:] VAGLIADOLIT — (View).   83 × 126 mm.
[The whole plate:] 38   178 × 126 mm.
[28] [C:] CAMPREDON Nella Catalogna — (Plan).   123 × 172 mm.
[29] [C:] MONT-LOUIS Fabbricato nel 1678. ... — (Plan).   123 × 180 mm.
[30] [C:] GIRONA nella Catalogna Descritta Dal P. Cosmografo Coronelli — (Plan).   128 × 170 mm.
[31] [C:] Contorin di PALAMOS, E GIRONA, Descritti Dal P. Cosmografo Coronelli — (Map).   129 × 170 mm.
[32] [C:] PALAMOS Nella Catalogna — (Plan).   128 × 171 mm.
[33] [T:] PIANTA DELLA CITTA DI CAPO DE QUIERS — (Map). 523   128 × 173 mm.
[34] [C:] CAPO DI QUIERS Preso dal P. Conty Maggio 1655 — (Map). 45   128 × 345 mm.
[35] [T:] ROSES — (Map).   126 × 177 mm.
[36] [C:] ROSES E CAPO FOLIO — 47 (Map).   125 × 177 mm.
[37] [C:] ROSES DESCRITTO DAL P. CORONELLI — (Plan).   131 × 172 mm.
[38] [C:] CASTILLON D'Ampurda Preso Luglio 1655 dal P. Conty — (Map). 49   130 × 372 mm.
[39] [C:] BARCELLOИA Descritta Dal P. Coronelli — (Plan).   141 × 257 mm.
[40] [C:] BARCELLONA — (View).   138 × 251 mm.
[41] [C:] MONJOVI — (Plan). 52   126 × 176 mm.
[42] [C:] Tortosa, Frontiera della Catalogna colla Valenza — (Plan). 53   124 × 174 mm.

[43] [C:] OSTALRIC NELLA CATALOGNA — (Plan). 54   126 × 175 mm.
[44] [C:] SALVATIERRA — (Plan). 44 (pro 55).   125 × 176 mm.
[45] [a] [T:] MARTIA — (View).   81 × 125 mm.
[b] [T:] MALAGA — (View).   80 × 125 mm.
[The whole plate:] 56   176 × 125 mm.
[46] [C:] Fortin fabricato nel 1704. in Vangheses — (Plan).   125 × 177 mm.
[47] [C:] FORTE GOJAN — (Plan). 58   125 × 176 mm.
[48] [C:] RIO VIGO NELLA GALLIZIA Colla disposizione dall Armata Francese attaccata dell Angloianda 22. Ottobre 1702. — (Map). 5[9]   124 × 349 mm.
[49] [C:] CASTRO — VIGO — [C:] ... P. Coronelli — (Plan). 61   122 × 358 mm.
[50] [C:] PROFILO DI VIGO, Visto d'Oriente colle sue Fortezze — (View). 60 (pro 62).   125 × 176 mm.
[51] [C:] VIGO VISTO DAL MARE — (View). 63   125 × 178 mm.
[52] [a] [T:] SANTANDER — (View).   84 × 124 mm.
[b] [T:] GRANATA — (View).   80 × 124 mm.
[The whole plate:] 64   177 × 124 mm.
[53] [T:] PUERTO DE LOS ALFAQUES — (Map). 65   126 × 176 mm.
[54] [T:] Puerto de Peniscola — (Map). 66   126 × 177 mm.
[55] [a] [C:] CASTEL BRANCO — (Plan).   122 × 85 mm.
[b] [C:] VILLA FARINA — (Plan).   123 × 85 mm.
[The whole plate:] 67   126 × 176 mm.
[56] [T:] REGNO DI VALENZA — [Two fortifications with empty cartouches]. 68   125 × 177 mm.
[57] [C:] FORTE AMORIN — (Plan).   126 × 176 mm.
[58] [a] [C:] ELVAS — 70 (Plan).   121 × 84 mm.
[b] [C:] PORTALEGRE — (Plan).   121 × 84 mm.
[The whole plate:]   125 × 170 mm.
[59] [C:] PORTO DI DENIA — (View). 71   125 × 175 mm.
[60] [T:] ALICANTE — (View). 72   125 × 174 mm.
[61] [C:] VALENZA — (View). 73   123 × 176 mm.
[62] [C:] Parte della Citta di VALENZA — (Plan). 75 (pro 74).   124 × 174 mm.
[63] [C:] ALCALA DE EBRO — (Plan). 75   123 × 174 mm.
[64] [C:] CASTELLO FOLLIT — (Plan). 76   125 × 176 mm.
[65] [C:] Ridotto á Sarriau de Bande fabbricato nel 1704. nella Gallizia — (Plan and profile). 77   125 × 176 mm.
[66] [C:] LA GUARDIA Frontiera della Gallizia col Portogallo — (Plan). 78   124 × 177 mm.
[67] [C:] Porto di BAJONA Nella Gallizia — (Map). 79   125 × 176 mm.
[68] [C:] BAJONA Nella Gallizia — (Plan). 80   123 × 176 mm.
[69] [C:] BAJONA NELLA GALLIZIA — (View). 81   125 × 176 mm.
[70] [C:] LERIDA — (Plan). 82   124 × 175 mm.

REGNO DI GALLIZIA

[71] [C:] CONFINI DI GALLIZIA, E PORTOGALLO CO' FORTINI Fabbricati nel 1705 — (Map).   120 × 355 mm.
[72] [C:] CASTELLO DI SARAGOZZA Anticamente Palazzo degli Inquisitori — (Plan). 85   125 × 173 mm.
[73] [C:] PORTO FERROL — (Map). 86   125 × 174 mm.
[74] [a] [T:] TOLEDO — [View]   80 × 123 mm.
[b] [T:] [SEVIGLIA] — [View]   83 × 123 mm.
[The whole plate:] 87   172 × 123 mm.
[75] [C:] LA CORUÑA Colle Nuove Fortificazioni — (Plan). 88   126 × 175 mm.
[76] [C:] LA CORUÑA Colle Nuove Fortificazioni — (Map). 88 (pro 89)   126 × 177 mm.
[77] [T:] I.BEOBIE, ó DE LHOS HOSPITAL DESTINATA PER LA PACE MDCLIX — (Plan). 90   102 × 153 mm.
[78] [T:] F.BIDASSOA, CONFINE TRA FRANCIA, E SPAGNA — (Map). 91   125 × 175 mm.
[79] [C:] FONTARABIE — (Plan). 123 × 177 mm.
[80] [C:] SOCCOVA — (Map). 93   125 × 176 mm.
[81] [C:] PORTO CORUNA, E RIO FEROL — (Map). 94   125 × 175 mm.
[82] [C:] PARTE OCCIDENTALE DELL'EUROPA, Rappresentante i Viaggi Maritimi Dei due valorosi

Campioni e gloriosissimi Eroi, COMPETITORE ALLA MONARCHIA SPAGNUOLA. E L'ombra centrale dell'Ecclisse Totale di XII. Maggio MDCCVI. Descritti dal P. General Coronelli ne' XXXXV. Tomi della Sua Biblioteca . — (Map). 610 × 451 mm.

Notes: All the maps are blank on the verso and uncoloured. Some of the plates are badly cropped, including [74], where the title of the lower view is completely missing. Some of the plates are bound upside-down. The maps in our copy do not quite correspond to the index. Plate [18] bears two views: Barcelona, with the number 51, and Cadiz. According to the index, Cadiz should be no.30, and there should be two views of Barcelona on plate 51, where our copy has only one view. Map [29] in our copy is 'MONT-LOUIS Fabbricato nel 1678. 2. Leghe distante da Puicerda'; according to the index the maps in this position should be '40. Puicerda nella Catalogna', which is wanting in our copy. Map [33] has the title 'Pianta della citta di Capo de Quiers' in capitals, with 'Forte de Signal' in lower case; according to the index, the map here should be '45. Forte Signale nella Catalogna per 2. Rami'. Map [34], 'CAPO DI QUIERS Preso dal P. Conty Maggio 1655,' has the number 45 engraved on the plate. Nordenskiöld's signature, with the year 1900, was originally on the inside of the front cover, but was lost when the binding was repaired. Armao describes this volume under no.67 (p.145 — 146).

Lit.: See vol. 1.

Vol. IX
SPAGNA, Delineata Dal P. Coronelli. [Parte II.] [1708]
[Half title:]
LA SPAGNA   18,5 cm obl.

[1]   [a] [T:] ALCANTARILLA — (View). 61 × 180 mm.
      [b] [T:] CABEÇAS — (View). 62 × 180 mm.
      [The whole plate:] 123 × 180 mm.
[2]   [a] [T:] BADAJOS — (Plan). 123 × 89 mm.
      [b] [T:] ALBURQUEQUE — (View). 123 × 83 mm.
      [The whole plate:] 125 × 180 mm.
[3]   [T:] Burgos, Capitale della Castiglia Vecchia — (View). 124 × 178 mm.
[4]   [T:] VALLADOLID — (View). 122 × 178 mm.
[5]   [T:] TOLEDO — (View). 124 × 180 mm.
[6]   [T:] Castello di Segovia, visto da dietro — (View). 125 × 179 mm.
[7]   [a] [T:] MONT-JOUY — (Plan). 61 × 88 mm.
      [b] [T:] BARCELLONA — (Plan). 61 × 87 mm.
      [c] [T:] PUICERDA — (Plan). 59 × 88 mm.
      [d] [C:] PALAMOS — (Plan). 59 × 87 mm.
      [The whole plate:] 124 × 179 mm.
[8]   [C:] LERIDA — (Plan). 124 × 178 mm.
[9]   [a] [C:] FILX — (Plan). 60 × 88 mm.
      [b] [C:] GIRONNA — (Plan). 60 × 86 mm.
      [c] [C:] TARRAGONA — (Plan). 61 × 88 mm.
      [d] [C:] TORTOSA — (Plan). 61 × 86 mm.
      [The whole plate:] 125 × 178 mm.
[10] [T:] Siviglia — (Plan). 124 × 178 mm.
[11] [a] [T:] SIVIGLIA — (View). 62 × 182 mm.
      [b] [T:] Monistero di S.Francesco, e Piazza di Siviglia. — (View). 61 × 182 mm.
      [The whole plate:] 123 × 182 mm.
[12] [a] [C:] Cordova — (View). 59 × 174 mm.
      [b] [C:] Torre dell'Oro, e Ponte di Siviglia — (View). 59 × 174 mm.
      [The whole plate:] 123 × 178 mm.
[13] [T:] Maniera di castigare i Becchi contenti, particolarmen.te a Siviglia — (View). 122 × 177 mm.
[14] [a] [C:] CITTA, E PORTO CADIZ — (View). 59 × 175 mm.
      [b] [C:] PALAZZO REAL DI CADIZ — (View). 58 × 175 mm.
      [The whole plate:] 125 × 179 mm.
[15] [T:] Pesca del Ton a Cadiz. — (View). 123 × 180 mm.
[16] [a] [C:] GIBRALTAR — (View). 59 × 176 mm.
      [b] [C:] VEGEL — (View). 59 × 176 mm.
      [The whole plate:] 123 × 180 mm.
[17] [a] [C:] S. jvan del Fortache. — (View). 59 × 175 mm.
      [b] [C:] Palacios — (View). 59 × 176 mm.
      [The whole plate:] 124 × 180 mm.
[18] [a] [T:] OSSUNA — (View). 63 × 180 mm.
      [b] [T:] MARCHENA — (View). 61 × 180 mm.
      [The whole plate:] 124 × 180 mm.
[19] [a] [T:] LEBRIXA — (View). 62 × 182 mm.
      [b] [T:] XERES DELLA FRONTERA — (View). 62 × 182 mm.
      [The whole plate:] 124 × 182 mm.
[20] [T:] JERENNA — (View). 124 × 179 mm.
[21] [T:] HARDALES — (View). 123 × 180 mm.
[22] [a] [T:] ZAHARA — (View). 59 × 176 mm.
      [b] [T:] BORNES — (View). 59 × 176 mm.
      [The whole plate:] 123 × 180 mm.
[23] [T:] GRANATA — (View). 123 × 177 mm.
[24] [a] [C:] Palazzo de' Re' Mori in Granata — (View). 59 × 174 mm.
      [b] [C:] Castello di Granata — (View). 59 × 174 mm.
      [The whole plate:] 123 × 178 mm.
[25] [T:] Casa Reale di Xeneralife e suo Parco fuori di Grenada — (View). 124 × 179 mm.
[26] [T:] Masmorras, Caverns di Grenada — (View). 124 × 179 mm.
[27] [T:] LOYA. — (View). 125 × 180 mm.
[28] [T:] ANTEQUERA — (View). 123 × 178 mm.
[29] [T:] CARTAMA — (View). 123 × 178 mm.
[30] [C:] MALAGA ... — (View). 123 × 178 mm.
[31] [a] [C:] Settenil — (View). 59 × 174 mm.
      [b] [C:] Velez de Malaga — (View). 59 × 174 mm.
      [The whole plate:] 124 × 178 mm.
[32] [T:] ALHAMA — (View). 124 × 180 mm.
[33] [T:] ALHAMBRE — (View). 123 × 178 mm.
[34] [T:] BILBAO — (View). 124 × 178 mm.
[35] [T:] SANTANDER — (View). 124 × 178 mm.
[36] [T:] Monte S. Adriano. — (View). 123 × 177 mm.
[37] [a] [T:] ARCHIDONA — (View). 62 × 182 mm.
      [b] [T:] ECIJA — (View). 62 × 182 mm.
      [The whole plate:] 124 × 182 mm.

PORTOGALLO Delineato, e Descritto Dal P. Coronelli
[Half title:] PORTOGALLO
[38] [C:] REGNO DI PORTOGALLO Dedicato Al Reuerendissimo Padre Don Paulo Antonio Zaccarelli Abbate Generale de Camaldulensi — [T:] Gioseppe Volcetta sculp. — (Map). 437 × 600 mm.
[39] [T:] COSTE MARITIME DEL PORTOGALLO — (Map). 124 × 178 mm.
[40] [C:] LISBONA — (Plan). 124 × 179 mm.
[41] [C:] CITTA DI LISBONA Metropoli Del Regno di Portogallo — (Plan). 129 × 167 mm.
[42] [C:] LISBONA — (View). 124 × 178 mm.
[43] [a] [C:] LISBONA P. — (Plan). 124 × 90 mm.
      [b] [C:] LISBONA V. — (View). 124 × 88 mm.
      [The whole plate:] 124 × 179 mm.
[44] [a] [T:] LISBONA — (View). 80 × 124 mm.
      [b] [T:] GOA — (View). 82 × 124 mm.
      [The whole plate:] 178 × 124 mm.
[45] [C:] S GIO DE LISBONA — (Plan). 141 130 × 173 mm.
[46] [a] [C:] BELEM — (View). 124 × 89 mm.
      [b] [C:] T. DI BELEM — (View). 124 × 87 mm.
      [The whole plate:] 124 × 176 mm.
[47] [a] [T:] CASCAES, E BELLEM. — (View). 62 × 181 mm.
      [b] [T:] TORRE DI BELLEM. — (View). 62 × 181 mm.
      [The whole plate:] 124 × 181 mm.
[48] [C:] PORT A' PORT — (Map). 123 × 178 mm.
[49] [C:] BRAGA Arcivesco vale Nel Portogallo — (Plan). 124 × 179 mm.
[50] [C:] FORTEZZA D'ALMEIDA — [C:] NEL PORTOGALL[O] — (Plan). 106 × 263 mm.
[51] [C:] COIMBRA — (View). 124 × 179 mm.
[52] [a] [T:] ELVAS — (Plan). 118 × 83 mm.
      [b] [T:] VILLA NOVA — (Plan). 118 × 83 mm.
      [The whole plate:] 124 × 177 mm.

[53] [a] [C:] Extremog,ó Stremotiú — [C:] nel Portogallo — (View). 60 × 176 mm.
[b] [C:] Villa Vitiosa — [C:] Nel Portogallo — (View). 58 × 176 mm.
[The whole plate:] 123 × 176 mm.

[54] [a] [C:] Evora ò Ebora — [C:] Vescovale Nel Portogallo — (View). 58 × 179 mm.
[b] [C:] Aronches, ò Arunci — [C:] Terra Nel Portogallo — (View). 60 × 179 mm.
[The whole plate:] 123 × 179 mm.

[55] [C:] SETUVAL — (Plan). 123 × 178 mm.
[56] [C:] SETUVAL — (Plan). 123 × 179 mm.
[57] [C:] [F]ORTEZZA D'EVORA Nel Portogallo — [C:] Descritto Dal P. Cosmografo Coronell[i] (Plan). 105 × 264 mm.
[58] [a] [C:] ESTREMOZ — (Plan). 122 × 83 mm.
[b] [C:] EVOPA — (Plan). 122 × 91 mm.
[The whole plate:] [T:] REGNO DI PORTOGALLO — 125 × 177 mm.

[59] [a] [C:] Olivenca ò Oliventia, — [C:] Citta Nel Portogallo — (Plan). 58 × 180 mm.
[b] [C:] Ferretra — [C:] Castella Nel Portogallo — (View). 61 × 180 mm.
[The whole plate:] 123 × 180 mm.

Notes: All the maps are blank on the verso and uncoloured. The volume number is given in the Indice: 'Parte II. della Spagna'. The plates have no numbers engraved on them, with the exception of [45], which bears the number 141, printed upsidedown. The plates are not in the order given in the Indice. Some of them are badly cropped, such as [57] where the 'i' of 'Coronelli' is missing, and which has been bound so that the 'F' of 'Fortezza' disappears into the binding. Many of the plates in this volume are not maps or views, but pictures of houses and other buildings. Nordenskiöld's signature is on the inside of the front cover, with the year 1900.
Lit.: Armao nr 68, p. 146, Fonzo, p. 360.

Vol. X wanting.

Vol. XI
CITTA, FORTEZZE, ED ALTRI LUOGHI PRINCIPALI, Alle Sponde del RENO, E d'altri Fiumi suoi Tributarj Descritti Dal P. Coronelli [1708].
[Engraved half title:]
IL RENO   18,8 cm obl.

[1] [a] [T:] FILISBURGO — (Plan). 25 × 45 mm.
[b] [T:] HUNINGEN — (Plan). 22 × 35 mm.
[c] [T:] TORNAL — (Plan). 25 × 28 mm.
[d] [T:] FORTE LUIGI — (Plan). 27 × 35 mm.
[e] [T:] SAN LUIGI — (Plan). 30 × 35 mm.
[f] [T:] CAMBRAI — (Plan). 30 × 28 mm.
[g] [T:] DONCNERCHEN — (Plan). 30 × 26 mm.
[h] [T:] BISANZON — (Plan). 31 × 32 mm.
[i] [T:] LONGWI — (Plan). 27 × 31 mm.
[k] [T:] LILE — (Plan). 22 × 26 mm.
[l] [T:] ARGENTINA — (Plan). 20 × 37 mm.
[m] [T:] NAMUR — (Plan). 25 × 45 mm.
[n] [T:] BONNA — (View). 25 × 60 mm. (Irregular maps around the half title).
[The whole plate:] 180 × 175 mm.

[2] [a] [T:] FRANCHENTAL — (Plan). 34 × 27 mm.
[b] [T:] LANDAU — (Plan). 40 × 30 mm.
[c] [T:] LINBURGO — (Plan). 22 × 33 mm.
[d] [T:] MASTRICH — (Plan). 32 × 55 mm.
[e] [T:] JULIERS — (Plan). 24 × 37 mm.
[f] [T:] FILIPPEVILLE — (Plan). 42 × 30 mm.
[g] [T:] MAGONZA — (Plan). 32 × 27 mm. (Irregular maps around the title).
[The whole plate:] 172 × 163 mm.

[3] [C:] CORSO DEL RENO PARTE SETTENTRIO: Dedicato All'Illustrissimo, et Eccellentissimo S. POLO QUERINI, Procuratore di S. Marco. in Venetia 1690 — (Map). 447 × 612 mm.

[4] [C:] CORSO DEL RENO, Parte Meridionale, Dedicato All'Illustrissimo, et Eccellentissimo S. GIROLAMO QUERINI, Procuratore di S.Marco. In Venetia 1690 — (Map). 451 × 613 mm.

[5] [C:] ORIGINE DEL F. RENO — (View). 124 × 180 mm.
[6] [a] [T:] STRASBURGO — (Plan). 20 × 35 mm.
[b] [T:] LILLE — (Plan). 25 × 25 mm.
[c] [T:] LUXENBURG — (Plan). 27 × 34 mm.
[d] [T:] BESANCON — (Plan). 30 × 32 mm.
[e] [T:] DONQUERQUE — (Plan). 30 × 25 mm.
[f] [T:] CAMBRAI — (Plan). 32 × 27 mm.
[g] [T:] CASAL — (Plan). 30 × 28 mm.
[h] [T:] PIGNEROL — (Plan). 27 × 33 mm.
[i] [T:] TOURNAY — (Plan). 27 × 25 mm.
[k] [T:] NANCY — (Plan). 20 × 37 mm. (Irregular maps).
[The whole plate:] 178 × 176 mm.

[7] [a] [T:] CREUTZENAC — (Plan). Oval 41 × 84 mm.
[b] [T:] REYSERLOUTRE — (View). Oval 41 × 88 mm.
[c] [T:] WORMFS — (Plan). Oval 37 × 83 mm.
[d] [T:] SPIRA — (Plan). Oval 37 × 88 mm.
[e] [T:] BACHARACH — (View). Oval 43 × 88 mm.
[f] [T:] OPPENHEIM — (View). Oval 42 × 88 mm.
[The whole plate:] 124 × 178 mm.

[8] [a] [C:] WORMS, ouero VORMES, — [C:] VORMACIA detta dà Latini — (View). Oval 52 × 176 mm.
[b] [C:] FRANCOFORTE al Meno — [C:] FRANCOFURTOM Ad Moenum — (View). Oval 51 × 177 mm.
[The whole plate:] 123 × 180 mm.

ELECTORES ECCLESIÆSTICE
[9] [C:] PARTE SETTENTRIONALE degli Stati Dell'ELETTORE DI COLONIA Descritta, e Dedicata Dal P. Coronelli, Cosmografo della Serenissima Repub: All'Illustrissimo, et Eccellentissimo Signore Lorenzo Soranzo, Sauio Grande, et c. — (Map). 448 × 618 mm.

[10] [C:] PARTE MERIDIONALE degli Stati DELL'ELET: DI COLONIA Descritta, e Dedicata Dal P. Coronelli Cosmografo della Serenissima Repub: All'Illustrissimo, et Eccellentissimo Sig. Lorenzo Soranzo Sauio Grande et c. — (Map). 447 × 618 mm.
[Inset:] [C:] CORS'O DEL RENO — (Map). 215 × 160 mm.

[11] [a] [C:] TREVIRI — (View). 60 × 84 mm.
[b] [C:] MAGONZA — (View). 59 × 84 mm.
[c] [C:] MONACO — (View). 57 × 84 mm.
[d] [C:] COLONIA — (View). 57 × 84 mm.
[The whole plate:] 124 × 178 mm.

[12] [C:] COBLENTS Dell' Elettorato di Treviri — (Map). 124 × 179 mm.
[13] [C:] COBOLENTS — (View). 126 × 180 mm.
[14] [C:] COBLENTZ — (Plan). T.II.8. 139 × 159 mm.
[15] [C:] BONNA OU BONNA — (Plan). T.2.II 137 × 182 mm.
[16] [C:] BONNA, Come attrovauasi Nel MDLXXXVII. — (Plan). 123 × 179 mm.
[17] [C:] MAGONZA, ò MAYANCE — (View). 140 × 437 mm.
[18] [C:] MULLHIN — (Plan). 123 × 178 mm.
[19] [T:] CITTA DI MAGONZA — (Plan). T.2.2 141 × 182 mm.
[20] [a] [T:] MAGONZA — (View). 87 × 123 mm.
[b] [T:] SPIRA — (View). 72 × 123 mm.
[The whole plate:] 177 × 123 mm.

[21] [a] [C:] SPIRA Città Imperiale — [C:] SPEYR detta dagli Abitanti — (View). Oval 50 × 175 mm.
[b] [C:] MAGONZA Seggio Elettorale — [C:] MENTZ detta dagli Abitanti — (View). Oval 50 × 175 mm.
[The whole plate:] 123 × 178 mm.

[22] [a] [C:] STENAY — [T:] Dedic: All' Illustrissimo Sig: Bertuccio Valier Patritio Veneto — (View). 128 × 430 mm.
[b] [C:] SPIRA — (View). 130 × 430 mm.
[The whole plate:] 258 × 430 mm.

[23] [C:] TREVIRI — (View). 124 × 179 mm.

[24] [a] [T:] CREUTZNACH — (View). 75 × 124 mm.
     [b] [T:] WORMES — (View). 75 × 124 mm.
     [The whole plate:] 177 × 124 mm.
[25] [a] [T:] OPPENHEIM — (View). 84 × 124 mm.
     [b] [T:] BACHARACH — (View). 74 × 124 mm.
     [The whole plate:] 178 × 124 mm.
[26] [C:] VESCOVATO DI LIEGE Dedicato Dal P. Cosmografo Coronelli, All'illustrissimo Signore Gote Gio: Antonio Baldini, — (Map). 441 × 608 mm.
[27] [C:] LIEGE — (Plan). 155 × 210 mm.
[28] [a] [C:] HUY — (Plan). 117 × 85 mm.
     [b] [C:] LIEGE — (Plan). 117 × 85 mm.
     [The whole plate:] 121 × 176 mm.
[29] [C:] HUY Attaccato nel MDLXXXXV — (View). 154 × 256 mm.

ELECTORIS PALATINI INSIGNIA
[30] [C:] DEL PALATINATO et ELETTORATO DEL RENO Parte Occidentale, Descritta Dal P. Coronelli Cosmografo della Serenissima Republica, Dedicata All'Eccellenza del Sig: Cauaiiere SILVESTRO VALIER Procvratore di S.Marco, ad uso Dell Accademia Cosmografica Degli Argonauti — (Map). 617 × 449 mm.
     [Inset:] [C:] Corso del Reno (Map). — 272 × 193 mm.
[31] [C:] DEL PALATINATO, et ELETTORATO DEL RENO Parte Orientale, Descritto Dal P. Coronelli Cosmografo della Sere.ma Repu.ca Dedicato All'Eccellenza del Sig: Cauaiier Siluestro Valier Procuratore di S.Marco, ad uso dell'Accademia Cosmografica degli Argonauti — (Map). 620 × 454 mm.
[32] [C:] Dusseldorff colle proposte del Conte Generale Matteo Alberti — (Plan). T.2 19 129 × 178 mm.
[33] [T:] EIDELBERGA — Dedicata All'Illustrissimo, et Ecc.mo Signore Il S.D.GIROLAMO ACQUAVIVA D'ARAGONA, Duca d'Atri, et c (View). 258 × 352 mm.
[34] [a] [C:] Neuberg — (View). 45 × 65 mm.
     [b] [C:] Spira — (View). 45 × 41 mm.
     [c] [C:] Wolfs Brunnen — (View). 45 × 65 mm.
     [The whole plate, which contains also three pictures:] 124 × 178 mm.
[35] [a] [T:] EIDELBRGA — (View). 50 × 56 mm.
     [b] [C:] EIDELBRGA — (View). 51 × 173 mm.
     [The whole plate, which contains also two pictures:] 125 × 178 mm.
[36] [a] [C:] Palazzo dell F. Palatino — (View). 51 × 65 mm.
     [b] [T:] Heidelberga — (View). 51 × 38 mm.
     [c] [C:] Heyligenberg — (View). 51 × 65 mm.
     [d] [C:] Brisac — (View). 64 × 85 mm.
     [e] [C:] Strasburgo — (View). 64 × 85 mm.
     [The whole plate:] 122 × 177 mm.
[37] [a] [T:] HEIDELBERGA — (View). 80 × 126 mm.
     [b] [T:] FRANCFORT — (View). 83 × 126 mm.
     [The whole plate:] 180 × 126 mm.
[38] [a] [C:] HEIDELBERGA — (Plan). 121 × 91 mm.
     [b] [C:] LIEHTEMBERG — (Plan). 121 × 83 mm.
     [The whole plate:] 123 × 178 mm.
[39] [C:] MANHEIM — (Plan). 124 × 178 mm.
[40] [a] [C:] FILISBURGO — (Plan). 123 × 82 mm.
     [b] [C:] MANHEIM — (Plan). 123 × 91 mm.
     [The whole plate:] 125 × 178 mm.
[41] [T:] KEYSERWERI — (Plan). 124 × 178 mm.
[42] [a] [C:] BENFELD — (Plan). 120 × 87 mm.
     [b] [C:] BEFORT — (Plan). 120 × 85 mm.
     [The whole plate:] 123 × 177 mm.
[43] [C:] CITTA DI FRIBURGO — (Plan). 123 × 178 mm.
[44] [C:] BASILEA — 124 × 179 mm.
     [a] (View). 35 × 176 mm.
     [b] (Plan). 84 × 176 mm.
[45] [C:] BASILEA — (Plan). 125 × 180 mm.
[46] [C:] SCAEUSEN — (Plan). 124 × 177 mm.
[47] [C:] SCAFFUSA — (View). 124 × 179 mm.
[48] [C:] CONSTANZA — (View). 123 × 177 mm.
[49] [C:] FRANCHENTAL — (Plan). 126 × 181 mm.
[50] [C:] WESSEL — (Plan). 123 × 178 mm.
[51] [C:] WESSEL — (View). 125 × 180 mm.
[52] [C:] EMBRICA EMMERICK — (View). 127 × 301 mm.
[53] [C:] SCHENCHENSCHANS — (Plan). 124 × 179 mm.
[54] [C:] RINSBRG — (View). 129 × 280 mm.
[55] [C:] RHINSBERG — (Plan). 122 × 177 mm.
[56] [a] [C:] ORSOY — (Plan). 121 × 91 mm.
     [b] [C:] RIMBERGH — (Plan). 121 × 92 mm.
     [The whole plate:] T.II.24 123 × 187 mm.
[57] [C:] HORSOY — (Plan). 123 × 178 mm.
[58] [C:] RAINFELTZ — (Plan). T.II.6. 139 × 180 mm.
[59] [C:] HAILBRON Nella Svevia — (Plan). 124 × 177 mm.
[60] [C:] REES — (Plan). 125 × 178 mm.
[61] [C:] FILISBURGO — (View). 76 × 379 mm.
[62] [T:] Filisburgo, ò Philisbourg — (View). 125 × 178 mm.
[63] [C:] FILISBURGO, Assediato Da M.Dolfino 10. Ottobre, e preso l. Novembre 1688 — (Plan). 177 × 376 mm.
[64] [C:] ALSACIA SUPERIORE, e sue Dipendenze, Descritta, e Dedicata Dal P. Maestro Coronelli, Lettore e Cosmografo della Serenissima Republica di Venetia All'Eminentissimo, e Reuerendiss: Principe Il Sig: Cardinale D' Estrees, Commandatore degli Ordini di S. Maesta, et c. — (Map). 446 × 611 mm.
[65] [C:] ALSATIA INFERIORE, Descritta, e Dedicata Dal P. Cosmografo Coronelli All'Eminentissimo, e Reuerendissimo Principe, IL S. CARDINALE D'ESTREES, Duca, e Pari di Francia Commandatore degli Ordini di S. Maestà etc. — (Map). 448 × 612 mm.
[66] [C:] STRASBURGO — (View). 124 × 180 mm.
[67] [C:] Cittadella Di Strasburgo — (Plan). 125 × 178 mm.
[68] [C:] FORTI, che diffendono il passaggio del Reno a Strasburgo — (Plan). 123 × 180 mm.
[69] [a] [C:] FORTE LUIGI — (Plan). 121 × 87 mm.
     [b] [C:] UNINGUE — (Plan). 121 × 87 mm.
     [The whole plate:] 122 × 178 mm.
[70] [a] [C:] PHALSBOURG — (Plan). 122 × 88 mm.
     [b] [C:] SCHELESTAT — (Plan). 122 × 86 mm.
     [The whole plate:] 124 × 178 mm.
[71] [C:] BRISAC ANTICO — 126 × 179 mm.
     [a] (View). 30 × 105 mm.
     [b] (Plan). 92 × 177 mm.
[72] [a] [C:] NUOVO BRISACH — (Plan). 121 × 92 mm.
     [b] [C:] LANDAU — (Plan). 121 × 82 mm.
     [The whole plate:] 123 × 179 mm.

Notes: All the maps are blank on the verso and uncoloured. The plates in our copy are bound in a different order to the one described by Armao. The large view of Stenay and Spira [22] is not listed in the index, nor is it mentioned by Armao. Armao describes the volume as 'Opera pure rarissima e affato nota'. He cites only two libraries which have the volume: Florence and Roma V.E. The words 'Teatro della Guerra del P. Coronelli' appear on the lover margin of the text pages, but nowhere else. Nordenskiöld's has written his initials, AEN, in pencil on the inside of the front cover.

Lit.: Armao nr 70, p. 149—150, Fonzo, p. 361.

Vol. XII wanting
Vol. XIII wanting

Vol. XIV
LA SERENISSIMA REPUBBLICA DI GENOVA, E REGNO SUO DI CORSICA Descritti, e Delineati Dal P. Coronelli ex-Generale de' Minori Conventuali [1708].
[Half title:]
IL GENOVESATO   18,7 cm obl.

[1] [T:] GENOVESATO — (Chart). 123 × 178 mm.
[2] [C:] COSTA LIGUSTICA da C.Melle á M.Argentato, I CORSICA, e circonvicine. — (Chart). 126 × 180 mm.
[3] [C:] COSTE MARITIME DEL GENOVESATO — (Chart). 130 × 327 mm.
[4] [C:] GENOVESATO Parte Occidentale Descritto, e Dedicato Dal P. Maestro Coronelli Cosmografo della Senenissima Republica di Venetia ALL' EMINENTISSIMO PRINCIPE IL S. CARDINALE FIESCHI Arcivescovo di Genova, & c. in Venetia ... — (Map). 443 × 611 mm.

[5] [C:] GENOVESATO, Parte Orientale Dedicato ALL EMINENTISSIMO PRENCIPE IL S. CARDINALE FIESCHI, Arcivescovo di Genova. Dichiaratione delle Note, e Blasoni delle Tauole del Genouesato Autt. P. Cosmografo Coronelli. — (Map). 444 × 616 mm.

[6] [C:] GENOVA — (View). 128 × 384 mm.

[7] [C:] CITTA DI GENOVA Dedicata All'Illustrissimo signore FRANCESCO MARIA MICONE Dal P. Cosmografo Coronelli ... — (Plan). 218 × 326 mm.

[8] [C:] GENOVA Descritta dal P. Coronelli — (Plan). 124 × 179 mm.

[9] [C:] SAN PIERO D' APENA — (Plan). 121 × 175 mm.

[10] [C:] SAUONA, Descritta, e Dedicata Dal P. Maestro Coronelli Lettore, e Cosmografo della Serenissima Republica di Venetia — (Plan). 262 × 439 mm.

REGNO DI CORSICA

[11] [T:] Isole di Corsica, e Sardegna con parte delle Coste di Barbaria — (Map). 124 × 178 mm. See [1] in this ed.

[12] [C:] CORSO — [C:] I CORSICA — (Map). 123 × 85 mm.

[13] [C:] ISOLA DI CORSICA, DESCRITTA, E DEDICATA DAL P. EX-GENERALE CORONELLI AL EMINENTISSIMO PRENCIPE IL S. CARDINALE FIESCHI, Arcivescovo di Genova. — (Map). 605 × 447 mm.

[14] [C:] AJAZZO — (Plan). 125 × 176 mm.

[15] [C:] CALVI Nell Isola di CORSICA della Republica di Genoua — (Plan). 128 × 170 mm.

[16] [C:] S. FIORENZO Nell Isola Di Corsica — (Plan). 128 × 171 mm.

[17] [C:] Isola Taulara della Seressima Repubblica di Genova, dove le Galere dalla S. Religione di S.Stefano presero gli 2. Ottobre 1628. due Dalere di Biserta — (Map). 126 × 177 mm.

[18] [C:] ISOLA, E CASTELLO DI GERBI Descritto, e Dedicato Dal P. Maestro Coronelli Cosmografo della Serenissima Republica di Venetia All Illustrissimo Signore Abbate D. GIOSEPPE FRANCESCO BIANCO Canonico della Catedrale di Mazara et c. — (Map). 221 × 296 mm. [Inset:] [T:] CASTELLO DI GERBI — (Plan). 88 × 110 mm.

LA TOSCANA

[19] [C:] FIORENZA — (Plan). 123 × 178 mm.

[20] [C:] FIORENZA — (View). 127 × 260 mm.

[21] [T:] CITTADELLA DI FIORENZA, — (View). 124 × 178 mm.

CARDINALES TUSCI

[22] [T:] SIENA Lat. SLNA — [T:] Arcivescovale dall.' A. 1459. — (View). 124 × 178 mm.

[23] [C:] CITTADELLA DI SIENA — (View). 124 × 177 mm.

[24] [C:] Duomo di Siena — (View). 125 × 180 mm.

[25] [T:] S. Miniato nella Toscana — (View). 123 × 179 mm.

[26] [C:] CITTA, e FORTEZZA DI LIVORNO Descritta, e Dedicata Dal P. Cosmografo Coronelli All' Illustrissimo Signore ANIBALE SASSO Conte di Quara Maestro di Camera di S.A.S. il Sig.or Prencipe Cesare d'Este — (Plan). 171 × 259 mm.

[27] [C:] PORTO E LAZZARETTO DI LIVORNO — (Plan). 122 × 177 mm.

[28] [T:] Pontremolese venduto l.A.1650. da' Spagnuoli al Gran Duca di Toscana — (Map). 124 × 177 mm.

REPUBBLICA DI LUCCA, Delineata Dal P. Generale Coronelli

[29] [C:] REPUBLICA DI LUCCA, Nella Toscana, Accresciuta di molte notitie, Dal P. Cosmografo Coronelli, e Lettore Publico, Dedicata A Monsig. Illustrissimo, e Reuerendis. FABBIO GUINIGI, Arciuescouo di Raueña, Prencipe etc. — (Map). 444 × 610 mm.

[30] [C:] LUCCA — (Plan). 124 × 178 mm.

ISOLA, E REGNO DI SARDEGNA Descritti e Delineali Dal P. Cosmografo Coronelli

[31] [C:] Isola è Regno di Sardegna Soggetta al Rè di Spagna Descritta Dal P. Maestro Coronelli Cosmografo della Serenissima Republica di Venetia Dedicata al Padre Reuerendiss. Cloche Maestro Generale dell'Ordine dè Predicatori — (Map). 607 × 446 mm.

[32] [a] [C:] IS. DI CAPRI — (View). 51 × 267 mm.
[b] [T:] ISOLA DI CAPRI — [C:] Dedicata All: Illustriss: Sig: AntM: Mainert Gouern. Gen: dello Stato di Melfi — (Map). 157 × 272 mm.
[The whole plate:] 207 × 272 mm.

[33] [C:] ISOLA D'ELBA, gia detta, ILVA, et ÆTHALIA, Descritta Dal P.Cosmografo Coronelli — (Map). 177 × 242 mm.

[34] [C:] PORTO LONGONE NELL'ISOLA ELBA — (Plan). 48 130 × 171 mm.

[35] [C:] PORTOLONGONE — (Map). 124 × 178 mm.

[36] [C:] COSMOPOLI, ò PORTOFERRAIO Nell Isola d Elba — (Plan). 124 × 179 mm.

[37] [C:] ORBITELLO — (Plan). 124 × 178 mm.

[38] [T:] ORBITELLO — (Plan). 123 × 178 mm.

[39] [C:] PIONBINO — (Plan). 129 × 173 mm.

[40] [C:] PIOMBINO — (View). 128 × 360 mm.

[41] [C:] PORTO ERCOLE Nel Mare di Toscana — (Plan). 128 × 174 mm.

[42] [C:] VILLAFRANCA — (Map). 127 × 180 mm.

[43] [C:] SANT-ERMO di Porto Ercole — (Plan). 126 × 173 mm.

Notes: All the maps are blank on the verso and uncoloured. The volume contains twelve portraits: after map [5]: LAURENTIUS FLISCUS JANUENSIS, ARCHYEPISCOPUS, S.R.E. PRÆSBYIER CARDINALIS, CREATUS XVII. MAIJ MDCCVI.; after map [9]: JOAN BAPTISTA SPINOLA JANUEN. Titulo S.Cesarei Præsbyter Cardinalis, S.R. Ecclesiæ Camerarius, creatus ab Innocent: XII.die XII.Dec. MDCXCV. Ætatis suae XLVII.; after LA TOSCANA: COSMO III. VI. GRAN-DUC Descritte dal P. Coronelli; after CARDINALES TUSCI: FRANCISCUS MARIA S.R.E. DIACONUS CARDINALIS MEDICES FLORENTINUS, CREATUS II. SEPTEMBRIS. M.DCLXXXVI. Ant. Luciani scul.Venet.; NICOLAUS S.R.E. EPISCOPUS CARDINALIS ACCIAJOLUS, FLORENTINUS, CREATUS DIE XXIX NOVEMBRIS, ANNO M.DCLXIX.; CAROLUS SANCTÆ ROMANÆ ECCLESIÆ CARDINALIS BICHIUS SENENSIS, CREATUS DIE. XIII. MENSIS FERUARIJ, ANNO MDCXC Ant: Luciam delin: et scul:; BANDINUS S.R.E. PRESBYTER CARDINALIS PANCIATICUS FLORENTINUS, S.CONGREGATIONIS CONCILIJ PRÆFECTUS, CREATUS III. FEBRUARIJ.MDCXC.; FRANCISCUS MARTELLUS FLORENT: PATRIARCHA HEROSOLYMIT. S.CONSULTÆ SECRETARIUS S.R.E. PRÆSBYTER CARDINALIS, CREATUS IN CONSISTORIO SECR. XVII. MAIJ MDCCVI.; LAURENTIUS CORSINUS FLORENTINUS ARCHYEPISCOPUS NICOMEDIENSIS, S.S.D.N. THESAURARIUS GENERALIS S.R.E. PRÆSPYTER CARDINALIS, CREATUS D.XVII. MAIJ, A. MDCCVI.; CAROLUS AUGUSTINUS FABRONUS PISTORIENSIS, UTRIUSQUE SIGNATURÆ REFERENDARIUS S.C. DE PROPAGANDA FIDE SECRET. S.R.E. PRESBITER CARDINALIS, CREATUS XVII. MAIJ MDCCVI.; after REPUBBLICA DI LUCCA: HOPATIUS PHILIPPUS SPADA, LUCENSIS, ARCHYEPISCOPUS, EPISCOPUS LUCÆ S.R.E. PRESBYTER CARDINALIS, CREATUS IN CONCISTORIO SECRETO XVII. MAIJ MDCCVI.; after map [36] ...FRIDERICUS GUALDUS ... HERMETICI ORBIS PRINCEPS ...
Some of the plates are bound upside-down. The words 'Teatro della Guerra del P. Coronelli' appear on the lower margin of the text pages, but nowhere else.

Lit.: Armao nr 73, p. 154—155, Fonzo p. 361.

Vol. XV
[Stato Ecclesiastico]   [1708?]   18,3 cm obl.

[1] [C:] ITINERAIRE D ITALIE, oú sont les Routes de Nice á Rome, par Genes, Lucques, et Flóréce, et de Rome á Venise par Lorete, A PARIS, Par le Pere Coronelli —

(Map). 150 × 222 mm.
[Insets:] [C:] Route de Venise en Allemagne — (Map). 65 × 54 mm. (Irregular). [C:] Route de Rome a Naples — (Map). 42 × 80 mm. (Irregular).

[2] [C:] ROMA. — (Plan). 123 × 179 mm.
[3] [C:] LA SABINA A. P. Coronelli — (Map). 125 × 181 mm.
[4] [C:] TIVOLI — (Plan). 126 × 179 mm.
[5] [C:] NUOVO ACQUIDOTTO DI CIVITAVECCHIA ... Raccomandatane la Fabbrica da Innocezo XII. à Sapientissimi Ordini del Celebre Cardinale Panfilio, e sollecitata della Generosità di S.E. — (Map). 121 × 179 mm.
[6] [T:] FORTI CESAREI A. OSTIA, RESI ALLE ARMI PONTIFIZIE XXIV. GENNAJO MDLVII. — (Map). 126 × 181 mm.
[7] [C:] PORTI Antico, e Moderno D'ANZO Descritti, e Delineati Per Ordine DI N.S. INNOCENZO XII. Dal P. Cosmograrfo Coronelli — 121 × 180 mm.
 [a] [T:] PORTO ANTICO D'ANZO — (Plan). 118 × 115 mm.
 [b] [T:] DARSENA Proposta dal P. Coronelli guista la di liú Stampata Relazione — (Plan). 118 × 60 mm.
[8] [C:] NETTUNO, Aliaś Navale Antiatum — (Plan). 124 × 179 mm.
[9] [C:] PIANTA ALZATA DE' PORTI CLAUDIANO, E TRAJANO — (Plan). 124 × 180 mm.
[10] [C:] PORTO TRAJANO — (Plan). 124 × 178 mm.
[11] [C:] Rovine di Porto Trajano — (Plan). 125 × 180 mm.
[12] [C:] TERRITORIO D'ORVIETO D.D. P. Coronelli — (Map). 125 × 180 mm.
[13] [C:] OPVIETO. — (Plan). 124 × 180 mm.
[14] [C:] ACQUA-PENDENTE D.D. Dal P. Coronelli — (Plan). 123 × 180 mm.
[15] [C:] VICOVARO Occupato dagli Imperiali e recuperato dalla S.Sede 13.Febbraio 1557. — (Plan). 125 × 181 mm.
[16] [T:] DUCATO DI CASTRO — (Map). 125 × 180 mm.
[17] [T:] Castro, assediato dalle Armi Pontificie, e reso, e spianato 2. Sett. 1649. — (Plan). 125 × 180 mm.

UMBRIA
[18] [C:] PERUGIA — (Plan). 124 × 179 mm.
[19] [C:] PERUGIA — (View). 124 × 178 mm.
[20] [C:] CASTIGLIONE de Marchesi Della Corgna — 122 × 178 mm.
 [a] (View). 28 × 175 mm.
 [b] (Plan and view). 92 × 175 mm.
[21] [C:] MARCHESATO MONTE S. MARIA D. Dal P. Coronelli — (Map). 125 × 181 mm.
[22] [C:] MARCHESATO DEL MONTE S. MARIA — (Map). 124 × 179 mm.
[23] [T:] Citta' di Castello, L. Tiphernum — (Plan). 124 × 180 mm.
[24] [T:] CITTA DI CASTELLO — (Plan). 124 × 181 mm.
[25] [C:] SACRA S.P.N. FRANCISCI BENEDICTIO SUPER PATRIAM ASSISII ... — (View). 124 × 178 mm.
[26] [C:] TERRITORIO DI MONTE-FALCO D.D. Dal P. Coronelli. — (Map). 123 × 180 mm.
[27] [C:] TODI D.D. P. Coronelli — (Map). 124 × 183 mm.
[28] [C:] DIOCESI DI NARNI — (Map). 123 × 178 mm.
[29] [C:] CIVITTELLA — (View). 124 × 178 mm.
[30] [C:] Il'F. Tevere da M. Tosto sin'à Ponte Felice. D. dal P. Coronelli. — (Map). 124 × 181 mm.
[31] [C:] NARNI A.Molini B.Muragli Nuova — (Plan). 123 × 178 mm.
[32] [C:] TERRITORIO DI TERNI — (Map). 124 × 181 mm.
[33] [C:] TERNI, Straboni INTERMNA — (Plan). 125 × 180 mm.
[34] [C:] ACQUIDOTTI DI SPOLETI — (View). 125 × 182 mm.
[35] [C:] TERRITORIO DI GUBBIO D.D. P. Coronelli — (Map). 126 × 182 mm.
[36] [C:] TERRITORIO DI NOCERA A. P. Coronelli. — (Map). 124 × 181 mm.

MARCA ANCONITANA
[37] [C:] MARCA D'ANCONA D.P. P. Coronelli. — (Map). 125 × 181 mm.
[38] [C:] TERRITORIO D. ANCONA D.D. P. Coronelli. — (Map). 123 × 181 mm.
[39] [C:] ANCONA — (Plan). 124 × 180 mm.
[40] [C:] MACERATA — (Plan). 122 × 176 mm.
[41] [C:] TERRITORIO DI PESARO — (Map). 122 × 178 mm.
[42] [C:] TERRITORIO DI MONTE FELTRO, E MARCHESATO S.AGATA — (Map). 123 × 178 mm.
[43] [C:] DIOCESE DT FANO — (Map). 123 × 180 mm.
[44] [C:] TERRITORIO DI FANO — (Map). 125 × 181 mm.
[45] [C:] Monte Nuovo, Diocisi di Sinigagila — 124 × 179 mm.
 [a] (View). 37 × 174 mm.
 [b] (Plan). 77 × 173 mm.
[46] [C:] TERRITORJ DI S.ANGELO IN VADO E D'URBANIA, E VICARIATO D'AMOLA D.D. P. Coronelli — (Map). 121 × 178 mm.
[47] [C:] S. ELPIDIO — (View). 120 × 180 mm.
[48] [C:] TERITORIO DI SINIGAGLIA E VICARIATO DI MONDAVIO P. Coronelli — (Map). 122 × 178 mm.
[49] [C:] STATO D'URBINO Delineato, e Descritto Dal P. Cosmografo Coronelli — (Map). 122 × 178 mm.
[50] [C:] TERRITORIO D'URBINO D.D. P. Coronelli — (Map). 125 × 181 mm.
[51] [C:] URBINO, PATRIA DI OLEMENTE XII. S.S.PONTEFICE — (View). 122 × 177 mm.
[52] [T:] URBINO — (Plan). 124 × 180 mm.
[53] [C:] TERRITORIO DI FERMO D.D. Del P. Coronelli — (Map). 125 × 181 mm.
[54] [a] [C:] FERMO — (Plan). 126 × 180 mm.
 [b] [C:] FIRMUM FIRMA FIDES, ROMANORUM COLONIA — (View). 125 × 180 mm.
 [The whole plate:] 126 × 363 mm
[55] [C:] TERRITORJ DI FOSSOMBRONE, E PERGOLA P. Coronelli D. — (Map). 126 × 181 mm.
[56] [C:] PERGOLA — (Plan). 127 × 179 mm.
[57] [C:] TERRITORIO DI CAGLI — (Map). 125 × 181 mm.
[58] [C:] CAGLI. ... — (Plan). 124 × 180 mm.
[59] [C:] URBANIA — (Plan). 124 × 179 mm.
[60] [C:] FOSSOMBRONE — (Plan). 124 × 180 mm.
[61] [C:] S. ANGELO IN VADO. — (Plan). 123 × 179 mm.
[62] [C:] SINIGAGLIA — (Plan). 123 × 180 mm.

Notes: All the maps are blank on the verso and uncoloured. The title-page is wanting. The volume does not correspond to Armao's description of any one of the three parts of Coronelli's Stato Ecclesiastico, which form vols. XV—XVII of the Teatro della Guerra. The maps and plates in this volume come partly from vol.XV and partly from vol.XVI. Before map [37] there is a portrait of JOSEPH VALLEMANUS FABRIANENSIS, ARCHIEPISCOPUS ATHENARUM, S. PALATIJ APOSTOLICI PRÆFECTUS, S.R.E. PRESBYTER CARDINALIS, CREATUS IN CONSISTORIO SECRETO XVII. MAIJ. MDCCVI IN SIMILI CONSISTORIO PUBLICATUS I. AUG. MDCCVII. Anti Luciani scul: The plates are unnumbered, but the text pages of the Istoria della citta'di Ricanati are numbered 1—20 and the folios are signed A—K. Nordenskiöld's signature, with the year 1900, is on the inside of the front cover.

Lit.: Armao nr 74, p. 155—157, Fonzo, p. 361.

Vol. XVI
LA ROMAGNA PROVINCIA DELLO STATO ECCLESIASTICO Descritto, e Delineato Dal P. Cosmografo Coronelli. [1708?]. 19,1 cm obl.

[1] [C:] ROMAGNA D.D. Dal P. Coronelli — (Map). 125 × 179 mm.
RAVENNA RICERCATA, ANTICO — MODERNA, Accresciuta di Memorie, Ed ornata di copiose Figure Dal P. GENERALE CORONELLI In profondo ossequio A' questa celebre Città, quasi dilettissima sua Patria, Ed a,' Prestantissimi di lei Patrizj, Suoi Signori, e Patroni Colendissimi.

[Half title:] RAVENNA RICERCATA
[2] [C:] TERRITORIO DI RAVENNA, cioè PARTE MERIDIONALE DI QUELL'ARCIVESCOVATO, Descritta, e Dedicata Dal Padre Maestro Coronelli, Lettore publico, e Cosmografo della S.S.Republica di Venetia, All'Illustrissimo, e Reuerendissimo Signore MONSIGNORE FABBIO GUINIGI Arciuescouo di Rauenna, e Prencipe et c. — (Map). 440 × 603 mm.
[Inset:] [T:] PLANO ELEVATO DELL' ANTICA CITTA DI RAVENNA — (Plan). Oval 161 × 230 mm.
[3] [T:] Trino Vrbs ipsa uocabula gloriatur, trigeminaque positione exultat idest. Prima Rauenna i. media Cesarea. 2. ultima clasbis .3. inter Urbem et Mare plana mollitie arenaque munita uectationibus apta. Iornand: de Reb. Goth: — (View). 126 × 171 mm.
[4] [C:] RAVENNA ANTICA — (View). 147 × 244 mm.
[5] [C:] RAVENNA Regolata da Fiumi Descrita, e Dedicata Dal P. Maestro VINCENZO CORONELLI Cosmografo Publico All'Illustrissimo Signor D.Vincenzo Buttrighelli — (Plan). 193 × 271 mm.
[6] [C:] FORTEZZA DI RAVENNA — (Plan). 124 × 179 mm.
[7] [C:] RAVENNA Col Montone diuertita e con l'altre Diuersioni proposte, e non praticate — (Plan). 126 × 168 mm.
[8] [T:] DIOCESE DI RIMINI NELLA ROMAGNA, Descritta dal P. Coronelli — (Map). 124 × 179 mm.
[9] [C:] REPUBBLICA DI S. MARINO — (Map). 123 × 178 mm.
[10] [C:] RIMINI — (Plan). 122 × 177 mm.
[11] [C:] FAENZA — (Plan). 121 × 178 mm.
[12] [T:] CESENA — (Plan). 123 × 179 mm.
[13] [C:] TERRITORIO D'IMOLA Descritto, e Dedicato Dal Padre Cosmografo Coronelli All'Illustriss: Sig:Abbate GIOSEPPE PIGHINI, Auditore della Dataria di N.Signore — (Map). 280 × 400 mm.
[14] [C:] IMOLA — (Plan). 122 × 176 mm.
[15] [T:] ROCCA D'IMOLA — (Plan). 123 × 177 mm.
Notes: All the maps are blank on the verso and uncoloured. The volume contains part of vol.II of Stato Ecclesiastico and part of vol.III (vols.XVI and XVII of the Teatro della Guerra). There are four portraits: preceding map [2]: PHILIPPUS ANTONIUS GUALTERIUS URBEVETANUS, ARCHIEPISCOPUS, EPISCOPUS IMOLENSIS, PRESBYTER CARDINALIS,CREATUS XVII. MAIJ MDCCVI; preceding folio L: Effigie di Dante che si uede nel di lui Sepolcro in Rauenna; following folio M: B. Petrus ex Honestis Raueniatensis Fundator sive Reformator Canonicæ Portuensis; and preceding map [8]: Reuerendissimus Pater Magister ANTONIUS PACINUS Rauennas,... 'AEN' is written in pencil on the inside of the front cover.
Lit.: Armao nr 74, p. 155—157, Fonzo, p. 361.

Vol. XVII wanting

Vol. XVIII
DUCATO DI FERRARA, Descritto, e Delineato Dal P. Cosmografo Coronelli. [1707?].
[Half titles:]
IL FERRARESE   GLI ARGONAUTI   19,3 cm obl.

[1] [C:] FERRARESA Descrito Dal P. Coronelli — (Map). 122 × 178 mm.
[2] [C:] VICO-ABENZA, Poi FERRARIOLA, Oggidi VOGHENZA. — (Plan). 123 × 179 mm.
[3] [C:] Ferrota, o Frata, prima d' essere spionata — (Plan). 123 × 179 mm.
[4] [C:] Ferrarola, o Ferrara Traspadana Nell'A. 698. Quando a'15. d'Agosto il Popolo passo' il Pò — (Plan). 123 × 181 mm.
[5] [T:] FERRARA Distrutta dalla Duchessa Mathilde d'Este nel MCI. Ristaurata nel MCV. nella forma seguente. — (Plan). 123 × 178 mm.
[6] [C:] FERRARA, come trovavasi L. Anno DCCLXVIII. — (Plan). 123 × 180 mm.
[7] [C:] FERRARA Come trovavasi L. Anno DCCCXXXIX. — (Plan). 122 × 178 mm.
[8] [C:] FERRARA Nel D CCCLXXX. ... — (Plan). 124 × 180 mm.
[9] [T:] FERRARA RISTAURATA NEL MCXVI. — (Plan). 124 × 178 mm.
[10] [C:] FERRARA Nel DCCCCXVI ... — (Plan). 122 × 178 mm.
[11] [T:] FERRARA — (Plan). 121 × 182 mm.
[12] [C:] FERRARA. — (Plan). 122 × 178 mm.
[13] [C:] CITTA, e CITTADELLA DI FERRARA, Descritta Dal P. Cosmografo Coronelli, e Dedicata Al Molto Reuerendo Padre M:GIACINTO BERNARDI Prouinciale, e Guardiáno de'Min:Con: — (Plan). 226 × 291 mm.
[14] [T:] FERRARA — (View). 110 × 472 mm.
[15] [T:] DUOMO DI FERRARA — (View). 124 × 179 mm.
[16] [C:] PORTA S. BENEDETTO In Ferrara — (View). 123 × 178 mm.
[17] [C:] PORTA DI S.BENEDETTO DI FERRARA — (Plan). 127 × 172 mm.
[18] [C:] PORTA S.GIORGIO DI FERRARA — (View). 124 × 180 mm.
[19] [T:] Porta Paula di Ferrara — (View). 122 × 180 mm.
[20] [C:] Cittadella di FERRARA. — (View). 130 × 221 mm.
[21] [C:] CITTADELLA DI FERRARA — (Plan). 126 × 181 mm.
[22] [C:] FORO D'ALIENO Oggioli LA FRATA. — (Plan). 123 × 178 mm.
[23] [C:] CONTORNI DI FERRARA — (Map). 124 × 180 mm.
[24] [C:] FIGARUOLO, LA STELLATA, COLLA DIAMANTINA — (Map). 123 × 179 mm.
[25] [C:] POLESINE DI FERRARA E SUE BONIFICAZIONI — (Map). 123 × 178 mm.
[26] [C:] PARTE DELLA S. MARTINA Del Duca di Modona — (Map). 123 × 179 mm.
[27] [C:] POLESINE S. GIORGIO da Ferrara Sm' á Marazo, e Longastrino — (Map). 121 × 178 mm.
[28] [C:] POLESINE DI FERRARA Ove potrebbesi introdurre in Ramo del Po' di Lombardia Nel pó di Ferrara — (Map). 123 × 178 mm.
[29] [C:] FORTI DELLA RESURREZIONE ó del Ponte di Lago Scuro fabbricati da Urbano VII nel 1645 poi demoliti — (Plans). 124 × 177 mm.
[30] [T:] Ponte di Lago-scuro, battuto da 29. Agosto 1643. sino 4. Settembre, co' Forti demoliti nell' A. 1645. — (Plan). 127 × 358 mm.
[31] [C:] Ponte di Lago-Scuro — (View). 125 × 357 mm.
[32] [C:] VILLA DEL CAPO DEL FIUME Descritta dal P. Coronelli — (Map). 124 × 179 mm.
[33] [C:] POLESINE DI CASAGLIA COLLE VALLI DI MARARA; E POGGIO, Descrtti Dal P. Coronelli — (Map). 123 × 178 mm.
[34] [C:] VALLE DI MARARA Colla Navigazione di BOLOGNA — (Map). 124 × 179 mm.
[35] [C:] TERRITORIO DI CENTO — (Map). 123 × 178 mm.
[36] [C:] CONTORNI DI CENTO, E PIEVE — (Map). 123 × 179 mm.
[37] [C:] TERRITORIO DELLA PIEVE e parte di quello DI CENTO — (Map). 122 × 179 mm.
[38] [C:] PIANTA DEL PANARO INTRODOTTO NEL PO L. ANNO MDCI. Delineato dal P. Coronelli — (Map). 123 × 178 mm.
[39] [C:] PROPOSTE PER LA DIVERSION DEL RENO Dell' Anno 1660. — (Map). 125 × 181 mm.
[40] [C:] GIARE DEL RENO Colla S.Martma, et c. — (Map). 121 × 179 mm.
[41] [C:] SERRAGLIO DI VIGARANO DELLA MAINARDA — (Map). 122 × 178 mm.
[42] [C:] VALLE DI CO' DI LUPO, E SUOI CONTORNI — (Map). 123 × 180 mm.
[43] [C:] BONIFICAZIONE DEL M. BENTIVOGLIO — (Map). 124 × 180 mm.

[44] [C:] LA S. MARTINA — (Map). 123 × 179 mm.
[45] [C:] BONDENO Fortificato dal Duca di Parma Nel MDCXLIII — (Plan). 101 129 × 176 mm.
[46] [C:] TERRITORIO DI BONDENO — (Map). 123 × 179 mm.
[47] [C:] PAESITRA LA ZENA, ED IL MOLINO DEL C MANZOLI — (Map). 122 × 177 mm.
[48] [C:] RIVIERA TRASPADANA DELLA TORRE DELLA FOSSA SIN' A MARARA — (Map). 123 × 178 mm.
[49] [C:] IL PO' DAL GAROFOLO ALLA POLLICELLA — (Map). 125 × 180 mm.
[Inset:] [T:] Pollicella, e sue Trincere nell' A.MDLIV. — (Plan). 30 × 54 mm.
[50] [C:] LA MESOLA COL PORTO DI GORO — (Map). 123 × 180 mm.
[51] [C:] FUSIGNANO MARCHESATO DÈ CALCAGNINI Descritto, e Delineató Dal P. Coronelli — (Map). 124 × 179 mm.
COMACCHIO
[52] [C:] FERRARA, ARGENTA, E COMACCHIO — (Map). 130 × 229 mm.
[53] [C:] VALLI DI COMACCHIO — (Map). 123 × 179 mm.
[54] [C:] COMACCHIO, PORTO DI MAGNAVACCA, E CANALE PALLOTTO Descritti dal P. Coronelli — (Map). 131 × 391 mm.
[55] [C:] COMACCHIO CITTA, Prima fosse fortificata — (Plan). 125 × 357 mm.
[56] [T:] CITTA DI COMACCHIO — (View). 93 × 258 mm.
[57] [C:] CITTA DI COMACCHIO — (View). 125 × 362 mm.
[58] [C:] PO NUOVO DI S ALBERTO — (Map). 123 × 180 mm.
[59] [C:] POLESINE D'ARIANO — (Map). 123 × 178 mm.
[60] [C:] PO' D' ARIANO, E PO' DELLE FORNACI — (Map). 122 × 178 mm.
[61] [C:] PO' D' ARIANO, E DELLE FORNACI — (Map). 112 × 429 mm.
[62] [C:] PORTO DI PRIMARO — (Map). 122 × 178 mm.
[63] [C:] POLESINE DI ROVIGO Stato Veneto con parte del FERRARESE — (Map). 123 × 178 mm.
[64] [C:] Pollicella, e sue Trincere dell' A.164[0] — (Plan). 123 × 179 mm.
IL BOLOGNESE PROVINCIA DELLO STATO ECCLESIASTICO Descritto, e Delineato Dal P. Cosmografo Coronelli
[65] [C:] BOLOGNA Città Dello Stato Ecclesiastico, Descritta Dal Padre Cosmografo Coronelli — [C:] Dedicata All'Illustrissimo Signore CESARE BIANCHETTI GAMBALONGA SENATORE, ET C. — (Plan). 265 × 357 mm.
[66] [T:] BOLOGNA — (Plan). 119 × 163 mm.
CARDINALES E' BONONIA
[67] [C:] FORTE URBANO Descritto Dal P. Cosmografo Coronelli — [C:] Dedicato All Erudito Signor e GIO: STRIDBECK — (Plan). 222 × 284 mm.
IL DUCATO DELLA MIRANDOLA
[68] [C:] FORTEZZA DE MIRANDOLA — (Plan). 124 × 178 mm.
[69] [C:] MIRANDOLA — (View). 93 × 305 mm.
[70] [C:] MIRANDOLA — (View). 130 × 305 mm.
[71] [C:] Mirandola, assediata, e presa dagli Imperiali nel [1705] — (Plan). 124 × 178 mm.
[72] [C:] LA COИCORDIA MARCHESATO Del Duca della Mirandola — (Plan). 124 × 179 mm.
Notes: All the maps are blank on the verso and uncoloured. Fonzo states that this vol.XVIII is a continuation of the Stato Ecclesiastico. The text pages are wrongly bound. The second leaf and the Indice delle chiese... in Ducato di Ferrara have been bound back to front, recto to verso, as can be seen from the catchwords. On the lower margins of these leaves are the words 'Teatro della Guerra del P. Coronelli'. Armao deals with this volume under no. 75 (pp. 157—158); he cites only one copy, in the Vatican library. There are eight portraits in the volume: preceding map [1]: LAURENTIUS CASONUS SARZANENSIS SANCTÆ ROMANÆ ECCLESIÆ PRÆSPYTER CARDINALIS, CREATUS XVII. MAIJ A. MDCCVI; preceding map [11]: TADDÆVS ALOYSIVS S.R.E. PRESBYTER CARDINALIS DEL VERME PLACENTINVS CREATVS. DIE XII. DECEMBRIS M.DC.XCV.; between maps [14] and [15]: Statua del Duca Ercole I disegnata dal Contugo, che doveua collocavsi nella Piazza di Ferrara; between maps [53] and [54]: Medaglia della Storico Giovanni Francesco Ferro Comacchiese and between maps [64] and [65]: NICOLAUS GRIMALDUS JANUENSIS VOTANS SIGNATURÆ GRATIÆ, S.C. EPISCOPORUM, ET REGULARIUM SECRET. S.R. E. DIACONUS CARDINALIS, CREATUS XVII. MAIJ M.DCCVI; preceding map [67]: JACOBUS S.R.E. PRESBYTER CARDINALIS A'BONONIA, EJUSDEMQUE CIVITATIS ARCHIEPISCOPUS, CREATUS XII. DECEMBRIS AN ! MDCLXXXXV. Ant. Luciani Ven: scul:; — SEBASTIANUS ANTONIUS S.R.E. PRESBYTER CARDINALIS TANARIUS, BONONIENSIS CREATUS DIE XII DECEMBRIS, ANNI MDCXCV.; ALEXANDER CAPRARA BONONIENSIS S.R.ROTÆ AUDITOR, ET REGENS POENITENTIARIÆ, S.R.E. PRESBYTER CARDINALIS, CREATUS IN CONSISTORIO SECRETO XVII. MAIJ MDCCVI. Ant: Luciani scul: — The two pages of text which should accompany Comaccio are wanting in our copy. There are two copies of the Indice at the end of the volume. On map [64] the last digit of the year is missing, and on map [71] the whole year; but both dates are given in full in the Indice, so they are supplied in brackets in the text. Under the view [30] the text reads 'Forti demoliti nell' A. 1645', but the Indice gives the date 1646. The initials 'A.E.N.' are written in pencil on the inside of the front cover.

Lit.: Armao nr 175, p. 157—158, Fonzo, p. 361.

Vol. XIX wanting

Vol. XX
REGNO DI NAPOL [1708?]   18,5 cm obl.

[1] [C:] COSTE D'ITALIA Da P. Ercole, a. C. delle Armi, e Parte della Sicilia e Sardegna — (Chart). 125 × 174 mm.
[2] [C:] PARTE SETTENTR: DEL REGNO DI NAPOLI ED ISOLE ADIACENTI — (Map). 316 × 453 mm.
[3] [C:] PARTE MERIDIONALE DEL REGNO DI NAPOLI ED ISOLE ADIACENTI — [C:] Dedicate All'Illustriss: et Eccellentiss: S. D. FERDINANDO ORONZIO MONFORTE Duca di Laurito Marchese di S' Giuliano, Prencipe Del S. R' Impero, e Gentilhuomo della Camera di S' M' Cesarea — (Map). 316 × 453 mm.
[4] [C:] SPIAGGE DA M. CIRCELLO A' C. DELLE ARMI — (Chart). 5 137 × 401 mm.
[5] [C:] LA CITTA DI NAPOLI — (View). 168 × 207 mm.
[6] [a] [C:] NAPOLI — (View). 62 × 252 mm.
[b] [C:] CHIAJA, o Strada Medina Coeli — (View). 60 × 252 mm.
[The whole plate:] 8 127 × 255 mm.
[7] [C:] Veduta dal Ponte della Maddalena Sin all Isola di Capri — (View). 9 88 × 378 mm.
[8] [C:] Veduta dalla Torre di Chiaja Sin al Monte Misseno — (View). 10 88 × 377 mm.
[9] [C:] Castello dell OVO — (View). 11 126 × 178 mm.
[10] [a] [C:] Castello dell'Ovo — [C:] In Napoli — (View). 60 × 170 mm.
[b] [C:] Altra Veduta di — [C:] Castello dell' Ovo — (View). 60 × 170 mm.
[The whole plate:] 123 × 175 mm.
[11] [a] [C:] Molo Grande — [C:] In Napoli — (View). 60 × 172 mm.
[b] [C:] Molo Picciolo — [C:] In Napoli — (View). 60 × 172 mm.
[The whole plate:] 13 124 × 175 mm.
[12] [a] [C:] Veduta della Strada — [C:] Del Porto — (View).

[b] [C:] Veduta di — [C:] Monte Oliveto — (View). 59 × 171 mm.
[The whole plate:] 17 123 × 174 mm.

[13] [a] [C:] Veduta della Sapienza — (View). 59 × 172 mm.
[b] [C:] Veduta di S.Giovanni — (View). 60 × 172 mm.
[The whole plate:] 18 124 × 175 mm.

[14] [a] [C:] Veduta di Resina — [C:] In Napoli — (View). 60 × 173 mm.
[b] [C:] Veduta della Torre — [C:] Del Greco — (View). 60 × 173 mm.
[The whole plate:] 19 125 × 175 mm.

[15] [a] [C:] Porta Alva — [C:] In Napoli — (View). 60 × 170 mm.
[b] [C:] Marcato Grande — [C:] In Napoli — (View). 58 × 170 mm.
[The whole plate:] 20 125 × 175 mm.

[16] [a] [C:] Piazza del Gesu' — [C:] In Napoli — (View). 59 × 172 mm.
[b] [C:] La Vicaria — [C:] In Napoli — (View). 58 × 171 mm.
[The whole plate:] 21 124 × 175 mm.

[17] [a] [C:] Porta Medina — (View). 58 × 171 mm.
[b] [C:] Veduta della Darsena — (View). 59 × 170 mm.
[The whole plate:] 22 123 × 173 mm.

[18] [a] [C:] Veduta de Camaldoli — (View). 59 × 174 mm.
[b] [C:] Veduta di S.Paolo — (View). 59 × 173 mm.
[The whole plate:] 23 124 × 176 mm.

[19] [a] [C:] Largo di S.Domenico — [C:] In Napoli — (View). 58 × 171 mm.
[b] [C:] Veduta della Sellaria — [C:] In Napoli — (View). 60 × 171 mm.
[The whole plate:] 24 124 × 174 mm.

[20] [a] [C:] Veduta della Carita' — [C:] In Napoli — (View). 58 × 171 mm.
[b] [C:] Veduta dell' Incoronata — [C:] In Napoli — (View). 59 × 171 mm.
[The whole plate:] 25 124 × 174 mm.

[21] [a] [C:] Prospetto del — [C:] Real Palazzo di Napoli — (View). 60 × 174 mm.
[b] [C:] Veduta del Largo — [C:] Del Castello — (View). 61 × 174 mm.
[The whole plate:] 27 125 × 176 mm.

[22] [a] [C:] Veduta di Portici — (View). 60 × 170 mm.
[b] [C:] Veduta di Poggio-Reale — (View). 58 × 170 mm.
[The whole plate:] 28 123 × 174 mm.

[23] [a] [C:] Vedu'a della Torre — [C:] Di Rouiglione — (View). 60 × 174 mm.
[b] [C:] Veduta della Torre — [C:] Dell' Annonciata — (View). 60 × 174 mm.
[The whole plate:]29 125 × 176 mm.

[24] [a] [C:] Studj Pubblici — [C:] In Napoli — (View). 60 × 175 mm.
[b] [C:] S. M. degli Angeli — [C:] In Napoli — (View). 60 × 174 mm.
[The whole plate:] 30 125 × 177 mm.

[25] [a] [C:] Sorrento — (View). 59 × 175 mm.
[b] [C:] Veduta del Piano — [C:] di Sorrento — (View). 59 × 175 mm.
[The whole plate:] 31 123 × 178 mm.

[26] [C:] TERRITORIO DI POZZUOLI ... — (Map). 126 × 176 mm.

[27] [a] [C:] Citta di Pozzuoli — [C:] Veduta Da Montenuovo — (View). 59 × 173 mm.
[b] [C:] Veduta del Molo — [C:] di Pozzuoli — (View). 59 × 173 mm.
[The whole plate:] 33 123 × 177 mm.

[28] [a] [C:] Veduta della Città — [C:] Di Pozzuolo — (View). 59 × 172 mm.
[b] [C:] Veduta della Grotta di — [C:] Pozzuoli di fuori — (View). 59 × 172 mm.
[The whole plate:] 34 124 × 174 mm.

[29] [a] [C:] Monte Misseno — [C:] Mare Morto — (View). 59 × 173 mm.
[b] [C:] Campi Elisj,o — [C:] Mercato di Sabbato — (View). 62 × 173 mm.
[The whole plate:] 35 125 × 177 mm.

[30] [a] [C:] Castel à Mare di Stabia — (View). 59 × 171 mm.
[b] [C:] Massa Lobrense — (View). 60 × 171 mm.
[The whole plate:] 38 124 × 175 mm.

[31] [a] [C:] Castello, e Porto di Baja — [C:] In Pozzuoli — (View). 60 × 170 mm.
[b] [C:] Lago d'Agnano — [C:] In Pozzuoli — 58 × 170 mm.
[The whole plate:] 45 125 × 175 mm.

[32] [a] [C:] Isola di Capri — [C:] Nel Sano di Baja. — (View). 60 × 173 mm.
[b] [C:] Isola di Nisita — [C:] Nel Seno di Baja. — (View). 59 × 172 mm.
[Inset:] [T:] Pianta di Nisita — (Map). 12 × 11 mm.
[The whole plate:] 47 125 × 175 mm.

[33] [a] [C:] Porto, e Fortezza di Baja — (View). 59 × 172 mm.
[b] [C:] Città, e Fortezza d'Isca — (View). 59 × 172 mm.
[The whole plate:] 49 124 × 174 mm.

[34] [C:] Piagge della Provincia di BARI, Colle Rastellate del 1691. Per l'Contaggio di Conversano — (Map). 50 127 × 394 mm.

[35] [Fortezza di Tarranto] (Plan). 163 × 272 mm.

[36] [T:] VEDUTA DELLA TERRAE MARINA DI PROCIDA — (View). 53 × 268 mm.

[37] [T:] ISOLE DI TREMITI, già dette INSULÆ DIOMEDÆ, Possedute nel Golfo di Venetia da Canonici Regolari Lateranensi Dedicate Al Reuerendissimo Padre Abbate D. Nicolò Bambaccari, Predicatore Celeberimo, et Accademico Argonauta — (View). 385 × 537 mm.

[38] [C:] Isola San Nicola La Maggiore dell'Isole Tremiti — (View). 383 135 × 182 mm.

[39] [C:] TREMITI — (View). 55 125 × 178 mm.

[40] [T:] DOMINIO, E DIOCESE DEL S. MONASTERO CASSINENSE — (Map). 124 × 178 mm.

[41] [C:] S. SEVERO IN PUGLIA — (Plan). 57 124 × 177 mm.

[42] [a] [T:] AQUILA — (View). 77 × 118 mm.
[b] [T:] SULMONA — (Plan). 83 × 118 mm.
[The whole plate:] 58 173 × 121 mm.

[43] [C:] ASCOLI, AMATRICE E NORSIA — (Map). 59 125 × 177 mm.

[44] [C:] TERAMO, E GIULIANOVA Città Dell Abbruzzo e loro Contorni — (Map). 60 126 × 177 mm.

[45] [C:] CIVITA DI PENNE, DI S. ANGELO, CHIETI, E PESCARA — (Map). 125 × 176 mm.

[46] [T:] GAETA — (View). 63 124 × 176 mm.

[47] [T:] TERRACINA — (View). 64 124 × 176 mm.

[48] [a] [T:] TERRACINA — (View). 80 × 124 mm.
[b] [T:] NOLA — (View). 82 × 124 mm.
[The whole plate:] 64 178 × 124 mm.

[49] [T:] FONDI — 65 124 × 176 mm.

[50] [C:] REGGIO NELLA CALABRIA — (View). 66 129 × 175 mm.

SICILIA E MALTA

[51] [C:] TRINACRIA hoggidi SICILIA, Desc^ritta, e Dedicata Dal P. Coronelli, Cosmografo della Serenissima Republica Al Sublime merito DEL PADRE ANDREA MASSA, Rettore della Compagnia di Gesú in Palermo — (Map). 448 × 606 mm.

[52] [C:] PARTE ORIENTALE DELLA SICILIA, E ITALIA DA C.PASSARO AL GOIFO DI VENEZIA — (Chart). 70 124 × 175 mm.

[53] [C:] FARO di MESSINA — (View). 127 × 173 mm.

[54] [C:] SCILLA, e CARIDDI nello Stretto di Messina, rappresentati Secondo il parere del P. Atanasio Chirchero. — (Map). 87 125 × 168 mm.

[55] [T:] Scilla, e Caridi nel Faro di Messina — (View). 87 124 × 175 mm.

[56] [C:] MESSINA, Metropoli della Sicilia Dedicato Al M.P.Carlo Trigona, della Compagnia di Gesú. — (View). 157 129 × 170 mm.

[57] [C:] MESSINA — (Plan). 124 × 178 mm.
[58] [C:] Nuova Cittadella di MESSINA — (Plan). 124 × 179 mm.
[59] [a] [C:] SIRACUSA MODERNA — (Plan). 121 × 84 mm.
[b] [C:] SIRACUSA ANTICA — (Plan). 121 × 88 mm.
[The whole plate:] 123 × 179 mm.
[60] [C:] MELAZZO — (View). 124 × 169 mm.
[61] [C:] CATANIA — (Plan). 126 × 171 mm.
[62] [C:] TRAPANI — (View). 124 × 166 mm.
[63] [C:] PALERMO — (View). 123 × 168 mm.
[64] [T:] PALERMO — (Plan). 327 128 × 170 mm.
[65] [C:] Prospettiua á Ponente di Mazara descritta dal P. Cosmografo Coronelli — (View). 81 × 283 mm.
[66] [C:] MELAZZO — (Plan). 124 × 178 mm.
ISOLA DI MALTA.
[67] [C:] ISOLA DI MALTA, olim MELITA, Descritta, e Dedicata Dal P.Coronelli Cosmografo della Serenissima Republica di Venetia, — (Map). 447 × 605 mm.
[68] [T:] CITTA, e FORTEZZA DI MALTA — (Plan). 127 × 168 mm.
[69] [C:] CITTA E FORTEZZA DI MALTA Colle Nuoue, e proposte Fortificationi Nel Laboratorio del P. Coronelli in Venetia 1688 — [C:] Dedicata All' Ill[mo] Signore Francesco Corner, Figlio Dell Ecc[mo] Sig: Gio: Corner, dal P. Coronelli Cos[m] della Serenissima Republica di Ven: — (Plan). 258 × 431 mm.

Notes: All the maps are blank on the verso and uncoloured. This volume contains not only Regno di Napoli but also Sicilia e Malta. The index lists all the plates in one sequence. Sicilia e Malta is not quite complete, according to the list given by Armao. He and Fonzo both cite only one copy of this volume, in the Marciana in Venice. According to Armao, Regno di Napoli is the last part of the Teatro della Guerra. Our collection lacks five of the volumes which he treats as parts of the Teatro: Isole Britanniche, Oxford and Cambridge, Germania, Ungheria and Lombardia. Complete sets of the Teatro are very rare. The section 'Isola di Malta' includes a portrait of FRA ADRIANO DI VIGNACURT XL GRAN MASTRO GEROSOLIMITANO Nato nel 1619 Eletto li 24 luglio 1690 F. Vin: Coronelli Cosm: pub: D.D.D. 1693, preceding map [67]. Maps [2] and [3] are each surrounded by 49 small coats-of-arms, and map [67] has a border of 62 coats-of-arms of Grand Masters of the Order of Malta. Fonzo treats the Teatro della Guerra as a whole in the 'Annotazioni sul TG' at the end of his article. Nordenskiöld has written AEN in pencil on the inside of the front cover.
Lit.: Armao nr 75, p. 157—158, nr 76, p. 158—159, Fonzo p. 361—363.

60 CORONELLI, VINCENZO [1707?]

ARCIPELAGO 17,8 cm.

[1] [C:] ARCIPELAGO — (Map). 5 126 × 177 mm.
[2] [C:] PARTE OCCIDENTALE DELL' EUROPA, ... — = (59) 1707:VIII:[82].
[3] [T:] PARTE MERIDIONALE DELL' ARCIPELAGO del P. Coronelli Cosmografo Publico — (Map). 445 × 602 mm.
[4] [C:] PARALELLO GEOGRAFICO DELL' ANTICO COL MODERNO ARCIPELAGO Per Iŝtruzione dell' Istoria dell' Isole contenute in esso OPERA Del P. Maestro Coronelli Cosmografo della Serenissima Republica di Venezia, ad uso dell' Accademia Cosmografica degli Argonauti, Dedicato All' Eccellenza del Signor GIO: BATTISTA DONA Sauio Grande, etc. già Bailo in Constantinopoli. — (Map). 446 × 604 mm.
[5] [T:] ISOLA e REGNO DI CANDIA ol. CRETA — (Map). 191 × 432 mm.
[6] [C:] CASTEL RUGGIO — (View). 65 127 × 178 mm.
[7] [C:] FOGGIE — (Map). 124 129 × 169 mm.
[8] [T:] Rouine di Fabbriche nel Scoglio Capra, ó Anticlare del Mare di Mandria — (View). 67 126 × 178 mm.
[9] [C:] CANALE DI COSTANTINOPOLI, Già detto BOSFORO TRACIO, Descritto Dal Padre Cosmografo Coronelli Secondo le Relationi di Monsieur Galland, Dedicato All' Illustrissima Signoro Agnese, Teresia, Figlia del' Eccellentissimo S. Paulo Donado Patritio Veneto, etc. ... — (Map). 256 × 438 mm.
[Inset:] [C:] CANALE DI COSTANTINOPOLI, Descritto dal P. Cosmografo Coronelli Secondo le Relationi DEL CONTE LUIGI FERDINANDO MARSILII — (Map). 121 × 168 mm.
[10] [C:] CANALE DI COSTANTINOPOLI Descritto dal P. Cosmografo Coronelli, Secondo le Relationi di Monsieur Galland — (Map). 126 × 168 mm.
[11] [C:] VISTA DE HELLESPONTO ET DELLA PROPONTIDE — (View). 123 × 171 mm.
[12] [C:] GALIPOLI — (View). 76 126 × 178 mm.
[13] [C:] SETTE TORRI — (View). 76 124 × 177 mm.
[14] [C:] CITTA, E PORTO DI COSTANTINOPOLI — (View). 130 × 174 mm.
[15] [C:] DARDANELLO DI CONSTANTINOPOLI — (View). 128 × 172 mm.
[16] [C:] DARDANELLO DI CONSTANTINOPOLI — (View). 92 127 × 180 mm.
[17] [C:] DARDANELLI di Gallipoli — (Map). 112 130 × 175 mm.
[18] [C:] ANDRIANOPOLI — (View). 14 131 × 175 mm.
[19] [T:] LE SAPIENZE — (View). 11 127 × 177 mm.
[20] [a] [T:] COSTE SETTENTRIONALI DI NEGROPONTE, E ISOLE DI SCHIRO, SCOPPELLO, E SCHIATTO, E GOLFO DI VOLO — (Map). 45 × 165 mm.
[b] [T:] PASSAGGI TRA L'ISOLE DELL' ARCIPELAGO PER VELEGGIARE A'NEGROPONTE, SCIO, E SMIRNE — (Map). 69 × 165 mm.
[The whole plate:] 12 125 × 177 mm.
[21] [C:] SATALIA — (View). 242 130 × 173 mm.
[22] [C:] PELAGVSE NELL' ARCIPELAGO — (View). 199 128 × 172 mm.
[23] [C:] MONTE SANTO — (View). 118 × 155 mm.
[24] [C:] SCOGILO DI PARIO — (View). 20 126 × 177 mm.
[25] [C:] ISOLA DI TINE — (View). 128 × 164 mm.
[26] [C:] TINE — (View). 122 × 157 mm.
[27] [C:] TINE — (Plan). 23 125 × 178 mm.
[28] [T:] I. ANTICLARE, ó CAPRA — (View). 24 127 × 178 mm.
[29] [C:] PROSPETTO DI VOLO — (View). 25 125 × 177 mm. See (54) 1687:[33].
[30] [C:] PIANTA DELLA FORT: DI VOLO — (Plan). 28 125 × 158 mm. See (54) 1687:[32].
[31] [C:] MEGARA — (View). 128 × 178 mm. See (54) 1687:[30].
[32] [C:] ISOLA DI RODI — (Map). 123 × 163 mm. See (56) 1688:[1].
[33] [C:] CITTA DI RODI — (Plan). 211 126 × 162 mm. = 1688:[2] with small alterations.
[34] [C:] RODI — (View). 30 126 × 178 mm.
[35] [T:] SUAZICH — (View). 126 × 178 mm.
[36] [C:] SUAZICH — 31 (View). 127 × 409 mm.
[37] [T:] ISOLE DELLE SIMIE — (Map). 226 128 × 160 mm. = 1688:[3] with small alterations.
[38] [T:] ISOLA DI PISCOPIA nel Mare di Rodi posseduta Dalla Prosapia Cornari Sin l'an 1572 — (Map). 125 × 164 mm. = 1688:[4] with small alterations.
[39] [T:] I DI NICARIA NELL' ARCIPEL: — (Map). 182 130 × 170 mm. = 1688:[14] with small alterations.
[40] [C:] ISOLA E FORTE DI CALAMO — (View). 280 124 × 160 mm. = See (56) 1688:[9].
[41] [C:] PORTO JERO GERO — (Map). 36 127 × 180 mm.
[42] [C:] I. DELOS — (View). 37 126 × 177 mm.
[43] [T:] ISOLA DI SANCHIO, ò LANGO — (Map). 221 127 × 164 mm. = 1688:[5] with small alterations.
[44] [C:] STANCHIÒ, ò STANGIÒ — (View). 228 126 × 165 mm. = 1688:[6] with small alterations.

[45] [a] [C:] I. MORGO, e ZINARA — (Map). 122 × 88 mm.
 [b] [C:] I. NICARIA, e PATMOS — (Map). 123 × 86 mm.
 [The whole plate:] 40   126 × 180 mm.
[46] [T:] ISOLA DI CALAMO NEL ARCIPEL — (Map). 123 × 162 mm. = 1688:[8] with small alterations.
[47] [C:] FORT DI LEMNO — (Plan). 128 × 164 mm.
[48] [C:] SCHIATO — (View). 241   128 × 170 mm.
[49] [C:] Parte dell Isola di NIXIA — (View). 18   126 × 161 mm.
[50] [C:] FORTEZZA DI LERO — (View). 120 × 167 mm. See 1688:[13].
[51] [T:] SDILLES GRANDE, olim RHENÆA INSULA SDILLES PICCIOLA — (Map). 126 × 162 mm.
[52] [C:] TORON — (View). 266   128 × 173 mm.
[53] [C:] CALOIERO dalla parte di Tramontana — (View). 120 × 162 mm. = 1688:[11] with small alterations.
[54] [C:] CALOIERO dalla parte d'Ostro — (View). 81   132 × 176 mm. = 1688:[12].
[55] [T:] CALOJERO D'ANDRO — (View). 51   128 × 177 mm.
[56] [T:] LI NISARY — (Map). 187   126 × 165 mm.
[57] [T:] LIMONIA   ISOLA CARCHI — (Map). 215   128 × 168 mm.
[58] [C:] S. GIORGIO DI SCHIRO — (Plan). 129 × 167 mm.
[59] [C:] TENEDO — (View). 126 × 177 mm.
[60] [C:] ISOLA DEL TENEDO — (Map). 125 × 166 mm.
[61] [C:] GOLFO DELLE SMIRNE — (Map). 125 × 168 mm.
[62] [C:] SMIRNE — (View). 58   123 × 287 mm.
[63] [C:] Isole, e Città possedute per puí di 2. Secoli da Patrizj Gusliniani Genovesi sino L. A. 1566, nell'Arcipelago — [T:] SCIO — (Map). 60   126 × 179 mm.
[64] [C:] CITTA, e FORTEZZA DI SCIO — (View). 112 × 252 mm.
[65] [T:] PORTO DI SCIO — (Plan). 125 × 175 mm.
[66] [C:] SCIO — (Plan). 124 × 180 mm.
[67] [a] [C:] CASTEL RUGGIO — (View). 59 × 177 mm.
 [b] [C:] CISME — (Plan). 59 × 176 mm.
 [The whole plate:] 125 × 180 mm.

Notes: All the maps are blank on the verso and uncoloured. This volume is in exactly the same style as those in the Teatro della Guerra, but Armao does not consider it to be part of the same series; Fonzo, however, includes it as part of the Teatro. Immediately before the Indice is a portrait of SULTAN ACHMET HAN I, Figliuoto d'Ibraim I, e Fratello di Mehemet IV, e di Solimano II, à cui Successe nell'Impero d'Oriente l'Anno MDCLXXXX li Giugno. Our copy is not bound according to the Indice. It is bound together with our second copy of Spagna (61), and the large map of Parte Occidentale dell'Europa belonging to Spagna has been bound as map [2] of the Arcipelago. All the maps in our copy of Isola di Rodi appear also in the Arcipelago, with a few small changes — e.g. there is only one copy of the view of Caloiero dalla parte d'Ostro. Three of the plates also appear in our copy of Morea (54). Armao records only one copy of this volume, in Padua; Fonzo mentions also a copy in Rome, in the Vitt. Em. colloc. Our copy was bound for Nordenskiöld, and bears the initials A.E.N. in gold on the spine. His signature, with the year 1897, appears in ink on the first blank leaf, with the pencil note :'af Coronelli kartor äro daterade 1693—1706'. [The maps of Coronelli are dated 1693—1706].

Lit.: Armao nr 84, p. 168—169, Fonzo, p. 362.

61 CORONELLI, VINCENZO   [1707]

[Teatro della guerra.]

Vol. VIII
SPAGNA   17,8 cm.

[1] [C:] LA SPAGNA Suddiuisa ... — 366 = 1693:[2].
[2] [C:] PARTE ORIENTALE DELLA SPAGNA ... — [Part I]. = 1707:VIII:[2].
[3] [C:] [Parte Orientale della Spagna.] — [Part II]. = 1707:VIII:[3].
[4] [C:] PARTE OCCIDENTALE DELLA SPAGNA, ... — = 1707:VIII:[4].
[5] [C:] POSTE DALLA SPAGNA A PARIGI — 11 = 1707:VIII:[5].
[6] [a] [T:] MADRID — ... 12 = 1707:VIII:[6].
[7] [a] [T:] BARCELLONA — ... 13 = 1707:VIII:[7].
[8] [a] [C:] MADRID ... — 14 = 1707:VIII:[8].
[9] [C:] MADRID... — 15 = 1707:VIII:[9].
[10] [T:] MONT — SERRAT — 21 = 1707:VIII:[10].
[11] [C:] Casa, e Camera ... — 22 = 1707:VIII:[11].
[12] [a] [C:] Passagio di Francia in Spagna nella Bijcaia — ... = 1707:VII:[13].
[13] [T:] SPAGNA DAL RIO DI SIVIGLIA ... — 23 = 1707:VIII:[12].
[14] [C:] GIBRALTAR — 27 = 1707:VIII:[16].
[15] [C:] GIBALTAR Attaccata DA' GALLO-HISPANI ... — 25 = 1707:VIII:[14].
[16] [C:] GIBALTAR Attaccato da 'Gallo Spani ... — 26 = 1707:VIII:[15].
[17] [C:] PARTE OCCIDENTALE DEL MEDITERRANEO — 28 = 1707:VIII:[17].
[18] [C:] ISOLA E PORTO DI CADIZE — 43 = 1707:VIII:[18].
[19] [a] [T:] CEUTA — ... 31 = 1707:VIII:[20].
[20] [T:] COSTA DI VALENZA, ... — 32 = 1707:VIII:[21].
[21] [T:] I. IVICA — 33 = 1707:VIII:[22].
[22] [T:] ISOLA DI MAIORICA — = 1707:VIII:[23].
[23] [a] [T:] BILBAO — ... 35 = 1707:VIII:[24].
[24] [a] [T:] CORDUBA — ... 36 = 1707:VIII:[25].
[25] [a] [T:] LOXA — ... 37 = 1707:VIII:[26].
[26] [a] [T:] ANTIQUERA — ... 38 = 1707:VIII:[27].
[27] [C:] CAMPREDON ... — = 1707:VIII:[28].
[28] [C:] PUICERDA Nella Catalogna — (Plan). 130 × 171 mm.
[29] [C:] GIRONA ... — = 1707:VIII:[30].
[30] [C:] Contorin di PALAMOS,... — = 1707:VIII:[31].
[31] [T:] PIANTA DELLA CITTA DI CAPO DE QUIERS — 523 = 1707:VIII:[33].
[32] [C:] PALAMOS ... — = 1707:VIII:[32].
[33] [T:] ROSES — = 1707:VIII:[35].
[34] [C:] CAPO DI QUIERS ... — 45 = 1707:VIII:[34].
[35] [C:] ROSES E CAPO FOLIO — 47 = 1707:VIII:[36].
[36] [C:] ROSES DESCRITTO ... — = 1707:VIII:[37].
[37] [C:] CASTILLON ... — 49 = 1707:VIII:[38].
[38] [C:] BARCELLOИA ... — = 1707:VIII:[39].
[39] [C:] BARCELLONA — = 1707:VIII:[40].
[40] [C:] MONJOVI — 52 = 1707:VIII:[41].
[41] [C:] Tortosa, Frontiera ... — 53 = 1707:VIII:[42].
[42] [C:] OSTALRIC ... — 54 = 1707:VIII:[43].
[43] [a] [T:] BARCELLONA — ... 51 = 1707:VIII:[19].
[44] [C:] SALVATIERRA — 44 = 1707:VIII:[44].
[45] [a] [T:] MARTIA — ... 56 = 1707:VIII:[45].
[46] [C:] Fortin fabricato nel 1704 ... — = 1707:VIII:[46].
[47] [C:] FORTE GOJAN — 58 = 1707:VIII:[47].
[48] [C:] RIO VIGO ... — 59 = 1707:VIII:[48].
[49] [C:] PROFILO DI VIGO, ... — 60 = 1707:VIII:[50].
[50] [C:] CASTRO — VIGO — 61 = 1707:VIII:[49].
[51] [C:] VIGO VISTO ... — 63 = 1707:VIII:[51].
[52] [a] [T:] SANTANDER — ... 64 = 1707:VIII:[52].
[53] [T:] PUERTO DE LOS ALFAQUES — 65 = 1707:VIII:[53].
[54] [T:] Puerto de Peniscola — 66 = 1707:VIII:[54].
[55] [a] [C:] CASTEL BRANCO — ... 67 = 1707:VIII:[55].
[56] [T:] REGNO DI VALENZA — 68 = 1707:VIII:[56].
[57] [C:] FORTE AMORIN — = 1707:VIII:[57].
[58] [a] [C:] ELVAS — ... 70 = 1707:VIII:[58].
[59] [C:] PORTO DI DENIA — 71 = 1707:VIII:[59].
[60] [T:] ALICANTE — 72 = 1707:VIII:[60].
[61] [C:] VALENZA — 73 = 1707:VIII:[61].
[62] [C:] Parte della Città di VALENZA — 75 = 1707:VIII:[62].

[63]	[C:] ALCALA DE EBRO — 75	= 1707:VIII:[63].
[64]	[C:] CASTELLO FOLLIT — 76	= 1707:VIII:[64].
[65]	[C:] Ridotto á Sarriau de Bande ... — 77	= 1707:VIII:[65].
[66]	[C:] LA GUARDIA ... — 78	= 1707:VIII:[66].

REGNO DI GALLIZIA

[67]	[C:] Porto di BAJONA ... — 79	= 1707:VIII:[67].
[68]	[C:] BAJONA ... — 80	= 1707:VIII:[68].
[69]	[C:] BAJONA NELLA GALLIZIA — 81	= 1707:VIII:[69].
[70]	[C:] LERIDA — 82	= 1707:VIII:[70].
[71]	[C:] PORTO FERROL — 86	= 1707:VIII:[73].
[72]	[C:] CONFINI DI GALLIZIA, ... —	= 1707:VIII:[71].
[73]	[C:] CASTELLO DI SARAGOZZA ... — 85	= 1707:VIII:[72].
[74]	[a] [T:] TOLEDO — ... 87	= 1707:VIII:[74].
[75]	[C:] LA CORUÑA ... — 88	= 1707:VIII:[75].
[76]	[C:] LA CORUÑA ... — 88 (pro 89).	= 1707:VIII:[76].
[77]	[T:] I. BEOBIE, ó DE LHOS HOSPITAL ... — 90	= 1707:VIII:[77].
[78]	[T:] F. BIDASSOA, ... — 91	= 1707:VIII:[78].
[79]	[C:] FONTARABIE —	= 1707:VIII:[79].
[80]	[C:] SOCCOVA — 93	= 1707:VIII:[80].
[81]	[C:] PORTO CORUNA, ... — 94	= 1707:VIII:[81].

Notes: All the maps are blank on the verso, and uncoloured. This copy of vol. VIII of the Teatro della guerra is bound together with our copy of the Arcipelago no (60); the map which appears as no. [82] in our other copy of Spagna is here bound as no. [2] in the Arcipelago. As can be seen, the order of the maps in the two volumes is rather different. No. [28] is wanting in our other copy, although it appears in the index. This copy has been half bound in leather for Nordenskiöld, with his initials A.E.N. in gold on the spine. On the title-page is inscribed 'Giovan. Battista Monti done a tito Sucher anno 1849', and on the new blank leaf at the beginning is Nordenskiöld's signature with the date 1897, in ink, followed by the pencil note 'af Coronelli kartor äro daterade 1693—1706'. [Coronelli maps were dated 1693—1706.] Nordenskiöld's bookplate is on the inside of the front cover.

Lit.: See the other copy (59).

62 CRUYS, CORNELIUS [1703 ?]

NIEUW PAS-KAART BOEK BEHELSENDE De Groote Rivier DON of TANAIS, na deselfs waaragtige gelegenheydt Strekking, en Cours, vande STADT WORONETZ, tot daar hy in Zee Valdt met zyn invloeiende Stroomen, Eylanden, Steden, Dorpen, Kloosters etc: daer benevens Een zeer Curieuse Paskaart vande AZOFSCHE ZEE, of PALUS MŒOTIS en PONTUS EUXINUS of SWARTE ZEE met alle haar Diepten, Droogtens, aangelegen Rivieren, Havens Steden etc. Zynde daar by gevoegdt Een Afbeelding der Doorgraving, Om den DON door de ILAFLA te Leyden inde WOLGA of ASTRACANSCHE Rivier Alles Zeer Nauw-keurig, en door eygene Ondervinding opgenomen gepeylt, afgemeeten, en opgedragen aan ZYN DOORLUGTIGE HOOGHEYD ALIXIUS PETREIDES ERF-PRINCE der Keyser-Ryken, Koning-Ryken, Vorstendommen en Heerschappyen zyns Heer Vaders, Zyne GROOTMAGTIGSTE CZAARSCHE MAIESTEYT, door CORNELIS CRUYS, vice Admiral van Hooghgemelte Zyner MAIESTEYTS Zee-Magten TOT AMSTERDAM by Hendrick Doncker, Boek Caert en Kunstverkoper inde Nieuwbrugh Steegh int Stuurmans gereetschap met Privilege.

Новая Чертежная Книга Содержашая Великую рѣку Донъ или Танаисъ поея истинному положению рашнрению и течению игорода Воронежа Даже Дотого гдѣ ѡная Вморе Впадаетъ Сосвоими Втекушими рѣками Островами, Городами, Деревнями, монастырями ипроч, Присемъ, Sѣло Любопытный Чертежъ, АЗОВСКОВО МОРЯ ИЛИ ЕЗЕРА МЕОТСКАГО И ПОНТА ЭѴХИНСКОГО или ЧЕРНОГО МОРЯ Совсѣми ихъ глубинами, мѣлями, принадежашими рѣками, пристанми городами, присемъ приложено ИЗОБРА- ЖЕНИЕ ПРОКОПА Воежеѣы илавлу В'Вести Камышенкою рѣкою В'Волгу или Вастраханскую рѣку яжебъ Тѣмъ илавлинскимъ наводнением В'Водити издону илавлою и камышенкою рѣками В'Великую рѣку ВОЛГУ КАРАБЛИ й протчие. водные суды Все сѣло Прилѣжно И собственным Изобрѣтанием собрано Мѣрою Оловянною Водяною Вымѣреной. Приписано йли Поручено ЕГО ПРЕСВѢТЛОМУ ВЫСОЧЕСТВИЮ АЛЕХИЮ ПЕТРОВИЧЮ НАСЛѢДСТВЕННОМУ, ПРИНЦУ КЕСАРСТВЪ, КОРОЛЕВСТВЪ, КНЖСТВЪ ГДРСТВЪ, ЕГО ГДРЯ ОТЦА ЕГО САМОДЕРЖАВНѢИШАГО ЦРСКОГО ВЕЛИЧЕСТВА Корнелиа Креиса Наего Вышереченного ВЕЛИЧЕСТВА Морскими силами Вицъ Адмирала. ВАМСТЕРДАМѢ ОѴГендрика Дункера Книгъ Чертежныхъ ХудожеСтвъ Продавца Бинбруской Улицѣ Вкормчем Ѡруди сприимлиею. [Novaja Čertežnaja Kniga Soderžašaja Velikuju rěku Don ili Tanais poeja istinnomu položeniju razšireniju i tečeniju izgoroda Voroneža Daže Dotogo gdě onaja Vmore Vpadaet Sosvoimi Vtekušimi rěkami Ostrovami, Gorodami, Derevnjami, monastyrjami iproč, Prisem, Dzělo Ljubopytnyj Čertež, AZOVSKOVO MORJA ILI EZERA MEOTSKAGO I PONTA EVKSINSKOGO ili ČERNOGO MORJA Sovsěmi ih glubinami, měljami, prinaležašimi rěkami, pristanmi gorodami, prisem priloženo IZOBRAŽENIE PROKOPA Voežeěy ilavlu V'Vesti Kamyšenkoju rěkoju V'Volgu ili Vastrahanskuju rěku jažeb Těm ilavlinskim navodnenim V'Voditi izdonu ilavloju i kamyšenkoju rěkami V'Velikuju rěku VOLGU KARABLI i protčie. vodiye sudy Vse sělo dzělo Priležno i sobstvennym Izobrětaniem sobrano Měroju Olovjannoju Vodjanoju Vyměrenoj. Pripisano ili Poruceno EGO PRESVETLOMU VYSOČESTVIJU ALEKSIJU PETROVIČJU NASLĚDSTVENNOMU, PRINCU KESARSTV, KOROLEVSTV, KNJAŽESTV GOSUDARSTV, EGO GOSUDARJA OTCA EGO SAMODERŽAVNÉIŠAGO CARSKOGO VELIČESTVA Kornelia Kreisa Nad ego Vyšerečennogo VELIČETVA Morskimi silami Vic Admirala. VAMSTERDAMĚ OUGendrika Dunkera Knig Čertežnyh HudožeStv Prodavca Binbruskoi Ulice Vkormčem Orudii sprivilieju.]

[Engraved half-title:]

Nauw-keurige Afbeelding Vande Rivier DON, of TANAIS, de AZOFSCHE ZEE of PALUS MŒOTIS, en PONTUS EUXINUS of SWARTE ZEE, Zynde daar by gevoegdt. Een afbeelding der doorgraving, om den DON, door de Rivier ILAFLA, te ley den in de WOLGA, Meest door Eygen Ondervindinge van de Heer CORNELIS CRUYS Vice Admiral der Zeemagten Zyner GROOTMAGTIGSTE CZAARSHE MAIESTEYT.

Прилѣжное Описание рѣки Дону йли Танаиса АЗОВСКОВО МОРЯ ИЛИ ЕЗЕРА МЕОТСКАГО ПОНТА ЭѴХИНСКОГО ЙЛИ ЧЕРНОГО МОРЯ, присемъ Приложено Изображение ПРКОПА воеже ИЛАВЛУ й'вести камышенкою рекаю В'ВОЛГУ йли вастраханскую рѣку яжебъ тѣмъ Илавлискимъ Наводнениемъ в'водити йздону илавлою и камышенкою рѣками В'ВЕЛИКУЮ РѢКУ ВОЛГУ КАРАБЛИ и протчие водные суды отболшия части собственнымъ йзобрѣтаниемъ ГДНА КОРНЕЛИА КРЕИСА НАДЪ ЕГО САМОДЕРЖАВНЕИШАГО ЦРСКАГО ВЕЛИЧЕСТВА Морскими Силами вицъ Адмирала [Priležnoe Opisanie rěki Donu ili Tanaisa AZOVSKOVO MORJA ILI EZERA MEOTSKAGO PONTA EVKSINSKOGO ILI ČERNOGO MORJA, prisem priloženo Izobražentie PRKOPA voeže ILAVLU v'vesti kamyšenkoju rěkaju V'VOLGU ili vastrahanskuju rěku jažeb těm Ilavliskim Navodneniem v'voditi izdonu ilavloju i kamyšenkoju rěkami V'VELIKUJU RĚKU VOLGU KARABLI i protčie vodnye sudy otbolšija časti sobstvennym izobrětaniem GOSPODINA KORNELIA KREISA NAD EGO SAMODERŽAVNEIŠAGO CARSKAGO VELIČESTVA Morskimi Silami vic Admirala]

tot Amsterdam By Hendrick Doncker, Boek, Caert en Kunstverkoper, inde Nieuw brugh steegh int Stuurmans gereetschap met Privilege.

Вамстердамѣ Ѹ Гендрика Дункера Книгъ Чертежныхъ художествъ Продавца Бинбруской Улицѣ Вкормчем Ѡруди Сприивилиею

[Vamsterdame Ou Gendrika Dunkera Knig Čertežnyh hudožestv Prodavca Binbruskoi Ulice Vkormčem Orudii sprivilieju.] 53 cm.

[1] De Opdoening der Landen hier onder Vertoond,... van ASOF,... naar Constantinopolen,... (62 profiles). Uncoloured.

[2] [C:] Nieuwe Seer Accurate, en Naauwkeurige CAART VANDE REVIER DE DON OF TANAIS Met aanwijsinge van alle der Selver Dieptens, Droogtens etc. afgemeeten in 't Iaar 1699, in tegenwoordigheŷd vanden Grooten Heer, Czaar, en Grootvorst PETER ALEXIOWITS door gods genade Keŷser van geheel Groot, Cleŷn, en Wit Rusland, Mitsgaders van veele Andre Oostelŷke, Westelŷke, en Noordelŷke Coninkrŷken, Heerschappŷen, Vorstendommen, en Landen sŷner Hoogwaarde Vader, en Voorvaderlŷke erve, Heer, en beheerscher Selfshouder mitsgaders altoos onverwinnelŷke en Vermeerder des Rŷks etc. etc. etc. Aenwien Dese Caart in alle Eerbiedigheŷd Werd opgedragen door sŷn Majesteŷts Alder Ootmoedigste en Gehoorsaamste Dienaar Cornelis Cruŷs Vice Admiraal van Hooghgemelte Sŷn Majesteŷts Zeemaght. ... — [C:] Tot AMSTERDAM By Hendrik Donker, ... — 512 × 585 mm.
[Inset:] [T:] ... Magazyn op Taganrock aen de Zee Zyde... — (View). 178 × 471 mm.

[3] [The River Don] 510 × 581 mm.
[Inset:] [T:] Aftekning van zyn Czaerze Mayesteyts Haven by Tagenrock... — 275 × 395 mm. (Irregular).

[4] 1, 2 [The River Don]
[C:] t Amsterdam by Hendrick Doncker in de Nieuwebrug-steegh ... — [Divided into two parts]. 598 × 517 mm.
[Inset:] [T:] NB, in dit Kaartje. Werd u Vertoont het begin van de Rivier Don en Woronis, en waer de Selfde R.re Haar Oorspronck neemen —
[C:] Означение Сие карты откудъ Начинается рѣки Донъ и Воронеж и Ока и процие рѣки [Označenie Sie Karty otkud Načinaetsja rěki Don i Voronež i Oka i procie reki] — (Map). 149 × 139 mm.

[5] 3, 4, 5 [The River Don]
[C:] t Amsterdam by Hendrick Doncker inde Nieuwebrug Steegh ... — [Divided into three parts]. 588 × 514 mm.

[6] 6, 7 [The River Don]
[C:] t Amsterdam by Hendrick Doncker inde Nieuwebrug Steegh ... — [Divided into two parts]. 592 × 515 mm.

[7] 8, 9 [The River Don]
[C:] t Amsterdam by Hendrick Doncker inde Nieuwebrugh Steegh ... — [Divided into two parts]. 585 × 510 mm.

[8] 10, 11 [The River Don]
[C:] t'Amsterdam by Hendrick Doncker inde Nieuwe brug Steegh ... — [Divided into two parts]. 583 × 512 mm.

[9] 12, 13 [The River Don]
[C:] t Amsterdam by Hendrick Doncker in de Nieuwe brug steegh ... — [Divided into two parts]. 586 × 512 mm.

[10] 14, 15 [The River Don]
[C:] t Amsterdam by Hendrick Doncker in de Nieuwebrug steegh ... — [Divided into two parts]. 588 × 509 mm.

[11] 16, 17 [The River Don]
[C:] t Amsterdam by Hendrick Doncker inde Nieuwebrug Steegh ... — [Divided into two parts]. 584 × 508 mm.

[12] 18 [C:] Nieuwe, en Seer Accurate Caert Vande DOORGRAVINGE om met Scheepen uyt de Rivier DE DON of TANAIS door de Spruyten of Revierties Jlafla en Camisinka inde Wolga, of Astrachansche Rivier en Caspicke Zee te Vaaren Waerinne werd vertoont de Reets gemackte damme en Sluysen, met aenwysinge der Plaetse, Waerde Resterende noch sullen gemaeckt werden.
Новая и прединая Ката О̃ Перекопе что̃ и̃ Донъ или Танаиса Караблямъ Илалое река до Камышенки а Камосщенкою рекою в Волгу, или АСтраханскую реку в Капуское Море входитъ, какъ вСе̃ Ка̃те оказуемъ да Гола Промылъ Пруды Воротъ вуканы̃ Мѣста посему Принаваемъ что здѣлано Будетъ В амстеда̃ у̃ Гендрика Ду̃ке В новоу Бру̃ Сте̃ Метъ Превилечи. [Novaja i predivnaja Karta O Perekope čto viz Don ili Tanaisa Karabljam Ilavloe reka do Kamyšenki a Kamossěnkoju rekoju v Volgu, ili AStrahanskuju reku v Kaspuskoe More vhodit, kak vSi Karte okazuem da Gola Promysl Prudy Vorot vukazan MEstah posemu Priznavaem čto zděłano Budet V amsterdamě u Gendrika Dunkera V novou Brug Steg Met Previleči]
t'Amster dam by Hendrick Doncker, in de Nieuwenbrug-steeg, ... — (Map). 500 × 579 mm.

[13] 19, 20 [The River Don]
[C:] t Amsterdam by Hendrick Doncker inde Nieuwe brug Steegh ... — [Divided into two parts]. 586 × 502 mm.

[14] 21, 22, 23 [The River Don]
[C:] t Amsterdam by Hendrick Doncker inde Nieuwebrug Steegh ... — [Divided into three parts]. 593 × 510 mm.

[15] 24, 25 [The River Don]
[C:] t Amsterdam By Hendrick Doncker inde Nieuwe brug Steegh ... — [Divided into two parts]. 586 × 507 mm.

[16] 26, 27 [The River Don]
[C:] t,Amsterdam by Hendrick Doncker inde Nieuwe brug steegh ... — [Divided into two parts]. 587 × 503 mm.

[17] [C:] Nieuwe Seer Accurate en Naauwkeurige Kaart van het PALUS MEOTIS en ASOFSCHE ZEE, met aenwysinge van alle der Selven dieptens, droogtens etc. Afgemeten int Jaer 1699. in tegenwoordigh: vanden Grooten Heer, Czaar, en Groot Vorst PETER ALEXIWITS, door Godes genã Keyser van geheel, groot, Kleyn, en Wit Rusland, mitsgaders van veele andere, Oostelyke, Westelyke, en Noordelyke Coninkryken, Heerschappyen, Vorstendommen, en landen Syner Hooghwaarde Vader, en Voorvaderlyke erve, Heer, en Beheerscher Selfs houder, Mitgaders althoos onverwinnelyke, en vermeerder des Rykx etc: etc: etc:, aan Wien dese Kaart in alle Eerbiedigheyd werd opgedragen door syn Majesteyts alder Ootmoedigste, en gehoorsaamste dienaer Cornelis Cruys, Viec̃ Admiraal van Hooghgemelte syn Majesteyts Zeemacht tot Amsterdam by Hendrick Doncker, inde Nieuw-Brug Steeg in't Stuurmans Gereetschap, ... — 511 × 595 mm.

[18] [C:] Nieuwe Accurate en Naauwkeurige Kaarte vande PONTUS EUXINUS Hodie MARE NIGRUM by de Russe genaamt ZORNO MORE, of de SWARTE ZEE. Mitsgaders de Hellespont, of Straat van Constantinopole in Groot besteck. tot Amsterdam by Hendrick Doncker, inde Nieuwen Brug steeg in t'Stuermans Gereetschap, ... — 506 × 588 mm.
[Inset:] [Hellespont] 214 × 287 mm.

Notes: All the maps are blank on the back and mounted on greyish paper. They are coloured, except where otherwise specified. Koeman lists this atlas under Doncker; the Library of Congress lists it under Cruys. On the engraved half-title is a portrait of Peter the Great sitting with a sword in his right hand, the left hand resting on a crown. This is Cruys's only known work, and it was already noted as very scarce in 1761, in Gerhard P. Müller's 'Sammlung Russischer Geschichte' (vol. 6 part 1). In the second edition of the 'Sammlung', vol. 5 p. 262, Müller states that the maps were made by 'Herrn General-Major von Sparreuter' under Cruys's direction. In the List of Geographical Atlases in the Library of Congress, vol. 6, Clara Le Gear provides some very informative notes about Cruys and the atlas. Our copy is bound in paper, with a leather spine. On the first blank leaf Nordenskiöld has written his name, with the date 1883. 'Dupl' is written in pencil on the inside of the front cover.

Lit.: Adelung, Die ältesten ausl. Karten, p. 45—49, Koeman vol. 4, p. 188, Don 15, LC List, vol. 6, p. 322, nr 9296, Müller, G.F., Sammlung, vol. 5, p. 262, Muller, F., Bibl. Neerl.-Russe, p. 140, nr 1043, Tiele p. 68, nr 285.

63 DANCKWERTH, CASPAR   1652

Newe Landesbeschreibung der Zweij Hertzogthümer Schleswich Vnd Holstein, Zusambt Vielen dabeij gehörigen Newen LandCarten, Die auff Ihr Königl= Maÿtt zu Dennemarck, Norwegen etc. Vnd Ihr Fürstl Dürchl. Beeder Regierenden Hertzogen zu Schleswich Holstein, etc. Aller= vnd Gnädigsten befehle Von dero Königl. Maÿtt. bestaltem Mathematico Iohanne Mejero. Hus. Cimbro. Chorographicè elaborirt, Dürch Casparum Danckwerth D. Zusammen getragen Vnd Verfertigt, Worin auch Das Alte Teütschland Kürtzlich beschriebben, mit begriffen ist. ... Anno 1652. Matthias et Nicolaus Petersen, fratres, Aurifices Husumenses sculpserunt.   47,5 cm.

[1] [C:] Newe Landtcarte Von denbeiden Hertzogthümbern SCHLESWIEG Und HOLSTEIN Zusamēn. Anno 1650. — [C:] Serenissimo et Potentissimo Principi ac Domino, Dn̄o. FRIDERICO III. Daniæ, Norwegiæ, Vandalorum, Gothorumq3 'Regi. V Duci Sleswici Holsatiæ, Stormariæ & Dithmarsiæ, Comiti in Oldenborg et Delmenhorst. Et Serenissimo, Celsissimoqúe Principi ac Domino,Dn̄o. FRIDERICO IV. Hæredi Norwegiæ, Duci Sleswici Holsatiæ, Storma= et Dithmarsiæ, Comiti in Oldenborg et Delmēhor= Dominis suis Clementissimis, Tabulam hanc Geographicam; Ducatuum Sleswici & Holsatiæ Conjunctim exhibitorum, subjectissimè Offert author Iohannes Mejerus, Husumensis. Matthias und Nicolaq Pet= Goldtschmide gebr: Hus: Cimb: sculps. — Before [1]. 415 × 585 mm. [Insets:] [T:] [Rypen.] — 38 × 67 mm. [T:] Sleswieg. — 52 × 67 mm. [T:] Flensborg. — 38 × 67 mm. [T:] Haderschleben. — 38 × 67 mm. [T:] Husum. — 35 × 67 mm. [T:] Tondern. — 41 × 67 mm. [T:] Sonderborg — 33 × 67 mm. [T:] Apenrade. — 36 × 67 mm. [T:] Eckernförde — 42 × 67 mm. [T:] Tonning — 51 × 67 mm. [T:] Hamburg. — 54 × 66 mm. [T:] Kiel. — 58 × 66 mm. [T:] Rendssborg — 48 × 66 mm. [T:] Itzehoa. — 64 × 66 mm. [T:] Oldesloh. — 51 × 66 mm. [T:] Krempe — 37 × 66 mm. [T:] Gluckstadt. — 52 × 66 mm. [T:] Ploen. — 34 × 66 mm. (All insets plans).

[2] [C:] ORBIS VETVS CVM ORIGINE MAGNARVM IN EO GENTIVM A FILIIS ET NEPOTIBVS NOE. — [T:] Christian Rothgiesser Husum sculpsit Año 1651. — [C:] Viris Perquàm Reuerendis Doctissiinis Excellentissimis Clarissimis-qúe Dn. Stephano Klotz SS. Theologiæ Doctori Regiæ Majest. in ducatibus Sleswico et Holsatia Superintendenti Generali Præposito Ecclesiarum Flensburgensium et Pastori Ecclesiæ Flensburgensis ad ædem S.Nicolai. longè meritissimo. et Dn. Iohanni Reinboth SS. Theologiæ Doctori. Seren. Celsit. in ducatibus Sleswico et Holsatia Superintendenti Generali Præposito, et Concionatori aulico, multò dignissimo Tabulam hanc propagationem generis humani adumbrantem l.m. ded. Casparus Danckwerth.D. — Between pp. 28 and 29. 432 × 529 mm.

[3] [C:] GERMANIA ANTIQVA AVSTRALIS Cum Contermina Galliæ parte et Rhætià, Vindeliciàque Nonico et Pannonia — [C:] Christian Rothgiesser Husum sculps. — [C:] Uenerandæ Antiquitatis Cultoribus Uniuersis Tabulam hanc dedicat Consecratque Casparus Danckwerth. D. — Between pp. 32 and 33. 397 × 565 mm.

[4] [C:] GERMANIA ANTIQVA SEPTENTRIONALIS Cum finitimis regionibus Scythicis et Sarmaticis ... — [T:] Christian Rothgiesser Husum. sculps — Between pp. 46 and 47. 427 × 537 mm.

[5] [C:] Newe Landtcarte Von dem Hertzogthumbe SCHLESWIEG. Anno i650. — [T:] Matthias undt Nicolaus Peters Goldts. gebr. Hus. sculps. — [C:] Serenissimo et Potentissimo, Principi ac Domino Dn. FRIDERICO III. Daniæ, Norwegiæ, Vandalorum, Gothorumq3 Regi, V.Duci Slesw= Holsatiæ, Stormariæ & Dithmarsiæ, Comiti in Oldenborg & Delinenhorst. Et Serenissimo Celsissimoque Principi ac Domino Dn. FRIDERICO IV. Hæredi Norwegiæ, Duci Sleswici, Holsatiæ, Stormariæ et Dithmarsiæ Comiti in Oldenburg et Delmenhorst, Dominis suis Clementissimis, Tabulam hanc Geographicam Ducatq Sleswicensis prorsus Novam subjectissimè Offert author Iohannes Mejer, Husum. — Between pp. 52 and 53. 419 × 550 mm.

[6] [C:] Nb̄dertheil des Hertzogthumbs SCHLESWIEG. Serenissimo, Celsissimoq3 Principi ac Domino Dn̄o Christiano vi Daniæ, Norwegiæ, Vandalorum Gothorumq3 Principi Electo, Duci Slesvici, Holsatiæ, Stormariæ & Dithmarsiæ, Comiti in Oldenburg. et Delmenhorst, Domino meo Clementissimo, Tabulam hanc Geographicam subjectissime Offert, author Iohannes Mejerus Husum= Cimber. — [C:] Matthias und Nicolaq Pet. Goldtschmide gebr. Hus. sculp — Between pp. 52 and 53. 408 × 607 mm.

[7] [C:] Landtcarte Vom Sudertheil des Hertzogthumbes SCHLESWIEG. Anno 1650. — [C:] Illustrissimo, Celsissimoq3 Principi ac Domino Dn̄o, Friderico, Sereniss.æ Nostræ Celsitud.is Natu maximo, Hæredi Norvegiæ, Duci Slesvici, Holsatiæ, Stormariæ et Dithmarsiæ, Comiti in

Oldenburg et Delmenhorst, Domino meo Clementissimo, Tabulam hanc, Australem Ducatus Slesvicensis partem exhibentem, Subjectissime Offert author Iohannes Mejerus, Husum = Cimb, Reg.æ Maj.ís Mathematicus. Matthias & Nicola9 Peters Goldtschmide gebr: Hus. sculp. — Between pp. 52 and 53. 406 × 613 mm.

[8] [C:] Landtcarte Vom Ostertheile des Ambtes HATERSLEBEN Genandt Baringsÿssell. — [T:] Matthias Vnd Clauss Petersen G S: gebr: Husumenss: sculps: — [C:] Viro digintate eminenti, Generoso, Magnifico ac Strenuo, Dn. Cajo Von Allfelde. Equiti aurato, Dn. in Mehlbeck, Saxdorff, &c. Ecclesiæ Sleswicensis Cathedralis Archidiacono, Reg.æ Maj.ís Consiliario Intimo, ac Senatori in Ducatib9 Sleswicô et Holsatiâ, præfectoq3 Haderslebiensi. Fautori suo Obseruando, hanc Diœcesis Baringsiliæ Tabulam Geographicam Officiosissimè dedicat, Author Iohannes Mejer9 Husum= Reg.æ Maj.ís Mathematicus. Anno 1649. — Between pp. 70 and 71. 405 × 537 mm.

[9] [C:] Westertheil des Amptes HADERSCHLEBEN Zusambt Riepen Und dem Löhmcloster. Anno 1649. — [C:] Illustri Magnifico ac Strenuo Dn.Dn. Gregorio Krabben. Equiti aurato Dn. in Tastlundt, Senatori Regni Daniæ prudentissimo, præfectoq3: Ripensi, & Generoso, Strenuo ac prudentissimo Viro, Dn. Ottoni Kraggen, Hæreditario in Trutzholm Serenissimi Daniæ Regis Secretatio magno. Præfectoq3 Cænobij Halsted & præfecturæ Haranger in Norvegia, Patronis suis benignissimis, Tabulam hanc Geographicam Officiosissimè dedicat author Iohannes Mejerus, Hus. Reg.æ Maj.ís Mathematicq. Matthias Und Clauss Petersen Goldtschmide. gebr: Husumens: schulps: — Between pp. 76 and 77. 413 × 534 mm.

[10] [a] [C:] Grundtriss der Stadt Vndt des Schlosses Ripen. Anno 1651. — (Plan). 133 × 244 mm.
[b] [C:] Grundtriss der Stadt Vndt des Schlosses Husum. [C:] Matthias & Nicola9 Peters Goldtschmide gebr Husum. sculp. — (Plan). 180 × 274 mm.
[Inset:] [C:] HUSUM ao 1651. — (View). 63 × 157 mm.
[c] [C:] Grundtriss der Stadt Haderschleben. Anno 1651. — (Plan). 124 × 245 mm.
[d] [C:] Grundtriss der Fehstung Tonningē. Anno 1651. ... — [C:] Viris amplissimis doctissimis prudentissimis prudentib9 et honestis, Civitatis Ripensis Haderslebiensis, Tunderensis, Husumensis et Tonningensis Consulib9 et Senatorib9 dignissimis, effigies horum oppidorum Officiose inscribit author Iohannes Mejer9 Husum, Reg.æ Maj.ís Mathematicq. — (Plan). 240 × 274 mm.
[e] [C:] Grundtriss der Stadt Vndt des Schlosses Tonderen. Anno 1651. — (Plan). 154 × 246 mm.
[The whole map:] Between pp. 78 and 79. 434 × 542 mm.

[11] [C:] Das Ambt TONDERN ohne Lundtofft Herde Anno 1648 — [C:] Christian Rothgiesser Husum sculps. — [C:] Viro Generoso Magnifico et Strenuo Dnō. Wolff Blohm. Sereniss. et Celsissimi Ducis Sleswici & Holsatiæ, in ducatib9 his Consiliario provinciali, præfectoq3 Tunderensi, Domino in Testorp & Seedorp. Fautori suo honorando, Tabulam hanc Geographicam officiosissime inscribit author Iohannes Mejerus Husum. Reg.æ Maj.ís Mathematicq — Between pp. 84 and 85. 436 × 590 mm.

[12] [C:] Landtcarte der, zu dem AMBTE TONDEREN gehörigen Marschländer. Anno 1657. ... Generoso, Strenuo ac Splendido, Dn. Hans Blohm. Sereniss. Nostræ Celsit. Supremo rei Venatoriæ præfecto, fautori suo observando, regionem hanc Præfecturæ Tonderensis Maritimam et uliginosam Officiose' dedicat author Iohannes Mejerus Reg.æ Maj.ís Mathematiq . — [T:] Matthias & Nicola9 Peters Goldtschmide. gebr. Hus. sculps. — Between pp. 86 and 87. 392 × 480 mm.

[13] [a] [C:] Landtcarte Von dem NORTFRIESLANDE in dem Hertzogthumbe Slesswieg, Anno 1651. Viro Nobilissimo, Strenuo ac Magnifico Dnō Christophoro Von der Lippe Ictō Regiæ Maj. Cancellario & Consiliario Intimo, Hæreditario in Sillimow & Swargen, fautori suo honorando, Tabulam hanc Frisiæ minoris Cimbricæ, Officiosissimè inscribit author Iohannes Mejerus Husum. Reg.æ Maj.ís Mathematiq . — [T:] Matthias & Nicola9 Peters Goltschmide. gbr. Husum. sculps. — 383 × 281 mm.
[b] [C:] Landtcarte Von dem Alten NORTFRIESLANDE. Anno jz40. Frisia Cimbrica Antiqua Dignitate Eminenti Nobili amplissimo et prudentissimo Viro. Dnō Henrico Von Hatten Ictō. Sereniss. Regiæ Majest. et Sereniss. Celsit. Consiliario jntimo, earundemq3 in ducatib9 Slesvico et Holsatià Cancellario provinciali Canonicoq3 Slesvicensi, fautori suo Observando, Officiosissimè dedicata authore Iohanne Mejero Husum. Cimb. Reg.æ Maj.ís Mathematico. — 383 × 276 mm.
[The whole map:] Between pp. 88 and 89. 393 × 571 mm.

[14] [C:] Nordertheil Vom Alt Nordt Friesslande. biss an das Iahr. i240. — [C:] ... Viro Nobili, Amplissimo et prudentissimo, Dn. Iacobo Preussern, ictō Serenissimæ Celsitudinis Consiliario, Supremi dicasterij Gottorpiensis Assessori et Secretario Intimo, Nec non Spectabili, doctissimo, Clarissimoq3 Viro, Dn. Adamo Oleario, LL. AA Magistro, Sereniss. Celsit. Bibliothecario et Mathematico aulico, fautorib9 suis plurimum honorandis, partem hanc Frisiæ Septentrionalis antiquæ, perofficiosé dedicat author, Iohannes Meier9 Husum. Reg.æ Maj.ís Mathematicq. Anno j649. Matthias Und Clauss Petersen, G S.gebr= Husumenss. sculps. — Between pp. 88 and 89. 413 × 541 mm.

[15] [C:] Landtcarte Uom Ampte APENRADE und Luntoft herde — [C:] Christian Rodtgiesser Husum sculpsit — [C:] Viro Dignitate Eminenti generoso ac Strenuo, Dn. Iohanni Friderico Uon Winterfelt, Dnō in Dalmien, Garlien, et Stressaw, Ecclesiæ Cathedralis Lubecensis Præposito Canonico et Thesaurario, Ecclesiæ Collegialis Eutinensis Decano. Sereniss. et Celsiss. Ducis Sleswici & Holsatiæ Consiliario Intimo, ac præfecto Apenradensi, Fautori suo plurimum honorando. Tabulam hanc Geographicam officiosissimè inscribit. Author Iohannes Mejer Husum Reg.æ Maj.ís Mathematicq. — Between pp. 92 and 93. 448 × 400 mm.
[Inset:] [C:] Grundtriss der stat APENRADE mit dem schloss BRVNDLVNDT Aō 1648 — (Plan). 150 × 115 mm.

[16] [C:] Landtcarte Von dem Furstenthumbe SONDERBORG Alss den Ländern Alssen Sundewitt Und Luxborg. aō 1649. ... — [C:] ... Matthis Peterss. Gs. & Claus P. Goldtschmide Unt gbr. Huss. Cimb. sculp. — [C:] Illustrissimis et Celsissimis Principibus ac Dominis Dn. Friderico, Dn. Philippo ac Dn. Iohanni Christiano, Hæredibus Norwegiæ, Ducibus Sleswici & Holsatiæ Stormariæ & Dithmarsiæ Comitibus in Oldenborg et Delmenhorst, Dominis suis Clementissimis Tabulam hanc Geographicam submissè Offert, author Iohannes Meier, Reg.æ Mai.ís Mathematicq, Husan9 — Between pp. 98 and 99. 427 × 566 mm.
[Inset:] [C:] Grundtriss der stadt undt d. slosses Sonderborg. ... — (Plan). 146 × 108 mm.

[17] [C:] Landtcarte Von dem Ambte FLENSBORG, ohne Nordgoessherde. Anno 1648. Matthias & Nicola9 Peters Goldtschmide. gebr. Husum. sculps. — [C:] Viris Nobilib9 amplissimis et prudentissimis, Dnō. Theodoro Lente Ictō, Reg. Maj. Dan. et Norweg. Consiliario Intimo et Secretario dexterrimo Et Dnō. Philippo Iulio Borneman Ejusdem Seren. Reg: Majest: Secretario Spectatissimo, Fautorib9 suis honorandis. Tabulam hanc quatuor Nomorum, Præfecturæ Flensborgensis perofficiosè inscribit, Author Iohannes Mejer9, Husum. Reg.æ Maj.ís Mathematicq. — Between pp. 102 and 103. 425 × 561 mm.
[Inset:] [T:] Grundtriss der stadt Flensborg — (Plan). 112 × 206 mm.

[18] [C:] Nordertheil des Amptes GOTTORFF. Anno 1649. — [C:] Matthias und Clauss Petersen, Goldtschmide, gebr. Hus. sculps. — [C:] Viro Nobilissimo, Strenuo ac Magnifico, Dn. Iohanni Adolpho Kielmann, ICtō Eximio, Com. pal. Cæs. et sac. Rom. Imperÿ Exempto, Sereniss. Celsitud Consiliario Intimo, Cancellario aulico, ac præsidi supremi dicasterÿ Gottorpiensis, præfectoq9 Barmstedensi, patrono suo Observando, Tabulam hanc Geographicam

Officiosissime' dedicat. author Iohannes Meier Husumens: Reg.æ Maj.¹ˢ Mathematicǫ. — Between pp. 108 and 109. 381 × 568 mm.

[19] [a] [C:] Newe Landtcarte Von der Insull Helgelandt Anno 1649. author Iohanness Mejerǫ Husum — 198 × 263 mm.
[b] [C:] HELGELADT. in annis Christi 800. i300. & i649. ... — [T:] Matthias Vnd Clauss Petersen, G S. gebr = Husumenss. sculps. — [C:] Viris Nobilibus, Amplissimis, doctissimis ac prudentissimis, Dn. Eberhardo Weidenkopff, IUD. Sereniss. Celsitud. Consiliario, ac supremi dioasterij Gottorpiensis assessori, Et Dn. Eilhardo Schachten, Sereniss. ac Celsissimi Ducis Sleswici et Holsatiæ, in supremo Dicasterio Gottorpiensi secreatario, fautoribǫ suis Observandis, Tabulam hanc Simul Chorographicam & Topographicam, perofficiosè dedicat author Iohannes Mejerǫ. Husum. Reg.æ Maj.¹ˢ Mathematicǫ — 208 × 264 mm.
[c] [C:] Grundtriss der stadt Slesswieg. Anno 1649. — (Plan). 234 + 292 mm.
[d] [C:] Grundtriss Von Dennewarcks wall Undt der Alten stadt Slesswieg Wij ess Anno ii54 gewesen — (Plan). 174 × 292 mm.
[Inset:] [C:] Grundtriss der Alten stadt Sleswieg. Anno ii54. — (Plan). 102 × 140 mm.
[The whole map:] Between pp. 108 and 109. 412 × 573 mm.

[20] [C:] Carte Von den Ländern ANGLEN Und SCHWANSEN. Anno i649. Viris Generosis Strenuis ac splendidis, Dn. Heinrico Brockdorff, Domino in Hemmelmarck Sereniss. ac Celsiss. Ducis Sleswici & Holsatiæ Tribuno militum fortissimo. et Dn. Nicolao Von Allfeldt, Hæreditario in Geltingen. Tabulam hanc Georaphicam per Officiosé dedicat author, Iohannes Meier. Husan. Reg.æ Mai.¹ˢ Mathematicǫ. — [T:] Matthis und Clauss Petersen Goldtschmide und gebr: Hus. Cimb. sculps: — Between pp. 124 and 125. 431 × 535 mm.

[21] [C:] Eigentlicher Abriss des SCHLEISTROMS mit denen darinbelegenen Heringzeunen ... — [T:] Christian Lorensen Rodtgiesser sculps. — [C:] Viris Generosis Strenuis & Splendidis Dñ. Heinrico Rumoer Hæreditario in Röste. Dn. Gerhardo Philippo Uon Alfeldt Hæredit. in Buckhagn. Dn. Wolff Uon der Wisch Hæredit.in Ohe. Tabulam hanc Geographicam Officiose dedicat. author Iohannes Mejer Husum. Reg.æ Maj.¹ˢ Mathematicǫ. Aõ 1649 — Between pp. 132 and 133. 422 × 639 mm.
[Numerous insets of the fishing grounds]

[22] [C:] Suderteill des Amptes GOTTORF. Generoso, Strenuo ac Splendido, Dn. Ernesto Christophoro a Gunteroth. Sereniss. Nostræ Celsit. Mareschallo Aulico, et Supremo rei Equestris præfecto etc. Patrono suo Observando, Tabulam hanc Geographicam Officiosissimè in scribit. author Iohannes Mejerus. Hus. Reg.æ Maj.¹ˢ Mathematicǫ. Anno j65i. — [C:] ... Matthis und Clauss Peters: Goldtschmide und gbr. sculp. Husumens. — Between pp. 134 and 135. 403 × 599 mm.
[Insets:] [C:] Grundtriss Von Fridrichstadt Anno 1649. ... — (Plan). 118 × 124 mm. [C:] Grundtriss der stadt Eckernförde ... — (Plan). 122 × 154 mm.

[23] [C:] Landtcarte Von Nordgoesherde Ambt Husum Lundenberg Vndt dem Nortstrande. ... Viro Generoso, Strenuo ac splendido Dn. Ludero Dessien, Sereniss. Celsit. Conjugis Serenissimæ, Aulæ magistro et præfecturæ Husumanæ directori, Hæreditario in Daschow & Suderholtz, Et Nobili amplissimo ac prudentissimo Viro Dn. Iohanni Wittemake, Centurioni Regio et Nomarchæ in Norgoesherde, fautoribǫ suis Colendis, Tabulam hanc Geographicam perofficiosè inscribit author Iohannes Mejerǫ Husumens. Reg.æ Maj.¹ˢ Mathematicǫ. Anno j649. — [T:] Matthias Vnd Clauss Petersen G S.gebr. Husumenss. sculps. — Between pp. 136 and 137. 427 × 604 mm.

[24] [C:] Landtcarte Von EŸDERSTEDE EVerschop Und Uthholm. Viris Nobilibǫ, amplissimis, doctissimis & prudentissimis Dn. Ioachimo Danckwerth, Hæreditario in Höyersworth, Sereniss. Celsit. Ærarÿ præfecto dexterrimo Integerrimo, Fautori suo Multis Nominibǫ Colendo Et Dñõ. Augusto Luth amico suo Magno, Tabulam hanc Chorographicam Eÿderostadiæ Officiosè dedicat author Iohannes Mejerus Husum. Reg.æ Maj.¹ˢ Mathematicǫ. Anno 1648. Matthias und Nicolaǫ Pet= Goldtschmide gebr. Husum sculps. — Between pp. 146 and 147. 424 × 614 mm.

[25] [C:] Snderteil Uom Alt Nord Friesslande biss an das Iahr i240. — [C:] Andres Lorensen Rothgiesir Husum sculps. — [C:] Viro Nobili amplissimo ac Prudentissimo Dn. Casparo Schwencken Præsidi Eiderstedensi Nec Non Honestis ac prudentibǫ Regionum Eidersted. Euerschop. et Vthholm Senatoribǫ Tabulam hanc Chorographicam officiosè dedicat author Iohannes Mejerus Husum. Reg.æ Maj.¹ˢ Mathematicǫ. — Between pp. 152 and 153. 422 × 608 mm.
[Inset:] [C:] Abriss Uon RVNGHOLTE Und Seinen Kirchspielen Anno i240. ... — 183 × 165 mm.

[26] [a] [C:] Geometrisch Grundtriss Uon der Insull Arroe Anno 1648 — [C:] Viro Generoso, Strenuo ac splendido Domino, Friderico Uon Buchwalde Equiti aurato, Hæreditario in Preissorth, siue Bulcke, Seekamp etc. Legato militari supremo fortissimo, Fautori suo. Tabulam hanc Chorographicam officiosissime dedic Author Iohannes Meier, Reg.æ Maj.¹ˢ Matemati — 181 × 290 mm.
[b] [C:] Geometrisch Grundriss Uon dem lande Femeren Anno 1648. — [C:] FEMBRIA Dignitate præcellenti, Nobili Amplissimo ac prudentissimo Viro, Dn. Balthasari Gloxin I.V.D. Sereniss. Cels. Consiliario, ac supremi dicastery Gottorpiensis assessori Canonicoq₃ Lubecensi Fautori suo inscripta ab Authore Iohanne Mejero Husum Reg.æ Maj.¹ˢ Mathematico — 218 × 286 mm.
[c] [C:] Landtcarte Uon dem DÆNISCHEN WALDE — 228 × 289 mm.
[d] [C:] Grundtris der Stat BORG mit Ihren feltscheiden — 187 × 140 mm.
[e] [C:] Grundtriss der Stat BORG Auf Femern Anno 1648 — [C:] Andres Lorensen Rodtgiesser Husum sculpsit. — (Plan). 187 × 132 mm.
[The whole map:] Between pp. 154 and 155. 435 × 601 mm.

[27] [C:] Newe Landtcarte Von dem Hertzogthumbe HOLSTEIN Anno i649. — [C:] Serenissimo et Potentissimo Principi ac Dño. Dn FRIDERICO III. Daniæ Norwegiæ, Vandalorum, Gothorumque Regi, V.Duci Sleswici, Holsatiæ, Stormariæ et Dithmarsiæ, Comiti in Oldenburg et Delmenhorst et Serenissimo, Celsissimoque Principi ac Domino Dn. Friderico IV. Hæredi Norwegiæ, Duci Sleswici, Holsatiæ, Storma et Dithmarsiæ, Comiti in Oldenborg et Delmennhorst, Dominis suis Clementissimis, Tabulam hanc recentem Ducatǫ Holsatiæ, Subiectissime Offert. Author IOHANNES MEIER Husumens. Matthias Und Clauss Petersen Goldtschmide gebr. Hus. sculps. — Between pp. 168 and 169. 421 × 621 mm.

[28] [C:] Landtcarte Uon den Ambtern RENDSBORG KIEL und BORDESHOLM Anno 1649. — [C:] Christian Lorensen Rodtgiesser Husum sculpsit. — [C:] Viris Generosis Strenuis ac splendidis Dnõ Heinrico Blohm Equiti aurato, Domino in Hagen etc. Regiæ Majest: Senatori in ducatibǫ Sleswico et Holsatia ac præfecto Rensburgensi. Et Dnõ Paulo Rantzow Dn. in Bothkamp Kohouede et Bienenbecke Sereniss. Celsit. in ducatibus Sleswico et Holsatia Senatori ac præfecto Kiloniensi Fautoribǫ, suis Colendis Tabulam hanc Geometricam officiocissime inscribit Author Iohannes Mejerǫ Husum Reg.æ Maj.¹ˢ Mathematicǫ — Between pp. 182 and 183. 411 × 623 mm.
[Inset:] [C:] Grundtriss der Stadt vnd des Schlosses Rendsburg Anno 1649. — (Plan). 127 × 153 mm.

[29] [a] [C:] Grundtriss der Stadt Vndt des Schlosses Kiell. Anno 1651. — (Plan). 200 × 268 mm.
[b] [C:] Grundtriss der Stadt Rendsburg mit seinen belägerung und Wercken. Anno 1645. — (Plan). 200 × 269 mm.
[c] [C:] Grundtriss der Stadt Itzehoa. Anno 1651. Viris Amplissimis, Doctissimis, prudentissimis, prudentibǫ et

honestis Civitatum Chilonÿ. Rendesburgi. Itzehoæ, & Oldesloæ, Consulib_9 et Senatorib_9 dignissimis effigies horum oppidorum Officiosè inscribit, author Iohannes Mejer_9 Husum. Cimb. Reg.^{æ} Maj.^{ls} Mathemati_9. Matthias & Nicola_9 Peters Goldschmide. gebr. Husum. sculps. — (Plan). 165 × 271 mm.
[d] [C:] Grundtriss der Statt Oldesloh. Anno 1641. ... — (Plan). 166 × 269 mm.
[The whole map:] Between pp. 188 and 189. 397 × 571 mm.

[30] [C:] Landtcarte Von dem Lande WAGEREN. Welches ist das Ostertheil Von HOLSTEIN. aō 1651. ... — [T:] Matthias & Nicola_9 Peters Goltschmide gbr. Hus. sculps: — [C:] Eminentissimo, Illustrissimo et Celsissimo Principi ac Domino. Dnō. Iohanni, Episcopo Lubecensi, Hæredi Norwegiæ, Duci Schlesswici, Holsatiæ, Stormariæ, et Dithmarsiæ, Comiti in Oldenborg et Delmenhorst, Domino suo Clementissimo, Tabulam hanctoti_9 Wagriæ subjectissimè Offert, Author. Iohannes Mejerus Hus. Reg.^{æ} Maj.^{ls} Mathematic_9. — Between pp. 194 and 195. 420 × 514 mm.
[Insets:] [C:] Grundtriss Oldenburg. añ 1651. — (Plan). 156 × 123 mm. [C:] Grundtriss Oldenburg. Anno 1320 — (Plan). 173 × 155 mm.

[31] [C:] Nordertheill Uon WAGEREN Worinnen auch die ämpter Cissmar Und Oldenborg. Anno 1649 Illustrissimo & Celsissimo Principi ac Domino, Dnō Ioachimo Ernesto, Hæredi Norwegiæ Duci Sleswici & Holsatiæ, Stormariæ & Dithmarsiæ Comiti in Oldenburg et Delmenhorst, Domino suo Clementissimo, Tabulam hanc Geographicam submisse offert author Iohannes Mejer. Husumens. Reg.^{æ} Maj.^{ls} Mathematic_9. — [T:] Christian Lorensen, Rodtgiesser sculps — Between pp. 204 and 205. 420 × 611 mm.
[Insets:] [C:] Grundtriss d. Statt Undt d. Schlosses PLÖEN. — 59 × 86 mm. [C:] Grundtriss Vom Flecken Preetze. — 116 × 68 mm. [T:] Grundriss Uon LVTKENBORG. — 60 × 95 mm. [C:] Grundtriss Uō HILLIGNHAVEN. aō 1649 — 60 × 84 mm. [T:] Grundtriss der Newstadt. — 81 × 106 mm. (All insets plans).

[32] [C:] Landtcarte Uom Süderntheil des WAGERLANDŜ Und ein theil Stormarn. Worinnen dass Stifft Lubeck. das Furstenthumb PLÖEN Und das Ambt Segeberg begriffen Anno 1650 — [T:] Andres Lorensen Rothgiesser Hus. sculps. — [C:] Viris Generosis, Strenuis ac splendidis Dn. Casparo Uon Buchwaldt Equiti aurato Reg. Maj. in ducatib_9 Sleswicô & Holsatiâ Consiliario ac præfecto Segebergensi, Domino in Pronstorp, Dn. Nicolao Uon Qúalen. Sereniss. Celsit. in ducatib_9 Sleswico & Holsatiæ Consiliario, præfecto_93 Cissmariensi et Oldenborgensi Domino in Sÿggen, Tabulam hanc Geographicam Officiosissime dedicat author Iohannes Mejerus Husum Reg.^{æ} Maj.^{ls} Mathematicus. — Between pp. 214 and 215. 418 × 624 mm.
[Insets:] [C:] Grundtriss der stadt Und d.Schloss Eutÿn aō i648. — (Plan). 75 × 112 mm. [C:] Grundris der stadt & schloss. segeberg aō i648. — (Plan). 65 × 112 mm. [T:] Segeberg Ieschnhagn — (View). 36 × 70 mm [T:] Grundriss Trauemünde — (Plan). 75 × 135 mm.

[33] [C:] Landtcarte Von dem Furstenthumbe STORMARN. Anno 1650. — [C:] Matthias & Nicola_9 Peters. Goldtschmide gebr. Hus. sculp. — [C:] Illustri Generossimoq_3 Comiti ac domino, Dnō Christiano, Sacri Romani Imperÿ Comiti in Rantzow, Dnō. in Breitenburg, Lindewith. et Giesingholm. Ecquiti aurato, Sereniss.^{æ} Reg.^{æ} Majest. Dan. ac Norweg: Consiliario intimo, ejusdemq_3 in ducatib_9 Sleswico & Holsatià Senatori ac Vicario honoratissimo Præfecto Langelandiæ, Dithmarsiæ Australis & Præfecturæ Steinborgensis, Dn. meo Clement. Tabulam hanc Stormariæ Submissè Offert author Iohannes Mejer_9. Husum. Reg.^{æ} Maj.^{ls} Mathematic_9. — Between pp. 240 and 241. 391 × 545 mm.

[34] [C:] Die Ämbter Trittow, Reinbeeck, Tremsbüttel Und Steinhorst Aō 1649. Dignitate Eminentib_9, generosis et Strenuis Viris, Dn. Christophoro Iohanni Uon Bulow, præposito monastery Veteris in Ducatu Bremensi, Sereniss. ac Celsiss. Ducis Sleswici & Holsatiæ Consiliario Intimo, præfectoq_3 Tremsbuttelensi et Steinhorsty. Et Dn. Friderico Uon Alfeldt Hæreditario in Sestermúhe, præposito monastery V̇terssen, Sereniss. nostræ Celsitudinis in Ducatib_9 Sleswico et Holsatiâ Senatori, et præfecto Trittouiensi, Fautorib_9 suis, Tabulam hanc Geographicam perofficiose inscribit. Author Iohannes Mejer Husum Reg.^{æ} Maj.^{ls} Mathematic_9 — [T:] Andres Lorensen Rodtgiesser Husum. sculps. — Between pp. 246 and 247. 430 × 579 mm.
[Inset:] [C:] Grundriss Uon OLDESCHLOH Anno 1382 ... — (Plan). 136 × 147 mm.

[35] [C:] Grundtriss der Edlen Weitberumbten Statt HAMBURG. Anno 1651. — [C:] Matthias & Nicola_9 Peters Goldtschmide. gebr. Hus. sculps. — [C:] Viris Magnificis, Nobilissimis, Amplissimis ac prudentissimis Dñis Consulib_9 Dn. Alberto Von Eitzen IuL. Dn. Iohanni Brandt IuL. Dn. Bartoldo Möller IuL. & Dn. Nicolao Iarre IuL. Dñis Sÿndicis Dn. Iohanni Christophoro Meurer IUD & Dn. Brodero Pauli. IUD. Totiq_3 amplissimo, senatui Inclÿtæ Civitatis Hamburgensis splendissimæ Vrbis Hamburgi effigiem hanc recentem Officiosissimè inscribit. Iohannes Mejerus Husum. Reg.^{æ} Maj.^{ls} Mathematicus. — (Plan). Between pp. 250 and 251. 400 × 567 mm.

[36] [C:] Landt Carte Uon der Grafschaft PINNEN BERG aō 1650. — [T:] Andres Lorensen Rodtgiesser Husum. sculps. — [C:] Viro Generoso, Strenuo ac Splendido. Dnō. Iasparo Von Orźen. Reg. Mai. Consiliario Intimo ac præfecto Pinnenbergensi. et Nobili amplissimo. Doctissimo ac prudentissimo Viro Dñō Francisco Stapel I.V.D. Consiliario regio et præsidi Pinnēbergensi. Fautorib_9 suis honorandis. Tabulam hanc Geographicam per officiosē inscribit. author Iohannes Mejer, Husum. Reg.^{æ} Maj.^{ls} Mathematic_9 — Between pp. 274 and 275. 419 × 540 mm.
[Inset:] [T:] Grundtris der statt Und Uehstung Krempe aō i648 ... — (Plan). 117 × 129 mm.

[37] [C:] Newe Landtcarte Von dem Ampte STEINBORG. Der Kremper, Vndt Wilstermarsch. Anno 1651. — [C:] Viro Nobilissimo, Magnifico ac Clarissimo Dñō. Theodoro Reinking Iᴄ̄to Eximio Com.pal. Cæs. &c: Sereniss. Regiæ Majest. Consiliario Intimo. Cancellario ac præsidi Supremi Gluckstadiensis, Hæreditario in Wellingsbuttel. Et. Nobili amplissimo ac prudentissimo Viro. Dnō. Iacobo Steinman Iᴄ̄to, Consiliario Regio & præfecturæ Steinborg: administratori dignissimo, Fautorib_9 suis Colendis. Tabulam hanc Geometricam Officiosissimè dedicat author Iohannes Mejerus. Husū. Reg.^{æ} Maj.^{ls} Mathematicus. Matthias & Nicola_9 Peters Goldtschmide gbr. Hus. sculps. — Between pp. 280 and 281. 404 × 570 mm.
[Inset:] [C:] Grundtriss der Vehstung Gluckstadt. ... — (Plan). 128 × 143 mm.

[38] [a] [C:] Landtcarte Von DITHMARSCHEN Anno 1559. — [C:] Dignitate præcellenti,Nobili, amplissimo, prudentissimoq_3 Viro Dñō. Reimaro Doren, Iᴄ̄to, Reg.^{æ} Maj.^{ls} Consiliario Intimo, Canonicoq_3 Slesvicensi. Fautori suo Observando. Tabulam hanc Dithmarsiæ Veteris, perofficiosè dedicat author Iohannes Mejer_9. Husum. Reg.^{æ} Maj.^{ls} Mathematicus. Anno 1651. — 406 × 303 mm.
[b] [C:] Landtcarte Von DITHMARSCHEN Anno 1651. ... — [C:] Matthias & Nicolaus Peters Goldtschmide.gbr. Hus. sculps. — [C:] Viro Nobili amplissimo, prudentissimoq_3 Dñō. Iohanni Helmens, IUL. Reg.^{æ} Maj.^{ls} Consiliario, Intimo Fautori suo honorando, Tabulam hanc Dithmarsiæ perofficiosè inscribit, Author Iohannes Mejer_9 Reg.^{æ} Maj.^{ls} Mathematicus. — 406 × 305 mm.
[The whole map:] Between pp. 288 and 289. 406 × 608 mm.

[39] [C:] Landtcarte Von dem Sudertheill DITHMARSCHEN. Anno 1648. Author Iohannes Mejer_9 Husum. Reg.^{æ} Maj.^{ls} Mathematicus. ... Matthias Undt Nicolaus Peters Goldtsch: gebr. Hus. sculps. — [C:] Viris Nobilib_9 amplissimis, doctissimis et prudentissimis. Dnō. Iacobo Braun.I.U.L. Dithmarsiæ Australis, Satrapæ Regio dignissimo, Ut et Dnō.Georgio Reichen, Iudicÿ provincialis Dithmarsiæ

Meridionalis, Assessori ac Secretario Regio experientissimo, Nec Non Doctissimis, Prudentib₉ & honestis ejusdem Iudiciÿ provincialis Dithmarsici Senatorib₉ Tabulam hanc Chorographicam perofficiosè incribit author. — Between pp. 298 and 299. 400 × 596 mm.
[Insets:] [C:] Grundtriss der Festung BRUNSBUTTEL. Anno 1644. — (Plan). 102 × 123 mm. [C:] Delineatio Urbis MELDORPIÆ. Anno 1500. — (Plan). 128 × 127 mm.

[40] [C:] Landtcarte Von dem Nordertheill Dithmarschen. Nobili, amplissimo, doctissimo ac prudentissimo, Dn. Iohanni Boje, UID. præsidi Dithmarsiæ septentrionalis, fautori suo, Et Honestis ac prudentib₉ Ejusdem Regionis Senatorib₉, Tabulam hanc Geometricam perofficiosè inscribit author Iohannes Mejer₉ Husum. Regæ Majˡˢ Mathematic₉. — [C:] ... Matthis Pet. & Clauss Peterss Goldtschmide Unt gb Hus. Cimb. sculp. — Between pp. 300 and 301. 400 × 591 mm.
[Insets:] [C:] Grundriss Von Wesslingburen. ... — (Plan). 100 × 91 mm. [C:] Grundriss Uon Lunden. aō 1648. — (Plan). 106 × 83 mm. [C:] Grundriss Von der Heÿde ... — (Plan). 125 × 143 mm.

Notes: All the maps are blank on the back and uncoloured. Our copy is in poor condition. On map [1] the insets of Rejpen and Tonning are damaged so that part of each is missing. Map [25] is cropped on left and right margins, cutting into the map itself. All the maps are by Johannes Mejer of Husum. Blaeu used them later in vols. I and III of the Atlas Major. See the notes in no (24) in this catalogue. The engraved title-page is by Matthias and Nicolaus Rothgiesser. It includes portraits of Frederik III and Frederik IV, S. Ansgarius Primus Archi Episc. Hamburg and S. Vicelinus Episcopus Aldenburgensis. On the title-page 'Me Iure possidet Lorentz Douglies' is written in old ink.
Lit.: BM, Maps vol. 4, c. 794, Jöcher vol. 2, c. 19, Tooley, Dictionary p. 92 and p. 364.

64 **DELISLE, GUILLAUME   1740—1750**

ATLANTE NOVISSIMO CHE CONTIENE TUTTE LE PARTI DEL MONDO, NEL QUALE SONO ESATTAMENTE DESCRITTI GL'IMPERJ, LE MONARCHIE, STATI, REPUBBLICHE, ec. DEL SIG. GUGLIELMO DE L'ISLE, VOLUME PRIMO; Al quale si premette la prima Parte della Introduzione alla Geografia. DEL SIG. SANSON DI ABBEVILLE Ove si spiegano i suoi principj, le varie Maniere onde viene rappresentata, i suoi termini, e l'uso che si deve far delle Carte. A SUA ECCELENZA IL SIG. CAVALIERE PIER ANDREA CAPELLO ELETTO AMBASCIADORE DELLA SERENISS. REPUBBLICA DI VENEZIA, ALLA SACRA IMP. MAESTA 'DI CARLO VI. IN VENEZIA, NELLA STAMPERIA DI GIAMBATISTA ALBRIZZI Q. GIROL. M D C C X L.
[Engraved half title:]
ATLANTE NOVISSIMO Del Sigʳ GUGLIELMO DE L'ISLE.
36,5 cm.

Vol. I
[1] [C:] MAPPAMONDO, O sia DESCRIZIONE GENERALE DEL GLOBO TERRESTRE ED ACQUATICO. — 293 × 353 mm. The hemispheres with 155 mm. diam.
[2] [C:] NUOVA CARTA DELL ASIA secondo le vltime osservazioni fata in AMSTERDAM apresso ISAC TIRION — 274 × 337 mm.
[3] [C:] NUOVA CARTA DELL' IMPERIO DELLA CHINA e dei Paesi circonvicini. NUEVA CARTA DE L'IMPERIO DE LA QUINA, y de las Tierras comarcanas ... — 244 × 319 mm.
[4] [C:] IMPERIO DEL GIAPPONE — 242 × 315 mm.
[5] [C:] ISOLE FILIPPINE LADRONES e MOLUCCOS o ISOLE delle SPEZIARIE come anco CELEBES &c. ... — 277 × 320 mm.
[6] [C:] ISOLE di SUNDA BORNEO SUMATRA IAVA GRANDE &c. ... — 274 × 359 mm.
[7] [C:] INDIA di la del Fiume Ganges overo di MALACCA SIAM CAMBODIA CHIAMPA KOCHINKINA LAOS PEGU AVA &c. — 278 × 353 mm.
[8] [C:] IMPERO DEL GRAN MOGOL — 278 × 350 mm.
[9] [C:] ISOLA CEILON — 274 × 348 mm.
[10] [C:] REGNO DI PERSIA — 288 × 360 mm.
[11] [C:] CARTA NUOVA dell' ARABIA — 276 × 338 mm.
[12] [C:] TARTARIA — 275 × 336 mm.
[13] [C:] IRAK ARABI KURDISTAN DIARBEK TURCOMANNIA SIRIA e PALESTINA ... — 269 × 331 mm.
[14] [C:] STATI DEL TURCO situati NELL' EUROPA ASIA ed AFFRICA — 278 × 340 mm.
[15] [C:] CARTA NUOVA DELL' EUROPA — 270 × 330 mm.
[16] [C:] NUOVA CARTA del EUROPA TURCHESCA Secondo l'ultime Osservazioni fata in AMSTERDAM apresso ISAAK TIRION ... — 281 × 334 mm.
[17] [C:] REGNO DI POLONIA DIVISO NEI SUOI PALATINATI — 281 × 334 mm.
[18] [C:] MOSCOVIA O RUSSIA ... — 273 × 329 mm.
[19] [C:] REGNO DI SVEZIA — 276 × 326 mm.
[20] [C:] REGNO DI DANIMARCA ... — 274 × 330 mm.
[21] [C:] NUOVA CARTA DEL POLO ARTICO — Circular map with 273 mm. diam.
[22] [C:] REGNO DI UNGHERIA, e della TRANSILVANIA — 273 × 318 mm.
[23] [C:] GERMANIA DIVISA IN DIECI CIRCOLI — 277 × 330 mm.
[24] [C:] REGNO DI BOEMIA, DUCATO DI SLESIA, MARCHESATO DI MORAVIA, e LUSAZIA — 278 × 322 mm.
[25] [C:] CIRCOLO di BAVIERA e di AUSTRIA — 275 × 319 mm.
[26] [C:] NUOVA CARTA DEL CIRCˡᵒ di SASSONIA SUPERʳᵉ Ovvero SASSONIA, MISNIA, VOIGTLAND, TURINGIA, ANHALT, LUSAZIA, BRANDENBURG, e POMERANIA & A AMSTERDAM da ISAC TIRION. ... — [T:] F.Polanzani scul. — 274 × 325 mm.
[27] [C:] CARTA DEL CIRCOLO DI SASSONIA INFERIORE, che contiene li Paesi di MEKELENBURG, LAVENBURG, HOLSTEIN, BREMA, e VERDEN, BRANSUIC, e LUNENBURGO, HANOVER, HILDESHEIM, HALBERSTAD, e MAGDENBURG, ... — 278 × 331 mm.
[28] [C:] CIRCOLO di FRANCONIA e di SVEVIA — 276 × 323 mm.
[29] [C:] CIRCOLI SUPERᴿᴱ ed INFERᴿᴱ DEL RENO annesso il DUCATO DI LORENA — 279 × 329 mm.
[30] [C:] CIRCOLO di WESTFALIA diviso ne' suoi VESCOVADI, PRINCIPATI, CONTÉE, &c. — 274 × 324 mm.
[31] [C:] CARTA NUOVA ED ACCURATA delle XVII PROVINCIE de' PAESI BASSI. in Amsterdam da Isac Tirion. — 277 × 329 mm.
[32] [C:] NUOVA CARTA del DUCATO DI LUCEMBURGO, e della CONTÈA DI NAMUR. in Amsterdam da ISAC TIRION. — 271 × 318 mm.
[33] [C:] NUOVA CARTA del DUCATO di BRABANTE, LIMBURGO, e della GHELDRIA SUPERʳᵉ in Amsterdam da Isac Tirion. — 275 × 329 mm.
[34] [C:] NUOVA CARTA delle CONTÉE DI FIANDRA, ARTOIS, ed HANNONIA. in Amsterdam da ISAC TIRION. — 270 × 319 mm.

Vol. II
ATLANTE NOVISSIMO CHE CONTIENE TUTTE LE PARTI DEL MONDO, NEL QUALE SONO ESATTAMENTE DESCRITTI GL' IMPERJ, LE MONARCHIE, STATI, REPUBBLICHE, ec. DEL SIG. GUGLIELMO DE L'ISLE, VOLUME SECONDO; ED ULTIMO Al quale si premette la seconda Parte della Introduzione alla Geografia. DEL SIG. SANSON DI ABBEVILLE; Ove si danno tutte le varie Divisioni

della Superficie del Globo Terrestre. A SUA ECCELLENZA LA SIGNORA ELEONORA CO: COLLALTO K.A CAPELLO. IN VENEZIA, NELLA STAMPERIA DI GIAMBATISTA ALBRIZZI Q. GIROL. M D C C L.
[Engraved half title:]
ATLANTE NOVISSIMO Del Sig.r GUGLIELMO DE L'ISLE.
36,5 cm.

[1] [C:] NUOVA CARTA dell' ISOLE BRITANNICHE divise nei tre Regni d'INGHILTERRA, di SCOZIA, e d'IRLANDA. — 269 × 329 mm.
[2] [C:] INGHILTERRA — 376 × 322 mm.
[3] [C:] SCOZIA — 372 × 314 mm.
[4] [C:] IRLANDA — 377 × 318 mm.
[5] [C:] NUOVA CARTA delle PROVINCIE UNITE data in luce in Amsterdam da ISAC TIRION. — 274 × 313 mm.
[6] [C:] NUOVA CARTA DELLA CONTEA DI OLANDA — 269 × 321 mm.
[7] [C:] CARTA GEOGRAFICA DEL REGNO DI FRANCIA — 320 × 362 mm.
[8] [C:] CARTA GEOGRAFICA DEL GOVERNO DELLA NORMANDIA ... — 321 × 416 mm.
[9] [C:] CARTA GEOGRAFICA DEL GOVERNO DELL'ISOLA DI FRANCIA — 326 × 422 mm.
[10] [C:] CARTA GEOGRAFICA del GOVERNO della BRETAGNA ... — 309 × 403 mm.
[11] [C:] CARTA GEOGRAFICA DEL GOVERNO DI GUIENNA E GUASCOGNA — 323 × 424 mm.
[12] [C:] CARTA GEOGRAFICA del GOVERNO della LINGUADOCCA — 321 × 422 mm.
[13] [C:] CARTA GEOGRAFICA DEL GOVERNO DELLA PROVENZA — 326 × 423 mm.
[14] [C:] NUOVA CARTA della SPAGNA — 281 × 352 mm.
[15] [C:] CARTA GEOGRAFICA del REGNO di PORTOGALLO — 388 × 327 mm.
[16] [C:] NUOVA CARTA dei XIII CANTONI degli SVIZZERI insieme coi loro ALLEATI e SUDDITI. — 270 × 325 mm.
[17] [C:] CARTA GEOGRAFICA GENERALE DELL'ITALIA — 320 × 430 mm.
[Inset:] [T:] IL REGNO DI SICILIA — 98 × 115 mm.
[18] [C:] CARTA GEOGRAFICA DEL DUCATO DI SAVOJA — 325 × 423 mm.
[19] [C:] CARTA GEOGRAFICA DELLO STATO DEL PIEMONTE — 328 × 426 mm.
[20] [C:] STATO DI MILANO E SUOI CONFINI. — 328 × 399 mm.
[21] [C:] CARTA GEOGRAFICA DEI TERRITORI DI PAVIA DI LODI E DI PIACENZA — 325 × 396 mm.
[22] [C:] CARTA GEOGRAFICA DEL GOVERNO DELLA LIGURIA O SIA DELLO STATO della REPUBLICA di GENOVA. — 330 × 402 mm.
[23] [C:] CARTA GEOGRAFICA del DUCATO di MANTOUA — 327 × 422 mm.
[24] [C:] CARTA GEOGRAFICA DELL' STATO VENETO IN'ITALIA — 327 × 426 mm.
[25] [C:] CARTA GEOGRAFICA DEL TERRITORIO BRESCIANO — 323 × 421 mm.
[26] [C:] CARTA GEOGRAFICA DEL TERRITORIO PADOVANO — 325 × 421 mm.
[27] [C:] CARTA GEOGRAFICA DEL TERRITORIO TREVIGIANO — 328 × 394 mm.
[28] [C:] CARTA GEOGRAFICA DELLA PROVINCIA DEL FRIULI — 324 × 422 mm.
[29] [C:] CARTA GEOGRAFICA del STATO della CHIESA — 326 × 424 mm.
[30] [C:] CARTA GEOGRAFICA DEL GRAN DUCATO DI TOSCANA — 326 × 424 mm.
[31] [C:] CARTA GEOGRAFICA DEL TERRITORIO SENESE — 326 × 423 mm.
[32] [C:] CARTA GEOGRAFICA DEL REGNO DI NAPOLI — 325 × 420 mm.
[33] [C:] CARTA GEOGRAFICA DELLA TERRA DI LAVORA O SIA DELLA CAMPAGNA FELICE — 326 × 426 mm.
[34] [C:] CARTA GEOGRAFICA DELL'ISOLA DI SICILIA — 325 × 423 mm.
[35] [C:] CARTA GEOGRAFICA DELL'ISOLA DI SARDEGNA — 327 × 422 mm.
[36] [C:] CARTA GEOGRAFICA del REGNO di CORSICA — 325 × 421 mm.
[37] [C:] CARTA GENERALE DELL'AFRICA — 327 × 426 mm.
[38] [C:] CARTA GEOGRAFICA DEL CAPO DI BUONA SPERANZA — 328 × 421 mm.
[39] [C:] CARTA GEOGRAFICA DELL'AMERICA SETTENTRIONALE — 323 × 421 mm.
[40] [C:] CARTA GEOGRAFICA DEL CANADA NELL'AMERICA SETTENTRIONALE — 326 × 423 mm.
[41] [C:] CARTA GEOGRAFICA DELLA FLORIDA NELL'AMERICA SETTENTRIONALE — 324 × 424 mm.
[42] [C:] CARTA GEOGRAFICA DEL MESSICO O SIA DELLA NUOVA SPAGNA — 324 × 423 mm.
[43] [C:] CARTA GEOGRAFICA DELLA AMERICA MERIDIONALE — 325 × 422 mm.
[44] [C:] CARTA GEOGRAFICA DEL BRESIL — 322 × 419 mm.

Notes: All the maps are blank on the back and uncoloured. The two parts are bound separately, the maps following the text in each. In vol. I the text consists of 12 unnumbered and 59 numbered pages; in vol. II, of 16 unnumbered and 79 numbered pages. The same engraved title-page appears in both volumes before the red and black letterpress title-page. The cartouche of map [20] in vol. II includes a medallion with a portrait of ATILA RE DEGLI UNNI. Our copy was damaged by water during World War II, but the maps are well preserved. Nordenskiöld's signature is on the inside of the front cover of each volume, with the dates 1901 (vol. I) and Jan 1901 (vol. II).

65 DELISHE, JOSEPH NICOLAS 1745

Russischer ATLAS, welcher in einer General-Charte und neunzehen Special-Charten das gesamte Russische Reich und dessen angräntzende Länder, nach den Regeln der Erd-Beschreibung und den neuesten Observationen vorstellig macht. Entworffen bey der Kayserl. Academie der Wissenschafften. ST. PETERSBURG 1745. 53 cm.

[1] № 1 [C:] LAPPONIA RUSSICA cum adjacentibus Regionibus. — 494 × 565 mm.
[2] № 2 [C:] TERRITORIUM ARCHANGELOPOLIN inter PETROBURGUM et VOLOGDAM. — 493 × 568 mm.
[3] № 3 [C:] DVCATVVM ESTONIAE et LIVONIAE TABVLA cum cursu Fluvii DWINAE. — 502 × 577 mm.
[4] № 4 [C:] MOSCOVIÆ GUBERNIUM cum Adiacentibus REGIONIBUS — 488 × 551 mm.
[5] № 5 [C:] TABULA GEOGRAPHICA GUBERNIUM SMOLENSCENSE Cum Parlibus KIOVIENSIS BELGORODENSIS et VORONICENSIS GUBERNII Complectens — 484 × 552 mm.
[6] № 6 [C:] TERRITORIUM MESENENSE et PUSTO-SERENSE Cum Adiacentibus INSULIS et TERRITORIIS. — 487 × 542 mm.
[7] № 7 [C:] TATARIA minor Cum Adiacentibus KIOVIENSI et BELGORODENSI GUBERNIIS. — 489 × 557 mm.
[8] № 8 [C:] PROVINCIARUM USTIUGÆ et CHLYNOVI nec non Territoriorum IARENSCENSIS VAGÆ USTIUGÆ SOLIWYTSCHEG DÆ et TOTMÆ Delineatio Geographica. — 473 × 547 mm.
[9] № 9 [C:] CASANIÆ REGNUM cum Adiacentibus PROVINCIIS et Parte FLUVII VOLGÆ. — 487 × 556 mm.
[10] № 10 [C:] Delineatio FLUVII VOLGÆ a Samara usque ad Tsaricin — 485 × 552 mm.

[11] № 11. [C:] TERRITORIUM PONTUM EVXINUM et MARE CASPIUM Interiacens CUBANIÆ et GEOGRGIÆ Delineationem Geographicam reliquamque Partem FLUVII VOLGÆ eiusque Ostium exhibens. — 484 × 552 mm.

[12] № 12 [C:] PARS SIBIRIÆ tractum inter SALINAS ad CAMAM et TOBOLIUM comprehendens. — 493 × 556 mm.

[13] № 13 [C:] UFFENSIS PROVINCIA cum adiacentibus Regionibus — 492 × 557 mm.

[14] № 14 [T:] PARTES FLUVIORUM PETSCHORÆ OBII et IENISEÆ UNA CUM EORUM OSTIIS IN OCEANUM SEPTENTRIONALIM SE EXONERANTIUM. — 504 × 556 mm.

[15] № 15 [T:] TRACTUS FLUVIORUM IRTISCH, TOBOL, IENISEAE ET TUNGUSAE CUM IPSORUM FONTIBUS, ADIACENTIBUSQUE ITIDEM ET INTERIACENTIBUS REGIONIBUS — 510 × 561 mm.

[16] № 16 [T:] PARS MARIS GLACIALIS OSTIUMQUE FLUVII LENÆ cum TERRITORIO SEPTENTRIONALI IAKUTENSI — 504 × 558 mm.

[17] № 17 [T:] IRKUTENSIS VICE PRÆFECTURA cum MARI BAIKAL et FONTE FLUVII LENÆ PARTIBUSQUE FLUVIORUM ARGUN et AMUR AC CIRCUMIACENTIBUS TERRITORIIS — 504 × 555 mm.

[18] № 18 [T:] TERRITORII IACUTENSIS PARS ORIENTALIOR cum MAXIMA PARTE TERRÆ KAMTSCHATKÆ — 501 × 556 mm.
[Inset:] [C:] Ora extrema borealior SIBIRIÆ orientem respiciens ... — 119 × 134 mm.

[19] [T:] OSTIUM FLUVII AMUR cum PARTE AUSTRALIORI TERRÆ KAMTSCHATKÆ VARIISQUE in OCEANO SITIS INSULIS INTER QUAS PARS EMINET IAPONIÆ — 511 × 560 mm.

[20] [C:] MAPPA GENERALIS TOTIUS IMPERII RUSSICI —
[C:] Сия Карта представляющая съ возможною исправностию въ подлинномъ видѣ Все пространство Россiйскiй Имперiи съ ея Губернiями и Провинцiями Начата по премудрому намѣренiю славнѣйшаго въ свѣтѣ Монарха Блаженныя и вѣчно достойныя памяти Государя Императора ПЕТРА ВЕЛИКАГО Когда чрезъ неусыпное Его Величества попеченiе между прочими изрядными науками трудъ по Географiи воспрiятъ былъ ко окончанiю же приведена при благополучномъ Государствованiи Великiя Его Дщери Всепресвѣтлѣйшiя Державнѣйшiя и непобѣдимѣйшiя Государыни Императрицы ЕЛИСАВЕТЪ ПЕТРОВНЫ Самодержицы Всероссiйскiя а нынѣ для показанiя свѣту тѣхъ земель и Народовъ которые подъ скипетромъ и покровомъ сея великодушныя Обладательницы и щедротнѣйшiя матери отечества благополучiе вѣка своего прославляютъ издается во всенародное употребленiе лѣта отъ Рождества Христова 1745.
[Sija Karta predstavljajuščaja s vožmoznoju ispravnostiju v podlinnom vide Vse prostranstvo Rossiiskija Imperii s eja Gubernijami i Provincijami Načata po premudromu namereniju slavneišago v světě Monarha Blažennyja i věčno dostojnyja pamjati Gosudarja Imperatora PETRA VELIKAGO Kogda črez neusypnoe Ego Veličestva popečenie meždu pročimi izrjadnymi naukami trud po Geografii vosprijat byl ko okončaniju že privedena pri blagopolučnom Gosudarstvovanii Velikija Ego Dsčeri Vsepresvětlěišija Deržavněisija i nepobědiměišija Gosudaryni Imperatricy ELISAVET PETROVNY samoderžicy Vserossiiskija a nyne dlja pokazanija světu těh zemel' i Narodov kotorye pod skipetrom i pokrovom seja velikodušnyja Obladatel'nicy i sčedrotněišija materi otečestva blagopolučie věka svoego proslavljajut izdaetsja vo vsenarodnoe upotreblenie lěta ot Roždestva Hristova 1745.] —
[C:] Imperii Russici, quam late patet fines et Prouincias uniuersas, tabula haec curatius designata iam tum capto consilio conatuque, ex quo PETRI MAGNI auspiciis inter reliquas egregias artes, quibus ad cultum humanitatis et elegantes gentes vocantur, geographiae quoque dari coepta est opera, nunc imperante et felicitatem publicam quotidie augente ELISABETHA PETRI FILIA negotio ea qua par erat, et quanta adhiberi potuit diligentia perfecto, exacte describit oculisque clare subiicit eidemque Augustae nostrae, optimae principi, parenti patriae dedicatur, et ut discere omnes possint, quas nunc terras urbes atque nationes ejus clementia et preuidentia beent, in communes usus publicatur A.P.C.N. M DCCXLV. — 560 × 970 mm.

Notes: All the maps are blank on the back and uncoloured. Map [19] has been badly cropped, so that the number is cut away. The general map is bound at the end of the atlas, as in indicated in the list of contents, but is unnumbered. Each map has two stamps on the back: a round black one, bearing the words 'Ex Bibl. Com. F. Széché nyi', and a square blue one, which cannot be deciphered completely from any of the 21 examples, but which seems to read 'MASODLAT A.M.N. MUZEUMI SZECH ORSZ'.... The atlas is bound in the original leather, with blind tooling. The word 'Dupli' has been written in pencil on the inside of the front cover. Nordenskiöld's signature is on the first blank leaf.

Lit.: CLC I:1154, nr 3109.

66 DONCKER, HENDRIK 1664

Nieuw Groot STUURMANS STRAETS-BOECK, INHOUDENDE De Middellantse Zee Met veel nootwendige Zee-Kaerten/ Opdoeningen van Landen/ Veranderingen in veeler Coursen en Distantien/ noyt voor desen soo klaerlijck uyt-gegeven. Vermeerdert en verbetert door verscheyde Liefhebbers van de Navigatie. Ende in 't licht ghebracht, T'AMSTERDAM, By Hendrick Doncker Boeckverkoper en Graadbooghmaker, inde Nieuwbrugsteeg In 't Stuurmans gereedschap, het derde huys vande nieuwe brugh, inde straet. [The dedication to Michiel de Ruyter dated] In Amsterdam, den 17. April, 1664.   44,5 cm.

[1] 1 [C:] Paskaert van 't Westelycke deel Der MIDDELANDSCHE ZEE. Nieulycx gedruckt en uytgegeven T'AMSTERDAM, By Hendrick Doncker Boekverkoper en Graadboogh maker inde Niewbrugsteegh In 't Stuurmans gereedschap. — Before Fol. I. B 403 × 506 mm.

[2] 2 [C:] Pas kaert van 't Oostelycke deel Der MIDDELANDSCHE ZEE. Nieuwlyx gedruckt en uytgegeven T'AMSTERDAM, By Hendrick Doncker Boekverkoper en Graadboogh maker inde Nieuwbrug steegh In 't Stuurmans gereedschap. — Before Fol. I. B 405 × 505 mm.

[3] 2 [C:] de Zee Custen van HISPANIEN Van Gibralter tot Caep S. Martin; als mede van BARBARIEN Van Seute tot C. de Tenes. t'Amsterdam, By Hendrick Doncker. — Before Fol. 1. B 396 × 517 mm.

Eerste Vertooninge VAN DE Beschrijvinge der See-Custen van Spaengien/ van Calis af door de Strate tot aen de Caep Sint Martijn: Als oock de Custe van Barbaryen tot 't Eylandt Tabarca.

[4] De Spaensche Cust van Malaga tot Modril. On Fol. I. B. 78 × 237 mm.

[5] 3 [C:] BARBARIEN tusschen C.de Tenes en C.de Rosa. t'Amsterdam. By Hendrick Doncker. — Between pp. 2 and 3. 384 × 506 mm.

[6] Almeria. On 3 B2 116 × 241 mm.

[7] [T:] Den Inwijck ofte Baye van de Stadt Cartagena, de reden, diepten en gelegentheyt des selfs. — On 4 148 × 220 mm.

[8] De Bay van Alger. On 6 160 × 222 mm.

[9] Zee-Kusten van Spaengien tot aen Cabo St. Martijn als mede van Barbaryen tot 't Eylandt Tabarca. (144 profiles). 8—17 D

[10] 4 [C:] VALENTIEN, ende Catalonia tusschen C. d. S.Martin ende C de Creos. als mede de Eylanden van Majorca Minorca ende Yvica. T'AMSTERDAM, By Hendrick Doncker. — Between pp. 16 and 17 D. 388 × 513 mm.

Tweede Tertooninghe, VANDE Beschrijvinge der See-Kusten van Valentien ende Catalonie/ tusschen Cabo de Sinte Martijn/ en de

Cabo de Creos: als mede van de havenen/ Reeden/ Diepten en Ondiepten ontrent de Eylanden Yvica/ Majorca/ en Minorca.

[11] Zee-Kusten tusschen de Cabo St. Martijn/ en Cabo de Creos/ als mede van de Eylanden van Yvica/ Majorca/ en Minorca. (66 profiles). 21 D3 — 24

[12] 5 [C:] LANGVEDOC. tusschen C. de Creos en C. delle Melle. t'Amsterdam, By Hendrick Doncker. — Between pp. 24 and 25 E. 396 × 510 mm.

[13] 6 [C:] SARDINIA en CORSICA. t'Amsterdam, By Hendrick Doncker — Between pp. 24 and 25 E. 396 × 515 mm.

Derde Vertooninghe, VANDE Zee-Kusten, tusschen Kaep de Creos, en Cabo Delle Melle, als mede de Eylanden van Corsica en Sardinia.

[14] De Baye van Marsilien. On 25 E 180 × 213 mm.

[15] Caerte ende Baye van de Eylanden van Eres. On 27 140 × 235 mm.

[16] Als men voor Eres op de Reede leydt, ontrent daer het kruysken geteeckent staet, soo verthoont haer de Bay, ende de Eylanden aldus. On 27 172 × 245 mm.

[17] De Baye van Villa Franca. On 29 E3 90 × 237 mm.

[18] De groote Bay van Caliari. On 31 165 × 240 mm.

[19] Zee-Kusten tusschen Cabo de Creos/ en Cabo Delle Melle als mede van de Eylanden van Corsica en Sardinia. (105 profiles). 32 — 40

[20] 7 [C:] ITALIEN. tusschen Caap della Mella en Ostia. t'Amsterdam, By Hendrick Doncker. — Between pp. 40 and 41 G. 392 × 515 mm.

[21] 8 [C:] ITALIEN Tusschen Ostia en het Faro van Messina. t'Amsterdam, By Hendrick Doncker. — Between pp. 40 and 41 G. 385 × 501 mm.

[Inset:] [T:] Puzzola Napolis I. ISCHIA — 124 × 181 mm.

De vierde Verthooninghe, VANDE Zee-Kusten van Italien, tusschen Cabo Delle Melle, ende Messina op Sicilien.

[22] De Stadt ende Haven van Savona. On 41 G 115 × 163 mm.

[23] Zee-Kusten van Italien/ tusschen Cabo Delle Melle/ en Messina. (50 profiles). 45 G3 — 48

De vyfde Verthooninghe. Beschrijvinge van de gelegentheyt van de Zee-Kusten van geheel Sicilien, Malta: Als mede van Barbaryen, van 't Eylandt Tabarca Oost-waert aen.

[24] De Haven van Messina. On 48 115 × 215 mm.

[25] 9 [C:] SICILIEN Barbarien van C. Rosa tot I. Querqueni en de Zuydlickste custen van Sardinien. t'Amsterdam, by Hendrick Doncker. — Between pp. 48 and 49 H. 392 × 516 mm.

[Inset:] [T:] TABARCA — 94 × 126 mm.

[26] De Haven van Palermo in Cicilien. On 49 H 102 × 225 mm.

[27] Trapano Vechio. De Reede voor Trapano. On 50 205 × 250 mm.

[28] Af-beeldinge van de Reede onder Galita. On 51 H2 60 × 190 mm.

[29] Gergento. On 53 100 × 250 mm.

[30] Ontwerp van de Haven van Malta. On 53 100 × 120 mm.

[31] Monte Gibello. On 54 158 × 120 mm.

[32] Zee-Kusten van geheel Cicilien/ Malta/ als mede van Barbaryen/ van 't Eylandt Tabarca/ Oost-waert aen. (112 profiles). 55 — 61 I3.

Seste Verthooninge, Vande Beschryvinge der Oostersche Zee-Kusten/ van Calabrien/ van Messina tot Otranto: Als mede de Havenen/ en Eylanden in de Golfe van Venetien/ tot aen Corfu.

[33] Ontwerp van de Bay van Taranto. On 62 230 × 195 mm.

[34] 10 [C:] Oost Zyde van CALABRIA T'AMSTERDAM, By Hendrick Doncker. — Between pp. 62 and 63. 394 × 520 mm.

[35] 11 [C:] Golfo van VENETIEN, nieulycx uytgegeven T'AMSTERDAM, By Hendrick Doncker Boeckverkooper en graadbooghmaker inde Nieuw-brug-steegh, In 't Stuurmans gereedschap. — Between pp. 62 and 63. 393 × 507 mm.

[36] Figuerlijcke af-beeldinge van de Reede voor de Stadt Galipoli in de Golfe van Taranto. On 63 125 × 155 mm.

[37] De Haven van Brundisi. On 63 220 × 155 mm.

[38] De Reede voor Barri On 64 90 × 97 mm.

[39] Af-deelinge van de Reede voor Ancona. On 65 K 90 × 220 mm.

[40] De Riviere van Ferrara ofte Goera. On 65 K 110 × 120 mm.

[41] Af-beeldinge van de Reede van Rovigno. On 66 110 × 205 mm.

[42] Af-beeldinge van de Haven S. Pedro. On 67 K2 115 × 135 mm.

[43] De Haven van Catarro. On 68 90 × 110 mm.

[44] Zee-kusten van Calabrien/ van Messina tot Otranto/ als mede in de Golfe van Venetien tot Corfu. (155 profiles). 69 K3 — 78

Sevende Verthooninghe. Beschryvinghe van de Eylanden Corfu/ Pachsu/ Antipachsu/ Cephalonia/ ende Zante/ mitsgaders van de West-kust van Morea/ tot aen de Cabo de Spiensa/ ofte hoeck van Modon.

[45] 12 [C:] CORFU en By-leggende plaatsen — Between pp. 78 and 79. 393 × 515 mm.

[46] 13 [C:] CAPHALONIA, Zante en de Cust van Morea tot aen de C. de Sapienza. t'Amsterdam, By Hendrick Doncker. — Between pp. 78 and 79. 380 × 507 mm.

[47] Zee-Kusten van de Eylanden van Corfu/ Pachsu/ Cephalodia en Zante/ als mede van de West-Kust van Morea/ tot aen de hoeck van Modon. (24 profiles). 79 — 81 M

[48] 14 [C:] MOREA. van Sapienza tot C. S. Angelo, t'Amsterdam, By Hendrick Doncker. — Between pp. 80 and 81 M. 394 × 517 mm.

[49] 15 [C:] CANDIA. met de Omleggende Eylanden t'Amsterdam, By Hendrick Doncker. — Between pp. 80 and 81 M. 396 × 513 mm.

Achtste Verthooninghe, Beschryvinghe der Zee-Kusten van Morea/ tusschen Modon en Cabo S. Angelo/ als mede van 't Eylandt Candia.

[50] Zee-Kusten van Morea/ van de hoeck van Modon tot Cobo S. Angelo/ als mede van 't Eylandt Candia. (74 profiles). 84 — 89 N

[51] 16 [a] [C:] NEGROPONTE en Omleggende Eylanden t'Amsterdam, By Hendrick Doncker. — 149 × 509 mm.

[b] [C:] ARCHIPELAGO en Negroponte — 247 × 509 mm.

[The whole map:] Between pp. 88 and 89 N. 399 × 509 mm.

[52] [C:] Paskaerte Van de ARCHIPELAGUSCHE ZEE. t'Amsterdam By Hendrick Doncker in de Nieubrughsteegh. — Between pp. 88 and 89 N. 396 × 508 mm.

Negende Verthooninge, VANDE Beschryvinghe hoe men door de See Archipelagus (ende de Eylanden daer in gelegen) sal zeylen/ als mede de gelegentheydt der Eylanden Schyro/ Schoppello/ Siatta/ en andere daer ontrent; Item de Noord-Kusten van Negroponte/ ende hoe men de Golfe van Uolo/ ende Zitoeni sal bezeylen.

[53] Het Eylandt Macronisi. On 90 10 × 115 mm.

[54] Dese Figuur verthoont de gelentheydt van de Haven in 't Eylandt Zea. On 90 158 × 215 mm.

[55] Kaerte van de Golfe van Engia ofte van Athenen. On 91 N2 165 × 241 mm.

[56] Beschrijvinge hoe men door de Zee Archepelagus/ (ende de Eylanden daer inne gelegen) zeylen sal. (46 profiles). 95 — 98

Thiende verthooninge. Beschryvinghe der Zee-kusten van Natolien/ tusschen Metelijn/ ende Constantinopolen/ begrijpende die Golfe van Constantinopolen/ ofte de Zee van Marmora/ als mede de Eylanden van Lemnos/ Tenedos/ Mavera/ en andere daer ontrent gelegen.

[57] Hoemen in de Haven van Lemnos sal zeylen. On 98 123 × 130 mm.

[58] 17 [a] [C:] Paskaarte van 't Eylandt Metelino En de gelegentheyt daer ontrendt. — 254 × 290 mm.

[b] [C:] LEMNOS. t'Amsterdam, By Hendrick Doncker. — 121 × 227 mm.

[c] [C:] TENEDOS — 133 × 227 mm.

[d] [C:] Golf van Constantinopolen — 160 × 521 mm.

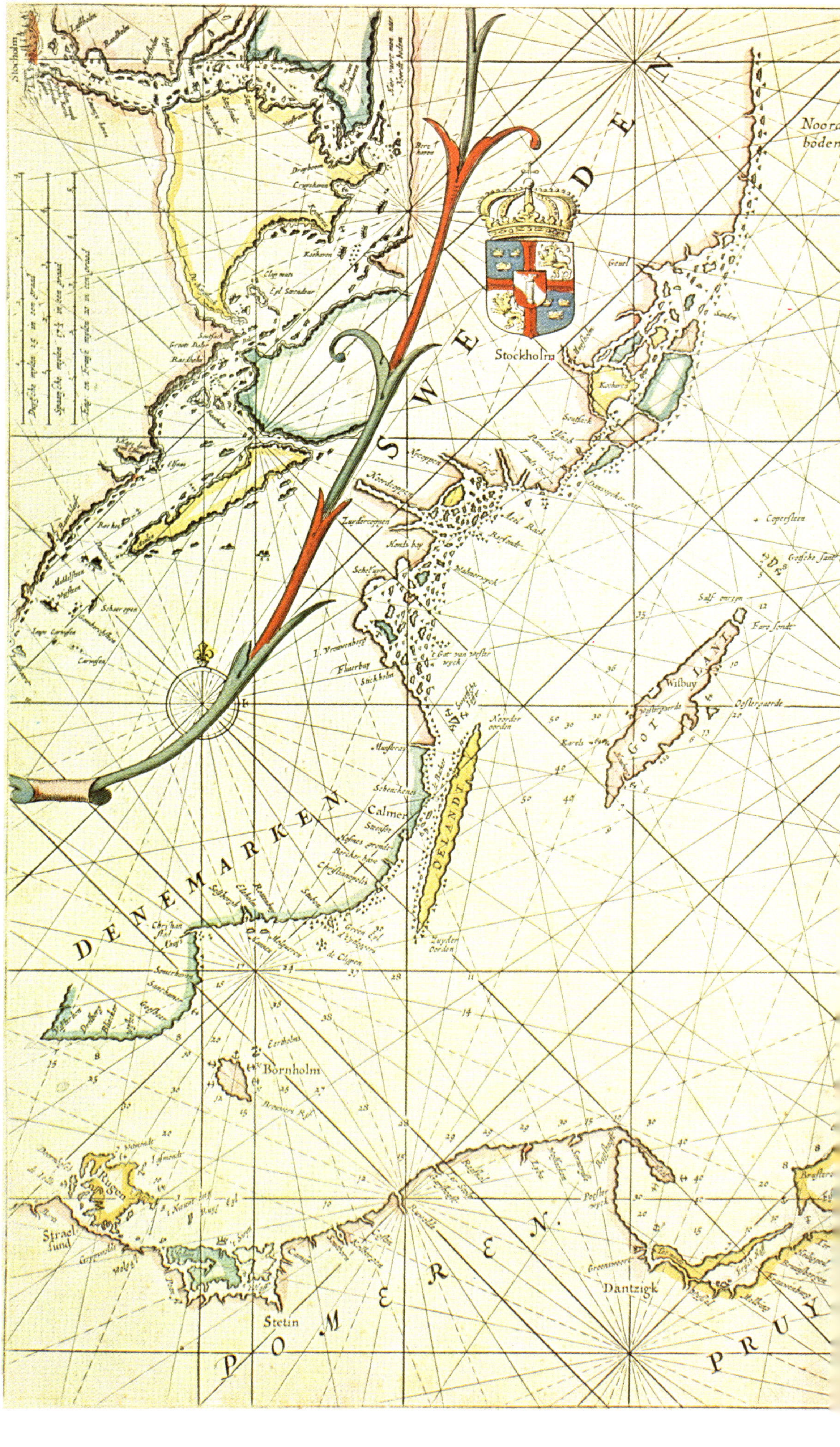
SWEDEN
Stockholm
Noordt bodem
DENEMARKEN
Calmer
OELANDT
GOTLANT
Wisbuy
Bornholm
Rugen
Strael sund
Stetin
Dantzigk
POMEREN
PRUY

Pas-Caart van de
OOST ZEE
Verthoonende
Alle de ghelegentheyt tusschen
't Eylandt Rugen en Wyborg.
Nieuwlyex uytgegeven
T'AMSTERDAM,
By Hendrick Doncker Boeckverko-
per en Graadboghmaker, inde Nieuwe-
brugh-steech, In 't Stuurmans
Gereedtschap 1664

[The whole map:] Between pp. 98 and 99   O2.   415 × 521 mm.
[59] [T:] Galipoli. — On 100   35 × 223 mm.
[60] Zee-Kusten van Natolia/ tusschen Metelijn/ ende Strate van Constantinopolen. (28 profiles).   102 — 104

Elfste verthooninghe, Beschrijvende de Wester Zee-Kusten van Natolia/ als de Haven van Smyrne/ ende Fogie Nova/ Item de Eylanden van Scio ofte Xio/ ende Metelino/ als mede van de Eylanden Rhodes ende Castel Rossa.

[61] 18 [C:] SMYRNE en de Eylanden Scio en Metelino t'Amsterdam, Bÿ Hendrick Doncker Inde Nieuw brughsteegh. — Between pp. 104 and 105   P   393 × 510 mm.
[62] [C:] De Haven van Metelijn. — On 105   P   230 × 200 mm.
[63] Af-beeldinge van de Eylanden ende Reede voor Fogie Nova. On 107   P2   115 × 240 mm.
[64] De West-Kusten van Natolia/ als mede de Zee-Havens. van Metelijn/ Smyrno/ Scio/ ofte Xio/ Rhodes/ en Castel Rossa. (22 profiles).   109   P3 — 110
[65] 19 [C:] 'T EYLANDT CYPRUS begrypende de Zuydelicste Zee Custen. — Between pp. 110 and 111.   392 × 510 mm.
[Inset:] [T:] ÆGYPTEN. —   173 × 239 mm.
[66] 21 [C:] Pas-Caert van de LEVANT ofte de Zee kusten van ÆGYPTEN, SORIA, CARAMANIA en 't Eylandt CYPRUS. t'Amsterdam, by Hendrick Doncker. — Between pp. 110 and 111.   408 × 507 mm.

Twaelfste Verthooninghe, Beschrijvinghe der Zee-Kusten van't Eylandt Cyprus/ de Lavant ofte Soria/ als mede van Egypten/ tusschen Damiata ende Alexandria.

[67] [T:] Schandroen Alexandrette.   Bay van Antioch. — On 112   182 × 225 mm.
[68] Aldus verthoont Tripoli. On 113   Q   125 × 230 mm.
[69] Bay van S^t. Jan d'Acare. On 114   116 × 153 mm.
[70] Af-beeldinghe van de Haven van Alexandrien. On 116   150 × 230 mm.
[71] Zee-Kusten van 't Eylandt Cyprus/ de Lavant ofte Soria. als mede van Egypten/ van Damiata tot Alexandria. (31 profiles).   117   Q3 — 120

Notes: All the large charts are blank on the back. The small charts and the profiles have text on the verso. All are uncoloured. The year on the title-page has been erased, and also on charts[1] 1, [2] 2 and [34] 10. Koeman describes this atlas under the numbers Don 47 A and Don 47 B. The contents of our copy corresponds with Don 47 A, but the title-page and the two following pages correspond with Don 47 B; folios A and A2 are the same as in Don 47 A. The Paskaert Van de ARCHIPELAGUSCHE ZEE is map 1 in Don 47 A, but it is bound after chart [51] 16 in our copy; it has no printed number in either example. According to Koeman all the charts bear Doncker's imprint; in our copy, it is lacking in charts [45] 12, Corfu, and [65] 19, Cyprus. Neither copy has a chart bearing the number 20. As Koeman states in his description of the Straets-Boeck (vol. 4, p. 186, Don 47 A), the charts are similar to those in the attases of Goos and Jacobsz, Theunis; their charts bear no imprint. The atlas is bound in old, worn vellum, with the title written in ink on the spine. Nordenskiöld's signature, with the year 1890, is on the inside of the front cover. There is an invoice from Frederick Muller in Amsterdam, dated 23 Avril 1890, which includes this atlas at the price of Fl.12.

Lit.: Koeman, vol. 4, p. 186—187, Don 47 A, Don 47 B., Tiele p. 78, nr 331.

67 DONCKER, HENDRIK   1666

DE ZEE-ATLAS OFTE WATER-WÆRELD, Vertoonende alle de ZEE-KUSTEN Van het bekende Deel des AERD-BODEMS, Met een generale beschrijvinge van dien. Seer dienstligh voor alle Schippers en Stuurlieden; mitsgaders Koop-lieden om op 't Kantoor gebruykt te werden. Nieuwelijks aldus uytgegeven. t'AMSTERDAM, By HENDRIK DONCKER, Boekverkooper, en Graat-boog-maker, in de Nieuwe-brug-steeg, in't Stuur-mans Gereetschap. ANNO 1666.   51 cm.

[1] [C:] NOVA TOTIUS TERRARUM ORBIS TABULA AUCTORE F. DE WIT. — [T:] t' Amsterdam bÿ Frederick de Wit in de Calverstraet inde Witte Paskaert, 1660. — (Map). 432 × 556 mm. The hemispheres with 262 mm. diam.
[Insets:] [C:] POLUS ARCTICUS. — (Celestial chart). Circular map with 101 mm. diam. [C:] POLUS ANTARCTICUS. — (Celestial chart). Circular map with 101 mm. diam. [C:] POLUS SEPTENTRIONALIS. — (Map). Circular map with 85 mm. diam. [C:] POLUS MERIDIONALIS. — (Map). Circular map with 85 mm. diam.
[2] 1 [C:] Pas-kaart van EUROPA met een gedeelte van de kust van Africa tot aen Cabo verde. Tot Amsterdam, By Hendrick Doncker inde Nieubrugsteegh. An.º 1665. — 422 × 513 mm.
[3] 3 [C:] Pas Caart van de ZUYDER-ZEE Texel, ende Vliestroom, als mede 't Amelander gat. t'Amsterdam, By Hendrick Doncker inde Nieuw brughsteegh in 't Stuurmans gereedschap. 1664. — 424 × 512 mm.
[4] [C:] Pas Caart van Texel tot aen de Hoofden, Vertoonende de Zee-Custen van Vrieslant, Hollant, Zeelant, Vlaenderen, en de Oost Kust van Engelant, als mede hoemen alle de selve Kusten en Havens uyt der Zee sal aendoen. T'AMSTERDAM, Bÿ Hendrick Doncker Boekverkoper en Graadbooghmaker, in de Nieubrugsteegh In't Stuurmans gereetschap. — 421 × 529 mm.
[5] 2 [C:] Pas Caart van de NOORT ZEE Verthoonende in zich alle de Custen en Havens daer rontom gelegen. Op nieuws aldus uytgegeven. TOT AMSTERDAM, By Hendrick Doncker Boeckverkooper en Graadboogmaker Inde Nieuwbrugh steegh in't Stuurmans gereedschap. Anno 1664. — 432 × 528 mm.
[6] [C:] PASCAART van de Zee-Custen van Ruslant, Laplant, Finmarcken, Spitsbergen en Nova-zemla. Nieuwlycx uytgegeven t'Amsterdam, bÿ Hendrick Doncker, inde Nieubrug steegh, in't Stuurmans Gereedtschap. A.º 1664. — 427 × 538 mm.
[Inset:] [T:] Archangel   De Eylanden van Podesemske — 115 × 142 mm. (Irregular).
[7] [C:] De Custen van Noorwegen, Finmarken, Laplandt, Spitsbergen, Ian Maÿen Eÿlandt, Yslandt, als mede Hitlandt, en een gedeelte van Schotlandt. 'tAmsterdam. Bÿ Hendrick Doncker ... — 429 × 527 mm.
[8] [C:] Pas-caerte van GROENLANDT, Yslandt, Straet Davids en Ian Mayen Eylant; hoemen de selvige van Hitlant en de Noord kusten van Schotlandt en Yrlandt beseylen mach. GEDRUCKT T'AMSTERDAM, Bÿ Hendrick Doncker ... — 422 × 520 mm.
[9] [C:] Pas Caart van de OOST ZEE Verthoonende Alle de ghelegentheyt tusschen 't Eylandt Rugen en Wyborg. Nieuwlycx uytgegeven T'AMSTERDAM, By Hendrick Doncker ... 1664 — 425 × 540 mm.
[Insets:] [T:] Stocholm — 137 × 235 mm. (Irregular). [T:] Coningsbergen   Dantzigh   Rygshooft — 156 × 250 mm. (Irregular).
[10] [C:] PAS-CAART van 'T CANAAL, vertoonende in 't Geheel Engelant, Schotlant, Yrlant, en een gedeelte van Vranckrÿk. Nieuwlycx uytgegeven T'AMSTERDAM, Bij Hendrick Doncker, ... Anno 1665. — 435 × 529 mm.
[11] [C:] PAS CAART VAN DE CANAAL tusschen Engeland en Vrancrijck. T'AMSTERDAM, By Hendrick Doncker, ... A.º 1661. — 423 × 535 mm.
[12] [C:] PASKAARTE om Achter YRLANT om te Zeylen, van Hitlant tot aen Heÿssant. Nieuwlycx uytgegeven t'Amsterdam, by Hendrick Doncker, ... — 435 × 531 mm.
[13] [C:] Pas Caert van 't in komen van de CANAEL; hoe men die sal aen doen als men uyt de West komt. t'Amsterdam, Bÿ Hendrick Doncker, ... Anno 1661. — 428 × 522 mm.
[14] [C:] Pas Caert van de BOCHT van Vranckrijck, Biscajen

en Galissen; tusschen Heyssant en C. de Finisterre. T'AMSTERDAM, Bÿ Hendrick Doncker, ... 1661. — 417 × 532 mm.

[15] [C:] Pas Caart van HISPANGIEN, Vertoonende de Custen van Granade, Andaluzie, Algarve, Portugael, Galissien en Biscaien; met een gedeelte van Vranckrÿck: streckende van Heÿsant tot de Straat van Gibraltar. NB. de Bocht van Vranckrÿck ingekort, en Verbetert, door A. en I. de Bree. T'AMSTERDAM, By Hendrick Doncker, ... — 435 × 535 mm.

[16] [C:] Nieuwe Pas-Caart; Vertoonende, hoe men uyt De CANAAL, de Custen van Portugael, Barbarÿen, de Canarische en Vlaemsche Eylanden beseylen zal. T'AMSTERDAM, By Hendrick Doncker, ... Anno 1661. — 431 × 531 mm.

[17] 1. [C:] Paskaert van 't Westelycke deel Der MIDDE- LANDSCHE ZEE. ... A? 1664. — = 1664:[1], but the year added.

[18] 2. [C:] Pas kaert van 't Oostelycke deel Der MIDDELANDSCHE ZEE. ... 1664. — = 1664:[2], but the year added.

[19] [C:] De Cust van BARBARIA, Gualata, Arguyn en Geneheo van Capo S. Vencent tot Capo Verde. Gedruckt tot Amsterdam. Bÿ Hendrick Doncker ... — 420 × 519 mm.

[20] 57 [a] [C:] De Cust van Barbaryen van out Mamora tot C. Blanco. — 156 × 509 mm.
[b] [C:] De Cust van Barbaryen van C.Blanco tot C. de Geer. — 147 × 509 mm.
[c] [T:] Punte del Gada Villa Franca — 102 × 113 mm.
[Inset:] [T:] De zuydhoec van 't Eylandt FAYAL — 50 × 50 mm.
[d] [C:] De Reede voor de Stadt Angra in 't eylandt Tercera — 102 × 211 mm.
[e] [C:] De Eylanden van Madera en Porto Santo. — 102 × 178 mm.
[The whole map:] 415 × 509 mm.

[21] 58 [C:] Canarische Eylanden Canaria, Teneriffa, Forteventura etc. t'Amsterdam, By Hendrick Doncker A? 1664. — 419 × 520 mm.
[Inset:] [C:] De tyhavens Porto de Naos ende P? de Cavallos aen de Zuydoostzyde van Lancerota. — 142 × 156 mm.

[22] [C:] Paskaart van GVINEA van C.Verde tot R.de Galion. t'AMSTERDAM. Bÿ Hendrick Doncker ... — 426 × 528 mm.

[23] [C:] PASCAART van de Zee-custen van Angola, en Cimbebas van Rivier de Galion tot C. de Bona Esperanca. tAmsterdam By Hendrick Doncker ... A? 1659. — 424 × 526 mm.
[Inset:] [T:] Bay de S. Martin Cabo de bona Esperanca — 70 × 141 mm. (Irregular).

[24] [The Indian Ocean from C. de Bona Esperança to CEYLON]. 583 × 444 mm.

[25] [The East Indian Islands, the coast of Asia from Ceylon to Japan and the North coast of Hollandia Nova]. 578 × 452 mm.

[26] [C:] Pascaerte vande CARIBISCHE Eylanden, vande Barbados tot aende Bocht van Mexico 'tAmsterdam, By Hendrick Doncker ... 428 × 533 mm.

[27] [Lesser Antilles from]MARGARITA [and] I. DE LA TRINIDAD [to] I. DE S.IUAN DE PUERTORICO.
[C:] T'AMSTERDAM. Bij Hendrick Doncker ... Anno 1658. — 441 × 540 mm.

[28] [C:] Pascaerte van BRAZIL, en NIEV NEDERLANDT. van Corvo en Flores tot de Barbados. 't Amsterdam By Hendrick Doncker ... — 430 × 537 mm.

[29] [C:] PASCAERT VAN NIEU NEDERLAND, Virginia en Nieu Engelant, Nieulycx uytgegeven T'AMSTERDAM Bÿ Hendrick Doncker ... 1660. — 441 × 540 mm.

[30] [C:] PASKAERT van BRASILIA van Pernambuco tot C. de S. Antonio. t AMSTERDAM Bÿ Hendrick Doncker. — 427 × 535 mm.

[31] [C:] Paskaarte van 't Zuÿdelÿckste Deel van AMERICA. van Cabo S.t Antonio, tot Caep de Hoorn, ende inde Zuÿd

Zee, tot B. de Tongoÿ. t Amsterdam. Bÿ Hendrick Doncker ... — 423 × 532 mm.

[32] [C:] Pascaart vertoonende de Zeecusten van Chili, Peru, Hispania Nova, Nova Granada, en California. 't Amsterdam By Hendrick Doncker ... — 428 × 539 mm.
[Insets:] [T:] YEDSO IAPAN — 120 × 105 mm. (Irregular). [T:] Islas de las Velas alias Ladrones. — 130 × 193 mm. (Irregular). [T:] ZEELANDIA NOVA. — 83 × 117 mm. (Irregular).

Notes: All the charts are blank on the back. The engraved title-page and the charts are coloured. The Register der Caerten van de Zee Atlas indicates 30 items, but the atlas has 32 charts. The two additional ones are [20] and [21], with the engraved numbers 57 and 58, which first appeared in the edition of 1665 and which are found inserted in a number of copies of the 1666 edition. Our copy corresponds partly with Koeman's Don 9 A, partly with Don 9 B. The title is that of Don 9 A, but it is not printed on a separate slip. The following text is the same as in Don 9 B. The date of the title-page has been altered from 1665 to 1666. Charts [2], [3], [17] and [18] are new; charts [5], [6], [7], [9], [12], [15] and [22] have been revised in some way. The year has been altered on chart [9], and visibly erased from charts [12] and [22]. Doncker's charts were the most up-to-date in the second half of the 17th century (Koeman 4, p. 151). There are similarities between them and the charts published by van Loon, Goos and Jacobsz, Theunis, but Doncker improved and corrected his original charts more often than did his contemporaries. Our copy is bound in old vellum with gold tooling. The number 73 is written in large black figures on the front cover. Nordenskiöld's bookplate is pasted to the inside of the front cover, and his signature with the year 1890 is on the first blank leaf. An invoice of Frederick Muller's, of Amsterdam, dated 23 Avril 1890, gives the price of this atlas as 24: — fl.

Lit.: Koeman vol. 4, p. 154 and 161, Don 9 A and B, Nederl. Hist. Scheepv. Mus., vol. 1, p. 47, Tiele p. 78, nr 328.

68 DONCKER, HENDRIK [1669]

LA ATLAS DEL MUNDO O EL MUNDO AGUADO. Enseña Todas las Entradas de los puertos y de las Costas halladas y conosidas DEL MUNDO. Con un Mostrasion y declarasion muy servisial para todas Capp[nes,] Maestres y Pilotoz Zamigos del arte. Nueuamente dado a la lus. En AMSTERDAM, Con HENRICQUE DONCQUER, Vendedor de Libroz, en el Señal del Graetboogmaquer, en la Calle primera pasanda la Puenta Nueva. 46,3 cm.

[1] [The world] [T:] N.P.Berchem invent. — [T:] I de Visscher sculpsit. — (Map). 450 × 560 mm. The hemispheres with 288 mm. diam.
[Insets:] [T:] POLUS ARCTICUS. — Circular map with 130 mm. diam. [T:] POLUS ANTARCTICUS. — Circular map with 130 mm. diam. See 1666:[1].

[2] 1 [C:] Pas-kaart van EUROPA ... — = 1666:[2], but the year erased.

[3] 2 [C:] Pas Caart van de NOORT ZEE ... — = 1666:[5], but the year erased.

[4] 3 [C:] Pas Caart van de ZUYDER-ZEE ... — = 1666:[3], but the year erased.

[5] 5 [C:] Zee-kaert van de EEMS, ELVE, Weser, Eyder en de Hever. als mede hoe de selvige gaten van Heylige-landt gelegen syn. — 421 × 529 mm.

[6] [C:] Paskaart van de Iutsche Cust, van Ees tot de Horn. Nieu verbetert door Recht Lutsen van den Hoogh 't Amsterdam, Bÿ Hendirck Doncker inde Nieuwe brughsteegh. — 444 × 546 mm.

[7] [C:] PASCAART van de Zee-custen van Ruslant, Laplant, Finmarcken, Spitsbergen en Novazemla, Nieulÿcx uytgegeven t'Amsterdam, Bÿ Hendrick Doncker, Boekverkoper en Graadbooghmaker, Inde Nieubrugh steegh, In 't Stuurmans Gereedschap. — 436 × 532 mm. See 1666:[6].

[8] [C:] De Custen van Noorwegen, ... — = 1666:[7].
[9] [a] [C:] Pas-Caert van IAN MAYEN EYLANDT, Vertonende Perfect alle de gelegentheyt van't selve. — 427 × 239 mm.
[b] [C:] Pas Caert van SPITSBERGEN, Nieuwlyx verbetert: 't Amsterdam, By Hendrick Doncker.— 427 × 289 mm.
[The whole map:] 427 × 531 mm.
[10] [C:] Pas-caerte van GROENLANDT, ... — = 1666:[8].
[11] [C:] Pas-Caart van de OOST ZEE, Verthoonende Alle de ghelegentheyt tusschen 't Eylandt Rugen en Wyborg. Nieuwelycx uytgegeven t'Amsterdam, by Hendrick Doncker ... — 438 × 520 mm. See 1666:[9].
[12] [C:] Pas-Caert van Texel tot aen de Hoofden, ... — = 1666:[4].
[13] 32 [C:] De Cust van HOLLANDT tusschen de Maes en Texel. — 427 × 521 mm.
[14] 33 [a] [C:] De TEXEL Stroom met de gaten van't Marsdiep. — 425 × 258 mm.
[Inset:] Caarte vande Reede end Haven van Medenblick ... Beschreven A⁰ 1641 ... 240 × 111 mm. (Irregular).
[b] [C:] Pas Caert van DE MASE Ende het Goereesche gat. t'Amstelredam, By Hendrick Doncker. — 425 × 271 mm.
[The whole map:] 428 × 532 mm.
[15] 34 [C:] De cust van ZEELANDT, bevatende de gaten van de Wielingen, ter Veere, Ziericzee, Brouwershave, Goeree, en de Maes. t'Amsterdam, By Hendrick Doncker. — 428 × 527 mm.
[16] 35 [C:] De Cust van VLAENDEREN van de Wielingen tot aen de Hoofden, met alle haer sanden en droogten. t'Amsterdam, By Hendrick Doncker. — 427 × 526 mm.
[17] [C:] PASCAART VAN DE CANAAL tusschen Engeland en Vrancrijck. ... — = 1666:[11], but the year erased.
[18] 37 [C:] Cust van VRANCKRYCK synde Normandien, en Picardien, van de Hoofden tot Ornay. t'Amsterdam By Hendrick Doncker. — 418 × 513 mm.
[19] 38 [C:] De Custen van ENGELANDT, tusschen Bevesier en Portland: oock hoese van Ornay gelegen zyn. — 427 × 526 mm.
[20] [C:] PAS-CAART van 'T CANAAL, vertoonende in 't Geheel Engelant, ... — = 1666:[10], but the year erased.
[21] [C:] Paskaarte om Achter Yrlant om te Zeylen, ... — = 1666:[12].
[22] [C:] Pas Caert van 't in komen van de CANAEL; ... — = 1666:[13], but the year erased.
[23] [C:] Pas Caert van de BOCHT van Vranckrijck, ... — = 1666:[14], but the year erased.
[24] 46 [C:] Pas Caart van HISPANGIEN, Vertoonende de Custen van Granade, Andaluzie Algarve Portugael, Galissien en Biscajen; met een gedeelte van Vranckryck; streckende van Heysant tot de Straet van Gibraltar. Verbetert door A.en I.de Bree. T'AMSTERDAM, By Hendrick Doncker, ... — 434 × 535 mm. 1666:[15], with small alterations and a new cartouche.
[25] [C:] Nieuwe Pas-Caart; Vertoonende hoemen uyt De CANAAL, de Custen van Portugael,... — = 1666:[16], but the year erased.
[26] 1 [C:] Paskaert van 't Westelycke deel Der MIDDELANDSCHE ZEE. ... — = 1664:[1].
[27] 2 [C:] Pas kaert van 't Oostelycke deel Der MIDDELANDSCHE ZEE. ... — = 1664:[2].
[28] [C:] De Cust van BARBARIA streckende van C.S.Vincent tot C.Verde. t'Amsterdam, by Hendrick Doncker. — 422 × 532 mm. See 1666:[19].
[29] 57 [a] [C:] De Cust van Barbaryen van out Mamora tot C.Blanco. — [b] [C:] De Cust van Barbaryen van C.Blanco ... — = 1666:[20].
[30] 58 [C:] Canarische Eylanden Canaria, Tenerifa, Forteventura etc. ... — = 1666:[21], but the year erased.
[31] [C:] Pas Caart van de VLAEMSCHE EYLANDEN. t'Amsterdam, By Hendrick Doncker, ... — 432 × 522 mm.
[32] [C:] Pas-Caart vande SOUTE EYLANDEN, ofte Ilhas de CABO VERDE. t'Amsterdam, By Hendrick Doncker, inde Nieubrugsteegh. — 432 × 526 mm.

[33] [C:] Paskaart van GVINEA van C.Verde tot R.de Galion. ... — = 1666:[22].
[34] [C:] Pas Caart van GAMBIA Vertoonende Rio Senega, C.Verde Rio Gambia en Rio Grande. Streckende van C.Blanco tot R.d'Nuña. t'Amsterdam, By Hendrick Doncker. — 430 × 525 mm.
[35] [C:] Pas Caert van GVINEA Vertoonende Sierra liona, Madre bombe en de Greyn cust van R.de Nunna tot C.das Palmas. t'Amsterdam, by Hendrick Doncker Inde Nieubrugsteegh. — 432 × 525 mm.
[36] [C:] Pas-Caert van GVINEA Vertoonende De Tand-kust, Qua Qua-kust en de Goud-kust. Van C.das Palmas tot R. da Volta. t'Amsterdam, By Hendrick Doncker Boeckverkoper. — 433 × 525 mm.
[37] [C:] Pas Caert van DE BOCHT VAN GVINEA, Vertoonende De Kust van Benin, Biafra en Gabon. van R. da Volta tot C.de lopo Gonzalves. t'Amsterdam, By Hendrick Doncker Boeckverkoper. — 434 × 524 mm.
[38] [C:] Pas Caert van CONGO en ANGOLA streckende van C.de lopo Gonzalves tot C.de Bras. t'Amsterdam, Gedruckt by Hendrick Doncker. Inde Nieuwbrugh steegh. — 432 × 525 mm.
[39] [C:] PASCAART van de Zee-custen van Angola en Cimbebas ... — = 1666:[23], but the year erased.
[40] [C:] PAS-CAERT van't Westelyckste Deel von OOST INDIEN, En de Eylanden daer onder begrepen, van C.de Bona Esperanca tot C.Comorin. t'Amsterdam, By Hendrick Doncker Boekverkoper en Graadbooghmaker inde Nieuwbrughsteegh. — 525 × 424 mm. See 1666:[24].
[41] [C:] PAS-CAERT van 't Oostelyckste Deel van OOST INDIEN, met alle de Eylanden daer onder gelegen, van Cabo Comorin tot aen Japan. t'Amsterdam, By Hendrick Doncker ... — 525 × 420 mm. See 1666:[25].
[42] [C:] DE GOLF van BENGALA. t'Amsterdam, By Hendrick Doncker ... — 432 × 520 mm.
[43] [C:] Pascaerte vande CARIBISCHE Eylanden, ... — = 1666:[26].
[44] [Lesser Antilles from] MARGARITA ... = 1666:[27], but the year erased.
[45] [C:] Pascaerte van BRAZIL, ... — = 1666:[28].
[46] [C:] Pas-Caert van TERRA NOVA, Nova Francia, Nieuw-Engeland en de groote Rivier van Canada. t'Amsterdam, By Hendrick Doncker, ... — 431 × 526 mm.
[47] [C:] PASCAERT VAN NIEU NEDERLAND, ... — = 1666:[29], but the year erased.
[48] [C:] PASKAERT van BRASILIA ... — = 1666:[30].
[49] [C:] Paskaarte van't Zuydelyckste Deel van AMERICA ... — = 1666:[31].
[50] [C:] Pascaart vertoonende de Zeecusten van Chili, ... — = 1666:[32].
[51] [C:] Pas-Caart van ZUYD-ZEE, tusschen California en Ilhas de Ladrones. t'Amsterdam, By Hendrick Doncker ... — 426 × 520 mm.

Notes: All the charts are blank on the back and uncoloured. The atlas has no index. The charts are undated, although dates have been erased from nos. [2], [3], [4], [7], [9a], [11], [17], [18], [20], [22], [23], [25], [26], [27], [30], [39], [44] and [47]. Koeman has deduced the date of the atlas by comparing the contents with dated Dutch editions. All Dutch charts of this period are very similar, although those by Doncker were more frequently up-dated and corrected than those by van Loon, Goos or Jacobsz, Theunis. Our copy of the 1669 Zee-atlas was damaged by water during World War II. It was bound for Nordenskiöld, with gold lettering on the spine. His bookplate is on the inside of the front cover.

Lit.: Koeman vol. 4, p. 154 and 162—163, Don 13, Tiele p. 78, nr 328.

69 DU BOIS, ABRAHAM 1729

LA GEOGRAPHIE MODERNE, Naturelle, Historique & Politique, dans une Methode Nouvelle & Aisée; Par le S.r ABRAHAM DU BOIS, Geographe, DIVISÈE EN QUATRE TOMES, Avec plusieurs Cartes & une Table des Matieres. TOME PREMIER, Contenant le Géographie génerale, ou les Principes de la Géographie, & partie de l'Europe. A LEIDE, Aux depens de PIERRE VANDER Aa, Marchand Libraire. MDCC XXIX.

25 cm.

Vol. I

[1] [C:] MAPPEMONDE. Suivant les Nouvelles Observations de Mess.rs de l'Academie Royale des Sciences, etc. Augmentées de Nouveau. A LEIDE Chez PIERRE VANDER AA. ... — Before Pag.1. 220 × 298 mm. The hemispheres with 155 mm. diam.

[2] [C:] GLOBE CELESTE. — (Celestial chart). Before Pag.1. 176 × 310 mm.

[3] [C:] L'EUROPE. Suivant les Nouvelles Observations de Mess.re de l'Academie Royale des Sciences, etc. Augmentées de Nouveau. A LEIDE, Chez PIERRE VANDER AA. ... — Between 38 a and Pag.39 221 × 295 mm.

[4] [C:] LE PORTUGAL Suivant les Nouvelles Observations de Mess.rs de l'Academie Royale des Sciences, etc. Augmentées de Nouveau. A LEIDE, Chez PIERRE VANDER AA. ... — Between pp. 42 and 43. 222 × 297 mm.

[5] [C:] L'ESPAGNE, Suivant des Nouvelles Observations de Mess.rs de l'Academie Royale des Sciences, etc. Augmentées de Nouveau. A LEIDE, Chez PIERRE VANDER AA. ... — Between pp. 48 and 49. 220 × 296 mm.

[6] [C:] LA FRANCE, Suivant les Nouvelles Observations de Mess.rs de l'Academie Royale des Sciences, etc. Augmentées de Nouveau. A LEIDE, Chez PIERRE VANDER AA. ... — Between pp. 98 and 99. 220 × 296 mm.

[7] [C:] CARTE DU GOUVERNEMENT DE L'ISLE DE FRANCE Suivant les Nouvelles Observations de Mess.rs de l'Academie Royale des Sciences, etc. Augmentées de Nouveau A LEIDE, Chez PIERRE VANDER AA. ... — Between pp. 102 and 103. 220 × 295 mm.

[8] [C:] CARTE DU GOUVERNEMENT D'ORLEANOIS. Suivant les Nouvelles Observations de Mess.rs de l'Academie Royale des Sciences, etc. Augmentees de Nouveau. A LEIDE, Chez PIERRE VANDER AA. ... — Between pp. 106 and 107. 221 × 296 mm.

[9] [C:] CARTE DU GOUVERNEMENT DE LYONNOIS, Suivant les Nouvelles Observations de Mess.rs de l'Academie Royale des Sciences, etc. Augmentées de Nouveau. A LEIDE, Chez PIERRE VANDER AA. ... — Between pp. 114 and 115. 221 × 296 mm.

[10] [C:] CARTE DU GOUVERNEMENT DE BRETAGNE, Suivant les Nouvelles Observations de Mess.rs de l'Academie Royale des Sciences, etc. Augmentées de Nouveau. A LEIDE, Chez PIERRE VANDER AA. ... — Between pp. 116 and 117. 220 × 296 mm.

[11] [C:] CARTE DU GOUVERNEMENT DE NORMANDIE, Suivant les Nouvelles Observations de Mess.rs de l'Academie Royale des Sciences, etc. Augmentées de Nouveau. A LEIDE, Chez PIERRE VANDER AA. ... — Between pp. 120 and 121. 220 × 296 mm.

[12] [C:] CARTE DU GOUVERNEMENT DE PICARDIE, Suivant les Nouvelles Observations de Mess.rs de l'Academie Royale des Sciences, etc. Augmentées de Nouveau. A LEIDE, Chez PIERRE VANDER AA. ... — Between pp. 122 and 123. 222 × 295 mm.

[13] [C:] CARTE DU GOUVERNEMENT DE CHAMPAGNE, Suivant les Nouvelles Observations de Mess.rs de l'Academie Royale des Sciences, etc. Augmentées de Nouveau A LEIDE, Chez PIERRE VANDER AA. ... — Between pp. 126 and 127. 220 × 295 mm.

[14] [C:] CARTE DU GOUVERNEMENT DE BOURGOGNE, Suivant les Nouvelles Observations de Mess.rs de l'Academie Royale des Sciences, etc. Augmentées de Nouveau. A LEIDE, Chez PIERRE VANDER AA. ... — Between pp. 128 and 129. 221 × 296 mm.

[15] [C:] CARTE DU GOUVERNEMENT DE DAUPHINÉ, Suivant les Nouvelles Observations de Mess.rs de l'Academie Royale des Sciences, etc. Augmentées de Nouveau. A LEIDE, Chez PIERRE VANDER AA. ... — Between pp. 132 and 133. 221 × 295 mm.

[16] [C:] CARTE DU GOUVERNEMENT DE PROVENCE, Suivant les Nouvelles Observations de Mess.rs de l'Academie Royale des Sciences, etc. Augmentées de Nouveau. A LEIDE, Chez PIERRE VANDER AA. ... — Between pp. 134 and 135. 221 × 295 mm.

[17] [C:] CARTE DU GOUVERNEMENT DE LANGUEDOC, Suivant les Nouvelles Observations de Mess.rs de l'Academie Royale des Sciences, etc. Augmentées de Nouveau. A LEIDE, Chez PIERRE VANDER AA. ... — Between pp. 138 and 139. 223 × 295 mm.

[18] [C:] CARTE DU GOUVERNEMENT DE GUYENNE ET GASCOGNE, Suivant les Nouvelles Observations de Mess.rs de l'Academie Royale des Sciences, etc. Augmentées de Nouveau. A LEIDE, Chez PIERRE VANDER AA. ... — Between pp. 140 and 141. 223 × 296 mm.

[19] [C:] L'ALSACE, Suivant les Nouvelles Observations de Mess.rs de l'Academie Royale des Sciences, etc. Augmentées de Nouveau. A LEIDE, Chez PIERRE VANDER AA. ... — Between pp. 148 and 149. 222 × 197 mm.

[20] [C:] CARTE D'ARTOIS, Suivant les Nouvelles Observations de Mess.rs de l'Academie Royale des Sciences, etc. Augmentées de Nouveau. A LEIDE Chez P.VANDER AA ... — Between pp. 152 and 153. 220 × 293 mm.

[21] [C:] LA SAVOYE, Suivant les Nouvelles Observations de Mess.rs de l'Academie Royale des Sciences, etc. Augmentées de Nouveau. A LEIDE, Chez PIERRE VANDER AA. ... — Between pp. 166 and 167. 220 × 296 mm.

[22] [C:] L'ITALIE, Suivant les Nouvelles Observations de Mess.rs de l'Academie Royale des Sciences, etc. Augmentées de Nouveau. A LEIDE, Chez PIERRE VANDER AA. ... — Between pp. 168 and 169. 220 × 296 mm.

[23] [C:] LE PIEMONT Suivant les Nouvelles Observations de Mess.rs de l'Academie Royale des Sciences, etc. Augmentées de Nouveau. A LEIDE Chez PIERRE VANDER AA. ... — Between pp. 172 and 173. 221 × 297 mm.

[24] [C:] SEIGNEURIE DE VENISE, Suivant les Nouvelles Observations de Mess.rs de l'Academie Royale des Sciences, etc. Augmentées de Nouveau. A LEIDE, Chez PIERRE VANDER AA. ... — Between pp. 184 and 185. 221 × 297 mm.

[25] [C:] LE GRAND DUCHÉ DE TOSCANE, Suivant les Nouvelles Observations de Mess.rs de l'Academie Royale des Sciences, etc. Augmentées de Nouveau. A LEIDE, Chez PIERRE VANDER AA. ... — Between pp. 192 and 193. 222 × 296 mm.

[26] [C:] L'ETAT DE L'EGLISE, Suivant les Nouvelles Observations de Mess.rs de l'Academie Royale des Sciences, etc. Augmentées de Nouveau. A LEIDE, Chez PIERRE VANDER AA. ... — Between pp. 194 and 195. 222 × 298 mm.

[27] [C:] LE ROYAUME DE NAPLES, Suivant les Nouvelles Observations de Mess.rs de l'Academie Royale des Sciences, etc. Augmentées de Nouveau. A LEIDE, Chez PIERRE VANDER AA. ... — Between pp. 200 and 201. 221 × 296 mm.

[28] [C:] L'ILE DE SICILE, Suivant les Nouvelles Observations de Mess.rs de l'Academie Royale des Sciences, etc. Augmentées de Nouveau. A LEIDE, Chez PIERRE VANDER AA. ... — Between pp. 206 and 207. 221 × 293 mm.

[29] [T:] L'ISLE DE MALTHE, Possedée par les Chevaliers, qui portent aujourdhuy ce nom, et ou le Grand Maistre de cet Ordre fait Sa Residence, elle est située dans la Mer Mediterranée entre la Barbarie et la Sicile. a 35. degrez 53 minutes de Latitude et a degr 30 min. de Longitude. selon les dernieres Observations, la plus grande partie des Geographes estime cette Isle estre d'Afrique — Between pp. 210 and 211. 171 × 274 mm.

[30] [C:] LA SUISSE, Suivant les Nouvelles Observations de Mess.rs de l'Academie Royale des Sciences, etc. Augmentées

de Nouveau, A LEIDE, Chez PIERRE VANDER AA ... — Pag 223. 220 × 297 mm.

[31] [C:] CARTE DE LORRAINE, Suivant les Nouvelles Observations de Messrs de l'Academie Royale des Sciences, etc. Augmentées de Nouveau. A LEIDE, Chez PIERRE VANDER AA. ... — Between pp. 244 and 245. 221 × 295 mm.

[32] [C:] L'ALLEMAGNE. Suivant les Nouvelles Observations de Messrs de l'Academie Royale des Sciences, etc. Augmentées de Nouveau. A LEIDE, Chez PIERRE VANDER AA. ... — Between pp. 246 and 247. 220 × 296 mm.

[33] [C:] CERCLE DE LA SOUABE SEPTENTRIONALE, Suivant les Nouvelles Observations de Messrs de l'Academie Royale des Sciences, etc. Augmentées de Nouveau. A LEIDE, Chez PIERRE VANDER AA. ... — Between pp. 248 and 249. 222 × 296 mm.

[34] [C:] CERCLE DE LA SOUABE MERIDIONALE, Suivant les Nouvelles Observations de Messrs de l'Academie Royale des Sciences, etc. Augmentées de Nouveau. A LEIDE, Chez PIERRE VANDER AA. ... — Between pp. 250 and 251. 222 × 297 mm.

[35] [C:] CERCLE DE BAVIERE, Suivant les Nouvelles Observations de Messrs de l'Academie Royale des Sciences, etc. Augmentées de Nouveau. A LEIDE, Chez PIERRE VANDER AA. ... — Between pp. 256 and 257. 222 × 296 mm.

[36] [C:] CERCLE D'AUTRICHE, Suivant les Nouvelles Observations de Messrs de l'Academie Royale des Sciences, etc. Augmentées de Nouveau. A LEIDE, Chez PIERRE VANDER AA. ... — Between pp. 260 and 261. 222 × 296 mm.

[37] [C:] CERCLE DE LA HAUTE SAXE, Suivant les Nouvelles Observations de Messrs de l'Academie Royale des Sciences, etc. Augmentées de Nouveau. A LEIDE, Chez PIERRE VANDER AA. ... — Between pp. 266 and 267. 224 × 296 mm.

[38] [C:] BRANDENBOURG ET POMERANIE, Suivant les Nouvelles Observations de Messrs de l'Academie Royale des Sciences, etc. Augmentées de Nouveau. A LEIDE, Chez PIERRE VANDER AA. ... — Between pp. 276 and 277. 224 × 295 mm.

[39] [C:] CERCLE DE LA BASSE SAXE Suivant les Nouvelles Observations de Messrs de l'Academie Royale des Sciences, etc. Augmentées de Nouveau. A LEIDE, Chez PIERRE VANDER AA. ... — Between pp. 282 and 283. 222 × 295 mm.

[40] [C:] LE DUCHÉ DE LUNEBOURG, Suivant les Nouvelles Observations de Messrs de l'Academie Royale des Sciences, etc. Augmentées de Nouveau. A LEIDE, Chez PIERRE VANDER AA. ... — Between pp. 282 and 283. 220 × 296 mm.

[41] [C:] CERCLE DE WESTPHALIE, Suivant les Nouvelles Observations de Messrs de l'Academie Royale des Sciences, etc. Augmentées de Nouveau. A LEIDE, Chez PIERRE VANDER AA. ... — Between pp. 296 and 297. 222 × 296 mm.

[42] [C:] L'EVECHÉ DE LIEGE, Suivant les Nouvelles Observations de Messrs de l'Academie Royale des Sciences, etc. Augmentées de Nouveau. A LEIDE, Chez PIERRE VANDER AA. ... — Between pp. 296 and 297. 222 × 296 mm.

[43] [C:] CERCLE DE FRANCONIE, Suivant les Nouvelles Observations de Messrs de l'Academie Royale des Sciences, etc. Augmentées de Nouveau. A LEIDE, Chez PIERRE VANDER AA. ... — Between pp. 304 and 305. 221 × 295 mm.

[44] [C:] CERCLE DU HAUT RHIN, Suivant les Nouvelles Observations de Messrs de l'Academie Royale des Sciences, etc. Augmentées de Nouveau. A LEIDE, Chez PIERRE VANDER AA. ... — Between pp. 310 and 311. 222 × 295 mm.

[45] [C:] LANDGRAVIAT DE HESSE, Suivant les Nouvelles Observations de Messrs de l'Academie Royale des Sciences, etc. Augmentées de Nouveau. A LEIDE, Chez PIERRE VANDER AA. ... — Between pp. 312 and 313. 222 × 296 mm.

[46] [C:] CERCLE ELECTORAL DU RHIN, Suivant les Nouvelles Observations de Messrs de l'Academie Royale des Sciences, etc. Augmentées de Nouveau. A LEIDE, Chez PIERRE VANDER AA. ... — Between pp. 318 and 319. 222 × 296 mm.

[47] [C:] L'ARCHEVECHE DE MAYENCE, Suivant les Nouvelles Observations de Messrs de l'Academie Royale des Sciences, etc. Augmentées de Nouveau. A LEIDE. Chez PIERRE VANDER AA. ... — Between pp. 320 and 321. 222 × 298 mm.

[48] [C:] L'ARCHEVECHÉ DE COLOGNE, Suivant les Nouvelles Observations de Messrs de l'Academie Royale des Sciences, etc. Augmentées de Nouveau. A LEIDE, Chez PIERRE VANDER AA. ... — Between pp. 320 and 321. 223 × 297 mm.

[49] [C:] L'ARCHEVECHE DE TREVES, Suivant les Nouvelles Observations de Messrs de l'Academie Royale des Sciences, etc. Augmentées de Nouveau. A LEIDE, Chez PIERRE VANDER AA. ... — Between pp. 320 and 321. 220 × 297 mm.

[50] [C:] LA BOHEME, Suivant les Nouvelles Observations de Messrs de l'Academie Royale des Sciences, etc. Augmentées de Nouveau. A LEIDE, Chez PIERRE VANDER AA. ... — Between pp. 332 and 333. 222 × 295 mm.

[51] [C:] LES XVII. PROVINCES DES PAYS BAS, Suivant les Nouvelles Observations de Messrs de l'Academie Royale des Sciences, etc. Augmentées de Nouveau. A LEIDE, Chez PIERRE VANDER AA. ... — Between pp. 348 and 349. 222 × 297 mm.

[52] [C:] CARTE DES PAYS BAS CATHOLIQUES, Suivant les Nouvelles Observations de Messrs de l'Academie Royale des Sciences, etc. Augmentées de Nouveau. A LEIDE, Chez PIERRE VANDER AA. ... — Between pp. 348 and 349. 221 × 294 mm.

[53] [C:] CARTE DU COMTE DE FLANDRE, Suivant les Nouvelles Observations de Messrs de l'Academie Royale des Sciences, etc. Augmentées de Nouveau. A LEIDE, Chez PIERRE VANDER AA. ... — Between pp. 350 and 351. 219 × 295 mm.

[54] [C:] CARTE DES COMTEZ de HAINAUT de NAMUR et de CAMBRESIS, Suivant les Nouvelles Observations de Messrs de l'Academie Royale des Sciences, etc. Augmentées de Nouveau. A LEIDE, Chez PIERRE VANDER AA. ... — Between pp. 354 and 355. 220 × 296 mm.

[55] [C:] LE DUCHÉ DE LUXEMBOURG, Suivant les Nouvelles Observations de Messrs de l'Academie Royale des Sciences, etc. Augmentées de Nouveau. A LEIDE, Chez PIERRE VANDER AA. ... — Between pp. 356 and 357. 221 × 296 mm.

[56] [C:] LE DUCHÉ DE LIMBOURG, Suivant les Nouvelles Observations de Messrs de l'Academie Royale des Sciences, etc. Augmentées de Nouveau. A LEIDE, Chez PIERRE VANDER AA. ... — Between pp. 356 and 357. 222 × 296 mm.

[57] [C:] CARTE DU BRABANT, Suivant les Nouvelles Observations de Messrs de l'Academie Royale des Sciences, etc. Augmentées de Nouveau. A LEIDE, Chez PIERRE VANDER AA. ... — Between pp. 358 and 359. 220 × 294 mm.

[58] [C:] LES PROVINCES UNIES DES PAYS BAS, Suivant les Nouvelles Observations de Messrs de l'Academie Royale des Sciences, etc. Augmentées de Nouveau. A LEIDE, Chez PIERRE VANDER AA. ... — Between pp. 362 and 363. 219 × 295 mm.

[59] [C:] LA HOLLANDE, Suivant les Nouvelles Observations de Messrs de l'Academie Royale des Sciences, etc. Augmentées de Nouveau. A LEIDE, Chez PIERRE VANDER AA. ... — Between pp. 366 and 367. 220 × 296 mm.

[60] [C:] LA ZELANDE, Suivant les Nouvelles Observations de Messrs de l'Academie Royale des Sciences, etc. Augmentees de Nouveau. A LEIDE, Chez PIERRE VANDER AA. ... — Between pp. 372 and 373. 221 × 297 mm.

[61] [C:] L'UTRECHT Suivant les Nouvelles Observations de Mess.rs de l'Academie Royale des Sciences, etc. Augmentées de Nouveau. A LEIDE, Chez PIERRE VANDER AA. ... — Between pp. 374 and 375. 221 × 295 mm.

[62] [C:] LA GUELDRE, Suivant les Nouvelles Observations de Mess.rs de l'Academie Royale des Sciences, etc. Augmentées de Nouveau. A LEIDE, Chez PIERRE VANDER AA. ... — Between pp. 376 and 377. 222 × 295 mm.

[63] [C:] L'OVER-ISSEL, Suivant les Nouvelles Observations de Mess.rs de l'Academie Royale des Sciences, etc. Augmentées de Nouveau. A LEIDE, Chez PIERRE VANDER AA. ... — Between pp. 378 and 379. 222 × 296 mm.

[64] [C:] LA GRONINGUE, Suivant les Nouvelles Observations de Mess.rs de l'Academie Royale des Sciences, etc. Augmentées de Nouveau. A LEIDE, Chez PIERRE VANDER AA. ... — Between pp. 380 and 381. 221 × 296 mm.

[65] [C:] LA FRISE, Suivant les Nouvelles Observations de Mess.rs de l'Academie Royale des Sciences, etc. Augmentées de Nouveau. A LEIDE, Chez PIERRE VANDER AA. ... — Between pp. 380 and 381. 223 × 298 mm.

[66] [C:] LES ISLES BRITANNIQUES, Suivant les Nouvelles Observations de Mess.rs de l'Academie Royale des Sciences, etc. Augmentées de Nouveau. A LEIDE, Chez PIERRE VANDER AA. ... — Between pp. 390 and 391. 220 × 295 mm.

[67] [C:] L'ANGLETERRE, Suivant les Nouvelles Observations de Mess.rs de l'Academie Royale des Sciences, etc. Augmentées de Nouveau. A LEIDE, Chez PIERRE VANDER AA. ... — Between pp. 392 and 393. 223 × 297 mm.

[68] [C:] L'ECOSSE, Suivant les Nouvelles Observations de Mess.rs de l'Academie Royale des Sciences, etc. Augmentées de Nouveau. A LEIDE, Chez PIERRE VANDER AA. ... — Between pp. 410 and 411. 223 × 297 mm.

[69] [C:] L'IRLANDE, Suivant les Nouvelles Observations de Mess.rs de l'Academie Royale des Sciences, etc. Augmentées de Nouveau. A LEIDE, Chez PIERRE VANDER AA. ... — Between pp. 418 and 419. 223 × 296 mm.

[70] [C:] SCANDINAVIE SEPTENTRIONALE OU COURONNES DU NORD Suivant les Nouvelles Observations de Mess.rs de l'Academie Royale des Sciences, etc. Augmentées de Nouveau. A LEIDE, Chez PIERRE VANDER AA. ... — Between pp. 434 and 435. 224 × 299 mm.

[71] [C:] SCANDINAVIE MERIDIONALE OU COURONNES DU NORD, Suivant les Nouvelles Observations de Mess.rs de l'Academie Royale des Sciences, etc. Augmentées de Nouveau. A LEIDE, Chez PIERRE VANDER AA. ... — Between pp. 434 and 435. 221 × 298 mm.

[72] [C:] LE DANEMARC, Suivant les Nouvelles Observations de Mess.rs de l'Academie Royale des Sciences, etc. Augmentées de Nouveau. A LEIDE, Chez PIERRE VANDER AA. ... — Between pp. 434 and 435. 219 × 296 mm.

[73] [C:] LA NORVEGUE, Suivant les Nouvelles Observations de Mess.rs de l'Academie Royale des Sciences, etc. Augmentées de Nouveau. A LEIDE, Chez PIERRE VANDER AA. ... — Between pp. 438 and 439. 223 × 294 mm.

[74] [C:] LA SUEDE, Suivant les Nouvelles Observations de Mess.rs de l'Academie Royale des Sciences, etc. Augmentées de Nouveau. A LEIDE, Chez PIERRE VANDER AA. ... — Between pp. 440 and 441. 220 × 294 mm.

[75] [C:] LA POLOGNE, Suivant les Nouvelles Observations de Mess.rs de l'Academie Royale des Sciences, etc. Augmentées de Nouveau. A LEIDE, Chez P. VANDER AA. ... — Between pp. 456 and 457. 221 × 295 mm.

[76] [C:] LA PRUSSE, Suivant les Nouvelles Observations de Mess.rs de l'Academie Royale des Sciences, etc. Augmentées de Nouveau. A LEIDE, Chez PIERRE VANDER AA. ... — Between pp. 466 and 467. 222 × 296 mm.

[77] [C:] LA MOSCOVIE MERIDIONALE, Suivant les Nouvelles Observations de Mess.rs de l'Academie Royale des Sciences, etc. Augmentées de Nouveau. A LEIDE, Chez PIERRE VANDER AA. ... — Between pp. 478 and 479. 222 × 296 mm.

[78] [C:] LA MOSCOVIE SEPTENTRIONALE, Suivant les Nouvelles Observations de Mess.rs de l'Academie Royale des Sciences, etc. Augmentées de Nouveau. A LEIDE, Chez PIERRE VANDER AA. ... — Between pp. 482 and 483. 221 × 295 mm.

[79] [C:] LA HONGRIE, Suivant les Nouvelles Observations de Mess.rs de l'Academie Royale des Sciences, etc. Augmentées de Nouveau. A LEIDE, Chez PIERRE VANDER AA. ... — Between pp. 488 and 489. 221 × 295 mm.

[80] [C:] TURQUIE en EUROPE, Suivant les Nouvelles Observations de Mess.rs de l'Academie Royale des Sciences, etc. Augmentées de Nouveau. A LEIDE, Chez PIERRE VANDER AA. ... — Between pp. 502 and 503. 222 × 297 mm.

[81] [C:] LA GRECE, Suivant les Nouvelles Observations de Mess.rs de l'Academie Royale des Sciences, etc. Augmentées de Nouveau. A LEIDE, Chez PIERRE VANDER AA. ... — Between pp. 514 and 515. 222 × 296 mm.

Vol. II
LA GEOGRAPHIE MODERNE, ... TOME SECOND, Contenant le reste de l'Europe. A LEIDE, Aux depens de PIERRE VANDER Aa, Marchand Libraire. MDCC XXIX.

[1] [C:] L'ASIE, Suivant les Nouvelles Observations de Mess.rs de l'Academie Royale des Sciences, etc. Augmentées de Nouveau. A LEIDE, Chez PIERRE VANDER AA. ... — Before p. 533. 221 × 294 mm.

[2] [C:] LA GRANDE TARTARIE, Suivant les Nouvelles Observatons de Mess.rs de l'Academie Royale des Sciences, etc. Augmentées de Nouveau. A LEIDE, Chez PIERRE VANDER AA. ... — Between pp. 554 and 555. 222 × 296 mm.

[3] [C:] TURQUIE EN ASIE, Suivant les Nouvelles Observations de Mess.rs de l'Academie Royale des Sciences, etc. Augmentées de Nouveau. A LEIDE, Chez PIERRE VANDER AA. ... — Between pp. 570 and 571. 223 × 296 mm.

[4] [C:] TERRE SAINTE, Suivant les Nouvelles Observations de Mess.rs de l'Academie Royale des Sciences, etc. Augmentées de Nouveau. A LEIDE, Chez PIERRE VANDER AA. ... — Between pp. 586 and 587. 221 × 297 mm.

[5] [C:] L'INDE DE ÇA LE GANGE, Suivant les Nouvelles Observations de Mess.rs de l'Academie Royale des Sciences, etc. Augmentées de Nouveau. A LEIDE, Chez PIERRE VANDER AA. ... — Between pp. 638 and 639. 223 × 296 mm.

[6] [C:] L'INDE DE LA GANGE, Suivant les Nouvelles Observations de Mess.rs de l'Academie Royale des Sciences, etc. Augmentées de Nouveau. A LEIDE, Chez PIERRE VANDER AA. ... — Between pp. 648 and 649. 222 × 296 mm.

[7] [C:] LA CHINE, Suivant les Nouvelles Observations de Mess.rs de l'Academie Royale des Sciences, etc. Augmentées de Nouveau. A LEIDE, Chez PIERRE VANDER AA. ... — Between pp. 662 and 663. 223 × 297 mm.

Vol. III
LA GEOGRAPHIE MODERNE, ... TOME TROISIÉME, Contenant l'Asie. A LEIDE, Aux depens de PIERRE VANDER Aa, Marchand Libraire. MDCC XXIX.

[1] [C:] L'AFRIQUE, Suivant les Nouvelles Observations de Mess.rs de l'Academie Royale des Sciences, etc. Augmentées de Nouveau. A LEIDE, Chez PIERRE VANDER AA. ... — Before p. 717. 220 × 296 mm.

[2] [C:] LE CAP DE BONNE ESPERANCE, Suivant les Nouvelles Observations de Mess.rs de l'Academie Royale des Sciences, etc. Augmentées de Nouveau. A LEIDE, Chez PIERRE VANDER AA. ... — Between pp. 770 and 771.

222 × 196 mm.

Vol. IV
LA GEOGRAPHIE MODERNE, ... TOME QUATRIÉME, Contenant l'Afrique, l'Amérique, & les Terres Inconnuës, Arctiques, & Antarctiques. A LEIDE, Aux depens de PIERRE VANDER Aa, Marchand Libraire. MDCC XXIX.

[1] [C:] L'AMERIQUE SEPTENTRIONALE, Suivant les Nouvelles Observations de Messrs de l'Academie Royale des Sciences, etc. Augmentées de Nouveau. A LEIDE, Chez PIERRE VANDER AA. ... — Between pp. 828 and 829. 221 × 295 mm.

[2] [C:] MEXIQUE OU NOUVELLE ESPAGNE, Suivant les Nouvelles Observations de Messrs de l'Academie Royale des Sciences, etc. Augmentées de Nouveau. A LEIDE, Chez PIERRE VANDER AA. ... — Between pp. 830 and 831. 222 × 296 mm.

[3] [C:] LA FLORIDE, Suivant les Nouvelles Observations de Messrs de l'Academie Royale des Sciences, etc. Augmentées de Nouveau. A LEIDE, Chez PIERRE VANDER AA. ... — Between pp. 842 and 843. 221 × 296 mm.

[4] [C:] CANADA ou NOUVELLE FRANCE, Suivant les Nouvelles Observations de Messrs de l'Academie Royale des Sciences, etc. Augmentées de Nouveau. A LEIDE, Chez PIERRE VANDER AA. ... — Between pp. 846 and 847. 222 × 296 mm.

[5] [C:] L'AMERIQUE MERIDIONALE, Suivant les Nouvelles Observations de Messrs de l'Academie Royale des Sciences, etc. Augmentées de Nouveau. A LEIDE, Chez PIERRE VANDER AA. ... — Between pp. 864 and 865. 221 × 296 mm.

[6] [C:] LE BRESIL, Suivant les Nouvelles Observations de Messrs de l'Academie Royale des Sciences, etc. Augmentées de Nouveau. A LEIDE, Chez PIERRE VANDER AA. ... — Between pp. 878 and 879. 222 × 296 mm.

Notes: All the maps are blank on the back and uncoloured. The title-page are printed in red and black. Each part has its own title-page, but the pagination is in one sequence throughout all four parts. The information given on the title-page does not altogether correspond with the actual contents of the separate parts: for example, the first part is said to include part of Europe, but in fact it covers the whole continent. The second part is said to contain 'le reste de l'Europe', but deals with Asia, as is stated before Chap. 1. The third part contains not Asia, as on the title-page, but Africa. The fourth part deals with America, and there is an additional section at the end covering 'Des terres polaires et inconnus, arctiques et antarctiques, septentrionales et australes'. The title-page also mentions the continuation of Africa. All the maps, with the exception of [29], L'Isle de Malthe, are signed 'A Leide, Chez Pierre Vander Aa'. All of them, except the celestial map and the map of Malta, are to be found in Pieter van der Aa's Nouvelle Atlas, 1714, which includes only one map not in Du Bois's Geographie: Le Duché de Brunswick. The Introduction à la Geographie, at the beginning of Part 1, includes two plates between p. 2 and 3, 'LE GLOBE CELESTE' and 'GLOBE TERESTRE', and between pp. 4 and 5 an armillary sphere, 'LA SPHERE ARTIFICIELLE'. Between p. 32 and 33 there is a plate with a beautiful wind rose, 'QUADRAN DE MER'. The copy in the Bibliothèque Nationale in Paris was printed in La Haye by J. Vanden Kieboom in 1736, and is in two volumes. Our copy is bound in one volume in contemporary binding with gold lettering on the spine. Nordenskiöld's signature, with the year 1898, is on the first blank leaf.
Lit.: Bibl. Nat. Paris, Cat. vol. 42, c. 433, Koeman vol. 1, p. 14—15, Aa 8.

70 DUDLEY, ROBERT 1646—1647

DELL'ARCANO DEL MARE, DI D. RVBERTO DVDLEO DVCA DI NORTVMBRIA, E CONTE DI VVARVICH, LIBRI SEI; Nel primo de'quali si tratta della Longitudine praticabile in diuersi modi, d'inuenzione dell'Autore, Nel Secondo, delle Carte sue generali, e de'Portolani rettificati in Longitudine, e Latitudine, Nel Terzo, della Disciplina sua Marittima, e Militare. Nel Quarto, dell'Architettura sua Nautica di Vascelli da querra, Nel Quinto, della nauigazione scientifica, e perfetta, cioè Spirale, ò di gran Circoli, Nel Sesto, delle Carte sue Geografiche, e Particolari. AL SERENISSIMO FERDINANDO SECONDO GRAN DVCA DI TOSCANA suo Signore. In FIRENZE, Nella Stamperia di Francesco Onofri. 1646. ...   43,5 cm.

Vol. I
DEL-L'ARCANO DEL MARE. TOMO PRIMO DIVISO NEL LIBRO PRIMO, E SECONDO.

No maps.

DEL-L'ARCANO DEL MARE, DEL DVCA DI NORTVMBRIA. LIBRO SECONDO.

[1] 8 [C:] Carta Terza generale di Europa. — [T:] AF^{O} Lucini Fecit. — Between pp. 12 and 13. 372 × 478 mm.

[2] 8 [C:] Carta prima Generale d'Affrica è par.^{e} d'America. — [T:] AF:Lucini Feci — Between pp. 16 and 17. 473 × 734 mm.
[Inset:] [T:] MARE DI ETHIOPIA. [and the coast from] C:das Palmas [to] Alanando — 186 × 245 mm.

[3] 6 [C:] Carta prima Generale d'America dell'India Occidētale è Mare del Zur. — [T:] AF$^{O}_{:}$ Lucini Feci — Between pp. 20 and 21. 484 × 697 mm.
[Inset:] [T:] AMERICA Maiestrale. — [T:] [From] C: Mendocino ò C: Corrientes [to] P$^{O}_{:}$ di S: Ipolito — 277 × 302 mm.

[4] 5 [C:] Carta terza Generale d'America. — [T:] AF: Lucini Feci — Between pp. 26 and 27. 466 × 758 mm.
[Inset:] [T:] Cili Patagoni Il Stetto di Magaglianes. Terra del Fuoco. — 279 × 247 mm.

[5] 9 [C:] Carta secon.^{a} Generale del'Asia. — [T:] AF: Lucini Fece — Between pp. 32 and 33. 482 × 372 mm.

[6] 7 [C:] Carta seconda Generale d'Affrica. — [T:] AF: Lucini Fece — Between pp. 34 and 35. 484 × 745 mm.
[Inset:] [T:] AFFRICA [from] Bocca del Mare Rosso [to] C: Falso. — 242 × 245 mm.

[7] 2 [C:] Carta prima Generale dell'Asia. — [T:] An^{o} Fr^{o} Lucini Fece. — Between pp. 38 and 39. 468 × 761 mm.

[8] 9 [C:] Asia carta diciasete piu moderna. — [T:] AF. Lucini Fecit. — Between pp. 52 and 53. 426 × 562 mm.

[9] 10 [C:] Carta terza Generale del'Asia. — [T:] AF: Lucini Fece — Between pp. 54 and 55. 465 × 382 mm.

[10] 11 [C:] Carta seconda Generale del'America. — [T:] AF: Lucini Feci — Between pp. 56 and 57. 447 × 372 mm.

[11] 12 [C:] Carta quarta generale. di Europa. — [T:] AF$^{O}_{:}$F$^{O}_{:}$ Lucini Feci: — Between pp. 58 and 59. 369 × 500 mm.

[12] 13 [C:] Carta quinta generale di Europa. — [T:] AF:Lucini Feci — Between pp. 58 and 59. 398 × 476 mm.

[13] 14 [C:] Carta sesta Generale del'Europa. — [T:] AF: Lucini Fece — Between pp. 60 and 61. 486 × 357 mm.

[14] [C:] Carta nonna Generale di Europa. — [T:] AF: Lucini Fece — Between pp. 60 and 61. 370 × 482 mm.

[15] [C:] Carta di Noruegia piu moderna. — [T:] AF$^{O}_{:}$ Lucini Fecit. — Between pp. 60 and 61. 500 × 370 mm.

Vol. II
DELL'ARCANO DEL MARE, TOMO SECONDO DIVISO NEL LIBRO TERZO, E QVARTO.

No maps.

Vol. III
DELL'ARCANO DEL MARE, DI D. RVBERTO DVDLEO DVCA DI NORTVMBRIA, E CONTE DI WARVICH. PARTE PRIMA DEL TOMO TERZO CONTENENTE IL LIBRO QVINTO, Nel quale si tratta della nauigazione scientifica, e perfetta, cioè Spirale, ... IN FIRENZE, Nella Stamperia di Francesco Onofri. 1647. ...   47,5 cm.

No maps.

DELL'ARCANO DEL MARE, DI D. RVBERTO DVDLEO ... PARTE SECONDA DEL TOMO TERZO CONTENENTE IL LIBRO SESTO, Nel quale si tratta delle Carte sue Corografiche, e Particolari. ... IN FIRENZE, Nella Stamperia di Francesco Onofri. 1647. ... [Colophon:] IN FIRENZE, Nella Stamperia di Francesco Onofri. ... MDX XXXXIIX.   54 cm.

[1] [C:] Vna Carta Generale del mare Mediterranio. Carta prima Generale d'Europa — [T:] AF: Lucini Fece. — 433 × 742 mm.

[2] [C:] Vna carta dell'Arcipelago, con parte del Mare mediterraneo uerso Leuante. Carta Seconda Geneale d'Euro[a] — [T:] AF. Lucini Fece. — 432 × 365 mm.

[3] [C:] Vna Carta del mare Oceano, cHe Comincia con il Capo S:Vincenzio in Portogallo, e Finisce con Iostretto di Gibilterra. Carta prima Particolare d'Europa I — [T:] AF: Lucini Fece. — 460 × 675 mm.

[4] [C:] Carta Particolare del mare Mediterranio che comincia con Io stretto di Gibilterra e Finisce con il Porto di Cartagena in Ispagna e del capo Falcone in Barberia. di Europa Carta II. — [T:] AF: Lucini Fece. — 466 × 754 mm.

[5] [C:] Carta particolare del mare Mediterraneo che Comincia con il capo Paulos e finisce con il capo di S.Martino in Ispagnse del capo Bogia in Barberia Euro[a] III. — [T:] AF: Lucini Fece. — 472 × 736 mm.

[6] [C:] Carta Particolare del mare Mediterraneo che cominca con il capo S.Martino e, finisce con il capo Dragone in Ispagna e, con Lisole di Maiorica, e, Minorica, e, ÿuica. di Europa carta quarta — [T:] AF: Lucini Fece. — 474 × 730 mm.

[7] [C:] Carta particolare del mare Mediterranneo che comincia con il capo Dragone in Jspagna e finisce con il capo Melle nella riuera di Genoua La Longitudine cominca da Lisolla di Picho e di Asores. di Europa Carta Quinta. — [T:] AF:LuciciFece — 465 × 737 mm.

[8] [C:] Europa. Carta quinta. seco[a]. — [T:] A[o].F[o].Lucini Feci. — 460 × 735 mm.

[9] [C:] Carta particolare del mare Mediterraneo che comincia con il capo Melle nella riuiera di Genoua e Finisce con Ciuita uecchia nelo Stat[o] del Papa La Longitudinc comincia da Lisolla di Picho di Asore[s] di Europa Carta Sesta. — [T:] AF: Lucini Fece. — 486 × 746 mm.

[10] [C:] Carta particolare della Jsolla di Sardinia e parte della Corsica La Longitudine comincia da Lisolla di Picho di Asores. di Europa carta Setima. — [T:] AF: Lucini Fece — 484 × 343 mm.

[11] [C:] Carta particolare del mare Mediterraneo che comincia con Ciuita uecchia è Finisce con il capo S:Maria in Calabria. La longitudine comincia da Lisola di Picho di Asores. di Europa Carta Ottaua. — [T:] AF: Lucini Fece. — 483 × 746 mm.

[12] [C:] Carta particolare del mare Mediterraneo che comincia con Budua in Dalmatia è Finisce con Corfu nelo Stato Venetiaõ La longitudine comincia da lIsola Picho di Asores Cartta Nona di Europa. — [T:] AF:Lucini Fece. — 421 × 322 mm.

[13] [C:] Carta particolare del mare Adriatico che comincia con il capo di Ancona è Finisce con l'Isola Lesina nello Isteso mare. La longitudine comincia da l'Isola di Picho di Asores. Carta X. di Europa — [T:] AF:Lucini Fece. — 483 × 699 mm.

[14] [C:] Carta particolare del mare Mediterraneo che comincia con il capo Spartiuento è Finisce con il cap[o] Matapan nella Morea. La longitudine comincia da l'Isola di Picco di Asores. Carta XI. di Europa. — [T:] AF: Lucini Fece. — 480 × 744 mm.

[15] [C:] Carta particolare del Arcipelago La longitudine comincia da l'Isola di Picco di Asores. Carta XII. di Europa. — [T:] AF:Lucini Fece. — 490 × 743 mm.

[16] [C:] Carta particolare del mare Mediteran[o] che comincia con il capo Gironda è Finisce con Antiochia in Soria. La longitudine comincia da l'Isola di Picco di Asores. Carta XIII. Euro[a]. — [T:] AF:Lucini Fece. — 433 × 372 mm.

[17] [C:] Carta particolare del mare Mediterraneo che comincia con l'Isola di Candia è Finisce con il capo Roxatim in Barberia La longitudine comincia da l'Isola di Picco di Asores. Carta. XIIII. d'Euro[a] — [T:] AF:Lucini Fece. — 478 × 750 mm.

[18] [C:] Carta particolare del mare Mediterraneo che comincia con il capo Teti e Finisce con Folselli in Barberia. La longitudine comincia da l'Isola di Picco di Asores. Carta. X.V. d'Euro[a] — [T:] AF:Lucini Fece. — 449 × 754 mm.

[19] [C:] Carta particolare del mare Mediterraneo che comincia con il Porto di tre Croce è Finisce con il capo Araso. La longitudine comincia da l'Isola di Picco di Asores. Carta X.V.I. d'Euro[a] — [T:] AF:Lucini Fece. — 484 × 757 mm.

[20] [C:] Carta particolare del mare Mediteranio che comincia con il capo Bogia è Finisce con il Porto di tre Croce. La longitudine comincia da l'Isola di Picco d'Asores Carta X.V.II. Euro[a]. — [T:] AF:Lucini Fece. — 423 × 372 mm.

[21] [C:] Carta particolare del Oceano che comincia con il capo S:Vincentio è Finisce con il capo Roxo in Portogallo La longitudine comincia da l'Isola di Picco d'Asores. di Europa Carta.X.V.III. — [T:] AF:Lucini Fece. — 460 × 379 mm.

[22] [C:] Carta particolare del Oceano che comincia con la costa di c.Roxo è Finisce con il capo di Mogera ni Portogallo. La longitudine comincia da l'Isola di Picco d'Asores di Europa Carta .X.V.IIII. — [T:] AF:Lucici Fece. — 482 × 369 mm.

[23] [C:] Carta particolare che comincia con il capo Mogera in Portogallo è Finisce con il capo di Coriano in Ispagna. La longitudine comincia da l'Isola di Picco d'Asores. di Europa Carta XX. — [T:] AF:Lucini Fece. — 476 × 375 mm.

[24] [C:] Carta particolare che comincia con il capo di Coriano è Finisce con il capo di Auiles in Ispagnia La longitudine comincia da l'Isola di Picco d'Asores. di Europa Carta .XXI. — [T:] AF:Lucini Fece — 465 × 742 mm.

[25] [C:] Carta particolare che comincia con il capo di Auiles è Finisce con il capo di Oringan in Biscaia sotto posto alla corona di Ispa[ia] La longitudine comincia da l'Isola di Picco d'Asores. di Europa Carta XXII. — [T:] AF:Lucini Fece. — 469 × 754 mm.

[26] [C:] Carta particolare che comincia con il capo di Oringan in Biscaia è Finisce con la costa di Alcason in Francia. La longitudine comincia da l'Isola di Picco d'Asores. di Europa Carta XXIII. — [T:] AF:Lucini Fece. — 467 × 370 mm.

[27] [C:] Carta particolare della costa di Guasconnia in Francia che comincia con il Fiume di Burdeaux è Finisce con l'Isola di Heÿs. La longitudine comincia da l'Isola di Picco d'Asores. di Europa Carta XXIIII. — [T:] AF::Lucini Fece. — 474 × 399 mm.

[28] [C:] Carta particolare della Brittania bassa in Francia che comincia con il capo Armentice à Finisce con il capo Forne. La longitudine comincia da l'Isola di Picco d'Asores. di Europa Carta XXV. — [T:] AF:Lucini Fece. — 475 × 747 mm.

[29] [C:] Carta particolare dell canale Fra Inghilterra è Francia che comincia con l'Isole di Sorlinges è Finisce con l'Isola di Garnseÿ. La longitudine comincia de l'Isola di Picco d'Asores. di Europa Carta .XXVI. — [T:] AF:Lucini Fece. — 486 × 748 mm.

[30] [C:] Carta particolare della costa d'Inghilterra è Francia che comincia con l'Isola di Garnesÿ e Finisce con il C:di Fecam nella costa di Normandia. La longitudine comincia da l'Isola di Picco d'Asores di Europa Carta .XXVII. — [T:] AF:Lucini Fece. — 487 × 385 mm.

[31] [C:] Carta particolare dell Mare di Ierlandia è parte di Inghilterr è della Iscotia. Lalongitudine comincia da l'Isola di Picco di Asores. di Europa Carta .XXVIII. — [T:] AF:Lucini Fece. — 486 × 766 mm.

[32] [C:] Carta particolare dell mare Oceano fra l'Ierlandia è l'Isole di Asores la longitudine comincia da l'Isola di Picco d'Asores di Europa Carta XXVIIII. — [T:] AF:Lucini

Fece. — 468 × 364 mm.

[33] [C:] Carta particolare dello stretto di Inghilterra tra Douer è Cales. con la costa intorno. La longitudine comincia da l Isola di Picho d'Asores. di Europa Carta XXX. — [T:] AF:Lucini Fece. — 458 × 362 mm.

[34] [C:] Carta particolare della bocca del Tamigi in Inghi.ta è Finisce à Ieÿstof nella Prouincia di Suffoleh. La longitudine comincia da l'Isola di Picho d'Asores. di Europa Carta XXXI. — [T:] AF:Lucini Fece. — 446 × 370 mm.

[35] [C:] Carta particolare della Costa di Inghilterra che comincia con Orfordness è Finisce con Flamborow heade. La longitudine Comincia da l'Isola di Picho d'Asores. di Europa Carta XXXII. — [T:] AF:Lucini Fece. — 467 × 363 mm.

[36] [C:] Carta particolare della costa di Inghilterra che comincia a Fÿleberg è Finisce con il C:di S:Tabs in Ischozia La longitudine Comincia da l'Isola di Picho d'Asores di Europa Carta XXXIII. — [T:] AF:Lucini Fece. — 475 × 357 mm.

[37] [C:] Carta particolare della costa di Scozia. che comincia con il C:di S: Tabs è Finisce con il c:d'Comar. La longitudine Comincia da l'Isola di Picho d'Asores di Europa Carta XXXIIII. — [T:] AF:Lucini Fece. — 482 × 349 mm.

[38] [C:] Carta particolare della costa di Scozia che comincia con il C:di Cromar è Finisce con l'Isole di Orcades. La longitudine Comincia da l'Isola di Picho d'Asores. di Europa Carta XXXV. — [T:] AF:Lucini Fece. — 488 × 378 mm.

[39] [C:] Carta particolare della costa di Zelanda è Frislanda è Olanda che comincia con il Porto di Newport è Finisce con Messelward La longitudine Comincia da l'Isola di Picho d'Asores. di Europa Carta XXXVI. — [T:] AF:Lucini Fece. — 475 × 761 mm.

[40] [C:] Carta particolare della costa di Zelanda è Frislanda è Olanda che comincia con il Porto di Newport è Finisce con Messelward. La longitudine Comincia da l'Isola di Pico d'Asores. Di Europa Carta XXXVI. seco.a — [T:] AF:Lucini Fece. — 464 × 753 mm.

[41] [C:] Carta particolare che comincia con il gran fiume Albis è contene parte del mare Baltico è Ientrata al sondo di Danemarca. La longitudine Comincia da l'Isola di Piccò d'Asores di Europa Carta XXXVII. — [T:] AF:Lucini Fece. — 482 × 759 mm.

[42] [C:] Carta particolare che comincia con la Iutlandia è contiene parte della costa di Suetzia è della Noruegia. Lalongitudine Comincia da l'Isola di Picho di Asores. di Europa Carta XXXVIII. — [T:] AF:Lucini Fece. — 482 × 748 mm.

[43] [C:] Carta particolare del mare Baltico che comincia con Colbergen è Finisce con il C:di VVestuesen in Prusia. La longitudine Comincia da l'Isola di Picco d'Asores. di Europa Carta XXXVIIII — [T:] AF:Lucini Fece. — 466 × 383 mm.

[44] [C:] Carta particolare del mare Baltico che comincia con il capo di Eleeholm in Suezia è Finisce con Padus in Liflandia. La longitudine Comincia da l'Isola di Picco d'Asores. di Europa Carta XXXX. — [T:] AF :Lucini Fece. — 484 × 755 mm.

[45] [C:] Carta particolare di Liuonia cor una particella della costa che comincia con LocKston è Finisce con il P.to Derliuen La longitudine Comincia da l'Isola di Picco d'Asores. di Europa Carta XXXXI. — [T:] AF:Lucini Fece. — 476 × 378 mm.
[Inset:] [In the C:] costa che comincia con LocKston è Finisce con il P.to Derliuen — 356 × 147 mm.

[46] [C:] Carta particolare dell fine del mare Baltico in sino all narue. La longitudine Comincia da l'Isola di Picho d'Asores. di Europa Carta XXXXII. — [T:] AF:Lucini Fece. — 483 × 748 mm.

[47] [C:] Carta particolare della entrata del mare Botnico ò Boddico. La longitudine Comincia da l'Isola di Picco d'Asores. di Europa Carta XXXXIII. — [T:] AF:Lucini Fece — 483 × 374 mm.

[48] [C:] Carta particolare della parte Australe della Noruegia La longitudine Comincia da l'Isola di Piho d'Asores. di Europa Carta XXXXIIII. — [T:] AF:Lucini Fece. — 485 × 372 mm.

[49] [C:] Questa carta contiene l'Isolle di Fero è di Shutland con la Noruegia Settentrionale. La longitudine Comincia da l'Isola di Pico d'Asores di EuroPa Carta XXXXV. — [T:] AF:Lucini Fece. — 486 × 742 mm.

[50] [C:] Carta particolare della costa di Finlandia con il capo dell Norto. La longitudine Comincia da l'Isola di Pico d'Asores. di Europa Carta XXXXVI. — [T:] AF:Lucini Fece. — 473 × 391 mm.

[51] [C:] Carta particolare del Mare Settentrionale di Moscouia è Russia con Iistreto di Wigats è Finisce con il Fiume Obÿ La longitudine Comincia da l'Isola di Pico d'Asores di Europa Carta XXXXVII — [T:] AF:Lucini Fece — 478 × 746 mm.

[52] [C:] Carta particolare della costa di nuoua Zembla. La longitudine Comincia da l'Isola di Pico d'Asores. di Europa Carta XXXXVIII. — [T:] AF:Lucini Fece. — 478 × 737 mm.

[53] [C:] Carta particolare della Terra di Grenlande gia incognita fu scoperta da Inglesi sino a, gradi 80: di latitudine. La longitudine Comincia da l'Isola di Pico d'Asores. di Europa Carta XXXXVIIII. — [T:] AF:Lucini Fece. — 483 × 742 mm.

[54] [C:] Carta particolare dell'Isole di Islandia è Frislandia, con l'Isolette di Fare. La longitudine Comincia da l'Isola di Pico d'Asores. di Europa Carta XXXXX. — [T:] AF:Lucini Fece. — 483 × 764 mm.

[55] [C:] Carta particolare della Gronlandia Orientale. La longitudine Comincia da l'Isola di Pico d'Asores. di Europa Carta LI. — [T:] AF:Lucini Fece. — 476 × 754 mm.

[56] [C:] Carta particolare della Meta Inconita con la Gronlandia Occidentale è dell'Estotiland Scop.to dall'Inglesi La longitudine Comincia da l'Isola di Pico d'Asores. di Europa Carta.LII. — [T:] AF:Lucini Fece — 466 × 753 mm.

[57] [C:] Carta particolare della Meta Incognita Australe con una parte della America Settentrionale. La longitudine Comincia da l'Isola di Pico d'Asores. di Europa Carta .L.III. — [T:] AF:Lucini Fece. — 452 × 370 mm.

[58] [C:] Carta particolare dello istreto è Mare iscoperto da Hen.o Hudson Ingilese nel. 1611. La longitudine Comincia da l'Isola di Pico d'Asores. Carta LIIII. d'Euro.a — [T:] AF:Lucini Fece — 711 × 478 mm.

PARTE SECONDA DEL LIBRO SESTO.

[59] [C:] Carta particolare che comincia con li stretto di Gibilterro è Finisce con il capo Gruer nella Barberia Occide͂.le La longitudine Comincia da l'Isola di Pico d'Asores. di Affrica Carta prima. — [T:] AF :Lucini Fece — 483 × 753 mm.

[60] [C:] Carta particolare dell'Isole d'Asores con l'Isola di Madera. La longitudine Comincia da l'Isola di Pico d'Asores. di Affrica Carta II. — [T:] AF:Lucini Fece. — 475 × 761 mm.

[61] [C:] Carta particolare della Barberia Occidentale che comincia con il capo Gruer è Finisce con il capo Matas. La longitudine Comincia da l'Isola di Pico d'Asores. di Affrica Carta .III. — [T:] AF:Lucini Fece — 476 × 742 mm.

[62] [C:] Carta particolare della Barberia Australe che comincia con il capo Matas è Finiscie con il C:Himilas con l'Isole di capo Verde La longitudine Comincia da l'Isola di Pico d'Asores. di Affrica Carta .IIII. — [T:] AF: Lucini Fece. — 478 × 750 mm.

[63] [C:] Carta dell Isole di Capo Verde con l'Isole dell'Indie occidentale, et parte della Terra ferma di Guiana La longitudine Comincia da l'Isola di Pico d'Asores. di Affrica Carta.V. — [T:] AF:Lucini Fece. — 480 × 752 mm.

[64] [C:] Carta particolare dell mare Oceano fra la costa di Guinea è la Brasilia. La longitudine Comincia da l'Isola di Pico d'Asores. di Affrica Carta.VI. — [T:] AF:Lucini Fece — 488 × 756 mm.

[65] [C:] Carta particolare che comincia con il fiume Iuntas nella Guinea è finisce con il capo di S:Dara è con l'Isola d'S:Tomaso. La longit.^{ne} Comi.^{ca} da l'Isola d'Pico d'Asores di Affica Carta .VII. — [T:] AF:Lucini Fece. — 470 × 752 mm.
[Inset:] [T:] Isola di.S.Tommaso os. Thome. [and the coast from] C:Formosa [to] C:di Gabon — 203 × 236 mm.

[66] [C:] Carta particolare che comincia con l'Isola di S:Tomaso ò Tome è C:^{c}d S:Clara è finisce con il c:d'Aldeas La longitud.^{ne} Comi.^{ca} da l'Isola di Pico d'Asores d'Affica Carta .VIII — [T:] AF:Lucini Fece. — 482 × 372 mm.

[67] [C:] Carta particolare del mare di Ethiopia con l'Isola di S:Elena è parte della Costa. La longitu.^{ne} Cominca da l'Isola di Pico d'Asores. d'Affrica Carta VIIII. — [T:] AF:Lucini Face. — 491 × 765 mm.

[68] [C:] Carta particolare che comincia con il capo Aldea è Finisce con il capo Degortam. La longitud.^{ne} Comi.^{ca} da l'Isola di Pico d'Asores di Affrica Carta X. — [T:] AF:Lucini Fece. — 482 × 374 mm.

[69] [C:] Carta particolare che comincia con il capo Degortam è con il capo Buona Speranza è finisce in Gradi 2: di latitudine Australe. La longitud.^{ne} Comi.^{ca} da l'Isola di Pico d'Asores. di Affrica Carta XI. — [T:] AF:Lucini Fece. — 473 × 739 mm.

[70] [C:] Carta particolare della parte Australle della Isola S:Lorẽzo con la terra ferma dirinpetto è Finisce con Gradi:6: di latitudine Australe. La longitud.^{ne} Comin:^{a} da l'Isola di Pico d'Asores. di Affrica Carta XII. — [T:] AF:Lucini Fece. — 477 × 761 mm.

[71] [C:] Carta particolare dell mare è Lindie con la parte Tramontana dè l'Isola S:Lorenzo. La longitudine Cominca da l'Isola di Pico d'Asores. di Affrica Carta XIII. — [T:] AF:Lucini Fece. — 478 × 385 mm.

[72] [C:] Carta particolare della parte Tramontana dell Isola di San lorenzo con la costa diripetto sin^o à Monbazza con l'Isole è Seccagne int.^{no} La longitudi.^{ne} Comin.^{ca} da l'Isola di Pico d'Asores. d'Affrica Carta XIIII. — [T:] AF:Lucini Fece. — 468 × 752 mm.

[73] [C:] Carta particolare dell Mare dell Indie con le Secaie è alcqune Isolle. La longitudine Comi.^{ca} da l'Isola di Pico d'Asores d'Affrica Carta.XV. — [T:] AF:Lucini Fece. — 475 × 383 mm.

[74] [C:] Carta particolare che comincia con il capo è l'Isola Mombazza è finisce con il capo Baduis La longitud.^{ne} Comi.^{ca} da l'Isola di Pico d'Asores. d'Affrica Carta XVI. — [T:] AF:Lucini Fece. — 466 × 382 mm.
[Inset:] [T:] [The coast from] C:Tangoua [to] G:di Lama — 166 × 123 mm.

[75] [C:] Carta particolare che cominca con il capo Baduis è finisce con il capo Cumana, è mostra la bocca del mare Rosso. La longitudine Cominca da l'Isola di Pico d'Asores. d'Affrica Carta. XVII. — [T:] AF:Lucini Fece. — 486 × 732 mm.

PARTE TERZA DEL LIBRO SESTO

[76] [C:] Carta particolare che comincia con il capo Dofar in Arabia è finisce con il capo Cintapora nell Indie. La longitudine Cominca da l'Isola di Pico d'Asores. d'Asia Carta Prima — [T:] AF:Lucini Fece. — 486 × 753 mm.

[77] [C:] Questa carta contiene la costa dell'India Orientale con la costa di Coromandell è l'Isola di Zeilan è finisce con la parte Tramont.^{na} di Sumatra. La longitudine Cominca da l'Isola di Pico di Asores. d'Asia Carta. II. — [T:] AF:Lucini Fece. — 487 × 760 mm.

[78] [C:] Carta particolare del mare d'India sino allo stretto di Sunda fra l'Isole di Sumatra è di Iaua magg.^{re} con altre Isolette è scog.^{li} scop.^{to}d'Inglesi La longitudine Cominca da l'Isola di Pico d'Asores. d'Asia Carta III. — [T:] AF:Lucini Fece. — 466 × 756 mm.

[79] [C:] Carta particolare del stretto di Sunda fra l'Isole di Sumatra è Iaua maggre. La longitudine Cominca da l'Isola di Pico d'Asores. d'Asia Carta IIII. — [T:] AF:Lucini Fece. — 471 × 367 mm.

[80] [C:] Carta particolare del'Golfo di Bengala è Pegu che comincia co^n il capo Masulipatan è finisce con la punta Domurco. La longitu.^{ne} Comin:^{a} da l'Isola di Pico d'Asores d'Asia Carta.V. — [T:] AF:Lucini Fece. — 475 × 746 mm.

[81] [C:] Carta particolare della Malacca con la costa sin'al Pegu è Camboia con l'Isole di Sumatra è Burneo parte Tramontana con molte altre Isole è Iso.^{te} Intorõ La longitu.^{ne} Comic.^{a} da l'Isola di Pico d'Asores. d'Asia Carta. VI. — [T:] AF:Lucini Fece. — 480 × 752 mm.

[82] [C:] Carta particolare del mare di Cocincina con la parte Australe della China La longi.^{ne} Comin.^{ca} da l'Isola di Pico d'Asores d'Asia Carta VII. — [T:] AF:Lucini Fece. — 462 × 377 mm.

[83] [C:] Carta particolare del'mare è costa di Manilia. La longitud.^{ne} Comincia da l'Isola di Pico d'Asores d'Asia Carta.VIII. — [T:] AF:Lucini Fece. — 466 × 372 mm.

[84] [C:] Carta particolare dello Stretto di Manilia nel Isole Filippine. La longitu.^{ne} Comin.^{ca} da l'Isola di Pico d'Asores. d'Asia Carta. VIIII. — [T:] AF:Licino Fece. — 480 × 759 mm.

[85] [C:] Carta particolare dell'Isole Fillipine è di Luzon. La longitu.^{ne} Comin.^{ca} da l'Isola di Pico d'Asores. d'Asia Carta.X. — [T:] AF:Lucini Fece. — 484 × 376 mm.

[86] [C:] Carta particolare dell'Isola Mindano parte Australe con Celebes è Gilolo parte Tramontana è con l'Isole di Molucchi è altre Isolette intorõ La longitu.^{ne} Comin.^{a} da l'Isola di Pico d'Asores d'Asia Carta XI. — [T:] AF:Lucini Fece. — 476 × 751 mm.

[87] [C:] Carta particolare dell'Isole di Ladrões con l'Isole di Gilolo è de Molucchi La longitud.^{ne} Comincia da l'Isola di Pico d'Asores. d'Asia Carta XII. — [T:] AF:Lucini Fece. — 471 × 374 mm.

[88] [C:] Carta particolare delle 6 Isole de Molucchi La longitu.^{ne} Comin.^{ca} da l'Isola di Pico d'Asores: d'Asia Carta XIII. — [T:] AF:Lucini Fece. — 475 × 373 mm.

[89] [C:] Carta particolare dell'Isole di Iaua magg.^{re} è minore con la parte Austr.^{le} del Isole di Sumatra è Burneo La longi.^{ne} Comin.^{ca} da l'Isola di Pico d'Asores. d'Asia Carta. XIII — [T:] AF:Lucini Fece. — 475 × 753 mm.

[90] [C:] Carta particolare dell'Isole Celebes è Giliolo parte Austr.^{le} è di Butto, Batuliar, Timor, Seram, Banda,è Amboina è altre Isolet^e La longitudine Comincia da l'Isola di Pico d'Asores. d'Asia Carta.XV. — [T:] AF:Lucini Fece. — 459 × 379 mm.

[91] [C:] Carta particolare d'una parte della co.^{ta} di China con l'Isola di PaKas, è altre Isole, sino alla parte piu Australe del'Giapone, La longitu.^{ne} Comin.^{ca} da l'Isola di Pico d'Asores. D'Asia Carta XVI — [T:] AF:Lucini Fece. — 479 × 768 mm.

[92] [C:] Carta particolare della Grande Isola del Giapone è di Iezo con il Regno di Corai et altre Isole in torno. La longitud.^{ne} Comin.^{ca} da l'Isola di Pico d'Asores d'Asia Carta .XVII. — [T:] AF:Lucini Fece. — 479 × 748 mm.

[93] [C:] Carta particolare della parte Orientale del'Isola di Iezo con li stretto fra America è la detta Isola. La longitu.^{ne}Comincia da l'Isola di Pico d'Asores. d'Asia Carta.XVIII. — [T:] AF:Lucini Fece. — 471 × 748 mm.

[94] [C:] Carta particolare della costa Australe scoperta dall'Olandesi. La longitud.^{ne} Comin.^{ca} da l'Isola di Pico d'Asores d'Asia Carta XVIIII. — [T:] AF:Lucini Fece. — 468 × 378 mm.

[95] [C:] Carta particolare dell'mare è Isole scoperte dal capit.^{no} Iacomo Maier Olandese nel.1617 con parte della nuoua Guinea La longitudine Comincia da L'Isola di Pico d'Asores. D'Asia Carta.XX. — [T:] AF:Lucini Fece. — 471 × 748 mm.

[96] [C:] Isole Scoperte da Iacomo le Maier Olandese nel 1617. La longitudine Comincia da l'Isola di Pico d'Asores. d Asia. Carta XXI — [T:] AF:Lucini Fece. — 460 × 359 mm.

[97] [C:] Isole nel mare di Sur scoperte nel.1617. La longitudine Comincia da l'Isola di Pico d'Asores. d'Asia Carta.XXII. — [T:] AF:Lucini Fece. — 481 × 745 mm.

[98] [C:] Carta particolare del mare del Sur che comincia con l'Isole di Salamone è finisicie con la costa di Lima nel'Peru La longitudine Comincia da l'Isola di Pico di d'Asores.

Asia Carta.XXIII — [T:] AF:Lucini Fece. — 480 × 763 mm.

PARTE QVARTA DEL LIBRO SESTO

[99] [C:] Carta particolare della terra nuoua con la gran Baia et il Fiume grande della Canida. La longitudine Conincia da l'Isola di Pico d'Asores D'America Car.ª prima — [T:] AF:Lucini Fece. — 486 × 741 mm.

[100] [C:] Carta particolare della nuoua Belgia è parte della nuoua Anglia. La longitudine Cominca da l'Isola di Pico d'Asores. D'America carta II — [T:] AF:Lucini Fece. — 471 × 382 mm.

[101] [C:] Carta particolare della Virginia Vecchia è Nuoua. La longitu.ne Comi.ca da l'Isola di Pico di Asores. D'America Carta .III. — [T:] AF:Lucini Fece. — 478 × 378 mm.

[102] [C:] Carta particolare della costa di Florida è di Virginia. La longitudine Cominca da lisola di Pico d'Asores. D'America Carta IIII. — [T:] AF:Lucini Fece. — 475 × 386 mm.

[103] [C:] Carta particolare del'Isola di Cuba è di Iamaica con il Capo della Florida è l'Isola Intorno. La longitu.ne Cominca da l'Isola di Pico d'Asores. D'America Carta.V. — [T:] AF:Lucini Fece. — 481 × 748 mm.

[104] [C:] Carta particolare dell'Isola Ispaniola è S:Gio.ni nel'India ocident.te con l'Isole Intorno La longitudine Cominca da l'Isola di Pico d'Asores. D'America Carta. VI. — [T:] AF:Lucini Fece. — 482 × 758 mm.

[105] [C:] Carta particolare della Baia di Messico con la costa. La longitudine Cominca da l'Isola di Pico d'Asores. D'America Carta.VII — [T:] AF:Lucini Fece. — 474 × 744 mm.

[106] [C:] Carta particolare del'India Occidentale ch.e contiene il Golfo di Veragua, la Baia di Honduras nel'mare del'Noort è parte del'mare di Zur la longitudine Comincia da l'Isola di Pico d'Asores. D'America Carta.VIII. — [T:] AF:Lucini Fece. — 485 × 746 mm.

[107] [C:] Carta particolare del'India occidentale che comincia con il Capo S: Romano nel'mare delNort, è finisce con il' Rio Coquele. La longitudine Cominca da l'Isola di Pico d'Asores. D'America Carta VIIII. — [T:] AF:Lucini Fece. — 475 × 745 mm.

[108] [C:] Carta particolare dell'India Ocidentale, con la terra ferma dal'capo di Paria sin al'capo S:Romano. La longitudine Cominca da l'Isola di Pico d'Asores. D'America Carta.X. — [T:] AF:Lucini Fece. — 484 × 742 mm.

[109] [C:] Carta particolare dell'Isola di Bermuda sin all'India occidentale et al'capo S:Romano della Florida. La longitudine Cominca da l'Isola di Pico d'Asores. D'America Carta.XI. — [T:] AF:Lucini Fece. — 476 × 747 mm.

[110] [C:] Carta particolare del'mare Occeano dal'Isole d'Asores di Flores, e Coruo Sin alla terra nuoua in America. La longitu.ne Comin.ca da l'isola di Pico d'Asores. D'America Carta.XII. — [T:] AF:Lucini Fece. — 479 × 376 mm.

[111] [C:] AL SER.MO FERDINANDO.II. GRANDVCA DI TOSCANA SVO SIGNORE Don Roberto Dudleo Duca di Northumbria. XIII. d'Ameri.ª — [T:] AF.L.F — 468 × 734 mm.

[112] [C:] ALLA SER.MA SIG.RA PRINCIP.SA D'VRBINO GRANDVCHESSA DI TOSCANA SVA SIG.RA D: Roberto Dvdleo Dvca di Northumbria XIIII. d'America. — AF.LF. 477 × 741 mm.

[113] [C:] Carta particolare dell'Ri.o d'Amazone con la costa sin al' fiume Maranhan. La longitu.ne Comin.ca da l'Isola di Pico d'Asores. D'America Carta. XVI. — [T:] AF:Lucini Fece. — 370 × 480 mm.

[114] [C:] Carta particolare della Brasilia Settentrionale. La longitudi.ne Comincia da l'Isola di Pico d'Asores. D'America Carta.XVI — [T:] AF:Lucini Fece. — 482 × 750 mm.

[115] [C:] Carta particolare della Brasilia, che comincia con il capo S:Antonio et finisce con il Porto del'Spirito Sancto. La longitu.ne Comin.ª da l'Isola di Pico d'Asores. D'America Carta.XVII. — [T:] AF:Lucini Fece. — 483 × 749 mm.

[116] [C:] Carta particolare che mostra il Capo buona Speranza con il mare uerso Pon.te è con lisole di Tristan d'Acunha è di Mart.n Vaz La longitudine Comincia da l'Isola di Pico d'Aasores. D'America Carta.XVIII. — [T:] AF:Lucini Fece. — 482 × 752 mm.

[117] [C:] Carta particolare della Brasilia Australe che comincia dal'Por.to: del'Spir.to Santo è finisce con il capo Bianco. La longitudi.e Cominc.ª da l'Isola di Pico d'Asores. D'America Carta. XVIIII — [T:] AF:Lucini Fece. — 470 × 374 mm.

[118] [C:] Carta particolare dell'Rio della Plata che comincia con la costa in Gradi.31. di lati.ne Australe, è Finisce con il capo S:Andrea. La longitu.ne Comi.ca da l'Isola di Pico d'Asores. D'America Carta.XX. — [T:] AF:Lucini Fece. — 478 × 739 mm.

[119] [C:] Carta particolare che comincia con il capo S:Andrea è finiscie con il capo Matas d'America. La longitudine Comincia da l'Isola di Pico d'Asores. D'America Carta XXI. — [T:] AF:Lucini Fece. — 482 × 365 mm.

[120] [C:] Carta particolare della costa di America Australe che comincia al C:di Matas sin al C:di Galegos. La longitu.ne Cominc.ª da l'Isola di Pico d'Asores D'America ca.ta XXII — [T:] AF:Lucini Fece. — 474 × 378 mm.

[121] [C:] Carta particolare dello Stretto di Magellano è di Maire. La longitudine Comincia da l'Isola di Pico d'Asores. D'America Carta.XXIII. — [T:] AF:Lucini Fece. — 482 × 749 mm.

[122] [C:] Carta particolare della costa di Chilue è di Chica è parte Australe di Cili. La longitudine Comincia da l'Isola di Pico d'Asores. D'America Carta.XXIIII — [T:] AF:Lucini Fece. — 473 × 371 mm.

[123] [C:] Carta particolare della costa di Cili. La longitudine Comincia da l'Isola di Pico d'Asores. D'America Carta.XXV. — [T:] AF:Lucini Fece. — 476 × 366 mm.

[124] [C:] Carta particolare della costa del'Peru parte Australe con parte di Cili. La longitud.ne Cominc.sa l'Isola di Pico d'Asores. D'America carta. XXVI. — [T:] AF:Lucini Fece. — 474 × 365 mm.

[125] [C:] Carta particolare del'Peru che comincia con il' rio Pigua è finisce con il' capo di Guanapo La longitudine Comincia da l'Isola di Pico d'Asores. D'America. Carta.XXVII. — [T:] AF:Lucini Fece. — 478 × 379 mm.

[126] [C:] Carta particolare del'Peru che comincia con il'capo di Guanapo è finisce con il' C:S:Francesco La longitudine Comincia da l'Isola di Pico d'Asores. D'America Carta. XXVIII — [T:] AF:Lucini Fece. — 481 × 750 mm.

[127] [C:] Carta particolare del mare del'Zur che comincia con il' capo S:Francesco nel'Peru è finisce con il'capo S:Lazaro nella nuoua Spagnia. La longitu.ne Comi.ca da l'Isola di Pico d'Asores. D'America Carta. XXVIIII — [T:] AF:Lucini Fece. — 486 × 749 mm.

[128] [C:] Carta particolare dell'mare del'Zur che comincia con il capo Lucar è finisce con Cagidos nella nuoua Spagnia, è la Baia di Honduras La longitu.ne Comin.ca da l'Isola di Pico d'Asores. Di America Carta XXX. — [T:] AF:Lucini Fece . — 478 × 749 mm.

[129] [C:] Carta particolare della parte ocidentale della nuoua Spagnia, è della California. La longitudine Comincia da l'Isola di Pico d'Asores. D'America Carta XXXI — [T:] AF:Lucini Fece. — 482 × 756 mm.

[130] [C:] Carta particolare della America è parte maestrale dal C:di Cedros. La longitudine Comincia da l'Isola di Pico d'Asores. D'America Carta XXXII. — [T:] AF:Lucini Fece. — 473 × 758 mm.

[131] [C:] Carta particolare dello stretto di Iezo fra l'America è l'Isola Iezo. La longitudine Comincia da l'Isola di Pico d'Asores D'America carta XXXIII — [T:] AF:Lucini Fece — 480 × 383 mm.

Notes: All the maps are blank on the back and uncoloured. The three volumes are divided into six books, two to a volume: books one, three, four and five contain no maps. The sixth book is divided into four parts. Following the general title-page in the first book, our copy contains a facsimile of the patent from Ferdinand II, grand duke of Tuscany, confirming Dudley in the title Duke of Northumberland.

The order of the maps in book two does not follow the numbering on the maps themselves, but is the same as that in the copy in the Library of Congress. The first plate of the fourth book, in vol. 2, is wanting. The List of Atlases in the Library of Congress (vol. 1, pp. 203—216) describes the atlas in great detail; our copy corresponds more closely with the Grenville copy in the British Library, mentioned in a note on p. 204 of the Library of Congress List. All the maps and plates are engraved by Antonio Francesco Lucini. (See Library of Congress, vol. 1, p. 207, and C. Broekema, Sir Robert Dudley, Arcano del Mare.) The three volumes are bound in old worn leather, with gold coats-of-arms on front and back covers. All three volumes have the bookplates of the Right Honble Constantine John Baron Mulgrave and of Nordenskiöld. Nordenskiöld's signature is in the Parte prima del tome terzo.

Lit.: BM Maps, vol. 5, c. 164, Broekema, C., Sir Robert Dudley, [1976], Hale, Dudley, List, vol. 1, p. 203—216, Nat. Mar. Mus., vol. 3, p. 386—387, 323, Nederl. Hist. Schneepsv. Museum, Catalogus d. Bibl., vol. 1, p. 46.

71   DU PINET, ANTOINE   1564

PLANTZ, POVRTRAITZ ET DESCRIPTIONS DE PLVSIEVRS VILLES ET FORTERESSES, TANT DE L'EVROPE, Asie, & Afrique, que des Indes, & terres neuues: Leurs fondations, antiquitez, & manieres de viure: Auec plusieurs Cartes generales & particulieres, seruans à la Cosmographie, iointes à leurs declarations: Deux tables fort amples, l'vne des chapitres, & l'autre des matieres contenuës en ce present liure. Le tout mis par ordre, Region par Region, par ANTOINE du PINET. A LYON, PAR IAN D'OGEROLLES, M. D. LXIIII.   33, 4 cm.

- [1] Carte Cosmographicque, ou vniuerselle description du Monde, auecq les Ventz selon leur propre nature & operation figurés. (Map). On 6—7   a4   190 × 275 mm.
- [2] La Carte & description d'Europe. (Map).   10—11   251 × 334 mm.
- [3] Description de Gaule. (Map). On 13   b   119 × 155 mm.
- [4] [C:] PARIS. — [C:] Iean d'Ogerolles. — (Plan). 22—23. 255 × 325 mm.
- [5] LA VILLE DE LYON, SON PLANT, SES FORteresses, & les principaux bastimend d'icelle.
  [C:] LYON. — [C:] Iean d'Ogerolles. — (View). 28—29. 252 × 320 mm.
- [6] Le vif pourtrait de la Cité de Bourdeaux.
  [C:] BOVRDEAVX — [C:] A LYON, Par Iean d'Ogerolles. 1563, — (Plan). 38—39   d4   259 × 294 mm.
- [7] PLANT ET MODENE DE L'ILLVSTRE ET antique Cité de Geneue.
  [C:] GENEVE. — [C:] Geneue Cité situee en terrouer fecund au pays Sauoye, iouxte l'yssue du Rosne, separant ses Ondes du Lac de Losane. — [C:] Iean d'Ogerolles. — (View). 50—51.   252 × 321 mm.
- [8] La Ville de Parpignan. (View). On 56   123 × 157 mm.
- [9] Pouctraict & description de Thionuille.
  [C:] THIONVILLE. — (View). On 61   f3   95 × 123 mm.
- [10] Des Isles d'Angleterre & d'Escosse, & de celle d'Irlandt. (Map). On 67   84 × 135 mm.
- [11] [C:] Limites & description du païs de Germanie. — (Map). 74 — 75   g4   297 × 390 mm.
- [12] La magniffique & puissante Cité de Berne. (View). On 79   101 × 157 mm.
- [13] Le vif pourtrait de la Cité de Treues. (View). 86—87   h4   237 × 331 mm.
- [14] Le vif pourtrait de la noble & Imperiale Cité de Franckfort.
  [C:] FRANCKFORT. — [C:] Iean d'Ogerolles. — (View). 96—97   i3   255 × 320 mm.
- [15] MONTPELLIER, Cité & Vniuersité, tenuë auiourd'huy pour premiere en la faculté de Medecine. (View). 104—105   k3   169 × 308 mm.
- [16] LA VILLE DE POYTIERS. (View). 112—113   l 3   245 × 398 mm.
- [17] Le vif pourtrait de la noble ville & Cité de Tours.
  [C:] TOVRS. — [C:] LA VILE DE TOVRS. — [C:] Iean d'Ogerolles. — (View). 120—121   m3   256 × 334 mm.
- [18] Carte d'Italie. (Map). On 126   158 × 128 mm.
- [19] POVRTRAIT DE LA SVPERBE CITE DE GENNES. (View). 128—129   n3   203 × 411 mm.
- [20] Le vif pourtrait de la noble ville & Cité de Parme.
  [C:] PARME. — [C:] PARMIA — [C:] La ville de Parme, representant par vraye figure sa situation, auec l'ordonnance de l'armee Papistique & Imperiale, mise deuant la ville, deffendue par les François. — [C:] Iean d'Ogerolles. — (View). 136—137   o3   254 × 323 mm.
- [21] POVRTRAIT ET DESCRIPTION DE PAVIE. (View). On 141   p   68 × 122 mm.
- [22] Description de la forteville de la Mirandole.
  [C:] MIRANDOLE. — [C:] LA MIRANDOLA — [C:] La ville de la Mirandole, representant à l'entour lassiegement de l'armee Papistique & Imperialle, contre les François, & ceux de ladite ville. — [C:] Iean d'Ogerolles. — (View). 142—143   p3   256 × 325 mm.
- [23] Description de la Cité de Florence.
  [C:] FLORENCE. — [C:] LA FIGVRE DE LA VILLE DE FLORENCE. — [C:] Iean d'Ogerolles. — (View). 160—161   r 3   252 × 321 mm.
- [24] Pourtrait de la magnifique Cité de Venise.
  [C:] VENISE. — [C:] Iean d'Ogerolles. — (View). 168—169   s3   262 × 327 mm.
- [25] Description de la Cité de Romme.
  [C:] ROMME. — [T:] Iean d'Ogerolles. — (View). 176—177   t3   260 × 325 mm.
- [26] Tyoli Ville fort ancienne, d'ou le Teuerone fort, & edifiee 300. ans auant Rome.
  [C:] TIOLI — (View). On 183   v2   125 × 157 mm.
- [27] Carte du Royaume de Naples.
  [C:] Regnū Neapolit. Mare mediterraneum — (Map). On 185   v3   154 × 129 mm.
- [28] La Cité Royale de Naples.
  [C:] NAPLES — [C:] Napoli — [C:] Iean d'Ogerolles. — (View). 186—187   v3   252 × 322 mm.
- [29] Carte & description du Royaume de Sicile. (Map). On 205   y   157 × 126 mm.
- [30] Carte & description de Sardaigne.
  [C:] SARDINIA INSVLA — On 213   157 × 127 mm.
- [31] PLANT DE LA PVISSANTE ET RENOMMEE CITE DE CALARIS VILLE CAPITALE DE L'ISLE DE SARDAIGNE.
  [C:] CALARIS SARDINIÆ CAPVT — (Plan). On 216   127 × 158 mm.
- [32] Carte & description du pays & Empire de Grece. (Map). On 225   z3   156 × 126 mm.
- [33] PLANT ET MODENE DE L'ILLVSTRE ET Imperiale Cité de Constantinoble.
  L'Illustre & Imperialle Cité de Constantinoble.
  [C:] CONSTANTINOBLE. — [C:] Iean d'Ogerolles. — (Plan). 246—247   B4   258 × 325 mm.
- [34] Pourtrait & description de l'antique & Illustre Cité de Ierusalem, iadis chef du Royaume de Iudee, & maintenant tenuë par les Turcz.
  [T:] Jerusalem — [T:] C̄ — (View). 252—253   C3   155 × 378 mm.
- [35] DV GRAND CAIRE ET DE LA MANIERE DE VIVRE DES HABITANS DICELVY.   (View). On 275   E4   65 × 112 mm.
- [36] DE LA FORTE ET IMPRENABLE CITE D'ALGER.
  [T:] argier — (View). On 289   G   145 × 180 mm.
- [37] Plant & Pourtraict de l'Illustre Cité de Cusco, ville Capitale du Royaume de Peru.
  [C:] IL CVSCHO CITTA PRINCIPALE DELLA PROVINCIA DEL PERV — (Plan). 292—293   G3   272 × 376 mm.
- [38] POVRTRAIT ET DESCRIPTION DE LA GRANDE CITE DE TEMIstitan, ou, Tenuctutlan, ou selon aucuns Messico, ou, Mexico, ville capitale de la Nueua Espaigne.   (Plan). On 297   H   163 × 161 mm.

Notes: All the maps have text on the verso, and are uncoloured.

No. [27] has part of a view on the verso. Some of the pages are wrongly numbered: map [1] has the page-numbers 6 and 7, but the pages on the back are numbered XVII and XX, and map [2] has the page-numbers 10 and 11 with 5 and 8 on the back, pp. 10 and 11 occur again in the correct place. Map [1] is the world map by Gemma Frisius, and map [2] is Münster's map of Europe, first printed in his edition of Ptolemy, Basiliae 1540. Many of the other maps are also by Münster, and appear in different editions of his Cosmographia, sometimes with minor differences. According to Bartsch (vol. 9, p. 207—208, no. 53) the initial Ċ on the map of Jerusalem, [34], stands for an unidentified engraver. Antoine du Pinet is not mentioned by Bagrow or by Bonacker, but Lister refers to him as a French cartographer and Tooley is familiar with the man and his work, stating that his views were later used by Braun and Hogenberg. The Nouvelle Biographie générale states that he was born in Besançon or Baume-les-Dames, and died in Paris in 1565 or 1566. He published many other works besides the one described here. Our copy is bound in old vellum. On the title-page is a stamp with the words 'BIBLIOTHÈQUE DU ROI PALAIS ROYAL'. On the inside of the front cover is a note in ink: 'Af Louis-Philips Bibliothek 1852', and Nordenskiöld's signature with the year 1894. A card, bearing the words 'Comte d'Eu. 28 ocbre 1736' in old ink, has been pasted in. On the inside of the back cover Nordenskiöld has written 'Köpt i Kjobenhavn Jan. 1894. 20 kr.' and 'Obs. ! p. 3 Les meilleurs Chartes Geographiques du jourd'huy. p. 13 Högtrafvande inledning.' [= bombastic introduction.]

Lit.: BM Maps, vol. 5, c. 212, Lister p. 160, Nouv. biogr. gén, vol. 15, c. 327—328, Tooley, Dictionary p. 125.

72 FER, NICOLAS DE 1725

L'ATLAS CURIEUX OU LE MONDE RÉPRÉSENTÉ DANS DES CARTES GENERALES ET PARTICULIERES DU CIEL ET DE LA TERRE DIVISÉ TANT EN SES QUATRE PRINCIPALES PARTIES QUE PAR ETATS ET PROVINCES ET ORNÉ Par des Plans et Descriptions des Villes Capitales et Principales et des plus Superbes Edifices qui les Embelisent, Comme sont les Eglises, les Palais, les Maisons de Plaisance, les Iardins, les Fontaines &c. Par de Fer. A PARIS, Chez I.F.Benar Gendre de l'Auteur ... 1725. Tome Ier.   28,5 cm. obl.

Vol. I

[1] [C:] PLANISPHERES GELESTE. Par Mr de la Hire, Professeur Royal et de l'Academie des Siences. Mis au jour par N. de Fer. ... — [C:] A PARIS, Chez le Sr de Fer. ... 1705. H.Van Loon fecit. — 4. 227 × 329 mm.
[Insets:] [T:] Soleil, Selon le P.Kircher. — [T:] La Lune, Selon Mr Cassini. — 2 circular maps with 48 mm. diam. [T:] Mars, Selon Mr Cassini. — [T:] Mercure. — [T:] Venus, Selon Mr Cassini. — [T:] Saturne, Selon Mr Cassini. — 4 circular maps with 21 mm. diam.

[2] [T:] MAPPE-MONDE OU CARTE GENERALE DE LA TERRE, Dressée Sur les Observations de M^{rs} de l'Academie Royale des Sciences. Par N. de Fer. ... A PARIS Chez l'Auteur, ... 1717. — 6. 224 × 335 mm.

[3] [C:] MAPPE-MONDE ou CARTE UNIVERSEL^{LE} Par N. de Fer ... — [C:] A PARIS Chez l'Auteur ... 1714. — [T:] C.Inselin Sculps. — 7. 225 × 336 mm.

[4] [C:] L'EUROPE Suivant les Nouvelles Observations de M^{rs} de l'Academie Royale des Sciences Par N. de Fer. ... A PARIS Chez l'Autheur ... 1717. — [C:] Dediée A NOSSEIGNEURS LES ENFANS DE FRANCE, Par ... de Fer. — 8. 223 × 329 mm.

[5] [C:] L'ASIE Suivant les Nouvelles Decouvertes dont les Point Principaux Sont Placez Sur les Observations de M^{rs} de l'Academie Royale des Sciences. Par N. de Fer. ... 1717. — [C:] Dediée A NOSSEIGNEURS Les Enfans de France. Par ... de Fer.... — 9. 228 × 318 mm.

[6] [C:] L'AFRIQUE Dressée Selon les dernieres Relat. et Suivant les Nouvelles decouvertes dont les Points Principaux Sont placez Sur Observations de M^{rs} de l'Academie Royale des Sciences. Par N. de Fer. A PARIS Chez l'Auteur ... 1717. ... — [C:] Dediée A NOSSEIGNEURS Les Enfans de France. Par ... de Fer. — 10. 224 × 312 mm.

[7] [C:] L'AMERIQUE, MERIDIONALE ET SEPTENTRIONALE Dressée selon les dernieres Relations et suivant les Nouvelles Decouvertes dont les points principaux sont placez sur les Observations de M^{rs} de l'Academie Royale des Sciences. Par N. de Fer. — [T:] A PARIS, Chez l'Autheur ... 1717. — [C:] C. Inselin Scripsit. ... — [C:] Dressée et Dediée A NOSSEIGNEURS ENFANS DE FRANCE. Par ... de Fer. ... — 11. 222 × 331 mm.

[8] [C:] LA FRANCE Ses Conquêtes, Ses Acquisitions & ses Bornes Par les derniers Traitez et dont les Points principaux Sont posés Suivant les Observat. de M^{rs} de l'Academie Royale des Sciences. par N. de Fer. — [T:] Inselin sculp. — [C:] Dediée A NOSSEIGNEURS LES ENFANS DE FRANCE. Par ... de Fer. ... A Paris Chez l'Autheur ... 1705. — 12. 219 × 316 mm.

[9] [C:] DESCRIPTION DE LA FRANCE Par rapport au Regne de Clovis et de ses Enfans ... — [T:] Gravé par Berey — 13. 202 × 287 mm.

[10] [C:] ENVIRONS DE PARIS Par N. de Fer. 1705. — [T:] P.Starck-man sc. — 14. 243 × 344 mm.

[11] [C:] LUTECE OU PREMIER PLAN DE LA VILLE DE PARIS Tiré De Cesar, de Strabon de l'Empere^{ur} Iulien, et d'Ammian Marcelin. — [C:] A PARIS Chez le Sr Danet gendre l'Auteur ... 1724. — 15. 216 × 274 mm.

[12] [C:] LUTECE Conquise par les François Sur les Romains, ou SECOND PLAN DE LA VILLE DE PARIS Tiré Du Misopogene de l'Empereur Iulien, d'Amian Marcelin, ... du Temple et des Vestiges de cette Ancienne Enceinte qui subsiste encor aujourd'huy ou que l'on a vu de nos jours. ... — [C:] A PARIS Chez le Sr Danet gendre de l'Auteur ... 1724. A.C. — (Plan). 16. 213 × 318 mm.

[13] [C:] TROISIEME PLAN DE LA VILLE DE PARIS Son étendue et les Bourgs dont elle étoit environée sous le Regne de LOUIS LE JEUNE VII. du nom Tiré Des Descriptions de Fortunat et de Gregoire de Tours, ... — [C:] A PARIS Chez le Sr Danet gendre de l'Auteur ... 1724. — [T:] A.C. — (Plan). 17. 212 × 320 mm.

[14] [C:] QUATRIEME PLAN DE LA VILLE DE PARIS Son Accroissement et l'etat ou elle étoit sous le Regne de PHILIPPE AUGUSTE, qui mourut l'an 1223. apres avoir regne 43. ans. TIRÉ de Rigord, de Knobelsderf, ... — [C:] A PARIS. Chez le Sr Danet gendre de l'Auteur ... 1724. — [T:] A.C. — (Plan). 18. 210 × 320 mm.

[15] [C:] CINQUIEME PLAN DE LA VILLE DE PARIS son accroissement, et sa Quatrième cloture Commancée sous CHARLES V. l'an 1367. et finie sous CHARLES VI. l'an

1383. Tiré, Des Devis et Marchez fait avec les Ouvriers, Des Procez Verbaux de Toisez et Reception des Ouvrages, des comptes rendus par ceux qui en eurent la conduite, De la Chronique de M. S.de St Denis et d'autres Titres et Manuscrits qui sont conservés en la Chambre des Comptes et dans les Bibliotheques — [C:] A PARIS Chez le Sr de Fer ... 1714. A.C. — (Plan). Uncoloured. 215 × 323 mm.

[16] [C:] SIXIEME PLAN DE LA VILLE DE PARIS Et Ses Accroissements, depuis le Commencement du Regne de CHARLES VII. l'an 1422. jusqu'a la fin du Regne d'HENRY III. l'an 1589. Tiré des lettres Patentes qui ont ordonné les Ouvrages, des Contrats passez avec les Entrepreneurs, des Registres de la Chambre des Comptes, de l'Histoire et des Memoires du tems. — [C:] A PARIS Chez le Sr Danet gendre de l'Auteur ... 1724. — [T:] A.C. — (Plan). 20. Uncoloured. 213 × 321 mm.

[17] [C:] SEPTIEME PLAN DE LA VILLE DE PARIS Son Accroissement et ses Embelissemens sous HENRY IV. et LOUIS XIII. depuis 1589. jusques en 1643. Tiré des Lettres Patentes ou Arrest du Conseil qui ont ordonné les Ouvrages, des Devis et Marchez faits avec les Entrepreneurs, et levé sur lieux oujls ont été construits, et ou la plus grande partie Subsistent encore. — [C:] A PARIS Chez le Sr Danet gendre de l'Auteur ... 1724. A.C. — (Plan). 21. Uncoloured. 212 × 317 mm.

[18] [C:] LA PLAN DE LA VILLE, CITÉ, ET UNIVERSITÉ DE PARIS. Capitale du Royaume de France. ... Suivant les Dérnieres Observations de M^{rs} de l'Acedemie Royale des Sciences. Par N de Fer. — [T:] H.van Loon sculp. — (Plan). 22. Uncoloured. 221 × 332 mm.

[19] [C:] PLAN DE LA CONDUITE DES EAÜES DES FONTAINES PUBLIQUES DE LA VILLE DE PARIS Par de Fer. 1716. — [C:] ... A PARIS. Chez de Fer ... 1716. — 41. Uncoloured. 222 × 318 mm.

[20] [C:] LE BOIS DE BOULOGNE. Prés Paris. ... Par N. de Fer. .. 1705. — 52 Uncoloured. 233 × 323 mm.

[21] [C:] PARC, IARDINS, CHATEAU, ET BOURG DE MEUDON Pres et au dessous de PARIS. Presentement A MONSEIGNEUR LE DAUPHIN. Presenté a Monseigneur, par son tres humble Serviteur et Geographe, de Fer. 1708. — [T:] A Paris chez G.Danet gendre de l'auteur ... — 53. Uncoloured. 450 × 489 mm.
[Inset:] [T:] Veüe du Chateau de MEUDON, du Côté de l'Entrée. — (View). 96 × 120 mm.

[22] [C:] PLAN GENERAL DES CHATEAUX ET VILLE DE S.^{T} GERMAIN EN LAYE. A Paris Chez le Sr de Fer ... 1705. ... — [T:] H.van Loon fecit — (Plan). 54. Uncoloured. 228 × 335 mm.

[23] [C:] PLAN DE LA FOREST DE LAYE, et de la Garenne du Vezinet, DU BOURG DE S.^{T} GERMAIN dit en Laye, DE LA VILLE DE POISSY et de tout ce qui est contenu dans cet Ance que forme la Riviere de Seine Par N. de Fer. ... — [C:] ... A PARIS A Paris chez G. Danet gendre de l'auteur ... — [T:] A.Coquart. scul. — 57. Uncoloured. 468 × 422 mm.

[24] [C:] PLAN GENERAL DE LA MACHINE DE MARLY ET DE SES ENVIRONS. Par de Fer. 1716. A PARIS ... — 69. Uncoloured. 218 × 315 mm.

[25] [C:] PLAN GENERAL DE MARLY. ... — [C:] a Paris chez G.Danet gendre de l'auteur ... — [T:] H.van Loon sculp. — (Plan). 71. Uncoloured. 384 × 283 mm.

[26] [C:] PLAN GENERAL DE CHANTILLY, Apartenant à S.A.MGR LE PRINCE DE CONDÉ, Son Bourg, Ses Jardins, Fontaines, Bosquets et Canaux, Situés à 8. lieües de Paris, entre Senlis et la Riviere d'Oyse. A Paris chez Sr de Fer ... 1705. [T:] A.Coquart Sculp.^{S} et Scrip.^{S} — (Plan). 75. Uncoloured. 241 × 337 mm.

[27] [C:] PLAN GÉNÉRAL DU PARC ET DU CHĀU DE LESTANG, ou est celuy de LA MARCHE, et de VILLENEUVE, apartenans á Monseig.^{r} de Chamillart. Mis au Jour par N. de Fer. — A.Coquart Sculpsit (Plan). 76. Uncoloured. 245 × 341 mm.

[28] [C:] BOURG, CHATEAU, ET IARDINS DE FONTAINE-BLEAU Situez au Midy et a 14. Lieues de Paris, au milieu de la Forest de Biere ditte aujourdhuy de Fontaine-Bleau Mis au jour par N. de Fer ... — [T:] A Parie chez G.Danet gendre de l'auteur ... — [T:] Gravé par C.Inselin. — (Plan). 77. Uncoloured. 406 × 319 mm.

[29] [C:] FOREST DE BIERE OU DE FONTAINE-BLEAU. ... Mis au Jour Par de Fer ... 1705. — [T:] A Paris chez G.Danet gendre de l'auteur ... — [T:] C.Inselin Sculps. — 78. Uncoloured. 425 × 422 mm.

[30] [C:] LES GOUVERNEMENTS GENERAUX DE L'ISLE DE FRANCE et DE CHAMPAGNE, ou se Trouvent LES GENERALITEZ DE PARIS ET DE CHAALONS. Par N. de Fer. .., A PARIS Chez l'Auteur ... 1705. — [T:] P.Starck-man Sculps. — 79. 245 × 355 mm.

[31] [C:] GOUVERNEMENT GENERAL DE PICARDIE, et Partie de celuy de l'Isle de France ou se trouve LES GENERALITEZ D'AMIENS ET DE SOISSONS. Par N. de Fer — [C:] A Paris Chez l'Auteur ... 1705 — [T:] P. Starck-man sculs. — 80. 245 × 352 mm.

[32] [C:] PLAN DE LA VILLE ET CITADELLE D'AMIENS Par de Fer. A Paris, ... 1716. — (Plan). 81. Uncoloured. 220 × 320 mm.

[33] [C:] GOUVERNEMENT GENERAL DE NORMANDIE Subdivisé en Ses Trois Generalitez De Roüen De Caen et D'Alençon Par N. de Fer ... — [C:] A PARIS chez l'Autheur ... — 82. 242 × 344 mm.

[34] [C:] PLAN DE LA VILLE ET DU CHATEAU DE CAËN en Normandie Mis aujour Par N. de Fer ... 1718. — [T:] P. Starck-man sculp. — (Plan). 83. 240 × 338 mm.

[35] [C:] Isle, Rocher, Ville, château et Abbaye du MONT S.^{T} MICHEL Situé aux confins de Normandie et de Bretagne. ... Par N. de Fer. Sur les Memoires de Mr de la Salle APARIS ... 1705. — A.Coquart F. 84. Uncoloured. 247 × 334 mm.

[36] [C:] PLAN DU MONT S.^{T} MICHEL Par N. de Fer. A PARIS. — (Plan). 85. Uncoloured. 222 × 320 mm.

[37] [C:] GOUVERNEMENT GENERAL DE BRETAGNE ou se trouve LA GENERALITÉ DE NANTES. Par N de Fer. ... A Paris Chez l'Auteur ... 1705. P. Starck-man Scs. — 86. 240 × 351 mm.

[38] [C:] PLAN DE NANTES Par de Fer 1716. — (Plan). 87. Uncoloured. 221 × 318 mm.

[39] [C:] LES PROVINCES, OU GOUVERNEMENTS, DE POICTOU, D'ANJOU, DU MAINE, DE TOURAINE, DE BERRI, DE BOURBONNOIS, DE NIVERNOIS, ET D'ORLEANS. ou se Trouvent LES GENERALITEZ DE POICTIERS. DE TOURS, DE BOURGES, et D'ORLEANS et Grande Partie de celle DE MOULINS. Par N. de Fer. ... A PARIS, Chez l'Auteur ... 1705. — 88. 240 × 334 mm.

[40] [C:] GENERALITEZ DE TOURS, ET D'ORLEANS et Grande Partie de celle de BOURGES. ou se trouvent LE MAINE, L'ANJOU et LA TOURAINE, L'ORLEANOIS, LE VENDOMOIS, LE PERCHE, LA BEAUCE, LE GASTINOIS, LE BLAISOIS, ET LE BERRI. Par N. de Fer. ... A Paris Chez l'Auteur ... 1705 — [T:] P. Starck-man Sculs. — 89 244 × 349 mm.

[41] [C:] PLAN DE LA VILLE D'ORLEANS A Paris Chez le Sr de Fer ... 1705 — (Plan). 90 Uncoloured. 241 × 337 mm.

[42] [C:] Les Jonctions des deux Grandes Rivieres de Loire et de Seine par le NOUVEAU CANAL D'ORLEANS et Celuy de BRIARE. PAR N. DE FER ... A Paris ... 1716. — P. Starck-man Sculpsit 91. 216 × 317 mm.

[43] [C:] PLAN DE LA VILLE ET DES FAUXBOURGS DE BOURGES Capitale de la Province de Berri Mis au jour par N. de Fer ... 1705 — (Plan). 92. Uncoloured. 228 × 332 mm.

[44] [C:] LES ENVIRONS DE LA ROCHELLE ET DE L'ISLE DE RÉ. Par N. de Fer ... A PARIS Chez l'Auteur ... 1715. — 93. 223 × 324 mm.

[45] [T:] LES GENERALITEZ DE BOURDEAUX, DE LA ROCHELLE, ET DE LIMOGES. Composez des Provinces D'AUNIS, DE SAINTONGES, D'ANGOUMOIS, DE LA MARCHE, DU LIMOSIN, DU PERIGORD, AGENOIS, BAZADOIS, GUIENNE, LES LANDES, COMDOMOIS, VRAYE GASCOGNE, ET LES PAYS DE SOULE ET DE

LABOUR, avec Le Gouvernement de la Basse Navarre et de Bearn. Par N. de FER ... A PARIS Chez l'Auteur ... — 96. 362 × 253 mm.

[46] [C:] GOUVERNEMENT GENERAL DE LANGUEDOC et Partie de celuy DE GUIENNE et GASCOGNE, ou se trouvent LES GENERALITEZ DE TOULOUSE DE MONPELIER, ET DE MONTAUBAN. Par N. de Fer. — [C:] ...A Paris Chez l'Auteur ... 1705. — [T:] P. Starck-man Scus. — 99   234 × 339 mm.

[47] [C:] LE CANAL ROYAL DE LANGUEDOC, Pour la Jonction des deux Mers, Ocean et Mediterranée. Par N. de Fer. — [T:] A PARIS Chez le S.r de Fer ... 1716. — [T:] P. Starck-man Sculp. — 101. Uncoloured.   224 × 324 mm. [Inset:] [C:] CARTE DE LA RIVIERE DORB Dans la quelle passe le Canal, et ou sont les Pilots, Digues et Chaussées pour Soutenir et Conduire les Eaux qui Servent au d. Canal. — 53 × 170 mm. (Irregular).

[48] [C:] GOUVERNEMENT DE PROVENCE, GENERALITÉ D'AIX. Par N. de Fer. ... — [C:] ... A Paris chez l'Auteur ... 1705. — 102   228 × 341 mm.'

[49] [C:] MARSEILLE Ville considerable de Provence fameux Port sur Mer Mediterranée Par N. de Fer. — [C:] A Paris Chez lAuteur ... 1705. — 103. Uncoloured.   228 × 304 mm.

[50] [C:] LES ENVIRONS DE MARSEILLE et de son Territoire Dressé sur les Lieux Par le C. de S. Et mis au jour par N. de Fer ... A Paris ... 1708. ... — 104.   234 × 339 mm.

[51] [C:] GOUVERNEMENT DE DAUPHINÉ, GENERALITÉ DE GRENOBLE. Par N. de Fer. ... a Paris chez l'Auteur ... 1705. — [T:] P. Starck-man Scs. — 105. 223 × 339 mm.

[52] [C:] GOUVERNEMENT GENERAL DU LIONNOIS GENERALITEZ DE LION ET DE RIOM ou se trouve LES PROVINCES D AUVERGNE LIONNOIS FOREZ ET BFAUJOLOIS Par N. de Fer. ... — 106.   233 × 353 mm.

[53] [C:] LION Ville tres Considerable du Royaume de france Située au conflans du Rosne et de la Saone ... A Paris Chez le S.r de Fer ... 1705. — 107. Uncoloured.   222 × 336 mm.

[54] [C:] SOUVERAINETÉ DE NEUCHATEL ET DE VALLANGIN. Dediée A Monseigneur le Prince de CONTI Par Son tres humble et tres Obeissant Serviteur de Fer. — [T:] APARIS Chez le S.r de Fer ... 1705. C. Inselin Sculps. — 108   226 × 336 mm.

[55] [C:] LES DEUX BOURGOGNES DUCHÉ ET COMTÉ. GENERALITÉ DE DIJON. La Bresse et la Principauté de Dombes. Par N. de Fer. ... A PARIS Chez l'Auteur ... 1705. — 109   251 × 350 mm.

[56] [C:] PLAN de l'Ancienne et Nouvelle Ville de DIJON — [C:] A PARIS Chez le S.r de Fer ... 1705. — (Plan). 110. Uncoloured.   237 × 338 mm.

[57] [C:] HAUTE ET BASSE ALSACE, SUNTGOU, BRISGOU, ET ORTENOU. Par N de Fer. — [T:] P. Starck-man Sculs. — 111.   357 × 238 mm.

[58] [T:] LES ENVIRONS DES DEUX BRISACHS. Par N. de Fer, ... — [C:] C. Inselin Sculpsit — 112. Uncoloured. 232 × 335 mm.

[59—60] [C:] LES ENVIRONS DES DEUX BRISACHS ET DE FRIBOURG Par N. de Fer ... — A Paris chez l'Auteur ... 1705.
[59] [T:] VIEUX BRISACH   NOUVEAU BRISACH — A.Coquart.sculp. 113.   237 × 337 mm.
[60] [T:] FRIBOURG — A. Coquart.sculp. 114. 237 × 336 mm.

[61] [C:] LES DUCHEZ, DE LORRAINE, ET DE BAR, ET LES EVÉCHÈZ DE METZ, TOUL, ET VERDUN. Par N. de Fer. ... A PARIS chez l'auteur ... 1705. — [C:] Gravé par P. Starck-man. — 115. 231 × 337 mm.

[62] [C:] LE PAIS MESSIN, SES DEPENDANCES, et Terre Adiacentes Sur les Memoirs de Jean Brioys. Par N. de Fer. ... 1705. APARIS Chez le S.r de Fer — [C:] H.van Loon fec. — 116.   276 × 371 mm.

[63] [C:] LE COURS DE LA SARE aux Environs de la Quelle se Trouve Diverses Provinces qui Composent LA PROVINCE DE LA SARE ou LORRAINE ALLEMANDE. Par N. de Fer. ... A.PARIS Chez l'Auteur ... 1705 Gravé Par P. Starck-man. — 117.   336 × 235 mm.

[64] [C:] VOYAGE D'ENEE, Tire de Virgile. Par N. de Fer. ... 1705. — [C:] ... A PARIS Chez l'Auteur ... — [T:] P.Starck-man Sc. — 118.   242 × 332 mm.

Vol. II
SUITE DE L'ATLAS CURIEUX
SUITE DE L'ATLAS CURIEUX PAR DE FER. Tome II. A PARIS Chez I.F.Benard Gendre du S.r Fer ... 1725.

[1] [C:] PAÏS BAS CATOLIQUES Connues sous le nom de FLANDRE. Par N. de Fer. — [C:] ... A PARIS Chez l'Auteur ... 1705. ... — [T:] Van Loon sculp. — 3.   213 × 323 mm.

[2] [C:] LA FLANDRE ESPAGNOLE, et LA FLANDRE HOLLANDOISE. Avec les Nouvelles LIGNES. Par N. de Fer. ... 1705. — [C:] Gravé par P. Starck-man. — 4.   252 × 352 mm.

[3] [C:] BRUSELLES Ville des Pais Bas Capitale du Brabant et Sejour Ordinaire du Gouverneur pour le Roy d'Espagne. A PARIS Chez le S.r de Fer, ... 1705. — (Plan). 5. Uncoloured. 219 × 314 mm.

[4] [C:] PLAN DES ENVIRONS DE DUNKERQUE, ET MARDICK AVEC LE NOUVEAU CANAL FAIT POUR L'ECOULEMENT DES EAUX DU PAYS A LA MER; ... — [T:] P. Starck-man F. — 6. Uncoloured. 252 × 331 mm.

[5] [C:] BATAILLE DE FLEURUS ou l'avantage fut remportée sur l'Armée des Confederez par celle du Roy, Commandée par M.r le Marechal Duc de Luxembourg le Premier de juillet 1690. Par de Fer. A PARIS. Chez l'Auteur ... 1715. — 7. Uncoloured.   226 × 328 mm.

[6] [C:] PLAN DES RETRANCHEMENS ET DU CAMP DE DENAIN, ou est marqué Le Passage de l'Armée du Roy a Neuville sur l'Escaut. ... Par N. de Fer ... A Paris chez l'Auteur ... 1715. — [T:] A PARIS Chez l'Auteur ... 1715. — 8 et 9. Uncoloured.   311 × 527 mm.

[7] [C:] ANVERS — [C:] LE MARQUISAT DU S.T EMPIRE Consistant en la Seule Ville D'ANVERS, et Son Territoire qui fait une des Provinces des Pais Bas, au Roy d'Espagne. ... A PARIS Chez le S.r de Fer, ... 1705 — [T:] Grave Par P. Starck-man. — (Plan). 10. Uncoloured.   243 × 339 mm.

[8] [C:] PARTIE SEPTENTRIONALE DU DUCHE'DE BRABANT ou se trouve le Quartier d Anvers &c. aux Espagnols, le Marq.t de Bergop-Zoom, La Baronnie de Breda Mairie de Bois le Duc &c. aux Hollandois. Par N. de Fer. ... — [T:] Gravé par P. Starck-man. — 11.   241 × 338 mm.

[9] [C:] LES ENVIRONS DE NAMUR, DE HUY, ET DE CHARLE-ROY, ou se trouve encore LA HASBAYE. Par N. de Fer. AParis ... — 12.   229 × 585 mm.

[10] [C:] LES ENVIRONS DE DINANT, DE PHILIPPEVILLE, ET DE CHARLEMONT, ou se Trouve encore LE CONDROS. Par N. de Fer ... A PARIS, Chez l'Autheur ... 1705. — [C:] H.van Loon Sculp. — 13. 219 × 587 mm.

[11] [C:] LA HAUTE GUELDRES ou Se trouvent les Environs de GUELDRES, VENLO, ET RUREMONDE Par N. de Fer. ... 1705. — [T:] C. Inselin sculps. — 14.   241 × 340 mm.

[12] [C:] LA PARTIE SEPTENTRIONALE DE LA SEIGNEURIE DE L'EVECHE'DE LIEGE et LE LIMBOURG Hollandois ou se trouvent les Environs de Maestricht Par N. de Fer ... 1705 — [T:] Gravé Par P. Starck-man. — 15   245 × 337 mm.

[13] [C:] LES PROVINCES UNIES DES BAÏS BAS . Connues sous le nom DE HOLLANDE. Par N. de Fer. ... A PARIS, ... 1705. — [C:] Van Loon Sculp. — 16.   228 × 331 mm.

[14] [C:] AMSTERDAM, Fameux Port de Mer. ... Par N. de Fer A PARIS. ... 1705. — H. van Loon fecit.   (Plan). 17. Uncoloured.   222 × 331 mm.

[15] [C:] LA HAÏE Sejour ordinaire de la Cour Hollandoise Par N. de Fer A PARIS Chez l'Auteur ... 1705. — [T:] C. Inselin fecit — (Plan). 18. Uncoloured.   223 × 331 mm.

[16] [C:] LES ISLES BRITANIQUES, ou sont les Royaumes

D'ANGLETERRE, D'ESCOSSE et D'IRLANDE. Par N. de Fer. ... A PARIS Chés l'Auteur ... 1705. — [T:] Vincent de Ginville fecit. — 20. 220 × 328 mm.
[Insets:] [T:] ISLES DE FERO — 54 × 34 mm. [T:] ISLES DE SHET-LAND — 54 × 34 mm.
[Under these titles, over both maps:] Ces Isles sont au Nord de l'Escosse et sous la Domination du Roy de la grande Bretagne.

[17] [T:] PLAN DES VILLES DE LONDRES ET DE WESTMINSTER et de leurs Faubourgs avec le Bourg de Southwark. Par de Fer ... 1705. — [T:] C. Inselin Sculps. — (Plan). 21. Uncoloured. 222 × 335 mm.

[18] [C:] L'ISLE DE WIGHT, Dressée sur les Derniers Memoires A Paris Chez N: de Fer ... — [T:] H. Van Loon sculp. — 22. 350 × 315 mm.
[Insets:] [T:] LES ISLES SORLINGUES, ou SILLEY. ... — 98 × 77 mm. [T:] TOR BAYE. ... — 98 × 77 mm.

[19] [C:] L'ALLEMAGNE, DIVISÉE PAR CERCLES. Par N. de Fer. ... A PARIS, Chez l'Autheur ... 1705. H. van Loon Sculpc. — 23. 217 × 328 mm.

[20] [C:] LES XIII. CANTONS DES SUISSES LEURS ALLIEZ ET LEURS SUJETS. Par N. de Fer. ... — [C:] A Paris Chez l'Auteur ... 1705. — [T:] C. Inselin Sculp — 24. 229 × 327 mm.

[21] [C:] PLAN DE LA BATAILLE DE FREDELINGUE Gagnée Sur les Imperiaux par l'Armée du Roy commandée par M.r le Marquis de Villars le 14.Octobre 1702. mis au jour par N. de Fer. ... A Paris ... — 26. Uncoloured. 232 × 340 mm.

[22] [T:] LES QUATRE VILLES FORÉSTIÉRES, Situées sur le Rhein, Sont du Cercle de Soüabe et A l'Empereur. Par N. de Fer. A Paris ... 1705. — [T:] A. Coquart. Sculp. — 27. Uncoloured. 254 × 353 mm.
[a] [T:] RHEINFELD Ville Forestieres — (Plan). 76 × 201 mm.
[b] [T:] SECKINGEN Ville Forestieres. — (Plan). 76 × 143 mm.
[c] [C:] CONSTANCE, est vne Ville du Cercle de Soüabe Située au bord du Rhein appartenant a l'Empereur. — (Plan). 152 × 202 mm.
[d] [T:] LAUFFENBURG Ville Forestieres. — (Plan). 86 × 143 mm.
[e] [T:] WALDSHUST Ville Forestieres. — (Plan). 65 × 143 mm.

[23] [T:] LE COURS DU RHEIN Depuis MAYENCE jusques a COBLENS. Ou se Trouvent Partie Des Estats de TREVES. De MAYENCE et DU PALATINAT Du RHEIN. les Comtes de CAZENELLENBOGEN et de SPANHEIM. &.c Par N. de Fer. ... — 28. 233 × 341 mm.

[24] [C:] LES ENVIRONS DE LANDAU Par N. de Fer, ... 1705. — [T:] C. Inselin Sculpsit. — 29 235 × 333 mm.

[25] [C:] LE COURS DU RHEIN, de puis Coblens Jusques a Cologne, ou se trouvent partie des Archevêchez et Electorats de Treves, et de Cologne, et partie des Duchez de Iuliers et de Berg. Par N. de Fer. ... A Paris Chez l'Auteur, ... 1705. — [T:] C. Inselin Sculpsit — 30. 232 × 334 mm.

[26] [C:] LE COURS DU RHEIN Depuis Cologne, Jusques a Rheinberg, ou se trouvent Le Bas Electorat de Cologne, Partie des Duchez de Iuliers, de Berg, et de Gueldres et le Comté de Meurs. Par N. de Fer. ... — [C:] A Paris Chez l'Auteur ... 1702. — 31. 231 × 328 mm.

[27] [C:] COLOGNE Ville Considerable Située Sur le bord Occidentale du Rhein Capit. de l'Electorat de meme nom. Par N. de Fer. ... — [T:] a Paris ... 1705. — (Plan). 32. Uncoloured. 229 × 347 mm.

[28] [C:] LE COURS DU RHEIN depuis Rheinberg jusque a Arnhem, ou se trouvent LE DUCHÉ DE CLEVES et partie de ce luy de la GUELDRES Espagnole et Hollandoise. Par N. de Fer. ... A PARIS Chez l'Auteur ... 1705. — 33. 227 × 332 mm.

[29] [C:] LE COURS DE LA MOSELLE Depuis l'Embouchure de la Saare jusques a Cocheim, ou se trouve LES ENVIRONS DE TREVE ET TRAEBACH. Par N. de Fer. ... A PARIS chez l'Auteur ... 1705. — 34. 232 × 327 mm.

[30] [C:] LE CERCLE DE SOUABE. Par N. de Fer. ... 1705. — [C:] A Paris Chez l'Auteur ... 1705. — [C:] P. Starck-man Sc. — 35 253 × 345 mm.

[31] [C:] CERCLE DE BAVIERE. Par N. de Fer ... A PARIS Chez l'Auteur ... 1705. — [T:] P. Starck-man Sculps. — 36. 246 × 338 mm.

[32] [T:] PLAN DE LA VILLE D'ULM. Ville Imperiale d'Allemagne du cercle de Souabe située sur le Danube. A PARIS Chez le S.r de Fer ... 1705 — (Plan). 38. Uncoloured. 247 × 345 mm.

[33] [C:] MUNICH, Ville Capitale des Etats de son Altesse Electorale de Baviere. ... — [T:] A PARIS Chez le S.r de Fer ... 1705. — A. Coquart. sculp. (Plan). 39. Uncoloured. 234 × 326 mm.

[34] [C:] LES ENVIRONS DE VIENNE en Autriche. Par N. de Fer ... A PARIS ... 1705. — 40 162 × 496 mm.

[35] [a] [T:] VEUË SEPTENTRIONALE DE VIENNE En Autriche. — (View). 123 × 334 mm.
[b] [T:] VEUË MERIDIONALE DE VIENNE En Autriche. — (View). 113 × 335 mm.
[The whole map:] A Paris chez le Sieur de Fer. ... 1705 L.G.Begule Sculpsit 41. Uncoloured. 240 × 337 mm.

[36] [C:] VIENNE capitale de l'Archiduché d'Autriche Residence ordinaire des Empereurs d'Occident de la Maison d'Autriche, ... Par N. de Fer. ... — [T:] A PARIS ... 1705. — (Plan). 42 Uncoloured. 245 × 338 mm.

[37] [C:] PLAN DE STRAALSUND Par de Fer 1716. — (Plan). 43. Uncoloured. 221 × 320 mm.

[38] [C:] ESTATS DES COURONNES DE DANNEMARK, SUEDE, ET POLOGNE sur la Mer Baltique. Dressés et Dediés ANOSSEIGNEURS LES ENFANS DE FRANCE. Par leurs tres humble et tres Obeissant Serviteur de Fer ... — 45. 431 × 346 mm.
[Inset:] [C:] DESCRIPTION DE L'ISLE DE HUENE ... — 80 × 100 mm. (Irregular).

[39] [C:] LE SUND ou DETROIT DU SOND Passage ordinaire des Vaisseaux qui entrent ou qui Sortent de la Mer Baltiq. En y payent un droit si considerable qu'il fait un des meilleurs et des plus gros reuenus du Roy de Dannemarq. Par N. de Fer ... — [T:] A Paris Chez l'Auteur ... 1705. — [T:] C. Inselin Sculpsit — 46. 328 × 219 mm.

[40] [C:] COPENHAGUE Ville Capitale du Royaume de Dannemarq et Sejour ordinaire du Roy. Située dans l'Isle de Seelande au Detroit du Sond ... Par N. de Fer. — [T:] A PARIS Chez le S.r de Fer ... 1705. — [T:] C.Inselin Sculps. — (Plan). 47. Uncoloured. 221 × 328 mm.

[41] [C:] ESTATS DE LA COURONNE DE POLOGNE Par de Fer 1717. — 48. Uncoloured. 218 × 314 mm.

[42] [T:] VARSOVIE — A. Coquart sculp. 49. Uncoloured. 232 × 336 mm.
[a] (Plan). 149 × 334 mm.
[Insets:] VEÜE DU CHATEAU DE LOWICZ (View). 35 × 85 mm. PLAN DU CHATEAU DE LOUWITZ OU LOWICL (Plan). 35 × 85 mm.
[b] (View). 75 × 335 mm.

[43] [C:] PLAN DE NARVA Assiegé par 80000. Moscovites, qui furent Attaqués et deffaits dans leurs lignes par CHARLES XII. Roy de Suede Commandant son Armée en personne a l'age de dix huit ans, le 30. Novembre 1705. — [C:] A PARIS, Chez le S.r De Fer, ... 1701. — [T:] Grave par van Loon. — (Plan). 50. Uncoloured. 228 × 339 mm.

[44] [C:] ESTATS DU GRAND DUC DE MOSCOVIE Dressée sur de Nouveaux Memoire par N. de Fer ... — 51 212 × 321 mm.

[45] [C:] LA HONGRIE LA TRANSILVANIE LA VALAQUIE LA MOLDAVIE & Par N. de Fer. ... A PARIS Chez l'Auteur ... 1717. — Rich 52. 224 × 320 mm.

[46] [C:] LA JOURNÉE DE POLTAWA EN UKRAINE, le 8.e juillet 1709. Entre l'Armée de sa Majesté Suedoise Charles XII. et celle de sa Majesté Csarienne Pierre I. Empereur de la grande Russie, dit Vulgairement Grand Duc de Moscovie. de Fer. 1714. — 53 Uncoloured. 228 × 330 mm.
[Inset:] [T:] le Bourg de Perewoloczna ... — 79 × 65 mm.

[47] [T:] LA MER NOIRE, Autrefois PONT-EUXIN, Appellée

[48] par les Turcs CARA-DENGHIS, Et par les Cosaques CZORNO-MORE Cette Carte a été tirée d'apres vn Manuscrit Turc fait a Caffa. Par de Fer ... — [T:] A PARIS Chez l'Auteur — 54 240 × 341 mm.

[48] [C:] ESPAGNE ET PORTUGAL Divisés en ses Principales parties ou Royaumes. Par N. de Fer. A PARIS, Chez l'Autheur ... 1705. — [T:] H. van Loon Sculp. — 55. 216 × 330 mm.

[49] [T:] MADRID, Ville Considerable de la Nouvelle Castille, Sejour ordinaire des Roys d'Espagne. Par N. de Fer ... — [C:] ... A PARIS Chez le Sr de Fer ... 1705. — (Plan). 56. Uncoloured. 221 × 325 mm.

[50] [C:] ROYAUME DE GALICE PROVINCE D'ESPAGNE Par N. de Fer ... A Paris Chez l'Auteur ... 1705. — 59. 234 × 325 mm.
[Insets:] [C:] PORT ET RADE DE VIGO en Galice Par N. de Fer. 1705. — [T:] C. Inselin Sculpsit. — 165 × 107 mm. [T:] LA VILLE ET LE PORT DE LA COROGNE — 49 × 107 mm.

[51] [C:] LES ASTURIES ET LA BISCAYE, LES ROYAUME DE NAVARRE, D'ARRAGON ET DE LEON, ET CELUY DE LA VIEILLE CASTILLE. Par N. de Fer ... — 60. 255 × 375 mm.

[52] [C:] L'ANDALOUSIE, LES ROYAUMES DE GRENADE, ET DE MURCIE, et Grande Partie de ceux DE LEON, DE CASTILLE, ET DE VALENCE. Par N. de Fer ... A PARIS Chez l'Auteur ... 1705. — [T:] P. Starckman Scs. — 61. 250 × 351 mm.

[53] [C:] PRINCIPAUTÉ DE CATALOGNE A Paris chez le Sr de Fer, ... — 62. 239 × 345 mm.

[54] [C:] CADIS son Port, sa Rade, et ses environs. ... Par N. de Fer. ... A PARIS ... 1705. — 63. 243 × 341 mm.

[55] [T:] LE FAMEUX DETROIT DE GIBALTAR. Par N. de Fer. — [T:] A Paris chez le Sr de Fer ... — [T:] C. Inselin Sculpsit. — 64. 230 × 310 mm.
[Inset:] [C:] COSTE D' ANDALOUSIE ET D'ALGARVE depuis CADIS Jusque au CAP. Sr VINCENT ... — 170 × 67 mm. (Irregular).

[56] [C:] Maison et Chambre Angelique de la Vierge Marie de MONT-SERRAT Située en Catalogne a Sept lieües et au Nord de Barcelone ... A PARIS Chez le Sr de Fer ... 1705. — (View). 67. Uncoloured. 222 × 334 mm.

[57] [C:] L'ISLE MAYORQUE Mis au jour par N. de Fer ... — [C:] A PARIS. Chez le Sr de Fer ... 1715. — 68. 234 × 340 mm.

[58] [C:] PLAN DE PALMA VILLE CAPITALE DE L'ISLE DE MAJORQUE. Mis au jour par N. de Fer. ... La plus grande Partie des dehors de la Place ne sont que Proiettes. 1715. — (Plan). 69. Uncoloured. 232 × 341 mm.

[59] [C:] LE PORT ET LA VILLE DE MAHON le Bourg et le Fort de St Philippe Dans l'Isle de Minorque l'vne des Isles de la Mer Mediterranée sur les Côtes d'Espagne Par de Fer ... — 70. Uncoloured. 220 × 324 mm.

[60] [C:] EMBOUCHURE DE LA RIVIERE DU TAGE Par N. de Fer. ... A PARIS, Chez l'Auteur, ... 1715 — 71. Uncoloured. 167 × 408 mm.
[Insets:] PALAIS ROYAL DE LISBONNE (View). 40 × 147 mm. LE CHÂTEAU DE BELEM. Pres Lisbonne dans la Riviere du Tage. (View). 40 × 147 mm.

[61] [C:] BATAILLE D'ALMANZA Dans le Royaume de Valence. ou l'Armée des Alliez fut deffaite par celle des deux Couronnes, le 25. Avril 1707. Par N. de Fer. — 72. Uncoloured. 223 × 324 mm.

[62] [C:] LES ROYAUMES DE PORTUGAL et D'ALGARVE Par N. de Fer ... a Paris Chez l'Auteur ... 1705. — [T:] P. Starck-man scus. — 73. 355 × 256 mm.

[63] [a] [T:] PALAIS ROYAL DE LISBONNE. — (View). 105 × 164 mm.
[b] [T:] LE CHATEAU DE BELEM. pres Lisbonne dans le Riviere du Tage — (View). 105 × 163 mm.
[C:] [T:] LISBONNE. — (Plan). 129 × 327 mm.
[The whole map:] A. Coquart sculp. 74. Uncoloured. 238 × 329 mm.

[64] [a] [T:] ELVAS. — (Plan). 231 × 165 mm.
[b] [T:] EVORA. — (Plan). 231 × 164 mm.
[The whole map:] A Paris chez Sr de Fer ... A. Coquart. Sculp. 75. Uncoloured. 252 × 350 mm.

[65] [a] [T:] OLIVENÇA. — (Plan). 224 × 160 mm.
[b] [T:] SETUVAL. — (Plan). 224 × 161 mm.
[The whole map:] A.Paris chez Sr de Fer ... A. Coquart. Sculp. 76. Uncoloured. 243 × 344 mm.

[66] [a] [C:] ESTREMOS Est vne Ville considerable de Portugal dans la Province d'Alentejo, partagée en haute et Basse Ville le côté de la Ville haute qui regarde le dedans de la basse ... — (Plan). 122 × 172 mm.
[b] [C:] VILLA VIÇIOSA ou Ville Plaisante est fort Ancienne de la Province d'Alentejo en Portugal ... — (Plan). 122 × 171 mm.
[c] [C:] S.^{T} IULIEN ou S.^{T} GIAÕ Est vne Forteresse considerable Située a l'Embouchure de la Riviere du Tage ... — (Plan). 121 × 172 mm.
[d] [C:] ARONCHES Est vne Ville forte de Portugal dans la Province d'Alentejo située sur la Caya. ... — (Plan). 121 × 171 mm.
[The whole map:] A. Coquart. Sculp. A.Paris chez le Sr de Fer ... 77. Uncoloured. 253 × 351 mm.

[67] [C:] L'ITALIE Par N. de Fer ... — [T:] A PARIS Chez l'Auteur ... 1705. — [T:] C. Inselin Sculp. — 78. 222 × 328 mm.

[68] [C:] LES ÉTATS DE SAVOYE Subdivisés en CHABLAIS, GENEVOIS, FAUSIGNY, TARANTAISE MORIENNE. et la VRAYE SAVOYE Par N de Fer ... 1705 — [T:] T. Rousseau Sculp. — 79 253 × 345 mm.

[69] [C:] ETAT DE LA REPUBLIQUE DE GENES Par N de Fer. ... 1705. Gravé Par P. Starck-man — 80. 157 × 368 mm.

[70] [C:] MILAN Ville des plus grandes, des plus riches, et des plus fortes d'Italie. Capitale du Duché de même nom, Sejour ordinaire du Gouverneur des Estats de Milan pour le Roy d'Espagne Par N. de Fer. — [T:] A PARIS Chez le Sr de Fer ... 1705. — [T:] C. Inselin Sculpsit — (Plan). 81. Uncoloured. 221 × 333 mm.

[71] [C:] LES ESTATS DU DUCHÉ DE MILAN Par N. de Fer. ... A Paris, Chez l'Auteur ... 1705. — [T:] Van Loon sculp. — 82. 213 × 322 mm.

[72] [C:] LES ENVIRONS DE MILAN. Par N. de Fer. ... A PARIS Chez l'Auteur ... 1705. — [T:] Vincent de Ginville Scripsit — 83. 226 × 341 mm.

[73] [T:] Frontieres DU MILANEZ, DU CREMONESE et DU LODESAN, au Roy d'Espagne. LE BERGAMAS, LE BRESSAN et LE CREMAS, a la Republique de Venise. ou sont remarquez. les Endroits ou les Armées des Alliez et des Imperiaux ont Campez en 1701 — Par N. de Fer. ... — [T:] C. Inselin Sculpsit. — 84. 227 × 338 mm.

[74] [C:] PLAN DE LA VILLE DE CREMONE, Comme elle etoit la Nuit du dernier de Janvier ou Premier de Fevrier 1702. pendant la quelle les Imperiaux y enterent qui en suitte en furent Chassez apres un Combat de Onze heures. Par N. de Fer, ... — [C:] A PARIS, Chez le Sr de Fer, ... 1705. — [C:] Van Loon fecit. — (Plan). 85. Uncoloured. 232 × 340 mm.

[75] [C:] LES DUCHEZ DE MANTOUE et de LA MIRANDOLE. Avec la plus grande partie des Territoire de VERONE BRESCIA, et de Cremone. Par N. de Fer. ... A Paris Chez l'Auteur ... 1705. — [C:] Cette Carte est tirée de Joannes Joansonius. et Gravée par van Loon. — 86 236 × 345 mm.

[76] [T:] LE SERAGLIO et les environs de MANTOÜE Par N. de Fer. — [C:] ... Par N. de Fer. ... 1705. Gravé par C. Inselin — 87 Uncoloured. 233 × 329 mm.

[77] [C:] MANTOÜE. Ville Considerable d'Italie Capitale d'un Duché de même nom, sejour ordinaire de son Prince et Siege d'un Evêque. Elle est située dans un Lac que forme les Eaux de la Riviere du Menzo, ou Mincio, ... Par N. de Fer. ... 1705. — [T:] H. van Loon fec. — 88. Uncoloured. 229 × 335 mm.

[78] [C:] LES DUCHEZ DE PARME ET PLAISANCE DE MODENE ET DE REGE. Par N. de Fer. A Paris Chez l'Autheur ... 1705. — [T:] C. Inselin Sculpsit — 89 236 × 350 mm.

[79] [C:] LES EMBOUCHURES DES RIVIERES DU PO ET DE L'ADIGE ou se trouvent LE FERRARESSE, LE BOULOGNESSE, et Partie de la Romagne. Par N. de Fer. ... — [T:] H. van Loon sculp. — 90. 229 × 336 mm.
[Inset:] [T:] LA REPUBLIQUE DE LUQUES, et la PRINCIPAUTÉ DE MASSE. — 133 × 123 mm.

[80] [C:] LES EVESCHÉS DE TRENTE, et de BRIXEN. LE COMTÉ DE TIROL et les Etats de la Republique de Venise dans le Fond du Golfe. Par N. de Fer. ... A PARIS, Chez l Auteur ... 1705. — 91 247 × 348 mm.

[81] [C:] LES ESTATS DE L'EGLISE, ET DE TOSCANE Par N. de Fer. ... 1705. — [T:] A PARIS ... — [C:] C. Inselin Sculps. — 92. 230 × 333 mm.

[82] [C:] LES ENVIRONS DE ROME Par N. de Fer ... A PARIS Chez l'Auteur ... 1705. — 93. 229 × 344 mm.

[83] [C:] PLAN DE LA VILLE DE ROME Par de Fer. A PARIS, Chez l'Autheur ... 1705. — (Plan). 94 Uncoloured. 231 × 297 mm.

[84] [T:] VENISE Ville Capitale de la plus Celebre et Illustre Republique de l'Europe. — [T:] Auertissement Le S.r de Fer a fait un grand Plan de Venise ... il se vend comme celuy cy, A PARIS Chez l'Auteur ... 1705. — (Plan). 96. Uncoloured. 213 × 331 mm.

[85] [C:] LES ENVIRONS DE LA VILLE DE NAPLES, Dans la Province de Labour, avec la Routte de cette Ville a Rome Par N. de Fer ... A PARIS chez l'Auteur ... — [T:] Vincent de Ginville Scripsit — 97. 226 × 338 mm.
[Inset as a part of the cartouche:] [T:] NOUVEAU PORT DE NETTUNO, Retabli par le Pape INNOCENT XII. en 1705. — 45 × 110 mm. (Irregular).

[86] [C:] LE ROYAUME DE NAPLES Par N. de Fer. ... A Paris, ... 1705. — [T:] Van Loon Sculpcit — 98. 223 × 334 mm.
[Inset:] [C:] L'ISLE DE SARDAGNE — 137 × 98 mm.

[87] [T:] NAPLES. — [T:] A PARIS Chez le S.r de Fer ... 1705. — (Plan). 99. Uncoloured. 222 × 331 mm.

[88] [C:] LES MERVEILLES DE POZZOLI ou POUZZOL CUME ET BAIA ou BAYES. Dans le Voisinage de Naples. Par N. de Fer. A Paris Chez l'Auteur ... 1705. ... — 100. Uncoloured. 222 × 329 mm.

[89] [T:] LE MONT VESUVE ou Montagne de Somma pres de Naples. — [T:] Par N. de Fer ... — (View). 101. Uncoloured. 227 × 334 mm.
[Inset:] [T:] COUPE DU MONT VESUVE. ... — 81 × 102 mm.

[90] [T:] LE MONT CASSIN Dessiné Sur les lieux par M.r de la Salle — [T:] A Paris Chez le S.r de Fer ... 1705. — (View). 102. Uncoloured. 234 × 328 mm.

[91] [C:] ISLE ET ROYAUME DE SICILE. Par N. de Fer ... — [C:] ... A PARIS Chez l'Autheur ... 1705. — [T:] H.van Loon sculp. — 103 226 × 334 mm.

[92] [C:] MESSINE Residence Ordinaire du Viceroy de Sicile. — (Plan). 104 Uncoloured. 225 × 333 mm.

[93] [a] [C:] CATANE et LE MONT GIBEL. en Sicile. — (Plan). 200 × 164 mm.
[b] [C:] PALERME. Capitale de Sicile. — (Plan). 200 × 164 mm.
[The whole map:] A PARIS Chez le S.r de Fer ... 1075 (pro 1705). 105 226 × 333 mm.

[94] [C:] GRECE MODERNE ou Partie Meridionale de la TURQUIE EN EUROPE. Divisée en Beglerbeglics ou Grands Gouvernements. Par N. de Fer. ... A PARIS, Chez l'Autheur ... 1705. — [T:] Van Loon Sculpsit — 106. 222 × 334 mm.

[95] [C:] VEÜE DE LA VILLE ET DU PORT DE CONSTANTINOPLE — (View). 107 Uncoloured. 228 × 331 mm.

[96] [T:] VEÜE DES DARDANELLES DE CONSTANTINOPLE — (View). 108 231 × 339 mm.

[97] [C:] LA PERSE, LA GEORGIE ET LA TURQUIE D'ASIE. Avec la partie Septentrionale DE L'ARABIE. Par N. de Fer ... 1705. — 109 229 × 336 mm.

[98] [T:] LE MEIDAN ou LA PIACE D'ISPAHAM en Perse — [T:] A. Coquart sculp — (View). 110 Uncoloured. 232 × 328 mm.

[99] [C:] LES VRAYS INDES dits GRANDS INDES OU INDES ORIENTALES Par N. de Fer. ... — [C:] ... A Paris Chez l'Auteur ... 1705. — [T:] C. Inselin Sculp. — 111. 228 × 315 mm.

[100] [C:] LA PARTIE ORIENTALE DE L'ASIE ou Se trouvent LE GRAND EMPIRE DES TARTARES CHINOIS et Celuy DU IAPON. Par N. de Fer ... A PARIS Chez l'Auteur ... 1705. — [C:] C. Inselin Sculpsit — 112. 231 × 329 mm.

[101] [C:] LES ISLES PHILLIPPINES et celles DES LARRONS ou de MARIANES, LES ISLES MOLUQUES et de LA SONDE, avec, LA PRESQUISLE DE L'INDE DE LA LE GANGE ou ORIENTALE Par N. de Fer, ... — [T:] A PARIS Chez l'Auteur ... 1705. — [C:] C. Inselin Sculpsit — 113. 223 × 335 mm.

[102] [C:] PLAN DE PONDICHERY a la côte de Coromandel Occupé par la Compagnie Royale des Indes Orientales. Mis au jour Par N. de Fer. ... A PARIS Chez le S.r de Fer ... 1705. — A. Coquart. Sculp. (Plan). 114. Uncoloured. 237 × 351 mm.

[103] [C:] LA TERRE SAINTE Tirée des Memoires de M. de la Ruë, Par N. de Fer ... 1705. — 233 × 307 mm.
[Inset:] [T:] Tabula Mansionum ad Caput 33. numer. LE PASSAGE-DU-PEUPLE SAINT par les Deserts de l'Arabie. — 80 × 100 mm. (Irregular).

[104] [C:] PLAN DU SAINT SEPULCHRE DE NÔTRE SEIG.R JESUS-CHRIST ... — 116
[Insets:] [C:] CARTE de la TERRE SAINTE avec les routes que N.S.J.C. á tenue par la Galilée, Samarie, Judée et Egypte. — 125 × 127 mm. [T:] Plan de la Ville de JERUSALEM. — (Plan). 94 × 141 mm.

[105] [C:] PARTIE ORIENTALE D'AFRIQUE ou se trouvent L'EGIPTE, LA NUBIE, L'ABISSINE, ET L'AJAN et partie DE LA NIGRITIE, DU GRAND DESERT ET DU BILDULGERID &c. ou se trouvent encore L ARABIE qui fait partie de l'Asie — ET LA MER ROVGE Par N. de Fer, ... — [T:] ... A Paris Chez l'Auteur ... 1705. — [C:] C. Inselin Sculpsit — 117. 225 × 323 mm.

[106] [C:] PARTIE OCCIDENTALE D'AFRIQUE ou se trouve les Isles Canaries, et du Cap Verd dans la Mer Atlantique les Etas du Roy de Maroc, les Royaumes d'Alger et de Tunis, le Biledulgerid, et le Saara, en BARBARIE. LA NIGRITIE, ET LA GUINEE. Par N. de Fer. ... — 118. 223 × 323 mm.

[107] [C:] PARTIE MERIDIONALE D'AFRIQUE ou se trouvent LA BASSE GUINÉE LA CAFRERIE, LE MONOMOTAPA, LE MONOEMUGI, LE ZANGUEBAR ET L'ISLE DE MADAGASCAR. Par N. de Fer ... — [C:] C. Inselin Sculps. — 119. 214 × 317 mm.

[108] [T:] CAP DE BONNE ESPERANCE Par N. de Fer. [T:] A PARIS Chez l'Auteur ... 1705. — 120. Uncoloured. 247 × 351 mm.
[a] (View). 110 × 332 mm.
[b] [T:] BAYE DE LA TABLE — 111 × 162 mm.
[c] [T:] LE FORT DU CAP DE BONNE ESPERANCE aux Hollandois — (Plan). 111 × 161 mm.

[109] [C:] LE CANADA, ou NOUVELLE FRANCE, la Floride, la Virginie, Pensilvanie, Caroline, Nouvelle Angleterre et Nouvelle Yorck, l'Isle de Terre Neuve, la Loüisane et le Cours de la Riviere de Misisipi. Par N. de Fer. ... A PARIS, Chez l'Auteur ... 1705. ... Van Loon sc. — 121. 232 × 339 mm.

[110] [C:] LES COSTES AUX ENVIRONS DE LA RIVIERE DE MISISIPI. Decouvertes par M.r de la Salle en 1683. et reconnues par M.r le Chevallier d'Jberville en 1698. et 1699. par N. de Fer, ... 1705. — Vincent de Ginville Sculpsit 122. 215 × 333 mm.

[111] [C:] Cette Carte DE CALIFORNIE et DU NOUVEAU MEXIQUE, est tirée de celle qui a ètè envoyée par un grand d'Espagne pour être communiquée a M.rs de l'Academie Royale des Sciences Par N. de Fer ... 1705. ... A Paris ... — [T:] C. Inselin Sculp. — 123. 223 × 336 mm.

[112] [C:] LE VIEUX MEXIQUE OU NOUVELLE ESPAGNE auec les costes DE LA FLORIDE Faisant partie de l'Amerique Septentrionale Par N. de Fer. ... AParis chez

l'Auteur ... 1705 — 124. 225 × 325 mm.

[113] PLAN DE LA FAMEUSE ET NOUVELLE VILLE DE MEXIQUE. Par N. de Fer 1715. (Plan). 125. Uncoloured. 221 × 333 mm.

[114] [C:] LES ISLES DE L'AMERIQUE Connue^s Sous le Nom D'ANTILLES, ou Sont les Isles de Cuba, St Domingue et Jamaique les Lucayes, les Caribes, et celles du Vent. Par N. de Fer. ... A PARIS, Chez l'Auteur ... 1705. — [T:] H van Loon sculp. — 126. 221 × 331 mm.

[115] [T:] L'ISLE S.^{T} DOMINGUE ou ESPAGNOLE. Decouverte en 1492. par les Espagnols. Dressée sur les Memoires de desfunt Mr de Cussy qui Commandoit dans la partie de l'Isle que les François possedent. Par N. de Fer. 1715. A PARIS. Chez l'Auteur ... — 127. 224 × 331 mm.

[116] [C:] L'ISLE DE LA JAMAIQUE, Divisée par Paroisses. Dressée sur des Memoires Anglois par le Sr de Fer ... a Paris chez l'Auteur ... A.P.D.R. — 128. 231 × 346 mm.

[117] [C:] L'ISLE DE LA MARTINIQUE A PARIS ... Chez le Sr de Fer ... 1704. — [T:] P. Starck-man Scs. — 129. 259 × 355 mm.

[118] [C:] PLAN DES VILLES, FORTS, PORT, RADE et Environs DE CARTAGENE Située dans l'Amerique Meridionale dans la Province de Terre Ferme appartenant aux Espagnols. Par N. de Fer ... 1705. — [T:] C. Inselin Sculpsit — 130 220 × 320 mm.

[119] [C:] LA TERRE FERME ET LE PEROU avec LE PAYS DES AMAZONES ET LE BRESIL Dans l'Amerique Meridionale Par N. de Fer. ... 1705. — [C:] ... Gravé par Charles Inselin — 131. 226 × 337 mm.

[120] [C:] LE CHILI et Les Provinces qui Composent Celle de RIO DE LA PLATA avec LES TERRES MAGELLANIQUE Par N. de Fer, ... — [T:] C. Inselin Sculpsit — 132. 222 × 334 mm.

[121] [C:] LE DETROIT DE MAGELLAN ... Par le Sr de Fer. A PARIS Chez l'auteur ... 1705. — [C:] Charles Inselin Sculpsit — 133. 225 × 336 mm.

Notes: All the maps are blank on the back, and are lightly coloured except where otherwise specified. The first edition of this atlas was published 1700—1705; this 1725 edition was published posthumously, and does not seem to be recorded, even in the Bibliothèque Nationale. Of the 1700—1705 edition, Lister states 'Most maps are eng. by Carolus Inselin, but no. X is eng. by van Loon.' In our copy 34 of the 185 maps are engraved by Inselin, 24 by P. Starck-man, 22 by A. Coquart, 21 by H. van Loon. Vincent de Ginville engraved 4 maps, and [C.A.] Berey, L.G. Begule and T. Rousseau each engraved one. The title-pages of both volumes are engraved by N. Guerard. One map, no. [75] in vol. 2, is 'tirée de Joannes Joansonius et Gravée par van Loon'. The name 'de Fer' is wanting on 13 maps, 10 of which bear the imprint of 'Sr Danet gendre de l'Auteur'. On map [2] in vol. 1 there are nine portrait medallions, representing Le Reverend Pere Tachard de la Compag. de Jesus Franc., Mr Cavilli de la Salle Francois., Mr Dampierre Anglois, Magellan Portuguais, Drac Anglois, Christophe Colomb Genois., Amerique Vespuce Florentin, Marc Paul Venitien, and Guillaume Schouten Hollandois. On maps [15] and [39] in vol. 2, C. Inselin's name is in reversed script. Map [43] depicts the battle of Narva, with the date 1705, but this is evidently a misprint as the battle was fought in 1700 and the map is dated 1701. In addition to the maps, both volumes contain a number of architectural plates. The volumes are bound in the original old leather, with scrollwork toolin. Nordenskiöld's signature is on the first blank leaf of each volume.

Lit.: BM Maps vol. 6, c. 28, (1705), Lister p. 150, Nouv. Biogr. Gen. vol. 17, c. 351—352.

73 FERRETTI, FRANCESCO 1580

DIPORTI NOTTVRNI, DIALLOGHI FAMILLIARI DEL CAP.^{O} FRANC.^{O} FERRETT^I CAV.^{RO} DELL'ORDINE DI SA.^{TO} STEFANO, CON LA DIMOSTRATIONE FIGVRALE INTAGLIATADA MICHELANGELO MARRELLI ANCONITANO; 1579 [Colophon:] STAMPATO IN ANCONA. Apresso Francesco Saluioni. 1580. 15 sm.

[1] [T:] RAGIONEVOL' FORMA ET VERA POSTVRA DEL'ISOLA DI RODI — [77] 130 × 88 mm.

[2] [T:] RAGIONEVOE' FORMA ET VERA POSTVRA DEL'ISOLA DI CANDIA — [79] 130 × 87 mm.

[3] [T:] RAGIONEVOL' FORMA ET VERA POSTVRA DEL'ISOLA DI CERIGO — [81] 132 × 86 mm.

[4] [T:] RAGIONEVOL' FORMA ET VERA POSTVRA DEL'ISOLA DI MILO — [83] 130 × 85 mm.

[5] [T:] RAGIONEVOL' FORMA ET VERA POSTVRA DEL'ISOLA DI TINO — [85] G 130 × 85 mm.

[6] [T:] RAGIONEVOL' FORMA ET VERA POSTVRA DEL'ISOLA DI ANDRIA — [87] G 2 130 × 86 mm.

[7] [T:] RAGIONEVOL' FORMA ET VERA POSTVRA DEL'ISOLA DI NECSIA — [89] G 3 130 × 84 mm.

[8] [T:] RAGIONEVOL' FORMA ET VERA POSTVRA DEL'ISOLA DI LANGO — [91] G 4 130 × 86 mm.

[9] [T:] RAGIONEVOL' FORMA ET VERA POSTVRA DEL'ISOLA DI CALOGERo — [93] 130 × 87 mm.

[10] [T:] RAGIONEVOL' FORMA ET VERA POSTVRA DEL'ISOLA DI CALAMO — [95] 131 × 87 mm.

[11] [T:] RAGIONEVOL' FORMA ET VERA POSTVRA DEL'ISOLA DI LEZZO — [97] 130 × 86 mm.

[12] [T:] RAGIONEVOL' FORMA ET VERA POSTVRA DEL'ISOLA DI PACTINO — [99] 130 × 86 mm.

[13] [T:] RAGIONEVOL' FORMA ET VERA POSTVRA DEL'ISOLA DI SAMO — [101] H 130 × 86 mm.

[14] [T:] RAGIONEVOL' FORMA ET VERA POSTVRA DEL'ISOLA DI STALIMINI — [103] H 2 130 × 86 mm.

[15] [T:] RAGIONEVOL' FORMA ET VERA POSTVRA DEL'ISOLA DI SCIO — [105] H 3 130 × 86 mm.

[16] [T:] RAGIONEVOL' FORMA ET VERA POSTVRA DEL'ISOLA DI METELLINO — [107] H 4 130 × 86 mm.

[17] [T:] RAGIONEVOL' FORMA ET VERA POSTVRA DEL'ISOLA DI SCHIZZO — [109] 130 × 85 mm.

[18] [T:] RAGIONEVOL' FORMA ET VERA POSTVRA DEL'ISOLA DI DROMO ET SERACHINO — [111] 130 × 87 mm.

[19] [T:] RAGIONEVOL' FORMA ET VERA POSTVRA DEL'ISOLA DI NEGROPONTE — [113] 130 × 81 mm.

[20] [T:] RAGIONEVOL' FORMA ET VERA POSTVRA DEL'ISOLA DI CIPRO — [117] I 128 × 85 mm.

[21] [T:] RAGIONEVOL' FORMA ET VERA POSTVRA DEL'ISOLA DI MALTA — [119] 127 × 85 mm.

[22] [T:] RAGIONEVOL' FORMA ET VERA POSTVRA DEL'ISOLA DI SICILIA — [121] I 3 127 × 84 mm.

[23] [T:] RAGIONEVOL' FORMA ET VERA POSTVRA DEL'ISOLA DI ELBA — [123] I 4 129 × 86 mm.

[24] [T:] RAGIONEVOL' FORMA ET VERA POSTVRA DEL'ISOLA DI CORSICA — [127] 130 × 85 mm.

[25] [T:] RAGIONEVOL' FORMA ET VERA POSTVRA DEL'ISOLA DI SARDEGNA — [129] 129 × 85 mm.

[26] [T:] RAGIONEVOL' FORMA ET VERA POSTVRA DEL'ISOLA DI MAIORICA — [131] 130 × 86 mm.

[27] [T:] RAGIONEVOL' FORMA ET VERA POSTVRA DEL'ISOLA DI MINORICA — [133] K 130 × 87 mm.

[28] [T:] RAGIONEVOL' FORMA ET VERA POSTVRA DEL'ISOLA DI INGLITERRA — [137] 130 × 85 mm.

Notes: All the maps have text on the verso and are uncoloured. All the plates follow exactly the same pattern: each is divided horizontally into two parts, the title of the map appearing in the upper section while the map itself is printed within a circle in the lower, square section. There are decorations in the four corners of the square. The leaves bearing maps on the recto are numbered only on the verso, but both sides are allowed for in the numbering. Two page-numbers, 78 and 82, have been duplicated in error. Our copy was bound by the Swedish bookbinder Hedberg, but the work is not up to his usual standard. Maps [7], [8], and [19] have been cropped on the right-hand side so that part of the circle is missing. Michelangelo Marrelli or Marelli was an Italian engraver who is mentioned by Thieme-Becker and Nagler. Nordenskiöld's signature is on the first blank leaf, and on the last blank leaf is the note in his hand: 'Denna upplaga utgafs med nytt tittelblad- ändrade dedikationer och nytt slutblad under titel: Ate Militare Del Capitano Francesco Ferretti Cavaglier di S. Stefano etc. ect. in Ancona, MDCVIII. Sjelfa texten i dessa båda arbeten är samma tryck o likaså kartorna.' [This edition was published with a new title-page, altered dedications and a new, printed final leaf, with the title: Ate Militare Del Capitano Francesco Ferretti Cavaglier di S. Stefano etc. etc. in Ancona, MDCVIII. The text itself is identical in both editions, and so are the maps.] This second edition is not in our collection.

Lit.: BM Gen. cat., vol. 72, col. 489, Nat. Mar. Mus. vol. 3, p. 23, nr 38, Nagler vol. 8, p. 320, Thieme-Becker vol. 24, p. 85, Tooley, Dictionary, p. 151.

74 FORESTI, JACOBUS PHILIPPUS BERGOMENSIS 1503

Nouissime hỹstoriar omniũ repercussiones. nouiter a Reuerendissimo patre Jacobo philippo Bergomēse ordinis Heremitarum edite: que Supplementum supplementi Cronicarũ nuncupantur. Incipiendo ab exordio mundi vsq in Annum salutis nostre.Mcccccij. [Colophon:] Explicit Supplementum Chronicarum Diligenter Et Accurate Reuisum Atq Correctũ. Venetiis Impressuz Per Albertinũ De Lissona Vercellēsem. Regnā: Leonardo Loredano Venetiarum Principe. A Natiuitate Christi.M.ccccc.iii. Die.iiii. Maii. Cuz Gratia Et Priuilegio:
32,3 cm.

[1] Terræ uniuersæ distinctio. (Map). On 7 88 × 132 mm. Two circular maps with 63 mm. diam.
[2] Cayrum. Mēphis: nũc ChayR̃ maxiã ciuitas appellata:... On 22 verso. 56 × 77 mm.
[3] Sodoma ciuitas apđ Arabiã. On 23 verso. 52 × 48 mm.
[4] Calcis etiã: Euboeæ insulæ ciuitas: quã Niceroponte nũc dicim[9]:... On 37 65 × 83 mm.
[5] GENVA VRBS MARITIMA. On 41 verso. 90 × 117 mm.
[6] THEBAE AEGYPTIACA CIVITAS. On 47 56 × 75 mm.
[7] CAPVA IN LABORIIS CIVITAS. On 83 65 × 83 mm.
[8] VRBS ROMA. On 91 verso. 117 × 140 mm.
[9] CIVITAS SYRACVSANA. On 93 verso. 56 × 80 mm.
[10] MEDIOLANVM CIVITAS CISALPINAE GALLIAE. On 119 verso. 146 × 145 mm.
[11] BRIXIA VRBS CISALPINAE GALLIAE. On 122 q2 60 × 74 mm.
[12] BONONIA CISALPINAE GALLIAE CIVITAS. On 127 56 × 76 mm.
[13] FLORENTIA ETHRVRIAE CIVITAS. On 128 68 × 87 mm.
[14] ALEXANDRIA CIVITAS EGYPTI. On 130 r2 65 × 83 mm.
[15] VTICA APHRICAE CIVITAS. On 156 u4 55 × 75 mm.
[16] VENETIAE CIVITAS REGIA. On 230 verso. 117 × 150 mm.
[17] RAGVSIVM DALMATIAE CIVITAS. On 231 verso. 58 × 79 mm.
[18] CENTVM ETHRVRIAE OPPIDVM. On 261 58 × 82 mm.
[19] PORTVS VENERIS OPPIDVM. On 291 verso. 57 × 81 mm.
[20] MEDIOLANVM CISALPINAE GALLIAE CIVITAS. On 300 = [10] in this ed.
[21] BRIXIA ITALIAE CIVITAS. On 373 verso. = [11] in this ed.
[22] GENVA MARITIMA CIVITAS. On 417 verso = [5] in this ed.
[23] GENVA MARITIMA CIVITAS. On 433 verso. = [5] in this ed.

Notes: The map and all the town views are coloured. The views described above are all true representations of the various towns, although simplified to show only the most characteristic features of each. There are very many other town views in the same style in the volume, but the same ones appear under different names and must be considered as types rather than accurate likenesses. The same view is used twice to illustrate Verona, and a third time for Damascus. Another appears twice under Bergomum, then under both Sparta and Spoletum. Constantinopolis, Napoli, Cayeta and Euboia are all the same, and so on. The author was born in Bergamo; he was a member of the Foresti family, but as a monk he used only the name Bergomensis. Jöcher refers to him by the latter name, but the Bibliothèque Nationale in Paris and the British Museum use Foresti. Our collection contains two other Latin editions without woodcuts, and a 1524 edition with woodcuts, described below. The 1503 edition is in a contemporary binding of vellum on wood, with blind tooling and metal clasps. There are many old manuscript notes on the verso of the first blank leaf, on the inside of the front cover and in several of the margins. The words 'Ex libris' are written on the title-page, but the following name has been erased. Nordenskiöld's signature, with the year 1876, is on the inside of the front cover, and there is a note in his hand on the inside of the back cover: 'Karta — f. 7, America — f. 8, ditto — f. 442'.

Lit.: Bibl. Nat. Paris, Cat. vol. 53, p. 472, BM Books, vol. 75, c. 532 Jöcher vol. 1, c. 997.

75 FORESTI, JACOBUS PHILIPPUS BERGOMENSIS 1524

SVPPLEMENTVM SVPPLEMENTI De le Chroniche del Venerando padre Frate Jacobo Philippo del ordine Heremitano Primo Authore. Vulgarizato & Hystoriato. Cum la Gionta per insino. 1524. [Colophon:] Finisse il Supplemento de le Croniche Vulgarizato & Hystoriato con la gionta per insino del anno.1524. del mese di Octobrio. Impresso in Venetia per Ioāne Francischo & Ioanne Antonio Fratelli di Rusconi. Regnante lo Inclyto Principe Andrea Griti. Nel anno del Signore.1524. del mese di Nouēbrio.
29,5 cm.

[1] La distinctione della terra. On V = 1503:[1].
[2] Chalci:cioe Negroponte citta. On XXXIII verso. 63 × 80 mm.
[3] Genua citta in Liguria. On XXXVII = 1503:[5], [22], [23].
[4] Thebe citta de Egypto. On XLI verso. = 1503:[6].
[5] Capua citta in Campagna. On LXVIII verso. = 1503:[7].
[6] La citta de Roma. On LXXV = 1503:[8].
[7] Siracusa citta nella Isola de Cicilia. On LXXVI verso. = 1503:[9].
[8] Milano citta dignissima in Francia Cisalpina. On XCVI verso. = 1503:[10], [20].
[9] Brixia citta in Francia Cisalpina. On XCVIII verso. = 1503:[11], [21].
[10] Vicentia citta bellissima. On XCIX 56 × 74 mm.
[11] Mantua citta nobilissima. On XCIX verso. 55 × 75 mm.
[12] Bononia citta degna & anticha. On CIII = 1503:[12].
[13] Fiorenza citta nobilissima in Toschana. On CIIII Oii = 1503:[13].
[14] Alexandria citta grandissima in Egypto. On CV verso. = 1503:[14].
[15] Vtica citta in Aphrica. On CXXV verso. = 1503:[15].
[16] Tiboli citta de Latini. Tiboli ouer Tiuoli ... On CL verso. 63 × 82 mm.
[17] El principio de Venetia citta Regia. On CLXXIX = 1503:[16].
[18] Ragusia citta in Dalmatia. On CLXXIX verso. = 1503:[17].
[19] Citta Vechia in Toschana. On CCII Ciiii = 1503:[18].

[20] Porte Venere Castello de Genoua. On CCXXIII verso. = 1503:[19].
[21] Milão citta Metropolitana: On CCXXIX verso. = 8 in this ed.
[22] Bologna citta in Romagna. On CCLVI verso. = [12] in this ed.
[23] Bressa citta in Lombardia. On CCLXXXIIII = [9] in this ed.
[24] Genoua citta Maritima. On CCCXXI s iii = [3] in this ed.
[25] Genoua citta maritima. On CCCXXXV = [3] in this ed.
[26] Genoua citta marittima. On CCCLXIIII = [3] in this ed.

Notes: The map and all the town views are uncoloured. The view of Chalci, [2], is different from the one in the 1503 edition, [4], although in each case the view is of that town only. Vicentia, [10], and Mantua, [11], are not in the 1503 edition, while the views of Cayrum and Sodoma are in the 1503 edition but not in the 1524 edition. The view of Tiboli, [16], is different from the one which appears in the 1503 edition under the heading Tyburtine = Tibur = Tiboli; this does appear in the 1524 edition, but as Eleusi citta. There are other views of Milan as well as those listed above, but they are all stylised ones which also occur elsewhere. This 1524 edition still contains many duplicate views.

This edition contains a new chapter dealing with the years 1503—1524. The vignette on the title-page is signed F.V. (= Florio Vavassore, see Nagler vol. 2, c. 908—910). The volume has been rebound, using the original vellum. Nordenskiöld's signature is on the first old blank leaf.

Lit.: See Foresti 1503.

76 GEDDA, PETTER 1694—1695

General Hydrographisk CHART-BOOK öfwer ÖSTERSIÖN, och KATTE-GATT, Till sin rætta Figur och Stoorleek, Landstræckningar, så wæl som Lângs- och Twers courser, Polihœgder och Længder, Grund och Bankar med mera, dem Siöfahrande till Nytta och Rættelse. Fôrst Aff Hans Konglige May[tts]. till Swerige Vice Amirals, Wâlb: Herr WERNER von ROSENFELTS, I några Åhr med Flÿt fattade Observationer. Jemwæl Sedermera Af âthskillige egne Tÿd effter annnn giorde Special Hydrographiske Chartor ihoopdragen Sammanfattat och Aftecknat Anno 1694. Aff PETTER GEDDA Styrmans-Capitein och Directeur œfwer Lotseriet under Hans Kongl. Maj. i Swerige. j' AMSTERDAM, Hoos ...   53,7 cm.

[1]   1 [C:] Wäxande Grad-Charta öfwer ÖSTER-SIÖN Ifrån Skagen till Norrebottn och Nÿenskantz ... — Blank on the back. = 1699:[1].

[2]   7 [C:] Special Passcharta Öfwer een Deel af ÖSTER-SIÖÖN, Nembl: den FINSKA-BOTTN med alla sina Couster och lägenheeter ifrån Kimitöö och Moösund intill Ändan wedh Nyenskantz med flÿt sammandragen och rÿtat med Privilegiô på 10.åhrs tÿd af Petter Gedda A[o]. 1695. — Map on the back. = 1699:[7].

[3]   8 [C:] [Special Passcharta Öfwer een Deel af ÖSTER-SIÖÖN, Altifrån Sandhamn till Rÿga ...] — Map on the back. = 1699:[8].

[4]   9 [C:] Några Små Pass-Chartor som uti Större bestick innehålla STOCKHOLMS-LEEDEN, ... — Blank on the back. = 1699:[9].

Notes: In this edition the title-leaf is blank on the verso. The following leaf, bearing the 'Påminnelse till læsaren' [Notice to the reader] has text on both sides; the next has the Privilegium on the recto and is blank on the verso. The last of the preliminary leaves bears the dedication to King Charles XI of Sweden, with the Register on the verso. With this text Nordenskiöld has collected four of Gedda's charts, mostly in very bad condition. Chart 1 is identical to that in our other two copies, but much of the bottom left-hand corner is missing. The next chart is the right-hand side of chart 7; its importance for Nordenskiöld is that the cartouche contains text which is wanting in the other copies. On the verso of this chart is the leaf-hand side of chart 8. The last of the four is chart 9, which is complete, but slightly torn along the right-hand border.

Lit.: See Gedda, Petter 1699.

77 GEDDA, PETTER 1699

[General Hydrographisk CHART-BOOK öfwer ÖSTERSIÖN, och KATTE-GATT, Till sin rætta Figur och Stoorleek, Landstræckningar, så wæl som Lângs-och Twers courser, Polihœgder och Længder, Grund och Bankar med mera, dem Siöfahrande till Nytta och Rættelse. Fôrst Aff Hans Konglige May[tts]. till Swerige Vice Amirals, Wâlb: Herr WERNER von ROSENFELTS, I några Åhr med Flÿt fattade Observationer. Jemwæl Sedermera Af âthskillige egne Tÿd effter annnn giorde Special Hydrographiske Chartor ihoopdragen Sammanfattat och Aftecknat Anno 1694. Aff PETTER GEDDA Styrmans-Capitein och Directeur œfwer Lotseriet under Hans Kongl. Maj. i Swerige. j' AMSTERDAM, Hoos]   54,5 cm.

[1]   1 [C:] Wäxande Grad-Charta öfwer ÖSTER-SIÖN Ifrån Skagen till Norrebottn och Nÿenskantz Efftеr Vice Ammiralen Walb.[ne] H.[r] Werner van Rosenfelts. så Wäl som egne, med flÿt giorde Observationer; efftеr några åhrs omkringfarande och Cousternas noga afpeÿlande nÿligen meflÿt sammandragen och afteknat at Petter Gedda. Anno 1694. — Gesnede door A: Winter   [C:] Serenissimo et Potentissimo Regi CAROLO XI.[MO] Svecorum, Gothorum, Wandalorumg. Regi Magno Duci Finlandiæ, etc: etc: Mappam hanc generalem hÿdrographicam Maris Balthici humillime offert. dicat dedicat Suæ Regiæ Majestatis Subjectissimus subditus P:Gedda. — 519 × 585 mm. [Inset:] [The Eastern part of the Gulf of Finland].   132 × 112 mm.

[2]   2 [C:] Wäxande Grad-Charta Öfwer NORRE-BOTTN Innehållandes alle Cousterne ifrån GEFLE. och ÅBO alt op till Tårneå, af de bästa Geometriska Charter så wäl som hans Kongh: Maÿs:[is] till Swerige för detta Ammirals Sal: Herr Hendrich Gerdtson Siöhielms Particulier Beskrÿfningar, med flÿt Saṁandragen och aftecknat med Kongh: May[s] Privilegiö på 10 Ahrs tÿd Af Petter Gedda. A[o]. 1695. — [C:] CAROLO Caroli XI. Svecorum, Gothorum, Wandalorumq[ue] Regis etc: etc: FILIO SERENISSIMO PRINCIPI SVECIAE HAEREDITARIO Mappam hancce Hydro-graphicam Sinus Bottnici, dicat dedicat Suæ Reg: Celsitudinis Devotissimus et Humillimus Servus P:Gedda. — 519 × 585 mm.

[3]   3 [C:] Special Passcharta Öfwer SKAGER-RACK, Uthwÿsandes rätta beskaffenheeten af Cousten ifrån Fredrikshall i Norrige alt till Landscrona afpeÿlat sammandragit och oprÿtat af Petter Gedda. Anno 1695. ... — [C:] Illustrissimo et Excelleutissimo Comiti Dno

IOHANNI WACHTMEISTER Sac:æ Reg:æ Maj:is Sueciæ Senatori, ut et Thalassiarcho etc: etc: Mappam hanc Hydrographicañ Humillimè offert suæ Excellentiæ Humillimus Cliens. P:Gedda. — 530 × 590 mm.
[Inset:] [T:] Marstrand — 90 × 135 mm.

[4] 4 [The Baltic Sea from] Orsund [to] Calmar [and fram] Damgard [to] Liba —
[C:] Illustrissimo Excellentissimo Comiti Dno FABIANO WREEDE, Sac:æ Reg:æ Maj:is Sveciæ Senatori, nec non Cameræ Præsidi etc: etc: Tabulam hanc hydro-graphicam humillimè dicat Excellentia suæ, Humillimus Servus P:Gedda. — [An empty cartouche]. 527 × 586 mm.

[5] 5 [C:] Special Passcharta Öfwer een Deel aff ÖSTER-SIÖÖN, Begynnandes ifrån Calmarsund intill Stockholm, innehållandes Iemwäl Öjarna Gottland och Öland, samandragen och affrytat med 10 Åhrs Privilegiö. Af Petter Gedda. A:o 1695. — [C:] Illutrissimo Excellentissimo Comiti Dno IACOBO IOHANNI HASTFER. ... Marschallo etc: etc: Tabulam hanc submisse præbet suæ Excellentiæ Humillimus Servus P:Gedda, — 533 × 586 mm.

[6] 6 [C:] Special Passcharta Öfwer een Deel af ÖSTER-SIÖÖN, Begynnandes ifrån Elsnabben att Vtwysa Stockholms-Skårgården medh Heela Cousten intill Gefle, samt och den Finska Skärgården till Åbo, jemwäl Heela Åland afteknat med Privilegiô af Petter Gedda. A:o 1695. — [C:] Illustrissimo atq₃ Excellentissimo Comiti Dno ERICO DAALBERG Sac:æ Reg:æ Maj:is Sveciæ Senatori, et Campi,Marschallo etc: etc: Mappam hanc Hydrographicam submisso animo attribuit suæ Excellentiæ Servus humillimus P:Gedda — 529 × 584 mm.

[7] 7 [The Gulf of Finland from] Kimito Ins. [and] DAGÖÖ [to] Inåå [and] Hariewalla — [An empty cartouche]. [C:] Illustrissimo et Excellentissimo Comiti Dno DIETRICO WRANGEL Sac:æ Reg:æ Maj:is Sveciæ senatori, etc: etc: Chartam hancce Hydrographicam perhumiliter exhibet suæ Excellentiæ Servus humillimus P:Gedda. — 529 × 592 mm.
[Inset:] [T:] [The Gulf of Finland from] Poika [and] Seeskär [to] Nyen-Skantz — 160 × 592 mm.

[8] 8 [C:] Special Passcharta Öfwer een Deel af ÖSTER-SIÖÖN, Altifrån Sandhamn till Ryga Innehållandes Iemwäl Moösund, samt Öjarna Ösel och Dagon, med een Deel af Gottland och den Curiske Wallen, delineerat med 10.Åhrs Privilegiö Af Petter Gedda. A:o 1695. — [C:] Generosissimo Baroni Dno IOHANNI CLERCK Sac:æ Reg:æ Maj:is Sveciæ Ammiraldo etc: etc: Hydrographicam hanc Tabulam humiliter tribuit Generosiss:mi Domini Observantissimus Servus P:Gedda. — 534 × 590 mm.

[9] 9 [C:] Några Små Pass-Chartor som uti Större bestick innehålla STOCKHOLMS-LEEDEN, samt BLEKINGS-CUSTEN, item OERESUND, så wäl som Farwattnet till STRALSUND, aftecknade med Kongh: May:s allernådigste Privilegiô på 10. åhrs Tyd af Petter Gedda A:o 1695. — [C:] Generosissimo Baroni Dno ERICO SIÖBLAD Sac:æ Reg:æ Maj:is Sveciæ Ammiraldo etc: etc: Mappam hanc Hydrographicam humili affectu offert Generosissimi Domini Addietissimus Servus P:Gedda 530 × 585 mm.
[a] STOCKHOLMS-LEEDEN 330 × 373 mm.
[b] (BLEKINGS-CUSTEN) 330 × 215 mm.
[c] (OERESUND) 202 × 303 mm.
[d] Farwattnet till STRALSUND 218 × 255 mm.

[10] 10 [C:] Special Passchartor Öfwer Fahrwatnet åth LYBECK Och WISMAR Item Köpenhamns-redd och Droogden Noch Dantziger-redd, Samt med Slytehamn på Gottland och Serlehamn Uppå OESEL; altsamans Medflyt observerat, samandragit och opsatt, med 10 Åhrs Privilegiö å. 1695. af Petter Gedda. — [C:] Generosissimo Dn. CORNELIO ANKARSTIERNA Sac:æ Reg:æ Maj:is Sveciæ Ammiraldo etc: Charta haecce hydrographica humiliter dedicatur â Generosiss:mi Domini Addictissimo Servô P Gedda — 530 × 585 mm.
[a] Fahrwatnet åth LYBECK Och WISMAR 343 × 282 mm.
[b] (Köpenhamns-redd och Droogden) 205 × 295 mm.
[c] (Danziger-redd.) 135 × 295 mm.
[d] [T:] WISMAR-REDD — 175 × 283 mm.
[e] Slytehamn på Gottland 175 × 207 mm.
[f] (Serlehamn Uppå OESEL) 155 × 84 mm.

[11] [C:] General Passcharta Öfwer ÖSTER-SIÖÖN och SKAGER-RACK, Uthwysandes alla Courserne på det aldranogaste och accurateste, som det uthi platt och efftter een medierat Compassens afwykningh görligit warit så efftter V:Ammiralens Wölh:ne H: Werner von Rosenfeldts, som Egne med flyt gion observationer, sammanfattat, och opteeknat af Petter Gedda. A:o 1695. [C:] Illustrissimo et Excellentissimo Comiti Dn:o NICOLAO BIELCKE, Sac:æ Reg:æ Maj:is Sveciæ Senatori, ut et Campi Marscallo etc: etc: Hydrographica hæctabula pariter dicatur á suæ Excellentiæ Humillimo Servo P.Gedda. — [C:] Illustrissimo Exellentissimq₃ Comiti Dn:o BENEDICTO OXENSTIERNA Sac:æ Reg:æ Maj:is Sveciæ Senatori, nec non ejusdem Collegy â Secretis Præsidi etc: etc: mappa hæcce dedicatur â suæ Excellentiæ Humillimo servo P:Gedda. — [C:] Illustrissimo atq₃ Excellentissimo Comiti Dn:o NICOLAO GYLDENSTOLPE. Sac:æ Reg:æ Maj:is Senatori, etc: etc: Charta hæcce Hydrographica similiter offertur â suæ Excellentiæ Humillimo servo P:Gedda. — 513 × 579 mm.
[Insets:] [T:] LADOGA SEE — 170 × 111 mm. [T:] CARLS-CRONA. — (View). 40 × 222 mm.

[12] [C:] Een ny Forbättrat General Passcharta ofwer NORR SIÖN. Rätt lagd efer Magnetens Ordi. Narie Wysande. A Niw Mendet General Chart of the NORT SEA. Drawn according the true Veruation of the Magnet. Een Niewe Verbeeterde Generale Passkaart van de NOORDT ZEE. Geleyt nae het Waare Wysen van den Magneet. ... Carl Eldberg Delineavit. L.van Anse Sculpsit: — 520 × 582 mm.
[Insets:] [T:] [From] Herwich [to] Crame — 87 × 196 mm. (Irregular). [T:] [The approach to] Götheborg — 130 × 87 mm. [T:] Giötheborg — (View). 43 × 163 mm. (Irregular).

Notes: The charts are mounted back-to-back on cardboard, the first being pasted to the inside of the front cover and the last, [12], to the inside of the back cover. All the charts are uncoloured. The collection contains two identical copies of this edition. They lack the title-page and the preliminary leaves. Gedda's atlas is the first Swedish sea-atlas, although it was actually engraved and printed in Amsterdam, as all the skilled engravers in Stockholm were at that time engaged upon another major project. The atlas was first published in Dutch and Swedish editions simultaneously, in the summer of 1695. This first edition contained only 10 charts; the other two were added for the 1699 edition. Nordenskiöld's signature is on the front cover of one copy; on the other are his initials A.E.N. with the year 1896, and on the cover in another hand 'Siö-Chartor'. Our collection has a third copy of this atlas, very incomplete but nonetheless interesting; it is described above under no. 76.

Lit.: Bratt, p. 68—70; Dahlgren-Richter p. 173—187; Ehrensvärd, Ulla, Introduction to the facsimile edition of Geddas atlas, Stockholm 1974, Koeman vol. 4, p. 190, Ged 1; Lang, p. 59—61.

78 Geographia Classica 1712

Geographia Classica: THE GEOGRAPHY OF THE ANCIENTS, So far describ'd as it is contain'd in the Greek and Latin Classicks. IN Twenty nine Maps of the Old World, and its several Kingdoms and Provinces: Wherein the chief Places mention'd in Homer, Virgil, Ovid, Lucan, Eutropius, Cornelius Nepos, Justin, Quintus Curtius, Sallust, Livy, Cæsar, Plutarch, Xenophon, Herodotus, and many other Ancient Authors are describ'd. To which is added, a Map of the Places mention'd in the Old and New Testaments. A Collection long wanted, and now Publish'd for the Use of SCHOOLS. LONDON, Printed for Christopher Browne at the West End of St.Paul's Church-Yard, and

Benj. Tooke at the Middle-Temple Gate: M DCCXII.   19,1 cm.

[1] 1 A Map of the Whole WORLD as far as it was known to the Antients.   147 × 226 mm.
[2] 2 [C:] The seat of the TROJAN WAR According to Dictis Cretensis and Dares Phrygius. — 156 × 226 mm.
[3] 3 [C:] THE NAVIGATION of VLYSSES according to Homer. — 157 × 227 mm.
[4] 4 [C:] THE Voyage of Æneas as Described by VIRGIL — 157 × 227 mm.
[5] 5 [C:] The Voyage of ÆNEAS as Described by DIONISIUS HALICARNASSEUS in his first Book — 156 × 227 mm.
[6] 6 [a] [C:] ITALY according to JUSTIN — 77 × 95 mm.
[b] [C:] GREECE according to JUSTIN — 77 × 92 mm.
[c] [C:] A MAP of the WORLD as far as it is described by JUSTIN — 81 × 228 mm.
[The whole map:]   158 × 228 mm.
[7] 7 [C:] THE INFANCY of the ROMAN EMPIRE according to Florus — 157 × 230 mm.
[8] 8 [C:] The ROMAN EMPIRE in its Youthfull Age according to Florus — 157 × 228 mm.
[9] 9 [C:] a Map of the ROMAN EMPIRE in its Maturity. — 157 × 230 mm.
[10] 10 [C:] The Expedition of HANNIBAL General of the CARTHAGINIANS according to Livy, & Cornelius Nepos. — 157 × 228 mm.
[11] 11 The ROMAN EMPIRE as it was in the time of JULIUS CÆSAR and it is described in his Commentaries, and in Silius Italicus.   133 × 227 mm.
[12] 12 [C:] GALLIA VETVS Ad Iulij Cæsaris comentaris C Browne Excudit. — 155 × 228 mm.
[13] 13 [T:] BÆTICA or the Southern Part of SPAIN as it is described by CÆSAR, de Bello HISPANICO. — 155 × 228 mm.
[14] 14 [C:] AFRICA. ex Bello Africano C.I.CÆSARIS — 157 × 228 mm.
[Inset:] [C:] ÆGIPTUS ex Bello Alexandrino C.I.Cæsaris — 58 × 62 mm.
[15] 15 A Map of EUROPE   ASIA & AFRICA as far as they are described in Lucan's Pharsalia   131 × 227 mm.
[16] 16 [C:] Antient GREECE and the adjacent ISLANDS according to Cornelius Nepos and others. — 182 × 241 mm.
[17] 17 [C:] GREECE and the Empire of Crœsus according to Herodotus. — 157 × 228 mm.
[18] 18 [C:] LYBIA according to HERODOTUS — 157 × 227 mm.
[19] 19 [C:] ÆGYPT As Described in the second Book of Herodotus. ... — 228 × 158 mm.
[20] 20 [C:] The Conquests of PYRRHUS King of the EPIROTS according to Plutarch. — 157 × 229 mm.
[21] 21 [C:] The Conquests of DEMETRIUS surnamed POLIORCETES — 155 × 227 mm.
[22] 22 [C:] The Expedition of Agisilaus King of Sparta according to Xenophon — 131 × 228 mm.
[23] 23 [C:] The Retreat of the ten Thousand Greeks according to Xenophon — 159 × 229 mm.
[24] 24 [C:] SYRIA and ASSYRIA According to the Description of Ptolomy and other Authors. — 157 × 226 mm.
[25] 25 [C:] SCRIPTURAL GEOGRAPHY Containing the Places mentioned in the OLD and NEW TESTAMENTS. — 157 × 331 mm.
[26] 26 A MAP of the places Mentioned in Eusebius'S Ecclesiastical History.   133 × 227 mm.
[27] 27 [C:] THE EMPIRE of CYRUS the GREAT first King of Persia — 157 × 227 mm.
[28] 28 [C:] THE PERSIAN EMPIRE Divided into Twenty Governments by Darius son of Histaspes — 157 × 227 mm.
[29] 29 [C:] The Expedition of ALEXANDER the GREAT according to Quintus Curtius, Arrian, and others. — 131 × 246 mm.

Notes: All the maps are blank on the back and uncoloured. Each plate is numbered twice, in the upper and lower right-hand corners. The numbers are in the parenthesis. The volume is bound in contemporary leather with blind tooling. On the title-page is the signature of Franciscus Blanching, with the words 'c m̃it Londini 1713', and on the blank leaf at the back are the words 'Ex libris Aldonizi Veraney'. Nordenskiöld's signature is on the inside of the front cover, with the year 1885.

Lit.: BMGC 83:756.

79 GOOS, PIETER   1658

DE Lichtende Colomne OFTE ZEE-SPIEGEL, Inhoudende De Zee-kusten van de Noordsche/ Oostersche/ en Westersche Schipvaert; vertoonende in vele nootsaecklÿcke Zee-Caerten/ alle de Havens/ Rivieren/ Baeyen/ Reeden/ Diepten/ en Drooghten; seer curieus op sijn behoorlÿcke Polus-hooghte geleght/ en versien met Opdoeninge der principaelste Landen/ en op wat Cours en Verheyt sy van malkanderen gelegen sÿn: Noyt voor desen so klaerlÿck uyt-gegeven/ en met groote vlÿt doorgaens vermeerdert en verbetert/ ten dienste van alle Zee-varende Persoonen. Als mede De Gelegentheyt van de Noordelijckste gelegen Landen, als van Yslant, de Straet Davis, Jan-Mayen Eylant, Beeren Eylant, Oudt Groenlant, Spits-bergen, en Nova Zembla: met veel Zee-Caerten en Opdoeningen versien. By een gebracht uyt ondersoeckinge van veel ervaren Stuer-luyden, Lootsen, en Liefhebberen der Navigatien. Met noch een Instructie ofte Onderwijs in de Konst der Zee-vaert/ als mede nieuwe Tafelen van des Sons en Sterren declinatie: Met een Almanach tot den Jare 1666. t'AMSTERDAM, Gedruckt by PIETER GOOS, Boeckverkooper op't Water, by de Nieuwe-brugh, in de Vergulde Zee-Spiegel. ANNO 1658.
[Half-title:]
DE Lichtende Colomne, OFTE Zee-spiegel, Inhoudende Eene Beschrijvinghe der See-Kusten Van de OOSTERSCHE en NOORDSCHE SCHIP-VAERT. Vertonende in veele nootsakelijcke Zee-Caerten alle de Havens/Rivieren/Baeyen/ Reeden/Diepten/ en Droogten; seer curieus op sijn behoorlijcke Polus-hooghte ghelegt/ en versien met de Op-doeninghe der principale Landen/ en op wat Cours en Verheydt sy van malkanderen ghelegen zijn: Noyt voor desen soo klaerlijck uyt-ghegheven/ en met groote vlijdt doorgaens vermeerdert en verbetert/ ten dienste van alle Zee-varende Personen. By-een ghebracht uyt ondersoeckinghe van veel ervaren Stier-luyden, Lootsen, en Lief-hebberen der Navigatien. TOT AMSTERDAM, By PIETER GOOS, op't Water by de Nieuwe-Brugh, in de Vergulde Zee-Spiegel, ANNO 1657.   45,3 cm.

Vol. I
[1] 1 [C:] Pascaart van EUROPA, Als mede een gedeelt vande cust van Africa. — Before I   A.   427 × 529 mm.
[2] 2 [C:] Pascaarte van de NOORT ZEE Vertonende van Caliz tot Dronten, als oock tusschen Doeveren en Hitlandt, T'AMSTERDAM. Bÿ Pieter Goos Plaetsnÿder op't water in De Vergulde Zee-Spiegel. A.º 1656. — Before I   A.   427 × 529 mm.
[3] 3 [C:] Pascaarte vande ZUYDER-ZEE, Texel, ende Vliestroom, als mede 't Amelander-gat. t'Amsterdam, Bÿ Pieter Goos op't Water inde Vergulde Zee Spiegel Anno 1657. — Before I   A.   429 × 524 mm.
Eerste Boeck der Nieuwe LICHTENDE ZEE-COLOMNE, OFTE ZEE-SPIEGEL. VAN DE Oostersche en Noordtsche Schip-vaert. ... Eerste Verthooninghe, Waer in De Zuyder-Zee/ Vlie-stroom/ Vlie en Amelander-gat.
[4] 4 [a] [C:] Pascaarte vande EEMSEN, Als de oude ofte wester Eems en de ooster Eems. — 432 × 253 mm.
[b] [C:] Pascaarte van't VLIE, Als mede een gedeelt van't Amelander gat. — 432 × 276 mm.
[The whole chart:] Between pp. 4 and 5   A 3.   432 × 532 mm.
[5] 5 [C:] Pascaerte Vande EEMS, ELVE, Weser, Eyder, en de Hever: als mede hoe die selvighe gaten van Heylighelandt gelegen syn. — Between pp. 4 and 5   A 3.   426 × 538 mm.

[6] Beschrijvinge van de Vliestroom. (3 profiles). On 5 A 3.

De Tweede Verthooninghe, Waer in: Van de Scholbalgh, Lauwers, Schille, beyde de Eemsen, de Weser, Elve, ende Eyder, oock andere Zee-gaten tusschen beyden.

[7] De Zee-gaten tusschen Scholbalgh en de Eyder. (13 profiles). On 11 B 2.

De Derde Verthooninghe, Waer in De Kusten vande West en Oostzijde van Jutlant: Mitsgaders de Beldt, tot voorby Lalant en Langelant tot aen Barts, en Meun.

[8] 6 [C:] Pascaerte Vande West en Oost-zyde van IVTLANDT, Als mede De Belt Mitsgaders De Zee-cust van Holster, Mekelenborg, en de Eylanden van Lalandt, Falster, ende Meun. — Between pp. 10 and 11 B 2. 431 × 707 mm.

[9] De Kusten van Jutlandt ende Beldt. (10 profiles). On 20

De Vierde Verthooninghe, Waer in Het Schager Rack, vande Paternosters tot Kol, en voorts door de Sondt tot Falsterbon, als mede de Sondt in 't groot.

[10] 7 [C:] Pascaarte vant SCHAGER-RACK vande Paternosters aen Kol, als mede de Sondt, oock hoe dese landen van Schagen gelegen zyn. — Between pp. 20 and 21 C 3. 429 × 534 mm.
[Inset:] [C:] De SONDT, met alle zyn gelegentheyt int groot. — 213 × 318 mm. (Irregular).

[11] [T:] Wt-Clippen ofte Paternosters   Eylant Masterlant — On 21 C 3 80 × 154 mm. (Irregular).

[12] [T:] Nydingh — On 22 45 × 214 mm. (Irregular).

[13] [T:] Kol, over dese 2 Warders Z.W. van u. — On 22 80 × 100 mm. (Irregular).

[14] 't Schager-Rack/ vande Pater-Nosters tot Kol/ als mede de Sondt. (6 profiles). On 27 D 2.

De Vijfde Verthooninghe Waer in: De Kusten van Noorweghen, vande Pater-Nosters tot der Neus.

[15] 8 [C:] Custen van NOORWEGEN, van Der Neus tot aen de Pater noster oock hoe de seluige Landen van Iutlant gelegen zyn. — Between pp. 28 and 29 D 3. 438 × 534 mm.

[16] [T:] De Haven van Maerdou. — On 29 D 3 118 × 140 mm. (Irregular).

[17] De Kusten van Noorweghen/ van de Pater-Nosters tot der Neus. (8 profiles). On 31—32

De Seste Verthooninge, Waer in De Kusten van Noorwegen, tusschen der Neus ende Schuytenes.

[18] 9 [C:] De Custen van NOORWEGEN Tusschen Der Neus en Schuitenes — Between pp. 32 and 33 E. 429 × 529 mm.

[19] 10 [C:] Pascaerte van 't Liedt van BERGEN, Beginnende van Schuitenes tot aen Bergen. — Between pp. 32 and 33 E. 434 × 642 mm.

[20] Aldus is het Lant van de Jedder gedaen/ ... (2 profiles). On 33 E

De Sevenste Verthooninghe, Waer in: Hoemen 't Liet van Bergen op sal zeylen.

[21] Aldus doet de Bock op/ als men bezuyden Schuytenes is voor dat Liet. Aldus is den Bergh Sijck gedaen/ alsmen benoorden Schuytenes is. (2 profiles). On 36

De Achtste Verthooninghe, Zijnde De Kusten van Noorwegen, tusschen Ieltefioert en de hooge Hoeck van Horrel.

[22] 11 [C:] De Cust van NOORWEGEN Vertoonde van Bergen tot aen de hoeck van Horrel. — Between pp. 36 and 37 E 3. 428 × 538 mm.

[23] De Kusten van Noorwegen/ tusschen Jeltefioert en de hooge Hoeck van Horrel. (12 profiles). On 37 E 3—38

De Negenste Verthooninghe, Hoemen 't Liet van Dronten op seylen sal.

[24] 12 [C:] Caarte van NOORWEGEN vande hoeck van Horrel tot aen Momendael, waer in begrepen wort het Liet van Dronten. — Between pp. 38 and 39. 426 × 526 mm.

[25] Hoe men 't Liet van Dronten op-seylen sal. (9 profiles). On 41 F — 42

De Thiende Verthooninghe, Waer in De Oost-cust van Engelandt, van de Riviere van Londen tot Welles.

[26] 13 [C:] Pascaarte van ENGELANT Van t' Voorlandt tot aen Blakeney waer in te sien, is de mont vande Teemse. — Between pp. 42 and 43 F 2. 428 × 541 mm.
[Inset:] [C:] Rivier van Londen. — 96 × 321 mm.

[27] De Oost-Cust van Engelant/ tusschen de Rivier van Londen en Welles. (5 profiles). On 46

[28] 14 [C:] De Cust van ENGELANDT tusschen Welles en 't Eylandt Coket — Between pp. 46 and 47. 427 × 533 mm.

[29] Aldus is 't gedaen langs de noord-kust van Engelandt/ tusschen Jarmuyen Krammer/ alsmen binnen de bancken deur seylt. (Profile). On 47

De Elfde Verthooninghe, Waer in De Custen van Engelant en Schotlant, tusschen Welles en Coggen-Eylandt.

[30] De Kusten van Engelant en Schotlant/ tusschen Welles en Coggen-Eylant. (3 profiles). On 50

De Twaefde Verthooninghe, Zijnde De Kusten van Engelant en Schotlant, tusschen Koggen Eylant en d'Orcades.

[31] 15 [C:] De Custen van SCHOTLANT met de Eylanden van Orcanesse, van eylandt Coket tot I. Sande. — Between pp. 50 and 51 G 2. 424 × 527 mm.

[32] De Kusten van Schotlant/ tusschen Coggen-Eylant en d'Orcades. (4 profiles).   On 52

De Derthiende Verthooninge, Zijnde De Zee-Kusten van Fayerhil, Hitlant, en de omleggende Eylanden; Als mede d'Eylanden Fero, en sommige Eylanden achter de noord-west-hoeck van Schotlant.

[33] 16 [a] [C:] Eylanden van HITLANDT ofte Schetlant, Fayer hil, en Fulo. — 212 × 527 mm.
[b] [C:] Eylanden van HEBRIDES gelegen achter de noord-west hoeck van Schotlant. — 212 × 267 mm.
[c] [C:] Eylandē van FERO ofte Farre. — 212 × 258 mm.
[The whole chart:] Between pp. 52 and 53 G 3. 426 × 527 mm.

[34] De Zee-kusten van Fayerhil/ Hitlandt/ Fero/ en d'Eylanden van Schotlant. (27 profiles). On 55 — 56

TWEEDE BOECK DER NIEUWE LICHTENDE ZEECOLOMNE, OFTE ZEE-SPIEGEL, VAN DE OOSTERSCHE en NOORTSCHE SCHIP-VAERT. Inhoudende De Beschrijvinge van de Zee-Custen Noorwegen, Finmarcken, Laplant, Russen, en de gantsche Witte Zee.

[35] 17 [C:] Pascaart Vande zeecusten van RVSLANT, Laplant, Finmarcken, en Spitzbergen. — Between pp. 56 and 57 H. 440 × 529 mm.

[36] 18 [C:] De Custen van NOORWEGH̄ tusschen Dronten en Tromsondt. — Between pp. 56 and 57 H. 430 × 246 mm.

De eerste Verthooninghe, Zynde De Custen van Finmarcken/ van Dronten/ tot 't Eylandt Trom-zondt.

[37] De Cust van Finmarcken/ van Dronten tot Tromzont. (12 profiles). On 57 H — 58

De tweede Verthooninghe, Van De Cust van Finmarcken, van 't Eylandt Sanien, of Trom-zont tot Kijn of de Noordt-Caep.

[38] 19 [C:] Caarte van FINMARCKEN van t' Eylandt Sanien tot Noordkyn. — Between pp. 58 and 59 H 2. 434 × 530 mm.

[39] De Cust van Finmarcken/ van 't Eylandt Tromzondt tot Noort-kijn. (27 profiles). On 59 H 2 — 60

[40] 20 [C:] De Custen van NOORWEGEN en Laplandt, vande Noord-kyn tot aen de Rivier van Kola. — Between pp. 60 and 61 H 3. 427 × 530 mm.
[Inset:] [T:] Het Eylandt Wardhuys — 115 × 154 mm.

[41] De Cust van Finmarcken/ van 't Eylandt Trom-zondt tot Noord-kijn. (4 profiles). On 61 H3

De derde Verthooninghe, Waer in zijn De Zee-Custen tusschen de Noordt-Caep, of Noordt-Kijn tot de Rivier van Kola.

[42] De Zee-Custen tusschen de Noordt-Kijn en de Rivier van Kola. (20 profiles). On 62 — 63

De vierde Verthooninghe, Van De Zee-Custen van Laplandt, tusschen de Riviere Kola en de Eylanden van Swetenoes.

[43] 21 [a] [C:] Het eylandt Kilduyn met de Reede nae 't leven ontworpen leggende op de hoochte van 69 graden 40 minuiten. — 126 × 181 mm.
[b] [C:] De Rivier van KOLA in 't groot besteck. — 126 × 357 mm.
[c] [C:] De Custe van LAPLANDT tusschen de Rivier van Kola en de eylandē van Swetenoes — 296 × 542 mm.
[The whole chart:] Between pp. 64 and 65   I. 428 × 542 mm.

[44] 22 [C:] Pascaarte Van de Mont van de WITTE ZEE, tot

aende Riuier Dwina al: Archangel toe. — Between pp. 66 and 67 I 2. 425 × 533 mm.
[Insets:] [T:] SWETENOES, met de Eylandekens daer ontrent gelegen nae't leven ontworpen — 120 × 245 mm. (Irregular). [T:] De Eylanden van LOMBASCHO na't leven ontworpen — 85 × 80 mm.

[45] De Zee-Custen tusschen de Rivier Kola/ en d'Eylanden van Swetenoes. (7 profiles). On 67 I 2

De vyfde Verthooninghe, Zynde De Kust van de Mondt van de Witte Zee.

[46] 23 [C:] Pascaarte van WITTE-ZEE begrypende de custen van Laplandt, van Warsiga tot aen Kandalox en de cust van Corelia tot aen de Riviere Dwina — Between pp. 68 and 69 I 3. 432 × 525 mm.

[47] XXIII [C:] Caerte van ARCHANGEL ofte de Rivier de Duina, soo wel van't Nieuwe als 't Oude diep. — Between pp. 68 and 69 I 3. 423 × 523 mm.

[48] Aldus is 't Landt gedaen tusschen Swetenoes en Orlogenes/ alsmen daer voorby seylt. (Profile). On 69 I 3

De seste Verthooninghe, Synde De Zee-Kusten van de Witte Zee, en de Rivier van Archangel in 't groot.

[49] 23¼ [C:] Pascaarte van GROEN-LANDT, Yslandt, Straet Davids en Ian Mayen eylandt, hoemen de selvige van Hitlandt en de Noortcusten van Schotlandt en Yrlandt beseylen mach. — Between pp. 70 and 71. 428 × 530 mm.

Derde Boeck der Nieuwe LICHTENDE ZEE COLOMNE, OFTE ZEE-SPIEGEL, VANDE OOSTERSCHE en NOORTSCHE SCHIP-VAERT. Inhoudende De Beschrijvinge van Yslandt, Groenlandt, ofte de Straet Davids, als mede de gelegentheydt van Jan Mayen Eylandt, en Spits-Bergen, voorders de streckinghe van Candenoes Oost-waerts aen door het Waygat, tot de Tartarische ofte Ys-Zee.

De eerste Verthooninghe, Zynde De gelegentheydt tusschen Hitlandt ende Yslandt/ en van daer na de Straet Davids/ of de hoeck van Out-Groenlandt nu genaemt Staten-hoeck.
No charts.

De tweede Verthooninghe, Zynde De Beschryvinghe van Jan Mayen Eylandt.

[50] De Noord-West-Hoeck.
[C:] De Noordwest hoec van IAN MAYEN Eylandt. — (View). On 75 K 2 151 × 205 mm.

[51] De Beschrijvinge van Jan Mayen Eylandt. (3 profiles). On 76

[52] [a] 23½ [C:] Pas-caert van IAN MAYEN EYLANT. Verthoonde alle de ghelegentheyt van alle bayen, inbochten, diepten en en drooghten. — 427 × 251 mm.
[b] 23¾ [C:] Pas-caerte van SPITSBERGEN met alle haer Rivieren, havens, bayen, sanden en drooghten, als mede Hoemen C. de Uytkyck op Spits-bergen van de Noord Caap en Beeren Eylandt bezeylen sal. — 427 × 250 mm.
[The whole map:] Between pp. 76 and 77 K 3. 427 × 505 mm.

De derde Verthooninghe, Zynde De gheleghentheydt van 't Beeren-Eylandt. 't Hoopen-Eylant, als mede van geheel Spitsbergen, soo veel als die tot noch toe benoorden ende beoosten bekent is.

[53] 22½ De Hollantsche ofte Mourits Bay. On 79 151 × 211 mm.

[54] Beschrijvinge van 't Beeren-Eylant/ en 't Hoopen Eylant. (2 profiles). On 81 L

De Vierde Verthooninge, Waer in sijn: De Beschrijvinghe van Orlogenes en Kaep de Candenoes tot aen de West-Kuste van Nova Sembla en't Waygat.
No charts.

Vierde Boeck der Nieuwe Lichtende Zee Colomne, OFTE ZEE-SPIEGEL. VAN DE OOSTERSCHE en NOORTSCHE SCHIP-VAERT. Inhoudende De Beschrijvinghe van de gantsche Oost-Zee. De Eerste Verthooninghe, Waer in sijn: De Zee-kusten van Valsterboen tot Schenckenes, ende van het Eylant Rugen tot Rijgshooft.

[55] 24 [C:] Pascaarte vande OOST-ZEE Van't Eylandt Rugen, ofte Bornholm tot aen Wyborg. T'AMSTERDAM. Bÿ Pieter Goos Plaetsnÿder op't water in De Vergulde Zee-Spiegel, A.º 1656. — Between pp. [84] and 85 L 3. 430 × 538 mm.

[56] 25 [C:] De Custen van DENEMARCKEN en Sweden van Valsterbon tot Schenckenes, Als mede de Custen van Pomeren van 't Eylant Rugen tot Rygshooft. — Between pp. [84] and 85 L 3. 436 × 528 mm.

[57] 't NIEUWE-DIEP.
[T:] EYLANDT RVGEN POMEREN — On 88 169 × 200 mm.

[58] 26 [C:] Caarte van PRVYSSEN en Coerlandt van Rugshooft tot der Winda — Between pp. 90 and 91 M 2. 431 × 529 mm.

[59] De Zee-Kusten tusschen Valsterboen en Schenckenes. Als mede van't Eylant Rugen tot Rijghs-hooft. (11 profiles). On 91 M 2

De Tweede Verthooninge, Waer in sijn: De Zee-Kusten tusschen Rijghs-Hooft en der Winda.

[60] De Zee-Kusten tusschen Rijghs-hooft ende Der Winda. (14 profiles). On 93 M 3

De Derde Verthooninge, Waer in sijn: De Zee-Kusten tusschen Der Winda en Revel, als mede de Eylanden van 't Alandts Haff.

[61] 27 [C:] Pascaarte van LIIFLANDT ende Oost-Finlandt, van der Winda tot aende hoeck van Alandt ende voort tot Revel. — Between pp. 94 and 95. 430 × 528 mm.

[62] De Zee-Kusten tusschen Der Winda en Revel/ (18 profiles). On 98 — 99 N 2

[63] 28 [C:] De Zeecusten van LIIFLANDT, ende Oost Finlandt, van Wolfs-oort tot aen Wyborgh. — Between pp. 98 and 99 N 2. 425 × 528 mm.

De vierde Verthooninghe, Zynde De Zee-Kusten tusschen Wolf, en 't uytterste van de Oost-Zee.

[64] Groot en Kleyn Wranger. On 99 N 2 116 × 152 mm. (Irregular).

[65] De Zee-Kusten tusschen 't Eylant Wolf en 't uyterste vande Oost-Zee. (9 profiles). On 102 and 103.

De Vijfde Verthooninge, Waer in sijn: De Zee-Kusten van Sweden, tusschen Oelandt, en Stockholm, als mede de Eylanden van Oelant en Gotlant, en't Liet van Stockholm in 't groot, en 't Gat van Vttoy.

[66] 29 [C:] Caarte van SWEDEN Van Oelandt tot aen Stocholm — Between pp. 102 and 103.

[67] 30 [a] [C:] Caarte van't gat van ABBO, ofte VTTOY. — 432 × 262 mm.
[b] [C:] Caarte van STOCHOLMSE Liet. — 432 × 257 mm.
[The whole chart:] Between pp. 102 and 103. 432 × 525 mm.

[68] De Zee-Kusten van Sweden/ tusschen Oelant en Stockholm. (4 profiles). On 108

Vol. II
Eerste Boeck der Nieuwe Lichtende Zee Colomne, OFTE ZEE-SPIEGEL. VANDE WESTERSCHE SCHIP-VAERT, Inhoudende De Beschrijvinghe der Zee-Kusten van Hollandt, Zeelandt en Vlaenderen, van Texel tot de Hoofden.

De Eerste Verthooninge, Waer in sijn: De Tessel-stroom en Gaten van Texel.

[1] 31 [C:] Cust van Hollant tusschen de Maes ende Texel. — Between pp. 2 and 3 (A) 2. 422 × 528 mm.

[2] 32 [a] [C:] De TEXEL Stroom met de gaten vant Marsdiep. — 430 × 261 mm.
[Inset:] [C:] Caarte vande Reede end Haven van Medenblick hoemen die comen soo van 't Wieringer als vriesch vlack beseylen mogen tot dienst en nut voor alle Zeevaren luyden, perfectelyc gemeten en afgepeylt, Beschreve A.º 1641 uyt speciale last van E.H.Burgermeesteren en de Regeerders der voorss. Stadt Medenblick. — 240 × 112 mm. (Irregular).
[b] [C:] Caarte van DE MASE; Ende het Goereesche gat. — 430 × 267 mm.
[The whole chart:] Between pp. 2 and 3 (A) 2. 430 × 534 mm.

De Tweede Verthooninge, Waer in is: De Hollantsche Kust, van Texel tot de Maes, als mede De Gaten van Texel, de Maes en 't Goereetsche gat.

[3] Texel/ Maes/ en 't Goereesche-Gat. (14 profiles). On 7 (B) 2.

De Derde Verthooninge, Waer in zijn: Al de Zee-Gaten, tusschen de Maes en de Wielingen, als van Brouwers-haven, Zierck-zee, Der Veer, en de Wielingen.

[4] 33 [C:] De Cust van ZEELANDT, Begrypende in sich de gaten, als vande Wielingen, ter Veere. Ziericzee, Brouwershaven, Goeree, en de Maes — Between pp. 8 and 9 (C). 429 × 529 mm.

[5] 34 [C:] De Cust van VLAENDEREN Beginnende vande Wielingen tot aen de Hoofden met alle haer sanden en droogten. — Between pp. 12 and 13 (D). 429 × 538 mm.

[6] De Zee-gaten van ter Veer ende Wielingen. (4 profiles). On 13 (D).

De Vierde Vertooninge, VVaer in sijn: De Cust van Vlaenderen, van de Wielingen tot de Hoofden, als ook de Cust van Engelant, van Doveren tot 't noord Voor-land.

[7] De Kust van Engelant van 't Voorlant tot Doveren. (4 profiles). On 18

Tweede Boeck der Nieuwe Lichtende Zee Colomne, OFTE ZEE-SPIEGEL. VANDE WESTERSCHE SCHIP-VAERT, Inhoudende De Beschrijvinghe van de Kusten van Vranckrijck, van Tresport tot Roscou: Ende Kusten van Engelant, van Fierley West aen tot Engelants-eyndt: 't Canaal van Brustou: Als mede de Zee-Kusten van Yrlant.

De Eerste Verthooninge, Waer in: De Kusten van Vranckrijck, Van Swartenes tot 't Eylant Ornay, en van Doveren tot Bevesier.

[8] 35 [C:] Pascaart vant CANAAL Begrypende in sich Engelandt, Schotlandt, en Jerlandt, als mede een gedeelt van Francryck. — Between pp. 18 and 19 (E) 2. 430 × 533 mm.

[9] 36 [C:] De Cust van NORMANDIE en Picardie. als mede een gedeelt in Engelandt tusschen de Hoofden ende Ornay. — Between pp. 18 and 19 (E) 2. 425 × 530 mm.

[10] De Cust van Normandye/ van Swartenes tot 't Eylandt Ornay. (12 profiles). On 22

De Tweede Verthooninge, Waer in zijn: De Cust van Bretaigne, van 't Eylandt Ornay tot het Eylandt van Heysandt.

[11] 37 [C:] De Custen van BRETAIGNE, Waer in vertoont wort alle gelegentheyt tusschen Caap de Hague en 't Eylant Heyssant. — Between pp. 22 and 23 (F) 2. 427 × 530 mm.

[12] S. MALO. [C:] De Haven van S. Malo — On 24   171 × 152 mm.

[13] 38 [C:] De Custen van ENGELANDT, tusschen Fierley en Poortlant, oock hoese van Ornay gelegen zyn. — Between pp. 26 and 27 (G) 2. 427 × 531 mm.

[14] De Cust van Bretaigne/ tusschen 't eylandt Orany/ en Heyzant. (6 profiles). On 27 (G) 2

De Derde Vertooninge. VVaer in sijn: De Cust van Engelandt van Bevesier tot Poortlandt.

[15] De Cust van Engelandt/ tusschen Bevesier en Poortlandt. (7 profiles). On 30

De vierde Verthooninghe, Zynde De Kust van Engelant, tusschen Poortlant en Lezart.

[16] TORBAY. On 30   71 × 98 mm.

[17] 39 [C:] De Custen Van Engelant tusschen de twee pointen van Poortlandt en Lezard. — Between pp. 30 and 31 (H) 2. 411 × 526 mm.

[18] De Cust van Engelandt tusschen Poosrtlant en Lezart. (20 profiles). On 32 — 34

De vijfde Verthooninghe, Zynde De Kusten van Engelant, van Lezart en Engelantseyndt, tot C. de Cornwal, de Sorrels, en het Canaal van Brustou.

[19] 40 [C:] Cust van ENGELANT, Van Lezard tot Engelands Eyndt, de Sorlinges, ende Canaal van Brestou, als mede hoe zy van Yerland gelegen syn. — Between pp. 34 and 35 (I) 2. 425 × 529 mm.
[Inset:] [T:] Sorlinges — 122 × 113 mm.

[20] De kust van Engel. van Lezart of Engelants-eynt tot kaep de Cornwal. De Sorrels/ ende Verkeerde Canael van Bristouw. (29 profiles). On 38 — 39 (K) 2

De seste Verthooninghe, Zynde De Zuyd-oost en Oost-Kust van Yrlant, tusschen Corckbegh en Hedenhoo ofte Hout.

[21] 41 [C:] De Zuyd Oost zyde Van YERLANDT Van Dubling tot aen t' Eylandt Corkbeg. — Between pp. 40 and 41 (L). 414 × 542 mm.

[22] Boven-landt ofte 't Hooge landt over den hoeck van Grenoort. 't Vlacke Voor-landt van Grenoort. (Profile). On 41 (L) 25 × 56 mm.

[23] De zuyd-oost en oost Cust van Yerlandt/ tusschen Corckbeg en Hedenhoo. (20 profiles). On 45 (M) — 47 (M) 2

[24] 42 [C:] De Noord-oost zyde van YERLANDT Van Caap de Hoorn tot aen Hedehde en als mede hoe t'van Schotlandt gelegen is. — Between pp. 46 and 47 (M) 2. 416 × 531 mm.

De sevenste Verthooninghe, Zynde De noord-oost Cust van Yerlandt, tusschen Hedenhoo of Hout, en Hoornhed, als oock Schotlandt daer tegen over.

[25] De noord-oost Cust van Yrlant/ tusschen Hedenho en Hoornhead; (11 profiles). On 50 —51 (N) 2

[26] 43 [C:] De Noordwest zyde van YERLANDT. Beginnende van Capo de Hoorn tot aen Schynes, ofte Slynehead. — Between pp. 50 and 51 (N) 2. 427 × 525 mm.

De achtste Verthooninghe, Zynde De noord-west Cust van Yerlandt, tusschen Hoornhead en Slynehead.

[27] De noord-oost Cust van Yrlant/ tusschen Hoornhead en Slynehead; (12 profiles). On 52 — 53 (O)

[28] 44 [C:] De west custen van YERLANDT Beginnende van Corckbeg tot aen Slynhooft. — Between pp. 52 and 53 (O). 429 × 531 mm.

De negenste Verthooninghe, Zynde De West-Hoeck en Zuyd-Cust van Yrlandt, tusschen Slynenead en Corck-Haven.

[29] De West-hoek en Zuyd-kust van Yrlant tusschen Slynehead en Corck haven. (42 profiles). On 56 — 59 (P) 2 59 (P) 2 with verso blank.

Derde Boeck der LICHTENDE ZEE-COLOMNE, OFTE ZEE-SPIEGEL. VAN DE WESTERSCHE SCHIP-VAERT: Inhoudende de Beschrijvinge van Vranckrijck/ Biscayen/ Galissien/ Portugael en Algarve/ van Heyssant tot de Strate van Gibralter.

De eerste Verthooninghe, Zynde De Kust van Vranckrijck, van Heysant en het Eylandt Boelyn.

[30] 45 [C:] De Custen van HISPANIA, als Andaluzia, Portugal, Gallissien, Biscajen, en een gedeelt van Vranckryck, beginnen van Heysant tot aen Larache. — Between pp. [60] and 61 (Q). 427 × 532 mm.

[31] 46 [C:] De Cust van Bretaigne van Heysandt tot aent Eylant Boelyn. — Between pp. [60] and 61 (Q). 427 × 533 mm.

[32] S. Matheus klooster. Conquets oort. (Profile). On 61 (Q)

[33] De Zee-kusten van Bretaignien tusschen Heysant en het eylandt Boeljin. (24 profiles). On 65 (R) — 66

De Tweede Verthooninge, Zynde De Cust van Poictou en Xantoigne, tusschen Boelyn en de Rivier van Bordeaux.

[34] 47 [C:] De Custen van POICTOU, XANTOIGNE En een gedeelt van Bretaigne van Boelyn tot aen de Rivier van Bourdeaux. — Between pp. 66 and 67 (R) 2. 420 × 525 mm.

[35] AFBEELDINGE van OLLONNE. On 68   162 × 226 mm.

[36] De Cust van Poictou en Xantoigne/ van Boelijn tot de Rivier van Bordeaux. (19 profiles) On 71 (S) 2 — 72

De derde Verthooninghe, Zynde De Beschrijvinge van de Rivier van Bordeaux; als mede van de selvige tot S. Sebastiaen ofte Konincx-Reede.

[37] 48 [C:] Caarte Vande Rivier van Bourdeaux tot aen Bayone en voorts aen Coninx rede. — Between pp. 72 and 73 (T). 414 × 530 mm.

[38] De Kust van Vranckrijck van de Rivier van Bordeaux tot Konincks-Reede. (11 profiles). On 74—75 (T) 2.

De vierde Verthooninghe, Zynde De Cust van Biscayen tusschen Konincks-Reede en het Eylandt Sint Cipriaen.

[39] 49 [a] [C:] Kust Van Biscayen tusschen Orio ende rio de Sella. — 205 × 524 mm.
[b] [C:] Kust Van Biscayen tusschen Rio de Sella en t'Eylant van S. Cyprian. — 205 × 524 mm.
[The whole chart:] Between pp. 74 and 75 (T) 2. 414 × 524 mm.

[40] De Cust van Biscayen van Konincks-Reede tot S. Cipriaen. (31 profiles). 78—80

De vijfde Verthooninghe, Zynde De Zee-Custen van Galissien en Portugall, tusschen 't Eylandt van S. Sipriaen en Camina.

[41] 50 [C:] Caarte Vande custen van Galissien tusschen 't Eylant van S. Ciprian en Camina — Between pp. 80 and 81 (X).   421 × 529 mm.
[42] De Kusten van Galissien en Portugall/ van S. Cypriaen tot Camina.   (31 profiles). 84—86

De seste Verthooninghe, Zynde De Zee-Kusten van 't Noordelijkste deel van Portugall, van Camina tot Pissage.

[43] 51 [C:] Cust van PORTVGAL t'Noordelyckste deel beginnende van Viana tot aen Pissage. — Between pp. 86 and 87 (Y 2).   404 × 510 mm.
[44] De Kust. van 't Noordlijkste deel van Portugall/ van Camina tot Pissage. (13 profiles). On 87 (Y 2)—88

De sevenste Verthooninghe, Zynde De Zee-Kusten van 't Zuydlijckste deel van Portugall van Pissage tot S. Uves ofte Setubal.

[45] 52 [C:] De Cust van PORTVGAEL Het Zuydlyckste deel, Beginnende van Pissage tot aen S. Vues alias Setubal. — Between pp. 88 and 89   (Z).   427 × 525 mm.
[46] De Kust. van 't Zuydelijkste deel van Portugall/ van Pissage tot S. Uves. (8 profiles). On 89 (Z) — 90

De achtste Verthooninghe, Zynde De Zee-Kusten Algarve en Andaluzia van S. Uves tot Palos ofte Clif.

[47] 53 [C:] Cust van ANDALVZIA, En Algarve, Beginnende van Capo de Spichel tot aen het Clif. — Between pp. 90 and 91 (Z2).   428 × 523 mm.
[48] De Kusten van Algarve en Andaluzia/ van S. Uves tot Polos ofte Clif.   (15 profiles). On 92 — 93 (Aa)

De negenste Verthooninghe, Zynde De Zee-Kusten van Andaluzien, van Polos tot door de Strate van Gibralter by Modril, ende de Kuste van Barbaryen daer tegen over. Als mede de Barbarische Kust van C. Spartel tot oudt Mamora.

[49] 54 [C:] Cust van HISPANGIEN Vande Rivier van Sivilien tot aen Malaga ende De cust van Barbarien van Out Mamora tot Penon de Velez. — Between pp. 92 and 93 (Aa).   397 × 528 mm.
[50] De Spaensche Cust van Malaga tot Modril. On 95 (Aa)2 74 × 235 mm. (Irregular).
[51] De Zee-Cust. van Andaluzia/ van Palos tot inde Straet voorby Modril. Als mede de Kusten van Barbarien daer tegen over. (6 profiles). On 97 (Bb) Verso blank.

Vierde Boeck der LICHTENDE ZEE COLOMNE, OFTE ZEE-SPIEGEL, VAN DE WESTERSCHE SCHIP-VAERT. Inhoudende De Custen van Barbarien/ Gualata// Arguyn/ Genehoe/ en de Vlaemsche ende Canarische Eylanden/ van de Straet van Gibralter tot Capo de Verde.

De eerste Verthooninghe, Zynde De Zee-Kusten van Barbarien, van Oudt Mamora tot Capo de Geer, als mede de Vlaemsche Eylanden.

[52] 55 [C:] De Cust van BARBARIA, Gualata, Arguyn, en Geneheo, van Capo S. Vincente tot Capo Verde. — Between pp. [98] and 99 (Bb) 2.   425 × 526 mm.
[53] 56 [a] [C:] de Cust van Barbaryen van out Mamora tot Capo Blanco. — 160 × 528 mm.
  [b] [C:] De Cust van Barbaryen van Capo Blanco Tot Capo de Geer. — 152 × 528 mm.
  [c] [C:] De Reede van Punte del Gada int Eylandt S. Michiels. — 114 × 120 mm.
  [Inset:] [T:] De zuydhoec vant Eylandt FAYAL. — 51 × 51 mm.
  [d] [C:] De Reede voor de Stadt Abgra int eylandt Tercera — (Plan). 114 × 217 mm.
  [e] [C:] De Eylanden van Madera en Porto Santo — 114 × 184 mm.
  [The whole map:] Between pp. [98] and 99 (Bb) 2. Verso blank.   436 × 528 mm.
[54] De Zee-Kusten van Barbarien/ van Mamora tot C. de Geer/ Als mede de Vlaemsche Eylanden. (18 profiles). 103 (Cc) 2—104

De tweede Verthooninghe, Zynde Van de Canarische Eylanden.

[55] 57 [C:] Caarte Voor een gedeelte der Canarise Eylanden als Canaria, Tenerifa, Forteventura, etc. — Between pp. 104 and 105 (Dd). 426 × 532 mm.
  [Inset:] [C:] De tyhavens Porto de Naos en Porto de Cavallos aen de Zuyd-oostzyde van Lãcerota — 145 × 158 mm.

[56] Van de Canarische Eylanden. (15 profiles). On 106—107 107 with verso blank.

Notes: All the large charts are blank on the back and all the charts in the text have text or map on the verso, except where otherwise specified. All are uncoloured. The two title-pages bear different dates: the engraved one is dated 1658, the letterpress one 1657. The title-page of vol. 2 is wanting in this copy. The title for the engraved title-page is printed on a separate slip and pasted in the appropriate space. Our copy corresponds with Koeman's Goos 22. Our copy does not have the error in pagination wich Koeman mentions in a note to Goos 22. The Zeespiegel was not Pieter Goos's own original work: he obtained the plates from Jacobsz, Theunis, and also largely copied his text. The charts did not normally bear Jacobsz.'s imprint, and Goos rarely signed his work. Only three of the charts in this atlas, 2, 3 and 24 (our maps [2], [3] and [56] bear Goos's imprint, with a date. According to Koeman there seems tot have been a certain amount of collaboration between Goos, Doncker and Jacobsz, Theunis. Our copy was bound in leather for Nordenskiöld, and his signature appears on the first blank leaf.

Lit.: Koeman vol. 4, p. 201, 204—207, Goos 17, Goos 22.

80 GOOS, PIETER   1673

L'ATLAS de la MER, Ou MONDE AQUATICQUE, Representant toutes les COSTES MARITIMES de l'Univers descouvertes & cogneues. Tres necessaire & commode Pour tous Pilotes, Maistres de Navire & Marchands. Mis nouvellement en Lumiere & Impriné. A AMSTERDAM, Chez PIETER GOOS, au miroir de la Mer. 1673.   53 cm.

[1] [C:] ORBIS TERRARVM NOVA ET ACCVRATISSIMA TABVLA. auctore PETRO GOOS. — [C:] Nieuwe WERELT KAERT uÿt gegeven tot AMSTELDAM bÿ Pieter Goos. — (Map). 440 × 543 mm. The hemispheres with 261 mm. diam.
  [Insets:] [The North and South Poles.] Circular maps with 102 mm. diam.
[2] [C:] Pascaart van EUROPA, Als mede een gedeelt vande cust van Africa. Gedruckt en uÿtgegeven, tot Amsterdam Bÿ Pieter Goos. — = 1658:I:[1] with very small alterations.
[3] [C:] Pascaart van de NOORT ZEE Verthoonende in zich alle de Custen en havens daer rontom gelegen. Op nieuws oversien en verbetert. Gedruckt tot Amsterdam, Bÿ Pieter Goos, op't Waater in De Vergulde Zee Spiegel bÿde N:brugh, Anno 1675 — [T:] Gesneden bÿ Geraerd Coeck. — 444 × 546 mm. See 1658:I:[2].
[4] [C:] Pas-Caart van de OOST ZEE Verthoonende Alle de ghelegentheydt tusschen 't Eylandt Rugen ende Wÿborg. Op nieuws oversien en verbeetert, t'Amsterdam By Pieter Goos op't water inde vergulde Zeespiegel 1673 — [T:] Gesneden bÿ Gerard Coeck. — 442 × 550 mm. See 1658:I:[56].
[5] [C:] Pascaarte vande ZUYDER-ZEE, Texel, ende Vliestroom, ... Anno 1666. — = 1658: I:[3], but the year altered.
[6] [C:] Pascaart van de NOORD ZEE, Van TEXEL, tot de HOOFDEN Nieulycx uijtgegeven t'Amsterdam, Bij Pieter Goos. — 443 × 548 mm.
[7] [C:] Cust van Hollant tusschen de Maes ende Texel. — = 1658:II:[1].
[8] [a] [C:] De TEXEL Stroom ... — [b] [C:] Caarte van DE MASE, ... — = 1658:II:[2].
[9] [C:] De Cust van ZEELANDT, Begrypende in sich de gaten, ... — = 1658:II:[4] with very small alterations.
[10] [C:] PASKAERT Van de Zeeusche en Vlaemsche Kusten, tonende alle drooghten, diepten, en ondiepten, tusschen 't eylandt Schouwen en de Hoofden, curieuselyck beschreven door Dirck Davidsz. — [Part I] 431 × 471 mm.
[11] [Paskaert van de Zeusche en Vlaemsche Kusten]. [Part

[12] [C:] Pascaarte van ENGELANT Van t'Voorlandt tot aen Blakeney ... — = 1658:I:[26].

[13] [C:] Pas-Caart vant CANAAL Vertoonende in 't Gheheel Engelandt, Schotlandt, Yrlandt, en een gedeelte van Vrancrÿck. Op nieus oversien en verbetert. — [C:] t'Amsterdam, By Pieter Goos. op't water by de N; brugh inde Zee-spiegel. 1675. — [T:] Gesneden bÿ Gerard Coeck. — 445 × 545 mm. See 1658:II:[8]. See 1658:II:[8].

[14] [C:] Het Canaal tusschen ENGELAND en VRANCRIICK. t'Amsterdam, Bij Pieter Goos. — 431 × 546 mm.

[15] [C:] Paskaarte om Achter YRLANDT om te Zeÿlen van Hitlant tot aen Heijssat Nieuwlycx Vytgegeven t'Amsterdam bij Pieter Goos op het waater in DeVergulde-Zee-spiegel Anno 1673 — 443 × 546 mm.

[16] [C:] Paskaerte van't in comen Van't CANAAL, hoemen dat sal aen doen, als men uyt de West comt. t'Amsteldam, bÿ Pieter Goos. — 441 × 536 mm.

[17] [C:] Paskaerte Vande BOCHT van Vranckrijck Biscajen en Galissen tusschen Heysant en C.de Finisterre — 446 × 544 mm.

[18] [C:] Pas-Caart van HISPANGIEN, Vertoonende de Custen van Granade, Andaluzie, Algarve, Portugael, Galissien, en Biscaien, met een gedeelte van Vranckrÿck; streckende van Heysant tot de Straet van Gibralter. Verbetert door A. en I.de Bree. T'AMSTERDAM, Bÿ Pieter Goos, op't Water, bÿ de N:brugh, in De Vergulde Zee-spiegel. A.º 1675. — 443 × 543 mm.

[19] [C:] Paskaerte Van't Westelyckste Der MIDDELANDSCHE ZEE. Gesneden gedruckt en uytgegeven t'Amsterdam by Pieter Goos, op't Water in de Vergulde Zee Spiegel. — 400 × 519 mm.

[20] [C:] PASKAERTE Van't Oostelyckste Der MIDDELANDSCHE ZEE Gesneden, Gedruckt, en Uytgegeven t'Amsterdam by Pieter Goos, op't Water inde Vergulde Zee Spiegel. — 400 × 519 mm.

[21] [C:] De Cust van BARBARIA, Gualata, ... — = 1658:II:[52].

[22] [a] [C:] de Cust van Barbaryen van out Mamora ... — [b] [C:] De Cust van Barbaryen van Capo Blanco ... — = 1658:II:[53].

[23] [C:] Caarte Voor een gedeelte der Canarise Eylanden als Canaria, ... — = 1658:II:[55].

[24] [C:] Pas-Caart van GVINEA en de Custen daer aen gelegen Van Cabo verde tot Cabo de Bona Esperanca. — 556 × 442 mm.

[25] [T:] PAS-KAARTE van de Zuyd-west-kust van Africa; van Cabo Negro tot beoosten Cabo de Bona Esperança. Nüwlyks besgreven en uyt-gegeven by Pieter Goos. t'Amsterdam — 296 × 526 mm. [Insets:] [The cost from:] Bay de S. Helena [to] Rio Dolçe 137 × 169 mm. [T:] Vlees bay A goa de S.Bras — 110 × 94 mm.

[26] [C:] Paskaerte Zynde t'OOSTERDEEL Van OOST INDIEN, met alle de Eylanden daer ontrendt geleegen van C.Comorin tot aen Iapan. t'AMSTERDAM, by Pieter Goos, op't Waeter in de Vergulde Zeespiegel. — 445 × 542 mm.

[27] [C:] Pascaerte Van't Westelycke Deel van OOST INDIEN, Van Cabo de Bona Esperanca, tot C.Comorin. TOT AMSTERDAM, Gedruckt by Pieter Goos, op't water inde Vergulde Zee spiegel. — 444 × 546 mm.

[28] [C:] Noordoost Cust Van ASIA van IAPAN tot NOVA ZEMLA. — 445 × 545 mm.

[29] [C:] De Zee Custen van Ruslant, Laplant, Finmarcken Spitsbergen en Nova Zemla. t'Amsterdam, By Pieter Goos op't water by de Nieuwe brugh in de Vergulde Zee Spiegel. — 444 × 545 mm. [Inset:] [C:] De Reviere Dwina, Ofte De Reviere van Archangel Soo het Nieuwe als 't Oude diep. — 220 × 210 mm. (Irregular).

[30] [C:] De Custen van Noorwegen, Finmarcken, Laplandt, Spitsbergen, Ian Mayen Eylandt, Yslandt, als mede Hitlandt, en een gedeelte van Schotlandt en Yrlandt. t'Amsterdam, By Pieter Goos op't Water inde Vergulde Zee-spiegel. — 446 × 543 mm.

[31] [C:] Pascaerte van GROEN-LANDT, Yslandt Straet Davids en Ian Mayen eylandt, hoemen de selvige van Hitlandt en de Noort custen van Schotlandt en Yrlandt beseylen mach. — 427 × 529 mm.

[32] [C:] PASKAERT Zijnde de Noordelijckste Zeekusten Van AMERICA Van Groenland door de Straet Davis en de Straet Hudson tot Terra Neuf. — 444 × 545 mm.

[33] [C:] Pascaerte vande Vlaemsche, Soute, en Caribesche Eylanden, als mede Terra Nova, en de Custen van Nova Francia, Nova Anglia, Nieu Nederlandt, Venezuela, Nueva Andalusia, Guiana, en een gedeelte, van Brazil — [T:] Abraham Deur fecit. — 446 × 545 mm.

[34] [C:] Pascaerte Van WESTINDIEN De Vaste Kusten En de Eylanden — 446 × 543 mm. [Inset:] [T:] Het Canael tusschen Havana aen Cuba eñ de Tortugas eñ Martyres aen Cabo de la Florida in Groot besteck — 110 × 184 mm.

[35] [C:] Pascaert Vande CARIBES EYLANDEN. Gedruckt t'Amsterdam by Pieter Goos. — 441 × 542 mm.

[36] [C:] Paskaart van BRASIL Van Rio de los Amazones, tot Rio de la Plata — 447 × 545 mm.

[37] [C:] Pascaerte van Het Zuydelijckste van AMERICA Van Rio de la Plata, tot Caap de Hoorn, ende inde Zuyd Zee, tot B.de Koquimbo. Nieuwlÿcks Vÿtgegeven Anno 1666 — 445 × 545 mm.

[38] [C:] Pascaerte Van NOVA HISPANIA CHILI, PERV, en GVATIMALA t'AMSTERDAM by Pieter Goos op't Waater inde Vergulde Zeespiegel A.º 1666 — 442 × 545 mm.

[39] [C:] Paskaerte Van NOVA GRANADA, en t'Eylandt CALIFORNIA. t'AMSTERDAM by Pieter Goos op't Waater inde Vergulde Zeespiegel A.º 1666 — 444 × 545 mm.

[40] [C:] Pascaerte Vande ZVYD-ZEE tussche California, en Ilhas de Ladrones. t'AMSTERDAM by Pieter Goos op't Waater inde Vergulde Zeespiegel Anno 1666 — 442 × 543 mm.

Notes: All the charts and the title-page are blank on the back and coloured. The charts are numbered in old ink on the verso from 1 to 42; nos, 34 and 35 are wanting, and no.20 is bound before no. 19. Nos. 1—5 have manuscript titles on the verso: 1. Carte Vniuersele, 2. Europe, 3. Mer du Nort, 4. Mer Baltique, 5. Mer du Zud. The title-page is dated 1673; maps [3] [13] and [18] are dated 1675. There are eight preliminary pages, containing a 'Brieve declaration Des parties, formes, & proprietés du Monde and on the last page 'L'ordre Que nous tenons en cet Atlas de la Mer'. These leaves are signed A, A2, B. This edition is the same as Koeman's Goos 11 B. His note reads 'A copy with French text, containing 41 charts, dated 1673 was mentioned by Hantzsch, no. 263.' After writing this, he saw our copy, and added the further note: 'a copy with 40 charts in the Nordenskiöld collection in the University Library, Helsinki.' Our copy seems to be the only known example of the French edition of 1673. Koeman lists all the charts in the atlas only under Goos 1 B; those in our copy are the same, except that we lack two of them, corresponding to the missing numbers mentioned above. Goos 1 B is the edition of 1666; many of our charts are new issues, with later dates. None of our charts have engraved numbers, but nine of Koeman's do. On charts [24] and [36] latitudes have been added in manuscript, and chart [34] also has a manuscript note in the right-hand margin. Most of the charts are copied from Doncker's Zee-atlas. Nordenskiöld bought this atlas from Frederick Muller in Amsterdam in 1890: Muller's invoice for 15 fl. is dated 23 April, and Nordenskiöld paid it on 14 May the same year. His signature, with the date 1890, is on the first blank leaf, and his bookplate is pasted to the inside of the front cover, with the number 339 C M in blue pencil.

Lit.: Nederl. Hist. Scheepv. Mus. Cat. bibl. vol. 1, p. 48, 1670 ed., Tiele p. 93, nr 399, 1670 ed., Koeman vol. 4, p. 196—197 Goos 1 B, p. 199, Goos 11 B.

81 GOSSELIN, PASCAL FRANÇOIS JOSEPH   1798

RECHERCHES SUR LA GÉOGRAPHIE SYSTÉMATIQUE ET POSITIVE DES ANCIENS; POUR SERVIR DE BASE À L'HISTOIRE DE LA GÉOGRAPHIE ANCIENNE. Par P.F.J. GOSSELIN, DE L'INSTITUT NATIONAL DE FRANCE. TOME PREMIER. A PARIS, DE L'IMPRIMERIE DE LA RÉPUBLIQUE. An VI.

[Half title:]
RECHERCHES SUR LA GÉOGRAPHIE SYSTÉMATIQUE ET POSITIVE DES ANCIENS.   30,7 cm.

Vol. I

[1] N°.I. [T:] HIPPARCHI SYSTEMA GEOGRAPHICUM Enucleabat GOSSELLIN M.D.CC.LXXXXIII. — Beaublé Scrip.t Chamoüin Sculp.t 230 × 419 mm.
[Inset:] [T:] Hipparchi Triangulorum mensura et delineatio — 55 × 98 mm.

[2] N°.II. [T:] HIPPARCHI SYSTEMA GEOGRAPHICUM PROJECTIONI EJUS SUBDITUM Auctore GOSSELLIN, M.DCC.LXXXXIII. — Chamoüin Sculp. Niodot Scrip. 230 × 413 mm.

[3] [a] N°.III. [T:] POUR LES RECHERCHES SUR LE PÉRIPLE D'HANNON Par P.F.J.GOSSELLIN. — 199 × 202 mm.
[Inset:] [T:] IBÉRIE   LIBYE — 73 × 58 mm.
[b] N°.IV. [T:] POUR LES RECHERCHES SUR LE PÉRIPLE DE POLYBE Par P.F.J.GOSSELLIN. — 199 × 203 mm.
[Inset:] [T:] IBÉRIE   LIBYE — 73 × 58 mm.
[The whole map:]Beaublé Scrip.t Chomoüin Sculp.t 199 × 405 mm.

[4] [a] N°.V. [T:] POUR LES RECHERCHES SUR LES CÔTES OCCIDENTALES DE L'AFRIQUE DE PTOLÉMÉE; ET SUR LES ISLES CONNUES PAR LES ANCIENS DANS L'OCÉAN ATLANTIQUE. Par P.F.J.GOSSELLIN. — 202 × 257 mm.
[Inset:] [T:] DÉTROIT D'HERCULE — 73 × 58 mm.
[b] N°.VI. [T:] CÔTES OCCIDENTALES DE L'AFRIQUE SELON PTOLÉMÉE — 202 × 120 mm.
[The whole map:] Chamoüin Sculps.t Beaublé Scrips.t 202 × 381 mm.

[5] [a] N°.VII. [T:] ORIENTALIUM AFRICÆ PARTIUM EX HODIERNIS PTOLEMÆI TABULIS DELINEATIO DUPLEX; Prior, lineis expressa, ex Tabulis græcis. Altera, punctis exarata, ex Tabulis latinis. — 198 × 132 mm.
[b] N°.VIII. [T:] ORIENTALES AFRICÆ PARTES, AD VERAM PTOLEMÆI DELINEATIONEM EX EJUSDEM PROLEGOMENIS RESTITUTÆ. Auctor GOSSELLIN. — 198 × 131 mm.
[c] N°.IX. [T:] POUR LES RECHERCHES SUR LES CÔTES ORIENTALES DE L'AFRIQUE — 198 × 160 mm.
[The whole map:] Chamoüin Sculps. Niodot Scrips. 198 × 427 mm.

[6] N°.X. [T:] POUR L'EXAMEN DES PRÉTENDUS VOYAGES DES ANCIENS AUTOUR DE L'AFRIQUE Par P.F.J.GOSSELLIN. — Chamouin Sculps. Niodot Scrips. 200 × 212 mm.

Vol. II
RECHERCHES SUR LA GÉOGRAPHIE ... TOME SECOND.
...

[1] N°.I. [T:] POLYBII INTERNUM MARE Enucleabat GOSSELLIN, M.DCC.LXXXXII. — Chamouin Sculps. Niodot Scrips. 237 × 166 mm.
[Inset:] [T:] Polybii Triangulorum mensura et delineatio — 62 × 148 mm.

[2] N°.II. [T:] MARINI TYRII SYSTEMA GEOGRAPHICUM. Enucleabat GOSSELLIN, M.DCC.XCI. — Chamouin Sculps.t Beaublé Scrips.t 227 × 480 mm.

[3] [a] N°.IV. [T:] SINUS ARABICUS EX TABULIS HODIERNIS PTOLEMÆI. — 244 × 198 mm.
[b] N°.V. [T:] POUR LES RECHERCHES SUR LE GOLFE ARABIQUE. Par P.F.J.GOSSELLIN. — 244 × 254 mm.
[Insets:] [The Northern part of the Golfe Arabique] 75 × 87 mm. [The Southern part of the Golfe Arabique] 95 × 105 mm. (Irregular).
[The whole map:] Chamouin Sculp.t Beaublé Scripsit 244 × 453 mm.

Notes: All the maps are blank on the back and uncoloured. They appear at the ends of the volumes. Plate III in vol. 2 is not map; its title is 'Pour les Recherches sur le Système Geographique de MARIN de Tyr'. Our collection has three volumes of Gosselin's 'Recherches'; the fourth is lacking. Vol. 3 was printed in 1813, and therefore does not come within the scope of this catalogue. The volumes are bound in boards, and have been badly damaged by water. Nordenskiöld's signature is on the blank leaf at the beginning of vol. 1.

Lit.: NBG 21:328—330.

82 GOTTFRIED, JOHANN LUDWIG   1695

Vermehrte ARCHONTOLOGIA COSMICA, Das ist Beschreibung aller Käiserthümer / Königreiche / und Republiquen der Welt / die keinen Höhern erkennen: Wie dieselbe in ihren Gräntzen und Anmarckungen begriffen / was darinnen für Provincien und Landschafften / stehende und fliessende Wässer / Städte und Vestungen / Commercien und Handthierungen sich befinden; Wie auch von der alten und neuen Einwohner Gebräuchen / Rechten und Gewonheiten / Frucht- und Unfruchtbarkeit dess Erdreichs: Ingleichem von der Potentaten Renten und Einkommen / Kriegs-Macht zu Wasser und Land / Religions- und Kirchen-Wesen / endlich auch ordentlicher Succession der Römischen Käiser / Könige / Fürsten und Herren: Alles auss glaubwürdigen Gründen und Zeugnüssen / von Anfang biss auff unsere Zeiten / in richtiger Ordnung abgefasset / und biss auff das Jahr 1694. continuiret: Auch mit richtigen Registern / und den vornehmsten in Kupffer gestochenen Land-Tafeln und Städten versehen / und von neuem zum Druck befördert Durch Matthæi Merians Sel. Erben. Gedruckt zu Franckfurt am Mayn / bey Johann Görlin. Im Jarh Christi M DC XCV.

[Half title:]
Vermerhte ARCHONTOLOGIA COSMICA.
[Engraved half title:]
ARCHONTOLOGIA COSMICA. FRANCOFURTI AD MOENUM. Impensis Matthæi Meriani hæredum.   34 cm.

[1] NOVA TOTIUS TERRARUM OBRIS GEOGRAPHICA AC HYDROGRAPHICA TABULA Wahre Bildtnüss des Gantzen Erden Kraÿses mit allen seinen theilen. (Map). Before I A 246 × 357 mm.
[Insets:] [The northern hemisphere] Circular map with 67 mm diam. [The southern hemisphere] Circular map with 67 mm diam.

[2] [C:] STATO DELLA CHIESA Con la Toscana Herrschafften der Röm: Kirchen, vnd Grosshertzogthumb Florentz. — (Map). Before I A 274 × 357 mm.

[3] [C:] ROMA. — [T:] Ant. Tempesta ad uiuã delineau. — [T:] M. Merian sculpsit. — (Plan). Between pp. 2 and 3. 307 × 710 mm.

[4] CIVITATIS AVENIONIS OMNIMQ VIARVM ET ÆDIFICIORVM EIVS PERFECTA DELINEATIO. 1635. [T:] M. Merian fecit. — (Plan). Between pp. 8 and 9. 257 × 340 mm.

[5] [C:] NOVA TOTIUS GERMANIÆ DESCRIPTIO. Teütschland. — (Map). Between pp. 66 and 67. 267 × 360 mm.

[6] [C:] Archiducatus Austriæ Superioris. Ober Österreich. Auctore Io: Bapt Suttinger — (Map). Between pp. 72 and 73. 300 × 276 mm.

[7] [C:] Archiducatus AUSTRIÆ. Vnter Österreich. — (Map). Between pp. 72 and 73. 292 × 378 mm.

[8] [T:] VIENNA AVSTRIÆ. — (View). Between pp. 72 and 73. 210 × 329 mm.

[9] [C:] Dass Läger, welches die Türckische Armee uor Wien 1683 geschlagen. — (Plan). Between pp. 72 and 73. 280 × 365 mm.
[Inset:] [A part of the siege]. 95 × 138 mm.

[10] [C:] ALSATIA INFERIOR — [T:] Frid. Hulsius Excudit — (Map). Between pp. 72 and 73. 196 × 292 mm.

[11] [T:] ARGENTINA. STRASSBURG. — (View). Between pp. 72 and 73. 238 × 386 mm.

[12] [C:] Grund-Riss der Statt und Vestung Strassburg nebst den Vorgelegten Citadellen wie auch die Schantzen am-in-und überm Rhein bey Keÿl welche Anno 1682 Ultimo Augustÿ mehrentheils verfertiget gewesen. — (Plan). Between pp. 72 and 73. 288 × 350 mm.
[Inset:] [T:] STRASBOVRG. — 80 × 162 mm.

[13] [C:] Wahre Contrafactur Der Vesten Statt vnd Passes Brÿsach. — (View). Between pp. 72 and 73. 190 × 352 mm.

[14] [T:] Eigentliche Contrafactur der Statt Costantz am Bodensee wie solche währender Belägerung Anno 1633. im wesen gestanden. — (Plan). Between pp. 72 and 73. 245 × 350 mm.

[15] [T:] Lindaw Im Bodensee. — (Plan). Between pp. 72 and 73. 177 × 312 mm.

[16] [C:] Die Statt Kempten Im Algäw. — (Plan). Between pp. 72 and 73. 187 × 312 mm.

[17] [C:] FRANCONIA. vulgo Franckenlandt. — (Map). Between pp. 72 and 73. 197 × 293 mm.

[18] [T:] FRANCOFVRTVM Franckfurt. — [T:] M. Merian fecit. — (Plan). Between pp. 72 and 73. 277 × 353 mm.

[19] [T:] HERBIPOLIS. Württzburg. — (View). Between pp. 72 and 73. 232 × 636 mm.

[20] [C:] WIRTENBERG DVCATUS. — [T:] Fridr. Hulsius Excudit. — (Map). Between pp. 72 and 73. 200 × 293 mm.

[21] [T:] Die Fürst: Statt Stuetgart. — (Plan). Between pp. 72 and 73. 211 × 327 mm.

[22] [T:] AUGVSTA VINDELICORUM. Augspurg. — [T:] M. Merian fecit. — (Plan). Between pp. 72 and 73. 200 × 305 mm.

[23] [T:] Vlm. — [T:] Merian fecit. — (Plan). Between pp. 72 and 73. 197 × 314 mm.

[24] [C:] BAVARIA DVCATUS. — (Map). Between pp. 72 and 73. 192 × 288 mm.

[25] [C:] MONACHIVM. München. — (Plan). Between pp. 72 and 73. 295 × 359 mm.

[26] [C:] PALATINATUS BAVARIÆ. — (Map). Between pp. 72 and 73. 192 × 290 mm.

[27] [C:] PALATINATUS RHENI. ... — (Map). Between pp. 72 and 73. 193 × 290 mm.

[28] Wahre Contrafactur der Churfürstlichen Residenz Statt Heidelberg.
[T:] HEIDELBERGA — (View). Between pp. 72 and 73. 249 × 363 mm.

[29] PROSPECT Des Churfürstlichen Pfältzischen RESIDENT Schlosses vnd Lustgartens zu Heidelberg. (View). Between pp. 72 and 73. 242 × 350 mm.

[30] [T:] FRANCKENTHAL. — (Plan). Between pp. 72 and 73. 225 × 255 mm.

[31] [T:] MANNHEIM — (Plan). Between pp. 72 and 73. 233 × 319 mm.

[32] [T:] Speÿer. — (View). Between pp. 72 and 73. 181 × 347 mm.

[33] [T:] WORMATIA. Wormbs. — (View). Between pp. 72 and 73. 205 × 676 mm.

[34] [C:] Wahre Bildnüss der Statt Maintz, sampt den newen Schantzen, Schiffbrucken vnd Leger, wie dieselbe Voriger Zeit im Wesen stund. ANNO 1633. — [T:] ARCHIEPISCOPALIS MOGUNTIA — [T:] M. Meriang ad viu: delineau: et sculp. — (View). Between pp. 72 and 73. 204 × 654 mm.

[35] [C:] TREVERIS. Trier. — (View). Between pp. 72 and 73. 214 × 345 mm.

[36] [T:] COLONIA AGRIPPINA. Cölln. — [T:] M. Merian fecit. — (Plan). Between pp. 72 and 73. 276 × 356 mm.

[37] [T:] LEODIUM. LIEGE. Lütich. — (Plan). Between pp. 72 and 73. 286 × 375 mm.

[38] [C:] Erfurt. — (Plan). Between pp. 72 and 73. 281 × 385 mm.

[39] [C:] Ober Sachsen. Lausznitz. vnd Meissen. — (Map). Between pp. 72 and 73. 260 × 361 mm.

[40] [a] [T:] Döblen. — (View). 129 × 373 mm.
[b] [T:] Dressden. — (View). 120 × 372 mm.
[The whole plate:] Between pp. 72 and 73. 250 × 372 mm.

[41] [T:] LEIPZIGK — (Plan). Between pp. 72 and 73. 280 × 355 mm.

[42] [C:] BRANDEBVRGVM MARCHIONATVS. Cum Ducatibus POMERANIÆ et MEKELENBVRGI — (Map). Between pp. 72 and 73. 288 × 385 mm.

[43] [C:] Chur.Fürstl. Resi St. Berlin: v. Cöln: [T:] Casp: Merian fec. — (View). Between pp. 72 and 73. 230 × 712 mm.

[44] [C:] DVCATVS BRVNSVICENSIS fereq$_3$ LVNÆBVRGENSIS Cum adjacentibus Episcopatib$_9$ Comit. Domin. etc. — (Map). Between pp. 72 and 73. 278 × 355 mm.

[45] [T:] F.B.L.Residents Statt Hannover — [T:] Conr. Buno Delineavit — [T:] Casp. Merian fec. — (View). Between pp. 72 and 73. 267 × 668 mm.

[46] [T:] BRUNSVICA. Braunschweig. — (View). Between pp. 72 and 73. 129 × 545 mm.

[47] [C:] BOHEMIA — (Map). Between pp. 72 and 73. 275 × 358 mm.

[48] [C:] MORAVIA MARCHIONATVS Auctore I.A.Comenio. — (Map). Between pp. 72 and 73. 269 × 344 mm.

[49] Wahrhaffte CONTRAFACTUR Der Weit Berühmbten Königlichen Haupt Statt Prag in Böhmen, wie solche Jetziger Zeit im wesen steht.
[T:] PRAGA — (View). Between pp. 72 and 73. 235 × 691 mm.

[50] [C:] WRATISLAVIA. Bresslaw. — (Plan). Between pp. 72 and 73. 287 × 363 mm.

[51] [C:] SILESIA DVCATUS A Martino Helwigio Nisseni descriptus. — (Map). Between pp. 72 and 73. 264 × 343 mm.

[52] [C:] GALLIA. LE ROYAVME DE FRANCE. Franckreÿch. — (Map). Between pp. 128 and 129. 272 × 357 mm.

[53] [T:] PARYS — [C:] Matth: Merian ad uivum delineau: — (View). Between pp. 130 and 131. 266 × 699 mm.

[54] [a] [T:] SILVANECTUM SENLIS. — (View). 88 × 311 mm.
[b] [T:] LEMOVICVM LIMOGES. — (View). 92 × 310 mm.
[The whole plate:] Between pp. 134 and 135. 188 × 311 mm.

[55] [T:] BOVRDEAVX. — [T:] Caspar Merian fe. — (View). Between pp. 136 and 137. 244 × 692 mm.

[56] [T:] ROTOMAGVS A^{o} 1655 ROVAN — (Plan). Between pp. 136 and 137. 346 × 413 mm.

[57] [T:] LYON — (View). Between pp. 156 and 157. 239 × 345 mm.

[58] [a] [T:] TROYE — (View). 110 × 352 mm.
[b] [T:] CHAALONS EN CHAMPAIGNE. — (View). 149 × 354 mm.
[The whole plate:] Between pp. 156 and 157. 268 × 354 mm.

[59] [C:] HISPANIA Regnum. — [T:] M. Merian fecit — (Map). Between pp. 184 and 185. 257 × 357 mm.

[60] [T:] HISPALIS UVLGO SEVILLIÆ VRBIS TOTO ORBE CELEBERRIMÆ PRIMARIÆ EFFIGIES HISPANIÆ QVE. — [T:] SEVILLIA — (View). Between pp. 184 and 185. 225 × 353 mm.

[61] [T:] BURGOS. — (View). Between pp. 188 and 189. 187 × 312 mm.

[62] [C:] PORTVGALLIA et ALGARBIA quæ olim LVSITANIA. Auctore Vernando Alvero Secco. — (Map). Between pp. 234 and 235. 283 × 370 mm.

[63] [T:] OLISIPPO. LISABONA. — (Plan). Between pp. 236 and 237. 280 × 364 mm.

[64] [C:] REGNO DI NAPOLI. — (Map). Between pp. 240 and 241. 273 × 356 mm.
[65] [T:] NEAPOLIS. — (Plan). Between pp. 240 and 241. 274 × 357 mm.
[66] [C:] SICILIA REGNVM. — [T:] M Merian fecit. — (Map). Between pp. 266 and 267. 270 × 358 mm.
[67] [C:] MANTVA DVCATVS. — (Map). Between pp. 276 and 277. 276 × 366 mm.
[68] [T:] MEDIOLANVM. — (Plan). Between pp. 276 and 277. 268 × 352 mm.
[69] [T:] GOA. — (Plan). Between pp. 294 and 295. 270 × 355 mm.
[70] [C:] AMERICA noviter delineata. — [T:] M. Merian fecit. — (Map). Between pp. 308 and 309. 279 × 361 mm.
[Inset:] [C:] Septentrionalissimas Americæ partes, Groenlandiam picta, Islandiam et adjacentes, quod Americæ tabulæ comodé comprebendi non potuerit peculiari hac tabella Spectatorib$_9$ exhibendas duximus. — (Map). 52 × 60 mm.
[71] [C:] MAGNÆ BRITANNIÆ et HIBERNIÆ TABVLÆ. Die Britannischen Inseln. — [T:] M. Merian fecit. — (Map). Between pp. 340 and 341. 270 × 355 mm.
[Inset:] [T:] Orcades Insulæ — (Map). 43 × 64 mm.
[72] [C:] Totius Regni HUNGARIÆ Maximæ que Partis DANUBII FLUMINIS una cum adjacentibus et finitimis REGIONIBUS — (Map). Between pp. 380 and 381. 309 × 591 mm.
[73] [T:] BVDA. Ofen. — (View). Between pp. 380 and 381. 196 × 327 mm.
[74] [T:] TOPOGRAPHIA REGIÆ LIBERÆQ$_3$ CIVITATIS POSONIENSIS UVLGO Pressburg HVNGARIÆ SVPERIORIS AD DANUBIVM SITA CVM ADIACENTI CASTRO, VBI SACRA REGNI HVNGARIÆ CORONA CONSERVATVR. — Between pp. 380 × 381 mm. 242 × 346 mm.
[75] [C:] POLONIA Regnum, et SILESIA Ducatus. — [T:] M. Merian fecit — (Map). Between pp. 392 × 393 mm. 272 × 350 mm.
[76] [T:] CRACOVIA. — (View). Between pp. 394 and 395. 201 × 389 mm.
[77] [C:] DANIA REGNVM. — (Map). Between pp. 410 and 411. 280 × 336 mm.
[78] [C:] HAFNIA METROPOLIS ET PORTVS CELEBERRIMVS DANIÆ. — [T:] COPPENHAGEN — (View). Between pp. 412 and 413. 197 × 339 mm.
[79] [C:] Tabula exantissima Regnorū SUECIÆ et NORVEGIÆ nec non MARIS UNIVERSI ORIENTALIS Terraeumq$_3$ adjacentium, summo studio ad Andrea Bureo Sueco. — Between pp. 424 and 425. 290 × 361 mm.
[80] [T:] STOCKHOLM. — (View). Between pp. 424 and 425. 194 × 330 mm.
[81] [C:] TABULA RUSSIÆ ex autographo, quod delineandum curavit Foedor filius Tzaris Boris desumta et ad fluvios Dwinam Zuchanaw alique loca quandum ex tabulis et notiÿs ad nos delatis fieri potuit amplificata aliâs dicta MOSCOVIA — (Map). Between pp. 436 and 437. 280 × 349 mm.
[Inset:] [T:] ARCHANGELSCKAGOROD. — 41 × 78 mm.
[82] [T:] MOSCVA — (Plan). Between pp. 438 and 439. 272 × 352 mm.
[83] [C:] LOTHARINGIA DVCATVS Vulgo LORRAINE. — (Map). Between pp. 448 and 449. 281 × 367 mm.
[84] [T:] NANCEIVM. NANCY. — (Plan). Between pp. 450 and 451. 232 × 351 mm.
[85] [C:] NOVA ITALIÆ DELINEATIO — (Map). Between pp. 456 and 457. 285 × 366 mm.
[86] [C:] SABAVDIA DVCATVS. SAVOYE. — (Map). Between pp. 456—457. 270 × 358 mm.
[87] [C:] TVRINO — (Plan). Between pp. 458 and 459. 183 × 255 mm.
[88] [C:] FLORENTIA. — (View). Between pp. 470 and 471. 216 × 343 mm.
[89] [T:] MANTOVA — (Plan). Between pp. 470 and 471. 246 × 349 mm.
[90] [C:] BELGII sive GERMANIA INFERIORIS. Nider-Teütschlandt. — (Map). Between pp. 486 and 487. 290 × 362 mm.
[91] [a] [T:] ANTWERPEN — (View). 118 × 530 mm.
[b] [T:] BRÜSSEL — (View). 148 × 531 mm.
[The whole plate:] Between pp. 486 and 487. 275 × 531 mm.
[92] [T:] AMSTERDAM — (View). Between pp. 486 and 487. 198 × 714 mm.
[93] [C:] Die Eÿdtgnoschafft Pünten vnd Wallis. HELVETIA cum Confinijs. — [T:] Hans Conrd Geiger Von Zürich. fecit Año 1637. — Between pp. 546 and 547. 272 × 351 mm.
[94] [T:] LVCERN. — (Plan). Between pp. 548 and 549. 211 × 351 mm.
[95] [T:] TIGURVM. Zürych. — (Plan). Between pp. 548 and 549. 268 × 350 mm.
[96] [T:] BERNA — [T:] Ioseph Plep figur: M:Merian sculp: — (Plan). Between pp. 548 and 549. 211 × 348 mm.
[97] [T:] Freÿburg In Vchtlandt. FRYBURGUM NUITONIÆ. — (Plan). Between pp. 548 and 549. 221 × 349 mm.
[98] [T:] BASILEA Basel. — (Plan). Between pp. 552 and 553. 265 × 354 mm.
[99] [T:] SCAFHUSIA. — [C:] Schaffhausen. — [T:] I. Caspar Lang inv. M. Merian sculp: — (Plan). Between pp. 552 and 553. 209 × 374 mm.
[100] Eigentliche Bildtnuss des Grossen Wasserbruchs oder Falls des Rheins Im Lauffen. Vera Delineatio Catarrhactarū Rheni ad Lauffen. (View). Between pp. 552 and 553. 195 × 282 mm.
[101] [T:] Landschafft vmb das Wildebadt Pfäffers — [T:] REGIO circa thermas Fabarias. — (Map). Between pp. 552 and 553. 256 × 180 mm.
[102] Wahre Contrafactur des Wunderlichen Bads Zu Pfäffers In Ober Schweytz, Effigios Æquarū Pfefers. [T:] M. Merian fecit. — (View). Between pp. 552 and 553. 265 × 183 mm.
[103] [T:] Baden Im Argöw. BADEN ARGOIÆ. — (View). Between pp. 552 and 553. 270 × 347 mm.
[104] [T:] Chur. CURIA RHÆTIÆ. — (View). Between pp. 552 and 553. 198 × 278 mm.
[105] [T:] VENETIA. — [T:] M. Merian fecit. — (Plan). Between pp. 598 and 599. 304 × 711 mm.
[106] [a] [T:] CANDIA — (View). 121 × 350 mm.
[b] [T:] CORPHV — (View). 128 × 350 mm.
[The whole plate:] Between pp. 610 and 611. 265 × 350 mm.
[107] [T:] GENVA. — (View). Between pp. 624 and 625. 205 × 390 mm.
[108] [T:] LVCA — (Plan). Between pp. 640 and 641. 254 × 371 mm.
[109] [T:] GENEUE. Genff. — (View). Between pp. 642 and 643. 229 × 341 mm.
[110] [a] [T:] RAGUSA. — (View). 116 × 305 mm.
[b] [T:] NEGROPONTE. — (View). 80 × 305 mm.
[The whole plate:] Between pp. 644 and 645. 206 × 305 mm.
[111] [C:] TVRCICVM IMPERIVM. Türckische Reÿch. ... — (Map). Between pp. 648 and 649. 272 × 353 mm.
[112] CONSTANTINOPOLITANÆ VRBIS EFFIGIES AD VIVUM EXPRESSA, QVAM TVRCÆ STAMPOLDAM VOCANT.
[T:] CONSTANTINOPOLIS. — [T:] M. Merian fecit. — (View). Between pp. 650 and 651. 206 × 697 mm.
[113] [T:] IERUSALEM. — (View). Between pp. 702 and 703. 184 × 336 mm.
[114] [C:] ALGIER — (Plan). Between pp. 716 and 717. 217 × 347 mm.
[115] [T:] ABRIS DER VESTUNG TRIPOLI IN BARBARIEN ... — (Plan). Between pp. 718 and 719. 273 × 386 mm.
[116] [T:] TVNES — (View). Between pp. 720 and 721. 199 × 367 mm.
[117] [C:] ÆTHIOPIA SVPERIOR vel INTERIOR vulgo ABISSINORVM sive PRESBITERI IOANNIS IMPERIVM. — (Map). Between pp. 724 and 725. 288 ×

375 mm.
[118] [C:] ÆTHIOPIA INFERIOR vel EXTERIOR MONOMOTAPA. — (Map). Between pp. 724 and 725 287 × 372 mm.
[119] [C:] PERSIA Sive SOPHORVM REGNVM — [T:] M. Merian fecit. — (Map). Between pp. 748 and 749. 268 × 346 mm.
[120] [C:] ISFAHAN. — (View). Between pp. 754 and 755. 293 × 380 mm.
[121] [C:] TARTARIA sive MAGNI CHAMI IMPERIORUM — (Map). Between pp. 818 and 819. 269 × 352 mm.
[122] [C:] CHINA Veteribus SINARVM REGIO nunc Incolis TAME dicta. — [T:] M. Merian fecit. — (Map). Between pp. 826 and 827. 271 × 343 mm.
[123] [C:] XVNTIEN alis QVINZAY. — (Plan). Between pp. 828 and 829. 181 × 256 mm.
[124] [C:] INDIA ORIENTALIS, ET INSVLÆ ADIACENTES. — [T:] M. Merian sculp: — (Map). Between pp. 854 and 855. 267 × 356 mm.
[125] [C:] nova descriptio AFRICÆ. — (Map). Between pp. 876 and 877. 270 × 362 mm.

Notes: All the maps are blank on the back and uncoloured. The double map of London is lacking. On maps [10] and [20] the name Fridr. Hulsius has been partially scraped away, but it is still quite legible. The introduction to this large historical-geographical work is signed by Johann Gottfried and Matthæus Merian. The form of the author's name varies. According to many reference works, among them the Allgemeine Deutsche Biographie, J.L. Gottfridt is Johann Philipp Abelin of Strasbourg, who translated and compiled a number of different works. About this one the ADB (vol. 1, p. 18) states; 'Auch die öfters aufgelegte "Archontologica cosmica" ist nur eine mit Zusätzen versehene Uebersetzung von des Petrus d'Avity "Monde" immerhin wenigstens besser als die damals fast allein gebrauchte Münster'sche Cosmographie.' CLC:I:12, no. 58, lists the book under Avity, P. d', and after 'verfasset durch Johann Ludwig Gottfried' states '[pseud. of J.P. Abelin]'; Frieda Gallati makes it clear in her work that Gottfried and Abelin are two different people. The volume is bound in old leather. Nordenskiöld's signature is on the blank leaf at the beginning, with the year 1880.

Lit.: Jöcher, I:19, II:1093, ADB:I:18, CLC:I:12, nr 58, IV:4, nr 4104, BM General catolouge of printed books, 89:545—46, BN, Paris Catalogue, V:844—45, Droysen, G., Arlanibaeus, Gogofredus, Abelinus. 1864, Gallati, F(rieda), "Der Königlich Schwedische in Teutschland geführte Krieg" Frauenfeld 1902.

83 GOUGH, RICHARD 1780

BRITISH TOPOGRAPHY. OR, AN HISTORICAL ACCOUNT OF WHAT HAS BEEN DONE FOR ILLUSTRATING THE TOPOGRAPHICAL ANTIQUITIES OF GREAT BRITAIN AND IRELAND. VOLUME I. LONDON, PRINTED FOR T. PAYNE AND SON, AND J. NICHOLS. MDCCLXXX. 27,5 cm.

Vol. I
[1] Pl. I. [a] [A part of Britain in the Peutinger table from Scheyb's correct edition.] [T:] Fig. 1. p. 57. — 233 × 133 mm.
[b] [An old sketch of the "four great Roman ways" from the Additamenta to Matthew Paris.] [T:] Fig.2. p.10. — 113 × 231 mm.
[c] [... a specimen of Chinese map-making, from a map of their coast from Lammo ... to Cochinchina.] [T:] Fig.3. p.59. — 117 × 230 mm.
[The whole plate:] p. 57. 237 × 238 mm.
[2] Pl. II. [Britannia, nunc dicta Anglia, quæ complectitur Scociam, Galeweiam & Walliam. From a MS. of Matthew Paris's history, in the King's library,] p. 62. 360 × 235 mm.
[3] Pl. III [a] [T:] Brittania insula Hibernia [from Benet college MS.D.xii.I.] — [T:] Fig.I.p.60. —
[b] [England from a manuscript of Higden's Polychronicon in the Royal Library in the British Museum.] [T:] Fig. II.p.61. —
[a] and [b] 230 × 126 mm.
[c] [Great Britain, from the 2d part of Matthew Paris's history in the Benet college MS.] [T:] Fig. III p.64. — 231 × 235 mm.
[The whole plate:] p. 64. 235 × 369 mm.
[4] Pl. IV [Great Britain from the MS. of Matthew Paris's Historia Minor in the Cotton library.] p. 67. 363 × 239 mm.
[5] Pl. V. [An engraved sketch of the map of Great-Britain from the Hereford world map.] Basire Sc. p. 74. 232 × 365 mm.
[Inset:] [T:] Britannia hybernia ox d des — [T:] p. 60. — 92 × 166 mm.
[6] Pl. VI [Great Britain supposed to be of the age of Edward III. Copy made by Mr. Basire.] p.76. Between pp. 80 and 81. 321 × 667 mm.
[7] Pl. VII [a] [The stations in England (London, Rochester, Canterbury, Dover) for a pilgrimage from England to the Holy Land, in a MS. of Matthew Paris's history, in the Royal Library.] [T:] Fig.1. — 326 × 105 mm.
[b] [The stations in England (London, Rochester, Canterbury, Dover) from a pilgrimage from England to the Holy Land, in a Matthew Paris MS. in the Benet college,] [T:] Fig. 2. — 352 × 85 mm.
[The whole plate:] p. 85. 367 × 235 mm.
[8] Pl. VIII [One third of the map of Scotland in the MS. of Harding's Chronicle in the Bodleian library.] p. 579. 332 × 239 mm. (This map is wrongly bound in our copy. See II: [1].)

Vol. II
BRITISH TOPOGRAPHY. ... VOLUME II

[1] Pl. VIII [Two thirds of the map of Scotland in the MS. of Harding's Chronicle in the Bodleian library.]
[a] 337 × 245 mm.
[b] 333 × 245 mm.
[The whole plate:] p. 579. 687 × 245 mm. See I:[8].

Notes: All the maps are blank on the back and uncoloured. This edition is a new, enlarged version of the Anecdotes of British Topography published in 1768. Where necessary, we have provided titles for the maps from the accompanying text. From the Directions to the binder on the last page of vol. 2 it can be seen that the three parts of the map of Scotland have been misbound. Our copy is in the original binding, with gilt tooling on the leather spine. Nordenskiöld's signature is on the first blank leaf of each volume; in vol. 1 he has added the date 'Dec. 1895'. In Frederick Müller's Catalogue Topographie ancienne, 1896, p. 26, no. 234, this work is priced at 25 fl.

Lit.: Bonacker p. 102, DNB 8:279, Enc. Brit. 10:555, NBG 21: 387—388.

84 GUICCIARDINI, LODOVICO 1567

DESCRITTIONE DI M. LODOVICO GVICCIARDINI PATRITIO FIORENTINO, DI TVTTI I PAESI BASSI, ALTRIMENTI DETTI GERMANIA INFERIORE. Con piu carte di Geographia del paese, & col ritratto naturale di piu terre principali. ... IN ANVERSA M. D. LXVII. Apresso Guglielmo Siluio, Stampatore Regio. 32,3 cm.

[1] [T:] LA DESCRITTIONE DI BELGICA CON LE SVE FRONTIERE — [C:] Omnis Belgica intra Rhenum, Matronam, Sequanā ac Oceanum, ... — [T:] C. D. Hooghe Fe. — (Map). Before 1 B Verso blank. 313 × 408 mm.

[2] DESCRITTIONE PARTICVLARE DI BRABANTE.
[C:] Descrittione particulare di Brabante. — (Map). 47 Fij 254 × 339 mm.

[3] DESCRITTIONE DI BRVSELLES.
BRVSELLES (Plan). H ij [On verso:] 56 246 × 345 mm.

[4] DESCRITTIONE DI BOLDVC.
[T:] BOLDVCH — (View). R [On verso:] 127 248 × 348 mm.

[5] DESCRITTIONE DI MALINES.
[T:] MALINES. — (View). V ij [On verso:] 150 244 × 341 mm.

[6] DESCRITTIONE D'HOLLANDA.
[C:] DESCRITTIONE PARTICVLARE D'HOLLANDA ET DEL PAESE D'VTRECHT. — (Map). Z ij [On verso:] 175 254 × 331 mm.

[7] DESCRITTIONE DI FIANDRA.
[C:] DESCRITTIONE PARTICVLARE DI FIANDRA. — (Map). Dd [On verso:] 216 256 × 347 mm.

[8] LA DESCRITTIONE DI GVANTO.
GVANTO. (Plan). 198 (pro 219). Ee ij 246 × 343 mm.

[9] DESCRITTIONE DI BRVGGIA.
[C:] BRVGAE — (Plan). Ff ij [On verso:] 224 247 × 346 mm.

[10] DESCRITTIONE D'HAINAVLT.
[T:] HAINAVLT — [C:] DESCRITTIONE PARTICVLARE DEL CONTADO D'HAINAVLT. — (Map). Kk [On verso:] 260 252 × 337 mm.

[11] DESCRITTIONE DI LIEGE.
[T:] LIEGE — (Plan). Nn ij [On verso:] 283 248 × 347 mm.

Notes: All the maps have text on the verso, except where otherwise specified, and are uncoloured. This edition was bound for Nordenskiöld, and bears the initials A.E.N. in gold on the spine. His bookplate is on the inside of the front cover. The entry in the Nordenskiöld collection catalogue indicates that Nordenskiöld purchased this volume from the Italian antiquarian bookseller Leo S. Olschki for the sum of 40 fr.

85 GUICCIARDINI, LODOVICO 1581

DESCRITTIONE DI M. LODOVICO GVICCIARDINI PATRITIO FIORENTINO, DI TVTTI I PAESI BASSI, ALTRIMENTI DETTI GERMANIA INFERIORE. Con tutte le carte di Geographia del paese, & col ritratto naturale di molte terre principali; Riueduta di nuouo, & ampliata per tutto piu che la meta dal medesimo autore. ... IN ANVERSA, Apresso Christofano Plantino, Stampatore Regio. M. D. LXXXI.
[Half title:]
Descrittione di tutti i paesi Bassi. 33,4 cm.

[1] [C:] DESCRIPTIO GERMANIAE INFERIORIS. — (Map). Before 1 A Blank on the back. 235 × 319 mm.

[2] DESCRITTIONE PARTICVLARE DI BRABANTE.
[C:] BRABANTIA. — (Map). 65 F 3 233 × 313 mm.

[3] [C:] LOVANIVM Brabanticarum vrbium caput, vnica Musarũ ac prestantissimarum artium sedes optatissimumq₃ domicilium. — (Plan). 73 G 232 × 316 mm.

[4] DESCRITTIONE DI BRVSELLES.
[C:] BRVXELLA fontium copia cœli amœnitate et ædificiorum splendore nobiliss. — (Plan). 77 H 232 × 317 mm. See 1567:[3].

[5] DESCRITTIONE D'ANVERSA.
[C:] ANTWERPIÆ NOBILISSIMI TOTIVS ORBIS TERRARV EMPORII TYPVS. ANNO .M.D.LXXXI. — (Plan). 87 I 4 234 × 318 mm.

[6] DESCRITTIONE DI BOLDVC.
[C:] TSHERTOGENBOSCH. — [C:] BVSCVMDVCIS oppidum ludo literario, et pugnaci populo nobile Horum arma superiorib. annis haud semel Geldrij sensere, cum qua gente vario certatum est euentu nostris hominibus In hac vrbe templum est Deiparæ sacrum, op visendo apparatu Hadrianus Barlandus. — (View). 185 V 230 × 311 mm. See 1567:[4].

[7] 12 [C:] BERGHẼ OP ZOOM. — (Plan). Between pp. 192 and 193. Blank on the back. 163 × 238 mm.

[8] [T:] Rÿnsberch. — [T:] Hũb. exc. ... — (Plan). Between pp. 196 and 197. Blank on the back. 180 × 271 mm.

[9] DESCRITTIONE DI MASTRICHT.
[C:] TRAIECTVM ad Mosam. — (Plan). 197 Y 233 × 317 mm.

[10] [C:] LIRA, elegans et amoenum Brabantiae Opp. adeo, vt multorum huius tractus nobilium in ocio degentiũ, a curis & turba iucundissimus sit recessus. — (Plan). 205 Z 3 232 × 314 mm.

[11] DESCRITTIONE DEL DVCATO DI LIMBORGO.
[C:] LIMBOVRG. — (View). 217 a 3 233 × 317 mm.

[12] DESCRITTIONE DI MALINES.
[T:] Mechelen. — [C:] Nitidissime ciuitatis Mechlineensis in meditullio Brabantie exactis: delineatio. — (Plan). 227 b 2 232 × 318 mm.

[13] [C:] GELRIA, ET ZVTFANIA. — (Map). 235 c 2 230 × 311 mm.

[14] [T:] NYMMEGEN. — [C:] NOVIOMAGĨ, siue Nouiomagum vulgo Nijmmegen inclyta quondam Francorũ Regia vrbs Gelriæ prima: — (Plan). 241 d 232 × 313 mm.

[15] DESCRITTIONE DI RVERMOND.
[T:] RVERMONDE — [C:] RVREMVNDA GELRIAE OPP — (Plan). 245 e 229 × 303 mm.

[16] DESCRITTIONE DI ZVTPHEN.
[T:] ZVTPHEN — (Plan). 249 f 233 × 313 mm.

[17] DESCRITTIONE DI ARNEM.
[T:] ARNHEM — [C:] ARNHEMIVM, GELRIAE IN RIPA RHENI OPP. — (Plan). 253 g 234 × 334 mm.

[18] 22 [T:] Gelria. — [An empty cartouche.] (Plan). Between pp. 256 and 257. Blank on the back. 163 × 238 mm.

[19] DESCRITTIONE DI DEVENTER.
[T:] Deuenter. — [C:] LIBERÆ ET HANSEATICÆ VRBIS DAVETRIESIS DELINEATIO — (Plan). 263 i 2 232 × 317 mm.

[20] 24. [C:] Vrbis Campensis ad isolam Fluuium icon. — [T:] CAMPEN. — (Plan). Between pp. 266 and 267. Blank on the back. 236 × 315 mm.

[21] 25. [C:] Swolla diu celebris meruit virtitubus Arma: Quæ Populum sortem nobilitare solent. Jnde salutisera vetere pietate fideque Jn Tripolim recepi fœdere digna fuit. — (Plan). Between pp. 266 and 267. Blank on the back. 232 × 313 mm.

[22] DESCRITTIONE DI FRISIA.
[C:] FRISIAE OCCIDENTALIS TYPVS. — (Map). 269 k 232 × 313 mm.

[23] DESCRITTIONE DI LEEWARDEN.
[C:] LEWARDVM, Occidentalis Frisiæ Opp: 1581 — (Plan). 279 m 2 230 × 313 mm.

[24] 28. [C:] FRANICHER. — (Plan). Between pp. 282 and 283. Blank on the back. 237 × 163 mm.

[25] DESCRITTIONE DI GRONINGHEN.
[C:] GRONINGA, opulenta, popolosa, et valide contra hostiles insultus munita Phrisię vrbs Ptolemeo Phileum, constructa et denominata à Grunno Anthenoris Regis Francorum frē, Anno ante incarnationem Christi, CCC LXXVII. vt Humbaldus scribit. — (Plan). 285 n 232 × 318 mm.

[26] DESCRITTIONE D'HOLLANDIA.
[C:] HOLLANDIAE CATTORVM REGIONIS TYPVS. — (Map). 297 p 231 × 313 mm.

[27] DESCRITTIONE DI DORDRECHT.
[C:] DORDRECHT. — (Plan). 305 r 231 × 313 mm.

[28] DESCRITTIONE DI HAERLEM.
[C:] Harlemum siue Herlemum vrbs Hollandiæ situ, et ædificiorum pulchritudine peramœna. — [T:] Harlem — (Plan). 309 s 253 × 335 mm.

[29] DESCRITTIONE DI DELFT.
[T:] DELFT. — [C:] Delphium, vrbs Hollandiæ cultissima ab eiusdem nominis fossa, vulgo Delft appellata. — (Plan). 313 t 233 × 316 mm.

[30] DESCRITTIONE DI LEIDEN.
[T:] LVGDVNVM BATAVORVM LEYDEN IN

[31] HOLLANT — (Plan). 319 v 2 243 × 330 mm.
DESCRITTIONE DI AMSTERDAM.
[T:] Amstelredamum. — (Plan). 325 x 233 × 316 mm.

[32] 35. [C:] La ville d'ENCHVSE situe en la Comte d'hollande cõe elle se cõporte a present — (Plan). Between pp. 328 and 329. Blank on the back. 233 × 319 mm.

[33] 41. [C:] Hoorn in Hollandt. — (Plan). Between pp. 328 and 329. Blank on the back. 233 × 327 mm.

[34] 42 [T:] Schoonhouẽ — (Plan). Between pp. 332 and 333. Blank on the back. 225 × 159 mm.

[35] [T:] ROTTERDAM — [An empty cartouche.] (Plan). Between pp. 334 and 335. Blank on the back. 257 × 343 mm.

[36] DESCRITTIONE DI HAIA.
[C:] Grauenhaghe, T'hoff van Hollant. — (Plan). 337 Aa 230 × 314 mm.

[37] DESCRITTIONE BRITTANICA.
[C:] RVINARVM ARCIS BRITANNICÆ APVD BATAVOS TYPVS. — [C:] Absoluta huius tabulę delinaitione Cãdidiss. spectator, misit ad me hanc vetustam inscriptionem Hubertus Goltzius,... Vale. Ab. Ortelius. — (View). 343 Bb 2 225 × 320 mm.

[38] 39 [T:] Briel. — (Plan). Between pp. 348 and 349. Blank on the back. 163 × 237 mm.

[39] DESCRITTIONE DI VTRECHT.
[C:] TRAJECTVM. — (Plan). 353 Cc 3 233 × 319 mm.

[40] DESCRITTIONE DI SILANDA.
[C:] ZELANDIÆ TYPVS. — (Map). 365 Dd 3 232 × 314 mm.

[41] DESCRITTIONE DI MIDDELBORGO.
[C:] MIDDELBVRGVM Selandiae Opp: situ opere et mercimoniis florentiss. — (Plan). 373 Ee 230 × 315 mm.

[42] [T:] VLISSINGHE Dlant Van Walcheren — (Plan). 377 Ff 229 × 321 mm.

[43] DESCRITTIONE DI FIANDRA.
[C:] FLANDRIA — (Map). 387 Hh 2 230 × 313 mm.

[44] DESCRITTIONE DI GVANTO.
[C:] GANDAVVM. — (Plan). 395 Ii 2 234 × 323 mm. See 1567:[8].

[45] DESCRITTIONE DI BRVGGIA.
[C:] BRVGÆ FLANDICARVM VRBIVM DECVS. — [C:] Brugæ vulgo Brugh vrbs ædificiorũ pulehritudine, magnificẽtiaq₃ nitore, ac forma elegantissima: celeberrimũ olim Emporium. — (Plan). 403 Kk 2 233 × 319 mm. See 1567:]9].

[46] DESCRITTIONE D'YPRI.
[C:] HYPRA flandriarum Ciuitatũ munitissima — (Plan). 413 Mm 232 × 319 mm.

[47] 50. [T:] SLVYS. — [C:] SLVSA teutonicæ Flandriæ opp: admodum elegans. — (Plan). Between pp. 416 and 417. Blank on the back. 235 × 313 mm.

[48] [T:] OOSTENDE. — [C:] Vraye delineation de la ville d'Ostende assiegee par le Ser.me Prince Albertus Archid. d'Austrie, Duc de Brabant, Conte de Flandres, etc. faict l'an 1602 le premier iour d'October. Ioan. Baptista Vrints excud. ... — (Plan). Between pp. 416 and 417. Blank on the back. 288 × 376 mm.

[49] [C:] GRAVELINGA, VRBS MARITIMA, OLIM PORTV AMPLISSIMO FAMOSA. — [T:] GREVELINGE. — (Plan). 419 Nn 2 226 × 301 mm.

[50] DESCRITTIONE DI LILLA.
[T:] Lille. — (Plan). 429 Pp 230 × 310 mm.

[51] [C:] DVACVM, Catuacorum vrbs, tam situ quam incolis et literarum studijs elegantissime ornata. — [T:] Douaỹ — (Plan). 433 Qq 228 × 310 mm.

[52] 55 [C:] TORNACVM. — (Plan). Between pp. [440] and [441]. Blank on the back. 233 × 320 mm.

[53] [T:] HVLST — (Plan). Between pp. 444 and 445. Blank on the back. 182 × 271 mm.

[54] DESCRITTIONE D'ALOST.
[C:] ALOSTVM Flandriæ Imperialis Caput. — [C:] AELST. — (Plan). 445 Ss 233 × 318 mm.

[55] DESCRITTIONE D'ARTOIS.
[C:] ATREBATVM REGIONIS VERA DESCRIPTIO. — (Map). 455 Vv 2 229 × 310 mm.

[56] LA VILLA D'ARAZZO.
[T:] ARRAS — (Plan). 461 Xx 235 × 319 mm.

[57] 60 [C:] LA VILLE DE CAMBRAY. — (Plan). Between pp. [470] and [471]. Blank on the back. 239 × 328 mm.

[58] DESCRITTIONE D'HAINAVLT.
[C:] HANNONIÆ COMITATVS DESCRIP. — (Map). 473 aa 230 × 311 mm.

[59] DESCRITTIONE DI MONS.
[C:] MONS. — [C:] MONS, Hannoniæ vrbs potens et ampla, a Carola Magno Metropolitano muneze et cæsareis priuelegijs donato, Trulsa flu. alluitur, propugnaculis et natura loci munitissima, Gens humana et opulenta, Saginariæ negatiatione dedita. — (Plan). 477 bb 229 × 314 mm.

[60] DESCRITTIONE DI VALENZINA.
[T:] VALENCHIENES — [C:] Valencena quondam cijgnorum vallis vrbs Han: per elegans et valde magnifica. — (Plan). 483 cc 2 229 × 319 mm.

[61] DESCRITTIONE DEL DVCATO DI LVZIMBORGO.
[C:] LVTZENBVRGENSIS DVCATVS VERISS DESCRIPT — (Map). 507 ff 2 230 × 313 mm.

[62] LA VILLA DI LVZIMBORGO.
[T:] LVTZENBOVRG. — [C:] Lutzenburgum Ducatus eiusdẽ nominis vetus et primaria vrbs, in superiorẽ et inferiorem situ mirabili, vallibus, et pcipitijs secatur Castro quondã, et Benedictⁿorũ coenobio Ducũ oratorio et sepulturę nucupato p̃slans — (Plan). 513 gg 229 × 314 mm.

[63] CONTADO DI NAMVRRA.
[C:] NAMVRCVM, COMITATVS. — (Map). 521 ii 233 × 313 mm.

[64] DESCRITTIONE DI NAMVRRA.
[C:] NAMVRCVM. — [C:] NAMVRCVM ad Mosæ flumen sita Ciuitas, ad viuum expressa. — (View). 525 kk 230 × 316 mm.

[65] DESCRITTIONE DEL VESCOVADO DI LIEGE.
[C:] LEODIENSIS EPISCOPATVS DELINEATIO. — (Map). 529 ll 228 × 307 mm.

[66] [C:] LIEGE — (View). 533 mm 229 × 310 mm.

[67] [C:] AQVISGRANVM, vulgo Aich Per antiqua Imperij vrbs, monumento Caroli Magni, Thermar prestantia et Memorabilis. — (Plan). 549 oo 228 × 309 mm.

Notes: All the maps have text on the verso, except where otherwise specified, and are uncoloured. There are maps from two different sources in this volume. Those with text on the verso and page-numbers seem to be original to the work; the seventeen maps which are blank on the back seem to have been inserted later, from some other volume. Twelve of these are numbered. On the verso of p. 439, DESCRITTIONE DI TORNAI, are the words 'Per causa della guerra non s'e ancor' potuto hauere il ritratto di questa Citta al naturale'; however, the map of TORNACVM follows, between pp. 440 & 441. It is numbered 55 (our no. is [52]) and is blank on the back. The same text is printed on the otherwise blank verso of p. 469, DESCRITTIONE DI CAMBRAI; this is followed by map [57], with the number 60. The cartouche of map [48] bears the date 1602, suggesting that it was inserted after the publication of the volume.
Following the title-page is the portrait: 'PHILIPPVS, O.G. HISPANIARVM SICILIÆ NEAPOLIS REX ARCHIDVX DAVSTRIÆ ETC.' The volume is in blue boards, with a black leather spine. Nordenskiöld's signature is on the first blank leaf.

86 GUICCIARDINI, LODOVICO 1633—1635

BELGICÆ, SIVE Inferioris Germaniæ, DESCRIPTIO: Auctore LVDOVICO GVICCIARDINO Nobili Florentino. EDITIO POSTREMA; Additamentis novis et Statu Politico regionum et urbium aucta, Earundemque iconismis illustrata. AMSTERDAMI, Apud GVILIELMVM BLAEV. M D C XXXV.

13,7 cm.

Vol. I
PARS PRIMA sive BELGICÆ DESCRIPTIO GENERALIS, Auctore LVDOVICO GVICCIARDINO Nobili Florentino. AMSTERDAMI; Apud GVILIELMVM BLAEV. M D C XXXV.

[1] [C:] INFERIOR GERMANIA — (Map). Before I A 94 × 130 mm.
[2] [C:] GALLIÆ BELGICÆ veteris accurata descriptio amico colendo d:o P Bertio I Hondius D:t — (Map). Between pp. 2 and 3. 93 × 134 mm.

Vol. II
PARS SECVNDA: DE BELGICA Regi Hispaniarum, &c. SVBDITA; Auctore LVDOVICO GVICCIARDINO NOBILI FLORENTINO. Additamentis passim insertis, & ad hæc tempora auctis. AMSTERDAMI Apud GVILIELMVM BLAEV. M D CXXXIII.

[1] [C:] BRABANTIA — (Map). Between pp. 90 and 91. 95 × 129 mm.
[2] [C:] LEVVEN. — (Plan). Between pp. 94 and 95. 108 × 131 mm.
[3] [C:] BRVSSEL. — [An empty cartouche.] (Plan). Between pp. 108 and 109. 108 × 130 mm.
[4] [C:] ANTWERPEN. — [Two empty cartouches.] (Plan). Between pp. 128 and 129. 107 × 130 mm.
[5] [C:] 's HERTOGENBOS. — (Plan). Between pp. 246 and 247. 107 × 131 mm.
[6] [C:] BERGEN, OP ZOOM. — [An empty cartouche.] (Plan). Between pp. 256 and 257. 107 × 131 mm.
[7] [C:] BREDA. — [An empty cartouche.] (Plan). Between pp. 260 and 261. 107 × 129 mm.
[8] [C:] MAESTRICHT. — [An empty cartouche.] (Plan). Between pp. 264 and 265. 107 × 130 mm.
[9] [C:] LIMBVRG. — [An empty cartouche.] (Plan). Between pp. 290 and M 13. 107 × 130 mm.
[10] [C:] MECHELEN. — [An empty cartouche.] (Plan). Before M 19. 108 × 130 mm.
[11] [C:] LIMBURGUM — (Map). Before 291. 92 × 129 mm.
[12] [C:] Lutzenburg — (Map). Before 291. 94 × 130 mm.
[13] [C:] LVTZENBVRG. — (Plan). Between pp. 292 and 293. 107 × 130 mm.
[14] [C:] FLANDRIA — (Map). Between pp. 304 and 305. 91 × 130 mm.
[15] [C:] GENT. — (Plan). Between pp. 312 and 313. 108 × 130 mm.
[16] [C:] OOSTENDE. — [An empty cartouche.] (Plan). Between pp. 342 and 343. 107 × 130 mm.
[17] [C:] LILLE, v. RYSSEL. — [An empty cartouche]. (Plan). Between pp. 380 and 381. 107 × 130 mm.
[18] [C:] DOVAY. — [An empty cartouche]. (Plan). Between pp. 384 and 385. 108 × 131 mm.
[19] [C:] TOVRNAY, v DOORNICK. — (Plan). Between pp. 388 and 389. 107 × 129 mm.
[20] [C:] ARTESIA — (Map). Between pp. 412 and 413. 91 × 130 mm.
[21] [C:] ARRAS, v. ATRECHT. — [An empty cartouche]. (Plan). Between pp. 412 and 413. 107 × 130 mm.
[22] [C:] HANNONIA — (Map). Between pp. 426 and 427. 91 × 130 mm.
[23] [C:] MONS, v. BERGEN IN HENEGOV. — [An empty cartouche] (Plan). Between pp. 428 and 429. 108 × 130 mm.
[24] [C:] NAMUR — (Map). Between pp. 464 and 465. 92 × 130 mm.
[25] [C:] NAMEN. — (Plan). Between pp. 466 and 467. 107 × 130 mm.
[26] [C:] Leodiensis Dioecesis — (Map). Between pp. 470 and 471. 93 × 129 mm.

Notes: All the maps are blank on the back and uncoloured. The maps are completely different from those in the 1567 and 1581 editions, both in size and in what they show. The volume is bound in old vellum, with holes indicating where the straps used to be. Nordenskiöld's signature is on the blank leaf at the beginning, with the year 1898.
Lit.: Bagrow p. 345, Bagrow, Catal. I:102—103.

87 GUTHRIE, WILLIAM 1779

A NEW Geographical, Historical, and Commercial GRAMMAR; AND PRESENT STATE OF THE SEVERAL KINGDOMS OF THE WORLD. ... TO WHICH ARE ADDED, I. A GEOGRAPHICAL INDEX, with the Names of Places alphabetically arranged. II. A TABLE of the COINS of all Nations, and their Value in ENGLISH MONEY. III. A CHRONOLOGICAL TABLE of remarkable Events from the Creation to the Present Time. BY WILLIAM GUTHRIE, Esq. ILLUSTRATED WITH A CORRECT SET OF MAPS, Engraved by Mr.KITCHIN, Geographer. The SIXTH EDITION, improved and enlarged; The ASTRONOMICAL PART by JAMES FERGUSON, F.R.S. LONDON: Printed for EDWARD and CHARLES DILLY, in the Poultry; and GEORGE ROBINSON, Pater-noster-Row, MDCCLXXIX. 21,4 cm.

[1] [C:] A New Map of the WORLD, Drawn from the latest Authorities By Tho:s Kitchin. — Frontispiece. The Western and Eastern hemispheres with 193 mm. diam.
[2] [C:] EUROPE Drawn from the best Authorities By T.Kitchin — Between pp. 64 and 65. 188 × 224 mm.
[3] [C:] SWEDEN DENMARK & NORWAY. Drawn from the best Authorities By T Kitchin — Between pp. 66 and 67. 188 × 224 mm.
[Inset:] [T:] ICELAND ISLE. Drawn to the same Scale. — 60 × 73 mm.
[4] [C:] RUSSIA OR MOSCOVY IN EUROPE Drawn from the latest Authorities, By Tho:s Kitchin Geo:r — Between pp. 102 and 103. 183 × 202 mm.
[5] [C:] SCOTLAND Drawn from the best Authorities By Tho:s Kitchin. — Between pp. 122 and 123. 188 × 222 mm.
[Inset:] [T:] Shetland Isles — 56 × 44 mm.
[6] [C:] ENGLAND and WALES Drawn from the best Authorities By Tho:s Kitchin. — Between pp. 174 and 175. 188 × 222 mm.
[7] [C:] IRELAND Drawn from the latest Authorities By Tho:s Kitchin Geo:r — Between pp. 350 and 351. 182 × 221 mm.
[8] [C:] FRANCE Drawn from the latest Authorities By Tho:s Kitchin Geo:r — Between pp. 372 and 373. 190 × 222 mm.
[9] [C:] GERMANY Drawn from the latest Authorities By Tho:s Kitchin Geo:r — Between pp. 412 and 413. 191 × 210 mm.
[10] [C:] POLAND LITHUANIA and PRUSSIA Drawn from the latest Authorities By Tho:s Kitchin Geog:r — Between pp. 450 and 451. 183 × 217 mm.
[11] [C:] SPAIN and PORTUGAL Drawn from the latest Authorities, By Tho:s Kitchin Geo:r — Between pp. 466 and 467. 190 × 222 mm.
[12] [C:] ITALY Drawn from the best Authorities By Tho:s Kitchin Geog:r — Between pp. 486 and 487. 187 × 223 mm.
[13] [C:] TURKY IN EUROPE & HUNGARY ... — Between pp. 506 and 507. 197 × 255 mm.
[14] [C:] ASIA Drawn from the best Authorities By T. Kitchin. — Between pp. 512 and 513. 187 × 224 mm.
[15] [C:] EAST INDIES from the best Authorities By Tho:s Kitchin Geo:r — Between pp. 544 and 545. 188 × 282 mm.
[16] [C:] AFRICA Drawn from the latest Authorities By Tho:s Kitchin Geo:r — Between pp. 586 and 587. 183 × 222 mm.
[17] [C:] NORTH AMERICA Drawn from the best Authorities By T. Kitchin. — Between pp. 614 and 615. 188 × 224 mm.
[18] [C:] WEST INDIES from the best Authorities By Tho:s Kitchin Geo:r — Between pp. 680 and 681. 176 × 343 mm.
[19] [C:] SOUTH AMERICA Drawn from the best Authorities

by T. Kitchin. — Between pp. 704 and 705. 186 × 222 mm.
Notes: All the maps are blank on the back and uncoloured. The first edition of this work was appeared 1770. In addition to the maps there is plate 'The Artificial Sphere' between pp. 16 & 17. The volume is bound in contemporary leather. Nordenskiöld's signature is on the first blank leaf at the beginning.

Lit.: Tooley, Dictionary p. 216.

88 HERMELIN, SAMUEL GUSTAV 1797—1807

Geographiske CHARTOR öfver Swerige, jämte BIFOGADE RITNINGAR, MED Hans Maj:t Konung GUSTAF den Fjerde ADOLPHS ALLERNÅDIGSTE TILLSTÅND utgifne Af Friherre S. G. Hermelin Första Afdelningen, DE NORRA LANDSORTER. STOCKHOLM 1797 58,2 cm.

[1] [C:] CHARTA öfwer SWERIGE med Tilgränsande Länder Kongl. Maj:t Konung GUSTAF IV. ADOLPH i underdånighet tilegnad af S. G. Hermelin. Sammandragen af C. E. Enagrius 1797 Graverad af Fredr. Akrel. — 542 × 575 mm.

[2] [T:] KARTA ÖFVER SVERIGE OCH NORRIGE UTGIFVEN AF Geografiska Inrättningen 1815. Sammandragen och författad af C. P. Hällström. — S. Anderson sc. 900 × 586 mm.
[Inset:] [T:] FINMARKENS AMT — 101 × 240 mm.

[3] [T:] CHARTA Öfver Wästerbottn och Svenske Lappmarcken. På Bergs Rådet, Friherre S. G. HERMELINS anstalt och omkostnad, efter äldre och nyare Chartor samt Observationer vid en Resa år 1795, Författad af Anton Swab, Bergmästare vid Stora Kopparberget och Ledamot af K. S. Vet. Acad., och af Clas Wallman Marckscheider vid K. Bergs-Colleg. Af den sistnämde vidare tilökad År 1796. — [T:] Graverad af Fr. Akrel — 530 × 565 mm.

[4] [T:] CHARTA öfver ÅNGERMANLAND, MEDELPAD och JÄMTLAND efter den af Landshöfdingen Friherre P A Örnsköld år 1771 utgifne Charta med Tilläggningar af Friherre S. G. Hermelin 1797. — [T:] Graverad af G. Broling. — 501 × 610 mm.

[5] [T:] CHARTA Öfver HERJEÅDALEN författad efter den af Landshöfdingen och Commendeuren HERR GREFVE F. A. U. CRONSTEDT lämnade Charta och efter Observationer vid en Resa år 1796, af A. SWAB Bergmästare, och C. M. ROBSAHM v. Not. vid K. Bergs Coll. på Bergs-Rådet Friherre S. G. HERMELINS Anstalt och Omkostnad, utgifven 1797. — 434 × 518 mm.

[6] [T:] Charta öfver GÄSTRIKLAND och HELLSINGLAND, Sammandragen, under Landshöfdingen och Commendeurens af Kongl Nordstjerne Orden Högwälborne Herr Grefve F. A. U. CRONSTEDTS inseende, af Ingenieuren Olof Insulander År 1796. Utgifven af Frih. S. G. HERMELIN. — [T:] Graverad af Fr. Akrel. — 598 × 554 mm.

GEOGRAPHISKE CHARTOR ÖFVER SWERIGE Utgifvne af Friherre S. G. Hermelin Tredje Afdelningen SVEARIKE. STOCKHOLM 1801.

[7] Utsigt af Stockholms Stad. Ritadt och graveradt af J. F. Martin. (View). On the title-page. Uncoloured. 221 × 401 mm.

[8] [C:] KARTA Öfver SWEARIKE och Norra Delen af SWERIGE UTGIFVEN AF Geografiska Inrättningen 1811. Författad af C. P. HÄLLSTRÖM — S. Anderson Sc. 916 × 569 mm.

[9] [T:] CHARTA ÖFVER STORA KOPPARBERGS HÖFDINGEDÖME ELLER DALARNE UTGIFVEN AF FRIHERRE S. G. HERMELIN Författad af C. P. HÄLLSTRÖM 1800. Graverad af Fr. Akrel. — 569 × 587 mm.

[10] [T:] CHARTA ÖFVER KOPPARBERGS, SÄTERS, NÄSGÅRDS OCH WÄSTER BERGSLAGENS Fögderier i Stora Kopparbergs Höfdingedöme UTGIFVEN AF FRIHERRE S. G. HERMELIN. Författad af C. P. HÄLLSTRÖM Geschworner 1800 — Graverad af Fr. Akrel. 580 × 610 mm.

[11] [T:] CHARTA ÖFVER WÄSTERÅS HÖFDINGEDÖME utgifven af FRIHERRE S. G. HERMELIN Efter äldre Chartor med Rättelser och Tilläggningar under Resor af BERGMÄSTAREN C. A. HJORT af ORNÄS och efter nyaste Astronomiska Observationer författad af C. P. HÄLLSTRÖM 1800. Graverad af Fr. Akrel — 561 × 600 mm.

[12] [C:] Charta öfver UPSALA HÖFDINGEDÖME utgifven af FRIHERRE S. G. HERMELIN. Författad af C. P. HÄLLSTRÖM. 1801. Graverad af Fredr. Akrel — 638 × 445 mm.

[13] [T:] CHARTA ÖFVER STOCKHOLMS HÖFDINGDÖME EFTER meddelta Chartor och Underrättelser af Öfver Ståthållaren Landshöfdingen öfver Stockholms Län Riddaren och Commendeuren af Kongl. M:ts Orden HÖGVÄLBORNE GREFVE HERR SAMUEL AF UGGLAS, och efter nyare Mätningar, Resor och Astronomiska Observationer författad af C. P. HÄLLSTRÖM. 1802 Utgifwen af FRIHERRE S. G. HERMELIN. S I Neele sc. Strand London. — 902 × 595 mm.

[14] [C:] Charta ÖFVER ÖREBRO Höfdingdöme UTGIFVEN AF FRIHERRE S. G. HERMELIN. Efter sammandragna geometriska Mätningar och flera Orters åren 1798, 1801 och 1802 astronomiskt bestämda Lägen. FORFATTAD AF C. P. HÄLLSTRÖM 1803. — S. I. Neele sc. Strand London 770 × 494 mm.

[15] [T:] CHARTA ÖFVER NYKÖPINGS HÖFDINGDÖME.

UTGIFVEN AF FRIHERRE S. G. HERMELIN. FÖRFATTAD AF C. P. HÄLLSTRÖM Premier Ingeniör. 1804. — Graverad af Sam. Anderson. 557 × 623 mm.
MED KONGL. MAJ:TS Nådigste Tillstånd, GEOGRAFISKE KARTOR öfver SWERIGE Utgifne af FRIHERRE S. G. HERMELIN. Tredje Afdelningen. GÖTARIKE. STOCKHOLM 1807.

[16] [T:] KARTA öfver GÖTARIKE eller Södra Delen af Swerige utgifven af FRIHERRE S. G. HERMELIN. Efter äldre och nyare Kartor samt Astronomiska Observationer, författad af C. P. HÄLLSTRÖM. 1807. — Graverad af C. G. Lundgren   848 × 580 mm.
[17] [T:] KARTA ÖFVER GÖTEBORGS OCH BOHUS LÄNS HÖFDINGDÖME Utgifwen af FRIHERRE S. G. HERMELIN Författad af C. G. FORSSELL. Und. Löjtn. vid Örlogs Flott.   1806 — Graverad af S. Anderson. 905 × 562 mm.
[18] [T:] KARTA öfver HALMSTADS HÖFDINGDÖME eller Halland UTGIFVEN AF Friherre S. G. Hermelin Författad efter Geometriska Kartor och under Resor gjorde Mätningar och Observationer af C. G. FORSSELL 1807 — [T:] Sam. Anderson Sc. — 840 × 607 mm.
[19] [T:] KARTA öfver CARLSTADS HÖFDINGDÖME eller Wärmeland. Utgifven af FRIHERRE S. G. HERMELIN Efter nya Astronomiska Observationer och sammandrag af Geometriska Mätningar Författad af C. P. HÄLLSTRÖM. 1808. Graverad af C. G. Lundgren. — 639 × 880 mm.
[20] [T:] KARTA öfver WÄRMELAND SÖDRA DELEN Utgifven af FRIHERRE S. G. HERMELIN. ... Graverad af C. G. Lundgren — 629 × 876 mm.
[21] [T:] KARTA öfver ELFSBORGS Höfdingdöme UTGIFVEN AF FRIHERRE S. G. HERMELIN Enligt nyaste Astronomiska Observationer samt under Resor förbättrade äldre Geometriska Kartor Författad af Carl G. Forssell. 1808. — S. Andersson S.   583 × 932 mm.
[22] [T:] KARTA öfver SKARABORGS Höfdingdöme. Utgifven af FRIHERRE S. G. HERMELIN. Efter Geometriska Kartor, nyaste Astronomiska Observationer och under Resor gjorda Rättelser; Författad af C. G. FORSSELL 1807. — S. Anderson Sc.   604 × 618 mm.
[23] [C:] KARTA öfver JÖNKÖPINGS KRONOBERGS och BLEKINGS HÖFDINGSDÖME Ufgifven af Friherre S. G. Hermelin Efter äldre Kartor och af Capt. C. G. Forssell under resor gjorda Rättelser FÖRFATTAD AF C. P. HÄLLSTRÖM CAPT. VID SJÖMÄTN. CORPSEN 1809. — Graverad af Sam. Anderson.   859 × 627 mm.
[24] [T:] KARTA öfver ÖSTERGÖTLAND utgifven af FRIHERRE S. G. HERMELIN. Efter den af Förste Landm. M. WALLBERG sammandragna Karta och enligt nyaste Astronomiska Ortsbestämmelser författad af C. P. HÄLLSTRÖM Capitaine vid Kongl. Sjömätn. Corpsen. 1810. — Graverad af C. G. Lundgren   597 × 638 mm.
[25] [T:] KARTA öfver GOTTLAND ELLER Wisby HÖFDINGDÖME utgifwen af FRIH.RE S. G. HERMELIN Författad af C. P. HÄLLSTRÖM Prem.r Ingeniör. 1805. — Graverad af E. Åkerlund och C. G. Lundgren —   895 × 579 mm.
[Inset:] [T:] GOTTSKA SANDÖ — 105 × 111 mm.
[26] [C:] KARTA ÖFVER MALMÖHUS OCH CHRISTIANSTADS HÖFDINGDÖMEN ELLER Skåne Utgifven af Geografiska Inrättningen 1812. Författad af C. P. HÄLLSTRÖM — NORRA DELEN Graverad af Edvard Personne.   508 × 914 mm.
[27] KARTA öfver SKÅNE   SÖDRA DELEN.   Graverad af Edvard Personne.   506 × 907 mm.
[28] [T:] KARTA ÖFVER KALMAR LÄN OCH Öland UTGIFVEN AF Geografiska Inrättningen 1818. Författad af C. P. HÄLLSTRÖM. — Graverad af C. G. Lundgren. 1166 × 583 mm.
GEOGRAPHISKE CHARTOR ÖFVER SWERIGE MED Hans Maj:t Konung GUSTAF IV. ADOLPHS Allernådigste Tilstånd UTGIFNE AF FRIHERRE S. G. HERMELIN. ANDRA AFDELNINGEN Storfurstendömet FINLAND STOCKHOLM 1799.
[29] Utsigt ifrån Wermasvuori åt Sjöarne Jokijärvi och Umolanselkä uti Hauho Sockn i Nylands och Tavastehus Höfdingedöme. Ritad af C. P. Hällström Graverad af J. F Martin (View). On the title-page. Uncoloured. 223 × 322 mm.
[30] [C:] CHARTA öfver STORFURSTENDÖMET FINLAND utgifwen PÅ FRIHERRE S. G. HERMELINS Anstalt och Omkostnad SAMMANDRAGEN OCH FÖRFATTAD AF C. P. Hällström Philos. Magister och Auscultant i Kongl BergsColl. 1799. Graverad af Fr. Akrel. — 540 × 580 mm.
[31] [T:] CHARTA öfver ULEÅBORGS HÖFDINGEDÖME På Friherre S G Hermelins Anstalt och Omkostnad författad enligt särskilde Chartor och Anmärkningar under Resor af C. P. HÄLLSTRÖM Auscultant i Kongl. Bergs Colleg. 1798. Graverad af Fr. Akrel. — 580 × 614 mm.
[32] [T:] Charta öfver WASA HÖFDINGEDÖME, utgifven af Friherre S G Hermelin. Författad af C. P. HÄLLSTRÖM Philos. Mag. och Ausc. vid K. Bergs Coll. 1798. — 551 × 622 mm.
[33] [T:] CHARTA öfver ÅBO OCH BJÖRNEBORGS HÖFDINGEDÖME UTGIFVEN AF Friherre S. G. Hermelin EFTER SÄRSKILDE CHARTOR FÖRFATTAD af C. P. HÄLLSTRÖM Auscultant i Kl. Bergs Coll. 1799. — Graverad af Fr. Akrel.   575 × 622 mm.
[34] [T:] Charta öfver NYLANDS och TAVASTEHUS samt KYMMENEGÅRDS Höfdingedömen utgifven af Friherre S G Hermelin och författad af C. P. HÄLLSTRÖM Auscultant i Kl. Bergs Coll., 1798. — 567 × 616 mm.
[35] [T:] Charta ÖFVER SAWOLAX OCH KARELENS ELLER KUOPIO HÖFDINGEDÖME UTGIFVEN AF Friherre S. G. Hermelin, FÖRFATTAD AF C. P. HÄLLSTRÖM. Graverad af Fr. Akrel. — 555 × 628 mm.

Notes: All the maps are blank on the back, and all are coloured except where otherwise specified. In this copy the second part is bound after the third. Hermelin's atlas was a private undertaking, but for some time it filled the place of an officially produced atlas. Carl Ritter, in his 'Erdkunde' (2 nd ed., vol.1, p.29), states that Hermelin's maps were the result of the mapmaker's own work combined with a critical use of earlier material. It is a remarkable atlas, of great importance in the development of Swedich cartography. The volume is bound in beautiful red morocco with gold tooling. A bookbinder's label, 'MELKER STATLANDER, Bokbindare i Stockholm, vid Österlånggatan, nära Slottsbacken', is pasted to the inside of the back cover.
Lit.: Bratt, p. 77—80, Lönborg, p. 193—218, Ritter, vol. 1, p. 29.

89 HERMELIN, SAMUEL GUSTAV   1797—1799

[Geographiske CHARTOR öfver Swerige, jämte BIFOGADE RITNINGAR, MED Hans Maj:t Konung GUSTAF den Fjerde ADOLPHS ALLERNÅDIGSTE TILLSTÅND utgifne Af Friherre S. G. Hermelin. ANDRA AFDELNINGEN Storfurstendömet FINLAND   STOCKHOLM 1799.]   62 cm.

[1] [C:] CHARTA öfver STORFURSTENDÖMET FINLAND ... — = 1797—1807:[30].
[2] [T:] Charta ÖFVER SAWOLAX OCH KARELENS ELLER KUOPIO HÖFDINGEDÖME ... — = 1797—1807:[35].
[3] [T:] Charta öfver NYLANDS och TAVASTEHUS samt KYMMENEGÅRDS Höfdingedömen ... — = 1797—1807: [34].
[4] [T:] CHARTA öfver ÅBO OCH BJÖRNEBORGS HÖFDINGEDÖME ... — = 1797—1807:[33].
[5] [T:] Charta öfver WASA HÖFDINGEDÖME, ... — = 1797—1807:[32].
[6] [T:] CHARTA öfver ULEÅBORGS HÖFDINGEDÖME ... — = 1797—1807:[31].

[Första Afdelningen, DE NORRA LANDSORTER.]
[7] [T:] CHARTA Öfver Wästerbottn och Svenske Lappmarcken ... — = 1797—1807:[3].

[8] [T:] CHARTA öfver ÅNGERMANLAND, MEDELPAD och JÄMTLAND ... — = 1797—1807:[4].
[9] [T:] CHARTA Öfver HERJEÅDALEN ... — = 1797—1807:[5].
[10] [T:] Charta öfver GÄSTRIKLAND och HELLSINGLAND,... — = 1797—1807:[6].

Notes: All the maps are blank on the back and coloured. The volume is not a published edition but a made-up collection of Hermelin maps. It is bound in blue boards, with a manuscript title on the front cover: 'Carter öfver Finland och Norrland'. It contains all the six maps of Finland that appear in the published edition, but in reverse order. The following four maps are from the first part of the atlas.

Lit.: See Hermelin 1797—1807.

90 HOMANN, JOHANN BAPTIST AND HEIRS 1710—1750

[Collection of maps without title-page.] obl. 54 cm.

[1] [C:] SAXONIÆ TRACTUS DUCATUM MAGDEBURGENSEM cum suo CIRCULO SALICO PRINC: ANHALTINUM HALBERSTADIENSEM finitimarumq$_3$ Regionum ELECTORATUS nempe BRANDENBURG: SAXONIÆ DUCATUS BRUNSVICENSIS etc. Partes Ostendens editus a Joh: Baptist: Homañi S.C.M. Geog. Filio NORIBERGÆ ... — 468 × 536 mm.
[Inset:] [T:] MAGDEBURG — (View). 86 × 218 mm.

[2] [C:] Potentissimo BORUSSORUM REGI FRIDERICO WILHELMO Majestate, Fortitudine Clementia Augustissimo Hancce LITHUANIAM BORUSSICAM in qva loca colonijs Salisburg. ad incolendum Regio nutu concessa chorographice exhibentur. D D D REGIAE SUAE MAIESTATIS Servi subjectissimi Homanniani Heredes Norib. A. M D CCXXXV. ... — [C:] ... Designante I.F.Betgen Mense Febr. 1733. — (The map is a continuation of [86]). 480 × 572 mm.
[Inset:] [C:] PLAN von der in Lithauen neu angelegten Stadt GUMBINNEN — (Plan). 160 × 215 mm.

[3] [C:] TABVLA MARCHIONATVS BRANDENBVRGICI ET DVCATVS POMERANIÆ quæ sunt Pars Septentrionalis CIRCVLI SAXONIÆ SVPERIORIS novissime edita A IOH. BAPTISTA HOMANNO Noriberg... — 419 × 525 mm.

[4] [C:] REGNUM BORUSSIÆ Gloriosis auspicijs Serenissimi et Potentissimi Prin FRIDERICI III PRIMI BORUSSIÆ REGIS, MARCH. ET ELECT. BRAN inauguratum die 18. Ian A. 1701. Geographice cum vicinis Regionibus adumbratum a IOH. BAPTISTA HOMANNO Norimbergæ ... — 478 × 568 mm.

[5] [C:] General-Carte der gesamten Königlichen Preussischen Länder. zu finden bei I.D.Schleuen Kupferstecher in Berlin. — 577 × 701 mm.
[Insets:] [T:] Berlin. — (View). 85 × 180 mm. [T:] Bresslau — (View).70 × 175 mm. [C:] Königsberg. — (View). 70 × 200 mm.

[6] [C:] MARCHIONATUS LUSATIÆ INFERIORIS BOHEMIÆ olim REGNO jam ELECT. SAXONIÆ subject in Circulos, Dynastias et Præfect: accuratissime distinctus calamo et sumtibus MATTH. SEUTTERI S.C.Maj. Geographi Aug. Vindel. — Tob:Conr. Lotter, sculps. 484 × 570 mm.

[7] [C:] TOTIUS MARCHIONATUS LUSATIAE tam superioris quam inferioris Tabula specialis in suos Comitatus et Dominatus distincta Revisa et aucta, â Viro Clarissimo Dom. Ioh. Hübnero et in lucem edita â Ioh Baptista Homanno S.C.M G. Norimbergæ ... — 478 × 568 mm.

[8] [C:] LUSATIAE SUPERIORIS Tabula Chorographica exacte tradita per IOH. GEORG. SCHREIBERUM & excusa studio. HOMANNIANORUM HEREDUM Noribergæ, Cum Pr. 1732. Cæsar et El. Saxon. — 437 × 550 mm.

[9] [C:] INSULÆ ET PRINCIPATUS RUGIÆ cum vicinis POMERANIÆ Littoribus Nova Tabula edita â IOH: BAPTISTA HOMANNO Sacræ Cæsareæ Majestatis Geographo Noribergæ ... — 482 × 577 mm.

[10] [C:] DUCATUS POMERANIÆ novissima Tabula in anteriorem et interiorem divisa, quatenus subsunt CORONIS SUECIÆ ET BORUSSIÆ cum insertis et adjacentibus Ditionibus exhibita a IOH. BAPTISTA HOMANN Noribergæ. ... — 486 × 567 mm.

[11] [C:] MEKLENBVRG DVCATVS Auctore Ioanne Laurenbergio. — [C:] AMSTELODAMI, Excudebat Ioannes Ianssonius. — Uncoloured. Text on the back. 362 × 475 mm.

[12] [C:] DUCATUS MEKLENBURGICI Tabula Generalis continens DUC. VANDALIÆ et MEKLENBURG COMITATUM ET EPISCOPATUM SWERINENSEM ROSTOCHIENSE et STARGARDIENSE DOMINIUM excudente IO. BAPTISTA HOMANNO Noribergæ ... — 485 × 569 mm.

[13] [C:] LUTZENBURGENSIS DUCATUS VERISS. DESCRIPT. Iacobo Surhonio Monta. Auct. — [C:] ... Anno 1646. — [T:] Visscher Excu — Uncoloured. 372 × 485 mm.
[Inset:] [T:] Luxenburgum. — (View). 40 × 70 mm.

[14] [C:] DUCATUS IULIACI & BERGENSIS Tabula Geographica, simul Ducatum CLIVIAE & MEURSIAE Principatum, nec non adjac-terrarum, inter quas' integer Duc at. LIMBURGENSIS exhibetur, fines complectens. Ex prototypo Iaillotiano delineata novisq$_3$ accessionibus auctior & emendatior reddita. Excudentibus Homañianis Heredibus, ... — 560 × 476 mm.
[Inset:] [T:] Nota. Quoniam spatii angustia prohibuit in mappa majore integrum Duc Bergens: repræsentare residuum ejus secundum eandem scalæ magnitudinem hic delineatum exhibemus — 82 × 68 mm.

[15] [C:] NOVA ET ACCURATA DUCATUS CLIVIÆ ET COMITATUS MARCHIÆ, CUM FINITIMIS PROVINCIIS DELINEATIO Cura et cælo MATTHÆI SEUTTERI. S.C.CATHOL. REGIÆ MAJEST. GEOGR. AUGUSTÆ VINDELICOR. — 488 × 569 mm.

[16] Carte geographique du COMTÉ INFERIEVR de CAZENELNBOGEN, mise au jour par les Heritiers de Homann. Avec Pr. Imperial. l'An 1745.
[C:] INFERIORIS COMITATVS CATTIMELIBOCENSIS delineatio geographica una cum confiniis Edentibus Homann. Her. C.P.S.C.M.G. A.^{o} 1745 — 400 × 556 mm.

[17] [C:] LANDGRAVIATUS HASSIÆ INFERIORIS nova Tabula, in qua præcipue DITIONES HASSOCASSELENSE ET COMITATUS WALDECK cum insertis et vicinis aliorū Statuum Præfecturis exhibentur à IOH.BAPT. HOMANNO Noribergiæ — 483 × 576 mm.

[18] HASSIAE SVPERIORIS ET WETTERAV. PARTIS DELINEATIO, CVM DESCRIPTIONE CASTRORVM PROPE GIESSAM ET CONIVNCTIONIS AD VRBAM TRAVNICI ET BATIANICI EXERCITVVM, SERENISSIMO PRINCIPI ac DOMINO, DN.^{o} LVDOVICO, HASSIAE LANDGRAVIO, PRINCIPI HERSFELDIAE, etc. etc. etc. humillime oblata a CHRISTOPH MAX. PRONNER, Excudentibus Homannianis Heredibus. A.^{o} 1746. ... 431 × 551 mm.
[Inset:] [C:] GIESSEN — (View). 70 × 150 mm.

[19] Karte der Gefürsteten GRAFFSCHAFT HENNEBERG, mit dem angränzenden FVRSTENTH. COBVRG u. andern GRAENZLAENDERN, nach authentischen Documenten und Nachrichten verfertiget, und in ihre Aembter eingetheilet. Herausgegeben von Homænnischen Erben. ... A. 1743.
[C:] S.R.I.COMITATVS HENNEBERG secundum Præfecturas & modernas Dynastias, una cum confini PR:COBVRGENSI geographice consignatus & in hac Tabula editus. — [C:] ... Mappa hæc ad fidem optimorum documentorum moderatore potissimum et directore illustri Domino Ioh. Iacobo Zinckio, Consiliario Aulico Meinungensi conciñata prodit studio et opera Homañianorum Heredum. A. 1743... — La CARTE du

Comté de HENNEBERG avec les pais confins du Principauté de COBVRG. Le tout subdivisé en ses Baillages et dressé selon les memoires les plus authentiques. ... A Nüremberg chez les Heritiers de Homañ. A.1743. ... I,G. Küsel delin. 469 × 553 mm.

[20] [C:] EPISCOPATUUM MONASTERIENSIS ET OSNABRUGENSIS UT ET COMITATUUM BENTHEIM, TECLENBURG, STENFORD, LINGEN, DIEPHOLT, DELMENHORST, RIETBERG etc. etc. novissima et accuratissima Designatio cura et sumptibus MATTHÆI SEUTTERI, S.C. ET REG. CATHOL. MAJEST. GEOGR. AUGUSTÆ VINDEL. — [T:] Tob. Con. Lotter sculp. — 566 × 488 mm.

[21] [C:] PROTOPARCHIÆ MINDELHEMENSIS Nova Tabula Geographica, Quam, Ob singularem erga Patriam Amorem, Perillustri ac Generoso Domino D.no Maximiliano Antonio L.B.de Zündt, Domino in Kintzingen, Kimpsenhausen, et Harkirchen, etc. etc. Sereniss. Elect. Bavariæ Camerario, et Consiliario Aulico: nec non Supremo Urbis, et Protoparehiæ Mindelh. Præf. et Granario. Patrono suo Gratiosissimo submissè dedicat IO. BAPTISTA HOMANN Sac. Cæs. Maj. Geographus torquatus, et Regiæ Boruss. Societatis Scientiarū membrum... (Norimbergæ.). ... — 482 × 576 mm.
[Inset:] [T:] Die Stadt MINDELHEIM gegen Mitternacht anzusehen — (View). 70 × 120 mm.

[22] [C:] ARCHIEPISCOPATUS et ELECTORATUS COLONIENSIS ut et DUCATUUM IULIACENSIS ET MONTENSIS nec non COMITATUS MEURSIAE Nova Tabula excudente IOHAN BAPTISTA HOMANNO Noribergæ. ... — 478 × 564 mm.

[23] [C:] NOVA TERRITORII ERFORDIEN[SIS] IN SUAS PRÆFECTURAS accurate divisi descriptio cui accedit ERFORDIÆ URBIS exterior Facies et Prospectus Auctore IOH. BAPT. HOMANNO Noribergæ ... — [C:] Revidit Fridericus Zollmannus A. 1717. — 477 × 574 mm.
[Inset:] [C:] DIE STADT ERFURT. — (View). 55 × 290 mm.

[24] [C:] RECENS ET ACCURATA DESIGNATIO EPISCOPATUS PADERBORNENSIS IN SUAS DIOECESES ET PRÆFECT. EXACTE DISTINCTI opera et sumptibus MATTHÆI SEUTTERI, GEOGR. CÆSAREI ET CHALCOGR. AUGUSTÆ VINDEL. ... — [T:] Tob.Con: Lotter, sc. — 485 × 542 mm.
[Inset:] [T:] PADERBORN. — (View). 75 × 400 mm.

[25] [C:] S. R. IMP. COMITATUS HANAU proprie sic dictus, cum singulis suis Præfecturis; ut et Comitatus SOLMS. BUDINGEN et NIDDA cumreliqua WETTERAVIA et vicinis Regionibus per FR. ZOLLMANNUM. A.C.S.S.V. curante IOH. CHR. HOMANNO. D.M. Noribergæ A.Dom MDCC XXVIII. ... — R.A. Schneider sculps. Furth. 478 × 554 mm.
[Inset:] [T:] Prospect der Stadt Hanau gegen Mittag anzusehen. — (View). 80 × 343 mm.

[26] [C:] CIRCULI WESTPHALIÆ in omnes suos STATUS ET PROVINCIAS accurate divisi Nova et exacta Tabula edita sumtibus IOH. BAPTISTÆ HOMAN Noribergæ. — 568 × 483 mm.

[27] [C:] S.R.I. PRINCIPATUS et EPISCOPATUS EISTETTENSIS cum omnibus suis Præfecturis et pertinentiis, tam in proprio, quam in alieno Territorio vicinorum Statuum sitis Geographicę exhibitus à IOHANNE BAPTISTA HOMANNO S.C.M.Geographo et Regiæ Scientiarum Societatis Berolinensis membro NORIMBERGÆ ... — Mense Iulio 1745 emendatior reddita. 482 × 566 mm.
[Inset:] [T:] Prospect der Hoch Fürstl. Bischöfflichen Haupt und Residenz-Stadt EICHSTETT samt dē Schloss S.t WILIBALDSBURG. — (View). 100 × 230 mm.

[28] [C:] DUCATUS FRANCIÆ ORIENTALIS Seu SAC.ROM.IMPerij PRINCIPATUS et EPISCOPATUS HERBIPOLENSIS Vulgo WÜRTZBURGENSIS cum omnibus suis Officiis et pertinentijs Geographice exhibitus á IOH. BAPT. HOMANN SAC.CÆS.MAJ. Geographo, et Regiæ Berolinēsis Societatis scientiarum membro Norimbergæ. ... — 477 × 560 mm.
[Inset:] [T:] Grundriss der Würtzbur. Stadt und Vestung KÖNIGSHOFEN. — (Plan). 77 × 94 mm.

[29] [C:] OLDENBVRG COMITATVS — [T:] Amstelodami Guiljelm.Blauew excudit. — [T:] E.Sijmonsz.Hamersveldt sculp. — Uncoloured. 373 × 490 mm.

[30] [C:] Ducatus: olim Episcopatus BREMENSIS et ostiorum ALBIS et VISURGIS Fluviorum, novissima Descriptio. — [C:] Nobilissimo Amplissimo Consultissimoque Viro D.CORNELIO DE GRAAF, Domino in Zuijdt Polsbroeck. Inclyti et Celeberrimi Amsterodamensium Emporii Consuli ac Senatori Dignissimo. Tabulam hanc Geographicam. D.D.D. Ioannes Ianssonius. — Uncoloured. 425 × 528 mm.

[31] [C:] NOBILIS FLUVIUS ALBIS maximâ curâ, ex varijs, famosisq_3 Autoribus collectus, et in lucem editus, a Nicolao Johannide Piscatore. 1657. — [C:] Amplissimis, Consultissimis, et Prudentissimis Viris Senatoribus, Consulibusq_3 Reipublicæ HAMBURGENSIS, hanc celeberrimi Fluminis ALBIS delineationem, summo studio ac nitore elaboratum, benevolo amino dat, dicat donat. Nicolaus Iohannides Piscator. — [Divided into two parts]. Uncoloured. 368 × 524 mm.
[Inset:] [C:] EMPORIUM HAMBURGUM — (View). 40 × 253 mm.

[32] ANDERER und MINDERE THEIL DES GANTZEN HOCHLÖBL. FRÄNCKISCHEN CRAISSES, MIT WELCHEM ZUGLEICH DAS ERTZ-STIFT und CHUR FÜRSTENTUM MAYNTZ SAMPT DENEN NOCH ÜBRIGE FRÄNCK: STAATEN als da seind die GRAFSCH. WERTHEIM REINECK und ERPACH nebst der angrentzenden NIDEREN CHUR PFALTZ am RHEIN in dieser Tafel angezeigt werden.
[C:] ELECTORATUS MOGUNTINUS ut et PALATIN: INFER. HASSIÆ & Fluminis Moeni aliqua pars exhibens simul Occid: Circ: Franconiae partes nimiru in finam part, Episc. Würtz: Comit. Werth: Reineck, Hohenl: & Erpach etc. Geogr: exhibitus. Conante IOH. BAPT. HOMANNO S.C.M.Geog. ... — 547 × 547 mm. See [79].

[33] [Ducatus Wurtenbergici]
[C:] DOMS Serenissimo Celsissimoq_3 Principi ac Domino Domino EBERHARDO LUDOVICO Duci Würtenbergiæ et Thecciæ Comiti Montisbelgardi, Dynastæ in Haydenheim etc Sac. Cæs. Maj. ac Rom. Imp. ut et Circuli Suevici Generali Mareschallo Campi et Generali Equitatus etc Domino suo Clementissimo Tabulam hanc in debitæ submissimis tesseram... D.D.D. Auctor ... Año 1710. — (The map is a continuation of [56]). 576 × 481 mm.
[Inset:] [T:] STUTTGART — (View). 30 × 95 mm.

[34] [C:] PARS VEDEROVIÆ PLVRIMAS DITIONES PRINC. et COM. NASSOVICOR. imprimis verô REGIONEM SCHWALBACENSEM Acidulis claram exhibens accuratè distincta á Ioh. Baptista Hohmanno S.C.M.Geographo Noribergæ ... — 465 × 552 mm.
[Insets:] [T:] Langen Schwalbach — (View). 60 × 107 mm.

[35] [C:] NASSOVIÆ PRINCIPATUS et ad cum spectantes Ditiones, cum adjacentib_9 Comitatibus, Dominiis et Præfecturis. intra Mosellam, Lahnum et citeriorem ac ulteriorem Rheni ripan sitis, summa cura et industria delineatus per MATTHÆUM SEUTTERUM, S.Cæs. et Cathol. Majest. Geographum August. Vindelic. — 494 × 575 mm.

[36] [C:] L'EVECHE ET L'ETAT DE LIEGE Avec les appartenances designées dans les pais voisins Delineation nouvelle et exacte Aux depens DE MATTHIEU SEUTTER, Geographe et Graveur Imperial D AUGSBOURG. ... — [T:] Tob: Con: Lotter, sculps. — 488 × 573 mm.

[37] [C:] Chorographia Territorii NAUMBURGO-CITIENSIS Episcopatus olim nomine celebris una cum magna Confiniorum parte exactissime designata a IOH: GEORG: SCHREIBERO Edita curis et impensis HOMANNIANORUM HEREDUM Norib: A.MDCCXXXII ... — 451 × 538 mm.

[38] [C:] TABULA GEOGRAPHICA in qua Serenissimi

Principis FRIDERICI Duc. Sax. Iuliæ, Cliviæ et Montium, nec non Angariæ et Westphaliæ PRINCIPATVS GOTHA, COBVRG ET ALTENBURG cum omnibus eorundem Præfecturis tam in Thuringia quam Misnia et Franconia sitis ostendentur à IOH. BAPTISTA HOMANNO Sacræ Cæsareæ Majestatis Geographo et Reg. Borussicæ Societ. Scientiaru Membro Norimbergæ. ... — 478 × 558 mm.
[Inset:] [T:] Die Hoch Fürstl: Residenz Stadt GOTHA. — (View). 45 × 125 mm.

[39] [C:] PRINCIPATVS ISENACENSIS cum adjacentibus vicinorum Statuum Ditionibus exhibitus à IOHANNE BAPT. HOMANNO... (Norimbergæ.) ... — 487 × 567 mm.

[40] [C:] COMITATUS STOLBERGICI ad Hercyniam ceterarumq$_3$ ad ILLUSTRISS. COMITES pertinentium Ditionum & terrarum ipsis adjacentium Geographica Descriptio. Edita curis Homannianorum Heredum. Norimbergæ ... — [T:] Nachricht: ... Stolberg den 22 Oct. 1736. I.F.Penther. ... — 481 × 569 mm.

[41] [C:] S.R.I. PRINCIPATUS FULDENSIS IN BUCHONIA cum adjacentibus quibusdam Regionibus adumbratus â IOH.BATPTISTA HOMANNO Sacræ Cæsareæ Majestatis Geographo Noribergæ. ... — 485 × 576 mm.

[42] [C:] DUCATUS BRUNSUICENSIS in tres suos Principatus CALENBERGICUMsc. GRUBENHAG. & GUELPHERBITANUM distincte divisi, nec non EPISCOPATUS HILDESIENSIS, PR.HALBER. Comitatus Schauenburgici, aliorumq$_3$ confiniorum exacta Tabula, edita cura IOH. BAPT. HOMANNI S.C.M. Geographi ... — 503 × 586 mm.

[43] = [42] in this ed. with small alterations.

[44] [C:] PRINCIPATVS BRANDENBVRGICO-CVLMBACENSIS vel BARVTHINVS Tabvla Geographica qvoad Partem Svperiorem expressvs. — 475 × 541 mm.
[Inset:] [T:] Marggræflich Brandenburg-Bayreutisches Amt LAVENSTEIN an denen Thüringischen Grænzen gelegen. — 67 × 80 mm.

[45] [C:] WALDECCIAE ac Finitimorum Dominiorum ITTERANI & CANSTEINIANI nec non insertæ Dioecesis EIMELRODENSIS accurata Tabula, excusa Per HOMANNIANOS HEREDES Noribergæ M D CC XXXIII. — [C:] CAROLO AVGVSTO FRIDERICO, S.R.I. PRINCIPI WALDECCIÆ Comiti Pirmontii et Rupis Rappoldi, Domino in Hoheneck et Gerolseck Dat Dicat Dedicat I. NICOLAI I.G.C.C. — 542 × 469 mm.

[46] [C:] ALSATIA tam SVPERIOR, quam INFERIOR una cum SVNDGOVIA, utraque in suos Status provinciales divisa & ex subsidiis veteribus Speklinianis æque ac recentioribus delineata Studio Homannianorum Heredum. — (The map is a continuation of [48]). 551 × 422 mm.

[47] [C:] LANDGRAVIATUS ALSATIAE tam SUPERIORIS quam INFERI cum utroque MARCHIONATU BADENSI ut et tractu Herciniæ Silvæ ac Ditione quatuor Urbium Silvestr editore IOH. BAPTISTA HOMANNO NORIBERGÆ ... — 574 × 478 mm.

[48] ALSATIA SVPERIOR una cum SVNTGOVIA (The map is a continuation of [46]). 547 × 419 mm.

[49] [C:] CHOROGRAPHIA ARGENTORATI ALSATIÆ METROPOLIS sculpta et excusa a MATTHÆO SEUTTERO S:C.M.Geogr. Aug.Vindel. ... — 490 × 576 mm.

[50] [C:] THEATRUM BELLI RHENANI AUSPICATIS MILITIÆ PRIMITIIS POTENTISSIMI ROMAN. ET HUNGA. REGIS IOSEPHI I. PII FELICIS AUGUSTI LANDAVIO GLORIOSE EXPUGNATO APERTUM io Septemb. Anno M D CCII Novâ Tabulâ repræsentatū à IOAN. BAPTISTA HOMAN NORIMBERGÆ ... — [C:] FLUVIORUM RHENI MOSÆ: AC MOSELLÆ Novissima Exhibitio qua Sacri tres Electoratus & Archiepiscop MOGUNTINUS, COLONIENSIS ET TREVIRENSIS PALATINATUS RHENI, ALSATIA ET LOTHARINGIA cum finitimis BELGII REGII & BATAVORUM Provincys accurate ostenduntur. — 562 × 482 mm.
[Insets:] [T:] LANDAW — (View). 40 × 95 mm. [T:] BENEVOLE SPECTATOR, Vt Tractum totius RHENI ab Origine usque ad Ostia ea, qua possibile esset amplitudine Ostenderemus, Duplicem illius Fontem in hoc quadratum spatium eadem Milliarium scalá redegimus. — 110 × 137 mm.

[51] [C:] Theatrum Belli ad RHENUM SUPERIOR. nec non Munimentorum tum Imperialium, tum Gallicorum ichnographica exhibitio accurate tradita Per Homannianos Heredes A. MD CCXXXIV. ... — 549 × 462 mm.
[Insets:] [T:] LANDAV — 132 × 93 mm. [T:] STRASBURG — 132 × 93 mm. [T:] NEU BREISACH — 132 × 93 mm. [T:] FORT LOVIS — 64 × 93 mm. [T:] HÜNNINGEN — 65 × 93 mm. [T:] MANHEIM — 115 × 93 mm. [T:] PHILIPPSBURG — 130 × 92 mm. [T:] ALT BREISACH — 138 × 92 mm. [T:] FREIBURG — 141 × 92 mm. (All insets plans).

[52] [C:] DUCATUS LUNEBURGICI et COMITATUS DANNEBERGENSIS accurata Descriptio primum edita à IOH. BAPT. HOMANNO. S.C.M. Geo De in recenter recusa et augmentata Noribergæ ... — 482 × 573 mm.

[53] CURSUS RHENI à BASILEA USQUE AD BONNAM III. SECT. EXHIBIT$_9$, à D.G. de L'ISLIO EDITUS PRIMUM, NUNC EMENDATIOR & AUCTIOR REDDIT$_9$ PER HOMANN. HERED. ... SECTIO III. seu SUPERIOR. in qua sistitur maxima pars ALSATIÆ, BRISGOVIÆ una cum alijs SUEVIÆ Tractibus confinibus. (The map is a continuation of [72] and [78]). 440 × 593 mm.

[54] [C:] S.R.I. CIRCULUS RHENANUS INFERIOR SIVE ELECTORUM RHENI complectens tres Archiepiscopatus MOGUNTINUM COLONIENSEM et TREVIRENSEM, PALATINATUM RHENI, Comit Beilstein Newenaer, Inf. Isenburg, et Reiferscheit repræsentatus à IOH BAPTISTA HOMANNO... Norimbergæ ... — 571 × 485 mm.

[55] [C:] S.R.I. CIRCULUS RHENANUS SUPERIOR in quo sunt LANDGRAVIATVS HASSO-CASSELENSIS DARMSTADIENSIS ET RHENOFELDENSIS ABBATIA FULDENSIS PRINCIPATUS WALDECK ET HIRSCHFELD Comitatus Nassau-Weilburg Usingen Wisbaden et Idstein Solmensis Hanoviensis Isenburgensis superior Witgenstein Hatzfeld Westerburg et Hachenburg URBES IMPERIALES: Franckfurt, Fridberg, Wetzlar et Gelenhausen ex conatibus Ioh. Baptistæ Homanni Norimbergæ ... — 486 × 569 mm.

[56] [C:] DUCATUS WURTENBERGICI cum Locis limitaneis, utpote maxima parte CIRCULI SUEVICI præsertim Utroq$_3$ MARCHIONATU BADNSI et SYLVA vulgo NIGRA. Viva et post omnes exactissima Deline per M. IOHANNEM MAJER Pastorem Walddorffensem opera IOH. BAPTISTÆ HOMANNI Norimbergæ ... — (The map is continuation of [33]). 575 × 479 mm.
[Insets:] [T:] TÜBINGEN — (View). 40 × 80 mm. [T:] SYLVÆ HERCINIÆ sive MARTIÆ pars superior, olim dicta EREMUS HELVETIORUM, cum Landgraviatu Nellenburg, Princip-Comitatu Fürstenberg, Situ Hohentwielæ et Civitatibus Sylvestribus &c. &c. — 101 × 328 mm.

[57] [C:] CIRCVLI SVEVIÆ MAPPA ex subsidijs Michalianis delineata & a D^{no} I.M. HASIO M.P.P. quoad accuratā singulorum Statuum determinationem emendata & ad LL. magis legitimæ project. reducta. Opus sumi Geographi posthumum, & adjuncta Tabula explanatoria editum, opera Homañianorum Heredum A.1743. — 513 × 541 mm.

[58] [C:] Ducatus LIMBVRG Amstelodami Sumptibus Corn̄: Dankero. — Uncoloured. 378 × 480 mm.

[59] Carte du CONSISTOIRE de WITTEBERG, avec ses Dioceses et Paroisses, dediée à Son ALTESSE ROIALE Monseigneur le PRINCE FREDERIC CHRETIEN LEOPOLD PRINCE ROIAL et ELECTORAL et DVC de SAXE$_{ss}$ par son tres-Soumis et tres-obeïssant serviteur Iean Ehrenfried Vierenklee l'An MDCCXXXXIXI.
[C:] REGIAE CELSITVDINI SERENISS. PRINCIPI AC DN̄O FRIDER.CHRISTIAN LEOPOLDO PRINC̄POL. et LITH̄. REḠ PRINC̄.ELECT̄.AC DVCI SAX̄ DN̄O. SVO LONGE.CLEMENTISS. CONSISTORII

WITTEBERGENSIS TABVLAM HANC GEOGRAPHICAM SVMMA MENTIS PIETATE CONSECRAVIT SVBIECTISSIMVS SERVVS IOANNES EHRENFRIED VIERENKLEE HOMAN.HERED. CVRA ET STVDIIS MDCCXXXXVIIII ... — 437 × 547 mm.

[60] Multis in locis augmentata. longeque priori Editione correctior facta hæc THURINGIÆ TABULA A.º D.1729 per Joh. Christ. Homannum M.D. et Phys:Ord: ...
[C:] LANDGRAVIAT[VS] THURINGIÆ TABULA GENER[A]LIS in suos PRINCIPATVS ET STA[TV]VS accurate divi[sa] per IOH.BAPT.HOMA[NNUM] Noriberg[æ]— Noviter hæc Tabula auctior & correctior reddita est studio Friderici Christiani Lesseri A.1738. Curantibus Homannianis Heredibus. Accedit jndex Topologicus mappæ accomodatus ejusdem Authoris locupletissimus. 477 × 573 mm.

[61] [C:] DUCATUS BREMAE et FERDAE Nova Tabula edita à IOH.BAPT.HOMANNO Norimbergæ ... — 482 × 561 mm.

[62] [C:] Typus Geographicus DUCAT. LAUENBURGICI Novus in suas Præfecturas ope probatorum documentorum divisus in superque Parergo Historico de diversis illius ab Henrici Leonis usq$_3$ ad hæc tempora Dominij Periodis adornatus et delineatus a IOH. BAPT. HOMANNI S.C.M. Geogr. FILIO Noribergæ ... Anno D. M D CC XXIX. — Rup Ad Schneider Sculp Furth. — 560 × 475 mm.
[Inset:] [T:] HADULORUM REGIO In Ducatu Bremensi sita Ditionis olim Lauenburgensis nunc vero sub sequestratione Sacr: Casar: Majestatis. — 130 × 141 mm.

[63] [C:] Delineatio aureae Sterilitatis Herciniensis, i.e. HERCINIÆ METALLIFERÆ accurata Chorographia, omnes simul fodinas & loca nativa minerarum, quæ ibi effodiuntur, addita nomenclatura, distincte exhibens. Edita curis Homannianorum Heredum. Norib. ... — 484 × 558 mm.

[64] [C:] Mappa Geographica CIRCULI METALLIFERI Electoratus Saxoniæ cum omnibus, quæ in eo comprehenduntur PRÆFECTURIS ET DYNASTIIS, quales sunt. I. Præf. Zwickavienses, II. Præf. Schwarzenbergens. III. Dyn. Hartenstein, IV. Glaucha, V. Præf. Lemsa, VI. Præf. Waldenburg, VII. Præf. Rochsburg, VIII. Præf.Penig, IX. Præf. Wechselburg, X. Præf. Chemnit, XI. Præf. Stollberg, XII. Præf Grunhayn, XIII. Præf. Wolckenstain, XIV. Præf. Lauterstein, XV. Præf. Augustopolit. XVI. Præf. Franckenberg, XVII. Præf. Nossen, XVIII. Præf. Freyberg, XIX. Præf. Grullenburg, XX. Præf. Frauenstein, XXI. Præf. Altenberg, XXII. Præf. Dippoldiswalda, Accedunt præfecturæ circuli Misnici XXIII. Præf. Pirnensis, cum Dyn. Lauenstein, XXIV. Præf. Loehmen, XXV. Præf. Hohenstein. cura MATTH.SEUTTER, GEOGR. CÆSAR. AUG.VIND. ... — Tob:Conr. Lotter sculpsit. [Part I]. 573 × 491 mm.

[65] [Mappa Geographica CIRCULI METALLIFERI Electoratus Saxoniæ...] [Part II]. 573 × 491 mm.

[66] [C:] DUCATUS SAXONIAE SUPERIORIS ut status ipsius antiquissimus fuit per secula X. priora, sc. post Chr. nat. ad Ann. 1000. usque ex historiæ Sax. monumentis compilatus, et geographice designatus per FRIDERICUM ZOLIMANNUM in publicum emissus ab HOMANNIANIS HEREDIBUS. Norib. A.1732 ... TAB. III. — 482 × 583 mm.

[67] [C:] DUCATUS SAXONIAE SUPERIORIS prout ipsius conditio fuit ab Anno 1000 usque ad A.1400. sive intra Seculum X.^{m} et XV.^{m} ex historia maxime mediae ætatis erutus, ac Geographice designatus per FRID. ZOLLMANN. A.C.S.U.S in lucem prolatus ab HOMANN HEREDIB. Norib. A.1732 ... TAB. II. — 477 × 555 mm.

[68] [C:] DVCATVS ELECTORAT$_9$ et PRINCIPAT$_9$ DVCVM SAXONIÆ prout illorum conditio hodierna est Geographice consignati per PHIL. HENR. et FRID. ZOLLMANN in lucem prolati ab HOMANNIANIS HEREDIBVS Geographis Norib. MDCCXXXI TAB.I. ... — 576 × 957 mm.

[69] [C:] CIRCULI SUPE. SAXONIAE PARS MERIDIONALIS sive DUCATUS, ELECTORATUS et PRINCIPATUS DUCUM SAXONIAE ex Zolmannianis et Zürnerianis subsidijs designata et edita Per Homannianos Heredes. A. M D CC XXX IV. ... — 477 × 555 mm.

[70] REGNI BORUSSIAE ET ELECTORATUS BRANDENBURGICI, ceterarumque, Quae FRIDIRICI, Reg.Bor. sceptro reguntur. nec non finitimarum Prŏv. DELINEATIO, ad Stationes Publicorum cursuum et veredariorum, quae ultra cc mill. Germ. in longitudinem patent cognoscendas accommodata: quasque Vtilitati Publicae instituas. Ejusdem REGIS Aug. Auspiciis, hereditario Jure. moderatur et regit Vir Ill.^{mus} JOANNES CASIMIRUS.S.R.I. COMES A WARTENBERG. REG. MAJEST. BORUSSOR Supremus Camerarius et Minister Status Primarius etc. etc. [T:] P.Schenk Excudit O.P. Regis Polon. et Elect. Saxon. — 478 × 604 mm.

[71] [C:] CIRCULUS SAXONIÆ INFERIORIS in omnes suos STATUS et PRINCIPATUS accurate divisus ex conatibus IOH. BAPT. HOMANNI NORIMBERGÆ ... — 471 × 555 mm.

[72] CURSUS RHENI à BASILEA USQUE AD BONNAM III. SECT. EXHIBITUS, a D. G. de L ISLIO EDITUS PRIMUM, NUNC EMENDATIOR & AUCTIOR REDDIT PER HOMANN. HEREDES. ... SECTIO II. seu MEDIA, quæ continet part. ELECT. PALAT. DUC. BIPONT. ALSATIÆ INFER. COMIT. RHINGRAF. DUC. WÜRTEMB. MARCH. BADENS (The map is a continuation of [53] and [78]). 429 × 592 mm.

[73] [C:] EXACTISSIMA PALATINATUS AD RHENUM TABULA IN QUA EPISCOPATUS WORMACIENSIS ET SPIRENSIS DUCATUS BIPONTINUS aliæq$_3$ complures Insertæ, adjacentes et finitimæ Regiones ostĕduntur conante IOH. BAPTISTA HOMAN Noribergæ ... — 484 × 565 mm.

[74] HAUT PALATINAT, ou la Partie Septentrionale du Cercle de BAVIERE
[C:] PALATINATUS BAVARIÆ vulgo DIE OBERE PFALTZ in omnes ejusdem STATUS ET PRÆFECTURAS accuratè divisus Auctore IOH. BAPTISTA HOMANNO Sac. Cæs. Maj. Geographo. Noribe ... — 477 × 559 mm.

[75] LA BASSE BAVIERE, divisée en 2: Regences: 1) de LANDSHUT, subdivisée en 21. Baillages: et la Regence de STRAVBING, subdivisée en 24. Baillages.
[C:] BAVARIAE PARS INFERIOR tam in sua REGIMINA GENERALIA quam in eorundem PRÆFECIVRAS PARTICVLARES accurate divisa. excudente IOH. BAPTISTA HOMANNO Norimbergæ ... — 475 × 575 mm.

[76] LA HAVTE BAVIERE, divisée en deux grandes Regences (1 de MUNCHEN, subdivisée en 38. Baillages; et 2) la Regence de BURCKHAVSEN, subdivisée en 21. Bailleges.
[C:] BAVARIÆ PARS SUPERIOR tam in sua REGIMINA PRINCIPALIORA quàm in eorundem PRÆFECTURAS PARTICULARES accuratè divisa Excudente IOH. BAPTISTA HOMANNO Norimbergæ. ... — 580 × 490 mm.
[Inset:] [C:] BURKHUSIENSIS DITIONIS Pars inferior pro supplemento tabulæ nostræ sub cadem milliarium scala hic in hoc quadratum spatium separatim redacta proponitur. — 217 × 177 mm.

[77] La Cercle de BAVIERE, qui comprend la Regence d'Amberg, le Palatinat de Neuburg et de Sulzbach, le Landgrafiat de LEICHTENBERG le tout compris sous le nom de HAUT PALATINAT; encote le Duché ou l'Electorat de haute et basse BAVIERE, le Duche de NEUBURG, lévêché de RATISBONNE, l'evêche de FREYSINGEN, l'evêche de PASSAU, l'Archevèche de SALTZBOURG, comme aussi la Prevauté de BERCHLOTSCADEN.
[C:] BAVARIÆ CIRCULUS et ELECTORAT$_9$ IN SUAS QUASQUE DITIONES tam cum ADIACENTIBUS QUAM INSERTIS REGIONIBUS accuratissime divisus per IO: BAPTISTAM HOMANNUM Norimbergæ 1728 — 549 × 472 mm.

[78] CURSUS RHENI À BASILEA USQUE AD BONNAM, III. SECTIONIBUS EXHIBITUS À DOMINO G: DE L'ISLE, GEOGR. REGIO PAR. EDITUS NUNC MULTIS MODIS AUCTIOR et EMENDATIOR REDDITUS, PER HOMANNIANOS HEREDES, NORIBERGÆ; ... SECTIO I. seu INFERIOR. IN QUA VIDERE EST PART. ELECT. COLON. MOGUNT. UNA CUM PARTE MOSELLÆ et MOENI NEC NON VEDEROVIÆ, COM. CATIMELIB. HANOV. SPANH. &c. ... (The map is a continuation of [53] and [72]). 455 × 597 mm.

[79] ERSTER UND GRÖSTER THEIL DES GANTZEN HOCHLÖBL: FRANCKISCHEN CRAISSES IN WELCHEM DIE BISTHUMER BAMBERG WÜRTZBURG UND AICHSTETT, die Marggr. CULMBACH und ONOLTZBACH das Hertzogt. COBURG, Fürstent. SCHWARTZENBERG, Graffsch. HOHENLO, CASTEL, LIMBURG und SEINSHEIM, das NÜRNBERGISCHE Gebiet und die Hälffte der angrenzenden OBERN PFALTZ mit vorgestelt werden.
[C:] CIRCULI FRANCONIÆ PARS ORIENTALIS ET POTIOR novissime delineata quam Illustrissimis Generosissimis ac Exellentissimis Dn Dn toti$_9$ CIRC. FRANCON. LEGATIS pro Salute publ. Norimbergæ congregatis Dominis suis Gratiosis humillimé D.D.D Io. BAPT. HOMANN NORIMBERGAE ... — 547 × 478 mm. See [32].

[80] LA BASSE SILESIE, qui comprend les Principautés de Schweidnitz, de Iauer, de Glogau, de Breslau, de Liegnitz, de Brieg, de Wolau, de Oels & de Sagan, dessinée par les Heritiers de Homann. l'An 1745.
[C:] DVCATVS SILESIAE TABVLA GEOGRAPHICA PRIMA, INFERIOREM EIVS PARTEM, seu NOVEM PRINCIPATVS, quorum insignia hic adjecta sunt, secundum statum recentissimum complectens. Ad mentem Hasiani avtographi majoris legitime delineata et edita curis Homann. Heredum. Norimb. ... A.º MDCCXXXXV. ... — 394 × 554 mm.

[81] LA HAUTE SILESIE, qui comprend les Principautés de Neise, de Munsterberg, de Iægerndorf, de Troppau, d'Oppeln, de Ratibor, de Teschen. dessinée par les Heritiers de Homann. l'An 1746.
[C:] DVCATVS SILESIAE TABVLA ALTERA SVPERIOREM SILESIAM exhibens ex mappa Hasiana majore desumta & excusa per Homañianos Heredes Norimb. A.º MD CCXXXXVI. ... — 392 × 553 mm.

[82] LE DVCHÉ DE SILESIE, suivant l'état présent. dressé par TOBIE MAIER, et publié par les Héritiers de Homann, á Nuremberg. 1749. ...
[C:] DVCATVS SILESIAE Tabula geographica generalis, statui hodierno, ei nempe qui post pacem Dresdensem locum obtinet, adaptata. iustaque Graduatione rectificata, per TOB. MAIER. Norimbergae Impensis HOMANNIANORVM HEREDVM. A. 1749. ... — 453 × 536 mm.

[83] Carte d'HONGRIE en general, contenant selon la Division ancienne & methodique, la HONGRIE en particulier, la CROATIE, la DALMATIE, la BOSNIE, la SERVIE, la BOULGARIE; la Principauté de TRANSYLVANIE, les Despotats de WALACHIE & de MOLDAV; le tout dressé sur le pied de l'ancienne et de la nouvelle Geographie par Mons. I.M.Hasius, Profess. des Mathemat.
[C:] HVNGARIAE ampliori significatu et veteris vel Methodicae, complexae REGNA: HVNGARIAE PROPRIAE, CROATIÆ DALMATIAE, BOSNIAE, SERVIAE, BVLGARIAE, CVMANIAE, PRINCIPATVM: TRANSSYLVANIAE, DESPOTATVS: WALACHIAE, MOLDAVIAE, [exclusis ab eadem alienatis GALITIA et LVDOMIRIRIA] in suas Provincias ac partes divisae et quoad IMPERANTES ex AVSTRIACIS, TVRCIS et VENETIS distinctae [juncta tamen propter coṁoditatem ROMANIA vel ROMELIA TVRCICA] TABVLA ex recentissimis pariter et antiquissimis relationibus et monumentis concinnata, ac secundum leges Projectionis Stereographicae legitimae descripta a I.M.HASIO, M.PP. Curantibus Homannianis Heredibus. ... 1744. — 465 × 578 mm.

[84] [C:] REGNI HUNGARIÆ Tabula Generalis ex Archetypo MÜLLERIANO S C M. Capit et Ing desumta, et in hane formam contracta Viis Veredariis aucta. Novissimæq$_3$ Pacis Passarovicensis Confiniis illustrata á IO. BAPT. HOMANNO Sac. Cæs. Maj. Geographo Norimbergæ. — 470 × 565 mm.

[85] DIE GEGEND um PRAG, oder der alte PRAGER KREYS, nebst den angränzenden Landschafften des Rakonizer, Boleslawer u. Kaurzimer Cr. Aus dem Müllerischen und andern Original genoṁen u. ans Tagslicht gestelt von Hom. Erb. ... A. 1742. Les ENVIRONS de PRAGVE, ou sont marqués les limites des Cercles et des Provinces selon la Carte de M^r· Müller et selon la Division ancienne del' Institution de CHARLES IV. Dessinés par les Heritiers d'Homañ. ... A. MDCCXLII. 492 × 588 mm.

[86] [LITHUANIA BORUSSICA] (The map is a continuation of [2]). 490 × 582 mm.

[87] [C:] TABULA GENERALIS MARCHIONATUS MORAVIÆ IN SEX CIRCULOS DIVISÆ quos MANDATO CÆSAREO accuratè emensus hac mappa delineatos exhibet Ioh. Christoph.Müller S.C.M. Capitan Editore Ioh. Bapt. Homanno Noribergæ. ... — 478 × 573 mm.

[88] Carte des ETATS DE BOHEME, avec le Souverain DVCE DE SILESIE; publiee par les Heritiers de Homañ. l'An 1748.
[C:] REGNI BOHEMIAE, DVC. SILESIAE, MARCHIONATVVM MORAVIAE et LVSATIAE Tabula generalis. ex mensurationibus geodeticis Mulleri, Wielandii aliorumque ad normam observationum astronomicarum adaptatis deprompta et designata, a Tob. Majero Mathem. Cult. Edentibus Homann. Heredibus Norimbergæ A. MDCCXXXXVII. ... — 478 × 542 mm.

[89] le Royaume de BOHEME divise en XII Cercles, appellés 1) Saatz, 2) Leitmeritz, 3) Bunzel, 4) Kœnigsgrætz, 5) Chrudim 6) Czaslau, 7) Kaurzim, 8) Rakonitz 9) Pilsen, 10) Beraun, 11) celui de Prachin, 12) celui de Bechin. d'ou appartient aussi la Comte de Glatz & le pays d'Eger, tire d'une Carte faite p. M Müller.
[C:] BOHEMIAE REGNUM in XII Circulos divisum cum COM. GLAC. et Distr. Egerano ceterisq$_3$ circumjacentibus terris ex Müllerianis aliisq$_3$ chorographicis subsidys delineatum nunc noviter revisum et emendatius Per Homannianos Heredes. ... — 473 × 550 mm.

[90] [C:] IMP. CAES. CAROLO VI. AVGVSTO PIO VICTORI GENTIS SVAE SIDERI FELICISSIMO CHOROGRAPHIAM HANC EXHIBENTEM PRIMAR. REGIONVM HABSPVRGICAR. SITVM POSITVMQ. BREVIBVS EXTERARVM DITIONVM INTERVALLIS VT PERMISTVM ET IMPLICATVM ITA VARIIS TVRBIS EXPOSITVM NEC NON VLTIMOS IMPERII GERM. TERMINOS PERPETVA TRANSITVVM OBSIDIONVM HIBERNORVM COACTIONVM VEXATIONE AGITATOS ANTIQVAE FIDEI ET INVICTAE TESTES PIETATIS SVPPLEX DICAT PROVINCIA BRISGOIA AVST. ANT. MDCCXVIII. ... IOH. BAPT. HOMANN S.C.M. GEOGR. edidit Noribergæ. — 575 × 485 mm. = 1762:[91].

[91] [C:] EPISCOPATUS HILDESIENSIS NEC NON VICINORUM STATUUM DELINEATIO GEOGRAPHICA. per GERHARD.IUST. ARENHOLDUM Hildesiensem Iur. et Math. Stud. opera Hæred. IOH. BAPTIST.HOMANNI S.C.M. Geographi Norimbergæ. ... — 477 × 557 mm.
[Inset:] [T:] ICHNOGRAPHIA HILDESIÆ. — (Plan). 98 × 102 mm. [T:] Scenographia Vrbis Hildesiæ ab occidente — (View). 57 × 210 mm.

[92] [C:] MOSELLÆ FLUMINIS TABULA SPECIALIS in qua ARCHIEPISCOPATUS et ELECTORATUS TREVIRENSIS in suas Præfecturas accurate divisus ut et EYFALIÆ TRACTUS ostenditur Sumtibus IOH. BAPTISTÆ HOMANNI ... (Noribergæ) ... — [T:] I.M.Seeligman fecit — 486 × 576 mm.

[93] [C:] COMITATUS PRINCIPALIS TIROLIS in quo EPISC. TRIDENTIN9 ET. BRIXENSIS Comitatus Brigantinus, Feldkirchiæ Sonnebergæ et Pludentii. accuratè exhibentur Editore IOH. BAPTISTA HOMANNO Sacræ Cæs. Majestatis Geographo Noribergæ ... — 483 × 578 mm.

[94] [C:] S.R.I. PRINCIPATVS et. ARCHIEPISCOPATUS SALISBURGENSIS cum Subjectis, Insertis, ac Finitimis Regionibus recenter et accuraté elucubratus per A.R.P.O. de G.O.S.B.S. in Michaël-Beyrn. operá IOH. BAPT. HOMANN Sac.Cæs.Maj.Geogra. Norimbergæ ... — 485 × 582 mm.
[Inset:] [T:] AUSTRIA SALISBURGENSIS. — 61 × 99 mm.

[95] [C:] Tabula DUCATUS CARNIOLIÆ VINDORUM MARCHIÆ et HISTRIÆ ex mente Illustr.^{mi} quondam I.B.VALVASORII concinnata et exhibita â IO. BAPT HOMANNO S.C.M.Geogr: Noribergæ ... — 483 × 581 mm.
[Insets:] [T:] Prospect der St. LAYBACH der Haupt Stadt in Herzogthum Crain — (View). 80 × 292 mm.
[T:] CIRKHNITZER SEE — 100 × 144 mm.

[96] [C:] Nova et accurata CARINIÆ DUCATUS Tabula geographica, in SUPERIOREM et INFERIOREM divisa cum insertis partibus, Archiepriscopatui Salisburgensi propriis, nec non Dynastiis aliquot, quæ tempere S.Henrici Imperatoris circa A. 1007 Episcopatui Bambergensi Donationis titulo accresserunt in lucem edita à IO.BAPT. HOMANNO S.C.M. Geographo Norimbergæ. ... — 491 × 584 mm.
[Insets:] [C:] DIE STADT CLAGENFURT — (View). 108 × 375 mm. [T:] Die Strassen aus Cärnthen in Crain über und durch den Berg Loibl. — (View). 100 × 97 mm.

[97] [C:] DUCATUS STIRIÆ NOVISSIMA TABULA ex ampliore mappa olim R.D.^{ni} GEORGII MATTH. VISCHER S.C.M. LEOPOLDI I. Glor^{ssæ} Mem^{æ} Geographi deducta, et in hac utiliore forma Curiosorum oculis exhibita à IOH. BAPTI. HOMANNO Noribergæ. ... — 478 × 559 mm.
[Inset:] [T:] GRÄTZ die Haubt-Statt des gantzen Hertzogthums — (View). 95 × 120 mm.

[98] [C:] SAC. ROM. IMPERII PRINCIPATUS & EPISCOPATUS BAMBERGENSIS Nova Tabula Geographica in qua non solum omnes ejusdem Toparchiæ, Officia et Præfecturæ proximæ et remotæ, sed etiam Dominatus Carinthiaci a SS. Imperatorib9 HENRICO et CUNEGUNDA præfato Episcopatui non tam titulo Dotis, quam Donationis annexi cum vicinis finitimorum quorundam S.R.I. Statuum confinijs exhibentur â Io. Bapt. Homanno S.C.M. Geographo ... (Norimbergæ) ... — 480 × 571 mm.
[Inset:] [C:] CARINTHIÆ BAMBERGENSIS TABVLA SPECIALIS continens Toparchias Villacensem, Wolffbergensem, Griffensem, Pleubergensem, et Strasriedensem — 130 × 147 mm.

[99] Carte du COMTÉ d'OTTINGVE, situé dans le Cercle de Suabe, & divisé én IV. Parties, qui sont la PRINCIPAVTÉ d'OTTINGVE, la Comté d'OTTINGVE-OTTINGVE, la Comté d'OTTINGVE-WALLERSTEIN, & la Comte d'OTTINGVE-BALDERN.
[C:] Mappa Geographica COMITATVS OETTINGENSIS in Circulo Suevico siti, prout ille continet PRINCIPATVM hodiernum OETINGENSEM ut & COMIT. OETINGANO. OETINGENSEM & OETINGANO-WALLERSTEINEN-SEM, & COMIT. OETING. BALDERENSEM, similiter Territoria vrbium Imperial. NORDL. DVNKELSBVHL & BOPFING atque alias adjac. regiones, Delineante M.F.C. & edentibus Homañianis Heredibus Norimb. 1744. ... — 485 × 527 mm.
[Inset:] [T:] Prosp. von Oettingen — c. 55 × 150 mm.

[100] [C:] Nova et accurata TERRITORII VLMENSIS cum DOMINIO WAINENSI Descriptio quam, revidente e curante IOHANNE CHRISTOPHORO LAUTERBACH Eiusdem Reipubl. Ulm. Ingeniero et Archit. in lucem edidit IOH. BAPTISTA HOMANN GEOGR. NORIBERGÆ. ... — 482 × 572 mm.
[Inset:] [C:] Grund und Abriss der ULMISCHEN HERRSCHAFFT ZU WAIN (3 Meil-wegs ober Ulm an der Iler gelegen) mit ordentlicher Verzeichnus der Hohen Obrigkeitlichen Gränzen Holzmarkungen und darin gehörigen Dörffern und Weilern nach dem gr. Original des Seel. Herrn Pfarrers zu Altheim M.Iohan Wolfgang Bachmayrs abgezeichnet. — 142 × 172 mm.

[101] Le CERCLE D'AVTRICHE consistant dans l'Archiduché d'Autriche le Duché de Stirie, de Carinthie, de Carniole, dans la Comté de Tyrol, et les Pais Autrichiens Anteriers dans la Souabe, avec ses confins dessiné avec justesse par Tobie Maier, Mathematicien, aux depens des Heritiers de Homann. 1747.
[C:] S.R.I. CIRCVLVS AVSTRIACVS quem componunt ARCHID. AVSTRIAE, DVCATVS STIRIAE, CARINTHIAE, CARNIOLIAE, COMIT. TYROLENSIS, ditionesque SVEVIAE austriacae, cum suis confiniis a Tobia Majero, Math. Cult. legitime designatus . Curantibus Homannianis Heredibus. ... A.º 1747. — 447 × 524 mm.

[102] LA BASSE AVTRICHE, qui se divise en 4. Quartieres, qui sont 1) la superieure Manhardsberg. 2) l'inférieure Manhardsberg 3) la superieure Wienerwald, 4) l'inférieure Wienerwald.
[C:] ARCHIDUCATUS AUSTRIAE INFERIORIS In omnes suas Quadrantes Ditiones divisi Nova et exacta Tabula è conatibus IO. BAPTISTAE HOMANNI Noribergæ. ... — 483 × 575 mm.

[103] [C:] ARCHIDUCATUS AUSTRIAE SUPERIORIS in suas Quadrantes Ditiones exacte divisi accuratissima Tabula ex amplissima Rey. Dn GEORG MATTH.VISCHER Sac. Cæs. Maj. (LEOPOLDINI Glor.^{mæ}Mem.) Geogra. desumta et exhibita à IOH. BAPTISTA HOMANNO Noribergæ. ... — [C:] LA HAVTE AVTRICHE, qui se divise en 4; Quartieres appelles 1) Muhl Viertel 2) Schwarz Viertel, 3) Haus Viertel 4) Traun Viertel. ... — 482 × 573 mm.

[104] CARTE CRITIQVE DE L'ALLEMAGNE, faite suivant un nouveau Dessein appuyé des monumens authentics du tems ancien et nouveau, avec une comparaison de celui de M^{r}· de l'Isle et de Homann. Dressée par M^{r}· Tob. Mayer, de la Societé cosmographique. Publiée par les Heritiers de Homann, l'an 1750.
[C:] GERMANIAE ATQVE IN EA LOCORVM PRINCIPALIORVM MAPPA CRITICA, ex latitudinum obseruationibus, quas hactenus colligere licuit, omnibus; mappis specialibus compluribus; itinerariis antiquis Antonini, Augustano et Hierosolymitano, adhibita circumspectione ac saniori crisi concinnata, simulque cum aliorum Geographorum mappis comparata a Tob. Mayero, societ. cosmograph. Norib. sodali. Impensis Homannianorum Heredum, Noribergæ 1750. ... — 452 × 538 mm.

[105] [C:] NEUE SÄCHSISCHE POST-CHARTE mit denen POST-WEGEN und STRASSEN wie viel Meilen die Stationes von ein ander liegen Gestochen von P.SCHENK Jun. in Amsterdam ... — [T:] NB: In vieles Verbessert und Nachgesehne mit vielen Stationes auff dass Accurateste, Anno 1734. — 501 × 589 mm.

[106] L'ALLEMAGNE, distinguée en ses Cercles & subdivisée en ses Etats, contenant son Etendue presente, rectifiée & methodiquement enluminee suivant les Elements de Geographie de Mr. Schatz, A. 1741 ...
[C:] IMPERII ROMANO-GERMANICI IN SVOS STATVS ET CIRCVLOS DIVISI TABVLA GENERALIS in Usus Iuventutis erudiendæ accommodata a IOH. BAPT. HOMANNO, S.C.M. Geographo. Reg. Boruss. Societ. Scient. Sodali Norimbergæ ... — 461 × 545 mm.

[107] POSTARUM SEU VEREDARIORUM STATIONES PER GERMANIAM ET PROVINCIAS ADIACENTES.
[C:] Neu-vermehrte POST-CHARTE durch gantz TEUTSCHLAND nach Italien, Franckreich, Niederland, Preussen, Polen, und Ungarn etc. von Herrn IOH. PETER NELL zu Damenacher Rom. Keys. Maj: Rath und Ober-Postverwalter in Prag sowol anfangs inventirt als anjetzo

viel vermehrt mit Fleis aber in Kupfer gebracht und verlegt von Iohann Baptist Homann in Nürnberg ... — [C:] Illustrissimo ac Exellentissimo Domino D^{no} CAROLO JOSEPHO S.R. Imp. Comiti á Paar,... Domino mihi Gratioso D D. Humillimus ac devotissimus Ioannes Pet. Nell S.C.M. Postar.^{m} Campestrium Magister. — 458 × 572 mm.

[108] [C:] HYDROGRAPHIA GERMANIÆ qua GEOGRAPHIAE NATURALIS ea pars quæ de Aquis celebrioribus, præsertim vero de Fluminibus Germaniæ agit, ex probatissimis quibusq$_3$ mappis et peculiaribus Regionum descriptionibus collecta exhibetur operâ IOH. BAPTISTÆ HOMANNI Noribergæ. ... — [C:] Perillustri et Generosissimo Domino D^{no} FRIDERICO CHRISTIANO S.R.I. Lib.Bar. ab EDELSHEIM ... Patrono suo maxumo hoc qualecunq$_3$ subcisivarum horarum opusculum dicat Phil. Henr. Zollmannus I.V.C. ... — 484 × 578 mm.

[109] [C:] Accurata UTOPIÆ TABULA Das ist Der Neuentdeckten SCHALCK-WELT, oder des so offtbenañten, und doch nie erkañten SCHLARRAFFENLANDES Neu erfundene lächerliche Land-tabelle Worinnen alle und jede Laster in besondere Königreiche, Provintzen und Herrschafften abgetheilet. Beyneben auch die nächst angräntzende Länder Der FROMMEN: des zeitlichen AUFF- und UNTERGANGS auch ewigen VERDERBENS Regionen samt einer Erklærung anmuthig und nutzlich vorgestellt werden durch Author anonymus. Prostat in Officina Homanniana. — 482 × 561 mm.

Notes: All the maps are blank on the back except map [11], which has text. All are coloured except maps [11], [13], [29—31] and [58]; these six share other features, being smaller than the other maps in the atlas and of Dutch origin, signed by Dutch map-makers. These maps can be found in Koeman as follows: map [11] in vol. 2, p. 349, Me 31A (14); map [13] in vol. 3, p. 160, Vis 2 (16); map [29] in vol. 1, p. 74, Bl 1 (17); map [30] in vol. 2, p. 442, Me 88B (25); map [31] in vol. 3, p. 178 (88). Map [58], with Sumptibus Corn: Dankero, does not appear to be in Koeman. The atlas can be considered as a Homann atlas since 85 of the 109 maps are signed by Johannes Baptista Homann, his son Johann Christoph, or by Homann's heirs. Map [13], by Visscher, is dated 1646, but none of the other maps has such an early date; many of them, however, including undated ones, appear to be later issues of earlier maps. Map [97], for example, by the Tyrolean Georg Mathias Vischer, belongs to his twelve-sheet map of Austria, first published in 1669. Some of the multi-sheet maps have been bound so that the sheets are separated by other maps. Four maps bear portraits in the cartouches: map [4] has a portrait of FRIDERICVS REX BORUSSIAE et El. Br.; map [28], DUCATUS FRANCIAE ORIENTALIS, has portraits of S. KILIANVS, S. BURCARDUS, PIPINUS Francorū Rex, and CAROLUS MAGNUS Rom. Imperator et Francorum Rex; map [33], the first sheet of the map of Würtemberg, has a portrait of Eberhard Ludwig, the Duke of Würtemberg. This map is also decorated with 38 coats-of-arms down the left-hand border; the other sheet, map [56], has a corresponding double row of 38 coats down the right-hand border. Map [94], ARCHIEPISCOPATUS SALISBURGENSIS, has a portrait of its archbishop Franciscus Antonius. Maps [5] and [68] bear portraits of unnamed royalty. The last map, [109], is not bound into the atlas but inserted loose at the end. This edition is the re-engraved one with a new cartouche (See Tooley, Geographical oddities, p. 20—21). The atlas is bound in the original boards, with a leather spine.

Lit.: Bagrow, Geschichte p. 369, Koeman vol. 1, p. 74, vol. 2, p. 442, vol. 3, p. 160 and p. 178, Sandler, Homännische Erben p. 393—402, 405—410, Sandler, J.B.Homann, p. 382—384, Sandler, Seutter, p. 8—9, Tooley, Oddities, p. 20—21, nr. 87.

91 HOMANN, JOHANN BAPTIST AND HEIRS 1720—1771

[Collection of maps without title-page.] obl. 54,3 cm.

[1] [C:] DIVERSI GLOBI TERR-AQVEI STATIONE VARIANTE ET VISU INTERCEDENTE, PER COLUROS TROPICORUM, PER AMBOS POLOS ET PARTICUL. SPHÆRÆ ZENITH IN PLANUM DELINEATI ORTHOGRAPHICI PROSPECTUS; [C:] QUIBUS ADDITÆ PRO MUTATIONE HORIZONTIS DIFFERENTES SPHÆRÆ POSITIONES EARUMQUE MUTUA CUM CIRC. COELESTIBUS CONVENIENTIA ET RELATIO; AUGUSTÆ VINDELICOR. CURA ET STUDIO MATTH. SEUTTERI, S.C.M.GEORGR. — 493 × 573 mm.
[a] [World] The hemispheres with 270 mm. diam.
[b] [C:] HEMISPHÆRIUM OBLIQUUM GLOBI TERRESTRIS — Circular map with 115 mm. diam.
[c] [C:] HEMISPHÆRIUM SEPTENTRIONALE GLOBI TERRESTRIS POLO ARCTICO CENTRUM ET ÆQUATORE HORIZONT REPRÆSENT — Circular map with 145 mm. diam.
[d] [C:] HEMISPHÆRIUM OBLIQUUM GLOBI TERRESTRIS — Circular map with 118 mm. diam.
[e] [C:] NOVI ORBIS OPTICA SUPERFICIES — Circular map with 112 mm. diam.
[f] [C:] HEMISPHÆRII MERIDIONAL. OPTICA FIGURA — Circular map with 94 mm. diam.
[g] [C:] HEMISPHÆRIUM MERIDIONALE GLOBI TERRESTRIS SEPTENTRIONALI IMMEDIATE OPPOSITUM — Circular map with 140 mm. diam.
[h] [C:] HEMISPHÆRII SEPTENTRIONA OPTICA FIGURA — Circular map with 94 mm. diam.
[j] [C:] VETERIS ORBIS OPTICA SUPERFICIES — Circular map with 112 mm. diam.

[2] [C:] PLANIGLOBII TERRESTRIS CUM UTROQ$_3$ HEMISPHÆRIO CÆLESTI GENERALIS REPRÆSENTATIO Quam ex novissimis probatissimisque recentium Geographorum scriptis concinnatam. multisq$_3$ phænomenis illustratam publice proponit IO. BAPT. HOMANN. Sac. Gæs. Maj. Geographus et Reg. Scientiarum Acadē. Berolinensis Socius, Norimbergæ. ... — 480 × 545 mm. The terrestrial hemispheres with 266 mm. diam., the celestial ones with 140 mm.

[3] [C:] PLANIGLOBII TERRESTRIS Mappa Vniversalis. Utrumq$_3$ Hemisphærium Orient et Occidentale repræsentans Ex IV. mappis generalibus Hasianis composita et adjectis ceteris hemisphæriis designata a G.M.Lowizio. Excudentibus Homãnianis Heredibus ... A. MDCCXXXXVI Fig. I. dicitur Hemisphaerium polare arcticum. Fig. II. Hemisphærium polare antarcticum. Fig. III. Hemisphærium Sphæræ obliquæ pro horizonte Norimberg. Fig. IV. ejus oppositum inferius cum Antipodibus Norimbergensibus. — [C:] MAPPEMONDE, qui represente les deux Hemispheres, savoir celui de l'Orient et celui de l'Occident, tirée des quatre Cartes generales de feu M. le Professeur Hasius, dressée par Mr G.M.Lowitz, et publiée par les Heritiers de Homann. ... l'An 1746. Fig. I. Hemisphere polaire Arctique. Fig. II. Hemisphere polaire Antarctique. Fig. III. Hemisphere de la Sphere oblique pour l'Horizon de Nuremberg. Fig. IV. Les Antipodes de Nuremberg. — 462 × 548 mm.
[a] [World] The hemispheres with 270 mm. diam.
[b] Fig.I. Circular map with 132 mm. diam.
[c] Fig.II. Circular map with 132 mm. diam.
[d] Fig.III. Circular map with 104 mm. diam.
[e] Fig.IV. Circular map with 104 mm. diam.

[4] L'EUROPE, dessinée Suivant les Regles le plus precises d'une nouvelle Projection Stereographique, tirée des Observations et des Relations les plus modernes et appuyée en divers endroits par des Monumens antiques dressée et divisée methodiquement par Iean Matthias Has, Profess. Ordin. des Mathematiques. Publiée par les Heritiers d'Homann. l'An 1743 ...
[C:] EUROPA Seduncum legitimas Projectionis

Stereographicæ regulas et juxta recentissimas observationes æque ac relationes adhibitis qvoq$_3$ veterum monumentorum subsidiis descripta et in partes suas methodicas X divisa à IOH. MATTH. HASIO Math. P.P.O. edita Curis Homannianorum Heredum. A. MDCCXXXXIII ... — [T:] I.C. Reinsperger inv: et sc: — 470 × 553 mm.

[5] [C:] MAGNÆ BRITANNIAE Pars Meridionalis, in qua REGNUM ANGLIÆ TAM IN SEPTEM ANTIQUA ANGLO-SAXONUM REGNA quam in omnes Hodiernas Regiones accurate divisum hic ostenditur, quam tabula ab ARCHETYPO VISCHERIANO desumptam exhibet IOH BAPT. HOMAN^9 Noribergæ. — 566 × 483 mm.

[6] [C:] MAGNÆ BRITANNIÆ Pars Septentrionalis qua REGNUM SCOTIÆ in Suas Partes et subjacentes Insulas divisum ACCURATA TABULA ex archetypo VISCHERIANO desumta exhibetur imitatore IOHAN. BAPT. HOMANNO Noribergæ. ... — 566 × 475 mm.

[7] [C:] HIBERNIÆ REGNUM tam in præcipuas ULTONIÆ, CONNACIÆ, LACENIÆ et MOMONIÆ, quam in minores earundem Provincias et Ditiones divisum ex prototypo GUIL. PETTY-VISCHERIANO deductu et exhibitum à IOH. BAPT. HOMANNO Noribergæ. ... — 568 × 479 mm.

[8] [C:] VRBIUM LONDINI et WEST-MONASTERII nec non Suburbii SOUTHWARK accurata Ichnographia, in qua viæ publicæ omnes et singulæ, plateæ majores et minores, vici, angiponti, porticulæ etc. una cum accessionibus AEdificiorum, quibus urbs usque ad A. 1736. novissime locupletata est, repræsentantur. Ad normam prototypi Londinensis edita curis Homannianorum Heredum. ... Neuester GRUNDRIS der STÆDTE LONDON und WEST-MÜNSTER, samt der Vorstadt SOUTHWARK, worinnen alle Haubt-Strassen, gross und kleine Gassen, so gar die meisten Ein- und Durchfahrten, wie auch, was man bis zu dem Jahr 1736. von neuen angebauet, accurat angezeiget werden. Getreulich aus dem Londonischen Original genomen und zum Stich befördert von Homænnischen Erben. Nürnb. ... — (Plan). (The map is a continuation of [9]). 503 × 579 mm.

[9] [VRBIUM LONDINI ...] (Plan). (The map is a continuation of [8]). 503 × 583 mm.

[10] [C:] REGNI DANIAE in quo sunt DUCATUS HOLSATIA ET SLESVICUM INSULÆ DANICÆ, PROVINCIÆ IUTIA SCANIA BLEKINGIA Nova Tabula edita à IO. BAPTISTA HOMANNO Noribergæ. at aucta secundum Geographiam novissimam Iohann Hübneri. I.U.L. — 482 × 573 mm.

[11] [C:] DANIÆ REGNUM CUM DUCATU HOLSATIÆ ET SLESVICI, NEC NON INSULÆ DANICÆ, ET IUTIA CUM PARTE SCANIÆ, EXCUS. OPERA ET STUDIO MATTHÆI SEÜTTERI S.CÆS. MAJ.GEOGR. AUG. — 498 × 578 mm.

[12] [C:] DUCATUS SLESVICENSIS in omnes ejusdem Generales et Particulares Præfecturas exactè divisi Nova tabula, edita à IOH. BAPTISTA HOMAÑO... (Norimbergæ.) ... — 485 × 567 mm.

[13] = [12] in this ed.

[14] [C:] TABULA GENERALIS IUTIAE, continens DIOECESES QUATUOR, ALBURGENSEM, WIBURGENSEM, RIPENSEM ET ARHUSIENSEM, quæ et sunt divisæ IN OMNIA SUA DOMINIA. novissimè edita à IOH. BAPT. HOMANNO Noribergæ. ... — 571 × 490 mm.

[15] [C:] INSVLÆ DANICÆ IN MARI BALTHICO SITÆ, utpote ZEELANDIA, FIONIA, LANGELANDIA, LALANDIA, FALSTRIA, FEMBRIA MONA, repræsentantæ et auctæ secundum Geographiam novissimam IOH: HÜBNERI. I.V.L. à IOH: BAPT. HOMANNO. ... — 487 × 568 mm.
[Inset:] [T:] DER SUND — (View). Oval 70 × 110 mm.

[16] [C:] TABULA GENERALIS TOTIUS BELGII qua PROVINCIÆ XVII. INFER. GERMANIÆ olim sub S.R.I. CIRCULO BURGUNDIÆ comprehensæ nunc in Varias Potentias tum liberas utpote PROV. VII. FOEDERATAS, tum reliquas HISPANIÆ et GALLIÆ Coronis subjectas, separata ostenduntur à JOHANNE BAPTISTA HOMANNO Norimbergæ. ... — 476 × 561 mm.

[17] [C:] ARENA MARTIS IN BELGIO. QUA PROVINCIÆ X. CATHOLICÆ INFERIORIS GERMANIÆ Cum vicinis Episcopatibus COLONIENSI ET LEODIENSI aliisque finitimis Regionibus novissime proponuntur à IO. BAPTISTA HOMANNO NORIMBERGÆ. ... — 484 × 559 mm.
[Inset:] [T:] LUTTICH — (View). Oval 32 × 85 mm.

[18] [C:] BELGII PARS SEPTENTRIONALIS communi nomine Vulgo HOLLANDIA nuncupata CONTINENS STATUM POTENTISSIMÆ BATAVORUM REIPUBLICÆ SEV PROVINCIAS VII. FOEDERATAS. exhibente IO. BAPTISTA HOMANNO NORIBERGÆ. ... — 481 × 562 mm.
[Insets:] [T:] Batavorum Coloniæ OCCIDENTAL. INDIIS Septentrionalis AMERICÆ implantatæ. — 77 × 172 mm. (Irregular). [C:] NIEW AMSTERDAM — (View). Oval 30 × 55 mm. [T:] INDIA ORIENTALIS Batavorum Commerciis. Potentia & Coloniis celeberrima. — 123 × 138 mm. [C:] BATAVIA — (View). Oval 30 × 70 mm. [T:] LEODIENSIS PARS GVLICK LIMBURG PARS — 67 × 45 mm.

[19] [T:] ACCURATERGRUNDRIS und PROSPECT der WELTBERUHMTEN HOLLANDISCHEN HAUPT und HANDELS-STADT AMSTERDAM edirt von IOHANN BAPTIST HOMANNS Kayserlichen Geographi seeligen ERBE in Nurnberg 1727. ... — (Plan). 485 × 575 mm.
[Inset:] [C:] Prospect der Vortrefflichen Kauff und Handels Stadt AMSTERDAM — (View). 108 × 430 mm. (Irregular).

[20] [C:] DUCATUS BRABANTIÆ Nova Tabula in qua LOVANII BRUXELLARUM MARCH S. IMPERII SYLVÆ DUCIS et MECHLINIÆ DOMINIA in suas quasq$_3$ minores Ditiones subdivisa ostenduntur a IOH BAPT HOMANNO Norimbergæ ... — 575 × 481 mm.

[21] [C:] NIEUWE KAART van de XVII NEDERLANDSCHE PROVINCIEN waar in aangewezen worden de landen door den KONING VAN VRANKRYK geconquesteerd als mede die van het HUIS VAN OOSTENRYK, van den KONING VAN PRUISEN en den STAAT DER VEREENIGDE NEDERLANDE alles v...s het laatste tractaat van Barriere uitgegen door REINIER en JOSUA OTTENS te AMSTERDAM. — 575 × 499 mm.

[22] [C:] COMITATUS FLANDRIÆ in omnes ejusdem subjacentes Ditiões cum adjacentibus accuratissime divisus sumtibus IOH. BAPT. HOMANNI Noribergæ. ... — 479 × 570 mm.

[23] le Royaume de BOHEME divisé en XII Cercles, appellés 1) Saatz, 2) Leitmeritz, 3) Bunzel, 4) Kœnigsræts, 5) Chrudim 6) Czaslau, 7) Kaurzim, 8) Rakonitz 9) Pilsen, 10) Beraun, 11) celui de Prachin, 12) celui de Bechin. d'ou appartient aussi la Comte de Glatz & le pays d'Eger, tiré d'une Carte faite p M.Müller.
[C:] BOHEMIÆ REGNUM in XII Circulos divisum ... — = 1710—1750:[89].

[24] LA BASSE SILESIE, qui comprend les Principautés de Schweidnitz, de Lauer, de Glogau, de Breslau, de Liegnitz, de Brieg, de Wolau, de Oels & de Sagan, dessinée par les Heritiers de Homann. l'An 1745.
[C:] DVCATVS SILESIAE TABVLA GEOGRAPHICA PRIMA, INFERIOREM EIVS PARTEM, ... — = 1710—1750:[80].

[25] = [24] in this ed. with small alterations.

[26] LA HAUTE SILESIE, qui comprend les Principautés de Neise, de Munsterberg, de Lægerndorf. de Troppau, d'Oppeln, de Ratibor, de Teschen. dessinée par les Heritiers de Homann. l'An 1746.
[C:] DVCATVS SILESIAE TABVLA ALTERA SVPERIOREM SILESIAM ... — = 1710—1750:[81].

[27] Geographische Verzeichnung des BVDISSINISCHEN CREISES in dem Marggrafthum OBER LAVSITZ, aus zuversichtlichen geodetischen Zeichnungen genomen und ans Licht gestellet von Homænnischen Erben. Anno 1746. Carte du CERCLE de BVDISSIN dans le Marggrafiat de la

HAVTE LVSACE, tirée des Morceaux geometriquement levés. Publiée par les Heritiers de Homann. l'An 1746. 427 × 464 mm.

[28] le CERCLE D'AVTRICHE consistant dans l'Archiduché d'Autriche le Duché de Stirie, de Carinthie, de Carniole, dans la Comté de Tyrol, et les Pais Autrichiens Anterieurs dans la Souabe, avec ses confins dessiné avec justesse par Tobie Maїer, Mathematicien, aux depens des Heritiers de Homann. 1747.
[C:] S.R.I. CIRCVLVS AVSTRIACVS ... — = 1710—1750: [101].

[29] Chorographia VI. milliarium Regionis circa Vrbem VIENNAM Austriacam, deprompta ex mappa majori Vischeriana, et ad praesentem statum, uti Dominium minus eminens A. 1734. se habebat, accommodata per Homannianos Heredes. A. 1748. ... 457 × 555 mm.

[30] [T:] PROSPECT und GRUND-RISS der KAYSERL. RESIDENZ-STADT WIEN mit negst anligender GEGEND und NEUEN LINIEN umb die VORSTÄDT. verlegts IOH. BAPT. HOMANN in NÜR — (Plan). 480 × 567 mm.
[Inset:] [T:] Prospect der Kayserl. Residenz-Stadt WIEN, wie solche von Mitternacht anzusehen. — (View). 105 × 320 mm.

[31] ANDERER und MINDERE THEIL DES GANTZEN HOCHLÖBL. FRÄNCKISCHEN CRAISSES, MIT WELCHEM ZUGLEICH DAS ERTZ-STIFT und CHUR FÜRSTENTUM MAYNTZ SAMPT DENEN NOCH ÜBRIGE̅ FRANCK: STAATEN als da seind die GRAFSCH. WERTHEIM REINECK und ERPACH nebst der angrentzenden NIDEREN CHUR PFALTZ am RHEIN in dieser Tafel angezeigt werden
[C:] ELECTORATUS MOGUNTINUS ... — = 1710—1750: [32]. See [39].

[32] [C:] MOSELLÆ FLUMINIS TABULA SPECIALIS ... — = 1710—1750:[92].

[33] = [32] in this ed. with a different cartouche and without the name Seeligman.

[34] [C:] CIRCULI SUPE. SAXONIAE PARS MERIDIONALIS ... — = 1710—1752:[69].

[35] = [34] in this ed.

[36] Multis in locis augmentata, longeque priori Editione correctior facta hæc THURINGIÆ TABULA A.º D. 1729 per Ioh. Christ. Homannum M.D. et Phys: Ord: ...
[C:] LANDGRAVIATVS THURINGIÆ TABULA GENERALIS ... — = 1710—1752:[60].

[37] [C:] TABULA MARCHIONATUS BRANDENBURGICI ET DUCATUS POMERANIÆ quæ sunt Pars Septentrionalis CIRCULI SAXONIÆ SUPERIORIS novissimè edita A. IOH. BAPTISTA HOMANNO Noriberg ... — 482 × 555 mm. See 1710—1752:[3].

[38] [C:] INSULÆ ET PRINCIPATUS RUGIÆ ... — = 1710— 1750:[9].

[39] ERSTER UND GRÖSTER THEIL DES GANTZEN HOCHLÖBL: FRANCKISCHEN CRAISSES IN WELCHEM DIE BISTHUMER BAMBERG WÜRTZBURG UND AICHSTETT, die Marggr. CULMBACH und ONOLTZBACH das Hertzogt. COBURG, Fürstent. SCHWARTZENBERG, Graffsch. HOHENLO, CASTEL, LIMBURG und SEINSHEIM, das NÜRNBERGISCHE gebiet und die Hälffte der angrentzenden OBERN PFALTZ mit vorgestellt werden.
[C:] CIRCULI FRANCONIÆ PARS ORIENTALIS ET POTIOR novissime delineata ... — = 1710—1750:[79]. See [31].

[40] = [39] in this ed.

[41] La Cercle de BAVIERE, qui comprend la Regence d'Amberg, le Palatinat de Neuburg et de Sulzbach, le Landgrafiat de LEICHTENBERG le tout compris sous le nom de HAUT PALATINAT; encote le Duché ou l'Electorat de haute et basse BAVIERE, le Duche de Neuburg, l'eveché de RATISBONNE, l'evêche de FREYSINGEN, l'evêche de PASSAU, l'Archevêche de SALTZBOURG, comme aussi la Prevauté de BERCHLOTSCADEN.
[C:] BAVARIÆ CIRCULUS et ELECTORAT9, ... — = 1710—1750:[77].

[42] = [40] in this ed.

[43] [C:] PALATINATUS BAVARIÆ vulgo DIE OBERE PFALTZ ... — = 1710—1750:[74].

[44] [C:] CIRCVLI SVEVIÆ MAPPA ex subsidijs Michalianis delineata & a D.ⁿᵒ I.M. HASIO M.P.P. quoad accuratā singulorum Statuum determinationem emendata & ad LL. magis legitimæ project reducta. Opus sum̃i Geographi posthumum, & adjuncta Tabula explanatoria editum, opera Homañianorum Heredum A.1743. — 513 × 549 mm.

[45] [C:] S.R.I. CIRCULUS RHENANUS SUPERIOR ... — = 1710—1750:[55].

[46] [C:] PARS VEDEROVIÆ PLVRIMAS DITIONES PRINC. et COM. NASSOVICOR. ... — = 1710—1750:[34].

[47] [C:] CIRCULI WESTPHALIÆ ... — = 1710—1750:[26].

[48] = [47] in this ed.

[49] [C:] DUCATUS IULIACI & BERGENCIS Tabula Geographica ... — = 1710—1750:[14].

[50] [C:] CIRCULUS SAXONIÆ INFERIORIS ... — = 1710—1750:[71].

[51] [C:] DUCATUS BRUNSUICENSIS ... — = 1710—1750: [43].

[52] [C:] DUCATUS MEKLENBURGICI ... — = 1710—1750: [12].

[53] = [52] in this ed.

[54] [C:] TABVLA GENERALIS HOLSATIAE complectens HOLSATIÆ DITHMARSIÆ STORMARIÆ ET VAGRIÆ DVCATVS edita à IOH. BAPT. Homanno NORIBERG: ... — 481 × 571 mm.

[55] = [54] in this ed.

[56] [C:] DUCATUS BREMAE et FERDAE Nova Tabula ... — = 1710—1750:[61].

[57] = [39] and [40] in this ed.

[58] [T:] PROSPECT und GRUNDRIS der des HEIL: RÖM.REICHS-STADT NÜRNBERG samt ihren LINIEN und GEGEND auf eine Meil wegs herumb edirt von IOH. BAP. HOMANN daselbst — 488 × 571 mm.
[Inset:] (View). 120 × 568 mm.

[59] = [44] in this ed.

[60] [C:] Novveav PLAN du CAROLSRVHE sur deux feuilles Dedié & presenté A SON ALTESSE SERENISSIME, MONSEIGNEVR LE PRINCE CHARLES AVGVSTE, MARGGRAVE, de Baade & Hochberg, Landgrave de Sausenberg, Comte de Sponheim & d'Eberstein, Seigneur de Roeteln, Baadeweiler, Lahr, Mahlberg,ₜₜ General Major de S.M.I. & du Cercle de Suabe, Com̃e aussi Colonel d'un Regiment d'Infanterie &c. &c. Par Ses très humbles & tres obèissans Serviteurs les Heritiers de feu Homann. Mich: Rössler sculps. Norimb: — [T:] Erstes Blat in welchem zu sehen Nº. 1. Die Gegend um Carolsruh 2 Der Grundriss 3 Der Prospect desselben verzeichnet von Iohann Iacob Baumeister Ingenieur Capitain bey Ihro Hochf. Durchl. Herz. Carl Alex. v. Wurt. A. 1737. — [T:] Feuille I.ʳᵉ Sur la quelle on voit Nº. 1. Les Environs. 2. l'Icnographie 3. & le Prospet du Chateau de Carolsruhe Designé par Iean Iacque Baumeister Capit. des Ingenieurs S.A.S. Msgr. CHARLES ALEX. Duc de Wurt. A. 1737. — 585 × 490 mm.
[a] [T:] N.ʳᵒ 1. — 185 × 118 mm.
[b] [C:] Grundriss N. 2. — (Plan). 187 × 327 mm.
[c] [C:] Prospect gegen Mittag N. 3. — (View). 188 × 417 mm.

[61] = [45] in this ed.

[62] [C:] ALSATIA tam SVPERIOR, quam INFERIOR una cum SVNDGOVIA,... — = 1710—1750:[46] and [48].

[63] [C:] S.R.I. CIRCULUS RHENANUS INFERIOR SIVE ELECTORUM RHENI ... — = 1710—1750:[54].

[64] [LAN]DGRAVIATVS HASSO-DARMSTATTINI & omnium eo spectantium Terrarum Repræsentatio geographica. sex Foliis tradita. Folium I.
[C:] SERENISSIMO PRINCIPI GLORIOSISSIME NVNC REGENTI DOMINO SVO CLEMENTISSIMO LVDOVICO VIII PRINCIPI PIO FELICI Tabulam hanc geographicam LANDGRAVIATVS HASSO-DARMSTADINI & omnium eo spectantium Comitatuum,

Regionum, Vrbium & Pagorum, nec non adjacentium Terrarum studiosissime designatam humillime D.D.D. Auctor devotissimus Christophorus Max. Pronner. Curantib₉ Homañianis Heredibus. A. 1751 — [T:] Ex Originali Proñeriano ad hanc Graduationem reduxit D.^{us} Tobias Majer P.P. Göttingens. — 442 × 518 mm.

[65] LANDGRAVIATVS HASSO-DARMSTATTINI & omnium eo spectantium Terrarum Repræsentatio Geographica Folium secundum. 441 × 517 mm.

[66] TERRÆ PRINCIPAT. HASSO-DARMSTADINI sitæ inter Fluovios Lahn et Fulda. Folium IV. 426 × 514 mm.

[67] TERRÆ PRINCIPATVS HASSO-DARMSTATTINI, ubi confines sunt Terris Principatus Nassoviensis, Siegen, Dillenburg, Dietz. Folium III. 432 × 512 mm.

[68] [T:] PLAN du MAYENCE, ville fort de Archeveché du meme Nom située sur le Bord du Rhin au Confluant du Mayn ... com͞e il s, est trouve avec ses nouveaux Ouvrages exterieurs l'An 1735. sous la Direction du General Maitre d'Artillerie Bar. de... Mis au jour par les Heritiers de feu M^r le Doct. Homann. ...
Accurater PLAN der CHURF. — ERTZBISCH Residenz Stadt MAYNZ ... wie sich solche dermahlen mit ihren neuen Wercken unter Direction des Herrn General Feld Zeugm. B. von .... befindet. Herausgegeben in der Hom. Off. ... — (Plan). 573 × 475 mm.
[Inset:] [T:] PROSPECT von MAYNZ — (View). 140 × 473 mm.

[69] = [47] and [48] in this ed. with small alterations.

[70] [C:] Vue de la Montagne de BROKEN située dans le Territoire du Comté de Wernigerode, qui est dans les forêts de Hartz. — [C:] PERSPECTIVISCHE VORSTELLVNG des berühmten BLOCKEN ODER BLOCKS-BERGS mit der jenigen Gegend, so weit solche von dem, der auf der Spitze des Berges stehet, gesehen werden kan. Gezeichnet A.⁰ 1732. von L.S.Bestehorn. herausgegeben von Homænn. Erben. 1749. ... — [T:] ... Nürnberg am Walpurgis-tag. 1751. — (View). 466 × 543 mm.

[71] = [50] in this ed.

[72] [C:] DUCATUS LUNEBURGICI et COMITATUS DANNEBERGENSIS accurata Descriptio ... — = 1710—1750:[52].

[73] [C:] EPISCOPATUS HILDESIENSIS NEC NON VICINORUM STATUUM DELINEATIO GEOGRAPHICA. ... — = 1710—1750:[91].

[74] = [34] and [35] in this ed.

[75] [C:] Denen HochEdelgebohrnen Magnificis HochEdlen Vesten u. Hochgelahrten auch Hochweisen HERREN, HERREN BVRGEMEISTERN, Proconsulibus, Baumeistern, Syndico, Stadt-Richtern und andern Hochansehnl. Assessoribus des Hochlöbl. Stadt-Regiments u. Deroselben Gerichte wird dieser GRVNDRISS DER STADT LEIPZIG ehrerbietigst gewiedmet von den Homaennischen Erben. ... A. 1749. — 507 × 543 mm.

[76] [C:] DUCATUS MEKLENBURGICUS in qúo súnt DUCATUS VANDLIÆ et MEKLENBURGI DUCATUS et COMITATUS SWERINENSIS ROSTOCHIENSE et STARGARDIENSE DOMIN Auctore F. de Wit ... — [T:] AMSTELODAMI ex Officina I. CÓVENS et C. MORTIER. — 489 × 564 mm. See [52] and [53] in this ed.

[77] = [37] in this ed.

[78] [C:] Die Königl. PREVS: u. Churf. BRANDENBVRG. RESIDENZ-STADT BERLIN entworfen von Iohann Fridrich Waltern zu Berlin 1737 u. nach dem grossen Original in diesen kleinen Form gebracht u. heraussgegeben von Homann. Erben. Regiae BORVSS. & Elector. BRANDENB. Sedis BEROLINI Ichnographia ex prototypo Walteriano majori Berolini edito in hanc minorem formam reducta, et excusa per Homānianos Heredes. — (Plan). 488 × 562 mm.
[Inset:] [T:] Prospect der Stadt BERLIN wie solche Nord-Westwärts anzusehen — (View). 130 × 558 mm.

[79] [T:] Prospect, Grundris und Gegent der Königl. Schwed. Vestung STRALSUND, wie solche den 15 Julij A⁰ 1715 von den Nordischen Hohen Allijrten ist belagert worden. Von (tit.) Herrn DANIEL HEER Königl. Poln. und Churf. Säx. Ingenieur-Major abgezeichnet, und von IOH. BAPT. HOMANN der Rom. Keis. Maj. Geographo in Nürnberg heraus gegeben. ... — 485 × 575 mm.
[Insets:] [C:] Vorstellung Verschiedener Attaques zur See und der Penemunder Schanz. — 305 × 245 mm. (Irregular). [T:] STRALSUND — (View). 110 × 571 mm.

[80] [T:] PROSPECT, GRUNDRIS und GEGEND der Polnischen vesten Reichs und Handels-Stadt DANTZIG und ihrem WERDER edirt von Io. Bapt. Homann S.C.M.Geog. in Nürnberg. ... — (Plan). 483 × 568 mm.
[Inset:] [C:] Prospect der Stadt DANZIG — (View). 85 × 348 mm.

[81] [C:] SAXONIÆ INFERIORIS CIRCULUS juxta Principatus et Status suos accurate delineatus cura et stilo MATTHÆI SEUTTERI S.C.M.GEOGR.AUG. — 494 × 577 mm.

[82] [C:] DUCATUS LUNEBURGICUS cum COMITATU DANNEBERGENSI juxta PRÆFECTURAS suas accurate designatus et mappa Geographica editus per MATTH. SEUTTER SAC. CÆS. MAJ. GEOGR. AUG. VIND. — 493 × 575 mm.

[83] [C:] CIRCULUS WESTPHALICUS IN SUAS PROVINCIAS ET DITIONES accurate distinctus et recentissime delineat. cura et cælo MATTH. SEUTTERI S.C.M.G. ... AUG. VINDEL. — [T:] G. Matthæus Seüter jun.sculpsit — 498 × 580 mm.

[84] [C:] PALATINATUS INFERIOR, sive ELECTORATUS PALATINATUS AD RHENUM cum adjacentibus ARCHI-EPISCOPATU MOGUNTINO, EPISCOPAT. SPIRENSI, ET WORMATIENSI, LANDGRAVIATU HASSO-DARMSTADIENSI ET PRINCIPAT. AC COMITATIBUS ALIIS, Cura et Studio MATTHÆI SEUTTERI, SAC. CÆSAR. ET REG. CATHOL. MAJEST. GEOGR. et Chalcographi AUGUSTANI. ... — 492 × 578 mm.

[85] [C:] DUCATUS IULIACENSIS, CLIVIENSIS et MONTENSIS ut et PRINCIPATUS MEURSIANI et COMITATUS ZUTPHANIENSIS novissima et accuratissima Delineatio, Opera et Impensis MATTHÆI SEUTTERI, S. CÆS. et REGIÆ CATHOL. MAJ. GEOGR. AUGUSTANI. — 568 × 495 mm.

[86] [C:] LANDGRAVIATUS THURINGIÆ juxta recentiss: designation: in suos PRINCIPATUS, STATUS, ET PRÆFECTURAS accuratissime divisus studio et impensis MATTHÆI SEUTERI GEOGR. CÆSAR. ET CHALCOGR. AUGUSTÆ VINDELIC. ... — [T:] Tob. Con. Lotter, sc. 485 × 575 mm.

[87] [C:] BORUSSIÆ REGNUM sub fortissimo Tutamine et justissimo Regimine Serenissimi ac Potentissimi Principis FRIDERICI WILHELMI lætissimis incrementis efflorescens cum adjacentib. Regionibus mappa Geographica delineatum Cura et sumtibus MATTH.SEUTERI, SAC. CÆS. MAJ. GEOGRAPHI. AUG. — 490 × 573 mm.
[Inset:] [C:] PRINCIPATUS NEOCOMENSIS seu NEUFCHATEL ad BORUSSIÆ REGEM Spectans — 153 × 117 mm.

[88] TABULA NOVA CIRCULI ELECTORALIS, RHENI, ad Usum Serenissimi BURGUNDIÆ DUCIS.
[C:] LE CERCLE ESLECTORALDU RHEIN divisé en tous les ESTATS qui le composent à l'Usage DE MONSEIGNEUR LE DUC DE BOURGOGNE, Par son tres Humble et tres Obeissant serviteur, H JAILLOT. — [C:] ... A AMSTERDAM Che R& J. OTTENS. — 593 × 454 mm.

[89] POSTARUM SEU VEREDARIORUM STATIONES PER GERMANIAM ET PROVINCIAS ADIACENTES.
[C:] Neu-vermehrte POST-CHARTE durch gantz TEUTSCHLAND ... — = 1710—1750:[106].

[90] [C:] BELLI ab obitu CAROLI VI. Imperatoris usqve ad pacem Dresdae d.25.Dec. MDCCXLV. Factam tam in GERMANIA quam BELGIO ob successionem AVSTRIACAM gesti THEATRVM geographice

delineatum a L. I. Krausio LL. cult. curantibus Homannianis Heredibus ... A. 1748. — [C:] Serenissimo PRINCIPI AC DOMINO DOMINO FRIDERICO MARGGRAVIO BRANDENBVRGI DVCI BORVSSIAE Silesiae, Magdeburgi, Cliviae, Iuliaci, Montium, Stetini, Pomeraniae, Cassubiorum, Vandalorum, Megapoleos & Crosnae. Burggravio Noribergae reliqu~ reliqu~ Circuli Franconici Supremo belli Duci et Præfecto trium legionum & cohortium Principi ac Domino longe clementissimo Tabulam hanc geographicam humillime consecrat Subjectissimus Laur. Iac. Kraus. — 472 × 1073 mm.

[91] [C:] AREA BELLI GERMANICI PRAESENTIS, In qua cum cura omnia illa loca designata inveniuntur, quæ ad hunc usque diem casus notabiliores insignia reddidere: Suorum Studiorum Promotori Nobiliss. et Generos. Domino D[no] Joh. Jennings ad Prætor. turm. Centurioni incluto Dedicata ab. A. Åkerman Reg. Soc. Lit. et Scient. Ups. Sculptore. Upsaliæ Mense Majo 1758. — 265 × 424 mm.

[92] Carte des ÉTATS DE BOHEME, avec le Souverain DVCE DE SILESIE; publiee par les Heritiers de Homañ. l'An 1748.
[C:] REGNI BOHEMIAE, DVC. SILESIAE, MARCHIONATVVM MORAVIAE et LVSATIAE Tabula generalis. ... — = 1710—1750:[88].

[93] [C:] GERMANIA AUSTRIACA complectens S.R.I. CIRCULUM AUSTRIACUM ut et reliquas in Germania Augustissimæ Domui Austr. devotas TERRAS HÆREDITARIAS Auctore IO BAPT HOMANN Noribergæ. ... — 483 × 568 mm.

[94] [C:] REGNI BOHEMIÆ, DUCATUS SILESIÆ, MARCHIONATUS MORAVIÆ et LUSATIÆ, Tabula Generalis sumtibus IOH. B. HOMANNI S.C.M. Geograph: Noribergæ. ... — 479 × 567 mm.

[95] = [94] in this ed.

[96] Kriegs-Expeditions-Karte in Böhmen I. Blat, in welchem die Haubtstadt PRAG mit der Französsischen und Sæchsischen Belagerüg und Eroberung, so den 26. Novembre 1741. geschehen, vorgestellet wird. Ans Licht gestellt von Homæñ Erben. A 1743. ... Carte des Expeditions de Guerre en Boheme, I.Feuille, dans laquelle se voit le Plan de la Ville de PRAGUE, assiegeé et prise par les Troupes auxiliaires de France et de Saxe en l'An 1741, le 26. Novembre. mise au jour par les Heritiers de Homan. l'An 1743. ... 478 × 573 mm.
[Insets:] [T:] Plan de l'Armée Françoise campeé sous PRAG en Iuin et Iuillet 1742. ... — [T:] Dessiné par Sinsart Ingenieur François — (Plan). 151 × 184 mm. [T:] Le meme Campement Dessiné par un autre Ingenieur. — (Plan). 132 × 195 mm.

[97] KRIEGS-EXPEDITIONS-CARTE von BOHMEN II. Blat, in welcher die Kriegs-Operationen von PRAG und EGER vorgestellet werden, nach Französ. Originalien heraus gegeben von Homæñ. Erben. A 1743. CARTE des EXPEDITIONS de la GVERRE en Boheme II Feuille representant les Operations de la Guerre devant d'Egra et de Prague et dressée sur les derniers Plans des Ingenieurs François A Norimberg par et chez les Heritiers de Homan l'A 1743. 432 × 531 mm.
[a] [C:] PLAN d'EGRA avec l'Attaque au mois d'Avril 1742. — (Plan). 150 × 207 mm.
[b] [T:] Vorstellung der STRASSE und Örter, durch welche sich die Franz. Armée aus Prag den 6 Decemb. 1742. über den Rakonitzer, Satzer- und Pilsner-Kreis nach Egra retirirt haben. ... Route, que M[r] le M. de Bel Isle a tenu dans la Retraite, qu'il a faite de Prag par les Cercles de Rakonitz, de Satz et de Pilsen a Egra. ... — 150 × 240 mm.
[c] [C:] KRIEGS-THEATRVM in den GEGENDEN von PRAG oder Situation der Französ. Armée als sich solche von Pisek aus unter dem Feld M. Broglio hieher retirirt, und die Oesterr. ihnen nachgefolget. ... — 275 × 390 mm.

[98] [T:] Carte des Expeditions de Guerre en Boheme, III feuille, dans la quelle se voit le Plan de l'Attaque et de la Defense de PRAG, l'an 1742 depuis le 28 Iuillet jusqu'au 13me du mois 7br. mise au jour par les Heritiers d'Homañ l'An 1743. ... — 424 × 500 mm.
[a] [T:] Abregé du Siege de PRAG... — [T:] Dessié par Sinsart, Ingenieur François. — 421 × 323 mm.
[b] [T:] Legende De l'Attaque De la Defense... — [T:] Dessine par M[r].Perizot Maitre des Desseins du Roi — 421 × 170 mm.

[99] [C:] REGNI BOHEMIAE CIRCULUS LITOMERICENSIS ex MÜLLERIANIS aliisque recentissimis subsidiis chorographice designatus ut et secundum statum politicum modernum expressus et in lucem editus ab HOMANNIANIS HEŘEDIBUS. 1774 ... — 475 × 567 mm.

[100] [C:] REGNI BOHEMIAE CIRCULUS BOLESLAVIENSIS, ex MÜLLERIANIS aliisque recentissimis subsidiis chorographice designatus ut et secundum statum politicum modernum expressus et in lucem editus ab HOMANNIANIS HEREDIBUS. 1770. ... — 506 × 509 mm.

[101] [C:] Novissima et Accuratissima HELVETIÆ RHÆTIÆ, VALESIÆ et PARTIS SABAUDIÆ TABULA ex Officina R. & I. Ottens, Amst: ... — 484 × 568 mm.

[102] CARTE de FRANCE, dressée par GVILLAVME DE L'ISLE, et accommodée par les Heritiers d'HOMANN. a l'instruction de la Jeunesse, Norimb. 1741 ...
[C:] REGNI GALLIAE seu FRANCIAE et NAVARRAE Tabula Geographica in usum Elementorum Geographiæ Schazianorum accoṁodata, Per Homannianos Heredes 1741 ... — 480 × 573 mm.

[103] EL REYNO DE ESPANNA dividido en dos grandes Estados DE ARAGON Y DE CASTILLA, subdividido en muchas Provincias, donde se halla tambien EL REYNO DE PORTUGAL.
[C:] REGNORVM HISPANIÆ et PORTVGALLIAE Tabula generalis de l'Isliana aucta et ad Usum Scholarum novissime accoṁodata á Ioh. Bapt. Homanno S.C.M.Geogr. Norimbergæ — 470 × 580 mm.

[104] NOVA REGNI HISPANIÆ ACCURATA DESCRIPTIO, AD USUM SERENISSIMI BURGUNDIÆ DUCIS
[C:] L'ESPAGNE Divisée en tous ses ROYAUMES, PRINCIPAUTÉS, &c à l'Usage de MONSEIGNEUR LE DUC DE BOURGOGNE Par son tres Humble et tres Obeissant Serviteur H. Iaillot A AMSTERDAM Chez R. & J. Ottens. — 452 × 592 mm.

[105] [T:] Neuester und exacter PLAN und PROSPECT von der STADT, VESTVNG, BAY und FORTIFICATION von GIBRALTAR, theils, wie es Lit: A: mit den Approchen der Spanier, die sie im letztern Krieg dafür gemacht, zu sehen, theils wie es Lit: B seit der letztern Belagerung 1727. von den Engelländern zu besserer Sicherheit mit neuen Fortifications-Werckern vermehrt, und fast unüberwindlich gemacht, von den Spaniern hingegen gegen die Land-Seyte zu bey etlichen Jahren her mit neuen Linien eingeschlossen worden, nach einem Englischen Original nebst deutlichen und vollständigen Anmerckungen accurat heraus gegeben von Homännischen Erben, Nürnberg A[o] 1733. ... — 471 × 565 mm.
[a] A [T:] GIBRALTAR ... — 224 × 333 mm.
[b] B [Gibraltar] 215 × 561 mm.
[c] [T:] Prospect von GIBRALTAR — (View). 110 × 228 mm.
[d] [T:] Prospect von CADIX — (View). 110 × 228 mm.

[106] Gli STATI d'ITALIA, secondo le Osservationi, fatte dalla Societa di Sc. di Parigi, dal R.P.Riccioli della S. die Gieusu ed., altri Astronomi, di prima geograficamente delineati dall'Eccell[mo] Sg[r] de l'Isle, ed accoṁodati agli Elementi Geografici, del Sg[r] Schaz; alle spese degl' Heredi d'Homan. L Año MDCCXLII.
[C:] ITALIA in suos STATVS divisa et ex prototypo de l'ISLIANO desumta Elementis insuper Geographiæ Schaziani accoṁodata Curantibus Homannianis Heredibus ... — 488 × 573 mm.

[107] = [106] in this ed. with small alterations.

[108] [C:] CURSUS FLUMINIS PADI vel PO per LONGOBARDIAM a fonte usque ad Ostia Cum fluv. Tanaro, Doria, Sessia, Tesino, Adda, Oglio &c. ut &

Statibus adjac. Pedemonty, Montisferr. Mediol. Mantuani, Parmensis, Ferrar. Dedicat$_9$ CLEMENTI XI. Pontif. M. ab IPSIUS Supr. Præf. Vigilum & Centur. Cohortis Prætoriæ Augustino Cerruti, Designatore & Auctore, nunc recusus ab Homannianis Heredibus. A. MDCCXXXV. — 510 × 580 mm.

[109] [C:] REGNI & INSVLAE SICILIAE Tabula geographica, ex Archetypo grandiori in hoc compendium redacta, studio Homannianorum Heredum. A.º 1747. ... Imperat CAROLI VI. ab Illmo Cte de Schmettau A.º 1719. 20. 21. factis. ... — 460 × 541 mm.

[110] Carta Geographica, la quale rappresenta lo Stato della Republica di GENOVA partita nella Riviera di Levante et di Ponente. Data in publico per gli Heredi d'Homann. ... 1743. Der STAAT von der Republic GENOVA, nach seiner Eintheilung in die ost u. west-Rivier geographisch vorgestellet und herausgegen von Hom. Erben A. 1743. ... 478 × 551 mm.
[Insets:] [C:] Ichnographia Genuæ quæ est status Genuensis urbs capitalis et Metropolitana. sita super Colli in medio fere Territorii. Dicitur superba ob splendidorum ædificiorum multitudinem Italis audit Genoa — (Plan). 13 × 185 mm. [C:] GENUA. — (View). 136 × 535 mm.

[111] = [110] in this ed.

[112] [C:] PIANTA di CREMONA, e delle altre Fortezze di MILANO come anco parte di quelle, che sono situate al fiume Po, disegnate con tutta diligenza secondo il vero Originale Appresso gli Eredi di Giovanni Christoforo Homann. Dottore di Medicina. ... PLAN von CREMONA und denen übrigen MAYLÆNDISCHEN, auch theils am Po Fluss gelegenen Vestungen, nach accuraten Originall. verzeichnet und zu finden in der Homæñisch: Officin. A:1734. ... — 483 × 561 mm.
[a] [T:] FORT DE FUENTES — (Plan). 124 × 131 mm.
[b] [T:] NOVARA — (Plan). 155 × 131 mm.
[c] [T:] PLAN DE CREMONE — (Plan). 200 × 290 mm.
[d] [T:] Chateau de SERAVALLE — (Plan). 114 × 132 mm.
[e] [T:] TORTONE avec l'Attaque. — (Plan). 167 × 132 mm.
[f] [T:] PLAN DE LA VILLE DE PAVIE — (Plan). 193 × 252 mm.
[g] [C:] CASAL, dit de St Vas, Ville Forte d'Italie Capitale du Monferrat, située sur la Riviere du Po, avec Titre d'Eveché, et de Cité, sa Citadelle est le meilleure d'Italie, et elle a souffert plusieurs sieges. — (Plan). 193 × 303 mm.

[113] [DIOCESI PADOVANA...] (The map is a continuation of [114] and [116]). 700 × 443 mm.

[114] [DIOCESI PADOVA...] [C:] All' Em.^{mo} e Reu:^{mo} Sig: Cardinal GIORGIO CORNARO Vescovo di PADOVA, Co: di Piove di Sacco &c. ... Padova Ii 28.Giugno 1720. Di Vostra Eminenza. Vmiliss.^{o} Dev.^{mo} et Osseq.^{mo} Serv.^{re} Paolo Bartolomeo Clarici. — (The map is a continuation of [113] and [116]). 695 × 458 mm.

[115] [C:] Ichnographia Urbis in TUSCIA primariæ FLORENTIÆ Scenographice simul excusa ab HOMANNIANIS HEREDIBUS ... MDCCXXXI. — (Plan). 491 × 575 mm.
[Inset:] [T:] Prospect der Stadt FLORENTZ. — (View). 148 × 553 mm.

[116] [C:] DIOCESI PADOVANA CON TUTTA LA SUA ESTENSIONE NE VICINI TERRITORI DI D. PAOLO BARTOLOMEO CLARICI — 700 × 464 mm. (The map is a continuation of [113] and [116]).

[117] [C:] NEAPOLIS REGNUM quo continentur APRUTIUM ULTERIUS ET CITERIUS, COMITATUS MOLISIUS TERRA LABORIS, CAPITANIATA PRINCIPAT. ULTERIOR ET CITERIOR BARIANUS ET HYDRUNTINUS AGER BASILICATA CALABRIA CITERIOR ET ULTERIOR cura et cælo MATTHÆI SEUTTERI SAC. CÆS. MAJ. GEOGRAPHI AUGUSTA VIND. — 579 × 497 mm.

[118] = [117] in this ed. but in the cartouche TOBIÆ CONRADI LOTTERI instead of MATTHÆ: SEUTTERI.

[119] [C:] REGIÆ CELSITUDINIS SABAUDICÆ STATUS in quo DUCATUS SABAUDIÆ PRINCIPATUS PEDEMONTIUM ET DUCATUS MONTISFERRATI in suas quasq$_3$ Ditiones & Territoria divisi cum finitimis Regionibus exhibentur Directione et Sumptibus IO BAPTISTÆ HOMANNI Norimbergæ ... — 494 × 562 mm.

[120] [C:] STATUS ECCLESIASTICI MAGNIQUE DUCATUS FLORENTINI Nova Exhibitio repræsentata a IO BAPT. HOMANNO Norimbergæ ... — 476 × 563 mm.

[121] [C:] DOMINII VENETI cum vicinis PARMÆ MUTINÆ MANTUÆ et MIRANDOL^æ STATIBUS Nova Descriptio, edita A IOH. BAPTISTA HOMANNO Sacræ Cæs. Majestatis Geographo Noribergæ. ... — 487 × 570 mm.

[122] [C:] NOUVELLE CARTE DE L'ISLE DE CORSE Apartenante a la Republique de GENES. Presentement divisée & Soulevée, sous les ordres du BARON de NEUHOFF, elu Roy sous le nom de THEODORE PREMIER, Levé sur les Lieux par le Capitaine I. VOGT, Donnée au jour par RENIER & IOSUÉ OTTENS. Geographes a Amsterdam. — 506 × 583 mm.

[123] [C:] IMPERII TVRCICI EVROPAEI TERRA, in primis GRAECIA cum confiniis, ad intelligendos Scriptores N.T. ceterosque graecos et latinos accommodata, In Vsum PRINCIPIS Iuventutis in heredem nati, DVCIS BRVNSVICO-LVNEBVRG CAROLI WILHELMI FERDINANDI adornavit Ioañes Christoph Harenberg Gen. Sch. Insp. et Reg. Scient. Societ. Berol. Sodal. Curantibus Homannianis Heredibus A. 1741. ... — 488 × 568 mm.

[124] [C:] Fluviorum in Europa principis DANUBII CUM ADIACENTIBUS REGNIS nec non totius GRÆCIÆ ET ARCHIPELAGI Novissima Tabula Authore IOH. BAPTISTA HOMANNO NORIMBERGÆ ... — 481 × 576 mm.
[Inset:] [T:] Cum integrum DANUBII TRACTUM in Tabula nostra superius una serie continuare non potuimus. Fragmentum istud tanquam partem pertinentem huc infra posuimus. —

[125] = [124] in this ed. with small alterations in the cartouches.

[126] = [125] in this ed.

[127] [C:] REGNUM BOSNIÆ, una cum finitimis CROATIÆ, DALMATIÆ, SLAVONIÆ, HUNG. et SERVIÆ partibus, adjuncta præcipuorum in his regionibus munimentorum ichnographia Curantibus Homañianis Heredibus Norib. ... REGNI SERVIÆ PARS, una cum finitimis VALACHIÆ & BULGARIÆ partibus, addita præcipuorum in his regionibus munimentorum & castellorum Ichnographia. Curantibus Homannianis Heredibus, Norib. ... — 606 × 1117 mm.
[a] [C:] Theatrum Belli inter Imperat CAROL.VI. et SULT. ACHMET IV. in partibus regnorum SERVIÆ et BOSNIÆ, ex avthenticis subsidys delineatum a Ioh. Fr. Öttingero Loc. ten. Imper. — 308—992 mm.
[b] [T:] Plan von USSITZA — (Plan). 67 × 106 mm.
[c:] [T:] BRODT — (Plan). 93 × 138 mm.
[d] [T:] WIHAZ — (Plan). 98 × 138 mm.
[e] [T:] ZWORNEK — (View). 98 × 138 mm.
[f] [T:] VALIOVA — (Plan). 93 × 138 mm.
[g] [T:] KRAKOIEVAZ — (Plan). 98 × 138 mm.
[h] [T:] SERAGLIO — (View). 100 × 138 mm.
[i] [T:] RATSCHA — (Plan). 146 × 134 mm.
[j] [T:] SABATZ — (Plan). 146 × 137 mm.
[k] [T:] BELGRAD — (Plan). 146 × 135 mm.
[l] [T:] ORSAVA — (Plan). 146 × 135 mm.
[m] [T:] WIDDIN — (Plan). 146 × 135 mm.
[n] [T:] NICOPOLIS — (Plan). 146 × 135 mm.
[o] [T:] NISSA — (Plan). 146 × 137 mm.
[p] [T:] CHATCHEK — (Plan). 146 × 136 mm.
[q] [T:] ZWORNIECK in R. Bosniæ. — (Plan). 92 × 116 mm.
[r] [T:] BANIALUCKA in R. Bosniæ. — (Plan). 92 × 106 mm.
[s] [T:] GRADISCA in Sclavoniæ. — (Plan). 92 × 105 mm.

[t] [T:] CARLSTADT in Croatia. — (Plan). 92 × 104 mm.

[u] [T:] PETERWARDIN in Sinnio Hung. — (Plan). 92 × 114 mm.

[v] [T:] TEMESWAR, in Hung. — (Plan). 92 × 110 mm.

[x] [T:] ESSECK ad fl. Trava. — (Plan). 92 × 103 mm.

[z] [T:] PANZOVA nel Banato. — (Plan). 92 × 103 mm.

[aa] [T:] VIPALANCKA ad Danub. — (Plan). 92 × 102 mm.

[bb] [T:] SERAGLIO in R. Bosniæ — (Plan). 92 × 115 mm.

[128] [C:] Accurata totius ARCHIPELAGI et GRÆCIÆ TABULA in qua omnes subjacentes Regiones et Insulæ per I Danckerts ... — 507 × 602 mm.

[129] [T:] Accurate Vorstellung der Orientalisch-Kayserlichen Haupt- und Residenz-Stadt CONSTANTINOPEL samt ihrer Gegend und zweyen berühmten Meer-Engen Bosphoro Thracio und Hellesponto oder dem freto der Dardanellen herausgegeben von IOHANN BAPTIST HOMANN. DER ROM. KAYS. MAJEST. Geographo in NÜRNBERG. ... — 485 × 574 mm.

[Insets:] [C:] Prospectivische Vorstellung der DARDANELLEN Vor CONSTANTINOPEL. — (View). 112 × 168 mm. [T:] Prospect der Türckisch: Haupt und Residentz-Stadt STAMBUL Oder CONSTANTINOPEL, von Mitternacht anzusehen. — (View). Uncoloured. 137 × 571 mm.

[130] [C:] MAPPA GEOGRAPHICA GRÆCIÆ SEPTENTRIONALIS HODIERNÆ sive Provinciarum MACEDONIÆ, THESSALIÆ et ALBANIÆ, in qua ultima Provincia Habitationes sitæ GENTIS MONTENEGRIANÆ in Comitatu ZENTANENSI expressæ sunt, unacum finitimis Regionibus atque Insulis, ex recentissimis novissimisque Subsidiis secundum normam legitimæ Projectionis in usum belli præsentis delineata. NORIMBERGÆ Cura HOMANNIANORUM HEREDUM. ... A<u>o</u> 1770. — D.A.Hauer sc. Norimb. 443 × 560 mm.

[131] [C:] REIPUBLICÆ ET STATUS GENERALIS POLONIÆ NOVA TABULA, COMPREHENDENS MAIORIS ET MINORIS POLONIÆ REGNI MAGNI DUCATUS LITHUANIÆ DUCATUS PRUSSIÆ, CURLANDIÆ, SAMOGITIÆ MASSOVIÆ VOLHYNIÆ PODOLIÆ RUSSIÆ UCRANIÆ et de MOSCOVIÆ PARS Accuratam Descriptionem. Amstelodami, apud R. et J.Ottens. in platoa Vulgo dicta, de Niuwedyk in signo Majpa Terra. — Jacob Keyser Sculptor 501 × 880 mm.

[132] Carte des Etats de la COVRONNE de POLOGNE, nouvellement dessinée par M<u>r</u>· Tob. Mayer et publiee par les Heritiers de Homann l'an MDCCL.

[C:] Mappa Geographica REGNI POLONIAE ex novissimis quotquot sunt mappis specialibus composita et ad LL. stereographicae projectionis revocata a Tob. Mayero S.C.S. Luci publicae tradita per Homannianos Heredes. Norimb. A. MDCCL. — 458 × 538 mm.

[133] [C:] MAPPA GEOGRAPHICA, ex novissimis observationibus repræsentans REGNUM POLONIÆ ET MAGNUM DUCATUM LITHUANIÆ, Cura et Sumptibus TOBIÆ CONRADI LOTTER Geogr. Aug. Vindel. 1759. — T. C. Lotter sculps 480 × 580 mm.

[134] [C:] Novissima et accuratissima MAGNI DUCATUS LITHUANIÆ in suos Palatinatus et Castellanias divisæ Delineatio, cura et impensis MATTHÆI SEUTTERI, S.Cæs. et Reg. Cathol. Majest. Geogr et Chalcographi Augustani. — [T:] Anjezò in Verlag bey Iohañ Michael Probst, Chalcogr. in Augspurg. — 491 × 567 mm.

[135] [C:] Die Königl. POLNISCHE u. PREUSISCHE Hansee- und Handels-Stadt DANTZIG, Poln. Gdansko, im Lande Pomerellien ... in einem richtigen PLAN und PROSPECT nebst Anzeige der Russ.-Saechssischen Belagerung A. 1734. entworfen u. herausgegeben von Homænnischen Erben, A. 1739 ...

Urbs Hanseatica BORUSSIÆ POLONICÆ, DANTISCUM, vel Gedanum, Polon, Gdansko, in Pomerellia sita, ... ichno- et Scenographice repræsentata, exhibens simul Russico, — Saxonicam, quæ A. 1734 contigit, obsidionem. Edentibus Hom. Heredibus. A.MDCCXXXIX. ... — (Plan). 478 × 544 mm.

[Inset:] [T:] PROSCPECT von DANTZIG — (View). Uncoloured. 145 × 540 mm.

[136] [C:] DVCATVVM LIVONIÆ et CVRLANDIÆ cum vicinis Insulis Nova Exhibitio Geographica editore IOH. BAPTISTA HOMANNO NORIMBERGÆ ... — 488 × 583 mm.

[137] [C:] Potentissimo BORUSSORUM REGI FRIDERICO WILHELMO Majestate, Fortitudine Clementia Augustissimo Hancce LITHUANIAM BORUSSICAM ... — = 1710—1750:[2].

[138] [C:] Tabula Geographica continens Despotatus WALLACHIÆ atque MOLDAVIÆ, Provinciam BESSARABIÆ Sub clientela Turcica, itemque Provinciam Polonicam PODOLIÆ, tamquam Regiones, in quibus bellum præsens geritur, ex HASIANIS aliisque novissimis Subsidiis secundum statum politicum recentissimum delineata, in lucem edita ab HOMANNIANIS HEREDIBUS 1769. ... — 472 × 567 mm.

[139] [C:] VKRANIA quæ et TERRA COSACCORVM cum vicinis WALACHIÆ, MOLDAVIÆ, MINORISq$_3$ TARTARIÆ PROVINCIIS exhibita à IOH. BAPTISTA HOMANNO Norimbergæ ... — 475 × 562 mm.

[140] = [139] in this ed.

[141] = [139] in this ed. with very small alterations.

[142] [C:] Theatrum belli Russorum Victoriis illustratum sive Nova et accurata TURCICARUM ET TARTARICUM Provinciarum intra fluvios Tyras s. Niester et Tanaim s. Don, ab Oram Ponti Euxini et in Peloponēso Taurica sitarum Designatio, manu et impensis TOB. CONRADI LOTTERI CHALC. ET GEOGR. AUG.VIND. — 490 × 573 mm.

[143] PLAN der fürnehmsten FINNISCHEN Vestungen aus Russischen u. Schwedischen Urkunden hergenoṁen. Ans Licht gestellt von Homannischen Erben A.1750.

[T:] PLAN des FORTERESSES les plus celebres situées dans la FINNLAND. Tiré des memoires les plus autenthiques des Russiens et des Suedois. Publié par les Heritiers de Homann l'An 1750 II. le feuille. — 419 × 538 mm.

[a] [C:] Grundriss und Gegend von Neustadt, Nystaedt, in Fiñland, allwo der Friede zwischen Russland uns Schweden An. geschlossen worden. ... — (Plan). 212 × 536 mm.

[b] [C:] Savolai oder Neuschloss, Nyschloss, eine Vestung in der Provintz Savolaxia in Fiñland (Russisch seit 1714) ... — (Plan). 200 × 267 mm.

[c] [C:] Anno 1714 Den 29 Iuly Ist die Vestung Neu Schloss eingenoṁen, vor alters Sawolay genañt ... — 200 × 267 mm.

[144] [C:] INGERMANLANDIÆ seu INGRIAE novissima Tabula luci tradita Per Homannianos Heredes Norib. A. MDCCXXXIV. ... — 467 × 548 mm.

[Inset:] [C:] S<u>t</u> Petersburg. — (View). 140 × 235 mm.

[145] [C:] INGRIA et CARELIA. I.Griṁel del. — Uncoloured. 595 × 447 mm.

[146] Tab. I. [C:] Планъ Императорскаго столичнаго города Санктпетербурга сочиненной въ 1737 году [Plan Imperatorskago stoličnago goroda Sanktpeterburga sočinennoj v 1737 godu]

Plan der Kayserl. Residentz Stadt St. Petersburg wie solcher A.º 1737 aufgenommen worden — G.I. Unvertzagt sculps. — Uncoloured. 393 × 608 mm.

[147] [C:] Ладожское озеро [Ladožkoe ozero]. Lacus Ladoga. Течение Невы рѣки изъ Ладожскаго озера къ Ст. Петербургу [Tečenie Nevy rěki iz Ladožskago ozera k St. Peterburgu]

Fluvius Newa e Lacu Ladoga Petropolin versus procurrens. I. Griṁel del. — Uncoloured. 449 × 602 mm.

[148] [C:] Ладожской Каналъ [Ladožskoj Kanal] CANALIS LADOGENSIS. I Griṁel del: — Uncoloured. 441 × 633 mm.

[149] [C:] Ладожское озеро и Финский заливъ съ прилѣжащи-

ми мѣстами [Ladožskoe ozero i Finskij zaliv s priležaščimi mĕstami]
Lacus Ladoga et sinus Finnicus cum interiacentibus et adiacentibus Regionibus. J.Grimmel del: — Uncoloured. 451 × 647 mm.

[150] [C:] Планъ Императорскаго столичнаго города Москвы сочиненной подъ смотрѣніемъ архитектора Ивана Мичурина въ 1739 году [Plan Imperatorskago stoličnago goroda Moskvy sočinennoj pod smotreniem arhitektora Ivana Mičurina v 1739 godu] — 502 × 520 mm.

[151] [C:] Финский заливъ отъ Кронштата до Санктпетербурга съ лѣжащими по берегам забавными домами [Finskoj zaliv ot Kronštata do Sanktpeterburga s ležaščimi po beregam zabavnymi domami]
Der Sinus Finnicus von Cronstad bis St. Petersbürg benebst den auf seinen Kusten befindlichen Lusthöfen. — [T:] I.Grimmel del. — Uncoloured. 459 × 610 mm.

[152] [C:] SPATIOSISSIMUM IMPERIUM RUSSIÆ MAGNÆ juxta recentissimas Observationes MAPPA GEOGRAPHICA accuratissime delineatum opera et sumtibus TOBIÆ CONRADI LOTTERI, Geogr. et Chalcogr. AUGUSTÆ VINDEL. — 494 × 567 mm.

[153] [C:] IMPERII RUSSICI et TATARIAE UNIVERSAE tam majoris et Asiaticæ qvam minoris et Europææ TABVLA ex recentissimis et probatissimis monumentis et relationibus conciñata, et ad legitimas projectionum Geographic. regulas plane exacta opera IOH. MATTHIAE HASII Math. P.P. juncta Sciagraphia explicationis ejusdem et descriptionis Russiæ et Tatariæ universæ Geographico - historicæ. Impensis Homannianorum Heredum Norib. A.1739. ... — [C:] ANNAE Magnæ Victrici RUSSORUM IMPERATRICI Septentrionis et Orientis Sideri benigno, Hostium domitrici, Scientiarum Nutrici, Vitam longævam, Famam æternam, Populum fidelem, Victoriam perpetuam, Fortunā obseqventissimā p. m. precatus mappam hanc humillime consecrat Autor subjectissimus — 475 × 555 mm.

[154] = [153] in this ed.

[155] [C:] NOVA DESCRIPTIO GEOGRAPHICA TATTARIÆ MAGNÆ tam orientalis quam occidentalis in particularibus et generalibus Territoriis una cum Delineatione totius Imperii Russici imprimis SIBERIÆ accurate ostensa. — [C:] SERENISSIMO ac POTENTISSIMO REGI SUECORUM GOTORUM et VANDALORUM etc. etc. etc. FRIDERICO PRIMO Domino suo Clementissimo Mappam hanc Geographicam quæ Divina sic dispensante Providentia Originem suam Occasione Captivitatis SIBERICAE traxit, devotissimo Corde et Obsequiosissima Mente offert, dicat, dedicatq$_3$ humillimus ac obedientissimus Servus et Subditus P.I.v.Strahlenberg — [C:] ... Philipp Ioh. v. Strahlenberg I.A.Matern P.I.Frisch sculpsit. ... — 650 × 995 mm.

[156] [C:] Recentissima ASIAE Delineatio, Qua IMPERIA, ejus, REGNA, et STATUS, Unacum novissimis RUSSORUM detectionib$_9$ circa MARE CASPIUM et TERRAM YEDSO alias dict per illor: Expedit: et Excursiones, factis sistuntur dirigente IOH. CHRISTOPH.HOMANNO M.D. ... Noribergæ. — [T:] BENEVOLE SPECTATOR ... Ioh. Bapt: Homanni ... — 478 × 569 mm.

[157] Carte de l'ASIE. projettée Stereographiquement, tirée des Relations et Observations, contenues dans les voyages modernes, de meme que dans les monumens des anciens, corrigée de tout ce qui sent la fable, et divisée en ses IX Parties methodiques par le Sr I.M.HASIVS. Prof. des Math. Recueilliée et dessinée sur ses morceaux posthumes par Aug. Gottl. Boehmius, Maitre es Arts. Aux Depens des Heritiers de Homann l'An. 1744 ...
[C:] ASIA secundum legitimas Projectionis Stereographicæ regulas et juxta recentissimas observation. et relationes, explosis aliorum fabulosis designationibus et narrationibus, adhibitis quoque veterum monumentis et recentiorum itinerariis descripta, et in partes suas methodicas IX divisa a I MATTH. HASIO M.P.P.O. nunc ex beate defuncti subsidiis et M.S.C.tis designata a M. August Gottlob Boehmio Impensis Homannianorum Hered. A. 1744 — 479 × 558 mm.

[158] Tabula ex novissimis Relationibus ad mentem de L'Islii, inprimis vero celeberrimi Geographi, D^{ni} I.M.Hasii Prof. Vitemb. delineata. A.1737.
[C:] IMPERIUM TURCICUM in EUROPA, ASIA ET AFRICA REGIONES PROPRIAS, TRIBUTARIAS, CLIENTELARESq$_3$ sicut et omnes eusdem BEGLIRBEGATUS SEU PRÆFECTURAS GENERALES exhibens Sumtibus IO. BAPTISTA HOMANNI Norimbergæ ... — 488 × 582 mm.

[159] [C:] IMPERIUM TURCICUM in EUROPA. ASIA ET AFRICA, REGIONES PROPRIAS, TRIBUTARIAS, CLIENTELARESq$_3$ sicut et omnes ejusdem BEGLIRBEGATUS SEU PRÆFECTURAS GENERALES exhibens Sumptibus IO. BAPTISTÆ HOMANNI Noribergæ ... — 480 × 555 mm.

[160] NOVA IMPERII TURCARUM TABULA, AD USUM SERENISSIMI BURGUNDIÆ DUCIS.
[C:] ESTATS DEL'EMPIRE DU GRAND SEIGNEUR DES TURCS, EN EUROPE, EN ASIE, et EN AFRIQUE, divisé en tous ses BEGLERBEGLICZ, ou GOUVERNEMENTS; où sont aussi remarqués les Estats qui luy sont Tributaires. Dressé sur les plus Nouvelles Relations. AL'USAGE DE MONSEIGNEUR LE DUC DE BOURGOGNE Par son tres Humble et tres Obeissant Serviteur H: IAILLOT — [C:] ... A AMSTERDAM Chez R. et J. OTTENS. — 445 × 608 mm.
[Inset:] [T:] ROYAUME D'ALGER BILEDULGERID — 105 × 154 mm.

[161] [C:] REGNI DAVIDICI et SALOMONÆI Descriptio Geographica cum vicinis regionibus SYRIÆ et ÆGYPTI, junctim per colores exhibens status diversos harum regionum, Ex veteribus Monumentis, in subsidium vocatis recentissimis observationibus, concinnata a IOH. MATTHIA HASIO Math.P. MAPPA PRINCIPALIS Schema I. — Prostat Noribergæ in Officina Homañiana Impensis Heredis Homann, I.M.F. 457 × 314 mm.

[162] [C:] REGNI DAVIDICI et SALOMONÆI Descriptio Geographica cum vicinis regionibus SYRIÆ et ÆGYPTI, junctim per colores exhibens status diversos harum regionum, Ex veteribus Monumentis, in subsidium vocatis recentissimis observationibus, concinnata a IOH. MATTHIA HASIO Math.P. MAPPA PRINCIPALIS Schema II. — Prostat Noribergæ in Officina Homañiana Impensis Heredis Homann. I.M.F. 457 × 314 mm.

[163] [C:] REGNI DAVIDICI et SALOMONÆI Descriptio Geographica cum vicinis regionibus SYRIÆ et ÆGYPTI, junctim per colores exhibens status diversos harum regionum, Ex veteribus Monumentis, in subsidium vocatis resentissimis observationbus, concinnata a IOH. MATTHIA HASIO Math.P. MAPPA PRINCIPALIS Schema III. — Prostat Noribergæ in Officina Homañiana Impensis Heredis Homann, I.M.F. 457 × 314 mm.

[164] LA PALESTINE ou LA TERRE SAINTE, distribuée en XII Tribus, etendue par les Rois DAVID et SALOMON jusqu'aux frontieres de Thapsac ou d'Orontes etc. dessinée par S. I.C.Harenberg, et donnée au Public par les Heritiers de Homann. ... l'An 1744.
[C:] PALÆSTINA seu TERRA olim SANCTA, tum duodecim tribubus distributa, tum a DAVIDE et SALOMONE usque ad terminos Thapsaci seu Orontis, Fert. fluvius magni, et quaqua versum dilatata con finibusque regionibus adjectis et Terra GOSEN ac serie itinerarū Isrælitarum ex ea usq$_3$ ad introitum p Iordanem exornata. Secundū monumenta veterū et recentiorū digessit ac delineavit, I.C.Harenberg Ediderunt Heredes Homañiani. A.1744 ... J.M. Seeligmann sc. — 459 × 548 mm.

[165] [C:] IUDÆA SEU PALÆSTINA ob sacratissima Redemtoris vestigia hodie dicta TERRA SANCTA prout olim IN DUODECIM TRIBUS DIVISA separatis ab invicem Regnis IUDA ET ISRAEL expressis insuper VI ultimi temporis ejusdem Terræ Provinciis collecta ex Tabulis Guil. Sansoný Christ^{ssmi} Regis Geogr. à IOH. BAPTISTA HOMANNO Norimbergæ... — 481 × 558 mm.

[Inset:] [T:] Populi Isräelitici ex Ægypto per Desertum in Terram Promissionis Canaan quadraginta annorum Iter Stationes et Profectio — 92 × 80 mm.
[166] [C:] CARTE de l'ASIE MINEVRE ou de la NATOLIE et du PONT EVXIN, tirée des Voyages et des Observations des Anciens et Modernes, et dressée suivant les principes d'une nouvelle Projection par S.^{r} HAS, P.P. imprimée aux depens des Heritiers de Homann. Nuremb. ... A.1743. ASIAE MINORIS Veteris et Novae, itemqve PONTI EVXINI et PALVDIS MAEOTIDIS Mappa vel Tabula, ad legitimae projectionis Stereographicæ normam, veterum acutorum et recentiorum itinerariorum ac Observationum fidem descripta a IOH. MATTH. HASIO, Math. Prof. editaqve cura & Impensis Homannianorum Heredum. A. 1743. ... — 490 × 580 mm.
[167] CARTE DE LA TURQUIE ASIATIQUE contenant la NATOLIE MODERNE divisée en ses Beglerbeys &.
[C:] TURCIA ASIATICA exhibens NATOLIAM MODERNAM, in suos Beglirbegatus divisam, itemque reliquos Beglirbegatus, sive Gubernationes et Præfecturas generales, in Regionibus GEORGIÆ, ARMENIÆ, MESOPOTAMIÆ, SYRIÆ et ARABIÆ sitos, una cum MARI NIGRO, MARI AZOWIENSI, MARI di MARMORA, et MARI ÆGEO, atque adjacentibus Insulis, ex novissimis Subsidiis ac relationibus ad normam legitimæ Projectionis in usum belli præsentis delineata. Impensis HOMANNIANORUM HEREDUM, Norimbergæ, 1771. ... — 458 × 527 mm.
[168] [C:] REGNI SINÆ vel SINÆ PROPRIÆ Mappa et Descriptio Geographica, ex mappis particularibus, quas Sinarum Rex CANGHI opera patrum Missionariorum e S.I. in provincias regni universi ejus rei gratia ablegatorum concinnari fecit, perfecta, Publicoque primum communicata in opere magnificentissimo R.P. du HALDE, et ab Anvillæo Gall: Reg: Geographo, in compendiosiorem hanc formam reducta, nunc secundum magis legitimas projectionis Stereographicæ leges reformata, studio IOH: MATTH: HASII. MATH: P:P. Impensis Homañiarorum Heredum. — 581 × 517 mm.
[169] [C:] GEOGRAPHICA NOVA ex Oriente gratiosissima, duabus tabulis specialissimis contenta quarum una MARE CASPIVM altera KAMTZADALIAM seu TERRAM JEDSO curiosè exhibēt Editore IO. BAPT HOMANN S.C.M. GEOGR Norimbergæ. — 485 × 575 mm.
[a] [T:] DAS CASPISCHE MEER wie solches auf Ihro Gros-Czaar. Maj. ordre durch einen erfarnen See-Capitain abgezeichnet und auf 200 Meillen wegs in die Lenge und 50 in die Breite befunden worden. — 485 × 250 mm.
[b] [T:] DAS LAND KAMTZADALIE sonst JEDSO mit der LAMSKISCH od PENSINSKISCHEN SEE, wie solche durch verschiedene Reisen der Russischen Cosacken und Zobel-fangern über Wasser und Land bestrichen und angemerkt worden. — 485 × 255 mm.
[170] [C:] PROVINCIARUM PERSICARUM KILANIÆ nempe CHIRVANIÆ DAGESTANIÆ aliarumque vicinarum regionum partium NOVA GEOGRAPHICA TABULA Ex Itinerario celeberrimi olim ADAMI OLEARII aliisq$_3$ recentioris Geographiæ ad miniculis desumpta à IO. BAPT. HOMANNO, Sac. Cæs. Maj. Geographo ejusque Filio. Noribergæ — R.A.S. 1728. 482 × 567 mm.
[Inset:] [T:] Prospect der Russischen Stadt und Vestung Tercki — (View). 90 × 138 mm.
[171] [C:] NOVA MARIS CASPII ET REGIONIS USBECK Cum Provincijs adjacentibus vera Delineatio In qua itinera Regia et alia notabiliora accurate denotantur Per A. Maas. 1735. Curatib$_9$ Homañianis Heredib. ... — [C:] Nota, ... Reductio mappæ hujus a majore in hanc minorem formam facta est per Iohannem Petrum van Ghelen. 1735. ... — 485 × 575 mm.
[172] [C:] OPULENTISSIMI REGNI PERSIÆ JUXTA SUAS PROVINCIAS recentissima et accuratissima Designatio, Studio et sumtibus MATTHÆI SEUTTERI, S.CÆS. ET REG. CATHOL. MAJ. GEOGR. AUG. ... — 500 × 579 mm.
[173] [C:] IMPERII PERSICI IN OMNES SUAS PROVINCIAS (tam veteribus quam modernis earundem nominibus Signatas) EXACTE DIVISI Nova Tabula Geographica, quam ex præcipuis OLEARII, TAVERNIERI, RELANDI aliorumque recentium Authorum Scriptis concinnatam Luci publicæ exponit IO. BAPTISTA HOMANN SAC. CÆS. MAI. Geographus. et Regiæ Borussicæ Scientiarum Societatis membrum NORIMBERGÆ ... — 485 × 577 mm.
[174] [C:] NIEUWE KAART van OOSTINDIE met alle desselfs omleggende Eylanden. etc. — 427 × 1030 mm.
[Inset:] [C:] ASIA — Oval 130 × 157 mm.
[175] IMPERIUM JAPONICUM PER SEXAGINTA ET SEX REGIONES DIGESTUM ATQUE EX IPSORUM JAPONENSIUM MAPPIS DESCRIPTUM PER MATTHÆUM SEUTTER, S. CÆS. ET REG. CATHOL. MAJ. GEOGR. AUGUSTAN. 468 × 575 mm.
[Inset:] [T:] CONSPECTUS URBIS NANGASACKI, et Insulæ ante illam sitæ, in qua sedes est Batavorum. — 143 × 213 mm.
[176] [C:] Peninsula INDIÆ citra Gangem, hoc est Orae celeberrimae MALABAR & COROMANDEL Cum adjacente Insula non minus celebratissima CEYLON Secundum prototypon De l'Islianum edita, insuperq$_3$ novissimis Observationibus correcta et notatis, qvae cuivis genti Europææ possidentur, terris et emporÿs, aucta, studio, Homannianorum Heredum Norib. M DCC XXXIII ... — 540 × 478 mm.
[177] [C:] AFRICÆ in Tabula Geographica Delineatio admentem Novissimorum eorumq$_3$ optimorum Geographorum emendata, Indicibus Vtilissimis aucta et ad usum Tyronum imprimis Geographicorum. Variis compendiosæ Methodi adminiculis accomodata. Opera A.F.ZÜRNERI Reg: Maj: Pol: et El: Sax: Provinciarum finiumq$_3$ Commissarii et Geographi ut et Reg: Soc: Sci: B.M. Ex Officina PETRI SCHENKII. in platea vulgo de Warmoes straat sub signo N.Visschers athlas. — 498 × 581 mm.
[178] [C:] AFRICA Secundum legitimas Projectionis Stereographicæ regulas et juxta recentissimas relationes et observationes in subsidium vocatis quoque veterum Leonis Africani Nubiensis Geographi et aliorū monumentis et eliminatis fabulosis aliorum designationibus pro præsenti statu ejus aptius exhibita à IOH. MATTHIA HASIO, M.P.P.O. h.t. Facult. Phil. in Acad. Witeb. Decano. Impensis Homannianorum Heredum. ... A. 1737. — Noribergæ in Officina Homanniana 467 × 564 mm.
[179] = [178] in this ed. but without Noribergæ in...
[180] ÆGYPTUS HODIERNA Ex itinerario Celeberrimi Viri, PAULI LUCÆ Franci desumta, ac novissime repræsentata à IOHANNE BAPTISTA HOMANN S.C.M. Geographo NORIMBERGÆ.
[C:] DAS HEUTIGE ÆGYPTEN aus der Reyssbeschreibung des berühmten H^n PAUL LUCAS gezogē, und mit folgenden Denckwürdigkeiten herausgegeben von IOHANN BAPT. HOMANN KEYSERL. GEOGR. in Nürnbg. — [T:] Ioannes Christophorus I.B Homanni Filius delineavit. ... — 557 × 469 mm.
[181] = [180] in this ed.
[182] [C:] Statuum MAROCCANORUM, REGNORUM nempe FESSANI, MAROCCANI, TAFILETANI et SEGELOMESSANI Secundum suas Provincias accurate divisorum, Typus generalis novus, ex variis recentioris Geographiæ adminicul depromptus et designatus a, IO. CHRIS. HOMANNO M.D. Noribergæ Anno 1728. ... — 479 × 555 mm.
[Insets:] [T:] Porto Santo INSULA MADERA Sub Lusitanis — 42 × 77 mm. [T:] Der Stadt MAROCCO græster Theil samt dessen Koeniglichen Hof — (View). 110 × 265 mm. [T:] Prospect der Königlichen Residens Stadt MEQUINETZ — (View). 110 × 267 mm.
[183] GVINEA propria, nec non NIGRITIÆ vel Terræ NIGRORVM maxima pars, Geographis hodiernis dicta utraq$_3$ ÆTHIOPIA INFERIOR, & hujus quidem pars australis ex delineationibus Anvillianis itineri Guineensi D.

de Marchais insertis secundum Leges projectionis stereographicæ Hasianæ designata & edita studio & labore Homannianorum Heredum Norimb. ... A.1743.
La GVINEE de meme que la plus grande Partie du Pais des NEGRES, appellées par les Geographes modernes ETHIOPIE INFERIEVRE & meridionale, tirées des morceaux geographiques de M.ʳ d'Anville, qu'il a inseres au Voyage du Chev. de Marchais, & puis desinées suivant les Loix de la nouvelle projection de feu M.ʳ le Prof. Has, par les Heritiers d'Homan. A. 1743. [T:] I.C. Reinsperger inc. et sc. — 458 × 555 mm.

[184] [C:] TOTIUS AMERICAE SEPTENTRIONALIS ET MERIDIONALIS NOVISSIMA REPRÆSENTATIO quam ex singulis recentium Geographorum Tabulis collectā luci publicæ accomodavit IOHANNES BAPTISTA HOMANN Sac. Cæs. Maj. Geog. e Reg. Boruss. Societ: Scientiarum membrum Norimbergæ ... — 483 × 566 mm.

[185] [C:] Recentissima NOVI ORBIS Sive AMERICÆ SEPTENTRIONALIS et MERIDIONALIS TABULA Per FRED. DE WITT. Amst: ... ex Officina R. & I. OTTENS. — 485 × 572 mm.

[186] [C:] NOVUS ORBIS SIVE AMERICA MERIDIONALIS ET SEPTENTRIONALIS, PER SUA REGNA, PROVINCIAS, ET INSULAS IUXTA OBSERVATIONES ET DESCRIPTIONES RECENTISS. DIVISA ET ADORNATA CURA ET OPERA MATTH. SEUTTER, SAC. CÆS. MAJ. GEOGR. AUG. VIND. — 496 × 575 mm.

[187] [C:] KRIGS THEATREN I AMERICA 1777. SEAT OF WAR IN AMERICA 1777. — Uncoloured. 235 × 380 mm.
[Inset:] [C:] NORTH AMERICA. — 103 × 131 mm. Irregular.

[188] [C:] AMERICA SEPTENTRIONALIS a Domino d'Anville in Galliis edita nunc in Anglia Coloniis in INTERIOREM VIRGINIAM deductis nec non Fluvii OHIO cursu aucta notisq₃ geographicis et historicis illustrata. Sumptibus Homannianorum Heredum Noribergæ. A.⁰ 1756. — 453 × 505 mm.

[189] [C:] Amplissimæ Regionis MISSISSIPI Seu PROVINCIÆ LUDOVICIANÆ â R.P. Ludovico Hennepin Francisc Miss IN AMERICA SEPTENTRIONALI Anno 1687. detectæ, nunc Gallorum Colonii et Actionum Negotiis toto Orbe celeberrimæ. Nova Tabula edita à IO. BAPT. HOMANNO S.C.M.Geographo Norimbergæ. ... — 483 × 577 mm.
[Inset:] [T:] Catarrhacta ad Niagaram. — (View). 83 × 85 mm.

[190] [C:] REGNI MEXICANI Seu NOVÆ HISPANIÆ LUDOVICIANÆ, N. ANGLIÆ, CAROLINÆ, VIRGINIÆ, et PENSYLVANIÆ nec non INSVLARVM ARCHIPELAGI MEXICANI IN AMERICA SEPTENTRIONALI accurata Tabula exhibita À IOH. BAPTISTA HOMANNO Noribergæ. ... — 475 × 572 mm.

[191] [C:] Typus Geographicus CHILI PARᴬGUAY FRETI MAGELLANICI &c. ex PPᵇ⁹ Alfonso d'Ovalle & Nicol. Techo nec non de Brouwer, Narbouroug, de Beauchesne &c. à Guiliel de l'Islio descript₉, in superque secundum recentiores du Frezier relationes rectificat₉; cui accedit Ichnographia Urb. cap. S Iago Editoribus Homannianis Heredibus. Norib. A.MDCCXXXIII ... — 477 × 557 mm.
[Insets:] [C:] PLAN DE LA VILLE DE SANTIAGO Capitale du Royaume de Chili située ... a 28 lieues du port de Valparaisso dans la Mer du Sud ... Ex Frezierio pag.88. — (Plan). 127 × 197 mm. [T:] Vue de la petite montagne de Sᵗᵉ Lucie — (View). 15 × 36 mm.

[192] [C:] DOMINIA ANGLORUM in præcipuis Insulis AMERICÆ ut sunt Insula S. CHRISTOPHORI ANTEGOA IAMAICA BARBADOS ex Insulis Antillicanis nec non Insulæ BERMUDES vel SOMMERS dictæ, singulari mappa omnia exhibita et edita ab Homannianis Heredibus. ... Die ENGLISCHE COLONIE-LÆNDER Auf den Insuln von AMERICA und zwar die Insuln S.CHRISTOPHORI ANTEGOA IAMAICA BARBADOS alles Antillische Insuln samt den Ins: BERMUDES sonst SOMMERS genāt, auf einem besondern Blat sæmtlₑ vorgestellet u. herausgegeben von Homænnischen Erben ... — 488 × 555 mm.
[a] [T:] Delineatio Insulæ Sᵀ CHRISTOPHORI alias I.KITTS ad fidem Prototypi Anglicani expressa curis Homann: Hered: — 112 × 276 mm.
[b] [T:] Insula ANTEGOA ad Fidem Prototypi Londinensis designata et excusa per Homannianos Heredes — 255 × 276 mm.
[c] [T:] INSULA BARBADOES in suas Parochias distincta, una cum Oris maritimis, Viis &c. ad fidem Anglicani Authoris delineata. ... — 218 × 273 mm.
[d] [T:] Insulæ BERMUDES in suas Tribus divisæ, cum omnibus Castellis et Fortalitijs, secundum exemplar Londinense delineatæ. — 116 × 276 mm.
[e] [T:] INSULA IAMAICA in suas Parochias divisa, et secundum Exemplar primitivum Londinense excusa. — 150 × 273 mm.

[193] [a] [C:] Neu und verbesserter PLAN der St. u. Hafens HAVANA auf der Ins. CVBA mit den Wasser-Tiefen, Sandbænckenn und Klippen nochmahlen über sehen v. Pʳ Chassereau Anno 1739. — Publicatum secundum sententiam Parlamenti Ian. 21. 1739. Ex Officina Th. Bowles Lonāini, & recusa Norimb. in Officina Homañiana (Plan). 233 × 278 mm.
[Inset:] (View). 65 × 122 mm.
[b] [T:] CARTAGENA in Terra firma Americæ sita, ichnographia repræsentata et recusa Norimbergæ ab Homan. Heredibus.
[C:] Neu und verbesserter PLAN des Hafens von CARTHAGENA in America, ... nach dem Entwurf des Pr. Chassereau, Archit. 1740. nach Engelland gebracht. und ans Liecht gegeben. — 230 × 280 mm.
[The whole map:] 478 × 280 mm.

[194] [C:] Mappa Geographica, complectens I. INDIÆ OCCIDENTALIS PARTEM MEDIAM CIRCVM ISTHMVM PANAMENSEM II. Ipsumq₃ Isthmum. III. Ichnographiam præcipuorum locorum & portuum ad has terras pertinentium. Desumta omnia ex Historia Insulæ S.Dominici & pro præsenti statu belli, quod est 1740 inter Anglos & Hispanos exortum, luci publicæ tradita ab Homannianis Heredibus. ... — 575 × 486 mm.
[a] [C:] CARTE DES ISLES L'AMERIQUE ET DE PLUSIEURS PAYS DE TERRE FERME situés audevant de ces Isles & autour de Golfe de Mexique. DRESSÉE Sur un grand nombre de Cartes particulieres, sur les instructions des Navigateurs et Voyageurs, sur les récits des Historiens Espagnols, qui fournissent des détails, qu'on n'a point fait entrer dans les Cartes. le tout s'accordant avec des Determinations les plus nouvelles & avec des Observations Astronomiques de Longitude de la Martinique, Sᵗ Dominque, la Jamaique, Carthagene et la Louysiane. PAR LE Sᴿ D ANVILLE Geographe Ordʳᵉ du Roi. mars 1731 — 295 × 486 mm.
[b] [T:] BAYE DE PANAMA — 135 × 138 mm.
[c] [T:] Delineatio munimenti et Portus S.AUGUSTINI. — 135 × 138 mm.
[d] [T:] Delineatio Portus Mexicani VERA CRUZ V.S. Crucis. — (Plan). 137 × 127 mm.
[e] [C:] Urbs capitalis Regni Mexicani dicta MEXICO — (View). 137 × 222 mm.
[f] [T:] Ichnographia Urbis SAN-DOMINGO ... — (Plan). 137 × 127 mm.

Notes: All the maps are blank on the back and coloured, except where otherwise specified. This collection of maps, now lying loose in what appears to have been the original binding, includes 41 maps signed neither by Homann nor by Homann's heirs. One of these, map [187], is dated 1777, but as it has nothing to do with the Homann maps it has not been included in the dating of the atlas. All the other maps appear in the Atlas Geographicus Major, vols. I—III. There are two or sometimes three copies of some of the maps. Maps [32] and [33], the two copies of Mosellæ Fluminis Tabula specialis, have very amusing differences in the cartouches. Many of the duplicates differ only in the colouring. Map [127], Regnum Bosniæ, una cum finitimis Croatiæ, Dalmatiæ, Slavoniæ, Hung. et Serviæ ... includes a war map, Theatrum belli inter Imperat. Carol VI et Sult. Achmet IV ... ; a western part has been pasted to this, which when unfolded covers three of the maps on the left-hand side [c, d and e]. On map [153] there is a portrait of the Empress Anna of Russia; map [87] has a portrait of an anonymous member of royalty in the cartouche. The seven Russian maps, [145—151], are described in Bagrow's History of Russian Cartography, ed. Henry W. Castner, part 5. On the view of Blocken, map [70], is the name L.S. Bestehorn; Sandler, using the form 'Bestehom', thinks that this hides the name August, Boehme. (Sandler, Homännische Erben, p. 401 n.1.) August Gottlieb Boehme or Boehmius was a cartographer who worked for Homann (Tooley, Dictionary, p. 42). Between maps [79] and [80] is inserted a 'Tabula Poliometrica Germaniae ac Praecipuorum quorundam locorum Europae. In der Homannischen Officin. Nürnberg A. MDCCXXXI'. Between maps [181] and [182] is an 'Orbis in Tabula, d.i. Geographische Universal Karte, I, II... entworfen von Iohann Gottfried Grossen. Exuderunt Heredes Homañiani Noribergæ'. Many of the maps bear manuscript notes about the latitude and longitude of places on them, and different numbers are written in old ink on the maps or their versos.

Lit.: Bagrow, Geschichte, p. 170—171, Bagrow-Castner, p. 182—184, 242, Sandler, Homännische Erben, p. 393—402, 405—410, Sandler, Seutter, p. 8-10.

92 HOMANN, JOHANN BAPTIST AND HEIRS 1736—1788

[Collection of maps without title-page.]   obl. 53,5 cm.

[1] [C:] EUROPE divisée en ses Empires, Royaumes et Républiques Par C.F. DELAMARCHE, Géographe,- et Successeur de ROBERT DE VAUGONDY Revue et Corrigée suivant les Nouvelles Divisions. A PARIS, Rue du Jardinet, N°.13, vis-à-vis celle de l'Eperon — Barriere Sculp. Dien Scripsit 493 × 669 mm.

[2] [C:] MAPPA DANIÆ NORVEGIÆ et SVECIÆ ex optimis mappis geogr. confecta et juxta recentiores observationes mathemat. delineata AUGUSTISSIMO MONARCHÆ CHRISTIANO SEPTIMO Regi Daniæ Norvegiæ Vandal. et Goth. Duci Slesv. Holsat. Storm. Ditmar. et Oldenb. subjectissime dedicata a C I Pontoppidan — 554 × 583 mm.

[3] [C:] KONGERIGET NORGE afdelet i sine fûre Stifter, nemlig AGGERSHUUS, CHRISTIANSAND, BERGEN-HUUS og TRONHIEM, samt underliggende Provstier. Med Kongelig Allernaadigst Tilladelse og Bevilling forfærdiget Aar 1761. af O: A: Wangensteën. Capitain ved det Norske Artillerie-Corps. — [T:] TAP Lingeling Iunior sculp: — 558 × 482 mm.
[Inset:] [C:] NORDLAND og FINMARKEN under TRONHIEMS STIFT — 162 × 237 mm.

[4] [C:] AGGERSHUUS STIFT, afdelet i sine Amter og Fogderier; Med Kongelig Allernaadigst Tilladelse og Bevilling 1762 forfærdiget og udgivet af O A Wangensteën Capitain ved det Norske Artillerie Corps. TAPLingeling Iun: sculp: 1762 & 1763 Hamb: 578 × 483 mm.

[5] [C:] Generalis et prorsus Nova DANIÆ REGNI Tabula Geographica, AUGUSTISSIMO MONARCHÆ, FRIDERICO QVINTO REGI DANIÆ, NORVEG:, WANDAL:, GOTHOR:, DUCI SLESV:, HOLSAT:, STORM:, DITM:, COMITI IN OLDENB: & DELMENH:, REGUM OMNIUM, PATRI & PASTORI SIMILLIMO, QVIA SIMUL ABSOLUTISSIMO & INDUL-GENTISSIMO, DEVOTA MANU E.P. OBLATA. A°. MDCCLXIII — [T:] Med Kongelig Allernaadigst Privilegium, for A.H.Godiche og hans Arvinger. 1766. — 620 × 515 mm.

[6] [C:] DUCATUS SLESVICENSIS ... — = 1720—1771:[12].

[7] [C:] TABVLA GENERALIS HOLSATIAE ... — = 1720—1771:[54].

[8] A General Map of GREAT BRITAIN and IRELAND with Part of Holland Flandres, France, &c. Agreable to Modern History By the Heirs of late M.ʳ Homann, at Nüremberg 1749. ...
[C:] REGNORVM MAGNAE BRITANNIÆ et HIBERNIAE MAPPA GEOGRAPHICA iuxta Observationes astronomicas recentiores denuo correcta et ad formam legitimæ projectionis reducta a Tobia Majero edentib₉ Homañianis Heredibus Norimbergæ aõ. 1749. — 466 × 539 mm.
[Inset:] [C:] Insulæ Schetlandicæ secundum eandem Scalam mappæ principalis hic ob folii augustiam seorsim adpositæ — 103 × 140 mm.

[9] [T:] THE KINGDOME OF MERCIE. — [C:] LA PLUS GRANDE PARTIE de la MANCHE, qui contient LES CÔTES D'ANGLETERRE et celles de FRANCE les BORDS MARITIMES de PICARDIE Aux depens de MATTHIEU SEUTTER ... — 487 × 567 mm.

[10] [C:] SEPTEM PROVINCIAE seu BELGIVM FOEDERATVM quod generaliter HOLLANDIA audit, speciali mappa delineatum, adhibitis in auxilium observationibus astronomicis nec non mensurationibus Snellii, Muschenbrokii etc. Auctore Tobia Mayero, Soc. Geogr. Sodali. Edentibus Homañianis Heredibus. A. 1748. — 471 × 516 mm.

[11] Carte des PAIS BAS CATHOLIQVES ou des X PROVINCES de l'Allemagne Inferieure etc. dessinée au juste selon les exactes observations Astronomiques et Operations Geometriques des Mess.ʸʳ Cassini, Snellius, Muschenbrok etc. dressée par S.ʳ Tobias Maier Mathematicien. Aux depens des Heritiers de Homann. l'An 1747. ...
[C:] BELGIVM CATHOLICVM seu DECEM PROVINCIAE GERMANIAE INFERIORIS cum confiniis GERMANIAE SVP. et FRANCIAE. Legitime omnia delineata et ad ductum observationum astronomicarum, nec non Geometricarum operationum a Cassinio Snellio Muschenbrokio aliisqve rite habitarum examinata studiosissime et representata a TOB. MAIERO Math. Cult. Edentibus HOMANNIANIS HEREDIB. A. 1747. — 472 × 554 mm.

[12] Carte des XVII. PROVINCES ou de L'ALLEMAGNE INFERIEVRE, dressée suivant la Projection stereographique, et appüyée par les mesures faites de Mess. Cassini, Snellius et Mouschenbrok, par M.ʳ Tob. Majer de la Societé geographique, et publiée par les Heritiers de Homann. l'An 1748.
[C:] BELGII UNIVERSI seu INFERIORIS GERMANIAE quam XVII PROVINCIAE, Austriaco, Gallico et Batavo Sceptro parentes constituunt, nova Tabula Geographica a Tobia Majero, Math. Cult. ad leges legitimae delineationis revocata Cura et Studio Homannianorum Heredum. ... A. 1747. — R.A.Schneider sculp. Furth. 470 × 525 mm.

[13] [C:] FLANDRIA MAXIMUS ET PULCHERRIMUS EUROPÆ COMITATUS, in suas Ditiones accurate distinctus, cura et sumtibus MATTHÆI SEUTTERI, S. CÆS. et CATHOLICÆ REGIÆ MAJ. GEOGRAPHI, AUGUSTÆ VINDEL. — 495 × 577 mm.

[14] CARTE de FRANCE dresséé par GVILLAVME DE L'ISLE et accommodée par les Heritiers d'HOMANN. a l'instruction de la Jeunesse Norimb. 1741
[C:] REGNI GALLIAE seu FRANCIAE et NAVARRAE ... — = 1720—1771:[102].

[15] [C:] Carte DE LA FRANCE, Divisée en Départemens et sous-divisée en Arrondissemens Communaux, avec Les Sièges des principales Autorités Administratives, Iudiciaires, Militaires & Eclésiastiques, Dessinée par HÉRISSON et Gravée par CHAMOUIN, Sous la Direction de J.B.SARRET, Auteur de la Description. Benizy scripsit. —
A PARIS Chez Chamouin, l'un des Editeurs, Rue de la

Harpe, N.ºs 20 et 242, vis-à-vis celle Serpente, dans la Porte Cochère, au fond de la Cour, a 12e Et chez Ch.^les Picquet, Géographe, Petit Hôtel de Bouillon, Quai Voltaire ou Malaquais, entre la Rue des Sts Pères et celle des Petits Augustins. 521 × 791 mm.

[16] EL REYNO DE ESPANNA dividido en dos grandes Estados DE ARAGON Y DE CASTILLA, subdividido en muchas Provincias, donde se halla tambien EL REYNO DE PORTVGAL.
[C:] REGNORUM HISPANIÆ et PORTUGALLIAE Tabula generalis de l'Islana, aucta et ad Usum Scholarum novissime accomodata à Ioh. Bapt. Homanno S.C.M.Geogr. Norimbergæ — 467 × 583 mm. See 1720—1771:[103].

[17] [C:] Carte nouvelle De L'ISLE de CADIX & du Detroit de GIBRALTAR Levée par Iean de PETIT cy devant Ingenieur & Architecte du Roy de France & dernierement Lieut. Colonel & Ingen. Ordin de Sa Maj. Polonoise, Publiée par Mr WEIDLER, Professeur des Mathem. a Witenberg en Saxe, de l'Academie Royale Britañ. & Prussieñe des sciences. Aux Depens des Heritiers du feu M. le Docteur Homann, Geographe — R.A.Schneider sculp. Furth. 563 × 480 mm.

[18] [C:] REGNUM PORTUGALLIÆ Divisum In Quinque Provincias majores & Subdivisum in sua quæque Territoria una cum REGNO ALGARBIÆ speciali mappa exhibitum Per Ioh. Bapt. Homannum S.Cæs. Maj. Geographum Norimbergæ ... —
Edita primum per I.B.Nolin nunc recusa per H.H. 1736. ... 592 × 463 mm.

[19] Gli STATI d'ITALIA, secondo le Osservationi, fatte dalla Societa di Sc. di Parigi, dal R.P.Riccioli della S. die Gieusu ed. altri Astronomi, di prima geographicamente delineati dall' Eccll.^mo Sg.^r de l'Isle, ed accomodati agli Elementi Geographici, del Sg.^r Schaz; alle spese degl'Heredi d'Homann. L Anno MDCCXLII.
[C:] ITALIA in suos STATVS divisa ... — = 1720—1771:[107].

[20] [C:] Novissima & exactissima TOTIVS REGNI NEAPOLIS TABVLA PRÆSENTIS BELLI STATVI ACCOMMODATA ET EXHIBITA A IOANNE BAPT: HOMANNO Norimbergæ. — 559 × 483 m. See 1720—1771:[117] and [118].

[21] [C:] REGNI & INSVLAE SICILIAE Tabula geographica, ... — = 1720—1771:[109].

[22] Les Etats de L'EGLISE & du GRAND DVCHE de TOSCANE, dressés par Mr Tob. Mayer, de la Soc. Geogr. chez les Herit. de Homann. l'An MDCCXLVIII. ...
[C:] STATVS ECCLESIASTICI nec non MAGNI DVCATVS TOSCANAE NOVA TABVLA GEOGRAPHICA secundum principia legitimæ Delineationis descripta a Tob. Majero, Societ. Geogr. Sodali curantibus Homannianis Heredibus Norimbergæ A. 1748. — 473 × 528 mm.

[23] [C:] DOMINII VENETI cum vicinis PARMÆ MUTINÆ MANTUÆ et MIRANDOL.^æ STATIBUS Nova Descriptio, ... — = 1720—1771:[121].

[24] CARTA GEOGRAFICA, la quale rappresenta lo Stato della REPVBLICA di GENOVA partita nella Riviera di Levante et di Ponente. Data in publico per gli Heredi d'Homann.
[C:] MAPPA GEOGRAPHICA STATVS GENVENSIS ex subsidiis recentissimis præcipue vero ex majori mappa du Chafrion, mediante legitime projiciendi methodo delineata a Tobia Majero Soc. Cosmogr. Sodali, in lucem proferentibus Homannianis Heredibvs. A.º 1749 — 473 × 553 mm.

[25] [C:] DUCATUS MEDIOLANI una cum Confinÿs accurata Tabula exhibitus auctus et emēdatus Per Ioh. Bapt. Homannum. — 467 × 578 mm.

[26] [C:] REGIÆ CELSITUDINIS SABAUDICÆ STATUS ... — = 1720—1771:[119].

[27] Tabula ad Geographiam Hübnerianam recentissime recognita nec minus passim auota et religionum simul distinctione illustrata per HOMANNIANOS HEREDES Anno 1732.
[C:] Potentissimæ HELVETIORUM REIPUBLICÆ CANTONES TREDECIM cum Foederatis et Subjectis Provinciis exhibiti A IOH. BAPTISTA HOMANNO Norimbergæ — 477 × 557 mm.

[28] ALLEMAGNE, distinguée en ses Cercles & subdivisée en ses Etats, contenant son Etendue presente, rectifiée & methodiquement enluminee suivant les Elements de Geographie de Mr. Schatz, ...
[C:] IMPERII ROMANO-GERMANICI IN SVOS STATVS ET CIRCVLOS DIVISI TABVLA GENERALIS ... — = 1710—1750:[106] with small alterations.

[29] [C:] Nouvelle Carte Geographique des Postes D'ALLEMAGNE et des Provinces limitrophes avec Privilege de S.M.I. aux fraix des Heritiers de Homan à Nurenberg. 1764. — [C:] Neue und vollständige POSTKARTE durch ganz DEUTSCHLAND und durch die angränzende Theile der benachbarten Länder zusammeñ getragen und ausgefertiget von FRANZ IOSEPH HEGER Churfürstlich Maynzischen und Fürstlich Taxischen Hofrath auch der Kayserl. Reichs Post Commissario. Mit Kayserl. allergnäd. Privilegio. Im Verlag bey denen HOMAENNISCHEN ERBEN in Nürnberg, 1764. — [C:] Eminentissimo ac Celsissimo Principi ac Domino Domino EMERICO IOSEPHO S. Sedis Moguntinæ ARCHI EPISCOPO S.R.I. per Germaniam Archi Cancellario Principi Electori Postarum Imperialium Protectori Principi ac Domino clementissimo D.D.D. Servus humillimus Francisc_9 Ioseph_9 Heger. — 765 × 943 mm.

[30] le CERCLE D'AVTRICHE consistant dans l'Archiduché d'Autriche le Duché de Stirie, de Carinthie, de Carniole, dans la Comté de Tyrol, et les Pais Autrichiens Anterieurs dans la Souabe, avec ses confins dessiné avec justesse par Tobie Maier, Mathematicien, aux depens des Heritiers de Homann. 1747.
[C:] S.R.I. CIRCVLVS AVSTRIACVS ... — = 1710—1750:[101].

[31] [C:] BAVARIÆ CIRCULUS et ELECTORAT_9 ... — = 1710—1750:[77].

[32] [C:] CIRCVLI SVEVIÆ MAPPA ... — = 1710—1750:[57].

[33] [C:] S.R.I. CIRCULUS RHENANUS SUPERIOR ... — = 1710—1750:[55].

[34] ANDERER und MINDERE THEIL DES GANTZEN HOCHLÖBL. FRÄNCKISCHEN CRAISSES, MIT WELCHEM ZUGLEICH DAS ERTZ-STIFT und CHURFÜRSTENTUM MAYNTZ SAMPT DENEN NOCH ÜBRIGE FRÄNCK: STAATEN als da seind die GRAFSCH. WERTHEIM REINECK und ERPACH nebst der angrentzenden NIDEREN CHUR PFALTZ am RHEIN in dieser Tafel angezeigt werden
[C:] ELECTORATUS MOGUNTINUS ... — = 1710—1750:[32]. See [37].

[35] [C:] EXACTISSIMA PALATINATUS AD RHENUM TABULA ... — = 1710—1750:[73].

[36] [C:] MOSELLÆ FLUMINIS TABULA SPECIALIS ... — = 1710—1750:[92].

[37] ERSTER UND GRÖSTER THEIL DES GANTZEN HOCHLÖBL. FRANCKISCHEN CRAISSES IN WELCHEM DIE BISTHUMER BAMBERG WÜRTZBURG UND AICHSTETT, die Marggr. CULMBACH und ONOLTZBACH das Hertzogt. COBURG, Fürstent. SCHWARTZENBERG, Graffsch. HOHENLO, CASTEL, LIMBURG und SEINSHEIM, das NÜRNBERGISCHE Gebiet und die Hälffte der angrenzenden OBERN PFALTZ mit vorgestelt werden.
[C:] CIRCULI FRANCONIÆ PARS ORIENTALIS ET POTIOR novissime delineata ... — = 1710—1750:[79]. See [34].

[38] [C:] DUCATUS LUNEBURGICI et COMITATUS DANNEBERGENSIS accurata Descriptio ... — = 1710—1750:[52].

[39] [C:] THEATRUM BELLI RHENANI ... — =

[40] [C:] 1710—1750:[50].
[40] [C:] CIRCULI WESTPHALIÆ ... — = 1710—1752:[26].
[41] [C:] CIRCULUS WESTPHALICUS ... — = 1720—1771:[83].
[42] [C:] DUCATUS IULIACI & BERGENSIS Tabula Geographica, ... — = 1710—50:[14].
[43] [C:] Vorstellung der Königlich Preussischen am Rhein liegenden Staaten, als der Hertzogthümer CLEVE, U: GELDERN, U: der Grafschaft MARCK, nebst den angräntzenden Ländern. — 310 × 393 mm.
[44] [C:] CIRCULUS SAXONIÆ INFERIORIS ... — = 1710—1750:[71].
[45] [C:] ELECTORATUS HANOVERANI cum ditionibus et præfecturis suis nova et accurata delin: curata a MATTH. SEUTTERO, GEOGR. CÆS. AUG. VIND. — Tob. Conr. Lotter sculps. 569 × 486 mm.
[46] [C:] DUCATUS BRUNSUICENSIS ... — = 1710—1750:[42].
[47] NOVA ELECTORATUS BRANDENBURGICI TABULA, EDITA PER I.P. FR. VON GUNDLING.
[C:] LAND-CHARTE DES CHUR-FÜRSTENTHUMS BRANDENBURG. AMSTERDAM, Bey JOHANNES COVENS und CORNELIUS MORTIER. ... — [T:] G.P.Busch sculpsit. — 473 × 600 mm.
[48] [C:] DUCATUS MEKLENBURGICI Tabula Generalis ... — = 1710—1750:[12].
[49] [C:] SAXONIÆ SUPERIORIS CIRCULUS, ob oculos sistens DUCATUM et ELECTORATUM SAXONIÆ MARCHIONATUM MISNIÆ, LANDGRAVIATUM THURINGIÆ, PRINCIPATUM ANHALTINUM SCHWARZENBURG, HALLENSEM COMITAT. MANSFELD. VOITLAND. &c. cum aliis insertis et adjacentibus Provinciis accurate delineatus Per MATTH. SEUTTER S.C.M. G. AUGUSTANUM — 492 × 573 mm.
[50] [C:] CIRCULI SUPE. SAXONIAE PARS MERIDIONALIS ... — = 1710—1750:[69].
[51] Multis in locis augmentata, longeque priori Editione correctior facta hæc THURINGIÆ TABULA A.º D. 1729 per Ioh. Christ. Homannum M.D. et Phys: Ord.
[C:] LANDGRAVIATUS THURINGIÆ TABULA GENERALIS ... — = 1710—1750:[60].
[52] [C:] TABVLA MARCHIONATVS BRANDENBVRGICI ET DVCATVS POMERANIÆ ... — = 1710—1750:[3].
[53] [C:] REGNUM BORUSSIÆ Gloriosis auspicys Serenissimi et Potentissimi Prin. FRIDERICI III PRIMI BORUSSIÆ REGIS, MARCH. ET ELECT. BRAN. inauguratum die 18. Ian A. 1701. Geographice cum vicinis Regionibus adumbratum a IOH. BAPTISTA HOMANNO Norimbergæ. — 477 × 564 mm. See 1710—1750:[4].
[54] [C:] SPATIOSISSIMUM IMPERIUM RUSSIÆ MAGNÆ juxta recentissimas Observationes MAPPA GEOGRAPHICA ... — = 1720—1771:[152].
[55] [C:] IMPERII RUSSICI et TATARIAE UNIVERSAE tam majoris et Asiaticæ qvam minoris et Europææ TABVLA ... — = 1720—1771:[153].
[56] [C:] AMPLISSIMA UCRANIÆ REGIO, PALATINATUS KIOVIENSEM ET BRACLAVIENSEM COMPLECTENS, CUM ADJACENTIBUS PROVINCIIS juxta recentissimam designationem æri incisa arte et sumtibus TOBIÆ. CONRADI. LOTTERI, GEOGRAPHI. AUGUSTÆ VINDEL. — 488 × 570 mm.
[57] [C:] Theatrum belli Russorum Victoriis illustratum sive Nova et accurata TURCICARUM ET TARTARICUM Provinciarum ... — = 1720—1771:[142].
[58] [C:] MAPPA GEOGRAPHICA ex novissimis observationibus repræsentans REGNUM POLONIÆ ET MAGNUM DUCATUM LITHUANIÆ, ... — = 1720—1771:[133], but without 1759.
[59] Carte des ETATS DE BOHEME, avec le Souverain DVCE DE SILESIE; publiee par les Heritiers de Homañ. 1 An 1748.
[C:] REGNI BOHEMIAE, DVC. SILESIAE, MARCHIONATVVM MORAVIAE et LVSATIAE Tabula generalis. ... — = 1710—1750:[88].
[60] [C:] BOHEMIA REGNUM juxta XII. Circulos divisum, cum Comitatu Glacensi et ditione Egrana, nec non confinibus Provinciis in mappa Geographica accuratissime delineatum per MATTHÆUM SEUTTER, Sac. Cæs. Maj. Geographü AUG. VIND. — 488 × 568 mm.
[Inset:] [T:] Prospect der Stadt CARLSBAD an dem Wege gegen den Buchberg von Nord Osten gegē Sud Westen anzusehen. — (View). 75 × 180 mm.
[61] [C:] SILESIÆ DUCATUS TAM SUPERIOR QUAM INFERIOR, JUXTA SUOS XVII MINORES PRINCIPATUS ET VI LIBERA DOMINIA DISTERMINAT. NOVA MAPPA GEOGRAPHICA ob oculos positus Cura et Sumtibus MATTH. SEUTTERI S.C.M.G. AUGUST. — 490 × 562 mm.
[Inset:] [T:] BRESLAW — (Plan). 78 × 98 mm.
[62] Carte d'HONGRIE en general, contenant selon la Division ancienne & methodique, la HONGRIE en particulier, la CROATIE, la DALMATIE, la BOSNIE, la SERVIE, la BOULGARIE; la Principauté de TRANSYLVANIE, les Despotats de WALACHIE & de MOLDAV; le tout dressé sur le pied de l'ancienne et de la nouvelle Geographie par Mons. I.M.Hasius, Profess. des Mathemat.
[C:] HVNGARIAE ampliori significatu et veteris vel Methodicae, complexae REGNA: ... — = 1710—1750:[83].
[63] [C:] NEUESTE KARTE DER KOENIGREICHE BOSNIEN SERVIEN CROATIEN UND SLAVONIEN Samt den angrænzenden Provinzen TEMESWAR, DALMATIEN, HERZEGOWINA, RAGUSA, STEYERMARK, KÆRNTHEN, KRAIN, FRIAUL, GRADISKA, UND ISTRIEN, einem grosen Theil von UNGARN, SIEBENBÜRGEN, MOLDAU, WALACHEI, BULGARIEN, ALBANIEN, MACEDONIEN, und einem Stück des KIRCHENSTAATS UND K[reichs] NEAPEL. Nach den besten Originalzeichnungen Charten, und Beschreibungen entworfen von Herrn Carl Schütz. 1788. — [T:] C.Schütz fec. — Zu finden in Wien bey Artaria Compagnie Kunsthaendlern auf dem Kohlmarkt. 485 × 726 mm.
[64] DER LAUF DES DONAU STROMS VON WIEN BIS IN DAS SCHWARZE MEER oder Neuester Kriegsschauplatz zwischen Oesterreich und der Pforte welcher das Koenigreich Ungarn. Sclavonien, Sirmien, Siebenbürgen, Bukowina, Croatien, Dalmatien, Bosnien, Servien, Bulgarien, die Walachei, Bessarabien, die Ukraine, Galizien, Mæhren, Oesterreich, und Steyermark & enthält. LE COURS DU DANUBE DEPUIS VIENNE JUSQU'À SON EMBOUCHURE DANS LA MER NOIRE ou nouvelle Carte du Theatre de la querre entre l'Autriche et la Turquie Contenant Le royaume de Hongrie, Esclavonie, Sirmie, Transylvanie, Bucovine, Croatie, Dalmatie, Bosnie, Servie, Valachie, Moldavie, Bessarabe, l'Ukraine, avec une partie de la Galicie, Moravie, Autriche, Stirie &. &.
Nach den besten Karten und Handzeichnungen entworfen und gestochen von F.Müller. ... zu finden in Wien bey Artaria Compagnie Kunsthändlern am Michaelerplatz. 337 × 508 mm.
[65] KRIEGSTHEATER ODER GRÆNZKARTE OESTERREICHS, RUSSLANDS, UND DER TÜRKEY, enthaltend Das Koenigreich Ungarn, Siebenbürgen, Moldau, Bessarabien, Walachey, Bulgarien, Servien, Bosnien, Sclavonien, Croatien, Albanien, Romanien, Macedonien, einen Theil Griechenlands, und des Archipelagus, die Dardanellen, das schwarze und asowische Meer, die Krim, Tatarey, Kuban, Circassien, &: &: Nebst einem Theil von Russland, Polen, Schlesien, Mæhren, Oesterreich, Steuermark &.
Nach den besten Karten und Handzeichnungen von C.Schütz entworfen 1788. Gestochen von F.Müller ... zu finden in Wien bey Artaria Compagnie Kunsthändlern am Michaelerplatz. 412 × 713 mm.
[66] [C:] KARTE der GEGEND um BELGRAD auf 15 bis 20 Meilen in Umkreis, nämlich von Futak Peterwardein Semlin gegen Sabatz Hassan Bassa Palanka Semendria Rama und Vypalanka, auf welcher alle Hauptstrassen und wie die Flüsse Donau Theis und Sau sich zusam̄en vereinigen, genau

angezeicht sind. in Wien bey Artaria Compagnie. — Nach den besten Originalzeichnungen gestochen von Mansfeld 1788. 481 × 684 mm.

[67] [C:] GRÆCIA NOVA et MARE ÆGEUM s. ARCHIPELAGUS, in qua Mappa MACEDONIA, ALBANIA, EPIRUS THESSALIA ET MOREA, cum circumjacentibus Insulis CORCYRA, CEPHALONIA, ZACYNTHOS, STALIMENE, METELINO, CHIOS, distinctæ exhibentur, opera et sumtibus TOBIÆ CONRADI LOTTERI, GEOGRAPHI AUGUSTÆ VINDEL. ... — 489 × 566 mm.

[68] [C:] REGNUM MOREÆ accuratissime divisum in PROVINCIAS SACCANIAM, TZACONIAM, CALISCOPIUM et DUCATUM CLARENSÆ; una cum INSULIS CEPHALONIA, ZACYNTHO CYTHERA, ÆGINA et SIDRA. sumptibus TOBIÆ CONRADI LOTTER, Geogr. et Chalcogr. AUGUSTÆ VINDEL. — Georg Friderich, Lotter sculpsit. 487 × 573 mm.

[69] N? 138. [C:] CARTE GÉNÉRALE ET POLITIQUE DE L'ASIE Par E. Mentelle, Membre de l'Institut National des Sciences et Professeur aux Ecoles Centrales du Département de la Seine; Et P.G. Chanlaire l'un des Auteurs de l'Atlas National. An VI. A PARIS CHEZ LES AUTEURS P.G.Chanlaire Rue Geoffroy-Langevin, N? 328. Et E.Mentelle Cour du Louvre, N? 7. — 318 × 419 mm.

[70] Tabula ex novissimis Relationibus ad mentem de L'Islii, imprimis vero celeberrimi Geographi, Dni I.M. Hasii Prof. Vitemb. delineata A. 1737.
[C:] IMPERIUM TURCICUM in EUROPA, ASIA ET AFRICA ... — = 1720—1771:[158].

[71] [C:] TERRA SANCTA SIVE PALÆSTINA exhibens non solum REGNA VETERA IUDA ET ISRAEL in suas XII. Tribus distincta, sed etiam eorundem diversarum ætatum conditionem et facta in Sacris Paginis indicata. MAPPA GEOGRAPHICA noviter adornata opera et Studio TOBIÆ CONRADI LOTTER Geographi AUG. VIND. 1759. — Matth: Albrecht Lotter, Sculps: Aug.V. — 478 × 577 mm.
[Inset:] [T:] Israelitarum ex Ægypto in promissam terram Canaan Peregrinatio et Mansiones per deserta, 40. ann. spatio confectæ. — 110 × 85 mm. See 1720—1771:[165].

[72] [C:] NATOLIÆ, olim ASIÆ MINORIS TABULA PER MATTH. SEUTTERUM — [C:] excudit in Aug. Vind. per MATTH. SEUTTERUM S.C.M.Geogr. — 468 × 545 mm.

[73] [C:] OPULENTISSIMI REGNI PERSIÆ JUXTA SUAS PROVINCIAS recentissima et accuratissima Designatio, ... — = 1720—1771:[172], but in the cartouche TOBIÆ CONDRADI LOTTERI instead of MATTHÆI SEUTTERI.

[74] [C:] Carte Nouvelle de l'Amerique Angloise contenant tout ce que les Anglois possedent sur le Continent de l'Amerique Septentrionale Savoir le Canada, la Nouvelle Ecosse ou Acadie, les treize Provinces unies qui sont: les quatres Colonies de la Nouvelle Angleterre 1. New Hampshire, 2. Massachusetsbaye, 3. Rhode-Island, & 4. Conecticut, 5 la Nouvelle York, 6 Nouvelle Iersey, 7. Pensilvanie, 8. les Comtés de Newcastle Kent et Sussex sur la Delaware, 9. Mariland, 10. Virginie, 11. la Caroline Septentrionale, 12 la Caroline Meridionale et 13. Georgie: avec la Floride. Gravée exactement d'après les determinations geographiques dernierement faites par Matthieu Albert Lotter à Augsbourg. — 592 × 489 mm.

[75] N? 155. [C:] CARTE GÉNÉRALE ET POLITIQUE DE L'AMERIQUE Par E. Mentelle, Membre de l'Institut National des Science et Professeur aux Ecoles Centrales du Département de la Seine; Et P.G. Chanlaire l'un des Auteurs de l'Atlas National. An VI. A PARIS CHEZ LES AUTEURS, P.G. Chanlaire Rue Geoffroy-Langevin N? 328 E.Mentelle Cour du Louvre N? 7. — 328 × 426 mm.

[76] N? 150. [C:] CARTE GÉNÉRALE ET POLITIQUE DE L'AFRIQUE Par E. Mentelle, Membre de l'Institut National des Sciences et Professeur aux Ecoles Centrales du Département de la Seine; et P.G. Chanlaire l'un des Auteurs de l'Atlas National. An VI. A PARIS CHEZ LES AUTEURS, P.G. Chanlaire Rue Geoffroy-Langevin, N? 328. Et E.Mentelle Cour du Louvre N? 7. — 321 × 426 mm.

[77] CARTE PARTICULIÉRE DE L'AMÉRIQUE SEPTENTRIONALE.
[C:] A MAP of the BRITISH EMPIRE in AMERICA with the FRENCH, SPANISH and the DUTCH SETTLEMENTS adjacent thereto by Henry Popple at Amsterdam Printed for I.COVENS and C.MORTIER. — J.Condet s. 490 × 481 mm.
[Insets:] [T:] FALL of NIAGARA — (View). 27 × 55 mm. [T:] MEXICO — (Plan). 25 × 55 mm. [T:] QUEBEC — (View). 25 × 55 mm. [T:] NEW YORK — (View). 25 × 55 mm. [T:] Placentia — 17 × 32 mm. [T:] Annapolis Royal — 10 × 32 mm. [T:] Boston — 27 × 32 mm. [T:] New York — 35 × 32 mm. [T:] Charles Town — 24 × 32 mm. [T:] Bermuda — 20 × 32 mm. [T:] S.Augustine — 15 × 15 mm. [T:] Provindence — 15 × 15 mm. [T:] Havana — 17 × 15 mm. [T:] S Jago — 17 × 15 mm. [T:] Kingston H[r] — 20 × 32 mm. [T:] Port Antonio — (Map). 30 × 32 mm. and (Plan). 11 × 10 mm. [T:] Port Royal in Martinica — 27 × 32 mm. [T:] Barbadoes — 20 × 16 mm. [T:] Antigua — 20 × 14 mm. [T:] Cartagene — 30 × 32 mm. [T:] Porto Bello — 30 × 32 mm. See [82] and [83].

[78] NOUVELLE CARTE PARTICULIÈRE DE L'AMERIQUE, OU SONT EXACTEMENT MARQUÉES une PARTIE de la BAYE D'HUDSON, le PAYS des KILISTINONS, la SOURCE de la GRANDE RIVIÈRE de MISSISIPI, le PAYS des ILLINOIS &c.
I. K. s. 577 × 527 mm.

[79] NOUVELLE CARTE PARTICULIÈRE DE L'AMERIQUE ou sont exactement marquées la Nouvelle BRETAGNE, le CANADA ou Nouvelle FRANCE, la Nouvelle ECOSSE, la Nouvelle ANGLETERRE, la Nouvelle YORK, la PENSILVANIE, MARY-LAND, la CAROLINE Septentrionale l'Ile de TERRE NEUVE, le GRAND BANC &c. I.Condet s. 574 × 525 mm.

[80] NOUVELLE CARTE PARTICULIÈRE de L'AMERIQUE ou sont exactement marquées les PROVINCES SUIVANTES comme la CAROLINE MERIDIONALE, la FLORIDE, la LOUISIANE, le MEXIQUE, le JUCATAN, le GUATIMALA, le DARIEN, & une Partie de CUBA.
[C:] A MAP of the BRITISH EMPIRE in AMERICA with the FRENCH, SPANISCH and the DUTCH SETTLEMENTS adjacent thereto by Henry Popple. at AMSTERDAM Printed for IOHN COVENS and CORNELIUS MORTIER. — 575 × 526 mm.

[81] NOUVELLE CARTE PARTICULIERE DE L'AMERIQUE OU SONT EXACTEMENT MARQUÉES LES ILES DE BERMUDE, LA IAMAIQUE, SAINT DOMINGUE, LES ANTILLES, LA TERRE FERME &c. I. Condet s. 572 × 523 mm.

[82] LES PRICIPALES FORTERESSES PORTS &c. DE L'AMÉRIQUE SEPTENTRIONALE.
[a] [C:] The Harbour of PLACENTIA — 81 × 149 mm.
[b] [C:] The Town and Harbour of CHARLES TOWN in SOUTH CAROLINA — 116 × 149 mm.
[c] [C:] FORT ROYAL in MARTINICA — 138 × 151 mm.
[d] [T:] CURACAO — 151 × 143 mm.
[e] [C:] The Harbour of ANAPOLIS ROYAL — 57 × 149 mm.
[f] [C:] HARBOUR of S[t] AUGUSTINE. — 74 × 74 mm.
[g] [C:] The Harbour of Providence. — 74 × 74 mm.
[h] [C:] The Island of BARBADOES. — 92 × 73 mm.
[i] [C:] ANTIGUA. — 92 × 76 mm.
[k] [C:] CARTAGENE on the Coast of NEW SPAIN. — 145 × 143 mm.
[l] [C:] BOSTON HARBOUR. — 141 × 149 mm.
[m] [C:] The HAVANA. — 83 × 73 mm.
[n] [C:] BAY of S[t] IAGO in CUBA. — 83 × 75 mm.

[o] [C:] KINGSTON HARBOUR in JAMAICA. — 102 × 145 mm.
[p] [C:] NEW YORK and PERTHAMBOY HARBOURS — 172 × 149 mm.
[r] [T:] A Plan of the Harbour of PORT ANTONIO in JAMAICA. — 150 × 150 mm.
[Inset:] [Port Antonio] (Plan). 66 × 46 mm.
[s] [C:] The BERMUDA or SUMMER ISLANDS. — 107 × 147 mm.
[t] [C:] HARBOUR of PORTO BELLO. — 156 × 150 mm.
[The whole map:] I.K.S. — 482 × 611 mm. See [77].

[83] [a] [C:] MEXICO. — (Plan). 120 × 271 mm.
[b] [C:] NEW YORK — (View). 120 × 266 mm.
[c] [T:] FALL of NIAGARA. — (View). 132 × 272 mm.
[d] [C:] QUEBEC. — (View). 132 × 266 mm.
See [77].

Notes: All the maps are blank on the back and coloured. The volume lacks a title-page; it begins with a plate 'SCHEMATISMVS GEOGRAPHIAE MATHEMATICAE, id est, repraesentatio figurarum, in quantum ad aliqualem globi terraquei et mapparum intelligentiam in gratiam juventutis erudiendae facere possunt, expositionem ipsarum tradente D$^{\underline{o}}$ Schazio in elementis Geographiae 1753. pro atlante scholastico conscriptis. Cura Homann. Heredum, Norimbergae Anno 1753.' More than half the maps are by Johannes Baptista Homann or his heirs, and the majority of the rest are by Seutter or Lotter. Short biographies of the Norwegian map-makers can be found in Engelstad's map catalogue, 'Norge i Kart gjennom 400 år'. The Popple maps, nos. [77—83], are from a Covens and Mortier atlas (Koeman, vol. 2, p. 60, C & M 8 (106—112)). 17 of the 18 maps on no. [82] are found reduced as insets on map [77], as are the four views from map [83]. Maps [69], [75] and [76] are inserted loosely into the volume. Map [15] bears a portrait of the Empress Anna of Russia. The atlas does not correspond with any of those described by Sandler; it is a made-up collection of maps which justifies treatment as a Homann atlas.

Lit.: Engelstad, p. 100 and 107, Koeman vol. 2, p. 60, C & M 8, maps (106—112), Sandler, Homann, and Homann heirs. Homann heirs.

93 **HOMANN, JOHANN BAPTIST** [1752?]

ATLAS NOVUS TERRARUM ORBIS IMPERIA, REGNA ET STATUS exactis Tabulis Geographice demonstrans, Opera IOHANNIS BAPTISTÆ HOMANNI Sacræ Cæs. Maj. Geographi, et Reg.^{iæ} Boruss. Societ. Scient. Membri NORIBERGÆ... ..
ATLAS COMPENDIARIVS QVINQVAGINTA SELECTARVM TABVLARVM GEOGRAPHICARVM HOMANNI, AD MENTEM RECENTIORVM GEOGRAPHORVM RECOGNITVS ET DISPOSITVS. ... Kleiner ATLAS von Homanns-Land-Karten/ Nach Anleitung Der neuesten Erd-Beschreibere verbessert und eingerichtet. ... Zu finden in Nürnberg in der Homännischen Officin. 52,3 cm.

[1] [C:] PLANISPHÆRIUM CÆLESTE. — (Celestial chart). Opera G.C.Eimmarti. prostat in Officina Homanniana. 484 × 566 mm. The spheres with 282 mm. diam.
[2] [C:] PLANIGLOBII TERRESTRIS CUM UTROQ HEMISPHÆRIO CÆLESTI GENERALIS REPRÆSENTATIO ... — = 1720—1771:[2].
[3] EL REYNO DE ESPANNA dividido en dos grandes Estados DE ARAGONY DE CASTILLA, subdividido en muchas Provincias, donde se halla tambien EL REYNO DE PORTVGAL.
[C:] REGNORUM HISPANIÆ et PORTUGALLIAE Tabula generalis ... — = 1736—1788:[16].
[4] CARTE de FRANCE, dressée par GVILLAVME DE L'ISLE, et accommodée par les Heritiers d'Homann. a l'intruction de la Jeunesse. Norimb. 1741 ...
[C:] REGNI GALLIAE seu FRANCIAE et NAVARRAE Tabula Geographica ... — = 1720—1771:[102].
[5] [C:] MAGNA BRITANNIA complectens ANGLIÆ, SCOTIÆ ET HIBERNIÆ REGNA in suas Provincias et Comitatus divisa repræsentante IO. BAPT. HOMANN NORIMBERG ... — 475 × 565 mm.
[6] [C:] TABULA GENERALIS TOTIUS BELGII qua PROVINCIÆ XVII. INFER. GERMANIÆ ... — = 1720—1771:[16].
[7] [C:] ARENA MARTIS IN BELGIO. QUA PROVINCIÆ X. CATHOLICÆ INFERIORIS GERMANIÆ ... — = 1720—1771:[17].
[8] [C:] BELGII PARS SEPTENTRIONALIS communi nomine Vulgo HOLLANDIA ... — = 1720—1771:[18].
[9] Tabula ad Geographiam Hübnerianam recentissime recognita nec minus passim aucta et religionum simul distinctione illustrata per HOMANNIANOS HEREDES. Anno 1732
[C:] Potentissimæ HELVETIORUM REIPUBLICÆ CANTONES TREDECIM ... — = 1736—1788:[27].
[10] Gli STATI d'ITALIA secondo le Osservationi, fatte dalla Societa de Sc. di Parigi dal R.P.Riccioli della S. die Gieusu ed, altri Astronomi, di prima geograficamente delineati dall'Eccell^{mo} Sg^{r} de l'Isle, ed accomodati agli Elementi Geografici, del Sg^{r}. Schaz; alle spese degl'Heredi d'Homañ. L Año MDCCXLII.
[C:] ITALIA ... — = 1720—1771:[106].
[11] [C:] REGIÆ CELSITUDINIS SABAUDICÆ STATUS in quo DUCATUS SABAUDIÆ PRINCIPATUS PEDEMONTIUM ET DUCATUS MONTISFERRATI ... — = 1720—1771:[119].
[12] [C:] DUCATUS MEDIOLANI ... — = 1736—1788:[25].
[13] [C:] STATUS ECCLESIASTICI MAGNIQUE DUCATUS FLORENTINI ... — = 1720—1771:[120].
[14] [C:] Novissima & exactissima TOTIVS REGNI NEAPOLIS TABVLA ... — = 1736—1788:[20].
[15] [C:] REGNORUM SICILIÆ ET SARDINIÆ nec non MELITÆ seu MALTÆ INSULA cum adjectis ITALIÆ et AFRICÆ LITORIBUS Nova Tabula Auctore IOH: BAPT: HOMANNO Geogra Norimbergæ ... — 485 × 574 mm.
[Insets:] [T:] CATANEÆ urbis eique vicini MONTIS ÆTNÆ in Sicilia prospectus — (Plan). 117 × 138 mm.
[T:] VALLETTA civitas Maltæ celeberrima, Melitensium Equitum Sedes primaria et propugnaculum adversus Turcas invictissimum. — 87 × 93 mm.
[16] L'ALLEMAGNE, distinguée en ses Cercles & subdivisée en ses Etats, contenant son Etendue presente, rectifiée & methodiquement enluminée suivant les Elements de Geographie de Mr. Schatz A. 1741 ...
[C:] IMPERII ROMANO-GERMANICI IN SVOS STATVS ET CIRCVLOS DIVISI TABVLA GENERALIS ... — = 1710—1750:[106] with small alterations.
[17] POSTARUM SEU VEREDARIORUM STATIONES PER GERMANIAM ET PROVINCIAS ADIACENTES
[C:] Neu vermehrte POST CHARTE durch gantz TEUTSCHLAND ... — = 1710—1750:[107].
[18] [C:] GERMANIA AUSTRIACA complectens S.R.I. CIRCULUM AUSTRIACUM ... — = 1720—1771:[93].
[19] La Cercle de BAVIERE, qui comprend la Regence d'Amberg, le Palatinat de Neuburg et le Sulzbach, le Landgrafiat de LEICHTENBERG le tout compris sous le nom de HAUT PALATINAT; encore le Duché ou l'Electorat de haute et basse BAVIERE, le Duche de NEUBURG, l'evêché de RATISBONNE, l'evêche de FREYSINGEN, l'evêché de PASSAU, l'Archevêche de SALTZBOURG, comme aussi la Prevauté de BERCHLOTSCADEN.
[C:] BAVARIÆ CIRCULUS et ELECTORAT$_9$ ... — = 1710—1750:[77].
[20] [C:] CIRCVLI SVEVIÆ MAPPA ... — = 1710—1750:[57].
[21] [C:] THEATRUM BELLI RHENANI ... — = 1710—1750:[50].
[22] ANDERER und MINDERE THEIL DES GANTZEN

HOCHLÖBL. FRÄNCKISCHEN CRAISSES, MIT WELCHEM ZUGLEICH DAS ERTZ-STIFT und CHURFÜRSTENTUM MAYNTZ SAMPT DENEN NOCH ÜBRIGE FRANCK: STAATEN als da seind die GRAFSCH. WERTHEIM REINECK und ERPACH nebst der angrentzenden NIDEREN CHUR PFALTZ am RHEIN in dieser Tafel angezeigt werden
[C:] ELECTORATUS MOGUNTINUS ... — = 1710—1750:[32]. See [25].

[23] [C:] EXACTISSIMA PALATINATUS AD RHENUM TABULA ... — = 1710—1750:[73].

[24] [C:] MOSELLÆ FLUMINIS TABULA SPECIALIS ... — = 1710—1750:[92].

[25] ERSTER UND GRÖSTER THEIL DES GANTZEN HOCHLÖBL: FRANCKISCHEN CRAISSES IN WELCHEM DIE BISTHUMER BAMBERG WÜRTZBURG UND AICHSTETT, die Marggr. CULMBACH und ONOLTZBACH das Hertzogt. COBURG, Fürstent. SCHWARTZENBERG, Graffsch. HOHENLO, CASTEL, LIMBURG und SEINSHEIM, das NÜRNBERGISCHE Gebiet und die Hälffte der angrenzenden OBERN PFALTZ mit vorgestelt werden.
[C:] CIRCULI FRANCONIÆ PARS ORIENTALIS ET POTIOR novissime delineata ... — = 1710—1750:[79]. See [22].

[26] [C:] CIRCULI WESTPHALIÆ ... — = 1710—1750:[26].

[27] [C:] DUCATUS IULIACI & BERGENSIS Tabula Geographica, ... — = 1710—1750:[14].

[28] [C:] CIRCULUS SAXONIÆ INFERIORIS ... — = 1710—1750:[71].

[29] [C:] DUCATUS LUNEBURGICI et COMITATUS DANNEBERGENSIS accurata Descriptio ... — = 1710—1750:[52].

[30] [C:] DUCATUS BRUNSUICENSIS ... — = 1710—1750:[42].

[31] [C:] TABVLA GENERALIS HOLSATIAE ... — = 1720—1771:[54].

[32] [C:] DUCATUS MEKLENBURGICI Tabula Generalis ... — = 1710—1750:[12].

[33] [C:] CIRCULI SUPE. SAXONIAE PARS MERIDIONALIS ... — = 1710—1750:[69].

[34] Multis in locis augmentata longeque priori Editione correctior facta hæc THURINGIÆ TABULA A. D. 1729 per Ioh. Christ. Homannum M.D. et Phys: Ord. ...
[C:] LANDGRAVIATUS THURINGIÆ TABULA GENERALIS ... — = 1710—1750:[60].

[35] [C:] TABULA MARCHIONATUS BRANDENBURGICI ET DUCATUS POMERANIÆ ... — = 1720—1771:[37].

[36] [C:] REGNI BOHEMIÆ, DUCATUS SILESIÆ, MARCHIONATUS MORAVIÆ et LUSATIÆ Tabula Generalis ... — = 1720—1771:[94].

[37] [C:] REGNI DANIAE in quo sunt DUCATUS HOLSATIA ET SLESVICUM, ... — = 1720—1771:[10] with small alterations.

[38] [C:] DUCATUS SLESVICENSIS ... — = 1720—1771:[12].

[39] [C:] REGNI POLONIÆ MAGNIQUE DUCATUS$_9$ LITHUANIÆ Nova et exacta tabula ad mentem STAROVOLCII descripta á IOH. BAPT. HOMANNO Sac. Cæs. Mai. Geographo Revisa et ad præsentem statum accomodata 1739. — 481 × 548 mm.

[40] [C:] REGNUM BORUSSIÆ ... — = 1710—1750:[4].

[41] [C:] IMPERII RUSSICI et TATARIAE UNIVERSAE tam majoris et Asiaticæ qvam minoris et Europææ TABVLA ... — = 1720—1771:[153].

[42] [C:] Fluviorum in Europa principis DANUBII CUM ADIACENTIBUS REGNIS ... — = 1720—1771:[125].

[43] [C:] VKRANIA quæ et TERRA COSACCORVM ... — = 1720—1771:[139].

[44] Tabula ex novissimis Relationibus ad mentem de L'Islii, inprimis vero celeberrimi Geographi, D^{ni} I.M.Hasii Prof. Vitemb. delineata.A.1737.
[C:] IMPERIUM TURCICUM in EUROPA, ASIA ET AFRICA ... — = 1720—1771:[158].

[45] [C:] Recentissima ASIAE Delineatio, ... — = 1720—1771:[156].

[46] [C:] IUDÆA SEU PALÆSTINA ob sacratissima Redemtoris vestigia hodie dicta TERRA SANCTA ... — = 1720—1771:[165].

[47] [C:] AFRICA Secundum legitimas Projectionis Stereographicæ regulas ... — = 1720—1771:[179].

[48] [C:] TOTIUS AMERICAE SEPTENTRIONALIS ET MERIDIONALIS NOVISSIMA REPRÆSENTATIO ... — = 1720—1771:[184].

Notes: All the maps are blank on the back and coloured. Our copy is incomplete: the 'Extractum Privilegii' and 'Introductio Geographica', listed at c. and d. in the index on the letterpress title-page, are both wanting, as are also maps 3, Europe, and 40, Regnum Sueciae. There is a German Register on the title-page, in addition to the Latin index. The coloured half-title is engraved by Mich. Rössler; it depicts part of a terrestrial globe, showing Europe and Africa. The maps are numbered in old ink on the recto, with a manuscript title in French; the first map is our no. [3], which is no. 4 of the complete volume and is numbered accordingly. In the cartouche of map [40] there is a portrait of 'FRIDERICVS REX BORUSIÆ, et El. Br.'; the words 'Rex Borusiae' replace some earlier title, no longer decipherable. The same cartouche contains also a small sketch-map of Brandenburg. The cartouche of map [41] contains a dedication to the Empress Anna of Russia, together with her portrait. The cartouche of map [5] contains the portrait of an unnamed person. All but two of the maps are signed by one of the Homanns or their heirs. Nordenskiöld's signature, with the date 1881, is on the first blank leaf.

Lit.: BM Maps, vol. 7, c. 623, Sandler, Die Homännischen Erben, p. 409.

94 HOMANN HEIRS 1753

ATLAS COMPENDIARIVS seu ita dictus SCHOLASTICVS MINOR in usum erudiendae juventutis adornatus. Excudentibus Homañianis Heredibus A. MDCCLIII.   55,2 cm.

[1] [C:] PLANIGLOBII TERRESTRIS Mappa Universalis Utrumq$_3$ Hemisphærium Orient et Occidentale repræsentans Ex IV. mappis generalibus, Hasianis, composita et adjectis ceteris hemisphærus designata a G. M. Lowizio Excudentibus Homann Heredibus. Cum Priv. S.Cæs.Maj. A MDCCXXXVI. Fig. I. dicitur Hemisphærium polare arcticum Fig. II. Hemisphærium polare antarcticum. Fig. III. Hemisphærium Sphæræ obliquæ pro horizonte Norimb. Fig. IV. ejus oppositum inferius cum Antipodibus Norimbergensibus. —
[C:] MAPPE-MONDE qui represente les deux Hemispheres savoir celui de l'Orient et celui de l'Occident tiree des quatre Cartes generales de feu M. le Profess. Hasius, dressée par M. G.M.Lowitz, et publiée par les Heritiers de Homann Avec Priv. de S.Maj.Imper l'An 1746. Fig. I. Hemisphere polaire Arctique. Fig. II. Hemisphere polaire Antarctique Fig. III. Hemisphere de la Sphere oblique pour l'Horizon de Nuremberg. Fig. IV. Les Antipodes de Nuremberg. — [T:] S. Dorn sculp. — 443 × 521 mm.
[a] [World] The hemispheres with 252 mm. diam.
[b] Fig. I. Circular map with 124 mm. diam.
[c] Fig. II. Circular map with 124 mm. diam.
[d] Fig. III. Circular map with 100 mm. diam.
[e] Fig. IV. Circular map with 100 mm. diam.
See 1720—1771:[3].

[2] L'EUROPE, dessinée Suivant les Regles le plus precises d'une nouvelle Projection Stereographique, tirée des Observations et des Relations les plus modernes et appuyée en divers endroits par des Monumens antiques. dresée et divisée methodiquement par Iean Matthias Has. Profess. Ordin. des Mathematiques, Publiée par les Heritiers d'Homann. l'An 1743 ...

[C:] EUROPA Secundum legitimas Projectionis Stereographicæ regulas et juxta recentissimas observationes æque ac relationes adhibitis queq3 veterum monumentorum subsidiis descripta et in partes suas methodicas X. divisa a IOH. MATTH. HASIO Math. P.P.O. edita Curis Homannianorum Heredum. — 460 × 535 mm. See 1720—1771:[4].

[3] L'ALLEMAGNE, distinguée en ses Cercles & subdivisée en ses Etats, contenant son Etendue presente, rectifiée & methodiquement enluminee suivant les Elements de Geographie de Mr. Schatz. A. 1741 ...
[C:] IMPERII ROMANO GERMANICI IN SVOS STATVS ET CIRCVLOS DIVISI TABVLA GENERALIS ... [T:] Dorn sc. — = 1710—1750:[106] with alterations.

[4] Carte des XVII. PROVINCES ou de L'ALLEMAGNE INFERIEVRE dressée suivant la Projection stereographique et appüyée par les mesures faites de Mess. Cassini, Snellius et Mouschenbrok, par M.r Tob. Majer de la Societé geographique et publiée par les Heritiers de Homann l'An 1748.
[C:] BELGII UNIVERSI seu INFERIORIS GERMANIAE quam XVII PROVINCIAE, Austriaco, Gallico et Batavo Sceptro parentes constituunt, nova Tabula Geographica a Tobia Majero Math. Cult. ad leges legitimae delineationis revocata Cura et Studio Homannianorum Heredum. ... A.o 1748. — 463 × 514 mm. See 1736—1788:[12].

[5] LA SVISSE, divisee en ses tréze CANTONS, ses Alliez et ses Sujets.
[C:] HELVETIA TREDECIM STATIBVS LIBERIS quos CANTONES vocant, composita. Una cum foederatis & subjectis Provinciis, ex probatissimis Subsidiis geographice delineata per D.M TOBIAM MAYERVM, Professorem Matth. Goettingensem. Luci publicae tradita ab HOMANNIANIS HEREDIBVS. Norimbergae A. 1751. — 419 × 534 mm.

[6] CARTE de FRANCE. dressee par GUILLAUME DE L'ISLE et accommodéé par les Heritiers d HOMANN a l'instruction de la Ieunesse Norimb. 1741.
[C:] REGNI GALLIAE seu FRANCIAE et NAVARRAE Tabula Geographica ... — = 1720—1771:[102] with small alterations.

[7] Gli STATI d'ITALIA secondo le Osservationi, fatte dalla Societa di Sc. di Parigi, dal R. P. Riccioli della S. die Gieusu ed; altri Astronomi, di prima geograficamente delineati dall'Eccell.mo Sg.r de l'Isle, ed accomodati agli Elementi Geografici, del Sg.r Schaz; alle spese degl' Heredi d'Homañ L Año MDCCXLII.
[C:] ITALIA in suos STATVS divisa ... — = 1720—1771:[106] with small alterations.

[8] A General Map of GREAT BRITAIN and IRELAND with Part of Holland, Flanders, France &c. Agreable to modern History By the Heirs of late M.r Homann, at Nuremberg.
[C:] MAGNA BRITANNIA complectens ANGLIAE, SCOTIAE et HYBERNIAE Regn in suas Prov. et Comitat. divisa et ex mappis Londinensibus designata per Homannianos Heredes. — 473 × 561 mm.
[Inset:] [C:] ORCADES INSVLÆ borealiores nec non Insul. SCHETLANDICÆ Secundum eandem mappæ principalis Scalam exhibitæ. — 140 × 160 mm. See 1736—1788:[8].

[9] Carte general d'ESPAGNE et de PORTVGAL divisée en ses provinces actuelles par D. T. Lopez, nouvellement dressée par F. L. G. à Nuremberg chez les Heret, de Homann l'an 1782.
[C:] Regnorum HISPANIÆ et PORTVGALLIÆ Tabula generalis ad statum hodiernum in suas Provincias divisa per D. T. Lopez in nonnullis emendavit F. L. Güssefeld. Edentibus Homannianis Hæredibus. MDCCLXXXII. ... — 460 × 589 mm.

[10] Carte des Etats de la COVRONNE de POLOGNE, nouvellement dessinee par M.r Tob. Mayer et publiee par les Heritiers de Homann. l'an MDCCLXXIII.
[C:] Mappa Geographica REGNI POLONIAE ex novissimis quotquot sunt mappis specialibus composita et ad L L. stereographica projectionis revocata a Tob. Mayero. S.C.S. Luci publicae tradita per Homannianos Heredes Norimb. A. MDCCLXXIII. ... — 440 × 504 mm. See 1720—1771:[132].

[11] [C:] Regnum BORUSSIAE Gloriosis auspicys Serenissimi et Potentissimi Princip FRIDERICI III PRIMI BORUSSIAE REGIS MARCH ET ELECT BRANDENBURG inauguratum die 18 Jan A 1701 Geographice cum vicinis Regionibus adumbratum a IOH BAPTISTA HOMANNO Norimbergae — 480 × 566 mm. See 1710—1750:[4].

[12] [C:] REGNI DANIAE in quo sunt DUCATUS HOLSATIA ET SLESVICUM ... — = 1720—1771:[10] with small alterations.

[13] [C:] SCANDINAVIA complectens SVECIÆ, DANIÆ et NORVEGIÆ REGNA ex novissimis subsidiis delineata et ad Leges Projectionis Stereographicae legitimae reducta ab AUGUSTO GOTTLOB BÖEHMIO Electoris Saxoniæ Cohortis Architecton Milit. Mathematico, Societatis oeconomicæ Lipsiensis membro honorario et Societatis Cosmographiæ Sodali Norimbergæ Cura HOMANNIANORUM HEREDUM. ... Anno 1776. — 477 × 546 mm.

[14] Carte generale d'Empire de Russie et de Tartarie grande et petite en Europe et Asie. — [C:] IMPERII RUSSICI et TATARIAE UNIVERSAE tam majoris et Asiaticæ quam minoris et Europææ TABVLA ex recentissimis et probatissimis monumentis et relationibus concinnata et ad legitimas projectionum Geographic. regulas plane exacta opera IOH. MATHIAE HASII Math. P. P. juncta Sciagraphia explicationis ejusdem et descriptionis Russiæ et Tatariæ universæ Geographico-historicæ. Impensis Homannianorum Heredum Norimbergæ ... — 467 × 534 mm. See 1720—1771:[106].

[15] Carte d'HONGRIE en general, contenant selon la Division ancienne & metodique, la HONGRIE en particulier, la CROATIE, la DALMATIE, la BOSNIE, la SERVIE, la BOULGARIE, la Principauté de TRANSYLVANIE, les Despotats de WALACHIE & de MOLDAV; le tout dressé sur le pied de l'ancienne et de la nouvelle Geographie par Mons. I. M. Hasius, Profess. des Mathemat.
[C:] HVNGARIAE ampliori significatu et veteris vel Methodicae complexae REGNA: ... — = 1710—1750:[83] with small alterations.

[16] [C:] IMPERII TVRCICI EVROPAEI TERRA, in primis CRAECIA ... — = 1720—1771:[123] with alterations.

[17] Carte de l'ASIE, projettée Stereographiquement, tirée des Relations et Observations, contenues dans les voyages modernes, de meme que dans les monumens des anciens, corrigée de tout ce qui sent la fable, et divisée en ses IX. Parties methodiques par le S.r I. M. HASIVS Prof. des Math. Recueilliée et dessinee sur ses morceaux posthumes par Aug. Gottl. Boehmius, Maitre es Arts aux Depens des Heritiers de Homann l'An. 1744.
[C:] ASIA secundum legitimas Projectionis Stereographicæ regulas... — [T:] Seb. Dorn sculps. — = 1720—1771:[157] with alterations.

[18] Carte de la TERRE SAINTE divisée selon les DOVZE TRIBVS D'ISRAEL revûe et augmentée par M.r Iean Christoph Harenberg Prevot et Professeur. Publiée par les soins des Heritiers de Homann. l'An 1750.
[C:] PALAESTINA in XII. TRIBVS divisa, CVM TERRIS ADIACENTIBVS denuo revisa & copiosior reddita Studio IOHANNIS CHRISTOPH. HARENBERGII Praep. S. Laur. Schening. Curantibus Homannianis Heredibus Norimb. A. 1750. — [C:] SERENISSIMO IVVENTVTIS PRINCIPI in spem successionis nato DOMINO, DOMINO CAROLO WILHELMO FERDINANDO progenito ex Ducibus Bruns vico-Luneburgicis, majorum gloria corusco, orbis delicio, Musarum honori dat, dicat, consecrat TANTO NOMINI Devotissimus Auctor. — 447 × 526 mm.
[Inset:] [T:] REGIVNCVLAE, in quas PALAESTINA olim fuit divisa, delineatae — 225 × 175 mm.

[19] [C:] AFRICA Secundum legitimas Projectionis Stereographicæ regulas et juxta recentissimas relationes et

observationes in subsidium vocatis quoque veterum Leonis Africani Nubiensis Geographi et aliorum monumentis et eliminatis fabulosis aliorum designationibus pro præsenti statu ejus aptius exhibita a IOH. MATTHIA HASIO M. P. P. O. h t. Facult. Phil. in Acad. Witeb. Decano Impensis Homannianorum Heredum. ... — [T:] D. A. Hauer sculp — 455 × 545 mm. See 1720—1771:[178].

[20] [C:] AMERICAE Mappa generalis Secundum legitimas projectionis stereographicæ regulas relationesque recentissimas et observationes sociorum Acad. reg: scquæ Parisiis est aliorumque auctorum necnon secundum mentem D. I. M. Hasii M. P P. in partes suas methodicas divisa nunc concinnata et delineata ab Aug. Gottl. Boehmio Phil Magistro In lucem proferentibus Homannianis Heredibus A. MDCCXXXVI. — 455 × 523 mm.

Notes: All the maps are blank on the back and coloured. The title-page is decorated with 28 coats-of-arms. Before the maps there is a table with the title: 'SCHEMATISMVS GEOGRAPHIAE MATHEMATICAE, id est, repraesentatio figurarum, in quantum ad aliqualem globi terraquei et mapparum intelligentiam in gratiam juventutis erudiendae facere possunt, expositionem ipsarum tradente D$\underline{o}$ Schazio in elementis Geographiae, 1753'. Sandler mentions this atlas on p. 405. There is a copy in the National Maritime Museum, Greenwich, which is described in the library's catalogue (vol. 3, part 1, p. 537); the entry states that most of the maps are from earlier atlases, but that two new ones are added. Map [9] in our copy, Regnorum Hispaniæ et Portugalliæ, is dated 1782, and replaces an earlier map of the same region by Seutter. Map [10] is a later issue of the map of Poland, dated 1773, and the map of Scandinavia, [13], is dated 1776; the title-page, however, still bears the date 1753. Nordenskiöld's signature is on the front cover.

Lit.: National Maritime Mus. Cat. vol. 3:1, Atlases, p. 357, Sandler p. 405.

95 HOMANN, JOHANN BAPTIST AND HEIRS 1762

ATLAS GERMANIAE SPECIALIS SEV SYSTEMA TABVLARVM GEOGRAPHICARVM, in qvibus IMPERIVM ROMANO-GERMANICVM generalibus repraesentationibus nec non ejus partes, quae sunt BOHEMICI STATVS ET CIRCVLI ditionesque in iis comprehensae, ecclesiasticae et seculares, nimirum Electoratus, Principatus, Comitatus etc. specialibus delineationibus exhibentur. Opus inceptum a IOH. BAPT. HOMANNO, et ad hunc usque diem ab Homannianis Heredibus studiose continuatum. Appellatum alias TOMVS SECVNDVS ATLANTIS MAIORIS. Prostat in Officina Homanniana. Norimbergae A. MDCCLIII. I.G. Ebersperger sculp.
[Title-page:]
Kurze Nachricht von dem neuesten Homännischen Atlas von Deutschland, von desselben Zuverlässigkeit / Art der Zusammensetzung/ Fortsetzung und Gebrauch/ auch übrigen dahin gehörigen Vorschlägen und Absichten/ deme beygefüget ist eine ausführliche Verzeichnis aller und jeder Reichs-Stände, wie sich selbige in die Reichskreise einthielen/ und bey den Kreisstägen ihr Sitz- und Stimm-Recht behaupten. Ans Licht gestellt von den Homännischen Erben in Nürnberg. M D C C L I I I.
[Engraved title-page:]
ATLAS HOMANNIAVS Mathematico-Historice delineatus. I.Iust.Preisler del. 1762. Andr. Hoffer sculps. 54,3 cm.

[1] L'ALLEMAGNE, distinguée en ses Cercles & subdivisée en ses Etats, contenant son Etendue presente, rectifiée & methodiquement enluminée suivant les Elements de Geographie de Mr. Schatz.
[C:] IMPERII ROMANO-GERMANICI IN SVOS STATVS ET CIRCVLOS DIVISI TABVLA GENERALIS ... — = 1710—1750:[106] with alterations.

[2] L'ALLEMAGNE, distinguée en ses Cercles & subdivisée en ses Etats, contenant son Etendue presente, rectifiée & methodiquement enluminée suivant les Elements de Geographie de Mr. Schatz.
[C:] GERMANIA ECCLESIASTICA seu IMPERIVM ROMANO-GERMANICVM in suas tam seculares quam Ecclesiastica ditiones concinnis coloribus peculiariter distinctum et exhibitum in Officina Homanniana. — 456 × 536 mm. = [1] in this ed. with a new text in the cartouche.

[3] [C:] Tabula Geographica TOTIUS GERMANIÆ qua DIFFERENTIUM IMPERII TRIUM RELIGIONUM STATUS ET DOMINIA diversis coloribus distincta exhibentur à IOH: BAPT: HOMANNO Sac: Cæs: Maj: Geographo et Reg: Borus: Societatis Scientiarum Membro. — 482 × 556 mm.

[4] [C:] GERMANIA BENEDICTINA qvæ in illa sunt Monasteria Ord. S. BENEDICTI monstrans, exacte ita delineata per P.R.C.P.W.C.B.S. excusa studio et sumtibus. HOMANNIANORUM HEREDUM Norib. A. M D C C XXXII. — 460 × 563 mm.
[Inset:] [C:] Appendix Monasteriorum Ord. S.Bened. quæ extant in Poloniâ et Lithuania. — 105 × 106 mm.

[5] POSTARUM SEU VEREDARIORUM STATIONES PER GERMANIAM ET PROVINCIAS ADIACENTES
[C:] Neu vermehrte POST CHARTE durch gantz TEUTSCHLAND ... — = 1710—1750:[107].

[6] [C:] HYDROGRAPHIA GERMANIÆ qua GEOGRAPHIAE NATURALIS ea pars quæ de Aquis celebrioribus,... — = 1710—1750:[108].

[7] CARTE CRITIQVE DE L'ALLEMAGNE, faite suivant un nouveau Dessein appujé des monumens authentiques du tems ancien et nouveau, avec une comparaison de celui de M^r de l'Isle et de Homann. Dressée par Mr Tob. Mayer, de la Société cosmographique. Publiée par les Heritiers de Homann l'an 1750.
[C:] GERMANIAE ATQVE IN EA LOCORVM PRINCIPALIORVM MAPPA CRITICA, ... — Videantur de hac mappa Ephemerides Cosmographicæ vel Kosmographische Nachrichten pag. 353. = 1710—1750:[104].

[8] Carte des ÉTATS DE BOHEME, avec le Souverain DVCE DE SILESIE, publiee par les Heritiers de Homañ, l'An 1748:
[C:] REGNI BOHEMIAE, DVC. SILESIAE, MARCHIONATVVM MORAVIAE et LVSATIAE Tabula generalis ... — = 1710—1750:[88].

[9] le Royaume de BOHEME divise en XII Cercles appellés 1) Saatz, 2) Leitmeritz, 3) Bunzel, 4) Kœnigsgrætz, 5) Chrudim 6) Czaslau 7) Kaurzim, 8) Rakonitz 9) Pilsen, 10) Beraun 11) celui de Prachin 12) celui de Bechin. d'ou appartient aussi le Comte de Glatz & le pays d Eger tire d'une Carte faite p. M Müller.
[C:] BOHEMIAE REGNUM in XII Circulos divisum ... — = 1710—1750:[89].

[10] DIE GEGEND um PRAG, oder der alte PRAGER KREYS, nebst den angränzenden Landschafften des Rakonizer, Boleslawer u. Kaurzimer Cr. Aus dem Müllerischen und andern Originalen genom̅en u. ans Tagslicht gestellt von Hom. Erb. A. 1742. Les ENVIRONS de PRAGVE, ou sont marqués les limites des Cercles et des Provinces selon la Carte de M^r· Müller et selon la Division ancienne de l'Institution de CHARLES IV: Dessinés par les Heritiers d'Homañ. A. MDCCXLII. = 1710—1750:[85].

[11] Carte du Diocese de BRESLAV, avec ses IV. Archidiaconats, subdivisés en ses Cercles Archipresbyteriales dessinée sous la Direction du bien reverend Sieur de Felbiger, par les Heritiers de Homann. l'An MDCCLI.
[C:] Reverendissimo et Celsissimo PRINCIPI ET DOMINO DOMINO PHILIPPO GOTTHARDO PRINCIPI DE SCHAFFGOTSCH Episcopo Wratislaviensi Principi Nissensi et Duci Gottkoviensi Ordinis nigrae aquilae Borussicae Equiti et Ducal. Canoniae ad D. Virg. in Arena Wraae Ord. S. August. Can. Reg. Lateran. ABBATI AC DOMINO universam Dioecesim suam in persona Clementissime visitanti pro perennatura pastoralis hujus

[12] sollicitudinis Canoniae quoq₃ Saganensi exhibitae memoria AMPLISSIMI EPISCOP. WRATISLAVIENSIS Tabulam hanc Geographicam profundissima cum Veneratione D. D. D. Subjectissimus Ignatius Felbiger, Ord. S. Aug. Can. Reg. ad D. Virg. Sagan. — 470 × 534 mm.

[12] LA COMTÈ DE GLATZ avec le Principauté de MVNSTERBERG dressée sur des dessins Autographes par Tob. Mayer, aux depans des Heritiers de Homann à Nüremberg. 1747.
[C:] COMITATUS GLACIENSIS Tabula Geogr. ex autographis delineationibus depromta Edentibus Homannianis Heredibus A. 1747. — 456 × 543 mm.

[13] [C:] TABULA GENERALIS MARCHIONATUS MORAVIÆ IN SEX CIRCULOS DIVISÆ ... — = 1710—1750:[87].

[14] 79 CIRCULI OLOMUCENSIS PARS BOREALIS. (The map is a continuation of [15].) 465 × 578 mm.

[15] 80 CIRCULI OLOMUCENSIS PARS AUSTRALIS
[C:] MARCHIONATÛS MORAVIAE CIRCULUS OLOMUCENSIS quem MANDATO CÆSAREO accuratè emensus hac mappa delineatum exhibet Io. Chr. Müller S.C.M. Cap. et Ingen: Editore Ioh. Baptista Homann Norimbergæ. — (The map is a continuation of [14]). 456 × 574 mm.

[16] 81 CIRCULI PREROVIENSIS PARS BOREALIS
[C:] MARCHIONATUS MORAVIÆ CIRCULUS PREROVIENSIS Quem MANDATO CÆSAREO accurate emensus hac mappa delineatum publice exhibet Io. Chr. Müller S.C.M. Capitan Editore Io. Baptista Homanno Noribergæ. — (The map is a continuation of [17]). 466 × 572 mm.

[17] 82. CIRCULI PREROVIENSIS PARS AUSTRALIS (The map is a continuation of [16]). 463 × 570 mm.

[18] 83. CIRCULI BRUNNENSIS PARS SEPTENTRIONALIS.
[C:] MARCHIONATÛS MORAVIÆ CIRCULUS BRUNNENSIS quem MANDATO CÆSAREO accuratè emensus hac mappa delineatum exhibet I. C. Müller S.C.M. Capit. et Ingen. Editore Ioh. Baptista Homanno Noribergæ. — (The map is a continuation of [19]). 475 × 595 mm.

[19] 84. CIRCULI BRUNNENSIS PARS MERIDIONALIS. (The map is a continuation of [18]). 473 × 592 mm.

[20] 85. [C:] MARCHIONATÛS MORAVIÆ CIRCULUS HRADISTIENSIS quem MANDATO CÆSAREO accurate emensus hac mappa delineatum exhibet Ioh. Christ. Müller S.C M. Capitan. Editore Ioh. Baptista Homanno Noribergæ. — 484 × 579 mm.

[21] 86 [C:] MARCHIONATUS MORAVIÆ CIRCULI ZNOYMENSIS ET IGLAVIENSIS quos MANDATO CÆSAREO accuratè emensus hâc Mappâ delineatos exhibet Io. Chr Müller S.C.M. Capitan Editore Io. Baptista Homanno Noribergæ. — 484 × 582 mm.

[22] [C:] TOTIUS MARCHIONATUS LUSATIAE tam superioris quam inferioris Tabula specialis ... — = 1710—1750:[7] with small alterations.

[23] [C:] LUSATIAE SUPERIORIS Tabula Chorographica ... — = 1710—1750:[8].

[24] Geographische Verzeichnung des BVDISSINISCHEN CREISES in dem Marggrafthum OBER LAVSITZ, aus zuversichtlichen geodetischen Zeichnungen genom̄en und ans Licht gestellet von Homænnischen Erben. Anno 1746. Carte du CERCLE de BVDISSIN dans le Marggrafiat de la HAVTE LVSACE, tirée des Morceaux geometriquement levés. Publiée par les Heritiers de Homann. l'An 1746. = 1720—1771:[27].

[25] LA PARTIE ORIENTALE DE MARGGRAVIAT DE LA HAVTE LVSACE L'AN 1753.
[C:] Geographische Verzeichnung des GOERLIZER CREISES mit dem QVEISS-CREISE welches zusammen ist der Ostliche Theil von dem Marggrafthum OBER LAVSIZ Herausgegeben von Homaennischen Erben. Anno 1753. — 510 × 451 mm.

[26] Le CERCLE D'AVTRICHE consistant dans l'Archiduché d'Autriche le Duché de Stirie, de Carinthie, de Carniole, dans la Comté de Tyrol, et les Pais Autrichiens Anterieurs dans la Souabe, avec ses confins dessiné avec justesse par Tobie Maier, Mathematicien, aux depens des Heritiers de Homann. 1747.
[C:] S. R. I. CIRCVLVS AVSTRIACVS ... — = 1710—1750:[101].

[27] [C:] ARCHIDUCATUS AUSTRIAE SUPERIORIS in suas Quadrantes Ditiones exacte divisi accuratissima Tabula ... — = 1710—1750:[103].

[28] LA BASSE AVTRICHE, qui se divise en 4. Quartiers qui sont 1) la superieure Manhardsberg 2) l'inferieure Manhardsberg 3) la superieure Wienerwald, 4) l'inferieure Wienerwald.
[C:] ARCHIDUCATUS AUSTRIAE INFERIORIS ... — = 1710—1750:[102].

[29] Chorographia VI. milliarium Regionis circa Vrbem VIENNAM Austriacam, deprompta ex mappa majori Vischeriana, et ad praesentem statum, uti Dominium minus eminens A. 1734. se habebat, accommodata per Homannianos Heredes. A. 1748. = 1720—1771:[29].

[30] [C:] DUCATUS STIRIÆ NOVISSIMA TABULA ... — = 1710—1750:[97].

[31] [C:] Nova et accurata CARINTHIÆ DUCATUS Tabula geographica, ... — = 1710—1750:[96].

[32] [C:] Tabula DUCATUS CARNIOLIÆ VINDORUM MARCHIÆ et HISTRIÆ ... — = 1710—1750:[95].

[33] [C:] COMITATUS PRINCIPALIS TIROLIS ... — = 1710—1750:[93].

[34] [C:] S. R. I. CIRCULUS RHENANUS INFERIOR SIVE ELECTORUM RHENI ... — = 1710—1750:[54].

[35] ANDERER und MINDERE THEIL DES GANTZEN HOCHLÖBL. FRÄNCKISCHEN CRAISSES, MIT WELCHEM ZUGLEICH DAS ERTZ-STIFT und CHURFÜRSTENTUM MAYNTZ SAMPT DENEN NOCH ÜBRIGE FRÄNCK: STAATEN als da seind die GRAFSCH. WERTHEIM REINECK und ERPACH nebst der angrentzenden NIDEREN CHUR PFALTZ am RHEIN in dieser Tafel angezeigt werden
[C:] ELECTORATUS MOGUNTINUS ... — = 1710—1750:[32]. See [67].

[36] [C:] MOSELLÆ FLUMINIS TABULA SPECIALIS ... — = 1710—1750:[92], but without I.M. Seeligman fecit.

[37] [C:] ARCHIEPISCOPATUS et ELECTORATUS COLONIENSIS ... — = 1710—1750:[22].

[38] [C:] EXACTISSIMA PALATINATUS AD RHENUM TABULA,...— = 1710—1750:[73].

[39—42] [C:] EIN THEIL des HUNDSRUCKS mit den angrænzenden Maynz- u. Trierischen Lændern in IV Sectionen Worinen die Marche u Lager der Kayserl. u. Reichs-Armee unter Com̄ando des Herrn General-Feld-Zeug-M. Grafen von SECKENDORF von Mayntz uber den Hundsruck nach der Mosel gegen Trier u. das Luxemburgische A.1735. vom M. Oct. biss zuer folgten Stillstand angezeiget. Mit Vorwissen hochged. Ihro Hochgr. Excell. aus Dero Cantzley com̄unicirt, u. in Verlag gegeben an die Homænnisch: Erben. —
[39] SECTIO. IV. 324 × 431 mm.
[40] SECTIO. III. 321 × 420 mm.
[41] SECTIO. II. 322 × 438 mm.
[42] SECTIO. I. 321 × 451 mm.

[43] [C:] CIRCULI SUPE. SAXONIAE PARS MERIDIONALIS... Per Homannianos Heredes. A. MDCCLVII. — = 1710—1750:[69], but the year altered.

[44] Mappa Geographica exhibens DVCATVM SAXONIAE Specialiter Sumtum, et qui Praerogativa Electorali gaudet, seu Circuli Electoralis nomine insignitur, Iunctis inserto tractu Gomern ex terris Burggr. Magdeburgici, nec non seudis Comit. Barby et Dynastiæ Baruth. Ex manuscriptis Delineationibus desumta et quatuor sectionibus in unum folium jungendis edita. Curis Homañianorum Heredum. Norimb. A.1752.
SECTIO I. cum parte Septentrionali versus Occidentem, ubi Praefectura Belzig, Praefectura Gomern et Comit. Barby cum parte boreali Circuli Vitembergensis, nec non confiniis Anhaltinis, Magdeburgius et mediae Marchiae

repræsentantur. (The map is a continuation of [45], [46] and [47]). 314 × 460 mm.

[45] Carte Geographique, ou on fait voir le DVCHE de SAXONIE nomē le CERCLE ELECTORALE, cest à dire, les Terres aux quelles la Dignité Electorale de Saxe est attacheè. Avec la Terre incorporèe de Gomern et les Terres feodales du Comtè de Barby et de la Dynastie de Baruth. Dessinèe suivant les Cartes msctes. Publièe par les Heritiers de Homañ 1752.
SECTIO II. cum parte Septentrionali versus Orientem, ubi videntur Praefectura Iuterbock, Praefectura Daahme, Dynastia Baruth cum boreali parte Praefect. Seidæ et circuli Vitemb. orientalis Cum confiniis mediæ marchiæ et Lusatiae inferioris. (The map is a continuation of [44], [46] and [47]). 313 × 458 mm.

[46] DVCATVS SAXONIAE, dicti CIRCVLI ELECTORALIS SECTIO III. vers. merid. et Occ. exhibens Praefecturam Bitterfeld et Praefecturam Graefenhainchen, cum maxima parte Circuli Witembergensis, et cum Confiniis Principatus Anhaltini, et Circuli Lipsiensis. Curis Homannianorum Heredum A. 1752.
[C:] Besondere Land Karte des HERZOGTH. od. CHVRKREISES SACHSEN Welcher aus den Aemtern Annaberg, Beltzig, Bitterfeld, Græfenhainchen, Liebenwerda, Pretsch Seyda, Schlieben, Schweiniz, Daame, Iuterbock, Gomēn u. Creis Amt Witemberg. zusamēn gesezet ist. Nebst den Grafsch. Barby u. Baruth wie auch die Herrsch. Sonnewalde. Ans Licht gestellt von Homaennischen Erben. A. 1752. ... — 314 × 462 mm. (The map is a continuation of [44], [45] and [47]).

[47] DVCATVS SAXONIAE, dicti CIRCVLI ELECTORALIS SECTIO IV. versus merid. et Orientem repraesentans Praefecturam Schweinitz, Praefecturam Annaburg, Praefecturam Schlieben, Praefecturam Pretzsch et Praefecturam Liebenwerda, cum parte Circuli Vitembergensis, una cum Dynastia Sonnenwalde et confiniis Lusatiae Superioris, nec non Circuli Missnensis. Curis Homannian. Heredum A. 1752. (The map is a continuation of [44], [45] and [46]). 313 × 459 mm.

[48] [C:] DUCATUS SAXONIAE SUPERIORIS prout ipsius conditio fuit ab Anno 1000 ... — = 1710—1750:[67].

[49] [C:] DUCATUS SAXONIAE SUPERIORIS ut status ipsius antiquissimus fuit per secula X priora, ... — = 1710—1750:[66].

[50] [C:] CARTE ITINERAIRE par le Pays de l'ELECTORAT DE SAXE faisant voir les GRANDS CHEMINS depuis LIPSIC jusqu' aux Villes les plus principales des Pays Circonvoisins, faite en faveur du Commerce & publièe par les soins des Heritiers de Homann. l'An 1752. ... —
[C:] HOHE HEERSTRASSE durch das Chur Fürst. SACHSEN. Wie selbige aus Polen u. Schlesien in die Lande Thüringen, Sachsen, Meissen u. so ferner gehen soll; ingeɭ wie Sie auf unterschiedɭ Art zu Wasser und Land umfahren wird. entworfen von I. C. K. Reichenb. Varisco 1728. — 456 × 562 mm.

[51] Carte du CONSISTOIRE de WITTEBERG, avec ses Dioceses et Paroisses, dediée à Son ALTESSE ROIALE Monseigneur le PRINCE FREDERIC CHRETIEN LEOPOLD PRINCE ROIAL et ELECTORAL et DVC de SAXE $_{gg}$ par son tres-soumis et tres-obeïssant serviteur Iean Ehrenfried Vierenklee l'An MDCCXXXXIX.
[C:] REGIAE CELSITVDINI SERENISS. PRINCIPI AC DNO FRIDER. CHRISTIANO LEOPOLDO ... — = 1710—1750:[59].

[52] Multis in locis augmentata longeque priori Editione correctior facta hæc THURINGIÆ TABULA A.º D. 1729 per Ioh. Christ. Homannum M.D. et Phys: Ord.
[C:] LANDGRAVIATVS THURINGIÆ TABULA GENERALIS ... — = 1710—1750:[60].

[53] [C:] NOVA TERRITORII ERFORDIENSIS IN SUAS PRÆFECTURAS accurate devisi descriptio Auctore IOH. BAPT. HOMANNO Noriberge Anno 1762. — 465 × 565 mm. See 1710—1750:[23].

[54] [C:] TABULA GEOGRAPHICA in qua Serenissimi Principis FRIDERICI Duc Sax. Iuliæ, Cliviæ et Montium, nec non Angariæ et Westphaliæ PRINCIPATVS GOTHA, COBVRG ET ALTENBURG ... — = 1710—1750:[38].

[55] [C:] PRINCIPATUS ISENACENSIS ... — = 1710—1750:[39].

[56] SECTIO SVPERIOR THVRINGIAE ORIENTALIS, in qva COMITATVS SCHWARZBVRGICVS SVPERIOR, DYNASTIAE BLANCKENHAYN, KRANICHFELD, REMDA, reliqva, cvm confiniis Dvcatus GOTHANI et OSTERLANDIAE geographice repræsentantur.
[C:] Regiæ Celsitudini Serenissimo Principi ac Domino FRIDERICO CHRISTIANO LEOPOLDO, Principi Regio Poloniæ et Lithuaniæ, Principi Electorali et Duci Saxoniæ, Iuliaci, Cliviæ et Montium, Angriæ quoque et Westphaliæ, Landgravio Thuringiæ, Marchioni Misniæ et Lusatiæ Superioris ac Inferioris, Burggravio Magdeburgico, Principi Comiti Hennebergensi, Comiti Marcæ, Ravensbergæ, Barby et Hanoviæ, Dynastæ Ravensteinii, Principi Electorali et Domino suo longe clementissimo THVRINGIAE ORIENTALIS Tabulam hanc Geographicam summa mentis devotione consecrat subjectissimus devotissimusque servus Iohannes Wilhelmus Zollmann. Curantibus Homannianis Heredibus. A. 1747. — Christ. Fridr. Oetinger sculps. Norib. 323 × 465 mm.

[57] SECTIO INFERIOR, DVCATVM VINARIENSEM, nec non ISENACENSIS Partes Boreales et Orientales, PRINCIPATVM QVERFVRTENSEM, ut et Territorium ERFVRTENSE, COMITATVM BEICHLINGEN, Balifiatum THVRINGIAE et alia repræsentans. 324 × 466 mm.

[58] [C:] Serenissimo Principi ac Domino, Domino ERNESTO FRIDERICO Duci Saxoniæ, Iuliaci, Cliviæ et Montium, nec non Angriæ et Westph, Landgrav. Thuringiæ, Marchioni Misniæ, Princ. Comiti Hennebergæ, Comiti Culenburgi, Marcæ et Ravenspergæ, Dño Ravensteinij etc etc. Principi ac Domino suo Clementissimo hanc EJUSDEM PRINCIPATUS SAXO-HILDBURGHUSIAM Novam et exactam tabulam submississime DDD. IOANNES BAPT. HOMANN S.C M. Geographus et Reg. Boruss. Societatis Scientiarum Memb. Norimbergæ. — 476 × 568 mm.
[Inset:] [C:] PLAN Der Hoch-Fürstlichen Residenz-Stadt HILDBURGHAUSEN. — (Plan). 174 × 225 mm.

[59] [C:] Chorographia Territorii NAUMBURGO-CITIENSIS Episcopatus ... — = 1710—1750:[37].

[60] [C:] COMITATUS STOLBERGICI ... — = 1710—1750:[40].

[61] [C:] Delineatio Geographica TERRITORII Celsissimorum S.R.I. COMITUM RUTHENORUM de PLAUEN utriusque Lineae Senioris nempe ac Iunioris partem VOGTLANDIAE olim ac hodie sic dictae constituentis. Impensis Homannianorum Heredum. — 477 × 538 mm.

[62] [C:] TABVLA MARCHIONATVS BRANDENBVRGICI ET DVCATVS POMERANIÆ ... — = 1710—1750:[3] with small alterations.

[63] [C:] DUCATUS POMERANIÆ novissima Tabula ... — = 1710—1750:[10].

[64] [C:] INSULÆ ET PRINCIPATUS RUGIÆ ... — = 1710—1750:[9].

[65] Die GRAFSCHAFT MANSFELD Königl. Preuss. und Churfürstl. Sächsischen Antheils mit allen darinnen befindlichen Städten, Dorfschaften, Kupferhütten, Bergwerks-Stollen, Berg-Gränzen und Holzungen.
[C:] COMITATVS MANSFELD prout ille juris hodie Saxonico-Electoralis et Magdeburgici, atque adeo secundum statum novissimum se habet, geographice ab anonymo delineatus. Ad normam legitimæ designationis reductus a Tob. Majero. Curantibus Homañianis Heredibus A. MDCCL. — Emendatior rèddita studio Domini Biringii reverendi & de Geographia patria bene merentis pastoris in terris Mansfeldensibus M.Aug. 1751. 447 × 531 mm.

[66] CARTE ITINERAIRE depuis DRESDE à WARSOVIE par deux Routes differentes. La seconde feuille pour un ATLAS DE VOYAGEVR, qu' on va construire à Nuremberg par les Heritiers de Homan. l'An 1751.
[C:] POLNISCHE REISE KARTE über die vornehmsten

Passagen von DRESDEN nach WARSCHAU auf zweyerley Wegen I) über Breslau, Peterkau und II) über Lissa, Kalicz Aus Zürnerischen u. andern Nachrichten geographisch entworffen von Homännischen Erben 1751. Zweytes Blat des REISE ATLAS. —
[a] 194 × 340 mm.
[b] 194 × 338 mm.

[67] ERSTER UND GRÖSTER THEIL DES GANTZEN HOCHLÖBL: FRANCKISCHEN CRAISSES IN WELCHEM DIE BISTHUMER BAMBERG WÜRTZBURG UND AICHSTETT, die Marggr. CULMBACH und ONOLTZBACH das Hertzogt. COBURG Fürstent. SCHWARTZENBERG, Graffsch. HOHENLO, CASTEL LIMBURG und SEINSHEIM, das NÜRNBERGISCHE Gebiet und die Hälffte der angrenzenden OBERN PFALTZ mit vorgestelt werden.
[C:] CIRCULI FRANCONIÆ PARS ORIENTALIS ET POTIOR novissime delineata ... — = 1710—1750:[79]. See 35.

[68] = [35] in this ed.

[69] [C:] SAC. ROM. IMPERII PRINCIPATUS & EPISCOPATUS BAMBERGENSIS Nova Tabula Geographica ... — = 1710—1750:[98].

[70] [C:] DUCATUS FRANCIÆ ORIENTALIS seu SAC. ROM. IMPerij PRINCIPATUS et EPISCOPATUS HERBIPOLENSIS Vulgo WÜRTZBURGENSIS ... — = 1710—1750:[28].

[71] [C:] S. R. I. PRINCIPATUS et EPISCOPATUS EISTETTENSIS ... — = 1710—1750:[27].

[72] [C:] PRINCIPATVS BRANDENBVRGICO-CVLMBACENSIS vel BARVTHINVS Tabvla Geographica qvoad Partem Svperiorem expressvs. delineata à Mathæo Ferdinand Cnopf et emendata de Paulo Daniel Longolio, edentibus Homannianis Heredibus. — ... = 1710—1750:[44] with a new text in the cartouche.

[73] Karte der Gefürsteten GRAFFSCHAFT HENNEBERG, mit dem angränzenden FVRSTENTH. COBVRG u. andern GRAENZLAENDERN, nach authentischen Documenten und Nachrichten verfertiget, und in ihre Aembter eingetheilet. Herausgegeben von Homännischen Erben in Nürnberg. A. 1743.
[C:] S. R. I. COMITATVS HENNEBERG secundum Præfecturas & modernas Dynastias ... — = 1710—1750:[19].

[74] La Comté de Hohenloh, avec les Pays, qui y confinent.
[C:] Serenissimis PRINCIPIBVS ac Dominis ab Hohenloh, Dynastis in Langenburg, nec non Celsissimis COMITIBVS ac Dominis ab Hohenloh et Gleichen, Dynastis in Langenb. et Cranchfeld etc. Dominis meis Clementissimis, COMITATVS HOHENLOICI Tabulam hanc Geographicam humillime dicat, dedicat Auctor devotissimus Ioh. Carolus Schapuzet. Excudentib$_9$ Homannianis Heredibus A. 1748. — 467 × 568 mm.
[Insets:] [C:] Die in der Land-Grafschft Thüringen liegende und dem Hochgræfl. Hauss Hohenloh-Neuenstein gehörige obere Grafschaft Gleichen. — 147 × 100 mm.
[C:] Die in Nieder Elsass liegende Hochfürstl. Hohenloh-Bartensteinische und Hochgræfl. Leiningische gemeinschaftliche Aempter Ober- und Nieder-Brunn. — 100 × 105 mm.

[75] [C:] COMITATUS LIMPVRGENSIS Mandato Speciali imperantium mensuratus & hac Tabula geographica comprehensus In lucem prodit Curis Homannianorum Heredum Norimb. 1749. — 447 × 525 mm.

[76] [C:] Geographica Descriptio MONTANI CUIUSDAM DISTRICTUS IN FRANCONIA in quo ILLUSTRISSIMORUM S R I COMITUM a GIECH PARTICULARE TERRITORIUM cum incorporatis Præfecturis Pagis ac Pertinentiis, quæ partim in suo proprio partim in alieno finitimorum S.R.I. utpote Circ. Franc. Directorum Principum Territorio sitæ sunt Auspiciis Illustrissimi S.R.Imp. Comitis ac Domini D^{ni} CAROLI GODOFREDI COMITIS à GIECH Dynastæ in Thurnavia et Buchavia æri incisa. — 481 × 561 mm.
[Inset:] [T:] THURNAU — (View). 68 × 151 mm.

[77] [C:] DELINEATIO NORDGOVIÆ VETERIS prout ejus facies SECULO XI. & XII. fuit, Geographice designata per IOHANNEM HENRICVM de FALCKENSTEIN C. A. B. O ac In Lucem emissa sumptibus Homannianorum Heredum Norib. 1733. — 460 × 558 mm.
[Inset:] [C:] Conspectus Fossæ Carolinæ pro conjungendo Danubio & Rheno. — 134 × 170 mm.

[78] La Cercle de BAVIERE qui comprend la Regence d'Amberg le Palatinat de Neuburg et de Sulzbach le Landgrafiat de LEICHTENBERG le tout compris sous le nom de HAUT PALATINAT: encote le Duche ou l'Electorat de haute et basse BAVIERE le Duche de NEUBURG, l'eveché de RATISBONNE, l'evèché de FREYSINGEN, l'evèché de PASSAU l'Archeveche de SALTZBOURG, comme aussi la Prevaute de BERCHLOTSCADEN
[C:] BAVARIÆ CIRCULUS et ELECTORAT$_9$ ... — = 1710—1750:[77].

[79] LA HAVTE BAVIERE, divisée en deux grandes Regences (1 de MUNCHEN, subdivisée en 38. Baillages; et 2) là Regence de BURCKHAVSEN, subdivisée en 21. Baillages.
[C:] BAVARIÆ PARS SUPERIOR ... — = 1710—1750:[76].

[80] LA BASSE BAVIERE, divisée en 2: Regences: 1) de LANDSHUT, subdivisée en 21. Baillages; et la Regence de STRAVBING, subdivisée en 24. Baillages.
[C:] BAVARIAE PARS INFERIOR ... — = 1710—1750:[75].

[81] HAUT PALATINAT, ou la Partie Septentrionale du Cercle de BAVIERE
[C:] PALATINATUS BAVARIÆ vulgo DIE OBERE PFALTZ ... — = 1710—1750:[74].

[82] [C:] Carte des ENVIRONS de MVNICH la Capitale de Baviere, dessinée suivant le dernier Etât, Nuremberg par les Heritiers de Homan.   KARTE von der GEGEND um MVNCHEN, der Haupt Stadt im Herzoghth: BAYREN, nach dem neuesten Staat entworfen u. herausgegeben von Homænischen Erben. A^o 1743. — 441 × 520 mm.

[83] [C:] S. R. I. PRINCIPATVS et ARCHIEPISCOPATUS SALISBURGENSIS ... — = 1710—1750:[94].

[84] [C:] CIRCVLI SVEVIÆ MAPPA ... — = 1710—1750:[57].

[85] LES COURS DE POSTES PAR LE CERCLE DE SUABE, come ils se presentent dans la Carte Geographique, publiée par les Heritiers de Homan, l'an 1752.
[C:] Special Post Karte durch den SCHWAEBISCHEN KREIS in welcher die Poststations Oerter, Strassen und Weiten Geographisch vorgestellt werden. Herausgegeben von Homännischen Erben. 1752. — 456 × 567 mm.

[86] [C:] DUCATUS WURTENBERGICI cum Locis limitaneis, ... — (The map is a continuation of [87]). = 1710—1750:[56].

[87] [Ducatus Wurtenbergici] ... (The map is a continuation of [86]). = 1710—1750:[33].

[88] Carte du COMTÉ d'OTTINGVE, situé dans le Cercle de Suabe, & divise én IV Parties, qui sont la PRINCIPAVTÉ d'OTTINGVE, la Comté d'OTTINGVE-OTTINGVE, la Comté d'OTTINGVE-WALLERSTEIN, & la Comte d'OTTINGVE-BALDERN.
[C:] Mappa Geographica COMITATVS OETTINGENSIS ... — = 1710—1750:[99].

[89] [C:] PROTOPARCHIÆ MINDELHEMENSIS Nova Tabula Geographica. ... — = 1710—1750:[21].

[90] Die GEGEND um NÖRDLINGEN, genandt das RIES, benebst dem PROSPECT u. GRUNDRIS der K. FR. Reichs St. NÖRDLINGEN. zu finden in der Homænn. Officin —
[C:] TRACTUS NORDLINGENSIS Germ. RIES dicti accurata Descriptio, adjecto Indice, cui Dominium cujusvis loci aliaque Iura competant, illustrata. Curātib. Homannianis Heredib$_e$ 1738. — 468 × 574 mm.
[Insets:] [T:] NORDLINGÆ Ichnographia. — (Plan). 83 × 80 mm. [Nörling] (View). 155 × 390 mm.

[91] [C:] IMP. CAES. CAROLO VI. ... — = 1710—1750:[90].

[92] [C:] Nova COMITATUS PAPPENHEIMENSIS Tabula cum finitimis diversorum Imperii statuum locis et tractibus,

nec non Dynastia BELLENBERG in Suevia sita. Curis et impensis Homañianorum Heredum. — 460 × 558 mm. [Insets:] [C:] Herrschafft BELLENBERG an der Iller in Schwaben liegend. — 104 × 140 mm. [T:] Prospect der Stadt PAPPENHEIM. — (View). 104 × 168 mm.

[93] [C:] Nova et accurata TERRITORII VLMENSIS cum DOMINIO WAINENSI Descriptio ... — = 1710–1750:[100].

[94] [C:] THEATRUM BELLI RHENANI ... — = 1710–1750:[50].

[95] CURSUS RHENI à BASILEA USQUE AD BONNAM III. SECT. EXHIBIT$_9$, à D.G. de L'ISLIO EDITUS PRIMUM, NUNC EMENDATIOR & AUCTIOR REDDIT$_9$ PER HOMANN HERED. SECTIO III. seu SUPERIOR. in qua sistitur maxima pars ALSATIÆ, BRISCOVIÆ una cum alijs SUEVIÆ Tractibus confinibus. (The map is a continuation of [96] and [97]). = 1710–1750:[53].

[96] CURSUS RHENI à BASILEA USQUE AD BONNAM III. SECT. EXHIBITUS; à D.G. de LISLIO EDITUS PRIMUM, NUNC EMENDATIOR & AUCTIOR REDDIT, PER HOMANN. HEREDES. SECTIO II. seu MEDIA, quæ continet part. ELECT. PALAT. DUC. BIPONT. ALSATIÆ INFER. COMIT. RHINGRAF. DUC. WÜRTEMB. MARCH. BADENS (The map is a continuation of [95] and [97]). = 1710–1750:[72].

[97] CURSUS RHENI À BASILEA USQUE AD BONNAM. III. SECTIONIBUS EXHIBITUS À DOMINO G. DE L'ISLE, GEOGR. REGIO PAR. EDITUS NUNC MULTIS MODIS AUCTIOR et EMENDATIOR REDDITUS, PER HOMANNIANOS HEREDES, NORIBERGÆ; SECTIO I. seu INFERIOR. IN QUA VIDERE EST PART. ELECT. COLON. MOGUNT. UNA CUM PARTE MOSELLÆ et MOENI NEC NON VEDEROVIÆ , COM. CATIMELIB. HANOV. SPANH. &c. (The map is a continuation of [95] and [97]). = 1710–1750:[78].

[98] [C:] S.R.I. CIRCULUS RHENANUS SUPERIOR ... — = 1710–1750:[55].

[99] [C:] Territorium Seculare EPISCOPATVS WORMATIENSIS Tabula Geographica delineatum, cui accedit Præfectura Palatinatus Alzey. Opera Homannianorum Heredum A. 1752. ... — 478 × 560 mm.

[100] [C:] Territorium Seculare EPISCOPATVS SPIRENSIS una cum terris adiacentibus ex delineationibus Bloedneri architecti militaris Würtembergici desumtum et exhibitum hac nova mappa Geographica. Excudentibus Homannianis Heredibus. 1753. ... — 481 × 549 mm.

[101] [C:] Vorstellung der LINIE u. INONDATION von BRUCHSAHL bis Ketsch, woselbst die Inondation in Rhein flieset u. ferner von da bis MANHEIM nebst denen Gegenden, u dem Campem. der Kayserl. u Reichs Armée 1735. Ingleichen von der Attaque PHILIPPSBURG, nebst den dabey gemachten Fortificat. werckern, welche währender Belagerung gemacht worden. Ausgefertigt in der Homännl — Officin. — [T:] G.F.Riecke Fähndr. del. —
[a] 336 × 547 mm.
[b] 336 × 121 mm.

[102] [C:] Die Gegenden des Rheins von SPEYER bis MAYNTZ nebst der Situation længst der Bergstrasse zwischen dem Rhein und dem Odewaldt dem Mayn und Necker. 1735. Imverlag Der Homænnischen Erben. — Sectio .I. (The map is a continuation of [103]). 315 × 454 mm.

[103] Les Environs du Rhin, depuis Spire iusque à Mayence, avec les pais adjecents de la Rue des Montagnes appellée BERGSTRASSE entre les Rivieres du Rhin, de Main, & de Neckar. Par et chez les Heritiers de Homañ à Norimberg. Sectio II. ... (The map is a continuation of [102]). 315 × 454 mm.

[104] [T:] Vorstellung des CAMPEMENTS der KAYSERL. u. REICHS-ARMEE zu BRUCHSAL, mit denen Inondationen u. neuen Linien 1735 in denen Gegenden von Ettlingen, bis Langenbruck. Ausgefertigt in der Homännle Officin — [T:] Levé par G.F.Riecke, Enseigne de S.A.S. Msg^r le Duc de Brounsvic & Lüneb. — (The map is a continuation of [105]). 245 × 435 mm.

[105] [T:] CAMPEMENT de l'Armée Imperiale à BRUCHSAL, ou l'on remarque les Inondations, & les Lignes tracées l'an 1735 dans les Terrains d'Ettlingen, de Durlach, jusqu'à Langenbruck. Mis au jour par les Heritiers de feu Ms^r le Docteur Homann. — (The map is a continuation of [104]). 247 × 435 mm.

[106] [T:] HERTZOGTHUM WESTPHALEN — Folium V. 380 × 514 mm.

[107] [C:] S.R.I. PRINCIPATVS FVLDENSIS IN BVCHONIA cum adjacentibus quibusdam Regionibus adumbratus a IOH. BAPTISTA HOMANNO. Sacræ Cæsareæ Majestatis Geographo. Norimbergæ. — (The map is a continuation of [108]). 370 × 511 mm. See 1710–1750:[41].

[108] [Principatus Fuldensis in Buchonia] (The map is a continuation of [107]). 367 × 500 mm.

[109] [C:] S.R.IMP. COMITATUS HANAU ... — = 1710–1750:[25] without Schneider.

[110] [C:] WALDECCIAE ac Finitimorum Dominiorum ITTERANI & CANSTEINIANI ... — = 1710–1750:[45].

[111] Carte geographique du COMTÉ INFERIEVR de CAZENELNBOGEN, mise au jour par les Heritiers de Homann. l'An 1745.
[C:] INFERIORIS COMITATVS CATTIMELIBOCENSIS delineatio geographica ... — = 1710–1750:[16].

[112] [C:] PARS VEDEROVIÆ PLVRIMAS DITIONES PRINC. et COM. NASSOVICOR. ... — = 1710–1750:[34].

[113] [T:] Abbildung der Keÿs^{rl} Freyen-Reichs-Wahl- und Handelstatt FRANCKFURT AM MAYN MIT IHREM GEBIET und Gräntzen. vorgestelt von IOH. BAPTIST HOMANN in Nürnberg. — 496 × 579 mm.
[Insets:] [Franckfurt] (View). 100 × 310 mm.

[114] [C:] CIRCULI WESTPHALIAE quo ad partem septentrionalem in suos Status ecclesiasticos & seculares divisi Tabula geographica edita sumtibus Homannianorum Heredum, Norimbergæ. A.^{o} 1761. ... — [T:] S.Dorn sc. — 570 × 485 mm. See 1710–1750:[26].

[115] [C:] DUCATUS IULIACI & BERGENSIS Tabula Geographica, ... — = 1710–1750:[14].

[116] Territorii EPISCOPATVS OSNABRVGENSIS Tabula geographica, olim á Ioh. Gigante Ludensi, D.Med. & Math. 1631. delineata, nunc vero revisa, et fere ubique emendata et in omnes suos districtus vel satrapias (Ambter) accurato divisa à Iohanne Henrico Meuschen, Osnabrugensi, Med.Pract. et rerum Naturalium Collectore. Reducente ad leges nostræ delineationis. D. Tob. Mayero, M.P. Cura et impensis Homannianorum Heredum. 1753. 470 × 418 mm.
[Inset:] [T:] DITIO RECKENBERGENSIS, Pars episcopatus Osnabrugensis, quam ob separatum ejus situm peculiari hoc schemate sub eadem scala adjungere visum est. — 162 × 136 mm.

[117] [C:] Tabula FRISIÆ ORIENTALIS olim Vbbonis Emmii Deinde Sansonis et Allardi studio nota cum variis Autographis denuo collata, aucta, innumerisque in locis emendata ab EHRENREICHIO GERHARDO COLDEWEY. D. SER: PR: OR: CONSILIARIO ADVOCATO FISCI ET ARCHIVARIO Ex Officina IOH: CHRISTOPH: HOMANNI MD. Noribergæ Anno Iubilæi secundi August: Confess: 1730. — [C:] Faustis Sub Auspiciis PATRIS PATRIAE Serenissimi Principis ac Domini Domini GEORGII ALBERTI Sacri Romani Imperii Principis ac Domini Imperantis Frisiae Orientali Domini Esenae Stedesdorfii et Wittmundae reliqua reliqua Pii Sapientis Felicis. — 486 × 579 mm.
[Insets:] [T:] EMDEN — (Plan). 97 × 110 mm. [T:] AURICH — (Plan). 64 × 92 mm. [T:] Facies DOLLARTI uti olim fuit, cujus magna pars pro ut mappa exhibet, divinis auspiciis ad continentem rediit. — 115 × 220 mm.

[118] [T:] Die GRAFSCHAFT PYRMONT mit den umliegenden Hañoverischen, Braunschweig. und Lippischen auch Paderbornischen Grænzländern, von dem Herrn

Hauptmann Overheide gezeichnet und herauss gegeben von Homäñischen Erben A.º 1752. [T:] La Comté de PYRMONT avec les Environs et les Confins des Païs d'Hañovre, de Brounsvic, de Paderborn, et de la Comte de Lippe, levée sur les Lieux par M.ʳ le Capit. Overheide, et publiée par les Heritiers de Homann. l'An 1752. corrigée par l'Auteur l'an 1753. — 452 × 557 mm.
[Inset:] [T:] Gegend des Schlosses und Neustadt Pyrmont, mit dem Mineral brunen aus dem punct P entworfen. — 92 × 180 mm.

[119] [C:] CIRCULUS SAXONIÆ INFERIORIS ... — = 1710—1750:[71].
[120] [C:] SAXONIÆ TRACTUS DUCATUM MAGDEBURGENSEM ... — = 1710—1750:[1].
[121] TABVLA GEOGRAPHICA meridionalium Regionum tam ELECTORALIVM quam DVCALIVM BRVNSVICO - LVNEBVRGENSIVM etc. edita Impensis Homannianis Heredibus, A.1762.
[C:] GEOGRAPHISCHE LAGE der südlichen BRAUNSCHWEIGISCHEN REICHSGEBIETE darinnen: Das HERZOGTHUM BRAUNSCHW. WOLFENBÜTTEL mit seinem FÜRSTENTH. BLANKENBURG und Amt WALKENRIED, Das FÜRSTENTH. CALENBERG mit seinem abgelegenen GÖTTINGISCHEN QUARTIER, Das HERZOGTHUM GRUBENHAGEN mit seinen ausserhalb liegenden Theilen, und endlich Der HARTZWALD deutlich vorgestellt werden. Alles benebst den angränzenden Ländern aus verschiedenen Hülfsmitteln und mit Zuziehung der öffentlichen Beschreibungen verzeichnet und heraus gegeben auf Kosten der Homannischen Erben. A. 1762. — 472 × 543 mm.
[122] [C:] Delineatio aureae Sterilitatis Herciniensis, i.e. HERCINIÆ METALLIFERÆ accurata Chorographia, ... Edita curis Homannianorum Heredum. Norimbergæ. — = 1710—1750:[63] with small alterations.
[123] [C:] EPISCOPATUS HILDESIENSIS NEC NON VICINORUM STATUUM DELINEATIO GEOGRAPHICA. ... — = 1710—1750:[91].
[124] [C:] DUCATUS LUNEBURGICI et COMITATUS DANNEBERGENSIS accurata Descriptio ... — = 1710—1750:[52].
[125] [C:] DUCATUS MEKLENBURGICI Tabula Generalis ... — = 1710—1750:[12].
[126] [C:] Typus Geographicus DUCAT. LAUENBURGICI ... — = 1710—1750:[62].
[127] [C:] TABVLA GENERALIS HOLSATIAE ... — = 1720—1771:[54].
[128] [C:] DUCATUS BREMAE et FERDAE Nova Tabula ... — = 1710—1750:[61].
[129] Carte de la Principauté de HALBERSTADT, y compris les pays incorporés, savoir la Comté de REINSTEIN & la Dynastie de DERENBURG avec les Territoires adjacents, lesquels sont l'Abbaye de QUEDLINGBOURG & la Comté de WERNIGERODE, la Principauté de Blankenbourg etc. Publiée par les soins des Heritiers de Homann l'an 1750.
[C:] Mappa specialis PRINCIPATVS HALBERSTADIENSIS una cum unitis cum eo terris COMITATVS REINSTEIN et Dynastiæ DERENBVRG, repraesentans simul Abbatiam QVEDLINGBVRG & Comitat. WERNIGERODE, nec non conterminum Principat. BLANCKENBVRG, Herciniam Anhaltinam et Dynastiam SCHAVEN. Delineata primum à G. Hier. RIESE, Architect milit. Borussico et Architecto provinciali Halberstadiensi Dein correctior reddita à Tobia Majero. Societ. Cosmogr. sodali. Curantibus Homannianis Heredibus Norimbergæ A. MDCCL. — 452 × 542 mm.
[130] Des REISE ATLAS erstes Blatt, in welchem die Landstrasse von Nurnberg nach Goettingen verzeichnet ist. (The map is a continuation of [131]). 347 × 246 mm.
[131] [C:] ITER MAYERIANVM ad MVSAS GOETTINGENSES Norimberga A. 1751. factum. Ex ipsius Collectione designavit Iohannes Andreas Friedericus Yelin, Philos. et Math. apud Goettingenses cultor. ATLANTIS ITINERARII Primum Specimen, ad imitandum aliis itinerantibus proponunt Heredes Homanniani. Ao. 1751. — (The map is a continuation of [130]). 347 × 246 mm.
[132] [C:] BELLI ab obitu CAROLI VI. Imperatoris usqve ad pacem Dresdae d. 25. Dec. MDCCXLV. Factam tam in GERMANIA quam BELGIO ob successionem AVSTRIACAM gesti THEATRVM geographice delineatum ... — (The map is a continuation of [133]). 468 × 543 mm. = 1720—1771:[90].
[133] [Belli ab obitu CAROLI VI...]
[C:] Serenissimo PRINCIPI AC DOMINO DOMINO FRIDERICO ... — (The map is a continuation of [132]). 470 × 546 mm. = 1720—1771:[90].

Notes: All the maps are blank on the back and coloured. The volume has three title-page. The engraved one is dated 1762, and signed 'I. Iust Preisler del. 1762 Andr. Hoffer sculps.' The Latin one is signed 'I.G. Ebersperger sculp.'; it depicts the imperial insignia, with the words 'Augustae Germanorum Majestati Sacrum'. Sandler (p. 397) states that these insignia appear on the engraved title-page. A small map of Germany is incorporated in the design. After the Latin title-page is the index, with the note 'Mappae Homannianae de Germania omnes hic extant continuatae usque ad annum 1752 inclusive.' Then follows the German title-page, and then the Anmerkungen, signed by 'Homännische Erben' and dated 'Nürnberg im Anfang des Jahrs 1754'. The number of each map, as it appears in the index, is written in old ink on the recto, with a short title in German. Before the maps is a table entitled: 'ORBIS IN TABULA PARS SECUNDA, d.i. Zweyter Theil der Geographischen Universal-Charte, vorstellend auf einem einzigen Blatt alle Crayse, Provinzen und vornehmste Örter des H. RÖMISCHEN REICHS, Teutscher Nation ... entworfen von Ioh. Gottfried Gross. Excuderunt Heredes Homañiani Noribergae.' In a cartouche on map [83] there is a portrait of 'Franciscus Antonius Archi-Ep. Salisb', and a small circular map of 'Hierarchia Salisburge...' On map [2] the title has been printed on a separate slip and pasted into the cartouche. Our volume is very similar to that described by Sandler (pp. 397—400); the slight differences between them suggest that some of the maps are of different states. Sandler's description of these atlases comes under the heading 'Der Homännische Verlag um 1760'. The latest date on a map in our copy is 1762 (map [53], Nov. Territorii Erfordiensis), which is also the date on the engraved title-page, so it is clearly a later edition than the one described by Sandler. The atlas is bound in old leather with blind tooling; the binding is in poor condition.

Lit.: Sandler, Homann, Sandler, Homännische Erben, p. 397—400.

96 HOMANN, JOHANN BAPTIST [1762?]

[Collection of town plans and views without title-page.]
                 obl 53,7 cm.

[1] [C:] Vue de la Montagne de BROKEN ... — = 1720—1771:[70], but without the text with 1751.
[2] [C:] Prospectus Sanctæ olim et celeberrimæ Urbis HIEROSOLYMÆ opera et impensis MATTHÆI SEUTTER S.CÆS. et REG. CATH. MAJ. GEOGR. et CHALCOGR. AUGUST. VIND. Prospect der vormals Heiligen und Welt Berühmten Stadt IERUSALEM durch Fleiss und in Verlag MATTHÆI SEUTTERS, IHRO KAYS, und KÖNIGL. CATHOL. MAJ. GEOGRAPHI u. KUPFERST. in AUGSPURG. — 483 × 569 mm.
[Inset:] [T:] IERUSALEM — (View). 157 × 558 mm.
[3] [T:] Verschiedene PROSPECTE der VORNEMSTEN STÄDTEN in PERSIEN samt vorderst einer unsern dem Caspischen Meer, dem Russischen Reich zugehörig, gelegenen Stadt, zu mehrerem Liecht und Erleuterung der neu-verfertigten Persianischen Land-Charten herausgegeben von IOHANN BAPTIST HOMANN, Der RÖM. KAYS. MAJ.ᵗ Geographo in Nürnberg. ... — 484 × 577 mm.

[a] [T:] ASTRACHAN, Die Haupt-Stadt des Russischen Königreichs gleiches namens. — (View). 111 × 141 mm.
[b] [T:] DERBENT. an der Caspischen See die gränz-Stadt, und Schlüssel des Reichs Persien. — (View). 111 × 140 mm.
[c] [T:] TEFLIS, die Haupt-Stadt in Gurgistan oder Georgien. — (View). 111 × 138 mm.
[d] [T:] KARS. — 111 × 140 mm.
[e] [T:] ERZERUM die Grantz-Stadt in Armenien. — 110 × 141 mm.
[f] [T:] BACCU. eine Stadt in Meden, an der Caspischen See. — 110 × 140 mm.
[g] [T:] SULTANIA ein Königliche Stadt in der Prov. Erack Atzem. — (View). 110 × 138 mm.
[h] [T:] SCHAMACHIA im Gebürg der Provincz Schirwan. — (View). 110 × 140 mm.
[i] [T:] ERIVAN die Haupt-Stadt in Armenia. — (View). 107 × 140 mm.
[k] [T:] SCHIRAS vor alters Persepolis, die Haupt-Stadt des gantzen Reichs, ietz nur in Farsistan. — (View). 107 × 140 mm.
[l] [T:] CANDAHAR Stadt und Vestung, an der Indianischen Gräntze des Reichs Persien. — 107 × 140 mm.
[m] [T:] Die Stadt ARDEBIL in Adirbeitzan. — 107 × 138 mm.
[n] [T:] Die Stadt KACHAN in Erack. — (View). 111 × 140 mm.
[o] [T:] Prospect der Königlich Persischen Haupt und Residenz-Stadt ISPHAHAN in der Prov. Erack oder Parthia. — (View). 111 × 285 mm.
[p] [T:] GAMRON oder BENDERABASSI. — (View). 111 × 140 mm.

[4] [C:] CONSTANTINOPOLIS amplissima, potentissima, et magnificentissima Urbs et sedes Imperatoris Turcici in Provincia Romania ad Bosphorum Thraciæ sita. CONSTANTINOPEL, die grössest, mächtigst u. Prächtigste Residenz Stadt des Türck. Kaysers in der Prov. Romanien am Bosph. Thracico gelegen. verlegt von M. Seutter, I.R.K. MAJEST. GEOGR. in AUGSP. — 485 × 565 mm.
[Inset:] [T:] Prospect der Türckischen Haupt und Residentz Stadt STAMBUL oder CONSTANTINOPEL von Mitternacht an zu sehen. — (View). 135 × 555 mm.

[5] [T:] Neuester und exacter PLAN und PROSPECT von der STADT, VESTVNG, BAY und FORTIFICATION von GIBRALTAR, ... — = 1720—1771:[105].

[6] [C:] HOLMIA celeberrima Metropolis et Sedes Regia REGNI SUECIÆ, accuratissima Ichnographia et Prospectibus ob oculos posita per MATTH.SEUTTER, SAC. CÆS. MAJEST. GEOGR. AUG. VIND. STOCKHOLM die vortreffliche Haupt und Residenz Statt dess KÖNIG REICHS SCHWEDEN, in einem accuraten Grund Riss ū Prospecten vorgestellt von MATTHÆUS SEUTTER, IHRO R.K.M.GEOGR. AUGSPURG. ... 483 × 565 mm.
[Insets:] [C:] Prospect des Königl. Schwedischen Residenz Schloss in STOCKHOLM, mit dem NORDER MALM. — (View). 88 × 554 mm. [C:] Prospect der Königlich. Strasse in STOCKHOLM, mit dem SÜDER MALM und Ritterholms Kirch. — (View). 87 × 554 mm.

[7] [T:] COPPENHAGEN die Königl. Dänische Haupt und Residenz Stadt, in GrundRiss heraus gegeben u. verlegt von MATTH, SEUTTER, I.R.K.M.G. in AUGSPURG. Plan de COPPENHAGUE, Capitale et Residence du Roy de Dennemarck gravée par MATTH. SEUTTER, Graveur d'AUGSBOURG, S.C.M.G. — [T:] Iohann Thomas Kraus delineavit. Aug. Vind. — 493 × 570 mm.
[Inset:] [T:] Prospect der Königl. Dænischen Haupt ū. Residentz Statt COPPENHAGEN. — (View). 98 × 560 mm.

[8] [VRBIUM LONDINI...] (The map is a continuation of [10] and [11]). 510 × 515 mm.

[9] [C:] The CITY GUIDE or A Pocket MAP of LONDON, WESTMINSTER And SOUTHWARK With yᵉ New Buildings to yᵉ Year 1746/7 — Printed for Tho: Bowles in Sᵗ. Pauls Church Yard, & Iohn Bowles at the Black Horse in Cornhill 243 × 493 mm.

[10] [VRBIUM LONDINI ...] (The map is a continuation of [8] and [11]). = 1720—1771:[9].

[11] [C:] VRBIUM LONDINI et WEST-MONASTERII nec non Suburbii SOUTHWARK accurata Ichnographia, ... — (The map is a continuation of [8] and [10]). = 1720—1771:[8].

[12] [C:] PLAN DE LA VILLE DE RHEIMS Par le Sʳ Daudet Geographe du Roy le Iʳ Octobre 1722. — [T:] Graué par G.j.B Scotin leieune — A Paris Chez de Mortain Mᵉ Peintre sur le pont Nôtre Dame pres la pompe aux belles Estampes ... Uncoloured. 324 × 448 mm.

[13] [C:] PLAN DE LA VILLE et Citadelᵉ D'AMIENS Capitale de la Picardie ... — [C:] ... A Paris chez Mʳ de Beaurin Geographe Ordinaire du Roy Qùay des Augustins proche la Pavée. Gravé par Incelin — Uncoloured. 247 × 328 mm.

[14] [C:] NOUVEAU PLAN DE DIEPPE Ville et Port de Mer de la Normandie, avec tous les nouveaux Ouvrages, et projets qui sont marqués sur le plan. il y à un Presidial qui relève de Rouën. AParis chez Mʳ Beaurin Geographe Ordinaire du Roy Quay des Augustins. — [C:] ... Gravé par Incelin — Uncoloured. 267 × 340 mm.

[15] [C:] PLAN DE LA VILLE ET CHÂTEAU DE S.MALO ... — [T:] a Paris chez le Sʳ de Beaurain Geographe ordinaire du Roi quay des Grands Augustins — Uncoloured. 271 × 416 mm.

[16] [C:] VEÜE et Perspective de la Ville de Reims du Coté du Chemin de Paris, par le Sʳ Daudet Geographe du Roy 1722. — [T:] A. Maison-neuve f. — Se Vend a Paris Chez de Mortain sur lepont N. Dame du Coté de la Pompe au belles Estampes ... (View). Uncoloured. 325 × 446 mm.

[17] [C:] VEUE DE LA HAUTE ET BASSE VILLE DE BOULOGNE SUR MER CAPITALE DU COMTÉ BOULONNOIS — Ph.Luto acolythus Bolonæus ad vivum delineavit an. 1725 Gravé par les soins de Sʳ de Beaurain Géographe du Roy et se vend chez luy a Paris quay des Augustins prés la rue pavée. A. Mutel. Sculpsit. (View). Uncoloured. 253 × 503 mm.

[18] [C:] PLAN DE LA HAUTE ET BASSE VILLE DE BOULOGNE Sur Mer CAPITALE DU COMTÉ BOULONNOIS ... — Uncoloured. 243 × 321 mm.

[19] [C:] ACCURATE VORSTELLUNG des neuesten PLANS der unter Französischer Bothmaesigkeit seit dem Crambresischen Frieden 1556. stehenden Bischöflichen HAUBTSTADT und VESTUNG METZ, so ehmalen auch die HaubtStadt im Königreich AUSTRASIEN gewesen, ... an das Tags Liecht gestellet und zu finden in der Homænn. Officin 1738. ... Accurata Repraesentatio ichnographica URBIS EPISCOPALIS in Ducatu LOTHARINGIÆ, dictae METÆ, antiquis DIVODURUM Mediomatricorum, quæ et olim Regni AUSTRASIÆ urbs capitalis fuit, Iuris Germanici pridem, Pace veró Cameracensi A. 1556. Gallis cessa, ... secundum statum recentissimum edita, prostat in Offic. Homanniana Norib. A. MDCCXXXIX. ... — [C:] ... Dessiné par F.W.Zollmann Lieut. des Ingen. — 465 × 550 mm.

[20] [C:] VERSAILLES Chateau de plaisance le plus delicieux et le plus magnifique dans l'Ile de France, bati par ordre de Louis XIV. Roj de France, et nom̄e ā cause de sa rare beauté la huitieme marveille du monde, Aux depens de Matth. Seütter, Geographe de sa Maj. Imp. et Catholique, Augsbourg. VERSAILLES das anmuthig ū: prächtigste Lust-Schloss in Isle de France, von Kön. Ludwig XIV erbauet, ū: wegē kostbarer Schönheit das achte Wunderwerck der Welt geneñet, verlegt v. M.Seütt. K.Geogr. — (View). 489 × 567 mm.

[21] [C:] CARTE TOPOGRAPHIQUE des ENVIRONS & du PLAN DE PARIS levée par Msʳ l'Abbé DELAGRIVE, & Copiée selon l'original Parisien par les Heritiers de feu Dʳ Homann. ... An. 1739. — [C:] KARTE VON DER GEGEND und GRUNDRIS der Stadt PARIS, von dem Herrn Abt DELAGRIVE verzeichnet und nach dem

Parisischen Original ins kleine gebracht und herausgegeben von Homænischen Erben. ... — 490 × 573 mm.

[22] [C:] PLAN DE LA VILLE ET DES ENVIRON DE DIJON Dedié A SON ALTESSE SERENISSIME MONSEIGNEUR LE DUC Par Son tres heumble et tres Obbeissant Serviteur de Beaurain Geographe Ordinaire du Roy — [C:] A PARIS Chez le Sieur de Beaurain Geographe Ordinaire du Roy Quay des Grands Augustins proche la Rue Pavée — 522 × 700 mm.
[Insets:] [C:] Les Environs DE DIJON — (Map). 148 × 154 mm. [C:] VEÜE DE DIJON — [T:] du Cotté de la vénue de Paris — (View). 52 × 415 mm. [T:] PLAN DU CHATEAU ET DU PARC DE LA COLOMBIERE Qui se trouve au bout du Cours de la porte S. Pierre, Situé sur la riviere d'Ouche éloigné de la ville de 680. toises. — Uncoloured. 120 × 170 mm.

[23] [C:] LA VILLE D'ORLEANS avec ses Environs, A Paris chez M.r de Beaurin Geographe Ordinaire du Roy Quay des Augustins proche la Rue Pavée. — [C:] DEDIÉE A SON ALTESSE ROYALE MONSEIGNEUR LE DUC D'ORLEANS Par Son tres humble et tres Obeiss. Serviteur de Beaurin G. du R. — Uncoloured. 241 × 301 mm.
[Inset:] [T:] LES ENVIRONS D'ORLEANS — (Map). 77 × 91 mm.

[24] [C:] ROÜEN. Ville Capitale de Normandie, Port de Mer sur la Riviere de Seine, ... Par N. de Fer: Geographe de sa Majesté Catolique et de Monseigneur le Dauphin. — [C:] ... A PARIS Chez le S.r Danet Gendre de l'Auteur sur le Pont Nôtre Dame a la Sphere Royale. ... 1724. — [T:] A.C.S. — Uncoloured. 399 × 554 mm.

[25] [C:] MAYLAND, die Haupt-Stadt des Herzogthumbs gleiches Nahmens, nebst beygefügten Plans der übrigen fürnehmsten Mayländischen Vestungen, edirt und zu finden in der Homännischen Officin. Anno 1734. ... — [C:] Pianta del Castello di MILANO. e suoi Attacchi cominciati li 15 Dec. 1733. — 478 × 567 mm.
[Insets:] [T:] Pianta de PIZZIGHITONE e Gera e suoi attacchi Seguiti l'anno 1733 li 18. Novemb. — 153 × 131 mm. (Irregular). [T:] NOVARA — 100 × 118 mm. [T:] LODI. — 75 × 80 mm. [T:] TORTONA. — 72 × 80 mm. [T:] La Citta di VALENZA. — 92 × 125 mm. [T:] MORTARA. — 90 × 116 mm. [T:] MANTUA — 133 × 170 mm. [T:] Il Piano del Prospetto del Castello di Milano — 133 × 170 mm.

[26] [C:] MELITE vulgo MALTA cum vicinis GOZA, quæ olim GAULOS, et COMINO insulis, uti exhibetur á NIC. de FER, nunc æri incisa per MATTH. SEUTTER, S.C.M. GEOGR. AUGUSTANUM. Sita est hæc insula inter Barbariam et Siciliam ... — (Map). 494 × 570 mm.
[Inset:] [T:] CITTA VALETTA — 147 × 167 mm.

[27] [C:] FIRENZA la Capitale di Toscana et la Residenza de gran Duchi appresso del fiume Arno Vene sono pochi simili in Italia riguardo della Grandezza, magnificenza, d egli edifici arte et pretiosita, sicche ottimomente merita il titalo della Bella. FLORENZ die Haupt Statt in Toscana u: Residenz selbiger Gross Herzogen an dem Fluss Arno, so an Grösse, magnifiq$_3$ Gebäuen, Kunst u Kostbarkeitē in Italiē wenig ihres gleichē hat u: dahero dē Tittul la Bella dass ist die Schöne, bestens meritirt. verlegt von MATTH. SEUTTER. S.C.M.GEOGR. in AUGSPURG — 488 × 566 mm.
[Inset:] [T:] FLORENZ. — (View). 134 × 555 mm.

[28] [C:] NEAPOLIS, Regni hujus maxima, ornatissima, siti amœnissima, multisq$_3$ castellis munita Metropolis et Emporium maritimum florentissimum, cum illustrissimis ædificiis delineata cura et cælo MATTHÆI SEUTTERI, SAC. CÆS. MAJEST. GEOGR. AUGUSTA VINDELICOR. — 491 × 570 mm.
[Insets:] [T:] Veduta del MOLO. — 90 × 140 mm. [T:] Veduta di CASTEL del OVO. — 90 × 140 mm. [T:] Veduta di CASTEL Nuovo. — 90 × 140 mm. [T:] Piazza del Mercato. — 90 × 140 mm. [T:] Veduta del l'Argo del Castello S.ELMO. — 90 × 140 mm. [T:] VESUVIUS M. — 90 × 140 mm. [Inset:] [T:] Montis Interioris conspectus. — 32 × 39 mm. [T:] Veduta del PALAZZO del VICE RE. — 90 × 140 mm. (All the insets views).

[29] [T:] VETERIS et MODERNÆ URBIS ROMÆ ICHNOGRAPHIA et ACCURATA DESIGNATIO, cura et sumtibus MATTHÆI SEUTTERI, S.C.M.Geogr. Augustani — 490 × 566 mm.
[Inset:] [T:] Die 7 Berge der Alten Statt ROM — 50 × 72 mm.

[30] [T:] LE SETTE CHIESE DI ROMA con le loro principali Reliquie, Stationi, et indulgenze. dato in luce da MATTEO SEUTTERO, scultore in rame in AUGUSTA. DIE SIEBEN KIRCHEN VON ROM, mit ihren vornehmsten Heiligthümern, Stationen und Ablass. heraus gegeben von MATTHÆO-SEUTTER, IHRO RÖM.KAJ.MAJ. GEOGR. AUGSP. — 495 × 575 mm.

[31] [T:] STETINUM celeberrima et munitissima Pomeraniæ Citerioris Metropolis ac Emporium florentissimum. Cura et sumtibus MATTHÆI SEUTTERI, Sac.Cæs. et Reg Cathol. Majest. Geogr. Aug. Vindel. STETTIN die Weitberühmtest und überaus Feste Haupt Stadt, auch florisanter Handels-Plaz in Vor Pomern Heraus gegeben und Verlegt von MATTH. SEUTTER, Kayserl. Geogr. in Augspurg. — 487 × 568 mm.
[Inset:] [T:] STETTIN IN POMMERN — (View). 120 × 557 mm.

[32] [C:] MAGDEBURGUM Ducatus cognominis Metropolis ad Albium, sub Ditione Regis Borussiæ, bene munitum ac florens Emporium, in qvo Tribunal Provinciale, Consistorium et Camera constituta. Operâ et cœlo MATTHÆI SEUTTERI, Chalc. Augustani. MAGDEBURG die Haupt Statt eines Herzogthumss gleiches Nahmens, an der Elb dem König in Preussen zuständig, eine Wohlfortificierte und florisante Handel Statt, in welcher die Magdeburgische Landes Regierung, Consistorium und Camer angelegt; Verfertigt von MATTHÆUS SEUTTER, Kupferste. in Augspurg. Ihro Röm. Kayserę; May: Geographo. — 496 × 570 mm.
[Inset:] [T:] MAGDEBURG — (View). 90 × 367 mm.

[33] [T:] PROSPECT und GRUND-RISS der KAYSERL. RESIDENZ-STADT WIEN ... — = 1720—1771:[30]. See [62].

[34] [C:] Eigentliche Verzeichnung der GEGEND UND PROSPECTEN der Hochfürstl. Bischöfflich: Haupt v. Residentz Stadt AICHSTÆDT zu finden BEY IOH: BAPT: HOMANNS SEEL. ERBE. in Nürnberg und edirt im Jahr 1730. ... — 482 × 562 mm.
[Inset:] [T:] PROSPECT DER HOCHFÜRSTL. BISCHÖFFLICH. HAVBT VND RESIDENTZ STADT AICHSTAEDT. — (View). 117 × 286 mm.

[35] [T:] DARSTELLUNG des GRUNDRISSES und PROSPECTES der Königl. Preussisch-Magdeburgischen und des Saal-Crayses Haupt Stadt HALLE, welcher daselbst auf Kosten und Verlag IOHANN BAPTISTÆ HOMANNS Der RÖM. KAYS. MAI. Geographi und Mitglids der Königl. Preuss. Societät der Wissenschafftē, ist ausgemessen und Geometrice verzeichnet worden von I.C.HOMANN, der Medicin und Mathematic Studioso. zufinden in NÜRNBERG bey dem Authore. ... — 471 × 568 mm.
[Inset:] [T:] Prospect der Stadt HALLE wie solche von Abend anzusehen — (View). 107 × 257 mm.

[36] [C:] Die Herzogl: HOLSTEIN-GOTTORP: Residenz-See- und Handelstadt KIEL Sambt dessen HAFEN in einem accuraten PLAN und PROSPECT entworfen Sereniss. Ducis HOLSATO-GOTTORPIENSIS Sedes et celebre Emporium KILONIUM una cum ejus PORTU ichno-et scenographice accurate delineatum Prostat in OFFICINA HOMAÑIANA ... — 547 × 470 mm.
[Insets:] [T:] PROSPECT, wie solcher von der Seyte des Seehafens anzusehen — (View). 71 × 232 mm. [T:] PROSPECT, wie solcher von der Land Seyte zu sehen — (View). 71 × 230 mm. [T:] KIELER HAAFEN oder FÖHR — (Map). 146 × 464 mm.

[37] [T:] PROSPECT und GRUNDRIS der KEISERL. FREYEN REICHS und ANSEE STADT HAMBURG.

samt ihrer GEGEND. edirt durch IOH. BAPT. HOMANN in Nürnberg — 484 × 581 mm.
[Insets:] [T:] Das Hamburgische Ampt Ritzenbuttel — (Map). 75 × 130 mm. [C:] Prospect der Stadt HAMBURG gegen Mittag anzusehen. — (View). 130 × 340 mm.

[38] [T:] Die Königl. POLNISCHE u. PREUSISCHE Hansee- und Handels-Stadt DANTZIG, ... — = 1720—1771:[135].

[39] [T:] ABBILDUNG der vornehmsten PROSPECTEN der Königl. Preusisch-Magdeb. u. des Saal-Creises Haupt-Stadt HALLE, wie solche daselbst nach wahrer Beschaffenheit derer Gebäuden selbst verzeichnet worden von einem dasigen Med^{nae}. e Mathem. Studioso. verlegts IOH. BAPT. HOMANN. Der Röm. Kays. Maj^{tt} Geographus und Mitglied der Königl. Preuss. Societät der Wissenschafften in Nürnberg. — (View). 460 × 546 mm.

[40] [C:] Tabula ichnographica CELLÆ ad Alleram PRINCIPUM LUNEBURGENSIUM quondam sedis calamo MATTHÆI SEUTTERI, S.C.Maj. Geographi Aug. Vindel. ZELL an der Aller der HERZOGE zu LÜNEBURG ehemalige Residenz. — 485 × 568 mm.

[41] [T:] LÜNEBURGUM ad flumen Elmenaw, ex ruderibus Bardovicensibus aucta, in societatem Hanseaticarum recepta, hodie in Ditione Regis Angliæ et Electoris Hanoveranensis posita Opera et sumptibus MATTH. SEUTTER SAC. CÆS. MAY. GEOGR. LÜNEBURG eine alte, ehemahls Herzoglich, nunmehro Churfürstl: Hanoverische wohlberühmte Statt in Nidersæchsischen Craÿs. ausgefertiget von MATTH. SEUTTER KEYSERL. GEOGR. IN AUGSPURG. — 492 × 563 mm.
[Inset:] [T:] LÜNEBURG — (View). 131 × 548 mm.

[42] [C:] GRUNDRISS DER STADT BRAUNSCHWEIG in welchem die Lage aller Herrschafftlichen und Publiquen Gebäuden, Mühlen, Brücken, Strassen und Gassen, ingleichen der Ein- und Ausflus des Ocker-Stroms, samt seinen Canälen zuersehen sind; zum Nuzen und Gebrauch vor Reisende ū: Fremde eingerichtet von M. COUNRADI, Ingenieur, und heraus gegeben von MATTH. SEUTTER, Kays. Geogr. in Augspurg — 485 × 564 mm.

[43] [C:] HAMBURGUM celeberrima libera Imperii et Hanseatica civitas ac oplentissimum Emporium, circa Ostium Albis ad Mare Septentr, S.C.M.G. HAMBURG eine Weltberühmte Freye Reichs und Hansee- auch reiche ū: Volkreiche Handels Statt an der Elb, nicht weit von der Nord See. Heraus gegeben u: verlegt von MATTHÆUS SEUTTER I.R.K.M.G. in AUGSP. — 494 × 572 mm.
[Inset:] [T:] HAMBURG. — (View). 145 × 562 mm.

[44] [C:] AUGSPURG DIE HAUPT-STADT UND ZIERDE DES SCHWÆBISCHEN CRAISES, SAMT DER UMLIGENDEN GEGEND IN DIE BREITE AUF 3 UND IN DIE LÄNGE AUF 1 1/2 STUND GERECHNET, Mit sonderbahrem Fleiss Verfertiget und Verlegt von MATTHÆO SEUTTER daselbst. I.R.K.M.G. —
[T:] Golffried Rogg del. — Melchior Rhein fecit. (Map). 491 × 566 mm.
[Inset:] [T:] Prospect dess Heil. Röm. Reichs freÿen Stadt AUGSPURG wie solche von Morgen her anzusehen. — (View). 125 × 553 mm.

[45] [T:] PROSPECTE des HARTZWALDS nebst accurater Vorstellung der auf selbigem gebräuchlichen BERGWERKS-MACHINEN Ertz- und Præge-Arbeiten, als ein Anhang zur Geographischen Charte des Hartzwalds heraus gegeben von Homæñischen Erben Nürnb. ... PROSPECTUS HERCINIENSES, una cum Iconibus MACHINARUM, et quæ porro circa VENAS eruendas, tundendas, urendas, lavandas, cribrandas et excoquendas, itemque circa duplicem monetandi modum notatu digna occurrunt, uti in Fodinis Herciniensibus in usu sunt, repræsentata omnia, et pro illustranda mappa Chorographica edita per Homanianos Heredes, Norib: ... — (Views). 477 × 588 mm.

[46] [T:] STRASBOURG, ville ancienne celebre et tres fortificeé, du Roy de France dans la Basse Alsace sur le Rhin, gravée aux depens de Matth. Seutter, S.C.M.Geogr. à Augsb. STRASBURG, eine Uhralte sehr Berühmte u. nun auch ungemein fortificirte Statt dem König in Franckr. gehörig in Unter Elsas am Rhein ligend, verfertigt ū. verlegts M. Seutter, I.R.K. Majest. Geogr. in Augspurg — [T:] Ioh. Thomas Kraus delin. — 490 × 569 mm.
[Inset:] [T:] STRASBURG — (View). 143 × 560 mm.

[47] = [46] in this ed. with small alterations.

[48] [C:] DIE HOCHFÜRSTLICHE RESIDETZ FRIEDENSTEIN UND HAUPT STADT GOTHA Verfertigt und verlegt von MATTHÆO SEUTTER IHRO RÖM. KAJSERL. MAJ. GEOGR. in AUGSP. — [C:] ... H.A.Koenig delineavit. — 489 × 568 mm.

[49] [C:] Scenographiae LIPSIACAE folium secundum. Accurante D^{no} Ioach. Ernesto Scheflero prodit in lucem In Officina Homanniana. ... A.^{o} 1749. ... — (Views). 409 × 411 mm.

[50] VRBIS LIPSIAE nec non ædificiorum in ipsa publicorum facies, graphice delineata per Ioach. Ernest. Scheflerum, Architect: Edentibus Homann. Heredibus ... A.^{o} 1749. fol. I. (Views). 410 × 550 mm.
[C:] Prospect von LEIPZIG wie solcher von Süd-Ost an zusehen. ... — 135 × 545 mm.

[51] [C:] Denen HochEdelgebohrnen Magnificis HochEdlen Vesten u. Hochgelahrten auch Hochweisen HERREN, HERREN BVRGEMEISTERN,... wird dieser GRVNDRISS DER STADT LEIPZIG ... — = 1720—1775:[75].

[52] [T:] DRESDA ad Albim, Saxoniæ Superioris Metropolis, ac magnifica Ducis Electoris et Regis Poloniæ Sedes Opera et Sumptibus MATTH. SEUTTERI, SAC. CÆS. MAY. GEOGR AUGUSTANI. DRESDEN an der Elb, eine Haupt-Stadt des Obern Sachsen, ū: Höchst vortreffliche Residentz des dasigen Churfürsten ū: Konigs in Pohlen ausgefertigt von MATTH. SEUTTER KAY. GEOGR. IN AUGSP. — 490 × 557 mm.
[Inset:] [T:] Die Königl. u. Churfürstl. Sächsische Haupt ū. Residentz Stadt und Vestung DRESDEN. — (View). 103 × 549 mm.

[53] PROSPECTUS NORIMBERGENSES. Prostant in Officina Homanniana. (Views). 472 × 556 mm.

[54] [T:] PROSPECT und GRUNDRIS der des HEIL: RÖM. REICHS-STADT NÜRNBERG ... — = 1720—1771:[58].

[55] [C:] GRUNDRIS der des Heil. Röm. Reichs Freyen Stadt NURNBERG Zu finden In der Homæñischen Officin. Anno 1732. ... — 482 × 566 mm.

[56] [T:] Accurater Prospect der HOCH.FURSTL. MARGGRAF BAADEN DURLACHISCHEN neu erbauten verwunderungs würdigē Residenz Stadt CARLSRUHE, verlegt v. M. SEUTTER. d. R.K.ū. K.C.M.GEOGR. in AUGSP. ... Representation exacte de CHARLESRUH, Residence admirable de S.A.S.MONSEIGNEUR le MARGGRAVE de BADE DURLACH, gravée aux depens de MATTH. SEUTER, GEOGRAPHE de sa MAJ. IMP. e CATHOL. á AUGSBOURG — 486 × 568 mm.

[57] [T:] Accurate Vorstellung der HOCH FÜRSTL. BISCHÖFFL. RESIDENZ und HAUPT-STADT WÜRTZBURG des Herzogthums Francken, wie solche unter Höchst Rühmlicher Regirung des jetzigen Hochwürdigsten Fürsten und Herren Herrn Ioh. Phil. Franz Gr. v. Schonborn mit vielen neu-erbauten herrlichen Palästen und Gebäuden vermehret worden. In Kupffer herausgegeben von I. B. Homann. Der Röm. Kais. Maj^{t} Geographo. und Mitglied der Königl. Preuss Societat der Wissenschafften. A.1723 in Nurnberg. ... — 485 × 578 mm.

[58] [T:] ULMA memorabilis ac permunita libera Imperii Civitas ad Danubium, ubi Ilara et Blavus ei miscentur, cura et impensis MATTH. SEUTTERI, S.Cæs. et Cathol. Reg. Maj. Geogr. Augustæ Vindel. ULM eine considerable Freye Reichs Statt in Schwaben, wo die Flüsse Iler u: Blau in die Donau fallen, verfertigt durch MATTHÆUM SEUTTER, Seiner Kayserl. u. Königl. Cathol. Majest. Geogr. in Augspurg. — 490 × 571 mm.
[Inset:] [T:] ULM gegen Sud West. — (View). 121 × 557 mm.

[59] [T:] Accurata recens delineata Ichnographia celeberrimæ liberæ Imperii Civitatis ac Sveviæ Metropolis AUGUSTÆ VINDELICORUM, Cura et sumtibus MATTH. SEUTTERI S.C.M.G. Augustani. Neu verfertigt accurater Grund Riss der Hochberühmten dess Heil: Röm: Reichs Freyen u: dess Schwäbischen Creises Haupt Statt AUGSPURG, in Kupfer gestochen und verlegt von M. SEUTTER, I.R.K.M.GEOGR. — [C:] Viris Perillustribus DOMINO IOANNI _ IACOBO HOLZAPFEL AB HERXHEIM et DÑO WOLFFGANGO IACOBO SULZERO SAC. CÆS. MAIEST. CONSILIARIIS ACTUALIBUS Inclytæ Reipublicæ Augustanæ Duum Viris Præfectis Splendidissimis, Dominis suis Gratiosis, Ichnographiam Urbis Augustæ Vindel. submisse offert ac consecrat devotiss. Civis et Chalcographus MATTHÆUS SEUTTER. — [T:] Ioh. Thomas Kraus Architectus et Perspectivicus delineavit — 496 × 572 mm.

[60] [T:] FRANCOFURTUM ad Mœnum, Libera Imperii, ut et Electioni et Coronationi Cæsarum Romanorum destinata Civitas, et florentissimum Germaniæ Emporium. per M. SEUTTER, S.C.et C.MAJ. GEOGR. ... FRANCKFURT am Mayn, eine Freye Reichs zu der Wahl und Crönung der Römischen Kaiser Bestimte und weit Berühmte florissante Handel Stadt. verlegt von M. SEUTTER RÖM. KAISERL. GEOGRAPH. ... — 492 × 575 mm.
[Inset:] [T:] FRANCKFURT am MAYN — (View). 103 × 355 mm.

[61] [T:] COLONIA AGRIPPINA antiquissima, maxima ac celeberrima Libera Imperii Civitas et Emporium florentissimum Autore MATTHÆO SEUTTER, SAC.CÆS. ET REG. CATHOL. MAY. GEOGR. AUGUST. CÖLLN am Rhein eine uhralte, sehr grose Hochberühmte freye Reichs- und florisante Handel-Statt. verfertigt und heraus gegeben von MATTHÆUS SEUTTER. KAYSRL. GEOGR. IN AUGSPURG — 486 × 560 mm.
[Inset:] [T:] AGRIPPINA CÖLLN am RHEIN — (View). 135 × 548 mm.

[62] [C:] WIEN DIE WELT BERÜHMTE KAYSERL. RESID. STADT nach ihrem PROSPECT u: GRUND RISS, samt anstossender GEGEND und NEUEN LINIEN um die VOR-STÄDTE. verfertigt und verlegts MATTH. SEUTTER in AUGSP. — 494 × 581 mm.
[Inset:] [T:] Prospect der Kayserl. Residenz Stadt WIEN, wie solche von Mitternacht anzusehen. — (View). 127 × 571 mm. See [33].

[63] [C:] MANHEIMIUM Munitissimum Oppidum et hodierno die Residentia Electoris Palatini, ad Confluentes Rheni et Nicri, juxta recentissimam delineationem edita per MATTHÆUM SEUTTER, S.CÆS. ET REG. CATHOL. MAJEST. GEOGRAPHUM, AUGUSTÆ VINDEL. — 489 × 565 mm.
[Inset:] [T:] Prospect der Chur Fürstl. Haupt und Residenz Statt MANHEIM. — (View). 145 × 554 mm.

[64] [T:] TREVERIS ad Mosellam, Metropolis et Sedes Archi-Episcopi et Electoris ejusdem, olim antiqvitate et Claritudine præcipua. Labore et sumptibus MATTHÆI SEUTTERI SAC. CÆS. MAY. Geographo. TRIER an der Mosel, die Haupt u: Residentz Statt des dasigen Ertz-Bischoff u: Chur Fürsten, ehemals wegen ihres Alterthum u: herrl. Zustands fast berühmt. verfertigt u: in Verlag bey M. SEUTTER, KAYS. MAY. Geogr. in Augsp. — 489 × 575 mm.
[Inset:] (View). 120 × 339 mm.

[65] [C:] ERFORDIAE primariae THVRINGIAE Vrbis novissima Ichnographia, cura & studio prodüt C. A. MOLITORIS CANTORIS ET CANONICI. Col: Eccl. B.M.V. Excudentibus Homañianis Heredibus, Norimbergæ. A.⁰ 1745. ... ERFVRTH, der Haupt Stadt in THVRINGEN neuester mit Fleiss verfertigter Grundriss, Ans Licht gestellt von Homænnischen Erben. — 503 × 555 mm.
[Inset:] (View). 122 × 551 mm.

[66] [C:] Eigentliche Abbildung und Prospecte derer Kirchen, Palläst, prächtigen publiqven Gebäuen u. Statuen so in der Königl. Preussich und Churfürstlich Brandenburgischen Residenz-Statt BERLIN anzutreffen. verlegt von MATTH. SEUTTER Kayserl. Geographo in Augspurg. — (Views). 484 × 557 mm.

[67] [T:] PLAN du MAYENCE, ville fort de l'Archeveché du meme Nom ... — = 1720—1771:[68].

[68] [C:] PROSPECTUS Principalis Waldeccensis Arcis et Novæ Urbis PYRMONTII, cum vicinis et adjacentibus Fontibus Mineralibus et finitimis locis, æri incisus et excusus per MATTHÆUM SEUTTER, S.Cæs. et Reg: Cath. Majest. Geogr. Augustæ Vind. — [T:] I. C. Otto delin. A.⁰1738. — (View). 491 × 567 mm.

[69] [a] t'Oude Hof in's Gravenhage waer K. CAREL III. zyn verblyf is geweest, Eyndelyk met de Gecombineerde vloot op de Adm: Rooke vertrocke. den 3 Ianuary 1704. Vetus Aula Hagae Comitis, in qua commoratus est CAROLUS III. Hispaniarum Rex, prius quam in Portugalliam trajiceret cum classe foederata. Pet: Schenk exc: Amst: C.P. (View). 142 × 185 mm.
[b] Landing van zyn M.ᵗ CAREL de III. Koning van Spanje: tot Lissabon in Portugael. den 7 Maert 1704. Appulsus CAROLI III Hispaniarum Regis ad Vrbem Lisbonam 7 Martii 1704. Pet: Schenk exc: Amst: C.P. (View). 142 × 185 mm.
[c] Held-haftige actie, vant' gecombineerde Leger onder de H. van Marlb. en P.ʳ L. van Baden, de Fransen en By'ren, in haer voordeel aen gegrepen, en geslagen. den 2 Iuly 1704. Pugna egregie pugnata, et res feliciter gestae a fortissimis Viris Duce Marleburgio, et Principe Badæo adversus Gallos. Pet. Schenk exc: Amst: C.P. (Map). 142 × 185 mm.
[d] Plan van Hochstett, van de Roemwaerdige Battailje onder het Commando der H.ʳ van Marlb: en P.ʳ Eug: tegens C. Byren en de G.ʳ Tallard. d'13 Aug: 1704. Planum oppidi Hogstadii, cum ibi feliciter pugnaretur auspicus Ducis Marleburgii et P.ʳ Eugenii, adversus Gallos et Bavaros. 1704. Pet: Schenk exc: Amst: C.P. 140 × 185 mm.
[e] [T:] AUGSBURG — Legers der Byersen, Fransen, en Geallieerden by Augsburg, soo als die gelegen hebben. den 15 en 23 Iuly 1704. Exercitus Gallorum, Bavarorum, et Foederatorum ad Augustam Vindelicorum, quomodo erant positi. 15 et 23 Iulii 1704. Pet: Schenk exc: Amst: C.P. (Map). 140 × 183 mm.
[f] GIBRALTER Verovert door de P.ʳvan Hessen Darmstadt, met de ontscheepte Militie van de Eng: en Holl: onder de Adm: Rooke en Callenberg. den 4.Aug: 1704. CALPE Capta a Principe Hassiae Darmstadi, Anglis et Batavis militibus e navibus egredi jussis, Ducibus Rookio et Callenbergio. 4 Aug 1704. Pet: Schenk exc: Amst: C.P. (View). 142 × 185 mm.
[g] Verwinning der Eng: en Holl: onder 't belyt van de Admiralen Rooke en Kallenberg, behaelt op de Fransen by Mallaga onder den G.ʳ van Toulouse. den 24 Aug: 1704. Victoria Anglorum et Batavorum Ducibus Rookio et Callenbergio adversus Gallos, Duce Tolosano ad Mallagam parta. 24 Aug: 1704. Pet: Schenk exc: Amst: C.P. 142 × 183 mm.
[h] [T:] LANDAU — Belegering der Stadt Landau, met aenwysinge, hoe verre dagelyks gevordert is, onder 't beleit des Roomschen Konings en P.ʳ L. van Baden. Overgegeven 'd 26 Nov: 1704. Obsessio urbis Landavii, docente hac tabella quantum indies profecerint foederati, auspiciis Romanorum Regis, et Principis Badaci. Pet: Schenk exc: Amst: C.P. 142 × 183 mm.
[i] GIBRALTER doorde Marquies 'd Villa Davias belegert. 'd 12 Nov: 1704 en door de Vies-Admiraal Leake met 20 Eng: en Holl: schepen, met Amonitie versien doen opbreken etc. CALPE obsessa ab Hispanis, qui Solvere obsidionem coacti sunt ab Anglis et Batavis, postquam illuc cum classe 20 navium venissent. Pet: Schenk exc: Amst: C.P. (Map). 142 × 185 mm.
[The whole plate:] Uncoloured. 490 × 580 mm.

[70] [T:] PLAN der Hochfürstl. Residenz- und Haubt-Stadt CASSEL in Nieder-Hessen nebst dem Hochfürstl. Lust-Garten auf der Aue. Herausgegeben von Homæñischen

Erben. A 1742. ... PLAN de la Ville Capitale de CASSEL en basse Hesse, levé nouvellement et mis au jour par les Heritiers d'Homann. — [T:] revidirt von Herrn Leopold Ingen.Hauptm. — 496 × 558 mm.
[Inset:] [T:] Prospect der Stadt CASSEL von Osten. — (View). 75 × 555 mm. [C:] Die Gegend von CASSEL — (Map). 105 × 111 mm.

[71] [T:] RATISBONA in media Bavaria ad Danubium sita, probe munita, et præter florentem mercaturam, ob continuata ab A.º 1662. Comitia per omnen Europam celebratissima Libera Imperii Rom. Civitas. excusa, et venum exposita à MATTH. SEUTTER CIVE AUGUSTANO SAC. CÆS. MAJEST. GEOGR. REGENSPURG eine mitten in Baijren an der Donau gelegene, wohl befestigte, und neben der guten Handelschafft, auch wegen des schon von A.º 1662. continuirlich daselbst gehaltenen Reichs Tages weltberühmte Freye Reichs Statt. herausgegeben von M. SEUTTER KAYSERL. GEOGR. IN AUGSP. — [T:] Johann Ulrich Krauss Architect delineavit — 495 × 569 mm.
[Inset:] [T:] REGENSPURG — (View). 105 × 277 mm.

[72] [C:] Prospectus illustriores celeberrimæ Archiepiscopalis Urbis SALISBURGENSIS, præsipuorumque in ea magnificorum ac admirabilium tam sacrorum quam profanorum ædificiorum, in Ornamentum Tabulæ Geographicæ æri incisi ac venum expositi a MATTHÆO SEUTTERO S.C.Maj. Geogr. Augusta Vind. Die vornehmste Prospect Der weltberühmten Erzbischöfflichen Statt SALZBURG, und derselben vornehmsten prächtig und wunderbahren so wohl geistlich als weltlichen Gebäuden, zu mehrerer Auszierung selbiger Landcharte in Kupfer gestochen und zum Verkauf dargelegt von MATTHÆUS SEUTTER I.R.K.M.G. in Augspurg. — (Views). 483 × 567 mm.
[T:] Die Hoch Fürstliche Haupt und Residentz STADT SALTZBURG, von Mitternacht anzusehen. — (View). 120 × 360 mm.

[73] [C:] BREMA. — [C:] BREMA libera R.I. urbs Ex ampliori G.M.L. delinatione In minutiorem hanc translata æriq₃ incisa â Casparo Schultzen. A.D.M. DC LXIV. — Uncoloured. 229 × 405 mm.

[74] [C:] MÜNCHEN, die weitberühmt, præchtig und wohl fortificirte Chur-Fürstl. Haupt u: Residenz Stadt des Herzogthums Bayern. verlegts MATTH. SEUTTER KAYS. GEOGR. in AUGSPURG. ... — 486 × 568 mm.
[Insets:] [T:] Die Churfürstliche Haupt und Residentz Stadt MÜNCHEN, wie solche von Mitternacht gegen Mittag anzusehen ist. — (View). 125 × 557 mm.
[T:] Prospect des Weitberühmten Chur Fürstl: Bayrischen Lust Schlosses Nümphenburg unweit München samt dem Vortrefflichen Lust Garten. — (View). 131 × 148 mm.

[75] [C:] CLAGENFURTUM Ducatus Carinthiæ Metropolis cura et impensis MATTHÆI SEUTTERI. Geogr. Cæsarei et Chalcogr. Augustæ Vindel. accuratiss delin. CLAGENFURT die Haupt Stadt des Herzogthums Kärnthen im Grundriss und Prospect heraus gegeben von MATTHÆUS SEUTTER, Kayserlichen Geographo und Kupfferstecher in Augspurg. — [T:] N.I.G.Surgant Geom. Provinc. delin. — 499 × 340 mm.
[Inset:] [T:] Prospect von CLAGENFURT der Haupt Stadt in Kärnthen. — (View). 82 × 340 mm.

[76] [C:] Die Kays. Residentz- u. Haubt-Stadt WIEN, nebst den Vorstætten in einem accuraten Plan u. Prospect entworfen und edirt von H.E. ... — 489 × 538 mm.
[Inset:] (View). 98 × 533 mm.

[77] [T:] WRATISLAVIA antiquissima et celeberrima DUCAT. SILESIACI Metropolis ac florentissimum Bonarum Artium et Mercium Emporium ad amnem Viadrum. BRESLAU die uhralte ū Hochberühmte Haupt Statt des Herzogth. Schlesien auch Vortrefflicher aufenthalt der Musen ū. florisanter Handels Plaz an dem Oder Strom. verlegts Matth. Seutter in Aug. — [T:] Der. Röm. Kaj. Maj. Geogr. — 494 × 571 mm.
[Inset:] [T:] BRESLAW — (View). 89 × 333 mm.

[78] [T:] SCENOGRAPHIA Urbium SILESIÆ Tab. X d.i. VORSTELLUNG der Stædte SCHLESIENS X. Tab: in welcher die Prospecte von den fürnehmsten Stædten des Fürstenth. OPPELN, nebst einigen andern Glogauischen und Stands-Herrschaftlichen zu sehen; verzeichnet von F.B. Werner, u. herausgegeben von Hom. Erben Nürnberg. ... — (View). 500 × 578 mm.
[a] [T:] KOSEL [Oppeln] — 153 × 147 mm.
[b] [T:] OPPELN. — 153 × 268 mm.
[c] [T:] CLOSTER CZARNOWANS [Oppeln] — 153 × 147 mm.
[d] [T:] KRAPITZ [Oppeln] — 150 × 157 mm.
[e] [T:] KOEBEN [Glog] — 150 × 175 m.
[f] [T:] NEVSTADT [Oppeln] — 150 × 157 mm.
[g] [T:] PRAVSNITZ in der Standts Herrschafft, Trachenberg — 152 × 155 mm.
[h] [T:] ENGELSBERG in der Herrschafft Freudenthal — 152 × 153 mm.
[i] [T:] FREYHAN in der Stands Herrschafft Militsch — 152 × 155 mm.

[79] [T:] SCENOGRAPHIA Vrbium SILESIÆ, Tab: IX. d.i. PROSPECTE der Stædte SCHLESIENS, IX.Tabell, in welcher die Stædte der Fürstenth. GLOGAU &c. vorgestellet werden, gezeichnet von F B.Werner, und edirt von Hom. Erben Nürnberg,... — (Views). 468 × 546 mm.
[a] [T:] RATIBOR Haubtst. des Fürstenth. dieses Nahmens. — 142 × 271 mm.
[b] [T:] OBER GLOGAV von vielen insgemein KLEIN GLOGAV benambset in das Fürstenth. Oppeln gehörig — 142 × 270 mm.
[c] [T:] FREYSTADT [Glogauisch] — 145 × 152 mm.
[d] [T:] ALTEN SCHŒNAV im HIRSCHBERGISCHEN. — 145 × 180 mm.
[e] [T:] GVRAV [Glog.] — 145 × 152 mm.
[f] [T:] GROS GLOGAV. — 142 × 268 mm.
[g] [T:] TROPPAV Haubtst. des Fürstenth. dieses Nahmens. — 142 × 268 mm.

[80] SCENOGRAPHIA URBIUM SILESIÆ TAB.VIII. das ist, VORSTELLUNG der Prospecte von den Stædten SCHLESIENS, Achte T. in welcher die fürnehmsten Stædte des Fürst. IAUER accurat vorgestellet werden, entworfen von F.B.Werner Siles. und ausgefertiget von Homænnischen Erben, Nürnberg 1739. ... (Views). 468 × 575 mm.
[a] [T:] Lauer — 154 × 267 mm.
[b] [T:] Hirschberg — 154 × 270 mm.
[c] [T:] Closter und Stadtel Liebethal — 150 × 160 mm.
[d] [T:] Warmbad — 150 × 160 mm.
[e] [T:] Lemberg vulgo Löwenberg — 150 × 155 mm.
[f] [T:] Buntzlau — 161 × 160 mm.
[g] [T:] Schmiedeberg — 161 × 253 mm.
[h] [T:] Greiffenberg — 161 × 155 mm.

[81] [C:] SCENOGRAPHIA URBIUM SILESIÆ TAB: VII. i e. VORSTELLUNG der PROSPECTE von den vornehmsten Stædten der Fürstenth. MÜNSTERB. IÆGERND. im H^Z· SCHLESIEN entworfen von F.B.Werner u. herausgegeben von HOMÆNNISCHEN ERBEN Nürnberg A. 1738 ... — (Views). 481 × 572 mm.
[a] [T:] MÜNSTERBERG [Haupst. des Fürstenth.] — 168 × 271 mm.
[b] [T:] FRANCKENSTEIN [Münsterberge.] — 168 × 273 mm.
[c] [T:] Das Fürstl. Stift und Closter CAMENTZ [Münsterb.] — 145 × 148 mm.
[d] [T:] IAEGERNDORF — 145 × 254 mm.
[e] [T:] Das Fürstl. Stift und Closter HENRICHAV [Münsterberge.] — 145 × 158 mm.
[f] [T:] SILBERBERG [Münsterberge.] — 158 × 148 mm.
[g] [T:] REICHSTEIN Ein Kayserl. freye Berg-Stadt, welches Bergwerk zum goldenen Esel genant, worvon den Schlesiern der Nahme Esels-fresser Schimpfweis gegeben worden. [Münsterberge.] — 158 × 160 mm.

[82] SCENOGRAPHIA URBIUM SILESIÆ TAB. VI. das ist, VORSTEL^LUNG der Prospecte von Stædten SCHLESIENS, Sechste Tabell, in welcher die Fürnehmsten

Stædte des Fürst. SCHWEIDNITZ accurat vorgestellet werden, entworfen von F.B.Werner Siles. und ausgefertiget von Homænnischen Erben, Nürnberg 1738. ... (Views). 457 × 584 mm.
- [a] [T:] REICHENBACH — 150 × 152 mm.
- [b] [T:] SCHWEIDNITZ — 150 × 270 mm.
- [c] [T:] SIRIGAV — 150 × 156 mm.
- [d] [T:] Schloss FÜRSTENSTEIN von Mittag — 150 × 152 mm.
- [e] [T:] LANDSHVT — 150 × 270 mm.
- [f] [T:] Das Schloss FÜRSTENSTEIN v. Morgen. — 150 × 156 mm.
- [g] [T:] FREŸBERG — 151 × 165 mm.
- [h] [T:] Privilegirte Gnaden-Kirche zur heiligen Dreyfaltigkeit vor Schweidnitz — 151 × 165 mm.
- [i] [T:] ZOBTEN — 151 × 168 mm.

[83] [C:] SCENOGRAPHIA URBIUM SILESIÆ TAB: V. i e. VORSTELLUNG der PROSPECTE von den vornehmsten Stædten der Fürstenth. LIEGNITZ u. TESCHEN im Herzogth. SCHLESIEN entworfen von F. B. Werner u. herausgegeben von HOMÆNNISCHEN ERBEN Nürnberg A. 1738 ... — (Views). 472 × 568 mm.
- [a] [T:] LIEGNITZ — 163 × 268 mm.
- [b] [T:] TESCHEN — 163 × 268 mm.
- [c] [T:] LÜBEN (Liegn.) — 151 × 161 mm.
- [d] [T:] GOLDBERG (Liegn.) — 151 × 161 mm.
- [e] [T:] FREYSTADTEL (im Teschnischen Fürstenthum.) — 151 × 167 mm.
- [f] [T:] GRADITZBERG [Liegn.] mit dem neuen darunter gelegenen Gräfl. Frankenberg. Schloss. — 152 × 161 mm.
- [g] [T:] PARCHWITZ (Liegn.) — 152 × 167 mm.

[84] [C:] SCENOGRAPHIA URBIUM SILESIÆ TAB. IV. das ist VORSTELUNG der Prospecte von den Stædten SCHLESIENS, Vierte Tabell in welcher die Fürnehmsten Stædte des Fürstenthums NEISE accurat vorgestellet werden, entworfen von F.B.Werner Siles. und ausgefertiget von Homænnischen Erben, Nürnberg 1738. ... — (Views). 492 × 567 mm.
- [a] [T:] NEIS. — 157 × 265 mm.
- [b] [T:] WARTA. — 157 × 147 mm.
- [c] [T:] HOTZENPLOTZ. — 157 × 150 mm.
- [d] [T:] OTTMACHAV. — 151 × 150 mm.
- [e] [T:] ZIEGENHALS. — 151 × 150 mm.
- [f] [T:] ZVCKMANTEL. — 151 × 150 mm.
- [g] [T:] Schloss Iohannisberg u. Stædtl Iauernig — 150 × 150 mm.
- [h] [T:] GROTKAV. — 150 × 150 mm.
- [i] [T:] PATSCHKAV. — 150 × 150 mm.

[85] [C:] SCENOGRAPHIA URBIUM SILESIÆ TAB: III i.e. VORSTELLUNG der PROSPECTE von den vornehmsten Stædten des Fürstenth. WOHLAU im Herzoght. SCHLESIEN, entworfen von F. B. Werner u. herausgegeben von HOMÆNNISCHEN ERBEN Nürnberg A: 1737 ... — (Views). 480 × 546 mm.
- [a] [T:] WOHLAV — 187 × 270 mm.
- [b] [T:] PROSPECT der Stadt RÜTZEN, im Wohlauischen Fürstenth. in Schlesien gelegen, alswo die Rütznische Crayss-Täge von desselben Herren Creyssständen in der so genanden Land-stube gehalten werden, welcher gestalt solcher Prospect A. 1736. sich præsentiret, sambt der Gegend wie weit selbige auf dem Schloss allda zu sehen. ... — [C:] Dem Hoch-u Wohlgebohrnē Herrn Herrn HANS FRIDERICH des H.R.Reichs Freyherrn von ROTH. Erb Herr̄ der Stadt Rützen wie auch der Gütter Irsingn klein Laurschütz, Hern Laurschütz der Rom. Kays. May. Hochmeritirt wirkl. Reichs Hof-Rath. humill. dedic. F B Werner — 187 × 270 mm.
- [c] [T:] STEINAV — 142 × 153 mm.
- [d] [T:] RAVDEN — 142 × 153 mm.
- [e] [T:] HERRN STADT — 142 × 153 mm.
- [f] [T:] Fürstlich Stifft u. Clost. Leubus — 142 × 153 mm.
- [g] [T:] Closter Gros-Strenz der PP. Carmeliter-Ordens in der Standts-Herrsch. Trachenberg — 142 × 153 mm.

[86] [T:] SCENOGRAPHIA Vrbium SILESIÆ, Tab: II. d.i. PROSPECTE der Sædte SCHLESIENS II.Tab: in welcher die Stædte der Fürstenth. BRESLAW und SAGAN vorgestellet werden, gezeichnet von F.B.Werner, und edirt von Hom. Erben. Nürnberg, ... — (Views). 463 × 500 mm.
- [a] [T:] BRESLAW — 142 × 290 mm.
- [b] [T:] Prospect der Insul S Iohannis oder Doms vor Breslau — 106 × 168 mm.
- [c] [T:] NAMSLAV (Bresl.) — 108 × 168 mm.
- [d] [T:] BRESLAV, von der Oder Seyten. — 145 × 290 mm.
- [e] [T:] NEVMARCK (Bresl.) — 108 × 168 mm.
- [f] [T:] SAGAN, wie es nach dem A. 1731 erlittenen grossen Brand anzusehen. — 147 × 290 mm.
- [g] [T:] LEOBSCHÜTZ, vulg. Lischwitz genandt (Iaegernd:) — 112 × 168 mm.

[87] [T:] SCENOGRAPHIA Vrbium SILESIÆ, Tab: I. d.i. PROSPECTE der Stædte SCHLESIENS, I. Tabell, in welcher die Stædte der Fürstenth. OELS und BRIEG vorgestellet werden, gezeichnet von F B.Werner, und edirt von Hom. Erben. Nürnberg, ... — (Views). 470 × 555 mm.
- [a] [T:] BRIEG — 151 × 275 mm.
- [b] [T:] OELS — 151 × 276 mm.
- [c] [T:] OLAV (Brieg) — 142 × 160 mm.
- [d] [T:] CL. TREBNITZ. (Oels.) — 72 × 160 mm.
- [e] [T:] IVLIVSBVRG. (Oels.) — 70 × 160 mm.
- [f] [T:] FESTENBERG (Oels.) — 143 × 160 mm.
- [g] [T:] NIMTSCH (Brieg) — 144 × 160 mm.
- [h] [T:] STREELEN. (Brieg) — 144 × 160 mm.
- [i] [T:] BERNSTADT (Oels) — 144 × 160 mm.

[88] = [44] in this ed. with small alterations.

[89] [C:] PRAGA celeberrima et maxima totius BOHEMIÆ Metropolis et Universitas florentissima ad Muldam Fl. PRAG die Berühmtest ū. grösseste Haupt-Stadt ū. florisanteste Universitæt des Königreichs BÖHMEN. Verfertiget ū. verlegt von M. SEUTTER, I.R.K.M.G. IN AUGSPURG. ... — 490 × 568 mm.
- [Inset:] [T:] PRAG — (View). 109 × 559 mm.

[90] = [45] in this ed.

[91] = [54] in this ed.

[92] [C:] Grundriss und Prospect des Welt-berühmten CARLSBAD, mit unterschiedlichen Gegenden accurat gezeichnet und ausgefertiget von Homännischen Erben. ... Anno 1733. — 488 × 574 mm.
- [a] [C:] Schönes Lust-Haus u. Spaziergang die Wiesen genandt im CARLSBAD. — (View). 112 × 188 mm.
- [b] [C:] Der sied heisse Brudel oder Ausbruch des mineralischen Wassers im CARLSBAD. — 112 × 187 mm.
- [c] [C:] Grundriss der Gassen und Gebäude in CARLSBAD. ... — 175 × 282 mm.
- [d] [C:] Angenehmer Prospect in der Stadt CARLSBAD gegen Mittag anzusehen ... — (View). 175 × 282 mm.
- [e] [T:] Wahrer Prospect des weit berühmten warmen Bads und Stadt CARLSBAD — (View). 191 × 568 mm.

[93] [C:] NIEUWE PLATTE GROND van 'S GRAVENHAGE MET DE PUBLICQUE GEBOUWEN opgedraagen aan DE EDELE ACHTBARE HEERE BURGERMEESTERS EN REGEERDERS DER SELVE STEDE. Door haar Edelheÿts Onderdanigste en gehoorsaamste Dienaresse Anna Beek. ... — [T:] J. Rousset delin: — Uncoloured. 472 × 578 mm. See [98].

[94] [T:] URBIS TRAIECTI AD RHENUM NOVISSIMA ET ACCURATISSIMA DELINEATIO APUD R. & J.OTTENS. — [C:] NOBILISSIMIS ET AMPLISSIMIS Civitatis Trajectinæ Consulibus et Senatoribus Hanc Novissimam et exactissimam Urbis Suæ Tabulam Humillime D.D.D. C. Specht — [T:] Jan V. Vianen. Fecit. — Uncoloured. 483 × 571 mm.

[95] [C:] PLAN DE MAESTRICHT ... [C:] A PARIS Chez S.r de Beaurain Geographe Ordin.re du Roy Quay des Augustins proche la Rue Pavée. — Uncoloured. 234 × 365 mm.

[96] [T:] AMSTER[DAM] — Uncoloured. (The map is a

continuation of [99]). 571 × 437 mm.
[Inset:] [C:] CAARTE VAN AMSTELLAND. — (Map). 205 × 160 mm.

[97] [C:] AMSTERDAM die Weltberühmte Haupt- und Handel Statt in Holland sowohl im Prospect als Grund-Riss auf das neuest und accurateste entworffen und verlegt von MATTH. SEUTTER Ihro Röm. Kajserl. Majest. Geogr. — [T:] in Augspurg — 492 × 576 mm.
[Inset:] [T:] AMSTERDAM. — (View). 101 × 362 mm.

[98] [C:] HAGA COMITUM, [Germ. GRAVEN-HAAG Gall. la Haye] Sedes ordinum Belgii foederati ichnographica & cumfacie ædificiorum ni ipsa publicorum repræsentata. Editoribus Homañianis Heredibus. ... — 504 × 563 mm.
[Inset:] [T:] PROSPECT von GRAVEN HAAG — (View). 96 × 559 mm. See [93].

[99] [T:] [AMSTER]DAM. — [C:] PLAN TRES EXACT DE LA FAMEUSE VILLE MARCHANDE D'AMSTERDAM Gravée et mis au jour Par HENRY DE LETH à l'enseigne du Pecheur — Uncoloured. (The map is a continuation of [96]). 567 × 438 mm.

[100] [T:] A TRUE PLAN OF BERGEN-OP-ZOOM With the Forts Lines and Country adjacent Also the Approaches of the FRENCH under Count Lowendahl who Opened the Trenches Iuly 5 1747 ... — Publish'd by I. Millan Whitehall Augst 31st 1747. Price 1^s Col^d 2^s — Uncoloured. 447 × 390 mm.

[101] [C:] A Genuine and Exact Plan of the Fortifications of BERGEN-OP-ZOOM with the Forts MOERMONT, PINSEN, and ROVER, and ẛ Line of STEENBERGE Also of The French Trenches and Attacks during ẛ Present Siege. Being an exact Copy of One lately sent from the Hague. — Printed for Tho: Bowles in St Pauls Church Yard & Iohn Bowles at the Black Horse in Cornhill. — Uncoloured. 273 × 399 mm.

[102] [T:] MARCHIONATUS SACRI ROMANI IMPERII. — [C:] Nobilissimo, Amplissimo, Prudentissimoq$_3$ Senatuj Urbis Antverpiæ, nec non Marchionatus Sacri Imperij, Viris Consultissimis Sapientissimisq$_3$, hanc Novam, et à quamplurimis mendis expurgatam totjus Territorij Tabulam, lubentissimo, devotissimoq$_3$ animo offert, dedicat, consecrat. Nicolaus Jansenius Piscator: — [T:] Ꝟisscher Excudebat — (Map). Uncoloured. 457 × 554 mm.
[Insets:] [T:] ANTWERPEN — (View). Oval 60 × 260 mm. [T:] ANTWERPEN — [C:] Sic se offert Antverpia Septimontio, Bredâ et Gravâ venienti Antwerpen, soomen komt van Sevenbergen Breda en de Graeff. — (View). Oval 48 × 128 mm. [T:] ANTWERPEN — [C:] Sic se offert Antverpia, Mechliniâ, Bruxelljs, et Lovanio venienti. Antwerpen soo men komt van Mechelen Bruxel en Leuven — (View). Oval 48 × 128 mm. [T:] Tabella hæc in gratiam Spectatorum addita ut Ostium Scaldis videant simul etiam propugnacula, Aggeres, Terras que à Mare absorptas. Dit Caertjen is hier by gevoecht om te vertonen den uytloop vande Schelde mitsgaders de schansen, dycken en t verdroncken lant daer aen leggende. — (Map). 80 × 160 mm.

[103] [a] [C:] HUY (wiens gesight inde voorige) verweerd vanden 26 May tot den 11 Iun. 1705. HOYA, Cronstromio gubernante, adversus Gallorum insultus, usque ad 11 Iun. defensa: 1705. P.Schenk exc. Amst: C.P. — 151 × 187 mm.
[b] [C:] ALBERQUERQUE, in Spanje, ontrent de grenssen van Portugal by Elvas, onderwerpt sich Koning Carel de III, den 10 Iun 1705. ALBUQUERQUA, in Lusitaniæ finibus, et haud procul ab Emerita, regi Carolo III sese subjecit, die 10 Iuny, 1705. P. Schenk exc: Amst: C.P. — (View). 151 × 190 mm.
[c] [C:] Ponty word geslagen, in de baey van Gibralter (sie deese ook in de voorige) van de vlooten der Geallieerde, den 20 Meert. 1705. Maritimo prælio in sinu Calpetano Galli á Foederatis devincuntur, die 20 Martii, 1705. P. Schenk exc: Amst: C.P. — (View). 151 × 187 mm.
[d] [C:] De Fransse, door Eugenius, aan den Adda by Cassano en Treviglio, geslagen, den 16 Aug. 1705. Galli, duce Eugenio, ad Adduam, prope Cassanum et Trevilium profligati, die 16 Aug. 1705. P. Schenk exc: Amst: C.P. — 151 × 187 mm.
[e] [C:] De Linien in Vlanderen, by het Fort S Philippe, tusschen Brugge en Gent, door den Baron Spar, gebrooken, den 4 Aug. 1705. Gallorum præcinctiones in Flandria, ad Munimentum Divi Philippi, divellit baro Sparrius, die 4 Aug. 1705. P. Schenk exc: Amst: C.P. — 151 × 190 mm.
[f] [C:] De Linien, in Braband, by Hillissem, ontrent Loven en Thienen, door Marlborough, gebrooken, den 18 Iul. 1705. Gallorum præcinctiones, in Brabantia, iuxta Hilleshemium, noctu perrumpit, ducesque capit Marlobrochius, die 18 Iul. 1705. P. Schenk exc: Amst: C.P. — 151 × 187 mm.
[g] [C:] HAGENAU in de Boven Elsas (welke ook inde voorige) by nacht van de Fransche de belegeraars gelaaten, den 5 Oct. 1705. HAGENOA (cuius munitiones ab hisce plane diversæ in superioribus) nocturno abitu deserta á Gallis, die 5 Oct. 1705. P. Schenk exc: Amst: C.P. — 147 × 187 mm.
[h] [C:] BARCELONA, aan de Middelandsche Zee, wel eer inder Carthaginenseren, Gothen, Sarazeenen en eindelyk der Franschen krygsmagt, onderwerpt sich koning Carel de III, den 14 Oct. 1705 BARCINOMEN Hisp. Tarraconensis urbem littoralem Hispanis eripiunt Galli, 1697; Gallis eripiunt Foederati tradantque regi Carolo III, die 14 Oct. 1705. P. Schenk exc: Amst:C.P. — 147 × 190 mm.
[i] [C:] LEEUWE, gemeenlyk Sout-Leeuwe, in Braband tusschen Thienen en S.Truyen, de Fransche ontweldigd, den 5 Aug. 1705. LEWIA ad Gefam torrentem (qui se in Geetam præcipitat) validum oppidum, Gallis extortum, die 5 Aug. 1705. P. Schenk exc: Amst: C.P. — 147 × 187 mm.
[The whole plate:] Uncoloured. 460 × 580 mm.

Notes: All the maps are blank on the back, and all are coloured except where otherwise, specified. This collection of town plans and views contains 40 maps by J.B. Homann, I.C. Homann or Homann's heirs, and 37 by Matthäus Seutter. The Homann maps are from the Städteatlas which forms vol.3 of the Homännischen Atlas geographicus Major. The British Library Map Library has two collections of town plans and views published by the Officina Homann; neither has a title-page, and both have been catalogued in the same way as our copy. Maps [12]—[18] and [95] are French maps in a individual style, forming a group quite different from the other maps in this collection. Maps [100—101] and [103] form another distinctive little group, quite different from the Homann and Seutter maps. A slip bearing a manuscript title in Swedish, 'Plan-Cartor', is pasted to the front cover of our copy.

Lit.: British Museum, Maps, vol. 7, c. 623, Sandler, Homännische Erben p. 400—402.

97 HONTERUS, JOHANNES 1530

IOANNIS HONTER CORONENSIS RVDIMENTORVM COsmographiæ libri duo. Quorū prior Astronomiæ, posterior Geographiæ principia, breuissime complectitur. Cœlorum partes, stellas cum flatibus, amnes, Regnaq́; cum populis, parue libelle tenes. [Colophon:] CRACOVIAE MATHIAS SCHARFENBERGIVS EXCVDEBAT. M.D.XXX. 15,7 cm.

[1] [World]
[T:] EVROPA AFRICA ASIA — Uncoloured. Text on verso. Circular map with 43 mm. diam.

Notes: The map appears on the title-page and after A5. According to Bagrow, Catal., I:111, the volume should also include a map entitled 'Vniversalis geographiæ typus', but this is wanting in our copy. The leaves are signed Aij — Aiiij, A5, B — Biiij; Bij is wanting. Nordenskiöld bought the volume unbound, in very fine old paper covers. He later had it bound in red leather, with gilt lettering, by Alfr. Lundin in Stockholm. On the inside of the back paper cover he has

98 HONTERUS, JOHANNES 1546

RVDIMENTA COSMOGRAPHICA. TIGVRI APVD FROSCHOuerum, Anno M.D.XLVI. 14 cm.

- [1] REGIONES ET NOMINA VENTORVM.
  [World] a 2 Circular map with 40 mm. diam. See 1530:[1].
- [2] [T:] VNIVERSALIS COSMOGRAPHIA — [T:] TIGVRI IVE .M.D.XLVI. — a 3 121 × 160 mm.
- [3] [T:] HISPANIA — 122 × 155 mm.
- [4] [T:] GALLIA — b 121 × 155 mm.
- [5] [C:] DANIAE ET PARTIS SVEDIÆ TYPVS — [T:] CK — Blank on the back. 185 × 223 mm.
- [6] [T:] GERMANIA. b 2 123 × 155 mm.
- [7] [T:] MAIOR POLONIA MINOR POLONIA — b 3 122 × 155 mm.
- [8] [T:] VNGARIA BOSNA DACIA THRACIA — 122 × 155 mm.
- [9] [T:] MACEDONIA ACHAIA PELOPONESVS — c 122 × 155 mm.
- [10] [T:] ITALIA — c 2 123 × 157 mm.
- [11] [T:] GALILAEA IVDAEA SYRIA MESOPOTAMIA CHALDAEA — c 3 123 × 155 mm.
- [12] [T:] ASIA MINOR — 122 × 157 mm.
- [13] [T:] ASIA — d 122 × 157 mm.
- [14] [T:] AFRICA — d 2 123 × 162 mm.
- [15] [T:] SICILIA — 122 × 77 mm.

Notes: All the maps, except [5], have maps on the verso, and they are all uncoloured. In this edition, America has been added to the circular map, [1]. The book was intended for use in schools, and the text of this edition is in hexameters, verse being easier to memorise than prose. Map [5], Daniae et partie Svediae typus, has been inserted between the two parts of Gallia; it is not original to the work. There are two plates before p. a2: CIRCVLI SPHAERAE CVM V. ZONIS, and ORDO PLANETARVM CVM ASPECTIBVS. The volume has been bound for Nordenskiöld, and bears his initials AEN in gold on the spine. His bookplate is on the inside of the front cover, and his signature on the first blank leaf. On the title-page is written in old ink: 'Fridericus Rechlinger est possessor huius libri 1595.' On the verso of the first blank leaf Nordenskiöld has written: 'Författad af Johannes Honterus. Kartan öfver Danmark och Södra Sverge finnes i något förstorad skala återgifven i Ortelius 1570. Den är sannolikt kopierad efter Marcus Jordani karta öfver Norden. — samt in häftad i Honteri Cosmografi utan att ursprungligen hafva tillhört arbetet.' (= Written by Johannes Honterus. Map of Denmark and southern Sweden reappears on a slightly larger scale in Ortelius, 1570. It is probably copied from Marcus Jordani's map of the north, and is inserted into Honterus's Cosmographica, to which, however, it does not belong.

Lit.: Bagrow p. 123 and 348, Bagrow, Catal., I:110—113, Facs. Atl., pp. 111—112.

99 HONTERUS, JOHANNES [1548?]

RVDIMENTORVM COSMOGRAphicorum Ioan. Honteri Coronensis libri III. cum tabellis Geographicis elegantissimis. De uariarum rerum nomenclaturis per classes, liber I. 16,2 cm.

- [1] REGIONES ET NOMINA VENTORVM.
  [World] = 1546:[1].
- [2] 1 [T:] VNIVERSALIS COSMOGRAPHIA — = 1546:[2].
- [3] 2 [T:] HISPANIA — = 1546:[3] with small alterations.
- [4] 3 [T:] GALLIA — = 1546:[4].
- [5] 4 [T:] GERMA[NIA] — = 1546:[6] with small alterations.
- [6] 5 [T:] MAIOR POLONIA MINOR POLONIA — = 1546:[7] with small alterations.
- [7] 6 [T:] VNGARIA BOSNA DACIA THRACIA — = 1546:[8] with small alterations.
- [8] 7 [T:] MACEDONIA ACHAIA PELOPON — = 1546:[9] with small alterations.
- [9] 8 [T:] ITALIA — = 1546:[10].
- [10] 9 [T:] GALILAEA IVDAEA SYRIA MESOPOTAMIA CHALDAEA — = 1546:[11].
- [11] 01 [T:] ASIA MINOR — = 1546:[12].
- [12] 11 [T:] ASIA — = 1546:[13].
- [13] 21 [T:] AFRICA — = 1546:[14].
- [14] [T:] SICILIA — = 1546:[15].

Notes: All the maps are blank on the back and uncoloured. The lower part of the title-page has been torn away, leaving the upper part of the name of the printer, Froschauer, but not his address or the date. The leaves bearing the maps have no signatures, but the maps themselves are numbered in the middle of the lower margin. Maps [11] and [13] are numbered 01 and 21 instead of 10 and 12. The leaves at the beginning as far as B 5, are very worn in the lower border. There are five blank leaves following the text section, before the maps. As in the edition of 1546, there are two plates CIRCVLI SPHAERAE CVM V. ZONIS and ORDO PLANETARVM CVM ASPECTIBVS; in this edition they are bound before the first map. The verso of the title-page bears part of an owner's stamp: VF or VE, in a simple wreath. The title-page bears the words 'Monastery S: Georgÿ Hercyn:syluæ' written in old ink.. The volume is unbound.

Lit.: See Honter 1530 and 1546.

100 HONTERUS, JOHANNES 1549

RVDIMENTORVM COSMOGRAPHICOrum Ioan. Honteri Coronensis libri III. cum tabellis Geographicis elegantissimis. De uariarum rerum nomenclaturis per classes, liber I. TIGVRI APVD FROSCHOuerum. Anno, M.D.XLIX.

Maps are wanting.

Notes: This 1549 edition of Honteri Rudimenta cosmographica, printed in Tiguri apud Froshonem, lacks all the maps. The volume was bound for Nordenskiöld, in boards with a leather spine. His signature is on the second blank leaf.

101 HONTERUS, JOHANNES 1552

RVDIMENTORVM COSMOGRAPHICOrum Ioan. Honteri Coronensis libri III. cum tabellis Geographicis elegantissimis. De uariarum rerum nomenclaturis per classes, liber I. TIGVRI APVD FROSCHOuerum. Anno, M. D. LII. 15,8 cm.

- [1] REGIONES ET NOMINA VENTORVM.
  [World] a 2 = 1546:[1]
- [2] [T:] VNIVERSALIS COSMOGRAPHIA — a 3 = 1546:[2] with small alterations.
- [3] [T:] HISPANIA — = 1546:[3] with small alterations.
- [4] [T:] GALLIA — b = 1546:[4] with small alterations.
- [5] [T:] GERMANIA — b 2 = 1546:[6] with small alterations.
- [6] [T:] MAIOR POLONIA MINOR POLONIA — b 3 = 1546:[7] with small alterations.

- [7] [T:] VNGARIA BOSNA DACIA THRACIA — = 1546:[8] with small alterations.
- [8] [T:] MACEDONIA ACHAIA PELOPONES — c = 1546:[9] with small alterations.
- [9] [T:] ITALIA — c 2 = 1546:[10] with small alterations.
- [10] [T:] GALILAEA IVDAEA SYRIA MESOPOTAMIA CHALDAEA — c 3 = 1546:[11].
- [11] [T:] ASIA MINOR — = 1546:[12].
- [12] [T:] ASIA — d = 1546:[13].
- [13] [T:] AFRICA — d 2 = 1546:[14].
- [14] [T:] SICILIA — = 1546:[15].

Notes: All the maps are backed by other maps; they are uncoloured. They appear at the end of the volume, following the text. The maps are the same as those in the 1546 edition, with occasional alterations to the lettering and the addition or erasure of some place-names. The volume was bound for Nordenskiöld by Alfr. Lundin of Stockholm; it bears his initials AEN in gold on the spine. His bookplate is pasted to the inside of the front cover, and his signature is on the first blank leaf, with the date 1896 and a few notes in old ink. On the second blank leaf is written, in old ink, 'Vt quisque est iur optimus, ita difficilime alios esse improbos suspicatur Cicero ad C. fratrem.'

Lit.: See Honter 1530, 1546.

102 HONTERUS, JOHANNES 1552

RVDIMENTORVM COSMOGRAPHICOrum Ioan. Honteri Coronensis libri III. cum tabellis Geographicis elegantissimis. De uariarum rerum nomenclaturis per classes, liber I. TIGVRI APVD FROSCHOuerum. Anno, M. D. LII. 17,2 cm.

Notes: This volume contains the same maps as the other 1552 edition in the collection. All the maps have maps on the verso and are uncoloured. They are bound at the beginning, before the text. The book is bound together with 'Berosi sacerdotis CHALDAICI, ANTIQUITATUM ITALIAE AC TOTIVS ORbis libri quinque... ANTVERPIAE ... M.D.LII.' It has a very beautiful vellum binding, mounted on wood, with blind tooling. There are numerous underlinings and other notes in old ink in the volume.

103 HONTERUS, JOHANNES 1561

Ioannis Honteri Coronensis, de Cosmographiæ rudimentis, & omnium propè rerum nomenclatura, Libri IIII. VNÀ CVM Tabellis Geographicis præcipuis. ADIECTIS Eiusdem Autoris tam Astronomiæ, quam Geographiæ principijs. Cœlorum partes, stellas cum flatibus, amnes, Regnaq; cum populis, parue Libelle tenes. [Colophon:] BASILEÆ, PER HENRICVM PETRI, ANNO DOMINI M. D. LXI. 15,7 cm.

- [1—2] ORBIS VNIVERSALIS DESCRIPTIO. & Hibernia.
  - [1] [World] 894—895 Pp 2 123 × 153 mm.
  - [2] [T:] HYBERNIA IRLAND — 896 124 × 78 mm.
- [3—4] HISPANIÆ TABVLA, & Maioricæ insulæ.
  - [3] [T:] HISPANIA — 898—899 Qq 2 123 × 152 mm.
  - [4] [T:] MAIORICA — 900 124 × 78 mm.
- [5—6] GALLIÆ TABVLA, & Angliæ.
  - [5] [T:] GALLIA — 902—903 Rr 2 123 × 154 mm.
  - [6] [T:] ANGLIA SCOTIA — 904 123 × 76 mm.
- [7—8] GERMANIÆ TABVLA, & Zelandiæ.
  - [7] [T:] GERMANIA — 906—907 Ss 2 124 × 153 mm.
  - [8] [T:] SEELANDIA SCANDIA — 908 120 × 77 mm.
- [9—10] ITALIÆ TABVLA, & Siciliæ insulæ.
  - [9] [T:] ITALIA — 910—119 (pro 911) Tt 2 123 × 152 mm.
  - [10] [T:] SICILIA — 912 121 × 78 mm.
- [11—12] GRÆCIÆ TABVLA, & Euboeæ insulæ.
  - [11] [T:] GRÆTIA — 914—915 Vu 2 123 × 152 mm.
  - [12] [T:] EVBOEA — 916 76 × 124 mm.
- [13—14] PALÆSTINÆ TABVLA, & Cypri insulæ.
  - [13] [T:] CANAAN — 918—919 Xx 2 124 × 153 mm.
  - [14] [T:] CYPRVS — 920 77 × 123 mm.
- [15—16] INDIÆ INTRA GANGEM TABVLA, & Iauæ minoris insulæ.
  - [15] [T:] CAMBAYA ORISSA DELLI DECAN — 922—923 Yy 2 121 × 154 mm.
  - [16] [T:] IAVA MAIOR — 924 122 × 75 mm.
- [17—18] INDIÆ EXTRA GANGEM TABVLA, & Taprobanæ insulæ.
  - [17] [T:] MACINIR regio CASCAR MANGAI regio CHINA BENGALA regio BERMA reg. AVA reg. PEGO regio SAMOTRÆ — 926—927 Zz 2 122 × 152 mm.
  - [18] [T:] TAPROBANA — 928 122 × 75 mm.
- [19—20] APHRICÆ TABVLA, & Mederæ insulæ.
  - [19] [T:] ÆTHIOPIA INTERIOR AFRICA EXTERIOR — 930—931 AA 2 122 × 153 mm.
  - [20] [T:] MÆDERA — 932 122 × 75 mm.
- [21—22] LIBYÆ TABVLA, & Melitæ insulæ.
  - [21] [T:] MAVRITANIA BARBARIA AFRICA minor LIBYA interior MELLIS — 934—935 BB 2 123 × 153 mm.
  - [22] [T:] MELITA — 936 123 × 77 mm.
- [23—24] ÆGYPTI TABVLA, & Cubæ insulæ.
  - [23] [T:] MARMARICA ÆTHIOPIA sub ÆGYPTO — 938—939 CC 2 124 × 153 mm.
  - [24] [T:] CVBA — 940 77 × 122 mm.

Notes: All the maps have maps on the verso and are uncoloured. This edition of Honterus, printed in Basel, belongs to the work: 'PROCLI DE SPHÆRA LIBER I. CLEOMEDIS DE MVNDO, siue circularis inspectionis meteororum Libri II. ARATI SOLENSIS PHÆnomena, siue Apparentia. DIONYSII AFRI DESCRIPTIO Orbis habitabilis. Omnia Græcè et Latinè ita coniuncta, ut conferri ab utriusq₃ linguæ studiosis possint. ADIECTIS Doctorum uirorum annotationibus. VNA CVM IO. HONTERI CORONENSIS De Cosmographiæ rudimentis duplici editione, ligata scilicet et soluta.... BASILEÆ, PER HENRICVM PETRI. [Colophon:] BASILEÆ, PER HENRICVM PETRI, ANNO DOMINO 1561.' The maps are not the same as those in the various Zürich editions; even the cordiform world map is a new one. On map [18] Taprobana is Sumatra, not Ceylon. The maps are in pairs, linked by a common title; the second map is on the verso of the first, and usually represents an island. According to Bagrow (Catal., I:112) these maps are not by Honterus.

The volume was bound for Nordenskiöld, and bears his initials A.E.N. in gold on the spine. His bookplate is on the inside of the front cover, and his signature on the first blank leaf. The second blank leaf bears the stamped signature of C.N. Antinori.

Lit.: Facs. Atl., 111—112, reproduction of maps p. 112, fig. 72 and p. 119, fig. 76, Bagrow, Catal., I:110—113.

104 HONTERUS, JOHANNES 1583

RVDIMENTORVM COSMOGRAPHICOrum Ioan. Honteri Coronensis libri III. cum tabellis Geographicis elegantissimis. De variarum rerum nomenclaturis per classes, Liber I. M. D. LXXXIII. 16,7 cm.

- [1] REGIONES ET NOMINA VENTORVM. [World] a 2 = 1546:[1].
- [2] [T:] VNIVERSALIS COSMOGRAPHIA — a 3 = 1546:[2] with small alterations.
- [3] [T:] HISPANIA — = 1546:[3] with small alterations.
- [4] [T:] GALLIA — b = 1546:[4] with small alterations.
- [5] [T:] GERMANIA — b 2 = 1546:[6] with small alterations.

[6]   [T:] MAIOR POLONIA   MINOR POLONIA — b 3 = 1546:[7] with small alterations.
[7]   [T:] VNGARIA BOSNA DACIA THRACIA — = 1546:[8] with small alterations.
[8]   [T:] MACEDONIA ACHAIA PELOPONESVS — c = 1546:[9] with small alterations.
[9]   [T:] ITALIA — c 2 = 1546:[10] with small alterations.
[10] [T:] GALILAEA IVDAEA SYRIA MESOPOTAMIA CHALDAEA — c 3 = 1546:[11].
[11] [T:] ASIA MINOR — = 1546:[12].
[12] [T:] ASIA — d = 1546:[13] with small alterations.
[13] [T:] AFRICA — d 2 = 1546:[14] with small alterations.
[14] [T:] SICILIA — = 1546:[15].

Notes: All the maps have maps on the verso, and are uncoloured. The work is printed on poor quality paper, and the print is sometimes very unclear. The title-page does not bear the printer's address. The title is surrounded by a decorative border. The volume is bound in new leather. On the verso of the first blank leaf, Nordenskiöld has pencilled 'Kartorna från samma stockar som 1546 uppl., men En och legender tryckta med losa typer'. [The maps are from the same plates as those in the 1546 edition, but some of the legends are type-set.]

Lit.: See Honter 1546.

105 HONTERUS, JOHANNES   1585

Ioannis Honteri Coronensis, de Cosmographiæ rudimentis, & omnium propè rerum nomenclatura, Libri IIII. VNÀ CVM Tabellis Geographicis præcipuis. ADIECTIS Eiusdem Autoris tam Astronomiæ, quàm Geographiæ principijs. Cœlorum partes, stellas cum flatibus, amnes, Regnaq̃3 cum populis, parue Libelle tenes. [Colophon:] BASILEAE PER HENRICVM PETRI, ANNO DOMINI M. D. LXXXV.   17 cm.

[1—2] ORBIS VNIVERSALIS DESCRIPTIO, & Hibernia:
   [1]   [World] 646—647   T 2 = 1561:[1].
   [2]   [T:] HYBERNIA IRLAND — 648 = 1561:[2].
[3—4] HISPANIAE TABVLA, & Maioricæ insulæ.
   [3]   [T:] HISPANIA — 650—651 V 2 = 1561:[3].
   [4]   [T:] MAIORICA — 652 = 1561:[4].
[5—6] GALLIAE TABVLA, & Angliæ.
   [5]   [T:] GALLIA — 654—655 X 2 = 1561:[5].
   [6]   [T:] ANGLIA   SCOTIA — 656 = 1561:[6].
[7—8] GERMANIAE TABVLA, & Zelandiæ.
   [7]   [T:] GERMANIA — 685—665 (pro 658—659) = 1561:[7].
   [8]   [T:] SEELANDIA SCANDIA — 660 = 1561:[8].
[9—10] ITALIAE TABVLA & Siciliæ insulæ.
   [9]   [T:] ITALIA — 662—663 Z 2 = 1561:[9].
   [10] [T:] SICILIA — = 1561:[10].
[11—12] GRAECIAE TABVLA & Eubœæ insulæ.
   [11] [T:] GRÆTIA — 666—667 Aa 2 = 1561:[11].
   [12] [T:] EVBOEA — 668 = 1561:[12].
[13—14] PALAESTINAE TABVLA, & Cypri insulæ.
   [13] [T:] CANAAN — 670—671 Bb 2 = 1561:[13].
   [14] [T:] CYPRVS — = 1561:[14].
[15—16] INDIAE INTRA GANGEM TABVLA, & Iauæ minoris insulæ.
   [15] [T:] CAMBAYA ORISSA DELLI DECAN — 674—675 Cc 2 = 1561:[15].
   [16] [T:] IAVA MAIOR — 676 = 1561:[16].
[17—18] APHRICAE TABVLA, & Mederæ insulæ.
   [17] [T:] ÆTHIOPIA INTERIOR   AFRICA EXTERIOR — 678—679 Dd 2 = 1561:[19].
   [18] [T:] MÆDERA — 680 = 1561:[20].
[19—20] INDIAE EXTRA GANGEM TABVLA, & Taprobanæ insulæ.
   [19] [T:] MACINIR CASCAR   MANGAI regio ... — 682—683 Ee 2 = 1561:[17].
   [20] [T:] TAPROBANA — 684 = 1561:[18].
[21—22] AEGYPTI TABVLA, & Cubæ insulæ.
   [21] [T:] MARMARICA ÆTHIOPIA sub ÆGYPTO — 686—687 Ff 2 = 1561:[23].
   [22] [T:] CVBA — 688 = 1561:[24].
[23—24] LIBYAE TABVLA, & Melitæ insulæ.
   [23] [T:] MAVRITANIA BARBARIA ... — 690—691 Gg 2 = 1561:[21].
   [24] [T:] MELITA — 692 = 1561:[22].

Notes: All the maps have maps on the verso and are uncoloured. Like the 1561 edition, this new edition, printed in Basel, belongs to the work PROCLI DE SPHAERA LIBER I ... BASILEAE, PER SEBASTIANVM HENRIC PETRI. The title-pages of the two editions are different. There are old manuscript notes in the margins of map [1]. The work is bound in old vellum, together with M. Erasmus Schmidt's Tractatus de Dialectis Graecorum... Wittenbergae 1621. Nordenskiöld's signature is on the first blank leaf.

Lit.: See Honter 1561.

106 HONTERUS, JOHANNES   1597

ENCHIRIDION COSMOGRAPHIAE: CONTINENS PRAECIPVARVM ORBIS REGIONVM DElineationes, elegantissimis tabulis expressas, solidisq́; declarationibus illustratas, Carmine Heroico, libris tribus: AVCTORE IHOANNE HONTERO Coronense. ACCESSIT Eiusdem liber de variarum rerum Nomenclaturis, in classes tributus. TIGVRI APVD IOHAN. VVOLPHIVM: ANNO M. D. IIIC.   16 cm.

[1]   REGIONES ET NOMINA VENTORVM. [World] a 2 = 1546:[1].
[2]   [T:] VNIVERSALIS COSMOGRAPHIA — a 3 = 1546:[2].
[3]   [T:] HISPANIA — = 1546:[3] with small alterations.
[4]   [T:] GALLIA — b = 1546:[4] with small alterations.
[5]   [T:] GERMANIA — b 2 = 1546:[6] with small alterations.
[6]   [T:] MAIOR POLONIA MINOR POLONIA — b 3 = 1546:[7] with small alterations.
[7]   [T:] VNGARIA BOSNA [DACIA] THRACIA — = 1546:[8] with small alterations.
[8]   [T:] MACEDONIA ACHAIA PELOPNESVS — c = 1546:[9] with small alterations.
[9]   [T:] ITA[LIA] — c 2 = 1546:[10] with small alterations.
[10] [T:] GALLIAEA IVDAEA SYRIA MESOPOTAMIA CHALDAEA — c 3 = 1546:[11] with small alterations.
[11] [T:] ASIA MINOR — = 1546:[12] with small alterations.
[12] [T:] ASIA -- d = 1546:[13] with small alterations.
[13] [T:] AFRICA — d 2 = 1546:[14] with small alterations.
[14] [T:] SICILIA — = 1546:[15].

Notes: All the maps have maps on the verso, and are uncoloured. The maps in this edition are mostly the same as those in the editions of 1546, 1548, 1552 and 1583, but on most of them a number of place-names have been removed, and on some the names have been reset. The volume is half bound in modern leather for Nordenskiöld, with the initials AEN in gold on the spine. Nordenskiöld's signature is on the first blank leaf.

Lit.: See Honter 1530 and 1546.

107 HORN, GEORG   1653

ACCURATISSIMA ORBIS ANTIQVI DELINEATIO. SIVE GEOGRAPHIA VETUS, SACRA, & PROFANA, Exhibens, Quicquid Imperiorum, Regnorum, Principatuum, Rerumpublicarum ab initio rerum ad praesentem usque Mundi statum fuit. Ad illustrandos tam sacros quam profanos Historicos Antiquos inprimis necessaria, CUI ADJUNXIMUS TABULAS PEUTINGERIANAS. Seriem Tabularum sequens pagina indicabit. AMSTELODAMI, Prostant apud JOANNEM JANSSONIUM, M DC LIII.   50,8 cm.

[1] [C:] ORBIS TERRARVM VETERIBVS COGNITI TYPVS GEOGRAPHICVS. — [An empty cartouche]. 400 × 503 mm.
[2] [T:] GEOGRAPHIA SACRA. — [T:] Ex Conatibus geographicis Abrahami Ortelij. — 357 × 474 mm.
[Inset:] ... ORBIS TERRARVM ... — Oval 61 × 101 mm.
[3] [C:] TABVLA ITINERARIA PATRIARCHARVM ABRAHAMI, ISAACI et IACOBI. — [C:] AMSTELODAMI, Apud Ioannem Ianssonium. — 378 × 520 mm.
[4] [C:] IUDÆÆ seu TERRÆ ISRAELIS Tabula geographica; in qua Locorum in Veteri et Novo Testamento celebratissimorum Situs accurate descripti. arte facta à Tilemanno Stella Sigenensi. — 354 × 483 mm.
[5] TRIBVS RVBEN, et GAD et partes orientales tribuum BENIAMIN, EPHRAIM, et DIMIDIÆ MANASSE intra Iordanem. 436 × 533 mm.
[6] [T:] Tribuum EPHRAIM, BENIAMIN, et DIMIDIÆ MANASSE intra Iordanem partes occidentales et partes septentrionalis DAN et IUDA. — 425 × 535 mm.
[7] [T:] TRIBVS ASER, et partes occidentales tribuum ZABVLON et ISACHAR. — 418 × 706 mm.
[8] [T:] DIMIDIA TRIBVS MANASSE Ultra Iordanem, TRIBUS NEPTALIM et partes orientales tribuum ZABVION et ISACHAR. — 434 × 706 mm.
[Inset:] [C:] PEREGRINATIO ABRAHÆ. — 132 × 210 mm.
[9] Pars maxima TRIBVS IVDA Versus orientem. 437 × 536 mm.
[Inset:] [C:] ITINERA ET MANSIONES DESERTI. — 142 × 216 mm.
[10] [T:] TRIBVS SIMEON et pars meridionalis TRIBVS DAN, et orientalis TRIBUS IVDA. — 418 × 537 mm.
[11] [C:] ÆGYPTVS ANTIQVA Divisa in Nomos Authore P. DUVAL Abbeviliense Regis Christianissimi Geographo. — [C:] A Monsieur Monsieur DOVIAT Sgr̃ de Montreuille, Con.er du Roy, et Maistre Ordinaire en sa Chambre des Comptes Par son Treshumble et obeisant Seruiteur P. DUVAL Geographe de sa Maieste. — 376 × 514 mm.
[12] [C:] ERYTHRAEI SIVE RVBRI MARIS PERIPLVS, OLIM AB ARRIANO DESCRIPTVS, NVNC VERO AB ABRAH. ORTELIO EX EODEM DELINEATVS. — [T:] Amstelodami, Sumptibus Ioannis Ianssonii. — 391 × 465 mm.
[Insets:] [T:] ANNONIS PERIPLVS. — [T:] [The northern hemisphere]. Circular maps with 76 mm. diam.
[13] [C:] AFRICAE PROPRIAE TABVLA. In qua, Punica regna uides, Tyrios, et Agenoris vrbem. — 370 × 513 mm.
[14] [C:] CYPRVS, Insula læta choris, blandorum et mater amorum. — [T:] Amstelodami, Sumptibus Ioannis Ianssonii. — 342 × 470 mm.
[15] [C:] CRETA Iovis magni, medio jacet insula ponto. Ex conatibus geographicis Abrahami Ortely. — [T:] Amstelodami, Sumptibus Ioannis Ianssonii. — 372 × 480 mm.
[16] [C:] HELLAS seu GRÆCIA Sophiani. — 362 × 494 mm.
[17] [C:] ATTICA, MECARICA, CORINTHIACA, BŒOTIA, PHOCIS, LOCRI. Ex Clarissimi D. T. VELII M. D. Delineatione. — [C:] Amstelodami Apud Joannem Janssonium. — 361 × 490 mm.
[18] [C:] ARGONAVTICA. — [T:] Petrus Kærius Cælavit Ætatis suæ 74. [1645] — 376 × 501 mm.
[Inset:] [T:] EVROPA. — 69 × 88 mm. [T:] THESSALIA DOLOPES LOCRI. — 70 × 70 mm. [T:] BITHYNIA. — 89 × 136 mm.
[19] [C:] AENEAE TROIANI NAVIGATIO Ad Virgilij sex priores Aeneidos. — [T:] Amstelodami, Sumptibus Ioannis Ianssonii. — 393 × 491 mm.
[Inset:] [C:] VLYSSIS ERRORES, ex Conatib. Geographicis Ab. Ortelij. — 108 × 207 mm.
[20] [C:] Tabula ITINERIS DECIES MILLE Græcorum sub Cyro contra fratrem suum Artaxerxem Regum Persarum; Eorumque Reditus sub Xenophonte; secundum ipsium Xenophontis Commentaria. Per P. du Val Abbevillensem, Geographum Regium. — [C:] A Haut et puissant Seigneur Messire FRANCOIS DE L'ISLE, seigneur de Mariuault, S Crespin, Ybouuiller, Aubouruille, Montagu, la Roue Alinuille, et autres lieux, Baron d'Ansouillé. par son tres humble et tres Obeissant Seruiteur P. du Val Geographe du Roy. — 411 × 491 mm.
[21] [C:] ALEXANDRI MAGNI MACEDONIS EXPEDITIO. — 365 × 467 mm.
[22] [C:] HISPANIÆ VETERIS DESCRIPTIO. Amstelodami Apud Joannem Janssonium. — [T:] Abraham Goos sculpsit. — 368 × 488 mm.
[Inset:] [T:] TARTESSIS. — 75 × 71 mm.
[23] [C:] GALLIA VETVS Ad Iulij Cæsaris commentaria. — [C:] AMSTELODAMI Apud Ioannem Ianssonium. — [T:] J. vanden Ende fec. — 353 × 434 mm.
[24] [C:] GALLIÆ VETERIS Typus. Amstelodami Apud Ioannem Ianssonium. — [C:] Nomenclaturæ et positionis locorum huius tabulæ testimoniæ, pete ex Thesauro nostro Geographico. — 390 × 490 mm.
[25] [C:] BELGII VETERIS TYPVS Ex Conatibus Geographicis Abrahami Ortelii. ... — [T:] Petrus Kærius Cælavit. 379 × 477 mm.
[26] [C:] Patriæ antiquæ INTER IULY et CAROLI MAGNI Cæsarum Romanorum Tempora Descriptio. — [C:] H wich inventor S. Sævrij Sculptor. — 383 × 469 mm.
[27] [C:] INSVLARVM BRITANNICARVM Acurata Delineatio ex Geographicis Conatibus ABRAHAMI ORTELLII. AMSTELODAMI apud Ioannem Ianssonium. — [T:] Petrus Kærius Cælavit. — 390 × 505 mm.
[28] [C:] ITALIÆ ANTIQVÆ Noua Delinatio. Auctore PHIL. CLUVERO. — [T:] Amstelodami Apud Joannem Janssonium. — 382 × 502 mm.
[29] [C:] ITALIA GALLICA sive GALLIA CISALPINA ex conatibus Geographicis Abrah. Ortelij. — [T:] Petrus Kærius Cælavit. — 345 × 461 mm.
[30] [C:] Nova & accurata TVSCIÆ ANTIQVÆ Descriptio Autore AB. ORTELIO. — [T:] Petrus Kærius Cælavit. — 343 × 490 mm.
[31] [C:] LATIVM. — 354 × 483 mm.
[32] [C:] Itala nam tellus GRÆCIA MAIOR ERAT OVID. IV. FASTOR. Hæc Italiæ pars nunc primum de prisca ærugine est abstersa et ejusmodi, ut videre licet, nitori reddita. — [T:] AMSTELODAMI, Excudit Joannes Janssonius. — 377 × 509 mm.
[33] [C:] INSVLAR ALIQVOT AEGAEI MARIS ANTIQVA DESCRIP. Ex Conatibus geographicis Abrahami Ortelij Antverpiani. — 430 × 491 mm.
[a] [C:] INSVLARVM, SARDINIÆ ET CORSICÆ Antiqua descriptio. — [T:] Amstelodami, Apud Ioannem Ianssonium. — 136 × 488 mm.
[b] [T:] TENOS RHENIA DELVS. — 96 × 123 mm.
[c] [T:] ICARIA. — 61 × 123 mm.
[d] [C:] EVBOEA, INSVLA. — 164 × 221 mm.
[e] [T:] SAMVS. — 96 × 123 mm.
[f] [T:] CIA et CEOS. — 61 × 123 mm.
[g] [T:] RHODVS. — 104 × 123 mm.
[h] [T:] CHIOS. — 104 × 107 mm.
[i] [T:] LEMNOS. — 104 × 107 mm.
[k] [T:] LESBOS. — 104 × 123 mm.
[34] [C:] SICILIÆ VETERIS TYPVS. Amstelodami, Apud Joannem Janssonium. — [T:] Abraham Goos sculpsit. — 375 × 482 mm.
[Inset:] [C:] Territorij Syracusani loca, incertæ positionis: Acrillæ, Echetla, Magella. — 136 × 93 mm.
[35] [C:] VETERIS PANNONIÆ UTRIUSQVE Nec non ILLYRICI Descriptio Geographica. — 376 × 473 mm.
[36] [C:] VETVS DESCRIPTIO DACIARVM Nec non MOESIARVM. ... — [T:] Petrus Kærius Cælavit. — 356 × 476 mm.
[37] [C:] ΠΟΝΤΟΣ ΕΥΞΕΙΝΟΣ. [PONTOS EUXEINOS]. PONTVS EUXINVS. Æquor fasonio pulsatum remige primum. Ex conatibus ABRAHAMI ORTELII. — [T:] Petrus Kærius Cælavit. — 372 × 480 mm.

[38] [C:] ΘΡΑΚΗ. [THRAKĒ]. THRACIAE VETERIS TYPVS. Ex conatibus Geographicis Abrah. Ortelij. — [T:] Petrus Kærius Cælavit. — 368 × 480 mm.
[39] [C:] DESCRIPTIO PEREGRINATIONIS D. PAULI, APOSTOLI, Exhibens Loca fere omnia tam in Novo Testamento quàm in Actis Apostolorum memorata: Operâ ABRAHAMI ORTELII. — [T:] Petrus Kærius Cælavit. — 362 × 507 mm.
[40] [C:] GERMANIÆ VETERIS Nova Descriptio. — [T:] Petrus Kærius Cælavit. — [T:] Apud Joan: Janssonium. — 375 × 470 mm.
[41] [C:] EVROPAM; sive CELTICAM VETEREM. Sic describere conabar Abrahamus Ortelius. — [T:] Evert Sijmons z. Hamers veldt sculpsit. — 351 × 468 mm.
[42] [C:] BRITANNIA prout divisa fuit temporibus ANGLO-SAXONVM, præsertim durante illorum HEPTARCHIA. — 416 × 312 mm.
[43] [C:] CAMBRIÆ TYPVS Auctore Humfredo Lhuydo Denbigiense Cambro-britanno. — 340 × 489 mm.
[44] [C:] IMPERIVM ROMANUM Auth. Phil. Briet e societ. Iesu. — 381 × 517 mm.
[Inset:] [T:] VMBRI. VESTINI. PELIGNI. VOLCI CAMPANI. — 110 × 258 mm.
[45] [C:] LVMEN HISTORIARVM. PER ORIENTEM, illustrandis Biblijs sacris, Martijrologio, & alijs mustis à FRAN. HAREIO concinnatum. — [T:] Petrus Kærius Cælavit. — 380 × 472 mm.
[Inset:] [T:] IVDÆAE amplior descriptio. — 227 × 111 mm.
[46] [C:] LVMEN HISTORIARVM per OCCIDENTEM ex conatibus FRAN. HARÆI Antuerpiæ. — [T:] P. Kærius Cælavit. — 378 × 478 mm.
[47—50][C:] TABVLA ITINERARIA ex illustri PEUTINGERORUM BIBLIOTHECA Quæ Augustæ Vindelicorum Beneficio MARCI VELSERI Septem-viri Augustani In Lucem edita. —
[47] [a] TABVLÆ PEVTINGERIANÆ SEGMENTVM PRIMVM, ab ostiis Rheni bonnam vique. 185 × 505 mm.
[b] SEGMENTVM SECVNDVM à Bonna vsque Marcomannos. 185 × 505 mm.
[The whole map:] 390 × 505 mm.
[48] [a] TABVLÆ PEVTINGERIANÆ SEGMENTVM III. à Marcomannis ad Sarmatas vsque. 185 × 505 mm.
[b] SEGMENTVM IV. à Sarmatis vsque ad Hamaxobios. 185 × 504 mm.
[The whole map:] 390 × 504 mm.
[49] [a] TABVLÆ PEVTINGERIANÆ SEGMENTVM V. à Sarmatis Hamaxobiis vsque ad Roxulanas. 185 × 507 mm.
[b] SEGMENTVM VI. à Sarmatis Roxulanis vsque ad Parnacos. 185 × 510 mm.
[The whole map:] 393 × 510 mm.
[50] [a] TABVLÆ PEVTINGERIANÆ SEGMENTVM VII à Parnacis vsque ad Paralocas Schythas. 185 × 504 mm.
[b] SEGMENTVM VIII à Paralocis Schythis vsque ad finem ASIÆ. 185 × 507 mm.
[The whole map:] 390 × 507 mm.
[51] [C:] IMPERIUM CAROLI MAGNI. — [T:] Amstelodami, sumptibus Ioannis Ianssonii. — 378 × 522 mm.

Notes: All the maps are blank on the back and uncoloured. The title-page is printed in red and black. The sixth map in the index, Palestina, sive Terra sancta, is lacking in this copy. It is a reduced version of the Situs Terræ Promissionis ... per Christianum Adrichomium Delphum, and appears in our copy of Adrichem's 'Theatrum Terræ Sanctæ et Biblicarum historiarum', Coloniæ Agrippinæ 1590, and in the 1593 edition. Map [42], Britannica, has seven illustrations down each border, representing the kings of the Anglo-Saxon heptarchy. Preceding the maps listed here, there is a wind map with two cartouches: [C:] TABVLA ANEMOGRAPHICA seu PYXIS NAVTICA Ventorum nomina sex linguis repræsentans, and [C:] AMSTELODAMI Apud Ioan. Ianssonium. The map is uncoloured, as are all the others. Map [26], Patriæ antiquæ ..., is referred to as Clivia vetus in the index. Koeman describes this atlas under J. Janssonius, Ja 2 and Ja 3. Ja 2 is the 1652 edition without the introduction by Georg Hornius, which is included in the 1653 edition. The title-page in our copy corresponds with that of Ja 2, except for one small difference of line division; otherwise the atlas is identical to the 1653 edition, Ja 3. In his short note on Hornius, Koeman points out that this atlas should not be confused with the sixth volume of the Janssonius Novus Atlas, which was not published until 1658, and which is an enlarged edition of the original Accuratissima Orbis Antiqui Delineatio. The atlas is bound in old vellum. Nordenskiöld's signature, with the date 1876, is on the inside of the front cover.

Lit.: Koeman, vol. 2, p. 151 and 185—187, Ja 2, Ja 3, Phillips, vol. 1, p. 3, nr 16.

108 HORN, GEORG   1677

ACCURATISSIMA ORBIS DELINEATIO Sive GEOGRAPHIA VETUS, SACRA & PROFANA. Exhibens, Quicquid Imperiorum, Regnorum, Principatuum, Rerumpublicarum, ab initio rerum, ad præsentem usque mundi statum fuit. Præmissa est INTRODUCTIO ad GEOGRAPHIAM ANTIQUAM. Qua ORBIS VETUS, GENTIUM MIGRATIONES, Populorum Origines, & quicquid Historias illustrare potest, breviter refertur. Authore GEORGIO HORNIO Historiarum in Acad. Lugduno-Batava, Professore. AMSTELODAMI, Apud JANSSONIO WAESBERGIANOS. Anno M D C LXXVII.   53,3 sm.

[1] [C:] ORBIS TERRARVM VETERIBVS COGNITI TYPVS GEOGRAPHICVS. — [C:] Nobilissimo Amplissimoq$_3$ Viro, D.^{no} FRANCISCO BANNINGIO COCQ, Equiti, D.^{no} in Purmerlant et Ylpendam, Consuli Reipublicæ Amstelodamensis. D. D. D. Iohan Ianssonius. — = 1653:[1], but dedication added.
[2] [T:] GEOGRAPHIA SACRA — = 1653:[2].
[3] [C:] TABVLA ITINERERIA PATRIARCHARVM ABRAHAMI, ISAACI et IACOBI. — = 1653:[3].
[4] [C:] IUDÆÆ seu TERRÆ ISRAELIS Tabula geographica; ... — = 1653:[4].
[5] [C:] PALESTINA, SIUE TERRÆ SANCTÆ DESCRIPTIO — [C:] Amstelodami excudebat Joannes Joansonius — 432 × 560 mm.
[Inset:] [T:] Ierusalem — (View).   55 × 63 mm.
[6] TRIBVS RVBEN, et GAD ... = 1653:[5] with small alterations.
[7] [T:] Tribuum EPHRAIM, BENIAMIN, et DIMIDIÆ MANASSE ... — = 1653:[6] with small alterations.
[8] [T:] VS ASER, et partes occidentales tribuum ZEBVLON ... — = 1653:[7] with small alterations and the left hand part left out.
[9] [T:] DIMIDIA TRIBVS MAN — [T:] TRIB — 433 × 347 mm. = 1653: lefthand parts of maps [8] and [7] with small alterations.
[10] [T:] ASSE Ultra Iordanem, TRIBUS NEPTALIM et partes orientales tribuum ZABVION et ISACHAR. — = 1653:[8] with small alterations and without the left hand part.
[11] Pars maxima TRIBVS IVDA Versus Orientem. = 1653:[9] with small alterations.
[12] [T:] TRIBVS SIMEON et pars meridionalis TRIBVS DAN, ... — = 1653:[10] with small alterations.
[13] [C:] DESCRIPTIO PEREGRINATIONIS D. PAULI, APOSTOLI, ... — = 1653:[39].
[14] [C:] ÆGYPTVS ANTIQVA ... — = 1653:[11].
[15] [C:] ERYTHRAEI SIVE RVBRI MARIS PERIPLVS, ... — = 1653:[12].
[16] [C:] AFRICAE PROPRIAE TABVLA. ... — = 1653:[13].
[17] [C:] CYPRVS, ... — = 1653:[14].
[18] [C:] CRETA ... — = 1653:[15].

[19] [C:] HELLAS seu GRÆCIA Sophiani. — = 1653:[16].
[20] [C:] ATTICA, MEGARICA, CORINTHIACA, ... — = 1653:[17].
[21] [C:] ARGONAVTICA. — = 1653:[18].
[22] [C:] AENEAE TROIANI NAVIGATIO ... — = 1653:[19].
[23] [C:] Tabula ITINERIS DECIES MILLE Græcorum ... — = 1653:[20].
[24] [C:] ALEXANDRI MAGNI MACEDONIS EXPEDITIO. — = 1653:[21].
[25] [C:] HISPANIÆ VETERIS DESCRIPTIO. ... — = 1653:[22].
[26] [C:] GALLIA VETVS ... — = 1653:[23].
[27] [C:] GALLIÆ VETERIS Typus. ... — = 1653:[24].
[28] [C:] BELGII VETERIS TYPVS ... — = 1653:[25].
[29] [C:] INSVLARVM BRITANNICARVM Acurata Delineatio ... — = 1653:[27].
[30] [C:] ITALIÆ ANTIQUÆ Noua Delinatio. ... — = 1653:[28].
[31] [C:] ITALIA GALLICA sive GALLIA CISALPINA ... — = 1653:[29].
[32] [C:] Nova & accurata TVSCIÆ ANTIQVÆ Descriptio ... — = 1653:[30].
[33] [C:] LATIVM — = 1653:[31].
[34] [C:] Itala nam tellus GRÆCIA MAIOR ... — = 1653:[32].
[35] [C:] INSVLAR ALIQVOT AEGAEI MARIS ANTIQVA DESCRIP. ... — = 1653:[33].
[36] [C:] SICILIÆ VETERIS TYPVS. ... — = 1653:[34].
[37] [C:] VETERIS PANNONIÆ UTRIUSQVE Nec non ILLYRICI Descriptio ... — = 1653:[35].
[38] [C:] ΠΟΝΤΟΣ ΕΥΞΕΙΝΟΣ. [PONTOS EUXEINOS]. PONTVS EUXINVS. ... = 1653:[37].
[39] [C:] VETVS DESCRIPTIO DACIARVM ... — = 1653:[36].
[40] [C:] ΘΡΑΚΗ. [THRAKĒ]. THRACIÆ VETERIS TYPVS. ... — = 1653:[38].
[41] [C:] GERMANIÆ VETERIS Nova Descriptio. — = 1653:[40].
[42] [C:] EVROPAM; sive CELTICAM VETEREM. ... — = 1653:[41].
[43] [C:] BRITANNIA prout divisa fuit temporibus ANGLO-SAXONVM, ... — = 1653:[42].
[44] [C:] CAMBRIÆ TYPVS ... — = 1653:[43].
[45] [C:] IMPERIVM ROMANUM ... — = 1653:[44].
[46] [C:] Patriæ antiquæ INTER IULY et CAROLI MAGNI ... — = 1653:[26].
[47] [C:] LVMEN HISTORIARVM. PER ORIENTEM, ... — = 1653:[45].
[48] [C:] LVMEN HISTORIARVM per OCCIDENTEM ... — = 1653:[46].
[49] [C:] IMPERIUM CAROLI MAGNI — = 1653:[51].
[50—53] [C:] TABVLA ITINERARIA ex illustri PEUTINGERORUM BIBLIOTHECA ... — = 1653:[47—50].
[50] [a] TABVLÆ PEVTINGERIANÆ SEGMENTVM PRIMVM, ab ostiis Rheni bonnam vsque. [b] SEGMENTVM SECVNDVM ... = 1653:[47].
[51] [a] TABVLÆ PEVTINGERIANÆ SEGMENTVM III. ... [b] SEGMENTVM IV. ... = 1653:[48].
[52] [a] TABVLÆ PEVTINGERIANÆ SEGMENTVM V. ... [b] SEGMENTVM VI. ... = 1653:[49].
[53] [a] TABVLÆ PEVTINGERIANÆ SEGMENTVM VII ... [b] SEGMENTVM VIII ... = 1653:[50].

Notes: All the maps are blank on the back and uncoloured. They are in a slightly different order from the 1653 edition. The TABVLA ANEMOGRAPHICA... is the same as in the 1653 edition, and appears in the same place in the volume. This copy includes the Palestina map, [5], lacking in our copy of the earlier edition. Map [9] is a curious combination of parts of two different maps; it is not present in the 1653 edition. The Hornius text is wanting. Koeman mentions two copies of this edition, each with 51 maps. In our copy maps [9] and [10] have been numbered separately by hand, although they are treated as one map in the index; the numbering therefore runs 1—54, the wind-map being no.1. The volume is bound in old leather, with blind tooling. On the inside of the front cover is the signature of Olov Nordenfeldt; Nordenskiöld's signature is on the first blank leaf, with the date 1897 d. 18de Maj.

Lit.: Koeman vol. 2, p. 186, Ja 6.

109 Isole famose ... [1571]

[Isole famose porti, fortezze, e terre maritime sottoposte alla Ser.ma Sig.ria di Venetia ad altri Principi Christiani, et al Sig.or Turco, nuouamēte poste in luce. In Venetia alla libraria del segno di S.Marco.] 26,2 cm.

[1] [C:] ISOLA DI CERIGO — 203 × 152 mm.
[2] [C:] NEGROPONTE Insula — 204 × 155 mm.
[3] [C:] SCIO. Chio antiquam.e detto Insula posta nello Arcipelago... — 212 × 161 mm.
[4] [C:] MOREA Peninsula prouinc.a principale della grecia, ... — 212 × 153 mm.
[5] [C:] PALMOSA ... — 203 × 157 mm.
[6] [C:] SAMO nello Arcipelago, ... — 204 × 151 mm.
[7] [C:] RHODI insula et Citta memorabile ... — 198 × 156 mm.
[8] [C:] CIPRO insula nobiliss. ... — 200 × 156 mm.
[9] [C:] Milo insula posta nel mare dello Arcipelago ... — 198 × 146 mm.
[10] [C:] METELIN Mitilene antiquant.e detta dala citta da Miletto figliolo di Phebo edificata ... — 224 × 165 mm.
[11] [C:] Scarpanto Carpanto antiquamente ... — 203 × 153 mm.
[12] [C:] Nicsia Nacso antiquam.e detta Isola posta nello Arcipelago ... — 199 × 148 mm.
[13] [C:] CANDIA uel Creta insula posta nel mare Mediterraneo ... — 192 × 157 mm.
[14] [C:] Corfu insula antiquamente detta Malena ... — 190 × 151 mm.
[15] [C:] SICILIA INSVLA — 149 × 212 mm.
[16] [T:] COSTANTINOPOLI — (Plan). [T:] Appresso Gioan Francesco Cam[otio] — 194 × 248 mm.
[17] [C:] TINE insula, et citta antiqua posta nello Arcipelago ... — 158 × 200 mm.
[18] [C:] CEFALONIA Insula posta sopra il mare Adriatico, ... — 151 × 205 mm.
[19] [C:] ZANTE insula posta nel mare Mediteraneo ... — 172 × 206 mm.
[20] [C:] SOPPOTO fortezza nella prou.a della Cimera ... — [C:] In Venetia apresso Giouan Franc. Camocio alla libraria della Piramide. — (View). 172 × 230 mm.

Notes: All the maps are blank on the back and uncoloured. This collection of island maps has no title-page, nor any other text-bearing page, but according to Nordenskiöld's note on the inside of the front cover the maps belong to a work entitled 'Isole famose'. The note reads: 'Kartor ur: Isole famose porti, fortezze, et terre maritime sottoposte alla Ser.ma Sig.ria di Venetia, ad altri Principi Christiani, et al Sig.or Turco, nuouvamente poste in luce. In Venetia alla libreria del Segno di S. Marco. Arbetet är anonymt red Franc. Camotio Venetiis. c. 1573.' Rodolfo Gallo, in his essay on Camocio in Imago Mundi VII, states that a complete volume of the Isole famose should contain 88 sheets, numbered consecutively. Our maps have no numbers. Gallo lists the 88 maps; 18 of ours are included. Our maps [1], ISOLA DI CERIGO, and [16], COSTANTINOPOLI, Appresso Gionn Francesco Cam[otio], are from a different edition of the Isolario, described by Gallo on p. 99. He discusses the date of publication, and concludes that it cannot have been published before August 1574, as one of the maps bears this date. The first map is pasted on a leaf of old paper. The text in the cartouche of map [5] is partly illegible. From map [8] onwards, the maps are placed on the left-hand side of the opening. Map [16], COSTANTINOPOLI, is badly cropped down both sides so that part of the legend under the text is missing, and the name Camocio is abbreviate to Cam. Nordenskiöld has pasted two letters from second-hand bookshops into the volume. The first is from Breslauer & Meyer in München, offering a copy of Isole famose for M 360; the other is from Leo S. Olschki in Verona, offering this particular collection for 18 Fr. Nordenskiöld's signature is on the first blank leaf.

Lit.: Bagrow, Geschichte, p. 336, Gallo, Imago Mundi VII, p. 93—102, Nordenskiöld, Facs. Atl. p. 118, Tooley, Dictionary p. 58.

Milliaria Hispanica communia

110 JACOBSZ, THEUNIS   1657

't Nieuwe en Vergroote Zee-Boeck/Dat is: des Piloots ofte Loots-Mans Zee-Spiegel. Inhoudende De Zee-Kusten van de Noordsche/ Oostersche ende Westersche Schip-vaert/ versien met veele noodwendige Zee-Caerten/Opdoeninge van Landen/ veranderingen in veele Courssen en Distantien/noyt voor desen soo klarlijck uytgegeven; Verbetert en vermeerdert met nieuwe Caerten ende Opdoeningen/soo in de Oost-Zee/als op andere plaetsen/ten dienste van alle Zee-varende Persoonen. Als mede een Nieuwe Beschrijvinge van Groenlant, Jan Mayen Eylant, 't Beeren-Eylant, Spits-Bergen, Nova Zembla, en 't Nieuw gevonden Lant. t'Samen-gebracht uyt ondersoeckinge van veel ervaren Stuer-Luyden/Lootsen ende Liefhebberen van de Navigatien. En in 't Licht gebracht DOOR THEUNIS JACOBSZ. Met noch een byvoeginge van een korte Instructie/ofte onderrechtingh in de Konst der Zee-vaert/als mede nieuwe Tafelen van des Sons en Sterren Declinatie/met een Almanack van IO. naest-volgende Jaren. t'AMSTELREDAM, Gedruckt by Jacob Theunisz, Boeck-verkooper op 't Water/in de Loots-Man/Anno 1657.   44,6 cm.

Vol. I
- [1]   1 [C:] Pascaart van EUROPA, Als mede een gedeelt vande cust van Africa. — Before I   A.   429 × 530 mm.
- [2]   2 [C:] Pascaarte van de NOORT ZEE Vertonende van Caliz tot Dronten, als oock tusschen Doeveren en Hitlandt, — Before I   A.   425 × 542 mm.
- [3]   3 [C:] Pascaarte vande ZUYDER-ZEE, Texel, ende Vliestroom als mede 't Amelander gat. — Before I A.   433 × 525 mm.

Eerste Boeck der Nieuwe LICHTENDE ZEE-COLOMNE, OFTE ZEE-SPIEGEL. Van de Oostersche en Noordtsche Schip-vaert. Inhoudende De Beschrijvinghe van de Noort-Zee, de Custen van Hollandt, Vrieslandt, Holsten, Jutlant, Meklenborgh en Denemarcken tot Valsterboen, en 't Eylant Rugen: als mede de Kust van Noorwegen tot Dronten, als oock d'Oost-zijde van Engelant ende Schotlant.
Eerste Verthooninghe, Waer in de Zuyder-Zee/ Vlie-stroom/ Vlie en Amelander-gat.
- [4]   4 [a] [C:] Pascaarte vande EEMSEN, Als de oude ofte wester Eems en de ooster Eems. —   431 × 277 mm.
  [b] [C:] Pascaarte van 't VLIE, Als mede een gedeelt van 't Amelander gat. —   431 × 253 mm.
  [The whole chart:] Between pp. 4 and 5   A 3   431 × 530 mm.
- [5]   5 [C:] Pascaerte Vande EEMS, ELVE, Weser, Eyder, en de Hever: als mede hoe die selvighe gaten van Heylighelandt gelegen syn. — Between pp. 4 and 5   A 3   428 × 541 mm.
- [6]   Beschrijvinge van de Vliestroom. (3 profiles)   On 5   A 3

De Tweede Verthooninghe, Waer in: Van de Scholbalgh, Lauwers, Schille, beyde de Eemsen, de Weser, Elve, ende Eyder, oock andere Zee-gaten tusschen beyden.
- [7]   De Zee-gaten tusschen Scholbalgh en de Eyder.   (13 profiles).   On 11   B 2

De Derde Verthooninghe, Waer in De Kusten vande Westen Oost-zijde van Jutlant: Mitsgaders de Beldt, tot voorby Lalant en Langelant tot aen Barts, en Meun.
- [8]   6 [C:] Pascaerte Vande West en Oost-zyde van IVTLANDT, Als mede De Belt Mitsgaders De Zee-cust van Holster, Mekelenborg, en de Eylanden van Lalandt, Falster, ende Meun. — Between pp. 10 and 11   B 2   431 × 705 mm.
- [9]   De Kusten van Jutlant ende de Beldt. (10 profiles).   On 20

De Vierde Verthooninghe, Waer in Het Schager Rack, vande Pater-nosters tot Kol, en voorts door de Sondt tot Falsterbon, als mede de Sondt in't groot.
- [10]   7 [C:] Pascaerte vant SCHAGER-RACK vande Pater-nosters aen Kol, als mede de Sondt, oock hoe dese landen van Schagen gelegen zyn. — Between pp. 20 and 21   C 3.   429 × 534 mm.
  [Inset:] [C:] De SONDT, met alle zyn gelegentheyt int groot. —   213 × 318 mm.   (Irregular).
- [11]   [T:] Wt-Clippen ofte Paternosters Eylant Masterlant — On 21   C 3   80 × 154 mm.
- [12]   [T:] Nydingh — On 22   45 × 214 mm. (Irregular).
- [13]   [T:] Kol over dese 2. Warders Z.W. van u. — On 22   80 × 100 mm. (Irregular).
- [14]   't Schager-Rack/ vande Pater-Nosters tot Kol/ als mede de Sondt.   (6 profiles).   On 27   D 2

De Vijfde Verthooninghe, Waer in: De Kusten van Noorwegen, vande Pater-Nosters tot der Neus.
- [15]   8 [C:] Custen van NOORWEGEN; van Der Neus tot aen de Pater noster oock hoe de seluige Landen van Iutlant gelegen zyn. — Between pp. 28 and 29   D 3.   438 × 534 mm.
- [16]   De Haven van Maerdou.   On 29   D 3   118 × 140 mm. (Irregular).
- [17]   De Kusten van Noorwegen/ van de Pater-Nosters tot der Neus.   (8 profiles).   On 31—32

De Seste Verthooninge, Waer in: De Kusten van Noorwegen, tusschen der Neus ende Schuytenes.
- [18]   9 [C:] De Custen van NOORWEGEN Tusschen Der Neus en Schuitenes — Between pp. 32 and 33 E.   429 × 529 mm.

[19] 10 [C:] Pascaerte van 't Liedt van BERGEN, Beginnende van Schuitenes tot aen Bergen. — Between pp. 32 and 33 E. 434 × 642 mm.
[20] Aldus is het Lant van de Jedder gedaen/ ... (2 profiles). On 33 E

De Sevenste Verthooninghe, Waer in Hoe men 't Liet van Bergen op sal zeylen.

[21] Aldus doet de Bock op/ als men bezuyden Schuytenes is voor dat Liet. Aldus is den Bergh Sijck gedaen/ alsmen benoorden Schuytenes is. (2 profiles). On 36

De Achtste Verthooninghe, Waer in De Custen van Noorwegen, tusschen Ie Ieltefioert en de hooge Hoeck van Horrel.

[22] 12 [C:] Caarte van NOORWEGEN vande hoeck van Horrel tot aen Momendael, waer in begrepen wort het Liet van Dronten. — Between pp. 36 and 37 E 3. 426 × 526 mm.
[23] 11 [C:] De Cust van NOORWEGEN Vertoonde van Bergen tot aen de hoeck van Horrel. — Between pp. 36 and 37 E 3. 428 × 538 mm.
[24] De Custen van Noorwegen/ tusschen Jeltefioerd en de hooge Hoeck van Horrel. (12 profiles). On 37 E3 — 38

De Negenste Verthooninghe, Waer in Hoe men 't Liet van Dronten op seylen sal.

[25] Hoe men 't Liet van Dronten op seylen sal. (9 profiles). On 41 F — 42

De Thiende Verthooninghe, Waer in De Oost-Cust van Engelandt, van de Riviere van Londen tot Welles.

[26] 13 [C:] Pascaerte van ENGELANT Van t'Voorlandt tot aen Blakeney waer in te sien is de mont vande Teemse. — Between pp. 42 and 43 F 2. 428 × 541 mm.
 [Inset:] [C:] Rivier van Londen — 96 × 321 mm.
[27] De Oost-Cust van Engelant/ tusschen de Rivier van Londen en Welles. (5 profiles). On 46
[28] 14 [C:] De Cust van ENGELANDT tusschen Welles en 't Eylandt Coket — Between pp. 46 and 47. 427 × 533 mm.
[29] Aldus is 't gedaen langs de noord kust van Engelandt/ tusschen Jarmuyen en Krammer/ alsmen binnen de bancken deur seylt. (Profile). On 47

De Elfde Verthooninge, Waer in De Custen van Engelant en Schotlant, tusschen Welles en Coggen-Eylandt.

[30] De Custen van Engelant en Schotlant/ tusschen Welles en Coggen Eylant. (3 profiles). On 50

De Twaelfde Verthooninghe, Waer in De Custen van Engelant en Schotlant, tusschen Koggen Eylant en d'Orcades.

[31] 15 [C:] De Custen van SCHOTLANT met de Eylanden van Orcanesse, van eylandt Coket tot I. Sande. — Between pp. 50 and 51 G 2. 428 × 530 mm.
[32] De Custen van Schotlant/ tusschen Coggen-Eylant en d'Orcades. (4 profiles). On 52

De Derthiende Verthooninghe, Waer in De Zee-Custen van Fayerhil, Hitlandt, en de omleggende Eylanden. Als mede d'Eylanden Fero, en sommige Eylanden achter de noord-west-hoeck van Schotlant.

[33] 16 [a] [C:] Eylanden van HITLANDT ofte Schetlant, Fayer hil, en Fulo. — 213 × 527 mm.
 [b] [C:] Eylanden van HEBRIDES gelegen achter de noord-west hoeck van Schotlant. — 212 × 266 mm.
 [c] [C:] Eylanden van FERO ofte Farre. — 212 × 259 mm.
 [The whole chart:] Between pp. 52 and 53 G 3. 428 × 527 mm.
[34] De Zee-kusten van Fayerhil/ Hitlandt/ Fero/ en d'Eylanden van Schotlant. (27 profiles). On 55 — 56

TWEEDE BOECK DER NIEUWE LICHTENDE ZEE-COLOMNE, OFTE ZEE-SPIEGEL, VAN DE OOSTERSCHE en NOORTSCHE SCHIP-VAERT. Inhoudende De Beschrijvinge van de Zee-Custen Noorwegen, Finmarcken, Laplandt, Russen, en de gantsche Witte Zee.

[35] 17 [C:] Pascaart Vande zeecusten van RVSLANT, Laplant, Finmarcken, en Spitzbergen. — Between pp. 56 and 57 H. 442 × 529 mm.
[36] 18 [C:] De Custen van NOORWEGH̄ tusschen Dronten en Tromsondt — Between pp. 56 and 57 H. 429 × 246 mm.

De Eerste Verthooninghe, Waer in De Custen van Finmarcken/ van Dronten/ tot 't Eylandt Trom-zondt.

[37] De Cust van Finmarcken/ van Dronten aen 't Eylandt Tromzont. (12 profiles). On 57 H — 58

De Tweede Verthooninghe, Waer in De Cust van Finmarcken, van 't Eylandt Sanien, of Trom-zont tot Kijn of de Noordt-Caep.

[38] 19 [C:] Caarte van FINMARCKEN van t'Eylandt Sanien tot Noordkyn — Between pp. 58 and 59 H 2. 436 × 528 mm.
[39] De Cust van Finmarcken/ van 't Eylandt Tromzondt tot Noordt-kijn. (27 profiles). On 59 H 2—60
[40] 20 [C:] De Custen van NOORWEGEN en Laplandt, vande Noord-kyn tot aen de Rivier van Kola. — Between pp. 60 and 61 H 3. 428 × 530 mm.
 [Inset:] [T:] Het Eylandt Wardhuys — 115 × 155 mm.
[41] De Cust van Finmarcken/ van 't Eylandt Tron-zondt tot Noord-kijn. (4 profiles). On 61 H 3

De Derde Verthooninghe, Waer in De Zee-Custen tusschen de Noordt-Kaep, of Noordt-Kijn tot de Rivier van Kola.

[42] De Zee-Custen tusschen de Noord-kijn en de Rivier van Kola. (20 profiles). On 62—63

De Vierde Verthooninghe, Waer in De Zee-Custen van Laplandt, tusschen de Riviere Kola en de Eylanden van Swetenoes.

[43] 21 [a] [C:] Het eylandt Kilduyn met de Reede nae 't leven ontworpen leggende op de hoochte van 69 graden 40 minuiten. — 126 × 182 mm.
 [b] [C:] De Rivier van KOLA in 't groot besteck. — 126 × 182 mm.
 [c] [C:] De Custe van LAPLANDT tusschen de Rivier van Kola en de eylandē van Swetenoes — 298 × 543 mm.
 [The whole chart:] Between pp. 64 and 65 I. 431 × 543 mm.
[44] 22 [C:] Pascaarte Van de Mont van de WITTE ZEE, tot aende Riuier Dwina al: Archangel toe. — Between pp. 66 and 67 I2. 425 × 534 mm.
 [Insets:] [T:] SWETENOES, met de Eylandekens daer ontrent gelegen nae 't leven ontworpen — 120 × 245 mm. (Irregular). [T:] De Eylanden van LOMBASCHO na 't leven ontworpen — 85 × 80 mm.
[45] De Zee-Kusten tusschen de Rivier Kola/ en d'Eylanden van Swetenoes. (7 profiles). On 67 I 2

De Vijfde Verthooninghe, Waer in: De Kust van de Mondt van de Witte Zee.

[46] 23 [C:] Pascaarte vañ WITTE-ZEE begrypende de custen van Laplandt, van Warsiga tot aen Kandalox en de cust van Corelia tot aen de Riviere Dwina — Between pp. 68 and 69 I 3. 431 × 525 mm.
[47] XXIII [C:] Caerte van ARCHANGEL ofte de Rivier de Duina, soo wel van 't Nieuwe als 't Oude diep. — Between pp. 68 and 69 I 3. 423 × 524 mm.
[48] Aldus ist Lant gedaen tusschen Swetenoes en Orlogenes/ alsmen daer voorby zeylt. (Profile). On 69 I 3.

De Seste Verthooninghe, Waer in: De Zee-Kusten van de Witte Zee, en de Rivier van Archangel int groot.

[49] 23¼ [C:] Pascaerte van GROEN-LANDT, Yslandt, Straet Davids en Ian Mayen eylandt; hoemen de selvige van Hitlandt en de Noortcusten van Schotlandt en Yrlandt beseylen mach. — Between pp. 70 and 71. 428 × 531 mm.

Derde Boeck der Nieuwe LICHTENDE ZEE COLOMNE, OFTE ZEE-SPIEGEL. VAN DE OOSTERSCHE en NOORTSCHE SCHIP-VAERT. Inhoudende de Beschrijvinghe van Yslandt, Groenlandt, ofte de Straet Davids, als mede de gelegentheyt van Ian Mayen Eylandt, en Spits-Berghen, voorders de streckinghe van Candenoes Oost-waerts aen door het Waygat, tot de Tartarische ofte Ys-Zee.

De Eerste Verthooninghe, Waer in: De gelegentheydt tusschen Hitlandt naer Yslandt/ en van daer na de Straet Davids/ of de hoeck van Out-Groenlant/ nu ghenaemt Staten-hoeck.
No charts.

De Tweede Verthooninge, Waer in: De Beschrijvinghe van Jan Mayen Eylandt.

[50] 21½ De Noord-West-Hoeck.
 [C:] De Noord-westhoec van IAN MAYEN Eylandt. — (View). On 75 K 2 151 × 205 mm.
[51] De Beschrijvinge van Jan Mayen Eylant. (3 profiles). On 76
[52] [a] 23½ [C:] Pas-caert van IAN MAYEN EYLANT.

Verthoonde alle de ghelegentheyt van alle bayen, inbochten, diepten en en drooghten. — 427 × 251 mm.

[b] 23¾ [C:] Pas-caerte van SPITSBERGEN met alle haer Rivieren, havens, bayen, sanden en droogten, als mede Hoemen C. de Uytkyck op Spits-bergen van de Noord Caap en Beeren Eylandt bezeylen sal. — 427 × 249 mm.

[The whole chart:] Between pp. 76 and 77 K 3. 427 × 503 mm.

De Derde Verthooninge, Waer in: De ghelegentheydt van 't Beeren-Eylandt, 't Hoopen-Eylandt, als mede van gheheel Spitsbergen, soo veel als die tot noch toe benoorden ende beoosten bekent is.

[53] 22½ De Hollantsche ofte Maurits-Bay. On 79 152 × 212 mm.

[54] Beschrijvinge van 't Beeren-Eylant/ en 't Hoopen Eylant. (2 profiles). On 81 L

De Vierde Verthooninghe, Waer in: De Beschrijvinghe van Orlogenes en Kaep de Candenoes tot aen de West-Kuste van Nova Sembla en 't Waygat.

No charts.

Vierde Boeck der Nieuwe LICHTENDE ZEE COLOMNE, OFTE ZEE-SPIEGEL. VAN DE OOSTERSCHE en NOORTSCHE SCHIP-VAERT. Inhoudende De Beschrijvinghe van de gantsche Oost-Zee. De Eerste Verthoninghe, Waer in: De Zee-Kusten van Valsterboen tot Schenckenes/ ende van het Eylant Rugen tot Rijgs-hooft.

[55] 24 [C:] Pascaarte vande OOST-ZEE Van 't Eylandt Rugen, ofte Bornholm tot aen Wyborg. — Between pp. [84] and 85 L 3. 430 × 539 mm.

[56] 25 [C:] De Custen van DENEMARCKEN en Sweden van Valsterbon tot Schenckenes, Als mede de Custen van Pomeren van 't Eylant Rugen tot Rygshooft. — Between pp. [84] and 85 L 3. 441 × 531 mm.

[57] 't NIEUWE-DIEP.
[T:] EYLANDT RVGEN   POMEREN — On 88 169 × 199 mm.

[58] 26 [C:] Caarte van PRVYSSEN en Coerlandt van Rygshooft tot der Winda — Between pp. 90 and 91 M 2. 431 × 526 mm.

[59] De Zee-Kusten tusschen Valsterboen en Schenckenes. Als mede. van 't Eylant Rugen tot Rijghs-hooft. (11 profiles). On 91 M 2

De Tweede Verthooninghe, Waer in: De Zee-Kusten tusschen Rijghs-Hooft en Der Winda.

[60] De Zee-Kusten tusschen Rijghs-hooft ende Der Winda. (14 profiles). On 93 M 3

De Derde Verthooninghe, Waer in: De Zee-Kusten tusschen Der Winda en Revel, als mede de Eylanden van 't Alandts Haff.

[61] 27 [C:] Pascaarte van LIIFLANDT ende Oost-Finlandt, van der Winda tot aende hoeck van Alandt ende voort tot Revel. — Between pp. 94 and 95. 431 × 526 mm.

[62] De Zee-Kusten tusschen Der Winda en Revel/ (18 profiles). On 98 — 99 N 2

[63] 28 [C:] De Zeecusten van LIIFLANDT, ende Oost Finlandt, van Wolfs-oort tot aen Wyborgh. — Between pp. 98 and 99 N 2. 425 × 533 mm.

De Vierde Verthooninghe, Waer in: De Zee-Kusten tusschen Wolf, en 't uytterste vande Oost-Zee.

[64] Groot en Kleyn Wranger. On 99 N 2 117 × 153 mm. (Irregular).

[65] De Zee-Kusten tusschen 't Eylant Wolf en 't uyterste vande Oost-Zee. (9 profiles). On 102 and 103

De Vijfde Verthooninghe, Waer in: De Zee-Kusten van Sweden, tusschen Oelandt, en Stockholm, als mede de Eylanden van Oelant en Gotlant, en 't Liet van Stockholm in 't groot, en 't Gat van Uttoy.

[66] 29 [C:] Caarte van SWEDEN Van Oelandt tot aen Stocholm. — Between pp. 102 and 103. 441 × 534 mm.

[67] 30 [a] [C:] Caarte van 't gat van ABBO, ofte VTTOY. — 431 × 262 mm.
[b] [C:] Caarte van STOCHOLMSE Liet. — 431 × 260 mm.
[The whole chart:] Between pp. 102 and 103. 431 × 524 mm.

[68] De Zee-Kusten van Sweden/ tusschen Oelant en Stockholm. (4 profiles). On 108

Notes: All the large charts are blank on the back; the smaller ones and the profiles have text on the verso. All the charts are coloured; the title-page is not. Koeman describes in detail the relationships of the family of chart-makers. Theunis (= Anthonie) Jacobsz added the epithet 'Lootsman' to his name to distinguish himself from other printers of the same name working at that time. His sons Jacob and Casparus used the family name Theunisz. Theunis Jacobsz's charts are in a completely new style, bearing no resemblance to the charts in pilots by Colom or Blaeu which were current at that time. His charts do not bear his imprint. Evidence of cooperation among publishers can be seen from the fact that in 1650 Pieter Goos brought out an edition of the Zee-Spiegel under his imprint, using charts printed from Jacobsz's plates, and that in 1651 Joannes Janssonius did the same, using his own imprint. (See Koeman, vol. 4 p. 270.) Our copies of Goos 1658 and Janssonius (117) 1653 contain the same charts and almost the same text as Jacobsz's Zee-Spiegel described here. The table of contents is the same in all three. The second part bound in with this copy of Jacobsz is by Jan Janssonius, 1653, and is treated under his name. Koeman mentions our copy in the 'Additions' to Jac 18, where he originally stated that no copy was known but that the edition was mentioned in the bibliography by Bierens de Haan, p. 139. Nordenskiöld bought the volume for 30 fl. from Frederik Muller in Amsterdam, in 1892. The invoice is dated 28 nov. 1892, and was paid on 19 Dec. the same year. The copy is bound in old vellum; it has been restored, but is not in good repair. Nordenskiöld's signature is on the first old blank leaf, with the date 1892.

Lit.: Koeman vol. 4, p. 223, p. 236; p. 236, Jac. 18, additional note; p. 270, M.Ja 2; Tiele, p. 120, nr 527.

111 JACOBSZ, THEUNIS 1666

LE GRAND & NOUVEAU MIROIR OU FLAMBEAU, De la Mer contenant la description de toutes les Costes Marines Occidentalles & Septentrionnalles, desmonstrant en plusieurs Cartes tres necessaire tous les Ports, fleuves, bayes, Rades, profondeurs & bancs chascun tres exactement couché selon leur vraye hauteur pollaire, & pourveu des descouvrements des terres principales, & à quel cours & distance elles sont situées les unes des autres. Jamais parcidevant si Clairement mis en lumiere & outrece augmenté & amandé pour bien & utilité de tous Mariniers & Navigateurs. Recueilly des Recherches de divers Experimentez Pilotes & Amateurs de la navigation. Avec une tres belle & necessaire instruction en l'art de la navigation & aussi pourveu d'Almanachs jusques en l'An 1672. Traduict de Flaman en François par PAUL YVOUNET. A AMSTERDAM. Imprimé chez JAQUES & GASPER ANTHOINE, Librairiers, demeurant sur l'eau au Pilotte. ANNO 1666.   45,8 cm.

Vol. I.

PREMIERE LIVRE, DE LA COLOMNE FLAMBOYANTE, DE LA Navigation Orientale & Septentrionale: CONTENANT La description de la Mer Septentrionale, les Costes de Hollande, Frise, Holsteyn, Jutlant, Mekelenbourg, & Danemarque jusques à Valsterboen, & l'Isle de Rugen, comme aussi la Coste de Norwege jusques à Dronten, comme pareillement la coste Orientale d'Angleterre & d'Escosse.

La premiere Demonstrance, EN LAQUELLE: Le Zuyder-Zee, le Fleuve de Flie, & les Trous de Flie & Amelant.

[1] 1 [C:] Pascaart van EUROPA, Als mede een gedeelt van cust van Africa. t Amsterdam, By Theunis Iacobsz op 't water inde Lootsman. — Before Fol: 1 A 431 × 524 mm. See 1657:I:[1].

[2] [C:] Pas Caart van de NOORT ZEE Verthoonende in zich alle de Custen en Havens daer rontom gelegen t'Amsterdam By Iacob Theuniss Loots-man Boeckverkoper en Graadboghmaker op t Water inde Loots-man. — Before

Fol: 1   A   435 × 521 mm. See 1657:I:[2].
- [3] 3 [C:] Pascaarte vande ZUYDER-ZEE, Texel, ende Vliestroom, als mede t Amelander -gat. t'Amsterdam, By Iacob Theunitz, boeck-verkooper inde Lootsman. — Before Fol: 1 A   423 × 530 mm. See 1657:I:[3].
- [4] 4 [a] [C:] Pascaarte vande EEMSEN Als de oude ofte wester Eems en de ooster Ems — 422 × 274 mm.
  [b] [C:] Pascaarte van't VLIE, Als mede een gedeelt van t Amelander gat 't Amsterdam, By Iacob Theunitz opt water in de Lootsman. 422 × 246 mm.
  [The whole chart:] Between pp. 4 and 5   A 3.   422 × 525 mm. See 1657:I:[4].
- [5] 5 [C:] Pascaarte vande EEMS, ELVE, Weser, Eyder, en de Hever: als mede hoe die selvighe gaten van Heylighelant ghelegen syn. t'Amsterdam. By Iacob Theunisz op't water inde Lootsman. — Between pp. 4 and 5   A 3.   422 × 523 mm. See 1657:I:[5].
- [6] Des Trous de Vlie & d'Amelant. (3 profiles). On 5   A 3 See 1657:I:[6].

La Deuxiesme Demonstration, EN LAQUELLE: Du Scholbalgh, Lauwers, Schille, les deux Eems, le Weser, Elbe, & l'Eyder, & autres trous de la Mer entre deux.
- [7] Les Trous de la Mer entre Scholbalgh & l'Eyder. (7 profiles).   On 10   See 1657:I:[8].
- [8] 6 [C:] Pascaerte Vande West en Oost cust van IUTLANT, Als mede DE BELT; Mitsgaders de zee-cust van Holster, Mekelenborg en de Eylanden van Lalandt, Falster ende Meun. 't Amsterdam, By Iacob Theunisz. op 't water in de Lootsman. — Between pp. 10 and 11   B 2   420 × 666 mm. See 1657:I:[7].

La Troisiesme Demonstration, EN LAQUELLE: Les Costes Occidentall & Oriental de Iutlant: aussi le Belt jusques à outre Lalant & Langelant.
- [9] Les Costes de Jutlant & le Belt. (7 profiles).   On 18   See 1657:I:[9].

La Quatriesme Demonstration, EN LAQUELLE: Comment on fera voile de Col dans le Sont, & de là par les Droogen ou Seches à Valsterboen. d'Avantage les Costes de Holsten, Mekelenborgh, & les Isles Meridionales de Danemarc. Du Belt jusques au Jelle.
- [10] 7 [C:] Pascaarte van SCHAGER-RACK, vande Paternosters als mede Maesterlant tot aen Kol, ooch hoe dese landen van Schagen gelegen zyn. 't Amsterdam, By Iacob Theunisz. op 't water inde Lootsman. — Between pp. 18 and 19   C 2   420 × 522 mm.
  [Inset:] [C:] De SONDT, met alle zyn gelegentheyt int groot. —   223 × 318 mm. (Irregular). See 1657:I:[10].
- [11] De Kol par le Sondt à Velsterboen, & les Isles Meridionales dans le Belt. (5 profiles). On 21   C 3—22 See 1657:I:[9] and [14].

La Cincquiesme Demonstration, EN LAQUELLE: Les Costes de Norwegen entre Aker-Sondt & Kol.
- [12] [T:] Escueils l'ancans en Mer, ou Pater-nosters. Isle. Maesterlant. — On 22   75 × 152 mm. (Irregular). See 1657:I:[11].
- [13] 8 [C:] Custen van NOORWEGEN, Van der Neus, tot aen de Pater nosters; oock hoe de selvige Landen van Iutlant gelegen syn. 't Amsterdam, By Iacob Theunisz. op't water inde Lootsman. — Between pp. 22 and 23.   420 × 522 mm. See 1657:I:[15].
- [14] [T:] Kol à l'endroit de cex deux Marques, Zúdouest de vous. — On 23   63 × 85 mm. See 1657:I[13].
- [15] Les Coste de Norwege, entre Akersondt & Kol. (3 profiles). On 26   See 1657:I:[14].

La Sixiesme Demonstration, EN LA QUELLE: Les Costes de Norwege entre Aker-Sont & Schaer-sont, & de Schaer-sont à Schuytenes.
- [16] 9 [C:] De Custen van NOORWEGEN Tusschen Der Neus en Schuitenes. 't Amsterdam, By Iacob Theunisz. op't water inde Lootsman. — Between pp. 26 and 27   D 2   422 × 527 mm. See 1657:I:[18].
- [17] Le Havre de Maerdou. On 27   D 2   120 × 145 mm. See 1657:I:[16].
- [18] Costes de Norwege entre Akersont & Schuytenes. (8 profiles). On 30   See: 1657:I:[17] and [20].

La Septiesme Demonstration, EN LAQUELLE: Le Liedt de Bergen, & la Coste de Norwege jusques à Stemmes-hest.
- [19] 10 [C:] Pascaerte van t Liedt van BERGEN Beginnende van Schuytenes tot aen Bergen. 't Amsterdam, By Iacob Theunisz. op t water inde Lootsman. — Between pp. 30 and 31.   418 × 627 mm. See 1657:I:[19].
- [20] La Liedt de Bergen, la Coste de Norwege jusques à Stemmesheft. (16 profiles). On 34 See 1657:I:[21], [24] and [25].

La Huictiesme Demonstrance, En laquelle: Le Liet de Dronten.
- [21] 11 [C:] De Cust van NOORWEGEN Vertoonde van Bergen tot aen de hoeck van Horrel t Amsterdam. By Iacob Theunisz. op't water inde Lootsman. — Between pp. 34 and 35   E 2   420 × 522 mm. See 1657:I:[23].
- [22] 12 [C:] Caerte van NOORWEGEN vande hoeck van Horrel tot aen Momendael, waer in begrepen wort het Liet van Dronten. — Between pp. 34 and 35   E2   422 × 522 mm. See 1657:I:[22].
- [23] Le Liedt de Dronten. (2 profiles). On 37

DEUXIESME LIVRE, DE LA COLOMNE FLAMBOYANTE, DE LA Navigation Orientale & Septentrionale: CONTENANT La description des Costes Marines de Norwege, Finmarck, Lapponie & toute là Mer Blanche.

La Premiere Demonstrance, EN LAQUELLE: La Costes de Norwege, depuis Dronten jusques au Noord-Caep, comme encore l'Isle de Iean Maeyen, & là terre de Spitsbergen nouvellement descouverte.
- [24] 17 [C:] PASCAART Van de Zee-custen van Ruslandt, Laplandt, Finmarcken Spitsbergen en Nova-zembla 't Amsterdam By Theunis Iacobsz op't water inde Lootsman. Op nieus oversien en verbetert — Between pp. 38 and 39.   428 × 547 mm. See 1657:I:[35].
- [25] 18 [C:] de Custen van FINMARCKEN tusschen Dronten en Tromsondt. 't Amsterdam By Iacob Theunisz op't water inde Lootsman. — Between pp. 38 and 39.   423 × 524 mm. See 1657:I;[36].
- [26] Costé de Norwege entre Dronten & le Noord-Caep. (23 profiles).   39—40 See 1657:I:[36].

La Deuxiesme Demonstrance, EN LAQUELLE: Les Costes de Mer entre le Noordt-Caep & Swetenoes.
- [27] 19 [C:] Caarte van FINMARCKEN, van't Eylant Sanien tot Noord-Kyn. 't Amsterdam; By Iacob Theunisz. op't water Inde Lootsman. — Between pp. 40 and 41.   F.   422 × 528 mm. See 1657:I:[38].
- [28] 20 [C:] de Custen van NOORWEGEN, en Laplandt, vande Noord-kyn tot aen de Rivier van Kola. 't Amsterdam, By Iacob Theunisz. opt water inde Lootsman. — Between pp. 40 and 41.   F.   422 × 528 mm.
  [Inset:] [T:] Het Eylandt Warhuys. — 114 × 158 mm. See 1657:I:[40].
- [29] 21 [a] [C:] Het eylant Kilduyn met de Rede ... — 122 × 170 mm.
  [b] [C:] de Rivier van KOLA in't groot besteck.   't Amsterdam, By Iacob Theunisz opt water inde Lootsman. — 122 × 348 mm.
  [c] [C:] de Custen van LAPLANT tusschen de Rivier van Kola en de eylande van Swetenoes. —
  [The whole chart:] Between pp. 40 and 41   F.   423 × 524 mm. See 1657:I:[43].
- [30] Les Costes de Mer entre Noordt Caep & Swetenoes. (24 profiles). On 44 — 45   F 3 See 1657:I:[42].
- [31] 22 [C:] Pascaerte van de Mont van de WITTE ZEE, tot aen de Rivier van Archangel. 't Amsterdam, By Iacob Theunisz, op't water in de Lootsman. — Between pp. 44 and 45   F 3.   420 × 523 mm.
  [Insets:] [T:] SWETENOES, met de Eylandekens daer ontrent gelegen. ...   115 × 195 mm. (Irregular).   [T:] de Eylanden van Lombascho ... — 85 × 78 mm. See 1657:I:[644].
- [32] 23 [C:] Pascaarte vande WITTE ZEE begrypende de custen van Laplant, van Warsiga tot Kandalox en de cust van Corelia tot aen de Riviere Dwina. 't Amsterdam; By Iacob Theunisz. inde Lootsman. — Between pp. 44 and 45 F 3.   425 × 530 mm. See 1657:I:[46].
- [33] 24 [C:] Caerte van ARCHANGEL ofte de Rivier de Duina, soo wel van 't Nieuwe als 't Oude Diep. 't Amsterdam, By

Iacob Theunisz, op 't water in de Lootsman. — Between pp. 44 and 45 F 3. 420 × 522 mm. See 1657:I:[47].

La Troisiesme Demonstrance, EN LAQUELLE: Les Costes de Mer & Havres de Swetenoes, & toute la Mer Blanche.

[34] 25 [C:] Pascaerte van GROEN-LANDT, Yslandt, Straet Davids en Ian Mayen eylandt; hoemen de selvige van Hitlandt en de Noortcusten van Schotlandt en Yrlandt beseylen mach. — [T:] 't Amsterdam by Iacob Theunisz op 't Water inde Lootsman. — Between pp. 48 and 49 G. 423 × 530 mm. See 1657:I:[49].

[35] 26 [a] [C:] Pas-caert van IAN MAYEN EYLANT, Verthoonde alle de gelegentheyt van alle bayen, inbochten, diepten en en drooghten. 't Amsterdam by Iacob Theunisz op 't water inde Lootsman. — 422 × 260 mm.
[b] [C:] Pas-caert van SPITSBERGEN met alle haer Rivieren, havens, bayen, sanden en droogten. als mede Hoe men C. de Uytkyck op Spits-bergen van de Noord Caap en Beeren Eylandt bezeylen sal. — 422 × 260 mm.
[The whole chart:] Between pp. 48 and 49 G. 422 × 525 mm.

[36] [C:] Pascaarte vande OOST ZEE Van t Eylandt Rugen of van de hoeck van Valsterbon tot aen Wyborg 't Amsterdam By Theunis Iacobsz op t water inde Lootsman. — Between pp. 48 and 49 G. 420 × 554 mm. See 1657:I:[55].

[37] 28 [C:] De Custen van DENEMARCKEN, en Sweden, van Valsterbon tot Schenckenes, als mede de custen van Pomeren van 't eylant Rugen tot Rygshooft. 't Amsterdam, By Iacob Theunisz. op 't water inde Lootsman. — Between pp. 48 and 49 G. 422 × 526 mm. See 1657:I:[56].

TROISIESME LIVRE, DE LA COLOMNE FLAMBOYANTE, DE LA Navigation Orientale & Septentrionale: CONTENANT La description de toute la Mer Orientale.

La Premiere Demonstration, EN LAQUELLE: Les Costes de Mer depuis Valsterboen jusques à Christianopel, & de l'Isle de Rugen à Rijghshooft.

[38] [C:] 'T NIEWE-DIEP — [T:] 'T EYLAND RUGEN POMEREN — On 51 G 2 158 × 169 mm. See 1657:I:[57].

[39] Les Costes de Mer depuis Valsterboen jusques à Christianopel, & d l'Isle de Rugen à Rijghs-hooft. (10 profiles). On 54 See 1657:I:[59].

La Deuxiesme Demonstrance, EN LAQUELLE: Les Costes de Mer entre Rijghs-hooft & Derwinde.

[40] 29 [C:] Caerte van PRVYSSEN en Coerlandt, van Rygshooft tot der Winda. 't Amsterdam, By Iacob Theunisz. op t water in de Lootsman. — Between pp. 54 and 55. 423 × 523 mm. See 1657:I:[58].

[41] Les Costes de Mer entre Rijghshooft & Derwinde. (9 profiles). On 55 See 1647:I:[60].

La Troisiesme Demonstrance, EN LAQUELLE: Les Costes de Mer entre Derwinde & le Bout de là Mer Orientale.

[42] 30 [C:] Pascaert van LYFLANT ende Oost-Finlandt, van der Winda tot aen de hoeck van Alandt ende voort tot Revel. — Between pp. 56 and 57 H. 420 × 523 mm. See 1657:I:[61].

[43] 31 [C:] de Zee-custen van LIIFLANDT, En Oost Finlandt, van Wolfs-oort tot aen Wyborgh 't Amsterdam. By Iacob Theunisz. op 't water inde Lootsman. — Between pp. 56 and 57 H. 422 × 522 mm. See 1657:I:[63].

[44] Grand & Petit Wranger. On 59 H 2 115 × 155 mm. (Irregular). See 1657:I:[64].

[45] Les Costes de Mer entre Der Winde & le Bout de la Mer Orientale, (24 profiles). On 62 — 63 See 1657:I:[65].

[46] 32 [C:] Caarte van SWEDEN Van Oelandt tot aen Stocholm; 't Amsterdam, By Iacob Theunisz. op 't water in de Lootsman. — Between pp. 62 and 63. 423 × 524 mm. See 1657:I:[66].

[47] 33 [a] [C:] Caarte van 't gat van ABBO ofte VTTOY, 't Amsterdam By Iacob Theunisz opt water inde Lootsman. — 420 × 260 mm.
[b] [C:] Caarte van STOCHOLMSE Liet. — 420 × 262 mm.
[The whole chart:] Between pp. 62 and 63. 420 × 523 mm. See 1657:I:[67].

La Quatriesme Demonstrance, EN LAQUELLE: De Isles d'Oelant & Godtlant: comme aussi les Costes de Suede jusques à outre Stockholm.

[48] Les Isles d'Oelandt & Godtlandt: &c. (4 profiles). On 68 See 1657:I:[68].

Vol. II

Le Premier Liure Du Grand & Nouveau Miroir OU FLAMBEAU DE LA MER, Tant de la NAVIGATION SEPTENTRIONALEE. QUE OCCIDENTALLE, Contenant la description des Costes Marines de Hollande, Zelande & Flandres depuis Tessel jusques au pas de Calais.

Premiere demonstration de Courans & Pertuis de Tessel.

[1] W 4 [a] [C:] De TEXEL Stroom en de Gaten van Marsdiep. — 428 × 265 mm.
[Inset:] [C:] Caarte van de Rede en Haven van Medenblick hoemen die comeñ soo van 't Wieringer als Vriesch vlak beseylen mogen tot dienst en nut voor alle zeevareñ luyden, perfectelyck gemeteñ en afgepeylt. Beschreven A^o 1659 uyt speciale last vañ E.H. Burgemeesteren en de Regeerders der voorss Stadt Medenblyck. — 240 × 110 mm. (Irregular).
[b] [C:] Caerte van DE MASE, Ende het Goereesche gat. 't Amsterdam, By Iacob Theunisz, op 't water in de Lootsman. — 428 × 265 mm.
[The whole chart:] Before 1 A. 428 × 536 mm.

[2] W 5 [C:] Cust van HOLLANT Tusschen de Maes ende Texel 't Amsterdam, By Iacob Theunisz opt water inde Lootsman. — Between pp. 2 and 3 A 2. 422 × 530 mm.

La deuxiesme Desmonstrance, En laquelle est Descritte la Coste de Hollande, de Texel, à la Muze comme aussy les entrées de Texel, la Muze & Goerée.

[3] Tessel, la Meuze & l'entrée de Goerée. (14 profiles). On 7 — 8

La troisiéme Démonstrance, Des Pertuis & entrées, entre la Meuze & les Wielingen, comme aussi de Delfshaven, Zierickzee, Derveer & les Wielingen.

[4] W 6 [C:] De Cust van ZEELAND, Begrypende in sich de Zee gaten, als van de Wielingen, Ter Veere, Ziericzee, Brouwers-haven, Goeree en de Maes. t'Amsterdam, By Iacob Theunisz op t'water inde Lootsman. — Between pp. 8 and 9 B. 423 × 524 mm.

[5] Les pertuis & entrées de Zierickzee, Brouwershaven & Wielingen. (4 profiles). On 14

La quatriesme Démonstration. En laquelle est comprise la Coste de Flandres, depuis les Wielingen jusques au Pas de Calais, comme aussi la Coste d'Angleterre de Douvres jusques au Voorlandt Septentrional.

[6] W 7 [C:] De Cust van VLAENDEREN, Beginnende vande Wielingen tot aende Hoofden; met alle haer sanden en droogten. t Amsterdam, By Iacob Theunisz. op 't water iñ Lootsman.. — Between pp. 14 and 15. 431 × 533 mm.

[7] 13 [C:] Pascaerte van ENGELANT vant Voorland tot aen Blakeney, waer in te sien is de mont vande Teemse. 't Amsterdam, By Iacob Theunisz, opt water inde Lootsman. Between pp. 18 and 19 C2. 420 × 526 mm.
[Inset:] [C:] Rivier van Londen — 95 × 318 mm. See 1657:I:[26].

[8] La Coste de Flandres, depuis les Wielingen, jusques au Pas de Calais. (3 profiles). On 19 C 2

La cinquiesme Démonstration. En laquelle est décrite la Coste Orientalle d'Angleterre, de la Riviere de Londres jusques à Welle.

[9] La Coste Orientalle d'Angleterre entre la Riviere de Londres & Welles. (6 profiles). On 23 See 1657:I:[27] and [29].

La sixiéme Démonstrance. Des Costes d'Angleterre & Ecosse, entre Walles, & l'Isle de Coggen.

[10] 14 [C:] de Cust van ENGELAND, tusschen Welles en 't Eylandt Cogge, 't Amsterdam, By Iacob Theunisz op 't water inde Lootsman. — Between pp. 24 and 25 D. 423 × 527 mm. See 1657:I:[28], with small differences.

[11] 15 [C:] De Custen van SCHOTLAND met de Eylanden van Orcanesse; van 't Eyland Coket tot I. Sande. 't Amsterdam, By Iacob Theunisz. op 't water in de Lootsman. — Between pp. 26 and 27 D 2. 417 × 522 mm. See 1657:I:[31].

[12] Les Costes d'Angleterre, & d'Ecosse, entre Welles & l'Islle de Coggen. (3 profiles). On 27   D 2   See 1657:I:[30].

La septiésme Démonstrance. Les Costes d'Angleterre & Ecosse, entre l'Isle de Coggen & les Orcades.

[13] 16 [a] [C:] Eylanden van HITLANT ofte Schetlant, Fayer hil en Fulo. 't Amsterdam By Iacob Theunisz op twater inde Lootsman. — 210 × 537 mm.
  [b] [C:] Eylanden van HEBRIDES gelegen achter de noordwest hoeck van Schotlandt — 213 × 262 mm.
  [c] [C:] Eylanden van FERO ofte Farre — 213 × 262 mm.
  [The whole chart:] Between pp. 28 and 29   D 3.   424 × 537 mm.   See 1657:I:[33].

[14] Les Costes d'Ecosse, entre l'Isle de Coggen & les Orcades. (4 profiles). On 29   D 3 See 1657:I:[32].

La huictiésme Démonstrance. Le Costes de Fayerhil, Hitlandt, & les Isles circonvoisines; comme aussi les Isles Fero, & quelques autres Isles derriere la poincte du Nord-Ouest d'Ecosse.

[15] Les Costes de Fayerhil, Hitlant, Fero, & les Isles d'Ecosse. (27 profiles). On 31 — 32   See 1657:I:[34].

Le deuxiésme Liure Du Grand & Nouveau Miroir OU FLAMBEAU DE LA MER, Tant de la NAVIGATION OCCIDENALLE QUE SEPTENTRIONALLE, Contenant la description des Costes Marines de France, de Tresport à Roscou, & les Costes d'Angleterre, de Fierley vers l'ouest jusques au bout Meridional d'Angleterre, comme aussi la Manche de Bristoc & Costes d'Irlande.

La premiere Démonstration. En laquelle est comprise les Costes de France, depuis le pas de Calais jusques à l'Isle d'Ornay, & de Douvre à Portlandt.

[16] W 8 [C:] PASCAART vant CANAAL. Begrypende in sich Engelandt, Schotlandt, en Jerlandt, als mede een gedeelt van Francryck Op nieu wt gegeven by Anthony Iacobsen jnde Loots-man — Between pp. 32 and 33 E.   432 × 550 mm.

[17] W 9 [C:] De Cust van NORMANDIE, en Picardie; als mede een gedeelt van Engeland, tusschen de Hoofden, Ornay ende Poortlant. 't Amsterdam, By Iacob Theunisz, op't water in de Lootsman. — Between pp. 32 and 33   E. 428 × 528 mm.

[18] La Coste de Normandie, Grinés, jusq̀ à l'Isle d'Ornay. (12 profiles). On 36

La deuxiésme Démonstration. Traictant des Costant de Bretaigne, de l'Isle d'Ornay, jusques à l'Isle de Ouessant.

[19] W 10 [C:] De Custen van BRETAIGNE, Waer in vertoont wort alle gelegentheyt tusschen Caap de Hague en 't Eylant Heyssant. 't Amsterdam, By Iacob Theunisz. op't water inde Lootsman. — Between pp. 36 and 37   E 3.   424 × 526 mm.

[20] Sᵗ·MALO.
  [C:] De Haven van S.Malo — On 38   170 × 170 mm.

[21] La Coste de Bretaigne entre l'Isle dOrnay & Ouessant. (6 profiles). On 40

La troisiéme Démonstration. De la Costé d'Angleterre de Bevesier jusques à Poortlant.

[22] W 11 [C:] De Custen van ENGELANDT Tusschen Fierley en Poortlant; ook hoese van Ornay gelegen zyn. t Amsterdam, By Iacob Theuniss. op't water inde Loots man. — Between pp. 40 and 41.   F.   424 × 523 mm.

[23] W 12 [C:] De Custen van ENGELANT Tusschen de twee pointen van Poortlandt en Lezard. — Between pp. 42 and 43   F 2.   427 × 536 mm.

[24] La Coste d'Angleterre, entre Bevesier & Poortlandt. (7 profiles). On 43   F 2

La quatriéme Démonstration. De la Coste d'Angleterre, entre Poortlandt & Lezart.

[25] TORBAY. — On 43   F 2   50 × 70 mm.

[26] La Coste d'Angleterre, entre Poortlant & Lezart. (23 profiles). On 45   F 3 — 46

La cinquiéme Démonstration. Estant la Coste d'Angleterre, de Lezart au bout d'Angleterre jusques au Cap de Cornuaille, les Sorlinges & le Canal de Bristocq.

[27] W 13 [C:] Cust van ENGELANT, Van Lezard tot Engelands eynd, de Sorlinges, ende Canael van Brestou, alsmede hoe 't van Yerland gelegen is. 't Amsterdam, By Iacob Theunisz. Boeck-verkoper opt water iñ Lootsman. — Between pp. 46 and 47.   427 × 535 mm.
  [Inset:] [T:] Sorlinges —   125 × 124 mm.

[28] Les Sorlingues, & le Canal de Bristouw. (29 profiles). On 50—52

La sixiésme Démonstration. Estant de la Coste du Sud-est & est d'Irlande, entre Corckbegh & Hedenhoo ou Hout.

[29] W 14 [C:] De Zuyd oost zyde van YERLANDT Van Dubling tot aen 't Eylandt Corckbeg. 't Amsterdam, By Iacob Theunisz op 't water inde Loots-man. — Between pp. 52 and 53 G3.   413 × 535 mm.

[30] La platte devan la Terre de Grenoort, du Chasteau de S. Margets à Grenoort. (Profile). On 54

[31] La Coste du Sudest & de l'Est d'Irlande, entre Corckbeg & Hedenhoo. (20 profiles). On 58—59   H 2

[32] W 15 [C:] De Noord oost zyde van YERLANDT Van Caap de Hoorn tot aen Hededhe; Als mede hoe 't van Schotlant gelegen is. 't Amsterdam By Iacob Theunisz, op't water in de Lootsman. — Between pp. 58 and 59 H 2.   415 × 535 mm.
  [Inset:] [T:] Vertoninghe vande Rivier van Dunbriton aende westzyde van Schotlant —   75 × 113 mm.

La septiésme Démonstrance, Qui est la Coste du nord d'Est d'Irlande, entre Hedenhoo ou Hout, & Hoornhed, comme aussi Ecosse vis à vis.

[33] La Costes du Nordest d'Irlande, entre Hedenho au hout & Hoornhed. (10 profiles). On 62 — 63

[34] W 16 [C:] De Noordwest zyde van YERLANDT Beginnende van Capo de Hoorn; tot aen Schynes, of Slynehead. t Amsterdam, By Iacob Theunisz op 't water inde Loots-man. — Between pp. 62 and 63.   424 × 527 mm.

La huictiésme Démonstrance. Estant la Coste du nordouest d'Irlande, entre Hedenhoo & Slynehead.

[35] La Coste du Nordest, d'Irlande, entre Hoornhead & Slynehead. (11 profiles)   On 64 — 65   I

[36] W 17 [C:] De west custen van YERLANDT, Beginnende van Corckbeg tot aen Slynhooft. 't Amsterdam, By Iacob Theunisz. op't water inde Lootsman. — Between pp. 64 and 65 I.   422 × 528 mm.

La neufiésme Démonstrance. La poincte Occidentalle & la Coste Meridionale d'Irlande, entre Slynehead & Korck-haven.

[37] La poincte Occidentalle, & la coste Meridionale d'Irlande, entre Slynehead & Corkhaven. (36 profiles). On 68—70

Le troiziésme Liure Du Grand & Nouveau Miroir OU FLAMBEAU DE LA MER, De la NAVIGATION tant SEPTENTRIONALLE, QUE OCCIDENTALLE. Contenant la description de France, Biscaye, Gallice, Portugal & Algarve, de Ouessant ou Destroit de Gibraltar.

La Premiere Demonstration de la Coste de France, de Ouessant jusques à Belle Isle.

[38] W 18 [C:] Pas Caart van HISPANGIEN, Vertoonende de Custen van Granada, Andaluzie, Algarve, Portugael, Galissien en Biscaien; met een gedeelte van Vranckryck: strecken̄ van Heysant tot de straet Gibralter. NB . de Bocht van Vranckryck ingekort en Verbetert, door A en I de Bree. T'AMSTERDAM, By Iacob Theunisz Boeck-verkoper, op t'water inde Lootsman. — Between pp. 70 and 71.   428 × 530 mm.

[39] W 19 [C:] De Zee-custen van BRETAIGNE van Heysandt tot aen Boelyn. 't Amsterdam; By Iacob Theunisz opt water in de Lootsman. — Between pp. 70 and 71.   425 × 528 mm.

[40] Cloistre S. Mathieu   Pointe du Conquet. (Profile). On 71

[41] Les Costes de Bretaigne entre Ouessant & Bel-Isle. (22 profiles). On 75   K 2 — 76

La deuxiésme Démonstrance, La Coste de Poictou, & Xainctonge, entre Bel-Isle & la Riviere de Bordeaux.

[42] W 20 [C:] De custen van SAINTOIGNE, Poictou, en eengedeelte van Bretaigne; van Boelyn tot aende Rivier van Bourdeaux. — Between pp. 76 and 77   K 3.   423 × 528 mm.

[43] DESCRIPTION D'OLLONNE. On 78   153 × 170 mm.

[44] La Coste de Poictou & de Xanictonge, de Belle-Isle jusques à la Riviere de Bourdeaux. (17 profiles). On 80 —81 L

La troisiésme Démonstrance. Estant la Description de la Riviere de Bourdeaux; comme aussi depuis icelle jusques à S.Sebastien ou Rade Royale.

[45] W 21 [C:] Caarte vande Rivier van BOVRDEAVX tot aen Bayone, ende voorts aen Gataria. — Between pp. 82 and 83 L 2. 425 × 530 mm.

[46] Les Costes de France, de la Riviere de Bourdeaux, jusques à la Rade Royale. (12 profiles). On 84

[47] W 22 [a] [C:] Cust van BISCAYEN tusschen Gatarya en Rio de Sella. 't Amsterdam, By Iacob Theunisz op 'twater inde Lootsman. — 207 × 526 mm.
[b] [C:] Cust van BISCAYEN Tusschen Villa Visioça ende C. de Ortegael. — 206 × 526 mm.
[The whole chart:] Between pp. 84 and 85 L 3. 418 × 526 mm.

La quatriésme Démonstration. Qui est la Coste de Biscaye, entre Gateria & l'Isle de S. Cyprien.

[48] La Coste de Biscaye, entre la Rade Royale, & S. Cyprien. (30 profiles). On 87—89 M

[49] W 23 [C:] Caerte van GALISSIEN Tusschen C. d. Ortegal, C. de Finis terre en Camina. 't Amsterdam. By Iacob Theunisz, Boeck-verkooper op't water inde Lootsman. — Between pp. 88 and 89 M. 418 × 527 mm.

La cinquiéme Démonstration. En laquelle sont les Costes Marines de Gallice, & Portugal entre l'Isle de S. Cyprien & Camine.

[50] La Coste Marine de Gallice, & de Portugal entre l'Isle de S. Cyprien & Camine. (28 profiles). On 93 M 3 — 95

[51] W 24 [C:] Cust van PORTVGAL 't Noordelyckste deel beginnende van Viana tot aen Pissage. — Between pp. 94 and 95. 418 × 524 mm.

La sixiéme Démonstration. Des Costes Marines les plus au nord de Portugal, de Camine au Passage.

[52] Marines les plus du nord de Portugal, de Camine au Passage. (13 profiles). On 96 — 97 N

[53] W 25 [C:] De Cust van PORTVGAEL Het Zuydlyckste deel, Beginnende van Pissage tot aen S. Vues alias Setubal. — Between pp. 96 and 97 N. 415 × 518 mm.

La septiésme Démonstration. Contenant les Costes Marines du sud de Portugal, du Passage jusques à S. Vval.

[54] La Coste de Gallice, & de Portugal entre l'Isle de S. Cyprien & Camine. (7 profiles). On 98 — 99 N 2

[55] W 26 [C:] De Cust van ANDALVZIA en Algarve, van Capo de Spichel tot aen het Clif. 't Amsterdam, By Iacob Theunisz, boeck-verkooper op 't water inde Loots man. — Between pp. 98 and 99 N 2. 422 × 532 mm.

La huictiésme Demonstration. Contenant les Costes Marines Dalgarue & Andaluzie de S. Vval à Palos ou Falaize.

[56] Les Costes d'Algarve & Andoulesie, de S. Vves à Palos ou Falaize. (15 profiles). On 100 — 101 N 3

[57] W 27 [C:] Cust van HISPANGIEN Vande Rivier van Sivilien tot Malaga; Ende van Barbarien, van Out Mamora tot Penon de Velez. 't Amsterdam, By Iacob Theunisz, Boeckverkooper op't water inde Lootsman. — Between pp. 100 and 101 N 3. 421 × 523 mm.

La neufiésme Démonstration. Des Costes Marines d'Andulouzie, de Polos jusques au destroit de Gibraltar prez Modril, & la coste de Barbarie à l'opposite, comme aussi la Coste de Barbarye du Cap de Spartel au vieil Mamore.

[58] La Coste d'Espagne de Malgue à Modril. — On 103 67 × 180 mm. (Irregular).

[59] Les Costes Andoulesie, de Palos dans le Destroit outre Motrie. Comme aussi les Costes de Barbaries ... (6 profiles). On 104

[60] W 28 [C:] De Cust van BARBARIA, Gualata, Argyun, en Geneheo, van Capo S. Vincente tot Capo Verde. 't Amsterdam By Anthonij Iacobssē, op water in den Lootsman, — Between pp. 104 and 105 O. 426 × 542 mm.

[61] W 29 [a] [C:] Cust van BARBARIEN Van Out Mamora tot aen Capo Blanco. — 208 × 528 mm.
[b] [C:] Cust van BARBARIEN; Van Capo Blanco tot Capo de Geer, 't Amsterdam By Iacob Theunisz, boeckverkooper op't water inde Loots-man. — 207 × 528 mm.
[The whole chart:] Between pp. 104 and 105 O. 420 × 528 mm.

La quatriéme Liure Du Miroir ou FLAMBEAU DE LA MER, CONTENANT LES COSTES MARINES De Barbarie, Gualete, Argun Genehoe, les Isles de Madere & de Canarie, du Destroit de Gibraltar au Cap de Verd.
La Premiere Démonstrance, CONTENANT Les Costes Marines de Barbarie depuis Vieil Mamore au Cap de Geer comme aussi les Isles de Madere.

[62] Les Costes Marines de Barbarie, de Mamora au Cap de Geer. (18 profiles). On 108—110

La deuxiésme Demonstration. Qui est des Isles de CANARIE.

[63] W 30 [C:] Pascaarte voor een gedeelte der CANARISE Eylanden, als Canaria, Tenerifa, Forteventura etc. 't Amsterdam By Iacob Theunisz. iñ Lootsman. — Between pp. 110 and 111. 422 × 531 mm.
[Inset:] [C:] Ty-havens van LANCEROTA las Porto de Naos, en Porto de Cavallos. — 120 × 158 mm.

[64] Des Isles de Canarie. (13 profiles). On 111 — 112

Notes: All the large charts are blank on the back; the smaller ones and the profiles have text on the verso. All are uncoloured. This copy corresponds with Koeman's Jac 33 and Jac 34. In his 'Additions' he mentions our copy with the note 'A complete copy, comprising parts I and II in the Nordenskiöld collection in the University Library, Helsinki. This is the only copy known with both parts combined with a general title-page dated 1666. The almanac covers the years 1666—1672.' As the two parts are combined, charts 1—3 occur once only, at the beginning of vol. 1, not in both parts ad described by Koeman. The date on the title-page has been altered by hand to 1669. The second part has no title-page. On the verso of the last preliminary leaf there is a 'Table, Pour la commodité de tous Amateurs de la Navigation...' which lists only the charts from vol. 2. The charts in vol. 1 are the same as those in the 1657 edition, but in a later state. The engraved number 27 is wanting on chart [36] in vol. 1. The charts are numbered differently in the two editions. The charts with the engraved numbers 13—16, which are in vol. 1 of the 1657 edition, are in vol. 2 of the 1666 edition, between charts W 7 and W 8 (our nos. [6] and [16]). On the first old blank leaf is written in old ink 'Ce liure apartiene a moy Samuel Thomas Je prie dieu dy Retenir quelque bonne Choze ≃ S Thõmaẽ,' followed by Nordenskiöld's signature. The volume has been bound for Nordenskiöld by Alfr. Lundin of Stockholm in new vellum with gold lettering. Nordenskiöld's bookplate is on the inside of the front cover.
See also notes to (110) 1657.

Lit.: Koeman, vol. 4, p. 223, pp. 247—249, Jac 33 and 34, Tiele p. 120 and Goos p. 92—93, nr 396, 398.

112 JANSSONIUS, JOANNES 1645

Vol. I
NOVUS ATLAS, Das ist Welt-beschreibung mit schönen newen ausführlichen Taffeln Inhaltende Die Königreiche vnd Länder des gantzen Erdtreichs. Abgetheilt In drey Theile. AMSTELODAMI, Apud Iohannem Ianssonium. ANNO MDCXXXXV   50,5 cm.

[1] Die Gantze Welt.
[C:] NOVA TOTIVS TERRARVM OBRIS GEOGRAPHICA AC HYDROGRAPHICA TABVLA. Auct: Henr:Hondio. — [C:] ... Amstelodami Excudit Ioannes Ianssonius. — [C:] Doctissimis Ornatissimisq$_3$ Viris D.D.Davidi Sanclaro, Antonio de Willon, et D.Martinio, Matheseos in illustris. Academia Parisiensi Professoribus eximiis in veræ amicitiæ μνημόσυνον [mnēmósunon] D.D. Henr. Hondius A.º 1641 — A 376 × 542 mm. The hemispheres with 280 mm. diam.

[2] Die Länder vnter POLVS ARCTICVS.
[C:] NOVA ET ACCVRATA POLI ARCTICI et terrarum Circum Iacentium DESCRIPTIO. — [C:] AMSTELODAMI, apud Ioannem Ianssonium. — C 408 × 515 mm.

[3] EUROPA.
[C:] EVROPA EXACTISSIME DESCRIPTA Auctore HENRICO HONDIO. 1641. — [C:] LVDOVICO XIII. GALLIARUM ET NAVARRÆ REGI CHRISTIANISSIMO. Europæ hanc Tabulam D D. HENRICUS HONDIVS — [T:] Amstelodami sumptibus Ioannis Ianssonii. — D   376 × 503 mm.

[4] Die Britannische Insuln/ der Alten Scribenten.
[C:] INSVLARVM BRITANNICARVM Acurata Delineatio ex Geographicis Conatibus ABRAHAMI ORTELII AMSTELODAMI apud Ioannem Ianssonium — [T:] Petrus Kærius Cælavit. — Engelland. E   391 × 511 mm.

[5] BRITANNIA.
[C:] MAGNÆ BRITANNIÆ et HIBERNIÆ Nova DESCRIPTIO Amstelodami, Apud Ioannem Ianssonium. — F   424 × 542 mm.
[Inset:] [C:] Orcades Insulæ.   65 × 56 mm.

[6] Das Königreich Irrland.
[C:] HIBERNIA REGNVM Vulgo IRELAND. — [T:] Amstelodami, Apud Ioannem Ianssonium. — Irrland. G   382 × 497 mm.

[7] Das Königreich Schottland.
[C:] SCOTIA REGNVM — [T:] Amstelodami, Apud Ioannem Ianssonium. — Schottland. H   381 × 497 mm.
[Inset:] [T:] ORCADES INSVLÆ. — 110 × 78 mm.

[8] Das Königreich Engeland.
[C:] ANGLIA REGNVM — [T:] Amstelodami, Apud Ioannem Ianssonium. — 2   I   385 × 491 mm.

[9] Das Königreich Schweden.
[C:] SVECIÆ, NORVEGIÆ, ET DANIÆ, Nova Tabula. — [T:] Amstelodami. Ioannes Ianssonius excudit. — Europa. N   468 × 546 mm.

[10] Eysslandt.
[C:] TABVLA ISLANDIÆ Auctore Georgio Carolo Flandro. — O   377 × 491 mm.

[11] Das Bischoffthoffthumb STAVANGRIA, vnd dessen angräntzende örther.
[C:] Nova et accurata Tabula EPISCOPATVVM STAVANGRIENSIS, BERGENSIS et ASLOIENSIS Vicinarumque aliquot territoriorum. — [T:] Amstelodami, apud Ioannem Ianssonium. — P   397 × 489 mm.

[12] Gothlandt.
[C:] GOTHIA — [T:] Amstelodami sumptibus Ioannis Ianssonii — Q   391 × 482 mm.

[13] Uplandt.
[C:] VPLANDIA. Amstelodami apud Ioannem Ianssonium. — R   358 × 487 mm.

[14] LIVONIA, oder Lieffland.
[C:] NOVA TOTIVS LIVONIÆ accurata Descriptio. Apud Joan: Janssonium. —   389 × 513 mm.

[15] Reussen vnd Moscaw.
[C:] NOVISSIMA RUSSIÆ TABULA Authore Isaaco Massa. Doctrina et humanitate prædito D. Isaaco Bernart, rerum quæ per Moscoviam maxime trahuntur mercatori peritissimo, hanc Moscoviæ tabulā dedicat affinis finis Hen. Hondius. — [T:] Amstelodami sumptibus Ioannis Ianssonii. — T   466 × 549 mm.

[16] Moscaw gegen Mitternacht vnd Auffgang.
[C:] RVSSIÆ, vulgo MOSCOVIA dictæ, Partes Septentrionalis et Orientalis. Auctore Isaaco Massa. — [C:] ... Iohannes Ianssonius Excudit. — 418 × 539 mm.

[17] MOSCOVIA AUSTRALIS. Oder/ Das theil der Moscaw/ welches gegen Mittag liget.
[C:] MOSCOVIÆ PARS AVSTRALIS. Auctore Isaaco Massa. — Moscaw   380 × 499 mm.

[18] Königreich Polen.
[C:] NOVISSIMA POLONIÆ REGNI Descriptio. — [C:] Nobiliss.^{o} & tam dignitate generis, quam Meritis in Patriam Honoratiss.^{o} Viro, D.^{no} NICOLAO PAHL, in celeberrimo Maris Balthici emporio, Vrbe GEDANENSI, Præconsuli & vicepræsidi, bonarum artium Patrono ac fautori observantiæ ergò D.D.D. IOANNES IANSSONIVS. — y   431 × 537 mm.

[19] Das Gross-Hertzogthumb Littaw/neben einigen andern daran-stossenden Provintzen.
[C:] MAGNI DVCATVS LITHVANIÆ Cæterarumq$_3$ Regionum illi adiacentium exacta descrip Illss^{mi} ac Excell!^{mi} Principis ac Dñi D.Nicolai Christophori Radziwil D.G.Olycæ ac in Nieswies Ducis,S.Rom.Imp. Principis in Szylowiec ac Mir comitis, et S.Sepulchri Hirosolimitani Militis etc. opera et cura in lucem edita — [T:] Sumptibus Ioannis Ianssonii. — z   435 × 539 mm.
[Inset:] [C:] Lectori Sal. Hunc Borysthenis tractum ... adjiciamus ... — 273 × 108 mm.

[20] Das Hertzogthumb Preussen.
[C:] PRUSSIA ACCURATE DESCRIPTA a Gasparo Henneberg Erlichensi. — [T:] Amstelodami, Apud Ioannem Ianssonium. — [T:] Sculpserunt Salomon Rogeri et E.S.Hamers-veldt. — Aa   375 × 487 mm.

[21] Von den Dreyen Werdern Am Hertzogthum Preussen.
[C:] TRACTUUM BORUSSIÆ, circa Gedanum et Elbingam/: ab incolis WERDER appellati/: cum adiuncta NERINGIA, nova et elaboratissima delineatio Authore Olao Ioannis Gotho. — [T:] Amstelodami Excud. Ioannes Ianssonius. — Bb   Verso blank.   413 × 484 mm.

[22] CRIMEA, Oder Die Przecopenser Tartarey/Vnd der Peninsul bey den Alten Taurica Chersonesus genant.
[C:] TAVRICA CHERSONESVS, Hodie PRZECOPSCA, et GAZARA dicitur. — Asia. Cc   380 × 498 mm.

[23] Dennemarck.
[C:] REGNI DANIÆ Accuratissima delineatio. — [C:] Nobilissimo Amplissimo, Consultissimoque Viro D. GERARDO SCHAEP, I.V.D. Inclÿti et Celeberrimi Amsterodamensium Emporii Consuli ac Senatori: et ad Ser: DANIÆ Regem Legato Dignissimo, D.D.D. Joannes Janssonius. — Dd   451 × 557 mm.

[24] SEELANDIA oder Seelandt in Dennemarck.
[C:] SELANDIÆ In Regno Daniæ Insulæ Chorographica Descriptio. — [C:] VIRO Illustri ac Generoso Dño GEORGIO SEEFELDO Hæreditario in REFFES, Regni Daniæ Senatori, ac Iudici provintiali Selandico, Domino ac Patrono plurimum honorando D.D.D. Ioannes Ianssonius. — [C:] Iohannes Ianssonius Excudit. — Dd 2   440 × 525 mm.

[25] LALANDIA oder Lalandt. FALSTRIA oder Falster.
[C:] LALANDIÆ et FALSTRIÆ Accurata Descriptio. — [C:] Iohannes Ianssonius Excudit. — Dd 3   Verso blank. 410 × 532 mm.

[26] FIONIA sampt ihren vmbligenden Inseln.
[C:] NOVA et accurata descriptio totius FIONIÆ vulgo FVNEN. — Dd 4   401 × 510 mm.

[27] IUTIA oder IVTLANDIA.
[C:] Totius IVTIÆ GENERALIS Accurata delincatio. — Dd 5   436 × 557 mm.

[28] Die Hertzogthumben Schlesswick vnd Holstein.
[C:] DUCATUS HOLSATIÆ NOVA TABULA — [C:] AMSTELODAMI, Sumptibus et typis eneis Ioannis Ianssonii. — Ee   377 × 508 mm.
[Insets:] [C:] Alluvies propè Detzbul, Incolis Inferioris Germaniæ, a Duce Holsatiæ concessa aggeribus cingi. Aenwas bij Detzbul den Nederlanders geconsenteert te bedycken van den Hartogh van Holsteyn. — 105 × 128 mm. [C:] Tabula Barmerensis, Meggerensis, et Noortstaepplerensis maris: Incolis Inferioris Germaniæ concessum hæc maria aggeribus cingere, et desiccare. — 105 × 128 mm.

[29] Alt Teutschland.
[C:] GERMANIAE VETERIS, typus. Ioannes Ianssonius Excud. — [T:] Petrus Kærius Cælavit. — [C:] DN. IACOBO MONAVIO SILESIO PATRICIO VRATISLAVIENSI, VIRO ET ERVDITIONE ET HVMANITATE ORNATISSIMO, ABRAHAMVS ORTELIVS HOC MVTVÆ AMICITIAE MONVMENTVM LIBENS DONABAT DEDICABATQV. — Ff   378 × 475 mm.

[30] Teutschland.
[C:] GERMANIÆ nova et accurata delineatio ... Amstelodami, ex officina Ioannis Ianssonii. — Gg   343 × 472 mm.

[31] Nieder Sachsen.
[C:] SAXONIA INFERIOR Joannes Janssonius Excudit. — Teutschlandt. Hh 372 × 455 mm.

[32] Der general Fluss die Elbe.
[C:] ALBIS Fluvius. Germaniæ celebris, A FONTIBUS AD OSTIA Cum fluminibus ab utroque latere in illum fluentibus, descriptus. — [C:] Amstelodami, Apud Ioannem Ianssonium. — [Divided into two parts]. Ii 388 × 492 mm.

[33] Beschreibung des Elbstroms.
[C:] NOBILIS FLUVIUS ALBIS maximá curá, ex variis, famosisq$_3$ Autoribus collectus, et in lucem editus. a IOANNE IANSSONIO Amstelodami. — [C:] Amplissimis, Consultissimis, et Prudentissimis Viris Senatoribus, Consulibusq$_3$ Reipublicæ HAMBURGENSIS hanc celeberrimi Fluminis ALBIS delineationem, summo studio ac nitore elaboratam, benevolo animo dat, dicat donat. Ioannes Ianssonius. — [Divided into two parts]. Teutschlandt Kk 366 × 516 mm.
[Inset:] [C:] EMPORIUM HAMBURGUM — (View). 54 × 254 mm.

[34] Das Hertzogthumb Lüneburg.
[C:] DVCATVS LVNEBVRGENSIS Adiacentiumq$_3$ regionum delineatio Auctore IOHANNE MELLINGERO. — [T:] Amstelodami, Apud Ioannem Ianssonium. — Teutschlandt. Ll 376 × 485 mm.

[35] Das Hertzogthumb Meckelnburg.
[C:] MEKLENBVRG DVCATVS Auctore Ioanne Laurenbergio. — [C:] AMSTELODAMI, Excudebat Ioannes Ianssonius. — Teutschlandt. Mm 362 × 477 mm.

[36] Pommern.
[C:] NOVA ILLVSTRISSIMI DVCATVS POMERANIÆ TABVLA antea Viro Cl.D.D.Eilhardo Lubino edita, nunc iterum correcta per Frid.Palbitzke Pomer. L.L.Studiosum. — [C:] ... AMSTELODAMI, Apud Ioannem Ianssonium — Teutschlandt. Nn 379 × 490 mm.

[37] Die Insel Rügen.
[C:] RVGIA INSVLA AC DVCATVS accuratissime descripta ab E.Lubino. ... — [T:] Ioannis Ianssonius Excudit — Teutschlandt. Oo 386 × 504 mm.

[38] Die Marck Brandenburg.
[C:] MARCHIONATUS BRANDENBURGICUS Authore Olao Iohannis Gotho, Gustaui Mag. R.S.Cosmographo. — [T:] Apud Ioannem Ianssonium. — [C:] Nobili ac Magnifico Domino Michaeli Blondo, Sacræ Regiæ Maiestatis Sueciæ apud Sereniss: Magnæ Britanniæ Regem Agenti. D.Dedicat H.Hondius. — Teutschlandt. Pp 478 × 551 mm.

[39] Ober Sachsen.
[C:] SAXONIA SVPERIOR — [T:] Amstelodami. Sumptibus Joannis Janssonii. — Teutschlandt Qq 381 × 498 m.

[40] Meissen.
[C:] Marchionatus MISNIÆ una cum VOITLANDIA. Authore Olao Ioannis Gotho S.R.M. Sueciæ Geographo. — [T:] Amstelodami Apud Joannem Janssonium. — [C:] Amplissimo Spectatissimo consultissimoque viro D. ANDREÆ BICKERO I.V.D.Reipub. Amstelodamensis Consuli et Senatori varys ad Reges POLONIÆ et SVECIÆ Legationibus Clarissimo Tab.hanc D.D.D. Henricus Hondius. — Teutschlandt. Rr 420 × 517 mm.

[41] Die Landgrafschafft Thüringen.
[C:] THURINGIA LANTGRAVIATUS. — [C:] Serenissimo, Fortissimoque Principi ac Domino D.BERHARDO Duci Saxoniæ, Iuliæ Clivorum, Montiumq$_3$ Lantgravio THURINGIÆ, March, Misniæ, Comiti Marcæ et Ravensbergæ Domino Ravesteini etc. Hanc accuratissimam totius Thuringiæ tabulam lubens consecrat dedicatque Henricus Hondius. — Teutschlandt. Ss 413 × 517 mm.

[42] Die Grafschafft Manssfeldt.
[C:] COMITATVS MANSFELDIÆ DESCRIPTIO. Auctore Tilemanno Stella Sig. — [T:] Amstelodami Apud Ioannem Ianssonium — Teutschlandt. Tt Verso blank. 377 × 485 mm.

[43] Das Ertz-bischthumb Magdenburg/ sampt den darbey gelegenen orthen.
[C:] PRINCIPATUS ANHALDINUS ET MAGDEBURGENSIS Archiepiscopatus. — [T:] Amstelodami Sumptibus Ioannis Ianssonii. — Teutschlandt. Vv 381 × 480 mm.

[44] Das Hertzogthumb Braunschweig.
[C:] Serenissimo PRINCIPI AC DOMINO, D. CHRISTIANO DUCI BRUNSVICENSI ET LUNEBURGENSI Hanc accuratissimam sui Ducatus Brunsuicensis Tabulam dedicat consecratq$_3$. Ioannes Ianssonius. — Teutschlandt. Ww 397 × 492 mm.

[45] Das Bisthumb Hildesheim.
[C:] EPISCOPATVS HILDESIENSIS DESCRIPTIO NOVISSIMA Authore Ioanne Gigante D.Med. et Math. — [C:] Amstelodami, Excudebat Ioannes Ianssonius. — Xx 404 × 443 mm.

[46] Der Westphalische Kreyss.
[C:] CIRCVLVS WESTPHALICVS, Sive GERMANIÆ INFERIORIS. — [T:] Ioannes Ianssonius Excudit. — 19 Teutschlandt. Yy 407 × 538 mm.
[Inset:] [T:] Hamborg — (Plan). 28 × 63 mm. (Irregular).

[47] Die gantze Fahrt von Amsterdam biss nach Hamburg, vber die Watten.
[C:] NIEUWE CAERTE waerinne vertoont wordt de gantsche Vaert van Amsterdam over de WATTEN tot de stadt Hamborch toe. Den liefhebberen enden reysendē luyden tot nut en vermaeck int coper gesneden door Ian Ianssen. — [Divided into two parts]. Zz 442 × 506 mm.
[Inset:] [C:] Op datmen de Elve tot Hamborg toe bequamentlyck soude connen sien, soo hebbē wy t gene daer noch aen resteerde hier neuen in desen hoeck op de selue streckinge en mate van onse caerte bygeuoegt. — 95 × 64 mm.

[48] [C:] EPISCOPATVS BREMENSIS cum Adiacentibus. — [T:] Per Gerardum Mercatorem ... — Blank on the back. 355 × 457 mm.

[49] Die Grafschafft Oldenburg.
[C:] OLDENBVRG COMITATVS — [T:] Amstelodami Ex Officina Ioannis Ianssoni. — Teutschlandt Bbb 372 × 485 mm.

[50] Ostfriessland.
[C:] TYPVS FRISIÆ ORIENTALIS. Auctore Vbbone Emmio. — [T:] Amstelodami, Excudebat Ioannes Ianssonius. — [T:] Sculpserunt Salomon Rogeri, et E.S. Hamersveldt. — Ccc 375 × 490 mm.
[Inset:] [C:] RIDERIÆ PORTIONIS facies, ante inundationem, quæ postea sinus maris facta est. — 117 × 99 mm.

[51] Das Bischthumb Osnabrück.
[C:] OSNABRVGENSIS EPISCOPATVS. Auctore Ioanne Gigante. — [T:] Amstelodami Apud Ioannem Ianssonium. — [C:] Reverendissimo et Illmo Principi ac Domino D^{no} FRANCISCO GVILIELMO Episc. OSNABRVGENSI S.ROM:IMP:PRIN: Comiti in Wartenberg etc. Principi suo longe clementissimo humillime offert IOANNES GIGAS MED.DOCT. — Teutschlandt. Ddd Verso blank. 367 × 477 mm.
[Insets:] [T:] OSENBRVGGE — (View). 54 × 166 mm. [C:] DISTRICTVS RECKENBERGENSIS. — 84 × 80 mm.

[52] Das Bischthumb Münster.
[C:] MONASTERIENSIS EPISCOPATVS. — [T:] Amstelodami, Apud Ioannem Ianssonium. — Teutschlandt. Eee 368 × 483 mm.

[53] Die Grafschafften BENTHEM Vnd STEINFURT.
[C:] COMITATVS BENTHEIM, et STEINFVRT. Auctore Ioanne Westenberg M.Doct. et Math. — [T:] Ioannes Ianssonius Excudit. — Teutschlandt. Fff Verso blank. 375 × 496 mm.

[54] Das Bischthumb Paderborn.
[C:] EPISCOPATVS PADERBORNENSIS descriptio nova Ioanne Gigante Ludense D.Med. et Math. Auctore. — [T:] Amstelodami Joannes Janssonius Excudit. —

Teutschlandt. Ggg 373 × 488 mm.
[55] Das Hertzogthumb Westphalen.
[C:] WESTPHALIA DVCATVS — [T:] AMSTELODAMI, Excudebat Ioannes Ianssonius. — Teutschlandt. Hhh 378 × 492 mm.
[56] Das Hertzogthumb Cleve.
[C:] CLIVIA DVCATVS ET RAVESTEIN DOMINIVM — Teutschlandt. Iii 378 × 496 mm.
[57] Das Hertzogthumb Gülich.
[C:] IVLIACENSIS ET MONTENSIS DVCATVS. De Hertoghdomen GVLICK en BERGHE. — Teutschlandt. Kkk 376 × 493 mm.
[58] Die Grafschafft von der Marck vnd Ravensberg.
[C:] COMITATVS MARCHIA ET RAVENSBERG. — Teutschlandt. Lll 378 × 492 mm.
[Inset:] [T:] RAVENSBERG COMITATVS. — 187 × 148 mm.
[59] Das Ertzbischthumb Cölln.
[C:] COLONIENSIS ARCHIEPISCOPATUS — [T:] Amstelodami, Apud Ioannem Ianssonium — Teutschlandt. Mmm 374 × 485 mm.
[60] [C:] RHENVS Fluviorum Europæ celeberrimus, cum MOSA, MOSELLA, et reliquis, in illum se exonerantibus fluminibus. — Blank on the back. 415 × 934 mm.
[61] Das Lütticher Gebiet.
[C:] DIOECESIS LEODIENSIS ACCURATA TABULA. Amstelodami. Sumptibus Ioannis Ianssonii. — [C:] Humanissimo viro Domino Ioanni le Roux, urbis Amstelodamensis mercatori fidelissimo, hanc Leodiensis Diæcesis tabulam benevolentiæ ergo Dedicat. Henricus Hondius. — Niederlandt Ooo 452 × 536 mm.
[62] Das Ertzbischthumb Trier.
[C:] ARCHIEPISCOPATVS TREVIRENSIS — [T:] Joannes Janssonius excudit. — Teutschlandt. Ppp 408 × 479 mm.
[63] Die Grafschafft Nassaw.
[C:] NASSOVIA COMITATVS — [T:] Amstelodami, Joannes Janssonius Excudit. — Teutschlandt. Qqq 376 × 489 mm.
[64] Grafschafft Waldeck.
[C:] WALDECK COMITATVS. — [T:] Amstelodami Apud Ioannem Ianssonium — Rrr 380 × 500 mm.
[65] Landgrafschafft Hessen.
[C:] HASSIA Landgraviatus. — Sss 445 × 552 mm.
[66] Beschreibung des Stiffts HIRSCHFELT.
[C:] TERRITORIVM ABBATIÆ HERESFELDENSIS. 't Stift Hirszfeldt. Apud Ioannem Ianssonium. — 15 Ttt Verso blank. 385 × 493 mm.
[67] Hertzogthumb Franckenlandt.
[C:] FRANCONIÆ Nova Descriptio. Iohannes Ianssonius Excud. — [C:] Reverendissim & Illustrissimo Principi ac Domino Dnō FRANCISCO, Episcopo Bambergensi & Wirceburgensi, Franciæ Orientalis Duci, Domino suo clementissimo, humillime offert Nicolaus Rittershusius U.I.D. — Vuu 415 × 533 mm.
[68] Das Fürstenthumb Hennenberg.
[C:] PRINCIPATUS HENNENBERGENSIS. — [C:] Humanitate et virtute prædito, D. SALOMONI DIERKENS, mercatori fidelissimo, in benevolentiæ testimonium Dedicat. Henricus Hondius. Amstelodami Sumptibus Iaonnis Ianssonii. — Teutschlandt. Www Verso blank. 372 × 493 mm.
[69] Die Graffschafft Wertheim/ neben den herumb liegenden Oertern vnd Gegenden.
[C:] COMITATVS WERTHEIMICI FINITIMARVMQVE REGIONVM NOVA ET EXACTA DESCRIPTIO. — [T:] Ioannes Ianssonius excudit — Teutschland. Xxx 380 × 501 mm.
[70] Das Gebiet der Stadt Franckfurth am Mayn.
[C:] TERRITORIVM FRANCOFVRTENSE — [C:] AMSTELODAMI, Apud Ioannem Ianssonium. — Teutschlandt. Yyy 377 × 488 mm.
[71] Pfaltz am Rhein.
[C:] PALATINATVS AD RHENVM — [T:] Joannes Janssonius Excudit — Teutschlandt. Zzz 398 × 509 mm.

[72] Die Grafschafft Erpach.
[C:] ERPACH COMITATUS. — [C:] AMSTELODAMI apud Ioannem Ianssonium. — [T:] Petrus Kærius Cælavit — Teutschlandt. aaaa Verso blank. 352 × 470 mm.
[73] Elsass.
[C:] VTRIUSQUÆ ALSATIÆ SUPERIORIS AC INFERIORIS NOVA TABVLA. — [T:] Amstelodami Sumptibus Ioannis Ianssonii. — Teutschlandt. Bbbb 385 × 542 mm.
[74] Das Bischthumb Strassburg.
[C:] TERRITORIUM ARGENTORATENSE. Ioannes Ianssonius Excudit. — [T:] Petrus Kærius Cælavit. — Teutschlandt. Dddd 376 × 489 mm.
[75] Hertzogthumb Würtenberg.
[C:] WIRTENBERG DVCATVS. — [T:] Per Gerardum Mercatorem... — [T:] Amstelodami, Excusum apud Ioannem Ianssonium. — Teutschlandt. Eeee 365 × 440 mm.
[76] Schwabenlandt.
[C:] TOTIVS SVEVIÆ novissima TABVLA — [C:] Amstelodami ex officina Ioannis Ianssonii. — Ffff 384 × 487 mm.
[77] Alemannia oder Ober Schwaben.
[C:] NOVA ALEMANNIÆ SIVE SVEVIÆ SVPERIORIS TABVLA. — [C:] ... Amstelodami, Apud Ioannem Ianssonium — Teutschlandt. Gggg 378 × 488 mm.
[78] Die Grafschafft Tirol.
[C:] COMITATUS TIROLENSIS. — [T:] Joannes Janssonius Excudit — Teutschlandt. Hhhh 399 × 513 mm.
[79] Fürstenthumb Trient.
[C:] TERRITORIUM TRIDENTINUM — [T:] AMSTELODAMI, Excudebat Ioannes Ianssonius. — Italia. Iiii 372 × 481 mm.
[80] Ober Pfaltz oder Ober Beyern.
[C:] PALATINATVS BAVARIÆ. — [T:] Per Gerardum Mercatorem ... — [T:] Apud Ioannem Ianssonium, — Teutschlandt. Kkkk 367 × 494 mm.
[81] Hertzogthumb Beyern.
[C:] BAVARIÆ Superioris et Inferioris nova descriptio. — [C:] Amstelodami Excudebat Ioannes Ianssonius — Llll 378 × 462 mm.
[82] Beschreibung Der Vmb die Stadt New = Marck in der Ober-Pfaltz gelegenen Landschafft.
[C:] TERRITORII NOVOFORENSIS IN SVPERIORE PALATINATU accurata descriptio Auct. Nicolao Rittershusio D. — Mmmm 402 × 508 mm.
[83] Das Nürnberger Gebiet.
[C:] TERRITORIVM NORIMBERGENSE. — [T:] Joannes Ianssonius Excudit. — [C:] Nobilissimis Amplissimis Consultissimisque Viris Dominis D Consulibus totique Senatui inclytæ reipublicæ Norimbergensis dedicabat. Joannes Ianssonius. — Nnnn 360 × 462 mm.
[Inset:] [T:] NVRNBERG — (Plan). 91 × 116 mm.
[84] Der Donawstrom.
[C:] DANVBIVS, FLVVIVS EUROPÆ MAXIMUS, A FONTIBUS AD OSTIA, Cum omnibus Fluminib[9], ab utroque latere, in illum fluentibus. — Teutschlandt. Oooo 410 × 958 mm.
[85] Das Königreich vnd Chur Böhmen.
[C:] BOHEMIA. — [T:] Amstelodami Apud Ioannem Ianssonium. — Teutschlandt. Pppp 403 × 468 mm.
[86] Die Obere Laussnitz.
[C:] LUSATIA SUPERIOR Auth. Bartholomæo Sculteto Gorlitio. — [T:] Amstelodami Sumptibus Ioannis Ianssonii. — Qqqq 380 × 488 mm.
[87] Die Grafschafft Glatz.
[C:] COMITATUS GLATZ Authore Iona Sculteto. Ioannes Ianssonius excudit. — 56 Teutschlandt. Rrrr Verso blank. 380 × 460 mm.
[88] Schlesien.
[C:] SILESIÆ DVCATVS Accurata et vera delineatio, VIRIS MAGNIFICIS AC GENEROSIS, D.Valentino a Stössel in Seppa Kawer. D.Sigismundo a Loss, in Simpsen Dammer. D.Caspari à Stosch. D.Davidi Gotfr a Stosch

[89] Nieder-Schlesien.
[C:] SILESIA INFERIOR, Sereniss. ac Celsiss. Principibus ac Dominis Dn. GEORGIO, Dn. LVDOVICO, Dn. CHRISTIANO, Fratribus, Ducibus Silesiæ Ligniciens. ac Bergensibus, Dominis gratiosissimis dicata à Jona Sculteto Sprotta-Silesio. — [T:] Johannes Janssonius Excud. — Teutschlandt. Ssss 2   415 × 508 mm.

Patruelibus in Gross et klein Tschirna. D.Gotfried ab Haugwitz in Brodelwitz, Ziebendorf EQUITIBUS. PATRONIS. Dicat Dedicatq₃ Ionas Scultetus Sprotta Silesius — [T:] AMSTELODAMI Sumptibus Ioannis Ianssonii. — Teutschlandt. Ssss   382 × 490 mm.

[90] Das Fürstenthumb GLOGAU Mit den daherumbliegenden Fürstenthümmern vnd Kräysen.
[C:] DVCATVS SILESIÆ GLOGANI Vera Delineatio Secundá curá ac labore confecta A Iona Sculteta Sprotta Silesio. — Teutschland. Tttt   415 × 529 mm.

[91] Das Hertzogthumb von Wolaw.
[C:] Ducatus SILESIÆ WOLANUS Authore Iona Sculteto Sprotta Silesio. — [T:] Ioannes Ianssonius excudit. —
[C:] Serenissimo et Celsissimo Principi ac Domino, D. GEORGIO RODVLPHO, DUCI SILESIÆ LIGNICIENSI, BREGENSI, WOLAVIENSI, GOLTBERGENSI, DOMINO SUO AC PRINCIPI CLEMENTISSIMO, Delineationem istam Ducatus WOLANI humillime D.D. Ionas Scultetus. — Vuuu   Verso blank.   390 × 484 mm.

[92] Das Hertzogthumb Bresslaw.
[C:] DUCATUS BRESLANUS sive WRATISLAVIENSIS. — [T:] Amstelodami. sumptibus Ioannis Ianssonii. —
[C:] Nobil. Ampl.ᵐᵒ & Consultissimo viro D. BERNHARDO GULIELMO NUSLERO, Celsissimo Lygio Bergensium Duci â Consilys ac secretis. Præcipuo operis huius Promotori. A Georgio Vechnero S.Th.D. et Iona Sculteto Sprotta Silesio. — 60 Teutschlandt. Wwww   397 × 492 mm.
[Inset:] [C:] BRESLAW totius SILESIÆ METROPOLIS. — (Plan).   124 × 195 mm.

[93] Das Hertzogthumb Lignitz.
[C:] Ducatus SILESIÆ LIGNICIENSIS. Serenissimo & Celsissimo PRINCIPI AC DOMINO D. GEORGIO RODVLFO Dvci Silesiæ Liginciensi Bregensi & Goldbergensi, Principi suo ac Domino gratiosissimo. Hanc Ducat. Lingiciensis tab. D.D. Ionas Scultetus Sil. — [T:] Amstelodami Sumptibus Joannis Janssonii. — Wwww 2   Verso blank.   390 × 476 mm.
[Inset:] [T:] FVRSTLICHE STADT LIGNITZ — (View).   53 × 154 mm.

[94] Beschreibung des Fürstenthumbs Grottkaw/ vnd des Bischthumbs Neiss.
[C:] DVCATVS SILESIÆ GROTGANVS cum Districtu Episcopali NISSENSI Delineatore IONA SCVLTETO, Silesio. — [T:] Amstelodami, Apud Joannem Janssonium. —
[C:] Generoso & Magnifico D. OTTONI HENRICO de Radschin, in Steina, Wolffsdorf, Gismansdorf, Zaupitz, &c. Operis huius Patrono præcipuo D. a IONA SCVLTETO Silesio. — Teutschlandt. xxxx   393 × 501 mm.

[95] Die Marckgrafschafft Mähren.
[C:] MARCHIONATVS MORAVIÆ Auct I.Comenio. — [T:] Amstelodami Excudit Ioannes Ianssonius. — Teutschlandt. Yyyy   382 × 537 mm.

[96] Das Ertzhertzogthumb Oesterreich.
[C:] AVSTRIA ARCHIDVCATVS Auctore Wolfgango Lazio. — [C:] AMSTELODAMI, Ioannes Ianssonius excudit. — Teutschlandt. Zzzz   362 × 532 mm.

[97] Das Bischthumb Saltzburg.
[C:] SALTZBVRG ARCHIEPISCOPATVS, et CARINTHIA DVCATVS. Auctore Ger.Mercatore. — [T:] Amsterdami Apud Ioannem Ianssonium — Teutschlandt. Aaaaa   374 × 490 mm.

[98] Steyermarck.
[C:] STIRIA — [T:] Per Gerardum Mercatorem... — Teutschlandt. Bbbbb   304 × 412 mm.

[99] Das Königreich Ungern.

[C:] HVNGARIA REGNVM. — [T:] Amsterdami Apud Iohannem Ianssonium. — Teutschlandt. Ccccc   419 × 507 mm.

[100] Siebenbürgen.
[C:] TRANSYLVANIA, SIBENBURGEN. ... Amstelodami, Apud Ioannem Ianssonium. — [T:] Per Gerardum Mercatorem ... — Teutschland.   335 × 426 mm.

[101] Kärnten/ Crain/ Isterreich vnd die Windische Marck.
[C:] KARSTIA, CARNIOLA, HISTRIA et WINDORVM MARCHIA. Ger. Mercatore Auctore — [C:] ... Ioannis Ianssonius excudit. — Teutschlandt. Eeeee   378 × 489 mm.

[102] Wallachia / Servia / Bulgaria vnd Romania.
[C:] WALACHIA SERVIA, BVLGARIA, ROMANIA — [T:] Per Gerardum Mercatorem ... — Teutschlandt. Ggggg   344 × 465 mm.

[103] Sclavonia / Croatia / Bosnia vnd ein Theil der Dalmacey.
[C:] SCLAVONIA, CROATIA, BOSNIA cum DALMATIÆ PARTE. — [T:] Per Gerardum Mercatorem... — Fffff   354 × 460 mm.

Notes: All the maps have text on the verso, except where otherwise indicated. The title-page and maps are all coloured. 'An de Günstigen Leser' is dated 1638. Map [1] has four portraits, one in each corner: JVLIVS CAESAR, CLAVDIVS PTOLOMAEVS ALE., GERARDVS MERCATOR Flander., and IVDOCVS HONDIVS Flander. Map [36] has a portrait of BVGISLAVS IVNIOR XIV POMERANIÆ DUX. This Janssonius atlas, which is a development of the Mercator-Hondius atlases, corresponds with the copy described by Koeman under Me 131 (1647) with the title-page as described in Me 134 (1649) except that our copy was printed in 1645, and the imprint has AMSTERDAMI instead of AMSTELODAMI. There are only minor differences between the two atlases. One distinction, which may serve to identify the one from which any particular map is taken, is that 'Teutschlandt' appears at the foot of each page with a 'dt' in our copy, in all but two maps, but with only 'd' in the copy described by Koeman. The title is printed on a separate slip and pasted in the appropriate place on the title-page, but the imprint is part of the engraved plate. The text on the title-page reads 'In drey Theile', but 'drey' has been crossed out and 'vier' written beneath in old ink. A number of the leaf signatures are also corrected in ink. The engraving on the title-page is the same as in Blaeu's Novus Atlas of 1635. The volume is in poor repair. It is bound in old vellum, with gold tooling. The volume formerly belonged in turn to various Swedes, as can be seen from the names written on the last blank leaf and on the inside of the front cover: Gustaf Adolph de la Gardie, Axel Vintsson Posse, Breant Alexander Rappe, A.R. Posse, Arvid Rutger Posse, Rutger JAV Brunnerus, Grefve Arvid Rutger Posse, Rappe Rutger Posse, Brunnerus (several times), Magister Brunnerus, De la Gardie af Christiernin, Breant Alex Rappe, af Christiernin, minister Krigsman. 'Arvid Rutger Posse' is written in the margin of map [8], and 'Esaias M. Tegnér' below the text on map [57]. Nordenskiöld has written his initials in red pencil on the inside of the front cover.

Lit.: Keuning, Joh. Janssonius, Koeman vol. 2, p. 475—477, Me 131 and Me 134.

113 JANSSONIUS, JOANNES   [1645?]

Vol. II
[Novus Atlas, Das ist Welt-Beschreibung mit schönen newen ausssführlichen Land-Tafeln. Zweite Theil: Inhaltende Niederlandt, Franckreich und Hispanien.]   50,5 cm.

[1] BELGIVM,Oder/Das Alte Niederland.
[C:] BELGII VETERIS TYPVS Ex Conatibus Geographicis Abrahami Ortelii HAC LITTERARVM FORMA VETVSTIORA PINXIMVS. Quæ paulo erant

recentiora his notauimus: Nulla autem antiquitate illustria, hoc charactere Recentissima vero, his vernaculis ab alys distinximus. — [T:] Petrus Kærius Cælavit. — A 377 × 491 mm.

[2] Niderlandt.
[C:] NOVA Totius BELGII Sive GERMANIÆ INFERIORIS accuratissima Delineatio. — [T:] Amstelodami. Apud Ioannem Ianssonium — I Niderlandt. A 443 × 545 mm.

[3] Das Hertzogthumb Brabandt.
[C:] NOVISSIMA ET ACCVRATISSIMA BRABANTIÆ DVCATVS TABVLA. — [C:] AMSTELODAMI, Sumptibus Ioannis Ianssonii — 6 Niderlandt. D 387 × 495 mm.

[4] Das erste theil von Brabant/ dessen Haupstadt ist Löven.
[C:] PRIMA PARS BRABANTIÆ cuius caput LOVANIVM Auctore Michaele Florentio a Langren Hispan. Regis Mathematico. — [C:] ... Amstelodami, apud Ioannem Ianssonium. — Niderlandt. F 410 × 525 mm.

[5] Das ander theil van Brabant/dessen Hauptstadt ist Brüssel.
[C:] SECVNDA PARS BRABANTIÆ cuius urbs primaria BRVXELLÆ Descr. Michaele Florentio a Langren Mathematico Regio — [C:] ... Amstelodami, Apud Ioannem Ianssonium. — Niderlandt. G 411 × 525 mm.

[6] Der dritte Theil von Brabant, dessen die erste Stadt ist Antorff/ eine Marckgrafschafft des Röm. Reichs.
[C:] TERTIA PARS BRABANTIÆ qua continetur MARCHIONAT.S.R.I. horum urbs primaria ANTVERPIA Ex Archetypo Michaelis Florenty a Langren Reg.Maj.Mathematico — [C:] ... Amstelodami, apud Ioannem Ianssonium. — Niderlandt. H 413 × 513 mm.

[7] Bergen op-Soom / Steinbergen / sampt andern allda gemachten Wercken.
[C:] TABVLA Bergarum ad Zomam Stenbergæ et novorum ibi operum Ad amussim fecit Franciscus van Schoten Math. Professor in Acad. Leidensi — 13 Niderlant. I 224 × 531 mm.
[Inset:] [T:] Castra Pinsii — (Plan). [T:] Apud Joannem Janssonium. — 84 × 103 mm.

[8] Das Castel bey Santfliet.
[C:] TABVLA Castelli ad Sandflitam, qua simul inundati agri, alluviones, fossæ, alvei, quæ Bergas ad Zomam et Antverpiam interjacent, annotantur. ... Amstelodami, Apud Ioan. Ianssonium. — Niderlandt. I 2 365 × 493 mm.

[9] Hertzogenbusch.
[C:] QVARTA PARS BRABANTIÆ cujus caput SYLVADVCIS. Willebordus vander Burght describ. — [C:] ... Amstelodami Sumptibus Ioannis Ianssonii. — Niderland. K 407 × 514 mm.

[10] Das Hertzogthumb Limburg.
[C:] DVCATVS LIMBVRGVM Auctore ÆGIDIO MARTINI. — [T:] Amstelodami Apud Ioannem Ianssonium. — Niderlandt. L 379 × 492 mm.

[11] Das Hertzogthumb Lützelburg.
[C:] DVCATVS LVTZENBVRGENSIS Nova et accurata DESCRIPTIO. — [T:] Amstelodami, Apud Ioannem Ianssonium. — Niderlandt. M 390 × 507 mm.

[12] Das Hertzogthumb Geldern / vnd die Grafschafft Sütphen.
[C:] DVCATVS GELDRIÆ novissima descriptio. — [T:] Joa[nnes] Janssonius excudit. — Niderlandt. 381 × 520 mm.

[13] Das Reich oder die Marckgrafschafft Nimwegen.
[C:] DVCATVS GELRIAE, pars prima Quæ est NEOMAGENSIS. — [T:] Amstelodami, apud Joannem Janssonium. — Nidergang. O 379 × 518 mm.

[14] Das zweyte Theil des Hertzogthumbs GELDERN, Welches ist das Gebiet von ROERMOND.
[C:] DVCATVS GELRIAE pars secunda Quæ est RVREMONDENSIS. — P 379 × 520 mm.

[15] Die Grafschafft Zütphen.
[C:] COMITATUS ZUTPHANIA Excudit Joannes Janssonius. — Niderlandt. Q 375 × 482 mm.

[16] Die Velaw.
[C:] DVCATVS GELRIAE pars Quarta Quæ est ARNHEMIENSIS, Siue VELAVIA. — [T:] Amstelodami, apud Joannem Janssonium. — Niderlandt. R 378 × 515 mm.

[17] Alt BATAVIA. Oder Ein Theil des Rheins zusampt der gantzen Maass.
[C:] DESCRIPTIO FLUMINUM RHENI, VAHALIS et MOSÆ a Rheno Berca ad Goricomium usque, comprehendens IMPERIUM NOVIOMAGENSE, BATAVIAM, TIELÆ et BOMELII INsulas, regionesque conterminas. — [C:] ... AMSTELODAMI Sumptibus Ioannis Ianssonii. — [Divided into two parts]. Niderlandt. S 372 × 494 mm.

[18] Der Grabe S. MARIÆ Welcher auch FOSSA EVGENIANA genennet/ Zwischen dem Rhein vnd Maass aussgeführt im jahr 1628.
[C:] FOSSA EUGENIANA quæ a Rheno ad Mosam duci cœpta est, Anno MDCXXVII ductu Comitis Henrici vanden Berge. — [C:] ... AMSTELODAMI Sumptibus Ioannis Ianssonii. — Niderland. T 368 × 495 mm.

[19] Die Grafschafft Flandern.
[C:] COMITATUS FLANDRIÆ Nova Tabula. Viro Doctissimo D. IOANNI D'HONDT cognato suo Medicinæ Doct. peritissimo Lub. Meritoq$_3$ dedicat H. Hondius. — [T:] Amstelodami apud Ioannem Ianssonium. — Niderlandt. V 409 × 527 mm.

[20] Duynkirchen.
[a] [C:] Pascaert vande Custe van Vlaenderen, van Walcheren tot Cales en Bouloigne in Vranckrÿck. Carte mariné dela Coste de Flandres, depuis l'isle de Walcheren en Zeelande, jusq$_3$ a Calais et Bouloigne de France. Amstelodami apud Ioannem Ianssonium. — (Chart). 111 × 510 mm.
[b] [C:] Afbeeldinghe vande vermaerde seehaven ende stadt van Duynkercken met der omliggende plaetsen sanden ende droochten, afgeteeckent door Capiteijn Pieter Codde van Enchuysen. — [C:] Pourtraict de la fameuse ville et havre de Duynckercke et places voisines, sables etc. faict par le Capitaine Pierre Codde d'Enchuyse. — (Chart). 318 × 513 mm.
[Insets:] [T:] DVNCKERCKE — (View). 43 × 216 mm. [T:] Cales — 40 × 137 mm.
[The whole map:] Niderlandt. 431 × 513 mm.

[21] Das Occidentalische theil Teutsch Flandern.
[C:] FLANDRIÆ PARS OCCIDENTALIS ... AMSTELODAMI, Sumptibus Ioannis Iãssonii. — Niderlandt. X 381 × 486 mm.

[22] Das Orientalische theil Flammisch Flandern.
[C:] PARS FLANDRIÆ orientalis; FRANCONATUM, insulam CADSANT etc. Civitatesq$_3$ Gandavum, Brugas, Slusam, Oostendam aliasq$_3$ continens. — [C:] Amstelodami, Sumptibus Ioannis Ianssonii. — Niderlandt. Y 394 × 499 mm.

[23] Welsch Flandern / In gemeiner Sprach FLANDRE WALLONNE.
[C:] FLANDRIA GALLICA Continens CASTELLANIAS Insulensem Duacensem Orchianensem Ciuitatem Dominiumq$_3$ TORNACENSE ... Amstelodami Ioannes Ianssonius exc. — Niderlandt. Z 399 × 494 mm.

[24] Reichs: vnd eigen Flandern.
[C:] FLANDRIÆ Partes duæ, quarum altera PROPRIETARIA, altera IMPERIALIS vulgo dicitur. — [C:] Nob.^{mo} Stren.^{mo} Prud.^{moq_3} Viro D. IACOBO WIITS Exercitus Ordinum Belgicæ Fœderatæ Ephoro, et Concilii militaris Præsidi, ac præsidiariorum militum in urbe Amsteldamensi Præfecto, Viro de patria ac Reip. hujus salute præclare merito, et indies merenti, D.D. Joannes Janssonius. — Niderlandt. Aa 411 × 519 mm.

[25] Die Grafschafft ARTESIA.
[C:] ARTESIA, COMITATVS ARTOIS. — [T:] Ioannes Ianssonius excud; — Niderlandt. Bb 378 × 496 mm.

[26] Die Grafschafft Hennegaw.
[C:] COMITATVVM HANNONIÆ ET NAMVRCI DESCRIPTIO. — [T:] Amstelodami Excudebat Joannes Janssonius. — Niderlandt. Cc 380 × 495 mm.

[27] Das Ertzbischoffthumb Cambray.

[C:] ARCIHIEPISCOPATVS CAMERACENSIS. Archevesche de CAMBRAY. — [T:] Amstelodami, Apud Johannem Ianssonium. — 13 Franckreich. Dd 384 × 493 mm.

[28] Die Grafschafft Namur.
[C:] NAMVRCVM COMITATVS Auctore Iohann. Surhonio. — [T:] Amstelodami, apud Joannem Janssonium. — Niederlandt. Ee 407 × 522 mm.

[29] Grafschafft Holland.
[C:] COMITATVS HOLLANDIÆ Nova Descriptio, Ex Optimis & novissimis Delineationibus designata. Amstelodami, Apud Joannem Janssonium — [T:] Geeraerd Coeck Sculpsit. — Niederlandt. FF 388 × 525 mm.

[30] Delfflandt / Schieland / vnd die beyliegende Inseln.
[C:] Novissima DELFLANDIÆ, SCHIELANDIÆ et circumiacentium insularum ut VOORNÆ, OVERFLACKEÆ, GOEREÆ, ISELMONDÆ, aliarumque tabula Auctore Balthazaro Florentio a Berckenrode AMSTELODAMI, Sumptibus Ioannis Ianssonii Anno 1641. — Niderlandt Gg 448 × 548 mm.

[31] Hollandt so gegen Mittag ligt / in gemein Süd-Hollandt.
[C:] Novissima Tabula INSVLAR. DORDRACENSIS, ALBLASSER, CRIMPER, CLVNDERT etc: Comprehendens item TERRITORIA VIANÆ, GORICOMII, LEERDAMI, ALTENÆ, HEVSDENÆ, ac Civitates S.Geertrudisbergam, Sevenbergam, Willemstadium, et circumjacentes Regiones ad Holl. pertinentes. Auct. Balth. Florentio a Berckenrode. ... Amstelodami, Sumptibus Ioannis Ianssonii — Niederland. Hh 447 × 547 mm.

[32] Rheinlandt.
[C:] RHINOLANDIÆ, AMSTELANDIÆ, et circumjacent. aliquot territoriorū, accurata desc. Auct. Balthazaro Flor. a Berckenrode. AMSTELODAMI. Sumptibus Ioannij Ianssonij. Anno 1641. — Niederland. Ii 450 × 545 mm.

[33] Nord-Hollandt Oder West-Friesslandt.
[C:] HOLLANDIÆ pars Septentrionalis, Vulgo WESTVRIESLAND en 'tnoorder quartier. — [T:] Iohannes Ianssonius Excud. — Niederland. Kk 446 × 546 mm.

[34] Die aussgetrockenete Meer in Hollandt / gemeinlich genannt die ZEYPE, BEEMSTER, PVRMER, WORMER, &c.
[a] [C:] DE ZYPE — [T:] Petrus Kærius Cælavit. — 167 × 229 mm.
[b] [C:] BEEMSTER — 167 × 230 mm.
[c] [C:] DE PURMER. Gemeten ende geteekent door Mr Lucas Jansen Sinck Anno 1622. — 167 × 153 mm.
[d] [C:] DE WORMER — 167 × 150 mm.
[e] [C:] CAERTE VAN WATERLAND Vertonende de gelegentheyt der Meeren onlangs bedyckt als Buycksloter Broecker en Belmer meer met de naest gelegen Steden. tot Amsterdam by Ian Iansz. — 167 × 152 mm.
[The whole map:] Ll 346 × 472 mm.

[35] Grafschafft Seeland.
[C:] ZEELANDIA Comitatus. — [C:] Nobiliss. Magnif.^{co} Fortissimoq$_3$ Domino, D. IOANNI DE KNVYT, Equiti et Domino in Veteri et Novo Vosmar: nomine præp. Ord. Belg. Fœd. ad Christianissimum Regem Gall. Legato; primario, et Nobilium nomine in Ampl. Ord. Zelandiæ Collegio, eorundemque Deputatorū Consilio, Assessori; nec non et Excellentiæ suæ, Illustrissimi Principis Auriaci, Consiliario Dignissimo. D.D. Joannes Janssonius. — Niederlandt. Mm 379 × 497 mm.

[36] Die Herrschafft Mecheln.
[C:] MECHLINIA DOMINIVM, et AERSCHOT DVCATVS Auctore Michaele Flor: a Langren Regis Catholici Mathematico. — [T:] Amstelodami, Apud Ioannem Ianssonium. — Niederlandt. Nn 405 × 510 mm.

[37] Das Stifft Vtrecht.
[C:] EPISCOP. VLTRAIECTINVS Auct. Balthazaro Florentio a Berkenrode. AMTSELODAMI, Apud Ioannem Ianssonium. — [C:] Evert Sijmonszoon Hamersveldt sculpsit — Niederlandt. Oo 372 × 484 mm.

[38] TRANSISALANIA, auff Teutsch / Ober-Yssel.
[C:] DITIO TRANS-ISULANA — [T:] IOANNES IANSSONIUS excud. — Niederlandt. PP 382 × 487 mm.

[39] Die Landschafft Drente.
[C:] DRENTIA COMITATVS. Transisulaniæ Tabula II. Auctore Cornelio Pynacker I.C. — [T:] Apud Joannem Janssonium. — [T:] A. van den Broeck fecit. — Niederland. Ss 385 × 527 mm.

[40] Westfriesslandt.
[C:] FRISIA OCCIDENTALIS Auctoribus Adriano Metio et Gerardo Freitag. Amstelodami, Ioannes Ianssonius Excudit — [T:] Sculpserunt E.S.Hamers-veldt et S.Rogeri. — Niederlandt. Tt 384 × 495 mm.

[41] Gröninger Landt.
[C:] GRONINGA DOMINIVM. Auctore Bartholdo Wicheringe. — [C:] Amstelodami, Excudebat Ioannes Ianssonius. — [T:] Sculpserunt Erardus Sim: Hamersveldt, et Sal: Rogeri. — Vu 378 × 495 mm.

[42] Franckreich so Strabo vnd andere alte Scribenten beschrieben.
[C:] GALLIÆ VETERIS Typus. Amstelodami Apud Ioannem Ianssonium. — A 390 × 491 mm.

[43] Franckreich / So allein auss dem Iulio Cæsare gezogen.
[C:] GALLIA VETVS Ad Iulij Cæsaris commentaria — [C:] AMSTELODAMI Apud Ioannem Ianssonium. — [T:] J. vanden Ende fec. — Franckreich. B 370 × 499 mm.

[44] Das Reich CAROLI MAGNI.
[C:] IMPERIUM CAROLI MAGNI — [T:] Amstelodami, sumptibus Ioannis Ianssonii. — Franckreich. C 368 × 524 mm.

[45] Das Königreich Franckreich.
[C:] GALLIÆ supra omnes in hac forma editiones locu pletissima et exactissima descriptio. auctore H. Hondius. ... — [T:] Amstelodami apud Ioannem Ianssonium — Franckreich. D 366 × 496 mm.

[46] Beschreibung der PICARDEY.
[C:] PICARDIA VERA ET INFERIOR — [C:] Illust.^{mo} atq$_3$ Excell.^{mo} Domino D. HERCULI DE CHARNACE, Equiti, Regis Christ.^{mi} a sanctiorib. consilÿs, Gubernatori vrbis, arcis et comitatus Claromontani, Exercituum suæ Ma^{tis} Marescalo, eiusdemq$_3$ ad D.D.Ordines foederatarum Provinciarum legato dignissimo. Henricus Hondius. — [T:] ... Amstelodami sumptibus Ioannis Ianssonii — [T:] Cornelis Cl. Duysend sculp. — Franckreich. E 389 × 541 mm.

[47] Die Provintz CALES Mit dem gewonnenen Land.
[C:] LE GOUVERNEMENT DE CALAIS & Païs Reconquis. — [T:] Amstelodami, Apud Ioannem Ianssonium. — [C:] Nobilissimo Strenuiss. et Spectatiss. viro D. CORN: DE GLARGES, Equiti S. Michaelis, D.^{no} ab. Ælæmes, Illust: ac Præpot: D.D.Ordinum Confederat. Belgiæ Provintiarum res Agenti in Gallia, Caleti Residenti Hanc tab: dat dicat. Ioann Ianssonius. — F 400 × 509 mm.

[48] Die Grafschafft BOULOGNE Vnd GVINES.
[C:] DESCRIPTIO BOLONIÆ PONTIEU Comit. S.Pauli Cum adjacentibus — [T:] Amstelodami, Apud Ioannem Ianssonium. — Franckreich. G 378 × 522 mm.

[49] VERMANDOIS.
[a] [C:] DESCRIPTIO VEROMANDVORVM Auctore Ioanne Suthonio Gallice VERMANDOIS. — Franckreich. H 383 × 253 mm.
[b] [C:] GOVVERNEMENT de la CAPPELLE par P. petit Bourbon. — 383 × 251 mm.
[The whole map:] Franckreich. H 383 × 515 mm.

[50] Schampanien.
[C:] CHAMPAIGNE et BRIE etc. — Franckreich. K 400 × 500 mm.

[51] Das Remische Hertzogthumb In gemeiner Sprach DVCHE PAIRIE Vnd Das Ertzbischthumb de Rheims.
[C:] DIOECESE DE RHEIMS, et le Païs de RETHEL. Par Iean Iubrien Chalonnois. — [T:] Amstelodami, Sumptibus Joannis Janssonij. — L 385 × 495 mm.

[52] Die Herrschafft RHETELOIS.
[C:] CARTE du Pais de RETELOIS. Faicte par Iehan Iubrien Chalonnois. 1641 — [C:] ... AMSTELODAMI Apud Ioannem Ianssonium. — Franckreich. M Verso blank. 375 × 498 mm.

[53] Das Fürstenthumb SEDAN vnd RAVCOVRT, Sampt der Vogtey DONGHERI.
[C:] La SOVVERAINETÉ de SEDAN et de RAVCOVRT, et la PREVOSTÉ de DONCHERI. ... — [C:] AMSTELODAMI Apud Ioannem Ianssonium. ... — [T:] Et se vendent a Paris chez Melchior Tauernier demeurant sur l'Isle du Palais — Franckreich. N 374 × 498 mm.

[54] Die Briensische Grafschafft / in gemeiner Sprach COMTE de BRIE.
[C:] LE PAIS DE BRIE. — [T:] Ioannes Ianssonius excudit. — Franckreich. 386 × 495 mm.

[55] Das Hertzogthumb Lothringen.
[C:] LOTHARINGIA DVCATVS Noua descriptio. AMSTELODAMI Apud Ioannem Ianssonium — Lothringen P 419 × 541 mm.

[56] [C:] LOTHARINGIA SEPTENTRIONALIS LORAINE vers le Sept.^{ion} — [T:] Amstelodami Apud Ioannem Ianssonium — Blank on the back. 371 × 496 mm.

[57] Metz /
[C:] TERRITORIVM METENSE. Auctore AB. FABERT Consule urbis Metensis. LE PAIS MESSIN. — [T:] Amstelodami, Apud Ioannem Ianssonium. — Franckreich. R 379 × 493 mm.

[58] [C:] LORRAINE, VERS LE MIDY. — [T:] Apud Ioannem Ianssonium. — Blank on the back. 371 × 493 mm.

[59] Das Theil des Königreichs So eigentlich Francia genennet wird.
[C:] AGER PARISIENSIS Vulgo L'ISLE DE FRANCE Fr. Guilloterius Bitur Viu. describ. et CL. V. PETRO Pithœo I.C. dedicabat. — T 328 × 467 mm.

[60] Das Gubernament L'ISLE de FRANCE, vnd sonderlich von HVREPOIS.
[C:] LE GOVVERNEMENT DE L'ISLE DE FRANCE Par Damien de Templeux Escuyer S.^{r} Du Frestoy. — 18 Franckreich V 407 × 510 mm.

[61] Das Hertzogthumb Vales, Auff Frantzösisch LA DUCHE DE VALOIS.
[C:] VALESIVM Ducatus. VALOIS. — [T:] Joannes Janssonius Excudebat. — [T:] A.van den Broeck fecit. — Franckreich. W 405 × 512 mm.

[62] GASTINOIS.
[C:] GASTINOIS et SENONOIS — [An empty cartouche.] [T:] Amstelodami apud Ioannem Ianssonium — Franckreich. X 381 × 492 mm.

[63] Die Graffschafft Bellovacum, Auff Frantzösisch BEAUVOISIS.
[C:] BEAUVAISIS Comitatus BELOVACIUM. — [T:] Amstelodami Apud Ioannem Ianssonium — Franckreich. X 2 373 × 501 mm.

[64] Das Hertzogthumb Normandien.
[C:] NORMANDIA DUCATUS. Ioannes Ianssonius excudit. — Franckreich. Y Verso blank. 379 × 524 mm.

[65] Die Herrschafft DE CAVX.
[C:] LE PAIS DE CAVX a Amsterdam imprimé ches Ioannem Ianssonium et se vendent a Paris ches Melchior Tavernier aupres du Palais. — Caux Z Verso blank. 372 × 494 mm.

[66] Belsia oder Beausse.
[C:] BELSIA Vulgo LA BEAVSSE. — Franckreich. Aa 379 × 497 mm.

[67] Die Grafschafften PERCHE vnd BLOIS.
[a] [C:] PERCHENSIS COMITATVS LA PERCHE COMTE — 393 × 234 mm.
[b] [C:] COMITATVS BLESENSIS, Auctore Ioanne Temporio. BLAISOIS. — 393 × 264 mm.
[The whole map:] Franckreich. Bb 393 × 509 mm.

[68] Hertzogthumb Berry.
[C:] BITVRICVM DVCATVS DVCHE DE BERRI. — [T:] Amstelodami. Apud Ioannem Ianssonium. — Franckreich. Cc 368 × 486 mm.

[69] Tours.
[C:] Touraine TURONENSIS Ducatus Amstelodami Apud Ioannem Ianssonium. — Ee 372 × 489 mm.

[70] Grafschafft Mans.
[C:] DIOCESE DV MANS Vulgo LE MAINE, ubi olim CENOMANI. — Franckreich. Ff Verso blank. 420 × 514 mm.

[71] Hertzogthumb Aniou.
[C:] ANIOV. — Franckreich Gg 426 × 559 mm.

[72] Das Hertzogthumb Britannien.
[C:] DUCHE de BRETAIGNE Dessigné par le Sieur Hardy Mareschal des logis du Roy, Avec Privilege de sa Maieste Amstelodami Apud Ioannem Ianssonium — [T:] Es se vendent aussi a Paris chez Melchior Tavernier demeurant sur L'Isle du Palais a la Sphere. — Franckreich. Hh 372 × 502 mm.

[73] Die Graffschafft Poictiers.
[C:] PICTAVIÆ DVCATVS DESCRIPTIO, Vulgo LE PAIS DE POICTOV. — [T:] Amstelodami, apud Ioannem Ianssonium. — Franckreich. Ii 377 × 519 mm.

[74] Das Loudunenser Gebiet.
[a] [C:] LOVDVNOIS. LAVDVNVM. — 371 × 330 mm.
[b] [C:] MIREBALAIS. — [C:] ... Amstelodami Excudebat Joannes Janssonius. — 371 × 156 mm.
[The whole map:] Franckreich. Kk 371 × 496 mm.

[75] Die Landschafft XANTONGE.
[C:] LA SAINTONGE uers le Septentrion auecq Le PAYS d'AULNIS et les Isles de RÉ et OLERON. — [T:] Par Mr Samson Geographe du Roy — Franckreich. Ll 445 × 555 mm.

[76] Die Landschafft XANTONGE.
[C:] LA SAINTONGE vers le Midy: Auecq LE BROVAGEAIS, TERRE d'ARVERT &c. — [T:] Par Mr Samson Geographe du Roy — Franckreich. Mm 439 × 564 mm.

[77] Die Insulen S. MARTINI Vnd OLERON. in gemeiner Sprach L'ISLE de RE.
[C:] INSVLÆ DIVI MARTINI et VLIARVS Vulgo L'ISLE DE RE et OLERON. — [T:] Amstelodami, Apud Ioannem Ianssonium. — Franckreich Nn 383 × 521 mm.

[78] Beschreibung von GVIENNE oder AQVITANIEN.
[C:] DESCRIPTION DV GVIENNE. Ioannis Ianssonius exc. — Franckreich. Oo 384 × 521 mm.

[79] Das Hertzogthumb D'AIGVILLON.
[C:] LE DVCHE DAIGVILLON Trace par le Sr du Vall. — [C:] Dedié A MADAME LA DVCHESSE D AIGVILLON Par le sieur Pierre du Vall domestique de Monseigneur le Marquis de St Sorlin Abbé de St Remy de Rheims. — Pp Verso blank. 401 × 512 mm.

[80] Bourdeaux.
[C:] BOVRDELOIS, PAYS DE MEDOC, ET LA PREVOSTE DE BORN. — [T:] Amstelodami excudit Joannes Janssonius — [T:] Evert Sijmonsz. HamersVeldt sculp. — Franckreich. Qq 374 × 497 mm.

[81] Das Fürstenthumb BEARN.
[C:] LE PAIS DE BEARN ... — [T:] Amstelodami Apud Ioannem Ianssonium. — [T:] Evert Sijmons z. Hamers veldt sculp. — Franckreich Rr 381 × 499 mm.

[82] Das Bissthumb D'AIRE.
[C:] L'EVESCHÉ D'AIRE tracé par le Sieur Pierre du Val Secretaire de Monseigneur l'Evesque d'Aire. — [C:] A MONSEIGNEVR L'EVESQVE D'AIRE MONSEIG-NEVR Ce trauail ajant esté dressé a vostre service, et de plus contenant les lieux qui vous recognoissent pour pasteur, passerá sous vostre protection, si vous l'avéz pour agreable, et sera un tesmoignage de la fidelité et affection que vous doibt. Monseigneur Vostre treshumble et tresaffectionne serviteur Pierre du Val. — Ss 436 × 538 mm.

[83] Langedock.
[C:] LANGVEDOC — [T:] Amstelodami Apud Ioannem Ianssonium. — 50 Franckreich. Tt 458 × 535 mm.

[84] Cadurch / In gemeiner Sprach QVERCY.

[C:] Quercy CADVRCIVM — [T:] Amstelodami. Apud Ioannem Ianssonium. — Franckreich. Vu 372 × 496 mm.

[85] Die Graffschafft PERIGORD.
[C:] LE Comte de PERIGORT. — [T:] Amstelodami Apud Ioannem Ianssonium — Franckreich. Xx 358 × 491 mm.

[86] Das Stifft SARLAT.
[C:] LE DIOCESE DE SARLAT DIOCOESIS SARLATENSIS — [T:] Delineabat Joannes Tardo, canonicus [Ecc]lesiæ Sarlati 162[5] — [T:] Amstelodami, Excudit Ioannes Ianssonius. — Franckreich. Yy 367 × 481 mm.

[87] LEMOVICIVM.
[C:] TOTIUS LEMOVICI ET Confinium provinciarū quantum ad dioecesin Lemovicensen spectant. NOVISSIMA & FIDISSIMA DESCRIPTIO. Ant. Jo. Fayano M.L. — [C:] ... Amstelodami Apud Ioannem Ianssonium. — [C:] NOBILISSIMO & ILLUSTRISSIMO, ANNETO DE LEVI DUCI de Vantadour: Franciæ Pari, et Provinciæ Lemovicesis Moderatori Prudētissimo. I.Fayanus Medic^9. S.P.D. ... — Franckreich. Zz 373 × 498 mm.
[Inset:] [T:] Plan de la Ville de Lymoges — (Plan). 119 × 96 mm.

[88] Das Hertzogthumb AVVERGNE.
[C:] LE Duche de AVVERGNE — [T:] Amstelodami Apud Ioannem Ianssonium. — Franckreich. Aaa 381 × 497 mm.

[89] Hertzogthumb Bourbon.
[C:] BORBONIVM DVCATVS. BOVRBONNOIS. — Franckreich. Bbb 381 × 498 mm.

[90] Das Hertzogthumb Nivers.
[C:] CARTE DV PAÏS et Duchè de NIVERNOIS — [C:] ... Amstelodami, Sumptibus Ioannis Ianssonii. ... — Franckreich Ccc Verso blank. 377 × 501 mm.

[91] LION, FOREST vnd BEAVIOLOIS.
[C:] LIONNOIS, FOREST, BEAVIOLOIS ET MASCONNOIS. — [T:] Amstelodami, Apud Ioannem Ianssonium. — Franckreich. Ddd 372 × 491 mm.

[92] [C:] VTRIVSQVE BVRGVNDIÆ, tum Ducatus tum Comitatus, DESCRIPTIO. Amsterdami Apud Ioannem Ianssonium. — Blank on the back. 383 × 498 mm.

[93] [C:] GOUVERNEMENT GENERAL du Duché de BOURGOGNE, Comté de BRESSE, Pays de BVGE VALROMEY, et GEX. &c. — [T:] Par Mr Samson Geographe du Roy — [T:] Amstelodami Apud Ioannem Ianssonium. — Blank on the back. 420 × 523 mm.

[94] CAROLOESIVM oder CHAROLOIS.
[C:] Les environs de L'ESTANG DE LONGPENDV, Comprenant vne grande partie du COMTÉ de CHAROLOIS. Par Iean van Damme S^r d'Amendale. — [T:] AVBroeck fecit. — [T:] Amstelod. Joannes Janssonius excud. — Franckreich. Ggg Verso blank. 378 × 500 mm.

[95] BRESSIA. Oder PAYS DE BRESSE.
[C:] BRESSIA Vulgo BRESSE — [T:] Amstelodami Apud Ioannem Ianssonium. — Franckreich. Hhh 397 × 529 mm.

[96] Das Fürstenthumb in gemeiner Sprach LA SOUVERAINETE DE DOMBES.
[C:] LA PRINCIPAVTE DE DOMBES. — [T:] J^a vanden Eynde sculpsit. — [T:] Amstelodami Apud Ioannem Ianssonium — Franckreich. Iii 350 × 458 mm.

[97] Delphinat.
[C:] NOVA et accurata Descriptio DELPHINATVS vulgo DAVPHINÉ Ioannes Ianssonius excudit. — Franckreich. Kkk 375 × 515 mm.

[98] Provintz.
[C:] Comté Et GOUVERNEMENT De PROVENCE — Franckreich. Lll 424 × 539 mm.

[99] Das Fürstenthumb Oranien.
[C:] La PRINCIPAVTÉ D'ORANGE et COMTAT de VENAISSIN Amstelodami Ex. Ioannes Ianssonius. — [T:] Evert Sijmons z. Hamers veldt sculp. — [C:] Illustrissimo Principi Domino FREDERICO HENRICO Dei gratia Arausionensium Principi, Comiti m Nassau etc. foederatarum Inferioris Germaniæ Provinciarum summo Gubernatori etc. benevolentiæ ergo DD! Iodocus et Henricus Hondij. — Franckreich. Mmm 375 × 497 mm.

[100] [C:] COMITATUS BURGUNDIÆ — [T:] AMSTELODAMI Sumptibus Ioannis Ianssonii. — Blank on the back. 419 × 538 mm.

[101] Das Hertzogthumb Saphoyen.
[C:] SABAVDIA DVCATVS. SAVOYE — [T:] Amsterdami. Apud Ioan: Ianssonium. — Franckreich. Ooo 378 × 496 mm.

[102] Genffer See.
[C:] LACVS LEMANNI LOCORVMQVE CIRCVMIACENTIVM ACCVRATISSIMA DESCRIPTIO. Auctore IACOBO GOVLARTIO GENEVENSI. Amstelodami. Apud Ioannem Ianssonium. — Ooo 2 409 × 514 mm.

[103] Schweitzerlandt.
[C:] HELVETIÆ RHETIÆ & VALESIÆ cum omnibus finitimis regionibus Tabula Vulgo Schweitzerland. — [T:] Amstelodami, Apud Ioannem Ianssonium. — ppp 414 × 534 mm.

[104] Das Bassler Gebiet.
[C:] TERRITORY BASILIENSIS NOVA DESCRIPTIO Ioannes Ianssonius Excudit. — [T:] Petrus Kærius Cælavit — Teutschland. Qqq 378 × 491 mm.

[105] Zürichgaw.
[C:] ZVRICHGOW et Basiliensis provincia — [T:] A. vanden Broeck fecit. — [T:] Amstelodami Apud Johannem Janssonium. — Rrr 380 × 498 mm.

[106] Wiflispurgergaw.
[C:] DAS WIFLISPVRGERGOW Gerardo Mercatore Auctore. — [T:] Ioannis Ianssonius excud: — Sss 380 × 496 mm.

[107] Argaw.
[C:] ARGOW cum parte merid. ZVRICHGOW Auctore Ger: Mercatore. ... — [T:] Johannes Janssonius excud. — Ttt 383 × 497 mm.

[108] Grawpündten.
[C:] Alpinæ seu Foederatæ RHÆTIÆ SUBDITARUMQUE ei Terrarum nova descriptio. Auctoribus Fortunato Sprechero à Berneck. Eq.aur. et I.V.D.Ret. AC PHIL. CLUVERIO. — [C:] Amstelodami Ex officina Ioannis Ianssoni. — [T:] Everardus Simonis Hamers-veldt Sculpsit. — Vvv 375 × 495 mm.

[109] Alt Spanien.
[C:] HISPANIÆ VETERIS DESCRIPTIO. Amstelodami Apud. Joannem Janssonium — [T:] Abraham Goos sculpsit. — Spanien. A 368 × 487 mm.
[Inset:] [T:] TARTESSIS. — 84 × 80 mm.

[110] Hispania.
[C:] TYPVS HISPANIÆ ab Hesselo Gerardo delineata et juxta annotationes Doctiss. D^{ni} Don Andreæ d'Almada S.Theologiæ Publici Professoris apud Coimbricenses emendatus — [T:] Amstelredami, Ex officina ære et sumptibus Ioannis Ianssonii — Spanien. 358 × 471 mm.

[111] Das Königreich NAVARRA.
[C:] NAVARRA REGNVM. — Spanien. C 411 × 496 mm.

[112] BISCAIA vnd GUIPUSCOA.
[C:] BISCAIA ET GVIPVSCOA CANTABRIÆ VETERIS PARS. — [T:] Amstelodami Apud Ioannem Ianssonium — Spanien E 375 × 488 mm.

[113] Königreich LEGIO, Vnd das Fürstenthumb ASTVRIAS.
[C:] LEGIONIS REGNVM et ASTVRIARVM PRINCIPATVS. — Spanien. E 374 × 482 mm.

[114] Das Königreich GALLICIA.
[C:] GALLÆCIA REGNVM, descripta a F.Fer.Ojea Ord.præd. et postmodum multis in locis emendata et aucta. — Hispanien. F Verso blank. 372 × 485 mm.

[115] Portugal vnd Algarbia.
[C:] PORTVGALLIA et ALGARBIA quæ olim LVSITANIA Auctore Vernando Alvero Secco. — [T:] Amstelodami Apud Ioannem Ianssonium. — Spanien. G 381 × 495 mm.

[116] Alt vnd New Castilien.

[C:] VTRIVSQVE CASTILIÆ nova descriptio. — Spanien. H 409 × 499 mm.

[117] ANDALVZIA.
[C:] ANDALVZIA continens SEVILLAM et CORDVBAM. — Hispanien. I 378 × 500 mm.

[118] Granaten.
[C:] GRANATA, ET MVRCIA REGNA. — Hispanien. K 375 × 493 mm.

[119] Das Königreich VALENTIA.
[C:] VAL[E]NTIA RE[G]NVM. Có[test]ani.Ptol. E[dent]ani Plin. — Hispanien. 350 × 476 mm.

[120] Das Königreich ARRAGONIA.
[C:] ... ARRAGONIA REGNVM. Auctore Joanne Baptista Labanna. — [C:] Amplissimo et Nobili Viro GASPARI CHARLE[S] Sacri Romani Imperij Equiti aurato [?] de Baerledoncq, cohortis liberæ Duci ref[?] Reg: Majestatis Catholicæ generali aggerun[?] — Hispanien. M 412 × 517 mm.

[121] Das Königreich CATALONIA.
[C:] CATALONIA — Spanien. N 381 × 483 mm.

[122] Die Balearische Insuln / MAIORCA vnd MINORCA.
[C:] INSVLÆ BALEARIDES et PYTIVSÆ. — [T:] E.Sijmons Hamers-veldt sculpsit. — [T:] Joannes Janssonius Excudit. — Spanien. Q 380 × 496 mm.

Notes: All the maps have text on the verso except where otherwise specified, and all are coloured. The title-pages of both parts of this volume are wanting. The volume almost corresponds with Koeman's Me 135A, vol. 2, but that is dated 1649, while this copy seems to belong to the 1645 edition. This is borne out by the differences between the two copies. One map in our copy, [56] Lotharingis Septentrionalis, is not in Koeman. The names in the signatures at the foot of the page are not found in Koeman's description, but in our copy they occur quite frequently. On a number of the maps part of the text is illegible, and is here supplied in brackets according to the text given in Koeman. Part of the upper left-hand corner of map [39] has been cut off. On map [72] the indication as to where the map is sold has been scraped away, but is still legible. The volume is in bad repair. It is bound in old vellum with gold tooling. Nordenskiöld has written his initials in red on the inside of the front cover.

Lit.: Keuning, Joh. Janssonius, Koeman vol. 2, p. 478—480, Me 135A.

114 JANSSONIUS, JOANNES 1645

Vol. III
NOVUS ATLAS, Das ist: Welt-Beschreibung / mit schönen newen Land-Taffeln. Begreiffende Italien / Asien / Africa vnd America. Dritter Theil. AMSTELODAMI, APUD I[ONNEM IANSSONIUM / ANNO 1645.] 50,5 cm.

[1] Alt ITALIEN.
[T:] ITALIA ANTIQVA PHILIPPO CLUVERO BORUSSO DESIGNATORE — [T:] Iodocus Hondius Excu. — [C:] Viro Antiqva domo Generoso ac Nobili: Omni Virtute pollenti et insigni: Rebusque gerundis Strenuo atq₃ Magnifico; Domino THEODORICO CLUVERO Domino hereditario in Hastede etc: Gentili meo Hoc Observantiæ piæ, amorisque religiosissimi Testamen Lubens animo, ac merito v.D.D. Philippus Cluverus. — Italien. A 358 × 488 mm.

[2] Italia oder Welschland.
[C:] ITALIA Nuouamente piu perfetta che mai per inanzi posta in luce, scolpita et con le suoi figure uiuamente rappresentate — [C:] Amstelodami apud Ioannem Ianssonium — B & C 367 × 491 mm.

[3] Herrschafft Venedig.
[C:] DOMINIUM VENETUM IN ITALIA — [T:] Amstelodami, Apud Ioannem Ianssonium. — [C:] Illustrissimorum, Potentissimorumq₃ DD:FÆDE- RATI BELGY ORDINUM ad SERENISSIMAM VENETORUM REMP: designato Legato D.D.GULIELMO BOREELIO, Duynbequy, Westhoviæ, etc: Domino: Celeberrimæ Ciuitati Amstelodamensium a Consylys et Pensionario D D.C. Henricus Hondius. — D 372 × 494 mm.

[4] Der Bergomensische Landkreyss / welchen sie nennen IL BERGAMASCO.
[C:] TERRITORIO DI BERGAMO — [T:] Amstelodami Ioannes Ianssonius, Excudit. — Italia. E 373 × 482 mm.

[5] Die Brixiensische Landschafft / welche sie nennen IL BRESCIANO.
[C:] TERRITORIO di BRESCIA et di CREMA — [C:] AMSTELODAMI, Apud Ioannem Ianssonium. — Italia. F 386 × 489 mm.

[6] Das Cremensische Gebiet / Sonsten IL CREMASCO. [On verso:] IL CADORINO
[a] [C:] TERRITORIO CREMASCO — 378 × 248 mm.
[b] [C:] IL CADORINO — [T:] Amstelodami, Ex Officina Ioannis Ianssonii. — 378 × 248 mm.
[The whole map:] Italia. G 378 × 496 mm.

[7] Der Veronische Landkreyss / Sonsten IL VERONESE.
[C:] TERRITORIO DI VERONA Amstelodami, Sumptibus Ioannis Ianssonii. — Italia. H 376 × 485 mm.

[8] Das Rhodiginische Gebiet.
[C:] POLESINO DI ROVIGO. — [T:] Amstelodami Sumptibus Ioannis Ianssonii. — Italia. I Verso blank. 370 × 480 mm.

[9] Das Vicenzische Gebieth.
[C:] TERRITORIO DI VICENZA — Italia. K 414 × 496 mm.

[10] Das Paduanische Gebieth.
[C:] TERRITORIO PADOVANO. — [T:] Amstelodami, Apud Ioannem Ianssonium — Italia. L 378 × 486 mm.

[11] Die Marck TREVISE.
[C:] TERRITORIO TREVIGIANO — [T:] Amstelodami Sumptibus Joannis Janssonii. — Italia. N 371 × 478 mm.

[12] Beschreibung Das Belluensisch: vnd Feltrinischen Bischoffthumbs.
[C:] IL BELLVNESE CON IL FELTRINO. — [T:] Amstelodami Apud Ioan: Ianssonium — Italia. O Verso blank. 378 × 485 mm.

[13] FORVM-IVLIVM, Auff Italianisch genannt FRIVLI.
[C:] Patria del FRIVLI olim FORVM IVLII — [C:] Amstelodami, Sumptibus Ioannis Ianssonii — P 369 × 479 mm.

[14] ISTRIA.
[C:] ISTRIA olim IAPIDIA — [T:] Amstelodami Sumptibus Ioannis Ianssonii. — Italia. Q 385 × 502 mm.

[15] Der Standt von MEYLAND.
[C:] STATO DI MILANO — Italia. R 409 × 532 mm.

[16] Das theil Meylandt am Gebürge oder Mitternacht.
[C:] PARTE ALPESTRE DELLO STATO DI MILANO Con il LAGO MAGGIORE DI LUGANO, É DI COMO — [T:] Amstelodami, Apud Ioannem Ianssonium — Italia. S 372 × 486 mm.

[17] Das Hertzogthumb MEYLAND.
[C:] DVCATO ouero TERRITORIO DI MILANO — [T:] Amstelodami, Apud Ioannem Ianssonium. — Italien. 372 × 485 mm.

[18] Das Theil MEYLAND Gegen Mittag.
[C:] TERRITORIO DI PAVIA, LODI, NOVARRA, TORTONA, ALESSANDRIA et altri vicini dello Stato di Milano. — [T:] Amstelodami. Excudebat Ioannes Ianssonius. — V 369 × 482 mm.

[19] Das Landgebiet CREMONÆ.
[C:] TERRITORIO di CREMONA — [T:] Amstelodami Sumptibus Ioannis Ianssonii. — Italia. W 370 × 483 mm.

[20] PIEMONT.
[C:] PRINCIPATUS PEDEMONTII, Ducatus AUGUSTÆ PRÆTORIÆ, SALUTII Marchionatus, ASTÆ, VERCELLARUM ET NICEÆ Comitatus Nova Tabula. — [C:] ... Amstelodami Ioannes Janssonius excudit. — Italia. X 410 × 528 mm.

[21] PIEMONT.

[C:] PIEMONTE ET MONFERRATO — Italia. Y Z 418 × 519 mm.

[22] Die Herrschafft VERCEIL.
[C:] SIGNORIA DI VERCELLI — [T:] Amsterodami apud Ioannem Ianssonium. — Italia. Bb 381 × 490 mm.

[23] Das Hertzogthumb MANTVA.
[C:] MANTVA DVCATVS — [C:] ... Amstelodami, Excudebat Ioannes Ianssonius. — Italia. Cc 345 × 463 mm.

[24] LIGURIA, Oder Der Standt Genua.
[C:] LIGVRIA, ò Stato della Republica di GENOVA. — Italia. Dd 378 × 525 mm.

[25] Der Standt Genua gegen Abend.
[C:] RIVIERA DI GENOVA DI PONENTE — Italia. Ee 424 × 523 mm.

[26] Der Standt Genna gegen Anffgang.
[C:] RIVIERA DI GENOVA DI LEVANTE — [T:] Amstelodami, Excudebat Ioannes Ianssonius — Italia. Ff 380 × 490 mm.

[27] CORSICA. [On verso:] SARDINIA.
[a] [C:] descriptio CORSICÆ Insulæ — 340 × 226 mm.
[b] [C:] descriptio SARDINIÆ Insulæ. — [T:] Per Gerardum Mercatorem — 340 × 226 mm.
[The whole map:] Gg 340 × 462 mm.

[28] RESPUBLICA LVCENSIS.
[C:] STATO DELLA REPUBLICA DI LUCCA. Amstelodami, sumptibus Ioannis Ianssonii — [T:] Everardus Simonis Hamers-veldt Sculpsit. — Italia. Hh 377 × 493 mm.

[29] ETRVRIA, Jetzo genant TOSCANA.
[C:] DOMINIO FIORENTINO — [T:] Amstelodami, Excudebat Ioannes Ianssonius — Italia. Ii 378 × 485 mm.

[30] Das Senensische Gebiet.
[C:] TERRITORIO DI SIENA con il Ducato di CASTRO — [T:] Amstelodami, Ioannes Ianssonius excudit — Italia. Kk 379 × 486 mm.

[31] Die Insel Ischia.
[C:] ISCHIA Isola olim ÆNARIA — [C:] ... Amstelodami Apud Ioannem Ianssonium. — Italia. Ll 350 × 452 mm.
[Inset:] [C:] ELBA ISOLA, olim Ilua. — 133 × 187 mm.

[32] Das Hertzogthumb PARMA vnd PLACENTIA.
[C:] DVCATO DI PARMA ET PIACENZA — [T:] Amstelodami, Sumptibus Ioannis Ianssonii. — Italia. Mm 378 × 484 mm.

[33] Das Hertzogthumb MUTINA Vnd RHEGIVM, Sampt den benachbarten Herrschafften.
[C:] DVCATO DI MODENA REGIO et CARPI Col Dominio della Carfagnana — [C:] ... Amstelodami, Apud Ioannem Ianssonium — Italia. Nn 390 × 487 mm.

[34] Der Kirchen Herrschafft.
[C:] STATO DELLA CHIESA CON LA TOSCANA — [T:] Amstelodami, Sumptibus Ioannis Ianssonii. — [C:] Humanissimo, fidelissimoq₃ viro Domino Gisberto Teulinck, Vrbis Amstelodamensis mercatori eximio; hanc, totius Dominii Ecclesiastici in Italia, novam tabulam, in amicitiæ testimonium dedicat consecratoq₃. Henricus Hondius. — Italia. Oo & Pp 413 × 520 mm.

[35] Das Hertzogthumb FERRARIA.
[C:] DVCATO DI FERRARA — [T:] Amstelodami Sumptibus Ioannis Ianssonii — Italia. Qq 367 × 476 mm.

[36] ROMANULA, vorzeiten genant FLAMINIA.
[C:] ROMAGNA olim FLAMINIA — [T:] Amstelodami, Sumptibus Ioannis Ianssonij — 34 Italia. RR 373 × 487 mm.

[37] Die Bononiensische Landschafft.
[C:] TERRITORIO DI BOLOGNA — [T:] Amstelodami, Apud Ioannem Ianssonium. — Ss 424 × 522 mm.

[38] Die Orivetanische Landschafft / Genant IL ORVIETANO.
[C:] TERRITORIO DI ORVIETO. — [T:] Amstelodami, Apud Ioannem Ianssonium. — Italia. Tt Verso blank. 380 × 486 mm.

[39] Die Perusinische Landschafft.
[C:] TERRITORIO PERVGINO — [T:] AMSTELO- DAMI Sumptibus Ioannis Ianss — Italia. Vv 372 × 490 mm.

[40] Das Hertzogthumb URBINUM.
[C:] DVCATO di VRBINO — Italia. Ww 376 × 486 mm.

[41] SABINA, Des H.Petri Patrimonium / Vnd Der Römische Landkreyss / vorzeiten LATIVM genant.
[C:] CAMPAGNA DI ROMA; olim Latium: PATRIMONIO DI S.PIETRO; et SABINA. — [T:] Amstelodami Excudebat Ioannes Ianssonius. — Italia. Xx 394 × 512 mm.

[42] UMBRIA, Oder Das Spoletanische Hertzogthumb.
[C:] VMBRIA overo DVCATO DI SPOLETO. — [T:] Amstelodami, Iohannes Ianssonius Excudit, — Italia. Yy 376 × 486 mm.

[43] Die Anconitanische Marck / vorzeiten genant PICENUM.
[C:] MARCA D'ANCONA olim PICENVM. — [C:] AMSTELODAMI, Ioannes Ianssonius excudit. — Italia. Zz 375 × 483 mm.

[44] Das Königreich Neapolis.
[C:] NEAPOLITANUM REGNUM — [T:] Amstelodami, Sumptibus Ioannis Ianssonii. — Italia. Aaa 423 × 515 mm.

[45] APRUTIUM, Sonsten genant ABRVZZO; Da die Samnites wohnen.
[C:] ABRVZZO CITRA, ET VLTRA. — [T:] Amstelodami, Apud Ioann. Ianssonium. — Italia. Bbb 375 × 486 mm.

[46] CAMPANIA FELIX, Jetzo genant TERRA DI LAVORO.
[C:] TERRA DI LAVORO, olim CAMPANIA FELIX — [T:] AMSTELODAMI, Ioannes Ianssonius Excudit. — Italia. Ccc 379 × 484 mm.

[47] Die Grafschafft MOLISO, sampt PRINCIPATO VLTRA.
[C:] CONTADO DI MOLISE et PRINCIPATO VLTRA — [T:] Amstelodami Apud Ioannem Ianssonium. — Italia. Ddd 378 × 485 mm.

[48] PRINCIPATUS CITERIOR, vorzeiten genant PICENTIA.
[C:] PRINCIPATO CITRA olim PICENTIA — [T:] Amstelodami Sumptibus Ioannis Ianssonii. — Italia. Eee 371 × 487 mm.

[49] CAPITANATA, Vor zeiten genant APVLIA DAVINA.
[C:] CAPITANATA, olim MESAPIÆ et IAPYGIÆ PARS. — [T:] Amstelodami, Apud Ioannem Ianssonium. — Italia. Fff 375 × 484 mm.

[50] Das Landt BARI, Vor zeiten genant APVLIA PEVCETIA.
[C:] TERRA DI BARI ET BASILICATA — [T:] Amstelodami, Apud Ioannem Ianssonium. — Ggg 377 × 491 mm.

[51] HYDRUNTUM, Sonsten TERRA DOTRANTO.
[C:] Terra di OTRANTO olim SALENTINA et IAPIGIA — [T:] Amstelodami, Iohannes Ianssonius Excud. — Hhh 371 × 483 mm.

[52] CALABRIA, Sonsten Gross Griechenlandt.
[C:] CALABRIA CITRA olim Magna Græcia. — [T:] Amstelodam Iohannes Ianssonius Excudit. — Italia. Iii 379 × 487 mm.

[53] CALABRIA.
[C:] CALABRIA VLTRA, olim Altera Magnæ Græciæ pars — [T:] Amstelodami, Apud Ioannem Ianssonium. — Italia. Kkk 383 × 489 mm.

[54] Kas Königreich Sicilien.
[C:] SICILIAE Regnum — [T:] Per Gerardum Mercatorem... — Europa. Lll 336 × 474 mm.

[55] Griechenland.
[C:] Nova Totius GRÆCIÆ descriptio. — [T:] Per Gerardum Mercatorem ... — Græcia. Mmm 360 × 465 mm.

[56] Macedonien EPIRUS vnd ACHAIA.
[C:] MACEDONIA EPIRVS et ACHAIA — [T:] Per Gerardum Mercatorem ... — Græcia. Nnn 353 × 427 mm.

[57] MOREA, Sonsten PELOPONNESUS.
[C:] MOREA olim Peloponnesus — [T:] Per Gerardum Mercatorem ... — Græcia. Ooo 335 × 413 mm.

[58] CANDIE.

[C:] CANDIA olim CRETA — [T:] Iohannes Ianssonius Excudit. — Græcia. Ppp 377 × 523 mm.

NOVUS ATLAS Das ist: Welt-Beschreibung/ mit allerhand schönen Land-Charten. Inhaltende Asien/ Africa vnd America. Dritten Theils Ander Stück. AMSTELODAMI, Apud IOANNEM IANSSONIUM. Anno MDCXXXXV.

[59] ASIA.
[C:] ASIA recens summa cura delineata Auct. Henr. Hondio. 1641. — [T:] Amstelodami, apud Ioannem Ianssonium. — [C:] Viro Clarissimo, et in omni disciplinarum genere exercitatissimo, D. Eylhardo Lubino S.S. Theologiæ Doctori, ejusdemq$_3$, in Academia Rostochiensi, Professori, hanc Asiæ Tabulam benevolentiæ ergò, dico et consecro. Henricus Hondius. — 373 × 495 mm.

[60] Das Türckische Reich.
[C:] TVRCICVM IMPERIVM ... — [T:] Ioannes Ianssonius excudit. — Asia. B 407 × 517 mm.

[61] Natolien oder klein Asien.
[C:] NATOLIA, quæ olim ASIA MINOR. — Asia. C 383 × 500 mm.

[62] Die Insel CYPRUS.
[C:] CYPRVS INSVLA. — 4 Europa. D 376 × 499 mm.

[63] Das Gelobte Landt
[C:] SITUS TERRÆ PROMISSIONIS. S.S. Bibliorum intelligentiam exacte aperiens per Chr.Adrichom. — [T:] Amstelodami, Sumptibus Ioannis Ianssonii. — [T:] Sculpserunt Everardus Sim. Hamers-veldt et Salomon Rogeri. — Asia. E 370 × 494 mm.

[64] Das Königreich Persien.
[C:] PERSIA, Sive SOPHORVM REGNVM. — Asia. F 373 × 486 mm.

[65] Tartarien.
[C:] TARTARIA sive MAGNI CHAMI IMPERIVM — Asia. G 381 × 497 mm.

[66] Das Chinensische Reich.
[C:] CHINA Veteribus SINARVM REGIO nunc Incolis TAME dicta. — [C:] ...Apud Ioannem Ianssonium. — Asia. H 406 × 496 mm.

[67] Indien gegen Auffgang.
[C:] INDIÆ ORIENTALIS NOVA DESCRIPTIO — [C:] AMSTELODAMI Ioannes Ianssonius excudebat — (Chart). Asia. K 386 × 502 mm.

[68] Das Reich des Grossen MOGOLIS.
[C:] MAGNI MOGOLIS IMPERIUM. — [T:] Amstelodami Apud Ioannem Ianssonium. — 8 Asia. L 365 × 493 mm.

[69] Die Indianische Insulen.
[C:] INDIA quæ ORIENTALIS dicitur, et INSVLÆ ADIACENTES. — [T:] Amstelodami, apud Ioannem Ianssonium. — [C:] Doctrina et virtute præstanti, D. CHRISTOPHORO THISIO, Mercatori fidelissimo, atq$_3$ ex participantium) SOCIETATIS INDIÆ ORIENTALIS) non minimo, Geographiæ amatori eximio, hanc INDIÆ ORIENTALIS tabulam emendatam dedicat. Henricus Hondius — (Chart). Asia. M 391 × 485 mm.

[70] Die Inseln MOLVCCÆ.
[C:] INSULARUM MOLUCCARUM Nova descriptio — [T:] AMSTELODAMI, Apud Ioannem Ianssonium. — (Chart). Asia. N 380 × 497 mm.

[71] AFRICA.
[C:] AFRICÆ nova Tabula. Auct: Heñ. Hondio. 1641. — [T:] Amstelodami, apud Ioannem Ianssonium — Africa. Aa 373 × 493 mm.

[72] Die Barbarey.
[C:] NOVA BARBARIÆ DESCRIPTIO Amstelodami. Apud Ioannem Ianssonium. — Bb 351 × 519 mm.

[73] Die Königreiche FESSANVM Vnd MAUROCANUM.
[C:] FEZZÆ ET MAROCCHI REGNA AFRICÆ CELEBERRIMA, describebat Abrah: Ortelius. — Africa. Cc 382 × 498 mm.

[74] GUINEA.
[C:] GVINEA — [T:] Amstelodami, Sumptibus Joannis Janssonij. — Africa. Dd 380 × 520 mm.

[75] Das Königreich der Abissiner.
[C:] ÆTHIOPIA SVPERIOR vel INTERIOR; vulgo ABISSINORVM sive PRESBITERI IOANNIS IMPERIVM. — Africa. Ee 381 × 491 mm.

[76] Nieder-Morenlandt.
[C:] ÆTHIOPIA INFERIOR, vel EXTERIOR. Partes magis Septentrionales, quæ hic desiderantur, vide in tabula Æthiopiæ Superioris. — Africa. Gg 378 × 497 mm.

[77] AMERICA.
[C:] AMERICA noviter delineata Auct: Henrico Hondio. 1641. — [T:] Amstelodami, Excudit Ioannes Ianssonius. — America. Aaa 374 × 498 mm.
[Insets:] [T:] Borealiores Americæ tractus cum hac tabula comprehendi ... et Polus Arcticus includitur. — 67 × 108 mm. [T:] TERRA AUSTRALIS INCOGNITA — 86 × 124 mm.

[78] America gegen Mitternacht.
[C:] AMERICA SEPTENTRIONALIS. — [C:] AMSTELODAMI, Excudit Ioannes Ianssonius. — 2 America. BBB 463 × 552 mm.

[79] New BELGICA Vnd New ANGLIA.
[C:] NOVA BELGICA ET ANGLIA NOVA — [C:] ... Amstelodami Johannes Janssonius Excudit — Ameriea. Ccc 384 × 502 mm.

[80] Die Landschafft Virginia.
[C:] NOVA VIRGINIÆ TABVLA — [C:] ... Amstelodami, ex officina Henrici Hondii. — America. Ddd 378 × 491 mm.

[81] Die Insel FLORIDA.
[C:] VIRGINIÆ partis australis, et FLORIDÆ partis orientalis interjacentiumq$_3$ regionum NOVA DESCRIPTIO. — Hispanien. Eee 383 × 502 mm.

[82] Bermudes.
[C:] Mappa ÆSTIVARVM Insularum, alias BARMVDAS dictarum, ... accurate descripta. — [C:] ... Amstelodami, Apud Ioannem Ianssonium — West-Indien. Fff 389 × 513 mm.

[83] New Hispanien.
[C:] NOVA HISPANIA, ET NOVA GALICIA. — America. Ggg 345 × 481 mm.

[84] Die West-Indischen Insuln an dem Mitternächtischen Meer / vor dem Golfo de Mexico; sampt noch etlichen andern Oertern / so auff dem festen Lande ligen.
[C:] INSVLÆ AMERICANÆ IN OCEANO SEPTENTRIONALI, cum Terris adiacentibus. — [T:] Amstelodami, Apud Ioannem Ianssonium. — (Chart). Hhh 375 × 518 mm.

[85] America gegen Mittag.
[C:] AMERICÆ PARS MERIDIONALIS Amstelodami Sumptibus Ioannis Ianssony. — 461 × 549 mm.

[86] TERRA FIRMA, NEVVA GRANADA, POPAYAN, &c.
[C:] TERRA FIRMA et. NOVUM REGNUM GRANATENSE et POPAYAN — [T:] Amstelodami Joannes Janssonius excudit — America. Kkk 373 × 490 mm.

[87] Königreich Peru.
[C:] PERV — [T:] AMSTELODAMI, Apud Ioannem Ianssonium. — America. Lll 375 × 487 mm.

[88] VENEZUELA.
[C:] VENEZUELA, cum parte Australi NOVÆ ANDALUSIÆ. — [C:] ... AMSTELODAMI, Ioannes Ianssonius Excudit. — [T:] Sculpserunt E.S.Hamers-veldt et S.Rogeri. — America. Mmm 372 × 489 mm.

[89] GUYANA.
[C:] GVIANA siue AMAZONVM REGIO — [C:] AMSTELODAMI, Ioannes Ianssonius excudit. — America. Nnn 370 × 486 mm.

[90] Die Landschafft Brasilien.
[C:] ACCURATISSIMA BRASILIÆ TABULA. Amstelodami Joannes Janssonius excudit. — America. Ooo 375 × 485 mm.
[Insets:] [T:] Baya de todos os Sanctos — 67 × 103 mm. [T:] Villa d'Olinda de Pernambuco — 67 × 102 mm.

[91] Die Provintz von RIO DE LA PLATA, Sampt den beyligenden Landen.

[C:] PARAGVAY, O PROV. DE RIO DE LA PLATA cum regionibus adiacentibus TVCVMAN et S.^{TA} CRVZ DE LA SIERRA. — [C:] AMSTELODAMI, Excudebat Ioannes Ianssonius. — America. Ppp 370 × 477 mm.

[92] CHILI.
[C:] CHILI. — [C:] AMSTELODAMI, Ioannes Ianssonius excudit. — America. 370 × 478 mm.

[93] FRETUM MAGELLANICUM.
[C:] FRETI MAGELLANICI ac novi FRETI vulgo LE MAIRE exactissima delineatio. — [T:] Lectori Meo. Descriptionem hanc novam freti Magellanici nobis communicavit clarissimus vir Bernardus Joannis Monasteriensis qui nove menses in peragratione huius freti impendit. sub duce Sebaldi de Waerdt Afbeelding der Straet Magellanes So als de selve van Mr Barent Iansz. Potgieter van Munster door eñ weder door bevaren eñ met syn Capiteyn Sebald de Waerd met groot pericul syns levens seer naerstig ondersocht is. — Rrr 380 × 490 mm.

[94] Der Polus Antarcticus gegen Mittag / Neben den Landschafften / welchebey / vnd vnter ihme gelegen seynd.
[C:] POLUS ANTARCTICUS. Ioannes Ianssonius excudit. — [An empty cartouche]. 434 × 491 mm.

Notes: All the maps have text on the verso except where otherwise specified. They are all coloured. The bottom right-hand corner of the title-page is wanting, so that the imprint is incomplete. The year of publication is lacking, but can be found on the title-page of the second part of the volume. The titles of both parts are printed on separate slips and pasted in the appropriate space, on the coloured title-pages, but the imprints are part of the engraved plates. Our titles differ from all of those given by Koeman for the different editions of the German Atlas, but he has no description for the 1645 edition, to which our copy must belong. The contents correspond with his Me 136A. The volume is in bad condition, as are the other wolumes of this atlas. They are all bound in old vellum gold tooling. Nordenskiöld has written his initials in red pencil on the inside of the front cover.

Lit.: Koeman vol. 2, p. 480—482, Me 136A.

115 JANSSONIUS, JOANNES   1647

Vol. IV
NOVUS ATLAS oder Welt-beschreibung in welcher ausssführlich abgebildet de Königreiche ENGELLAND SCHOTLAND vnd IRLAND. Dass Vierdte Theil. AMSTELODAMI, Apud Ioannem Ianssonium. ANNO M DC XLVII.   50,5 cm.

[1] BRITANNIA.
[C:] INSVLARVM BRITANNICARVM Acurata Delineatio ex Geographicis Conatibus ABRAHAMI ORTELII AMSTELODAMI. apud Ioannem Ianssonium — [T:] Petrus Kærius Cælavit. — I A 390 × 507 mm.

[2] BRITANNIA.
[C:] MAGNÆ BRITANNIÆ et HIPERNIÆ Nova DESCRIPTIO ... — 15 E = 1645:I:[5].

[3] BRITANNIA.
[C:] [Britannia prout divisa fuit temporibus Anglo-Saxonum, præsertim durante illorum Heptarchia.] — 73 V The right half of the map wanting. The left part 417 × 263 mm.

[4] BRITANNIA.
[C:] ANGLIA REGNVM — 87 Aa = 1645:I:[8].

[5] CANTIVM.
[C:] CANTIVM Vernacule KENT. — [T:] Amstelodami Apud Ioannem Ianssonium. — 105 Ff 381 × 499 mm.

[6] CANTIUM. [On verso:] DIE REGNI. SUSSEX.
[C:] SUTHSEXIA. vernacule SUSSEX. — [T:] Amstelodami Apud Ioannem Janssonium — 119 Kk 377 × 508 mm.

[7] SUTH-REY.
[C:] SURRIA. vernacule SURREY. — 129 Nn 380 × 499 mm.

[8] DIE ATTREBATIER. BARK-SHIRE.
[C:] HANTONIÆ COMITATUS Cum BERCHERIA. — [T:] Amstelodami Apud Joannem Jãssonium. — 133 Pp 437 × 549 mm.

[9] WILSHIRE.
[C:] WILTONIA sive COMITATVS WILTONIENSIS. Anglis WIL SHIRE. — [T:] Amstelodami Apud Ioannem Ianssonium — 149 Vu 396 × 496 mm.

[10] SOMERSET-SHIRE.
[C:] SOMERSETTENSIS COMITATVS: Somerset Shire. — [T:] Amstelodami Apud Joannem Janssonium — 157 Zz 376 × 498 mm.

[11] DIE DVROTRIGES. DORSET-SHIRE.
[C:] COMITATVS DORCESTRIA. Vulgo Anglice DORSET SHIRE. — [T:] Amstelodami Apud Joannem Janssonium — 169 Ddd 377 × 493 mm.

[12] DANMONII
[C:] DEVONIÆ DESCRIPTIO. The DESCRIPTION of DEVON-SHIRE Amstelodami Apud Ioannem Ianssonium. — 175 Fff 378 × 486 mm.

[13] CORNVVALLIA vulgò CORNWALL.
[C:] CORNUBIA. sive CORNWALLIA. — [T:] Amstelodami Excudebat Ioannes Ianssonius — 181 Hhh 376 × 505 mm.

[14] GLOCESTER-SHIRE.
[C:] GLOCESTRIA DVCATVS, cum MONVMETHENSI Comitatu. GLOCESTER SHIRE & MONMOVTH SHIRE. — 191 Lll 406 × 513 mm.

[15] OXFORD-SHIRE.
[C:] OXONIUM Comitatus Vulgo OXFORD SHIRE. — 203 Ppp 379 × 486 mm.

[16] CATTIEUCHLANI. BUCKINGHAM-SHIRE.
[C:] BUCKINGAMIÆ COMITATVS cum BEDFORDIENSI; vulgo BUCKINGAMSHIRE and BEDFORDSHIRE. — [T:] Amstelodami Apud Ioannem Janssonium. — 211 Sss 402 × 504 mm.

[17] CATTIEUCHLANI. [On verso:] HERTFORD-SHIRE.
[C:] MIDDELSEXIÆ cum HERTFORDIÆ COMITATU: Midlesex & Hertford Shire. — [T:] Amstelodami Apud Joannem Janssonium. — 217 Vuu 434 × 547 mm.

[18] ESSEX.
[C:] ESSEXIÆ DESCRIPTIO. The DESCRIPTION of ESSEX. AMSTELODAMI, Sumptibus Ioannis Ianssonii. — 235 Bbbb 378 × 490 mm.

[19] SUFFOLKE. SOVTH-FOLKE, oder SUFFOLKE.
[C:] SUFFOLCIA vernacula SUFFOLKE. — [T:] Ioannes Ianssonius Excudit. — 245 Eeee 378 × 495 mm.

[20] NORTH-FOLKE.
[C:] NORTFOLCIA; vernacule NORFOLKE. — [T:] Amstelodami, apud Ioannem Ianssonium. — 253 Hhhh 378 × 488 mm.

[21] CAMBRIDGE-SHIRE.
[C:] COMITATIS CANTABRIGIENSIS; vernacule CAMBRIDGE SHIRE. — [T:] Amstelodami Apud Joannem Janssonium. — 261 Llll 411 × 515 mm.

[22] HVNTINGDON-SHIRE.
[C:] HVNTINGDONENSIS COMITATVS HUNTINGTON SHIRE. — 267 Nnnn 392 × 494 mm.

[23] Beschreibung des überschwembdten Landes THE FENNES genandt / welches in Engelland an den Grentzen nachfolgender Schiren oder Graffschafften / als da seynd ... lieget.
[C:] A general Plott and description of the Fennes and surounded grcunds in the sixe Counties of Norfolke, Suffolke, Cambridge, with in the Isle of Ely, Huntington, Northampton and Lincolne etc. — [C:] ... AMSTELODAMI, Sumptibus Ioannis Ianssonii. — [C:] ILLUSTRISSIMIS, MAGNIFICIS, ET GENEROSIS DOMINIS, DOMINIS. ... Vestris Amplitudinibus in omnibus seruire paratus Henricus Hondius. — 271 Engelland. Pppp 433 × 553 mm.

[24] CORITANI. NORTHAMPTON-SHIRE.
[C:] COMITATVS NORTHANTONENSIS vernacule NORTHAMTON SHIRE. — 273 Qqqq 385 × 511 mm.

[25] NORTHAMPTON-SHIRE [On verso:] LEICESTER-

SHIRE.
[C:] LEICESTRENSIS COMITAVS cum RVTLANDIÆ. Vulgo Leicester & Rutland Shire. — [T:] Amstelodami Ex. Joannes Janssonius — 279 Ssss 434 × 548 mm.

[26] RVTLAND-SHIRE. [On verso:] LINCOLNE-SHIRE.
[C:] LINCOLNIA COMITATVS Anglis LYNCOLNE SHIRE. — 285 Vvvv 394 × 496 mm.

[27] NOTTINGHAM-SHIRE.
[C:] COMITATVS NOTTINGHAMIENSIS; Sive NOTTINGHAM SHIRE. — 295 Zzzz 372 × 478 mm.

[28] NOTINGHAM-SHIRE [On verso:] DARBY-SHIRE.
[C:] COMITATVS DARBIENSIS. — 297 Aaaaa 380 × 492 mm.

[29] CORNAVII. WARWICK-SHIRE.
[C:] WIGORNIENSIS Comitatus cum WARWICENSI; nec non CONVENTRIÆ LIBERTAS. — [T:] Amstelodami Apud Ioannem Ianssonium. — 301 Ccccc 425 × 523 mm.

[30] STAFFORD-SHIRE.
[C:] SALOPIENSIS COMITATVS cum STAFFORD-IENSI. SHROPSHIRE & STAFFORDSHIRE. — 311 Fffff 423 × 531 mm.

[31] CHES-SHIRE.
[C:] CESTRIA COMITATVS PALATINVS. THE COUNTYE PALATINE OF CHESTER. — 321 Iiiii 378 × 496 mm.

[32] CHES-SHIRE. [On verso:] Süd-WALLIA.
[C:] PRINCIPATVS WALLIÆ PARS AVSTRALIS: Vulgo SOUTH-WALES. — [T:] Amstelodami Apud Joannem Janssonium. — 327 Lllll 408 × 522 mm.

[33] HEREFORD-SHIRE.
[C:] HEREFORDIA COMITATVS vernacule HEREFORD SHIRE — [T:] Amstelodami Apud Ioan. Ianssonium. — 331 Nnnnn 375 × 496 mm.

[34] RADNOR-SHIRE.
[C:] RADNORIENSIS COMITATVS Vulgo The Countie of RADNOR. — [T:] Amstelodami Apud Ioannem Ianssonium. — 335 Ppppp 372 × 479 mm.

[35] SILVRES. [On verso:] DIMETÆ. CAERMARDEN-SHIRE.
[C:] PENBROCHIA Comitatus et Comitatus CAERMARDINVM. Amstelodami Apud Ioannem Ianssonium. — 341 Rrrrr 379 × 514 mm.

[36] CARDIGAN-SHIRE.
[C:] CERETICA; sive CARDIGANENSIS Comitatus; Anglis CARDIGAN SHIRE. — [T:] Amstelodami Apud Joannem Janssonium. — 347 Ttttt 377 × 500 mm.

[37] Nord-WALLIA.
[C:] PRINCIPATVS WALLIÆ PARS BOREALIS Vulgo NORTH WALES. — [T:] Amstelodami Apud Ioannem Ianssonium. — 349 Vvvvv 401 × 510 mm.

[38] ORDEVICES. [On verso:] MONTGOMERY-SHIRE.
[C:] MERVINIA; et MONTGOMERIA Comitatus. — 351 Xxxxx 376 × 493 mm.

[39] YORCK-SHIRE.
[C:] DVCATVS EBORACENSIS. Anglice YORKSHIRE. — 363 379 × 486 mm.

[40] WEST-RIDING.
[C:] DVCATVS EBORACENSIS PARS OCCIDENTALIS; THE WESTRIDING OF YORKE SHIRE. — 365 Ccccc 409 × 495 mm.

[41] WEST-RIDING. [On verso:] EAST-RIDING.
[C:] DVCATVS EBORACENSIS PARS ORIENTALIS. THE EASTRIDING of YORKE SHIRE. — 375 Ffffff 376 × 499 mm.

[42] YORCK-SHIRE. [On verso:] NORTH-RIDING.
[C:] DVCATVS EBORACENSIS PARS BOREALIS. THE NORTHRIDINGE of YORKESHIRE. — 379 Hhhhhh 380 × 492 mm.

[43] RICHMONT-SHIRE. [On verso:] Bisthumb DVRHAM.
[C:] EPISCOPATVS DVNELMENSIS Vulgo The Bishoprike of DVRHAM. — [T:] Amstelodami Apud Joannem Janssonium — 389 Lllllll 403 × 506 mm.

[44] Bissthumb DVRHAM. [On verso:] LANCA-SHIRE.
[C:] LANCASTRIA PALATINATVS Anglis LANCASTER & LANCAS SHIRE. — [T:] Amstelodami Apud Joannem Janssonium. — 395 Nnnnnn 374 × 499 mm.

[45] WEST-MORE-LAND.
[C:] CUMBRIA & WESTMORIA. Vulgo Cumberland & Westmorland. — [T:] Amstelodami Apud Joannem Janssonium — 403 Qqqqqq 418 × 536 mm.

[46] OTTADINI. NORTH-HVMBER-LAND.
[C:] COMITATVS NORTHVMBRIA vernacule NORTHUMBERLAND. — [T:] Amstelodami Apud Joannem Janssonium — 421 Xxxxxx 402 × 492 mm.

[47] INSULÆ BRITANNICÆ. Die Insul WIGHT.
[a] [C:] MONA INSVLA Vulgo ANGLESEY. — 212 × 263 mm.
[b] [C:] MONA INSVLA Vulgo THE ISLE OF MAN. — 212 × 263 mm.
[c] [C:] VECTIS INSVLA Anglice THE ISLE OF WIGHT. — [T:] Amstelodami Apud Ioannem Ianssonium. — 211 × 532 mm.
[The whole map:] 435 Bbbbbbb 447 × 550 mm.

[48] INSULÆ BRITANNICÆ.
[a] [C:] HOLY ILAND. — 195 × 248 mm.
[b] [C:] GARNSEY. — 195 × 248 mm.
[c] [C:] FARNE. — 195 × 248 mm.
[d] [C:] IARSEY. — 195 × 247 mm.
[The whole map:] 445 Eeeeeee 407 × 513 mm.

[49] Das Königreich SCHOTLAND.
[C:] SCOTIA REGNVM — I A = 1645:I:[7].

[50] LAVDEN, Oder LOTHIEN.
[C:] PROVINCÆ LAUDEN seu LOTHIEN et LINLITOUO — 5 c 362 × 537 mm.

[51] Beschreibung Der ORCADVM Vnd der Insel Schottland.
[C:] ORCADVM et SCHETLANDIÆ INSVLARVM accuratissima descriptio. — [T:] AMSTELODAMI. Sumptibus Ioannis Ianssonii — 37 m 374 × 486 mm.
[a] [C:] ORCADES. — 363 × 200 mm.
[b] [C:] SCHETLANDIA — 363 × 266 mm.

[52] Die Orcadische Insulen. [On verso:] Die Insel Vnd Königreich HIBERNIA Ins gemein Irrland genandt.
[C:] HIBERNIA REGNVM Vulgo IRELAND. — 39 n = 1645:I:[6].

[53] MOMONIA auff English MOUNSTER.
[C:] PROVINCIA MOMONIÆ. The PROVINCE of MOVNSTER. — [T:] Amstelodami, Sumptibus Joannis Janssonÿ. — 47 q 379 × 487 mm.

[54] LAGENIA Oder LEINSTER.
[C:] COMITATVS LAGENIÆ The COVNTIE of LEINSTER. — [T:] Amstelodami, Apud Joannem Janssonium. — 49 r 379 × 487 mm.

[55] LAGENIA oder LEINSTER. [On verso:] CONNACHTIA Oder CONACHT.
[C:] PROVINCIA CONNACHTIÆ The PROVINCE of CONNAVGT Amstelodami Excudebat Joannes Janssonius. — 51 s 380 × 490 mm.

[56] CONACHT. [On verso:] VLTONIA Oder ULSTER.
[C:] PROVINCIA VLTONIÆ The PROVINCE of VLSTER — [T:] Amstelodami, Apud Joannem Janssonium — 53 t 379 × 487 mm.

Notes: All the maps have text on the verso and are coloured. The title is printed on a separate slip and pasted over the Latin text on the title-page. The German text lacks the words 'Durch Johan Janssen' which Koeman gives in his description of this edition. There are other minor differences between the text of the title in our copy and that described by Koeman. The 'Register und Ordnung...' is bound at the end of the volume. According to Koeman pp. 446—452 are without signatures, but in our copy they are signed Fffffff, Fffffff2, Ggggggg. The maps of England are beautifully decorated with coats-of-arms. Map [3], which is incomplete, has historical illustrations down the left-hand border. Keuning's only note on this edition is that 6 maps of Scottish counties have been added. The volume is bound in old vellum with gold tooling. It is in poor repair. Nordenskiöld has written his initials on the inside of the front cover.

Lit.: Keuning, Janssonius p. 71, Koeman vol. 2, p. 491, Me 162, and p. 486—489, Me 152.

116 JANSSONIUS, JOANNES   1657

Vol. V
HET VYFDE DEEL Des GROOTEN ATLAS, Vervattende De Water-Weereldt / OFTE Een naerstige Beschrijving van alle Zeen des gantschen Aerdt-bodems: Ontdeckt door de heedendaeghsche Ship-vaert. AMSTELODAMI, Apud Joannem Ianssonium. 1657.   51,5 cm.

[1] BESCHRYVINGE van den POLUS ARCTICUS, En onder den selven leggende Landschappen.
[C:] NOVA ET ACCVRATA POLI ARCTICI et terrarum Circum Iacentium DESCRIPTIO. — ... 45 N = 1645:I:[2].

[2] MAR DEL NORT. Ofte Beschryvinge van de groote Noord-Zee, ...
[C:] MAR DEL NORT. — 47 O   430 × 558 mm.

[3] [C:] CAPITANIÆ DE CIRII, et PARNAMBVCO. — Between pp. 48 and 49 P. Blank on the back.   440 × 540 mm.

[4] [C:] CAPITANIARUM DE PHERNAMBVCA, ITAMARACA, PARAIBA, ET RIO GRANDE NOUA DELINEATIO. — Between pp. 48 and 49 P.   Blank on the back.   446 × 559 mm.

[5] Beschryvinge van het Eylandt CUBA, JAMAYCA, EN HISPANIOLA.
[C:] INSVLARVM HISPANIOLÆ et CVBÆ Cum Insulis circum jacentibus accurata delineatio. — 53 Q   408 × 526 mm.

[6] Beschryvinge van S.JUAN de PUERTO RICO, En alle de CARIBISCHE EYLANDEN.
[C:] INSVLA S.IUAN DE PUERTO RICO CARIBES; Vel CANIBALUM Insulæ. — 55 R   402 × 513 mm.

[7] De GROOTE ÆTHIOPISCHE ZEE, Met de Africaensche en VVest-Indische daer aen stootende Custen, ...
[C:] MAR DI ÆTHIOPIA Vulgo OCEANUS ÆTHIOPICUS. — 57 S   433 × 553 mm.

[8] MAR D'INDIA, OFTE, De Oost-Indische ZEE, ...
[C:] MAR di INDIA — 69 Y   435 × 553 mm.

[9] Beschriijvinge van de Oost-Indische Zee. [On verso:] BESCHRYVINGE van het Eylandt CEYLON.
[C:] INSVLA ZEILAN, olim TAPROBANA; nunc incolis TENARISIM. — 75 Aa   410 × 510 mm.

[10] BESCHRYVINGE van GOLFO de BENGALA.
[C:] SINUS GANGETICUS; Vulgo GOLFO DE BENGALA Nova descriptio. — 77 Bb   468 × 541 mm.

[11] [C:] INSVLARVM BANDANENSIVM Novissima delineatio. AMSTELODAMI; Apud Ioan: Ianssonium. — [T:] I. van Loon delin: et sculp. — Between pp. 82 and 83 Dd.   Blank on the back.   439 × 520 mm.

[12] [C:] Insula BORNEO et occidentalis pars CELEBIS cum adjacentibus Insulis. — Between pp. 82 and 83 Dd.   Blank on the back.   418 × 525 mm.

[13] [C:] SVMATRÆ ET INSULARUM LOCORUMQUE NONNULLORUM CIRCUMIACENTIUM TABULA NOUA. — Between pp. 82 and 83 Dd.   Blank on the back.   420 × 519 mm.

[14] [C:] INSULÆ IAVÆ Cum parte insularum BORNEO SVMATRÆ, et circumjacentium insularum novissima delineatio. — Between pp. 84 and 85 Ee.   Blank on the back.   418 × 517 mm.

[15] De ZUYD-ZEE, Of het MARE PACIFICUM. Van de Spaensche MAR DEL ZUR genoemt. ...
[C:] MAR DEL ZVR Hispanis MARE PACIFICUM. — 85 Ee   435 × 540 mm.

[16] Den POLUS ANTARCTICUS, En de onder den selven gheleghene Landtschappen, nevens de daer aenstootende Zee-en.
[T:] TERRA AUSTRALIS INCOGNITA — 97 Ii   432 × 491 mm.   The hemisphere with 430 mm. diam.

[17] De Zee-Custen in FINMARKEN, LAPLAND, RUSLAND, NOVA ZEMBLA, EN SPITS-BERGEN, alwaer de Walvisschen gevangen worden.
[C:] Pascaart Vande ZEE-CUSTEN Van Finmarcken, Laplant, Ruslant, Nova Zembla en Spitsbergen, hoe alle Havens, Rivieren, en Droogten van malcanderen in hare courssen en distantien gelegen zyn, alles op haer rechte situatie geleyt, veel verbetert nu nieulyx beschreṽ. T'AMSTERDAM door Ian Ianssen
TABULA HYDROGRAPHICA Oræ Maritimæ seu LITTORUM Finniæ, Laplandiæ, Russiæ, Novæ Zemblæ et Spitsbergii, omnium ibidem Portuum, Fluviorum, Breviumq₃ situs distantiasq₃ exhibens, in sua cujusque Elevatione: multo quam antè emendatior novissimo discripta. Amstelodami a Ioanne Ianssonio. — [C:] T'AMSTELREDAM By Ian Ianssen op t'water inde Pascaart. — 101 Ll   438 × 551 mm. See 1653:I:[35].

[18] [C:] Typus Maritimus GROENLANDIÆ; Islandiæ, Freti Davidis, Insulæ Iohannis Mayen, et Hitlandiæ, Scotiæ, et Hiberniæ litora maritima septentrionalia. — Between pp. 102 and 103 Mm.   Blank on the back.   425 × 530 mm. See 1653:I:[49].

[19] BESCHRYVINGE VAN WAYGATS, Of De NASSAUSCHE STRATE.
[C:] NOVA ZEMLA, Waygats, Fretum Nassovicum, et Terra Samoiedum singula omnium emendatissimè descripta. — 107 Nn   401 × 503 mm.

[20] [C:] SPITZBERGA. — Between pp. 108 and 109 Oo. Blank on the back.   410 × 512 mm.

[21] Beschryvinge van JAN MAYEN EYLANDT.
[C:] INSULÆ IOHANNIS MAYEN Cum universo situ Sinuum et Promontoriorum. Nova descriptio. — 111 Pp   402 × 511 mm.

[22] Beschryvinge des MARIS BALTHICI, Of der OOST-ZEE.
[C:] Pascaart Vande OOST-ZEE Vertoonende in sich, alle gelegentheden vañ Custen van Denemarcken, Sweden, Pomeren, Pruyssen, Courlant, Lyflant en Finlant, alles op syn rechte hoogte distantien ende courssen geleyt.
TABULA HYDROGRAPHICA Maris BALTICI Exhibens accuratam Littorum Daniæ, Sueciæ, Pomeraniæ, Borussiæ, Courlandiæ, Livoniæ et Finniæ faciem in sua cujusque Poli Elevatione, distantia et situ; novissimè discripta. AMSTELODAMI Apud Ioannem Ianssonium. — [C:] T'AMSTELREDAM By Ian Ianssen. — 113 Qq   423 × 545 mm. See 1653:I:[55].

[23] BESCHRYVINGE Van de NOORD-ZEE, En de Custen, dewelcke van de selve bespoelt worden.
[C:] Pascaart vande NOORT-ZEE Waer in vertoont wort, de ware distantien en streckingen van alle havens en droogtē gelegen tusschen Calis ende Dronten, als mede tusschen Doeveren en Hitlandt, alles op syn behoorlycke Polus hoochte geleyt.
TABVLA HYDROGRAPHICA OCEANI BOREALIS; in qua Omnium Portuum et brevium, inter Caletum et Drontium, interque Davernum et Hitlandiam, veri situs et distantiæ exhibentur; novissime descripta. AMSTELODAMI A Ioanne Ianssonio — 123 Tt   432 × 550 mm. See 1653:I:[2].

[24] AFBEELDINGE der Noord-Custen des Koninckrijcks Vranckrijck, En der Zuyd-Custen van Enghelandt, Dewelcke den CANAEL begrijpen. Als oock mede, De Oost-Custen van Enghelandt, Schotlandt, en alle de Custen van Yerlandt.
[C:] Pascaart Vant CANAAL Tusschen Engelant en Vrancryck, alsmede geheel Jerlant en Schotlant, waer in men claer can sien de rechte distantien en courssen tusschen alle havens en droogtē, alles op syn ware hoogten geleyt.
TABULA HYDOGRAPHICA FRETI seu CANALIS quod est Inter Angliam et Galliam, nec non Hiberniam et Scotiam, in qua longitudines latitudinesq₃ omnium Portuum breviumque, in sua cujusque poli Elevatione graphicè depinguntur novissime discripta. Amstelodami a Ioanne Ianssonio — 137 Zz   430 × 548 mm. See 1653:II:[8].

[25] BESCHRYVINGE der CUSTEN van de Koninckrijcken

NOVA ET ACCVRATA
POLI ARCTICI
et terrarum Circum
Iacentium
DESCRIPTIO.

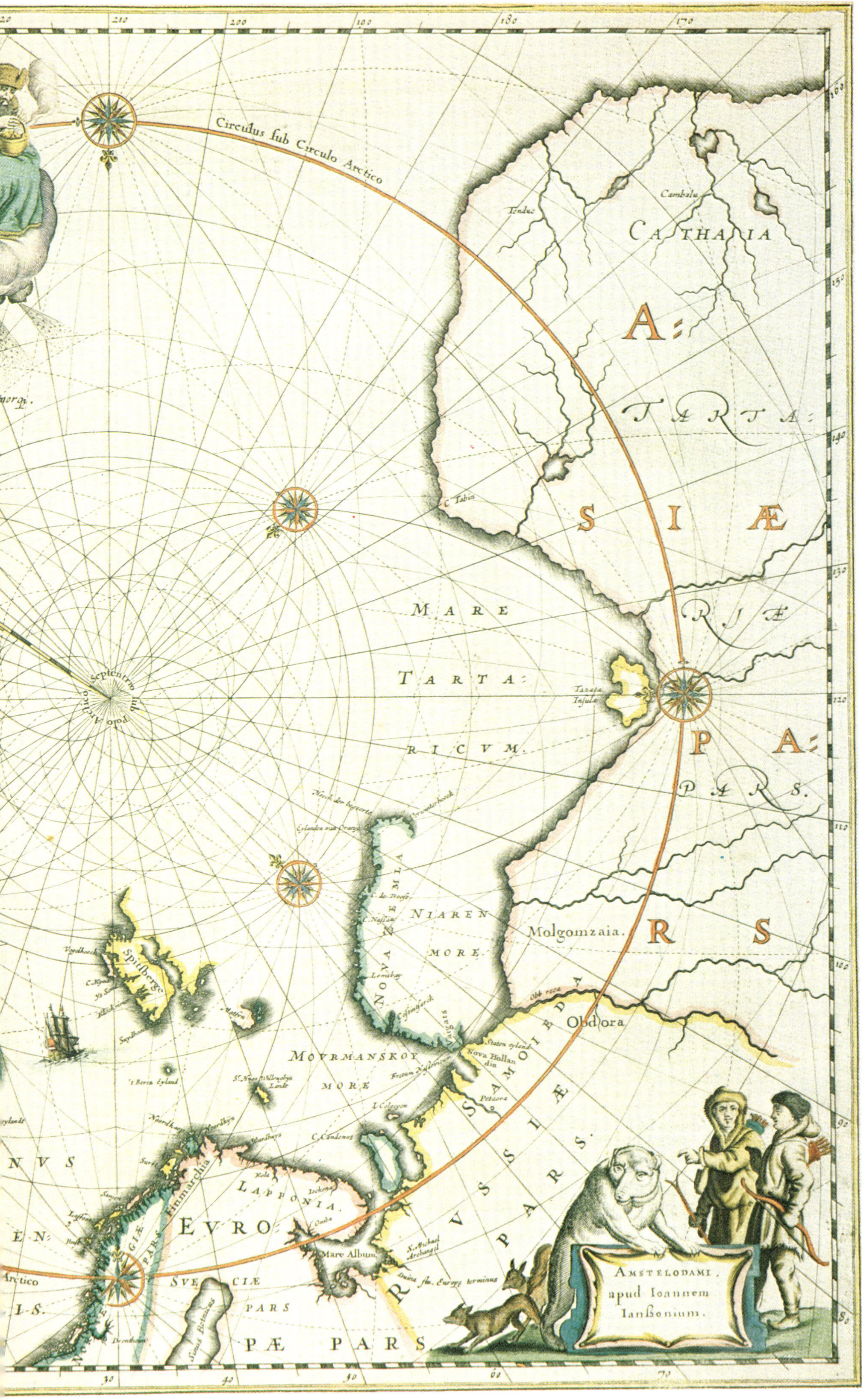
Circulus sub Circulo Arctico
Cambalu
Tenduc
CATHAIA
A:
TARTA:
SIÆ
RIÆ
PA:
PARS.
RS
MARE
TARTA:
RICVM.
Tazata Insula
C. Tabin
Molgomzaia.
Obdora
NOVA ZEMLA
NIAREN MORE.
Spitsberge
MOVRMANSKOY MORE
SAMOIEDA
RVSSIÆ PARS.
LAPPONIA.
EVRO
SVECIÆ PARS
PÆ PARS
Finmarchia
Mare Album
S. Michael Archangel
Duina flu. Europæ terminus
AMSTELODAMI, apud Ioannem Ianssonium.

VRANCKRYCK en SPANGIEN, dewelcke aen de groote West-zee leggen.
[C:] Pascaart Vande CUSTEN Van Andaluzia, Portugal, Gallissien, Biscajen, en een gedeelt van Vranckryck, beginnen̄ van Heysant tot aende mont vande straat van Gibraltar, alles op syn ware distantien courssen en Polus hoogte geleyt.
TABULA HYDROGRAPHICA de ORIS Andalusiæ, Portugalliæ, Galliciæ, Biscajæ et aliqua Galliæ parte; incipiendo ab Heysant usq$_3$ ad littus maritimum Gibraltar: omnia cum veris suis distantis et cursibus ad altitudinem Poli directa. AMSTELODAMI Apud Ioannem Ianssonium — 151 Ddd 431 × 545 mm. See 1653:II:[30].

[26] BESCHRYVINGE des MARIS ATLANTICI, OFTE Der Zee-Custen tusschen de Caep S.Vincent in Spangien, en Cabo Verde in Africa; Als oock mede, Der Canarische, Cabo Verdische, en Vlaemsche Eylanden.
[C:] PASCAART, Waer in men claarlyck zien can, alle havens rivieren drooghten, gelegen tusschen C.S.Vincent en C.Verde, zoo mede inde Flaemsche, Canarische en Soute Eylanden, alles op zyn behoorlycke distantien streckingen en polus hoogte geleyt.
TABULA HYDROGRAPHICA Vby clarissime perspicinutur omnes portus, flu: et vada jacentia inter Cap. S.Vincentii et Cap. Verde una cum insulis Asores (alias Flandricæ) et Canaria utpote salsedine resertis. Omnia cum suis lineis et Polorum distantiis exquisite designata. — [T:] t'Amstelredam by Ian Ianssen. — 157 Fff 417 × 537 mm. See 1653:II:[52].

[27] [C:] INSVLÆ FLANDRICÆ, olim ASORES DICTÆ. — [T:] Amstelodami, Apud Ioannem Ianssonium. — Between pp. 158 and 159 Ggg. Blank on the back. 424 × 531 mm.

[28] [C:] INSVLÆ CANARIÆ, olim FORTVNATÆ DICTÆ. — [T:] Amstelodami, Apud Ioannem Ianssonium. — Between pp. 158 and 159 Ggg. Blank on the back. 425 × 532 mm.

[29] [C:] INSULÆ DE CABO VERDE, Olim HESPERIDES, Sive GORGADES: Belgice DE ZOUTE EYLANDEN. — Between pp. 160 and 161 Hhh. Blank on the back. 435 × 551 mm.

[30] DE MIDDELLANDSCHE ZEE, Met alle haer Eylanden, en de daer aenstootende soo wel Europæische, als Africaensche, en Asiatische CUSTEN.
[C:] Pascaarte Van't westlyckste deel vande MIDDELLANDSCHE-ZEE, Waer in vertoont wort, de ware gelegentheden van alle rivieren, haven, Capen droogtē en bayen, alles synde op hare streckingen en distantien geleyt.
Tabula Hydrographica de partibus Occidentalioribus MARIS MEDITERRANEI In qua veri situs omnium flumium, portium, promontoriorum, vadorum, sinuumq$_3$ secundum longitudinem suam positi exhibent AMSTELODAMI, Apud Ioan. Ianssonium. — 161 Hhh 414 × 533 mm.

[31] Met alle haer Eylanden en de daer aenstootende Custen.
[C:] INSVLÆ MELITÆ Vulgò MALTÉ Nova et accurata Descriptio. — 183 Ooo 406 × 510 mm.
[Inset:] [T:] La cité Valette — (Plan). 133 × 183 mm.

[32] Verklaringe der tweede PAS-CAERT van de MIDDELLANDTSCHE ZEE.
[C:] Pascaarte Van't Oostelyckste deel vande MIDDELANSCHE ZEE Vertonende in sich de ware gelegentheden van alle Capen, havens, rivieren, bayen en droogtē, zynde alles op zyn behoorlycke streckingen en distantiē geleyt.
TABULA HYDROGRAPHICA de partibus Orientalioribus MARIS MEDITERRANEI, Exhibens verum situm omnium Promontoriorum, portuum, fluminum, sinuum, vadorumque secundum exactam cujusque longitudinem et distantiam descriptorum. AMSTELODAMI Apud Ioannem Ianssonium. — 195 Sss 415 × 543 mm.

[33] Van de Middellandtsche Zee. [On verso:] Beschrijvinge der Custen van MORLACA en DALMATIA...
[C:] IADERA, SICVM et ÆNONA Vulgo ZARA, SIBENICO et NONA cum Insulis adjacentibus. in Parte DALMATIÆ Boreali. — [T:] Amstelodami, Apud Ioannem Ianssonium. — 205 Xxx 419 × 527 mm.

Notes: The maps have text on the verso except where otherwise specified; there are ten new ones, all blank on the back, inserted between numbered pages. All the maps are coloured. The title is printed on a separate slip and pasted in the appropriate place on the coloured, engraved title-page, which is signed 'D V Bremden sculp'. The second part of the atlas, 'Tweede Deel', with 89 pages and 10 maps, is wanting, although it is included in the 'Register'. The new maps are not listed in the 'Register', this fifth volume of Janssonius's Atlas corresponds with Koeman's Me 170, but the maps are in a different order. On p. 39 L there is a wind map: TABVLA ANEMOGRAPHICA, SIVE COMPASSUS, AVT PIXI NAVTICA. Dat is: De Tafel der Winden, of des ZEE-COMPASSES, Met sijne beschrijvinge en verklaringe.
[C:] TABVLA ANEMOGRAPHICA seu PYXIS NAVTICA Ventorum nomina sex linguis repræsentans. — [T:] AMSTELODAMI Apud Ioan Ianssonium. —
Some of the maps have Spanish text, some have Latin and Dutch legends, and map [31], Malta, has French text, but for the most part the maps have Dutch text. Like the other volumes of this atlas, this volume is bound in old vellum with gold tooling. Nordenskiöld's signature is on the inside of the front cover, with his bookplate. In another hand is the pencil inscription: 'Is het deel van den atlas van Janssonius, op de Zeevaert betrekkelijk. Besonderlijk voll voor het Noordent.'

Lit.: Keuning, Janssonius p. 81—84, Koeman vol. 2, p. 496, Me 170, and p. 493—494, Me 164, Nederl. Hist. Scheepv. Mus. Cat. bibl. vol. 1, p. 45.

117 JANSSONIUS, JOANNES   1653

Vol. I
DE Lichtende Colomne, OFTE Zee-spiegel, Inhoudende Eene Beschrijvinghe der See-Kusten Van de OOSTERSCHE en NOORTSCHE SCHIP-VAERT. Vertoonende in veele nootsaeckelijcke Zee-Caerten alle de Havens/Rivieren/Baeyen/ Reeden/Diepten/ en Drooghten; seer curieus op sijn behoorlijcke Polus-hooghte geleght/ en versien met de Op-doeninghe der principale Landen/ en op wat Cours en Verheydt sy van malkanderen gelegen zijn: Nout voor desen soo klaerlijck uyt-ghegheven / en met groote vlijt doorgaens vermeerdert en verbetert/ ten dienste van alle Zee-varende Persoonen. By-een ghebracht uyt ondersoeckinghe van veel ervaren Stier-luyden, Lootsen, en Lief-hebberen der Navigatien. t'AMSTERDAM. By JAN JANSZ. Boeck-Verkooper op 't Water, in de Pas-Caert, ANNO 1653.

[Engraved title-page:]
DE Lichtende Columne OFTE ZEE- SPIEGEL, Inhoudende De Zee-kusten van de Noordsche/ Oostersche/ en Westersche Schip-vaert/ vertoonende in veele nootsaeklijcke Zee-Caerten alle de Havens/ Rivieren/ Baeyen/Reeden/Diepten/en Droghten; seer curieus op sijn behoorlijcke Polus-hooghte gelegt/en versien met de Opdoeninge der principaelste Landen/ en op wat Cours en Verheyt sy van malkanderen gelegen sijn: Noyt voor desen so klaerlijck uyt-gegeven/en met groote vlijt door-gaens vermeerdert en verbetert/ ten dienste van alle Zee-varende Persoonen. Als meede De Gelegentheyt van de Noordelijckste gelegen Landen, als van Yslant, de Straet Davids, Jan-Magen Eylant, Beeren Eylant, Oudt Groenlant, Spitsbergen, en Nova Zembla: met veel Zee-Caerten en Opdoeningen versien. By een gebracht uyt onder-soeckinge van veel ervaren Stuer-luyden, Lootsen, en Lief-hebberen der Navigatien. Met noch een Instructie ofte Onder-wijs in de Konst der Zee-vaerdt/ als mede nieuwe Tafelen van des Sons en Sterren declinatie: Met een Almanach tot den Jare 1661. t'AMSTERDAM: Gedruckt by JAN JANSZ, Boeck-verkooper op het Water, in de Pas-Caert, ANNO 1651.   45,7 cm.

Eerste Boeck der Nieuwe LICHTENDE ZEE-COLOMNE, OFTE

ZEE-SPIEGEL. VAN DE Oostersche en Noordtsche Schip-vaert. Inhoudende De Beschrijvinghe van de Noort-Zee, de Custen van Hollandt, Vrieslandt, Holsten, Jutlant, Meklenborgh en Denemarcken tot Valsterboen, en 't Eylant Rugen: als mede de Kust van Noorwegen tot Dronten, als oock d' Oost-zijde van Engelant ende Schotlant.

Eerste Verthooninghe, Waer in De Zuyder-Zee/ Vlie-stroom/ Vlie en Amelander-gat.

[1] 1 [C:] Pascaart van EUROPA, Als mede een gedeelt vande cust van Africa. — Before 1 A. 425 × 522 mm.

[2] 2 [C:] Pascaarte van de NOORT ZEE Vertonende van Caliz tot Dronten, als oock tusschen Doeveren en Hitlandt. — Before 1 A. 422 × 540 mm.

[3] 3 [C:] Pascaarte vande ZUYDER-ZEE, Texel, ende Vliestroom als mede 't Amelander gat. — Before 1 A. 426 × 522 mm.

[4] 4 [a] [C:] Pascaarte vande EEMSEN. Als de oude ofte wester Eems en de ooster Eems. — 428 × 272 mm.
[b] [C:] Pascaarte van 't VLIE, Als mede een gedeelt van 't Amelander gat. — 428 × 251 mm.
[The whole chart:] Between pp. 4 and 5   A 3. 428 × 526 mm.

[5] 5 [C:] Pascaerte Vande EEMS, ELVE, Weser, Eyder, en de Hever: als mede hoe die selvighe gaten van Heylighelandt gelegen syn. — Between pp. 4 and 5   A 3. 425 × 536 mm.

[6] Beschrijvinge van de Vliestroom. (3 profiles). On 5   A 3

De Tweede Verthooninghe, Waer in: Van de Scholbalgh, Lauwers, Schille, beyde de Eemsen, de Weser, Elve, ende Eyder, oock andere Zee-gaten tusschen beyden.

[7] De Zee-gaten tusschen Scholbalgh en de Eyder. (11 profiles). On 11   B 2

De Derde Verthooninghe, Waer in De Kusten vande West en Oostzijde van Jutlant: Mitsgaders de Beldt, tot voorby Lalant en Langelant tot aen Barts, en Meun.

[8] 6 [C:] Pascaerte Vande West en Oost-zyde van IVTLANDT, Als mede De Belt Mitsgaders De Zee-cust van Holster, Mekelenborg, en de Eylanden van Lalandt, Falster, ende Meun. — Between pp. 10 and 11   B 2. 432 × 710 mm.

[9] De Kusten van Jutlant ende de Beldt. (10 profiles). On 20

De Vierde Verthooninghe, Waer in Het Schager Rack, vande Pater-nosters tot Kol, en voorts door de Sondt tot Falsterbon, als mede de Sondt in 't groot.

[10] 7 [C:] Pascaarte vant SCHAGER-RACK vande Paternosters aen Kol, als mede de Sondt, oock hoe dese landen van Schagen gelegen zyn. — Between pp. 20 and 21   C 3. 425 × 528 mm.
[Inset:] [C:] De SONDT, met alle zyn gelegentheyt int groot. — 215 × 315 mm. (Irregular).

[11] [T:] Wt-Clippen ofte Paternosters Eylant Masterlant — On 21   C 3   80 × 160 mm. (Irregular).

[12] Nydingh   On 22   45 × 214 mm. (Irregular).

[13] [T:] Kol over dese 2. Warders Z. W. van u. — On 22   80 × 100 mm. (Irregular).

[14] 't Schager Rack/ vande Pater-Nosters tot Kol/ als mede de Sondt. (6 profiles). On 27   D 2

De Vijfde Verthooninghe, Waer in: De Kusten van Noorwegen, vande Pater-Nosters tot der Neus.

[15] 8 [C:] Custen van NOORWEGEN; van Der Neus tot aen de Pater noster oock hoe de seluige Landen van Iutlant gelegen zyn. — Between pp. 28 and 29   D 3. 428 × 532 mm.

[16] De Haven van Maerdou.   On 29   D 3   120 × 140 mm. (Irregular).

[17] De Kusten van Noorwegen/ van de Pater-Nosters tot der Neus. (8 profiles). On 31 — 32

De Seste Verthooninge, Waer in: De Kusten van Noorwegen, tusschen der Neus ende Schuytenes.

[18] 9 [C:] De Custen van NOORWEGEN Tusschen Der Neus en Schuitenes — Between pp. 32 and 33   E. 425 × 525 mm.

[19] 10 [C:] Pascaerte van 't Liedt van BERGEN, Beginnende van Schuitenes tot aen Bergen. — Between pp. 32 and 33   E. 431 × 637 mm.

[20] [T:] Aldus is het Lant van de Jedder gedaen/ ... — (2 profiles). On 33   E

De Sevenste Verthooninghe, Waer in Hoe men 't Liet van Bergen op sal zeylen.

[21] Aldus doet de Bock op/ alsmen bezuyden Schuytenes is voor dat Liet. Aldus is den Bergh Sijck gedaen/ alsmen benoorden Schuytenes is. (2 profiles). On 36

De Achtste Verthooninghe, Waer in De Custen van Noorwegen, tusschen Ieltefioert en de hooge Hoeck van Horrel.

[22] 11 [C:] De Cust van NOORWEGEN Vertoonde van Bergen tot aen de hoeck van Horrel. — Between pp. 36 and 37   E 3. 427 × 534 mm.

[23] De Custen van Noorwegen/ tusschen Jeltefioerd en de hooge Hoeck van Horrel. (12 profiles). On 37   E 3 — 38

De Negenste Verthooninghe, Waer in Hoe men 't Liet van Dronten op seylen sal.

[24] 12 [C:] Caarte van NOORWEGEN vande hoeck van Horrel tot aen Momendael, waer in begrepen wort het Liet van Dronten. — Between pp. 38 and 39. 425 × 522 mm.

[25] Hoe men 't Liet van Dronten op seylen sal. (9 profiles). On 41   F — 42

De Thiende Verthooninghe, Waer in De Oost-Cust van Engelandt, van de Riviere van Londen tot Welles.

[26] 13 [C:] Pascaarte van ENGELANT Van t' Voorlandt tot aen Blakeney waer in te sien is de mont vande Teemse. — Between pp. 42 and 43   F 2. 426 × 539 mm.
[Inset:] [C:] Rivier van Londen. — 96 × 319 mm.

[27] De Oost-Cust van Engelant/ tusschen de Rivier van Londen en Welles. (5 profiles). On 46

[28] 14 [C:] De Cust van ENGELANDT tusschen Welles en 't Eylandt Coket — Between pp. 46 and 47. 425 × 528 mm.

[29] Aldus is 't gedaen langs de noord-kust van Engelandt/ tusschen Jarmuyen en Krammer/ alsmen binnen de bancken deur seylt. (Profile). On 47

De Elfde Verthooninge, Waer in De Custen van Engelant en Schotlant, tusschen Welles en Coggen-Eylandt.

[30] De Custen van Engelant en Schotlant/ tusschen Welles en Coggen Eylant. (3 profiles). On 50

De Twaelfde Verthooninghe, Waer in De Custen van Engelant en Schotlant, tusschen Koggen Eylant en d'Orcades.

[31] 15 [C:] De Custen van SCHOTLANT met de Eylanden van Orcanesse; van eylandt Coket tot I. Sande. — Between pp. 50 and 51   G 2. 425 × 532 mm.

[32] De Custen van Schotlant/ tusschen Coggen-Eylant en d'Orcades. (4 profiles). On 52

De Derthiende Verthooninghe, Waer in De Zee-Custen van Fayerhil, Hitlandt, en de omleggende Eylanden. Als mede d'Eylanden Fero, en sommige Eylanden achter de noord-westhoeck van Schotlant.

[33] 16 [a] [C:] Eylanden van HITLANDT ofte Schetlant, Fayer hil, en Fulo. — 212 × 521 mm.
[b] [C:] Eylanden van HEBRIDES gelegen achter de noord-west hoeck van Schotlant. — 212 × 266 mm.
[c] [C:] Eylanden van FERO ofte Farre. — 212 × 256 mm.
[The whole chart:] Between pp. 52 and 53   G 3. 426 × 521 mm.

[34] De Zee-kusten van Fayerhil/ Hitlandt/ Fero/ en d'Eylanden van Schotlant. (27 profiles). On 55 — 56

TWEEDE BOECK DER NIEUWE LICHTENDE ZEE-COLOMNE, OFTE ZEE-SPIEGEL, VAN DE OOSTERSCHE en NOORTSCHE SCHIP-VAERT. Inhoudende De Beschrijvinge van de Zee-Custen Noorwegen, Finmarcken, Laplandt, Russen, en de gantsche Witte Zee.

De Eerste Verthooninghe, Waer in De Custen van Finmarcken/ van Dronten/ tot 't Eylandt Trom-zondt.

[35] 17 [C:] Pascaart Vande zeecusten van RVSLANT, Laplant, Finmarcken, en Spitzbergen. — Between pp. 56 and 57   H. 438 × 527 mm.

[36] 18 [C:] De Custen van NOORWEGH tusschen Dronten en Tromsondt — Between pp. 56 and 57   H. 427 × 245 mm.

[37] De Cust van Finmarcken/ van Dronten aen 't Eylandt Tromzont. (12 profiles). On 57   H — 58

De Tweede Verthooninghe, Waer in De Cust van Finmarcken, van' Eylandt Sanien, of Trom-zont tot Kijn of de Noordt-Caep.

[38] 19 [C:] Caarte van FINMARCKEN van t'Eylandt Sanien tot Noordkyn — Between p. 58 and 59   H 2.   439 × 533 mm.
[39] De Cust van Finmarcken/ van't Eylandt Tromzondt tot Noordt-kijn. (27 profiles). On 59   H 2—60
[40] 20 [C:] De Custen van NOORWEGEN en Laplandt, vande Noord-kyn tot aende Rivier van Kola. — Between pp. 60 and 61   H 3.   425 × 526 mm.
[Inset:] [T:] Het Eylandt Wardhuys —   115 × 152 mm.
[41] De Cust van Finmarcken/ van't Eylandt Trom-zondt tot Noord-kijn. (4 profiles). On 61   H 3
De Derde Verthooninge, Waer in De Zee-Custen tusschen de Noordt-Kaep, of Noordt-Kijn tot de Rivier van Kola.
[42] De Zee-Custen tusschen de Noord-kijn en de Rivier van Kola. (20 profiles). On 62—63
De Vierde Verthooninghe, Waer in De Zee-Custen van Laplandt, tusschen de Riviere Kola en de Eylanden van Swetenoes.
[43] 21 [a] [C:] Het eylandt Kilduyn met de Reede nae 't leven ontworpen leggende op de hoochte van 69 graden 40 minuiten. —   126 × 181 mm.
[b] [C:] De Rivier van KOLA in't groot besteck. —   126 × 356 mm.
[c] [C:] De Custe van LAPLANDT tusschen de Rivier van Kola en de eylandē van Swetenoes —   297 × 542 mm.
[The whole chart:] Between pp. 64 and 65   I.   428 × 542 mm.
[44] 22 [C:] Pascaarte Van de Mont van de WITTE ZEE, tot aende Riuier Dwina al: Archangel toe. — Between pp. 66 and 67   I 2.   424 × 528 mm.
[Insets:] [T:] SWETENOES, met de Eylandekens daer ontrent gelegen nae 't leven ontworpen —   120 × 245 mm. (Irregular).   [T:] De Eylanden van LOMBASCHO na 't leven ontworpen —   85 × 80 mm.
[45] De Zee-Kusten tusschen de Rivier Kola/ en d'Eylanden van Swetenoes. (7 profiles). On 67   I 2
De Vijfde Verthooninghe, Waer in: De Kust van de Mondt van de Witte Zee.
[46] 23 [C:] Pascaarte vañ WITTE-ZEE begrypende de custen van Laplandt, van Warsiga tot aen Kandalox en de cust van Corelia tot aen de Riviere Dwina — Between pp. 68 and 69   I 3.   428 × 521 mm.
[47] XXIII [C:] Caerte van ARCHANGEL ofte de Rivier de Duina, soo wel van't Nieuwe als 't Oude diep. — Between pp. 68 and 69   I 3.   421 × 521 mm.
[48] Aldus ist Lant gedaen tusschen Swetenoes en Orlogenes/ alsmen daer voorby zeylt. (Profile). On 69   I 3
De Seste Verthooninghe, Waer in: De Zee-Kusen van de Witte Zee, en de Rivier van Archangel int groot.
[49] 23¼ [C:] Pascaerte van GROEN-LANDT, Yslandt, Straet Davids en Ian Mayen eylandt; hoemen de selvige van Hitlandt en de Noortcusten van Schotlandt en Yrlandt beseylen mach. — Between pp. 70 and 71.   426 × 528 mm.
Derde Boeck der Nieuwe LICHTENDE ZEE COLOMNE, OFTE ZEE-SPIEGEL. VAN DE OOSTERSCHE en NOORTSCHE SCHIP-VAERT. Inhoudende De Beschrijvinghe van Yslandt, Groenlandt, ofte de Straet Davids, als mede de gelegentheyt van Ian Mayen Eylandt, en Spits-Berghen, voorders de streckinghe van Candenoes Oost-waerts aen door het Waygat, tot de Tartarische ofte Ys-Zee.
De Eerste Verthooninghe, Waer in: De gelegentheydt tusschen Hitlandt naer Yslandt/ en van daer na de Straet Davids/ of de hoeck van Out-Groenlant/ nu ghenaemt Staten-hoeck.
No charts.
De Tweede Verthooninge, Waer in: De Beschrijvinghe van Jan Mayen Eylandt.
[50] [a] 23½ [C:] Pas-caert van IAN MAYEN EYLANT. Verthoonde alle de gelegentheyt van alle bayen, enbochten, diepten en en drooghten. —   423 × 248 mm.
[b] 23¾ [C:] Pas-caerte van SPITSBERGEN met alle haer Rivieren, havens, hoemen, sanden en droogten als mede Hoemen C. de Uytkyck op Spits-bergen van de Noord Caap en Beeren Eylandt bezeylen sal. —   423 × 248 mm.
[The whole chart:] Between pp. 72 and 73   K.   423 × 498 mm.
[51] 21½ De Noord-West-Hoeck.

[C:] De Noord-westhoec van IAN MAYEN Eylandt. — (View). On 75   K 2   151 × 208 mm.
[52] De Beschrijvinge van Jan Mayen Eylant. (3 profiles). On 76
De Derde Verthooninge, Waer in: de ghelegentheydt van't Beeren-Eylandt, 't Hoopen-Eylandt, als mede van gheheel Spits-bergen, soo veel als die tot noch toe boenoorden ende beoosten bekent is.
[53] 22½ De Hollantsche ofte Maurits-Bay. On 79   154 × 212 mm.
[54] Beschrijvinge van 't Beeren-Eylandt/ en 't Hoopen Eylant. (2 profiles). On 81   L
De Vierde Verthooninge, Waer in: De Beschrijvinghe van Orlogenes en Kaep de Candenoes tot aen de West-Kuste van Nova Sembla en 't Waygat.
No charts.
Vierde Boeck der Nieuwe LICHTENDE ZEE COLOMNE, OFTE ZEE-SPIEGEL. VAN DE OOSTERSCHE en NOORTSCHE SCHIP-VAERT. Inhoudende De Beschrijvinghe van de gantsche Oost-Zee.
De Eerste Verthooninghe, Waer in: De Zee-Kusten van Valsterboen tot Schenckenes/ ende van het Eylant Rugen tot Rijgs-hooft.
[55] 24 [C:] Pascaarte vande OOST-ZEE Van't Eylandt Rugen, ofte Bornholm tot aen Wyborg. — Between pp. [84] and 85   L 3.   426 × 530 mm.
[56] 25 [C:] De Custen van DENEMARCKEN en Sweden van Valsterbon tot Schenckenes, Als mede de Custen van Pomeren van 't Eylant Rugen tot Rygshooft. — Between pp. [84] and 85   L 3.   438 × 525 mm.
[57] 't NIEUWE-DIEP.
[T:] EYLANDT RVGEN   POMEREN — On 88   169 × 200 mm.
[58] 26 [C:] Caarte van PRVYSSEN en Coerlandt van Rygshooft tot der Winda — Between pp. 90 and 91   M 2.   431 × 528 mm.
[59] De Zee-Kusten tusschen Valsterboen en Schenckenes. Als mede. van 't Eylant Rugen tot Rijghs-hooft. (11 profiles). On 91   M 2
De Tweede Verthooninghe, Waer in: De Zee-Kusten tusschen Rijghs-Hooft en Der Winda.
[60] De Zee-Kusten tusschen Rijghs-hooft ende Der Winda. (14 profiles). On 93   M 3
De Derde Verthooninge, Waer in: De Zee-Kusten tusschen Der Winda en Revel, als mede de Eylanden van 't Alandts Haff.
[61] 27 [C:] Pascaarte van LIIFLANDT ende Oost-Finlandt, van der Winda tot aende hoeck van Alandt ende voort tot Revel. — Between pp. 94 and 95.   425 × 520 mm.
[62] De Zee-Kusten tusschen Der Winda en Revel/ (18 profiles). On 98 — 99   N 2.
[63] 28 [C:] De Zeecusten van LIIFLANDT, Ende Oost Finlandt, van Wolfs-oort tot aen Wyborgh. — Between pp. 98 and 99   N 2.   423 × 523 mm.
De Vierde Verthooninghe, Waer in: De Zee-Kusten tusschen Wolf, en 't uytterste vande Oost-Zee.
[64] Groot en Kleyn Wranger. On 99   N 2   117 × 153 mm. (Irregular).
[65] De Zee-Kusten tusschen 't Eylant Wolf en 't uyterste vande Oost-Zee. (9 profiles). On 102 and 103.
De Vijfde Verthooninghe, Waer in: De Zee-Kusten van Sweden, tusschen Oelandt, en Stockholm, als mede de Eylanden van Oelant en Gotlant, en 't Liet van Stockholm in't groot, en 't Gat van Uttoy.
[66] 29 [C:] Caarte van SWEDEN Van Oelandt tot aen Stocholm. — Between pp. 102 and 103.   441 × 527 mm.
[67] 30 [a] [C:] Caarte van't gat van ABBO, ofte VTTOY. —   432 × 262 mm.
[b] [C:] Caarte van STOCHOLMSE Liet. —   432 × 259 mm.
[The whole chart:] Between pp. 102 and 103.   432 × 526 mm.
[68] De Zee-Kusten van Sweden/ tusschen Oelant en Stockholm. (4 profiles). On 108

Vol. II
DE Lichtende Golomne, OFTE Zee-spiegel, Inhoudende Eene Beschrijvinghe der See-Kusten Van DE WESTERSCHE SCHIP-

VAERT. Vertoonende in veele nootsaeckelijcke Zee-Caerten alle de Havens/ Rivieren/ Baeyen/ Reeden/ Diepten/ en Drooghten; seer curieus op sijn behoorlijcke Polus-hooghte geleght/ en versien met de Op-doeninghe der principale Landen/ en op wat Cours en Verheydt sy van malkanderen gelegen zijn: Noyt voor desen soo klaerlijck uyt-ghegheven/ en met groote vlijt doorgaens vermeerdert en verbetert/ ten dienste van alle Zee-varende Persoonen. By-een ghebracht uyt ondersoeckinghe van veel ervaren Stier-luyden, Lootsen, en Lief-hebberen der Navigatien. t'AMSTERDAM. By JAN JANSZ. Boeck-Verkooper op 't Water, in de Pas-Caert, ANNO 1653.

Eerste Boeck der Nieuwe LICHTENDE ZEE COLOMNE, OFTE ZEE-SPIEGEL. VANDE WESTERSCHE SCHIP-VAERT, Inhoudende De Beschrijvinge der Zee-Kusten van Hollandt, Zeelandt en Vlaenderen, van Texel tot de Hoofden.
Eerste Verthooninge, Waer in: De Tessel-stroom en Gaten van Texel.

[1] 31 [C:] Cust van Hollant tusschen de Maes ende Texel. — Before I (A). 417 × 520 mm.
[2] 32 [a] [C:] De TEXEL Stroom met de gaten vant Marsdiep. — 426 × 259 mm.
 [Inset:] [C:] Caarte vande Reede end Haven van Medenblick hoemen die comen soo van 't Wieringer als Vriesch vlack beseylen mogen tot dienst en nut voor alle Zeevaren luyden, perfectelyc gemeten en afgepeylt. Beschreve A.º 1641 uyt speciale last van E.H.Burgemeesteren en de Regeerders der vorss. Stadt Medenblick. — 240 × 117 mm. (Irregular).
 [b] [C:] Caarte van DE MASE, Ende het Goereesche gat. — 426 × 264 mm.
 [The whole chart:] Between pp. 2 and 3 (A)2. 426 × 527 mm.

De Tweede Verthooninghe, Waer in De Kust van Hollant, van Texel tot de Maes, als mede de Gaten van Texel, de Maes en 't Goereetsche gat.

[3] Texel/ Mase/ en 't Goereesche-Gat. (14 profiles). On 7 (B)2

De Derde Verthooninge, Waer in: Al de Zee-Gaten, tusschen de Maes en de Wielingen, als van Brouwers-haven, Zierck-zee, Der Veer, en de Wielingen.

[4] 33 [C:] De Cust van ZEELANDT, Begrypende in sich de gaten, als vande Wielingen, ter Veere, Ziericzee, Brouwershaven, Goeree, en de Maes — Between pp. 8 and 9 (C). 426 × 522 mm.
[5] 34 [C:] De Cust van VLAENDEREN Beginnende vande Wielingen tot aen de Hoofden met alle haer sanden en droogten. — Between pp. 12 and 13 (D). 425 × 532 mm.
[6] De Zee-gaten van ter Veer ende Wielingen. (4 profiles). On 13 (D)

De Vierde Vertooninge, Waer in: De Cust van Vlaenderen, van de Wielingen tot de Hoofden, als oock de Cust, van Engelant van Doveren tot 't noord Voor-landt.

[7] De Kust van Engelant van 't Voorlant tot Doveren. (4 profiles). On 18

Tweede Boeck der Nieuwe LICHTENDE ZEE COLUMNE, OFTE ZEE-SPIEGEL. Vande Westersche Schip-vaert, Inhoudende De Beschrijvinge van de Kusten van Vranckrijk, van Tresport tot Roscou: En de Kusten van Engelant, van Fierley West aen tot Engelants-eynt: 't Canaal van Brustou: Als mede de Zee-Kusten van Yrlant.
De Eerste Verthooninge, Waer in: De Kusten van Vranckrijck, Van Swartenes tot 't Eylant Ornay, en van Doveren tot Bevesier.

[8] 35 [C:] Pascaart vant CANAAL Begrypende in sich Engelandt, Schotlandt, en Jerlandt, als mede een gedeelt van Francryck. — Between pp. 18 and 19 (E)2. 426 × 526 mm.
[9] 36 [C:] De Cust van NORMANDIE en Picardie als mede een gedeelt in Engelandt tusschen de Hoofden ende Ornay. — Between pp. 18 and 19 (E)2. 422 × 521 mm.
[10] De Cust van Normandye/ van Swartenes tot 't Eylant Ornay. (12 profiles). On 22

De Tweede Vertooning, Waer in: De Cust van Bretaigne, van 't Eylandt Ornay tot het Eylandt van Heysandt.

[11] 37 [C:] De Custen van BRETAIGNE, Waer in vertoont wort alle gelegentheyt tusschen Caap de Hague en t'Eylant Heyssant. — Between pp. 22 and 23 (F)2. 424 × 525 mm.
[12] S. MALO.
 [C:] De Haven van S.Malo — On 24 170 × 201 mm.
[13] 38 [C:] De Custen van ENGELANDT, tusschen Fierley en Poortlant; oock hoese van Ornay gelegen zyn. — Between pp. 26 and 27 (G)2. 423 × 522 mm.
[14] De Cust van Bretaigne/ tusschen 't eylandt Ornay/ en Heyzant. (6 profiles). On 27 (G)2

De Derde Vertooninghe, Waer in: De Cust van Engelant van Bevesier tot Poortlant.

[15] De Cust van Engelandt/ tusschen Bevesier en Poortlandt. (7 profiles). On 30

De Vierde Verthooninge, Waer in: De Cust van Engelant, tusschen Poortlant en Lezart.

[16] TORBAY. On 30 70 × 98 mm. (Irregular).
[17] 39 [C:] De Custen Van Engelant tusschen de twee pointen van Poortlandt en Lezard. — Between pp. 30 and 31 (H)2. 406 × 523 mm.
[18] De Cust van Engelant tusschen Poortlant en Lezart. (20 profiles). On 32—34

De Vijfde Verthooninghe, Waer in: De Kusten van Engelant, van Lezart en Engelants-eynt, tot C. de Cornwal, de Sorrels, en het Canaal van Brustou.

[19] 40 [C:] Cust van ENGELANT, Van Lezart tot Engelands Eyndt, de Sorlinges, ende Canaal van Brestou, als mede hoe zy van Yerland gelegen syn. — Between pp. 34 and 35 (I)2. 420 × 520 mm.
 [Inset:] [T:] Sorlinges — 121 × 111 mm.
[20] De kust van Engel. van Lezart of Engelants-eynt tot kaep de Cornwal, De Sorrels/ en de Verkeerde Canaal van Bristouw. (29 profiles). On 38—39 (K)2

De Seste Verthooninge, Waer in: De Zuyd-oost en Oost Kust van Yrlant, tusschen Corckbegh en Hedenhoo ofte Hout.

[21] 41 [C:] De Zuyd Oost zyde Van YERLANDT Van Dubling tot aen t'Eylandt Corkbeg. — Between pp. 40 and 41 (L). 406 × 528 mm.
[22] Boven-landt ofte 't Hooge landt over den hoeck van Grenoort. 't Vlacke Voor-landt van Grenoort. (Profile). On 41 (L)
[23] De zuyd-oost en oost Cust van Yerlandt/ tusschen Corckbeg en Hedenhoo. (20 profiles). On 45 (M) — 47 (M)2
[24] 42 [C:] De Noord-oost zyde van YERLANDT Van Caap de Hoorn tot aen Hedehde en als mede hoe t' van Schotlandt gelegen is. — Between pp. 46 and 47 (M)2. 414 × 527 mm.

De Sevenste Vertooninghe. Waer in: De noord-oost Cust van Yerlandt, tusschen Hedenhoo of Hout, en Hoornhed als oock Schotlandt daer tegen over.

[25] De noord-oost Cust van Yerlandt/ tusschen Hedenho en Hoornhead; Als oock mede Schotlandt daer tegen over. (11 profiles). On 50 — 51 (N)2
[26] 43 [C:] De Noordwest zyde van YERLANDT Beginnende van Capo de Hoorn tot aen Schynes, ofte Slynehead. — Between pp. 50 and 51 (N)2. 424 × 518 mm.

De Achtste Vertooninge, Waer in: De noord-west Cust van Yerlandt, tusschen Hoornhead en Slynehead.

[27] De noord-oost Cust van Yerlandt/ tusschen Hoornhead en Slynehead; (12 profiles). On 52 — 53 (O)
[28] 44 [C:] De west custen van YERLANDT Beginnende van Corckbeg tot aen Slynhooft. — Between pp. 52 and 53 (O). 428 × 525 mm.

De negenste Verthooning, Waer in: De West-Hoeck en Zuyd-Cust van Yerlandt tusschen Slynehead en Corck-Haven.

[29] De West-hoeck en Zuyd-kust van Yerlandt tusschen Slynehead en Corck-haven. (42 profiles). On 56—59 (P)2 59 (P)2 with verso blank.

Derde Boeck der LICHTENDE ZEE COLUMNE, OFTE ZEE-SPIEGEL VAN DE WESTERSCHE SCHIPVAERT. Inhoudende De Beschrijvinghe van Vranckrijck/ Biscayen/ Galissen/ Portugael en Algarve/ van Heyssant tot de Strate van Gibralter.
De Eerste Verthooninge, Waer in: De Kust van Vranckrijck, van Heysant en het Eylandt Boelyn.

[30] 45 [C:] De Custen van HISPANIA, als Andaluzia, Portugal, Gallissien, Biscajen, en een gedeelt van Vranckryck, beginnen van Heysant tot aen Larache. — Between pp. [60] and 61 (Q). 426 × 529 mm.

[31] 46 [C:] De Cust van Bretaigne van Heysandt tot aent Eylant Boelyn. — Between pp. [60] and 61 (Q). 424 × 526 mm.

[32] S. Matheus Klooster. Conquest-Oort. (Profile). On 61 (Q)

[33] De Zee-kusten van Bretaignien tusschen Heysant en het eylandt Boelijn. (24 profiles). On 65 (R) — 66

De Tweede Verthooninge, Waer in: De Cust van Poictou en Xantoigne, tusschen Boelyn en de Rivier van Bordeaux.

[34] 47 [C:] De Custen van POICTOU, XANTOIGNE En een gedeelt van Bretaigne van Boelyn tot aen de Rivier van Bourdeaux. — Between pp. 66 and 67 (R)2. 420 × 522 mm.

[35] AFBEELDINGE van OLLONNE. On 68 163 × 224 mm.

[36] De Cust van Poictou en Xantoigne/ van Boelyn tot de Rivier van Bordeanx. (19 profiles). On 71 (S)2 — 72

De Derde Verthooninge, Waer in: De Beschrijvinge van de Rivier van Bordeaux; alsmede van de selvige tot S.Sebastiaen ofte Konincx-Reede.

[37] 48 [C:] Caarte Vande Rivier van Bourdeaux tot aen Bayone en voorts aen Coninx rede. — Between pp. 72 and 73 (T). 414 × 527 mm.

[38] De Cust van Vranckrijck van de Rivier van Bordeaux tot Konincks-Reede. (11 profiles). On 74 — 75 (T)2

De Vierde Verthooninge, Waer in: De Cust van Biscayen tusschen Konincks-Reede en het Eylandt Sint Cipriaen.

[39] 49 [a] [C:] Kust Van Biscayen tusschen Orio ende rio de Sella. — 204 × 523 mm.
[b] [C:] Kust Van Biscayen tusschen Rio de Sella en t'Eylant van S.Cyprian. — 205 × 523 mm.
[The whole chart:] Between pp. 74 and 75 (T)2. 414 × 523 mm.

[40] De Cust van Biscayen van Konincks-Reede tot S.Cipriaen. (31 profiles). 78—80

De Vijfde Verthooninge, Waer in: De Zee-Custen van Galissien en Portugall, tusschen 't Eylandt van S.Sipriaen en Camina.

[41] 50 [C:] Caarte Vande custen van Galissien tusschen 't Eylant van S.Ciprian en Camina. — Between pp. 80 and 81 (X). 421 × 529 mm.

[42] De Kusten van Gallissien en Portugall/ van S.Cypriaen tot Camina. (31 profiles). 84—86

De Seste Verthooninghe, Waer in: De Zee-Kusten van 't Noordlijckste deel van Portugall van Camina tot Pissage.

[43] 51 [C:] Cust van PORTVGAL t'Noordelyckste deel beginnende van Viana tot aen Pissage. — Between pp. 86 and 87 (Y2). 404 × 511 mm.

[44] De Kust. van 't Noordlijckste deel van Portugall van Camina tot Pissage. (13 profiles). On 87 (Y2) — 88

De Sevenste Verthooninghe, Waer in: De Zee-Kusten van 't Zuydlijckste deel van Portugall van Pissage tot S.Uves ofte Setubal.

[45] 52 [C:] De Cust van PORTVGAEL Het Zuydlyckste deel, Beginnende van Pissage tot aen S.Vues alias Setubal. — Between pp. 88 and 89 (Z). 427 × 525 mm.

[46] De Kust. van 't Zuydelijkste deel van Portugall van Pissage tot S.Vves. (8 profiles). On 89 (Z) — 90

De Achtste Verthooninghe, Waer in: De Zee-Kusten Algarve en Andaluzia van S.Uves tot Palos ofte 't Clif.

[47] 53 [C:] Cust van ANDALVZIA, En Algarve, Beginnende van Capo de Spichel tot aen het Clif. — Between pp. 90 and 91 (Z2). 425 × 521 mm.

[48] De Kusten van Algarve en Andaluzia/ van S.Vves tot Polos ofte Clif. (15 profiles). On 92 — 93 (Aa)

De Negenste Verthooninghe, Waer in: De Zee-Kusten van Andaluzien van Palos tot door de Strate van Gibralter by Modril, ende de Kuste van Barbaryen daer tegen over. Als mede de Barbarische Kust van C.Spartel tot oudt Mamora.

[49] 54 [C:] Cust van HISPANGIEN Vande Rivier van Sivilien tot aen Malaga ende De cust van Barbarien van Out Mamora tot Penon de Velez. — Between pp. 92 and 93 (Aa). 397 × 526 mm.

[50] De Spaensche Cust van Malaga tot Modril. On 95 (Aa) 2 74 × 240 mm. (Irregular).

[51] De Zee-Cust. van Andaluzia van Palos tot inde Straet voorby Modril. Als mede de Kusten van Barbarien daer tegen over. (6 profiles). On 97 (Bb). Verso blank.

Vierde Boeck der LICHTENDE ZEE-COLUMNE, OFTE ZEE-SPIEGEL. VAN DE WESTERSCHE SCHIPVAERT. Inhoudende De Custen van Barbarien/ Gualata/ Arguyn/ Genehoe/ en de Vlaemsche ende Canarische Eylanden van de Straet van Gibralter tot Capo de Verde.

De Eerste Vertooninge, Waer in: De Zee-Kusten van Barbarien van Out Mamora tot Capo de Geer, als mede de Vlaemsche Eylanden.

[52] 55 [C:] De Cust van BARBARIA, Gualata, Arguyn, en Geneheo, van Capo S. Vincente tot Capo Verde. — Between pp. [98] and 99 (Bb)2. 425 × 521 mm.

[53] 56 [a] [C:] de Cust van Barbaryen van out Mamora tot Capo Blanco. — 158 × 524 mm.
[b] [C:] De Cust van Barbaryen van Capo Blanco Tot Capo de Geer. — 152 × 524 mm.
[c] [C:] De Reede van Punte del Gada int Eylandt S.Michiels — 114 × 119 mm.
[Inset:] [T:] De zuydhoec vant Eylandt FAYAL. — 15 × 50 mm.
[d] [C:] De Reede voor de Stadt Angra int eylandt Tercera — (Plan). 114 × 216 mm.
[e] [C:] De Eylanden van Madera en Porto Santo — 114 × 184 mm.
[The whole chart:] Between pp. [98] and 99 (Bb)2. Verso blank. 435 × 524 mm.

[54] De Zee-Kusten van Barbarien/ van Mamora tot C. de Geer/ Als mede de Vlaemsche Eylanden. (18 profiles). 103 (Cc)2 — 104

De Tweede Verthooninghe, Waer in: Van de Canarische Eylanden.

[55] 57 [C:] Caarte Voor een gedeelte der Canarise Eylanden als Canaria, Tenerifa, Forteventura, etc. — Between pp. 104 and 105 (Dd). 424 × 530 mm.
[Inset:] [C:] De tyhavens Porto de Naos en Porto de Cavallos aen de Zuyd-oostzyde van Lacerota — 144 × 156 mm.

[56] Vande Canarische Eylanden. (15 profiles). On 106 — 107 107 with verso blank.

Notes: All the large charts are blank on the back. The smaller charts and the profiles have text on the back, except where otherwise specified. All the charts and profiles are uncoloured. None of the charts in either part bear any imprint. The engraved title-page has the date 1651, the secondary title-page has 1653. In his 'Additions and Corrections', in a note to M. Ja 2, Koeman mentions a copy with these dates, but does not give a location for it. On the title-page of vol. 2 is an engraving of ships, signed with the monogram, = Christoph van Sichem senior or junior; in this case probably junior (see Nagler). Tiele mentions a copy with the date 1652 on the secondary title-page. The edition described here is almost identical to Pieter Goos's atlas of the same name, printed in 1658. The charts are the same, and there are only minor differences in the text. The plates were originally by Theunis Jacobsz (see Koeman, vol. 4 p. 270) and his Nieuwe en Vergroote Zee-Boeck of 1657 also contains these same charts. In our copy of his atlas the second part is by Janssonius, and is the same as vol. 2 of the atlas described here, except that some of the maps have been bound in a different order. The atlas has been bound for Nordenskiöld in leather. His signature is on the first old blank leaf.

Lit.: Koeman vol. 4, p. 270, M.Ja 2, Nagler, Monogrammisten vol. 2, p. 309—12, nrs 803—806, Tiele p. 122, nr 536.

118 JANSSONIUS, JOANNES 1653

Vol. II
DE Lichtende Colomne, OFTE Zee-spiegel, Inhoudende Eene

Beschrijvinghe der See-Kusten Van DE WESTERSCHE SCHIP-VAERT. Vertoonende in veele nootsaeckelijcke Zee-Caerten alle de Havens/ Rivieren/ Baeyen/ Reeden/ Diepten/ en Drooghten; seer curieus op sijn behoorlijcke Polus-hooghte gheleght/ en versien met de Op-doeninghe der principale Landen/ en op wat Cour en Verheydt sy van malkanderen gelegen zijn: Noyt voor desen soo klaerlijck uyt-ghegheven/ en met groote vlijt doorgaens vermeerde t en verbetert/ ten dienste van alle Zee-varende Persoonen. By-een ghebracht uyt ondersoeckinghe van veel ervaren Stier-luyden, Lootsen, en Lief-hebberen der Navigatien. t'AMSTERDAM. By JAN JANSZ. Boeck-Verkooper op 't Water, in de Pas-Caert, ANNO 1653.

Notes: This copy of vol. 2 of Janssonius's Zee-Spiegel of 1653 is bound together with vol. 1 of Theunis Jacobsz's Zee-Boeck of 1657 (110). Our collection also has a complete copy of both volumes of Janssonius's atlas. The copies of vol. 2 are identical except that some of the charts are bound in a different order: in this copy, chart 31 [1] follows p. 2; charts 55, 56 and 57 are numbered [52], [53] and [55] in the complete atlas (117), [54] being profiles, while in this copy these profiles are no. [52], and charts 55, 56 and 57 are numbered [54], [55] and [53] respectively, and are bound between pages 104 and 105 (Dd). The maps are coloured. See also notes to (117), 1653.

119 JODE, CORNELIS DE 1593

SPECVLVM ORBIS TERRÆ ANTVERPIÆ Sumptibus Viduæ et Ḥẹredū Gerardi de Iudæis. [Colophon:] VIDVA ET HÆREDES GERARDI DE IVDÆIS, SVIS SVMPTIBVS HOC OPVS GEOGRAPHICVM CVRAVERE IMPRIMI APVD ARNOLDVM CONINX, ANTVERPIÆ, ANNO M.D.XCIII.
47,2 cm.

Vol. I

[1] VNIVERSI ORBIS, TABVLA I.
[C:] TOTIVS ORBIS COGNITI VNIVERSALIS DESCRIPTIO. Cui etiam eandem orbis terræ delineationem, duorum circulorum capacitate, huius descriptionis mundi longitudinem documento admirantibus, adiecimus. A.º M.D.LXXXIX. Qui cupit ingentem gratis cognoscere mundum, / Hec percurrat, iter tunq₃ tabella dabit. / Quam nunc Iudœus, reddendam censuit illr: / Prisca cui placido pectore lecta fuit. — [T:] Gerardus Iudoeus excudeb. — [T:] Hanc orbis vniuersalē descriptionem Corn: de Iudoejs Antverpien. pridie Calend. Noueb. in alma Academia duacēsi, Aº 1589. pfecit. — Fol. I. A 345 × 508 mm.
[Insets:] [The Western and Eastern hemispheres]. Two circular maps with 106 mm. diam.

[2] VNIVERSI ORBIS TABVLA II.
[C:] HEMISPHETIV̄ AB ÆQVINOCTIALI LINEA, AD CIRCVLV̄ POLI ARCTICI. — [C:] HEMISPHERIV̄ AB ÆQVINOCTIALI LINEA, AD CIRCVLV̄ POLI ATARCTICI. — Fol. 2 B Verso blank. 319 × 521 mm. The hemispheres with 264 mm. diam.

[3] AMERICA SEV NOVVS ORBIS.
[C:] BRASILIA ET PERVVIA. Ad Strenuū et Magnificū Dn̄m. D. TheoDoricū Echter a Mespelbrū, Sac. Cæs. Maies.ti & Reuerēdiss. Principi, Episc. Herbipolēsi, primū a consilijs. &c. — Fol. 3. C 356 × 421 mm.

[4] AFRICA.
[C:] AFRICAE VERA FORMA, ET SITVS. — [C:] Cosmographiæ Studiosis S. ... Formis hæredum Gerardi de Iode — Fol. 4 D 324 × 450 mm.

[5] BARBARIAE TABVLA.
[C:] BARBARIA pars APRICÆ, Compræhendens præcipua Loca Versus littora MARIS MEDITERRANEI — Fol. 5 E 353 × 454 mm. [Divided into two parts].

[6] ASIÆ VNIVERSALIS ENARRATIO.
[C:] ASIA, PARTIVM ORBIS MAXIMA. — Fol. 6. F 373 × 463 mm.

[7] EVROPA.
[C:] NOVA TOTIVS EVROPAE TABVLA ex magnis Gerardi de Iudæis P. desumpta. Generoso atq₃ magnifico Dn̄o. D. TheoDorico Echter a Mespelbrū, Cæs. Maiestat. et Reueredis̄s. Princip. Episcopi Herbipolēsis, a Consilijs primo, dedicata. A. M.D.CXIII. — [T:] Formis heredū Gerardi de Iode. — Fol. 7. G 327 × 442 mm.

[8] ASIAE PRIMA PARS SIVE PERSICVM REGNVM.
[C:] PRIMÆ PARTIS ASIÆ acurata delineatio habens nomina antiqua et recentia continens Turcici Imperij magnam partem ac Sophorum seu Persarum Regnum obseruatis Ubiq₃ cū longitudinis tū latitudinis gradib[9] Autore Iacobo Castaldo pedemontano. Gerhardus de Iode excudebat. — [T:] Ioannes à Deutecū Lucas à Deutecū fece. — Fol. 8. H 301 × 506 mm.

[9] ASIAE SECVNDA PARS SIVE ARABIA.
[C:] SECVNDÆ PARTIS ASIAE, typus, qua oculis subijciuntur itinera nautarum qui Calecutium Indiæ mercandorum aromatum causa frequentant, ac eorum quoq₃ qui terrestri itinere adeunt Suacham, Laccam, in domino Præto Iani, nec non eorum qui Aden et Ormum inuisunt, et Balsaram quoque castrum, supra Euphratem fluuium situm, omnia suis gradibus subiecta, cum longitudinis tum latitudinis Iacobo Castaldo Pedemontano authore. Gerhardus de Iode excudebat. — [T:] Ioannes à deutecum, Lucas à deutecum, fecerunt. — Fol. 9. I 323 × 505 mm.

[10] ASIAE TERTIA PARS SIVE INDIA.
[C:] TERTIAE PARTIS ASIAE quæ modernis India orientalis dicitur acurata delineatio Autore Iacobo Castaldo Pedemontano. Gerardus de Iode excudebat. Ioannes à Deutecum Lucas à Deutecum Fecerunt. — Fol. 10. K 326 × 500 mm.

[11] CHINA QVAE ET SINA.
[T:] CHINA REGNVM — [C:] In China auem habent ... Collectore Cornelio de Iudeis Antverp. — KK 2 360 × 456 mm.

[12] AMERICAE PARS BOREALIS.
[C:] AMERICÆ PARS BOREALIS, FLORIDA, BACCALAOS, CANADA, CORTEREALIS. A Cornelio de Iudæis in lucē edita. — [C:] Generoso, atq₃ Magnifico Dn̄o, Dn̄o THEODORICO ECHTER, à Mespelbrū, Sacr. Cæsar. Maiest.ti, et Reuersmo. Principi, Episcopo Herbipolensi a consilijs primo. &c. Cornelius de Iudæis Antverp. D.D. Aº MDLXXXXIII. — Fol. 11 L 362 × 503 mm.

[13] QVIVIRAE REGNVM.
[C:] QVIVIRÆ REGNV̄, cum alijs versus Boreā. — Fol. 12. M 346 × 234 mm.

[14] [On verso:] NOVÆ GVINEÆ TABVLA.
[C:] NOVÆ GVINEÆ Forma, & Situs. — 345 × 214 mm.

[15] PALESTINÆ VEL TERRAE SANCTÆ TAB. I.
[C:] TERRÆ SANCTÆ, quæ Promissionis terra, est Syriæ pars ea, quæ Palæstina uocatur, descriptio, per Tylmannū Stellam. Gerardus de Iode excudebat. — [T:] Ioannes à Deutecum, Lucas à Deutecum Fecerunt. — Fol. 13. N 303 × 511 mm.
[Inset:][T:] CIVITAS HIERVSALEM — (View). 90 × 252 mm.

[16] PALESTINAE VEL TERRAE SANCTÆ TAB. II.
[T:] DESCRIPTIO et SITVS TERRÆ SANCTÆ ALIO NOMINE PALESTINA MVLTIS PRECIARIS HISTORYS ET MIRACVLIS VTRIVSQ₃ TESTAMĒTI A CHRISTO SALVATORE nobilitata. — [C:] Habes hic Beneuole lector ... Excudebat Antwerpiæ Gerardus de Jode — Fol. 14. O Verso blank. 334 × 509 mm.

[17] NATOLIA SEV IMPRIVM TVRCICVM.
[C:] NATOLIAM modern dicunt eam partem quam Asiam minorem appellauere veteres. — [C:] TVRCIA TVRCICIVE IMPERII seu Solij mannorum regni pleraque pars, nunc recens summa fide ac industria elucubrata. — [T:] Ioannes à Deutecum fecit. — Fol. 15. P 380 × 510 mm.

[18] GRAECIA.
[C:] Videbis totius Gręciæ limites diuisos per mōtes flumina

et maria, nominib. hodiernis, ad hunc modū. ... — Fol. 16. Q 386 × 513 mm.

[19] SICILIA INSVLA.
[a] [C:] SICILIA INSVLA MARIS Inferi. iuxta Mamertinum fretum. — 141 × 189 mm.
[b] [C:] CORSICA, OLIM CYRNVS INSVLA maris Ligustici. — [T:] SARDINIA TVRRHEnis maris Insula. — 114 × 188 mm.
[c] [T:] PYTHIVSÆ INSVLÆ maris Balearici. — [T:] MAIORICA ET MINORICA SARDOI maris Insulæ. — 78 × 188 mm.
[d] [C:] CYPRVS INSVLA MARIS SYRIACI iuxta Issicum sinum sita. — 141 × 294 mm.
[e] [C:] CANDIA, OLIM AERIA, CVRETIS MACARON ET CRETA DICTA Insula Libijci maris. — 114 × 194 mm.
[f] [T:] MELITA AFRICI seu Sicculi maris Insula. — [T:] MITYLENE AEGEI MARIS Insula in Adramitteno sinu. — 77 × 294 mm.
[The whole map:] Fol. 17. R 366 × 508 mm.

[20] ITALIA.
[C:] ITALIÆ TOTIVS ORBIS OLIM DOMATRICIS NOVA ET EXACTISS DESCRIPITO IACOBO CASTALDO AVCTORE Antuerpiæ celabat Gerardus de Jode anno 77... — Fol. 18. S 362 × 515 mm.

[21] REGNVM NEAPOLITANVM.
[C:] Ioannes à deutecum. f. NEAPOLITANI REGNI exacta ac diligens delineatio Authore Pyrrho Ligorio. Gerardus de Iode excudebat. — Fol. 19. T 374 × 514 mm.
[Inset:] [T:] NAPOLI — (View). 88 × 232 mm.

[22] MARCHIA TARVISINA. [On verso:] TERRITORIVM ROMANVM.
[a] [C:] PADVANI AGRI EIVSQVE VRBIVM VICORVM CASTRORVM MONTIVM FLVMINVM AD VIVVM EXPRESSIO — 376 × 261 mm.
[b] [C:] VRBIS ROMANE TERRITORIVM PRÆTER circumiacentium Vicmarumqué Ciuitatum Castrorum Villarum montiumqué situm etiam Viarū publicarum fluminum tijpum oculis subijciens — 376 × 242 mm.
[The whole map:] Fol. 20. V 376 × 510 mm.

[23] THVSCIA. FORVM IVLIVM. ET CORFV INSVLA.
[a] [C:] FORI IVLII QVAM FRIVL VOCANT HISTRIÆQ SS Venetorum senatui parentium ditionum Verus ac germanus tijpus — 366 × 241 mm.
[Inset:] [C:] CORFV Insula maris Adriatici Republicæ Venetæ parens. — 121 × 223 mm.
[b] [C:] TVSCIAE INSIGNIS ITALIÆ prouinciæ Vera ac elegans chorographia autore Hieronimo Bellarmato — 366 × 247 mm.
[The whole map:] Fol. 21. X 366 × 512 mm.

[24] PARMAE ET PLAISANTIAE DVCATVS.
[a] [T:] MARCÆ ANCONITANÆ SEV PICOENI AGRI Typus chorographicus. — 134 × 241 mm.
[b] [T:] VERA ET FIDELIS descriptio Comitatus Zaræ et Sebenici: vti impressa est olim Venetijs à Paulo Forlano — [T:] Ioannes à Dotinckum.f. — 131 × 217 mm.
[c] [C:] PARMÆ AC PLAISANTIÆ AMOENISSIMI DVCATVS typus elegans et acuratus, nunq$_3$ ante hac editus. — [T:] Ioannes à deutecū.f. — 245 × 487 mm.
[The whole map:] Fol. 22. Y 390 × 487 mm.

[25] GALLIA.
[C:] GALLIÆ Amplissimi Regni tabula. — Fol. 23. Z 305 × 446 mm.

[26] PEDEMONTANA REGIO, [On verso:] BITVRIGVM REGIO, SEV DVCATVS.
[a] [C:] BITVRIGVM prouinciæ quæ Berrij Vulgo dicitur Chorographica descriptio. — [T:] Ioannes à Deutecum, Lucas à Deutecum, Fecerunt. — 345 × 252 mm.
[b] [C:] PEDEMONTANÆ totius prope Italiæ fertilissimæ Regionis Vna cum suis finitimis elegantissimo descriptio. — 342 × 245 mm.
[The whole map:] Fol. 24 AA 342 × 508 mm.

[27] BVRGVNDIA.
[C:] COMITATVS BVRGVNDIÆ CVM MAGNA PARTE DVCATVS EIVSDEM NOVA ET ACCVRATISSIMA DESCRIPTIO — [T:] Antuerpiæ Excudebat Gerar. de Iode. — Fol. 25. BB 347 × 463 mm.

[28] VEROMANDVORVM TRACTVS, ET SABAVDIÆ.
[a] [C:] Typus Corographicus Veromanduæ partis Galliæ Belgicæ. — 345 × 227 mm.
[b] [C:] SABAVDIAE DVCATVS, SEV NARBONENSIS GALLIAE PARTIS, VERA GERMANAQVE DELINEATIO. — [T:] Ioannes à Deutecum, Lucas à Deutecu, fecerunt. — 345 × 213 mm.
[The whole map:] Fol. 26. CC 345 × 457 mm.

[29] CALETENSES ET BOLONIENSES. [On verso:] LIMANIA.
[a] [C:] LIMANIAE Topographia — 343 × 201 mm.
[b] [C:] BOLONIENSIVM DITIONIS ET CALETENSIVM EXACTA descript. — 343 × 241 mm.
[The whole map:] Fol. 27. DD 343 × 448 mm.

[30] ANDEGAVENSIS DVCATVS.
[C:] EXACTA NOVAQVE DESCRIPTIO DVCATVS ANDEGAVENSIS QVEM VVLGARI NOMINE Le Duche d'Aniou INDIGITANT — [T:] Ioannes à Doetinckū fecit. — Fol. 28. EE 346 × 445 mm.

[31] CENOMANIA, QVAE VVLGO DICTA LE MAYNE.
[T:] NOVA ET INTEGRA CÆNOMANIÆ DESCRIPTIO Vulg. la Mans. — [C:] Pour mieulx intendre, lecteur benigne, ... Prostant Antverpiæ apud Gerardum de Iode. — Verso blank. Fol. 29. FF 343 × 465 mm.

[32] HISPANIA.
[T:] Noua Descriptio Hispaniæ. Pirrho Ligorio Neap. Auctore. — [T:] Ioannes à duetecū Lucas à duetecū fecerunt. — Fol. 30. GG 380 × 507 mm.

[33] LVSITANIA.
[C:] PORTVGALLIAE QVÆ OLIM LVSITANIA VERNANDO ALVARO SECCO AVTORE RECENS DESCRIPTIO. Gerard. de Iode, excud. — [T:] Ioannes à deutecum, Lucas à deutecum, fecerunt. — Fol. 31. HH 315 × 524 mm.

[34] ANGLIA, SCOTIA, ET HYBERNIA.
[C:] ANGLIAE SCOTIAE ET HIBERNIE NOVA DESCRIPTIO. — Fol. 32. II 348 × 498 mm.

[35] GVIPVSCOA PROVINCIA, ET COMITATVS VENAYSCINENSIS.
[C:] COMITATVS. VENAYSCINENSIS NOVA DISCRIPTIO — Fol. 33. KK 298 × 241 mm.

[36] [On verso:] GVIPVSCOA PROVINCIA.
[C:] NOVA ET EXACTISSIMA DESCRIPTIO nobilis poruinciæ GVIPVSCOVÆ in partibus Hispaniæ sitæ — XXVI 353 × 256 mm.

Vol. II
[Germania Geographicis Tabulis Illustrata. Per Cornelium de Iudaeis Antverpianū.]

[1] GERMANIAE VNIVERSALIS TABVLA I.
[C:] GERMANIAE TOTIVS, NOSTRAE EVROPAE CELEBERRIMAE REGIONIS, DESCRIPTIO SINGVLARIS. — [T:] Gerardus de Iode excudebat. — Fol. 3. Dd 378 × 526 mm.

[2] SVETIA, GOTHIA ET NORVVEGIA.
[C:] A.º 1570 SEPTENTRIONALIV̄ REGIONVM SVETIÆ GOTHIÆ NORVEGIÆ DANIÆ et terrarum adiacetium recens exactaque descriptio per Liuinum algoet Auctorem Gerardus de Iode excudebat. Ioannes à Duetecū Lucas à Duetecū fecerunt — Fol. 4. Ee 370 × 498 mm.

[3] DANIAE REGNI ET HOLSATIÆ DVCATVS.
[C:] DANORVM MARCHIÆ SEV CIMBRICI REGNVM CONTINENTIS IVTIÆ DVCATVM ac Codanis sinus Insulas chorographica delineatio — Fol. 5. Ff 318 × 250 mm.

[4] [On verso:] HOLSATIA.
[C:] CHOROGRAPHICA DVCATVVM HOLSATIÆ SCHLESWICÆ ET STORMARIÆ delineatio. 324 × 250 mm.

[5] PRVSSIA.

[C:] PRVSSIÆ REGIONIS SARMATIÆ EVROPÆ NOBIBIlissimæ Noua et Vera descriptio — Fol. 6. Gg 362 × 496 mm.

[6] POMERANIA ET DIETHMARSIA.
[T:] POMERANIÆ Vtriusq$_3$, continentis præter Wolgastensem seu Barthiẽsem Stetinensemq$_3$ ducatus Rugium Insulam, prouincias ex Vandalico solo captas tijpus Geographi — Fol. 7. Hh 159 × 456 mm.

[7] [On verso:] DIETMARSIA.
[C:] THIETMARSORVM SIMBRICÆ CHERSONESI POPVLORVM foedis delineato Autore Petro Boekel — 144 × 228 mm.

[8] SAXONIA REGIO.
[T:] SAXONVM REGIONIS QVATENVS EIVS GENTIS IMPERIVM NOMENQVE olim patebat, recens germanaq$_3$ delineatio, Christiano Schrotenio authore. Gerardus de Iode excudebat. — [T:] Ioannes à Deutucũ. f. — Fol. 8. Ii 328 × 454 mm.

[9] LIVONIA ET MOSCOVIA DVCATVS.
[a] [C:] LIVONIÆ PROVINCIÆ AC EIVS Confinium Verus et elegans tỹpus Iõ Portantius Cosmographus Delinea. — [T:] Ioannes à Deutecũ, Lucas à Deutecũ Fecerunt. — 322 × 244 mm.
[b] [C:] MOSCOVIÆ MAXIMI AMPLISSIMI QVE DVCATVS chorographica descriptio Authore Anthonio Iankinsono Anglo — 322 × 253 mm.
[The whole map:] Fol. 9. Kk 322 × 504 mm.

[10] POLONIÆ REGNVM.
[C:] POLONIÆ AMPLISSIMI REGNI. . TYPVS GEOGRAPHICVS — Fol. 10. Ll 377 × 493 mm.

[11] BOHEMIAE REGNVM.
[T:] CHOROGRAPHIA INSIGNIS REGNI BOHEMIÆ, AVTHORE IOANNE GRIGVIGERO. — [T:] Ioannes à Deutecũ Lucas à Deutecũ Fecerunt. — Fol. 11. Mm 320 × 520 mm.

[12] MORAVIA SEV MORAVANIA.
[C:] MARAVANIÆ SEV MORAVIÆ MARCHIONATVS. Singulari fide ac diligentia Chorographice delineatus — Fol. 12. Nn Verso blank. 368 × 459 mm.

[13] MORAVIAE ET SILESIAE TABVLA.
[T:] SILESIÆ DVCATVS TYPICE descriptus per — Fol. 13. Oo 364 × 243 mm.

[14] [On verso:] DVCATVS OSVVIECZIMENSIS ET ZATORIENSIS.
[T:] DVCATVS. OSWIECZIM̃E.ET.ZATORIẼSIS — 348 × 248 mm.

[15] HVNGARICI REGNI, CVM TRANSILVANIA.
[T:] HVNGARIÆ TOTIVS VTI EX COMPLVRIBVS ALIORVM GEOGRAPHICIS CHARTIS à Matthia Zinthio Norico delineata est recens editio. — [T:] Ioannes à Deutecũ Lucas à Deutecum fece. — Fol. 14. Pp 295 × 490 mm.

[16] AVSTRIA, DVCATVS.
[C:] AVSTRIÆ DVCATVS. SEV PANNONIÆ SVPERIORIS CHOROGRAPHIA GERMANA SVMMA FIDE AC INDVSTRIA ELABORATA a Wolfgango Lazio — Fol. 15. Qq 377 × 521 mm.

[17] AVSTRIAE DVCATVS ONASVM.
[C:] Beschreibung des Erczherzġtumb Oesterreich ober Enns durch Augustin hirsuogel — [T:] Tzo Antorff by Gehard de Iode Anno 1583 — Fol. 16. Rr Verso blank. 377 × 487 mm.

[18] ILLYRICI SEV SCLAVONIÆ TABVLA.
[T:] MYSIAM HANC SVPERIOREM DACIÆ QV[E] PARTEM, LIBVRNIAM DALMATIAMQVE ac Sauiam, seu Saui fl ripas Bessi qui nunc Bosni dicti ex inferiori Mỹsia a [Bu]lgaris eiecti occuparunt possidentque: ac Getarum gentes creduntur. — [C:] ILLIRICI SEV SCLAVONIÆ, CONTINENTIS Croatiam, Carniam, Istriam, Bosniam, eisquæ conterminas prouincias, recens ac emendatus typus. Auctore Augustino Hirsvogelio. — Fol. 17. Ss 303 × 519 mm.

[19] CROATIAE TABVLA.
[C:] CROATIÆ, & circumiacentiũ Regionũ versus Turcam nova delineatio. Reverendiss$^{mo.}$ in Christo Patri ac Dño. D. LÆVINO TORRENTIO, Episcopo Antverpiẽsi. Dño. & Præsuli suo. Cornelius de Iudæis D. D. — [T:] Formis hæredũ Gerardi de Iode. — Fol. 18. Tt Verso blank. 335 × 412 mm.

[20] STYRAEMARCHIAE ET CARINTHIÆ DVCATVS.
[C:] STIRÆ MARCHIÆ DVCATVS SEV TAVRIScorum Noricorum sedis acuratus ac elegans tỹpus Chorographicus. — [C:] CARINTHIÆ DVCATVS VEL IVLIARVM alpium tractus vera ac genuina delineatio geographica. — Fol. 19. Vv Two circular maps with 295 (260) mm. diam. 351 × 520 mm.

[21] TIROLENSIS ET CARNIOLÆ COMITATVS.
[a] [T:] TIROLENSIS COMITATVS Seu partis Rhetiæ Alpestris insignis descriptio Chorographica. — 346 × 281 mm.
[b] [C:] CARNIOLÆ CHAZIOLÆQ$_3$ DVCATVS. NEC NON,ET.GORITIÆ COMITATVS, prouintiarum Norici ac Illirici vera propriaq$_3$ delineatio. — 346 × 222 mm.
[The whole map:] Fol. 20. Xx 346 × 516 mm.

[22] SALTZBVRGENSIS ET TREVERENSIS EPISCOPATVS.
[C:] SALTZBVRGENSIS EPISCOPATVS seu Iuuauiensis diæceseos Chorographia acuratissima elaborata ab Marco Setznagel Saltzburgensis. Gerardus de Iode excudebat. — [T:] Ioannes à Deutecum Lucas à Deutecum fecerunt. — Fol. 21. Yy 352 × 247 mm.

[23] [On verso:] TREVERENSIS EPISCOPATVS.
[C:] TREVIRENSIS EPISCOPATVS EXACTISSIMO DECRIPTIO PER IOHANNEM A SCILDE — [T:] Ioannes á Doetinckum fecit. — 328 × 238 mm.

[24] HELVETIAE SEV SVICIAE TABVLA.
[C:] HELVETIAE SEV SVICIAE QVAE MVLTIS CONFOEDERATORVM TERRA DICITVR PRIMAE GERMANORVM PROVINCIAE GALLIAE ITALIAEQVAE CONTIGVAE CHOROGRAPHIA VERA ET ELEGANS AVTORE — [T:] Ioannes à Deutecum Lucas à Deutecum fecerunt. — Fol. 22. Zz 392 × 519 mm.

[25] SVEVIAE TABVLA.
[C:] SVEVIAE vtriusq$_3$ cum Germanicæ tum Rethicæ Martianorumque nemorũ tỹpus chorographicus verus ac Germanus. Authore — Fol. 23. Aaa 371 × 422 mm.

[26] VALESIA, ET TERRITOR. BASILIENSE.
[a] [C:] VALESIÆ PROVINCIÆ MONTANÆ, ITALIAM, Galliam, ac Germaniam discernentis non minus vera quam elegans chorographiæ, Auctore Ioanne Schalbeter. — 125 × 485 mm.
[b] [C:] BASILEÆ INCLYTAE Rauracorum Vrbis, ac eiusdem circumuicini agri situs exactissima delineatio, Authore Sebastiano Munstero — 256 × 481 mm.
[The whole map:] Fol. 24. Bbb 390 × 485 mm.

[27] BAVARIAE DVCATVS.
[C:] BAVARIAE VTRIVSQVE CVM INFERIORIS TV̄ SVPERIORIS VERA ET AD AMVSSIM DESCRIPTIO. — [T:] Ioannes à Deutecũ.f. — Fol. 25. Ccc. 347 × 455 mm.

[28] VVIRTEMBERGENSIS DVCATVS ET PALATINATVS SVPERIOR.
[a] [C:] WIRTENBERGENSIS DVCATVS ELEGANS DELINEATIO. AVTORE GEORGIO GARNER. — Circular map with 266 mm. diam. 368 × 276 mm.
[b] [C:] PALATINATVS SVPERIORIS SEV BAVARIAE VERA DESCRIPTIO. AVTORE ERHARDO REYCH. — 368 × 253 mm.
[The whole map:] Fol. 26. Ddd 368 × 523 mm.

[29] TRACTVS DANVBII, TABVLA I.
[C:] NOVA EXACTISSIMAQVE DESCRIPTIO DANVBII, (qui alias Ister cognominatur) fluminis permagni totoq$_3$ terrarũ orbe celebratissimi:qui in Sueuiæ uilla Donestingen ad Nigram syluam oriens, longo tractu uersus orientem per Austriam , Vngariam, Seruiam, Vualachiam et Bulgariam fluens, multis amnibus in se receptis, in mare Ponticũ uel Euxinũ tandem deuoluitur: unà simul adiecta diligentissima delineatione totius Imperij Turcici & regnorũ,

ditionū urbiumq₃, quas idem iuratus hostis, sæua tyrannide superans Christianos, occupauit. Per Christianum Sgrothonū, Reg.Ma^ts Geograph. — [T:] Ioannes à Deutecum, Lucas à Deutecum Fecerunt. — Fol. 27. Eee 331 × 494 mm.

[30] TRACTVS DANVBII, TABVLA II.
[T:] Gerardus de Iode excudebat. Ioannes à Deutecū. Lucas à Deutecum. fecerunt. — Fol. 28. Fff 334 × 491 mm.

[31] TVRINGIAE COMITATVS, ET MISNIÆ MARCHIONATVS.
[a] [C:] TVRINGIAE COMITATVS PROVINCIALIS Verus ac germanus typus. Autore Johanne Mellingero Hallens. — 298 × 252 mm.
[b] [C:] MISNIAE MARCHIONATVS diligens et acurata delineatio Autore Bartholomæo Sculteto Gor — 298 × 250 mm.
[The whole map:] Fol. 29. Ggg 298 × 504 mm.

[32] FRANCIA ORIENTALIS.
[C:] FRANCOnia, nobilissim⁹ Germaniæ ducatus. — [C:] Amice Lector exhibentur hic tibi amplissimi Episcopat⁹ HERBIPOLENSIS, et BAMBERGENSIS, nonnullis in locis emendati castigatiq₃. — Fol. 30. Hhh 344 × 455 mm.

[33] PALATINATVS RHENI.
[C:] PALATINATVS Rheni, & circūiacentes Regiones, Alsatica, Witēbergica, Zweitbrucksēsis. — Fol. 31. Iii 335 × 426 mm.

[34] HESSIAE SEV CATTORVM TABVLA.
[C:] HESSIAE SEV CATTORVM NOBILISSIMORVM AC BELLICOSISSIMORVM populorum sedis genuinus nec Vngue' ante hac Visus typus Geographicus — [T:] Ioannes à Deutecum f. — Fol. 32. Kkk 354 × 460 mm.

[35] TRACTVS RHENI, TABVLA I.
[C:] Tractus Rhenanus multos olim Romanus labōres peperit Cuius initiū occupant Heluetij, olim Gall, nunc Alemani, reliquū ad Oceanū & Sequanā vsque fortiss. ... — [T:] Gerardus de Iode excudebat Anno Dn⁰ 1569 — Fol. 33. Lll 337 × 456 mm.

[36] TRACTVS RHENI, TABVLA II.
[C:] Austrasia, recentiorib. seculis dicta, nunc in varia diuisa est dominia, vtpote Lotharingiam Palatinatum, Bipontium, Treuirim, &c^e — Fol. 34. Mmm 339 × 452 mm.

[37] TRACTVS RHENI, TABVLA III.
[C:] INFERIORIS GERMANIÆ PARS. Habes in hac tabella, amice Lector, bonam inferioris Germaniæ partē, vnā cum cunctis eius amnibus, celebratissimoq₃ flumine Rheno. Qui tandē in tres claros se' scindens riuos, nimirū, Vahalim, Lequam, & Issulam, amittit natiuum nomen Rheni, olim apud oppidum Leidam in mare solitus exonerari. Excudebat Gerardus de Jode. — Fol. 35. Nnn 338 × 456 mm.

[38] MANSFELDIE COMITATVS.
[C:] MANSFELDIÆ COMITATVS DILIGENS ET ACVRATVS TYPVS — Fol. 36. Ooo 333 × 250 mm.

[39] [On verso:] CLIVENSIS ET IVLIACENSIS DVCATVS.
[C:] CLIVENSIS ET IVLIACENSIS DVCATVM nouus ac Verus typus. geographicus — 332 × 253 mm.

[40] VVESTPHALIAE TABVLA.
[C:] REITERATA EPISCOPATVS MONASTERIENSIS GEOGRAPHICA DESCRIPTIO CVI ADDITA EST ET OSNABRVGENSIS PER GODEFRIDIV MASCHOP EMBRICĒSEM COSMOGRAP. Godefridus Maschop Embricensis ad lectorem ... A⁰ 1569. — [T:] Ioannes a Deutecum Lucas à Duetecum fecerunt. — Fol. 37. Ppp 352 × 451 mm.

[41] [On verso:] VVALDECCENSIS COMITATVS.
[C:] WALDECCENSIS COMITATVS NOVA DESCRIPTIO — Fol. 38. Qqq 319 × 252 mm.

[42] LOTHARINGIA.
[C:] LOTHARINGIA DVCATVS. — [T:] Gerar. de Iode excudebat. — Verso blank. Fol. 40. Sss 354 × 494 mm.

[43] BELGICAE TABVLA.
[C:] GERMANIA INFERIOR. Gallia Belgica dicta, continens Hispaniarum Regis Provincias Septentrionales. Formis Hæredum Gerardi de Iode. — Fol. 41. Ttt 344 × 436 mm.

[44] LVTZENBVRGENSIS DVCATVS.
[C:] LVTZENBVR-GII Montuosissimi ac saltuosissimi ducatus Neustria seu Westerichiæ prouinciæ tijpus elegans et Verus nec Vnquā antehac Visus — Fol. 42. Vvv 370 × 455 mm.

[45] LEODIENSIS EPISCOPATVS.
[T:] EPISCOPATVS LEODIENSIS IN SE CONTINENS DVCATV̄^M BOVILLONENSEM MARCHIONATV̄^M FRANCIMONTENSEM ET COMITATVM BORCHLONENSEM ET HASBANIÆ CVM ALIQVOT BARONATIB₉ — [T:] Iohan.a Schilde Authore — Fol. 43. Xxx 316 × 503 mm.

[46] GELDRIAE DVCATVS, TABVLA.
[C:] GELDRIA. En tibi, amice Lector, ... Excudebat Antuuerpiæ Gerardus de Iode, Nouomagensis. — [T:] Ioannes à Duetecū Lucas à Duetucum fecerunt. — Fol. 44. Yyy 366 × 487 mm.

[47] FRISIA ORIENTALIS.
[C:] FRISIAE ORIENTALIS noua et exacta descriptio Auctore Laurentio Michaelis ab Hagen Karchen anno 1579 Gerar de Iode exeudebat — Fol. 45. Zzz 362 × 499 mm.

[48] HOLLANDIAE COMITATVS.
[C:] HOLLĀDIÆ INTEGRA COMITA. DESCRIPT. — [C:] Bescriuinge van dat vermarde en vruchtbaer graefscap van Hollant Met dat geheele lant van Vtrecht, ... te wetē a⁰ 1520. 1552. 1562. — Fol. 46. Aaaa 333 × 477 mm.

[49] ZELANDIAE TABVLA.
[C:] AV BENING LECTEVR SALVT Tv Vois icij amij lecteur le Paijs De Zelaande auecq les Leius Circonvoijssins & la quelle est enclos De la Grand Mere Occeane & auec la distance des villes & bourgaiges Selon le vraije art De Geometrie — Fol. 47. Bbbb 336 × 462 mm.

[50] BRABANTIÆ DVCATVS.
[C:] BRABANTIÆ BELGARVM PROVINCIÆ RECENS EXACTAQVE DESRIPTIO ... — Fol. 48. Cccc 350 × 492 mm.

[51] FLANDRIAE COMITATVS.
[C:] EXACTISSIMA FLANDRIÆ DESCRIPTIO, Flandria Galliæ Belgicæ prouincia celeberrima... — Fol. 49. Dddd 364 × 491 mm.

[52] ARTESIA.
[C:] ARTOIS Atrebatum regionis vera descriptio Johanne Surhouio montano Hanno: Auctore — Fol. 50. Eeee 370 × 467 mm.

[53] HANNONIA.
[C:] HANNONIÆ COMITATVS DESCRIPTIO — [T:] Antuerpiæ Excudebat Gerardus de Iode — Fol. 51. Ffff 359 × 503 mm.

Notes: All the maps have text on the verso, except where otherwise specified, and they are uncoloured. The two volumes are bound together. The first leaf of vol. 1 bears an extract from Boëtius on the recto, and on the verso an engraved portrait of Bishop Neidhard of Bamberg, to whom the atlas is dedicated. The title-page of vol. 2 is missing; the volume begins with fol. 1 Bb. Vol. 2 fol. 39 Rrr is also missing; according to Koeman, Jod.2:(73), the map on this folio should be 'Frisia orientalis'. This map appears in our copy as map [47], on fol. 45 Zzz, where Koeman describes a map (Jod.2:(79)) Frisiae Provinciae Tabula. Frisiae Antiquissimae. Trans. Rhenum. Provinci. Et. Adianentium Regionum Nova et Exacta descriptio; this map is wanting in our copy. The text in the cartouche on map [49] 'ZelandiæTabula' differs from that in Koeman's Jod.2:(81), where it is "Zelandia inferioris Germaniae Pars..." In other respects, our copy corresponds to Koeman's Jod.2.
Map [50] in vol. 2, "Brabantiæ Ducatus", is much smaller than the other maps in the volume. Map [10], vol. 2, bears a portrait of "SIGISMYN.III. D.G. REX Pol. Mold. XXXVII. prox. hæres REGIS Suæd."
The atlas is bound in old leather with gilt tooling.

Nordenskiöld's bookplate and signature, with the date 1889, are on the inside of the front cover.

Lit.: Fern. Van Ortroy, L'Oeuvre cartographique de Gérard et de Corneille de Jode. Gand 1914. Université de Gand. Recueil de travaux publ. par La Faculté de philosophie et lettres. Fasc. 44, Koeman vol. 2, p. 205—212.

Literature

Adelung, Friedrich von, Ueber die älteren ausländischen Karten von Russland. Beiträge zur Kenntniss des Russischen Reiches von K.E. v. Baer und Gr. v. Helmersen. 4. Bd. St. Petersburg 1841.

Allgemeine deutsche Biographie. Herausg. von Rochus v. Liliencron und F.X. Wegele. 1—56. Leipzig 1875—1912.

Almagià, Roberto, Vincenzo Coronelli e i suo globi. — Il. P. Vincenzo Coronelli dei frati minori conventuali 1650—1718. Nel III centenario della nascita. (Roma 1951) p. 80—87.

Armao, Ermanno, Vincenzo Coronelli. Cenni sull uomo e la sua vita. Catalogo radionato delle sue opere lettere. Fonti bibliografiche. Indici. Firenze 1944. — Biblioteca di bibliografia italiana 17.

Bachmann, Friedrich, Die alten Städtebilder. Ein Verzeichnis der graphischen Ortsansichten von Schedel bis Merian. 2. unveränderte Auflage. Stuttgart 1965.

Bagrow, Leo, Essay of a Catalogue of Map-Incunabula. — Imago mundi 7 (1951) pp. 106—109.

Bagrow, Leo, Die Geschichte der Kartographie. Berlin 1951.

Bagrow, Leo, A history of the Cartography of Russian. 1: up to 1600. 2: up to 1800. Edited by Henry W. Castner. Ontario 1975.

Bagrow, Leo, A Ortelii Catalogus cartographorum. 1—2. Gotha 1928—1930. Ergänzungsheft Nr 199 und Nr 210 zu "Petermanns Mitteilungen" aus Justus Perthes' Geographischer Anstalt. Gotha 1928—1930.

Beans, Georg H., Some notes from The Tall Tree Library. — Imago mundi 7 (1951) pp. 89—92.

Bonacker, Wilhelm, Kartenmacher aller Länder und Zeiten. Stuttgart 1966.

Bonasera, Francesco, Vincenzo Coronelli, geografo, cartografo, costruttore di globi. — Il. P. Vincenzo Coronelli dei frati minori conventuali 1650—1718. Nel III centenario della nascita. (Roma 1951) p. 39—79.

Bratt, Einar, En krönika om kartor över Sverige. Stockholm 1958.

The British Museum. Catalogue of printed maps, chartes and plans. Photolithographic edition, complete to 1964. 1—15. London 1967.

The British Museum. General catalogue of printed books 1—263. Photolithographic edition to 1955. London 1965—1966.

Broekema, C., Sir Robert Dudley. Arcano del Mare (1661). C. Broekema. Antiquarian Bookseller. [Catalogue.] Amsterdam [1976].

Brown, Lloyd A., The story of maps. Boston 1949.

Brunet, Jacques Charles, Manuel du libraire de l'amateur de livres. 1:1, 2—5. Paris 1860—1864.

Castellani, Carlo, Catalogo ragionato delle più rare o più importanti opere geografiche a stampa che si conseovano nella biblioteca del Collegio Romano. Roma 1876.

Dahlgren, Per & Richter, Herman, Sveriges sjökarta. Lund 1944. — Statens sjöhistoriska museum. Handlingar 1.

Destombes, Marcel, Catalogue des cartes gravées au XVe siècle. Union géographique internationale. — Rapport de la Commission pour la Bibliographie des cartes anciennes, 2. Paris 1952.

Destombes, Marcel, Mappemondes A.D. 1200—1500. Catalogue préparé par la commission des Cartes Anciennes de l'Union Géographique Internationale. Monumenta cartographica vetustioris aevi. A.D. 1200—1500. I. Mappamundi. Redacteurenchef Marcel Destombes. Amsterdam 1964. — Imago mundi. Suppl. 4. 1964.

Ehrensvärd, Ulla, Introduction to the facsimile edition af Petter Geddas Sjökarteatlas. Stockholm 1947.

Engelstad, Sigurd, Norge i kart gjennom 400 år. Med opplysninger om dem som utformet kartbildet. In inledning av Kristian Nissen. — J.W. Cappelens antikvariat. Katalog 15. Oslo 1952.

Ersch, Joh. Sam. & Gruber, J.G., Allgemeine Enzyklopädie der Wissenschaften und Künste in alphabetischer Folge. 1—21. Leipzig 1818—1825.

Fiorini, Matteo, Sfere terrestri e celesti di autore italiano oppure fatte o conservati in Italia. Roma 1899.

Fonzo, Lorenzo di, La produzione letterarie del P. Vincenzo Coronelli, O.F.M. Conv. (1650—1718). — Il. P. Vincenzo Coronelli dei frati minori conventuali 1650—1718. Nel III centenario della nascita. (Roma 1951) pp. 342—472.

Graesse, Joh.Georg Theod., Trésor de livres rares et précieuxs. 1—7. Suppl. Dresden 1859—1869.

Günther, Siegmund, Jakob Ziegler, ein bayerischer Geograph und Mathematiker. Ausbach und Leipzig 1896. — Forschungen und Kultur- und Literaturgeschichte Bayerns 4.

Günther, Siegmund, Johannes Honter, der Geograph Siebenbürgens. — Acta cartographica 20 (1975) pp. 301—321.

Günther, Siegmund, Peter und Philipp Apian, zwei deutsche Mathematiker und Kartographen. Prag 1882. — Abhandl. der Köningl. Böhm. Gesellschaft der Wissenschaften VI Folge. II:4.

Hain, Ludovicus, Repertorium bibliographicum in quo libri omnes ab arte typographica incenta usque ad A. MD. Typis Experessi enumerantum 1—2 & Supplement. Stuttgart 1826—1838 & London 1895—1898.

Jöcher, Christian Gottlieb, Allgemeine Gelehrten-Lexicon. 1—4. Leipzig 1750.

Keunig, Johannes, Blaeu's Atlas. — Imago mundi 14 (1959) pp. 74—89.

Keunig, Johannes, The "Civitates" of Braun and Hogenberg. — Imago Mundi 17 (1963) pp. 41—43.

Keunig, Johannes, Hessel Gerritsz. — Imago mundi 6 (1950) pp. 49—66.

Keunig, Johannes, The History of an Atlas. Mercator-Hondius. — Imago mundi 4 (1947) pp. 37—62.

Keunig, Johannes, The Novus Atlas of Johannes Janssonius. — Imago mundi 8 (1951) pp. 71—98.

Keunig, Johannes & Donkersloot-De Vrij, Marijke, Willem Janz. Blaeu. A biography and history of his work as a cartographer and publisher. Amsterdam 1973.

Koeman, C., Bibliography of terrestrial, maritime and celestial atlases and pilot books, published in the Netherlands up to 1880. — Atlantes Neerlandici. 1—5. Amsterdam 1967—1971.

Koeman, C., Joan Blaeu and his Grand Atlas. Introduction to the facsimile edition of Le Grand Atlas, 1663. Amsterdam 1970.

Koeman, C., A catalogue by Joan Blaeu. A facsimile with an accompanying text. Amsterdam 1967.

Koeman, C., Collections of maps and atlases in the Netherlands. Their history and present state. Leiden 1961. — Imago mundi. Suppl. 3.

Leithäuser, Joachim G., Mappae mundi. Die geistige Eroberung der Welt. Berlin 1958.

Lister, Raymond, How to identify old maps and globes with a list of cartographers, engravers, publishers and printers concerner with printed maps and globes from c. 1500 to c. 1850. London 1965.

Lynam, Edward, Floris Balthasar, Dutch map-maker, and his sons. — The Geographical journal 70 (1926) pp. 158—161.

Lönborg, Sven, Sveriges karta tiden till omkring 1850. Uppsala 1859.

Müller, Gerhard F., Sammlung Russischer Geschichte. [2. Herausgabe.] 1—5. Offenbach am Main 1777—1779.

Muris, Oswald & Saarmann, Gert, Der Globus im Wandel der Zeiten. Eine Geschichte der Globen. Berlin 1961.

Nagler, G.K., Die Monogrammisten. Fortgesetzt von A. Andresen & C. Clauss. 1—5. München & Leipzig 1879.

National Maritime Museum. Catalogue of the Library. 3: 1—2. London 1971.

The National Union Catalog. Imprints. 1. Mansel 1968.

Nederlandsch Historisch Sheepvaart Museum. Catalogus der Bibliotheek. 1—2. Amsterdam 1960.

Nordenskiöld, A.E., Facsimile-atlas to the early history of cartography with reproductions of the most important maps printed in the XV and XVI centuries. Transl. from the Swedish original by Johan Adolf Ekelöf and Clements R. Markham. Stockholm 1889.

Nordenskiöld, A.E., Periplus. An essay on the early history of charts and sailing-directions. Transl. by Francis A. Bather. Stockholm 1897.

Nordenskiöld, A.E., Vegas färd kring Asien och Europa. 1—2. Stockholm 1881.

Nouvelle biographie générale depuis les temps les plus reculés jusqua nos jours. 1—46. Paris 1855—1866.

Phillips, Philip Lee, A list of geographical atlases in the Library of Congress. 1—4. Washington 1909—20. 5—6. Compiled by Clara Egli Le Geer. Washington 1958—63.

Poggendorff, J.C., Biographisch-literarisch Handwörterbuch zur Geschichte der exacten Wissenschaften. 1—21. Leipzig 1863.

Ritter's geographisch-statistisches Lexicon über die Erdteile... 6., gänzlich umgearbeitete, stark vermehrte und verbesserte Auflage. Unter Redaction von Dr. Otto Henne-AmRhyn. I—II. Leipzig 1874.

Sandler, Christian, Die Homännischen Erben. — Acta cartographica 5 (1969) pp. 370—423.

Sandler, Christian, Johan Baptista Homan. — Zeitschrift der Gesellschaft für Erdkunde zu Berlin. Herausgegeben Prof. Dr. W. Koner. 21 (1886) pp. 328—386.

Sandler, Christian, Matthäus Seutter und seine Landkarten. — Mitteilungen des Vereins für Erdkunde zu Leipzig (1894) pp. 1—38.

Skelton, R.A., County atlases of the British Isles 1579—1850. — Map collectors' series. London 1964, 1965.

Skelton, R.A., Introduction to the Facsimile edition of Braun & Hogenberg. Civitates Orbis Terrarum 1572—1618. Amsterdam 1965.

Thieme, Ulrich & Becker, Felix, Allgemeine Lexicon der bildenden Künstler von der Antike bis zur Gegenwart. 1—36. Leipzig 1907—1947.

Tiele, P.A., Nederlandsche Bibliographie van Land- en Volkenkunde. — Bijdragen tot eene Nederlandsche Bibliographie uitgegeven door het Frederik Muller-Fonds. Amsterdam 1884.

Tooley, R.V., A dictionary of mapmakers including cartographers, geographers, publishers, engravers, etc. from earliest times to 1900. 1—6. London 1965.

Tooley, R.V., Geographical oddities or curious, inginions and imaginary maps and miscellaneous plates published in atlases. Map collectors' circle. London 1965—1971.

Tooley, R.V., Leo Belgicus. An illustrated list. London 1963.

Wallis, Helen, Introduction to Vincenzo Coronelli, Libro dei globi Venici 1693 (1701). Amsterdam 1969.

Appendix to the work: Ann-Mari Mickwitz & Leena Miekkavaara, The A.E. Nordenskiöld Collection in the Helsinki University Library. Annotated catalogue of maps made up to 1800. 1. Helsinki 1979.

The final bibliography covering the whole work will be published in the vol. III.

Helsingin yliopiston monistuspalvelu 1979.